# New England Furniture at Winterthur

# New England Furniture at Winterthur

## Queen Anne and Chippendale Periods

**Nancy E. Richards**
**and**
**Nancy Goyne Evans**

WITH
WENDY A. COOPER
AND
MICHAEL S. PODMANICZKY

RESEARCH ASSISTANCE BY
CLARE G. NOYES

**A Winterthur Book**

*Distributed by University Press of New England*

Generous funding for research and publication was provided by the Henry Luce Foundation, Inc., the Chipstone Foundation, and the Croll Foundation.

Content Editor:   Lisa L. Lock

Copy Editor:     Teresa A. Vivolo

Designed and produced by Laing Communications Inc., Redmond, Wash., Sandra J. Harner, Art Director

Copyright 1997, The Henry Francis du Pont Winterthur Museum, Inc.

Printed in Canada

Library of Congress Cataloging-in-Publication Data

Richards, Nancy (Nancy E.)
    New England furniture at Winterthur : Queen Anne and Chippendale
periods / by Nancy Richards and Nancy Goyne Evans ; with Wendy A.
Cooper and Michael S. Podmaniczky ; research assistance by Clare G.
Noyes.
        p.    cm. — (A Winterthur book)
    Includes bibliographical references and index.
    ISBN 0-912724-38-2 (cloth)
    1. Furniture—New England—Styles—Catalogs.   2. Decoration and
ornament—New England—Queen Anne style—Catalogs.   3. Decoration
and ornament—New England—Chippendale style—Catalogs.
4. Furniture—Delaware—Winterthur—Catalogs.   5. Henry Francis du
Pont Winterthur Museum—Catalogs.     I. Evans, Nancy Goyne.
II. Cooper, Wendy A.   III. Podmaniczky, Michael S.   IV. Title.
NK2410.R5   1997
749.214'074751'1--dc21                                                                    96-46794
                                                                                                        CIP

Frontispiece: Desk, New Hampshire, 1790–1815 (see No. 199).

# Contents

# Director's Foreword

I REMEMBER, AS A STUDENT DURING THE 1960S, inching my way into a dressing room adjacent to the Cecil Bedroom at Winterthur to view a magnificent desk-and-bookcase from Boston (No. 206). Its imposing scale, ambitious design, and flamboyant carving caught my eye. Yet few visitors could appreciate the grandeur of the enormous casepiece wedged into the crowded corner of a minor room. Guides knew little about the desk; Joseph Downs provided only a brief description and picture of it in his comprehensive catalogue of the Winterthur furniture collection. The piece was largely overlooked, but it was a favorite of mine. Happily, new attention has been focused on this masterpiece during the last decade. It represents the work of a talented British immigrant who may well have introduced the blockfront form to Boston. His design skills and construction techniques were exceptional. And of his many outstanding surviving products, none is finer than this desk-and-bookcase. Indeed many students of furniture consider it Boston's best piece of colonial case furniture.

The opening of the Galleries at Winterthur in 1992 offered the opportunity to celebrate the desk's newfound prominence. It now introduces the special exhibition "Perspectives on the Decorative Arts in Early America." For the first time, everyone can enjoy the extraordinary quality of this American masterwork.

The recent research on the desk-and-bookcase reflects the ongoing reevaluation of New England furniture. Building on a foundation of early scholarship beginning with Irving Lyon's seminal volume of 1891, *The Colonial Furniture of New England*, the current generation of collectors, dealers, and curators has amassed an impressive array of information on such topics as the introduction of English styles to New England, regional differences within New England cabinetmaking, and construction techniques of individual craftsmen. These discoveries have led us to reassess the extraordinary collection at Winterthur.

In 1952 Downs commenced a new era in furniture scholarship with his landmark catalogue *American Furniture: Queen Anne and Chippendale Periods in the Henry Francis du Pont Winterthur Museum*. We are now pleased to present Downs's New England pieces augmented with current information and, in addition, to share with you the many outstanding objects acquired by Winterthur since the publication of his book. This new catalogue results from the collaboration of several individuals. Nancy E. Richards and Nancy Goyne Evans, Winterthur's former senior curator and registrar respectively, have written the majority of entries. Curator of furniture Wendy A. Cooper offered her expertise on the desks in the collection; Clare G. Noyes added her insights on many of the tables, stands, and fire screens; and conservators Gregory J. Landrey, Michael S. Podmaniczky, and Mark J. Anderson assessed the condition of nearly every object. In addition, Podmaniczky and Evans prepared the case studies that appear at the end of the volume.

We seek to acquaint you with one of Winterthur's greatest treasures—its outstanding collection of New England furniture. We hope you will find the information an invaluable resource as well as a compelling lure to visit Winterthur—whether for the first or fiftieth time— to enjoy the beauty of New England's craft legacy.

*Dwight P. Lanmon*

# Acknowledgments

New England Furniture IS THE CULMINATION of the hard work, dedication, and contributions of many individuals and groups over many years. The authors gratefully acknowledge all those who shared their time, knowledge, advice, skills, and expertise.

The most helpful gift a scholar can be given is time—time to learn, time to do research, and time to write. The time for initial research and writing was made possible through a generous grant from the Luce Fund for Scholarship in American Art, a program of the Henry Luce Foundation. Luke Beckerdite, executive director of the Chipstone Foundation, helped secure a grant to fund research and production. David D. Croll of the Croll Foundation donated much-needed funds at the final stages of research and writing.

No project of this scope and size is an individual effort. Many staff members, both present and former, have contributed to the preparation of this publication. William S. Ayers and Janis Watson provided guidance through the hazardous journey of grant preparation. From the library, Eleanor McD. Thompson, Allison C. Thorp, Bert R. Denker and his staff, Heather A. Clewell, Paul B. Hensley, Beatrice K. Taylor, and E. Richard McKinstry and his staff were all unfailing in their assistance. Art handlers Douglas K. MacDonald, James A. Albanese, Mary K. Quinn, William G. Strootman, Erik Zuber, H. Mack Truax II, and James Schneck moved each piece of furniture in and out of the collection for examination and photography. Alberta Brandt, Susan Newton, Jennifer Menson, and Grace Eleazer in the Registration Office provided much-needed assistance along the way. Herbert L. Crossan III, who produced the photographs for this book, is owed a great debt of thanks. His ability to clearly capture the material is a major component in its success. His photographs will render the catalogue useful long after subsequent scholarship revises the text.

Gregory J. Landrey, Michael S. Podmaniczky, and Mark J. Anderson, furniture conservators, examined each piece of furniture on the basis of construction and condition. Richard K. Wolbers provided finish analysis of the painted and japanned objects. Debora D. Mayer, Kory Berrett, Don B. Heller, and Janice H. Carlson generously shared their technical expertise to assist in dating and evaluating objects in the catalogue. A special note of thanks goes to Harry A. Alden, who performed the hundreds of wood analyses included here. His assistance in identifying woods not previously associated with eighteenth-century New England cabinetmaking and his enthusiasm for the project enriched the final product tremendously. The curatorial staff over the years shared their expertise in their own fields; Donald L. Fennimore and Robert F. Trent graciously made available unpublished research.

Over the years several talented research assistants, both formal and informal, have contributed enormously to this study. For their observations, insights, and patience in tracking down the myriad details necessary for such a catalogue and, most of all, for their ongoing enthusiasm, special thanks are extended to Paula Fogarty and Elizabeth Laurent, who worked on the project in the very early stages, to Bradley Brooks, who incorporated the study of New England furniture into his internship, and to Jean M. Burks and Clare G. Noyes, who were part of the formal research team.

The research for this catalogue was aided enormously by the generous cooperation of colleagues at other institutions, owners of private collections, and dealers who willingly shared not only their collections but also their knowledge. For the luxury of examining and studying their collections in great detail, thanks are extended to: David Barquist, Yale University Art Gallery; Michael K. Brown, Bayou Bend Collection, Museum of Fine Arts, Houston; Edward S. Cooke, Jr., Museum of Fine Arts, Boston; Robert P. Emlen, John Nicholas Brown Center; Jeannine Falino, Museum of Fine Arts, Boston; Elizabeth Pratt Fox, Connecticut Historical Society; Donna-Belle Garvin, New Hampshire Historical Society; Morrison H. Heckscher, Metropolitan Museum of Art; William N. Hosley, Jr., Wadsworth Atheneum; Penelope Knowles, Lyman Allyn Museum; Deanne Levison, Israel Sack, Inc.; Jack Lindsay, Philadelphia Museum of Art; Thomas Michie and Christopher Monkhouse, Museum of Art, Rhode Island School of Design; Milo M. Naeve, Art Institute of Chicago; Karin Peterson, Antiquarian and Landmark Society; Candy Pissaro, Rhode Island Historical Society; Benjamin C. Reed, Jr., Newport Restoration Foundation; Albert Sack, Israel Sack, Inc.; Jayne Stokes, Milwaukee Art Museum; Susan Strickler, Worcester Art Museum; Gerald W. R. Ward, Museum of Fine Arts, Boston; David Wood, Concord Museum; and Philip Zea, Historic Deerfield. Other experts graciously shared their long experience in the field and patiently answered the seemingly endless questions that arise in the preparation of a manuscript. While it is not possible to thank each person individually, their contributions are gratefully acknowledged here.

Gary Kulik, deputy director of Library and Academic Programs, was instrumental in bringing this long-awaited book to the light of day. And finally, editor Lisa L. Lock and copyeditor Teresa A. Vivolo ably managed the herculean task of coordinating this complex project. The time and effort they invested in ensuring a unified and fluent text and their tireless attention to detail reflect their dedication and professionalism. Many thanks also to Susan Randolph for her expert handling of the production of this elegant volume.

# Introduction

*Brock Jobe*

"For Antiquarians one of the most important events of recent years is the publication this spring of the book *American Furniture, Queen Anne and Chippendale Periods,* by Joseph Downs, curator of the Henry Francis du Pont Winterthur Museum," announced the editor of *Antiques* in May 1952. Four years before, Downs and his friend and colleague Charles Montgomery had been lured to Winterthur by du Pont to prepare a card catalogue and book on his immense collection of Americana. Du Pont, who had decided to convert his great house into a museum, wanted to have a publication on the collection ready when he opened the doors. "It is anticipated," wrote Downs on September 27, 1948, that "the book will comprise several volumes and be the most important work in the field of American antiques." The goal was worthy but overly ambitious. The size of the collection proved daunting, and Downs was unable to meet du Pont's deadline. Rather than bring out a multivolume work immediately, Downs chose to concentrate on what both he and du Pont considered the heart of the collection, the eighteenth-century furniture in the Queen Anne and Chippendale styles. The resulting work became an immediate landmark. Only one catalogue of a museum furniture collection—Edwin Hipkiss's treatment of the Karolik Collection at the Museum of Fine Arts, Boston—had appeared previously. Downs's study is far more extensive in its scale and scholarship. "The superb collection of Queen Anne and Chippendale furniture at Winterthur," he noted, "provides an opportunity without parallel to observe the finest expression of eighteenth-century craftsmanship as it developed in the northern, middle, and southern colonies."[1]

Downs's approach to the catalogue reflects the interests of collectors and curators of the time. In a lengthy introduction he explores five topics. The first, "Cabinetmakers—Their Work and Their Times," surveys the most prominent colonial communities from Portsmouth to Charleston and presents their leading craftsmen and patrons. "Terminology of Furniture" contrasts the period descriptions of furniture (such as highboy or lowboy) with those created by collectors over the past century. "Regional Characteristics" summarizes the distinctive traits of furniture made in individual towns along the Atlantic coast. Although brief, Downs's overview had few peers. Regionalism had just become a subject of keen interest, and few publications had sought to codify the features associated with the furniture of different areas. "Furniture Exports and

Imports" identifies the importance of the export trade, particularly the shipment of furniture from New England to ports along the Atlantic coast and the importation of furniture from England to America. "Woods" provides a glossary of popular furniture woods beginning with mahogany and black walnut, the favorite woods for stylish furniture of the period, continuing through less expensive native hardwoods and concluding with the conifers white and yellow pine, red and white cedar, and bald cypress.

Downs followed the introduction with 388 concise entries, each accompanied by a large black and white illustration. Every entry includes the date, origin, maker (when known), measurements, and principal wood. Secondary woods are frequently cited for case furniture but rarely for other forms. More extensive analysis varies from piece to piece. Distinctive traits that tie an object to a particular town, shop, or owner warranted a remark; unusual or noteworthy design features sometimes also prompted a comment; but construction or condition issues barely received notice. Contemporary inventories and newspaper accounts add insights into the function of a form during the eighteenth century.

Downs's seminal volume remains a standard reference for anyone interested in American furniture. It has been reissued three times, spreading information about Winterthur and its exceptional collection of American furniture to every corner of the country. Collectors still find it a useful visual guide to the primary features of the Queen Anne and Chippendale styles. Yet today, forty-five years after its initial publication, the value of the volume has diminished. Its pages no longer encompass all the museum's eighteenth-century furniture; like any true collector, du Pont did not give up his acquisitive habits once the museum was open. He continued to make occasional purchases until the day he died—April 11, 1969—and even left instructions to his executors to buy certain pieces if they should ever become available. Curators have followed his lead, adding judiciously to the collections over the past quarter century. Charles Hummel highlighted many of these later accessions in a series of three articles in *Antiques*.[2] It was his work that spurred interest in a more thorough treatment. In 1980 Hummel and Nancy Richards, then senior curator, settled upon a regional format, focusing first on the New England collection. This book, *New England Furniture at Winterthur*, evolved from that decision. The new catalogue builds upon the scholarship of Downs; it includes nearly every piece of New England furniture that he presented and adds another seventy objects acquired since 1952. New information redefines the importance of many objects. Some that were once considered genuine are now labeled as fakes or restorations; the altered pieces, still of educational value, are discussed at the end of the volume in a select appendix of case studies. Other objects are reattributed. A "deception bed" (Downs, *American Furniture*, fig. 10) ascribed to Philadelphia and a side chair tied to New York (Downs, *American Furniture*, fig. 106) are reassigned to Boston. A blockfront chest (Downs, *American Furniture*, fig. 167) supposedly from Massachusetts and a drop-leaf breakfast table (Downs, *American Furniture*, fig. 307) thought to be from Rhode Island are now linked to Portsmouth, New Hampshire. In some entries, recent research more finely pinpoints the origin of an object. The discovery of a maker's inscription on a Connecticut blockfront chest of drawers (Downs, *American Furniture*, fig. 172) connects it to little-known cabinetmaker James Higgins of East Haddam, and the origin of a Connecticut desk-and-bookcase can be narrowed to the Norwich area through construction techniques and a solid history of ownership there.

As a current compendium of the collection, replete with this revised information based on recent research, *New England Furniture at Winterthur* will be an invaluable resource for those who have relied on Downs's ambitious but dated volume. Yet the new catalogue is far more than a corrected version of Downs's work. Since 1952, a generation of scholars has reshaped our understanding of early New England furniture. Many have been associated with Winterthur—

some as curators, others as research fellows or graduate students in the Winterthur Program in Early American Culture. Their contributions map in far more detail than did Downs the furniture industry of New England. They depict a trade dominated by artisans in major seaports from Portsmouth to New Haven. Of these communities, none had greater impact than Boston. According to a visitor in 1750, "the Artificers in this Place Exceed Any upon ye Continent And are here also Most Numerous as Cabinet Makers, Chace & Coach Makers . . . &C." The remark, which speaks to both the quality of workmanship and quantity of workers in Boston, is verified by surviving furniture and documentary evidence. More than 560 furnituremaking craftsmen found employment along the waterfront and winding streets of colonial Boston, more than five times the number in Newport, Rhode Island, the next largest New England community.[3] The Boston artisans were also the most specialized. In addition to joiners, cabinetmakers, turners, and chairmakers, Boston supported such luxury tradesmen as carvers, japanners, upholsterers, chair caners, and looking-glass makers. These workmen collaborated on sophisticated products for the homes of the mercantile aristocracy. Two ambitious pieces of case furniture in the Winterthur collection—a high chest made for Joshua Loring (see No. 160) and desk-and-bookcase owned by Josiah Quincy (see No. 206)—demonstrate the cooperative process. Cabinetmaker John Pimm constructed the case for Loring's chest, a carver fashioned the shells on the drawer fronts, a turner made the drops beneath the skirt, and a japanner (probably Robert Davis or his apprentice Stephen Whiting) gilded the shells and applied the brilliant painted decoration in imitation of oriental lacquer. Quincy's desk, though equally extravagant in its decoration, involved fewer participants: principally, a gifted but unidentified cabinetmaker and carver, John Welch. It did, however, require a key decorative element from another source: the mirrored glass for the doors was imported from England.

Boston had its greatest impact in the upholstery trade. The town supported nearly fifty upholstery shops during the colonial era; no other New England community contained more than one or two, and most had none. Boston upholsterers nearly monopolized the New England market for elegant beds and stuffed seating furniture. The business accounts of one Boston upholsterer, Samuel Grant, document the extent of the trade. From his shop at the Crown and Cushion on Union Street, he produced thousands of chairs not only for affluent customers in Boston but also for shipment to clients in distant locations along the Atlantic coast. His most ornate chairs for export, as well as those shipped by other upholsterers, have recently received careful study by Leigh Keno (see No. 27). Although traditionally attributed to New York or Newport manufacture, these examples have been reassigned to Boston and take their place among the best of Boston colonial furniture.

Like the case furniture owned by Loring and Quincy, Grant's furniture required the work of several specialists. He hired chairmakers and carvers to construct chair frames or bedsteads and cornices. Apparently he upholstered the frames himself, but for beds he turned to a sailmaker for the canvas bottom that supported the mattress; he employed a journeyman to make the mattress, bolster, and pillows; and he relied on seamstresses in his shop to fabricate the rest of the bed hangings.

During the second half of the eighteenth century, Boston's prominent craft position began to recede. Flourishing seaports such as Portsmouth, Newburyport, Salem, and Newport attracted growing numbers of artisans who sought success through local markets as well as the export trade. Inland communities, especially along the Connecticut River, also benefited from prosperous conditions. Clusters of craftsmen working in a similar manner stimulated the development of regional centers of furnituremaking. The appearance of furniture in each area arose from a combination of factors, including craft training, impact of a competitor, influence of a pattern book or imported piece of furniture, and the preferences of a patron. These conditions led to varied interpretations. In Portsmouth, Royal Governor John Wentworth's patronage of a British-trained cabinetmaker during the late 1760s fostered widespread acceptance of London rococo design throughout the town, while residents in the Hartford area embraced a version of Philadelphia design introduced by cabinetmaker Eliphalet Chapin after four years in Pennsylvania.

Whether in Portsmouth or Hartford, Boston or Newport, furniture design in eighteenth-century New England owed its inspiration to British models; the Germanic or Dutch influences found on furniture of the middle colonies were virtually nonexistent. French-inspired characteristics appear on only a small number of Newport items. Colonial tastemakers clearly looked to London for the latest fashions, and these styles reached New England through immigrant craftsmen, imported furniture, and, after midcentury, pattern books. During the 1720s, imported cane chairs with gracefully shaped cabriole legs introduced native artisans in Boston to the new Queen Anne style. By 1729 Grant had sold an upholstered chair with a "New fashion round seat." The next year, he produced a couch with "horsebone feet," the earliest period term for the cabriole leg. In 1732 a Boston japanner recorded the sale of a high chest with scrolled pediment. The curving contour of the round seat, cabriole leg, and pediment document the arrival of the new style; over the next decade it flourished in New England ports. Yet Queen Anne taste did not remain static, particularly in Boston. "Modern" elements of London design were quickly absorbed into the native vocabulary. Chairs with broader proportions, more intricately shaped splats, and small ball-and-claw feet (No. 27) were in production by the late 1730s. At the same time, shaped facades had begun to supplant japanned ornament and veneering in popularity on case furniture. Within a decade the first signs of a new style, termed *Chippendale* or *rococo*, had taken root when craftsmen referred to the sale of chairs with Marlborough (straight) legs. However, the primary elements of the fashion—interlaced strapwork splats, asymmetrical carving, more delicate parts, and squared elements (for example, trapezoidal rather than compass seats)—did not reach New England until after midcentury. The publication of Thomas Chippendale's *Gentleman and Cabinet-Maker's Director* encouraged the international popularity of the English rococo. However, in New England, a less expensive volume of London designs by Robert Manwaring, published in 1765, proved to be a more influential guide for craftsmen.[4] Yet neither design book had the impact of imported furniture. English chairs, in particular, were favored possessions of New England's wealthiest patrons and served as models for local artisans. The splat of virtually every Boston rococo chair known today is based on London precedents. Although the introduction of the Queen Anne and Chippendale styles can be precisely pinpointed, their demise is much more difficult to document; both fashions remained popular into the early nineteenth century. A pedimented high chest made by Brewster Dayton of Stratford, Connecticut, in 1784 (see No. 166) repeats a standard formula of the 1750s. The rural products of the Dunlaps in central New Hampshire display such Queen Anne features as cabriole legs and round feet. And even in the urban environment of Newport, Adam S. Coe built a classic Chippendale sofa as late as 1812 (see No. 98).

*New England Furniture at Winterthur* incorporates an impressive array of new scholarship. Its findings revise and amplify the notable contribution made by Downs some forty-five years ago. The impact of urban communities, especially Boston, as well as the pervasiveness of regionalism attract fresh attention. The importance of the export trade and the role of specialists, particularly the upholsterer, also receive careful consideration. The variety of New England furniture—in form, in origin, and in ornament—is amply demonstrated. Throughout this comprehensive undertaking, the unmistakable imprint of one man, Henry Francis du Pont, shines forth. His love of materials, eye for detail, and interest in the best permeates the pages. Here too one finds du Pont's ultimate goal of furthering knowledge in a topic he considered underappreciated by the sharing of his collections with the public. His words of introduction for Downs's catalogue of 1952 remain equally viable today. "Looking back on it now," he wrote, I am "glad that I have been able to preserve in some degree the evidences of early life in America, and I am gratified to feel that others too may find my collection a source of knowledge and inspiration."

---

Brock Jobe is deputy director for Collections, Conservation, and Interpretation at Winterthur.

[1]  [Alice Winchester], Preface to Joseph Downs, "A Selection of American Furniture," *Antiques* 61, no. 5 (May 1952): 424. Joseph Downs to H. F. du Pont, September 27, 1948, Winterthur Archives. Downs, *American Furniture*, p. xi.

[2]  Charles F. Hummel, "Queen Anne and Chippendale Furniture in the Henry Francis du Pont Winterthur Museum, Part I," *Antiques* 97, no. 6 (June 1970): 896–903; "Part II," *Antiques* 98, no. 6 (December 1970): 900–909; "Part III," *Antiques* 99, no. 1 (January 1971): 98–107.

[3]  Charles M. Andrews, ed., *Some Cursory Remarks Made by James Birket in his Voyage to North America, 1750–1751* (New Haven: Yale University Press, 1916), p. 24. Brock Jobe and Myrna Kaye, *New England Furniture, The Colonial Era: Selections from the Society for the Preservation of New England Antiquities* (Boston: Houghton Mifflin Co., 1984).

[4]  See, for example, the side table made by John Goddard and pictured in *John Brown House Loan Exhibition*, pp. 52–53. On the Boston japanner, see Brock Jobe, "The Boston Furniture Industry, 1720–1740," in *Boston Furniture*, pp. 42, 48. Robert Manwaring, *The Cabinet and Chair-Maker's Real Friend and Companion* (London: Henry Webley, 1765); Morrison H. Heckscher, "English Furniture Pattern Books in Eighteenth-Century America," in Luke Beckerdite, ed., *American Furniture 1994* (Milwaukee, Wis.: Chipstone Fndn., 1994), pp. 193–94.

# Notes to the Catalogue

NEW ENGLAND FURNITURE AT WINTERTHUR IS A RECORD of the museum's holdings from the Queen Anne and Chippendale periods. Intended as a reference and research resource, it is inclusive rather than selective in nature. The objects are arranged in sections of related functions and forms. Within each section, the objects are grouped by shared stylistic features. The order of presentation is an artificial one relying less on chronological progression than on the opportunity for comparison of related forms.

Authorship of discrete sections can be assigned as follows: "Seating Furniture" by Nancy Goyne Evans, couch forms in this section by Nancy E. Richards with Wendy A. Cooper; "Beds" by Nancy E. Richards with Wendy A. Cooper; "Tables" by Nancy E. Richards with Wendy A. Cooper and Clare G. Noyes; "Stands and Fire Screens" by Nancy E. Richards with Clare G. Noyes; "Dressing Tables and High Chests of Drawers" by Nancy Goyne Evans; "Chests of Drawers, Bureau Tables, and Chests-on-Chests" by Nancy Goyne Evans, bureau chests in this section by Nancy E. Richards with Clare G. Noyes; "Desks and Desk-and-Bookcases" by Wendy A. Cooper; "Looking Glasses and Dressing Glasses" by Nancy Goyne Evans; and "Case Studies" by Nancy Goyne Evans and Michael S. Podmaniczky.

Sources referenced more than ten times in the catalogue are given in short-title form throughout. For complete references, see the Short-Title Bibliography.

## Inscriptions or marks

All chalk, pencil, or ink inscriptions, signatures, labels, and pencil or scribe shop marks that appear on the object are faithfully transcribed; illegible inscriptions also are noted. Old index or present catalogue numbers are not included.

## Construction

Specific information on the methods of joinery are included. Directions (left or right) are presumed to be those as seen by the viewer.

## Condition

The present state of the object noting losses, restorations, replacements, and alterations is recorded, including details of upholstering techniques and materials. Finish is recorded under Materials.

## Dimensions

All dimensions are recorded in inches, taken to the nearest sixteenth of an inch; metric equivalents are given in centimeters. In addition to the overall dimensions, other relevant measurements are included for each specific form to permit comparison. For consistency, objects are measured on the left side and across the front. On seating furniture, the seat height is measured to the top edge of the framing member. If the seat rail is covered by upholstery, the measurement is taken on the inside of the framing member. The depth of the seat rail is measured from the front of the front seat rail to the back of the rear seat rail, at the center, beneath the rails. On frame tables, the width and depth of both the top and the frame are given; with round tables and stands, the dimensions of the top are those of the diameter with the grain and across the grain. On case furniture, the width and depth are given for the case's individual units.

## Materials

In most cases, the woods cited in the catalogue have been identified by microscopic analysis. Noted are the few exceptions where removal of a sample of veneer was not possible. The primary wood is listed first. Original secondary woods are included, noting their location. Occasionally a replacement secondary wood also will be identified. Where no location is specified, the interior elements are all of the same kind of wood. Included as a reference are the common and the botanical names for the woods cited in the catalogue:

| | |
|---|---|
| ash | *Fraxinus* sp. |
| bald cypress | *Taxodium* sp. |
| basswood | *Tilia* sp. |
| beech | *Fagus* sp. |
| birch | *Betula* sp. |
| butternut | *Juglans* sp. |
| cedar, Atlantic white | *Chamaecyparis thyoides* |
| cedar, Northern white | *Thuja* sp. |
| cherry | *Prunus* sp. |
| chestnut | *Castanea* sp. |
| elm | *Ulmus* sp. |
| fir | *Abies* sp. |
| hickory | *Carya* sp |
| mahogany | *Swietenia* sp. |
| maple, soft | *Acer* sp. |
| maple, hard | *Acer* sp. |
| oak, red | *Quercus* sp. (Erythrobalanus) |
| oak, white | *Quercus* sp. (Leucobalanus) |
| pine, white | *Pinus* sp. |
| pine, yellow | *Pinus* sp. |
| pine, red | *Pinus* sp. |
| poplar/aspen/cottonwood | *Populus* sp |
| red cedar | *Juniperus* sp. |
| red gum | *Liquidambar* sp. |

| | |
|---|---|
| sabicu or "horseflesh" | *Lysiloma* sp. |
| spruce | *Picea* sp. |
| sycamore | *Platanus* sp. |
| tulip-poplar | *Liriodendron* sp. |
| walnut, American black | *Juglans nigra* |

All entries also include the identification of the current finish and any old finish that can be isolated using enzyme testing. Upholstery descriptions (including place of origin and date) are provided where applicable.

### Exhibitions

References are listed in chronological order.

### Publications

Each publication in which an object has been discussed and (almost) always illustrated is listed chronologically. This section includes exhibition catalogues.

### Provenance

History of ownership is recorded in as much detail as is known, including original and former owners. Where provenance is by tradition rather than documentation, this is noted.

### Accession history

Information on how and when an item entered the museum's collection is given, including identification of dealers.

# The Catalogue

# Seating Furniture

HENRY FRANCIS DU PONT ASSEMBLED the core of his New England Queen Anne and Chippendale seating furniture collection before he opened Winterthur as a public museum. He acquired more than half the chairs and other seating forms represented in this catalogue from the late 1920s through the late 1940s. Dealers were du Pont's principal source for antiques, but he also bought at auction through agents and directly from private individuals, some of them fellow collectors. After Winterthur Museum opened in 1951, du Pont continued to take an active part in the acquisition process, making independent purchases or selecting objects in concert with museum staff and providing the purchase funds. This acquisition method accounts for more than a quarter of the seating furniture described in the following pages. Of the remaining 20 percent, a few chairs were gifts to the museum by independent donors, and the rest were purchased with museum acquisition funds both before and after du Pont's death in 1969.

The Winterthur collection of New England Queen Anne and Chippendale seating furniture is comprehensive. Construction dates range from the late 1720s through the end of the century. Many forms are represented: side chairs and armchairs, low chairs with short legs, children's chairs, roundabout chairs, easy chairs, upholstered armchairs and side chairs, and sofas and couches. Almost two-thirds of the seating furniture consists of standard armchairs and side chairs for adults. Armchairs, including the low forms, make up about 13 percent of this group, a good representation for a relatively uncommon form. Furniture with extensive upholstery accounts for 18.5 percent of the catalogue and includes easy chairs, upholstered-back side chairs and armchairs, and sofa-type seats. The number of upholstered examples is augmented substantially by the addition of chairs with upholstered loose seats and over-upholstered seat frames.

The catalogue incorporates every New England center of chairmaking in the period under discussion: eastern Connecticut, Newport and coastal Rhode Island, Boston and northeastern Massachusetts, and Portsmouth and vicinity. Representation within each region ranges from fair to excellent. Portsmouth and New Hampshire examples form a reasonable 8 percent of the seating catalogue, given the newness of New Hampshire furniture studies and the still limited identification of the early products. The Connecticut seating group is almost twice as large. Rhode Island seating furniture under earlier guidelines would have formed a substantial 20 percent of the seating catalogue; however, new research and thinking about coastal New England chairs has caused many examples formerly attributed to Newport to be reassigned to Boston.

Further augmenting the Boston group are other chairs previously associated with New York City. Thus, Boston area seating furniture forms a substantial 69 percent of the sample, leaving a mere 8 percent for objects still linked with Rhode Island.

Vernacular furniture is, at best, tentatively defined, but for purposes of this study it comprises most of the examples with woven bottoms (rush or splint), or 18 percent of the seating furniture. The body of formal, joined furniture that constitutes the larger segment of the collection is by no means entirely of urban origin. At least ten chairs have a rural or semirural orientation, as identified by the presence of exaggerated or distorted proportions and features. From the standpoint of style, the seating is almost equally divided between Queen Anne and Chippendale patterns. Elements of the William and Mary style are present in some of the vernacular chairs and in a small group of Boston and Portsmouth chairs that introduce features of the new Queen Anne style. Attributes of the Queen Anne and Chippendale styles are mixed in still other examples. Rounded shoulders, slim solid splats, or pad feet may be combined with squared shoulders, broad pierced splats, or claw feet. Many styles made to serve a local market also doubled as trade commodities to other regions of New England, rural and urban.

Forests and fisheries sustained the New England economy in the eighteenth century. Products of the land and sea formed the foundation upon which coastal and near coastal centers of commerce were established, such as Portsmouth, New Hampshire; Boston and northeastern Massachusetts; Newport and Providence, Rhode Island; Norwich and, eventually, Hartford, Connecticut. Gradually, astute merchants expanded the product base by including chairs and cabinetwares produced by a growing community of skilled woodworking craftsmen and by encouraging development of regional and inland markets and trading centers.

As demand increased, furniture craftsmen looked for ways to expand their production. Specialization was one answer, but concentration on a single skill, such as cabinetmaking, turning, carving, or upholstery, was possible only in urban areas of sufficient size to support a division of labor. Standardization of elements that were interchangeable among chair patterns—stiles, rails, front feet, and stretchers—was another way to reduce construction time. Many craftsmen, particularly those in nonurban areas, pursued auxiliary trades and businesses to supplement their income. Some were farmers, landlords, innkeepers, or storekeepers. Others practiced related woodworking skills, laboring at times as house or ship carpenters, coffinmakers, or wheelwrights. Still others became skilled in parallel trades, such as clockmaking and masonry, or served their communities as town officials.

Throughout the eighteenth century, British furniture design was the principal influence that shaped American production. Skilled immigrants, many of them from London, brought the latest urban or provincial patterns and occasionally left telltale evidence of their English training in the construction methods they used. American merchants imported furniture for speculation or personal use through English agents or made direct purchases in London. English design books such as Thomas Chippendale's *Gentleman and Cabinet-Maker's Director* (1762), George Hepplewhite's *Cabinet-Maker and Upholsterer's Guide* (1789), William Ince and John Mayhew's *Universal System of Houshold Furniture* (1762), or Robert Manwaring's *Cabinet and Chair-Maker's Real Friend and Companion* (1765) were also a source for American furnituremakers, exerting greater influence than heretofore suspected. Seven pieces of seating furniture in this catalogue are linked directly or closely with engraved plates in these design books. Other chair patterns of New England origin represent the indirect influence of English design books through furniture produced in other American centers, principally New York and Philadelphia.

Regional domestic influences on New England furniture were equally strong as those of English origin. New York seating furniture had considerable impact on design in Rhode Island

and eastern Connecticut and influenced some work produced in Massachusetts. Philadelphia patterns also have their counterparts in New England, and Philadelphia construction techniques are prominent in chairs produced by Eliphalet Chapin in the Connecticut River valley. Within New England, stylistic exchanges effected by migrating craftsmen or through bonds of marriage or blood relationship sometimes make it difficult to distinguish among vernacular seating from northeastern Massachusetts and southern New Hampshire, chairs made in Newport and eastern Connecticut, and seating furniture produced in Providence and Newport. Even standard regional indicators, such as primary and secondary woods, construction techniques, splat patterns, and the interpretation of individual elements, can be inconclusive in this period of growth and improved transportation and communication.

The New England collection of Queen Anne and Chippendale seating furniture at Winterthur covers a full range of design associated with these style periods, from the square-cornered cabriole leg to the straight Marlborough support, from the solid splat to the pierced banister, from the plainly interpreted chair to the ornamented one. Predominant in the collection are the "bread-and-butter" patterns: the solid-splat yoke-top Queen Anne chairs, the owl's-eye–banister Chippendale chairs, and the later straight-leg cross-slat chairs.

Considered first in the catalogue are chairs produced in northeastern Massachusetts during the late 1720s and early 1730s, a period when Boston solidified its position as the commercial and cultural center of New England. Deriving inspiration from English prototypes, urban craftsmen began to introduce new seating furniture designs in the 1720s that exchanged rectilinear lines for curvilinear ones. The contoured, or "crooked," back, which provided comfort and an aesthetically pleasing profile, replaced the straight, rigid William and Mary–style back support. Simple yoke-shape crest pieces and vase-shape splats became common, and curved "horsebone" legs with squared corners quickly evolved into graceful, rounded cabriole supports. Another important innovation was the introduction of loose, or slip, seats, a less expensive upholstery option than over-the-rail covers. Plain swelled and columnar stretcher turnings took the place of William and Mary–style braces, but the long, modeled, scroll-end arm common at the beginning of the century was retained.

Boston craftsmen refined and integrated the features of the new Queen Anne–style chair during the 1730s; they also introduced the compass, or rounded, seat as an alternative to the rectangular form. Most seats are plain, with only a low arch along the bottom edge of the front and side rails. A few rectangular seats are embellished with sawed S curves and a scallop in the front rail. Bold baroque features dominate the backs of some chairs: pronounced hooplike shoulders; prominent carved and pierced tops; salient swelled and lobed splats. Stain or resin with color, rather than paint, was the common surface finish for this joined furniture. Leather was the popular seat covering, although stout woolens, which were more expensive, were favored in some households.

Early Queen Anne chairs of eastern Connecticut origin are identified by the provincial quality of their features, such as attenuated backs, ornamented front *and* side seat rails, and baluster-turned side stretchers. Even in chairs of exaggerated feature, such as these, craftsmen paid considerable attention to design unification, which they addressed primarily through the repetition of motifs and profiles. New London County was the principal economic and cultural center of the region before the revolutionary war, and furniture produced there influenced production well beyond the county borders.

The shell as an ornamental device came into prominence in Queen Anne chairs of mature design produced from the late 1730s. Examples are either finely ribbed or deeply channeled and have plain or carved-scroll bases; sometimes they are enhanced by pendent ornament. Sweep back posts that conform to the splat profile were an ornamental alternative to the straight posts of standard 1730s design. This change led to the gradual widening of the back to the broad, squared profile of the Chippendale style. Even after the squared back was introduced in New England about midcentury, vestiges of the Queen Anne style sometimes remained, as indicated in chairs with attenuated backs and solid splats.

A mixture of styles is particularly common in vernacular seating furniture that dates after the middle of the century. Some woven-bottom chairs are completely turned; others are joined and turned. The squared and attenuated backs of these chairs may be accented by peaks and projecting tips in the crest or a pierced heart in the splat. Occasionally, pad feet support baluster-turned legs.

The double-loop, or owl's-eye, splat was an early, if not the earliest, design in the new Chippendale style to be introduced in New England in the mid eighteenth century, and it was by far the most popular pierced pattern until after the Revolution. Examples in the Winterthur collection show variety in ornamentation and feature: from plain to carved backs, from claw-foot cabriole legs to Marlborough supports, from over-the-rail upholstery to loose-seat covers. Both urban and nonurban chairmaking is represented, with side chairs the most common form.

In the decades spanning the Revolution, other interlaced-strap and pierced-splat chairs entered the New England furniture market. Boston consumers could choose between chairs constructed with stretcher-framed or stretcherless bases. A range of other options was also available: plain versus carved surfaces; Gothic splats with motifs including trefoils, quatrefoils, and lancets; carved-knee claw-foot cabriole legs or beaded Marlborough supports with or without open leg brackets; carved work accompanied by stipple-, gouge-, or punchwork accents; loose-seat or over-the-rail upholstery. Because leather was practical and moderately priced, it was frequently chosen for chair seats.

Boston and Boston-area chairs without stretchers probably represent, to some degree, a new dimension in consumerism. With several chair parts interchangeable from one pattern to another—legs, back posts, seat frames—and labor and material costs trimmed through elimination of the leg braces, cabinetmakers could produce chairs more quickly and economically. The savings passed on to the consumer likely stimulated trade and encouraged furnituremakers to stockpile small quantities of parts for quick assembly. The practice represented a stage in marketing between "bespoke" work (the construction of chairs from start to finish only upon receipt of an order) and the development of wareroom marketing in the early nineteenth century.

Notable for the simplicity of their designs are chairs of Portsmouth, New Hampshire, origin that are framed with vertical, slot-pierced splats and eastern Massachusetts chairs of pierced cross-banister pattern. The Portsmouth chair was made in substantial numbers from local materials, its popularity based as much on its modest cost as on its stylish yet restrained design. The Massachusetts chairs are somewhat more ornamental; their back posts are molded to complement the front legs, and the horizontal members are modestly carved. Some chairs have serpentine-front or hollow (saddle) seats that echo the curves of the back slats.

Roundabout chairs of New England origin in the Winterthur collection are divided between joined and turned examples. Of particular note in this group of furniture is the use of turned work of uncommon form and the introduction of special features, including extension headpieces. Roundabout chair construction used cherry as a primary wood in both formal and vernacular examples, although black walnut was more common in the upholstered examples. Birch and maple were other choices for woven-bottom chairs. Compass-shape seats added a measure of leg comfort to joined chairs; cushions could be used to soften woven seats. Consumers occasionally purchased a pair of roundabout chairs, and in some households roundabouts were part of a suite of seating furniture. Although householders of the colonial and early federal periods placed the roundabout in many locations throughout the home, an important function of this specialized piece of furniture was as a desk chair.

Easy chairs in the Winterthur collection range in design from an early cabriole-leg chair with horizontal, scrolled arms to the vertical-scroll styles and a late eighteenth-century example supported on Marlborough legs that features the new "saddle cheek" back illustrated in Hepplewhite's *Cabinet-Maker and Upholsterer's Guide* in a plate dated 1787. The easy chair was a joint production of the chairmaker and the upholsterer. The frame was relatively inexpensive because the use of fine wood, such as mahogany or walnut, was confined to the undercarriage. Special features in some frames include leaf-carved knees, flat stretchers, and unusual hooflike rear feet. By contrast, the stuffing materials and finish cover of the seat and upper structure were costly. Most easy chairs were "bespoke" work.

Durable woolen fabrics, such as harateens and moreens, were the most common finish covers on easy chairs made before the revolutionary war. Householders chose red, green, yellow, and occasionally blue. A few needlework covers have survived, but they were uncommon even during the period of their principal fabrication, from the 1740s to the 1770s. Leather was used infrequently on easy chairs until after the war, a period when cotton covers replaced woolen cloth as the principal choice. Some chairs were "Stuft in Canvas," that is, finished with undercovers only to receive slip cases that could be easily removed for washing.

Thomas Chippendale, commenting on stuffed furniture, noted that the upholstered seating furniture of a room was usually "covered with the same stuff as the Window-Curtains."[1] As in England, affluent colonial householders heeded that advice. Probate and other records of individuals of substance list the "chamber," or bedroom, as the principal location for easy chairs in American (and English) homes. The covers are generally similar in type and color to those on other chairs in the room and to the bed and window hangings.

Back stools, or armless chairs with upholstered backs and seats, were uncommon in eighteenth-century New England, as indicated by the few chairs that survive and the paucity of manuscript references to the form. The chair had a long pre-eighteenth-century history in Europe, and there, as in America, use of the form was limited to households of more prosperous members of society. American back stools range in period from William and Mary styles to late Chippendale designs with Marlborough legs. Among Queen Anne and Chippendale examples, consumer options included walnut and mahogany primary construction and seats upholstered loose or over the rails. A few back stools were made in sets; others were framed with short legs and used in bed chambers as seats for dressing. Sometimes householders purchased a low back stool en suite with an easy chair.

The history of the upholstered armchair parallels that of the back stool. It too was an expensive piece of furniture because it required a considerable amount of stuffing material and woven fabric to cover the frame. Pictorial evidence and the number of extant pre-federal examples describe a more extensive use of this seating form in America than the back stool. Householders placed upholstered armchairs in bedrooms, parlors, and dining rooms. The terminology that identifies this form in late eighteenth-century documents is variable. "Lolling chair," a name more common in the federal period, appears in Boston records as early as 1758. The term *French Chairs* is used in Ince and Mayhew's *Universal System of Houshold Furniture* in 1762 and Manwaring's *Cabinet and Chair-Maker's Real Friend and Companion* in 1765.

Long, stuffed seats accommodating one or more people—couches, settees, and sofas—have a history equally long as the chair. The long-seat styles popular in the eighteenth century evolved to recognizable form during the seventeenth century. English furnituremakers introduced the cabriole leg early in the eighteenth century, and high, scrolled, stuffed arms in the French style were probably introduced before 1750. Chippendale included several sofas in this style in the 1762 edition of the *Director*, the plates for which were engraved in 1759. Boston craftsmen soon added flaring rear feet without stretchers in a style duplicating that in a distinctive group of joined chairs produced locally, and Marlborough supports followed.

Couches made in the form of an extended chair with a framed back, or rest, at one end were in limited use in New England from as early as the seventeenth century. Wealth and leisure were implicit in the presence in a household of this form—a "bed" on which to rest fully clothed. A location on the main floor of a dwelling indicates the importance attached to owning a couch. The chair-style long seat kept pace with the dictates of fashion in the chair market during the early eighteenth century. By midcentury the comfort and opulence of fully stuffed, long furniture became the preferred option.

Early references to upholstered settees and sofas in America date to the 1750s. Examples with high, scroll arms were made into the postrevolutionary years and a few even into the early nineteenth century. The high cost of a sofa limited its purchase to a small affluent segment of society. Among identified owners in the late eighteenth century are a colonel, a governor, two signers of the Declaration of Independence, the first president of the United States, and wealthy merchants in Boston, Providence, and Philadelphia. Period documents indicate that some sofas were made en suite with a set of chairs, and others were upholstered to complement the seating in a room. The range of fabrics available for finish covers was similar to that for easy chairs: worsteds, silks, leathers, and cottons in colors of blue, green, red, and yellow.

*NGE*

---

[1] Thomas Chippendale, *The Gentleman and Cabinet-Maker's Director* (1762; reprint 3d ed., New York: Dover Publications, 1966), p. 3.

## 1 ♦ Side chair
Boston, Massachusetts
1728–35

In the early 1720s the popular straight-back (angled, or canted) "Boston chair," which had a leather seat and back panel and a block-and-baluster–turned base, was updated in several ways. Both straight-back chairs, such as this one, and early crook-back examples (see No. 2, fig. 1) had post faces run with moldings that were duplicated in chisel-carved crests. The new contoured-back feature, influenced by contemporary English cane chairs, was representative of a series of design innovations by the growing population of chairmakers in Boston. As a result, consumers could choose from a heterogeneous selection of chairs in which old and new elements were liberally intermixed.[1]

The vase-shape splat, or banister, was introduced to English seating furniture around 1710, although it was almost two decades before the pattern was adopted by American chairmakers. The flared-neck profile of the splat of this chair resembles a Chinese vase. The common sawed pattern (see No. 3), has been modified by the addition of a tall ogee base, probably introduced to simulate the carved wooden pedestals used to display such vases.

The front legs are the most distinctive feature of this chair. Horsebone supports, some with carved Spanish feet and more with squared feet that are continuous with the legs, appeared in the English market around 1700. Samuel Grant, a prosperous Boston upholsterer and importer, first listed "horsebone feet" (meaning legs) in a bill dated November 21, 1730. Although Grant was probably not the first Boston craftsman to employ squared cabriole legs, the date is reasonably close to their introduction in the city. Short, stumpy horsebone legs with Spanish feet appear on a number of Boston easy chairs made in the 1730s. The most common bracing system in chairs with horsebone legs consists of four turned stretchers with the crosspieces

positioned at the back and forward of center. The long baluster turnings in the side stretchers of this chair date stylistically earlier than the columnar form that became increasingly common in the 1730s (see No. 5).[2]

Neither eccentric nor transitional, this chair represents only one of many attempts by Boston craftsmen to stay abreast of the times in the rapidly changing furniture market of the 1720s and 1730s. Although Benno Forman dated this example rather closely to 1730–32 based upon the front legs, the many variants in the market framed with square cabrioles suggest a broader date range.

NGE

---

**Inscriptions or marks:** *Chiseled on inside rear seat rail:* "II".

**Construction:** The molded crest is supported on rectangular tenons at the sawed and molded post tops (pinned) and splat. The inset crest panel is flush with the splat face. The crest back is chamfered only along the curved edges; the crown and base are straight. A rectangular tenon secures the splat in the forward half of the molded stay rail. The splat edges are deeply rounded at the back, where light, vertical plane marks are visible on the broad surface. The stay rail is tenoned into the back posts. The back-post beading and molding terminate in high arches just above seat level; below, the post corners are chamfered in 4" sections. The seat rails are joined to the posts and legs with rectangular tenons (pinned); the rounded top lip is applied with nails and mitered at the front corners. The interior frame is rabbeted to receive a loose seat. Below the rabbet the front rail is heavily tooled in a deep chamfer. The rear feet are shaved to a cant on the forward faces. The front legs, which extend into the front seat corners, are deeply incised around the outside edges to form beads. The inset Spanish feet are carved from solid wood and chamfered at the inside corners from the foot pads up the legs. The side stretchers join the legs with rectangular tenons (pinned); the medial and rear stretchers are round tenoned into the adjacent members.

**Condition:** Both crest-post joints are cracked on the front surfaces through the pins. Some pins are replaced. Both inside front seat corners have sustained wood losses; the pin is exposed at the left joint. Cracks and repairs occur at the front leg extensions. The left rear foot is cracked on the forward outside corner below the side stretcher.

**Dimensions:**

| | | |
|---|---|---|
| H. | 45⁷/₈ in. | 116.5 cm |
| H. (seat) | 17¹/₄ in. | 43.8 cm |
| W. (crest) | 14³/₄ in. | 37.5 cm |
| W. (seat front) | 19 in. | 48.2 cm |
| W. (seat back) | 14⁷/₈ in. | 37.7 cm |
| W. (feet) | 21¹/₈ in. | 51.1 cm |
| D. (seat) | 15¹/₂ in. | 39.3 cm |
| D. (feet) | 19¹/₂ in. | 49.5 cm |

**Materials:** *Microanalysis:* Primary: soft maple group. *Finish:* muddied, medium reddish brown color in resin, probably over light reddish brown stain. *Upholstery:* floral patterned blue silk; France, 1740–60.

**Exhibitions:** "Change and Choice in Early American Decorative Arts," IBM Gallery of Science and Art, New York, December 12, 1989–February 3, 1990.

**Publications:** Forman, *American Seating Furniture*, fig. 170.

**Accession history:** Bequest of H. F. du Pont, 1969. 66.1311

---

1. For a London contoured-back cane chair, see Jobe, *Portsmouth Furniture*, cat. no. 76.

2. Forman, *American Seating Furniture*, p. 286; for easy chairs, see cats. 90–92.

## 2 ◆ Side chair
### Boston, northeastern Massachusetts, or coastal New Hampshire
### 1730–60

The overall design of this chair, an amalgam of elements from the old and new fashions in seating, was one of several patterns first produced in Boston or vicinity in the early 1730s. The chair has a close mate in the Winterthur collection that differs only in the larger size of the center front stretcher turnings (fig. 1).

A prominent feature is the vigorously shaped front rail of the rabbeted seat frame, a holdover, like the turned front legs and carved feet, from the William and Mary style. The same interrupted double-ogee profile appears at the front of a Spanish-foot easy chair once owned by Samuel Franklin of

Boston, a cousin of Benjamin Franklin. No. 1, a contemporary chair with this feature, represents an advance in the design of the base with the introduction of "horsebone legs" and a medial stretcher. Both No. 1 and this chair were made to receive loose, or slip, seats. Rabbeted frames fitted with removable upholstered bottoms were introduced to England from Holland during the reign of William and Mary. The ease and economy with which worn or soiled covers could be replaced made this form popular.[1]

Molded posts were first used in cane chairs produced after 1710 in Boston. The crook back (see fig. 1) was a new feature in leather-back chairs of the 1720s. The broad, carved-yoke crest introduced with the latter form coordinates better with a wide, straight-edge leather back panel than the illustrated narrow, ogee splat; however, the yoke top was

Fig. 1. Side chair, Boston, 1730–60.
Soft maple; H. 42 1/4 in. (107.3 cm),
H. (seat) 17 3/4 in. (45.1 cm),
W. (seat) 18 1/2 in. (47.0 cm),
D. (seat) 14 1/4 in. (36.2 cm).
(Winterthur 66.1303)

Fig. 2. Detail of No. 2, left front foot bottom.

four-piece molding mitered at the front corners and applied with nails. The side and rear stretchers are secured with mortise-and-tenon joints; the front stretcher is round tenoned into the legs. The front feet are cased on the forward and outside faces.

**Condition:** Surfaces are considerably nicked and marred, and there is substantial worm damage. The splat is cracked at the lower right corner. Many seat and stretcher joints are newly pinned. The loose seat is new, although the red morocco cover is aged. The loose-seat frame rests on nailed strips of wood inset within the chair frame but not original to it. The first loose seat was probably made of rush woven with exposed wooden blocks at the corners. The seat probably rested on a single interior ledge at the frame back and recessed ledges inside the front corner blocks.

**Dimensions:**

| | | |
|---|---|---|
| H. | 42 1/4 in. | 107.3 cm |
| H. (seat) | 17 3/4 in. | 45.1 cm |
| W. (crest) | 14 3/8 in. | 36.5 cm |
| W. (seat front) | 18 7/8 in. | 47.9 cm |
| W. (seat back) | 14 1/2 in. | 36.8 cm |
| W. (feet) | 19 5/8 in. | 49.8 cm |
| D. (seat) | 14 in. | 35.5 cm |
| D. (feet) | 18 5/8 in. | 47.3 cm |

**Materials:** *Microanalysis:* Primary: soft maple group. *Finish:* black paint over a reddish brown coat (probably resin with color).

**Accession history:** Bequest of H. F. du Pont, 1969. 66.1305

---

1. The Franklin easy chair is illustrated in Elizabeth Bidwell Bates and Jonathan L. Fairbanks, *American Furniture: 1620 to the Present* (New York: Richard Marek Publishers, 1981), p. 79. Use of the loose seat is discussed in Macquoid and Edwards, *Dictionary*, 3:359.

2. Forman, *American Seating Furniture*, cats. 54, 55, 75. For contour-back leather chairs of both types mentioned, see Jobe and Kaye, *New England Furniture*, nos. 91b, 91c.

an important stylistic advance over the tall crown of many contemporary leather chairs (see No. 1).[2]

This yoke-top chair and its mate were constructed as medium-priced yet stylish seating. The splats are roughly finished on the backs and asymmetrical in the longitudinal halves. The seat rails were carelessly framed, producing angles noticeably askew. The original bottoms probably were made of rush woven around loose-seat frames secured by molded strips nailed to the tops of the seat rails, a less expensive treatment than either leather or fabric covers. The partially turned base is a type common from the beginning of the century, although the rounded front stretcher tips with knife-edge flanges appear to be copied from contemporary leather chairs. The carved feet are pieced on the outside faces (fig. 2), a cheaper construction technique than

working a leg billet of larger dimension to accommodate the flare of the foot.

Chairs of this pattern appear to have been exported from Boston and vicinity along with the area's better-known leather seating and had a substantial impact on a group of chairs produced in Portsmouth, New Hampshire, and possibly in northeastern Massachusetts (see Nos. 17–19).

NGE

---

**Construction:** The carved and molded crest is supported on rectangular tenons at the contoured and molded post tops (pinned) and splat. A rectangular tenon secures the splat in the stay rail. The rear splat face is roughly finished. The stay rail, which is molded along the bottom edge, is tenoned into the back posts. The seat rails are joined to the posts and legs with rectangular tenons (pinned). The rail tops are finished with a shallow, rounded,

## 3 ◆ Side chair
### Probably northeastern Massachusetts
### 1730–70

Furniture historians have long grappled with the thorny problem of establishing guidelines for identifying local patterns in the large number of New England rush-bottom chairs represented by this example. To date no one has succeeded because chairs firmly documented to makers are practically unknown. Chairs similar to this chair have been ascribed through family histories to southern New Hampshire, northeastern and central Massachusetts, and coastal and inland Connecticut. About 1776 Prudence Punderson (1758–84) of Preston, Connecticut, near Norwich, stitched a needlework picture portraying Saint James in which a chair of this type is prominently displayed, further emphasizing the ubiquity and longevity of the pattern (fig. 1). Through the end of the century New England household inventories commonly list painted, rush-bottom vase-back seating.[1]

The basic characteristics of the pattern are turned William and Mary–style bases updated by Queen Anne–type crook backs, simple

**Fig. 1.** Prudence Punderson, "Saint James," Preston, Conn., ca. 1776. Needlework; H. 8 in. (20.3 cm), W. 7 in. (17.7 cm). (Connecticut Historical Society, Hartford)

vase-shape splats, and carved and molded yoke crests. Woven rush seats indicate that the original cost was modest. The crest is a variation of the one in No. 2; here the saddled midsection is narrower and the arched shoulders broader. Chairs with flared-top splats such as this one and as depicted by Punderson are the most common. Broad or narrow ogee-top splats, such as in No. 2, are occasional features. In either type, the base of the splat is much simpler than that illustrated in No. 1.

The greatest variation in chairs of this style occurs in the undercarriage, which is usually turned with bud- or cone-shape elements at the leg tops. The buds are generally small, the cones may be large or small, and the vase turnings beneath them vary in length and diameter. This chair has a bud-type leg.

Two dozen narrow yoke-top chairs from a large group of similar seating furniture have been associated with particular areas by family

or recovery histories. Chairs with bud turnings and slim side stretchers (generally two to a side) and chairs with large leg cones and sawed stretchers at the back or sides are ascribed to Massachusetts, except for an odd chair in each category that has a southern New Hampshire history. Chairs with small leg-top elements that vary from a cone to a bud, along with two turned side stretchers of the pattern illustrated, but with the bottom one being larger, have Connecticut histories. Because the sample is small, the suggested criteria for determining provenance may not stand the test of time; however, they provide a starting point. The attributions are further strengthened by comparing this chair with a companion armchair (No. 4).[2]

*NGE*

**Construction:** The carved and molded crest is supported on rectangular tenons at the sawed and molded post tops (pinned) and splat. A rectangular tenon secures the splat in the molded stay rail. The rear splat surface is roughly chamfered, top and bottom, adjacent to the tenons. The stay rail is tenoned into the back posts. The flattened seat rails (*lists* in period terminology) are rounded on the outside; the front member is terminated by the corner blocks. The rails are joined to the posts and front corner blocks with rectangular tenons. The front legs are round tenoned into the corner blocks; the stretchers are similarly joined to the posts and legs. The rear legs are canted on the forward faces below the side stretchers. The front feet are one piece with the legs.

**Condition:** The splat is repaired at the upper joint; the lower right spur is chipped. The inside face of the right post is sliced off below the stay rail. The top surface of the front stretcher is worn; the lower surface is gouged at the ball turnings. The feet are scuffed.

**Dimensions:**

| | | |
|---|---|---|
| H. | 42 in. | 106.6 cm |
| H. (seat) | 17 3/4 in. | 45.1 cm |
| W. (crest) | 14 1/8 in. | 35.9 cm |
| W. (seat front) | 18 15/16 in. | 48.1 cm |
| W. (seat back) | 13 7/8 in. | 35.2 cm |
| W. (feet) | 19 3/4 in. | 50.2 cm |
| D. (seat) | 14 in. | 35.5 cm |
| D. (feet) | 17 7/8 in. | 45.4 cm |

**Materials:** *Microanalysis:* Primary: poplar. Secondary: ash (stretcher). *Finish:* dark brown paint with colorless resin; colorless resin on seat.

**Provenance:** According to the last private owner, the chair was "brought to Wisconsin from Pennsylvania many years ago" (Laura Barber to H. F. du Pont, March 5, 1930, Winterthur Archives).

**Accession history:** Purchased by H. F. du Pont from Laura Barber, Waukesha, Wis., 1930. Bequest of H. F. du Pont, 1969.
58.1576

1. Homer Eaton Keyes, "A Study in Differences," *Antiques* 22, no. 1 (July 1932): 6–7. For a similar chair with double-spool–turned leg tops attributed to Samuel Gaylord, Jr., of Hadley, Mass., see *Great River*, cat. 123.

2. The sample upon which the regional criteria are based comprises: Massachusetts, bud tip: Peter Benes, *Old-Town and the Waterside* (Newburyport, Mass.: Historical Society of Old Newbury, 1986), cat. 20; Fales, *Furniture of Historic Deerfield*, figs. 52, 53; Katharine Bryant Hagler, *American Queen Anne Furniture, 1720–1755* (Dearborn, Mich.: Henry Ford Museum and Greenfield Village, 1976), p. 6; Keyes, "Study in Differences," fig. 1 right; *American Antiques from Israel Sack Collection*, 10 vols. (Washington, D.C.: Highland House, ca. 1969–), 4:878, 999; 7:1760. Massachusetts, large cone, sawed stretchers: Fales, *Furniture of Historic Deerfield*, figs. 55, 56; Fitzgerald, *Three Centuries*, fig. III-4; Lura Woodside Watkins, "Antiques with a History," *Antiquarian* 7, no. 2, part 1 (September 1926): 38; Kane, *Three Hundred Years*, no. 73; *American Antiques from Sack Collection*, 4:999; Robert W. Skinner, "Americana" (June 16, 1990), lot 79. Connecticut: Jobe and Kaye, *New England Furniture*, no. 92; Kane, *Three Hundred Years*, nos. 75, 76; Keyes, "Study in Differences," fig. 1 left; *New London County Furniture, 1730–1850* ([Litchfield, Conn.: Litchfield Historical Society, 1969]), no. 9; Trent with Nelson, "A Catalogue of New London County Joined Chairs," no. 41; Kevin M. Sweeney, "Furniture and Furniture Making in Mid Eighteenth-Century Wethersfield, Connecticut," *Antiques* 125, no. 5 (May 1984): 1162, fig. 13.

## 4 ◆ Armchair
### Northeastern Massachusetts
### 1730–70

The crook back was first introduced to the Boston furniture market as a variation on the high-crowned leather-covered chair of the 1720s. Block-and-turned legs with short balusters on rings, scroll arms of bell-shape cross section, and Spanish feet had come into fashion at the turn of the century. The balusters below the arms of this chair also derive from turned profiles of circa 1700, although the immediate prototypes are found in crowned, leather armchairs of the 1720s. The profile is not as vigorous as those of 1720s chairs, and the adjacent rings and spools have been rearranged. The front stretchers are also comparable in profile to 1720s and earlier work, although here, as in No. 3, turned stretchers have replaced sawed side braces.

The side stretchers are an adaptation of the front brace, redesigned to fit a shorter space.[1]

Armchairs of this pattern were probably made as companion pieces to side chairs in the style of No. 3. The two have many features in common: stretchers, feet, short leg balusters, bud tips at the seats or arms, and molded, crook backs. Even the long balusters immediately above and below the seat are interrelated. Those in the armchair are attenuated and accompanied by spools and extra rings to span the greater distance between the leg blocks and arms. A rush-seated armchair of close pattern that was illustrated in 1914 by Mary Northend in the parlor of the Abraham Adams house in Newbury reinforces the northeastern Massachusetts origin of these examples.[2]

This armchair may originally have had a rush seat—the common material for chairs of this type. Splint seats were cheaper, but they were also less durable and more destructive to the clothing of the sitter.

*NGE*

**Construction:** The carved and molded crest is supported on rectangular tenons at the sawed and molded post tops and splat (all pinned). A rectangular tenon secures the splat in the molded stay rail, which is tenoned into the back posts. The arms are attached to the back posts with vertical rectangular tenons; the joints appear to be secured by nails inserted from the back, countersunk, and the holes filled with a composition material. The arms are supported on round tenons at the front posts. The back-post molding extends a considerable distance below the seat. The roughly rounded, shaved seat rails are round tenoned into the posts and legs. Similar joints secure the legs and stretchers.

**Condition:** Nail repairs occur at the crest joints; the right arm is spliced at the upper back. The left rear post is considerably gouged on several faces between the seat and the upper side stretcher. The rear legs are pieced out about 2" at the bottom (a 1930 photograph shows casters on the rear legs); the left front foot is repaired on the front face. The front stretcher has some wear, and the grain is raised; the side stretchers are also worn. The splint seat is considerably broken and worn but has been in place a long time, as indicated by striped patterns on the seat rails.

**Dimensions:**

| | | |
|---|---|---|
| H. | 44 1/6 in. | 111.9 cm |
| H. (seat) | 17 3/4 in. | 45.1 cm |
| W. (crest) | 16 5/16 in. | 41.4 cm |
| W. (seat front) | 22 in. | 55.9 cm |
| W. (seat back) | 16 5/8 in. | 42.2 cm |
| W. (arms) | 26 3/8 in. | 67.0 cm |
| W. (feet) | 24 1/16 in. | 61.1 cm |
| D. (seat) | 16 1/4 in. | 41.3 cm |
| D. (feet) | 21 in. | 53.3 cm |

**Materials:** *Microanalysis:* Primary: soft maple group (arms); poplar (front legs). Secondary: ash (seat rail). *Finish:* dark brown paint over reddish brown paint; colorless resin.

**Accession history:** Purchased by H. F. du Pont before February 20, 1930. Bequest of H. F. du Pont, 1969. 59.2385

1. Forman, *American Seating Furniture*, cats. 53–55, 64, 75, 76, 78, 79.

2. Mary H. Northend, *Historic Homes of New England* (Boston: Little, Brown, 1914), facing p. 88 top.

## 5 ◆ Armchair
### Boston, Massachusetts
### 1728–40

A broader splat and crest saddle distinguish the back of this chair from No. 4. The seventeenth-century–style scroll arms are also less vigorous than No. 4 in the outward thrust. The forward supports, turned with large conical tips and well-rounded balusters, represent a profile used in cane- and leather-back chairs of the early eighteenth century. The striking new feature of this chair is the squared pattern of the cabriole legs with conforming feet and incised beading—the "horsebone feet" first identified in Boston records by upholsterer Samuel Grant in November 1730 (see No. 1).[1]

The change in leg design was accompanied by a simpler but equally effective bracing system and two new stretcher profiles. The front stretcher was moved to a medial position, which required the introduction of blocks in the side braces in which to socket the tips. Turned columns adjacent to the blocks and moderately swelled and tipped crosspieces helped to lighten the undercarriage. The new pattern was borrowed from the vocabulary of William and Mary design; there, columns are featured elements in the back posts of cane-, leather-, and banister-back chairs. The medial and rear stretchers are simplifications of the slim, double-baluster turnings common at the sides of early vase-splat chairs (see Nos. 3, 4), although the profile also is present in English formal seating of the early eighteenth century. The rear legs were visually lightened in the new system with the introduction of chamfers in the upper parts. A joined seat frame was used to receive a nailed cover of leather or cloth, adding a measure of luxury to this new-fashioned chair.[2]

NGE

**Construction:** The carved and molded crest is supported on rectangular tenons at the sawed and molded post tops (pinned) and splat. The back surface is flat with modeling at the wing tips and chamfers at the arches, top and bottom. The splat is canted at the edges, front to back, and tenoned into the molded stay rail; the stay rail is tenoned into the back posts. The arms are attached to the back posts with vertical rectangular tenons and supported on round tenons at the front posts, which form continuous units with the legs. The seat rails are joined to the posts and leg blocks with rectangular tenons. The rear legs are chamfered on all corners between the seat and rear stretcher; the feet are canted on the forward faces and chamfered at the front corners. The squared cabriole front legs are incised with beads on the outside edges and up the center; the knees never had brackets. The side stretchers are joined to the legs with vertical rectangular tenons (pinned); the medial and rear stretchers are round tenoned into the adjacent members.

**Condition:** Composition material fills a gouge at the right rear post-crest joint. The splat base is cracked, front and back. The right rear arm joint is repaired from the outside with a large pin and composition material. The top of the left arm scroll is repaired with a large rectangular patch. The right arm support is cracked at the inside base and at the outside surface of the spool and ring. The arm support and medial stretcher joints are reglued. The medial stretcher face is cracked at the left end. The right knee is scraped on the outside surface.

**Dimensions:**

| | | |
|---|---|---|
| H. | 40³/₄ in. | 103.5 cm |
| H. (seat) | 15⁵/₈ in. | 39.7 cm |
| W. (crest) | 17¹/₂ in. | 44.4 cm |
| W. (seat front) | 22⁷/₈ in. | 58.1 cm |
| W. (seat back) | 17³/₄ in. | 45.1 cm |
| W. (arms) | 23¹/₈ in. | 58.7 cm |
| W. (feet) | 23¹/₂ in. | 59.7 cm |
| D. (seat) | 17¹/₈ in. | 43.5 cm |
| D. (feet) | 20⁷/₈ in. | 53.0 cm |

**Materials:** *Microanalysis:* Primary: birch (front leg); cherry (rear leg). *Finish:* medium yellowish brown to reddish brown color in resin. *Upholstery:* modern leather.

**Exhibitions:** "Change and Choice in Early American Decorative Arts," IBM Gallery of Science and Art, New York, December 12, 1989–February 3, 1990.

**Accession history:** Bequest of Dr. and Mrs. Newberry Reynolds, Princeton, 1943. 71.603

1. A cane chair with similar arm supports is illustrated in Forman, *American Seating Furniture*, cat. 56; see p. 286 for Samuel Grant reference.

2. For cane-, leather-, and banister-back chairs with columnar posts, see Forman, *American Seating Furniture*, cat. 53, figs. 152, 153.

## 6 ◆ Armchair
**Boston, Massachusetts**
**1730–40**

This armchair is similar to No. 5 in the scrolled arms, conical-tipped front posts, over-the-rail upholstery, and stretcher system; however, the substitution here of rounded, lathe-turned cabriole legs for sawed, square-edge supports produced a stylish Queen Anne, saddle-crested chair. This change brought about a shift in orientation from rectilinear to curvilinear design. In No. 5 the strong vertical emphasis of the back posts and splat is reinforced by the selection of slim legs squared at the corners, but curved shapes are given prominence in this chair in the rounded leg surfaces and feet, swelled stretchers, post balusters, arm scrolls, and crest and splat shoulders.

Of the many heterogeneous designs available in Boston in the early 1730s, this chair is one of the more outstanding from an aesthetic perspective, particularly in the proportions and profiles of the undercarriage. Samuel Grant, the Boston upholsterer who first wrote of squared "horsebone feet" in November 1730, billed another customer fourteen months later for leather chairs with maple frames and "hor[se] bone round feet"—the turned cabriole style of No. 6.[1]

The use of knee blocks to form smooth transitions between legs and seat frames was uncommon in the early 1730s. The squared-cabriole chairs lack them, although incised beads minimize the abrupt termination of the knees (Nos. 1, 5). The maker of this chair further addressed this problem by modeling the inner knee faces and attaching William and

Mary–style circular bosses. The connection lacks complete unity, however, and the applied turning is purely ornamental; it is also rare. Circular bosses appear on two other Boston chairs, two slate-top dressing tables, and two low stools (one probably of English origin). Use of this ornament in English seating furniture is also confirmed by its appearance on a settee and a variety of chairs dating to the early 1700s, suggesting that a model, albeit an old-fashioned one, was in Boston for imitation.[2]

*NGE*

---

**Construction:** The carved and molded crest is supported on rectangular tenons at the sawed and molded post tops and splat (all pinned). The back edges of the splat are chamfered. A rectangular tenon secures the splat in the molded stay rail (pinned), which is tenoned into the back posts. The arms are attached to the back posts with vertical rectangular tenons at flattened post surfaces and supported on round tenons at the front posts. The front legs and posts are a continuous unit, except for the addition of knee bosses, which are probably glued on. The seat rails are joined to the posts and leg blocks with rectangular tenons. The rear legs are chamfered on all corners between the seat and side stretchers; the feet are canted on the forward faces and lightly chamfered at the front corners. The side stretchers are joined to the legs with vertical rectangular tenons (pinned); the medial and rear stretchers are round tenoned into the adjacent members.

**Condition:** Nail holes along the length of the arms suggest that they were padded at a later date. The seat rails are patched, and many tack holes are on the inside surfaces. The left front foot pad is partially replaced; the discs beneath the pads are worn almost smooth.

**Dimensions:**

| | | |
|---|---|---|
| H. | 43 1/4 in. | 109.8 cm |
| H. (seat) | 18 in. | 45.7 cm |
| W. (crest) | 16 3/4 in. | 42.5 cm |
| W. (seat front) | 23 1/2 in. | 59.7 cm |
| W. (seat back) | 17 1/4 in. | 43.8 cm |
| W. (arms) | 24 3/8 in. | 61.9 cm |
| W. (feet) | 24 3/4 in. | 62.9 cm |
| D. (seat) | 17 in. | 43.2 cm |
| D. (feet) | 21 in. | 53.3 cm |

**Materials:** *Microanalysis:* Primary: soft maple group. *Finish:* black paint over other dark coats; colorless resin. *Upholstery:* modern leather.

**Publications:** Downs, *American Furniture*, fig. 23. Jay E. Cantor, *Winterthur* (New York: Harry N. Abrams, 1985), p. 136.

**Accession history:** Bequest of H. F. du Pont, 1969. 54.509

---

1. Forman, *American Seating Furniture*, p. 286; see also Forman, "Delaware Valley 'Crookt Foot' and Slat-Back Chairs," *Winterthur Portfolio* 15, no. 1 (Spring 1980): 63–64. The existence of many chairs with squared and incised cabriole legs and simplified Queen Anne backs, which appear to have been exported from Boston to eastern Connecticut in considerable numbers, suggests that the style persisted as a cheap alternative to fully modeled legs well after the introduction of the rounded support. Examples once owned by Jonathan Trumbull furnish the Trumbull House in Lebanon, Conn. (Information courtesy of Robert F. Trent.)

2. The chairs with circular bosses are owned by Henry Ford Museum and Greenfield Village, Dearborn, Mich., and SPNEA, Boston; for the dressing tables, see Edith Gaines, "Collectors' Notes," *Antiques* 82, no. 1 (July 1962): 78; 1 stool is privately owned, the other is pictured in the Robert Wemyss Symonds Collection, no. 59.826, DAPC, Visual Resources Collection, Winterthur Library. For knee bosses on English seating furniture, see Hinckley, *Directory*, ills. 3, 4, 5, 8; Herbert Cescinsky and George Leland Hunter, *English and American Furniture* (Garden City, N.Y.: Garden City Publishing Co., 1929), p. 106; Cescinsky, *English Furniture*, 1: figs. 58, 59. A high chest in a transitional William and Mary–Queen Anne style also is embellished with knee bosses; see Kirk, *American Furniture*, fig. 555.

## 7 ◆ **Side chair**
Boston, Massachusetts
1730–65

---

If the painted, vase-back rush-bottom chair was the fashionable, inexpensive option of the early 1730s, the walnut side chair was the last word in sophisticated, contemporary seating furniture. The cost of a chair was about 37s. Development of the pattern can be followed in the accounts of Samuel Grant, Boston upholsterer and merchant, who first described "horsebone feet," or cabriole legs, in November 1730. Reference to "cushion," or loose, seats followed the next October. By January 1732 Grant was selling maple chair frames with horsebone "round" feet and leather cushion seats. Since seat shapes were not specifically noted, they probably were the standard trapezoidal shape. In 1734 Grant first described chair frames with "compass," or rounded, seats, so called because chairmakers laid out the curves of their templates with compasses. The crook back, also a feature of this chair, had been introduced to Boston chairs in the early 1720s. Visual corroboration of the Queen Anne style in Boston around 1730 occurs in John Smibert's 1732 portrait of Mrs. Andrew Oliver and her young son, in which Mrs. Oliver sits in a vase-back chair with a slightly raised crest that is related to the saddled form of this chair.[1]

Grant produced more than two thousand chairs during the 1730s, some in the older, leather-back style but an increasing number in the new-fashioned loose-seat cabriole-leg style with the distinctive saddled crest, vase back, and hollow plinth. The stretchers are slimmer than earlier patterns, and the curved brackets provide a smooth transition between the front knees and rails. The common rail embellishment is a sawed flat arch, but alternatives included a fancy, scalloped front rail (see No. 10) and over-the-rail upholstery (see No. 8). The flat foot, with its deeply cushioned pad, is uncommon. The cabriole-leg chair was exceedingly popular in Massachusetts, and in time craftsmen in eastern Connecticut and Portsmouth, New

Hampshire, and vicinity produced close interpretations (see No. 20, fig. 1).[2]

Benno Forman attributed this chair to the Boston shop of John Leach after comparing it with a Leach family chair made in this style; however, the differences seem greater than the similarities. The feet are not the same, and the Leach chair has a rectangular seat scalloped at the front rail. A survey of Boston-type saddle-crested chairs indicates that compass bottoms with plain, flat-arched rails may have been more common than plain, rectangular seats. The latter are frequently scalloped at the front. Walnut chairs appear to have been more popular with householders than painted maple frames.[3]

NGE

**Inscriptions or marks:** *Chiseled on front seat-rail rabbet:* "V".

**Construction:** The crest is supported on rectangular tenons at the flat-faced, contoured post tops (pinned) and splat. The crest saddle is lightly blocked and rounded at the back above the splat; the lower arches are lightly chamfered. The splat is canted at the edges, front to back, and tenoned into the plinth. The plinth is hollow on the front and side faces, finished with a top bead, and nailed to the back rail. The rear post corners are chamfered from crest to seat. The compass-shape seat is rounded at the top lip and sawed in flat, tooled arches at the bottom. An inside rabbet, broad in the forward part, supports the loose-seat frame. The seat rails are joined to the posts and front leg extensions with rectangular tenons (pinned). The rear legs are chamfered on all corners between the seat and rear stretcher; the feet are canted on the forward faces and chamfered at the front corners. The cabriole front legs have rounded knees and ³/₄" cushioned disks beneath the pad feet; the plain ogee knee brackets are attached with nails. The side stretchers are joined to the legs with vertical rectangular tenons (pinned at rear); the medial and rear stretchers are round tenoned into the adjacent members.

**Condition:** The crest ends have glued and patched age cracks. The left knee brackets are chipped at the upper front corner and defaced at the bottom side edge. The plinth has been glued. The right front foot is slightly chipped around the toe. The lower surface of the medial stretcher is pitted; the rear stretcher is cracked at the left end. The original

loose-seat frame is strengthened with supplemental rails mounted inside the frame. The seat retains its old webbing and linen sacking.

**Dimensions:**

| | | |
|---|---:|---:|
| H. | 40 in. | 101.6 cm |
| H. (seat) | 16⁷/₈ in. | 42.9 cm |
| W. (crest) | 14³/₄ in. | 37.5 cm |
| W. (seat front) | 20¹¹/₁₆ in. | 52.5 cm |
| W. (seat back) | 15 in. | 38.1 cm |
| W. (feet) | 21⁵/₈ in. | 55.0 cm |
| D. (seat) | 17 in. | 43.1 cm |
| D. (feet) | 19⁷/₈ in. | 50.5 cm |

**Materials:** *Microanalysis:* Primary: American black walnut. Secondary: soft maple group (loose-seat frame). *Finish:* medium brown color in resin. *Upholstery:* modern brown leather.

**Exhibitions:** "The Cut of the Cloth," Tri Delta Antiques Show, Dallas, March 28–31, 1985. "Change and Choice in Early American Decorative Arts," IBM Gallery of Science and Art, New York, December 12, 1989–February 3, 1990.

**Publications:** Downs, *American Furniture,* fig. 155. Forman, *American Seating Furniture,* fig. 156.

**Accession history:** Bequest of H. F. du Pont, 1969. 54.523

1. Forman, *American Seating Furniture,* pp. 285–87; Brock Jobe, "The Boston Furniture Industry, 1720–1740," in *Boston Furniture,* pp. 43, 47. Mrs. Oliver was the wife of the future lieutenant governor and secretary of the province of Massachusetts.

2. Jobe, "Boston Furniture Industry," pp. 33, 42; Brock Jobe, "The Boston Upholstery Trade, 1700–1775," in Cooke, *Upholstery,* p. 78. For Connecticut examples, see Trent with Nelson, "A Catalogue of New London County Joined Chairs," nos. 2, 3, 26, fig. 5; for a Portsmouth example, see Jobe, *Portsmouth Furniture,* cat. no. 79.

3. Forman, *American Seating Furniture,* fig. 156; Benno M. Forman to registrar, December 30, 1977, memorandum, folder 54.523, Registration Office, Winterthur; for the Leach family chair, see Jobe, "Boston Furniture Industry," fig. 33. For comparable British chairs, see Kirk, *American Furniture,* figs. 784, 789, 790, 795, 808, 809, 815, 834; Cescinsky, *English Furniture,* 1: figs. 65, 66.

## 8 ◆ Side chair
Boston, Massachusetts
1730–65

The characteristic features of this early Queen Anne–style chair are clear. The splat notches between the baluster and the squared, broadly defined ogee top are shallow and pointed. The columnar turnings of the side stretchers are straight-sided, terminating abruptly at the forward blocks; the bulbous form behind the front legs is short and stocky (fig. 1). Narrow chamfers are present on the forward corners of the rear feet. The plain, conical, medial-stretcher tips are of moderate size. Those in the rear brace are faced with inside rings, a variation of moderate occurrence. The front leg curve is comparable to that of other Boston vase-back chairs, but the pad foot is unusually delicate. The chair is distinguished from standard examples by two more uncommon features: the rounded segments in the lower back legs that replace the usual chamfered blocks and the over-the-rail upholstery of the compass seat.

This chair was constructed with an opening between the back rail and plinth so that the cover is carried completely over the back rail. The principal cover choices in the mid eighteenth century were leather—the most common material—and stout woolen fabrics. One or two rows of ornamental brass nails provided a finish. When leather was selected, a wide border of the same material occasionally provided an extra facing along the rails. Sometimes the leather strip was continued beyond the side rails onto the outer faces of the back posts, as old nail holes in this chair indicate (see fig. 1). The nailing pattern also demonstrates that the modern stuffing is too thick and the domed top surface too high in comparison to the original treatment. Neither a leather strip nor brass nails were used across the back rail where the cover was drawn under the rail and tacked.[1]

Leather was in demand for stuffed and loose seats from the 1730s to the 1770s because it was durable, practical, and less expensive than fabric coverings. Boston upholsterer Theodore Wheelwright's 1750 shop inventory included a "Bundle Black & Red Leather" as well as textiles such as cheney and harateen, two popular worsteds, which he offered in green, blue, and crimson. Moreen was a related worsted cloth, and on his circa 1765 trade card, Boston's Ziphion Thayer itemized crimson moreen, cheneys, and yellow and green harateen along with other upholstery goods. These fabrics were available both plain and ornamented with watered or embossed patterns.[2]

*NGE*

**Construction:** The crest is supported on rectangular tenons at the flat-faced, contoured post tops (pinned) and splat. The crest saddle is lightly blocked and rounded at the back above the splat; the arches are chamfered, top and bottom. The splat is canted at the edges, front to back, and tenoned

**Fig. 1.** Detail, right side undercarriage.

into the plinth. The plinth is hollow on the front and side faces, finished with a narrow top bead, and chamfered at the back edges of the side sweeps. Deeper than is common, it is mortised into the back posts independent of and slightly above the rear seat rail. The rear post corners are chamfered from crest to seat. The thick, compass-shape seat rails are joined to the posts and front leg extensions with rectangular tenons; the frame is squared on the interior. The rear legs are rounded between the seat and stretchers; the feet are canted on the forward faces and chamfered at the front corners. The cabriole front legs have rounded knees and disks beneath pad feet; the plain ogee knee brackets are attached with nails. The ankle backs are flattened above and below the stretcher joints. The side stretchers are joined to the legs with vertical rectangular tenons; the medial and rear stretchers are round tenoned into the adjacent members.

**Condition:** The crest is cracked at the left post joint and repaired. Filled nail holes form a rectangular pattern on the side post faces at seat level. A spline repair was made between the splat and plinth at the back. The disks beneath the pad feet are almost worn away.

**Dimensions:**

| | | |
|---|---|---|
| H. | 39³/4 in. | 101.0 cm |
| H. (seat) | 16 in. | 40.6 cm |
| W. (crest) | 14⁵/8 in. | 37.1 cm |
| W. (seat front) | 21 in. | 52.4 cm |
| W. (seat back) | 15 in. | 38.1 cm |
| W. (feet) | 21⁵/8 in. | 55.0 cm |
| D. (seat) | 17¹¹/16 in. | 44.9 cm |
| D. (feet) | 21¹/8 in. | 53.7 cm |

**Materials:** *Microanalysis:* Primary: soft maple group. *Finish:* medium brown color in resin; refinished. *Upholstery:* green silk damask; Europe, 1740–80.

**Accession history:** Bequest of H. F. du Pont, 1969. 54.543

---

1. I am indebted to Robert F. Trent for reviewing the upholstery process with me.

2. For chairs with original over-the-rail leather covers in place, see Dean A. Fales, Jr., "Hosmer Family Furniture," *Antiques* 83, no. 5 (May 1963): 549, fig. 3; Brock Jobe, "The Boston Upholstery Trade, 1700–1775," in Cooke, *Upholstery*, figs. 57, 60, 66. Andrew Passeri and Robert Trent, "The Wheelwright and Maerklein Inventories and the History of the Upholstery Trade in America, 1750–1900," in *New England Furniture*, pp. 333–39; Florence Montgomery, *Textiles in America, 1650–1870* (New York: W. W. Norton, 1984), pp. 199, 256–57, 300–303; Jobe, "Boston Upholstery Trade," p. 67.

## 9 ◆ Side chair

Boston, Massachusetts, or vicinity
1730–65

---

The lowest-priced fashionable Boston vase-back chair was made of painted maple and had a plain rectangular frame with a loose seat. A step up in quality was the varnished walnut chair of similar description. More expensive options were compass-bottom chairs with loose or fixed stuffed seats (see Nos. 7, 8). This example is one of six walnut, plain, vase-back Boston-style chairs in the Winterthur collection. Many Boston shops made vase-back chairs during the 1730s, each using its own splat template. Although the shapes produced are essentially similar, tracings indicate that subtle variations are present. Variables include the length and curve of the ogee top, the overall length and bottom width of the baluster, and the breadth and proportions

of the base. Although four chairs in the Winterthur group are classified as a set, the splats of only two are an exact match. The remaining chairs originally were parts of two other sets.

Vase-back chairs with cabriole legs and rectangular seat frames made for loose, or "cushion," seats were in the Boston market by the early 1730s; such chairs were identified in several 1732 accounts of Samuel Grant, a prosperous city upholsterer. Grant, like others of his specialty, purchased finished frames from local chairmakers, provided the upholstery, and vended the completed product on his own account.[1]

Stuffing a loose-seat frame in a Queen Anne chair began with tacking two strips of webbing across the length of the loose-frame top and one or two strips across the width to form an interwoven pattern. A coarse sackcloth, generally of linen, was tacked in place over the webbing and usually stuffed with grasses and sometimes a skimmer of horsehair or tow. An undercover tacked to the frame sides held the stuffing in place. Installation of a finish cover, which was secured to the frame bottom, completed the process. Leather, a relatively inexpensive material, was the most popular choice because textiles for upholstery—mainly worsted cheneys, harateens, and moreens—were imported and, therefore, more expensive.[2]

Two other options in vase-back seating were available to Massachusetts consumers. One chair was relatively inexpensive; the other was priced at the top of the consumer market. Economy-minded householders could purchase rush-bottom chairs similar to this chair but modified by a stay rail (lower-back cross rail) to support the splat. The turned base of No. 3 was retained, sometimes modified by the substitution of sawed stretchers at the sides and back. A more expensive choice was the upholstered chair with large ball-and-claw feet. The rarity of that Boston form today suggests it was an uncommon option in the eighteenth century.[3]

NGE

---

Inscriptions or marks: *Chiseled on front seat-rail rabbet:* "II".

Construction: The crest is supported on rectangular tenons at the flat-faced, contoured post tops (pinned) and splat. The crest saddle is lightly blocked at the back and the arches chamfered, top and bottom. The splat is canted at the edges, front to back, and tenoned into the plinth. The plinth is hollow on the front and side faces, finished with a top bead, and nailed to the back rail. The rear post corners are chamfered from crest to seat. The seat rails are slightly rounded at the top lip and sawed in flat, tooled arches at the bottom. An interior rabbet supports the loose seat frame. The rails are joined to the posts and front leg extensions with rectangular tenons (pinned). The rear legs are broadly chamfered on all corners between the seat and the rear stretcher; the feet are canted on the forward faces and broadly chamfered at the front corners. The cabriole front legs have rounded knees and disks beneath pad feet; the plain ogee knee brackets are attached with nails. The side stretchers are joined to the legs with vertical rectangular tenons (pinned at rear); the medial and rear stretchers are round tenoned into the adjacent members.

Condition: Age cracks across the crest-saddle face are filled with composition material. Cracks occur in the left back post, left front leg extension, and left stretcher (inside face). The left outside knee bracket is broken off at the upper rear corner. The medial and right side stretchers are gouged on the bottom surface; the right stretcher is also chipped on the outside face.

Dimensions:

| | | |
|---|---|---|
| H. | 38 7/8 in. | 98.7 cm |
| H. (seat) | 16 15/16 in. | 43.0 cm |
| W. (crest) | 14 5/8 in. | 37.1 cm |
| W. (seat front) | 19 3/4 in. | 50.1 cm |
| W. (seat back) | 15 1/8 in. | 38.4 cm |
| W. (feet) | 21 5/8 in. | 55.0 cm |
| D. (seat) | 16 1/4 in. | 41.3 cm |
| D. (feet) | 20 3/8 in. | 51.7 cm |

Materials: *Microanalysis:* Primary: American black walnut. *Finish:* medium brown color in resin. *Upholstery:* modern brown leather.

Accession history: Bequest of H. F. du Pont, 1969. 64.1008

---

1. The Grant accounts are quoted in Forman, *American Seating Furniture,* pp. 286–87.

2. Brock Jobe, "The Boston Upholstery Trade, 1700–1775," in Cooke, *Upholstery,* pp. 83–85.

3. For a rush-bottom chair, see Randall, *American Furniture,* no. 140; for a ball-and-claw–foot vase-back chair, see National Council of Girl Scouts, *Loan Exhibition of Eighteenth- and Early Nineteenth-Century Furniture and Glass* (New York: By the council, 1929), cat. 571.

## 10 ◆ Side chairs
### Boston, Massachusetts
### 1732–65

Recent scholarship has identified the pivotal role of Boston merchants in establishing the "London style" in joined seating furniture in the American colonies during the second quarter of the eighteenth century. Boston was the acknowledged colonial leader in overseas and coastal commerce by the 1730s, and the shipbuilding trades flourished in the city. In the search for viable commodities to maintain their position of leadership, local merchants turned to the city's chairmaking community, which responded with fashionable, but simplified, adaptations of current London designs in the early "Queen Anne" (late baroque) style (see Nos. 7–9). Boston chairs were soon being marketed successfully along the entire eastern seaboard, from Newfoundland to the West Indies.[1]

Ornamental specimens of the early Queen Anne Boston chair, which is identified by its saddled crest; plain, slim vase splat; and thin, pad-foot cabriole legs, have scalloped frames at the seat front replacing flat-arched rails (see Nos. 7, 9). The scalloped-front chair appears to have been almost as popular with consumers as the plain one. The prevailing scalloped-front form is the side chair, although from the numbers of armchairs known, it is apparent that many customers ordered suites of chairs containing both. Walnut was the preferred wood; maple is present in a one to three ratio. Scalloped-front chairs of the pattern illustrated were popular in eastern Massachusetts; merchants and sea captains also carried scalloped-front chairs to Rhode Island as ordered or venture cargo. Connecticut craftsmen were responsible for making a few adaptations in cherrywood.[2]

These three maple, scalloped-front chairs illustrate eastern Massachusetts Queen Anne design in its subtle variations. The genesis of the Massachusetts scalloped-rail form was the

crook-back chair with squared cabriole legs produced from before 1730 (see Nos. 1, 2). The crests of these three chairs compare in plan and modeling; from the back, the left chair is noticeably blocked at the saddle. The splat of the same chair is longer at the top element and decidedly more boxy. The top curves of the center chair bulge more, and those of the right chair have the character of a shallow bowl because the voids between the baluster and ogee are deeply cut. The splat edges in this chair are also less canted than in the other two. From left to right, the size of the foot pads increases. The transition from ankle to foot is more abrupt in the center chair, and the pad top is flatter. The knees of the right chair are slightly larger than the others.

The back contours of these chairs, which include the posts and splat, are reasonably similar (fig. 1). All side seat rails are sawed with flat arches, but the center and right chairs have an ogee return at the back. The rounded segment in the rear legs of the center chair is considerably less common than the squared segment with chamfered corners of the other two. Three different finishing techniques are evident in the rear feet: (from left to right) a canted forward face with adjacent chamfered corners; a blunt, vertical rear surface with a

slightly rounded forward face; and a canted forward face with squared corners. The side stretchers are the most complex units. All are block-and-columnar–turned but vary in subtle ways. The center and right chairs, which are close in design, have pronounced flares in the columns with deep cuts at the bases. The bulbous element at the front is heavy in the left chair and slimmer with a bulging base in the other two chairs. Immediately behind this element is a large, flaring cone—a profile that is repeated at the narrow end of the column to the left of the neck ring. The cones on the left chair have deep, flat-sided bases; in contrast, those on the center and right chairs are terminated by spreading feet. Almost 150 craftsmen worked in the furniture trades in Boston between 1730 and 1750, many of them involved directly in chairmaking, a fact that helps to explain the variety of detail encountered in the product.[3]

*NGE*

---

**Inscriptions or marks:** (Left) *Notched into the front seat-rail rabbet:* 2 V-shape cuts (representing number 2 in a set); (Center) *Chiseled on front seat rail and front loose-seat rail:* "XII"; (Right) *Chiseled on front seat-rail rabbet:* "I".

**Construction:** (Left) The crest is supported on rectangular tenons at the flat-faced, contoured post

tops (pinned) and splat. The face is cheeked at the ends and hollow at the saddle. The rear surface is blocked at the saddle, rounded at the base, and chamfered at the arches, top and bottom. The splat is canted at the edges, front to back, and tenoned into the plinth. The plinth is hollow on the front and side faces, finished with a top bead, and nailed to the back rail. The rear post corners are chamfered from crest to seat. The seat rails, which are sawed in ogees with a lunette at the front and flat arches at the sides, are tool-marked along the bottom. The top lip is rounded, and an inside rabbet supports the loose-seat frame. The rails are joined to the posts and front leg extensions with rectangular tenons (pinned). The rear legs are chamfered on all corners between the seat and rear stretcher; the feet are canted on the forward faces and broadly chamfered at the front corners. The front pad feet, which have narrow inset platforms behind the ankles, are without bottom disks; the plain ogee knee brackets are attached with nails and tooled on the bottom. The side stretchers are joined to the legs with vertical rectangular tenons (pinned); the medial and rear stretchers are round tenoned into the adjacent members.

(Center) Construction is similar to the left chair, but the back crest surface is not blocked at the saddle nor rounded at the saddle base. The rear legs are round in section between the seat and the rear stretcher. The rear feet flare backward and are squared on all corners. One-inch sections at the lower outside backs have been shaved to flat,

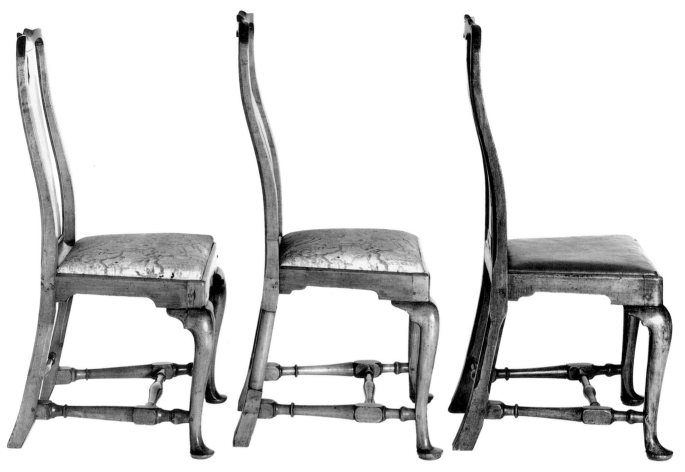

**Fig. 1.** Side profiles.

vertical surfaces. The front pad feet rest on shallow disks.

(Right) Construction is similar to the left chair, but the back crest surface is not blocked at the saddle. The splat edges are only slightly chamfered, front to back. The rear feet are canted on the forward faces, but the front corners are not chamfered. The front pad feet rest on wafer-thin disks.

**Condition:** (Left) The face of the left crest-and-post joint is repaired with a patch; a deep scratch marks the lower right face. A long crack occurs on the right post face at the side rail joint; minor cracks are present in the front leg extensions. The side bracket of the right knee is patched. The loose-seat frame is old but not original.

(Center) The crest is cracked and repaired at the left post joint; the back of the joint is chipped. A crack at the right front knee bracket has been repaired. The side stretcher joints are reinforced with nails at the inside front. The right front ankle is damaged with surface blemishes, and the outside 1/3 of the foot pad has been replaced.

(Right) The overall condition is poor. The crest ends are cracked (the left one through) and repaired at the back with wooden patches continuing onto the posts. Considerable insect damage occurs on the seat rails, lower back posts, right side stretcher, and left front foot. The damage has weakened the left front foot and caused wood losses at the back of the right rear foot. Most joint pins are renewed. The

right rear stretcher block has a sizable loss on the bottom surface. The loose-seat frame is modern.

**Dimensions:**

Left

| | | |
|---|---|---|
| H. | 40 in. | 101.6 cm |
| H. (seat) | 17 in. | 43.1 cm |
| W. (crest) | 14 1/2 in. | 36.9 cm |
| W. (seat front) | 20 1/4 in. | 51.4 cm |
| W. (seat back) | 15 in. | 38.1 cm |
| W. (feet) | 22 in. | 55.9 cm |
| D. (seat) | 16 7/16 in. | 41.7 cm |
| D. (feet) | 21 1/8 in. | 53.7 cm |

Center

| | | |
|---|---|---|
| H. | 42 in. | 106.7 cm |
| H. (seat) | 17 11/16 in. | 44.9 cm |
| W. (crest) | 14 3/8 in. | 36.5 cm |
| W. (seat front) | 19 3/4 in. | 50.2 cm |
| W. (seat back) | 15 in. | 38.1 cm |
| W. (feet) | 22 1/8 in. | 56.2 cm |
| D. (seat) | 16 1/2 in. | 41.9 cm |
| D. (feet) | 21 3/8 in. | 54.3 cm |

Right

| | | |
|---|---|---|
| H. | 41 3/4 in. | 106.1 cm |
| H. (seat) | 17 5/8 in. | 44.7 cm |
| W. (crest) | 14 1/2 in. | 36.9 cm |
| W. (seat front) | 20 1/4 in. | 51.4 cm |
| W. (seat back) | 15 1/8 in. | 38.4 cm |
| W. (feet) | 21 7/8 in. | 55.5 cm |
| D. (seat) | 16 3/8 in. | 41.5 cm |
| D. (feet) | 21 1/2 in. | 54.6 cm |

**Materials:** *Microanalysis:* (Left) Primary: soft maple group. Secondary: white pine group (loose-seat frame). (Center) Primary: soft maple group. Secondary: soft maple group (loose-seat frame). (Right) Primary: soft maple group. *Finish:* (Left, center) orange color in resin; refinished. (Right) mottled honey to light brown color in resin. *Upholstery:* (Left, center) roller-printed cotton with bright blue birds on a patterned beige ground; probably United States, 1830–50. (Right) modern leather.

**Accession history:** (Left, center) Purchased by H. F. du Pont at Israel Sack sale, American Art Association Anderson Galleries, New York, October 15–17, 1931, lots 104, 105. Bequest of H. F. du Pont, 1969. (Right) Bequest of H. F. du Pont, 1969. 59.838, 59.837, 64.997

1. Keno, Freund, and Miller, "Very Pink of the Mode," pp. 266–306.

2. For scalloped-front armchairs, see Randall, *American Furniture*, no. 138; Katharine Bryant Hagler, *American Queen Anne Furniture, 1720–1775* (Dearborn, Mich.: Henry Ford Museum and Greenfield Village, 1976), p. 16. Keno, Freund, and Miller, "Very Pink of the Mode," p. 267.

3. Keno, Freund, and Miller, "Very Pink of the Mode," p. 269.

## 11 ♦ Armchair
### Northeastern Massachusetts
### 1732–65

Low chairs with arms are rare. Although the seat breadth of this chair is less than average for an armchair, the side-rail design indicates that the chair has always had arms. The side rails are rounded along the top lip, as is the front rail, except immediately adjacent to the arm posts where the lip is squared for about one-quarter inch on either side of the posts (fig. 1). A related loose-seat walnut example has several variant features that serve to illuminate the range: a flat-arched front rail, rounded modeling in place of angular contours in the arms, squared-base arm supports, and slimmer braces supporting the legs.[1]

Except in seat height, this chair is closely related to Massachusetts plain and scalloped-rail maple and walnut armchairs of standard height. Of particular note for comparative purposes are the splat, front rail, leg, and stretcher profiles (see Nos. 7, 10 left). Two standard-height side chairs with similar splats, one with a shaped front rail, have traditions of family ownership in the Boston area. A shaped front rail of similar curve is seen occasionally in English seating.[2]

*NGE*

**Construction:** The crest is supported on rectangular tenons at the flat-faced, contoured post tops (pinned) and splat. The face is cheeked at the arches; the rear surface is slightly blocked at the center saddle, rounded at the saddle top, and chamfered at the arches. The splat is canted at the edges, front to back, and tenoned into the plinth. The plinth is hollow on the front and side faces, finished with a top bead, and nailed to the back rail. The rear post corners are chamfered from crest to seat. The arms are attached to the back posts with vertical rectangular tenons secured at the outside with wooden pins and on the inside possibly with metal sprigs. The arms are supported on rectangular

tenons at the front (pinned). The posts are rabbeted into the side seat rails, each joint secured from the outside with a countersunk screw and the hole filled with a wooden plug. Two additional screws secure each support from the inside rail surfaces. The seat rails, which are sawed in ogees with a lunette at the front and flat arches with ogee returns at the sides, have tool marks along the bottom. The top lip of the rails is rounded, and an inside rabbet supports the loose-seat frame. The rails are joined to the posts and front leg extensions with rectangular tenons (pinned, except the back rail). The rear legs are chamfered on all corners between the seat and rear stretcher; the

feet are canted on the forward faces and lightly chamfered at the front corners. The flattened front pad feet with inset rims around the backs were possibly once supported on shallow disks. The ogee-shape knee brackets are tooled on the bottoms and attached with nails. The side stretchers are joined to the legs with vertical rectangular tenons (pinned); the medial and rear stretchers are round tenoned into the adjacent members.

**Condition:** The left arm scroll is broken and repaired with a spline at the break and a large pin inserted from the forward face. The left seat rail is

**Fig. 1.** Detail, left seat rail and arm-support base.

split. The inside front seat corners are braced with modern diagonal struts held by screws; there is no evidence of original corner blocks. The undersurface of the medial stretcher is gouged. The loose-seat frame is modern.

**Dimensions:**

| | | |
|---|---|---|
| H. | 38 in. | 96.5 cm |
| H. (seat) | 12³/₄ in. | 32.4 cm |
| W. (crest) | 17¹/₈ in. | 43.5 cm |
| W. (seat front) | 21¹/₁₆ in. | 53.5 cm |
| W. (seat back) | 17¹/₂ in. | 44.5 cm |
| W. (arms) | 27⁷/₈ in. | 70.8 cm |
| W. (feet) | 22³/₈ in. | 56.8 cm |
| D. (seat) | 17⁵/₁₆ in. | 43.8 cm |
| D. (feet) | 20 in. | 50.8 cm |

**Materials:** *Microanalysis:* Primary: American black walnut. Secondary: white oak group (loose-seat frame). *Finish:* medium light brown to medium brown color in resin. *Upholstery:* coarsely woven block-printed cotton in red and black on a beige ground; France, 1770–90.

**Publications:** Downs, *American Furniture*, fig. 22. Marshall B. Davidson, ed., *The American Heritage History of Colonial Antiques* ([New York]: American Heritage Publishing Co., [1967]), fig. 168. Bishop, *Centuries and Styles of the American Chair*, fig. 77. Kirk, *American Chairs*, fig. 100. Kirk, *American Furniture*, fig. 792.

**Accession history:** Purchased by H. F. du Pont from King Hooper Mansion, Marblehead, Mass., 1933. Bequest of H. F. du Pont, 1969. 58.2594

---

1. The other low, loose-seat walnut armchair is illustrated in *American Antiques from Israel Sack Collection*, 10 vols. (Washington, D.C.: Highland House, ca. 1969–), 1:138.

2. For standard-height Massachusetts armchairs of similar design, see Randall, *American Furniture*, no. 138; *American Antiques from Sack Collection*, 1:101; David Stockwell advertisement and George E. Schoellkopf advertisement, *Antiques* 94, no. 2 (August 1968): 125; and 111, no. 6 (June 1977): 1139. For related side chairs with Massachusetts family histories, see Kirk, *American Chairs*, fig. 99; Kane, *Three Hundred Years*, no. 53. For an English shaped-skirt example, see Macquoid and Edwards, *Dictionary*, 1:257, fig. 94.

## 12 ◆ Side chair
Northeastern Massachusetts
1730–65

---

This design, which comprises an eclectic selection of elements present on early eighteenth-century Boston chairs, is an unusual, possibly unique, pattern. The splat is similar to that in No. 6. Both chairs also have curved backs, although this example is updated with the introduction of a new, uncarved crest and back posts with flattened surfaces. The curved line of the fashionable contoured back continues uninterrupted to the feet, which are canted on the forward surfaces, as is common, and lightly chamfered on all four corners. The corner chamfering of the rear foot is a subtle feature that came into use in formal Boston and regional seating following the introduction of the contoured back, although when present it is usually confined to the forward corners of the feet (see No. 9). The front stretcher tips,

turned with inner rings and disks, provide a second link with No. 6 and with the more advanced interpretations of the early Queen Anne Boston chair (Nos. 8, 10, 11), which have similar elements in the rear stretcher.

The rectilinear qualities of this chair are reinforced by the sawed, rectangular stretchers, a characteristic found in leather seating furniture. Influences from leather, cane, and banister-back chairs are combined in the front turnings. Tripartite stretchers are common in Boston chairs from the early eighteenth century, but the bold interpretation on this chair, accented by large, conical tips, derives more immediately from the leather chair with a crook back. Block-and-turned legs with short balusters supported on disks also date from the early 1700s, but baluster-shape *feet* appear as early as the late 1600s on low-back chairs upholstered with leather, turkey work, or serge. The baluster turnings on this chair are compressed versions of those in No. 2. The rush seat emphasizes the utilitarian function intended for this chair, although the choice of material did not preclude the addition of a cushion or pillow.[1]

The nomenclature and function of chairs with low seats have been debated for years. *Slipper chair* has been a popular name since the late nineteenth century, although the period term is *low chair*. Samuel Grant, a Boston upholsterer, sold a "Low chair horse bone feet" in January 1732 en suite with an easy chair. Both were popular eighteenth-century seating forms used in the bedchambers of the affluent, a custom transmitted from England.[2]

The term *low chair* continued in common use throughout the eighteenth century, as demonstrated in household inventories and craftsmen's shop accounts; however, references to low chairs are absent from mid eighteenth-century English design books. Instead these volumes illustrate designs for "Dressing Chairs" and "Dressing Stools," and the names are often prefaced by the adjective "Ladys." Although there is no indication that these seats were framed with any but standard-height legs, making them suitable for use at a dressing table, it seems reasonable to speculate that in practice some were reduced in height between the floor and the seat to produce low chairs. As such, the seats would have been at a convenient level for the actual task of clothing the body.[3]

NGE

---

**Construction:** The crest is supported on rectangular tenons at the flat-faced, contoured post tops (pinned) and splat. The face is cheeked; the back is slightly blocked at the center saddle, which has a chamfered base. The splat face is flush with the crest but inset slightly at the mortise-and-tenon joint at the stay rail. The splat is canted at the edges, front to back. The ogee-and-bead–molded stay rail is tenoned into the back posts. The back-post corners are square from crest to feet; the feet are chamfered on all four corners and canted on the forward faces. The bladelike seat rails tenon into the back posts; the front member is terminated by the corner blocks. The turned front legs and stretchers are round tenoned into the adjacent members. The side and rear stretchers are joined to the legs with rectangular tenons (pinned).

**Condition:** The upper right splat tip is broken and repaired; the lower right tip is cracked. The rush seat was replaced in the twentieth century.

**Dimensions:**

| | | |
|---|---|---|
| H. | 35 1/2 in. | 90.2 cm |
| H. (seat) | 12 1/16 in. | 30.6 cm |
| W. (crest) | 15 1/8 in. | 38.4 cm |
| W. (seat front) | 20 in. | 50.8 cm |
| W. (seat back) | 15 1/4 in. | 38.7 cm |
| W. (feet) | 20 1/16 in. | 50.9 cm |
| D. (seat) | 16 1/8 in. | 40.9 cm |
| D. (feet) | 19 1/8 in. | 48.5 cm |

**Materials:** *Microanalysis:* Primary: soft maple group. *Finish:* light brown color in resin.

**Accession history:** Purchased by H. F. du Pont from Harry Arons, Ansonia, Conn., 1963. Bequest of H. F. du Pont, 1969.
63.92

---

1. Forman, *American Seating Furniture*, cats. 45–47, 54–56, 63–65, 78–81, fig. 153.

2. Forman, *American Seating Furniture*, p. 360.

3. For use of the term *low chair*, see John and Thomas Gaines account book, 1707–60, Downs collection; William Barker account books, vol. 1 (1750–72) and vol. 2 (1753–66), Rhode Island Historical Society, Providence; estate of Andrew Oliver, "Sale of Sundry Effects at Auction," 1774, Hutchinson-Oliver papers, Massachusetts Historical Society, Boston; George Macy (1776), Dinah Jenkins (1788), Zebulon Butler (1790), Benjamin Coffin (1794), and Nathaniel Folger (1800) estate inventories, Registry of Probate, Nantucket Co., Mass., probate record books 3, 4. William Ince and John Mayhew, *The Universal System of Houshold Furniture* (1762; reprint, Chicago: Quadrangle Books, 1960), pls. 34, 35; Robert Manwaring, *The Cabinet and Chair-Maker's Real Friend and Companion* (London: Henry Webley, 1765), pls. 16–18. Robert Manwaring and others, *The Chair-Maker's Guide* (London: Robert Sayer, 1766), pls. 11, 30; [George] Hepplewhite, *The Cabinet-Maker and Upholsterer's Guide* (1794; reprint 3d ed., New York: Dover Publications, 1969), pl. 17.

## 13 ◆ Armchair and side chair
Boston, Massachusetts
1735–45

Formal American Queen Anne–style chairs
such as these with baroque, hooplike shoulders
in the crests and upper posts, have long been
associated with Newport (see No. 14). In most
examples the legs are braced by flat stretchers;
the straight-sided back splats are contoured
(spooned) in profile. The walnut-veneered
splats are further ornamented by a narrow
band of stringing, composed of one dark string
flanked by two light strings, adjacent to an
outer, broad cross-banded border. Richly
veneered furniture became popular in affluent
Boston society during the 1720s. Similar
ornament was used to embellish expensive,
high-style case furniture of the William and
Mary style. Most seats in chairs of this type
are upholstered over the rails, and the legs
have carved knees.[1]

The straight splat is rare in American
chairmaking and relatively uncommon in
English work. The pattern was introduced to
the English furniture market during the first or
second decade of the eighteenth century and
was constructed in Boston by the early 1730s.
The transfer likely occurred through the
importation of fashionable English chairs or,
possibly, through the arrival of an immigrant
English craftsman.

The English version usually has a curved
profile—the "bended back" of early eighteenth-
century records—and many such splats are
combined with a plain yoke crest, rather than
hoop shoulders. Development of the bended
back appears to have taken place in China.
Some Chinese chairs probably were imported
directly to Europe during the late seventeenth
century, since both the Dutch and Portuguese
had established an extensive network of
Eastern contacts.[2]

Some English contour-back chairs with
straight-sided splats are close imitations of the

oriental models. The designs of a few chairs
are even augmented by baroque-inspired
hoop shoulders, which were the prototypes
for the Boston chair backs. The flat stretchers
derive from a slightly more advanced English
design—the contour-back chair with a fancy
vase-shape splat. Many such chairs are
upholstered over the rails; in some cases
the tacking line is arched at the knee tops,
as on the side chair. The deeply carved knees
of the two chairs are more characteristic of
contemporary, high-style English work than
American carved examples, suggesting that the
ornamental work was executed by a carver of
English background or one knowledgeable in
English practice (figs. 1, 2).[3]

The chairs appear to be products of the
same shop. The proportional relationships
are similar, although in actual dimensions the
armchair is broader, deeper, and taller overall,
while the side chair is characteristically taller
through the seat and legs. Other features are
comparable: back contours, splat veneers,

carved legs, and side and rear stretchers. The fancy, medial stretchers of both chairs are replacements; the profile should correspond with that of No. 14. The arms of the larger chair are ornamented with unusual, carved beads extending from the inside surfaces at the arm-and-back–post joints to tiny, scrolled terminals at the outside top surfaces (fig. 3).[4]

NGE

**Construction:** (Armchair) The crest, of pronounced lateral curve, is supported on a horizontal rectangular tenon at the splat; the crest ends are joined to the post tops at vertical connections within the arches. The rear surface is rounded at the saddle base and arched ends, the surface continuing into the loops formed with the posts. The splat edges are canted, front to back, the bevel running out in points at plinth level. The splat face is veneered. The central figured panel is formed of two vertical pieces of matched wood. The string border comprises two light and a centered dark string; the broad, outer, cross-banded border is mitered at the four corners. The splat base is seated in a deep rabbet in the back face of the rear seat rail and nailed twice. The hollow, beaded-top plinth, which is nailed to the rear seat rail, is a three-sided shell removable for upholstery purposes. The deeply contoured back posts are chamfered at the rear corners from crest to seat. The arms are butted against the back posts to form right-angle rabbets pinned or nailed from the outside back and pinned again from the inside front arm surfaces. Small carved beads beginning at the inside lower back corners of the arms arch across the joint tops and swing forward 3 1/4" along the outside edges, terminating in tiny scrolls. The arms are supported on rectangular tenons at the front posts (pinned, both faces). The posts are rabbeted into the side seat rails and secured with pins and two or three countersunk screws in plugged holes. The seat rails are joined to the posts and front leg extensions with rectangular tenons. The rear legs are chamfered on all corners between the seat and side stretchers. The feet are canted on the forward faces and chamfered at the front corners. The high-relief–carved front knee brackets are applied, the vertical joints partially rounding with the scrolls. The flat side stretchers are joined to the legs with vertical rectangular tenons; the front legs are flattened at the joints. The medial stretcher is rabbeted into the side braces and nailed. The rear stretcher is round tenoned into the back legs.

(Side chair) The back construction and contour, seat-rail construction, lower back-post features, and knee-bracket design are the same as that of the armchair, except that small blocks are applied to the bottoms of the front and side seat rails at the knees to form flat arches. The side stretcher joints are similar; horizontal rectangular tenons secure the medial stretcher joints (pinned).

**Condition:** (Armchair) The crest-splat joint is broken out at the front and the piece reglued. The left crest-post joint is repaired, front and back; the right joint is repaired at the back. The splat face is defaced and cracked near the bottom; the veneer has been reglued at the lower left. The rabbet joint at the rear rail is repaired. The plinth face has been reworked, almost obliterating the top front bead.

The inside rear corner of the left arm is broken out and reglued; the inside forward corner of the right arm support is replaced at seat level. Long vertical repairs mark the forward outside corners of the back posts at seat level. The rear seat rail is reinforced with a screw-held block across the entire inside width; plugged screws reinforce the rear seat rail and plinth joint. The top 1/2" of each side rail is renewed. Small rail blocks, which probably once flanked the front knees, are missing. The medial stretcher was replaced about the late nineteenth century and is incorrect in profile; it is attached with cut nails (the chair probably once had a curved crosspiece of the pattern shown in No. 14).

(Side chair) The crest and post joints are cracked and repaired with nails; a small new piece of wood is set into the back of the right joint. The back surfaces of the splat and rear seat rail are roughened and somewhat defaced. The splat is split above the seat rail, and sections of cross-banded veneer have been replaced. The plinth is cracked at the right end. The right arch return of the front seat rail is restored. Evidence of an earlier pattern of decorative nails occurs on the front and side faces of the back posts adjacent to the present cover. A large, broken triangular piece has been reattached to the left front foot; the bottom disks of both feet are worn. The medial stretcher, a replacement, may be an old part from another chair; its surface color and texture differ substantially from that of the side stretchers (the chair probably once had a curved crosspiece of the pattern shown in No. 14). The joints are repaired with nails and new pieces of wood.

**Dimensions:**

Armchair

| | | |
|---|---|---|
| H. | 43 1/2 in. | 110.5 cm |
| H. (seat) | 17 in. | 43.1 cm |
| W. (crest | 16 3/4 in. | 42.5 cm |
| W. (seat front) | 23 in. | 58.4 cm |
| W. (seat back) | 17 in. | 43.1 cm |
| W. (arms) | 28 3/8 in. | 72.1 cm |
| W. (feet) | 24 3/8 in. | 61.9 cm |
| D. (seat) | 18 3/8 in. | 46.7 cm |
| D. (feet) | 23 1/2 in. | 59.7 cm |

Side chair

| | | |
|---|---|---|
| H. | 40 1/4 in. | 102.2 cm |
| H. (seat) | 18 1/2 in. | 47.0 cm |
| W. (crest | 14 1/8 in. | 35.9 cm |
| W. (seat front) | 20 in. | 50.8 cm |
| W. (seat back) | 14 1/2 in. | 36.8 cm |
| W. (feet) | 21 1/4 in. | 54.0 cm |
| D. (seat) | 16 in. | 40.6 cm |
| D. (feet) | 20 7/8 in. | 53.0 cm |

**Materials:** *Microanalysis:* (Armchair) Primary: American black walnut. Secondary: soft maple group (seat rails, splat). (Side chair) Primary: American black walnut. Secondary: soft maple group (front and rear seat rails); mahogany (replaced medial stretcher); white pine group (splat). *Finish:* (Armchair) variegated medium dark, yellowish brown color in resin; (Side chair) medium yellowish brown color in resin. *Upholstery:* (Armchair) green silk with gold and beige flowers in a compound weave; Europe, 1740–80; (Side chair) modern leather.

**Publications:** (Armchair) Kirk, *American Chairs,* fig. 154. (Side chair) Bishop, *Centuries and Styles of*

**Fig. 1.** Detail of side chair, right knee.

**Fig. 2.** Detail of armchair, right knee.

**Fig. 3.** Detail of armchair, right arm bead.

the American Chair, fig. 86. Fitzgerald, *Three Centuries*, fig. III-36.

**Provenance:** (Armchair) The armchair is said to have been owned originally by Capt. John Holland (b. 1758) and his wife Sarah May and to have descended in either the Holland or the Beal families of Boston and Rhode Island. Ex coll.: Rev. James Holland Beal.

**Accession history:** (Armchair) Museum purchase from Israel Sack, Inc., New York, 1959, funds gift of H. F. du Pont. (Side chair) Bequest of H. F. du Pont, 1969.
59.69, 58.2221

1. Ulysses G. Dietz, "The Cecil Bedroom Chairs: A Problem in Attribution (Newport and Beyond)" (typescript, 1978, Registration Office, Winterthur); see also *John Brown House Loan Exhibition*, cat. 2; Katharine Bryant Hagler, *American Queen Anne Furniture, 1720–1775* (Dearborn, Mich.: Henry Ford Museum and Greenfield Village, 1976), p. 27, bottom. Keno, Freund, and Miller, "Very Pink of the Mode," pp. 266–306, esp. p. 276.

2. Robert W. Symonds, "The Chair with the 'Bended Back,'" *Antique Collector* (July/August 1951): 155–61; Nicholas Grindley, *The Bended-Back Chair* (London: Barling, 1990); Robert C. Smith, "China, Japan, and the Anglo-American Chair," *Antiques* 96, no. 4 (October 1969): 552–58; Robert Hatfield Ellsworth, *Chinese Furniture: Hardwood Examples of the Ming and Early Ch'ing Dynasties* (New York: Random House, 1971), pls. 2, 23, 25, figs. 10, 11, cats. 3–5, 8–10, 14–20, 23; Wang Shixiang, *Classic Chinese Furniture* (London: Han-Shan Tang, 1986), pls. 37, 38, 45, 46, 48–51, 54–56. Also of significance was the enormous Dutch trade in blue and white porcelain and lacquerware, objects with surfaces that were frequently ornamented with scenes of oriental life and depictions of household furnishings suitable for copying; see Reinier Baarsen, "The Court Style in Holland," in Baarsen et al., *Courts and Colonies*, pp. 15, 17, 18.

3. Cescinsky, *English Furniture*, 1:52–55; Kirk, *American Furniture*, pp. 240–41; Macquoid and Edwards, *Dictionary*, 1:253–56; Symonds, "Chair with the 'Bended Back,'" pp. 155–56; Robert Wemyss Symonds Collection, nos. 59.463, 59.464, 59.549, DAPC, Visual Resources Collection, Winterthur Library.

4. A similar armchair that appears to be of the same set is in the Henry Ford Museum and is illustrated in Hagler, *American Queen Anne Furniture*, p. 27, bottom; the same chair was advertised by Jess Pavey of Birmingham, Mich., without upholstery, exposing the seat frame with the small rail blocks intact; see Jess Pavey advertisement, *Antiques* 76, no. 5 (November 1959): 371. The presence of small rail blocks on both the Henry Ford Museum armchair and the Winterthur side chair suggests strongly that the Winterthur armchair originally had rail blocks flanking the front knees. An old photograph of the armchair covered with "needlepoint" upholstery arched at the knee tops and extending over small, flanking rail blocks reinforces that theory; see John T. Kirk, *Early American Furniture* (1970; reprint, New York: Alfred A. Knopf, 1981), fig. 111. Apparently, the armchairs were once together because the Henry Ford Museum chair has the same incorrect medial stretcher replacement as the Winterthur armchair, and it has lost the veneer from the front surface of the splat.

## 14 ◆ Side chair
### Boston, Massachusetts
### 1735–50

Stylistically, this side chair dates later than No. 13 right because of the introduction of a vase-shape splat. The severity of the earlier design has been relieved further by a compass seat—a horseshoe shape that became fashionable in the 1730s. The outline of the seat is repeated in the flat stretchers. Like No. 13 right, chairs of this pattern with hoop shoulders long have been ascribed to Newport; they can now be assigned to Boston with certainty.[1]

Examples of the vase-back chair with hoop shoulders are uncommon but exceed in number those with straight-sided splats. Armchairs are conspicuously absent from the vase-back group. Compass seats, beaded scrolls at the knees, and flat stretchers further identify this pattern variation. Flat stretchers are specifically identified in the Boston accounts of Samuel Grant from 1742 and later, strengthening a Boston provenance for the chairs and suggesting a moderate date range for the use of this feature. Variation occurs in the front seat rail and knee curve. The three rail patterns are: a flat arch, as illustrated; a central astragal flanked by long oxbows; and a small, centered astragal flanked by short ogees ending in cusped C curves. The latter style is accompanied by long, flat knees of a type more common in English than American work. English hoop-crested chairs updated with vase-shape splats are only slightly more common than American examples; most are stretcherless or have turned braces.[2]

The cabriole leg, like the bended back, appears in Chinese furniture, particularly in low tables, stools, stands, and beds, some datable to the fifteenth century. The curved leg generally is terminated at the bottom by a small scroll or an angular or rounded pad. Viewed in profile, some of the rounded Chinese pads are surprisingly like the front feet of this chair. In Western cabinetwork, however, the more immediate inspiration for the leg curve appears to have been the popular, baroque S scroll used in architecture and furnishings throughout most of the seventeenth century. This style is rooted in classical antiquity, and the curved figure likely derived from an animal leg. Designs for baroque tables with ponderous, sometimes fantastic S-shape supports produced in Amsterdam as early as 1655 were still fashionable on the Continent and in England at the turn of the century. Daniel Marot, a French Huguenot in the service of William III, Prince of Orange, published a comparable design about 1700. His supports for seating furniture are simpler. Some are tight S scrolls; others bulge at the knees with moderately straight supports below, not unlike the line formed by the hoop shoulders and posts shown here (see No. 94, fig. 1). Some bulging knees are lined with a bead and scroll of the type illustrated, possibly marking the introduction of such ornament in seating furniture. After 1710 the exaggerated knee was gradually modified to the popular cabriole form. Walnut chairs with squared cabriole legs ordered in 1714 by Edward Dryden for Canons Ashby in Northamptonshire, England, from Thomas Phill, upholsterer of London, were described as "frames of ye newest fashion."[3]

Both the flared-neck splat (see Nos. 3, 4, 6) and the ogee-top figure, seen here, are derived from the profiles of Chinese vases. Comparable shapes appeared in Continental and English tin-glazed earthenwares beginning in the late seventeenth century.

NGE

---

**Inscriptions or marks:** *Chiseled on front seat-rail rabbet and front loose-seat rail:* "II".

**Construction:** The crest, with a pronounced lateral curve, is supported on a horizontal rectangular tenon at the splat; the crest ends are joined to the post tops at vertical connections within the arches. The rear surface is chamfered at the arched ends, top and bottom, the chamfer continuing into the loops formed with the posts. The splat is slightly canted at the edges, front to back, and tenoned into the plinth. The plinth is deeply hollowed on the front and side faces, finished with a top bead, and nailed to the rear seat rail. The deeply contoured back posts are chamfered at the rear corners from crest to seat. The seat rails are joined to the posts and front leg extensions with rectangular tenons (pinned). The rear legs are chamfered on all corners between the seat rails and rear stretcher; the feet are canted on the forward faces. The front knee scrolls and beads are cut from solid wood; the knee brackets are applied. Scribe lines detail the upper edges of the pad feet. The flat side stretchers are joined to the legs with vertical rectangular tenons; the front legs are flattened at the joints. Horizontal rectangular tenons secure the medial stretcher joints. The rear stretcher is round tenoned into the back legs.

**Condition:** A repair occurs at the left crest and post joint. Surface imperfections mark the splat top, front and back. The right front leg extension is damaged and repaired; the left extension is cracked. All the knee blocks are reattached with double screws. There is a minor repair at the left rear rail joint. The rear feet are chipped and gouged; other damage occurs on the inside surface of the left rear leg between the seat rail and stretchers.

**Dimensions:**

|  |  |  |
|---|---|---|
| H. | 41³⁄₈ in. | 105.1 cm |
| H. (seat) | 17⁷⁄₈ in. | 45.4 cm |
| W. (crest) | 15 in. | 38.1 cm |
| W. (seat front) | 20¹⁄₂ in. | 52.1 cm |
| W. (seat back) | 15 in. | 38.1 cm |
| W. (feet) | 21⁵⁄₈ in. | 54.9 cm |
| D. (seat) | 16³⁄₄ in. | 42.5 cm |
| D. (feet) | 21¹⁄₄ in. | 54.0 cm |

**Materials:** *Microanalysis:* Primary: American black walnut. Secondary: soft maple group (loose-seat frame). *Finish:* medium dark reddish brown color in resin over reddish brown stain. *Upholstery:* dark green and beige cut, uncut, and voided silk velvet; Europe, 1700–1740.

**Publications:** Ralph E. Carpenter, Jr., *The Arts and Crafts of Newport, Rhode Island, 1640–1820* (Newport: Preservation Society of Newport County, 1954), no. 17. Charles F. Hummel, "Queen Anne and Chippendale Furniture in the Henry Francis du Pont Winterthur Museum, Part 2," *Antiques* 98, no. 6 (December 1970): 902–4; figs. 6, 7.

**Provenance:** Ex coll.: Dr. and Mrs. Daniel Bruce Moffett.

**Accession history:** Museum purchase from John S. Walton, Inc., New York, 1959, funds gift of H. F. du Pont.
59.3

---

1. A set of 6 chairs similar to this chair has a history in the Eddy family of Warren, R.I., and on that basis the chairs were assigned to the cabinetmaker Job Townsend when sold from the Israel Sack collection in 1932. One piece of furniture retained by the family was said to be labeled, although documentation has never been published; American Art Association Anderson Galleries, "Colonial and Early Federal Furniture, Silver, and Porcelains from the Israel Sack Collection" (January 9, 1932), lot 80. Recent research by Leigh Keno and associates identifies Boston as the origin of this pattern; see Keno, Freund, and Miller, "Very Pink of the Mode," pp. 266–306.

2. For the Grant reference, see Keno, Freund, and Miller, "Very Pink of the Mode," p. 278. The date of the reference to flat stretchers, February 3, 1741/42, has been misinterpreted as 1741 in the text of this article; the date should be read as 1742, according to the "old style," or Julian, calendar, which was in effect in Britain and the American colonies until 1752. For the astragal-oxbow skirt pattern, see Greenlaw, *New England Furniture*, no. 52; for the astragal-ogee skirt pattern, see *American Antiques from Israel Sack Collection*, 10 vols. (Washington, D.C.: Highland House, ca. 1969–), 6:1650.

3. Geoffrey Beard and Christopher Gilbert, eds., *Dictionary of English Furniture Makers, 1660–1840* (London: Furniture History Society, 1986), p. 694. Robert Hatfield Ellsworth, *Chinese Furniture: Hardwood Examples of the Ming and Early Ch'ing Dynasties* (New York: Random House, 1971), figs. 40–44; Wang Shixiang, *Classic Chinese Furniture* (London: Han-Shan Tang, 1986), pls. 17–19, 65, 73, 75, 76, 126, 128. An illustration of a Chinese cabriole-leg chair complete with hoop elbows is part of the detail of an embroidery in the Manchoukuo National Museum, Mukden, Manchuria; see Ole Wanscher, *The Art of Furniture: Five Thousand Years of Furniture and Interiors* (London: George Allen and Unwin, 1966), p. 245. Reinier Baarsen, "Court Style in Holland," and Gervase Jackson-Stops, "The Court Style in Britain," in Baarsen et al., *Courts and Colonies*, figs. 3, 13, 56, 57, cats. 139–41; John Gloag, *The Englishman's Chair: Origins, Design, and Social History of Seat Furniture in England* (London: George Allen and Unwin, 1964), pp. 87–89, pl. 6; Peter Ward-Jackson, *English Furniture Designs of the Eighteenth Century* (London: Victoria and Albert Museum, Her Majesty's Stationery Office, 1958), pp. 32–33, nos. 4–6; Robert C. Smith, "China, Japan, and the Anglo-American Chair," *Antiques* 96, no. 4 (October 1969): 557–58. For chairs with exaggerated knees, see Macquoid and Edwards, *Dictionary*, 1:256, figs. 91, 92; p. 258, fig. 98; p. 261, figs. 106, 107. Nicholas Grindley, *The Bended-Back Chair* (London: Barling, 1990).

## 15 ◆ Side chair
Boston, Massachusetts
1735–45

This innovative and daring chair design is notable for its eclectic mix of features associated with Boston chair production of the 1730s, all of which have direct antecedents in English furniture. The chairmaker, after choosing slim cabriole legs, front and back, elected in a bold move to eliminate the stretchers. Throughout the design, ogee curves perfectly complement one another at the splat, sweeps of the back posts, sides of the seat, skirt front, legs, and knee brackets.

The earliest elements of the design—the vaselike splat and the saddled crest—became part of the vocabulary of Boston chair design in the early 1730s (see Nos. 9–12). The rounded, or compass, seat, this one flattened instead of rounded across the front, was in the market before the mid 1730s (see No. 7). Introduction of the sweep, or incurved, back posts probably followed shortly (see No. 24). The claw foot came into use in London during the 1710s, but it may have been the late 1730s before Boston chairmakers adopted the fashion. Scroll-lined knees and scalloped front rails were other customer options that added premiums to the basic cost of a framed chair. The sawed pattern of the front rail was one of the more complex designs available—it appears occasionally in standard, saddle-crested stretcher-base chairs (see No. 10) and in some of the hoop-shouldered flat-stretcher chairs (see No. 14).[1]

Augmenting these features are two uncommon ones on this chair, the first of which is the elongated, tonguelike beaded ornament of the knees. Its use in the side chair may be limited to two patterns—vase-back chairs without stretchers, as illustrated, and vase-back chairs with flat stretchers. The ornament also appears in a double-scroll–arm easy chair with standard columnar and swelled stretchers and in a roundabout chair.[2]

The other notable feature is the cabriole-style rear legs. The outside cheeks of the knees, like the inside cheeks of the back sweeps, were formed by the addition of rounded pieces of wood. Flared and blocked feet were the usual accompaniment of stretcherless chairs. In unbraced undercarriages the feature is aesthetically necessary to provide a graceful transition between the feet and the floor. The chisel mark "XII" inside the front seat rail indicates that this chair was one of a set of at least a dozen, a remarkable number for so unusual a design.[3]

Both the basic and the special features of this chair can be found in English furniture dating to the first quarter of the eighteenth century. Rounded back stiles, introduced there at an early date, appear to have been inspired by Chinese furniture. The cabriole leg may spring from the same source, in part. A japanned English chair of about 1710–20 with rounded stiles, rear cabrioles, and a contoured back also has a shaped rod-style crest piece of a type common in Chinese furniture. Chairs of this general description could have been among the furnishings imported from England by wealthy Bostonians in the 1720s. Low Chinese tables with blocked-foot cabriole legs may have been the models for English prototypes that inspired this feature in American chairs. Scroll-lined front knees, shaped front rails, compass seats, and claw feet were part of the continuing transfer of English design to America. Even the beaded tongues on the knees of this chair have an English source—a flat-stretcher side chair and a stretcherless easy chair.[4]

Until recently chairs of this general description were linked with New York and Rhode Island. New research and thinking about Boston's role in the coastal furniture trade has led to reassignment of the pattern to that center. Clouding the picture through the years has been the New York provenances associated with many of these chairs. For instance, Winterthur's chair was assigned to New York as early as 1950 when the bill from the vendor listed a provenance "from a descendant of Charles Morgan, early New York merchant." By contrast, a closely related chair with the same beaded knee ornament in the Museum of Fine Arts, Boston, has a long history of ownership in New Hampshire. Both areas, however, traded extensively with Boston in the eighteenth century.[5]

*NGE*

---

**Inscriptions or marks:** *Chiseled on front seat-rail rabbet:* "XII".

**Construction:** The crest is supported on rectangular tenons at the contoured and rounded post tops and splat (pinned). The rounded face is cheeked at the ends and hollow at the saddle. The rear surface is flat across the center and rounded at the arches. The contoured splat is deeply canted at the slightly rounded edges, front to back, and rabbeted into the back face of the plinth where it is held in place by four sprigs in a horizontal row. The plinth is hollow on the front and side faces, finished with a flattened bead (worn) at the top, and nailed to the back rail. The inner cheeks of the back-post sweeps are pieced. The posts are rounded on all surfaces above the blocks at the seat frame. The seat rails are sawed in flat arches at the sides and in a scalloped pattern at the front; the front edge is tool-marked along the bottom. The top lip is rounded, and an inside rabbet supports the compass-shape loose-seat frame. The rails are joined to the posts and front leg extensions with rectangular tenons (pinned). Interior triangular corner blocks (modern) are held with two screws each. The rear legs, which are squared and rounded, are pieced out with cheeks at the upper outside faces and supported on squared feet that flare outward and backward. The knees of the cabriole legs and adjacent brackets are lined with carved ogee and C scrolls that flank an elongated, beaded V-shape central ornament. The carved feet have apple-shape balls, two-knuckle toes, and webs between the toes. The knee brackets are held in place with glue.

**Condition:** A vertical hairline crack occurs on the face of the splat in the upper right corner. The right seat-rail joints are reinforced with additional pins. The left front leg extension has a hairline crack and a long vertical patch. Hairline cracks also occur in the right leg extension; one extends down into the knee. The interior corner blocks are new. The rear leg brackets have been reinforced with several small sprigs. The loose-seat frame is modern.

**Dimensions:**

| | | |
|---|---|---|
| H. | 40 1/2 in. | 102.9 cm |
| H. (seat) | 17 1/4 in. | 43.8 cm |
| W. (crest) | 14 7/8 in. | 37.8 cm |
| W. (seat front) | 20 1/8 in. | 51.1 cm |
| W. (seat back) | 15 1/4 in. | 38.7 cm |
| W. (feet) | 21 3/4 in. | 55.2 cm |
| D. (seat) | 16 7/8 in. | 42.8 cm |
| D. (feet) | 21 in. | 53.3 cm |

**Materials:** *Microanalysis:* Primary: American black walnut. Secondary: Douglas fir (seat blocks). *Finish:* surface refinished. Present finish medium reddish yellow brown color in resin. *Upholstery:* pieced white cotton (discolored) resist-dyed in 2 shades of blue in pattern of leaves, fruit, and woody vines with a large owl; probably England, ca. 1760.

**Exhibitions:** East Side Antiques Show, New York, January 22–30, 1982.

**Publications:** Downs, *American Furniture*, fig. 107. John A. H. Sweeney, *Winterthur Illustrated* (New York: Chanticleer Press for the Henry Francis du Pont Winterthur Museum, 1963), p. 37. Bishop, *Centuries and Styles of the American Chair*, fig. 92. Kirk, *American Chairs*, fig. 166.

**Provenance:** Descended in the family of Charles Morgan, a New York merchant.

**Accession history:** Purchased by Winterthur Museum from Ginsburg and Levy, Inc., New York, 1950.
58.960

---

1. For a chair with a similar front seat rail, see Kirk, *American Chairs*, fig. 164.

2. For other chairs with beaded knee ornament, see Kirk, *American Chairs*, fig. 158; *John Brown House Loan Exhibition*, cats. 5, 6; Randall, *American Furniture*, no. 133; Bernard and S. Dean Levy, Inc., *Catalogue VI* (New York: By the company, 1988), p. 42; Sotheby's, "Important Americana" (October 22, 1995), lot 126; Northeast Auctions, "New Hampshire Auction" (November 4, 5, 1995), lot 678.

3. For other chairs with cabriole rear legs, see Randall, *American Furniture*, no. 133; Sotheby's, "Important Americana"; Northeast Auctions, "New Hampshire Auction."

4. For English design sources, see Kirk, *American Furniture*, figs. 779, 780, 784–86, 788, 789, 794, 795, 800, 805, 810, 812, 815, 828, 1149. Macquoid and Edwards, *Dictionary*, 1: figs. 88–91. For Chinese design sources, see Kirk, *American Furniture*, fig. 1267; George N. Kates, *Chinese Household Furniture* (1948; reprint, New York: Dover Publications, 1962), pls. 62, 78, 79, 86, 87. For English sources for the beaded tongues on the knees of the chair, see Kirk, *American Furniture*, figs. 812, 1149.

5. Keno, Freund, and Miller, "Very Pink of the Mode," pp. 266–306; Ginsburg and Levy, bill to Winterthur Museum, December 1, 1950, folder 58.960, Registration Office, Winterthur; Randall, *American Furniture*, no. 133.

## 16 ◆ Side chair

Northeastern Massachusetts, probably Boston

1730–35

Long, slim, sometimes spare, lines are characteristic of a group of chairs that may represent the earliest expression of the full Queen Anne style in Boston—when the basic design was in place but had not been fully refined. Characteristic of emerging styles, elements in different stages of development often appear together, the choice varying from one chair (or set) to another. The critical points of reference here are the splat, front seat rail, legs, and side stretchers.

Comparison of this chair with the fully mature Queen Anne example in No. 9 points up significant differences in the splat. The long ogee at the top creates awkward negative

spaces in the flanking voids, which form exaggerated "bird's heads." The splat proper lacks the slim waist of the advanced design, and the base is much simpler. The pattern appears to be a blending of two profiles from the late 1720s (see Nos. 2, 5, 6). The front rail also is a hold-over from an earlier period, with the awkward gap between the ogees eliminated (see Nos. 1, 2).

The legs of this chair are unusually slim and attenuated without much curve at the knee. The flatness through the center on the outside surface was addressed in other chairs within the group. Some of those chairs also have knees lined with scrolls in the manner of Nos. 14 and 15. The same chairs chronicle the advance of the foot design from the disk of this chair to the saucer-shape pad of No. 14 to the ball-and-claw of No. 15. The stretcher-based chairs with lined knees in the sample

group are all designed with block-and-baluster turnings in the side braces, a form more common in the 1720s (see No. 1). By contrast, the side stretchers in this chair have been converted to the columnar style that became part of standard Boston Queen Anne design during the early 1730s. Columnar stretchers and full pad feet are features of a lone armchair fitted with the exaggerated ogee-headed splat of this group. The ogees of the front rail are more attenuated than those in the side chairs, a result of the broader dimensions of this seating form.[1]

The twentieth-century inscription accompanying this chair, which outlines a tradition of ownership in the Gov. Gurdon Saltonstall family of Connecticut, is typical of the attractive legends that frequently enhance antique furniture. Sometimes the "facts" can be verified, frequently not, and occasionally the truth lies somewhere between fact and fiction. Genealogical records indicate that Governor Saltonstall's daughter Katherine married Thomas Brattle of Boston, not Thomas Clap, president of Yale College. However, Mary Haynes Saltonstall, widow of the governor's son Roswell (or Rosewell), did become Clap's second wife. Also to be considered is why Saltonstall, a Connecticut resident, presented a family member with a set of Massachusetts chairs and how his death in 1724 can be reconciled with the 1735–45 date range for the chair. The history accompanying a related, though more sophisticated, pair of Boston chairs sold at auction in 1924 alleges that the furniture originally belonged to William Ellery (1727–1820) of Newport, a signer of the Declaration of Independence, and gives a line of descent in the Stedman family of an Ellery son-in-law. On the surface, this is a more plausible tradition, since historical and genealogical data corroborate the basic information. The chairs likely reached Newport in the coastal trade.[2]

NGE

**Inscriptions or marks:** *Inside the front seat rail:* "This chair was one of a set formerly owned by/ Gurdon Saltonstal, Governor of the Colony of/ Connecticut (1707–1724) and by him given to his daughter Catherine, as part of her wedding/ outfit, when she married President Clapp of/ Yale College" typed on modern paper label.

**Construction:** The delicate crest is supported on rectangular tenons at the flat-faced contoured post tops (pinned) and splat. The crest face is cheeked at the ends; the saddle back is blocked and the arches chamfered, top and bottom. The splat is canted at the edges, front to back, and tenoned into the plinth. The plinth is hollow on the front and side faces, finished with a top bead at the front only, and nailed to the back rail. The rear post corners are chamfered from crest to seat. The side seat rails are sawed in flat arches with ogee returns at the back; the front rail is shaped with double ogees.

The top lip is rounded and the bottoms lightly tooled; an inside rabbet supports the loose-seat frame. The front and side rails and the knee brackets are narrowly chamfered on the inside edges. The rails are joined to the posts and front leg extensions with rectangular tenons (pinned). The rear legs are chamfered on all corners between the seat and rear stretcher; the feet are canted on the forward faces. The front legs are slim; the small pad feet have narrow back ledges and remnants of disks. The ogee knee brackets are tooled on the bottoms and attached with nails. The side stretchers are joined to the legs with vertical rectangular tenons (pinned); the medial and rear stretchers are round tenoned into the adjacent members.

**Condition:** The upper right corner tip of the splat has been restored. The plinth is cracked in the upper part at both ends and secured with nails. The right seat rail is cracked at the rear joint; filled nail holes occur on the front rail at the left end. The rails are newly pinned on the inside. The side knee brackets are replaced, and the front brackets appear to have been taken off and reattached. A vertical crack occurs in the right front knee adjacent to the front bracket; the outside half of the foot is replaced. The left leg is patched at the front adjacent to the stretcher mortise. Modern glides have been attached to the front feet. A large chip is missing from the neck ring of the right stretcher. The loose-seat frame is modern.

**Dimensions:**

| | | |
|---|---|---|
| H. | 42³/₁₆ in. | 107.1 cm |
| H. (seat) | 17 in. | 43.1 cm |
| W. (crest) | 14³/₈ in. | 36.5 cm |
| W. (seat front) | 19³/₄ in. | 50.2 cm |
| W. (seat back) | 15 in. | 38.1 cm |
| W. (feet) | 20¹/₈ in. | 51.1 cm |
| D. (seat) | 16¹/₄ in. | 41.3 cm |
| D. (feet) | 19⁷/₈ in. | 50.5 cm |

**Materials:** *Microanalysis:* Primary: soft maple group. Secondary: hard maple group (rear seat rail). *Finish:* muddied medium light brown color in resin with traces of earlier light blue-green paint. *Upholstery:* crimson wool; Europe, 1725–75.

**Accession history:** Purchased by H. F. du Pont from Williams Antique Shop, Old Greenwich, Conn., 1951. Gift of H. F. du Pont, 1951. 51.26

---

1. For related chairs in this group, see Rodriguez Roque, *American Furniture*, no. 51; *John Brown House Loan Exhibition*, cat. 3; Trent with Nelson, "A Catalogue of New London County Joined Chairs," no. 27; Warren, *Bayou Bend*, no. 37; Monkhouse and Michie, *American Furniture*, cat. 101; Kirk, *American Chairs*, figs. 161, 165. For the armchair, see Teina Baumstone advertisement, *Antiques* 67, no. 4 (April 1955): 285.

2. *New England Historical and Genealogical Register* (Boston: Samuel G. Drake, 1853), 7:248–49; 8:317–18; 25:79–81. For information on Thomas Clap and Gurdon Saltonstall, see *Dictionary of American Biography*, ed. Allen Johnson and Dumas Malone (New York: Charles Scribner's Sons, 1930), 4:116–17, 16:317–18. For the William Ellery chairs, see American Art Association Anderson Galleries, "Colonial Furniture: The Superb Collection of Mr. Francis Hill Bigelow" (January 17, 1924), lot 142. William Ellery estate inventory, March 6, 1820, Probate Court, Newport Co., R.I. (microfilm, Downs collection).

## 17 • Side chair
**Portsmouth, New Hampshire, or vicinity, or possibly northeastern coastal Massachusetts**
**1732–60**
**Probably a member of the Gaines family**

A group of carved- and pierced-top chairs, numbering two dozen or more examples, appears to have originated in the Piscataqua region of New Hampshire, and perhaps the vicinity of Ipswich, Massachusetts. This chair and its mate (fig. 1) in the Winterthur collection along with Nos. 18 and 19 represent three distinct, although closely related, patterns in the group. The unusual hollow-top crest with carved scrolls derives from early eighteenth-century Boston chairs (fig. 2), which in turn reflect contemporary English design. Since the mid nineteenth century, chairs of this general pattern have been

attributed to John Gaines III (1704–43) of Portsmouth, as identified by a direct descendant who owned four side chairs. The set is still owned by the family.[1]

About 1724 Gaines arrived in Portsmouth from his native Ipswich, Massachusetts, where he had probably trained with his father, John II (1677–1748), a turner and chairmaker. John's younger brother Thomas I (1712–61) also appears to have trained with the father and joined his business in 1736. Following his apprenticeship, it is possible that Thomas worked for several years in Portsmouth with his brother.[2]

Given the nineteenth-century identification of the Gaines family seating and its possession by descendants, it is plausible that chairs of this and related patterns were made by John III; however, there seem to be too many variants for one shop to have

**Fig. 1.** Side view of mate chair, 1732–60. Soft maple; H. 41 3/8 in. (105.1 cm), H. (seat) 17 1/4 in. (43.8 cm), W. (seat) 18 1/8 in. (46.0 cm), D. (seat) 14 1/8 in. (35.9 cm). (Winterthur 58.1513)

**Fig. 2.** Side chair, Boston, 1695–1705. Red maple, red oak; H. 38 3/8 in. (97.5 cm), H. (seat) 18 1/2 in. (47.0 cm), W. (seat) 17 3/4 in. (45.1 cm), D. (seat) 14 3/8 in. (36.5 cm). (Winterthur 59.2115)

produced them all. The stylish yet provincial designs may represent a broader local production in top-line painted or varnished seating for a limited clientele. Perhaps some chairs were also produced in Ipswich, where an existing account book used by John II, and later Thomas I, describes the shop's most expensive seating as "carved back," "Carved top," and "Crown top" chairs. The terms may in part be interchangeable. Features were probably altered gradually since the chairs were produced from 1726 to 1741. Prices ranged from 10s. to 18s., the higher figures probably identifying "great," or arm, chairs. Early carved chairs could have had plain, rectangular panels at the center back. Family members likely remained in close touch, which suggests that it would be difficult to distinguish between Ipswich and Portsmouth production. The two communities are only about thirty miles distant overland, and an easier passage existed by water; it is perhaps significant that

John III owned a one-third interest in a schooner at his death in 1743.[3]

Many features that appear in Gaines-type chairs are relatively standard within the group: the block-and-compressed baluster legs with carved Spanish feet; the large, tripartite front stretchers and distinctive "sausage"-turned rear braces; the plain, sawed side stretchers; the half-circular front seat-rail pendants; the flat side-rail arches; and the crook back (see fig. 1) with molded posts and rounded shoulders. Variation occurs in the crests and splats. The hollow-top crest of this chair with coarsely carved leafage, scrolls, and piercings is interpreted in broad form, the scrolls ending above pins that secure the crest to the posts (fig. 3). In a narrow version, the central hollow is shorter and the scrolls terminate short of the posts. This splat with its "points" and "hooks" almost certainly dates later than the standard rounded and lobed version (see No. 217). Chairs without the lobed splat

either have stay rails mounted close to the back seat rail or a plinth—construction forms that represent stylistic advances in early Queen Anne chair design. Examples include No. 19 and side chairs with rectangular drops in the front rail and vase splats close in pattern to that of No. 2.[4]

*NGE*

---

**Inscriptions or marks:** *Chiseled on inside front seat rail:* "I".

**Construction:** The carved and pierced crest is supported on rectangular tenons at the contoured and molded post tops (pinned) and splat. The splat is canted at the edges, front to back, and tenoned into the molded stay rail, which is tenoned into the back posts (pinned). The seat rails are joined to the posts and leg blocks with rectangular tenons (pinned, except at back rail). A bead finishes the lower edge of the front rail. Recessed quarter-round ledges have been formed at the inside corners of the upper leg blocks, and a ledge is applied with rosehead nails to the inside back rail. The front feet are carved from solid wood. The side stretchers are joined to the legs with vertical rectangular tenons (pinned); the front and rear stretchers are round tenoned into the legs.

**Condition:** The crest-post joints are damaged and repaired. Nicks, punctures, and irregularities occur on most surfaces. The upper front leg blocks are defaced, and the right inside ledge is partially broken away, exposing a round tenon. The left and front seat rails are cracked at the leg joint. A series of nail holes on the outside front- and side-rail

**Fig. 3.** Detail of No. 17, crest.

edges indicates that the chair was partially overupholstered at one time. The left tip of the front stretcher is nailed from behind the leg block. Splits on the lower left and right leg blocks are repaired. The left front foot pad is pieced at the back, and the front carving is chipped. The loose rush seat is a modern replacement.

**Dimensions:**

| | | |
|---|---|---|
| H. | 41 1/4 in. | 104.8 cm |
| H. (seat) | 17 7/8 in. | 45.4 cm |
| W. (crest) | 13 1/2 in. | 34.3 cm |
| W. (seat front) | 18 3/8 in. | 46.7 cm |
| W. (seat back) | 14 in. | 35.5 cm |
| W. (feet) | 21 1/4 in. | 54.0 cm |
| D. (seat) | 13 15/16 in. | 35.4 cm |
| D. (feet) | 19 1/2 in. | 49.5 cm |

**Materials:** *Microanalysis:* Primary: soft maple (right front leg; left seat rail). Secondary: white pine group (rear seat-rail support); chestnut (loose-seat frame). *Finish:* streaked dark brown color in resin (mahoganized).

**Accession history:** Bequest of H. F. du Pont, 1969. 54.514

---

1. Although the 2 Winterthur chairs vary subtly, they probably are a pair. The chiseled numbers "I" and "IIII" appear inside the front seat rails. A similar chair in the Metropolitan Museum of Art is marked "VI," suggesting that a set of at least 6 once existed; Helen Comstock, "An Ipswich Account Book, 1707–1762," *Antiques* 66, no. 3 (September 1954): 191 lower left. The English prototype is illustrated in Forman, *American Seating Furniture*, fig. 171; Charles W. Brewster, *Rambles about Portsmouth*, 2d ser. (Portsmouth, N.H.: Lewis W. Brewster, 1869), p. 355; Stephen Decatur, "George and John Gaines of Portsmouth, N.H.," *American Collector* 7, no. 10 (November 1938): 6; Jobe, *Portsmouth Furniture*, pp. 295–300.

2. Comstock, "Ipswich Account Book," pp. 188–90. Robert E. P. Hendrick, "John Gaines II and Thomas Gaines I, 'Turners' of Ipswich, Massachusetts" (Master's thesis, University of Delaware, 1964), pp. 8–66, 78–94, apps. L, N, Y, AA. Based upon an analysis of accounts and sales, Hendrick noted a drop in the Gaines's shop production between 1732 and 1736, the period following Thomas's training with his father but preceding his entry into the family business. Thomas could have worked elsewhere during these years.

3. John Gaines II and Thomas Gaines I account book, 1707–60, Downs collection; Hendrick, "John Gaines II and Thomas Gaines I," p. 47.

4. A related side chair with narrow crest is illustrated in *The Decorative Arts of New Hampshire: A Sesquicentennial Exhibition* (Concord: New Hampshire Historical Society, 1973), fig. 50. For the pair of side chairs with rectangular drops, see Israel Sack advertisement, *Antiques* 135, no. 2 (February 1989): inside front cover.

## 18 ◆ Armchair
Portsmouth, New Hampshire, or vicinity, or possibly northeastern coastal Massachusetts
1730–60
Probably a member of the Gaines family

The patterns used for the crest, splat, and front seat rail of this chair vary significantly from those of No. 17 and the more common group profiles represented by No. 217. In the center of the rounded and molded crest is a large, carved, foliated C scroll (fig. 1). Related elements of molded and carved form are common in Boston cane-, leather-, and banister-back chairs dating to the early eighteenth century.[1]

Of closer comparison is the carved-top banister-back chair produced by a craftsman working within the same chairmaking group (fig. 2). Features of that chair that also appear

in No. 17 and this chair are the arms, arm supports, legs, turned stretchers, and feet. The two large C scrolls in the crest approximate in size and character the scroll centered in this crest, and the voluted scroll ends and crescent-shape gouges are similar in precise detail. John Gaines II recorded banister-back chairs in his Ipswich, Massachusetts, accounts beginning in 1717 and specially noted "banister backs bent" in 1725. At this date the term *bent back* probably identified a chair with turned and raked back posts, such as that in figure 2.[2]

The centered carving on this crest is a focus that draws the eye down the sawed, contoured back splat. The splat profile appears to be a new design but is actually a modification of the standard pattern (see No. 217). Above the large, inverted baluster that forms the principal element, the flared neck is terminated by large points. The baluster base is modified by a second pair of

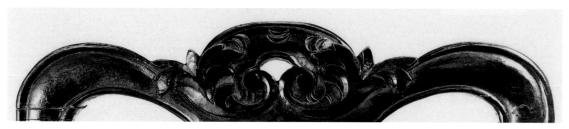

**Fig. 1.** Detail, crest.

rounded lobes above a typical high-mounted, molded stay rail, which sometimes varies subtly in profile in related chairs. Considerable evidence of hand tooling with a chisel in the form of shallow vertical and horizontal gouges marks the surfaces of the splat, front and back.

The vigorous scroll pattern of the front seat rail has the character of an ornate, painted or cloth-covered cornice of the type fashionable in the early eighteenth century. Like the chair rails with circular drops (see No. 17), the lower edge is beaded. To date this is the only example of the scrolled-rail pattern known.

The arms are a commanding feature of Gaines-type chairs, although undulating scrolled rests with carved grips were not new. They appear on seventeenth-century European chairs and are common on Boston great chairs of the early eighteenth century, but the difference in the arms on Gaines-type chairs is their heroic size. Placement of the arm supports above the front legs is an alternative treatment to setting them back along the side rails (see No. 217). The profiles of the arm supports are similar to those in No. 217 and the banister-back chair, which also shares in part the compressed ball-and-double-spool turning of the legs.[3]

Two other carved-crest variants are known in Gaines-type turned chairs. A side chair is ornamented with a high, centered and pierced lunette containing four carved, converging, cometlike scrolls. Its rounded-baluster splat and front skirt with a half-circular drop follow the standard group profile. A second side chair has a larger, more complex pierced crest comprising a molded, yoke-shape top supported on C scrolls, leafage, and a central ruffled ornament. The modified splat has large pointed projections at the bases of the neck and baluster. The rush bottom is woven around seat rails that are tenoned into the legs.[4]

NGE

---

**Construction:** The carved and pierced crest is supported on rectangular tenons at the molded post tops (pinned) and splat. The rear crest surface is

chamfered, top and bottom, except at the joint with the splat; the central piercing is beveled. The splat is heavily tooled on both surfaces and, with the back posts, is deeply contoured in the vertical plane. A rectangular tenon secures the splat and molded stay rail, which is tenoned into the back posts. The arms, molded to a bell shape with broad bases chamfered at the edges, are secured by rectangular tenons at the back posts (pinned) and round tenons at the front posts. The thick seat rails are joined to the legs and posts with rectangular tenons (pinned). The front seat rail is beaded at the lower edge and deeply chamfered toward the inside. Considerable evidence of hand tooling occurs on other interior edges and surfaces. The loose rush

seat, which is supported on recessed ledges cut into the front leg blocks and on applied triangular blocks at the rear corners, is fixed in place by thin "clamshell" facings nailed to the rail tops and extending beyond the inside edges. The side stretchers are joined to the legs with vertical rectangular tenons; the front and back stretchers are round tenoned into the legs. The front feet are carved from solid wood.

**Condition:** The crest and post joints are broken and repaired. A diagonal crack at arm level in the left back post is repaired. The rear seat rail is a replacement. Small angle irons reinforce the side rail and stretcher joints with the legs. The rear corner blocks in the seat frame are modern; the

**Fig. 2.** Armchair, probably by a member of the Gaines family, Portsmouth, N.H., and vicinity, or northeastern coastal Massachusetts, 1720–40. Maple; H. 44 1/8 in. (112.1 cm), H. (seat) 16 1/2 in. (41.9 cm), W. (seat) 22 in. (55.8 cm), D. (seat) 16 1/2 in. (41.9 cm), W. (arm) 26 in. (66.0 cm). (Winterthur 54.515)

loose rush seat is a replacement. The nailed rail-top facings may be replacements.

**Dimensions:**

| | | |
|---|---|---|
| H. | 43 in. | 109.2 cm |
| H. (seat) | 17⁵/₈ in. | 44.8 cm |
| W. (crest) | 17³/₈ in. | 44.1 cm |
| W. (seat front) | 24¹¹/₁₆ in. | 62.7 cm |
| W. (seat back) | 17¹/₂ in. | 44.4 cm |
| W. (arms) | 29¹/₄ in. | 74.3 cm |
| W. (feet) | 26³/₄ in. | 68.0 cm |
| D. (seat) | 16⁷/₈ in. | 42.9 cm |
| D. (feet) | 21³/₈ in. | 54.3 cm |

**Materials:** *Microanalysis:* Primary: hard maple group (front seat rail); soft maple group (front leg, loose-seat frame); maple (arms, crest, and front stretcher by macroidentification). Secondary: cherry (applied rail strips). *Finish:* streaked dark brown color in resin (mahoganized).

**Exhibitions:** "Accessions 1960," Winterthur Museum, Winterthur, Del., December 21, 1960–February 1, 1961.

**Publications:** *Accessions 1960* (Winterthur, Del.: Winterthur Museum, 1960), fig. 5. Dean A. Fales, Jr., *American Painted Furniture, 1660–1880* (New York: E. P. Dutton, 1972), fig. 40. Bishop, *Centuries and Styles of the American Chair,* fig. 73.

**Accession history:** Museum purchase from John S. Walton, Inc., New York, 1960, funds gift of H. F. du Pont.
60.102

---

1. An armchair at Chipstone has a similar carved crest but in other features is comparable to standard examples within the general group; see Rodriguez Roque, *American Furniture,* no. 75. For early Boston chairs, see Forman, *American Seating Furniture,* cats. 54, 56, 61, 62, 65–67.

2. John Gaines II and Thomas Gaines I account book, 1707–60, Downs collection. By the 1730s furniture nomenclature may have broadened, as suggested in scattered accounts relating to the chair production of John Gaines III of Portsmouth. The term *banister back* may have described both chairs framed with multiple slim uprights (see fig. 2) and chairs with large, single, central splats. Price would distinguish the 2 in records; the single splat chair was the more expensive; see Jobe, *Portsmouth Furniture,* p. 43.

3. For the European and Boston armchairs, see Forman, *American Seating Furniture,* figs. 120, 121; cats. 56, 64, 80.

4. For the lunette-top chair, see *American Antiques from Israel Sack Collection,* 10 vols. (Washington, D.C.: Highland House, ca. 1969–), 1:98, fig. 289. For the yoke-top chair, see Rodriguez Roque, *American Furniture,* no. 46.

## 19 ◆ Side chair
**Portsmouth, New Hampshire, or vicinity or possibly northeastern coastal Massachusetts**
**1735–60**
**Probably a member of the Gaines family**

Stylistically this chair is the latest of the Gaines-type designs. The old block-and-turned Spanish-foot supports have been replaced by slim, rounded cabriole legs with pad feet; the ogee curves are repeated in the front seat rail. Rounded back stiles complement the legs, and a plinth is substituted for the stay rail at the splat base. Four turned stretchers are typical of the new Queen Anne style. The sausagelike rear stretcher of earlier Gaines patterns has been retained; the front stretcher has been repositioned between the side braces and

redesigned to harmonize with the rear brace. Design subtleties include flared transitions between the posts and crest, stepped rear arches in the side seat rails, and small hocks behind the front ankles (fig. 1).[1]

The most commanding features of this chair are in the upper structure. The splat profile, a duplicate of that in No. 17, is a later stylistic development than the standard, rounded and lobed splats of other Gaines-type chairs (see No. 217). Like No. 18, the surfaces of the splat are heavily tooled. The crest is unique to the cabriole-leg chairs (fig. 2). The carved shell within a shell is part of the vocabulary of Queen Anne design, but the leaf pendants are holdovers from the William and Mary style. The evolution of this design is unclear, but direct inspiration may have come from English chairs in the early

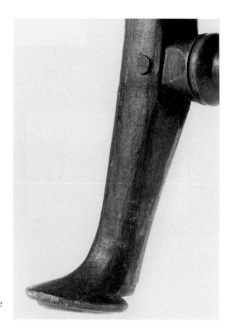

**Fig. 1.** Detail, right front ankle with hock.

**Condition:** The right post joint with the crest is broken and repaired at the back. The upper right corner of the splat is cracked and repaired; the upper left corner is defaced. A narrow strip is broken off the lower front edge of the plinth. The left front knee bracket is replaced; the left foot is restored at the front and the disks beneath both front feet are worn. The loose-seat frame, which has a new front rail, is old but may not be original to this chair.

**Dimensions:**

| | | |
|---|---|---|
| H. | 40 3/8 in. | 102.5 cm |
| H. (seat) | 17 1/4 in. | 43.8 cm |
| W. (crest) | 13 7/8 in. | 35.2 cm |
| W. (seat front) | 18 3/4 in. | 47.6 cm |
| W. (seat back) | 14 1/2 in. | 36.8 cm |
| W. (feet) | 20 7/8 in. | 53.0 cm |
| D. (seat) | 15 5/8 in. | 39.7 cm |
| D. (feet) | 19 7/8 in. | 50.5 cm |

**Materials:** *Microanalysis:* Primary: maple (rear leg, seat rail). *Finish:* streaked dark brown color in resin (mahoganized). *Upholstery:* red wool velvet; Europe, 1675–1725.

**Publications:** Charles F. Hummel, "Queen Anne and Chippendale Furniture in the Henry Francis du Pont Winterthur Museum, Part 2," *Antiques* 98, no. 6 (December 1970): 900–901.

**Accession history:** Purchased by H. F. du Pont from Teina Baumstone, New York, 1955. Gift of H. F. du Pont, 1958.
55.120

Georgian style with centered vase splats sometimes accompanied by canework between the splat and posts. A few such chairs have carved shells in the crest flanked by leaf sprays. Looking glasses of early Queen Anne style with sawed and pierced crests are another possible source.[2]

Several Portsmouth commercial records of the early 1730s provide insights on production in the woodworking shop of John Gaines III and illuminate the scope and nature of his chair trade. Gaines had accounts with leading community merchants John Moffatt and William Pepperrell (later Sir William Pepperrell). To pay Moffatt for merchandise, Gaines supplied him with rush-bottom chairs by the dozen or half dozen and frequently delivered them directly to one of Moffatt's sailing vessels. The chairs, moderately priced at 5s. 6d. and 6s. apiece, were often identified as black or "bla[ck] Varnisht." Unpainted, or "white," chairs were priced at 3s. 6d. The furniture must have been common, slat- or banister-back seating without arms, since 10s. was the charge for a "Great" chair with arms and surface finish.[3]

Considerably more expensive chairs acquired from Gaines and valued at 20s. or 25s. apiece are itemized in the accounts beginning in 1735. Seats were still made of rush, according to Moffatt's records, and Pepperrell described "banister Chairs," a term that at first appears to identify seating similar to figure 2 in No. 18. However, a single vertical splat, such as the one in this chair and those in Nos. 17 and 18, was also known as a banister in the early eighteenth century. The price indicates a sophisticated design, one that included carved work; the quantities supplied further suggest that the chairs were side chairs. The 5s. differential may describe

the transformation of No. 17 into this fashionable shell-carved cabriole-leg chair.[4]

*NGE*

---

**Inscriptions or marks:** *Chiseled on inside front seat rail:* "VIII" *inverted.*

**Construction:** Considerable evidence of tool marks occurs on the front legs and all elements above the seat. The carved and pierced crest is supported on rectangular tenons at the contoured and rounded post tops (pinned) and splat. The crest is flat on the back, and the edges are chamfered; the surfaces around the piercings and along the top edge are tooled. The splat is secured to the plinth by a rectangular tenon. The plinth is hollow on the front and side faces, finished with a top bead, and nailed to the rear seat rail. The seat rails are joined to the posts and legs with rectangular tenons (pinned). The loose-seat frame is supported on front corner blocks and interior rabbets at the front and side rails. The front feet are elevated on shallow disks; hocks occur behind the ankles. The knee brackets are attached with rosehead nails. The rear legs are chamfered on all corners between the seat rails and the rear stretcher. The feet are sharply canted on the forward faces. The side stretchers are joined to the legs with rectangular tenons (pinned); the medial and rear stretchers are round tenoned into the adjacent members.

1. To date, 3 chairs of this pattern are known: this example is chisel-marked "VIII" on the inside front seat rail; a companion chair at the MFA, Boston, bears the number "VII" (see Randall, *American Furniture*, no. 132); and another chair, now in the Currier Gallery of Art, Manchester, N.H., is marked "XII," indicating that at least 12 chairs were in the original set (see Eleanor H. Gustafson, "Museum Accessions," *Antiques* 133, no. 5 [May 1988]: 1082).

2. For Queen Anne prototypes, see Macquoid and Edwards, *Dictionary*, 1:255, fig. 88; Helena Hayward, ed., *World Furniture: An Illustrated History* (New York: McGraw-Hill Book Co., 1965), fig. 462; for looking-glass prototype style, see Downs, *American Furniture*, fig. 248.

3. John Moffatt ledger, 1725–50, New Hampshire Historical Society, Concord (photocopy, Downs collection).

4. Moffatt ledger. William Pepperrell account sheet, 1734–39, Miscellaneous Manuscripts 17A-4, New Hampshire Historical Society, Concord (photocopy, Downs collection).

**Fig. 2.** Detail, crest.

## 20 ◆ Side chair
Norwich, Connecticut
1735–60
Attributed to the Lathrop shops

This side chair is one of a group of nine Connecticut chairs that appears to be the product of two shops connected with the Lathrop family of woodworkers. Four of these, at the Metropolitan Museum of Art, have seat rail interiors notched to identify numbers two, three, four, and six of an original set. They have their original seat covers worked in crewels with hillocks, human and animal figures, and exotic floral forms. A fifth chair from this set was advertised for sale in 1977. Robert F. Trent has attributed the five chairs to the Lathrop-Royce cabinet shops of Wallingford, Connecticut.[1]

Other members of the extended Lathrop family pursued their trades in Norwich, where the remaining chairs, comprising three from a larger set and probably a fourth (this chair), almost certainly originated. The loose-seat frames of the three-chair set, originally owned by Col. Simon (d. 1774) and Martha (d. 1775) Lathrop, are inscribed with the date "June 17, 1756," the name "Elizabeth Lothrop," and the chair number within the set. Speculation is that daughter Elizabeth Lathrop (d. 1763) worked the original, flame-patterned Irish-stitch seat covers. The Lathrop inventories identify a set of "7 worked chairs," which were divided between the Lathrop's daughters Eunice Huntington (d. 1803) and Martha Cogswell (d. 1795), sisters of Elizabeth. During the period when the chairs were made, two Lathrop family members were active woodworkers in Norwich—William (d. 1778) and Zebediah (d. 1783).[2]

This side chair was thought to stand alone because it is the only one of the known nine that has side rails tenoned through the rear posts in the Philadelphia manner. It has now been determined that the irregularly shaped "through tenons" of the chair constitute

repairs caused by the original mortise holes being chopped too deeply and the tenons of the side rails breaking through the back posts. In other features the chair can be compared with those in the Norwich group, but because the original loose-seat frame is missing, it cannot be determined if the chair was inscribed by Elizabeth Lathrop. These four Norwich chairs, in turn, differ substantially from the Wallingford group, namely in the breadth of the saddle crest, the profiles of the splat and turnings, and the size of the front feet. Four unusual features, however, are common to all nine chairs: a bead across the plinth base, triangular-shape knee brackets applied to the seat-rail faces, angular cabriole legs, and rear side-rail returns in the form of small quarter rounds. The Wallingford chairs retain an old, if not original, surface finish,

which consists of reddish brown paint lightly streaked with black or dark brown to imitate the figure of mahogany—a rare survival.[3]

The Queen Anne style may have been introduced to Norwich around 1735 by William Manley, a cabinetmaker from Massachusetts. Local craftsmen, the Lathrops in particular, would have adopted the new style to remain competitive in the affluent society created by Norwich's commercial prosperity. The flat rear stretchers of all nine Lathrop chairs, which were common in earlier Boston regional work, suggest such influence (see No. 2). New to Boston chairs of the early 1730s was the tall, narrow, "bended back" with a vase-shape splat, interpreted here in somewhat attenuated form. A residual local feature present in the entire Lathrop group is the tripartite medial stretcher; the profile is

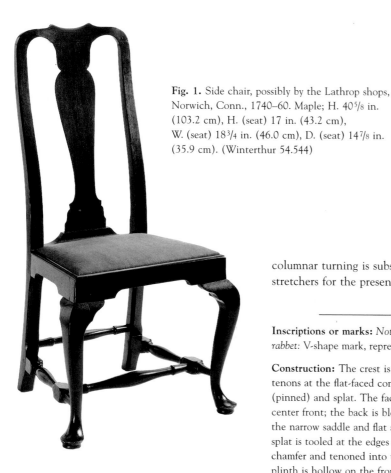

**Fig. 1.** Side chair, possibly by the Lathrop shops, Norwich, Conn., 1740–60. Maple; H. 40⅝ in. (103.2 cm), H. (seat) 17 in. (43.2 cm), W. (seat) 18¾ in. (46.0 cm), D. (seat) 14⅞ in. (35.9 cm). (Winterthur 54.544)

similar to the front braces in regional banister-back chairs produced from the 1720s. The stay rails of the banister-back chairs are also sawed in double ogees of broad sweep, which may have influenced the seat-rail design. On the whole, the somewhat unsure handling of the undercarriage and the choice of elements—a bold medial stretcher, flat rear stretcher, rectangular rear legs, squared cabriole legs, and deep, ogee-shape rails—suggest that the Queen Anne style in Norwich cabinetwork was initiated with this pattern.[4]

A significant advance in the Queen Anne design appears in another chair that may also have been a product of the Lathrop shops (fig. 1). The chair has been updated to the classic Boston design developed during the 1730s by the introduction of an ogee-top splat and a broader saddle in the crest. The splat base has been enlarged and the plinth broadened; the shallow seat rails are sawed with plain, flat arches. The stretchers are lighter than the earlier braces and updated, although the basic character of the side turnings is the same. The knee brackets are attached in the usual manner beneath the rails, instead of on the rail faces. Chamfers have been introduced to the back legs between the rails and stretchers and on the forward corners of the feet in the Boston manner. Points of similarity between the two Norwich chairs are the front curve of the cabriole legs at the ankles and pad feet and the thick, squared profile of the upper leg. In a still later chair design of Norwich origin a Boston-style

columnar turning is substituted in the side stretchers for the present baluster form.[5]

NGE

---

**Inscriptions or marks:** *Notched into the front seat-rail rabbet:* V-shape mark, representing number 1 of a set.

**Construction:** The crest is supported on rectangular tenons at the flat-faced contoured post tops (pinned) and splat. The face is cheeked at the center front; the back is blocked and chamfered at the narrow saddle and flat at the ends. The narrow splat is tooled at the edges with a narrow, rounded chamfer and tenoned into the plinth. The low plinth is hollow on the front and sides and nailed to the back rail; a bead is formed at the front base. The back posts are square-cornered from top to bottom. The deep seat rails are rounded at the top lip, rabbeted on the interior to support the loose-seat frame, and lightly tooled on the bottom edges. The front and side rails are sawed with broad double ogees; the rear side-rail returns terminate in quarter rounds. The rails are joined to the posts and front leg extensions with rectangular tenons (pinned), those at the side backs extending partially through the rear post surfaces (faulty construction). The cabriole front legs have creased knees. The pad feet, which are saucer-shaped and scribed with a line around the back, are supported on disks. The small triangular knee brackets are secured with glue and nails to the front faces of the rails. The side stretchers are joined to the rear legs with rectangular tenons (pinned) and to the front legs with round tenons (pinned). The medial stretcher is round tenoned into the adjacent members; the rear stretcher is joined to the back legs with vertical rectangular tenons.

**Condition:** The splat is gouged at the center back; the joint mortises are large, permitting the splat to skew at the base. The back seat rail is cracked and slightly defaced. Composition material fills part of the broken mortise in the right post. The back of the left front leg is split adjacent to the stretcher. The loose-seat frame is old but not original.

**Dimensions:**

| | | |
|---|---|---|
| H. | 43⅛ in. | 109.5 cm |
| H. (seat) | 18 in. | 45.7 cm |
| W. (crest) | 15½ in. | 39.4 cm |
| W. (seat front) | 19 in. | 48.2 cm |
| W. (seat back) | 15½ in. | 39.4 cm |
| W. (feet) | 20⅞ in. | 53.0 cm |
| D. (seat) | 15 1/16 in. | 38.2 cm |
| D. (feet) | 18½ in. | 47.0 cm |

**Materials:** *Microanalysis:* Primary: soft maple group (right front and left rear legs). Secondary: hard maple group (rear rail); white pine group (loose-seat frame). *Finish:* variable, medium reddish brown color in resin. *Upholstery:* Irish-stitch needlework in crewel yarns on canvas in a carnation-like polychrome pattern; probably America, 1730–75.

**Exhibitions:** "Legacy of a Provincial Elite: New London County Joined Chairs, 1720–1790," Connecticut Historical Society and Lyman Allyn Museum, Hartford and Norwich, October 1, 1985–February 28, 1986.

**Publications:** Downs, *American Furniture*, fig. 102. Marshall B. Davidson, ed., *The American Heritage History of Colonial Antiques* ([New York]: American Heritage Publishing Co., [1967]), fig. 172. Florence M. Montgomery, "A Pattern-Woven 'Flame Stitch' Fabric," *Antiques* 80, no. 5 (November 1961): 455, fig. 6. Trent with Nelson, "A Catalogue of New London County Joined Chairs," p. 93, fig. 16; pp. 99–100, no. 25.

**Accession history:** Purchased by H. F. du Pont from William B. Goodwin, Hartford, Conn. Bequest of H. F. du Pont, 1969.
58.2220

1. Heckscher, *American Furniture*, cat. no. 5. Based upon a nineteenth-century note in a needlework pocketbook, the chairs (and the pocketbook) possibly descended in the Southmayd family of Middletown, Conn. Salander Galleries, Inc., advertisement, *Antiques* 111, no. 5 (May 1977): 940; the whereabouts of the sixth chair in this set is unknown. Trent with Nelson, "A Catalogue of New London County Joined Chairs," pp. 79–85.

2. The group of 3 is divided among 2 private collections and the Henry Ford Museum, Dearborn, Mich.; 1 chair is still owned by a descendant of the first owners, Col. Simon Lathrop and his wife Martha Lathrop of Norwich; for the other privately owned chair, see Christie's, "Important American Furniture, Silver, Folk Art, and Decorative Arts" (October 21, 1989), lot 392; for the Ford Museum chair, see Katharine Bryant Hagler, *American Queen Anne Furniture, 1720–1755* (Dearborn, Mich.: Henry Ford Museum and Greenfield Village, 1976), fig. 29. Trent, "New London County Joined Chairs," pp. 17–18; Trent with Nelson, "A Catalogue of New London County Joined Chairs," pp. 79–80, 87–93. In 1964 Houghton Bulkeley identified 3 chairs similar to the Winterthur chair still owned by private families in eastern Connecticut and Boston. The chairs descended from a single source, said to be the Williams family of Lebanon, Conn. Some link with the Lathrop family is suggested but cannot be verified. Most, if not all, of these chairs appear to be independent of those described in the known group of 9.

3. Heckscher, *American Furniture*, cat. no. 5, p. 41.

4. Trent, "New London County Joined Chairs," pp. 32–34; Trent with Nelson, "A Catalogue of New London County Joined Chairs," pp. 79–80, 113–17.

5. Trent with Nelson, "A Catalogue of New London County Joined Chairs," pp. 94–95, 97–100. The attribution of fig. 1 to the Lathrop shops is based on the descent of 5 such chairs from Gen. Israel Putnam (d. 1790), whose second wife was Deborah Lathrop (d. 1777), niece of Simon and Martha Lathrop. In reviewing the dates of Deborah's 3 marriages—1738, 1755, and 1767 (to Putnam)—it seems likely that she acquired the chairs on or before her second marriage to furnish her Brooklyn, Conn., house, later the residence of General Putnam. Deborah's father, Samuel Lathrop, was first cousin to cabinetmaker William Lathrop. Upholstery evidence indicates that green wool plush was the original cover of the loose seats.

## 21 ◆ Side chair
### East Hartford or Norwich, Connecticut
### 1740–60

Since its purchase in 1960, this chair has been linked with a craftsman named Cheney because that name is inscribed in chalk on the loose-seat frame. Benjamin Cheney of East Hartford was identified as early as 1933 as an eighteenth-century woodworker and furnituremaker. A recent reappraisal of documents relating to Cheney suggests he was a carpenter, as indicated in land deeds and by his woodworking tools and part ownership of a sawmill. Upon reexamination of the chair, Robert F. Trent concluded that the name was added in the nineteenth century or later, a hypothesis confirmed when it was learned that "Cheney" was the name of the last private owner of the chair. Although an attribution to

Benjamin Cheney is no longer valid, the exact origin of the chair remains unsettled. Bernard Levy found a similar signature on a chest-on-chest he purchased from Mrs. James Campbell Cheney of Manchester, Connecticut, the former owner of the chair.[1]

The most distinctive feature of this chair is the pair of spurs, or cusps, located on the splat just below the center. This ornamental detail, which originated in British chairmaking during the second quarter of the eighteenth century, was broadly distributed and remained in the American furniture vocabulary until near the close of the century. Solid splats with this feature, and some of pierced pattern, were produced in most major American furniture centers, including Philadelphia, New York, eastern Connecticut, Newport, and Boston. Trent has also noted this feature in the furniture of Bermuda, another colonial British

trade center. Although many chairs with spurs are made of walnut or mahogany, eastern Connecticut chairmakers favored cherry.[2]

The precise eastern Connecticut origin of straight-backed (canted), spurred-splat compass-bottom chairs with chamfered rear legs and three turned outside stretchers is yet to be resolved. A strong tradition of furnituremaking existed in Norwich, the cultural and commercial center of New London County and vicinity. Features of this chair that link it to Norwich seating furniture include the chamfered rear legs, three-stretcher brace, and angular sweep of the front feet. Gov. John Pitkin (1694–1769), who owned an armchair of this pattern, was a resident of East Hartford, although he had strong political connections and support in New London County, and his deputy governor was a county resident. Several side chairs also have firm East Hartford histories. Because maritime and overland commerce between Norwich and East Hartford was well established and subtle variations within the pattern indicate that more than one shop was responsible for production, it is possible that chairs of this description were made in both Norwich and East Hartford. A second armchair was once owned by Mary Waring, daughter of Capt. Henry and Hannah (Ferris) Waring. Census records locate the family in Greenwich and Stamford, coastal towns in Fairfield County easily accessible to Norwich or East Hartford by water.[3]

This tall, slim, almost austere Connecticut chair is much more subtle in design than initial examination suggests. The seemingly disparate parts are interrelated through a series of recurring motifs and rhythms. The rounded profile of the crest shoulders is repeated in the upper splat lobes, the seat corners, and the bulging knees. The spurs at mid back are inverted at the splat base and reinterpreted as cusped knee brackets below the seat. The flat arches at the splat sides between the spurs and the base are repeated in the crest and seat rails. An alternative, but uncommon, seat pattern is the trapezoidal frame shaped with a central astragal flanked by long ogees in the front rail.[4]

*NGE*

---

**Inscriptions or marks:** *Chiseled on front seat-rail rabbet:* "I". *On loose-seat frame:* "T Cheney" or "I Cheney" in chalk.

**Construction:** The crest is supported on rectangular tenons at the flat-faced canted post tops (pinned) and splat. The face is cheeked at the ends; the back is flat with a wide chamfer across the saddle base and at the arches, top and bottom. The splat is sharply canted at the edges, front to back, and tenoned into the plinth. The plinth is hollow on the front and side faces, finished with a narrow top bead, and nailed to the back rail. The rear post corners are deeply chamfered from crest to seat. The compass seat is rounded at the top lip, and an inside rabbet supports the loose-seat frame. The front and side rails are sawed in flat arches, roughly tooled; vertical tool marks occur on the inside surface of the back rail. The rails are joined to the posts and front leg extensions with rectangular tenons (pinned). The rear legs are chamfered on all corners from seat to base. The back-post faces are shaved to vertical surfaces at rail level. The front knee brackets are secured with nails. The stretchers are round tenoned into the legs. Scribe lines are centered in the right side and rear stretchers.

**Condition:** Cracks are present at the left ends of the crest and plinth. A narrow chamfer at the base of the back rail may be a damage repair. The right front leg extension is cracked and repaired with a spline. Age cracks occur in the right knee; the left side knee bracket is replaced. The disks beneath both pad feet are worn. Some pins are replaced.

**Dimensions:**

| | | |
|---|---|---|
| H. | 42 1/16 in. | 106.9 cm |
| H. (seat) | 16 7/8 in. | 42.8 cm |
| W. (crest) | 15 1/4 in. | 38.7 cm |
| W. (seat front) | 20 1/2 in. | 52.0 cm |
| W. (seat back) | 15 1/2 in. | 39.4 cm |
| W. (feet) | 21 1/2 in. | 54.6 cm |
| D. (seat) | 16 1/2 in. | 41.9 cm |
| D. (feet) | 18 15/16 in. | 48.1 cm |

**Materials:** *Microanalysis:* Primary: cherry. Secondary: soft maple group (loose-seat frame). *Finish:* light reddish brown color in resin. *Upholstery:* block-printed polychrome cotton with "Indienne"-style floral forms; France, 1780–1800.

**Exhibitions:** "Accessions 1960," Winterthur Museum, Winterthur, Del., December 21, 1960–February 1, 1961. "Legacy of a Provincial Elite: New London County Joined Chairs, 1720–1790," Connecticut Historical Society and Lyman Allyn Museum, Hartford and Norwich, October 1, 1985–February 28, 1986.

**Publications:** *Accessions 1960* (Winterthur, Del.: Winterthur Museum, 1960), fig. 6, pp. 11–12. John T. Kirk, "The Distinctive Character of Connecticut Furniture," *Antiques* 92, no. 4 (October 1967): 528, fig. 8. Kirk, *American Chairs*, fig. 187. Trent with Nelson, "A Catalogue of New London County Joined Chairs," no. 16.

**Accession history:** Museum purchase from David Stockwell, Inc., Greenville, Del., 1960. 60.107

---

1. *Accessions 1960* (Winterthur, Del.: Winterthur Museum, 1960), fig. 6, pp. 11–12. Penrose R. Hoopes, "Notes on Some Colonial Cabinetmakers of Hartford," *Antiques* 23, no. 5 (May 1933): 171–72. Trent with Nelson, "A Catalogue of New London County Joined Chairs," no. 16. Bernard Levy to Robert F. Trent, January 7, 1986, folder 60.107, Registration Office, Winterthur.

2. For British examples with spurs, see Edgar G. Miller, Jr., *American Antique Furniture: A Book for Amateurs*, 2 vols. (Baltimore: Lord Baltimore Press, 1966), 1: figs. 53, 56; Kirk, *American Furniture*, figs. 832, 841, 842, 859, 891, 893; Hinckley, *Directory*, ill. 270. For American examples, see Kirk, *American Furniture*, figs. 833, 838, 890, 892; Downs, *American Furniture*, figs. 103, 121, 122; Jobe and Kaye, *New England Furniture*, nos. 108, 122; Kirk, *American Chairs*, figs. 52, 56, 57, 60, 61, 135, 147, 148, 180; *American Antiques from Israel Sack Collection*, 10 vols. (Washington, D.C.: Highland House, ca. 1969–), 4:920; Warren, *Bayou Bend*, nos. 41, 45, 46, 48, 75; Trent with Nelson, "A Catalogue of New London County Joined Chairs," p. 67.

3. Trent, "New London County Joined Chairs," pp. 15–22; Trent with Nelson, "A Catalogue of New London County Joined Chairs," pp. 67–69, 72–75, nos. 20, 21, 28, 31, fig. 16. For the Waring chair, see Bernard and S. Dean Levy, Inc., *In Search of Excellence* (New York: By the company, n.d.), p. 16.

4. For a chair of trapezoidal seat plan, see *American Antiques from Sack Collection*, 2:526.

## 22 ◆ Side chair
Fairfield County, Connecticut
1740–75

This chair and a mate in the Winterthur collection have long been without a firm regional attribution. The chair back (crest, splat, and posts) is a close copy of the standard Boston vase-back pattern of Nos. 7 and 9. When splat tracings of this chair and No. 7 are compared, this pattern is found to be slightly longer through the baluster and slimmer overall. Even the splats of this chair and its mate are not exact in every detail. The lengths vary by half an inch, even though the splats were produced from the same template. Because the discrepancies are confined to the base and ogee top, the reduction occurred in the framing process. Further comparison of the splat tracings from this chair and its mate indicates that the chairmaker who scribed the pattern on his maple chair stock let the

template slip during one tracing; thus the base curves of the two splats do not line up exactly.

Substantial deviation from standard southern New England regional seating types is manifest in the undercarriage of this chair. The side balusters, which have necked bases, are variants of the normal bulbous pattern (fig. 1). More unusual are the features of the front legs, including heavy knees, vertical creases, and distinctive pads. The ankles and feet are united abruptly with little transition from the tight curves of the lower legs to the flat tops of the pads. An extensive search of pictorial source materials has produced only a few pieces of furniture with the same rare foot: a cabriole-leg star-inlaid dressing table with strong William and Mary styling; a high chest of drawers ascribed to the Hartford area; a small, drop-leaf table with a family history in the town of Fairfield, Connecticut; and another vase-splat saddle-crested Queen Anne

side chair with a Fairfield County family history. Three other high chests of drawers with similar or related feet have been associated in recent furniture studies with Stratford, Woodbury, and the lower Housatonic River valley.[1]

Although this chair and the chair that descended in a Fairfield County family have little more than similar feet and upper back features in common, distinctly provincial characteristics associate them with Connecticut chairmaking and especially with coastal Connecticut work as produced from Fairfield County to New London County. The thick knees, squared legs, conical and baluster stretcher elements, and thin cross braces of this chair (see fig. 1) and the cusped knee brackets and extended side-rail returns of the Fairfield County family chair are features also present in New London County work. Of further note, the creased-leg feature of this chair also occurs on the drop-leaf table and high chest of drawers from Woodbury. Evidence for the Connecticut attribution of this chair is strong; the ascription to Fairfield County seems justified.[2]

NGE

Inscriptions or marks: *Chiseled on front seat-rail rabbet:* "IIII".

**Construction:** The molded crest is supported on rectangular tenons at the flat-faced contoured post tops (pinned) and splat. The crest saddle is rounded

**Fig. 1.** Detail, left side undercarriage.

at the back; the arches are chamfered, top and bottom. The slim splat is flat at the edges and tenoned into the plinth. The plinth is hollow on the front and side faces, finished with a top bead, and nailed to the back rail. The rear post corners are chamfered from crest to seat. The flat-arched seat rails are finished with a prominent applied bead at the upper edge and an interior rabbet. The rails are joined to the posts and front leg extensions with rectangular tenons (pinned). The rear legs are chamfered on all corners between the rails and rear stretcher. The front legs are marked by sharp creases down the front, back, and side faces. The large, flat-topped pad feet are supported on large disks. The slim side stretchers are round tenoned into the front legs and joined to the back legs with rectangular tenons (pinned); the medial and rear stretchers are round tenoned into the adjacent members.

**Condition:** The right rear crest joint with the post is damaged. A horizontal spline repair occurs at the lower splat back, and the lower forward edge of the plinth is damaged. All knee brackets appear to be replaced; lighter wood surfaces on the seat rails indicate that the original brackets were wider and thicker. The left front leg extension is cracked at the side pin. The medial and right side stretchers are nicked on the lower surfaces. The right tip of the medial stretcher is too small for the mortise, although the opposite side fits well; the problem appears to be an original mistake.

**Dimensions:**

| | | |
|---|---|---|
| H. | 40$^7$/$_{16}$ in. | 102.8 cm |
| H. (seat) | 17$^{11}$/$_{16}$ in. | 44.9 cm |
| W. (crest) | 14$^7$/$_8$ in. | 35.9 cm |
| W. (seat front) | 20$^3$/$_4$ in. | 52.7 cm |
| W. (seat back) | 14$^3$/$_4$ in. | 37.5 cm |
| W. (feet) | 22 in. | 55.9 cm |
| D. (seat) | 17$^3$/$_{16}$ in. | 43.6 cm |
| D. (feet) | 21$^1$/$_2$ in. | 54.6 cm |

**Materials:** *Microanalysis:* Primary: soft maple group. *Finish:* light brown color in resin with evidence of former darker coat removed. *Upholstery:* modern brown leather.

**Accession history:** Bequest of H. F. du Pont, 1969. 58.1739

1. For the dressing table and Hartford-area high chest of drawers, see *American Antiques from Israel Sack Collection,* 10 vols. (Washington, D.C.: Highland House, ca. 1969–), 4:959; 2:387; for the drop-leaf table and Queen Anne side chair, see *Connecticut Furniture,* nos. 164, 231; for the Stratford high chest of drawers, see Edward S. Cooke, Jr., "The Work of Brewster Dayton and Ebenezer Hubbell of Stratford, Connecticut," *Connecticut Historical Society Bulletin* 51, no. 4 (Fall 1986): 217; for the Woodbury high chest of drawers, see Edward S. Cooke, Jr., *Fiddlebacks and Crooked-backs: Elijah Booth and Other Joiners in Newtown and Woodbury, 1750–1820* (Waterbury, Conn.: Mattatuck Historical Society, 1982), fig. 25; for the Housatonic River valley high chest of drawers, see Jobe and Kaye, *New England Furniture,* no. 41. Stratford lies within Fairfield County; Woodbury is just outside. The Housatonic River forms the boundary between Fairfield and New Haven counties.

2. Trent with Nelson, "A Catalogue of New London County Joined Chairs," cats. 5, 6, 15, 16, 20–23, 25, 46, 49, 50, fig. 16; see also Nos. 20, 21 in this volume. Trent, *Hearts and Crowns,* nos. 27, 63, 65, 67, 73.

## 23 ◆ Side chair
Boston, Massachusetts
1735–60

Until recently, one of the challenges that faced modern furniture historians was the regional assignment of New England Queen Anne shell-crested chairs with solid splats such as that illustrated here and in No. 24. Reliable criteria to identify Newport and Boston production have been difficult to establish given the close communication that existed between the two communities beginning in the early eighteenth century. Records document substantial commercial interaction, although Boston, which was more than twice the size of Newport by 1750, established an aggressive coastal furniture trade early in the century, especially in chairs. An equally vigorous pattern of furniture exportation was developed at Newport by the 1750s, if not earlier; however, the principal

products of this trade were tables and case furniture, especially desks. New evidence and a reevaluation of the old documentation now indicate strongly that Boston dominated the seating furniture trade in Rhode Island until midcentury to the virtual exclusion of chair production in that region.[1]

This chair, which represents one small subgroup of shell-crested chairs with back posts that are straight in the frontal plane, is part of a larger body of Queen Anne seating furniture dominated by sweep back posts that conform to the splat curves (see No. 24). The shell pattern further limits the subgroup size; the modified scallop with its finely ribbed flutes is relatively rare (fig. 1). Less than a dozen chairs carved with a shell of this type have been published. Most are made of walnut, and none have histories of ownership. Even within this small group there are variations: straight (canted) and contoured

**Fig. 1.** Detail, crest shell.

backs (in profile); compass and rectangular seats; flat-arched and scalloped front rails; round-tipped medial stretchers and block-ended braces.[2]

The finely ribbed shell remained a choice in seating furniture for several decades. Some of the so-called owl's-eye chairs have a closely related shell, the shape modified somewhat due to the double-sweep crest design (see No. 31). The turned braces in the support structure of this chair are those introduced a few years earlier in the saddle-crested Queen Anne chair with a plain baluster splat (see Nos. 7, 8, 10). The splat here represents an advance over the earlier pattern, with its deeply incut shoulders forming volutes. The T-shape neck between the volutes, which supports the ogee-shape splat head, is common to the entire shell-crested group, although it is not always as carefully defined.[3]

*NGE*

---

**Inscriptions or marks:** *Chiseled on inside front seat rail:* "I".

**Construction:** The crest is supported on rectangular tenons at the flat-faced contoured post tops and splat. The finely ridged shell is carved from solid wood. The crest face is slightly cheeked at the arches; the back is chamfered at the arches and center base. The splat is canted at the edges, front to back, and tenoned into the plinth. The plinth is hollow on the front and side faces, finished with a top bead, and nailed to the back rail. The rear post corners are chamfered from crest to seat. The compass seat is rounded at the lip and sawed in flat, tooled arches at the bottom. An interior rabbet,

forming a rectangular opening, supports the loose-seat frame. The rails are joined to the posts and front leg extensions with rectangular tenons (pinned). Small 1/2"-by-1/2" vertical glueblocks flank the interior faces of the front leg extensions below the rabbet. The back legs are chamfered on all four corners between the seat and rear stretcher; the feet are canted on the forward faces and chamfered at the front corners. A small ledge occurs at the backs of the front pad feet. The side stretchers are joined to the legs with vertical rectangular tenons (pinned at back). The creased-tip medial and rear stretchers are round tenoned into the adjacent members.

**Condition:** The left front rail joint is reinforced with a modern metal brace. The interior front glueblocks are not original. Modern nails and screws secure three knee brackets. The outside knee bracket of the left front leg, which consists of two pieces of wood, is replaced. A crack in the left front leg extension is repaired. The forward tips of the front feet are worn, and the face of the left rear leg is cracked above and below the stretcher joint.

**Dimensions:**

| | | |
|---|---|---|
| H. | 38 13/16 in. | 98.7 cm |
| H. (seat) | 16 3/4 in. | 42.5 cm |
| W. (crest) | 15 1/2 in. | 39.3 cm |
| W. (seat front) | 20 15/16 in. | 53.2 cm |
| W. (seat back) | 15 3/16 in. | 38.6 cm |
| W. (feet) | 22 1/16 in. | 56.0 cm |
| D. (seat) | 17 in. | 43.2 cm |
| D. (feet) | 20 5/8 in. | 52.4 cm |

**Materials:** *Microanalysis:* Primary: American black walnut. *Finish:* medium yellowish brown color in resin. *Upholstery:* solidly worked crewel embroidery in a fanciful pattern of animals, insects, and flowers surrounding a female figure; probably Massachusetts, 1740–70.

**Exhibitions:** "Beyond Necessity: Art in the Folk Tradition," Brandywine River Museum, Chadds Ford, Pa., September 17–November 20, 1977.

**Publications:** Downs, *American Furniture*, fig. 101.

**Accession history:** Bequest of H. F. du Pont, 1969. 58.2219

---

1. Jobe and Kaye, *New England Furniture*, pp. 3–46; Margaretta Markle Lovell, "Boston Blockfront Furniture," in *Boston Furniture*, pp. 114–25; Forman, *American Seating Furniture*, pp. 284–87; Jeanne Vibert Sloane, "John Cahoone and the Newport Furniture Industry," in *New England Furniture*, pp. 88–98; Keno, Freund, and Miller, "Very Pink of the Mode," pp. 266–306.

2. For other chairs with this shell, see *American Antiques from Israel Sack Collection*, 10 vols. (Washington, D.C.: Highland House, ca. 1969–), 6:1544, 7:1846; Ralph E. Carpenter, Jr., *The Arts and Crafts of Newport, Rhode Island, 1640–1820* (Newport: Preservation Society of Newport County, 1954), no. 9; Craig and Tarlton advertisement, *Antiques* 98, no. 6 (December 1970): 839; Northeast Auctions, "New Hampshire Auction" (November 5–6, 1994), lot 487; Northeast Auctions, "New Hampshire Auction" (March 3, 1996), lot 679.

3. The backs in a closely related group of chairs vary from this pattern in the absence of the crest shell; a few have totally rounded back posts and some a scalloped front seat rail. Other chairs in this group have shells comparable to that in No. 24. Two chairs have histories: one is said to have descended from Joshua Otis, Jr., and Mary Otis (m. 1769) of Scituate, Mass. (see *American Antiques from Sack Collection*, 1:60); the other from Elizabeth Lord Eliot (m. 1760) (see Elisabeth Donaghy Garrett, "American Furniture in the DAR Museum," *Antiques* 109, no. 4 [April 1976]: 751, fig. 3); see also William H. Eliot, Jr., comp., and William S. Porter, ed., *Genealogy of the Eliot Family* (New Haven: George B. Bassett, 1854), pp. 68, 74.

## 24 ◆ Side chair (one of four)
Boston, Massachusetts
1740–65

Shell-crested Queen Anne chairs distinguished by sweep back posts that conform to the splat contours have been identified only recently as Boston products. Previously, many chairs of this pattern were assigned to Rhode Island, based on their long associations there with local families. Boston merchants shipped quantities of joined chairs acquired from the city's chairmakers to coastal markets, of which Rhode Island was a principal one. The chair was also popular in the home market, although no documented examples are known. Of those chairs with traditions of ownership, more are associated with Massachusetts than Rhode Island families. Two basic splat patterns occur: the plain, attenuated, volute-shouldered baluster of this chair and a similar one with prominent opposing lobes near the base. In early interpretations of the sweep-post style, the slim ogee-top splat common to Massachusetts chairs of the early 1730s is retained (see No. 7). All three splats appear in both pad-foot and ball-and-claw examples. Generally, the crest shell of the sweep-post group is similar to that illustrated—a deeply channeled, fluted pattern on a double-volute base. The same shell is also more common in the straight-post chair group than the finely ribbed shell of No. 23.[1]

The earliest sweep-post chairs have pad feet. The seat frames are either rectangular with a scalloped front (a lunette flanked by ogees) or compass shape with flat arches. Rare variants include a scalloped-front example with a pierced splat and a compass-seat chair without flat arches. Heavy, columnar-turned side stretchers are common throughout the group, regardless of the foot type. The medial and back stretchers in the pad-foot chairs are

similar to those of No. 23—long, swelled turnings flanked by conical tips.[2]

The seat shape of the fully developed volute-splat claw-foot chair is a compass with flat arches. The turned medial stretcher is heavier than in the pad-foot chair, its ends formed of blocks and large rings or swells that visually balance the large front claws. The carved-foot profiles are variable, ranging from compressed to square to long oval patterns; most are webbed between the multijointed toes. The knees are ornamented with vertical scallop shells and pendent bellflowers of a fairly standard pattern that differs substantially from the broad horizontally oriented crest shell (figs. 1, 2). The existence of at least one pair of chairs having gilded shells and the popularity of that enrichment in japanned and other furniture of the early eighteenth century suggests that this

embellishment was a more common customer option than is now apparent.[3]

The most distinctive feature of the group represented by this chair is the inward sweep of the back posts. The curved line, which introduced a new and stylish figure to the Queen Anne chair, complements the ogees of the splat, seat frame, and legs. The common method of constructing sweep back posts was to piece out the projecting inside cheeks in order to save expensive stock, such as walnut or mahogany. The pattern was fashionable in Britain beginning in the 1710s, along with the elongated scallop shell and pendent bellflower at the knees. There are subtly different American versions of the sweep. In this chair type the inside lower curve begins at or slightly below the bottom of the baluster. In the second version, the inside break begins well below the baluster near the splat base;

**Fig. 1.** Detail, right front knee shell and pendant.

**Fig. 2.** Detail, crest shell.

those chair backs tend to be broader, minimizing the verticality of the chair. The pad-foot and early claw-foot chairs generally belong to the first group.[4]

Documentation providing insights into the dimensions of the Boston chair trade is found in claims submitted to the city by several members of the woodworking community for losses sustained in the great Boston fire of March 1760. William Freeland, a joiner, had twelve mahogany "Compass Seat Carved Feet" chairs under construction when the disaster occurred. Chairmakers Henry Perkins and John Perkins were similarly employed making compass-seat chairs. Henry's timber stock included maple, mahogany, and walnut. Some of the walnut was described as "feat Stuf," probably referring to four-by-four-inch stock suitable for producing cabriole legs with pad or claw feet. John lost "220 wallnot Feet for Chairs" in the conflagration.[5]

NGE

---

**Inscriptions or marks:** *Chiseled on front seat rail and loose-seat frame:* "XI".

**Construction:** The crest is supported on rectangular tenons at the straight, flat-faced post tops and splat. The shell is carved from solid wood. The crest face is cheeked at the arches; the back is rounded at the arches, chamfered at the center base, and tooled with depressions behind alternating shell flutes. The splat is canted at the edges, front to back, and tenoned into the plinth. The plinth is hollow on the front and side faces, finished with a top bead, and nailed to the back rail. The inner cheeks of the back-post sweeps are pieced. The upper post backs are rounded to the sweeps where the surface is flat with chamfered corners. The outside chamfer terminates 1½" higher than the inside chamfer. The compass-shape seat is rounded at the top lip and sawed in flat, tooled arches at the bottom. An

internal rabbet, forming a rectangular opening, supports the loose-seat frame. The rails are joined to the posts and front leg extensions with rectangular tenons (pinned, except back rail). Brackets at the rear side and back rails are nailed in place. The rear legs are chamfered on all corners between the brackets and the rear stretcher. The feet are canted on the forward faces and chamfered at the front corners. The front leg shells and pendent husks are carved in low relief; the knee brackets are attached with nails. The side stretchers are joined to the legs with vertical rectangular tenons (pinned, side rear); horizontal rectangular tenons secure the medial stretcher. The creased-tip rear stretcher is round tenoned into the back legs.

**Condition:** The right rear rail bracket is replaced. The left stretcher is cracked and chipped on the inside face; an additional pin secures the joint with the back leg.

**Dimensions:**

| | | |
|---|---|---|
| H. | 39 in. | 99.0 cm |
| H. (seat) | 16½ in. | 41.9 cm |
| W. (crest) | 16 in. | 40.6 cm |
| W. (seat front) | 20¾ in. | 52.7 cm |
| W. (seat back) | 15⅛ in. | 38.4 cm |
| W. (feet) | 21⅜ in. | 54.3 cm |
| D. (seat) | 16¾ in. | 42.5 cm |
| D. (feet) | 20 in. | 50.8 cm |

**Materials:** *Microanalysis:* Primary: American black walnut. Secondary: soft maple group (loose-seat

frame). *Finish:* medium light yellowish brown color in resin. *Upholstery:* modern brown leather, although fragments of eighteenth-century red wool were found beneath old rosehead nails.

**Accession history:** Purchased by H. F. du Pont from Israel Sack, Inc., Boston and New York, 1929. Bequest of H. F. du Pont, 1969.
60.719.1

---

1. Keno, Freund, and Miller, "Very Pink of the Mode," pp. 266–306.

2. For a photograph of a pierced-splat chair, see no. 70.3883, DAPC, Visual Resources Collection, Winterthur Library; for the compass-seat chair, see C. L. Prickett advertisement, *Antiques* 132, no. 2 (August 1987): 224.

3. For a pair of gilded-shell chairs, see Leigh Keno advertisement, *Antiques* 136, no. 3 (September 1989): 368. A carved vertical shell similar to the one on the knees that extends down into the splat is a rare Boston crest variation; see *John Brown House Loan Exhibition*, cat. 8.

4. For English sweep-post chairs, see Macquoid and Edwards, *Dictionary*, p. 252, fig. 85; p. 255, fig. 86. Other examples are in the Robert Wemyss Symonds Collection, nos. 59.453, 59.475, 59.494, 59.508, 59.511, 59.526, DAPC, Visual Resources Collection, Winterthur Library. For broad-back chairs with lower sweeps, see Albert Sack, *Fine Points of Furniture: Early American* (New York: Crown Publishers, 1961), p. 23.

5. Boston Fire Documents and Correspondence, vol. 2, pp. 34, 79, 81, Boston Public Library, Boston.

## 25 ◆ Side chair (one of a pair)
Boston, Massachusetts
1740–55

This chair, like that in No. 15, has been assigned to Boston after a long association with New York cabinetmaking. The material of the splat beneath the walnut veneer is birch, a wood long associated with northeastern New England but uncommon in New York chairs. The splat, the central decorative feature of the chair, represents a logical advance in profile from that of No. 24, with the introduction of two lobes at the base of the vase complementing those at the top. The sweeps of the posts emphasize the strong curves of the central feature. This chair, numbered "VII" inside the front seat rail, has a mate (also at Winterthur) numbered "X" that defines the minimum size of the original set. One other chair with identical features throughout, probably also from the same set,

has been located. Winterthur's chair represents one of many Queen Anne–style pattern variations produced in the busy cabinet and chair shops of Boston for the coastal trade during the 1730s and 1740s. Variety in element profile and ornament from set to set seems to have been the norm and accounts for the difficulty in finding exact mates among surviving chairs.[1]

This chair represents the blending and Americanization of several British designs that entered the market in the early eighteenth century. The blocked-end medial stretcher with its large knobs, introduced in English seating furniture before 1720, became one of the signatures of Boston chairmaking. The trifid-type foot on the front legs is a rare design on both sides of the Atlantic; introduced in England during the second quarter of the century, it may have spawned Irish as well as American imitations. One of its distinctive characteristics is the ledge that

separates the foot proper from the platform (fig. 1). This support lacks the definition and detail, however, of the trifid foot produced in Philadelphia.[2]

The double-lobed splat in British chairmaking may date no earlier than the 1730s; it also had its Irish provincial copies. Compared to other interpretations, the clean simple lines of the Boston pattern are distinctive. Isolated shells with or without pendent drops, as introduced to the front legs of this chair, also have their models in British chairmaking. Less common in American work dating before 1750 is the crest shell accompanied by supplementary carving. This one is sensitively executed with flanking, scrolled-leaf sprigs (fig. 2). It relates generally to a more ornate interpretation in a set of chairs associated with wealthy Boston merchant Charles Apthorpe.[3]

Boston chairs fitted with double-lobed splats are a diverse group, with mixed and matched elements. Crest shells are varied in pattern and are usually unaccompanied by other ornament. A shell may be absent from the front knees, or the knees may be lined with a long, thin, carved scroll (see No. 15) or bracketed with a large uncarved scroll (see No. 26). Round pads or ball-and-claw feet are often substituted for the trifid terminal. A chair with claw feet and a variant shell in the crest is chisel-marked "Boston" on its loose-seat frame. A tipped stretcher sometimes substitutes for the knobbed one, or stretchers may be absent altogether. Occasionally, the rear leg is rounded between the seat and the side stretchers.[4]

This chair and its mate retain their original chisel-marked loose-seat frames, which have their original upholstery foundations. Still in place are the webbing, mounted in a two-by-two pattern; linen sackcloth; stuffing of grass and Spanish moss; and linen undercover (mostly retacked). An even rarer survival are the remnants of twine at the crossings of the

**Fig. 1.** Detail, right front foot.

webbing used to keep the support from shifting under the weight of a sitter.

NGE

**Inscriptions or marks:** *Chiseled on front seat-rail rabbet and loose-seat frame:* "VII".

**Construction:** The crest is supported on rectangular tenons at the straight, flat-faced post tops and splat. The shell is carved in high relief from the solid wood; the small scrolls and leafy floral sprigs are executed in low relief. The flat crest face is cheeked at the arches; the back is rounded at the arches, flattened through the center, and tooled at the center top with ribs and flutes to a 1" depth. The splat is canted at the tooled edges, front to back, and tenoned into the plinth; the front face is veneered with figured wood. The plinth is hollow on the front and side faces, finished with a flattened top bead and nailed to the back rail. The inner cheeks of the back-post sweeps are pieced. The upper post backs are rounded at the top and then flattened from above the pieced cheeks through the seat framing. The compass-shape seat is rounded at the top lip and sawed in flat arches at the bottom. An internal rabbet supports the loose-seat frame. The rails are joined to the posts and front leg

extensions with rectangular tenons (pinned). The rear legs are chamfered on all corners between the seat frame and stretchers. The feet are canted on the forward faces and chamfered at the front corners. The front leg shells are ribbed and fluted in low relief; the pendent bellflowers bear lightly tooled striations. The knee brackets are glued, nailed twice, and heavily tooled on the bottom. The shallow trifid feet are supported on high conforming platforms, the two separated visually by a narrow ledge around the outside. The side stretchers are joined to the legs with vertical rectangular tenons (pinned, side rear); horizontal rectangular tenons secure the medial stretcher (pinned). The conical-tipped rear stretcher round tenons into the back legs.

**Condition:** The outside tip of the lower right splat lobe was broken off and reattached behind the veneer; age cracks are present in the veneer. The pins for the side seat rails are new. A narrow vertical spline of wood 1⁵/₈" long is inserted at the center face of the left leg extension. The rear pins of the side stretchers are new; the columnar ring of the right stretcher is chipped on the top surface, and the blocks are defaced on the lower surface. Overall there are surface blemishes and nicks.

**Dimensions:**

| | | |
|---|---|---|
| H. | 39¹/₄ in. | 99.7 cm |
| H. (seat) | 17³/₈ in. | 44.1 cm |
| W. (crest) | 15 in. | 38.1 cm |
| W. (seat front) | 20⁷/₈ in. | 53.0 cm |
| W. (seat back) | 15⁵/₁₆ in. | 38.9 cm |
| W. (feet) | 21⁷/₈ in. | 55.6 cm |
| D. (seat) | 17¹/₂ in. | 44.4 cm |
| D. (feet) | 21⁷/₈ in. | 55.6 cm |

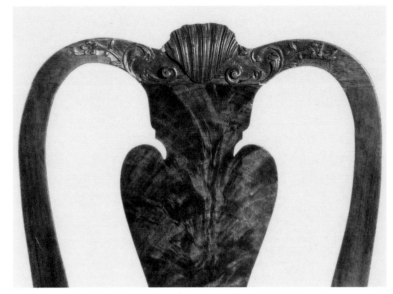

**Fig. 2.** Detail, crest.

**Materials:** *Microanalysis:* Primary: walnut. Secondary: birch (splat backing); maple (loose-seat frame). *Finish:* medium dark reddish brown color in resin. *Upholstery:* original loose-seat frame retains its original stuffing materials of linen cloth, dried grass, and Spanish moss; modern white and blue resist-dyed cotton slipcover.

**Accession history:** Purchased by H. F. du Pont from John S. Walton, Inc., New York, 1952. Gift of H. F. du Pont, 1952.
52.66.2

---

1. The chair with identical features is in the Museum of the City of New York; see Keno, Freund, and Miller, "Very Pink of the Mode," fig. 29.

2. For British prototypes, see Macquoid and Edwards, *Dictionary*, 1:254, fig. 84; Kirk, *American Furniture*, figs. 782, 784, 789, 795, 810, 823, 918.

3. For British prototypes, see Macquoid and Edwards, *Dictionary*, 1:255, fig. 86; p. 257, fig. 95; p. 263, figs. 116, 117; p. 264, fig. 121; Kirk, *American Furniture*, figs. 791, 805, 809, 819–22, 824, 827, 828, 831, 832. For an Apthorpe chair, see Heckscher, *American Furniture*, cat. No. 22.

4. For variant patterns in the double-lobed splat-style chair, see *American Antiques from Israel Sack Collection*, 10 vols. (Washington, D.C.: Highland House, 1969–), 2:337, 3:605; William Voss Elder III and Jayne E. Stokes, *American Furniture, 1680–1880, from the Collection of the Baltimore Museum of Art* (Baltimore: By the Museum, 1987), cat. no. 8; Ginsburg and Levy advertisement, *Antiques* 55, no. 6 (June 1949): 417; Heckscher, *American Furniture*, cat. nos. 8, 21; Ronald A. DeSilva advertisement, *Antiques* 108, no. 5 (November 1975): 889; Kirk, *American Chairs*, figs. 169, 170. For the Boston-marked chair, see Moses, *Master Craftsmen*, fig. 1.50.

## 26 ◆ Side chair
### Boston, Massachusetts
### 1735–50

A classic splat profile in Queen Anne chairs with unpierced backs is one with a bold, bulging, apple-shape element supported on a short baluster. The element has prototypes in English chairs, although the pattern is uncommon. Of the three English chairs noted, all have shell-carved knees of the general type found in No. 27, and one has both a double-ogee plinth and a crest shell closely similar to those in this chair. The primary wood is walnut.[1]

Boston chairs in the general style of this chair, featuring a high-relief unpierced shell in the crest, have more similarities than differences. They share the following: a bulging splat flanked by conforming posts, a double-ogee bead at the plinth top, a compass seat, tapered rear legs terminating in blocked feet, and uncarved, volute-type knee brackets. Variable features appear in the crest, knees, and front feet. By far the most common shell is the one illustrated, with bold ribs and flutes underscored by a hollow serpentine ribbon tipped by tiny volutes. In almost half the surveyed chairs with this shell, the crest is further carved with delicate sprigged ornament of the general type in No. 25. An alternative shell on two chairs (or sets of chairs) of the thirteen surveyed is more finely ribbed, supported on long opposing C scrolls, and accompanied by sprigged carving.[2]

Few chairs of this pattern are plain at the knees, as in this example. Of the sample, 85 percent are embellished with a carved elongated shell and pendent drop at the knee. About one-third of the shells are underlined with a voluted ribbon of the general type found in the crest. The two chairs in the sample with plain knees also have trifid feet. The common terminal is a deeply webbed claw grasping a ball.[3]

Chairs with apple-shape splats likely were introduced to the Boston chair market in the mid to late 1730s. With their boldly sawed, figured-veneer banisters and ornamental accompaniments, they stand in sharp contrast to the leanly defined, inverted-baluster saddle-top chairs that were the bread and butter of the trade (see Nos. 7, 9). Veneered-splat chairs appealed to a high-end market whose members were principally men of wealth.

Although the history of Winterthur's chair is not known, several of the other chairs (or sets) surveyed have known backgrounds. At least four are associated with families who resided in New York city or state, a factor that led in the early part of the twentieth century to the assignment of the pattern to that area. Radcliffe Baldwin of New York City owned an original set of twelve chairs. Other chairs descended in the Yates family of Schenectady, among whose owners Joseph C. Yates

(1768–1837) was mayor of that city and governor of the state. Another chair is said to have been owned in the Roosevelt family.[4]

A chair chisel-marked "IIII" on the front rail that descended from John Aspinwall (1707–74), a wealthy merchant and landholder in New York City, to the last private owner probably represents a larger original set. Aspinwall could have ordered and taken delivery of the chairs in person during one or more of his known voyages to Boston; several business associates also owned Boston furniture. The shell in Aspinwall's chair, like that in Winterthur's chair, has a baroque character, and the splat is veneered with figured walnut. The legs are more elegantly styled with carved shells and claw feet. Although Aspinwall died in 1774, the turmoil of the war years delayed the filing of his probate inventory until 1786. Between Aspinwall's New York City house and his country seat in Flushing (Queens borough), appraisers itemized a total of eighty-three chairs. Some are identified as vernacular seating, and twenty-six others were made of mahogany. The listing that is the best candidate for describing the veneered-splat walnut chair reads: "6 Red Bottom'd Chairs & 1 Elbow'd d[itt]o." The chairs were located in the "back Parlour." Three more red-bottomed chairs were kept in Mrs. Aspinwall's room and two others in a room occupied by Paschal N. Smith, who probably was a business partner of Aspinwall (all may have been part of the same set). The seat covers likely were a worsted fabric. Another group of leather-bottom chairs, the color reported once as black, was divided between the properties.[5]

A set of chairs with a Boston history provides additional insights on the types of seat covers used on the walnut-splat chairs. The set, today divided among three institutional collections, retains its original needlework covers with large, polychrome flowers on a mustard ground. By tradition, the chairs descended in the Fayerweather-Bromfield families, a history reinforced by the inscription "Cap^n Fayerweather" on one of the seat frames. Merchant John Fayerweather (1685–1760) was the father of Margaret Fayerweather (1732–61), the presumed needleworker who in 1749 married merchant Henry Bromfield (1727–1820) of Boston and London.[6]

NGE

**Inscriptions or marks:** *Chiseled on front seat-rail rabbet:* "V".

**Construction:** The crest is supported on rectangular tenons at the straight, flat-faced post tops and splat. The shell is carved in high relief from the solid wood. The flat crest face is slightly cheeked at the arches; the back is rounded at the arches and along the center bottom, flattened behind the shell, and deeply notched at the top behind the shell ribs. The contoured splat is deeply canted at the tooled edges, front to back, and tenoned into the plinth; the front face is veneered with figured wood. The plinth, carved with a double-ogee bead across the top and one piece with the rear seat rail, is hollow on the front and side faces. The angular inner cheeks of the back-post sweeps are pieced. The post backs are rounded from the top into the low sweeps, flattened, then blocked at the seat framing. The compass-shape seat is rounded at the top lip; an internal rabbet supports the loose-seat frame. The rails are joined to the posts and front leg extensions with rectangular tenons (pinned). The interior corner blocks are rectangular. The rear legs are squared and rounded and supported on squared feet that flare outward and backward. The front legs are rounded to the feet, except for a small section at the lower back, which is flattened to form three small panels extending through the foot platforms. The shallow trifid feet are supported on high conforming platforms, the two separated visually by a narrow ledge around the outside. The uncarved scrolled knee brackets are glued in place and faced on the back with small tenoned and glued blocks. The backs of the side rails are fitted with two-part brackets nailed in place; the back rail has small ogee brackets nailed in place.

**Condition:** The splat has a small piece of veneer replaced on the left side edge of the bulbous upper element. Small triangular pieces of wood broke out of the back posts and were reglued: inside the left post at the crest joint and on the rear face of the right post at the crest. Vertical stress cracks appear in the posts: left post, inside face at the back seat rail; right post, outside face from the sweep through the seat block and onto the upper leg where it curves onto the forward face. A horizontal stress crack occurs on the upper rear corner of the left side rail. The rear sweep of the right rear foot broke off and was replaced. The rear seat blocks have been replaced; the front ones, which could be original, were remounted. The scrolled bracket on the left side face of the left front leg is a replacement. The loose-seat frame is modern.

**Dimensions:**

| | | |
|---|---|---|
| H. | 38 1/8 in. | 96.8 cm |
| H. (seat) | 16 1/2 in. | 41.9 cm |
| W. (crest) | 16 5/8 in. | 42.2 cm |
| W. (seat front) | 21 in. | 53.3 cm |
| W. (seat back) | 15 1/2 in. | 39.4 cm |
| W. (feet) | 21 1/4 in. | 54.0 cm |
| D. (seat) | 18 5/8 in. | 47.3 cm |
| D. (feet) | 21 1/2 in. | 52.1 cm |

**Materials:** *Microanalysis:* Primary: walnut. Secondary: maple (splat backing). *Finish:* medium dark reddish brown color in resin. *Upholstery:* quilted and pieced white cotton (discolored) resist dyed in 2 shades of blue in pattern of woody vines with leaves of various types; probably England, ca. 1770.

**Accession history:** Purchased by H. F. du Pont from John S. Walton, Inc., New York, 1952. Gift of H. F. du Pont, 1952.
52.140

1. Kirk, *American Furniture*, figs. 803, 805; Keno, Freund, and Miller, "Very Pink of the Mode," fig. 3.

2. For chairs in the survey, see Bishop, *Centuries and Styles of the American Chair*, fig. 90 (alternative shell); Rollins, *Treasures of State*, cat. no. 11; Kirk, *American Chairs*, fig. 131; Fales, *Furniture of Historic Deerfield*, fig. 80; John L. Scherer, *New York Furniture at the New York State Museum* (Alexandria, Va.: Highland House, 1984), fig. 5; *American Antiques from Israel Sack Collection*, 10 vols. (Washington, D.C.: Highland House, 1969–), 5:1166; Sotheby Parke Bernet, "Fine Americana" (September 26, 1981), lot 431; Bernard and S. Dean Levy, Inc., *Catalogue IV* (New York: By the company, 1984), p. 20; Bernard and S. Dean Levy, Inc., *"Opulence and Splendor": The New York Chair, 1690–1830* (New York: By the company, 1984), p. 4; Northeast Auctions, "Annual Summer New Hampshire Auction" (August 3–4, 1996), lot 580; Comstock, *American Furniture*, no. 158; Ginsburg and Levy advertisement, *Antiques* 93, no. 3 (March 1968): 281 (alternative shell).

3. For the second chair with plain knees, see *American Antiques from Sack Collection*, 5:1166.

4. For a Baldwin chair, see Ginsburg and Levy advertisement; for the Yates family chair, see Scherer, *New York Furniture*, fig. 5; on the Roosevelt chair, see *American Antiques from Sack Collection*, 1:22 upper left.

5. For the Aspinwall chair, see Rollins, *Treasures of State*, cat. no. 11. John Aspinwall inventory, New York, 1774/86, Downs collection.

6. For 2 Fayerweather-Bromfield chairs, now in the Brooklyn Museum, see *American Antiques from Sack Collection*, 2:433; for a chair (1 of 2) from the set in the MFA, Boston, see Museum of Fine Arts, Boston, *Paul Revere's Boston, 1735–1818* (Boston: By the Museum, 1975), no. 104; for a chair (1 of 2) from the set at Historic Deerfield, see Fales, *Furniture of Historic Deerfield*, fig. 80.

## 27 ◆ Side chair
Boston, Massachusetts
1735–50

The cost of this chair when new was greater than that of No. 26, although they share many features. For this chair, the customer exercised his option to order "extras" in the form of carving: an intricate, undercut foliated shell in the crest; shells on the knees; and ball-and-claw feet. The crest shell is an unusual one in American chairs and perhaps even rarer in English design because only one example of this general profile has been located. In recent scholarship, shells of this type have been associated with John Welch, the preeminent Boston carver from the 1730s until 1780. The inspirational source for Welch's shell may lie outside English seating furniture. Separated from the crest line in its elevated position, the shell has the quality of a heraldic crest or cartouche of the type found on English

looking glasses dating from the late seventeenth century to the 1730s. Shells, leaves, canopies, and pierced crowns featured in raised, central locations on glass frames produced an effect comparable to that in the carved chairs. Early eighteenth-century Boston newspapers chronicle a brisk trade in imported English looking glasses.[1]

The best-known group of pierced-shell chairs is the set of eight handed down through seven generations in the female line of the Apthorp family. The first owners were Charles (1698–1758) and Grizzell Eastwick (1707–96) Apthorp of Boston, according to a nineteenth-century label pasted inside the frame of chair "I" in the set. Charles Apthorp was a British official and a substantial merchant. His relationship with Samuel Grant, a Boston upholsterer and supplier of seating furniture for local consumption and exportation, is well documented in Grant's accounts. The accounts

also establish links between Apthorp and carver John Welch. Apthorp, in turn, supplied Grant with imported English textiles for his business. Fragments of original upholstery on the loose seat of the labeled chair indicate that the original cover was a pale yellow silk damask.[2]

The Apthorp and Winterthur chairs differ in several obvious and a few subtle ways. The greatest difference is the presence of stretchers in the Apthorp group, the pattern similar to that in No. 82. The ankles in the front legs of the Apthorp chairs angle forward more acutely, and the tops of the claws are flatter and more squared. Small squared fins flank the base of the shell on the knees of the Apthorp chair, and the carving lacks a pendent drop. The carved work on both crests follows the same general plan—an elevated shell, supporting scrollwork, and flanking leafage— but the two exhibit substantial differences in choice of elements (fig. 1). The shell on Winterthur's chair is lower, broader, and angled farther backward. The leafy supports are replaced in the Apthorp chairs with arched, imbricated (scaled) strapwork that stands free of its base except at several supporting contact points. The flanking foliage forms long slender vines with small leaves.[3]

Craftsmen produced at least six variants on the Apthorp chair, the subtle differences occurring in the crest. Examples of three of them are in the Winterthur collection— this chair, another side chair, and a pair of armchairs that descended in the Stephanus Van Cortlandt family of New York. Other New York family owners were the Schuylers and Van Rensselaers. Current speculation is that some chairs may have been period copies of imported Boston chairs made in New York City. An unusual addition to this pattern group is a side chair that has a plain vase-shape splat of the type in No. 24. Stretchers brace the legs, and the knees are leaf-carved. The crest shell and imbricated strapwork are close in design to those elements in the

**Fig. 1.** Detail, crest.

Apthorp chairs, but the flanking foliage is more frondlike than vinelike.[4]

Dating of the chairs in the Apthorp group is based on information in the accounts of Samuel Grant, which begin in 1728. First in appearance is a reference to a "New fashion round seat," in October 1729, indicating that the Queen Anne style had been newly introduced in Boston. The reference "4 doz: Leathr chairs claw feet" (priced at 27s. each in March 1733) appears to signal the entrance of the ball-and-claw foot into the furniture market. That interpretation of the reference as published is flawed, however. Price and quantity and other references in Grant's accounts suggest that these were traditional turned frames with leather covers, a popular export commodity in Boston. "Leather . . . Cushn Seats" (loose seats) increased the price of the same chairs by a shilling (see Nos. 1, 2). With the addition in 1732 of "hor[se]bone round feet" (cabriole legs, probably with pad feet) to a maple frame with a cushion seat, there was a substantial increase in unit price to 40s. per chair. Clearly, the 27s. chairs with "claw" feet of 1733 were something other than carved walnut, Queen Anne ball-and-claw–foot chairs with veneered splats. The claws referred to could have been Spanish feet, which with their fluted toes approximate claws. Carved ball feet probably were not introduced until later in the decade at the earliest. Reinforcing this interpretation is the appearance of flat stretchers (the type of braces in the Apthorp chairs) in Grant's accounts only in 1742 (not 1741, as reported). Given Grant's meticulous method of recording chair sales, it seems unlikely that flat-stretcher chairs had been in the market for more than a few years at that time. In sum, the design sequence recorded in the craftsman's accounts suggests a range of 1735–50 for these unusual chairs.[5]

*NGE*

**Inscriptions or marks:** *Chiseled on front seat-rail rabbet:* "VIII". *Chiseled on loose-seat frame:* "III".

**Construction:** The crest is supported on rectangular tenons at the straight, flat-faced post tops and splat. The ribbed and striated shell and flanking foliage are carved in low to exceptionally high relief. The shell, which is elevated on a leafy pedestal, is positioned above the crest top with pierced openings below. The flat crest face is cheeked at the arches; the back is rounded except at the piercings below the shell, which are chamfered and heavily tooled. The splat is deeply canted at the edges, front to back, and tenoned into the plinth; the front face is veneered with figured wood. The plinth, carved with a double-ogee bead across the top, is hollow on the front and side faces and is one piece with the back rail. The angular inner cheeks of the back-post sweeps are pieced. The post backs are rounded from top to seat. The compass-shape seat is rounded at the top lip; an internal rabbet supports the loose-seat frame. The rails are joined to the posts and front leg extensions with rectangular tenons (some pinned). Small triangular blocks are glued into the rear corners; large triangular blocks at the front are held with two rosehead nails each. The rear legs are square at the seat rails and side-rail returns, then squared and rounded to the squared feet, which flare outward and backward. The front leg shells are ribbed and fluted in low relief; the pendent bellflowers are slightly hollowed. The front legs are entirely rounded. The carved feet have two-joint toes. The uncarved scrolled knee brackets are nailed and probably glued in place. The backs of the side rails are fitted with two-part brackets. A conical-tipped rear stretcher is round tenoned into its adjacent members.

**Condition:** The splat veneer has much surface crizzling and is patched in several places near the bottom. The beaded face of the plinth at the front of the mortise broke off and was reattached. Probably the only original knee block is that at the right front; the others are of variable age. Differences in surface color in the two-part side rear rail returns and an imperfect fit suggest that the lower pieces may have been replaced when some of the knee brackets were restored. The left front interior corner block is defaced but may be original; the right one bears circular saw marks. The rear blocks have some age but may not be original. The surface finish is in poor condition; it was once flaking but has been stabilized with a resin finish. The loose-seat frame is old but not original to this chair.

**Dimensions:**

| | | |
|---|---|---|
| H. | 38 1/8 in. | 96.8 cm |
| H. (seat) | 16 1/2 in. | 41.9 cm |
| W. (crest) | 16 7/8 in. | 42.9 cm |
| W. (seat front) | 21 in. | 53.3 cm |
| W. (seat back) | 15 1/2 in. | 39.4 cm |
| W. (feet) | 21 1/2 in. | 54.6 cm |
| D. (seat) | 18 in. | 45.7 cm |
| D. (feet) | 21 5/8 in. | 54.9 cm |

**Materials:** *Microanalysis:* Primary: walnut. Secondary: maple (splat backing; loose-seat frame). *Finish:* medium dark reddish brown color in resin (see **Condition**). *Upholstery:* modern white and blue resist-dyed cotton slipcover.

**Publications:** Keno, Freund, and Miller, "Very Pink of the Mode," fig. 36.

**Accession history:** Gift of H. F. du Pont, 1965. 63.615.2

1. For an English chair with a related shell and the looking-glass prototypes, see Macquoid and Edwards, *Dictionary*, 1:255, fig. 88; 2:315–36, figs. 13, 34, 40, 55, 56, 60, 61, 64; for another looking glass, see Downs, *American Furniture*, fig. 248. Keno, Freund, and Miller, "Very Pink of the Mode," 289–90; Dow, *Arts and Crafts in New England*, pp. 97, 106–7, 127.

2. Heckscher, *American Furniture*, cat. no. 22; Keno, Freund, and Miller, "Very Pink of the Mode," pp. 271–85.

3. Heckscher, *American Furniture*, cat. no. 22.

4. For the other Winterthur chairs, see Downs, *American Furniture*, figs. 26, 106; for the Schuyler chair, see Bernard and S. Dean Levy, Inc., *"Opulence and Splendor": The New York Chair, 1690–1830* (New York: By the company, 1984), p. 5; for the Van Rensselaer chair, see John S. Walton advertisement, *Antiques* 66, no. 2 (August 1954): 80; for the remaining variant, see *American Antiques from Israel Sack Collection*, 10 vols. (Washington, D.C.: Highland House, 1969–), 7:2007; for the vase-splat chair, see Bernard and S. Dean Levy, Inc., *Catalogue VI* (New York: By the company, 1988), pp. 50–51. Current thinking is that the armchair (1 of a pair) cited above in Downs (*American Furniture*, fig. 26), was made in New York City in the eighteenth century based on a Boston prototype.

5. For the references from the Samuel Grant accounts, see Forman, *American Seating Furniture*, pp. 286–87, 335, 338; for the Grant account interpretations, see Keno, Freund, and Miller, "Very Pink of the Mode," pp. 275, 278.

at the center with chamfers, top and bottom. The crest arches and projections are rounded, the latter scrolling backward slightly. The flat-faced splat is incised with short lines below the center to define the strap ends as scrolls. The figure-eight crossings at the center are modeled in low relief. The splat edges are slightly canted, front to back, and the piercings are rounded-canted; the splat is tenoned into the plinth. The plinth is hollow at the front and side faces, finished with a top bead, and nailed to the back rail. The upper post backs are rounded to the sweeps, where the surface is flat; the sweep cheeks are one piece of wood with the posts. The compass-shape seat is rounded at the top lip and sawed in low, flat arches. An interior rabbet, forming a rectangular opening, supports the loose-seat frame. The rails are joined to the posts and front leg extensions with rectangular tenons (pinned, twice at the side back). The rectangular rear legs are angled twice on the forward faces—below the seat rails and below the side stretchers. Narrow, tapered chamfers mark the forward corners. The front pad feet are supported on tall disks; each knee bracket is held with two rosehead nails. All stretcher tips are round tenoned into the adjacent members, except those at the side back, which are joined to the rear legs in rectangular tenons (pinned through).

**Condition:** The splat is cracked through in the lower section at several points. A thin spline at the plinth base extends from side to side on the forward face. Angle irons strengthen the inside front corners of the seat rail; other irons have been removed from the back corners. A vertical crack on the outside right post at the rail pins extends onto the front face above the rail. All rear rail and stretcher pins are replaced. A vertical crack is centered in the right front leg extension. Wood imperfections have caused cracks in the right front knee; the left knee is also cracked. The back feet are restored with triangular pieces at the inside (right foot) and back (left foot) faces.

**Dimensions:**

| | | |
|---|---|---|
| H. | 35³/₄ in. | 90.8 cm |
| H. (seat) | 14¹/₂ in. | 36.8 cm |
| W. (crest) | 21³/₄ in. | 55.2 cm |
| W. (seat front) | 21¹/₄ in. | 54.0 cm |
| W. (seat back) | 16³/₈ in. | 41.6 cm |
| W. (feet) | 22¹¹/₁₆ in. | 57.6 cm |
| D. (seat) | 17¹/₂ in. | 44.4 cm |
| D. (feet) | 21 in. | 53.3 cm |

**Materials:** *Microanalysis:* Primary: mahogany. *Finish:* medium to dark brown color in resin with slight reddish cast. *Upholstery:* floral patterned gold silk damask; Europe, 1725–50.

**Accession history:** Gift of H. F. du Pont, 1960. 59.2644

## 28 ◆ Side chair
Rhode Island, possibly Newport
1765–95

Exaggerated shoulders and embryonic crest tips are indications that this chair is a provincial product, even if made in Newport. In context the design dates after the early, narrow Queen Anne sweep back of No. 24 and the introduction of the interlaced, shell-less pattern of No. 46. The broadly interpreted back arch likely derives from New York chairmaking of the mid eighteenth century; the splat design is associated with a later date. The double figure-eight motif was first popular in the English chair market at midcentury. Massachusetts interpretations followed a few years later (see No. 58), providing a general dating frame for this chair. In 1762 William Ince and John Mayhew included a figure-eight splat in their design book, attesting to the continued popularity of the pattern.[1]

The strong visual impact of this low chair is due to the pierced work of the splat, although the splat surface is restrained. The carved "ears" and shell of the crest appear to be superfluous afterthoughts. "Low" chairs for bedchambers were produced by shortening the legs of standard designs (see Nos. 11, 12). Incised on the front-rail rabbet is the number "II." A matching chair at the Van Cortlandt House, New York City, is marked "IIII" on the rabbet. Clearly, a set numbering at least four low chairs once existed, a rare occurrence in the history of American furniture. The Van Cortlandt House chair was acquired in 1933 from sisters who had received it from relatives in New Bedford, Massachusetts, a city located near the Rhode Island border.[2]

*NGE*

**Inscriptions or marks:** *Chiseled on front seat-rail rabbet:* "II".

**Construction:** The crest is supported on rectangular tenons at the flat-faced canted posts (pinned) and splat. The central shell and end projections are one piece of wood with the crest. The shell is placed on the top surface, and the scroll beneath it is carved on the crest face. The flat crest face is slightly cheeked at the arched ends; the back surface is flat

1. For English chairs, see Kirk, *American Furniture*, figs. 1000, 1002–4, 1006; William Ince and John Mayhew, *The Universal System of Household Furniture* (1762; reprint, Chicago: Quadrangle Books, 1960), pl. 9 lower left.

2. Information on previous ownership of the Van Cortlandt chair is given on the backs of 2 old photographs; see folder 59.2644, Registration Office, Winterthur; other general information was obtained in telephone conversations with Van Cortlandt House staff in 1990.

## 29 ◆ Side chair

Eastern Massachusetts
1755–75

The basic Queen Anne saddle-crested chair so common in eastern Massachusetts from the 1730s to the Revolution (see No. 7) was updated sometime in the early 1750s with the introduction of a Chippendale-style crest. An arch was substituted for the saddle, and the rounded shoulders were replaced by carved, projecting tips emphasizing the rectilinear qualities of the chair back. Of particular note in this chair is the manner in which the posts taper inward to form a narrow top, a profile held over from Queen Anne styling (see No. 16). Other features also remained the same: the slim, ogee-top splat (here with a simplified base); the compass seat with flat arches; the columnar side stretchers and conical-tipped cross braces; and the plain cabriole legs. The short, flat pad feet of this chair are similar to those of No. 8. The maple frame was likely finished originally in a dark brown color and the loose seat covered with leather, a material more appropriate to a simple painted frame than the rich textile illustrated here. The current yellowish brown grained surface, which was probably applied in the late nineteenth century and meant to imitate burl walnut, likely refurbished a worn and damaged original surface. Interior woodwork painted to simulate the natural grain in wood was popular at the time the chair was painted. The detail in the mottled finish is accented by the restrained lines of the early Chippendale form.[1]

Ogee-crested chairs were popular in England before 1750, although the simple profile of this chair appears to have been uncommon there. Plain, uncarved, cabriole-leg examples made in New England were framed with either a compass or rectangular seat and the ogee splat of this chair or the solid banister of No. 24. Among more elaborate ogee-crested patterns, which are embellished with pierced-strapwork splats and carved ornament, several have eastern Massachusetts family histories associating them with the communities of Andover, Boston, Charlestown, Hingham, and Salem. Rush-seated block-and-turned chairs with ogee crests and pierced splats were also relatively common in the region from before the Revolution; many examples still exist in small institutional collections throughout Essex County.[2]

*NGE*

---

**Inscriptions or marks:** *Chiseled on front seat-rail rabbet and loose-seat frame:* "II". *On loose-seat frame:* "150 years old 1859/ —MHB—" in pencil.

**Construction:** The crest is supported on rectangular tenons at the flat-faced canted posts (pinned) and splat. The crest face is prominently cheeked at the arches, and each terminal is carved with opposing ogee channels separated by a narrow declivity. The rear edges are chamfered, except at the tips; the lunette chamfer runs out at the peak. The splat, which is deeply inset at the crest back, is canted at the edges, front to back, and tenoned into the plinth. The plinth is hollow on the front and side faces, finished with a top bead, and nailed to the back rail. A flattened area marks each post face at seat level; the rear post corners are chamfered from crest to seat. The compass-seat frame is rounded at the lip and sawed in flat, tooled arches at the bottom. An interior rabbet forming a rectangular opening supports the loose-seat frame. The rails are joined to the posts and front leg extensions with rectangular tenons (pinned). The rear legs are chamfered on all corners between the seat and rear stretcher; the feet are canted on the forward faces and chamfered in broad Vs at all corners. The plain, circular pad feet are defined by low ledges at the back; the knee brackets are nailed in place. The side stretchers are joined to the legs with vertical rectangular tenons (pinned at rear). The creased-tip medial and rear stretchers are round tenoned into the adjacent members. The old and probably original loose-seat frame is tenoned and pinned.

**Condition:** The seat frame has been reinforced with angle irons at the inside back joints. The right side knee bracket is replaced. The left side stretcher is gouged on the bottom surface in several places; the right stretcher-column collar is chipped on the outside face (but covered with the yellowish brown paint). The left front foot is chipped at the outside corner; the right foot pad is broken and reattached. The grained surfaces show modest wear and tear.

**Dimensions:**

| | | |
|---|---|---|
| H. | 39³/4 in. | 101.0 cm |
| H. (seat) | 17³/16 in. | 43.7 cm |
| W. (crest) | 16⁵/8 in. | 42.2 cm |
| W. (seat front) | 20 in. | 50.8 cm |
| W. (seat back) | 15 in. | 38.1 cm |
| W. (feet) | 20¹/4 in. | 51.7 cm |
| D. (seat) | 16¹/2 in. | 41.9 cm |
| D. (feet) | 19 in. | 48.2 cm |

**Materials:** *Microanalysis:* Primary: hard maple group (legs, stretchers); soft maple group (seat rails). Secondary: soft maple group (loose-seat frame). *Finish:* old but not original surface finish consisting of a straw-colored base grained in medium light and dark brown paint, probably to imitate burl walnut; resinous outer coat. *Upholstery:* coarse, twill-woven, floral silk damask; Europe, 1725–75.

**Exhibitions:** "Accessions 1960," Winterthur Museum, Winterthur, Del., December 21, 1960–February 1, 1961.

**Accession history:** Museum purchase from Roland B. Hammond, North Andover, Mass., 1960. 60.190

---

1. A pair of chairs identical to this example retains original loose leather seats and a brown finish that may be original; see Florene Maine advertisement, *Antiques* 79, no. 2 (February 1961): 143. For a splat-back roundabout chair presumed to retain the original cedar graining, see Fales, *Furniture of Historic Deerfield*, fig. 63. That chair's diagonal-banded simulated-wood figure was an alternative to the mottled ground of this chair.

2. For the chairs with family histories in Massachusetts communities, see Greenlaw, *New England Furniture*, no. 54; Randall, *American Furniture*, nos. 143, 148, 151, 152; Kane, *Three Hundred Years*, no. 125; Jobe and Kaye, *New England Furniture*, no. 124. For representative rush-seated chairs, see Fales, *Furniture of Historic Deerfield*, fig. 83; Jobe and Kaye, *New England Furniture*, no. 125.

## 30 ◆ Side chair
### Eastern Massachusetts
### 1755–85

Nineteen chairs from a study group numbering more than one hundred in the double-loop, or owl's-eye, pattern are associated by family history or early twentieth-century ownership with eastern Massachusetts, thus providing additional support for the traditional assignment of this pattern to the region. Chairs made in this fully developed Chippendale design were as plentiful in the late colonial marketplace as the earlier Queen Anne ogee-splat chair (see No. 7). The large sample size permits a comprehensive overview of production and ornament range from the early pad-foot chairs to the late straight-leg examples.[1]

This chair back is an excellent example of the fully developed owl's-eye pattern (fig. 1). The simplest splats are flat on the front surface; others are lightly modeled at the central loops. Splats with carved work in the central volutes are more common than plain ones, and many examples are also carved in the upper volutes. When defined, the narrow crescents extending from the upper slots into the crest generally have plain, rounded surfaces; some are detailed with gouges. The beaded ornament on this chair is rare, as is the fully modeled crest face. Often the arch centered in the crest is plain; occasionally it is carved with foliate ornament on a punchwork ground. The most popular crest treatment was the carved, fluted shell with coarsely or finely delineated ribs. In this example, the shell surface is carved with tapered reeds, a less popular treatment; a few shells are fanlike.[2]

Square seat frames are dominant in the owl's-eye group; compass seats are rare. Most front rails are plain, without flat or scalloped arches, and are shallow in vertical depth

Fig. 1. Detail, splat and crest shell.

Fig. 2. Frame without upholstery.

(fig. 2). Over-the-rail upholstery became popular in Massachusetts seating furniture during the Chippendale period, and about one in three examples in the one-hundred–plus sample are treated in this manner. In this chair, the front leg extensions are raised in peaks at the forward corners of the frame above seat level, a constructional device intended to secure the stuffed rolls used at the seat edges to define and stabilize the upholstery. Another common design feature is the creased cabriole knee flanked by small, plain brackets that produce an uninterrupted line to the rails; a cusped bracket is unusual. Leaf-carved knees are present in about two of five examples; several knees are further embellished with centered punchwork. A few Rhode Island chairs in the owl's-eye pattern have shell-carved knees. The beads on the knees of this chair terminate in tiny volutes, a pattern that is unique within the sample (fig. 3).[3]

Stylistically, the thin pad foot on a thick cushion base is the earliest cabriole-leg terminal within the sample (see No. 7). A few chairs in the punchwork-crest subgroup have pad feet incised with ribs; other pads are saucer shaped. The expensive carved claw apparently was the most popular cabriole terminal with customers, given the numbers that survive. Stretchers appear on two of every three cabriole-leg chairs in the study group; the conical-tipped cross brace is more common than the block-ended one. Stretcherless chairs with blocked rear feet are represented by one in four examples. In general, chairs without stretchers are considered to be more fully developed than those with braces. In this case, however, the greater number of stretcherless chairs have pad rather than claw feet. Rounding out the style

group are a few later, straight-leg chairs braced by rectangular stretchers.[4]

As in other seating, the side chair is the principal form. This example is the only low chair in the sample. The double chair, or two-seated settee, is represented by three examples, all with stretchers, claw feet, and leaf-carved knees. A cherrywood couch, or daybed, on pad feet appears to be of eastern Connecticut provenance.[5]

NGE

—————————

**Construction:** The crest is supported on rectangular tenons at the flat-faced canted posts and splat. The face is modeled at the arches and precisely ribbed at the shell; the rear surface is rounded at the top and chamfered along the bottom edge and outside tips. The splat face is lightly modeled at the loops, incised at the volutes, and channeled at the inner edges of the upper piercings. Each narrow upper slot is terminated by a bead and three gouged crescents. The splat is slightly canted at the edges and piercings, front to back, and tenoned into the back seat rail. The three-sided plinth, which is hollow on the front and side faces and finished with a top bead, is nailed to the back rail. The rear post edges are chamfered from crest to seat. The seat rails are joined to the posts and front leg extensions with vertical rectangular tenons (pinned at back posts). The front leg extensions are finished with triangular peaks at the front corners. The rear legs have short chamfers on all corners between the seat and rear stretcher. The feet are canted on the forward faces and chamfered at the front corners; chamfers at the rear corners extend to the rear stretcher. The front knees are creased at the center and the edges are carved with a voluted bead extending from the brackets to the ankles. The brackets are nailed in place; the claws have three-knuckle toes. The side stretchers are joined to the legs in vertical rectangular tenons (pinned at back); horizontal

Fig. 3. Detail, left front leg.

rectangular tenons secure the medial stretcher to the side blocks. The collared rear stretcher tips are round tenoned into the adjacent members.

**Condition:** The plinth was replaced in 1964. Plugged nail holes (which extend across the outside of the rear seat rail, up the front and back faces of the posts, and across the crest back, with short returns on the face) identify the introduction of a later cover and padding. New pieces of wood about 3/8" deep face the top surface of the back rail flanking the splat. Stress cracks occur in the rail and lower splat at the back. Four large triangular corner blocks, double-screwed in place, have been added to the interior seat frame. The right front leg is gouged across the center front face; the bottoms of all feet are worn. The medial stretcher is defaced with gouges and scrapes. The seat is upholstered over the rails.

**Dimensions:**

| | | |
|---|---|---|
| H. | 34 in. | 86.3 cm |
| H. (seat) | 14³/4 in. | 37.5 cm |
| W. (crest) | 20 in. | 50.8 cm |
| W. (seat front) | 22 in. | 55.8 cm |
| W. (seat back) | 16¹/2 in. | 41.9 cm |
| W. (feet) | 23⁵/8 in. | 60.0 cm |
| D. (seat) | 17⁷/8 in. | 45.4 cm |
| D. (feet) | 20³/4 in. | 52.7 cm |

**Materials:** *Microanalysis:* Primary: mahogany. Secondary: soft maple group (seat rails). *Finish:* variegated medium yellowish brown color in resin. *Upholstery:* pale blue-green silk (faded) with brocaded floral clusters; Europe, 1750–85.

**Provenance:** Descended in the Snow, Pecker, Hall, and Thayer families of the Boston–Medford–Hingham, Mass., area.

**Accession history:** Museum purchase from Winsor White, Duxbury, Mass., 1964.
64.109

---

1. For the 19 chairs or settees with Massachusetts family or early collection histories, see Jobe and Kaye, *New England Furniture*, nos. 109–11, 113; *American Antiques from Israel Sack Collection*, 10 vols. (Washington, D.C.: Highland House, ca. 1969–), 1:147 (now attributed to George Bright by Jobe and Kaye), 1:243, 3:623; Greenlaw, *New England Furniture*, no. 54; Randall, *American Furniture*, no. 143; C. L. Prickett advertisement, *Antiques* 136, no. 1 (July 1989): 19; Jonathan Fairbanks, "A Decade of Collecting American Decorative Arts and Sculpture at the Museum of Fine Arts, Boston," *Antiques* 120, no. 3 (September 1981): 602, pl. 12; American Art Association Anderson Galleries, "American Furniture from the Collection of Benjamin Flayderman" (April 17–18, 1931), lot 310; Warren, *Bayou Bend*, nos. 73, 94; Kane, *Three Hundred Years*, no. 125; Fales, *Furniture of Historic Deerfield*, fig. 96; Helen Comstock, "American Furniture in California," *Antiques* 65, no. 1 (January 1954): 57, fig. 16; Mary H. Northend, *Historic Homes of New England* (Boston: Little, Brown, 1914), opp. p. 117.

2. For foliate ornament on a punchwork ground, see No. 218; for a fanlike shell, see Jobe and Kaye, *New England Furniture*, no. 113.

3. For punchwork embellishment, see Gregory R. Weidman, *Furniture in Maryland, 1740–1940: The Collection of the Maryland Historical Society* (Baltimore: By the society, 1984), cat. 7.

4. For an incised pad foot, see Greenlaw, *New England Furniture*, no. 54.

5. For the settees, see Fairbanks, "Decade of Collecting," p. 602, pl. 12; *American Antiques from Sack Collection*, 3:623; Warren, *Bayou Bend*, no. 94. For the daybed, see Fales, *Furniture of Historic Deerfield*, fig. 97.

## 31 ◆ Armchair
### Eastern Massachusetts
### 1755–85

---

The finely ribbed and fluted crest shell of this chair (fig. 1) is distinctly different from the precisely styled ornament of No. 30. The pattern was introduced to the marketplace during the late Queen Anne period (see No. 23). The rest of the crest is relatively plain, with only carved tips and recessed, gouge-carved crescents below the shell. The splat has only two carved volutes instead of four, but the two ornaments coordinate well with the volutes carved into the side faces of the arm scrolls. The general austerity of the design is continued in the plain leg surfaces. The bulging knees with subtle angular reverses above the ankle tops are characteristic of eastern Massachusetts work. A block-ended medial stretcher is used in the understructure in place of the older but still popular conical-tipped Queen Anne brace. In view of the

several economies apparent in this chair, it is surprising that the customer chose carved claw feet and over-the-rail upholstery; the latter especially was a fairly expensive option in terms of labor and materials. From the previous survey (see No. 30), it is clear that the armchair is rare in this pattern. The arm design is used in other contemporary Massachusetts seating furniture.[1]

The pierced and looped splat of this chair is one of several early Chippendale-style New England designs that closely resemble English prototypes. Robert Manwaring illustrated two chairs drawn to this general pattern in *Cabinet and Chair-Maker's Real Friend and Companion* of 1765 and another the following year in *The Chair-Maker's Guide*, although the latter American version was probably in the market earlier. As stated by Manwaring, his designs were guides to "all the most APPROVED PATTERNS" in the London market, suggesting that the transfer occurred through previous direct furniture importation. Indeed, several English claw-foot, stretcherless owl's-

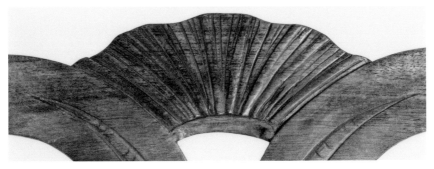

**Fig. 1.** Detail, crest shell.

eye chairs are hardly distinguishable from American counterparts. The English seating may be identified by the molded faces of the back posts, although chairs with other splat patterns introduced slightly later in Boston often have molded posts (see No. 57).[2]

Private individuals as well as merchants imported English furniture. Direct evidence of this practice is sparse, but the existence of almost identical designs on both sides of the Atlantic testifies to the traffic. Philip Bell, a London cabinetmaker, is known to have exported furniture to private Virginia customers. A Charleston merchant's notice of January 1759 describes a cargo of "mahogany, walnut, and Windsor chairs" on the *Prince of Orange* on a voyage from London. Additional proof of the trade occurs in the Boston inventory of John Spooner, Esq., dated in 1765: "6 London made black walnut chairs 8/ , 4 New England made ditto 8/." Robert W. Symonds, who studied the English export furniture trade to America, tabulated almost 44,000 items of cabinet- and upholsteryware entering the colonies between 1760 and 1767. A partial list of furnishings sold by Massachusetts governor Francis Bernard in 1770 indicates that furniture requirements were substantial in the households of leading American merchants, professional men, and officials. The list comprised six sets of "Leather bottom Chairs," twelve "Mohogo carv'd frame Chairs with crimson damask bottoms," a set of "Yellow bottom Chairs," and six "Red bottom Chairs"—a total of at least sixty chairs.[3]

*NGE*

---

**Construction:** The crest is supported on rectangular tenons at the flat-faced canted posts and splat. The flat crest face is cheeked through the outer arches; the tips are carved. The shell is carved with flutes and fine gouges above a narrow bead with tiny volute ends. The flat rear surface is rounded at the upper and lower edges, except at the chamfered center base and the blunt tips. The flat splat face, which is marked with an incised line between the central loops and the pierced pedestal, is shallowly carved at the lower volutes. The crescents in the

points above the narrow upper slots are rounded and gouged. The splat is slightly canted at the edges and piercings, front to back, and tenoned into the back seat rail. The three-sided plinth, which is hollow on the front and side faces and finished with a top bead, is nailed to the back rail. The rear posts are rounded at the back from crest to seat. The flat, curved arms are contoured slightly, with an outward slope near the back. The forward scrolls are carved with volutes at either side. The arms are joined to the back posts in right-angle rabbets held by screws concealed by wooden plugs. Short vertical extensions near the front are supported on the curved and molded arm-post tops. The post bases are rabbeted to the side seat rails and secured with single screws from inside the rails. The seat rails are joined to the posts and front leg extensions with vertical rectangular tenons (pinned at back posts). The rear legs are chamfered on all corners between the seat rails and rear stretcher. The feet are canted on the forward faces and broadly chamfered at the front corners. The front knees have sharp creases at the center that curve inward abruptly above the ankles; the brackets are nailed in place. The claws have three-knuckle toes; the rear toe is short and enlarged. The side stretchers are joined to the legs in vertical rectangular tenons; horizontal rectangular tenons secure the medial stretcher to the side blocks. The collared rear stretcher tips are round tenoned into the adjacent members.

**Condition:** The splat is cracked and repaired through the upper loop; 3/4" facing pieces are inset below the shell. Pieced repairs also mark the crest back at the same joint. The splat back is gouged and defaced at the loops and near the lower right corner. The rear seat rail is restored on the upper inside surface. The arm and arm-post joints are repaired with inset facing pieces on the inside surfaces and a short new section at the left post top. Plugged screws in the arm tops are part of the repairs. The seat is upholstered over the rails.

**Dimensions:**

| | | |
|---|---|---|
| H. | 38 1/8 in. | 96.8 cm |
| H. (seat) | 17 1/2 in. | 44.4 cm |
| W. (crest) | 23 1/4 in. | 59.1 cm |
| W. (seat front) | 25 in. | 63.5 cm |
| W. (seat back) | 19 in. | 48.2 cm |
| W. (arms) | 29 1/8 in. | 74.0 cm |
| W. (feet) | 26 3/4 in. | 67.9 cm |
| D. (seat) | 19 3/4 in. | 50.2 cm |
| D. (feet) | 24 in. | 60.9 cm |

**Materials:** *Microanalysis:* Primary: mahogany. Secondary: soft maple group (seat rails). *Finish:* variegated medium yellowish brown color in resin. *Upholstery:* watered blue wool moreen; England, 1750–1800.

**Publications:** Downs, *American Furniture*, fig. 56. Kirk, *American Chairs*, fig. 109. Victoria Kloss Ball, *Architecture and Interior Design: Europe and America from the Colonial Era to Today* (New York: John Wiley and Sons, 1980), p. 212, fig. 5.34.

**Provenance:** Ex coll.: Norvin H. Green, Tuxedo Park, N.Y.

**Accession history:** Purchased by H. F. du Pont from the Norvin H. Green sale, Parke-Bernet, New York, November 29–December 2, 1950, lot 650, via Charles Woolsey Lyon, Inc., New York. Gift of H. F. du Pont, 1952.
52.234

---

1. Jobe and Kaye, *New England Furniture*, no. 116; *American Antiques from Israel Sack Collection*, 10 vols. (Washington, D.C.: Highland House, ca. 1969–), 3:623; Warren, *Bayou Bend*, no. 94. For the only other owl's-eye–pattern armchair located for the survey, see Mary Northend Collection, no. 576, DAPC, Visual Resources Collection, Winterthur Library.

2. Robert Manwaring, *The Cabinet and Chair-Maker's Real Friend and Companion* (London: Henry Webley, 1765), pl. 4 right; pl. 5 left. Robert Manwaring and others, *The Chair-Maker's Guide* (London: Robert Sayer, 1766), title page and pl. 36 right. For English owl's-eye chairs, see Jobe and Kaye, *New England Furniture*, no. 109a; Kirk, *American Furniture*, fig. 849.

3. *South Carolina Gazette* (Charleston), January 19–27, 1759; John Spooner, Esq., estate inventory, 1765, Suffolk County Probate Court, Boston (microfilm, Downs collection); the Bernard furniture is listed in *Boston News-Letter*, August 30, 1770, as quoted in Dow, *Arts and Crafts in New England*, pp. 124–25. On Bell, see Wallace B. Gusler, *Furniture of Williamsburg and Eastern Virginia, 1710–1790* (Richmond: Virginia Museum, 1979), p. xviii. Robert W. Symonds, "The English Export Trade in Furniture to Colonial America, Part 2," *Antiques* 28, no. 4 (October 1935): 156.

## 32 ◆ Side chair (one of pair)
Eastern Massachusetts
1770–1800

The most austere owl's-eye chairs are those
with straight, or Marlborough, legs and plain,
rectangular stretchers. Apart from the sawed
profile of the flat-surfaced splat and the carved
crest terminals, the ornament of this chair is
confined to beading around the seat frame,
down the front legs, and along the leading
edges of the stretchers. The original covering
of the loose seat was probably leather, a
material in keeping with the simplicity of the
design. Still plainer examples of the owl's-eye
chair have bottoms of rush or occasionally
splint woven over the rails or around a loose-
seat frame. Curiously, armchairs are common
in the woven-seat group in contrast to the
rarity of arms in more formal designs.[1]

Other straight-leg owl's-eye chairs have
seats upholstered over the rails. The best
documented chair was made by George Bright
of Boston in 1770 for Jonathan Bowman of
Pownalborough, Maine, now in the collection
of the Society for the Preservation of New
England Antiquities. It retains the original
leather covering and ornamental brass nails
applied to three sides of the seat frame in an
open box pattern with vertical returns at the
corners. A chair at the Metropolitan Museum
of Art, also with the original leather upholstery
intact, is embellished with a carved crest shell
and carved volutes, like the Bowman chair. Its
serpentine-front seat has original brass nailing
in a pattern similar to the Bowman design but
includes an extra row of nails along the top
edge of the seat.[2]

The chair at the Metropolitan Museum
of Art is further enriched by molded surfaces
on the Marlborough front legs; the forward
supports in a Rhode Island chair with a nearly
identical splat are enhanced by finely executed
stop fluting. Bright's bill of 1770 documents
that the Marlborough leg was fashionable in

the prerevolutionary period, a date reinforced
by John Singleton Copley's 1769 portrait
of Boston merchant Isaac Smith. Smith is
seated in an overupholstered, Marlborough-
leg, mahogany chair, which appears to have a
black leather-covered seat with brass nailing.
Although Marlborough legs are mentioned
as early as 1746 in the Boston accounts of
upholsterer Samuel Grant, the style appears
to have first become popular in the city only
during the 1760s.[3]

NGE

---

**Inscriptions or marks:** *Notched into front seat-rail
rabbet:* 3 gouges, representing number 3 in a set.

**Construction:** The crest is supported on rectangular
tenons at the flat-faced canted posts and splat. The
slightly rounded crest face is cheeked at the outer
arches; the tips are carved, but the central lunette is

plain. The rear surface is flat with rounded edges at
the center top, arches, and outside tips; the center
bottom edge is canted. The splat surfaces are flat,
and the edges and piercings are canted, front to
back; the base tenons into the plinth. The plinth
is hollow on the front and side faces, finished with
a low top bead, and glued to the back rail. The rear
post corners are chamfered from crest to seat. The
seat frame is molded with a narrow, flat lip and an
outside quarter-round bead; a narrow interior rabbet
supports the loose-seat frame. The rails are joined to
the posts and front leg extensions with rectangular
tenons (pinned). The back legs are sawed with two
angles on the forward faces. The front corners of the
feet are chamfered, the interior chamfers extending
to the upper leg angles. The front legs are almost
square, with chamfers at the inside back corners;
the outside front corners are beaded. The side and
back stretchers are joined to the legs with vertical
rectangular tenons. The medial stretcher is
dovetailed into the side stretchers from the bottom.

A quarter-round bead embellishes the outside upper edges of the side and rear stretchers and the forward edge of the medial stretcher.

**Condition:** The top forward edge of the right crest arch has been restored with a long, narrow piece of wood. A 2 1/2" vertical crack is present at the top forward face of each front leg. The rear stretcher is a replacement, which is secured with round pins from the side surfaces of the rear legs. The medial-side stretcher joints have been reinforced with nails driven in from the bottom surface. Overall the surface finish is chipped, mottled, and streaked. The loose-seat frame is new.

**Dimensions:**

| | | |
|---|---|---|
| H. | 37 5/8 in. | 95.6 cm |
| H. (seat) | 16 5/8 in. | 42.2 cm |
| W. (crest) | 18 3/4 in. | 47.6 cm |
| W. (seat front) | 21 in. | 53.3 cm |
| W. (seat back) | 16 1/8 in. | 41.0 cm |
| W. (feet) | 21 1/8 in. | 53.6 cm |
| D. (seat) | 17 1/2 in. | 44.4 cm |
| D. (feet) | 19 7/8 in. | 50.5 cm |

**Materials:** *Microanalysis:* Primary: mahogany. Secondary: white oak group (modern loose-seat frame). *Finish:* clouded, medium light to medium yellowish brown color in resin; flaking. *Upholstery:* green silk damask; Europe, 1700–1740.

**Accession history:** Bequest of H. F. du Pont, 1969. 59.2315

1. For woven-bottom owl's-eye chairs, see Monkhouse and Michie, *American Furniture*, cat. 116; Fales, *Furniture of Historic Deerfield*, figs. 106, 107; Jairus B. Barnes and Moselle Taylor Meals, *American Furniture in the Western Reserve, 1680–1830* (Cleveland: Western Reserve Historical Society, 1972), cat. 14. David F. Wood, ed., *The Concord Museum: Decorative Arts from a New England Collection* (Concord, Mass.: By the museum, 1996), cat. 33.

2. For the Bowman chair, see Jobe and Kaye, *New England Furniture*, no. 113; for the Metropolitan Museum of Art chair, see Heckscher, *American Furniture*, cat. no. 16.

3. Jules David Prown, *John Singleton Copley, 1738–1815* (Washington, D.C.: National Gallery of Art, 1965), pl. 7. The chair may have been Smith's rather than an artist's prop; his estate inventory listed a set of 8 mahogany leather-bottom chairs in a dining area valued at £7.4.0, or 18s. per chair; Isaac Smith estate inventory, 1787, Suffolk County Probate Court, Boston (microfilm, Downs collection); Jobe and Kaye, *New England Furniture*, p. 391.

## 33 ◆ Side chair
### Probably Norwich, Connecticut
### 1760–69

The designs of this chair and No. 21, with its tall, narrow back and attenuated splat, are unmistakably related. Although a pierced splat has been substituted here for the solid banister of No. 21, other features are similar: the cabriole pad-foot legs, the cusped knee brackets, a three-stretcher bracing system, the flat-arched compass seat, and the saddled crest. Both chairs are associated with Connecticut by family history or previous ownership.

The pierced-splat chair appears to be identical to two chairs given to the Wadsworth Atheneum in Hartford by direct descendants of William Pitkin (1694–1769), governor of Connecticut. Upon close examination this chair was found to bear a darkened red-bordered gummed label located on the bottom of the right front corner block inscribed in black ink "Julia J. Pitkin." Unusual crescent-shape identification marks applied with a chisel to the front rails and loose-seat frames of all three chairs further identify them as a set.[1]

Uncommon, even rare, features dominate the design of this chair. The three-stretcher bracing system is unusual in American furniture. The use of this structure in eastern Connecticut (see No. 21) probably reflects the influence of Boston furnituremaking since similar braces appear in a chair of the hoop-shouldered veneered-splat group represented in No. 13. Hoop shoulders and three-stretcher braces are also present in early eighteenth-century British chairs, but again they are rare. From the design and construction of No. 21 to the production of this side chair, a low step was added to the flat, compass-seat arches.

**Fig. 1.** Armchair, Philadelphia, 1755–85. Mahogany, yellow poplar; H. 38¼ in. (97.2 cm), H. (seat) 17 in. (43.2 cm), W. (seat) 24⅜ in. (61.9 cm), D. (seat) 19⅝ in. (49.8 cm), L. (arms) 31 in. (78.7 cm). (Winterthur 57.666)

**Fig. 2.** Detail of No. 33, loose-seat frame bottom.

This subtle feature sometimes occurs in New York work but is more common in Philadelphia chairmaking. Eliphalet Chapin of East Windsor, Connecticut, who trained in Philadelphia, also used the stepped arch in his first Connecticut chairs, which date from the early 1770s (see No. 48).[2]

The splat silhouette of the Pitkin chairs is almost certainly a blending of several ideas by the maker. Foremost is the close association of the design with the Massachusetts looped splat (see Nos. 30, 31). Although scrolled in a reverse direction, the owl's eyes have much the same character. Beneath the loops, or eyes, the small, pedestal-top volutes are adapted from the upper strapwork of the same Massachusetts pattern and inverted. The introduction of a quatrefoil base and relocation of the loops at the banister top, however, make the design distinctly different from Massachusetts examples. The overall effect is that of Gothic tracery, although the allusion was perhaps unintentional. The circumstance is plausible, however, since copies of the third edition (1762) of Thomas Chippendale's *Director*, which included examples of furniture in the "Gothick" taste, were owned in Boston in 1768 and in Newport, where a volume descended in the Goddard family of cabinetmakers. It seems likely, too, that the chairmaker was reasonably familiar with Philadelphia or English chair design, or both. Splat counterparts fashioned

with clustered piercings near the banister top and a three-part pedestal rising from a quatrefoil appear in seating produced in both places (fig. 1).[3]

This chair is remarkable in that the loose-seat frame and upholstery foundation are original. The stuffing, which appears to be horsehair, may have been renewed, as the original undercover has been trimmed around the edges and retacked (fig. 2). The six sickle-shape marks that identify the seat as original to the chair frame are just visible on the inner edge of the front rail beneath the modern "#5."

During the 1770s the narrow, rounded Queen Anne back shown here was replaced by a rectangular framework with a serpentine top. The modified splat had a broader connection with the crest and a slightly shorter pedestal, and Marlborough legs and rectangular stretchers were substituted in the base. These chairs have been attributed to Norwich cabinetmaker Felix Huntington. A variant splat in a similar frame was introduced at the same time. It included a pointed quatrefoil in the base like that in figure 1, a deeply split Y in the pedestal, additional strapwork in the loops, and a small, cutout diamond and two small, spadelike figures at the top that resemble the upper central element in the Queen Anne chair. The chair was purchased from the Gen. Jabez Huntington house in Norwich in 1922 by

Edith Huntington Wilson, providing a definite Norwich orientation for the seating group.[4]

*NGE*

---

**Inscriptions or marks:** *Chiseled on front seat-rail rabbet and inside face of front loose-seat rail:* "IIIIII"; *On lower surface of right front corner block:* "Julia J. Pitkin" *in black ink, on old white, red-bordered gummed label.*

**Construction:** The crest is supported on rectangular tenons at the flat-faced canted posts (pinned) and splat. The face is cheeked near the ends. The rear surface is blocked across the saddle, which is chamfered at the lower edge; the arches are rounded-chamfered, top and bottom. The splat is plain; the edges and piercings are flat at the front and lightly chamfered at the back. The splat is tenoned into the plinth. The plinth is hollow on the front and side faces, finished with a low, stepped top bead, and nailed to the back rail; the plinth-front overhang is deep. The rear post corners are broadly chamfered from crest to seat. The compass seat is rounded at the lip; a deep, broad, interior rabbet supports the loose-seat frame. The front and side rails are sawed in flat, stepped arches and roughly tooled. The rails are joined to the posts and front leg extensions with rectangular tenons (pinned, twice at back rail). The rear legs are chamfered on all corners between the seat and base. The knee brackets are secured with nails. The well-worn front feet may never have had bottom disks; a scribe line defines the pad at the ankle back. All stretchers are round tenoned into the adjacent members.

**Condition:** A small crack occurs at the left front of the crest-post joint. A longer crack is centered in the left front leg extension. The knee bracket at the right side rail is mutilated. Interior seat blocks were added to the frame circa 1900. Most joints have been reglued in recent years; minor blemishes and damaged areas have been retouched. The feet are well worn at the bottom, front and back. The loose-seat frame constructed with pinned rectangular tenons retains its original upholstery foundation, comprising twill-woven linen webbing, a linen sackcloth, and a linen undercover. The stuffing (possibly horsehair) may be original. Fragments of a late nineteenth-century leather cover are present under an outer covering.

**Dimensions:**

| | | |
|---|---|---|
| H. | 42 1/8 in. | 107.0 cm |
| H. (seat) | 17 in. | 43.2 cm |
| W. (crest) | 14 3/4 in. | 37.5 cm |
| W. (seat front) | 20 7/8 in. | 53.0 cm |
| W. (seat back) | 15 3/8 in. | 39.1 cm |
| W. (feet) | 21 3/4 in. | 55.2 cm |
| D. (seat) | 17 in. | 43.2 cm |
| D. (feet) | 19 in. | 48.2 cm |

**Materials:** *Microanalysis:* Primary: cherry. Secondary: soft maple group (loose-seat frame). *Finish:* medium yellowish brown color in resin. *Upholstery:* oilcloth resembling leather; United States, 1920–50.

**Exhibitions:** "Legacy of a Provincial Elite: New London County Joined Chairs, 1720–1790," Connecticut Historical Society and Lyman Allyn Museum, Hartford and Norwich, October 1, 1985–February 28, 1986.

**Publications:** Trent with Nelson, "A Catalogue of New London County Joined Chairs," cat. 46, pp. 135, 140–41.

**Accession history:** Purchased by H. F. du Pont from Mrs. T. B. O'Toole, Wilmington, Del., 1955. Gift of H. F. du Pont, 1958.
55.133.1

1. For the Pitkin chairs, see *Connecticut Furniture*, no. 233; Philip Johnston, "Eighteenth- and Nineteenth-Century American Furniture in the Wadsworth Atheneum," *Antiques* 115, no. 5 (May 1979): 1026, pl. 11 right; Trent with Nelson, "A Catalogue of New London County Joined Chairs," cat. 46. A corner chair with this splat is known in a private Hartford collection.

2. For a Boston 3-stretcher chair, see *John Brown House Loan Exhibition*, cat. 2; for a British 3-stretcher chair, see Kirk, *American Furniture*, fig. 801. For New York and Philadelphia chairs with stepped, flat arches, see Kirk, *American Chairs*, figs. 45, 66, 67, 78, 139.

3. Thomas Chippendale, *The Gentleman and Cabinet-Maker's Director* (1762; reprint 3d ed., New York: Dover Publications, 1966), pls. 10 right (Philadelphia prototype), 11 left, 12 right, 17 left, 34c, 85, 97, 100; Jobe and Kaye, *New England Furniture*, p. 45 n. 60.

4. For rectangular-back chairs, see Trent and Nelson, "A Catalogue of New London County Joined Chairs," cats. 51–53; see also pp. 163–64. A pair of rectangular-back chairs attributed to Huntington have a history of descent in the Devotion family to which Huntington was related; see Lance Mayer and Gay Myers, eds., *The Devotion Family: The Lives and Possessions of Three Generations in Eighteenth-Century Connecticut* (New London, Conn.: Lyman Allyn Art Museum, 1991), fig. 7, pp. 18–20. Jabez and Felix Huntington were cousins; for the Jabez Huntington chair, see *Connecticut Furniture*, no. 246.

## 34 ◆ Side chair
### Eastern Connecticut
### 1780–1810

The provinciality of this owl's-eye, cherrywood chair is manifest in the breadth and proportions of the splat. The upper volutes and vertical slots are elongated, giving them greater prominence than in Boston chairs (see No. 31). The centered double loop is reduced in width and the curves altered to an inverted heart form. The pointed loop top has a greater rise than the prototypes, producing larger, oval-shape volutes within the loops. The tall, solid pedestal base further modifies the usual silhouette. The only surface embellishments on the chair are the molded legs and carved crest terminals. The substantial vertical depth of the seat frame is in striking contrast to other chairs of the period.

The loop variation of the splat, identified by the centered volutes of oval form, is common to a number of chairs with local eastern Connecticut histories. A set at the Putnam House in Brooklyn, Connecticut, descended from Col. Daniel Putnam. Chairs with central crest arches and two tiers of slots in the splat pedestal beneath the double loop are also associated with Windham County families.[1]

*NGE*

**Inscriptions or marks:** *Chiseled on top of rear seat rail beneath plinth:* "IIII".

**Construction:** The crest is supported on rectangular tenons at the flat-faced canted posts and splat (pinned). The face is slightly rounded; the tips are carved. The rear surface is flat with rounded edges, except for the blunt tips and a chamfer at the center base. Both splat surfaces are flat; the edges and piercings are only slightly canted, front to back. The base tenons into the back seat rail. The three-sided removable plinth, which is hollow on the face and sides and finished with a top bead, bears no evidence of nail holes. The rear posts are rounded at the back from crest to seat. The seat rails are joined to the posts and front leg extensions with vertical rectangular tenons. The back legs are sawed with two angles on the forward faces. The outside back corners are lightly rounded; the inside forward corners are chamfered from above the upper bends through the feet. The almost square front legs are molded with double channels on the outside faces and a bead at the outside forward corners. The inside rear corners are broadly chamfered. The plain side, rear, and medial stretchers are joined to the adjacent members with vertical rectangular tenons.

**Condition:** The plinth is now secured to the splat base with a modern screw; it probably was fastened originally with glue. Outside stress cracks occur on the back seat rail. A knot imperfection is located at midpoint on the back face of the left rear leg. The medial stretcher extends through the side stretchers, exposing the horizontal rectangular tenons. The treatment suggests that the brace was repaired or restored. Overall, surfaces are smooth and slick and appear to have been sanded prior to refinishing; only minor nicks and blemishes appear. The seat is upholstered over the rails.

**Dimensions:**

| | | |
|---|---|---|
| H. | 38³/₈ in. | 97.5 cm |
| H. (seat) | 16⁷/₈ in. | 42.9 cm |
| W. (crest) | 20¹/₂ in. | 52.1 cm |
| W. (seat front) | 20¹/₂ in. | 52.1 cm |
| W. (seat back) | 16¹/₂ in. | 41.9 cm |
| W. (feet) | 20¹/₄ in. | 51.4 cm |
| D. (seat) | 16¹/₂ in. | 41.9 cm |
| D. (feet) | 18¹/₂ in. | 47.0 cm |

**Materials:** *Microanalysis:* Primary: cherry (front legs, rear seat rail). Secondary: soft maple group (front and side rails). *Finish:* variegated medium yellowish brown color in resin (probably modern with old residue). *Upholstery:* blue-gray cut, uncut, and voided silk velvet; Europe, 1750–1800.

**Accession history:** Bequest of H. F. du Pont, 1969. 59.2313

---

1. Information about eastern Connecticut ownership of chairs with this general splat pattern was provided by Robert F. Trent.

## 35 ◆ Side chairs
**Northeastern Massachusetts or Newport, Rhode Island**
**1755–80**

Little has been written about a small group of chairs, comprising both formal and vernacular examples, distinguished by crests with beaklike ends and splats with pierced and beaded slots (left). These distinctive features may appear together or singly in combination with standard patterns. The divided attribution is based on family association and design. A side chair, part of an original set with needlework bottoms, once furnished a Boston area home. Chairs with Rhode Island associations include a pair from the Davenport family of Newport and Middletown and two armchairs believed to have descended from Christopher Champlin, Sr., a Charlestown resident who had business and family connections in Newport. In comparing the chairs of

Massachusetts provenance with those linked to Rhode Island, differences in design are apparent. The Boston chairs have up-to-date crest pieces in the Chippendale style and heavy knees appropriate to the post-1750 period (see No. 31); the beaded splat is slender with a plain neck and low base. The Rhode Island family chairs and the examples shown here have heavier splats with more intricate tops and bases. The beaklike crest is a variation of one first introduced on rush-seat furniture about 1730, based on a European prototype. The slender cabriole legs with high knees are a Boston feature current during the second quarter of the eighteenth century, a period when Boston merchants exported many chairs to Rhode Island. In short, the features suggest that the beak-crested chairs may be Rhode Island adaptations of urban Boston models. Walnut was the common choice of wood in both places.[1]

**Fig. 1.** Detail, rear surface of side chair splat (from set of six), northeastern Massachusetts or Newport, R.I., 1750–75. Walnut; H. 38¹/₂ in. (97.8 cm), H. (seat) 17¹/₈ in. (43.5 cm), W. (seat) 20⁷/₈ in. (52.7 cm), D. (seat) 16¹/₈ in. (41.0 cm). (Winterthur 51.64.5)

The same splat and crest patterns were popular for vernacular seating furniture with rush seats and block-and-turned bases and remained so into the period of the straight, or Marlborough, legs. Other variants have club-shape (tapered, cylindrical) legs with pad feet. Areas associated with the vernacular chairs include Rhode Island, eastern Connecticut, and the southeastern New Hampshire/Massachusetts border region (see No. 38). Maple is the principal wood of these chairs; a few examples are known in cherry or birch.[2]

Beaklike crests crown several Rhode Island–ascribed formal chairs with baluster-shape splats of alternative design. The pair of cabriole-leg, low armchairs from the Champlin family probably is the earliest in date; the chairs have solid splats and large forward-scrolling arms reminiscent of the William and Mary style. Pierced beads were a modest design alternative to the slotted banister of No. 35

left (fig. 1). In a variant with solid beads, chairmakers introduced tiny, upright, carved scrolls to the splat shoulders above the outside slots. Pierced, beaded splats also appear in English formal seating and in chairs produced in Philadelphia.[3]

The right chair, a beak-crested example similar to the left chair, except for the splat baluster, has bold splat shoulders sawed to form large volutes. The pattern, consisting of two long slots without beads separated by an elongated diamond, is comparable in size to the left chair. Several chairs of this pattern have ball-and-claw feet. Other claw-foot Rhode Island chairs with similar pierced splats have arched Queen Anne crests, with and without carved shells, and back posts that conform to the splat outline. Later examples have squared-tip, serpentine crests and straight front legs. Features generally common to the early formal chairs of this pierced-splat design are compass-

shape seats, cabriole legs terminated by rounded pad feet, block-and-columnar–turned side stretchers, and slim cross braces with conical tips in the Massachusetts style.[4]

*NGE*

**Inscriptions or marks:** (Left) *Chiseled on front seat-rail rabbet and loose-seat frame:* "I"; (Right) *Chiseled on front seat-rail rabbet:* "I"; *Chiseled on front loose-seat rail:* "III".

**Construction:** (Left) The crest is supported on rectangular tenons at the post tops (pinned) and splat. The face is blocked slightly at the posts; the rear surface is chamfered across the top and at the arches and tips. The splat is slightly canted at the edges, front to back, and tenoned into the plinth. The backs of the piercings are finished with chamfers, except at the rounded tops, which are channeled. The plinth is hollow on the front and side faces, finished with a top bead, and nailed to the back rail. The rear post corners are chamfered from crest to seat. The seat rails are joined to the posts and front leg extensions with rectangular tenons (pinned). The rear legs are chamfered on all corners between the seat and rear stretcher, and the chamfer tips are marked, top and bottom, by prominent scribe lines on the forward and inside post faces. The rear feet are canted on the forward faces. The knee brackets of the front legs are secured with nails. The side stretchers are joined to the legs in vertical rectangular tenons (pinned); the medial and rear stretchers are round tenoned into the adjacent members.

(Right) Construction is the same as in the left chair, except the rear crest surface is not chamfered across the top, the splat edges and piercings are straight from front to back, and there are no prominent scribe marks at the points of the rear leg chamfers.

**Condition:** (Left) Cracks appear as follows: crest, right center; splat, top center through to back; back posts, inside faces above the rear seat rail. The left side knee block is replaced, and the adjacent rail area is repaired with a new piece of wood. The left rear leg is cracked from side to side on the forward face below the side stretcher. Cracks occur on the inside right stretcher face at the rear joint, forward block, and bud terminal. The disks beneath the front feet are worn.

(Right) A small patch is set into the inside surface of the left back post near the top. A long crack on the right post face extends upward from the seat rail. A long gouge on the lower rear splat surface is repaired with composition material. The splat and plinth joint is repaired with a spline inserted from the back. The top third of the plinth face, including the bead, has been restored, introducing an incorrect ogee profile to the coved upper face. The seat rails and stretchers are mostly repinned. The side rail returns at the back posts are new and possibly do not reflect the original scheme. The left rail is cracked through and repaired above the return. The right side knee bracket is broken at the lower corner and

reglued. The left side stretcher is cracked through at the back ring turning and poorly repaired; the medial stretcher is defaced on the lower surface. Part of the right front corner of the loose-seat frame is replaced.

**Dimensions:**
Left

| | | |
|---|---|---|
| H. | 38 in. | 96.5 cm |
| H. (seat) | 17 in. | 43.1 cm |
| W. (crest) | 18 in. | 45.7 cm |
| W. (seat front) | 20¾ in. | 52.7 cm |
| W. (seat back) | 15¼ in. | 38.7 cm |
| W. (feet) | 22⅛ in. | 56.2 cm |
| D. (seat) | 16¾ in. | 42.5 cm |
| D. (feet) | 20 in. | 50.7 cm |

Right

| | | |
|---|---|---|
| H. | 38⅜ in. | 97.5 cm |
| H. (seat) | 17 in. | 43.1 cm |
| W. (crest) | 18 in. | 45.7 cm |
| W. (seat front) | 20¾ in. | 52.7 cm |
| W. (seat back) | 15⅜ in. | 39.1 cm |
| W. (feet) | 21⅛ in. | 53.6 cm |
| D. (seat) | 16⅞ in. | 42.9 cm |
| D. (feet) | 19¾ in. | 50.2 cm |

**Materials:** *Microanalysis:* (Left) Primary: American black walnut. Secondary: soft maple (loose-seat frame). (Right) Primary: American black walnut. Secondary: soft maple group (loose-seat frame). *Finish:* (Left) medium brown color in resin over red stain; (Right) dark medium brown color in resin over red stain. *Upholstery:* (Left and right) modern leather.

**Publications:** (Left) Downs, *American Furniture*, fig. 104. Kirk, *American Chairs*, fig. 178. Fitzgerald, *Three Centuries*, p. 6, fig. IV-14.

**Accession history:** (Left) Purchased by H. F. du Pont from Harry Arons, Ansonia, Conn., 1952. Gift of H. F. du Pont, 1952. (Right) Bequest of H. F. du Pont, 1969.
52.241.2, 64.1091

1. For the Boston chair, see Randall, *American Furniture*, no. 147. For the Davenport family chair, see Jobe and Kaye, *New England Furniture*, fig. I-42 left; see also Joseph K. Ott, "Lesser Known Rhode Island Cabinetmakers: The Carliles, Holmes Weaver, Judson Blake, the Rawsons, and Thomas Davenport," *Antiques* 121, no. 5 (May 1982): 1163, fig. 10. For the Champlin chair, see Joseph K. Ott, "Some Rhode Island Furniture," *Antiques* 107, no. 5 (May 1975): 940, fig. 1. Nutting, *Furniture Treasury*, no. 2237. For English chairs, see Kirk, *American Furniture*, figs. 774, 775. Keno, Freund, and Miller, "Very Pink of the Mode," pp. 292–96.

2. For a block-and-turned–leg chair, see Jairus B. Barnes and Moselle Taylor Meals, *American Furniture in the Western Reserve, 1680–1830* (Cleveland: Western Reserve Historical Society, 1972), cat. 8. For a Marlborough-leg chair, see Fales, *Furniture of Historic Deerfield*, fig. 11. For a club-leg chair ascribed to Rhode Island, see Kathleen Eagen Johnson, "The Fiddleback Chair," *Art and Antiques* 5 (September–October 1981): 80; for a closely related chair, see Chesterfield Antiques advertisement, *Antiques and the Arts Weekly*, March 2, 1990, p. 122; for a cylindrical-leg Rhode Island variant, see Monkhouse and Michie, *American Furniture*, cat. 96. For Connecticut chairs, see Trent, *Hearts and Crowns*, nos. 65–71; Northeast Auctions, "Important Americana and Folk Art" (November 6–7, 1993), lot 479.

3. For a Champlin family chair, see Ott, "Some Rhode Island Furniture," p. 940, fig. 1. For a pierced-bead chair, see Ralph E. Carpenter, Jr., *The Arts and Crafts of Newport, Rhode Island, 1640–1820* (Newport: Preservation Society of Newport County, 1954), no. 18. For scrolled splat variants, see Ott, "Lesser Known Rhode Island Cabinetmakers," p. 1163, fig. 10; Jobe and Kaye, *New England Furniture*, fig. I-42 left. For English and other American-produced beaded-splat formal seating, see Kirk, *American Furniture*, figs. 1009–11, 1013, 1014.

4. For ball-and-claw-foot beak-crested chairs, see no. 70.3863, DAPC, Visual Resources Collection, Winterthur Library; American Art Association Anderson Galleries, "American Furniture from the Collection of Benjamin Flayderman" (April 17–18, 1931), lot 135. For shell-carved chairs, see Kirk, *American Chairs*, fig. 172; Rodriguez Roque, *American Furniture*, no. 52. For a straight-leg chair, see *Litchfield County Furniture, 1730–1850* ([Litchfield, Conn.: Litchfield Historical Society, 1969]), no. 13.

**Fig. 1.** Detail, splat face.

## 36 ◆ Side chair

Newbury, Massachusetts, or vicinity
1770–1800

Rush-bottom chairs with distinctive, double-peak crests and heart-shape splats appear to have originated in Newbury, Massachusetts, and vicinity. A variant pattern with modified crest tips and a solid, flared-neck splat is also part of this group. Histories associated with chairs of both designs that are based on family traditions or early twentieth-century photographs of chairs in situ extend the association to the neighboring towns of Newburyport, West Newbury, and Byfield. Several other chairs have family histories in adjacent New Hampshire, including this example.[1]

A similar pierced-splat chair owned by the Society for the Preservation of New England Antiquities at the Tristram Coffin I

House in Newbury was the gift of a Coffin family descendant in 1929. In view of that connection an item in the September 25, 1784, Nantucket inventory of Silvanus Coffin is of more than passing interest. Among the household furnishings, which included a "large Green Chair" (Windsor) and "fram'd bottom" seating, were "6 Newberry Chairs" that passed to the widow as part of her estate allowance.[2]

Tristram Coffin I, founder of the Coffin family in America, settled first in Haverhill, moved in 1648 to Newbury, and became one of the original proprietors of Nantucket in 1680. Silvanus, who died in February 1783, was a fifth-generation descendant. His Newbury chairs could have been acquired in the early 1770s when he and his bride, Elizabeth Hussey, set up housekeeping. Several observations are pertinent: because Newbury chairs were readily identifiable well outside Newbury, the pattern was distinctive and

could have been this unusual design; the coincidence of family ownership seems more than incidental given Nantucket's maritime orientation and the continued Newbury residence of successive generations of the Coffin family; and there may have been a small, established coastal trade in Newbury chairs, with Nantucket being one of several (or many) retail outlets.[3]

Constructed as moderately priced but fashionable seating, this late eighteenth-century chair has an updated back on an outmoded base. The composite crest consists of a Queen Anne yoke flanked by sweep ends that terminate in Chippendale-style projecting tips. The chair is remarkable for its precision styling, beginning with the well-defined crest points and continuing to the splat baluster with its T-bridge top, deeply cut scrolls, and centered heart. A particularly unusual feature of the splat is the chamfering on the *forward* edges and openings (fig. 1). The Spanish feet are modeled with grooves of mechanical quality. Subtle differences in turned work within this group suggest that more than one shop produced the pattern.[4]

NGE

Construction: The crest is supported on rectangular tenons at the post tops (pinned) and splat. The splat is lightly chamfered at the front edges and piercings and tenoned into the stay rail. The stay rail is tenoned into the back posts. The post backs, rear legs, and front leg blocks are chamfered at the edges. The oval seat rails are round tenoned into the back posts and front seat blocks (pinned); the blocks are part of the front rail. Round tenons secure the front legs to the seat blocks and the stretchers to the posts and legs. The front feet are carved from solid wood.

Condition: The upper part of the left front leg is cracked on the inside face. The right front foot is chipped at the outside back corner.

Dimensions:

| | | |
|---|---|---|
| H. | 41 in. | 104.1 cm |
| H. (seat) | 18 1/8 in. | 46.0 cm |
| W. (crest) | 16 3/8 in. | 41.6 cm |
| W. (seat front) | 14 1/2 in. | 36.8 cm |
| W. (seat back) | 14 1/8 in. | 35.9 cm |
| W. (feet) | 18 5/8 in. | 47.3 cm |
| D. (seat) | 14 1/2 in. | 36.8 cm |
| D. (feet) | 18 in. | 46.1 cm |

Materials: Microanalysis: Primary: soft maple group (front legs, seat frame, stretchers); poplar (left rear post). Finish: light coat of dark brownish black paint or color in resin over light resinous coat of brown; yellowish coat of resin on seat.

Provenance: History of ownership in the Jamison family of Dunbarton, N.H.

Accession history: Bequest of H. F. du Pont, 1969. 61.1772

1. Jobe and Kaye, New England Furniture, no. 127. Peter Benes, Old-Town and the Waterside (Newburyport, Mass.: Historical Society of Old Newbury, 1986), pp. 47–49; an interior photographic view on p. 48 with peaked-crest chairs is identified as the home of George William Adams, Byfield, although the same view pictured in Mary H. Northend, Historic Homes of New England (Boston: Little, Brown, 1914), facing p. 89, is described as the Abraham Adams house, Newbury.

2. Silvanus Coffin estate inventory, September 25, 1784, Probate Court, Nantucket Co., Mass., Probate Record Book 3; Jobe and Kaye, New England Furniture, no. 127.

3. Louis Coffin, ed., The Coffin Family (Nantucket, Mass.: Nantucket Historical Assoc., 1962), pp. 92, 197.

4. A chair of variant design with an almost identical splat has a more typical Chippendale-style crest piece that is a broader, uncarved version of that in No. 29. The turned base features short columnar elements at the top of the front legs and pad feet at the bottom. Single swelled-and-tipped stretchers brace the sides and back, and a William and Mary–style stretcher at the front. Antiques Dealers' Association of America, Eighth Annual Antiques Show, loan exhibition, White Plains, N.Y., September 10–11, 1994, as illustrated in Antiques and the Arts Weekly, September 9, 1994.

## 37 ◆ Side chair
Probably Goffstown or Bedford, New Hampshire
1770–92
Attributed to Maj. John Dunlap (1746–92) or possibly to Lt. Samuel Dunlap (1752–1830)

A small, possibly unique, group of four chairs that includes this example has long been associated with southern New Hampshire and the Dunlap family of cabinetmakers. Two chairs in the group, owned by the Metropolitan Museum of Art were found in Goffstown, west of Manchester, where Maj. John Dunlap worked from about 1769 to 1777 before moving down the road one mile to Bedford (township). From 1773 to 1779, John's brother Lt. Samuel Dunlap worked with him before resettling in Henniker, some twenty miles away.[1]

The design of this chair is markedly similar in several decorative features to casework documented or attributed to the Dunlap brothers. The fourteen-section carved ornament on the crest (fig. 1) and seat front—designated a "sunrise fan" by Charles S. Parsons in his extensive study of the Dunlap craftsmen—is identical, except in size, to a fan common to many tall Dunlap casepieces (fig. 2). The tight S curves of the splat piercings, which are repeated in the outer profiles of the chair splat and in the seat rail, appear as horizontal, molded scrolls in the front skirts of the cases. The central splat feature, a heart above a diamond, also occurs in Dunlap casework, where a small heart on a stem is centered between the S scrolls of the front skirt (see fig. 2). In a further comparison the central astragal arch of the chair crest can be linked to pairs of

**Fig. 1.** Detail, crest center and splat.

**Fig. 2.** Detail, chest-on-chest attributed to Maj. John Dunlap, Bedford, N.H., 1777–92. H. 83 1/2 in. (212.1 cm), W. 40 1/2 in. (102.8 cm), D. 20 in. (50.7 cm). (New Hampshire Historical Society, Concord)

**Fig. 3.** Detail, chest-on-chest-on-frame attributed to Maj. John Dunlap, Goffstown or Bedford, N.H., 1769–92, or Lt. Samuel Dunlap, Goffstown, Henniker, or Salisbury, N.H., 1773–ca. 1800. H. 78 1/2 in. (199.3 cm), W. 41 in. (104.1 cm), D. 21 1/2 in. (54.6 cm). (Private collection; Photo, New Hampshire Historical Society)

skirt-front astragals in other tall Dunlap cases (fig. 3).[2]

The sawed, carved, and pierced elements of the Dunlap chair are confined within a tall, rigidly straight frame composed of posts, stay rail, front legs, and forward stretcher. The contrast between the rectilinear and curvilinear elements is marked. Heightening the effect are the molded surfaces of the straight elements, which are patterned with triple reeds flanked by broad channels. The projecting, molded crest tips, which in appearance are extensions of the posts, are an effective counterbalance to the prominent centered crown.

The original color of this chair was probably Prussian blue—the paint layer beneath the current dark and flaking outer coat. The Metropolitan Museum of Art's chairs have lost their original finish, and the fourth chair, which is at Chipstone Foundation, is covered with "old and much-darkened green paint." All four chair seats are covered with late eighteenth-century American crewel embroidery in a bold floral pattern. From the similarity of the measurements, frames, and stitchery, the chairs appear to constitute a set; however, the two Metropolitan Museum examples are made of cherry, and the other two are maple. It could be suggested that the chairs are from two sets; however, the distinctive character of the crewel embroidery, the use of solid seat boards rather than open frames, and the presence of animal-hide undercovers beneath the embroidery of all provide strong evidence for the single-set theory.[3]

*NGE*

---

**Construction:** The carved crest is supported on rectangular tenons at the post tops (pinned) and splat. The crest tapers in thickness from top to bottom and is shouldered on the back surface. The shell and splat face are flush. The splat, which also tapers from top to bottom, is tenoned into the stay rail plinth (pinned); the back edges and piercings are lightly chamfered. The thick stay rail and plinth are one piece of wood, the latter hollow on the face and beaded at the front of the crown. The stay rail is secured to the back posts with rectangular tenons (pinned). The posts, stay rail, and stretcher faces are molded with centered, triple reeds flanked by broad, shallow channels. The seat rails are joined to the legs and posts with rectangular tenons (pinned). The shell in the front rail, which is comparable to that in the crest, is only lightly carved at the center. The bottom edges of the front and side rails are marked by heavy tooling; the smooth back rail is molded with a narrow ogee on the outside lower edge. The rear feet are canted on the forward faces. The front and side stretchers are joined to the legs and posts with rectangular tenons (pinned);

the rear stretcher is round tenoned into the back posts. Molded strips, which are mitered at the front corners and applied with cut nails to the rail tops, secure the cushion seat.

**Condition:** Surfaces are marked by irregularities and paint losses. A crack in the right side of the splat has been repaired. Parts of the front and right rail moldings were replaced. The legs are worn at the upper front corners and gouged in the lower parts. Other gouges appear on the rear faces of the lower back posts. The right leg is cracked. The seat board is planed and oxidized on the lower surface.

**Dimensions:**

| | | |
|---|---|---|
| H. | 45 in. | 114.2 cm |
| H. (seat) | 16³/₈ in. | 41.6 cm |
| W. (crest) | 20⁵/₈ in. | 52.4 cm |
| W. (seat front) | 21⁵/₈ in. | 54.9 cm |
| W. (seat back) | 16 in. | 40.6 cm |
| W. (feet) | 21⁷/₈ in. | 55.5 cm |
| D. (seat) | 14³/₄ in. | 37.4 cm |
| D. (feet) | 17 in. | 43.1 cm |

**Materials:** *Microanalysis:* Primary: soft maple group. *Finish:* dark outer paint, dry and flaking, over earlier coat of Prussian blue. *Upholstery:* The seat board is covered with worn, floral-and-vine–patterned crewel embroidery on brown linen; America, 1740–1800. The original cover is now lined with modern muslin and attached with modern nails; beneath the cover and lining is a layer of cotton padding. Nailed directly to the seat board, which is hollowed in the center, is the original animal-hide undercover, the stuffing probably consists of hair clippings.

**Exhibitions:** "Beyond Necessity: Art in the Folk Tradition," Brandywine River Museum, Chadds Ford, Pa., September 17–November 20, 1977.

**Publications:** Downs, *American Furniture*, fig. 157. *Dunlaps and Their Furniture*, fig. 77. Bishop, *Centuries and Styles of the American Chair*, fig. 212. Dean A. Fales, Jr., *American Painted Furniture, 1660–1880* (New York: E. P. Dutton, 1972), fig. 111. Fitzgerald, *Three Centuries*, fig. VII-27.

**Accession history:** Bequest of H. F. du Pont, 1969. 60.1054

---

1. *Dunlaps and Their Furniture*, figs. 78a, b, pp. 1–22.

2. For asymmetrically shaped, skirt-front astragals in Dunlap cases, see *Dunlaps and Their Furniture*, figs. 16, 30, 34.

3. Rodriguez Roque, *American Furniture*, no. 65; the Chipstone chair may originally have been painted Prussian blue—pigment that when improperly compounded is fugitive and sometimes turns green. In addition, old yellowed varnish can camouflage a blue base. For the Metropolitan Museum of Art chairs, see Heckscher, *American Furniture*, cat. no. 19.

## 38 ◆ Side chair
**Southeastern New Hampshire, possibly Plaistow or Essex County, Massachusetts
1770–1800
J. F. Bly (owner)**

J. F. Bly, whose name is branded on the underside of the rear stretcher of this chair and its mate, has long been presumed to be the maker (fig. 1). Charles S. Parsons, who compiled extensive notes on New Hampshire furnituremakers, found a James Bly in Plaistow provincial deeds identified variously as a carpenter, housewright, innholder, husbandman, and yeoman (but not as a furnituremaker) from 1752 into the 1760s. Earlier deeds indicate that Bly was a landholder in the neighboring Massachusetts communities of Amesbury, Newbury, and Haverhill between 1739 and 1742 and perhaps later.[1]

A recent review of Plaistow land and probate records confirms Bly's principal

yeoman status and identifies a homestead farm, livestock, and husbandry utensils. The presence of axes, an adz, a crosscut saw, plane irons, and wedges in the estate records addresses Bly's adjunct trade as housewright and carpenter. The farm passed first to son Moses (b. 1752) and then by parcels to Moses's youngest son, Josiah Peabody Bly (b. 1791). Moses's 1844 estate records lack an inventory, but land records indicate that he was principally a farmer. An informal inventory of Josiah Peabody's estate lists a blacksmith shop and tools and a brickyard with a supply of timber to fire a kiln.[2]

None of the Bly family members mentioned appear to have made furniture, and the sons of Josiah Peabody Bly, the fourth generation, were born in the 1820s and 1830s—too late to have made chairs in the style of this example. However, this generation produced a candidate whose initials fit the brand—Josiah Franklin Bly (b. 1833),

**Fig. 1.** Detail, brand.

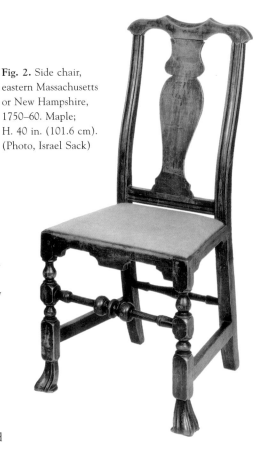

youngest son of Josiah Peabody. In 1856, shortly after attaining his majority, Josiah Franklin was described in a deed as a "trader," an occupation in which a name brand was often useful. By 1866 he lived in Salem, Massachusetts; two years later he was a resident of neighboring Danvers. The brands on the Bly chairs were applied with a hot iron that charred the wood, suggesting they were placed there long after the wood had thoroughly dried.[3]

How Josiah Franklin Bly acquired the pair of chairs that bear his brand can only be speculated upon. The furniture may have been owned by his forebears but was certainly not made by anyone in the direct Bly family line. The chairs possibly came from a collateral line or the family of Bly's wife, Matilda Welch Porter. It is also possible that Bly bought the chairs at a local sale when he set up housekeeping or at any time thereafter. No other Bly family members have been located whose given names fit the initials of the brand.

The support structure of the Bly chair, composed of turned and sawed elements and carved Spanish feet, is not far removed from Boston work of the 1720s and 1730s. The double-spool elements of the front leg tops are a variation of the usual baluster turnings. The back features—the crest, splat, and posts—are associated with formal Queen Anne and Chippendale seating furniture and date to the second half of the century. The splat design is a basic northeastern Massachusetts profile (see No. 6), broadened and pierced. The astragal-shape aperture base is a subtle feature, more common in formal seating. Flat back posts represent a stylistic advance over the crowned, molded surfaces common earlier. An almost imperceptible outward flare at the post tops is continued into the hollows of the crest tips. The unusual top piece is terminated by rounded, projecting beaklike points rather than common squared tips that curve upward.

The crest is related to a top piece associated with Portsmouth chairmaking (see No. 59), although an arch is substituted in this chair for the long central depression, or yoke, of that pattern. A pair of eastern Massachusetts

or New Hampshire chairs of midcentury, which have saddle-centered crests with prominent beaklike tips (fig. 2), appears to be more closely linked. The ogee-top vase splats supported in low stay rails are flanked by molded, crooked back posts. The Spanish-foot, turned bases resemble No. 17, with the substitution of a hollow-cornered, rectangular drop in the front rail, as found in some Gaines-type chairs. The same vase-splat pattern appears in another pair of side chairs that have an identical base, the back crowned by a familiar pierced, carved, and saddled Gaines-type crest.[4]

*NGE*

---

**Inscriptions or marks:** *Branded, in serif letters, on underside of rear stretcher:* "J.F.BLY".

**Construction:** The crest is supported on rectangular tenons at the canted post tops (pinned) and splat. The thin splat, lightly chamfered on the back at the outside edges and piercings, is tenoned into the molded stay rail; the stay rail, in turn, is tenoned into the back posts (pinned). The post faces are flattened at seat level. The rounded, bladelike seat rails are round tenoned into the back posts and the front seat blocks, which form the ends of the front rail. The front legs are round tenoned into the seat blocks. The front stretcher is similarly attached to the legs. The side and rear stretchers are joined to the legs and posts with rectangular tenons (pinned). The front feet are carved from solid wood.

**Condition:** The crest is slightly defaced at the center front, tips, and left joint with the post; cracks appear at the lower center back. The stay rail is cracked at the left front. Gouges occur on the front seat blocks, front stretcher turnings, and left leg baluster; the front stretcher is slightly worn. The rectangular stretchers and lower back posts are marked by gouges and irregularities. The rush seat is worn and has minor losses.

**Dimensions:**

| | | |
|---|---|---|
| H. | 37 in. | 94.0 cm |
| H. (seat) | 17 3/8 in. | 44.1 cm |
| W. (crest) | 17 5/16 in. | 44.0 cm |
| W. (seat front) | 19 3/8 in. | 49.2 cm |
| W. (seat back) | 14 1/8 in. | 35.9 cm |
| W. (feet) | 19 3/8 in. | 49.2 cm |
| D. (seat) | 14 3/8 in. | 36.5 cm |
| D. (feet) | 17 1/4 in. | 43.8 cm |

**Materials:** *Microanalysis:* Primary: soft maple group. Finish: traces of wine red and dark brown finish now coated by a low-sheen, colorless resin; colorless resin on seat over light brownish red and white paint; the seat blocks appear to have been painted white at one time to match the seat.

**Accession history:** Purchased by H. F. du Pont from Jane Wilson, Old Saybrook, Conn., 1954. Bequest of H. F. du Pont, 1969.
54.2.1

---

1. Charles S. Parsons, comp., notebook of New Hampshire Joiner-Cabinetmakers, 1981, DAPC, Visual Resources Collection, Winterthur Library.

2. James Bly, Moses Bly, and Josiah Peabody Bly land and estate records, 1758–1864, Registries of Deeds and Probate, Rockingham Co., N.H. Brickmaking was a profitable venture in parts of Plaistow, where there were large deposits of clay; Priscilla Hammond, comp., "Vital Records of Plaistow, N.H., 1726–1871" (New Hampshire Historical Society, 1937, typescript), pp. 8, 26, 44, 55, 66, 92; "200th Anniversary Celebration, Town of Plaistow, N.H., 1749–1949" [Plaistow, N.H.: 1949].

3. Hammond, "Vital Records," p. 93; Josiah Franklin Bly land records, 1855–74, Registry of Deeds, Rockingham Co., N.H.

4. A prototype for the beak-ended crest in fig. 2 occurs in British seating furniture; for 2 turned-base chairs with more exaggerated beak-ended crests and splat profiles identical to that in No. 1, see Kirk, *American Furniture*, figs. 774, 775. The pair of vase-splat chairs with the Gaines-type crest is illustrated in *American Antiques from Israel Sack Collection*, 10 vols. (Washington, D.C.: Highland House, ca. 1969–), 8:2236.

## 39 ◆ Armchair
Southeastern New England, probably
coastal Rhode Island or vicinity
1780–1810

This unusual armchair, with elements derived
from both formal and vernacular furniture,
is an amalgam of regional influences based
principally on Rhode Island furniture design.
The features with the strongest affinity to
Rhode Island work are the splat, arm posts,
front stretcher, and front feet.

The Chippendale-style crest with a
central arch flanked by long ogees was popular
throughout New England. Formal Rhode Island
examples are both carved and uncarved,
and the profile also is part of the regional
vocabulary of vernacular design. The Dominys
of neighboring Long Island and chairmakers
along the Connecticut coast employed
modified versions. The bold, broad splat
balanced by flaring necks, top and bottom,
appears to derive from a heart-shape loop-
pierced banister in formal Rhode Island
chairs with similar crests. Models also occur
in regional vernacular furniture.[1]

Boston design seems to have influenced
the chairmaker when he formed the arms,
which are slimmer and straighter than the
prototypes and finished at the front with
pronounced creases and cushioned sides
rather than carving (see No. 6). The rests
are supported on columnar posts with urn
bases borrowed directly from the pedestals of
Rhode Island candlestands and tea tables. The
baluster-shape post tips immediately above the
columns are derived from regional vernacular
furniture, specifically a group of Rhode Island
Windsor armchairs. The conical tips of the
front stretcher formed with inside, modeled
collars are like those in a group of cross-
stretcher high- and low-back Windsors made
in the 1760s in Newport, including twelve
chairs purchased for the Redwood Library in

1764. Precise bulbous elements, such as
those at the stretcher center, are present in
Rhode Island Windsors dating to the 1780s
and 1790s.[2]

The front feet, turned with sloping pads,
are an unusual feature. While block-and-turned
chairs with pad feet are not uncommon, this
particular profile is rare. Whether it derives
from a formal or vernacular regional pattern
is unclear. Rush-bottom club-foot chairs
produced in New York City, on Long Island by
the Dominys, and along the Connecticut coast
may be the prototypes. A related foot appears
on a so-called spider-leg breakfast table of
Newport origin. That design actually provides
a closer model because the pads appear to rest
within a low saucer on a disk base, somewhat
similar to those on this chair. In any event,
the craftsman who produced this uncommon
"great chair" gave eclecticism full reign and
still created a workable design.[3]

Only one other chair with features closely
linked to this one has been noted. A rush-

bottom maple armchair in the Bayou Bend
collection, Houston, has similar arms with
cushioned scrolls and a tipped front stretcher
marked by bulbous turnings also scribed with
centered lines. Also comparable are the
columnar arm posts, compressed front leg
balusters, and plain, cylindrical rear stretcher.
Although supported on carved Spanish feet in
place of Queen Anne-style pad feet, the ankles
of the Bayou Bend chair, like those of this
chair, are connected to the leg blocks with
small, ringlike collars (fig. 1).[4]

*NGE*

**Construction:** The crest is supported on rectangular
tenons at the flat-faced canted posts (pinned) and
splat. The crest face is slightly cheeked at the
arches, and the terminals are shaved to fine creases
at the tips. The rear edges are chamfered, except at
the tips. The splat, which is tenoned into the stay
rail, is flat at the front edges and chamfered at the
back. The plain stay rail, with a narrow bottom-
front chamfer, is joined to the posts with rectangular

tenons (pinned). The rear post corners are chamfered from crest to base, and the post faces are marked by a flattened area at seat level. The arms are U shaped with chamfers at the bottom edges extending to the "pillowed" forward scrolls, which are centered with sharp ridges. The arms are secured by rectangular tenons at the back posts (pinned) and round tenons at the front posts (pinned). The rounded rectangular seat rails are round tenoned into the posts. The rear legs are chamfered on the forward corners from seat to base. The front post turnings are detailed, and the leg blocks are lightly chamfered on all corners. A ring separates the front feet from the leg blocks; the forward-sloping pads are supported on wafer-thin disks. All stretchers are round tenoned into the adjacent members. The front stretcher balls are centered with double incised lines.

**Condition:** Some pins appear to be renewed. Overall, surfaces bear minor nicks and blemishes. The coarse rush seat is not original.

**Dimensions:**

| | | |
|---|---|---|
| H. | 42 in. | 106.7 cm |
| H. (seat) | 16½ in. | 41.9 cm |
| W. (crest) | 19½ in. | 49.5 cm |
| W. (seat front) | 22 in. | 55.8 cm |
| W. (seat back) | 16 in. | 40.6 cm |
| W. (arms) | 22⁵/₁₆ in. | 56.6 cm |
| W. (feet) | 23⅛ in. | 58.7 cm |
| D. (seat) | 16⅛ in. | 41.0 cm |
| D. (feet) | 19¼ in. | 48.9 cm |

**Materials:** *Microanalysis:* Primary: hard maple group. Secondary: ash (stretchers). *Finish:* deep brown color in resin; clear resin on seat top and edges.

**Publications:** Marshall B. Davidson, ed., *The American Heritage History of Colonial Antiques* ([New York]: American Heritage Publishing Co., [1967]), p. 230, fig. 330.

**Accession history:** Purchased by H. F. du Pont from Milford Antique Shop, Milford, Conn., 1952. Gift of H. F. du Pont, 1952.
52.153

---

1. For formal Rhode Island chairs with similar crests, see Kirk, *American Chairs*, figs. 175, 176; for vernacular chairs, see Dean F. Failey, *Long Island Is My Nation: The Decorative Arts and Craftsmen, 1640–1830* (Setauket, N.Y.: Society for the Preservation of Long Island Antiquities, 1976), fig. 226; Trent, *Hearts and Crowns*, nos. 72, 73. For formal chairs with related but pierced splats, see Ralph E. Carpenter, Jr., *The Arts and Crafts of Newport, Rhode Island, 1640–1820* (Newport: Preservation Society of Newport County, 1954), no. 4; Harold Sack and Deanne Levison, "Queen Anne and Chippendale Armchairs in America," *Antiques* 137, no. 5 (May 1990): 1173, pl. 8; for vernacular chairs, see Trent, *Hearts and Crowns*, no. 63; *Connecticut Furniture*, no. 221.

2. For Rhode Island stands and tables, see Carpenter, *Arts and Crafts of Newport*, nos. 54, 78, 79; *John Brown House Loan Exhibition*, cat. 33. For Windsor armchairs, see Nancy Goyne Evans, *American Windsor Chairs* (New York: Hudson Hills Press in association with the Henry Francis du Pont Winterthur Museum, 1996), figs. 6-1, 6-2, 6-35, 6-37, 6-141, 6-142. George Champlin Mason, *Annals of the Redwood Library and Athenaeum, Newport, Rhode Island* (Newport: Redwood Library, 1891), p. 53.

3. For a Dominy club-foot chair, see Failey, *Long Island Is My Nation*, no. 226; for the "spider-leg" table, see Bernard and S. Dean Levy, Inc., *An American Tea Party: Colonial Tea and Breakfast Tables, 1715–1783* (New York: By the company, 1988), cat. 12.

4. Warren, *Bayou Bend*, no. 215.

**Fig. 1.** Detail, left front foot.

terminology and price structure with turned seating ascribed to Milford suggests this was a "black" chair that sold for 4s. 6d. A companion armchair probably cost 6s. New Haven County inventories attest to the popularity of black chairs in the region. Joiner James Deneson owned two at his death in 1775, which, valued at 4s. apiece, may have been almost new, but five "poorer" black chairs were worth only a little more than 1s. 1d. apiece. Other local owners of black chairs in the mid 1770s include several farmers, a widow, a merchant, and a minister.[2]

The longevity of the banister-back chair is demonstrated by the existence of variations produced into the early nineteenth century in New York State and perhaps coastal Connecticut. David Coutant of New Rochelle stamped such a chair during the 1790s. A chair marked by Thomas Kinsela of Schenectady dates between 1800 and the chairmaker's death in 1822 when dozens of chair frames stood in the shop along with "53 Bundles flags," or rush.[3]

NGE

## 40 ◆ Side chair
Probably Milford, Connecticut
1760–90
Possibly John Durand (1735–80) or
Samuel Durand I (1738–1829)

Banister-back seating is not generally associated with the style periods today termed *Queen Anne* and *Chippendale*. Except for the reeded vertical back elements, however, this chair is identical to one featuring the more typical solid splat of the Queen Anne style (see No. 41). The pattern represents a fourth-generation interpretation of a tall design that originated in the seventeenth-century English cane chair, which was exported to America. Reinterpreted early in the eighteenth century as a fashionable, leather-upholstered chair

in Boston, the general design was soon modified again to produce an auxiliary line of inexpensive, rush-bottom seating with turned, split banisters and coarsely carved crests, or crowns. A plain crown topped the first molded-banister interpretations but generally was replaced during the third quarter of the century with the hollow crest shown here.[1]

This chair is one from a group associated with coastal Connecticut and further attributed in recent years to the Durand family of Milford. Several similar or related chairs have strong histories of ownership in Milford families. Although John Durand kept an account book between 1760 and his death in 1780, his use of generalized chair terms precludes precise identification of shop production. Comparison of account-book

**Construction:** The crest and stay rail are joined to the back posts with rectangular tenons. Narrow tenons secure the banisters to the crest and stay rail. The seat rails and stretchers are round tenoned into the legs; the socket points are marked by lightly scribed lines.

**Condition:** The surface has been scraped to remove former coats of paint, leaving the structural elements considerably defaced. The left back-post baluster collar is chipped. All four legs are scratched and gouged; the front stretchers are somewhat worn.

**Dimensions:**

| | | |
|---|---|---|
| H. | 41¹⁄₂ in. | 105.4 cm |
| H. (seat) | 16⁷⁄₈ in. | 42.9 cm |
| W. (crest) | 14¹⁄₂ in. | 36.8 cm |
| W. (seat front) | 14¹⁄₄ in. | 36.2 cm |
| W. (seat back) | 14¹⁄₄ in. | 36.2 cm |
| W. (feet) | 19¹⁄₂ in. | 49.5 cm |
| D. (seat) | 13⁵⁄₈ in. | 34.6 cm |
| D. (feet) | 14³⁄₄ in. | 37.4 cm |

**Materials:** *Microanalysis:* Primary: soft maple group. Secondary: ash (front bottom stretcher); yellow poplar (crest). *Finish:* black paint and clear resin over bare scraped wood.

**Accession history:** Gift of Mrs. Reginald Rose, Oyster Bay, N.Y., in memory of her mother, Mrs. Henry Horton Benkard, 1974. 74.39

1. Trent, *Hearts and Crowns,* pp. 30–54.

2. Benno M. Forman, "The Crown and York Chairs of Coastal Connecticut and the Work of the Durands of Milford," *Antiques* 105, no. 5 (May 1974): 1147–54; "Collectors' Notes," *Antiques* 106, no. 6 (December 1974): 1033; Trent, *Hearts and Crowns,* pp. 49–54, nos. 36, 47, 50. John Durand account book, 1760–83, Milford Historical Society, Milford, Conn. (microfilm, Downs collection). Edward Cooke, Jr., also noted the popularity of "black" chairs, many identified with slat backs, in neighboring Stratford; Edward Strong Cooke, Jr., "The Selective Conservative Taste: Furniture in Stratford, Connecticut, 1740–1800" (Master's thesis, University of Delaware, 1979), pp. 24–33. For transcription of New Haven Co., Conn., inventories, see Alice Hanson Jones, *American Colonial Wealth: Documents and Methods,* 3 vols. (New York: Arno Press, 1977), 2:502, 507, 534, 542, 563, 576.

3. Thomas Kinsela estate records, 1822–23, Surrogate Court, Schenectady Co., N.Y. Trent (*Hearts and Crowns,* nos. 47–50), demonstrates the longevity of the banister-back chair in coastal Connecticut; for Coutant (Coutong) and Kinsela chairs, see Roderic H. Blackburn, "Branded and Stamped New York Furniture," *Antiques* 119, no. 5 (May 1981): 1135, fig. 11; 1139, fig. 16.

## 41 ◆ Side chair

Probably Milford, Connecticut
1760–90
Possibly John Durand (1735–80) or
Samuel Durand I (1738–1829)

This simple splat-back chair, which is contemporary with the banister-back chair of No. 40, was likely produced in the same shop. The turned work is identical, and the hollow crest is varied only as necessary to accommodate a central splat. The two chairs would have been similarly priced. This is the "york" chair that was new to coastal Connecticut in the 1750s. John Durand of Milford first recorded this pattern, priced from 4s. to 4s. 6d., in his 1762 accounts. As the name suggests, the york chair, with a Queen Anne–style splat, was adapted from seating produced in neighboring New York, which had many commercial ties with coastal Connecticut. The york chair was purely a turner's product. Connecticut patrons who were more style conscious could purchase the "crooked-back" (contoured) cherry or maple splat chair—a pattern that combined a sawed, modeled back and yoke crest with a turned base and rush seat.[1]

The overall dimensions of the splat- and banister-back chairs are nearly identical, although the verticality of one is emphasized by the central splat and the horizontality of the other by a row of flat, vertical slats. As the york chair gained popularity during the 1760s and early 1770s, the banister-back chair began to fade from the market. Jireh Bull of Milford, perhaps a tailor by trade, preferred york chairs: in 1774 he owned fifteen side chairs of this description, six of which were well worn, having lost their rush bottoms. With the postrevolutionary years came further changes in furniture fashions, and by the 1790s the Windsor was the popular vernacular chair in New England, overshadowing all other styles.[2]

NGE

**Construction:** The crest and stay rail are joined to the back posts with rectangular tenons. Narrow tenons secure the splat to the crest and stay rail. The rear splat edges are chamfered. The seat rails and stretchers are round tenoned into the legs, the socket points marked by lightly scribed lines. Raised, turned bosses circumscribed by incised lines ornament the front leg tops. The back posts taper at the bottom to form feet.

**Condition:** The splat is broken at the upper left corner and repaired. The pin securing the crest and right back-post joint is missing. Nails reinforce the rail and stretcher joints at the legs. The upper front stretcher is worn on the top surface. The right rear post is deeply gouged at the inside base. The rush seat is slightly damaged.

**Dimensions:**

| | | |
|---|---|---|
| H. | 41³/₄ in. | 106.1 cm |
| H. (seat) | 16³/₄ in. | 42.5 cm |
| W. (crest) | 14¹/₄ in. | 36.2 cm |
| W. (seat front) | 18 in. | 45.7 cm |
| W. (seat back) | 13¹³/₁₆ in. | 35.1 cm |
| W. (feet) | 19¹/₈ in. | 48.5 cm |
| D. (seat) | 13¹/₄ in. | 33.6 cm |
| D. (feet) | 14¹/₄ in. | 36.2 cm |

**Materials:** *Microanalysis:* Primary: soft maple group. Secondary: hickory (stretcher). *Finish:* transparent black resin over brick-red primer or undercoat.

**Publications:** Benno M. Forman, "The Crown and York Chairs of Coastal Connecticut and the Work of the Durands of Milford," *Antiques* 105, no. 5 (May 1974): 1151, fig. 5.

**Accession history:** Museum purchase from Lillian B. Cogan, Farmington, Conn., 1972. 72.428

1. Both Benno Forman and Robert Trent identified this rush-seated pattern as a "red chair," based on terminology in the Durand accounts. Benno M. Forman, "The Crown and York Chairs of Coastal Connecticut and the Work of the Durands of Milford," *Antiques* 105, no. 5 (May 1974): 1151, fig. 5; Trent, *Hearts and Crowns*, p. 64. However, analysis of Durand's chair pricing structure (see No. 42) and information provided by Edward Cooke in his Stratford furniture study indicate that this was a "york" chair. Edward Strong Cooke, Jr., "The Selective Conservative Taste: Furniture in Stratford, Connecticut, 1740–1800" (Master's thesis, University of Delaware, 1979), pp. 29, 31–32. The appearance of the york chair in coastal Connecticut in the 1750s is confirmed in Forman, who cites an entry for "6 New Fashion york chairs" in the December 1, 1757, inventory of Capt. Joseph Blackleach of Stratford; Forman, "Crown and York Chairs," p. 1148; "Collectors' Notes," *Antiques* 106, no. 6 (December 1974): 1033. John Durand account book, 1760–83, Milford Historical Society, Milford, Conn. (microfilm, Downs collection).

2. Alice Hanson Jones, *American Colonial Wealth: Documents and Methods*, 3 vols. (New York: Arno Press, 1977), 2:519–22.

## 42 ◆ Side chair

**Probably Milford, Connecticut**
**1760–1800**
**Possibly John Durand (1735–80) or Samuel Durand I (1738–1829)**

The "red" chairs made in quantity and recorded by John Durand from the early 1760s until his death in 1780 were probably of this type. In previous publications highlighting Durand's work, the pattern has been identified as a "york" chair; however, Durand's pricing structure does not support this hypothesis. The chairmaker generally sold red chairs for 6s. to 7s. apiece. Most of the increase over the 4s. to 4s. 6d. cost of black chairs (see No. 40) and york chairs (see No. 41) was due to the labor-intensive pattern of the turned front legs. The large billet of wood required to

accommodate the knee and foot necessitated the removal of a considerable amount of material to shape the slim top cylinder and ankle. The craftsman also had to rechuck the lathe to turn the pad foot.[1]

Durand's model for the red chair was the turned, pad-foot chair with heavy, trumpet-shape front legs made in New York City, the Hudson River valley, and on Long Island (fig. 1). The pattern probably was popular in New York shortly after midcentury. Some New York chairs are stamped on the leg tops by makers working as late as the 1780s and 1790s. Nathaniel Dominy V of East Hampton, Long Island, made similar chairs with slightly later features during the early nineteenth century.[2]

The heavy, turned leg of the red chair, which is a direct descendent of the William and Mary trumpet-shape leg, was a moderately priced substitute for the cabriole leg. Slat- and spindle-back chairs with related but frequently less stylish legs were made in England's North Country, but whether such production predates American use of this support in the eighteenth century is debatable. Certainly the straight "cabriole" leg appears on American tables of early date (see Nos. 109, 111 right, 112).[3]

Coastal Connecticut red chairs are distinguishable from their New York prototypes by the substitution of double-ball turnings for the cone-and-ball at the post tops and a bulbous front stretcher without a central disk. New York seat fronts were framed either with corner blocks (see fig. 1) or cylindrical leg extensions. Connecticut chairs were constructed in the latter pattern.

NGE

**Fig. 1.** Side chair, New York, 1760–1800. Soft maple group; H. 40 1/8 in. (101.9 cm), H. (seat) 17 1/4 in. (43.8 cm), W. (seat) 19 3/4 in. (50.1 cm), D. (seat) 16 in. (40.6 cm). (Winterthur 58.1019)

**Construction:** The flat-faced crest is supported on round tenons in the turned back posts (pinned) and on a long, narrow rectangular tenon at the splat. Rectangular tenons secure the splat to the stay rail (pinned) and the stay rail to the posts. The rear splat edges are chamfered. The seat rails and stretchers are round tenoned into the legs, the socket points marked by lightly scribed lines. Raised, turned bosses ornament the front leg tops, and narrow collars mark the ankles above the raised pad feet. The back posts are rounded slightly to form feet.

**Condition:** The splat is cracked at the upper right corner and along the lower edge. The left front leg is cracked on the rear face below each stretcher socket; minor insect damage occurs on the foot. The top of the front stretcher and the upper backs of the posts are considerably worn. The rush seat is broken in several places.

**Dimensions:**

| | | |
|---|---|---|
| H. | 40 3/16 in. | 102.1 cm |
| H. (seat) | 16 1/2 in. | 41.9 cm |
| W. (crest) | 15 7/8 in. | 40.3 cm |
| W. (seat front) | 18 1/8 in. | 46.3 cm |
| W. (seat back) | 15 in. | 38.1 cm |
| W. (feet) | 21 1/16 in. | 51.9 cm |
| D. (seat) | 15 1/4 in. | 38.7 cm |
| D. (feet) | 16 1/4 in. | 41.3 cm |

**Materials:** *Microanalysis:* Primary: soft maple group. *Finish:* black paint over red primer; traces of bright yellow paint on seat.

**Provenance:** The chair descended in the Prindle family near Milford, Conn. It was owned by Horatio Nelson Prindle (1800–1848); his granddaughter; and her daughter, Marion Northrop, who was the last private owner (1977).

**Accession history:** Museum purchase from Lillian B. Cogan, Farmington, Conn., 1977. 77.193

1. John Durand account book, 1760–83, Milford Historical Society, Milford, Conn. (microfilm, Downs collection); Benno M. Forman, "The Crown and York Chairs of Coastal Connecticut and the Work of the Durands of Milford," *Antiques* 105, no. 5 (May 1974): 1148, 1152–53; Trent, *Hearts and Crowns*, pp. 60–64; Michael J. Ettema, "Technological Innovation and Design Economics in Furniture Manufacture," *Winterthur Portfolio* 16, nos. 2/3 (Summer/Autumn 1981): 199–200.

2. Roderic H. Blackburn, "Branded and Stamped New York Furniture," *Antiques* 119, no. 5 (May 1981): figs. 10, 12, 13. Albany chairmaker James Chesney illustrated a "Fiddle-Back" (red) chair in an *Albany Chronicle* advertisement dated April 10, 1797. Charles F. Hummel, *With Hammer in Hand: The Dominy Craftsmen of East Hampton, New York* (Charlottesville: University Press of Virginia for the Henry Francis du Pont Winterthur Museum, 1968), pp. 262–63.

3. William Cotton, "Vernacular Design: The Spindle Back Chair and Its North Country Origins," *Working Wood* (Spring 1980): 40–50; B. D. Cotton, *The Chair in the North West: Regional Styles in the Eighteenth and Nineteenth Centuries* (Burnley, Eng.: Towneley Hall Art Gallery and Museums, 1987).

## 43 ◆ Side chair
Possibly Milford, Connecticut
1785–1810
Possibly the Durand family

This design is a late eighteenth-century version of the york chair. The ogee-top splat, a profile associated with New York vernacular work, closely resembles the one in the trumpet-leg chair (see No. 42). Other shared features of the two are the tripartite front stretchers, yoke-type crests, and double-ball configuration of the upper back posts. The post tops of this chair have been streamlined to the point of suggesting bonelike articulations. This feature is found in larger form in rush-seated chairs associated with New London, Connecticut; a slim version appears in the posts of an uncommon, coastal Connecticut fan-back Windsor side chair dating to the 1790s. Baluster feet are frequently linked with Milford

area chairs (see Nos. 40, 41), but unlike the early examples, the rings that divide these front legs are sandwiched between narrow hollows, and the front feet and lower back-post balusters are capped with knife-edge disks. The sharply tapered back toes first appeared in this period. Overall, the slim, severe lines of this chair are in keeping with the simple elegance of the new federal style introduced following the revolutionary war.[1]

Samuel Durand II (1762?–1838), son of Samuel I, made york chairs as late as 1816, advancing his price from 4s. 6d. to 6s. apiece. A faded label inscription on the crest back associates this chair with Meriden, Connecticut, a community twenty-five miles inland from Milford but well within the resettlement area for families whose size outgrew the local neighborhood by the early nineteenth century. The chair may have been taken to Meriden sometime after

its construction in the Milford area, or it may have been made in Meriden by a chairmaker who had trained on the coast.[2]

NGE

---

**Inscriptions or marks:** *Attached to back of crest:* "1772/ Johnson/ Meriden" in black ink on modern, darkened paper label.

**Construction:** The flat-faced crest is supported on round tenons in the turned back posts (pinned) and on a long, narrow rectangular tenon at the splat. A rectangular tenon secures the splat and stay rail. The molded stay rail is joined to the posts with rectangular tenons; faint scribe lines mark the tops and bottoms of the mortise holes. The seat rails and stretchers are round tenoned into the legs, the socket points marked by lightly scribed lines. Raised, turned bosses circumscribed by incised lines ornament the front leg tops. The back posts taper at the bottom to form feet.

**Condition:** Both back-post baluster collars are chipped on the rear surface. The spool at the center of the front stretcher is chipped on the face. A shredded gouge occurs on the outside surface of the right rear post above the foot.

**Dimensions:**

| | | |
|---|---|---|
| H. | 40⁵/₈ in. | 103.2 cm |
| H. (seat) | 17⁵/₈ in. | 44.8 cm |
| W. (crest) | 14³/₄ in. | 37.5 cm |
| W. (seat front) | 17¹/₂ in. | 44.4 cm |
| W. (seat back) | 13³/₄ in. | 34.9 cm |
| W. (feet) | 18³/₁₆ in. | 46.2 cm |
| D. (seat) | 13¹/₈ in. | 33.4 cm |
| D. (feet) | 14 in. | 35.6 cm |

**Materials:** *Microanalysis:* Primary: soft maple group. Secondary: ash (side stretcher). *Finish:* transparent brown color in resin over an earlier dark red.

**Publications:** Benno M. Forman, "The Crown and York Chairs of Coastal Connecticut and the Work of the Durands of Milford," *Antiques* 105, no. 5 (May 1974): 1153, fig. 8.

**Accession history:** Museum purchase from Lillian B. Cogan, Farmington, Conn., 1972. 72.429

---

1. Benno M. Forman, "The Crown and York Chairs of Coastal Connecticut and the Work of the Durands of Milford," *Antiques* 105, no. 5 (May 1974): 1153, fig. 8; Trent, *Hearts and Crowns*, nos. 38–40, 65, 66, 68. Nancy Goyne Evans, *American Windsor Chairs* (New York: Hudson Hills Press in association with the Henry Francis du Pont Winterthur Museum, 1996), fig. 6-176.

2. Samuel Durand II daybook, 1806–38, Milford Historical Society, Milford, Conn. (microfilm, Downs collection).

## 44 ◆ Side chair
### Guilford-Branford, Connecticut
### 1790–1810

Chairs framed with this simple but graceful heart-pierced crown have long been associated by family ownership and tradition with the coastal Connecticut towns of Guilford and Branford near New Haven. The earliest local chairs with this crest, which date to about the mid eighteenth century, have turned, split banisters across the back. In a second design from the area, which also preceded this chair, a splat replaced the banisters, and the finials were refined to the urn-shape profile shown here.[1]

Differences between the second and the illustrated designs are based in the turnings. Long, angular back-post balusters accompanied by ball turnings centered between hollows were exchanged for this pattern, which places an elongated, well-rounded baluster above a short one. Wafer-thin disks replaced thick rings in the front legs, and turnings became lighter overall. Two features remained constant: the front stretcher profiles and the blocked upper back posts. The splat is a modified version of that in No. 41. The back feet taper sharply, a form common in late eighteenth-century turned chairs. The round-top front feet are a refinement of a shape used occasionally in earlier Connecticut chairs. The longer, slimmer profile approximates that of the round spade terminal in federal-style formal seating and tables.[2]

This back pattern probably was identified as a york chair in period documents; "fiddleback" was an alternative term. Samuel Durand II of neighboring Milford priced york and fiddleback chairs at 6s. apiece, which was also the average cost of a Windsor, the most popular painted chair in the New England furniture market in the 1790s.[3]

*NGE*

**Construction:** The crest and stay rail are joined to the back posts with rectangular tenons. Faint scribe lines on the posts mark the tops and bottoms of the mortise holes. The crest heart is roughly pierced and rounded outward, front and back. Narrow tenons secure the splat to the crest and stay rail. The seat rails and stretchers are round tenoned into the legs, the socket points marked by lightly scribed lines. The rounded front leg tops are circumscribed by incised lines. The back posts taper at the bottom to form feet.

**Condition:** The right back-post baluster collar is chipped on the face. The rear seat rail is nailed at the left rear leg. The front stretchers are somewhat worn.

**Dimensions:**

| | | |
|---|---:|---|
| H. | 43 7/8 in. | 111.5 cm |
| H. (seat) | 17 1/2 in. | 44.4 cm |
| W. (crest) | 14 in. | 35.6 cm |
| W. (seat front) | 17 3/4 in. | 45.1 cm |
| W. (seat back) | 14 in. | 35.6 cm |
| W. (feet) | 18 11/16 in. | 47.5 cm |
| D. (seat) | 13 5/8 in. | 34.6 cm |
| D. (feet) | 14 in. | 35.6 cm |

**Materials:** *Microanalysis:* Primary: soft maple group (legs). Secondary: ash (side stretchers). *Finish:* streaked transparent medium brown resin; colorless resin on seat.

**Accession history:** Gift of Lillian B. Cogan, Farmington, Conn., 1974.
74.134

1. Trent, *Hearts and Crowns*, nos. 30, 60–62; James R. Lindsay, *Pictorial Guilford: A New England Town in Photographs* (Guilford, Conn.: Guilford Historical Society, 1977), as reviewed in *Antiques and the Arts Weekly*, March 25, 1977. Kane, *Three Hundred Years*, no. 87.

2. Trent, *Hearts and Crowns*, nos. 60–62; for front feet, see nos. 26, 44, 56, 62, 69, 75.

3. Samuel Durand II daybook, 1806–38, Milford Historical Society, Milford, Conn. (microfilm, Downs collection).

## 45 ◆ Side chair
### Boston, Massachusetts
### 1755–85

Although the interlaced-strap pattern was popular in New England, it was less common than the owl's-eye design (see Nos. 30, 31); the variants are also less numerous. Two basic splat types identified by the pedestal patterns appear: a fret pierced by triple, vertical, round-top slots punctuated by beads across the center, as illustrated, and a Y strap within flanking borders, sometimes pierced with a small diamond at the base (see No. 46). The principal silhouette of the crest is the central lunette flanked by ogees generally terminated by carved tips. A few lunettes are carved as ribbed shells; most are plainer, with low-relief carving delineating the strap crossing only. Frequently, two small diamonds pierce the crest at the splat top. The diamonds are often positioned at the bases of small, modeled crescent tips of plain surface as illustrated; a few surfaces are gouged. A central lunette forming an open arch is a rare crest variant. Chairs with molded post faces are uncommon, and in this respect the style relates closely to owl's-eye seating. Both designs were in the market slightly earlier than other strap-back patterns in which molded posts are more common.[1]

A compass bottom, as seen in this chair, is generally encountered less frequently than the square seat; the ratio is, perhaps, one to two. Loose seats appear to outnumber frames upholstered over the rail by three to one, although the interlaced splat was probably introduced before the over-upholstered seat was common. The usual support is the cabriole leg, the terminals about equally divided between pad and claw feet. A few cabinet shops turned out straight-leg examples at the end of the style period. Interlaced-strap pattern chairs made in New England originated principally in Massachusetts.

Far fewer examples can be assigned to Rhode Island. Connecticut chairs, except for a pattern variation ascribed to members of the Chapin family, are uncommon. Some chairs associated with Connecticut through family history were made elsewhere, as is the case with this chair. The presumed original owner, a shipping merchant in the Fairfield area, could have acquired his set of chairs (this one is no. 5) directly at the source.[2]

One group of Massachusetts interlaced-strap chairs, represented by this example, has slim cabriole legs with high bulging knees, rear legs chamfered between the feet and seat, and conical-tipped cross stretchers. Comparable Rhode Island chairs, which are few in number, have cabriole legs squared off on the inside faces, unchamfered rear legs, and round-tipped cross stretchers. A second group of Massachusetts interlaced-strap chairs is stretcherless, and the rear legs end in flaring feet.[3]

The interlaced-strap pattern is also common in Philadelphia and New York joined chairs, but the silhouettes are sufficiently different and can be easily distinguished from New England seating. A few chairs of the pattern were also made in Portsmouth, New Hampshire; Virginia; and Charleston, South Carolina. The American interlaced-strap pattern was copied or adapted directly from British seating, although close prototypes are absent from design books. British models also served to foster design interest among Spanish and Portuguese chairmakers on the Continent.[4]

*NGE*

---

**Inscriptions or marks:** *Chiseled on front seat-rail rabbet:* "V".

**Construction:** The crest is supported on rectangular tenons at the flat-faced canted posts and three small tenons at the splat. The crest face, which is cheeked near the terminals, is carved in low relief at the central straps and crescents; the outer tips are carved in long ogee channels divided by a central declivity. The back is flat at the tips and central lunette, rounded along the ogee arches and lunette top, and chamfered at the center bottom piercings. The splat is lightly modeled on the face where the long straps cross and intersect with adjacent members; the upper volutes are carved. The splat edges and piercings are slightly canted, front to back, and lightly chamfered at the back surfaces; the base is tenoned into the plinth. The plinth is hollow on the front and side faces, beaded at the top, and nailed to the back rail. The posts are rounded at the upper back and chamfered at the lower back corners. The compass-seat frame has a rounded, sloping top lip; a broad interior rabbet, forming a rectangular opening, supports the loose-seat frame. The bottom surface is tooled at the flat front and side arches. The rails are joined to the posts and front leg extensions with vertical rectangular tenons (pinned, side front and side back only). The back legs are chamfered on all corners between the rails and the rear stretcher; the feet are canted on the forward faces and chamfered at the front and outer back corners. A narrow ledge marks the backs of the front pad feet, which are supported on high disks. The ankle backs are flat and scribed with mortising guides. The knee brackets are nailed on. The side stretchers are joined to the legs with vertical rectangular tenons (pinned at back). The creased-tip medial and rear stretchers are round tenoned into the adjacent members.

**Condition:** The splat top is cracked through at the center front. Vertical cracks occur in the left front leg extension at the rails. The right front knee bracket has been replaced. The medial and right side stretchers are gouged on the outer surfaces; the pad-foot disks are worn at the front. The loose-seat frame is modern.

**Dimensions:**

| | | |
|---|---|---|
| H. | 38¼ in. | 97.2 cm |
| H. (seat) | 16¾ in. | 42.5 cm |
| W. (crest) | 20⅛ in. | 51.1 cm |
| W. (seat front) | 20⅞ in. | 53.0 cm |
| W. (seat back) | 15⅜ in. | 39.1 cm |
| W. (feet) | 20½ in. | 52.1 cm |
| D. (seat) | 17⅝ in. | 44.7 cm |
| D. (feet) | 20¾ in. | 52.7 cm |

**Materials:** *Microanalysis:* Primary: American black walnut. *Finish:* medium light yellowish brown color in resin. *Upholstery:* yellow silk bourette; Europe, 1725–1800.

**Provenance:** Descended in the Bradley family of Greenfield (now known as Greenfield Hill), near Fairfield, Conn. Samuel Bradley was a prominent merchant engaged in the coastal shipping trade.

**Accession history:** Museum purchase from Mrs. Louis Moorehouse, Charleston, S.C., 1956. 56.32

---

1. For chairs with a Y-shape splat, see John S. Walton advertisement, *Antiques* 86, no. 1 (July 1964): 4. Molded posts appear on a few Massachusetts chairs with a variant splat that introduces an open diamond at the central strap crossing, in the New York style; Jobe and Kaye, *New England Furniture*, no. 116.

2. For a straight-leg chair, see Ralph E. Carpenter, Jr., *The Arts and Crafts of Newport, Rhode Island, 1640–1820* (Newport: Preservation Society of Newport County, 1954), no. 8. Family histories link several Massachusetts chairs with Hingham, Haverhill, Newburyport, and Shrewsbury; see (respectively) Randall, *American Furniture*, no. 149; David Stockwell advertisement, *Antiques* 90, no. 2 (August 1966): 131; Peter Benes, *Old-Town and the Waterside* (Newburyport, Mass.: Historical Society of Old Newbury, 1986), cat. 173; American Art Association Anderson Galleries, "American Furniture from the Collection of Benjamin Flayderman" (April 17–18, 1931), lot 337. A modified interlaced-strap pattern appears in chairs made in Norwich, Conn., possibly by Felix Huntington: 1 chair was recovered in 1922 from the Jabez Huntington house in Norwich; Kirk, *American Chairs*, fig. 201. Trent with Nelson, "A Catalogue of New London County Joined Chairs," nos. 54, 55.

3. For a Rhode Island chair with the named features, see Moses, *Master Craftsmen*, fig. 2.3. For a stretcherless Massachusetts chair, see *American Antiques from Israel Sack Collection*, 10 vols. (Washington, D.C.: Highland House, ca. 1969–), 1:41.

4. For Philadelphia and New York chairs, see Kirk, *American Chairs*, figs. 65, 67–73, 139–44; for a Portsmouth chair, see Jobe, *Portsmouth Furniture*, fig. 89c; for Virginia chairs, see Wallace B. Gusler, *Furniture of Williamsburg and Eastern Virginia, 1710–1790* (Richmond: Virginia Museum, 1979), figs. 23, 24; for a Charleston chair, see John Bivins and Forsyth Alexander, *The Regional Arts of the Early South: A Sampling from the Collections of the Museum of Early Southern Decorative Arts* (Winston-Salem, N.C.: By the museum, 1991), p. 93, cat. 31; for British chairs, see Kirk, *American Furniture*, figs. 854–57, 864, 865, 867; Hinckley, *Directory*, ill. 273; for a Spanish example, see Horace Wesley Ott, "Spanish Furniture of the Eighteenth Century," *Antiquarian* 13, no. 4 (November 1929): 45; for a Portuguese example, see Robert C. Smith, "Portuguese Chippendale Chairs," *Antiques* 82, no. 1 (July 1962): 57.

## 46 ◆ Side chair (one of a pair)
Newport, Rhode Island
ca. 1791–92

This chair is part of a sizable group of Rhode Island seating furniture first produced during the 1760s and fashioned with broad backs that are closer to contemporary New York design than to New England work. The genesis of the pattern is a Massachusetts chair of solid splat with sweep back posts and a prominent, fluted crest shell (see No. 24). There follows a diamond-pierced Y-strap splat (see No. 35 right) of Massachusetts or Newport origin in a similar back with a large, T-shape bridge forming the splat top. The next variant, illustrated here, introduces an interlaced top above the Y-strap splat. The back posts can be straight or sweeped in the frontal plane. Sweep posts are rare and may be confined to this pair

(which was part of an original set numbering at least six) and a richly embellished pair with flute-carved posts and a crest shell. All seats are compass-shape with flat arches. The rectangular rear legs are slightly flared, and the stretchers, both tipped and blocked, are delicate in size. Only in the carved chairs is the pattern varied by the introduction of curved stretchers (see No. 14). The sweep-post chairs have claw feet; the straight-post chairs are supported on pads raised on disks. The knees are uncarved. Slight variations appear in the crest; the triangular piercings of the straight-back chairs are slightly larger than in this design or are solid with modeled triangles.[1]

Several straight-post interlaced-splat chairs with pad feet are linked to Providence. The loose-seat frames of two chairs are inscribed in ink with abbreviations for that city. Another chair is said to have been owned by a General

James of Providence, probably Maj. Gen. Charles Tillinghast James (b. 1805) of the Rhode Island militia. This sweep-post chair and its mate, however, were described in 1951 by the last private owner as having descended in the Bangs family of Newport. The chairs were accompanied by a penciled note written by Mary Ellery Jennison Bangs, the last owner's grandmother: "This chair is one of a set given to my mother MGE before she was married in 1815—made for my grandmother KE - before she was married in 1792 in Newport—from maho[g]any wood grown on the plantation of her brother James Almy—in Nassau NP West Indies—now mine/ MEB." Bangs's mother, Mary Gould Ellery (MGE), married Samuel Jennison of Worcester, who later became first librarian of the American Antiquarian Society. The grandmother, Katharine Almy Ellery (KE), was the wife of Edmund T., both of Newport. The Ellerys were the daughter-in-law and son of William Ellery, delegate to the First Continental Congress and a signer of the Declaration of Independence.[2]

Information on James Gould Almy (b. 1772) is limited, but the tradition of his providing wood for his sister's set of chairs is significant. Microanalysis has identified the primary wood of this chair as sabicu (*Lysiloma* sp.), a dense tropical hardwood known in the eighteenth century as "horseflesh" and not unlike mahogany in appearance. The ornamental quality of the mottled figure in the wood and the rich reddish color could indeed have prompted Almy to present his sister with a sabicu log to make her dowry furniture. In summary it seems reasonable to suggest that the sets represented by this chair and the more richly ornamented examples, all with sweep backs and claw feet, were made in Newport, while the straight-post chairs were products of neighboring Providence.[3]

Providence and Newport shared close commercial ties, enhanced by the ease of water travel along Narragansett Bay. As Newport fell into decline following the Revolution, however, Providence began a long period of expansion and development. As early as 1756, six of the community's leading cabinetmakers joined in an agreement to regulate the "Price of Joinery Work." Such aggressive action likely laid the groundwork for the community's flourishing postrevolutionary furniture industry and its emerging independence from Newport as a style center.[4]

The Rhode Island interlaced chair back is distinctly different from the cross-loop patterns common in other coastal American regions, from eastern Massachusetts to the South. Parallels occur in British seating furniture, and design-book sources are promising. De La Cour, a French engraver working in England, produced a few chair designs, dating to 1743, that include patterns for interlaced strapwork backs that may have influenced the later published works of Robert Manwaring and Thomas Chippendale. In fact, a chair-back design in the 1762 edition of Chippendale's *Director* was possibly integral to the development of this chair pattern: its rounded back is laced with scrolls that turn in and out.[5]

The loose seats are original to this chair and its mate, and the needlework is likely original to the frames, although the covers have been removed on several occasions for repairs and cleaning and the edges have been trimmed and the canvas reattached in new holes. The set of covers was probably worked by Katharine Almy as a young girl in the 1780s, before the chairs were constructed: "Amy" is written in black ink in an eighteenth-century hand on the loose-seat frames of both chairs. This phonetic spelling probably followed the local pronunciation of the family name. Young women in affluent households were encouraged to be industrious and proficient with the needle, however by the time these covers were stitched, the practice of placing needlework covers on furniture had begun to wane.[6]

NGE

---

**Inscriptions or marks:** *Chiseled on front seat-rail rabbet (centered) and on front loose-seat rail:* "IIII". *On front rail of loose seat:* "Amy" *in black ink.*

**Construction:** The crest is supported on rectangular tenons at the flat-faced canted posts and splat. The flat crest face is slightly cheeked at the posts; the back surface is rounded, including the piercings and center base. The flat-faced splat is slightly modeled at the upper central straps; the back surface is flat with a narrow chamfer around the outside. The edges and piercings are slightly canted, front to back; the base is tenoned into the plinth. The plinth is hollow on the front and side faces; there is no top bead or evidence of nails (probably glued). The posts are rounded on the backs through the sweeps and flat below those points; the sweep cheeks are not pieced. The compass-seat frame has a thick, rounded and sloping top lip; a broad interior rabbet, forming a rectangular opening, supports the loose-seat frame. The front and side rails are sawed in flat arches, which bear diagonal rasp marks. The rails are joined to the posts and front leg extensions with rectangular tenons (pinned, twice at side backs). Small, single or double glueblocks support the interior corners. The rectangular rear legs are angled twice on the forward faces. The small, front claw feet have long, slim, three-knuckle toes that extend into the ankles as sinews. The side stretchers are joined to the rear legs with vertical rectangular tenons (pinned) and to the front legs with round tenons. The medial and rear stretchers are round tenoned into the adjacent members (rear stretchers pinned).

**Condition:** All knee brackets have been replaced, and new 1/8" facing pieces have been added to the bottoms of the adjacent rails. Cracks in the front leg extensions extend down into the knees. The side stretcher joints with the front legs are now nailed from the outside. The original loose-seat frame is tenoned and pinned.

**Dimensions:**

| | | |
|---|---|---|
| H. | 37 3/4 in. | 95.9 cm |
| H. (seat) | 17 3/8 in. | 44.1 cm |
| W. (crest) | 15 15/16 in. | 40.5 cm |
| W. (seat front) | 20 1/8 in. | 51.1 cm |
| W. (seat back) | 15 1/4 in. | 38.7 cm |
| W. (feet) | 21 1/8 in. | 53.6 cm |
| D. (seat) | 16 1/2 in. | 41.9 cm |
| D. (feet) | 20 3/8 in. | 51.7 cm |

**Materials:** *Microanalysis:* Primary: sabicu. Secondary: soft maple group (loose-seat frame). *Finish:* medium yellowish brown color in resin. *Upholstery:* tent-stitched canvaswork in crewel yarns on fine linen with silk accents; America, 1760–85.

**Publications:** Susan Burrows Swan, *Plain and Fancy: American Women and Their Needlework, 1700–1850* (New York: Holt, Rinehart, and Winston, 1977), p. 93, pl. 13 (textile). Jay E. Cantor, *Winterthur* (New York: Harry N. Abrams, 1985), p. 15 (textile). Nancy Goyne Evans, "A Pair of Distinctive Chairs from Newport, Rhode Island," *Antiques* 145, no. 1 (January 1994): 186–93.

**Provenance:** Descended in the Bangs family of Newport, R.I., to Ruth Sturgis, the last private owner.

**Accession history:** Museum purchase from Feralyn G. Watson Antiques, Sturbridge, Mass., 1959, with funds given by H. F. du Pont. 59.83.1

---

1. For carved sweep-post chairs, see Ralph E. Carpenter, Jr., "Discoveries in Newport Furniture and Silver," *Antiques* 68, no. 1 (July 1955): 44–45; for straight-post chairs, see Kane, *Three Hundred Years*, no. 122; Ralph E. Carpenter, Jr., *The Arts and Crafts of Newport, Rhode Island, 1640–1820* (Newport: Preservation Society of Newport County, 1954), no. 14.

2. For the Providence inscribed chairs, see Kane, *Three Hundred Years*, no. 122; Kirk, *American Chairs*, fig. 173. For the James chair, see Carpenter, *Arts and Crafts of Newport*, no. 14; see also *Who Was Who in America* (Chicago: A. N. Marquis Co., 1963), p. 275. The penciled note is in folder 59.83.1, .2, Registration Office, Winterthur. *New England Historical and Genealogical Register* (Boston: Samuel G. Drake, 1854), 8:318, 320; 14:288.

3. At age 20 James Almy married Martha Matilda Bowles of Christ Church Parish, New Providence; Gladys E. Bolhouse, former curator of manuscripts, Newport Historical Society, Newport, R.I., to author, November 15, 1991, folder 59.83.1, Registration Office, Winterthur. For a discussion of sabicu, see Eleanor H. Gustafson, "Collectors' Notes," *Antiques* 135, no. 5 (May 1989): 1102, 1106.

4. Eleanore Bradford Monahon, "Providence Cabinetmakers," *Rhode Island History* 23, no. 1 (January 1964): 1–4.

5. For De La Cour, Manwaring, and Chippendale designs, see Peter Ward-Jackson, *English Furniture Designs of the Eighteenth Century* (London: Victoria and Albert Museum, Her Majesty's Stationery Office, 1958), nos. 19, 101 lower right, 176. Thomas Chippendale, *The Gentleman and Cabinet-Maker's Director* (1762; reprint 3d ed., New York: Dover Publications, 1966), pl. 16 lower left.

6. This chair and its mate are discussed in more detail in Nancy Goyne Evans, "A Pair of Distinctive Chairs from Newport, Rhode Island," *Antiques* 145, no. 1 (January 1994): 186–93.

## 47 ◆ **Side chair** (one of a pair)
Newport, Rhode Island
1770–90

Plate 9 from Robert Manwaring's *Cabinet and Chair-Maker's Real Friend and Companion* published in London in 1765 illustrates two chair-back designs that were successfully adapted for production by American chairmakers. One pattern appears to have been limited to use in eastern Massachusetts; the other, illustrated here, was interpreted by both British and American craftsmen (fig. 1). Philadelphia, New York, and English chairmakers favored the cabriole leg for their double-loop–pattern chairs. Rhode Island craftsmen chose the Marlborough support. Unlike artisans in other regions, many Rhode Island chairmakers also appear to have been directly inspired by Manwaring's engraving in designing a flaring fan in the center of the crest (a fan-shape void in the Manwaring pattern) rather than reproducing a more common ornament such as a shell or leaf. Virtually all American and most British interpretations of this double-loop pattern are constructed with a double-ogee crest rail terminating in projecting tips, usually carved. A few British chairmakers placed the double-loop splat in a broad, round-shouldered Queen Anne back. Rhode Island production appears to be about equally divided between loose-seat and over-the-rail upholstery.[1]

Incorporated in the design of this chair are all the classic features of the Rhode Island pattern. The cushioned fan in the crest is finely crosshatched, and each small block is centered with a dot (fig. 2). Below the fan tip, a small diamond has a punchwork border of triangles (although sometimes this element is pierced instead). Both pairs of volutes are carved. The H-form pedestal beneath the central volutes has a recessed inner band adjacent to the piercing, which is bordered by a double row of punchwork triangles that reflect light like the facets in a bright-cut silver spoon. The emphasis on fine-line patterning and subtle accents continues in the stop fluting of the front legs.

In an even more sophisticated variation of this Rhode Island pattern, a small pierced oval framed by C scrolls with carved leafage above and below is centered between the upper volutes. Tapered bands of gadrooning extend from the crest tips into the upper splat straps and volutes, which are shorter and thicker than those illustrated here. The baluster portion of the splat is lighter and without cusps, or spurs, and a Y-shape strap is centered in the pedestal. One set of six side chairs has an unsubstantiated history of ownership by Joseph Wanton (d. 1790) of Newport, who became governor of Rhode Island in 1769 with the support of the Brown family of Providence. Four similar chairs, with and without arms, descended in the King family of Newport. Several chairs of the crosshatched type in the John Brown house loan exhibition of 1965 were claimed to have had Providence family associations, but details were not provided.[2]

This chair and its mate have a firm history only from the early twentieth century, but they could have been in the donor's family earlier. If such were the case, the chairs were probably associated with the Minturn and West families of Bristol, Rhode Island, a peninsular community midway between Providence and Newport.

In a plainer version of the double-loop–pattern chair, a simple, three- or four-lobe shell is substituted for the crosshatched ornament of the crest, and all other carving or modeling is eliminated from the back decoration, except for the carving in the crest tips. The stop fluting of the Marlborough legs is replaced by molded surfaces. Four chairs of this pattern are owned by a direct descendant of John Brown of Providence, who acquired

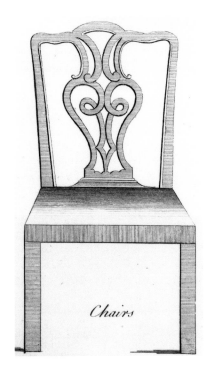

**Fig. 1.** From Robert Manwaring, *The Cabinet and Chair-Maker's Real Friend and Companion* (London: Henry Webley, 1765), pl. 9 right.

**Fig. 2.** Detail, crest center and splat.

much of his furniture in Newport. Accounts dated 1760 record the purchases of two furniture lots, both containing chairs, one from the shop of John Goddard. If the inherited chairs were part of either purchase, then the plain pattern was in the market first, and its design was based on an actual English chair rather than the design-book engraving of 1765.[3]

Some of the ornament in the double-loop chairs, such as the crosshatching, stop fluting, lobe-carved shells, and gadrooning, can be closely correlated with that on case work of known Newport origin, including several pieces of furniture labeled by John Townsend (1732–1809) and a gadroon-carved bureau table inscribed in chalk by Daniel Goddard (b. 1747). Without doubt, the balance tips in favor of Newport, rather than Providence, as the origin of this group of chairs.[4]

NGE

**Inscriptions or marks:** *Chiseled on front seat-rail rabbet and front loose-seat rail:* "V".

**Construction:** The crest is supported on rectangular tenons at the flat-faced canted posts and on three tenons at the splat. The rounded crest face is carved at the tips; the central ornament is cushioned and incised with lines and dots. The rear surface is flat at the center with a chamfer, top and bottom; the ogee ends are rounded along the top and bottom

edges. The splat face is flat, except for four small carved volutes, the crest-ornament extension, the large central loops, and the gougework border in the pedestal. The splat edges and piercings are slightly canted, front to back; the base is tenoned into the plinth. The plinth is hollow on the front and side faces, finished with a top bead, and nailed to the back rail. The post backs are rounded from crest to seat. The seat frame has a rounded-canted lip; an interior rabbet supports the loose-seat frame. The rails are joined to the front posts and leg extensions with vertical rectangular tenons (pinned, double at the side backs); scribe marks are visible at some joints. The rear feet are canted on the forward faces and chamfered at the front corners with the inside chamfers continuing to the back rail. The squared front legs are stop fluted on the outside faces and chamfered on the inside back corners. The side and rear stretchers are joined to the legs in vertical rectangular tenons (pinned, at side stretchers); the medial stretcher is dovetailed into the side stretchers from the bottom.

**Condition:** The crest tips are chipped on the back surface. The rear seat rail is patched at the upper right corner. The large, interior triangular seat blocks are replacements or additions. The medial stretcher is replaced but follows the original pattern, as indicated in the mate chair; nails secure the dovetails. New pins appear in the side and front rails and in the side stretchers. The loose-seat frame is original.

**Dimensions:**

| | | |
|---|---|---|
| H. | 37³⁄₈ in. | 95.0 cm |
| H. (seat) | 16³⁄₄ in. | 42.5 cm |
| W. (crest) | 21 in. | 53.3 cm |
| W. (seat front) | 20 in. | 50.8 cm |
| W. (seat back) | 15³⁄₈ in. | 39.1 cm |
| W. (feet) | 19¹⁄₂ in. | 49.5 cm |
| D. (seat) | 16¹⁄₈ in. | 41.0 cm |
| D. (feet) | 19¹⁄₈ in. | 48.6 cm |

**Materials:** *Microanalysis:* Primary: mahogany. Secondary: soft maple group (loose-seat frame). *Finish:* medium yellowish brown color in resin; refinished. *Upholstery:* gold silk damask; Europe, 1700–1750.

**Publications:** Kirk, *American Chairs,* fig. 182. Kirk, *American Furniture,* fig. 939.

**Provenance:** According to 1 of the donors, Mrs. William K. Wallbridge, the chairs were in her family home in Litchfield, Conn., when her mother died in 1919. Mrs. Wallbridge's mother was Gertrude Minturn (b. 1850; m. Col. George Bliss Sanford, 1874), daughter of Jonas and Abigail (West) Minturn of Bristol, R.I. (See also **Provenance** of No. 180.)

**Accession history:** Gift of Mr. and Mrs. William K. Wallbridge, Short Hills, N.J., 1958. 58.18.2

1. For New York, Philadelphia, and English examples, see Kirk, *American Chairs,* figs. 77, 78, 146–48; for British examples of this splat pattern within rounded Queen Anne backs, see Cescinsky, *English Furniture,* 2: figs. 23–25.

2. For examples of gadroon-carved chairs, see Ralph E. Carpenter, Jr., *The Arts and Crafts of Newport, Rhode Island, 1640–1820* (Newport: Preservation Society of Newport County, 1954), no. 4; 66.2664, DAPC, Visual Resources Collection, Winterthur Library; Israel Sack advertisement, *Antiques* 136, no. 6 (December 1989): inside front cover; Harold Sack and Deanne Levison, "Queen Anne and Chippendale Armchairs in America," *Antiques* 137, no. 5 (May 1990): 1173, pl. 8. On Wanton, see John S. Walton advertisement, *Antiques* 63, no. 2 (February 1953): 88; for the King family history, see Joseph Downs, "The Furniture of Goddard and Townsend," *Antiques* 52, no. 6 (December 1947): 430, fig. 9. *John Brown House Loan Exhibition,* cat. 12.

3. For shell-crested chairs, see Greenlaw, *New England Furniture,* no. 57; Wendy A. Cooper, "The Purchase of Furniture and Furnishings by John Brown, Providence Merchant, Part 1," *Antiques* 103, no. 2 (February 1973): 330, fig. 6, see also p. 333 for Brown's accounts of Newport furniture.

4. Moses, *Master Craftsmen,* figs. 1.39, 1.49, 2.3, 2.6a, 2.7 (labeled), 3.18 (labeled), 3.79b, 3.80, 3.81, 4.5–5a, 5.8, 5.24, 6.13 (inscribed), 7.18–18a; pl. 21.

## 48 ◆ Side chair

East Windsor or vicinity or possibly
Hartford, Connecticut
1770–85
Eliphalet Chapin (1741–1807) or Aaron
Chapin, or another area craftsman

Of the three interlaced-splat chair patterns
ascribed to the Chapin craftsmen of East
Windsor, Connecticut, two are represented
in the Winterthur collection—the design
illustrated in this chair and the one in No. 49.
Although this pattern, identified by crossed
straps that loop outward, was reasonably
common in Massachusetts, chairs of this
design were produced in far fewer numbers
in Rhode Island and Connecticut, where the
largest group is associated with the Chapin
cousins, Eliphalet and Aaron. Philadelphia
and New York craftsmen produced their own
versions of the interlaced splat. The long,
central ellipse of the Philadelphia chair
terminates abruptly in the arms of the Y,

which rise from the pedestal to form large
C scrolls. The ellipse straps of the Connecticut
chair, in contrast, are carried outward in
bulging loops that end in volutes, giving the
appearance of owl's eyes turned inside out
(see Nos. 30, 31). Although the splats differ
somewhat, certain construction points in the
Philadelphia and central Connecticut chairs
are the same. The undercarriages do not
have a bracing system, and the rear legs are
rounded stumps. The flat arches of the seat
rails are sawed with an extra shallow step
above the coves, and the side-rail tenons
pass completely through the back posts, where
they are exposed on the rear surface. Exposed
tenons are otherwise rare in New England
chairs. The two-piece vertical-grain corner
blocks within the seat frame are also typical
of Philadelphia construction.[1]

A review of Eliphalet Chapin's life
(1741–1807) provides some insights into the
introduction of Philadelphia construction
techniques to central Connecticut. The young

woodworker attained his majority in 1762
after serving an apprenticeship in the
cabinetmaking trade, possibly with his second
cousin Joseph Pease, Jr. (b. 1728), of Suffield.
Sometime after his training, possibly as early
as 1762, Chapin appears to have moved further
south in the Connecticut River valley to the
larger town of East Windsor to work as a
journeyman in one of several prosperous
shops located there. An ill-fated association
with a local woman who bore his child in
March 1767 caused Chapin to quit the region
for Philadelphia in 1766 or 1767, where
he remained for two to three years. Long
before documents corroborating Chapin's
Pennsylvania residency were published, the
Philadelphia character of his work was well
recognized. Chapin appears to have returned
to East Windsor by October 1769, when the
first of several business transactions dating to
that year and the next was recorded in the
accounts of Ebenezer Grant, an East Windsor
merchant. In 1771 Chapin purchased a house
lot and erected a dwelling in the First Parish of
East Windsor (the site location is now South
Windsor), where he maintained a successful
business until the end of the century. He
married in 1773, and the following year his
second cousin Aaron Chapin, who had just
completed his training, came to work as a
journeyman. Aaron remained until 1783 when
he moved to Hartford. Thus, both men, if not
additional family members and other local
woodworkers, were responsible for producing
the sizable body of cherrywood seating
furniture still extant, of which this chair and
No. 49 are representative. As early as 1937
it was recognized that "the curvature of the
front legs and the shape of the feet" in Chapin-
ascribed chairs "are so specific as almost to
qualify as the maker's signature." Equally
telling are the features of the chair backs.[2]

Design analysis of seventeen Chapin-type
chairs (or pairs of chairs) in this interlaced
splat pattern revealed basic features and subtle

**Fig. 1.** Detail, crest shell.

**Fig. 2.** Detail, right front foot.

variations. The crests of all but three chairs are centered with shells having eight to ten radiating lobes, as illustrated (fig. 1). Eight lobes, the most common number, occur on four of the five armchairs in the group. The fifth armchair, like two of the side chairs, has a Rhode Island–type five-lobe shell with intervening, shouldered flutes, generally in the style of No. 49. The shell tip is part of the splat top in about two-thirds of the examples. The splat directly below the shell has a curious, unexplained fissure. Behind the fissure the crest is extended onto the rear splat surface. All crests have projecting tips carved with high-shouldered, double flutes separated by a declivity.[3]

Only about one-third of the chairs in the group have carved splat volutes; the carved work is executed in low-relief pinwheels or high-relief coils. All the five-lobe fluted-shell chairs exhibit this detail. Although the straps forming the ellipse and loops are crossed from left to right in this chair, the common figure is a right-to-left lap executed in low relief. Less than half of the group is modeled in low relief at the top of the ellipse and at the pedestal arms; the remaining chairs are plain. The large bead at the plinth top is repeated in the lip of the seat frame. The base of the frame is sawed in flat, stepped arches in the Philadelphia manner (see also No. 33). Another feature exhibiting strong Philadelphia influence is the squared claw with its thick, jointed toes and short, stubby, triangular nails (fig. 2). In summary, the variable character of Chapin-type chair backs suggests that use of the design extended beyond the shop operated by Eliphalet with the assistance of Aaron to the production of other East Windsor and

area craftsmen, some of them kinsmen, who had trained or worked with the former Philadelphia journeyman or who simply copied a salable product.

Family histories connected with five groups of interlaced-splat chairs (including this example) describe a range of ownership extending along the Connecticut River valley from Deerfield in central Massachusetts to Middletown in southern Connecticut. A pair of chairs at the Yale University Art Gallery, which represents an original set of twelve, was made in 1781 for Alexander King of East Windsor, brother-in-law to Aaron Chapin. King's chairs, like this one, are made of cherry; mahogany is employed only rarely. William and Russel Stoughton, blacksmiths of East Windsor who had business dealings with the Chapins, explained the reason in their accounts: "to drawing mahogany logs from the river to the mil." The trouble of procuring mahogany, the substantial expense of the material, and the added cost of hauling the logs overland from the river likely were sufficient reasons to discourage both craftsman and customer.[4]

*NGE*

---

**Inscriptions or marks:** *Incised on inside rear seat rail:* "III". *On paper label, thumbtacked to inside rear seat rail:* "Obtained by me in Nov. 1937 (through M. R. Tynam, of/ Middletown, Conn.) from home of Alfred C. Ward, ex-/ Postmaster of Middletown, who stated that: —/ His grandmother, a Southmead (b. before 1820), had it from / her mother—chair never out of the family's possession in Middletown/ from time of Mr. Ward's great grandmother until Nov. 1937./ —Except for minor variations, chair is replica of one shown in/ Nutting II, 2192. Also

another shown in Antiques =/ 1 of set of 12 of which 2 were purchased by Dr. Irving Lyon, and/ placed in Garvan Collection at Yale - These chairs all/ ascribed to ELIPHALET CHAPIN (1760–1780s) =/ one of the great cabinetmakers of Connecticut/ Meade Minnigerode [sp.?] -/ November 25, 1937."

**Construction:** The crest is supported on round tenons at the flat-faced canted posts and a rectangular tenon at the splat. The crest face is contoured at the ogee ends, which terminate in projecting, carved tips scrolled backwards. The reeded shell is carved in high and low relief, the lower tip continuing onto the splat. The crest back is flattened at the shell and the ogees, which are rounded, top and bottom. The center back is scalloped at the top; the rounded bottom forms a ³/₄" extension onto the splat. The splat is lightly modeled on the face where the long straps cross and intersect with adjacent members. The edges and piercings are slightly canted, front to back; the base is tenoned into the plinth. The plinth is hollow on the front and side faces, finished with a large, thumb-molded bead at the top, and nailed to the back rail. The post backs are rounded from crest to seat. The seat frame has a large quarter-round lip; a narrow interior rabbet supports the loose-seat frame. The bottom arches are stepped. The rails are joined to the posts and front leg extensions with vertical rectangular tenons, which pierce through the back posts. The back rail is double pinned at either side. The interior corners are strengthened by large, quarter-round vertical-grain blocks (the front ones, two-part), each held by two rosehead nails. The back legs are rounded, top to bottom. The front claw feet comprise half-spherical balls with short, stumpy, two-joint toes that terminate abruptly in short triangular nails. The knee brackets are nailed twice.

**Condition:** The splat has a vertical break at the lower central loop crossing, which is repaired with a wooden splint. The left post is cracked at the front and back both above and below the through tenon. Multiple nail holes along all rail bottoms indicate the presence of former dust covers. The loose-seat frame is modern.

**Dimensions:**

| | | |
|---|---|---|
| H. | 38 1/2 in. | 97.8 cm |
| H. (seat) | 16 1/8 in. | 41.0 cm |
| W. (crest) | 22 1/2 in. | 57.1 cm |
| W. (seat front) | 21 1/8 in. | 53.7 cm |
| W. (seat back) | 16 1/2 in. | 41.9 cm |
| W. (feet) | 22 5/8 in. | 57.4 cm |
| D. (seat) | 16 3/4 in. | 42.5 cm |
| D. (feet) | 20 1/4 in. | 51.4 cm |

**Materials:** *Microanalysis:* Primary: cherry. Secondary: white pine group (seat blocks). *Finish:* medium dark reddish brown color in resin with remnants of an older similar finish. *Upholstery:* block-printed polychrome cotton with "Indienne"-style floral forms; France, 1780–1800.

**Publications:** Philip D. Zimmerman, "Regionalism in American Furniture Studies," in Gerald W. R. Ward, ed., *Perspectives on American Furniture* (New York: W. W. Norton for the Henry Francis du Pont Winterthur Museum, 1988), pp. 26–28, fig. 6.

**Provenance:** Descended in the Southmead family of Middletown, Conn.; owned by Alfred C. Ward, Middletown, Conn., when purchased by Meade Minnigerode (sp.?) of Middletown, Conn., in 1937 (see **Inscriptions or marks**).

**Accession history:** Purchased by H. F. du Pont from John S. Walton, Inc., New York, 1954. Gift of H. F. du Pont, 1958.
54.21

1. For the third interlaced, Chapin-type chair, along with related Philadelphia and New York chairs, see Kirk, *American Chairs*, figs. 69–72, 137–40, 197, 198.

2. Homer Eaton Keyes, "More Evidence for Eliphalet," *Antiques* 31, no. 1 (January 1937): 11; Joseph Lionetti and Robert Trent, "New Information about Chapin Chairs," *Antiques* 192, no. 5 (May 1986): 1082–95; Emily M. Davis, "Eliphalet Chapin," *Antiques* 35, no. 4 (April 1939): 172–73; Henry Maynard, "Eliphalet Chapin the Resolute Yankee, 1741–1807," *Connoisseur* 170, no. 684 (February 1969): 129. Philip Zea, "Furniture," in *Great River*, cat. 109.

3. For the chairs constituting the analysis group, see the following: Kane, *Three Hundred Years*, nos. 117–19; Kirk, *American Chairs*, fig. 196; "Museum Accessions," *Antiques* 107, no. 6 (June 1975): 1060; Elisabeth Donaghy Garrett, "American Furniture in the DAR Museum," *Antiques* 109, no. 4 (April 1976): 754, fig. 8; Heckscher, *American Furniture*, cat. no. 10; Fales, *Furniture of Historic Deerfield*, p. 56; Philip Johnston, "Eighteenth- and Nineteenth-Century American Furniture in the Wadsworth Atheneum," *Antiques* 115, no. 5 (May 1979): 1020, pl. 5; *Connecticut Furniture*, no. 238; Joseph K. Kindig III, *The Philadelphia Chair, 1685–1785* (York, Pa.: Historical Society of York County, 1978), fig. 38; Sotheby Parke Bernet, "Estate of Mabel Brady Garvan" (June 7, 1980), lot 160; for the Garbisch collection sale, see Sotheby Parke Bernet advertisement, *Antiques* 117, no. 5 (May 1980): 939; Lionetti and Trent, "New Information," p. 1086, fig. 8; Sotheby's, "Important Americana" (January 24–27, 1990), lot 1225.

4. Davis, "Eliphalet Chapin," p. 174. For the 4 remaining groups of chairs with family histories, see Kane, *Three Hundred Years*, no. 117; Lionetti and Trent, "New Information," p. 1086, figs. 8, 9; Garrett, "American Furniture in DAR Museum," p. 754, fig. 8; Fales, *Furniture of Historic Deerfield*, p. 56. The King chairs were purchased from Alexander's daughter in 1877 by Hartford antiquarian Dr. Irving W. Lyon, who is reputed to have seen the original bill of sale; Zea, "Furniture," cat. 109.

## 49 ◆ Side chair
East Windsor or vicinity or possibly Hartford, Connecticut
1775–90
Eliphalet Chapin (1741–1807) or Aaron Chapin, or another area craftsman

Chairs designed with crest curves and fluted tips similar to those in the Chapin-ascribed chair of No. 48 but ornamented with an unusual, X-centered splat are framed using the same Philadelphia through-tenon construction. The splat of this chair is an original Connecticut River valley pattern that probably derived from several sources. The upper loops are an adaptation of the interlaced splat (see No. 48) or owl's-eye patterns (see No. 30). A pierced quatrefoil like that at the splat base is common in joined seating originating in Philadelphia, the city where Eliphalet Chapin of East Windsor, Connecticut, worked as a journeyman for several years during the late 1760s. One Philadelphia quatrefoil-pierced

pattern also has a small X within an astragal-ended aperture at the center back in imitation of a design first published in the 1754 edition of Chippendale's *Director*.[1]

Robert Manwaring's *Real Friend and Companion* (1765) illustrates two Chinese fret patterns with backs dominated by large, bold Xs from corner to corner. Further study reveals that the central feature of one fret pattern, a large, concave diamond (fig. 1), also appears at the center of the Chapin design. Of additional interest, Manwaring centered a small shell in the chair crest; of even greater significance are the double-S brackets of the chair legs. Chapin used almost identical brackets on a set of straight-leg X-back chairs made for the Grant-Marsh family, which are documented to the chairmaker's shop in the accounts of Ebenezer Grant of East Windsor. Apparently, Chapin was also influenced by other Manwaring designs in the creation of this chair back. An engraving for a "parlor chair" may have been the source of the quatrefoil and its flanking

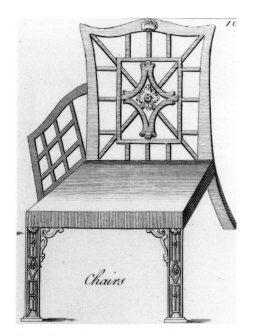

**Fig. 1.** From Robert Manwaring, *The Cabinet and Chair-Maker's Real Friend and Companion* (London: Henry Webley, 1765), pl. 10 right.

brackets, although the quatrefoil was a popular motif in Philadelphia chairs with Gothic-style splats. A design with a looped center (see No. 47, fig. 1) could have inspired the double, opposing C straps of the splat top immediately below the shell. Whereas this chair back has a shell in the crest, the Chapin bracket-leg chair for the Grant-Marsh family is designed with an open bridge without a shell, like that in No. 47, fig. 1. The overall evidence suggests strongly that Chapin owned a copy of Manwaring's designs.[2]

Like the interlaced-splat chairs represented by No. 48 and ascribed to the Chapin craftsmen or their followers, chairs of the pattern shown here are varied somewhat in decorative detail, based on the study of a fifteen-sample group. The support structures were designed in two patterns; the earliest is comparable to No. 48 in all features—leg curves, carved claws, and rear stumps—and includes three armchairs in the sample. The second, or Marlborough-style support, dates slightly later. Crest shells are varied from lobed to fluted-and-lobed patterns. Among the former, the number of lobes appears to have increased from eight or ten to twelve when the support structure was updated to the straight-leg pattern. Early fluted shells were carved with five-shouldered lobes in the Boston–Rhode Island style; later examples have six lobes with the intervening flutes generally plain (fig. 2). The crest of the Grant-

Marsh family chair has an undecorated open arch in place of a shell and cusped crest tips. The modeled crescent tips flanking the shell are featured in all chairs except a rare example with tapered legs substituted for straight Marlbourgh "feet." If the splat is not pierced directly below the shell, the carving is generally extended into the long, triangular cavity between the upper central straps, as illustrated; the carved shell tip is usually longer in the straight-leg chairs than in the cabriole-leg examples.[3]

Other splat variation is modest. The central X is positioned either in front of or behind the other strapwork, although a rear orientation is slightly more common. In one example the crossings are variable, but whether this is by design or mistake is unclear. The upper tips of several Xs are beaded, including those in this chair. Plinth and seat-frame tops in the cabriole-leg chairs are finished with large, thumb-molded beads (see No. 48). The straight-leg design has a low, stepped bead at the plinth and an outside bead at the flattened seat lip. The lip bead is continued down the outside forward corners of the front legs. Moderately shallow seat rails complement the Marlborough support structure, replacing the earlier deep rails finished with flat, stepped arches (see No. 48). Most chairs in the pattern have loose seats; a few are upholstered over the rails. Cherry is again the favored wood, although three chairs in this group are mahogany, including one of the three armchairs. Two groups have family histories. A cherrywood armchair is alleged to have been made as wedding furniture for Anna Barnard (m. 1772) of Northampton, Massachusetts. Ebenezer Grant of East Windsor bought a set of six chairs and other furniture from Eliphalet Chapin for his daughter Ann in 1775, when she married the Rev. John Marsh; the Marlborough-leg chair with brackets descended in the Marsh family.[4]

An unusual feature of Chapin seating furniture, but one difficult to investigate

**Fig. 2.** Detail, crest center and splat.

because the chairs must be partially disassembled or X-rayed, is the use of round tenons and mortises for crest and forward arm joints in place of standard, rectangular elements. Two side chairs in the style of No. 48 with family histories were found to have round-tenon joinery. One is a chair from the extensive Grant-Marsh family purchase from Eliphalet Chapin. The other is one of a pair of chairs at Yale University Art Gallery, New Haven, purchased in 1877 by antiquarian Dr. Irving W. Lyon from the daughter of the first owner. A diamond-back chair from the Grant-Marsh family purchase is also joined with round tenons. Recent X-ray examination has revealed that the crest-post joints of this chair and those of No. 48 are also secured by round tenons. This construction is rare in New England and New York eighteenth-century joined seating and uncommon in Philadelphia work. Although the case for ascribing the round-tenon chairs to the Chapins is strong, it does not necessarily follow that such chairs were made exclusively by the Chapin cousins. Other area workmen could have copied this feature just as they copied the chair patterns and the through-tenon construction of the side seat rails.[5]

NGE

**Inscriptions or marks:** *Chiseled at center of front seat-rail rabbet:* "II".

**Construction:** The crest is supported on round tenons at the flat-faced canted posts and on three rectangular tenons at the splat. The crest face, which is rounded and contoured, is centered with a carved and molded shell extending onto the splat; the crescent points and projecting crest tips are also carved. The crest back is flat through the center and into the ogees, which are rounded, top and bottom, near the ends; the tips and center base are also rounded. The shell back is chamfered and scalloped. The flat splat face is incised and modeled below the shell and lightly carved at the top beads of the X. Modeling occurs at the strap crossings with the X, the tiny outside center volutes, and the quatrefoil. The splat edges are flat and the piercings slightly canted, front to back; the base is tenoned into the plinth. The plinth is hollow on the front and side faces, finished with a low, stepped top bead, and glued to the back rail. The post backs are rounded from crest to seat. The seat frame has a broad, flattened lip with a narrow, incised, quarter-round outside bead. A narrow interior rabbet and four contoured-face triangular corner blocks held by screws and glue support the loose-seat frame. The rails are joined to the posts and front leg extensions with vertical rectangular tenons; the side-rail tenons extend through the rear posts. Only the back rail is pinned. The rectangular rear legs are chamfered on the inside forward corners, top to bottom. The rectangular front legs, which are chamfered on the inside back corners, have incised beads down the outside front corners similar to that at the seat lip. The side and rear stretchers are joined to the legs with vertical rectangular tenons; only the rear stretcher is pinned. The medial stretcher is dovetailed into the side stretchers from the bottom.

**Condition:** The splat straps are cracked through in five places, the breaks visible from the back. Splines repair the breaks on the front splat surface; a small triangular piece is also inset near the upper right X arm. A long, deep scratch occurs on the upper left back-post face. An internal screw repairs a break in the upper right back post several inches below the crest joint. The outside right rail lip is patched near the back. A thin spline is inserted at the rear plinth and splat joint. The corner blocks inside the rails are replaced. The loose-seat frame is modern.

**Dimensions:**

| | | |
|---|---|---|
| H. | 38 1/8 in. | 96.8 cm |
| H. (seat) | 16 in. | 40.6 cm |
| W. (crest) | 22 in. | 55.8 cm |
| W. (seat front) | 21 in. | 53.3 cm |
| W. (seat back) | 16 1/4 in. | 41.3 cm |
| W. (feet) | 20 7/8 in. | 53.0 cm |
| D. (seat) | 16 5/8 in. | 42.2 cm |
| D. (feet) | 18 7/8 in. | 47.9 cm |

**Materials:** *Microanalysis:* Primary: cherry. Secondary: white pine group (rear seat rail). *Finish:* medium light reddish brown color in resin. *Upholstery:* block-printed polychrome cotton with "Indienne"-style floral forms; France, 1780–1800.

**Publications:** Downs, *American Furniture*, fig. 128. Bishop, *Centuries and Styles of the American Chair*, fig. 206. Nancy Goyne Evans, "A Sense of Style: Design Sources for Windsor Furniture, Part 1," *Antiques* 133, no. 1 (January 1988): 292, fig. 16.

**Accession history:** Museum purchase from John S. Walton, Inc., New York, 1951.
54.534

1. Joseph Lionetti and Robert Trent, "New Information about Chapin Chairs," *Antiques* 192, no. 5 (May 1986): 1082–95; for the Philadelphia chair and its Chippendale design source, see Joseph K. Kindig III, *The Philadelphia Chair, 1685–1785* (York, Pa.: Historical Society of York County, 1978), fig. 62.

2. Robert Manwaring, *The Cabinet and Chair-Maker's Real Friend and Companion* (London: Henry Webley, 1765), pls. 9, 10; for the Grant-Marsh chair, see Lionetti and Trent, "New Information," fig. 12.

3. The chairs constituting the rest of the analysis group are in Philip Johnston, "Eighteenth- and Nineteenth-Century American Furniture in the Wadsworth Atheneum," *Antiques* 115, no. 5 (May 1979): 1012, pl. 7; Lionetti and Trent, "New Information," fig. 12; William Voss Elder III and Jayne E. Stokes, *American Furniture, 1680–1880, from the Collection of the Baltimore Museum of Art* (Baltimore: By the museum, 1987), cat. no. 19; *Connecticut Furniture*, nos. 241, 242; Fales, *Furniture of Historic Deerfield*, figs. 101, 102; Thomas D. Williams and Constance R. Williams advertisement, *Antiques* 77, no. 60 (June 1960): 551; Ruth Davidson, "Museum Accessions," *Antiques* 98, no. 3 (September 1970): 374; "Wethersfield: Living with Antiques," *Antiques* 86, no. 4 (October 1964): 466; Rodriguez Roque, *American Furniture*, no. 56; *American Antiques from Israel Sack Collection*, 10 vols. (Washington, D.C.: Highland House, ca. 1969–), 2:389, 391; "Connecticut Valley [Furniture]: Chapin Type," *Antiques* 70, no. 3 (September 1956): 227. For a Rhode Island shell, see Moses, *Master Craftsmen*, p. 277 top; the Grant-Marsh family chair is illustrated in Lionetti and Trent, "New Information," fig. 12; cusped crests are delineated in Manwaring, *Cabinet and Chair-Maker's Real Friend and Companion*, pls. 8 right, 11 right, 14 left, 15 left, 35 right.

4. Ebenezer Grant's account book entry for the Eliphalet Chapin furniture is illustrated in Lionetti and Trent, "New Information," fig. 7.

5. For round-tenon construction investigation results, see Lionetti and Trent, "New Information." Lyon reportedly saw the original bill of sale for the set of chairs, which was dated in 1781 by Eliphalet Chapin and addressed to Alexander King of East Windsor. King was a brother-in-law of Aaron Chapin, Eliphalet's second cousin and co-worker in the East Windsor shop until he moved to Hartford in 1783; Kane, *Three Hundred Years*, no. 117.

## 50 ◆ Side chairs
Boston, Massachusetts
1760–90

The interlaced chair splat with a quatrefoil base was a relatively common Massachusetts pattern. These two chairs, which have almost identical splats, illustrate the stylistic variety; examples with cabriole and Marlborough legs were about equally popular. The cabriole-leg style was further varied by omitting the stretchers and introducing typical Massachusetts flared back feet. The medial braces in stretcher chairs are turned in several patterns. The ring ends shown here are sometimes replaced by short, bulbous vases. Conical tips are rare in the center brace but common in the rear stretcher. The straight-leg chairs are beaded at the outside corners of the front supports; some also have beaded stretchers. Open leg brackets are rare, although some undoubtedly have fallen off over the years. Solid blocks of oxbow profile are more common, and some chairs were made without brackets. Over-the-rail upholstery appears on

chairs of both leg types. The armchair and roundabout chair are rare forms in this pattern, as they are in many formal designs.

Differences in construction details and secondary woods indicate that the chairs in this splat group were produced in more than one shop. There are also subtle differences in the carving, although the work is amazingly consistent and rich in quality. A leafy spray of acanthus with a pendent drop is centered in the crest; the arches are ruffled (fig. 1). The small leafy scrolls on stemlike beads at the outer splat straps have an organic quality. The leaf carving of the cabriole knees is consistent with that in other Boston-area chairs. The introduction of straight legs to chairs of this pattern speaks to the longevity of the design.

Six chairs or chair sets within this group have background histories in the greater Boston area. Chairs at the Museum of Fine Arts, Boston, descended in the Lane and Lamb families of that city. The Thomas Lamb (ca. 1753–1813) armchair is stamped with the

initials "S.F.," presumably those of Samuel Fiske, a Boston cabinetmaker who appears to have worked with Stephen Badlam of neighboring Dorchester early in his career. The stamps of both men occur together on several pieces of Boston furniture. A set of six side chairs at the Metropolitan Museum of Art, one of which has the inscription "Boston Massachusetts" penciled on the seat rail, was owned by H. Eugene Bolles of Boston sometime prior to 1909. Another side chair, owned in Worcester before 1917, is purported to have belonged to Gov. Caleb Strong (1745–1819) of Northampton, Massachusetts. Chairs that descended in the Longfellow family, comprising at least two different straight-leg sets, were used in family homes in Cambridge, Massachusetts, and Portland, Maine. The chairs at the Longfellow National Historic Site, Cambridge, were photographed in a downstairs hall in 1870 and inventoried there in 1912. The Portland chairs, which probably were transported from Boston, are

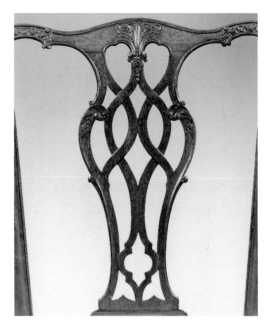

**Fig. 1.** Detail of left chair, center crest and splat.

somewhat different in that they have plain, uncarved backs and molded front legs. One chair is still covered in the original over-the-rail leather upholstery embellished with two rows of brass nails.[2]

Another pair of chairs has a Maryland history. They are associated with the Lloyds and Tilghmans of Baltimore and Easton as gifts to the family in the early twentieth century from an elderly Miss Etting, daughter of Solomon Etting, an importer. The Etting family was for several generations in the mercantile business, raising speculation that the pair of chairs represents furnishings shipped by or to them from a Boston craftsman or merchant factor in the eighteenth century.[3]

NGE

---

**Inscriptions or marks:** (Left) *Incised on front seat-rail rabbet:* "V". (Right) *Chiseled on front seat-rail rabbet:* "IIII".

**Construction:** (Left) The crest is supported on rectangular tenons at the canted posts and splat. The slightly rounded face is cheeked at the outer arches and carved with low-relief ornament and beading. The flat rear center surface is rounded at the top and chamfered at the bottom; the arches are rounded. The splat face is flat with low relief carved ornament and beads, modeled strap crossings and quatrefoil edges, and a central peaked ridge. The side edges and piercings are canted, front to back; the base is tenoned into the plinth. The plinth is hollow on the front and sides, finished with a top bead, and nailed twice at each end to the back rail. The post faces are serpentine-molded with flanking beads; the backs are rounded, crest to seat. The flat lip of the seat frame is finished with an outer quarter-round bead; narrow interior rabbets support the loose-seat frame. Triangular corner blocks are held in place with domed-head nails; scribe lines on the front block tops guided the craftsman in making the cuts to accommodate the front leg extensions. The rails are joined to the posts and front leg

extensions with vertical rectangular tenons (pinned). The rear legs are canted on the forward surfaces; all corners are chamfered between the rails and stretchers. The forward corners of the feet are broadly chamfered to points. The creased front knees are carved with channeled and incised leafage. The two-knuckle toes have medium-length nails; the side toes angle backward sharply. The knee brackets, which are nailed twice, are narrowly chamfered on the inside edges. The side stretchers are joined to the legs with rectangular tenons (pinned, rear); the medial and side stretcher blocks are joined with horizontal tenons. The rear stretcher is round tenoned into the back legs.

(Right) The joints and surfaces of the crest, splat, plinth, and posts correspond to those in the left chair, except that the crest face is flat and the plinth is glued to the back rail. The seat frame, which is shaped and joined like that in the left chair, has no corner blocks. The rear legs are canted on the forward surfaces. The forward corners of the back feet are chamfered, the inside chamfers continuing almost to the seat. The front legs are beaded on the outside forward corners and narrowly chamfered on the inside back corners; the brackets are nailed in place. All stretchers, except the back one, are crowned on the top surface. The side and rear stretchers are joined to the legs with vertical rectangular tenons (pinned); the medial stretcher is dovetailed into the side stretchers from the bottom.

**Condition:** (Left) The crest is nicked at the upper right edge. The splat is cracked and repaired along the left side from the top scroll to the plinth; a small chip is missing from the base at the lower left front. A vertical crack occurs in the left front leg extension above the front pin. The right rear foot has a deep gouge on the inside face; the left rear foot is chipped on the inside back corner. The forward toe of the right front foot is bruised. The loose-seat frame is modern.

(Right) Worm damage occurs on the left rear crest face. A modern cleat is fastened to the inside rear seat rail to supplement the rabbets of the interior frame. The left corner of the front rail is

cracked and defaced. The left front knee bracket has one new nail. Both front legs are worn at the beaded corners near the bottom. The seat-front and undercarriage surfaces are considerably nicked and marred. The loose-seat frame is modern.

**Dimensions:**
Left

| | | |
|---|---|---|
| H. | 36 13/16 in. | 93.5 cm |
| H. (seat) | 16 1/4 in. | 41.3 cm |
| W. (crest) | 20 in. | 50.8 cm |
| W. (seat front) | 21 1/2 in. | 54.6 cm |
| W. (seat back) | 16 1/8 in. | 41.0 cm |
| W. (feet) | 23 7/16 in. | 59.5 cm |
| D. (seat) | 17 1/4 in. | 43.8 cm |
| D. (feet) | 21 1/2 in. | 54.6 cm |

Right

| | | |
|---|---|---|
| H. | 36 3/4 in. | 93.3 cm |
| H. (seat) | 16 1/2 in. | 41.9 cm |
| W. (crest) | 19 3/8 in. | 49.2 cm |
| W. (seat front) | 21 1/4 in. | 53.9 cm |
| W. (seat back) | 16 1/8 in. | 41.0 cm |
| W. (feet) | 21 1/4 in. | 53.9 cm |
| D. (seat) | 17 1/8 in. | 43.5 cm |
| D. (feet) | 20 1/4 in. | 51.4 cm |

**Materials:** *Microanalysis:* (Left) Primary: mahogany. Secondary: white pine group (corner blocks). (Right) Primary: mahogany. *Finish:* (Left) medium light brown color with reddish cast, in resin. (Right) medium reddish brown color in resin. *Upholstery:* (Left) modern green silklike fabric. (Right) gold silk damask; Europe, 1740–70.

**Publications:** (Left) Downs, *American Furniture,* fig. 156.

**Accession history:** (Left) Purchased by H. F. du Pont from I. Winick, New York, 1949. Gift of H. F. du Pont, 1960. (Right) Bequest of H. F. du Pont, 1969.
59.2639, 64.662

---

1. For examples representative of the features and forms discussed, see Ginsburg and Levy advertisement and Kenneth Hammitt advertisement, *Antiques* 66, no. 2 (August 1954): 87, and 88, no. 4 (October 1965): 473; Anne Farnam, "Furniture at the Essex Institute, Salem, Massachusetts," *Antiques* 111, no. 5 (May 1977): 959, fig. 4; Walter Muir Whitehill, Brock Jobe, Jonathan Fairbanks, "Foreword," in *Boston Furniture,* p. xiii. For roundabout chairs of this pattern, see *American Antiques from Israel Sack Collection,* 10 vols. (Washington, D.C.: Highland House, ca. 1969–), 2:311; Fales, *Furniture of Historic Deerfield,* fig. 105. Newman Greenough, Esq., of Boston, owned "Mahog'y fram'd Chairs" with a "Round Chair" en suite. Greenough's side chairs were appraised at 30s. each and the round chair at 40s.; Newman Greenough, Esq., estate inventory, 1781, Suffolk County Probate Court, Boston (microfilm, Downs collection).

2. For chairs with histories of ownership, see Randall, *American Furniture,* no. 150; Whitehill, Jobe, and Fairbanks, "Foreword," p. xiii; Heckscher, *American Furniture,* cat. 17; Morse, *Furniture of the Olden Time,* p. 190; no. 82.1067, DAPC, Visual Resources Collection, Winterthur Library; Laura Fecych Sprague, ed., *Agreeable Situations: Society, Commerce, and Art in Southern Maine, 1780–1830* (Kennebunk, Maine: Brick Store Museum, 1987), cat. 57. Samuel Fiske (d. 1797) was later in partnership with his son William (b. 1770). Appropriately, a federal-style shield-back chair is branded by both men.

3. For the Maryland-owned chairs, see no. 74.5322, DAPC, Visual Resources Collection, Winterthur Library; folder 59.2639, Registration Office, Winterthur.

## 51 ◆ Side chair (one of a pair)
Great Britain or eastern Massachusetts
1760–90

Although the splat of this chair is comparable in pattern to the banisters of the chairs in No. 50, it is housed in a larger frame with stouter members and displays other notable differences. Overall, the features of this chair strongly suggest a British origin. A close comparison of the splat with those produced in Boston reveals that this design has oval rather than heart-shape top piercings, larger carved volutes, a lancet-tipped central ellipse, creases in the quatrefoil and central cross straps, differences in stem length above and below the quatrefoil, and base piercings without peaks. The same variations appear in the splats of British chairs of similar pattern. Of particular note are the distinctive lancet and the creases, elements that appear consistently in British work. In its dimensions, the splat is broader and the straps thicker than those in known Massachusetts examples.[1]

Except for the lobed ends, the crest curves are similar to those of the chairs in No. 50, but there the resemblance ends. The valancelike leaf carving at the center and the opposing S scrolls at the tips are uncommon, both in American and British work. Among American chairs of various splat patterns, several of New York origin are carved with related leaf forms; one crest is even terminated by opposing S scrolls of a comparable profile. The quatrefoil-splat variation shown here, however, is unknown in New York chair work. Thus, it would appear to be pure coincidence that this chair and its mate were acquired by a previous owner in Poughkeepsie, a Hudson River valley community north of New York City.[2]

The corner blocks in the seat frame of this chair and its mate are replacements or additions, eliminating the possibility that provenance could be established through the secondary woods. Beaded seat frames and legs are common to both British and American

joined seating. Here, however, the backward cants of the rear legs, particularly at the feet, are less pronounced than comparable angles in American work. These relatively straight legs, marked by long, inside chamfers from seat to floor, also lack the sharp chamfers of the rear feet common to many Massachusetts chairs (see Nos. 30, 31, 50).

Constructing a Marlborough frame was a relatively straightforward task. Hired shop hands were usually paid on a piecework basis. Through most of the eighteenth century, basic and extra charges for labor were generally determined through verbal agreements between workmen and shop masters. By the close of the century, printed price books were available in some large cities and provincial centers in Britain and America. As described in the Norwich (England) price book of 1801, "Chairs . . . of all kinds, are started as plain as possible, that any pattern of back, top, &c. may be introduced in same." The "patterns," or embellishments, added to the plain frame constituted customer options and were charged

according to a "table of extras" accompanying each basic chair description. A typical frame of the type illustrated here began with a "plain banister and pedestal" (plinth), plain seat rails and stretchers, "plain Marlbro' feet" (front), and "single pitch back feet." (A pitch is a canted, or angled, surface on the forward face of a back leg.) Charges for piercing the banister, or "cutting holes," were calculated per hole. "Working an ovalo, or quarter round," on the seat-frame lip or the plinth top accounted for other charges. Double, as opposed to single, pitches in the back legs cost several shillings more. Sophisticated extras, such as molded back posts and carving, elevated a chair from the category of "common" to that of "best."[3]

*NGE*

Construction: The crest is supported on rectangular tenons at the canted posts and splat. The rounded face is carved with low-relief ornament and beading; the lower beading is incised and channeled. The flat, center rear surface is rounded at the top and bottom, continuing into the arches. The splat face is flat with volutes carved in low relief and modeled strap crossings; peaked ridges occur in the quatrefoil and at the bases of the upper cross straps. Hollow channels form narrow C scrolls at the upper and lower outside splat edges. The side edges and piercings are canted, front to back, with narrow chamfers around the back edges. The splat base is tenoned into the plinth. The plinth is hollow on the front and side faces, finished with a low top bead, and glued to the back rail. The post faces are ogee-molded with flanking beads; the backs are rounded, crest to seat. The flat lip of the seat frame is finished with an outer quarter-round bead; narrow interior rabbets support the loose-seat frame. The seat rails are joined to the posts and front leg extensions with vertical rectangular tenons. The rear legs are canted on the forward surfaces; the inside corners are chamfered, top to bottom. The front legs are beaded on the outside front corners and chamfered on the inside rear corners. The thin, rectangular stretchers are crowned on the top surfaces. The side and rear stretchers are joined to the legs with rectangular tenons; the medial stretcher is dovetailed into the side stretchers from the bottom.

**Condition:** The center crest back is marked by a horizontal gouge; minor nicks and dents occur on the seat frame and understructure. A stress crack on the left front leg extends from the inside front corner of the foot to the stretcher. Small replacement corner blocks glued inside the seat frame are augmented by large facing blocks, each held with two screws; together the new blocks form large triangles. The slip seat is modern.

**Dimensions:**

| | | |
|---|---|---|
| H. | 38 7/16 in. | 97.6 cm |
| H. (seat) | 16 3/8 in. | 41.6 cm |
| W. (crest) | 21 in. | 53.3 cm |
| W. (seat front) | 21 5/8 in. | 54.9 cm |
| W. (seat back) | 17 7/8 in. | 45.4 cm |
| W. (feet) | 21 3/4 in. | 55.3 cm |
| D. (seat) | 17 7/8 in. | 45.4 cm |
| D. (feet) | 20 3/4 in. | 52.7 cm |

**Materials:** *Microanalysis:* Primary: mahogany. *Finish:* medium brown color with reddish cast, in resin; carving somewhat darker; crazed surfaces. *Upholstery:* peach silk-and-linen brocatelle; Europe, 1725–55.

**Provenance:** Ex coll.: Mrs. Henry H. Benkard, New York, 1929.

**Accession history:** Purchased by H. F. du Pont from the Mrs. Henry H. Benkard Sale, Anderson Galleries, New York, 1929. Bequest of H. F. du Pont, 1969.
57.510.1

1. For British chairs with splat variations, see Kirk, *American Furniture*, figs. 899, 901–3; Cescinsky, *English Furniture*, 2: figs. 251, 255, 256; F. Lewis Hinckley, *A Directory of Antique Furniture* (New York: Crown Publishers, 1953), fig. 799; Hinckley, *Directory*, fig. 283; Sotheby's, "Important English Furniture, Decorations, Clocks, and Carpets" (October 29, 1983), lot 58.

2. For New York chairs, see Downs, *American Furniture*, fig. 148; Bishop, *Centuries and Styles of the American Chair*, figs. 171, 178.

3. *Norwich Chair Makers' Price Book* (Norwich, Eng., 1801), as reproduced in Gerry Cotton, "'Common' Chairs from the Norwich Chairmakers' Price Book of 1801," *Regional Furniture* 2 (1988): 68–69, 74, 84.

## 52 ◆ Side chairs
Boston, Massachusetts
1760–75

The trefoil splat is among the most ornamental of the Chippendale-period patterns made in Boston. Close models exist in English chairs; however, both English and American examples are uncommon, suggesting that production was limited. Design-book sources provide only general prototypes for the principal elements of this splat—the trefoil of the top and the central lancet contained within the trefoil and its tall supporting bracket. Chippendale published four splat designs with pierced lancets, and William Ince and John Mayhew published one. The trefoil as a principal element in chair backs is less common in design books. Ince and Mayhew's book and Robert Manwaring's book both illustrate one. The English prototype for this chair appears to have been produced independently by a capable craftsman/designer probably working in London.[1]

With regard to interpretation and dating, there are parallels between the trefoil-splat chairs and the chairs in No. 50, representatives of a pattern that was also produced with cabriole and Marlborough supports. The cabriole bases are closely related, from the knee and claw carvings to the stretcher turnings. The Marlborough supports are also basically similar, but in this design, handsome, rope-carved beads are substituted for plain beads at the outside forward corners. Here, the same ornament appears in the chair backs of both the cabriole and Marlborough patterns, which are crowned by cusp-tip crests closely modeled after English prototypes. Although the two crests are about equal in length, the proportions vary; the central arch in the cabriole-leg chair is 1/2 inch longer. Subtle differences in the crest tips include the size of the rounded projection and the character of the carved work. Close comparison of the back carving reveals the hands of two artisans or the work of one man produced at different times (figs. 1, 2). The

than thirty years after Quincy's death, the chairs were moved to the family homestead at Braintree, where by the 1880s they furnished the east and west parlors. Two additional sets of straight-leg chairs of this splat pattern are known. One side chair has pierced brackets at the front legs, and an armchair has bold, forward-scrolling arms; both are upholstered over the rail. The desk-and-bookcase of No. 206 and the pair of looking glasses in No. 214 are also associated with the Quincy family.[4]

Mahogany chairs are uncommon in Boston inventories until the late 1760s, although at least three of the city's furnituremakers were framing mahogany chairs in their shops at the time of the great fire in 1760. Even when listed in inventories, mahogany chairs are rarely described further, except for the seat covers, and leather was a common choice, judging by the number of examples mentioned during the 1770s. The range of fabric covers and colors in the same period is modest but varied. Haircloth, the first choice after leather, was sturdy and practical. Both crimson and green damask are mentioned, probably the worsted variety rather than silk. Two relatively uncommon seat coverings listed are yellow russel, a stout-woven damask that was frequently calendared to give it a lustrous finish, and patch, an Indian printed cloth. Chairs bottomed with "Check," or "Furniture Check Cotton," are listed occasionally, with blue and white the frequent color choice.[5]

*NGE*

---

**Inscriptions or marks:** (Left) *Incised on front seat-rail rabbet:* "VIII". *Inside front seat rail:* "Property of Estelle M. Godfrey [?]" in faded ink, on aged, blue-bordered paper label. *Incised on loose-seat frame:* "III".

**Construction:** (Left) The crest is supported on rectangular tenons at the flared posts and splat. The slightly rounded face is cheeked at the outer arches and carved with low-relief ornament. The flat back surface is slightly blocked through the center and rounded, top and bottom. The splat face is flat, with low-relief carving and volutes. The edges and piercings are canted, front to back; the base is tenoned into the plinth. The plinth is hollow on the front and sides, finished with a low top bead, and glued to the rear seat rail. The flat-faced back posts are rope-carved at the outside edges; the backs are rounded, crest to seat. The flat lip of the seat frame is finished with an outer quarter-round bead; narrow interior rabbets support the loose-seat frame. The rails are joined to the back posts and front leg extensions with vertical rectangular tenons (pinned). The rear legs are canted on the forward surfaces; the feet are broadly chamfered to points on

---

central crest ornament in the cabriole-leg chair is delineated more carefully and has a base of slightly different design; overall, it is also somewhat larger. The lower beads of the pendent leaves within the trefoil are absent in the Marlborough-leg chair. The same variations that differentiate the crest carvings are present in the leaves that overlap the lancets. The volutes in the straight-leg chair have been carefully carved with an extra half turn in the scroll, but the floret centered below does not quite fill the space allotted to it. A subtle feature of both chairs is the diminutive trefoil on a stalklike projection at the splat base. The trefoil-splat pattern represents the epitome of Boston chairmaking in the Chippendale style, a style that is marked by delicacy and relative simplicity.[2]

The cabriole-leg chair was originally part of a set that numbered at least eight chairs. The furniture traditionally descended in the De Wolf family of Boston and Bristol, Rhode Island. Two chairs are at Winterthur, and two more are in the Museum of Art,

Rhode Island School of Design; a fifth is privately owned. A sixth chair now in the Metropolitan Museum of Art was acquired at the Mrs. J. Amory Haskell sale in 1944; the auction catalogue ascribed a Salem origin. The pattern appears to have been copied in the vicinity of York, Maine (part of Massachusetts until 1820), where the home of Jonathan Sayward was furnished with a set of six plain chairs without carving. Sayward also owned a set of plain, owl's-eye chairs (see No. 31) made locally. As a merchant, Sayward was familiar with the Boston market; he also served in the Massachusetts legislature as a York representative from 1766 to 1768, a period when both patterns were popular in the Massachusetts capital.[3]

The Marlborough-leg chair is one of five in institutional collections from an original set that probably numbered eight chairs and was owned by the wealthy Quincy family of Boston. Josiah Quincy, Jr., and his bride, Abigail Phillips, acquired the chairs in 1769 for their Short Street residence. In 1806, more

all corners. The creased front knees are carved with channeled and incised leafage; the knee brackets are nailed twice. The two-knuckle toes have medium-length nails; the side toes angle backward sharply. The side stretchers are joined to the legs with rectangular tenons (pinned, rear); the medial and side stretcher blocks are joined with horizontal tenons. The rear stretcher is round tenoned into the back legs.

(Right) The joints and surfaces of the crest, splat, and upper back posts are similar to the left chair, except that the center rear crest surface is flat rather than blocked and the plinth is nailed rather than glued to the rear seat rail. The seat rails are joined to the posts and front leg extensions with vertical rectangular tenons (pinned, side rear and back). The interior seat frame is strengthened by two large triangular corner blocks at the back corners and open braces notched into the rails at the front. The rear legs are canted on the forward surfaces; the inside forward corners are chamfered, top to bottom. The feet are chamfered on the remaining three corners. The front legs are cable-beaded on the outside forward corners; the inside rear corners are chamfered, top to bottom. The rectangular stretchers are flat on the top surface. The side and rear stretchers are joined to the legs with vertical rectangular tenons (pinned); the medial and side stretchers are joined with horizontal tenons.

**Condition:** (Left) The left rear crest-post joint is cracked across the back. The top and inside faces of the right stretcher column are defaced. The birch loose-seat frame is numbered "IIII," the chair frame, "VII." The loose-seat frame in a mate chair is made of maple; its number, "VII," corresponds to that on the chair rabbet. The present loose-seat frame, therefore, may be from another set.

(Right) A long horizontal stress crack on the crest face extends from the center of the right arch to the tip. The plinth ends are cracked and defaced with many holes, some patched. The triangular rear corner blocks, which are secured with screws, are old but probably not original. The top of the front rail is somewhat shattered from nail holes.

**Dimensions:**

Left
| | | |
|---|---|---|
| H. | 38 in. | 96.5 cm |
| H. (seat) | 16⅝ in. | 42.2 cm |
| W. (crest) | 22⁵⁄₁₆ in. | 56.6 cm |
| W. (seat front) | 21⅞ in. | 55.5 cm |
| W. (seat back) | 17⅛ in. | 43.5 cm |
| W. (feet) | 23⅝ in. | 60.0 cm |
| D. (seat) | 17⅞ in. | 45.4 cm |
| D. (feet) | 21⅞ in. | 55.5 cm |

Right
| | | |
|---|---|---|
| H. | 38¾ in. | 98.4 cm |
| H. (seat) | 17 in. | 43.2 cm |
| W. (crest) | 22⁷⁄₁₆ in. | 57.0 cm |
| W. (seat front) | 21⅝ in. | 54.9 cm |
| W. (seat back) | 17¼ in. | 43.8 cm |
| W. (feet) | 21½ in. | 54.6 cm |
| D. (seat) | 18½ in. | 47.0 cm |
| D. (feet) | 22⅛ in. | 56.2 cm |

**Fig. 1.** Detail of left chair, center crest and splat.

**Fig. 2.** Detail of right chair, center crest and splat.

**Materials:** *Microanalysis:* (Left) Primary: mahogany. Secondary: birch (loose-seat frame). (Right) Primary: mahogany. Secondary: birch (rear seat rail); soft maple group (front and side rails); beech (front corner braces); basswood (rear corner blocks). *Finish:* (Left) variegated medium dark brown color with reddish cast, in resin. (Right) variegated medium to medium dark reddish brown color in resin. *Upholstery:* (Left) blue and white cotton furniture check; probably England, 1760–1820. (Right) modern blue wool.

**Exhibitions:** (Right) "Beyond Necessity: Art in the Folk Tradition," Brandywine River Museum, Chadds Ford, Pa., September 17–November 20, 1977.

**Publications:** Charles F. Hummel, "Queen Anne and Chippendale Furniture in the Henry Francis du Pont Winterthur Museum, Part 2," *Antiques* 98, no. 6 (December 1970): 901–3; figs. 3–5. (Left) Mary Ellen Hayward Yehia, "Ornamental Carving on Boston Furniture of the Chippendale Style," in

*Boston Furniture*, p. 218. (Right) Bishop, *Centuries and Styles of the American Chair*, fig. 186.

**Accession history:** (Left) Purchased with its mate (not illustrated) by H. F. du Pont from the estate of Reginald M. Lewis, Easton, Md., 1961. Gift of H. F. du Pont, 1964. (Right) Purchased by H. F. du Pont from Edmund Quincy, Boston, 1953. Gift of H. F. du Pont, 1953.
61.140.1, 53.166.3

**Provenance:** (Left) With its mate, said to have descended in the De Wolf family of Boston and Bristol, R.I. Ex coll.: Reginald M. Lewis. (Right) By tradition, part of a set of 8 acquired by Abigail Phillips and Josiah Quincy, Jr., in 1769, at the time of their marriage. Some years after Quincy's death (1775), the chairs were moved from Boston to the Quincy House at Braintree, Mass., where photographs of the interior taken about 1880 (SPNEA archives, Boston) show 1 chair in the east parlor and 3 others in the west parlor. The presumed descent of the chair was from Abigail and Josiah Quincy to their granddaughter Abigail Phillips Quincy (1803–93); to her nephew Josiah Phillips Quincy (1829–1910); to his son Josiah Quincy (1859–1919) and Quincy's widow; to Edmund Quincy, the last family owner.

1. For an English prototype, see Cescinsky, *English Furniture*, 2:237. William Ince and John Mayhew, *The Universal System of Houshold Furniture* (1762; reprint, Chicago: Quadrangle Books, 1960), pl. 9 lower right; pl. 10 upper right; Robert Manwaring, *The Cabinet and Chair-Maker's Real Friend and Companion* (London: Henry Webley, 1765), pl. 5 left; Thomas Chippendale, *The Gentleman and Cabinet-Maker's Director* (1762; reprint 3d ed., New York: Dover Publications, 1966), pl. 14; pl. 16 upper right.

2. For an English model, see Cescinsky, *English Furniture*, 2:237.

3. For the RISD chairs, see "Museum Acquisitions," *Newsletter of the Decorative Arts Society* 3, nos. 3/4 (Summer/Fall 1994): 5. Heckscher, *American Furniture*, cat. no. 14; Parke-Bernet Galleries, "The Americana Collection of the Late Mrs. J. Amory Haskell, Part 2" (May 17–20, 1944), lot 753; Jobe and Kaye, *New England Furniture*, pp. 110, 400–402.

4. The remaining chairs from this set are at the Metropolitan Museum of Art (Heckscher, *American Furniture*, cat. no. 15), the SPNEA, Boston (Jobe and Kaye, *New England Furniture*, no. 117), and the Tryon Palace Restoration, New Bern, N.C. Josiah Quincy, Jr., estate inventory, Boston, 1775, Quincy papers, Massachusetts Historical Society (copy of inventory courtesy of the SPNEA). For the bracket-leg side chair and the armchair, see Lockwood, *Colonial Furniture*, 2: figs. 568, 83 (supplement).

5. Boston Fire Documents and Correspondence, 1760, Boston Public Library; Florence Montgomery, *Textiles in America, 1650–1870* (New York: W. W. Norton, 1984), pp. 318, 336–37; for relevant inventories see Nathaniel Rogers (1770), John Spooner (1771), Charles Hamock (1773), Andrew Oliver (1774), William Molineaux (1775), Robert Auchmuty (1779), Henderson Inches (1780), and John Williams (1782) estate inventories, Suffolk County Probate Court, Boston (microfilm, Downs collection).

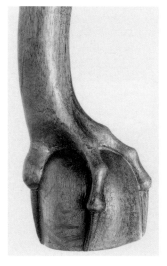

**Fig. 1.** Detail, right front foot.

## 53 ◆ **Side chair** (one of a pair)
Eastern Massachusetts
1760–85

This chair and its mate, probably once part of a set numbering six chairs, have a unique splat design. An extensive search has yielded no close prototype in American or British chairmaking. The pierced pattern is best classified with the owl's-eye chairs, yet it is distinctly different. The small, carved volutes, which are positioned at the loop tops instead of the terminals, face rather than oppose one another. Instead of forming a separate unit, the loops are part of the vase-shape baluster. The design is "streamlined," yet provincial. The two solid, lobed elements placed at the top connection with the crest are less than graceful. Pierced strapwork, such as appears in Nos. 30 and 31, would have enhanced and better integrated the upper back design.

Standard Massachusetts chairmaking practice within the scope of Chippendale design is reflected in several features of this chair: the carved sweeps at the crest tips; the shallow seat rails; the stretcherless base with blocked rear feet; and the slim, creased front legs with knee brackets continuing the leg curves into the rails. The heavy, Y-shape splat strap (see Nos. 35 right, 46) with flanking beads (see No. 35 left) and the carved feet, consisting of slim ankles, high-domed balls, and long, well-knuckled toes interact strongly with Rhode Island chairmaking. The nails projecting beyond the toe ends are extraordinarily long (fig. 1). The carved feet are close in form to the claws of a Boston turret-corner card table, which descended in the family of the Boston patriot Mercy Otis Warren (1728–1814). The quarter-round rear side-rail returns of the chair, which are a rarity, are fastened in place with tenons and one of two pins that pierce the side faces of the back posts at seat level, an indication that the blocks were part of the original design (fig. 2). Due to repairs, restoration, and multiple nail holes on the block edges, it is difficult to determine whether the returns were always covered by the upholstery material.[1]

*NGE*

**Construction:** The crest is supported on rectangular tenons at the flat-faced canted posts (pinned) and splat. The face is slightly rounded with backward sweeping, carved tips. The rear surface is flat with rounded tips and top; the lower edges are chamfered. The splat face is lightly modeled at the loops with volutes carved in low relief; the back surface is flat,

**Fig. 2.** Detail, left rear side rail and return.

with triangular chamfers at the bottom corners. The outside edges are slightly canted; the piercings are deeply canted, front to back. The splat is tenoned into the back rail. The three-sided plinth is hollow on the front and side faces, finished with a top bead, and nailed to the back rail. The post backs and sides are rounded from crest to seat. The seat rails and the large quarter-circle returns at either side back are joined to the posts and leg extensions with rectangular tenons. The back rail is pinned once at each side; the side rails are pinned twice at the posts (one pin at the rail return). The interior corners are braced by large triangular blocks; the rear blocks are secured with rosehead nails. The rounded rear legs are square in section and flare back at the base to form blocked, rectangular feet. The creased-knee cabriole front legs are supported on high-domed ball feet with slim, three-knuckle claws and long nails. The shorter rear claws relate closely to those in No. 57. The knee brackets are secured with rosehead nails.

**Condition:** The chair back was upholstered at one time. Filled nail holes extend up the posts, front and back, and along the crest at the upper back and center front. The right rear side rail return is replaced; the left return appears original except for a bottom piece under the leather. The rear, corner seat blocks appear to have been reattached, using rosehead nails; the front seat blocks are old replacements. A new wooden inset at the bottom of the left side rail extends from the front corner block halfway back along the bottom surface. Interior rectangular notches cut in the side and front rails are evidence of former brace-type repairs.

**Dimensions:**

| | | |
|---|---|---|
| H. | 38 in. | 96.5 cm |
| H. (seat) | 16 1/2 in. | 41.9 cm |
| W. (crest) | 18 1/2 in. | 47.0 cm |
| W. (seat front) | 21 in. | 53.3 cm |
| W. (seat back) | 16 1/8 in. | 41.0 cm |
| W. (feet) | 22 1/4 in. | 56.4 cm |
| D. (seat) | 18 in. | 45.7 cm |
| D. (feet) | 20 1/2 in. | 52.1 cm |

**Materials:** *Microanalysis:* Primary: mahogany. Secondary: soft maple group (seat rail). *Finish:* medium yellowish brown color in resin. *Upholstery:* modern leather ornamented with pre-1830s brass upholstery nails with cast heads and square shanks.

**Publications:** John A. H. Sweeney, *The Treasure House of Early American Rooms* (New York: Viking Press, 1963), p. 48.

**Accession history:** Purchased by H. F. du Pont from Harry Arons, Ansonia, Conn., 1954. Gift of H. F. du Pont, 1958.
54.91.3

---

1. For a Rhode Island chair with a comparable carved foot, see Moses, *Master Craftsmen*, fig. 1.49; for the Warren card table, see *American Antiques from Israel Sack Collection*, 10 vols. (Washington, D.C.: Highland House, ca. 1969–), 8:2260–61.

## 54 ◆ Side chairs
### Northeastern Massachusetts
### 1760–85

The pierced splat with long, pointed, rounded, and squared apertures accented by small diamond shapes was copied in several American colonial furniture centers from English prototypes. In Philadelphia, a scallop shell in the crest was the usual accompaniment. Rhode Island cabinetmakers placed the splat in a broad, round-shouldered, late Queen Anne sweep back. The design proved the most popular in Massachusetts where a crest ornament carved in low relief is the principal supplementary feature.[1]

Histories that associate several chairs or sets of chairs in the Massachusetts group with Marblehead, Chelsea, Gloucester, and Salem place the pattern firmly in the Boston and Essex County region. Nineteenth-century collector Ben Perley Poore, a part-time resident of Indian Hill Farm in West Newbury, owned a chair of this pattern. A chair that differs from the left chair only by the addition of a carved drop on the splat below the crest ornament was once the property of Katrina Kipper, proprietor of the Queen Ann Cottage in Boston during the second quarter of the twentieth century.[2]

Most Massachusetts chairs of this pattern are embellished with carved ornament,

although a few examples are plain, except for the modeled crest tips and claw feet. The C-scroll–bordered central ornament of the right chair with the pendent drop and winglike leafage (fig. 1) appears to be a close copy of an English pattern. Carved work originating in northeastern Massachusetts is often embellished with patterned grounds, here composed of stipples. Like its English model, the right chair also has leaf-carved crest terminals with the decoration spilling onto the upper posts. In contrast to the prototype, however, the splat is plain. Leafy splat decoration comparable to that in the English model appears in the left chair. The crest ornament on this chair is a variation of the motif centered in the punchwork ground of the right chair (fig. 2). Other chairs appear to conform to the general models described. Crest-rail profiles were sawed to one of three patterns: the two illustrated and a plain serpentine figure. Although the two crest patterns shown here appear unrelated, manipulation of the template for the left chair probably produced the "new" silhouette on the right.[3]

More than half the chairs in this pierced-splat group have carved knees, some creased at the center. The knee carvings of both chairs are accompanied by patterned grounds. The stippling on the right chair is limited solely to the bracket tips adjacent to the seat rails. The

**Fig. 1.** Detail of right chair, crest rail.

star-punched ground of the left chair is more extensive, covering most of the flat area on the brackets and continuing onto the upper knees (fig. 3). Stretchers are uncommon on chairs of this pattern. Most back legs are slender with flared feet, in the English fashion; some feet are slightly blocked, as on the left. Over-the-rail upholstery, a more expensive option than an upholstered loose seat, was popular in Massachusetts during part of the third quarter of the eighteenth century and later. More than half the examples in this group are upholstered in this manner. Economy had given way to fashion.

NGE

---

**Inscriptions or marks:** (Left) *Chiseled on front seat-rail rabbet:* "V".

**Construction:** (Left) The crest is supported on rectangular tenons at the flat-faced canted posts and splat. The crest face is flat at the center and cheeked near the tips. The carving is executed in

low relief. The crest back is flat at the center and rounded at the ends and lower center back; the center top is rounded and shallowly lobed. The flat splat is slightly canted at the edges and piercings, front to back, carved in low-relief in the upper section, and tenoned into the plinth. The plinth is hollow on the front and side faces and finished with a flattened top bead; the absence of nail holes suggests it was probably originally glued to the rear seat rail. The flat-faced canted back posts are rounded on the back surfaces, crest to seat. The rectangular tenons of the seat rail are pinned twice at the back and side back joints and once at the front and side front joints. The flat rail lip has a quarter-round bead at the outer edge. The interior frame is finished with narrow rabbets at the front and sides to support the loose-seat frame; a small, vertical, quarter-round glueblock remains at the left rear corner. The tapered rear legs are blocked at the feet on the outside surfaces. The creased knees are carved with leafage in low relief and further embellished with a star-punched ground at the bracket tops and upper leg corners. The claw feet have delicate three-knuckle toes with short nails. The knee brackets are applied with small

**Fig. 2.** Detail of left chair, crest and splat.

**Fig. 3.** Detail of left chair, left front knee carving and punchwork.

rosehead nails; ogee brackets at the side rear rails are attached with nails.

(Right) The crest is supported on rectangular tenons at the flat-faced canted posts and splat. The crest face is flat at the center and cheeked near the tips. The low-relief–carved ornament, which extends onto the splat, has a deeply stippled center ground; crescent-shape gouges accent the flanking leafage. Related leaf carving embellishes the crest ends and upper post faces. The crest back is flat at the center, rounded at the ends, and lightly chamfered at the center base; the center top is rounded and shallowly lobed. The flat splat is slightly canted at the edges and piercings, front to back, and tenoned into the rear seat rail. The three-sided plinth is hollow on the front and side faces and beaded at the top; it is not fastened to the rear seat rail. The posts are rounded on the back surfaces, crest to seat. The seat rails are joined to the posts and leg extensions with vertical rectangular tenons (pinned, on the rear faces of the back posts). Interior triangular corner blocks are secured with two rosehead nails. The tapered rectangular rear legs flare backward at the feet. The front legs are carved in low relief at the knees with incised and grooved leafage and tiny volutes. Stippling occurs at the upper tips of the knee brackets. The claws have delicate three-knuckle toes with medium-length nails; the side talons rake backward. The knee brackets are applied with single rosehead nails. The small ogee-shape brackets at the back rail and rear side rails are secured with two dome-head nails each.

**Condition:** (Left) The splat is cracked through and repaired at the top and bottom of the long, upper-left aperture. The left leg extension is cracked vertically through the front joint pin. The small right rear corner block has been restored; large triangular blocks held by two screws have been added at the front corners. A small chip is missing from the left front ball foot at the outside surface; the right ball is cracked in the same place. The loose-seat frame is upholstered.

(Right) The center base of the crest is cracked on the face where a piece broke out and was reapplied. The left crest and post joint is cracked and repaired. The splat has been restored along the right side from the top lobe and upper right aperture through the lower right aperture. A through crack occurs left of center between the upper and lower apertures. The plinth is a modern restoration. The rear leg brackets may be early replacements; both side-rear leg brackets are cracked through and reattached. The interior rear corner blocks, which are old but possibly not original, have unusual rounded forward lips on the bottom surface; the

right block has worm damage. The left rear foot has a triangular replacement piece at the inside rear corner running down to the outside rear corner. The right rear foot is cracked on the forward face from the center bottom upward toward the inside corner. The seat is upholstered over the rails.

**Dimensions:**

Left

| | | |
|---|---|---|
| H. | 37⅞ in. | 96.2 cm |
| H. (seat) | 16¾ in. | 42.5 cm |
| W. (crest) | 21⅛ in. | 53.6 cm |
| W. (seat front) | 21⅛ in. | 53.6 cm |
| W. (seat back) | 16¾ in. | 42.5 cm |
| W. (feet) | 23½ in. | 59.7 cm |
| D. (seat) | 16¼ in. | 41.3 cm |
| D. (feet) | 21¾ in. | 55.2 cm |

Right

| | | |
|---|---|---|
| H. | 38 in. | 96.5 cm |
| H. (seat) | 17⅛ in. | 43.5 cm |
| W. (crest) | 21⅝ in. | 54.9 cm |
| W. (seat front) | 21⅝ in. | 54.9 cm |
| W. (seat back) | 17 in. | 43.2 cm |
| W. (feet) | 23½ in. | 59.7 cm |
| D. (seat) | 17½ in. | 44.4 cm |
| D. (feet) | 21½ in. | 54.6 cm |

**Materials:** *Microanalysis:* (Left) Primary: mahogany. Secondary: beech (rear seat rail). (Right) Primary: mahogany. Secondary: maple (seat rails); white pine (corner blocks). *Finish:* (Left) medium reddish brown color in resin; (Right) medium dark brown color in resin. *Upholstery:* (Left and right) watered blue wool moreen; England, 1750–1800.

**Publications:** Downs, *American Furniture*, figs. 153, 154. (Left) Kirk, *American Chairs*, fig. 115. (Right) Kirk, *American Furniture*, fig. 890.

**Accession history:** (Left) Purchased for the museum by H. F. du Pont from John S. Walton, Inc., New York, 1951. (Right) Purchased for the museum by H. F. du Pont from Maurice Rubin, Colonial Antique Shop, Boston, 1951.
51.64.8, 51.77.1

---

1. Philadelphia and Rhode Island examples are in Philip H. Bradley advertisement, *Antiques* 109, no. 4 (April 1976): 670; Kirk, *American Chairs*, fig. 180.

2. Family, collector, and dealer histories are given in Jobe and Kaye, *New England Furniture*, no. 108; Morse, *Furniture of the Olden Time*, pp. 186–87; no. 66.1350, DAPC, Visual Resources Collection, Winterthur Library.

3. For plain examples, see Jobe and Kaye, *New England Furniture*, no. 108; Dean Wilson Antiques advertisement, *Antiques* 106, no. 3 (September 1974): 417; for the English prototype, see Kirk, *American Furniture*, fig. 891.

## 55 ◆ Side chair
Northeastern Massachusetts,
probably Boston
1760–90

The Gothic revival in eighteenth-century architecture and furniture design was primarily allusive rather than architecturally accurate. Thus, from the 1750s into the 1770s Gothic furniture motifs, such as pointed arches and cusps, trefoils and quatrefoils, and clustered columns, were simply interpreted using conventional chair frames. Thomas Chippendale included Gothic designs in the first and subsequent editions of the *Director*, beginning in 1754. Interest in the new style was manifest in American seating by 1760. In this design, which follows an English pattern, conventional rounded-end apertures have been gothicized with the addition of lancet tips, then stacked in two tiers to produce a delicate tracery.[1]

The double-tiered lancet splat appears to have been confined in American chair production to Massachusetts. A small number of chairs, all with similar splats framed in molded and carved, round-shouldered backs, are associated with four distinct sets of seating furniture. One set of six chairs that descended in the family of James Swan (1754–1830), a prominent Boston merchant and entrepreneur, varies from this example only in the use of straight rather than flared back feet. This chair, numbered "I" inside the seat rail, appears to be from the same set as a pair of chairs offered for sale several decades ago. Chairs from the remaining two sets, a side chair and armchair, are fashioned with straight, or Marlborough, front legs and rectangular stretchers. The straight-leg side chair, owned in Worcester at the beginning of the twentieth century, has simple, open brackets between the front legs and the seat rail and an upholstered loose seat. The armchair, which is upholstered over the

rails, descended in a Newburyport family. Of particular note, the arms are in the federal rather than Chippendale style, indicating a relatively late construction date.[2]

English chairs with splats of the illustrated pattern differ somewhat from comparable American seating. Variable features include heavier frames, serpentine seat fronts, square stretchers set diamondwise in straight-leg chairs, and more elaborate leg brackets. Some English examples have more ornate surface decoration; others are plainer than the American chair. The English design also appears to have inspired an elaborate Iberian interpretation.[3]

NGE

---

**Inscriptions or marks:** *Chiseled inside rear seat rail:* "I".

**Construction:** The crest is supported on rectangular tenons at the backward flaring posts (pinned) and splat. The face is slightly rounded and embellished with low-relief carving. The back surface is flat with rounded upper and lower edges; gouged V cuts at the lower center correspond to the three openings at the splat top. The tiny scrolls at the edge of the crest top and the apertures of the splat are formed in small cones tapered from front to back. The splat face (and adjacent crest) is modeled in low relief at the aperture tips, top and center. The side edges and piercings of the splat are canted, front to back; the base is tenoned into the plinth. The plinth, which is hollow on the face and sides and has a low top bead, is formed in one piece with the back seat rail. The post faces are molded with a serpentine crown flanked by beads; the back surfaces are rounded, crest to seat. The seat rails are joined to the post and leg extensions with rectangular tenons (pinned, twice at the back and side backs and once at the front and side fronts). The flat seat lip has a quarter-round bead at the outer edge. The interior frame is finished with narrow 3/16" rabbets at the front and sides to support the loose-seat frame; a horizontal line is incised across the inside back rail at rabbet level. The interior frame is strengthened by small triangular corner blocks; the front blocks were originally held by two small screws. Long, thin, ogee brackets at the side rear rails are tenoned into the back posts (held by the lower pins) and nailed to the rails; the inner edges are chamfered. The tapered rear legs are rectangular in section and flare backward at the feet. The front knee brackets were originally held by two screws apiece; the inside edges are chamfered. The knees are creased. The claws have knobby, two-knuckle toes with medium-length nails; the side toes rake backward.

**Condition:** The splat is cracked through at the left between the upper and lower apertures. The left seat rail has a 5" horizontal crack from the front joint backward. Many of the seat-rail joints are repinned. A long vertical crack on the inside face of the right back post extends above and below the back rail. The interior rear corner blocks are modern; the front blocks have been renailed. The right front knee is cracked vertically left of the crease; the left leg is cracked vertically on the outside face. The loose-seat frame is modern.

**Dimensions:**

| | | |
|---|---|---|
| H. | 37⅞ in. | 96.2 cm |
| H. (seat) | 16¾ in. | 42.5 cm |
| W. (crest) | 21⁷⁄₁₆ in. | 54.4 cm |
| W. (seat front) | 22⅜ in. | 56.8 cm |
| W. (seat back) | 17¾ in. | 45.1 cm |
| W. (feet) | 23⅝ in. | 60.0 cm |
| D. (seat) | 18½ in. | 47.0 cm |
| D. (feet) | 22¼ in. | 56.5 cm |

**Materials:** *Microanalysis:* Primary: mahogany. Secondary: white pine group (front glueblocks). *Finish:* variegated medium reddish brown color in resin.

**Publications:** Downs, *American Furniture*, fig. 155.

**Accession history:** Museum purchase from Charles Woolsey Lyon, New York, 1951. 54.532

---

1. Thomas Chippendale, *The Gentleman and Cabinet-Maker's Director* (London: By the author, 1754); (2d ed., London: By the author, 1755); (3d ed., London: By the author, 1762).

2. Chairs from the set of 6 are in the collections of the Museum of Fine Arts, Boston, the Yale University Art Gallery, and a private owner; Randall, *American Furniture*, no. 155; Kane, *Three Hundred Years*, no. 111. The pair is in *American Antiques from Israel Sack Collection*, 10 vols. (Washington, D.C.: Highland House, ca. 1969–), 2:350; for the side chair, see Morse, *Furniture of the Olden Time*, pp. 193–94; for the armchair, see Peter Benes, *Old-Town and the Waterside* (Newburyport, Mass.: Historical Society of Old Newbury, 1986), p. 163.

3. For English chairs, see Kirk, *American Furniture*, figs. 883–85, 887; Rosenbach Co. advertisement, *Antiques* 11, no. 6 (June 1927): 443; for Iberian chairs, see Hinckley, *Directory*, ill. 265; Helen Comstock, "Bicentennial of the Director," *Antiques* 67, no. 3 (March 1955): 227.

## 56 ◆ **Side chair** (one of a pair)
### Northeastern Massachusetts
### 1762–85

This chair and its mate, probably once part of a larger set, are the only examples of this Gothic-arch splat located to date. The absence of even a small body of related American work speaks to the rarity of the pattern. Exact British examples are also unknown, although an elaborately carved side chair with a related splat also based on a plate from Chippendale's *Director* is at Arundel Castle, Sussex.[1]

The back component of this chair is a faithful copy of a Chippendale design except for the supporting plinth; a plain bead and hemispherical-shape cutout are substituted for gadrooning and C scrolls (fig. 1). The slightly more rectilinear back frame was common in Massachusetts, although the carver included both the central ruffled leaf and beaded crest edges of the engraving. The leaf carving of the knees has been executed in the typical Massachusetts style with incised veining,

cross gouges, and a finely stippled background (fig. 2). The stuffed seat frame originally may have been brass nailed to better finish and define the lower edges.

Although genealogical information on the splat back of the mate to this chair provides documentation of family descent (fig. 3), actual identification remains elusive. When that splat was cracked along the left side, perhaps about 1890, three small wooden cross pieces were added to the back for reinforcement. Initials and dates, which chronicle ownership from 1791 to 1890, are stamped into the wooden surfaces. Unfortunately, the owners of the chairs are not further identified. The splat repair is unusual and the documentation method rare in the study of American seating furniture. Family histories generally are confined to paper labels or inked/penciled inscriptions on the bare wood of the seat frame.

*NGE*

---

**Construction:** The crest is supported on rectangular tenons at the flat-faced canted posts and splat.

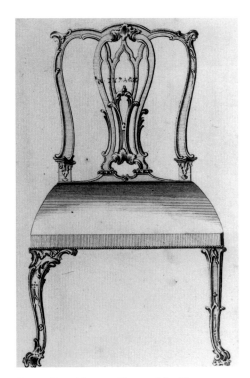

Fig. 1. From Thomas Chippendale, *The Gentleman and Cabinet-Maker's Director* (3d ed., London: By the author, 1762), pl. 14 right.

The flat face is slightly cheeked at the ends and embellished with low-relief carving. The back surface is flat at the center, rounded at the center top and ends, and rounded-chamfered at the center base. The small C-scroll tips that project beyond the crest and splat edges form small tapered cones, front to back. The splat face is carved and beaded in low relief; the side edges and piercings are canted, front to back. The base is tenoned into the rear seat rail. The three-sided plinth is marked by a hemispherical break at the center. The face and sides are hollow, the large, two-part top bead overhangs the edges, and the ends are nailed to the rear seat rail. The back posts are rounded on the rear surface, crest to seat. The seat rails are joined to the posts and leg extensions with rectangular tenons (double-

pinned, back and side back). The interior frame is strengthened with four triangular corner blocks, each held with four rosehead nails. Small, side-rear ogee brackets tenon into the rear legs (pinned) and are nailed once. The back legs, which are round in section, flare at the squared feet. The creased front knees are carved with leafage in low relief surrounded by fine punchwork. The plain, V-shape reserves at the knee centers are detailed with punchwork borders of large, spaced dots. The knee brackets were originally glued in place. The claws have three-knuckle toes with medium-length nails.

**Condition:** Nail holes appear at the upper back edge and bottom surface of the rear seat rail and at the outside post faces adjacent to the side rails where upholstery was once attached. Reinforcing nails have been added to three interior corner blocks. A screw secures the right side-rear rail return, and wire nails reinforce some knee brackets. There are surface losses to the finish.

**Dimensions:**

| | | |
|---|---|---|
| H. | 36³/4 in. | 93.3 cm |
| H. (seat) | 16¹/4 in. | 41.3 cm |
| W. (crest) | 19³/8 in. | 49.2 cm |
| W. (seat front) | 21¹/2 in. | 54.6 cm |
| W. (seat back) | 16³/4 in. | 42.5 cm |
| W. (feet) | 23 in. | 58.4 cm |
| D. (seat) | 17³/4 in. | 45.1 cm |
| D. (feet) | 20⁷/8 in. | 53.0 cm |

**Materials:** *Microanalysis:* Primary: mahogany. Secondary: soft maple group (side seat rails); birch (rear seat rail); white pine group (corner blocks). *Finish:* medium light to medium dark brown color in resin. *Upholstery:* blue silk taffeta of floral pattern brocaded on a compound weave; France, 1730–60.

**Accession history:** Purchased by H. F. du Pont from John S. Walton, Inc., New York, 1952. Bequest of H. F. du Pont, 1969.
65.1624.1

---

1. For the British example, see Macquoid and Edwards, *Dictionary,* 1:280, fig. 172; the British chair is a copy of pl. 14 left in Thomas Chippendale, *The Gentleman and Cabinet-Maker's Director* (1762; reprint 3d ed., New York: Dover Publications, 1966).

Fig. 2. Detail, right front knee.

Fig. 3. Detail, rear surface of side-chair splat, eastern Massachusetts, 1762–85. (Winterthur 65.1624.2)

## 57 ◆ Side chair
Boston or Salem, Massachusetts
1765–85

Few chairs without documentation to a maker can be dated as accurately as this one. In 1765 a design for a "Parlor Chair" with an identical splat embellished by carving was published in Robert Manwaring's *Cabinet and Chair-Maker's Real Friend and Companion* (fig. 1). On January 1, 1767, the *Boston News-Letter* announced the sale of this title by storekeepers Cox and Berry, who described the contents of the volume as "upwards of 100 new and beautiful Designs of all sorts of chairs." This promotion, modified from the book's title page, apparently intrigued one or more area craftsmen. Perhaps within a few months, the first of three or more sets of chairs in this pattern was made for speculation or to customer order. The most faithful copies of the Manwaring splat, and thus the most ornamental, consist of a partial set of chairs at the Metropolitan Museum of Art and a single example that retains its original linen undercover and stuffing of hair and grass. One set of seven, which includes this chair, and one or more additional groups have plain backs except for modeled volutes, although the knee carving has been retained.[1]

Recent comprehensive studies of mid eighteenth-century Boston furniture, which identify the work of a number of highly skilled, frequently anonymous carvers and the work of several lesser craftsmen, indicate that the carving on this chair is mechanical and less modeled than the best examples (fig. 2). The leafy forms on the leg tops are executed in a gouged technique composed mainly of closely spaced, thin grooves. Small, triangular reserves below the seat corners are subtly defined by borders of punchwork triangles. The feet are notable for their long-nailed rear talons, which are closely related to those in No. 53. The clean, flowing lines of the back

legs are common in Boston work and have their prototypes in British chairmaking. Molded surfaces, such as those on the back posts, appear on some of the best Boston carved chairs of the revolutionary period. Here, they seem somewhat pretentious flanking a basically unadorned splat. Does the plain splat represent a customer's option to economize, or was the set of chairs already framed and standing in the cabinetmaker's shop ready for upholstery when a patron stopped in and decided to buy? A second set of chairs, represented by an example at Colonial Williamsburg, appears to differ from the set represented here only in the knee carving. The leaves are better modeled, a different punched figure borders the reserves, and fine stippling surrounds the leaf tips. It is possible that both sets of chairs originated in the same shop, with the carved work subcontracted to different workmen, and both sets could have been produced specifically for

speculation. The highly carved set represented by the Metropolitan Museum of Art chairs, on the other hand, was bespoke work. Because this pattern appeared nowhere else in America or, apparently, in Britain, and since the chairs are relatively few in number, the suggestion that they were the product of a single enterprising craftsman is a viable one.[2]

The over-the-rail upholstery common to all chairs with this splat represented a substantial expense, especially in addition to the mahogany construction. The chair at Colonial Williamsburg, which has been photographed in the bare seat frame, presumably serves as a model for the rest. The front corners, formed by extending the legs, are finished with small, triangular peaks above the rail tops (see No. 30, fig. 2). The additional wood of the peaks helped to protect the delicate mortise joints from tack punctures. The upholstery, which is easily crushed from use, was also stabilized, since

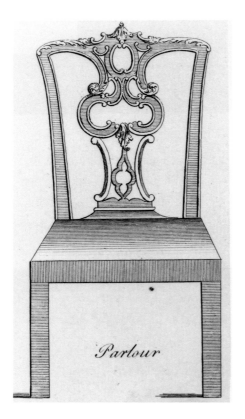

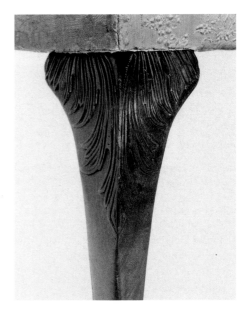

Fig. 2. Detail, left front knee carving.

the peaks anchored stiff grass rolls that were tacked to the rail tops to provide shape and rigidity. The upholsterer was guided by the peaks in gauging the stuffing height and the backward slope, or fall-in, from the front rail to the removable three-sided plinth. A distinct line of nail holes along the lower rail edges, each hole surrounded by a circle, indicates that the finish cover was embellished with a row of ornamental brass nails. Most chairs of this pattern had small brackets in the angles between the side seat rails and the back legs; many are now covered with upholstery fabric, although this may not have been the original intent. The brackets of this chair are tenoned into the back posts, which suggests that the framer recognized the vulnerability of a plain glue joint to secure an exposed mahogany bracket when upholstery is closely nailed along the lower rail edge. Of further note is the slightly recessed outside surface of the back seat rail in relation to the flanking posts, a condition noted in a similar chair at the Museum of Fine Arts, Boston. Here, the wood of the back rail is birch; there it is pine. Speculation is that a thin veneer of mahogany originally covered these surfaces.[3]

One chair in this group descended in the Dane family of Andover; another was handed down in the Pickman-Loring family, the first owner identified as Clark Gayton Pickman of Salem, who died in 1781. The Winterthur chair is the only chair of its set of seven that is inscribed. "Bottumd June 1773/ by WVE Salem" appears inside the back rail, but the upholsterer has not been identified in records.[4] Presumably, the notation was made when the chair was first upholstered rather than during subsequent work.

NGE

---

**Inscriptions or marks:** *Inverted on inside front rail:* "Bottumd June 1773/ by WVE Salem" in ink.

**Construction:** The crest is supported on rectangular tenons at the canted posts and on partially exposed rectangular tenons at the splat. The face is slightly rounded, with a bead scribed along the top edge that continues down the outside post faces; the flat back is rounded at the top and chamfered at the bottom. The splat face is flat, modeled only at the volutes. The edges and piercings are canted, front to back, and the base is tenoned into the back rail. The back-post faces are molded with a serpentine crown flanked by beads; the rounded back surfaces are squared slightly at the crest. The three-sided plinth is hollow on the front and side faces, finished with a top bead, and nailed to the back rail. The rails are joined to the front posts and leg extensions with vertical rectangular tenons (pinned, back and

side rails). Shallow ogee returns at the rear corners of the side rails are tenoned into the rear legs. The triangular interior corner blocks are cut with the grain oriented horizontally. The rounded rear legs are square in section and flare backward at the base in blocked, rectangular feet. The creased-knee cabriole front legs are supported on domed ball feet with slim, three-knuckle claws and long nails; the shorter rear toes relate closely to those in No. 53. The flattened, low-relief knee carving, which is accented by incised and channeled veining, has a plain-surface V-shape reserve at the center top bordered by a line of small punchwork triangles. The knee brackets are attached with internal screws, the holes plugged.

**Condition:** The splat back is marked by minor nicks and blemishes. The left end of the plinth is split due to nailing. All seat rail tops are cracked and split from successive nailings; the bottom edges are punctured by many nail holes. The side-rail returns at the back posts are considerably defaced and deteriorated on the bottom and interior surfaces from over-upholstery. The back posts are cracked at the side rail pins; a third pin has been added at the

right side. The splat has been chamfered slightly at the lower back surface to form a flush joint with the back rail, which is slightly inset from the adjacent posts. The surface, probably once veneered, is now refinished and colored to disguise the alteration. Modern screws and nails secure the seat blocks. The wooden plugs of the knee brackets are new. The finish on the splat face is considerably lighter than that on other parts of the chair, due to cleaning or wear.

**Dimensions:**

| | | |
|---|---|---|
| H. | 37 1/2 in. | 95.3 cm |
| H. (seat) | 17 1/2 in. | 44.4 cm |
| W. (crest) | 19 1/2 in. | 49.5 cm |
| W. (seat front) | 22 1/2 in. | 57.1 cm |
| W. (seat back) | 17 1/4 in. | 43.8 cm |
| W. (feet) | 23 3/4 in. | 60.3 cm |
| D. (seat) | 17 3/4 in. | 45.1 cm |
| D. (feet) | 21 1/4 in. | 54.0 cm |

**Materials:** *Microanalysis:* Primary: mahogany. Secondary: maple (front seat rail); birch (side and rear seat rails); white pine (seat-frame blocks). *Finish:* medium to medium dark brown color in resin. *Upholstery:* gold floral pattern-on-pattern, compound-weave silk; Europe, 1770–1800.

**Exhibitions:** "Change and Choice in Early American Decorative Arts," IBM Gallery of Science and Art, New York, December 12, 1989–February 3, 1990.

**Publications:** Kirk, *American Chairs*, fig. 113.

**Accession history:** Museum purchase from Israel Sack, New York, 1956.
56.52

---

1. *The Boston News-Letter* advertisement is transcribed in Dow, *Arts and Crafts in New England*, pp. 222–23. The text on Manwaring's title page actually reads: "upwards of One Hundred new and useful Designs for all Sorts of Chairs." One of the Metropolitan Museum of Art chairs is in Heckscher, *American Furniture*, cat. no. 84. The chair with original stuffing is in the Massachusetts Historical Society, Boston; see Mary Ellen Hayward Yehia, "Ornamental Carving on Boston Furniture of the Chippendale Style," in *Boston Furniture*, fig. 152.

2. Yehia, "Ornamental Carving," and Luke Beckerdite, "Carving Practices in Eighteenth-Century Boston," in *New England Furniture*; for British chairs, see Kirk, *American Furniture*, figs. 1028, 1029; for the Colonial Williamsburg chair, see Greenlaw, *New England Furniture*, no. 55. In Boston, where specialization was common within the furniture trade, the shop master often found it cheaper to commission carved work outside the shop than maintain a specialist on the premises; see Beckerdite, "Carving Practices," p. 138.

3. Robert F. Trent and Michael Podmaniczky provided insights on upholstery and construction techniques. See also Wallace Gusler, LeRoy Graves, and Mark Anderson, "The Technique of Eighteenth-Century Over-the-Rail-Upholstery," in Cooke, *Upholstery*, p. 90.

4. The Dane family chair is in Greenlaw, *New England Furniture*, no. 55; for the Pickman family chair, see Heckscher, *American Furniture*, cat. no. 13. Information on the set of 7 chairs is in a letter from Harold Sack to Charles F. Montgomery, July 12, 1956, folder 56.52, Registration Office, Winterthur.

## 58 ◆ Side chair
**Boston, Massachusetts**
**1760–85**

---

Splats with diamond-centered figure eights were common in British chairmaking during the third quarter of the eighteenth century. Although a few examples were produced in Pennsylvania and the South, the American center for interpretation of this general pattern was eastern Massachusetts, principally Boston. Several chairs have family histories that link them to that urban center. Judging by the body of furniture that survives, the design was popular. Like the owl's-eye splat, the pattern was interpreted as a double-back settee and a roundabout chair.[1]

The size of the group, about twenty chairs, facilitates a survey of basic features and customer options. With one exception, the splat surface modeling is the same throughout: the drapery swag is formed by two curved channels; the centered swag bead and lower bead are rounded; the central and lower central straps are delineated in low relief; and the diamond points are cushioned and rounded backward. The earliest chairs stylistically are those with scored pad feet elevated on cushioned pads. Plain crests, posts, and knees are the usual accompaniments of pad feet, although one example has stop-fluted back posts. Similar posts were introduced to uncarved chairs with claw feet. Frequently, chairs with two or more plain elements (crests, posts, or knees) are further linked through a subtle splat feature—pairs of small, projecting, uncarved scrolls flanking the top drapery and terminating the base curves above the plinth, as illustrated in this chair. In British chairmaking, small, dependent, wooden tassels, like that beneath the drapery, are sometimes supported by the scrolls flanking the drapery. Some American chairs have scroll-tipped knee brackets that visually integrate the upper and

lower structures. The splat curves are also echoed in the sharply creased knees. Although the urn-style splat and simply carved drapery swag suggest that this pattern originated in postwar neoclassical design, a solid splat of similar profile appears in Philadelphia Queen Anne work, and both Philadelphia and English chairs with carved drapery were in the prerevolutionary furniture market.[2]

A substantial number of chairs with diamond-centered figure-eight splats are carved with leaflike ornament that covers the crest arch and the knees; occasionally one of the two areas is plain. Stop-fluted back posts and small splat scrolls are generally absent from these chairs. The block-and-columnar–turned stretcher system, common to many Boston chairs (see No. 52 left), is present only in one carved example. Several chairs have solid crests carved with fanlike leafy ornament similar to that in No. 54 left instead of an oval aperture and drapery. The leafy pendant that replaces the swag relates to the crest ornament of the chairs in No. 52 but is smaller and more restrained.[3]

The asymmetrical knee carving of this chair is distinctive (fig. 1). The center front, diagonal C scroll with gougework border, ruffled leafy arc, long acanthus pendant, and flanking elements is a highlight of Boston carved ornament in the prerevolutionary period and may be the work of a single artisan. The same pattern appears on a sizable and varied group of furniture, consisting of two matched settees, a card table, three armchairs, and nineteen side chairs representing three splat patterns. The highly stylized hairy-paw feet of this chair can be seen on several side chairs with similar splats as well as five Boston chairs with "fringed" and pierced splats.[4]

The asymmetrical knee carving was copied directly and with reasonable fidelity from an English prototype. An armchair at Winterthur (fig. 2) was in a Brookline, Massachusetts, house when photographed about 1900. A side chair with a similar splat at the Museum of Fine Arts, Boston, was reputedly brought to

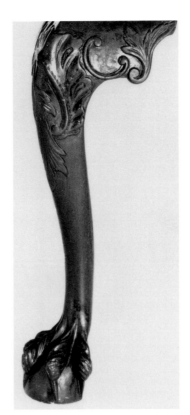

**Fig. 1.** Detail, right front leg.

America about 1750, where it was owned by William Phillips of Boston. These English chairs were also the inspiration for the hairy-paw feet of this chair, although the American carved work is an interpretation rather than a copy. Also noteworthy are the stop-fluted back posts of the English chairs, since stop fluting is present on several examples in the American group.[5]

In reviewing the eclectic combinations of features that appear in the diamond-back chairs and in the whole body of Boston seating with flared rear feet (Nos. 53–58), it becomes fairly obvious that the city's chairmaker-entrepreneurs were consciously developing new directions in marketing techniques. While not inexpensive to purchase, mahogany, flared-foot, stretcherless chairs were more economical to produce, in terms of material and labor, than the heavier block-and-turned–stretcher chairs (see Nos. 50 left, 52 left). Splat designs range from the unique (see Nos. 53, 56) to the popular, shown here and including the owl's-eye examples (see No. 31). Ornament frequently is spare; further embellishment is provided by molded back posts. When additional carved ornament is present, it generally is more extensive on the crest than the splat; the front knees may be carved or plain (see Nos. 54 right, 55), although carved knees also appear on chairs with plain backs

(see No. 57). In the chair shown here the overly elaborate knees and feet seem out of character with the plain back components. The same supports are better integrated in another Boston example embellished with a carved splat and crest tips and stop-fluted back posts.[6]

What is to be learned from making these comparisons and exploring the range of options? Whose choices do the selections represent—the chairmakers' or the consumers'? Without a comprehensive body of Boston chairmaking records for the second half of the eighteenth century (none of which are known to exist), definite answers cannot be framed. It is possible, however, to speculate. Most components, such as seat rails, back posts, and front legs, were reasonably interchangeable. Crest pieces were designed to fit either broad or narrow splat tops. Some chairmakers probably stockpiled finished or semifinished components in moderate quantity for quick assembly and surface finishing to facilitate and expedite customer orders. The practice represented a level of retail activity that lay somewhere between bespoken work, the prevailing custom of undertaking work from beginning to end only upon receipt of an order, and warehouse merchandising, which in America was primarily an early nineteenth-century development. Boston stretcherless seating as a body of furniture is likely a reflection of both customer choice and craft innovation. Examples with eclectic combinations of elements may represent customer choices dictated by component availability.

*NGE*

**Inscriptions or marks:** *Chiseled on inside face of rear seat rail:* "VII". *On deteriorated green and black, early twentieth-century paper label glued to inside rear seat rail:* "AYRE & CO.'S/ [Have]rhill, [Me]dford and Bosto[n]/ EXPRES[S]/ 36 Court Square, [?] K[?]Y AND 107 ARCH STRE[ETS,]/ BOSTON".

**Construction:** The crest is supported on rectangular tenons at the flared posts and splat. The flat face is

**Fig. 2.** Armchair, England, 1750–70. Mahogany, beech; H. 37 1/4 in. (94.6 cm), W. (seat) 25 1/2 in. (64.8 cm), D. (seat) 20 1/2 in. (52.1 cm). (Winterthur 51.80)

carved at the tips; the flat back surface is deeply rounded, top and bottom, including the pierced arch. The flat splat face is modeled at the drapery channels, the central strap crossings, and the beads below the drapery and above the plinth. The pointed central diamond tips are cushioned and rounded backward. The splat edges and piercings are round-canted, front to back; the base is tenoned into the plinth. The plinth is hollow on the front and sides, finished with a top bead, and glued to the rear seat rail. The back posts are flat on the front surface and rounded on the back, crest to seat. The shallow seat rails are joined to the back posts and front leg extensions with rectangular tenons (pinned). The flat top lip is finished with a quarter-round bead at the outside edge. The interior frame has narrow rabbets at the front and sides to support the loose-seat frame and triangular blocks at the corners. The rear seat rail is veneered on the outside face. Long, slim ogee brackets at the rear corners of the side rails are tenoned into the back posts (pinned, inside and out) and also secured with screws. The inner bracket edges are narrowly chamfered, and the outside lower corners are marked with small, triangular, spooned chisel cuts. The tapered rectangular legs flare backward at the feet. The front knees are carved in low to medium-high relief; two screws secure the knee brackets, which are deeply chamfered on the inside edges. The feet are carved as hairy claws with five toes, the carved work extending onto the back faces.

**Condition:** The right crest-post joint is cracked at the back, and the crest tip is repaired with a small facing piece extending from the inside top to the front face. The left crest tip is cracked and repaired. The central drapery is cracked through and repaired with a spline. Long cracks occur in the left seat rail

at the joints (including the bracket) and at the center through to the inside surface. The right rear corner bracket and the rear seat rail are cracked on the bottom surfaces. The right front leg extension is cracked vertically near the corner. The four interior corner blocks, which are held with screws and wire nails, are replacements or additions, although three probably date 1880–1920. The loose-seat frame is modern.

**Dimensions:**

| | | |
|---|---|---|
| H. | 36 7/8 in. | 93.6 cm |
| H. (seat) | 16 5/8 in. | 41.9 cm |
| W. (crest) | 20 1/2 in. | 52.1 cm |
| W. (seat front) | 21 5/8 in. | 54.9 cm |
| W. (seat back) | 16 1/2 in. | 41.9 cm |
| W. (feet) | 23 1/2 in. | 59.7 cm |
| D. (seat) | 17 1/2 in. | 44.4 cm |
| D. (feet) | 22 in. | 55.8 cm |

**Materials:** *Microanalysis:* Primary: mahogany; mahogany veneer (outside rear seat rail). Secondary: white oak group (rear seat rail). *Finish:* medium reddish brown color in resin. *Upholstery:* gold silk damask; Europe, 1740–70.

**Publications:** Downs, *American Furniture*, fig. 151. Mary Ellen Hayward Yehia, "Ornamental Carving on Boston Furniture of the Chippendale Style," in *Boston Furniture*, p. 211.

**Accession history:** Purchased by H. F. du Pont from Ginsburg and Levy, New York, 1950. Gift of H. F. du Pont, 1952. 52.242

---

1. For British examples, see Kirk, *American Chairs*, fig. 74; Cescinsky, *English Furniture*, 2:183; Hinckley, *Directory*, ills. 119, 120; Robert Wemyss Symonds Collection, DAPC, Visual Resources Collection, Winterthur Library; for Pennsylvania and southern examples, see Kane, *Three Hundred Years*, nos. 99, 101; Kirk, *American Chairs*, fig. 224. A chair said to have been bought at 1 of the sales of John Hancock's household furnishings is now in the Rhode Island School of Design; see Monkhouse and Michie, *American Furniture*, cat. 113. For a pair of chairs with the same provenance, see Robert W. Skinner, "Fine Americana" (June 5, 1993), lot 50. A chair reputedly given by John Hancock to a friend is now in the Daughters of the American Revolution Museum; see Elisabeth Donaghy Garrett, "American Furniture in the DAR Museum," *Antiques* 109, no. 4 (April 1976): 752, fig. 6. A set of 6 chairs was originally owned by Joseph Willard, president of Harvard College (1781–1804); see Parke-Bernet Galleries, "Important Early American Furniture and Silver: Collection of George M. Curtis" (May 14–15, 1948), lot 273. For roundabout chairs, see Teina Baumstone advertisement, *Antiques* 99, no. 1 (January 1971): 44; Jobe and Kaye, *New England Furniture*, no. 115.

2. For scored pad-foot chairs, see Jobe and Kaye, *New England Furniture*, p. 393; *American Antiques from Israel Sack Collection*, 10 vols. (Washington, D.C.: Highland House, ca. 1969– ), 9:2478; for a plain claw-foot chair, see Heckscher, *American Furniture*, cat. no. 11; for a British chair with pendent tassels, see Lockwood, *Colonial Furniture*, 2:89; for solid urn splats and drapery-carved ornament, see Kirk, *American Chairs*, figs. 47, 74, 75.

3. The carved example with block-and-columnar–turned stretchers is in the Henry Ford Museum; see Kirk, *American Chairs*, fig. 118. For a solid-crest chair, see Kane, *Three Hundred Years*, no. 100.

4. Heckscher, *American Furniture*, cat. no. 83 (settee); Luke Beckerdite, "Carving Practices in Eighteenth-Century Boston," in *New England Furniture*, p. 136 (card table); Kane, *Three Hundred Years*, nos. 97, 98 (armchair, side chair); *American Antiques from Sack Collection*, 4:1080–81 (side chair). A "fringed"-splat chair descended in the Marquand family of Boston; see Sotheby's, "Important American Furniture and Related Decorative Arts" (February 1, 1991), lot 771. A dining table now at Chipstone has related, although not identical feet; see Rodriguez Roque, *American Furniture*, no. 135. Of closer pattern are the feet on a desk labeled by Benjamin Frothingham of Charlestown, Mass., at Historic Deerfield; see Fales, *Furniture of Historic Deerfield*, fig. 464.

5. Identification of the English armchair in fig. 2 as being in the Beck family house in Brookline, Mass., based on a photograph of ca. 1900, is in Barry A. Greenlaw to Charles F. Hummel, December 17, 1975, folder 51.80, Registration Office, Winterthur. The dealer who sold the chair to Winterthur purchased it from the estate of Frederick Beck about 1951. The English side chair is in Museum of Fine Arts, Boston, *Paul Revere's Boston, 1735–1818* (Boston: By the museum, 1975), p. 50. Probate records from the 1760s and 1770s provide documentation of the use of English seating furniture in Boston households; John Spooner, Esq., and Edward Clarke estate inventories, 1765 and 1771, Suffolk County Probate Court, Boston (microfilm, Downs collection).

6. For an owl's-eye-pattern chair with flared rear feet, see Greenlaw, *New England Furniture*, no. 54. The better-integrated design similar to this chair is in *American Antiques from Sack Collection*, 4:1080–81.

## 59 ◆ Side chair
Portsmouth, New Hampshire
1760–90

This chair, a recognized Portsmouth pattern, is one of a partial set of three (two now privately owned), all of which retain the original leather seat covers, stuffing, and brass nailing. The crest forms an unusual profile, combining angular, low-arched ends with a depressed center section. The splat is a plain, tapered board pierced with vertical slots. Virtually identical crests crown the backs of a sizable number of turned vernacular chairs and a few joined examples constructed in New London County, Connecticut, where the common splat was an inverted baluster with a flared neck and base (fig. 1). These chairs were in the market by 1770 and perhaps as early as the late 1760s; Norwich was the local chairmaking center.[1]

Studying chairs framed with this crest provokes two obvious questions. The first has been addressed only in a cursory manner; the second has been ignored: What was the design source for this atypical, angular crest? What was the relationship between the seating furniture produced in Portsmouth and in New London County? The rectilinearity of the angular-crest pattern has been likened to Chinese design, and indeed there are parallels of a modified type. A related profile of inverted form is sometimes employed in the aprons, and occasionally in the stretchers, of Chinese tables of varying size and height and also in stands, stools, and couches; even Chinese lanterns are occasionally framed with members of this shape. Chinese chairs are frequently constructed with horizontal elements of raised-and-recessed profile that form aprons beneath seats and foot rests. A few chairs have slim, sticklike crests of the

same silhouette. The raised central sections of these cross pieces (which have a recessed profile that relates to this chair when inverted) are generally hollowed in a rounded, upward slope and curved laterally, while the end sections are slightly cheeked on the forward faces. This basic lateral crest curve was adapted from Chinese design for English seating in the new "Queen Anne" style in the early eighteenth century. The first English chairs framed with angular, depressed-center crests relate well to the eastern prototypes. In the manner of the Chinese models, the backs are rectilinear: the crests are square-cornered (but without pointed projections) and, like the back posts, have a slim, rounded, tubular appearance; the splats are straight sided and usually contoured in the side profile.[2]

The same lateral crest curve was introduced to the formal joined chair in America, where Boston was an important center that influenced furniture design in the communities and regions surrounding it, including southern New Hampshire. The early, shell-less Queen Anne profile (see Nos. 8, 11) was the basic prototype for the new angular figure of the Portsmouth chair, although at least one local craftsman had direct knowledge of the English early eighteenth-century depressed-center crest pattern, probably from work experience in England. Henry Golden, a London upholsterer, is known to have arrived in Portsmouth in 1763, and Robert Harrold, a cabinetmaker, followed about 1765. They were just two representatives of a small group of immigrant woodworkers in the community. Further innovation introduced the beaklike crest tips more in keeping with the rectilinear profiles of Chippendale-style design. It is perhaps cogent to observe that the new top line is almost exactly duplicated in the Queen Anne crest when standing behind the chair and looking down on the top piece. The figure

**Fig. 1.** Side chair, New London County, Conn., probably Norwich, 1770–80. Maple, yellow poplar; H. 37¹/₄ in. (94.6 cm), W. (seat) 21¹/₄ in. (54 cm), D. (seat) 16³/₈ in. (41.6 cm). (Connecticut Historical Society, Hartford)

forms a hollow center and raised ends, all defined by sharp ridges (fig. 2).[3]

The slotted, or fretted, splat accompanying the angular Portsmouth chair crest has direct prototypes in English design. A small, double–chair-back settee with splats of this type is known to have furnished the Boston home of Josiah Quincy, Sr., from about 1748, when the newly wealthy merchant purchased the long seat in England. The American adaptation, which is supported on Marlborough-type front legs, was probably in the local market by the 1760s. On occasion, local vernacular seating was also framed with the Portsmouth crest and a solid, tapered splat. As appropriate in inexpensive seating, the bottoms of these chairs are rushed, and the front legs and stretcher are turned. Carved Spanish feet sometimes complete the design. Tapered splats, some carved, some unpierced, were also reasonably popular with Virginia and coastal North Carolina chairmakers and consumers.[4]

The unusual nature of the angular crest precludes the possibility that New London County chairmakers developed their design independent of the Portsmouth model. Given the more advanced state of the furniture craft in Portsmouth during the 1760s and the known size and scope of the coastal and overseas furniture trade from the Piscataqua district (Portsmouth), there is little doubt that influence flowed in a southerly direction. Figures available from British customs' records from January 5, 1768, to January 5, 1773, show that 4,145 chairs were exported from the

**Fig. 2.** Detail of No. 10 left, profile of crest from above at rear.

Piscataqua district, but few chairs entered the same port as inward cargo. Chairs were shipped to destinations all along the North American coast and to the islands of the Caribbean. Some chairs undoubtedly entered the port of New London at the mouth of the Thames River, about twelve miles downstream from Norwich. Fragmentary customs' records for New London account for 113 chair imports from 1768 to 1773. Only half that number was exported during the same period. The importation or venture sale of just one set of Portsmouth angular-crest chairs at the Connecticut port would have been sufficient to stimulate local interest. It was the Connecticut vernacular seating trade that benefited most from the new design. Retaining the angular top piece and baluster splat of the joined chair (see fig. 1), area chairmakers substituted turned uprights and braces and introduced a rush seat.[5]

Leather seems to have been the popular covering for Portsmouth chairs with angular crests. Although the dark brown cover of this chair is considerably deteriorated and the stuffing somewhat collapsed, the basic plan of

the original seat remains intact. The webbing inside the seat frame has been replaced; however, the initial pattern of two crosswise and two front-to-back webs is indicated by light markings on the bottom of the original, deteriorated sackcloth. Probably during the late nineteenth century, the decorative brass-head nails were brightened with a coat of gilt paint, which has a granular appearance; some of the finish was slopped onto the surrounding leather. The survival of these original fittings provides important documentation for better understanding and interpreting eighteenth-century household furnishings.[6]

*NGE*

---

**Construction:** The crest is supported on rectangular tenons at the canted post tops (pinned) and splat. The rear crest surface has a ¹/₄" chamfer along the bottom edge; the top edge, beginning at the post tops, is sharply rounded. The thin splat, which is flat on the face and flush with the crest front, is deeply inset at the upper back. The side edges and slots are canted, front to back, except across the center back, where the slot tips are gouged with thumbprint depressions, and at the lower back, where the slot

**Fig. 3.** Detail of No. 59, rear surface of splat.

ends are channeled to the plinth (fig. 3). The splat base tenons into the plinth, which is hollow on the front and side faces, finished with a top bead, and nailed to the back rail. The rear post corners are chamfered from crest to seat on the inside and from crest to floor on the outside. The rails are joined to the posts and front leg extensions with rectangular tenons (pins are visible at the back and side back). The back legs are sawed with two angles on the forward faces. The front corners of the feet are chamfered, the interior chamfers extending to the upper leg angles. The front legs are almost square, with beads at the outside front corners and chamfers at the inside back corners. The stretchers are joined to the legs with vertical rectangular tenons (pinned, except the front). A quarter-round bead finishes the outside upper edges of all stretchers.

**Condition:** The post return at the left end of the crest is cracked horizontally across the forward and inside faces; the right return is cracked vertically on the inside face. Minor nicks and blemishes mark the back of the crest. A small chip is missing from the splat back at the top of the upper right slot. The rear surface of the left post has a long shallow, vertical gouge (smoothed) at and below seat level, which is accompanied by many small horizontal cracks, possibly due to imperfections in the wood. Minor cracks also occur along the lower surface of the rear stretcher, and long and short cracks mark the inside and lower surfaces of the right stretcher. A small knot has fallen out of the lower inside surface of the front stretcher near the right end. The beads embellishing the outside upper edges of the stretchers are almost worn away on the front and right braces, except at the ends. The dark brown-colored leather seat cover is original, as are the linen sackcloth and stuffing. The webbing has

been replaced. The leather is deteriorated: fine cracks cover the entire surface; severe cracks are present through the center; and a patch is in place above the left front leg. Several of the original brass nails are missing or replaced; gilt paint was applied at a later date.

**Dimensions:**

| | | |
|---|---|---|
| H. | 36³/4 in. | 93.4 cm |
| H. (seat) | 17¹/4 in. | 43.8 cm |
| W. (crest) | 18³/4 in. | 47.6 cm |
| W. (seat front) | 21¹/4 in. | 54.0 cm |
| W. (seat back) | 15³/4 in. | 40.0 cm |
| W. (feet) | 19³/4 in. | 50.2 cm |
| D. (seat) | 16⁵/8 in. | 42.2 cm |
| D. (feet) | 21¹/4 in. | 54.0 cm |

**Materials:** *Microanalysis:* Primary: cherry. Secondary: birch (rear seat rail); soft maple group (front seat rail). *Finish:* medium light yellowish to reddish brown color in resin (not original).

**Accession history:** Gift of Thomas A. Gray, 1991. 91.45

1. Jobe, *Portsmouth Furniture*, pp. 313–15. Portraits of the Reverend and Mrs. Ebenezer Devotion of neighboring Scotland, Conn., painted in 1770 by Winthrop Chandler, depict the New London County version of the angular-crest chair. Two years later other family members were shown in similar chairs; Trent with Nelson, "A Catalogue of New London County Joined Chairs," pp. 145–53.

2. Robert Hatfield Ellsworth, *Chinese Furniture: Hardwood Examples of the Ming and Early Ch'ing Dynasties* (New York: Random House, 1971), pl. 2, fig. 11; cats. 2, 6, 7, 9, 19, 23, 25, 66, 93, 94, 105, 106, 109, 112, 113. George N. Kates, *Chinese Household Furniture* (New York: Dover Publications, 1948), pls. 44, 46, 48, 51, 60, 77, 85–87, 89, 91, 111, 112. Nicholas Grindley, *The Bended-Back Chair* (London: Barling, 1990), fig. 18. Hinckley, *Directory*, ills. 15, 17, 18.

3. Jobe, *Portsmouth Furniture*, pp. 37, 41, 313.

4. Kirk, *American Chairs*, figs. 1018–22; Macquoid and Edwards, *Dictionary*, 1:270–71, figs. 136, 137, 140; Hinckley, *Directory*, pp. 76–77; Nutting, *Furniture Treasury*, no. 2170; Jobe and Kaye, *New England Furniture*, nos. 107, 126. The Portsmouth pattern is associated with the households of the prominent Langdon and Wendell families and the merchants John Saltar and Oliver Briard, who branded their armchairs; Myrna Kaye, "Marked Portsmouth Furniture," *Antiques* 113, no. 5 (May 1978): 1103, fig. 6; Jobe, *Portsmouth Furniture*, p. 315 n. 6. Northeast Auctions, "New Hampshire Auction" (November 16–17, 1991), lot 678; Wallace B. Gusler, *Furniture of Williamsburg and Eastern Virginia, 1710–1790* (Richmond: Virginia Museum, 1979), figs. 61, 62; John Bivins, Jr., *The Furniture of Coastal North Carolina, 1700–1820* (Winston-Salem, N.C.: Museum of Early Southern Decorative Arts, 1988), figs. 5.109–.113, 6.116, 6.117, 6.121, 6.128, 6.129.

5. For Portsmouth customs' statistics, see Brock W. Jobe, "An Introduction to Portsmouth Furniture of the Mid-Eighteenth Century," in *New England Furniture*, p. 165; for New London customs' statistics, see "Ledger of Imports and Exports: America, 1768–73," Board of Customs and Excise, Public Record Office, London. Trent, *Hearts and Crowns*, pp. 80–84.

6. Jobe and Kaye, *New England Furniture*, p. 317 n. 3.

## 60 ◆ Armchair
Boston, Massachusetts, or Great Britain
1765–85

This design is more closely allied with the Gothic style than any chair discussed so far (see Nos. 33, 50–52, 55, 56). Several derivative Gothic elements favored in varying degrees by mid eighteenth-century British and American chairmakers are combined—the quatrefoil, the lancet arch, and the small, winglike figure (splat base voids). The heavy modeling of the front legs is suggestive of cluster columns. The two-tiered arrangement of the splat, with its mullionlike vertical bars that appear to imitate the divisions between lights in a Gothic cathedral window, is a more evocative disposition of elements than those of previous designs. The splat is a close copy of the British prototype and, if American, is rare in joined seating. One mate is known; several closely related chairs are ascribed to Philadelphia.[1]

British chairs with two-tiered tracery splats have other features that are closely imitated in the design of this chair: the crest and upper splat carving; the triple-reeded back posts; the short, stumpy arm grips; and the saddled, or hollow, seat. Modeled legs with fancy beading, blocked feet, and carved, solid brackets also occur in some British prototypes.

The applied, beaded strips of wood attached to the bottom surfaces of the over-upholstered seat rails are a rarity in American seating and uncommon in British chairs. Original moldings were lost from many chairs over the years due to successive changes of upholstery. In 1762, when illustrating and commenting on two designs for "French Chairs" with upholstered seats and backs and open arms, Thomas Chippendale suggested that a "little Moulding, round the Bottom of the Edge of the Rails, has a good Effect."[2]

Tiered-lancet splats were sufficiently popular in British chairmaking that many variations were produced. A three-over-two lancet pattern supported on a low-arched base

appears in the 1762 edition of Chippendale's *Director*. Also worthy of note is the influence of the British pattern on Continental chairmaking; the tiered-lancet style spawned a number of North German imitations.[3]

Although the background histories of this lancet-back armchair and its mate are unknown, a New England origin has been suggested through analysis of the woods that supplement the primary construction material, which is mahogany. The front and rear seat rails are maple; birch is present in the side rails. The same combination of woods was used in the rails of Nos. 52 right, 56, and 57. Maple is a common secondary wood in British seating furniture, however, and birch is found upon occasion. Differentiating between American and European species is at best inconclusive. Further pursuit of a link with Boston-area production is based on the choice of design motifs. Related, though not identical, carved ornament is centered in the crests of Nos. 50 and 55, the latter of which also has

low-relief–modeled lancet tips like those flanking the crest ornament in this example. Ridged bars similar to those in the mullions are found in the backs of the chairs in No. 50, and quatrefoil and inverted wing-shape voids appear in the splats of the same chairs. The nubby arm grips, flowing carved foliage of the arm supports, and carved figure in the knee brackets appear to have their prototypes in an English armchair (see No. 58, fig. 2) which, with other examples, may have been owned in Boston in the eighteenth century and was closely copied by one or more Boston chairmakers.

In evaluating the suitability of a piece of furniture for a prominent collection of Americana, many factors are taken into account, and considerations vary from case to case. Outstanding qualities of this chair include the richness of the surface decoration and the relationship of the parts to the whole in producing a balanced, harmonious design. The rarity of the pattern, if the chair is

American, is particularly germane. Of additional consideration are the close links established with British chairmaking, which provide a basis for further study of design transmission. Always looming large in the evaluation process, however, is the condition of an object. Here, the condition is moderate to poor: there are many cracks and damaged areas, and the repairs are extensive. Overall, serious questions arise about the validity of such a chair in the Winterthur collection. Although this example presumably met selection criteria when purchased sometime prior to 1951, poor condition alone would preclude its acquisition today, no matter how rare and unusual the pattern.

*NGE*

---

**Construction:** The crest is supported on rectangular tenons at the flared posts and at eight points across the splat top. The slightly rounded face is carved in low relief with leafy ornament and beading; the back surface is rounded and shaped along the center bottom edge to complete the upper splat piercings. The splat face is carved in low relief across the top, creased at the center quatrefoils and base, and modeled in volutes at the lower corners. The splat bars are ridged vertically, above and below the quatrefoils. The splat edges and piercings are almost straight, front to back; the base is tenoned into the rear rail. The low, saddled, three-sided plinth is hollow on the front and sides, finished with a gadrooned molding at the top, and nailed to the rear seat rail. The back posts are molded with three heavy tapered reeds rising from a base "block"; the rear surfaces are rounded, crest to seat. The ogee-curved arms are rabbeted to the back posts at the front and outside faces, the joints secured with screws inserted diagonally from the back and concealed by composition material. The front tips are supported on rectangular tenons at the arm-post tops and were probably pinned originally from the inside. Low-relief–carved leafy ornament at each arm tip is centered by a floret; a ruffled leaf along the outside edge is terminated by a small volute at the back. The ogee curve of the arms is repeated in the rounded supports; the blocked support bases are rounded at the edges and contoured horizontally on the outside faces. The supports are dovetailed into the seat rails and each is secured by two screws inserted from the outside and concealed by composition material. Low-relief–carved leaves embellish the forward faces. The seat rails are joined to the back posts and front leg tops with rectangular tenons; the rear rail is pinned. The front and rear

rails are saddle-contoured. The beaded wooden borders below the upholstery at the front and side rails are applied with nails. The rear legs are canted on the forward faces below the side stretchers; the flared back surfaces are terminated by rounded heels. The inside forward corners are chamfered, top to bottom. The straight front legs are ogee molded on the outside faces and carved with heavy bead-and-reel moldings at the outside forward corners. The low, blocked feet are shaped to resemble the legs and are nailed on from the bottom. The four leaf-carved brackets appear to have been glued in place originally. The rectangular stretchers have crowned tops. The side and back braces are tenoned into the legs; the medial stretcher is dovetailed into the side stretchers from the bottom.

**Condition:** The crest is cracked through left of the center ornament and repaired with small pieces of wood and pins, mostly from the back. The left tip was broken off and is reattached; the right tip is cracked diagonally on the face into the inside joint surface. The splat is cracked through at the upper left volute neck and at all connections between the central quatrefoils. A large chip mars the rear surface of the right quatrefoil. Unexplained tool marks on the splat face above the plinth stand out in marked contrast to the finished surfaces of the surrounding wood. The left end of the plinth is cracked and renailed. The left back-post and side-rail joint is damaged by a crack extending several inches above and below the rail on the forward post face and continuing onto the side face where two countersunk screws concealed by composition material repair the break. Both arms and supports are extensively damaged. The arm- and back-post joints are reset; the left one is repaired with a spline and probably a new internal screw. The left elbow is cracked and repaired with pins on the inside face. The arm support bases, which are loose in their joints, are reattached to the side rails with two outside screws concealed by composition material. Two screws on the inside rails reinforce the joints at points where former repairs are visible. The right support base block is cracked at the forward inside corner. Multiple cracks damage the beaded strip applied to the bottom of the right rail; the front rail strip has been slightly shortened. The left front leg bracket has been altered by reducing the height and depth. The applied front feet (held by nails driven in from the bottom) have been in place a long time, although the attachment method is atypical of period practice. Nail evidence suggests that the left front foot was replaced in the nineteenth century. The theory is reinforced by the presence of chisel marks on the inside corner of the leg adjacent to the foot, indicating that the chamfer was enlarged

to correspond with that on the foot. The dovetail joints securing the medial brace to the side stretchers have been repaired; cracks occur in the side stretchers at the joints and beyond. The rear stretcher has a crack at the outside left end and a wood loss at the right joint. Both rear legs are cracked on several faces at stretcher level. The rounded heel in the left rear leg is absent in the right leg. An old wood loss occurs at the inside back corner of the right rear leg.

**Dimensions:**

| | | |
|---|---|---|
| H. | 37 3/8 in. | 94.9 cm |
| H. (seat) | 15 3/8 in. | 39.1 cm |
| W. (crest) | 23 11/16 in. | 60.1 cm |
| W. (seat front) | 22 7/8 in. | 58.1 cm |
| W. (seat back) | 19 1/4 in. | 48.9 cm |
| W. (arms) | 27 1/4 in. | 69.2 cm |
| W. (feet) | 23 | 58.4 cm |
| D. (seat) | 20 1/2 in. | 52.1 cm |
| D. (feet) | 22 3/4 in. | 57.8 cm |

**Materials:** *Microanalysis:* Primary: mahogany. Secondary: soft maple group (front and rear seat rails); birch (side seat rails). *Finish:* deep brown color with reddish cast, in resin. *Upholstery:* white silk with brocaded vines and floral forms in a diagonal pattern; Europe, 1745–75.

**Publications:** Downs, *American Furniture*, fig. 46.

**Accession history:** Bequest of H. F. du Pont, 1969. 59.1882

---

1. For British prototypes, see Kirk, *American Furniture*, fig. 987; Alice Winchester, ed., *The Antiques Treasury* (New York: E. P. Dutton, 1959), p. 70. The mate is in the Diplomatic Reception Rooms, U.S. Department of State, Washington, D.C.; see Fitzgerald, *Three Centuries*, fig. IV-7; one Philadelphia-ascribed chair is at Winterthur, acc. 70.1429; another is in Hornor, *Blue Book*, pl. 321.

2. Kirk, *American Furniture*, fig. 987; Sotheby Parke Bernet, "Collection of Rebekah Harkness" (May 19, 1979), lot 180; Cescinsky, *English Furniture*, 2:233; Winchester, *Antiques Treasury*, p. 70. Thomas Chippendale, *The Gentleman and Cabinet-Maker's Director* (1762; reprint 3d ed., New York: Dover Publications, 1966), p. 3, pl. 19.

3. For British variations, see Cescinsky, *English Furniture*, 2:232–33; Kirk, *American Furniture*, figs. 992, 993. Chippendale, *Director* (1762), pl. 14, center. Adaptations are illustrated in Herbert Cescinsky and George Leland Hunter, *English and American Furniture* (Garden City, N.Y.: Garden City Publishing Co., 1929), p. 134; Victoria and Albert Museum, *English Chairs* (2d ed.; London: Her Majesty's Stationery Office, 1965), pl. 82; Sotheby's, "Important English Furniture, Decorations, and Clocks" (December 13, 1986), lot 170. For German chairs, see Hinckley, *Directory*, ills. 264, 270; G. M. Ellwood, *English Furniture and Decoration, 1680–1800* (London: B. T. Batsford, 1909), p. 73.

## 61 ◆ Side chairs
Eastern Massachusetts
1780–1800

The cross-slat chair, a popular vernacular type from the sixteenth century, was first adapted to formal seating in England about the early 1760s. New England chairmakers may have introduced imitative patterns before the revolutionary war, but most American production of this design dates from the postwar years through the end of the century. The style is identified in a Connecticut price list issued in 1792 by the Hartford Society of Cabinetmakers: a "Chair with two cross slats and top rail." Philadelphia cabinet and chairmakers described a "Splat back chair with three cross Splatts" in their price book of 1795, just two years after local appraisers identified "9 Cross backed Mahogany Chairs" in the household of Jonathan Dickinson. From as early as 1792, a stock woodcut illustrating a dropleaf table, chest of drawers, and cross-slat side chair directed readers' attention to cabinetmakers' advertisements in New England

newspapers. In the meantime, interest in chairs with horizontal back members had continued through the 1780s in Britain, where a 1786 estimate-book drawing by the Gillows firm of Lancashire depicts a two-slat example titled "A Riddle [perforated] Back Chair of soft wood."[1]

Several features of the Massachusetts cross-slat chairs can be linked directly to surface ornament used in chairs with vertical splats. The crest-top bead was introduced to Chippendale-style seating in the 1760s (see Nos. 50, 52, 55, 56). Carved ornament comparable to the leafy scrolls in these two chairs appears in the crest tips of the chairs in No. 52. Back posts molded on the surface to a bold serpentine figure—an occasional customer option in prerevolutionary work (see Nos. 50, 55, 57)—proved a more frequent choice with the introduction of cross slats. New to the Massachusetts furniture market with the cross-slat chair was the Marlborough leg molded to the same serpentine figure. Prerevolutionary Marlborough styles are plain or ornamented with a simple corner bead, another indication

that the cross-slat chair was primarily a postwar pattern. Reinforcing the assumption is the presence of serpentine-molded, tapered legs in Massachusetts neoclassical chairs. A few cross-slat examples have tapered legs, but the square support appears to have remained the popular choice through the end of the century. The rectangular stretchers bracing these legs are often crowned on the top surface in the English manner—a rare feature in prerevolutionary American work (see Nos. 50 right, 60).[2]

Seven or eight pierced cross-slat patterns are associated with New England chairmaking. Of these the crowned anthemion, shown here, is the most ornate. Although the design has an English prototype, the anthemion in the British model is generally pierced between each leaf rather than once at the center. Several versions of the anthemion without the crown were probably referred to as the *Honey suckle pattern*, a term that appears in both the 1795 Philadelphia price book and a comparable volume published the following year in New York. Neither of two identified

Philadelphia patterns that fit this description
is crowned. New York cross-slat chairs are
unknown, although cabinet- and chairmaker
Joseph Cox, a new arrival to the city from
London, advertised "rail back chairs" in
1771. Chairs with two cross slats were more
common than three-slat examples, possibly
due to the price difference, although from an
aesthetic viewpoint, the latter are the more
successful. The serpentine-front seat with
over-the-rail upholstery, as illustrated, was a
popular choice for the cross-slat chair. The
use of brass nails adds richness and visual
definition. The distinctive nailed borders are
also critical in unifying the upper and lower
structures of a design visually oriented on the
horizontal line.[3]

Several crowned-anthemion chairs have
known New England associations. A two-slat
side chair with a serpentine seat front at the
Museum of Fine Arts, Boston, was once part
of the household furnishings of the Reverend
Dr. Daniel C. Sanders (1768–1850) of
Medfield, Massachusetts. A member of the
Hubbard family of Concord owned a pair
of two-slat chairs before 1871. Another pair
of chairs of variant pattern was owned by
the Robbins family of neighboring Milton,
Massachusetts; sometime before 1917 a related
cross-slat chair was in the possession of a
Salem resident.[4]

The right chair is branded with the name
"W PORTER" on the back rail (fig. 1), a
practice rare in formal seating furniture. The
stamp could be that of a maker, owner, or
upholsterer. A William Porter of Charlestown,
Massachusetts, has been identified as a
cabinetmaker in a marriage record of 1806.
If the marriage was Porter's first, the late date
casts doubt on his connection with the chair.
A more likely candidate is William Porter of
Boston, a distiller who was listed in the first
city directory of 1789 and for many years
thereafter; his widow was named in the 1816
volume. Porter's occupation as a distiller
suggests that he owned one or more brands
with which to stamp the containers that held
his products. The same tool could have been
used to mark his furniture.[5]

*NGE*

---

**Inscriptions or marks:** (Right) *Branded on underside
of rear seat rail:* "W PORTER" *in serif letters.*

**Construction:** (Left) The crest is supported on
rectangular tenons at the flared back posts (pinned).
The crest face is carved in low to medium-high relief
with a top bead, leafy tips, and crownlike ornament.
The flat back surface is rounded, top and bottom.
The cross slats, which are carved in the manner of
the crest, are tenoned into the back posts; the backs,
edges, and piercings are almost flat. The post faces
are serpentine molded and flanked by beads; the
backs are rounded. The rails are joined to the posts
and front leg extensions with rectangular tenons
(pinned). A facing strip nailed to the upper surface
of the rear seat rail is molded like the back posts.
The rear legs are canted on the forward faces and
narrowly chamfered on the inside forward corners
from near the top to the bottom. The squared front
legs are molded on the outside surfaces like the
back posts. The crowned rectangular stretchers are
tenoned into their adjacent members at the sides
and back; the medial stretcher is dovetailed into the
side braces from the bottom.

(Right) The joint construction and surface
shaping of the crest, cross slats, and posts correspond
to that in the left chair, except the crest face is
slightly cheeked between the center and the tips,
and the cross slats have slightly rounded top edges
and piercings that are slightly canted, front to back.
The post faces are serpentine molded and flanked by
beads; the backs are rounded. The rails are joined to
the posts and front leg extensions with rectangular
tenons. The exposed back rail is narrowly chamfered
at the bottom outside edge; a facing strip nailed to
the upper edge is scribed with a bead at the front
and back. The side rails are narrowly chamfered at
the bottom inside edges. Tool marks appear on the
inside faces of the side and front rails. The rear legs
are lightly canted on the forward faces. The inside
forward corners are chamfered, top to bottom; the
outside forward corners are chamfered only below
the side stretchers. The squared front legs are
molded on the outside surfaces in the manner of
the back posts. The crowned rectangular stretchers
are tenoned into the adjacent members at the sides
and back; the medial stretcher is dovetailed into the
side braces from the bottom.

**Condition:** (Left) The left rear crest surface is
cracked horizontally and repaired with a small nail.
The facing strip on the top of the back rail is
cracked at the left end. The front and side seat rails
have been cut out in rabbets on the upper inside

faces to the depth of about ¹/₂". Evidence of saw
use indicates that the chair was disassembled. The
purpose of the rabbets is unclear, since the rails
are unfinished to receive upholstery. Nailing has
caused the right side rail to crack from the top
into the side faces and the front rail to split at the
ends. A reinforcing cross piece applied with screws
(modern) to the inside face of the back rail butts
against the side rails. The side rails are reinforced
from the post backs with large screws concealed by
wooden plugs. A crack at the inside center face of
the rear stretcher continues to the lower right end.
Cracks are present on the lower surface and interior
rear joint of the right side stretcher.

(Right) Four spaced screw or nail holes in the
faces of the crest and cross slats extend through
to the back surfaces of the slats. The facing strip
on the top of the back rail is cracked at both ends.
Several previous upholstery covers were drawn
over the back rail and nailed to the rail bottom,
as indicated by holes and nails; nail holes are also
visible on the bottoms of the other rails. The left
inside corner of the front rail is split. The left front
leg is chipped at the back of the foot, and the beads
are slightly defaced.

**Dimensions:**

Left

| | | |
|---|---|---|
| H. | 40¹/₂ in. | 102.9 cm |
| H. (seat) | 17¹/₄ in. | 43.8 cm |
| W. (crest) | 19³/₈ in. | 49.2 cm |
| W. (seat front) | 20¹/₂ in. | 52.1 cm |
| W. (seat back) | 16³/₈ in. | 41.6 cm |
| W. (feet) | 20³/₈ in. | 51.7 cm |
| D. (seat) | 17⁵/₁₆ in. | 44.0 cm |
| D. (feet) | 18¹⁵/₁₆ in. | 48.1 cm |

Right

| | | |
|---|---|---|
| H. | 37¹/₂ in. | 95.2 cm |
| H. (seat) | 16¹/₈ in. | 41.0 cm |
| W. (crest) | 19 in. | 48.2 cm |
| W. (seat front) | 21¹/₈ in. | 53.6 cm |
| W. (seat back) | 16¹/₂ in. | 41.9 cm |
| W. (feet) | 21¹/₈ in. | 53.6 cm |
| D. (seat) | 18³/₁₆ in. | 46.2 cm |
| D. (feet) | 19³/₄ in. | 50.1 cm |

**Materials:** *Microanalysis:* (Left) Primary: mahogany.
Secondary: soft maple group (side and front seat
rails); birch (rear seat rail). (Right) Primary:
mahogany. Secondary: soft maple group (seat
frame); hard and soft maple groups (stretchers).

*Finish:* (Left) variegated medium dark brown color in resin; crazed and chipped surfaces. (Right) medium brown color in resin with darker residue from former finishes. *Upholstery:* (Left and right) green silk damask; Europe, probably Italy, 1700–1750.

**Publications:** Bishop, *Centuries and Styles of the American Chair,* figs. 227, 231. (Right) Montgomery, *American Furniture,* no. 12.

**Accession history:** (Left) Bequest of H. F. du Pont, 1969. (Right) Purchased by the Museum from John S. Walton, Inc., New York, 1962. 58.2353, 62.161

---

1. For the Connecticut price list, see *Great River,* cat. 318. The 1795 Philadelphia price book is quoted in Montgomery, *American Furniture,* no. 11. The Dickinson inventory is quoted in Robert F. Trent, "Mid-Atlantic Easy Chairs, 1770–1820: Old Questions and New Evidence," in Luke Beckerdite, ed., *American Furniture 1993* (Milwaukee, Wis.: Chipstone Fndn., 1993), p. 206. The Gillows drawing is in Kirk, *American Furniture,* fig. 1042. For British examples, see Jobe and Kaye, *New England Furniture,* no. 130; Hinckley, *Directory,* ills. 304, 305, 308, 309, 311; Kirk, *American Furniture,* figs. 1032–37, 1040, 1041. Samuel Kneeland and Lemuel Adams of Hartford used the stock woodcut illustration to introduce their new business in the autumn of 1792. The same image was used 12 years later when Pelatiah Bliss advertised at Springfield, Massachusetts; Phyllis Kihn, comp., "Connecticut Cabinetmakers, Part 1," *Connecticut Historical Society Bulletin* 32, no. 4 (October 1967): 141; Gail Nessell Colglazier, *Springfield Furniture, 1700–1850: A Large and Rich Assortment* (Springfield, Mass.: Connecticut Valley Historical Museum, 1990), p. 14.

2. For neoclassical Massachusetts seating, see Montgomery, *American Furniture,* nos. 25, 27, 34, 35, 107, 111, 114; for tapered-leg, Massachusetts cross-slat chairs, see Robert W. Skinner, "American and European Furniture and Decorative Arts" (August 18, 1990), lot 29C.

3. The honeysuckle-pattern quotations are from Montgomery, *American Furniture,* no. 11, p. 103; the Joseph Cox advertisement is quoted in William MacPherson Hornor, Jr., "A Survey of American 'Wing Chairs,'" *International Studio* 99, no. 410 (July 1931): 72. Other New England pierced cross-slat patterns are in Jobe and Kaye, *New England Furniture,* nos. 131–33; Randall, *American Furniture,* nos. 156, 157; Joseph Lionetti and Robert Trent, "New Information about Chapin Chairs," *Antiques* 192, no. 5 (May 1986): 1089, fig. 14; *New London County Furniture,* no. 101. For an English prototype, see Jobe and Kaye, *New England Furniture,* no. 130; for Philadelphia chairs, see Heckscher, *American Furniture,* cat. no. 62; Montgomery, *American Furniture,* no. 82; Hornor, *Blue Book,* pls. 367, 368.

4. An early twentieth-century photograph shows the chair owned by Sanders standing in the parlor at the Norwood, Mass., home of descendants who were parents of the donor; Jonathan Fairbanks, "A Decade of Collecting American Decorative Arts and Sculpture at the Museum of Fine Arts, Boston," *Antiques* 120, no. 3 (September 1981): 607, pl. 16. A Hubbard chair is in David F. Wood, ed., *The Concord Museum: Decorative Arts from a New England Collection* (Concord, Mass.: By the museum, 1996), cat. 28. The Robbins chair is cited in Jobe and Kaye, *New England Furniture,* no. 131 n. 3; for the Salem-owned chair see Morse, *Furniture of the Olden Time,* p. 196, ill. 177. Mary H. Northend photographed crowned-anthemion cross-slat chairs in northeastern Massachusetts and New Hampshire homes at the beginning of the twentieth century when collecting materials for her publications extolling "old houses" of the colonial period; Mary H. Northend Collection, no. 363, DAPC, Visual Resources Collection, Winterthur Library.

5. Montgomery, *American Furniture,* no. 12; folder 62.161, Registration Office, Winterthur. Boston city directories, 1789–1816, Downs collection.

## 62 ✦ **Side chair** (one of four)
Eastern Massachusetts
1780–1800

---

The saddled, or concave, seat was uncommon in late eighteenth-century American chair-making despite its use over a period of several decades spanning the late Chippendale and federal styles. Saddled, upholstered bottoms are found more frequently in English seating, especially the cross-slat styles. The period term for the concave rail form was "hollow seat," as listed in the *Journeymen Cabinet and Chair Makers' New-York Book of Prices* published in 1796. The Massachusetts provenance of this chair, one of a set of four, is confirmed by the character of the crowned anthemions (see No. 61), here unpierced, and the presence of birch in the seat rails.[1]

In addition to identifying period terminology, American price books provide insights on the cost of furniture construction. The Hartford Society of Cabinetmakers price list of 1792 set the labor charge for a chair with two cross slats below the top rail and a frame to receive a loose seat at 21s. "Chair frames to cover over the rails" were 2s. less, since the side and front rails could be left in a semifinished state. Extra charges, as described in the New York price book, included such items as sawing "holes" in, or piercing, the top rail and "cross splatts," shaping the seat rails to hollow form, bracing the understructure with stretchers, "moulding . . . the feet" (legs), and carving.[2]

The leather seat covers on this chair and its mates are original. The brown surface has possibly faded from black, although the dark brown hue seems well preserved at the side edges where there would have been the least wear and abrasion. The original webbing and sack cloth are in place, and the grass stuffing next to the sack cloth appears to be undisturbed. The nailing pattern and most of the domed brass nails are original. The nail heads bear tinted lacquer in imitation of gilding.[3]

Examples of eastern Massachusetts cross-slat chairs that can be closely dated are unknown. Stylistic evidence (see No. 61) suggests that the pattern may have been introduced in America just before the Revolution but became popular only during the 1780s. This hypothesis seems to be corroborated by documentation that accompanies several Philadelphia cross-slat chairs. In 1783, cabinetmaker Thomas Tufft supplied Dr. George and Deborah (Norris) Logan with a dozen mahogany chairs having "open Backs" for the dining room at Stenton, their Germantown mansion. Tufft's contemporary Jacob Wayne constructed six mahogany "slatt back chairs" for Capt. Thomas Mason in 1790, as described in a surviving bill of sale.[4]

*NGE*

---

**Construction:** The crest is supported on rectangular tenons at the slightly flared back posts. The flat face is carved with a top bead, leafy tips, and a central crownlike ornament, all in low to medium-high relief. The back surface is flat across the center and rounded, top and bottom. The cross slats, which are carved in the manner of the crest, are tenoned into the back posts. The backs are flat; the edges and piercings are canted slightly, front to back. The post faces are serpentine molded and flanked by beads; the backs are rounded. The seat is saddled, or hollow. The rails are joined to the posts and front legs with rectangular tenons. A facing strip nailed to the upper surface of the rear seat rail is beaded on the front edge. The rear legs, which are slightly canted on the forward faces below the seat, are almost vertical below that point; the feet flare slightly at the back. The inside forward corners of the back legs are chamfered, top to bottom; the outside corners are chamfered below the side stretchers. The squared front legs are molded on the outside faces like the back posts. The crowned rectangular stretchers are tenoned into the adjacent members at the sides and back; the medial stretcher is dovetailed into the side braces from the bottom.

**Condition:** The facing strip on the top of the back rail is cracked near the left end. The medial stretcher joints have been repaired with composition material; the side stretchers are probably reglued. The leather seat cover is coarsely cracked and damaged by two center splits and small surface losses. Circular marks on the leather surrounding some nails indicate that the fasteners have been reset and, in some cases, replaced using period nails. Surrounding most nails are deposits of polish residue that has interacted with the metal and produced corrosion.

**Dimensions:**

| | | |
|---|---|---|
| H. | 37 3/8 in. | 94.9 cm |
| H. (center seat) | 15 5/8 in. | 39.6 cm |
| W. (crest) | 19 1/4 in. | 48.9 cm |
| W. (seat front) | 21 1/2 in. | 54.6 cm |
| W. (seat back) | 16 5/8 in. | 42.2 cm |
| W. (feet) | 21 3/8 in. | 54.3 cm |
| D. (seat) | 17 3/4 in. | 45.1 cm |
| D. (feet) | 19 5/8 in. | 49.8 cm |

**Materials:** *Microanalysis:* Primary: mahogany. Secondary: birch (side and front seat rails). *Finish:* medium brown color with reddish cast in resin. *Upholstery:* original dark brown leather cover, interior stuffing, and brass-headed nails; eastern Massachusetts, 1780–1800.

**Publications:** Montgomery, *American Furniture*, no. 11.

**Accession history:** Museum purchase from Jack Partridge, Tavern Antique Shop, Norwalk, Conn., 1959.
59.126

---

1. For British examples, see Kirk, *American Furniture*, figs. 1032–34, 1036, 1037, 1039; Hinckley, *Directory*, ills. 308, 309. The 1796 New York price book is quoted in Montgomery, *American Furniture*, p. 103.

2. The Hartford price book is reproduced in *Great River*, cat. 18; the New York price book is quoted in Montgomery, *American Furniture*, p. 103.

3. Donald L. Fennimore, *Metalwork in Early America: Copper and Its Alloys from the Winterthur Museum* (Winterthur, Del.: By the museum, 1996), entry 318.

4. Examples from both sets of Philadelphia chairs were in the possession of descendants of the original owners in the early twentieth century; Hornor, *Blue Book*, pls. 101, 289, pp. 96, 189, 223. The term *open Backs* refers to the pierced cross members of the chair back, the language derived from the craft of the vernacular chairmaker, which describes three-back, four-back (and so on) solid-slat chairs with rush seats.

## 63 ◆ Side chair
### Eastern Massachusetts
### 1785–1800

The back of this chair is virtually identical to those pictured in Nos. 61 and 62. Indeed, the entire rear structure from the crest to the feet appears to be interchangeable with the joined-chair backs. The only significant alteration in the understructure is the location of the forward cross stretcher between the front legs instead of the side braces. Structural stability dictated this modification. Thin socketed frames that receive rush seats are considerably more fragile than those secured with mortise and tenon, and a rush seat is not as durable as one stuffed and covered with leather. A partial remedy was to coat the rush with paint or resin to stiffen and stabilize the fibers. Here, light brown pigment was added to the resin, and although this woven bottom is not original, the coated treatment duplicates period practice.

This is the only crowned-anthemion cross-slat chair with a rush seat located to date. Several other rush-bottom, pierced cross-slat patterns are represented by pairs or sets of chairs, but the numbers are limited. Rush seats are even less common in formal chairs of neoclassical pattern, unlike the rush-bottom, solid and pierced vertical-splat styles of earlier decades that are relatively common (see Nos. 3, 17, 36, 38). The decline in popularity of formal rush seating furniture was due in part to the growing affluence of a broad segment of American society in the postrevolutionary period. The primary factor, however, was the introduction and almost immediate popularity of a new type of seating—the fancy, painted chair with a rush or cane bottom. The bright colors, painted motifs, and ornamental profiles common to these chairs had broad appeal and soon established fancy seating as the principal furniture in the middle-class parlor.[1]

NGE

**Construction:** The crest is supported on rectangular tenons at the canted posts. The flat face is carved

with a top bead, leafy tips, and a central crownlike ornament, all in low to medium-high relief. The tips are somewhat crudely carved. The back surface is completely rounded, and the piercings are slightly canted, front to back. The cross slats, which are carved in the manner of the crest, are tenoned into the back posts. The backs are flat; the piercings are almost flat, front to back. The post faces are serpentine molded with flanking beads; the backs are rounded. The bladelike seat rails, which are rounded at the outside edges, are round tenoned into the posts and front seat blocks. The blocks are part of the serpentine-shape front seat rail. The rear legs are canted on the forward surfaces; the inside front corners are chamfered, top to bottom. The squared front legs are molded on the outside surfaces like the back posts. The inside back corners are canted, top to bottom. The rectangular stretchers are crowned on the top surface and tenoned into the adjacent members (pinned, inside and out).

**Condition:** Stress cracks mark the outside faces of the rear stretcher at the right side and the back of the left side stretcher. A strand of rush is missing from the seat at the center of the front quadrant.

**Dimensions:**

| | | |
|---|---|---|
| H. | 38 in. | 96.5 cm |
| H. (seat) | 18 in. | 45.7 cm |
| W. (crest) | 19 1/4 in. | 48.9 cm |
| W. (seat front) | 21 11/16 in. | 55.1 cm |
| W. (seat back) | 16 3/8 in. | 41.6 cm |
| W. (feet) | 20 1/8 in. | 51.1 cm |
| D. (seat) | 17 3/4 in. | 45.1 cm |
| D. (feet) | 19 5/8 in. | 49.8 cm |

**Materials:** *Microanalysis:* Primary: soft maple group. *Finish:* medium light yellowish brown color in resin with traces of dark brown color remaining; refinished.

**Publications:** Montgomery, *American Furniture*, no. 13.

**Accession history:** Museum purchase from John S. Walton, Inc., New York, 1960. 60.215

1. For rush-bottom chairs constructed in other cross-slat patterns, see Jobe and Kaye, *New England Furniture*, nos. 132, 134, 135, fig. 133a; Fales, *Furniture of Historic Deerfield*, fig. 117; for formal-pattern, neoclassical chairs with rush bottoms, see Fales, *Furniture of Historic Deerfield*, fig. 135; Kirk, *American Furniture*, fig. 1057.

## 64 ◆ Side chair
**Eastern Connecticut, probably New London County or southern Windham County**
**1780–1800**

The eastern Connecticut origin of this chair is suggested by the interrelationship of several elements of the design with that of seating furniture ascribed by family tradition and circumstantial evidence to this region: the plain, beaded-corner Marlborough legs; the open segmental leg brackets; and the rigid, barlike cross slats of the chair back. This example, which has a tall, lean back and simple crest profile is distinctive among comparative chairs, which have lower backs, posts sawed to a gentle outward flare, and serpentine crests terminated by spurred scrolls. (The profile of the spurred scrolls is similar to that of the mid-splat cusps in No. 21 when inverted.) One of the spurred-scroll

cross-slat chairs descended in the Howard family of Hampton.[1]

By extension, the Howard family chair relates to other joined seating associated with Windham and New London county families, including those of Gen. Jabez Huntington (1719–86) of Norwich, Nathaniel Hebard (1741–1803) of Lebanon, and the Devotions of Scotland. All of these chairs are framed with spurred-scroll crests, beaded Marlborough legs, and open segmental leg brackets. They differ from Winterthur's chair in having vertical splats shaped to one of several patterns. One pattern is similar to that in No. 33, a chair linked with the Pitkin family of eastern Connecticut. Both the Hebard and Devotion family chairs are of this splat pattern.[2]

The tall, exaggerated back of Winterthur's chair identifies it as a provincial expression of the late Chippendale style. The chair was recovered in Colchester, which is about fifteen miles west of Norwich. Few eastern

Connecticut chairs are as tall as this example. No. 33 comes within an inch of matching it, and several contemporary woven-bottom chairs surpass its 42⅞-inch height. Because of the high back, it has been suggested that the chair was made for ceremonial use in a church or fraternal lodge. The former seems plausible; the latter appears unlikely. Organizational rank and authority are traditionally symbolized in dress and the occupancy of a seat of authority, which frequently would be elevated, high-backed, and fitted with arms. This chair lacks the arms of authority.[3]

The tall back is just one exaggerated feature. The open brackets linking the front legs and seat rail are also scaled to a size out of proportion with the rest of the chair, making the seat appear unusually low. The severity of line that dominates the design is continued in the plain crest with swept-back tips. The utilitarian appearance of this chair suggests that the original, loose-seat cover was leather.

NGE

---

**Inscriptions or marks:** *Chiseled on inside front seat rail:* "II".

**Construction:** The crest is supported on rectangular tenons at the back posts (pinned). The crest face is flat except at the rounded tips and at the center, where the top rounds backward. The back surface is flat; the top is flat from either side of the arch to the tips. The cross slats tenon into the back posts. The slats and crest are contoured laterally. The back posts, which are contoured, or "spooned," vertically, are flat on all surfaces. The rails are joined to the posts and front leg extensions with rectangular tenons (pinned twice). The seat frame is rounded at the sloping top lip and rabbeted at the inside front and sides to support a loose-seat frame. The lower outside rail edges are finished with a bead at the front and sides. A complex molded facing strip, consisting of beads and a broad cove, is nailed to the upper surface of the rear seat rail. The rear legs are canted on the forward faces; the feet flare backward slightly at the heels. The front legs are square in section and beaded down the outside forward corners. The nailed, open brackets butt against the front legs but are notched into the front rail bead. The rectangular stretchers are tenoned into the adjacent members at the sides and back (pinned); the medial stretcher is dovetailed into the side braces from the bottom. The stretchers are beaded on the forward and outside top edges except for the rear brace.

**Condition:** Both crest joints have minor cracks on the forward faces. The seat rails and stretchers are partially repinned and reglued. The left front leg top, cracked through vertically, has sustained some wood loss and is repaired with composition material and two wooden pins. The right front leg top is cracked vertically at the pins. An interior crack occurs at the right end of the rear seat rail. The loose-seat frame is modern.

**Dimensions:**

| | | |
|---|---|---|
| H. | 42 7/8 in. | 108.9 cm |
| H. (seat) | 16 1/2 in. | 41.9 cm |
| W. (crest) | 20 1/2 in. | 52.1 cm |
| W. (seat front) | 20 3/8 in. | 51.7 cm |
| W. (seat back) | 15 1/2 in. | 39.4 cm |
| W. (feet) | 20 1/8 in. | 51.1 cm |
| D. (seat) | 15 3/16 in. | 38.5 cm |
| D. (feet) | 17 7/8 in. | 45.4 cm |

**Materials:** *Microanalysis:* Primary: cherry. *Finish:* medium reddish brown color in resin. *Upholstery:* block-printed polychrome cotton with "Indienne"-style floral forms; France, 1780–1800.

**Exhibitions:** "Legacy of a Provincial Elite: New London County Joined Chairs, 1720–1790," Connecticut Historical Society and Lyman Allyn Museum, Hartford and Norwich, October 1, 1985– February 28, 1986.

**Publications:** Trent with Nelson, "A Catalogue of New London County Joined Chairs," pp. 166–67.

**Accession history:** Museum purchase from Harry Arons, Ansonia, Conn., 1957. 57.103.4

1. Trent with Nelson, "A Catalogue of New London County Joined Chairs," pp. 170–75.

2. For the Huntington chairs, see *American Antiques from Israel Sack Collection*, 10 vols. (Washington, D.C.: Highland House, ca. 1969–), 2:375; for the Hebard chair, see Trent with Nelson, "A Catalogue of New London County Joined Chairs," pp. 154–55, 162–64; for the Devotion chair, see Lance Mayer and Gay Myers, eds., *The Devotion Family: The Lives and Possessions of Three Generations in Eighteenth-Century Connecticut* (New London, Conn.: Lyman Allyn Art Museum, 1991), p. 20.

3. For a discussion of this chair and an example of a taller woven-bottom chair, see Trent with Nelson, "A Catalogue of New London County Joined Chairs," no. 49, pp. 166–67.

## 65 ◆ Child's armchair
### Southern coastal New England
### 1760–85

Substantial numbers of children's chairs are recorded in the accounts of woodworking craftsmen, although precise descriptions are usually omitted. The standard chair had a rush seat and several cross slats at the back. The purchase price varied with time, place, and currency fluctuations, but 2s. to 3s. was the average standard charge throughout the eighteenth century for a child's plain chair. Although details are usually lacking, customer cost reflected such choices as chair style, use of arms, and type of finish. A charge for weaving the rush seat was sometimes not included in the basic price. The terms *child's chair*, *small chair*, and *little chair* were all applied to the diminutive seat: Robert Craig's description of a "Childs little Chare" sold from his Leicester, Massachusetts, shop in 1758 documents this terminology.[1]

In New England, members of the Gaines family of chairmakers made children's seating as early as 1726 in Ipswich, Massachusetts. Their little chairs were priced at 2s. 6d. or 3s. The cost can be compared with side chairs for adults, which sold for about 5s. 6d. for three-slat backs, 6s. for four-slat backs, and 9s. for banister backs. A new "bottom" for a child's chair woven of rush cost one customer 10d. in 1731.[2]

Between 1738 and 1748, Philadelphia chairmaker Solomon Fussell recorded moderate but steady orders for children's seating. A gauge of his activity and anticipated future sales is an outside supplier's delivery to Fussell in 1739 of "500 Children Chair List." This stockpile of parts probably lasted for several years and was equally suitable for use in side chairs, armchairs, and highchairs. Four lists were required to provide the framework for one woven seat. Only once did Fussell describe a chair in detail: "To one 4 Slat Childs Chair." The cost was 3s. 6d.; therefore

**Fig. 1.** From Robert Manwaring, *The Cabinet and Chair-Maker's Real Friend and Companion* (London: Henry Webley, 1765), pl. following preface.

Fussell's standard 3*s*. chair probably had a three-slat back. Fussell, like other craftsmen, sometimes sold his seating without any finish on the wood; such chairs were referred to as "white." Some seating was stained, some was painted. Other chairs were brushed with "Colour" mixed in varnish.[3]

Thomas Pratt of Malden, Massachusetts, and Elijah Pember of Ellington, Connecticut, numbered chairs for children among their furniture output during the 1750s. A contemporary, Isaiah Tiffany of Lebanon and Norwich, Connecticut, also offered small chairs "with Rockers." An unusual reference in any account is a "childs grat chare," although the number of surviving examples suggests that children's great chairs, that is, chairs with arms, were not uncommon. Elizabeth Luckis, a widow of Boston, had a "Child's arm Chair straw Bottom" in her household in 1766, perhaps for use by her grandchildren. William Barker of Providence, Rhode Island, constructed a child's armchair the same year for his wealthy patron John Brown. Rarities sold by Barker in 1753 and 1771 were described as "little chare[s] banester backt." The Proud family of Providence, spanning two generations of chairmakers, also offered a broad selection of children's seating, ranging from the side chair to the highchair, from the rocking chair to the Windsor. Eastward, along the coast at Dartmouth, Massachusetts, where Lemuel Tobey sold "Little" chairs for 2*s*. 5*d*., local demand appears to have been limited to children's slat-back side chairs.[4]

This child's great chair is unusual in several respects. The sawed back posts are more sophisticated than the turned back posts that are common to most rush-bottom vase-back chairs. The Chippendale-type crest dates the chair later than the front turnings and Spanish feet would indicate. Block-and-cylinder–type posts are rare in seating furniture dating after the early eighteenth century. The profile was common during the late seventeenth century in the back legs of caned chairs and in a few early banister-back and leather chairs. Boston

was the New England center for the cane-seat and related early chair trades, although a panel-back chair covered originally with leather or a textile and supported on four modified block-and-cylinder–type legs is attributed to Thomas Salmon of Stratford, Connecticut. That chair, which was owned during the early eighteenth century in neighboring Milford, could have relevance to this study, since a southern coastal New England provenance for the child's chair is suggested by supplemental features.[5]

The rare design of the front post on this chair may reflect the introduction of a new influence rather than the persistence of an older tradition. In a double-page engraving of architectural orders following the preface to his *Cabinet and Chair-Maker's Real Friend and Companion* of 1765, Robert Manwaring delineated both tuscan and ionic columns with shafts divided by large, square, dressed stones (fig. 1)—a decorative Mannerist embellishment that produces a sequence of alternating blocks and cylinders closely comparable to the front legs of the child's chair. Manwaring's work was well known in New England (see Nos. 47, 49, 57). The possibility that this source, or a related one, influenced the design of the child's chair should not be overlooked.[6]

Several features in particular suggest that the child's chair originated along the southern New England coast. The full-swelled high-shouldered baluster turnings beneath the arms have counterparts in Connecticut and Rhode Island chairmaking. Vase-shape splats with broad tops are common in the "york" chair, a

rush-bottom, turned- or club-leg seat made in New York City and environs and along the Connecticut coast (see Nos. 41, 42). Closer comparisons occur in the vase splats of rush-bottom chairs made in the Housatonic River valley of Connecticut. One style has an ogee top above a broad baluster; another has an elongated baluster with a short, stepped and rounded base, as illustrated here. The scroll arms and boldly turned front stretcher of this chair are late survivals of the William and Mary style. The central stretcher elements are repeated in the base turnings of the arm posts.[7]

*NGE*

---

**Construction:** The crest is supported on rectangular tenons at the flat-faced canted posts (pinned) and splat. The crest face is cheeked near the ends, and the tips are rounded backward; the rear surface is blocked at the saddle, which is chamfered at the base. The splat is flush with the crest and stay rail; the outside edges are canted, front to back. The back surface is planed vertically and tooled, top and bottom, to fit the mortises. The splat is tenoned into the stay rail. The plain stay rail, which is joined to the posts with rectangular tenons, is slightly inset at the back. The arms are secured by rectangular tenons (pinned) at the back posts and round tenons at the front posts (pinned). The seat rails, which are flat with rounded outer faces, are tenoned into the posts and legs. The rear legs are canted on the forward surfaces below the stretchers. The carved Spanish feet are one piece with the block-and-turned front legs. The stretchers are round tenoned into the adjacent members.

**Condition:** The left crest-post joint is patched on the face; the right end of the crest is cracked through at the same point. Wooden pins and metal sprigs secure the damaged areas. The right arm joint with the forward post is cracked on the outside surface. A blemish is present on the outside surface of the right back post below the seat. The rear stretcher is gouged along the bottom surface and is possibly reglued at the joints. Moderate wear occurs on the side stretchers; the front stretcher is less worn. Several front leg blocks and adjacent surfaces are marred by gouges. The forward and outside surfaces of the left front foot have been restored. The front feet may have had pads originally. Minor wormhole damage appears on the front legs and left rear foot. Strands of rush are missing from the seat front at the center right and near the right arm post.

**Dimensions:**

| | | |
|---|---|---|
| H. | 28 in. | 71.1 cm |
| H. (seat) | 9 3/8 in. | 23.8 cm |
| W. (crest) | 13 1/16 in. | 33.2 cm |
| W. (seat front) | 14 1/2 in. | 36.8 cm |
| W. (seat back) | 11 1/2 in. | 29.2 cm |
| W. (arms) | 15 7/8 in. | 40.3 cm |
| W. (feet) | 15 3/4 in. | 40.0 cm |
| D. (seat) | 10 3/4 in. | 27.3 cm |
| D. (feet) | 12 13/16 in. | 32.5 cm |

**Materials:** *Microanalysis:* Primary: soft maple group (right rear leg); ash (front stretcher by macroidentification). *Finish:* medium brown color in resin; residue of a darker surface coat.

**Accession history:** Bequest of H. F. du Pont, 1969. 66.1313

1. Robert Craig account book, 1757–81, Old Sturbridge Village, Sturbridge, Mass.

2. John Gaines II and Thomas Gaines I account book, 1707–60, Downs collection. Among general repairs noted in craftsmen's accounts, bottoming was the most common.

3. Solomon Fussell account book, 1738–48, Stephen Collins Papers, Library of Congress, Washington, D.C.

4. Isaiah Tiffany account book, 1746–67, Connecticut Historical Society, Hartford; Elizabeth Luckis estate inventory, 1766, Suffolk County Probate Court, Boston (microfilm, Downs collection); William Barker account books, vol. 1 (1750–72), vol. 2 (1753–66), and vol. 3 (1763–67), Rhode Island Historical Society, Providence; Lemuel Tobey account book, 1773–ca. 1777, Old Sturbridge Village, Sturbridge, Mass.; Thomas Pratt account book, 1730–68, Downs collection; Elijah Pember account book, 1758–67, Downs collection; William Proud, Daniel Proud, and Samuel Proud ledger, 1772–ca. 1825, Rhode Island Historical Society, Providence.

5. For cane-seat and other chairs with block-and-cylinder–type legs, see Forman, *American Seating Furniture*, cats. 52–56, 62, 64; Kirk, *American Furniture*, figs. 714–16, 719, 721, 725–31, 736, 739. For the Salmon chair, see Trent, *Hearts and Crowns*, no. 8.

6. Robert Manwaring, *The Cabinet and Chair-Maker's Real Friend and Companion* (London: Henry Webley, 1765), following preface.

7. For chairs with full-swelled baluster turnings, see *Connecticut Furniture*, no. 223; Pat Guthman advertisement, *Antiques and the Arts Weekly*, January 25, 1991, p. 14; Nancy Goyne Evans, *American Windsor Chairs* (New York: Hudson Hills Press in association with the Henry Francis du Pont Winterthur Museum, 1996), figs. 6-40, 6-41, 6-116, 6-133; for york chairs, see Trent, *Hearts and Crowns*, nos. 33, 34, 38–41; for Housatonic River valley chairs, see Edward S. Cooke, Jr., *Fiddlebacks and Crooked-backs: Elijah Booth and Other Joiners in Newtown and Woodbury, 1750–1820* (Waterbury, Conn.: Mattatuck Historical Society, 1982), figs. 3, 13.

## 66 ◆ Roundabout chair
### Southeastern New England
### 1740–75

Among the large number of turned roundabout chairs still in existence, this one appears to have no exact counterpart. The features, which are a reflection of various regional influences, suggest a reasonably early construction date. Upon acquisition, it was suggested that the chair originated in Portsmouth, New Hampshire, although the stylistic features favor a more southern origin. Cherry is the principal wood, and while used occasionally in New Hampshire furniture, it is more common in southeastern New England. Of the small number of chairs constructed with a double-baluster-and-cylinder post sequence above the seat, several have related double-baluster stretchers, and one is further braced at the lower leg blocks by southeastern New England–type cross stretchers. Flared-top balusters with carefully turned collars

and bases, as illustrated, were part of the vocabulary of Rhode Island and eastern Connecticut vernacular seating design. There are also strong Massachusetts influences represented here in the ogee-top splats (see No. 7), the carved Spanish feet with prominent toes and bulging heels, and the block-and-turned work in general (see Nos. 3, 4).[1]

This chair, remarkable for its large size, is unusual in several other respects. It is one of a few roundabout seats supported on four Spanish feet, as opposed to a single carved foot and three turned supports. Although vase splats are not uncommon in corner seating, this early narrow pattern is rare. The splats are supported in plinths sawed as part of the stay rails, which are bowed to complement the curved arm rails. The arms are terminated by unusual, cresent-shape grips instead of circular flat scrolls. Overall, the turned work is of excellent quality.[2]

The round, low-back chair was probably introduced to the American home in the early eighteenth century. John Gaines II's Ipswich, Massachusetts, shop accounts for 1736, 1740, and 1743 identify writing and barber's chairs, the latter possibly fitted with a back extension to support the head. Rather than supporting a writing leaf, like the later Windsor writing chair, the round-back seat had broad, low arms, which permitted the writer to draw the chair under the fall of a desk while retaining elbow support. Several other common names also describe this distinctive chair. Philadelphia craftsman Solomon Fussell identified a "Corner Chair" in 1744. John Banister, a Newport, Rhode Island, merchant, purchased a "Round about Chair" from William Love in 1750. "Compas Chair" may have been the local term in Malden, near Boston, where Thomas Pratt sold one such seat in 1756. "Round" and "round back" were other names, although the term *roundabout* was the most widely used.[3]

The "Round Back Flag Bottom Chair" listed in the Portsmouth, New Hampshire, estate of Anglican clergyman Arthur Browne (1773), was the popularly priced version of the roundabout. Framed chairs made of mahogany or walnut had loose bottoms upholstered in a variety of materials; leather and haircloth are mentioned in the 1776 confiscated Boston estate of Richard Lechmere. Household locations for the roundabout chair varied. Sitting or dining parlors sometimes contained a low-back chair, particularly if there was a desk or bookcase desk in the room, but they also appeared in entryways, bedrooms, and kitchens. A broad spectrum of society purchased and used the roundabout chair. Besides merchant owners, records name lawyers, sea captains, a sugar refiner, a retailer, a house carpenter, a cordwainer, and a victualler.[4]

*NGE*

---

**Construction:** The tall, narrow crest with long curved ends is molded to an ogee contour on the forward face and rounded behind the central projection. The crest is attached to the arm rail with nails driven up from the rail bottom 2" from either end. The sawed arm rail is formed by two sections that met originally in a lap joint at the center back; the forward ends are terminated by large, flat, hooklike scrolls. The upper edges are rounded slightly, front and back. The rail is supported on round tenons at the post tops. The splats, which are joined to the arm rails and the stay-rail plinths with rectangular tenons, are flat at the front edges and chamfered at the back. The stay rails are attached with rectangular tenons to the post blocks (partly pinned) and bowed to simulate the rail curve. Round tenons secure the rounded rectangular seat rails and turned stretchers to the post and leg blocks. The left front rail is continuous with the front seat block, into which is socketed the round tenon of the front leg. The feet are carved from solid wood.

**Condition:** The crest is loose at the right end. The left arm mortise probably broke through the top surface of the arm rail; the hole is repaired with composition material. A truncated pyramid-shape piece of wood is set into the bottom surface of the center-back rail joint. The rail face is split above the left splat. Wood losses occur at both of the heavily glued splat-rail joints. The upper tips of the right splat and lower tips of the left splat are replaced. Both splats are cracked through near the center bottom. The seat-level block of the rear post is patched at the front. The front seat rails are slightly skewed. Both left rear side stretchers appear to be old replacements; their overall diameters and central rings are noticeably smaller than the others. The back corner of the lower left leg block was broken off and reattached. All the feet are repaired with facing pieces at the pads; the left and rear feet have new front toes. The rush seat, which is old, worn, and sagging, is probably not original. Tack holes along the edges and across the seat block indicate that an upholstery layer was introduced at some time.

**Dimensions:**

| | | |
|---|---|---|
| H. | 34³/₄ in. | 88.2 cm |
| H. (seat) | 17¹/₈ in. | 43.5 cm |
| W. (crest) | 12¹/₂ in. | 31.7 cm |
| W. (seat, across center) | 26¹/₄ in. | 66.7 cm |
| W. (arms) | 30⁵/₈ in. | 77.8 cm |
| W. (feet, across center) | 31⁵/₈ in. | 80.3 cm |
| D. (center seat) | 23⁷/₈ in. | 60.6 cm |
| D. (feet, front to back) | 28³/₈ in. | 72.1 cm |

**Materials:** *Microanalysis:* Primary: cherry. Secondary: ash (right rear seat rail). *Finish:* black paint with clear resin; surface crackled, chipped, and repainted in many places with flat black.

**Accession history:** Purchased by H. F. du Pont from Lillian B. Cogan, Farmington, Conn., 1951. Gift of H. F. du Pont, 1951.
51.42

---

1. For baluster-cylinder post sequences on roundabout chairs, see John S. Walton advertisement, *Antiques and the Arts Weekly*, November 7, 1975; Nathan Liverant and Son advertisement, *Maine Antique Digest*, September 1982; Lewis M. Scranton advertisement, *Maine Antique Digest*, August 1983; see also Nutting, *Furniture Treasury*, no. 1835. Similar carved feet appear on Boston chairs; see Forman, *American Seating Furniture*, cats. 54, 56. A related york, or yoke-back, armchair with a narrow, ogee-top splat, double-baluster-and-cylinder turnings under the arms, and probably crescent-shape arm terminals could have been produced in the same or a neighboring shop as the roundabout chair; see *Antiques and the Arts Weekly*, September 28, 1990, p. 70 upper left.

2. For roundabout chairs with 4 Spanish feet, see *American Antiques from Israel Sack Collection*, 10 vols. (Washington, D.C.: Highland House, ca. 1969–), 1:57; Fales, *Furniture of Historic Deerfield*, fig. 63; Sotheby's, "Important Americana: The Bertram K. Little and Nina Fletcher Little Collection, Part 1" (January 29, 1994), lot 186.

3. Solomon Fussell account book, 1738–48, Stephen Collins Papers, Library of Congress, Washington, D.C.; John Banister receipt book, 1748–68, Newport Historical Society, Newport, R.I. (microfilm, Downs collection); Thomas Pratt account book, 1730–68, Downs collection; John Gaines II and Thomas Gaines I account book, 1707–60, Downs collection. A "round" chair is itemized in the 1768 inventory of Ebenezer Pierpoint of Roxbury, Mass., as quoted in Cummings, *Rural Household Inventories*, p. 219; a "round back" chair is listed in Joshua and Abraham Lunt (Newbury, Mass.) account book, 1736–72, Peabody Essex Museum, Salem, Mass.

4. Browne inventory, as quoted in Jane C. Giffen, "A Selection of New Hampshire Inventories," *Historical New Hampshire* 24, nos. 1/2 (Spring/Summer 1969): 54–59; Richard Lechmere confiscated estate, 1776, Massachusetts State Archives, Boston (photostat, Downs collection). Owner occupations and household locations for roundabout chairs are listed in estate inventories of Mrs. Mary Hubbard, 1779; John Eliot, 1772; Capt. David Malcolm (merchant), 1769; William Skinner, Benjamin Andrews, and Newman Greenough (lawyers), 1760, 1778, 1781; Richard Humphrys and Nicholas Gardiner (sea captains), 1759, 1782; John Baker (sugar refiner) 1780; Joseph Wheeler (retailer), 1761, all in Suffolk County Probate Court, Boston (microfilm, Downs collection); see also inventories of Consider Leeds (cordwainer), 1772, and John Shirley (victualler), 1773, as quoted in Cummings, *Rural Household Inventories*, pp. 253, 255–56; Jethro Spooner (house carpenter) inventory, 1769, Town Council Book, 1768–71, Newport Historical Society.

**Construction:** The ogee-ended crest is attached to the arm rail with eight rosehead nails (originally nine) driven up from the rail bottom; single nails extending from each ogee tip down through the rail are clinched over. The sawed arm rail is comprised of two sections that are butted at the center back. The forward ends are terminated by large, flat, circular scrolls, and the top edges are chamfered on the exposed surfaces. The rail is supported on round tenons at the post tops (pinned from outside). Round tenons also secure the rounded rectangular seat rails and the stretchers to the chamfered post and leg blocks. The left front rail is continuous with the front seat block, into which is socketed the reduced round tenon of the front leg. The flaring, creased ankles of the pad feet are separated from the leg blocks by rings. A back ledge and deep disk are common to each foot.

**Condition:** The left crest end, which is marked by multiple cracks, is broken through at the rise of the ogee. The front seat block is cracked on the forward faces; another crack occurs in the right seat-post block. The left rear seat rail has been reset at the back joint; an old, partially visible mortise hole is plugged. Since the seat appears level, the repair may represent an original mistake. The rush seat is old but not original; a central strand is broken out of the left rear quadrant.

**Dimensions:**

| | | |
|---|---|---|
| H. | 30 1/8 in. | 76.5 cm |
| H. (seat) | 16 3/4 in. | 42.5 cm |
| W. (crest) | 19 1/4 in. | 48.9 cm |
| W. (seat, across center) | 27 3/4 in. | 70.5 cm |
| W. (arms) | 28 3/4 in. | 73.0 cm |
| W. (feet, across center) | 23 7/8 in. | 60.6 cm |
| D. (center seat) | 24 in. | 61.0 cm |
| D. (feet, front to back) | 27 in. | 68.6 cm |

**Materials:** *Microanalysis:* Primary: birch. *Finish:* 2 coats or more of dark brown color in resin over brick-red stain; seat coated with thin light brown resin.

**Publications:** Downs, *American Furniture*, fig. 59. Bishop, *Centuries and Styles of the American Chair*, fig. 116.

**Accession history:** Purchased by H. F. du Pont from Charles R. Morson, New York, 1929. Bequest of H. F. du Pont, 1969.
58.1503

1. For Connecticut turned chairs, see Trent, *Hearts and Crowns*, nos. 13–17, 23, 42, 56, 58; for southern New England furniture employing birch, see Monkhouse and Michie, *American Furniture*, cat. 116; Jobe and Kaye, *New England Furniture*, nos. 53, 73, 129.

2. Stephen Fullerton inventory of losses, Boston Fire Documents and Correspondence, 1760, vol. 2, p. 38, Boston Public Library, Boston; Andrew Oliver inventory, as quoted in Alice Hanson Jones, *American Colonial Wealth: Documents and Methods*, 3 vols. (New York: Arno Press, 1977), 2:968; Mary Pease estate inventory, 1793, Registry of Probate, Nantucket County, Mass., Probate Record Book 4.

## 67 ◆ Roundabout chair
### Southeastern New England, probably coastal Rhode Island
### 1760–1800

Almost as unusual as the rush-bottom roundabout chair with four Spanish feet (see No. 66) is the turned corner seat with four circular pad supports. Linking this chair closely with the armchair of No. 39, and thus pinpointing its origin, are the post profiles below the arms (modified by the substitution of a ring turning for the urn) and the compressed-baluster-on-ring and block sequence beneath the seat. The pad feet are different, however. The corner-chair supports are shaped to a pattern common in formal seating furniture (see No. 10 center and right). Similar stretchers of long, double-baluster form centered by an oval turning occur with some frequency in rush-bottom work ascribed to neighboring coastal Connecticut. Birch, the construction material, is generally identified with northern New England, although the wood is found occasionally in chairs associated with the southern region, where it is employed as a secondary material in cabinetwork.[1]

Rush bottoms in roundabout chairs are usually not identified in estate inventories and other records. Among the items "Lost in the Shop" of chairmaker Stephen Fullerton during the great Boston fire of March 20, 1760, were two seats described only as "Roundbout Chairs," although the presence of "1000 Bondels of flagg" (rush) in the shop indicates the principal focus of Fullerton's work. Fourteen years later Andrew Oliver's "Straw Bottom Chair" valued at 4s. was described primarily because it was furnished with a "Cushing." As a single chair listed in conjunction with a "Black Walnut Desk & Book Case," the appraisers identified its function. The "Mans Round Chair" in the Nantucket estate of widow Mary Pease probably served the same purpose. Valued at 5s., it also had a rush seat. Although the Pease parlor was furnished with a large looking glass, an eight-day clock, and several mahogany tables in addition to a "Mehogany Swell'd Desk," the seating furniture of this room, the *best* in the house, was considerably less pretentious. Accompanying the roundabout chair were six "Red Joiners Chairs" and a "Great Black Chair," all probably fitted with

## 68 ◆ Roundabout chair

Eastern Connecticut, probably New
London County
1750–75

This chair is purported to have "descended in the families of William Williams, a signer of the Declaration of Independence from Connecticut, and Governor Jonathan Trumbull of Connecticut." While original ownership in the Williams or Trumbull families is unsubstantiated, possession of the chair by several generations of descendants named McClellan suggests that such a connection is plausible. Faith Williams (1775–1838), daughter of William Williams and granddaughter of Governor Trumbull, married lawyer John McClellan (1767–1858) of Woodstock, Connecticut, in 1796. About 1833 the McClellan house was destroyed by fire, although McClellan's one-room law office (now re-erected at Old Sturbridge Village, Massachusetts), which stood in the yard, escaped the conflagration. A new home was erected in 1833. A family history related two generations later by grandson Dr. George E. McClellan, who occupied the homestead, states that furnishings for the new house were "brought from Lebanon," Connecticut, from the residence of the Williams and Trumbull families. At George McClellan's death in the mid twentieth century, most of the "many Trumbull and Williams items" that filled his home passed to a grandson.[1]

The dealer from whom this roundabout was acquired claims to have first seen the chair in the George McClellan home during a visit in the 1940s or early 1950s. That dealer bought the chair in 1973 at an auction of the estate of Charles Woolsey Lyon, also a dealer, whose label appears beneath one arm terminal. The auction catalogue lists the provenance of the chair as Dr. George McClellan, but whether Lyon acquired the chair from McClellan or his heir is unclear.[2]

The close association of this roundabout chair with two eastern Connecticut families reinforces its regional attributes. The distinctive, oval-bottom, elongated balusters supporting the arm rail are similar to those in several other roundabouts ascribed to Connecticut or Rhode Island. Some chairs are constructed of cherry, as is this example. Of particular significance is the existence of another cherrywood roundabout chair of extension-top, square-seat, and box-stretcher design attributed to Connecticut that resembles the Winterthur chair in overall form. Differing elements of that chair include solid splats with plain bases; an inverted ogee top crest; columnar posts beneath the arm rail and crest; a heavy, rectangular front leg; and block-and-cylinder–turned side and rear legs. Another chair, one with a low back and said to be constructed of walnut but otherwise

virtually identical to the Winterthur chair, appears to have originated in the same shop. Were the materials alike, it could be suggested that the two chairs were made originally as a pair.[3]

The extension uprights of this chair vary significantly in design from the posts that support the arm rail. The upper back appears to be an early addition, possibly constructed during the lifetime of the original owner, since the construction techniques are consistent with eighteenth- and early nineteenth-century work. This speculation is reinforced by the existence of the walnut chair without a back extension. The extension splat is similar to those below the arm rail, the height and breadth modified slightly to fit a taller, narrower space. Although the crest is a mirror image of the rail cap on the arms (also probably an addition), the inverted profile is unusual and awkward. It is possible that the back alteration was carried out at the same time the seat frame was modified. Two opposing interior cleats originally supporting a loose-seat frame were rabbeted near the ends to receive a board (now missing) cut with a central hole to accommodate a chamber vessel. The chair currently has an extra-stuffed seat mounted on a solid board that was perhaps produced at the same time. Clearly, the purpose of the alteration was to modify a piece of household furniture to serve a new specialized function as a chair for an invalid or an elderly family member. The interior fitting provided convenience; the seat, comfort; and the extension top, a headrest and a support for a draped textile to ward off drafts.

A few roundabout chairs were fitted originally as close stools, or commode chairs. Normally, a lid accompanied the interior board and chamber vessel, and frequently deep skirts extended from the seat rails to conceal the interior "convenience." Such chairs were used in the bedroom. Many close stools are not further described in documents, although there is no mistaking the appearance of the chair in John Simpson's household. The Boston merchant died in 1764 possessed of "1 Round about Clost stool Chair & pan" valued at 15s.[4]

NGE

---

Inscriptions or marks: *Beneath right arm terminal:* "c. w. lyon/ 75178" typed, on modern white gummed label; accompanied by an indecipherable mark in blue ink.

Construction: The inverted, ogee-ended extension crest is supported on rectangular tenons at the post and splat tops. The crest face is rounded to the upper back edge; the back surface is flat. The flat-faced extension splat is curved laterally to conform to the crest and rail curves. The edges are canted, front to back; broad vertical plane marks are visible on the back surface. The straight upper posts are flat at the front and sides and rounded slightly at the back. The posts and splat are joined with rectangular tenons to

the heavy ogee-ended back rail on the arms, which is rounded on the face and flat at the top and back. Nine rosehead nails secure the back rail to the arms from the bottom. The two sections of the flat arm rail, which are butted at the center back, are chamfered at the top edges; the large forward terminals, or scrolls, are more oval than round. The flat-faced splats of the lower back have canted edges, front to back, and are tenoned into the arm rail and plinths. The plinths are hollow on the front and side faces, finished with low, stepped top beads, and nailed to the back seat rails. The posts are round tenoned into the arm rail. All joints are pinned from the outside rail surface; the end posts are also pinned at the inside. The rectangular seat frame is finished with a half-round top lip; interior cleats, secured by two wrought nails each, support the loose-seat frame. The rails are joined to the post and front leg blocks with rectangular tenons (pinned). The stretchers are joined to the legs at the lower blocks with rectangular tenons (pinned outside and inside). The interior corners of the blocks are scribed on both faces to mark the mortise slots. The outside top edges of the stretchers are defined with a narrow bead.

Condition: The extension top probably is not part of the original chair fabric; however, it was added at an early date. Minor cracks occur at or near many joints. Open rectangular slots 3 1/2" to 4" long were cut in the left rear and right front interior seat-frame cleats near either end, presumably to accommodate a board supporting a chamber pot. The slots have partially exposed the original nails securing the cleats. Small pierced holes centered in the bottom of each foot appear to have been made by modern glides. The loose-seat frame, which is not original, is made from a thick heavy board of dry, aged wood and is deeply stuffed. Under the brownish red leather outer cover is an undercover.

Dimensions:

| | | |
|---|---|---|
| H. | 45 5/8 in. | 115.9 cm |
| H. (seat) | 17 1/4 in. | 43.8 cm |
| W. (crest) | 17 5/8 in. | 44.8 cm |
| W. (seat, across center) | 24 1/4 in. | 61.6 cm |
| W. (arms) | 28 3/4 in. | 73.0 cm |
| W. (feet, across center) | 26 1/4 in. | 66.7 cm |
| D. (center seat) | 24 1/2 in. | 62.2 cm |
| D. (feet, front to back) | 26 1/4 in. | 66.7 cm |

Materials: *Microanalysis:* Primary: cherry. Secondary: chestnut (inner front rail); white pine group (loose-seat frame). *Finish:* (top extension) medium reddish brown color in resin; (chair) medium dark brown color in resin.

Provenance: The chair is alleged to have been originally owned by William Williams (1731–1811) and his wife Mary Trumbull, daughter of Gov. Jonathan Trumbull. It purportedly passed to their daughter Faith, who married John McClellan, a lawyer in Woodstock, Conn. The chair descended to their son, John McClellan, and to his son, George E. McClellan. It was sold at the Charles Woolsey Lyon estate auction at Sotheby Parke Bernet in 1973 and purchased at the sale by Lillian Blankley Cogan.

Accession history: Purchased by Winterthur Museum from Lillian Blankley Cogan, Farmington, Conn., 1974.
74.1

---

1. Sotheby Parke Bernet, "Eighteenth- and Nineteenth-Century American Furniture: From the Estate of the Late Charles Woolsey Lyon" (March 3, 1973), lot 152; Dorothy Putnam McClellan to Lillian Blankley Cogan, February 6, 1974, folder 74.1, Registration Office, Winterthur. For the McClellan law office, see John Obed Curtis, "The Buildings at Old Sturbridge Village," *Antiques* 114, no. 4 (October 1979): 898, fig. 4.

2. Lillian Blankley Cogan to Charles F. Hummel, December 29, 1973, folder 74.1, Registration Office, Winterthur; Sotheby Parke Bernet, "Eighteenth- and Nineteenth-Century American Furniture," lot 152.

3. For other roundabout chairs with oval-bottom balusters, see Jobe and Kaye, *New England Furniture*, no. 106; Rodriguez Roque, *American Furniture*, nos. 83, 84 (the provenance of no. 83 is the Lord and Burr families of Lyme, Conn.); Bernard and S. Dean Levy advertisement, *Antiques* 118, no. 1 (July 1980): 9; no. 75.265, DAPC, Visual Resources Collection, Winterthur Library (this chair was purchased in Connecticut by a former owner); Trent with Nelson, "A Catalogue of New London County Joined Chairs," no. 45 (this chair is said to have belonged to William Pitkin [1694–1769], a governor of Connecticut). For the tall cherrywood roundabout chair that resembles this chair, see "Shop Talk," *Antiques* 78, no. 6 (December 1960): 544. For the low roundabout walnut chair, see Scott Bassoff and Sandy Jacobs advertisement, *Antiques and the Arts Weekly*, August 2, 1991.

4. Hornor, *Blue Book*, pp. 199–200. John Simpson estate inventory, 1764, Suffolk County Probate Court, Boston (microfilm, Downs collection).

## 69 ◆ Roundabout chair
Connecticut, vicinity of Newtown
and Woodbury
1770–90

A small group of furniture, associated in recent decades with the lower Housatonic River valley, is identified in part by several unusual, shared leg features. The group consists primarily of tall chests and dressing tables. This roundabout chair, a form heretofore unreported, can now be added to that group. Typical of this furniture are prominent rounded knees flanked by hooklike brackets secured to the faces of the adjoining frame. A distinctive bead, terminated by a small roundel at the top and a faceted square at the bottom, borders most upper legs and brackets (fig. 1). Whether the feet are formed as pads or claws, the ankles are distinguished by curves that are deeply hollow and sloped in the New York manner. The feature is accentuated in this example by the long forward sweep of the center front toe. The resulting claw is perhaps the most aesthetically pleasing support in the group.

The same curve, with the addition of the bulge at the knee, is echoed in the long profile of the back splats, providing good visual compatibility between the upper and lower structures of the chair. The flaring tops and cusped bases of the back splats have prototypes in Housatonic River valley rush-bottom seating.[1]

Many pieces of Housatonic River valley furniture carved with the illustrated bead at the knee are framed with the same stepped, flat-arch skirt flanked (and divided) by deep cavettos. This chair is related to still other furniture from the region bearing distinctive features, such as flat, squared, and lobed feet, large hollow shells centered in the base molding, and small rosettes in the corner pilasters. The lamb's-tongue bases in the corner pilasters of a desk-and-bookcase in this group with the features described (see No. 202) have triangular profiles similar to those formed by the ogee tips terminating the crest rail in the roundabout chair. A particularly subtle feature of the chair is the rounded lip, or bead, along the entire upper back edge of the arms and crest (fig. 2). The forward termini of the

**Fig. 1.** Detail, side profile of rear leg, right side.

bead are tight volutes carved on the top surfaces of the "cushioned" arm pads. Smaller but similarly rounded pads appear in a corner chair with squared feet and flat-arched seat rails relating to Housatonic River valley work. Use of cushioned arm pads is widespread, however. Chairs of eastern Connecticut and Rhode Island origin sometimes have similar terminals with volute-carved tops.[2]

In a recent study of Housatonic River valley furniture, Edward S. Cooke, Jr., has shown that life in the region was steeped in traditional, conservative values, particularly as reflected in the social and economic development of Newtown, where farming was an important supplement to craft activity. Gradually, some communities, of which Woodbury is representative, adopted a more progressive outlook and began to reap the economic and cultural rewards that interaction in a broad, regional market provided. In still another development, which occurred well before the mid eighteenth century, craftsmen from the densely populated coastal communities began moving inland, carrying their traditions with them. All of these influences and a natural increase in the population of the region created more demand for consumer goods, which is reflected in the furniture.[3]

Although the background history of this chair is unknown, related furniture is associated with Housatonic River valley families. A key piece is a high chest of drawers, which by tradition was made for Hannah Grant of Newtown about the time of her marriage in 1769. It has bead-carved knees and claw feet that relate closely to the roundabout chair. A tall chest with similar features but shorter legs descended in the Stiles family of neighboring Southbury. Another tall chest, purchased from an old Woodbury estate at the turn of the twentieth century, has pad feet and a variant bead carved at the knees. Among a small group of dressing tables with related bead-carved knees and pad or claw feet, one is reputed to have come from the Johnson family of Newtown. A second table, probably made in the same town, has an association with a New Haven family.[4]

*NGE*

---

**Inscriptions or marks:** *Incised on both front rail rabbets near the front leg:* "X".

**Construction:** The short, ogee-ended crest is attached to the arm rail with three screws entering from the rail bottom—one at each end and one left of center through the long center-back lap joint formed by the two parts of the arm rail. The crest face is ogee contoured; the straight back surface is molded at the top with a lip that approximates a beaded edge. The beading is continued along the back edge of the arm rail to the front terminals. The terminals are large, domed scrolls with carved central volutes on the top surfaces. The arm faces are rounded to the crest ends. The plain splats are flat at the front edges, chamfered at the back edges, and tenoned into the arm rail and seat plinths. The posts, which are square-cornered except for a forward chamfer, are joined to the arm rail with rectangular tenons pinned once from the rail back. The low plinths, which are hollow on the front and side faces, are glued to the seat rails; the front edges extend beyond the rails. The rectangular seat frame is finished at the front rails with a narrow flat lip and a large outside bead. Rabbets inside the front rails and an irregular, tooled vertical interior block at the center back fastened with three rosehead nails support the loose-seat frame. Both rabbets are incised with an X near the front leg, presumably an

**Fig. 2.** Detail, right arm rail and rail cap.

assembly mark rather than a set number. The rail bottoms are sawed in flat arches with stepped and coved (cavetto) returns at the ends; the edges are slightly rough or tooled at the arches and scored with double kerf marks at the coved returns (behind the knee brackets). The rails are joined to the post and leg blocks with vertical rectangular tenons, which are pinned outside, except at the center front and right front. Double pins on the interior frame at either end of the right rear and left front rails (one only at the center back) are located in horizontal channels gouged in the rail faces. The lower pins are on a level with the rail returns. The high-cheeked knees and glued knee brackets of the cabriole legs are carved with flat beads at the edges, terminating in small roundels at the top and squared facets at the bottom. The ankles are deeply curved. The feet are shaped in long forward sweeps, which are terminated by squared, knuckled toes with recessed nails; the balls are apple shaped.

**Condition:** The left arm terminal is cracked through at a diagonal break above the post and repaired with a pin, glue, and composition material. An iron strap held by screws reinforces the bottom surface. The interior block at the center seat back is possibly an old replacement. Hairline cracks are present in several post-rail joints. A screw at the inside top of the left leg secures a crack extending down from the rear corner of the leg block. Five of the eight knee brackets are replacements: front leg (left); left leg (right); rear leg (left); right leg (both, one cracked). Insect damage occurs in the ball of the front foot and on the underlip of the right rear rail plinth. Remnants of an old paper label handwritten in black ink are glued to the inside face of the left front rail. Double nail holes on the bottom surfaces of the left rear and right front rails at the arch ends suggest that a commode frame was once in place, although not part of the original construction. The loose-seat frame was once covered with rush. The corner blocks have been cut down at the outside

edges, but the marks of the rush strands remain on the wood. The rush was probably painted white or cream color, as indicated by a residue on the plinth faces. Whether the rush seat was original to the chair or a later addition cannot be determined. The webbing of the seat frame is old, but uneven discoloration indicates it was removed from something else. The sackcloth, while discolored, is probably of nineteenth-century date. The modern leather seat cover is the only one placed on the frame since the rush was removed.

**Dimensions:**

| | | |
|---|---|---|
| H. | 31 in. | 78.7 cm |
| H. (seat) | 18 in. | 45.7 cm |
| W. (crest) | 15³/4 in. | 40.0 cm |
| W. (seat, across center) | 25 in. | 63.5 cm |
| W. (arms) | 29 in. | 73.6 cm |
| W. (feet, across center) | 29¹/4 in. | 74.3 cm |
| D. (seat) | 24³/4 in. | 62.9 cm |
| D. (feet) | 29¹/4 in. | 74.3 cm |

**Materials:** *Microanalysis:* Primary: cherry (front leg, left rear rail, loose-seat frame). Secondary: yellow poplar (seat-frame block). *Finish:* variegated dark reddish brown color in resin.

**Accession history:** Bequest of H. F. du Pont, 1969. 64.574

---

1. For the tall chests and 5 dressing tables in this group, see Edward S. Cooke, Jr., *Fiddlebacks and Crooked-backs: Elijah Booth and Other Joiners in Newtown and Woodbury, 1750–1820* (Waterbury, Conn.: Mattatuck Historical Society, 1982), figs. 7, 8, 32; Jobe and Kaye, *New England Furniture,* no. 41; *Connecticut Furniture,* no. 176; Fales, *Furniture of Historic Deerfield,* fig. 442; Ward, *American Case Furniture,* cat. 104; "Living with Antiques: The William Peters House," *Antiques* 105, no. 1 (January 1974): 142, pl. 5. For New York prototype feet, see Downs, *American Furniture,* figs. 65, 66; Warren, *Bayou Bend,* no. 87; for rush-bottom seating, see Cooke, *Fiddlebacks and Crooked-backs,* figs. 4, 5, 11–13.

2. The Housatonic River valley, which extends inland from Stratford on the coast, was readily accessible by way of Long Island Sound to the extensive trading region encompassed by this long body of water—from New York City to Cape Cod. For related Housatonic River valley furniture, see Cooke, *Fiddlebacks and Crooked-backs,* figs. 26, 28, 29; the squared-foot roundabout chair is illustrated in *Litchfield County Furniture, 1730–1850* (Litchfield, Conn.: Litchfield Historical Society, 1969), no. 12; for a Connecticut roundabout chair, see Rodriguez Roque, *American Furniture,* no. 84.

3. Cooke, *Fiddlebacks and Crooked-backs.*

4. The Grant high chest is owned by Connecticut Historical Society; see *Connecticut Furniture,* no. 90. The Stiles family tall chest, now at Colonial Williamsburg, is one of many pieces attributed without foundation to the local Booth family; see Greenlaw, *New England Furniture,* no. 82. For the second tall chest, now at SPNEA, see Jobe and Kaye, *New England Furniture,* no. 41. For the Johnson family dressing table, see Ward, *American Case Furniture,* cat. 104; for the New Haven family dressing table, see *Connecticut Furniture,* no. 176. See also J. A. Herdeg, "A Lower Housatonic River Valley Shop Tradition: An Analysis of Six Related Dressing Tables," *Connecticut Historical Society Bulletin* 56, nos. 1/2 (Winter/Spring 1991): 38–56.

## 70 ◆ Roundabout chair

Southeastern coastal New England,
from southern Massachusetts to
eastern Connecticut
1750–80

Although this chair has been ascribed in
the past to Massachusetts, regionally diverse
features within the design suggest that the
influence may be broader. Massachusetts
characteristics dominate the upper structure,
but Connecticut–Rhode Island features are
present in the undercarriage. The combination
points to a coastal origin where furniture
distributed by water to an interregional market
often had considerable impact on local design.

One feature that appears with frequency in
Massachusetts corner chairs is a pronounced
"elbow," rounded or pointed, positioned
between the arm terminal and the heavy
back rail. In this chair the broad elbows are
rounded. The columnar posts that support
these arms are turned with bulging vaselike
tips, another feature common in Massachusetts
chairs. The transition from tip to column is
abrupt, and only a thin ring separates the
column base from the seat block. Most posts
are enhanced to a greater degree with small
connector turnings; the starkness of this
example likely identifies it as a nonurban
product. Broad, lobed splats are common to
Massachusetts seating. The banisters of this
chair are balanced, top and bottom, because
the base and neck are the same size and have
the same profile (inverted). The center front
leg is particularly narrow across the knee. Of
greater interest, however, are the straight legs;
the profiles shift abruptly from round stock at
the top to contoured ankles and small pad
feet. A cherrywood corner chair ascribed to
Rhode Island and a maple and cherry example
with a Hartford provenance also have this
unusual feature. The profiles of the cross
stretchers relate generally to the silhouettes
of the arm posts.[1]

Written and visual evidence indicates that
roundabout chairs were sometimes produced

en suite with other formal household seating.
A large set of fourteen horsehair-covered
chairs owned in Portsmouth, New Hampshire,
in the late eighteenth century but originating
in the Boston area probably consisted of
twelve parlor chairs and two roundabouts. A
side chair and a corner chair from this suite,
owned by the Society for the Preservation
of New England Antiquities, Boston, have
pierced and carved splats like that of No. 58.
Six mahogany side chairs and "one Round
Chair" in the owl's-eye pattern (see No. 31)
enumerated together in 1781 appear to have
made a parlor set in the Boston home of
Newman Greenough, Esq. The side chairs
were valued at £1.10.0 apiece, the roundabout
chair, at £2.[2]

*NGE*

---

**Construction:** The ogee-ended crest is attached to
the arm rail with three countersunk screws entering

from the rail bottom. The crest face is rounded
to the upper back edge; the back surface is flat,
except at the ends where deep, U-shape channels
are terminated by small scrolls at the top edge. The
two-piece, flat arm rail with rounded-chamfered top
edges is butted at the center back; the bottom edges
are narrowly chamfered. The arms are terminated
at the front by small circular pads and broadened
adjacent to the crest to form rounded elbows. The
flat-faced splats are canted at the edges, front to
back, and tenoned into the arm rail and plinths. The
plinths are hollow on the front and side faces,
finished with top beads, and nailed to the back seat
rails. The posts are round tenoned into the arm rail.
The compass-shape seat frame is finished with a
rounded top lip, interior rabbets at the front rails
to support the loose-seat frame, and corner blocks
fastened with rosehead nails. The bottom edges are
sawed in flat arches and chamfered on the inside.
The rails are joined to the post blocks and front leg
extension with rectangular tenons (pinned). The
side and rear legs are continuous with the upper
posts. The creased-tip cross stretchers are round

tenoned into the legs. The double-rabbet joint at the center crossing is secured with a screw from the bottom.

**Condition:** Age cracks appear at the center crest back. A crack through the arm rail to the left of the back joint is secured with a screw from the bottom; the inside left arm terminal is defaced by worm damage. The right splat is cracked through at the upper right and lower left corners and glued. The flat-arch rail returns immediately flanking the front leg are restored (left) or cracked and defaced (right). The front leg-extension joint is repaired. A deteriorating knot is located in the right post block at the lower right corner. Cracks occur in the front and side legs at the stretcher sockets. The rear leg block is cracked at the lower inside edge, and a piece is missing. The interior front corner block is now secured with a screw, although the block appears to be original. The knee brackets have been attached with one or two screws. While all appear old, there is considerable variation in depth; the right front bracket may be an old replacement. Traces of disks are present beneath the pad feet. The loose-seat frame is modern.

**Dimensions:**

| | | |
|---|---|---|
| H. | 30 1/2 in. | 77.5 cm |
| H. (seat) | 17 1/4 in. | 43.8 cm |
| W. (crest) | 16 1/4 in. | 41.3 cm |
| W. (seat, across center) | 22 3/8 in. | 56.9 cm |
| W. (arms) | 27 1/4 in. | 69.2 cm |
| W. (feet, across center) | 24 1/2 in. | 62.2 cm |
| D. (seat) | 21 1/2 in. | 54.6 cm |
| D. (feet, front to back) | 25 5/8 in. | 64.1 cm |

**Materials:** *Microanalysis:* Primary: American black walnut. Secondary: red pine group (all corner blocks). *Finish:* medium brown color in resin. *Upholstery:* nineteenth-century red morocco leather pieced with a seam across the center; Europe or United States, 1800–1900.

**Accession history:** Gift of H. F. du Pont, 1960. 58.2428

1. For Massachusetts chairs, see *American Antiques from Israel Sack Collection*, 10 vols. (Washington, D.C.: Highland House, ca. 1969–), 4:1066; Bernard and S. Dean Levy, Inc., *Catalogue VI* (New York: By the company, 1988), p. 39. For Connecticut and Rhode Island chairs, see John Kenneth Byard advertisement, *Antiques* 72, no. 2 (August 1957): 97 (provenance given in Visual Resources Collection, Winterthur Library); Florene Maine advertisement, *Antiques* 85, no. 4 (April 1964): 367.

2. On the Portsmouth-owned chairs, see Jobe and Kaye, *New England Furniture*, nos. 114, 115. Newman Greenough, Esq., estate inventory, 1781, Suffolk County Probate Court, Boston (microfilm, Downs collection).

## 71 ✦ Roundabout chair
Southeastern New England, possibly Boston, Massachusetts, or vicinity
1745–75

The choice of cherrywood for the primary elements of this chair suggests a broad assignment to southeastern New England, although the chair has strong stylistic links to Boston. Prominent among the features now associated with that urban center are webbed claw feet of the pattern illustrated. This type of claw was first current in the city during the 1740s. Two other features of this chair that have Boston prototypes are the ogee knee brackets of pronounced pointed base and the baluster splat with its broad top and slim waist (see No. 14). The simple splat base, formed of small points and quarter rounds, recalls Boston work in the early Queen Anne style (see Nos. 4–6). Less clearly connected with Boston work is the use of cherrywood as the primary construction material. Cherry was

a more frequent choice among nonurban chairmakers and their customers. The principal material of the fashionable Boston chair from the 1730s to the 1750s was walnut, whether the furniture was made for local sale or export. The door remains ajar, however. Correspondence in the papers of Caleb Davis, a Boston merchant, indicates that cherrywood had once been common in the city but that by 1784 the local cabinetmakers had "done working in that Kind of wood."[1]

Two factors suggest that this roundabout chair in the Boston style may be the product of a more southerly region in New England— the cherrywood of its construction and the profiles of the arm supports. A second chair with related features—arms, posts, splats, cross stretchers, contoured seat front—is also made of cherrywood. A chair with identical posts and closely related cross stretchers is made of cherry supplemented, as is this chair, with maple. In other respects, the features are different, although that chair also has strong links with Boston design: the slot-pierced splats are a modification of the pattern in No. 35, and the intricately sawed skirts of the seat rails relate closely to a pattern in a hoop-shouldered flat-stretcher side chair of the type in No. 14.[2]

This third roundabout chair is part of the antiques collection of the Hartford (Connecticut) Steam Boiler Inspection and Insurance Company. In the eighteenth century the chair belonged to Mary Seymour, wife of Thomas Seymour (1735–1829), the first mayor of Hartford. A few years after Thomas Seymour's death, a grandson-in-law affixed to the back of the chair a brass plate giving the family history.[3]

The Winterthur chair also has a strong association with Connecticut and a distinguished history. The roundabout was acquired early in the twentieth century by pioneer collector George Smith Palmer (1855–1934), a Norwich resident until 1904 when he moved to neighboring New London. In 1928 Palmer sold his New London mansion and much of the collection to his long-time friend Israel Sack, who sent the collection to auction that same year. The chair, misidentified as mahogany, was described as a "transition type library chair of fine design." Henry Francis du Pont purchased the roundabout for the then-substantial sum of $1,600 and exhibited it in the landmark Girl Scouts loan exhibition the following year.[4]

*NGE*

---

**Construction:** The ogee-ended crest is attached to the arm rail with six countersunk screws entering from the rail bottom. The crest face is rounded to the upper back edge. The back surface is flat, except at the ends where deep V-cuts are terminated by small scrolls at the top edge. The two-piece flat arm rail with broadly chamfered top edges is butted at the center back; the bottom edges are narrowly chamfered. The forward terminals are large, circular pads. The flat-faced splats have deeply canted edges, front to back, and are tenoned into the arm rail and plinths. The plinths are hollow on the front and side faces; finished with low, stepped top beads; and nailed to the back seat rails. The posts are round tenoned into the arm rail. The compass-shape seat frame is finished with a rounded-sloping top lip, interior rabbets at the front rails to support the loose-seat frame, and corner blocks. The bottom edges of the front rails are sawed in flat arches; the rear rails have facing boards on the interior surfaces. The rails are joined to the post blocks and front leg extension with rectangular tenons (pinned). The side and rear legs are continuous with the upper posts. The knee brackets are double nailed. The three-knuckle claw toes are terminated by medium-length nails. The cross stretchers, which are secured at the center by a double rabbet, are round tenoned into the legs.

**Condition:** The right splat is cracked through and repaired at the upper left cheek and ogee. Four new interior corner blocks are secured by screws. The right rear rail may originally have had a full-width inner cleat mounted on the lower half to augment the two interior rabbets supporting the loose-seat frame; nail-hole and color evidence support this theory. The loose-seat frame is modern.

**Dimensions:**

| | | |
|---|---|---|
| H. | 35 3/8 in. | 89.9 cm |
| H. (seat) | 17 1/2 in. | 44.4 cm |
| W. (crest) | 22 3/4 in. | 57.8 cm |
| W. (seat, across center) | 25 1/4 in. | 64.2 cm |
| W. (arms) | 31 5/8 in. | 80.3 cm |
| W. (feet, across center) | 30 1/8 in. | 76.5 cm |
| D. (seat) | 24 1/4 in. | 61.6 cm |
| D. (feet, front to back) | 30 1/8 in. | 75.5 cm |

**Materials:** *Microanalysis:* Primary: cherry. Secondary: hard maple group (outer left rear rail); white pine group (inner left rear rail). *Finish:* medium dark brown color in resin; finely crackled. *Upholstery:* gold silk, floral pattern damask; Europe, 1730–60.

**Exhibitions:** "Loan Exhibition of Eighteenth- and Early Nineteenth-Century Furniture and Glass," National Council of Girl Scouts, New York, September 25–October 9, 1929.

**Publications:** National Council of Girl Scouts, *Loan Exhibition of Eighteenth- and Early Nineteenth-Century Furniture and Glass* (New York: By the council, 1929), cat. 553. Downs, *American Furniture*, fig. 63.

**Provenance:** Ex coll.: George S. Palmer, New London, Conn.

**Accession history:** Purchased by H. F. du Pont at the Palmer collection sale, Anderson Galleries, New York, October 20, 1928, lot 308. Gift of H. F. du Pont, 1960.
59.3385

---

1. Keno, Freund, and Miller, "Very Pink of the Mode," pp. 266–306, and esp. figs. 16 (feet) and 30 (knee brackets). Caleb Davis to and from Bergwin, Jukes, and London [Wilmington, N.C.], 1784, Caleb Davis Papers, Massachusetts Historical Society, Boston.

2. The second roundabout chair is in Bernard and S. Dean Levy, Inc., *Catalogue IV* (New York: By the company, 1984), p. 18. The third chair is in Sue M. Brander, "Thomas Seymour's Chair: A Silent Witness to History," *Antiques and the Arts Weekly*, February 24, 1995, p. 48.

3. Brander, "Thomas Seymour's Chair." Anderson Galleries, "The George S. Palmer Collection" (October 12, 1928), lot 308. National Council of Girl Scouts, *Loan Exhibition of Eighteenth- and Early Nineteenth-Century Furniture and Glass* (New York: By the council, 1929), cat. 553.

4. Anderson Galleries, "The George S. Palmer Collection" (October 12, 1928), lot 308. Trent with Nelson, "A Catalogue of New London County Joined Chairs," no. 45; *New London County Furniture*, pp. 1–2; NCGS, *Loan Exhibition*, cat. 553.

## 72 ◆ Roundabout chair
Boston, Massachusetts
1745–75

In the development of Queen Anne–style seating furniture, the saddle-crested lobed-splat design bridged the gap between the plain, vase-back pattern (see No. 10) and the lobed splat with a shell-centered crest (see No. 24). The sweep posts of the roundabout extension top and the vigorous profile of the splats are features that associate this chair with Boston craftsmanship. Sometimes the knees of cabriole front legs in low-backed roundabouts of this general pattern are carved with elongated shells and pendent bellflowers. The other three legs are frequently straight-tapered supports with stubby pad feet, as in this example; they are also found on small tables (see No. 111 left). The elements of the arm post and the cross-stretcher turnings have a general relationship. The posts are a variation of the columnar pattern in No. 67, and the cross-stretcher turnings are based on the block-and-columnar–turned side stretchers in Queen Anne seating (see Nos. 10, 24).[1]

Pattern variants in columnar-post roundabout chairs with heavy, solid splats include angular banisters, banisters with extra lobes at the base, and ogee-top vase splats. Some chairs have four cabriole legs; the feet can be claws or pads. Chairs with three tapered legs also have either claw or pad front feet. Roundabouts framed with compass-shape seat rails sweeping in and out at the sides introduced greater comfort for the sitter than the angular and rigid square frame (see No. 69).[2]

Basic material for the history surrounding this chair is found on a paper label under the seat rail. Joseph Haven, an early owner, was born in Portsmouth, New Hampshire, in 1757, the son of Samuel Haven, minister of the Second Congregational Church, and Mehitable Appleton of Cambridge, Massachusetts, who were married in 1753.

In 1784 Joseph (d. 1829), a merchant, married Eliza Wentworth (d. 1813) and then in 1814 married his second wife, Sarah Greenleaf Appleton (d. 1838), widow of Nathaniel W. Appleton, a physician of Boston. The physician and Haven were first cousins, having a common grandfather in the Reverend Doctor Nathaniel Appleton, father of Mehitable Appleton. Haven had no children. By terms of his will, the furniture remaining in his dwelling house at the death of his wife, Sarah, was to pass to his niece Elizabeth Haven Thacher (1798–1879).[3]

NGE

Inscriptions or marks: *Chiseled on right front seat-rail rabbet:* "II". *On underside of left rear seat rail:* "Large Round about Chair/ with Top, Belonged to Elizabeth/ Wentworth, wife of Joseph Haven/ Grandmother Thacher's Uncle" *in black ink, on deteriorated, blue-bordered, gummed paper label.*

**Construction:** The extension crest is supported on rectangular tenons at the post and splat tops. The crest face is rounded at the center and flat at the ends. The flattened crest back is slightly blocked at the center, rounded at the center base, and chamfered at the arches. The splat is curved laterally and canted at the edges, front to back; the lower back surface is tooled above the rail. The sweep posts, which are tenoned into the heavy back rail, have flat faces and chamfered back edges. The ogee-ended back rail is rounded on the face and flat at the back. Deep modified V-cuts near the upper back corners are terminated by end scrolls. The heavy rail is secured to the arms by six rosehead nails driven in from the bottom. The two-piece flat arm rail is butted at the center back and pinned once from the rear surface into the center back post; the forward terminals are long circular pads. The flat-faced lower back splats are canted at the edges, front to back, and cross planed on the back surfaces. The splats are tenoned into the arm rail and plinths. The plinths are hollow on the front and side faces, finished with low top beads, and nailed to the back seat rails. The posts are round tenoned into the arm rail (pinned, inside front and outside center back). The compass-shape seat frame is finished with a rounded-sloping top lip, interior rabbets at the front rails to support the loose-seat frame, and triangular corner blocks attached with nails. The bottom edges are sawed in flat arches. The rails are joined to the post blocks and front leg extension with rectangular tenons (double pinned, except at outside back of right post). The front knee bracket and leg-block brackets are nailed in place. The straight legs are continuous with the upper posts. The cross stretchers, which are secured at the center by a double rabbet, are round tenoned into the legs.

**Condition:** The extension splat is cracked at the top right and the base. The upper right extension post and crest joint is repaired with two facing pieces on the inside and back surfaces, extending onto the front. Deep gouges mark the rear face of the left arm rail at the ogee terminal of the heavy back rail; short cracks appear near the ends of the backward scrolling lips of the same rail. The inside face of the right arm rail is marked by a small triangular gouge near the back post. The upper 1/2" of the lower left back splat is pieced out, continuing into the mortise. The lower left corner of the right splat was broken off and restored; the entire left lobe was broken off vertically and reattached. A vertical crack occurs on the rear face of the left post. The rear corner block, the only original interior brace, is roughly chamfered on the forward edges and was originally secured with two rosehead nails (now renailed). The left front knee bracket was replaced some time ago. The remaining brackets show wood loss and deterioration; the inner surfaces vary somewhat, suggesting they are not all of the same period. The slip-seat frame is modern.

**Dimensions:**

| | | |
|---|---|---|
| H. | 44 5/8 in. | 113.3 cm |
| H. (seat) | 16 1/2 in. | 42.2 cm |
| W. (crest) | 16 1/2 in. | 41.9 cm |
| W. (seat, across center) | 23 1/4 in. | 59.0 cm |
| W. (arms) | 29 7/8 in. | 75.8 cm |
| W. (feet, across center) | 25 1/8 in. | 63.8 cm |
| D. (seat) | 22 1/8 in. | 56.2 cm |
| D. (feet, front to back) | 26 1/4 in. | 66.7 cm |

**Materials:** *Microanalysis:* Primary: American black walnut. *Finish:* medium dark reddish brown color in resin. *Upholstery:* Irish-stitch canvaswork in a modified diamond pattern; America or England, 1725–75.

**Publications:** Downs, *American Furniture*, fig. 64. Comstock, *American Furniture*, no. 154. John A. H. Sweeney, *Winterthur Illustrated* (New York: Chanticleer Press for the Henry Francis du Pont Winterthur Museum, 1963), p. 35.

Marshall B. Davidson, ed., *The American Heritage History of Colonial Antiques* ([New York]: American Heritage Publishing Co., [1967]), fig. 162. Bishop, *Centuries and Styles of the American Chair*, fig. 118.

**Accession history:** Purchased by H. F. du Pont from Israel Sack, Inc., probably in Boston. Bequest of H. F. du Pont, 1969.
58.2216

1. Roundabout chairs with top extensions are uncommon. Like the low roundabouts, they were expensive seats of specialized function—a low walnut corner chair retailed in 1741 in Boston cost 43 percent more than a walnut side chair with a rectangular seat and 26 percent more than a compass-seat chair; see Jobe and Kaye, *New England Furniture*, p. 360. For a low roundabout with a shell-carved front knee, see John S. Walton advertisement, *Antiques* 120, no. 6 (December 1981): 1258.

2. For listed pattern variants, see *American Antiques from Israel Sack Collection*, 10 vols. (Washington, D.C.: Highland House, ca. 1969–), 4:1007, 1100; Walton advertisement; Moses, *Master Craftsmen*, fig. 6.6; Nutting, *Furniture Treasury*, no. 2071.

3. Clifford K. Shipton, comp., *Biographical Sketches of Those Who Attended Harvard College in the Classes 1746–1750* (Boston: Massachusetts Historical Society, 1962), 12:382, 834, 390; Josiah Adams, comp., *The Genealogy of the Descendants of Richard Haven, of Lynn, Massachusetts* (Boston: William White and H. P. Lewis, 1843), pp. 18, 32; Isaac Appleton Jewett, comp., *Memorial of Samuel Appleton, of Ipswich, Massachusetts* (Boston: By the author, 1850), p. 4. A Portsmouth, N.H., federal-style settee at Winterthur, 1 of a pair, bears a label that gives a similar family history; see Jobe, *Portsmouth Furniture*, cat. no. 97. Joseph Haven will, 1829, Rockingham Co. Probate Court, Portsmouth, N.H.

## 73 ◆ Roundabout chair
Newport, Rhode Island
1760–90

The splat of this roundabout chair is a variant of a Rhode Island side chair banister (see No. 46). The double C scrolls are tighter and contained entirely within the splat rather than extending partially into the crest. Among a group of six or more surviving roundabout chairs with similar banisters, several are convincingly ascribed to Newport through circumstantial evidence. A pair of chairs was owned originally by John Brown (1736–1803), who by the 1790s was described as "the richest merchant in Providence." The loose seats of the chairs are inscribed in ink "Brown" and "John Brown," respectively. The furniture passed from Brown to his daughter Sarah, who married Karl Herreshoff in 1783. One chair is still owned by a direct descendant; the second was sold in recent decades by another descendant. Still another chair was displayed in 1953 at a loan exhibition of Newport-attributed furniture, when it was described as being "associated with Newport families."[1]

Brown, like his three merchant brothers, had close business connections in Newport. Business accounts and correspondence indicate that he purchased furniture from John Goddard, and he undoubtedly also patronized other Newport shops. An important and exceptional feature that links this chair and the others in the group with Newport cabinetmaking is the blocked compass seat with tight ogee curves that sweep across the front. They are similar to those in a documented Goddard tea table made for Jabez Bowen in 1763 (see No. 123 left). The profile is repeated in the sweep posts of No. 46.[2]

Further comparison of the chairs in this roundabout group identifies several variations. Three chairs have knuckle-type arm scrolls,

including this chair. One of the three has arms that are highly modeled behind the knuckles. In another, the columnar posts that support the arms are similar to those of this chair. The supports in the remaining chairs are shaped to an ogee profile similar to the leg curve but inverted. The splats of these chairs are contoured in the side plane to complement the curves of the arm supports. Only the Brown family chairs have four-claw feet; one other example has a single claw at the front. The large pad feet, as represented here and in several chairs with tall disks beneath the pads, are typical of Rhode Island production after 1750 as it evolved from Boston design of

earlier decades (see Nos. 10 center and right, 14, 35, 45). None of the roundabout chairs has stretchers.

Although it is unknown whether this chair once had a mate chair, evidence indicates that some householders, including Brown, purchased their roundabout chairs in pairs. The practice is further corroborated in the Newport cabinetmaking accounts of Benjamin Baker, who posted a charge to the account of Ebenezer Romrell on August 21, 1760, for "2 Roondeboote Chairs of mehogni." Of further note, probate inventories sometimes list more than one roundabout chair in a household. Some of these chairs likely were mates, although the brevity of most estate documents generally precludes a positive determination.[3]

NGE

---

**Inscriptions or marks:** *Inside right front seat rail:* "No. 1454/ Jonassen[?]/ HAVENS & WILDE" in ink, on preprinted and hand-written red-bordered, gummed paper label.

**Construction:** The ogee-end crest is attached to the arm rail with six spaced wooden pins driven in from the bottom along the back edge and by two recessed screws at the front that flank the center back post. The crest face is rounded to the upper back edge; the back surface is marked by a broad shallow channel. The two-piece flat arm rail with slightly rounded top edges is joined in a short lap at the center back. The forward-scroll knuckles, formed from two pieces of wood, are carved with volutes in the side faces. The flat-faced pierced splats are incised at the tops, bottoms, and crossings of the straps. The splat edges are flat; the piercings are only slightly canted, front to back. The splats are tenoned into the arm rail and plinths. The plinths are hollow on the front and side faces, finished with top beads, and nailed to the back seat rails. The posts are round tenoned into the arm rail and pinned once from the outside surface. The blocked compass-shape seat frame is finished with a rounded-sloping top lip, interior rabbets at the front rails to support the loose-seat frame, and corner blocks. The bottom edges are sawed in flat arches. The rails are joined to the post blocks and front leg extension with rectangular tenons (double-pinned at blocks, single-pinned at front leg). The side and rear legs, which are continuous with the upper posts, are creased at the front, back, and sides; the forward leg is rounded at the knee. The knee brackets are attached with nails.

**Condition:** The chair is in poor condition. The center back arm-rail joint is cracked, repaired, and patched with composition material (front). The rail is cracked through diagonally above the right splat and poorly repaired. The center back post is mutilated at the top. A crack behind the right arm terminal extends through the post joint. Both scroll returns are reattached with double nails. The left splat base is repaired with a thick spline across the back and at the front ends. The upper right volute of the right splat is cracked through and repaired. The left post top is cracked and repaired. Extra

pins reinforce most seat-rail joints; all the blocks, which are mortised, are cracked. The seat lip is mutilated in several places. The modern internal corner blocks are attached with screws and conceal any evidence of former blocks. All the knee brackets are reattached with additional nails. The brackets are similar in exterior patina, although differences in internal surfaces suggest that some are early replacements. The brackets flanking the front knee are mutilated at the edges. Cracks occur in the right and rear knees. The rear foot has a two-piece glued restoration reattached with a central pin. The right and left foot pads are restored at the outer one third and on the complete undersole, although the restoration shows considerable wear. The loose-seat frame is modern.

**Dimensions:**

| | | |
|---|---|---|
| H. | 29⁷/₈ in. | 75.9 cm |
| H. (seat) | 17¹/₁₆ in. | 43.3 cm |
| W. (crest) | 18¹/₈ in. | 46.0 cm |
| W. (seat, across center) | 23¹/₈ in. | 58.7 cm |
| W. (arms) | 29 in. | 73.6 cm |
| W. (feet, across center) | 26¹/₈ in. | 66.4 cm |
| D. (seat) | 22 in. | 55.8 cm |
| D. (feet, front to back) | 26 in. | 66.0 cm |

**Materials:** *Microanalysis:* Primary: American black walnut. *Finish:* mottled medium light to dark brown color in resin. *Upholstery:* gold silk damask of floral pattern; Europe, 1725–50.

**Publications:** Downs, *American Furniture*, fig. 68.

**Accession history:** Gift of H. F. du Pont, 1960. 59.2641

---

1. Wendy A. Cooper, "The Purchase of Furniture and Furnishings by John Brown, Providence Merchant, Part 1," *Antiques* 103, no. 2 (February 1973): 331; Ralph E. Carpenter, Jr., *The Arts and Crafts of Newport, Rhode Island, 1640–1820* (Newport: Preservation Society of Newport County, 1954), no. 20. On the Brown chairs, see *American Antiques from Israel Sack Collection*, 10 vols. (Washington, D.C.: Highland House, ca. 1969–), 4:966–67; Cooper, "Purchase of Furniture," p. 338, pl. 1; for the third chair with close Newport associations, see Carpenter, *Arts and Crafts of Newport*, no. 20. For the remaining chairs in the group, see Rodriguez Roque, *American Furniture*, no. 82; Moses, *Master Craftsmen*, fig. 1.54.

2. Cooper, "Purchase of Furniture," pp. 333–34.

3. Benjamin Baker account book, 1760–ca. 1788, Newport Historical Society, Newport, R.I.

## 74 ◆ Roundabout chair
### Boston, Massachusetts
### 1760–90

---

Sophistication of design has long been a criterion in collecting and evaluating antique seating furniture and cabinetwork. In ranking this roundabout chair within its specialized class, the tall seat scores high marks, with its ornamental sawed and turned elements, lofty stature, and well-planned proportions. However, close examination highlights another issue for consideration—condition. This chair has been restored and enhanced, a circumstance that substantially compromises the integrity of the object.

The extension-top splat has been replaced, and carved volutes and modeling have been introduced to the originally plain surfaces of the pierced banisters below the arm rail. This restoration and enhancement were probably carried out together during the late nineteenth century, since the carved volutes on all three splats are diminutive and executed with little refinement of technique (fig. 1). The poor quality of the surface decoration stands in sharp contrast to the exquisitely designed and modeled, double-ogee plinths at the lower splat bases. Examination of the rear surface of the extension splat highlights a second problem (fig. 2). Contrary to eighteenth-century practice, the entire back is crudely tooled and sharply beveled, eliminating most flat surfaces. The splat is exceptionally thick—a full inch—in contrast to other contemporary work, which measures three-quarters of an inch or less. The board is secured to the crest with tenons at the upper corners; however, the crest mortise extends across the full width of the central section (fig. 3). Clearly, the original extension splat was unpierced at the top and had a broad, one-piece tenon. Repairs to the crest and the extension-post joints seem to indicate that the original splat was damaged beyond repair. The design of a related extension-top corner chair in the Museum of Art, Rhode Island School of Design (RISD), Providence, suggests that the first extension splat was similar in pattern to the lower splats, which are solid across the top.[1]

Until recently, opinion on the origin of this chair and the RISD chair was divided between Newport, Rhode Island, and New York City. Based on newly published research, these chairs now may be safely assigned to Boston. Knee brackets with well-defined scrolls and cusps and banister plinths bordered by prominent double-ogee beads also appear on a select group of high-style Boston Queen Anne chairs, which, until recently were thought to have originated in New York City, based on family histories (see Nos. 26, 27). The double-ogee plinth feature is uncommon in American chairmaking and was probably copied directly from English prototypes where the design was first used in side chairs and armchairs with solid splats. De La Cour in the mid 1740s and Manwaring in 1765 published chair designs that include a double-ogee plinth. The interlaced-strap pattern of the splats also originated in England. The turnings in this chair relate closely to Boston work. The posts, which may be compared with those in No. 72, are varied only in the upper tips; the cross stretchers are identical.[2]

NGE

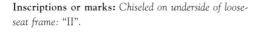

**Inscriptions or marks:** *Chiseled on underside of loose-seat frame:* "II".

**Construction:** The extension crest is supported on rectangular tenons at the posts (pinned from rear) and splat tops. The crest face is rounded at the center and flat at the ends; the back is slightly blocked at the center with a lightly chamfered center base and rounded ends. The splat is curved laterally and has deeply canted edges and piercings, front to back (some edges are hollow, some rounded). The volutes at the strap ends are crudely carved with little modeling; the strap crossings and

lower edges are only lightly delineated. The sweep posts, which are tenoned into the heavy back rail and pinned from the back, have flat faces and rounded backs that extend below the sweeps. The ogee-ended, heavy back rail is rounded on the face to an upper stepped ledge and is flat at the back. Large V-shape channels near the upper back corners are terminated by end scrolls. The rail was probably fastened to the arms originally with small wrought nails, possibly six, driven in from the bottom. The two-piece flat arm rail with slightly rounded top edges is butted at the center back; the forward terminals are large circular pads. The splats in the

lower chair back have canted edges and piercings, front to back. The faces are volute-carved and modeled. The splats are tenoned into the arm rail and plinths. The plinths are hollow on the front and side faces, finished with double-ogee top beads of rounded projecting lip, and double nailed to the back seat rails. The posts, which are round tenoned into the arm rail, are continuous with the legs. The compass-shape seat frame is finished with a rounded-sloping top lip, interior rabbets at the front seat rails to support the loose-seat frame, and flat arches at the bottom. The back rails are about 2" thick, and the inside bottom edges are chamfered. A triangular

Fig. 1. Detail, lower left splat and plinth.

Fig. 2. Detail, extension splat, rear surface.

Fig. 3. Detail, rear center bottom crest surface.

corner block at the inside back is held in place with four rosehead nails (the side blocks are modern). The rails are joined to the post blocks and front leg extension with rectangular tenons (pinned, except at left front and left side front). The knee brackets are attached with nails. The foot pads have low disks on the bottoms and a narrow ledge at the ankle back. The cross stretchers, which are secured at the center by a double rabbet, are round tenoned into the legs.

**Condition:** The crest joints are repaired with splines at the left extension post and the right straps of the splat, front and back; the splat joint is also pinned. A short crack occurs at the lower center left crest face; the center back has been reshaped. Composition material fills the extension-post joints at the bottom and upper left back; small wooden replacement pieces also appear at the top and bottom of the left post. The replacement extension splat is thick (1"), crudely shaped and tooled at the back, and poorly carved and modeled; it has some age. A through vertical crack is present below the upper left joint, and a knot disfigures the center base. The upper tenons of the extension splat fill only part of the original full-width crest mortise. The splat back is flush with the crest and heavy back rail instead of being inset. The back rail is patched at both joints with the extension posts and is newly pinned. Four screws (?) concealed by plugs appear to reinforce the back rail joint with the arms from the bottom in addition to the original wrought nails. The rail is cracked diagonally, front to back, to the right of the center post and repaired with nails; a spline fills a gap at the center butt joint. The lower back splats are somewhat worn but are not well carved or modeled and are thinner (3/8")

than usual. The left splat is repaired with a small wooden piece and composition material at the lower center, front to back. The center post is marked by shallow face cracks at the upper tip and the lower column, extending into the block. The left plinth is pieced out about 3/8" at the left end. The left and right interior corner seat blocks are modern. The front block is missing, but the presence of light-colored wood indicates that one was once in place. The left rear seat rail is split at the inside center and marked by stress cracks. Subtle differences occur in the knee brackets, but possibly all are original. The forward pad foot is cracked halfway across the front from the right side. The loose-seat frame, chisel-marked "II," is old but probably not original to this chair, as there is no corresponding chisel mark on the chair frame.

**Dimensions:**

| | | |
|---|---|---|
| H. | 44 in. | 111.7 cm |
| H. (seat) | 16 1/8 in. | 40.9 cm |
| W. (crest) | 17 1/8 in. | 43.5 cm |
| W. (seat, across center) | 26 1/4 in. | 66.7 cm |
| W. (arms) | 29 3/4 in. | 75.6 cm |
| W. (feet, across center) | 28 1/2 in. | 72.4 cm |
| D. (seat) | 25 in. | 63.5 cm |
| D. (feet, front to back) | 28 1/4 in. | 71.7 cm |

**Materials:** *Microanalysis:* Primary: American black walnut. Secondary: white pine group (rear inside corner block); soft maple group (loose-seat frame). *Finish:* variable golden to medium brown color in resin. *Upholstery:* floral-stamped blue wool velvet; Europe, 1700–1750.

**Publications:** Downs, *American Furniture*, fig. 67.

**Provenance:** An old photograph of the chair is inscribed on the reverse: "High Back Corner Arm Chair of conventional pattern, i e four duck feet, but of unusual depth of material throughout. Note reverse curve molding at foot of twin splats, width of knees, and exceptional turnings. Both Mr. Nutting who found it and Mr. Erving express the belief that it is the finest of the type that has come under their observation. The wood is walnut. This piece is to go to Penn [now Philadelphia] Museum if not sold to some collector. Can you use it . . . if so wire me Milford. Absolutely guaranteed American and antique. W R Secord." (Inscribed photograph, folder 58.2217, Registration Office, Winterthur.)

**Accession history:** Purchased by H. F. du Pont from William R. Secord, West Hartford and Milford, Conn., 1928. Bequest of H. F. du Pont, 1969. 58.2217

1. For the RISD chair, see Monkhouse and Michie, *American Furniture,* cat. 105.

2. For related English chairs, see Kirk, *American Chairs,* fig. 192; Kirk, *American Furniture,* fig. 805. For De La Cour's design, see Peter Ward-Jackson, *English Furniture Designs of the Eighteenth Century* (London: Victoria and Albert Museum, Her Majesty's Stationery Office, 1958), pl. 19 bottom row, third from left. Robert Manwaring, *The Cabinet and Chair-Maker's Real Friend and Companion* (London: Henry Webley, 1765), pl. 4 left.

## 75 ◆ Roundabout chair
Northeastern Massachusetts
1760–85

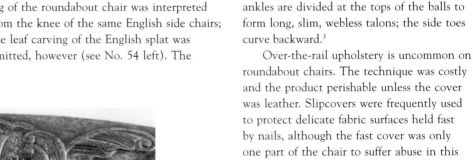

This chair can be identified as a Boston or vicinity product through several prominent features, namely the patterns of the pierced splat, rail ornament, and claw foot. The profiles of the turned arm posts and cross stretchers are also strong indicators of a northeastern Massachusetts origin. The stretchers are identical to those in Nos. 72 and 74, and the posts are generally comparable. Straight side and rear legs with diminutive pad feet appear in roundabout seating throughout southern New England (see Nos. 70, 72).[1]

Splats pierced with long, narrow apertures of squared, pointed, and rounded end appear in a small number of chairs first produced during the third quarter of the eighteenth century in Massachusetts, Rhode Island, and Philadelphia. The pattern, complete with projecting cusps at midpoint, represents a direct transmission of British chairmaking design to American colonial centers. The slots in this example are reduced in length to compensate for the low back, and the short banisters also include tiny pierced holes, which are absent from the splats of side chairs made in this pattern (see No. 54).[2]

The carved, C-scroll–bordered ornament on a ground of punched circles centered in the crest (fig. 1) is closely related to the principal ornament in a Massachusetts side chair (see No. 54 right). The British prototype also has

a central carved oval ornament flanked by a mantle of winglike foliage. The similarities are too close to be coincidental. The leafy knee ornament between carved volutes on the front leg of the roundabout chair was interpreted from the knee of the same English side chairs; the leaf carving of the English splat was omitted, however (see No. 54 left). The

carved claw on the front leg of the roundabout chair is close in pattern to the front feet of an eastern Massachusetts armchair with a diamond-centered interlaced splat. The slim ankles are divided at the tops of the balls to form long, slim, webless talons; the side toes curve backward.[3]

Over-the-rail upholstery is uncommon on roundabout chairs. The technique was costly and the product perishable unless the cover was leather. Slipcovers were frequently used to protect delicate fabric surfaces held fast by nails, although the fast cover was only one part of the chair to suffer abuse in this upholstery technique. Holes in seat rails, cracks at joints, and damaged leg brackets were also part of the toll of periodic nailings.

*NGE*

**Fig. 1.** Detail, crest.

**Construction:** The ogee-end crest is attached to the arm rail with six rosehead nails driven in from the

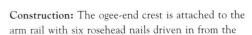

rail bottom. The crest face is rounded to the upper back edge and centered with carving on a circle-punched ground that extends onto the arm rail. The back crest surface is flat, except at the ends, where deep V-shape channels are terminated by small scrolls at the top edge. The two-piece flat arm rail with rounded-chamfered top edges is butted at the center back. The forward terminals are circular pads. The flat-faced splats have canted edges and piercings, front to back, and are tenoned into the arm rail and rear seat rails. The three-sided plinths are hollow on the front and side faces and finished with low, stepped top beads; they were nailed originally to the back seat rails (now held with screws). The posts are round tenoned into the arm rail; those at the sides are pinned from the outside surface. The seat rails are joined to the leg blocks and front leg extension with rectangular tenons (pinned). The back rails are 1 3/4" thick; the front rails are 1 1/4" thick. The side and rear legs are continuous with the upper posts; the knee and leg brackets are attached with nails. The front knee carving is coarse and flanked by shallow scrolls. The two-knuckle talons of the claw foot have short nails; the side talons are curved backward. The three small pad feet are scribed around the ankle backs. The cross stretchers, which are secured at the center by a double rabbet, are round tenoned into the legs.

**Condition:** One of the original nails securing the crest to the arm rail is missing. Short cracks in the ogee ends are repaired with nails. A sizable gap occurs at the center back where the two arm sections meet, causing the carving to misalign with that above it on the crest rail. A diagonal facing piece is set into the left arm rail surface above the post tip. A small chip has broken out of the upper left rear corner of the left splat. Shallow splines have been inserted behind the splats at the joints with the rails; the splat tenons are now secured in the mortises with nails driven in through the rails. The plinths are now attached with modern screws. Horizontal cracks occur on the inside surface of the left front seat rail. The right rear leg bracket is pieced but appears to be original. The right front knee bracket is broken off behind the scroll, and the piece is missing. The stretcher tips are now nailed to the legs.

**Dimensions:**

| | | |
|---|---|---|
| H. | 32 1/4 in. | 81.9 cm |
| H. (seat) | 16 in. | 40.6 cm |
| W. (crest) | 19 1/8 in. | 48.5 cm |
| W. (seat, across center) | 23 1/4 in. | 59.0 cm |
| W. (arms) | 28 1/2 in. | 72.4 cm |
| W. (feet, across center) | 24 5/8 in. | 62.6 cm |
| D. (seat) | 23 1/4 in. | 59.0 cm |
| D. (feet, front to back) | 26 3/8 in. | 67.0 cm |

**Materials:** *Microanalysis:* Primary: American black walnut. Secondary: soft maple group (seat rails). *Finish:* evidence of original brick-red primer and old dark brown resin found in pores; refinished in medium yellowish brown to reddish brown color in resin. *Upholstery:* green silk damask; Europe, 1700–1750.

**Publications:** American Art Association Anderson Galleries, "Important American Antiques from the King Hooper Mansion" (December 7–8, 1928), lot 233. Parke-Bernet Galleries, "New England Furniture and Decorations: Property of Blin W. Page" (January 26–27, 1945), lot 93. Charles F. Hummel, "Queen Anne and Chippendale Furniture in the Henry Francis du Pont Winterthur Museum, Part 2," *Antiques* 98, no. 6 (December 1970): 901, fig. 2.

**Provenance:** Ex colls.: Israel Sack, Blin W. Page.

**Accession history:** Purchased by H. F. du Pont from John S. Walton, Inc., New York, 1952. Gift of H. F. du Pont, 1952.
52.147

1. Jobe and Kaye, *New England Furniture*, no. 115; Trent with Nelson, "A Catalogue of New London County Joined Chairs," cat. 45.

2. For Rhode Island and Philadelphia side chairs, see *John Brown House Loan Exhibition*, cat. 11; *American Antiques from Israel Sack Collection*, 10 vols. (Washington, D.C.: Highland House, ca. 1969–), 3:749; for a British prototype, see Kirk, *American Furniture*, fig. 891.

3. The British prototype is illustrated in Kirk, *American Furniture*, fig. 891; for the Massachusetts chair with similarly carved claws, see Jobe and Kaye, *New England Furniture*, no. 116.

## 76 ◆ Roundabout chairs
### Southeastern coastal New England
### 1765–90

The body of turned work that provided models for eighteenth-century New England makers of vernacular chairs to draw upon had its immediate roots in high-style seating furniture produced in Boston and vicinity from the late seventeenth century through the early eighteenth century. Baluster turnings with bulging bodies and short, flaring necks, such as those in these two chairs and in other vernacular examples (see Nos. 3, 4, 17, 18, 36, 38, 39, 41), were prominent features of the cane-seat chair almost from the introduction of the new construction in Boston, New England's principal commercial center. Also part of the standard design vocabulary were short, conical connector elements beneath the arms and seat and double-baluster braces with tipped ends. The same shapes were associated with early leather and banister-back chairs produced in Boston (see No. 17, fig. 2). The prototypes for all these elements exist in English turned seating furniture.[1]

Although not as obvious, the profile and sequence of elements in the long extension spindles of the right chair also have late seventeenth-century roots. The button top, ringed neck, and elongated baluster are adapted from the conical pillars common in the backs of English and New England seating furniture of the period (see No. 17, fig. 2; No. 18, fig. 2). The profile of these spindles is notable for the long, rounded body of the baluster, an interpretation that appears to have originated along the southeastern New England coast. A group of turned vernacular chairs with provenances between New Haven and Saybrook, Connecticut, have round-bottom balusters as the principal central back units.[2]

By the second half of the eighteenth century, the type of thick-neck baluster in the posts and legs of both of these chairs was more commonly identified with turned work executed in coastal Connecticut and

Rhode Island (see No. 66) than with furniture originating in the Boston area. Examples appear frequently in Windsor furniture dating to the postrevolutionary period. The profile is particularly prominent in turned chairs produced by the Tracy family of New London County, Connecticut.[3]

Few woven-bottom roundabout chairs are distinguished by the presence of ornamental back slats sawed in double-ogee curves on the top edge. The profile is somewhat more common in the crests and stay rails of banister- and vase-back chairs. New England joined side chairs with this feature in the seat rails are illustrated in Nos. 16 and 20. Windsor chairs with double-ogee crests were made in the border area shared by Connecticut and Rhode Island. The hook-type arm profile of the tall roundabout is another indication that the chairs originated in the southern coastal region (fig. 1). A pierced vase-back rush-bottom chair ascribed to Fairfield County, Connecticut, has comparable elbows. That chair is framed with a double-ogee crest and a front stretcher that is a larger version of those in the low roundabout chair shown here.

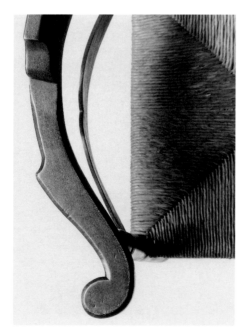

**Fig. 1.** Detail of right chair, top of arm rail, left side.

Derivative elbows can be found in Windsor chairs associated with Rhode Island. Further confirmation derives from the front leg in the tall chair, which is true poplar (*Populus* spp.)— an uncommon furniture wood also found in a small group of Windsor chairs associated with Rhode Island and the Connecticut–Rhode Island border region.[4]

First use of the double-ogee curve in Western seating furniture dates to the beginning of the eighteenth century when a few English hoof-foot cabriole-leg chairs with straight-sided back splats and molded serpentine crests in the Chinese taste were constructed with ogee-shape front rails. Eventually, other forms including tables and joined cases were designed with double-ogee curves at the frame edges. These sweeping contours can be found in oriental furniture dating to the end of the Ming Dynasty (1368–1644). Armchairs and side chairs are embellished with these graceful curves as are the skirts of tables, stands, and other forms. Although the craze for things oriental, especially porcelains, was strong in western Europe from the sixteenth century, oriental influence did not affect seating furniture until the beginning of the eighteenth century, aside from the use of cane. Most writers on the subject generally agree that there is little evidence that actual Chinese furniture was readily available for copying, and the eclectic use of oriental features in Western furniture seems to substantiate this viewpoint. Porcelains, screens, and other materials depicting Asian life and culture in the surface decoration likely were the vehicles of the transfer. Formal furniture was produced initially; vernacular interpretations followed later.[5]

*NGE*

**Construction:** (Left) The crest is secured to the arm rail with six spaced rosehead nails driven up from

rail edges are narrowly chamfered, top and bottom. The bowed and shaped back slats are tenoned into mortises in the long posts. The broad, flattened seat rails are joined to the posts with roughly shaped round tenons. The right front seat rail is continuous with the front seat block. The front leg is tenoned into the seat block, which is chamfered on the outside bottom edges and rounded at the top edges. The long posts and front leg are scribed with faint lines marking the mortises. The front leg is double grooved at the top element and double scored at the baluster body; similar markings appear on the arm posts. The stretchers, which are slightly rounded at the ends, are tenoned into the legs.

**Condition:** (Left) Modern wire nails secure the crest at the ogee ends, the arm rail at the outside forward edges, and the seat rails and some of the stretcher tips at the long posts. The tenon tops of both arm posts have broken through the top surface of the arm rail. A star crack marks the point where a cut nail secures the arm rail at the center back post. A wooden pin securing the right seat-rail tenon from the top of the front seat block appears to be a later addition; the seat block is cracked. The tops of all front stretchers are moderately worn; the upper left front stretcher is split. The left back and right front seat rails have been augmented in height by the addition of extra strips of wood placed on the tops to create an even frame all around and a slightly recessed seat well. The back of the left front leg cylinder is cracked adjacent to the upper stretcher. The inside face of the lower right front stretcher is splitting between the heartwood and sapwood due to differences in shrinkage. The original feet are worn away; small, circular disks remain on the front and right leg bottoms. The rush seat is not original but has been in place a long time; the pattern is ahistorical.

(Right) The second extension-top spindle from the left is a replacement. The right spindle is pinned from the back, top and bottom, with modern metal sprigs. The long posts are slightly cracked, defaced, or irregular at both ends of the left slat. The front seat block is cracked, and a piece is broken out of the lower rear surface. Many small brads repair the crack, and a new pin has been driven in from the right front edge to secure the leg top. All long posts are slightly cracked on the front faces at the joints with the seat rails; other cracks occur at the stretcher joints. The lower parts of all legs are considerably worn and defaced. Caster holes are present on all leg bottoms; metal caster plates remain on the center and left front legs. Some stretchers are nicked and splintered. The rush seat has some age but is not original.

the rail bottom and one wooden pin located left of the post near the back edge. The crest, which is rounded on the face to the upper back edge, is flat at the back and has ogee curves at the ends. The arm rail is sawed in two parts butted at the center back and terminated by large, plain, almost circular pads at the front. The rail is supported on the post tenons, which are pinned with cut nails on the inside surfaces at the center back and on the outside surface behind the arm terminals. The bowed and shaped back slats are tenoned into mortises in the long posts. The broad, flattened seat rails are joined to the posts with small rounded-square tenons. The left front rail is continuous with the front seat block. The front leg is tenoned into the seat block and pinned from the left face. The long posts and front leg are scribed with faint lines marking the

tops and bottoms of all mortises. The stretchers are round tenoned into the adjacent members.

(Right) The laterally curved extension crest, which is rounded on the face, is flat at the back and has ogee curves at the ends; it is supported on the tenons of the five turned spindles. The bottom is narrowly chamfered on all edges. The base of each spindle baluster is scored once and the bottom bead scored twice. The spindles tenon into the heavy back rail, which is rounded on the face, is flat at the top and back, and has ogee curves at the ends. The upper back and ogee edges are narrowly chamfered. The back rail is secured to the arm rail with six large rosehead nails driven up from the rail bottom. The two-piece flat arm rail is butted at the center back (pinned from rear); narrow, vertical splines in the joint, front and back, appear to be original. The

**Dimensions:**

Left

| | | |
|---|---|---|
| H. | 28³/₈ in. | 72.1 cm |
| H. (seat) | 16¹/₈ in. | 40.9 cm |
| W. (crest) | 17¹/₄ in. | 43.8 cm |
| W. (seat, across center) | 24¹/₄ in. | 61.6 cm |
| W. (arms) | 26⁵/₈ in. | 67.6 cm |
| W. (feet, across center) | 24¹/₂ in. | 62.2 cm |
| D. (center seat) | 23¹/₂ in. | 59.7 cm |
| D. (feet, front to back) | 24 in. | 60.9 cm |

Right

| | | |
|---|---|---|
| H. | 42¹/₄ in. | 107.3 cm |
| H. (seat) | 15³/₄ in. | 40.0 cm |
| W. (crest) | 13 in. | 33.0 cm |
| W. (seat, across center) | 22¹/₄ in. | 56.5 cm |
| W. (arms) | 28⁷/₈ in. | 73.3 cm |
| W. (feet, across center) | 24¹/₂ in. | 62.2 cm |
| D. (center seat) | 24 in. | 60.9 cm |
| D. (feet, front to back) | 23³/₄ in. | 60.3 cm |

**Materials:** *Microanalysis:* (Left) Primary: soft maple group (right leg). Secondary: hickory (stretchers, cross slats). (Right) Primary: soft maple group (post, arm rail, rail cap, spindle, crest). Secondary: cottonwood (*Populus*) (front leg), ash (cross slat, stretcher). *Finish:* (Left) remnants of dark brown paint over brick-red primer or wash; bare surfaces have patina from use. (Right) medium dark brown color with remnants of old dark brown paint or resin; many crackled surfaces. Rush seat coated with tan-colored resin.

**Accession history:** Bequest of H. F. du Pont, 1969. 66.1235, 66.1203

---

1. For early Boston and English examples with prototype turnings, see Forman, *American Seating Furniture*, figs. 126, 127, 152–54; cats. 53, 56, 59, 60, 64, 78, 79; Kirk, *American Furniture*, figs. 712, 721, 724, 728.

2. For prototypes for long spindles, see Forman, *American Seating Furniture*, cats. 53, 64, 67; fig. 173; Kirk, *American Furniture*, figs. 713, 718; for coastal Connecticut chairs with related spindles, see *Connecticut Furniture*, nos. 200–202.

3. Woven-bottom chairs with thick-neck balusters are in Trent, *Hearts and Crowns*, nos. 19–22, 24, 67, 68, 72.

4. For double-ogee crests or stay rails, see *Connecticut Furniture*, nos. 217, 223; Trent, *Hearts and Crowns*, nos. 28, 29; the Fairfield County chair in Trent, *Hearts and Crowns*, no. 63. For Windsor chairs, see Nancy Goyne Evans, *American Windsor Chairs* (New York: Hudson Hills Press in association with the Henry Francis du Pont Winterthur Museum, 1996), figs. 6-43–45, 6-96, 6-98, 6-99, 6-101, 6-133, 6-134.

5. For an English chair in the Chinese taste, see Kirk, *American Chairs*, fig. 153; for English and American tables and cases, see Kirk, *American Furniture*, figs. 600, 619, 1272, 1299; *Connecticut Furniture*, no. 161; Fales, *Furniture of Historic Deerfield*, fig. 311; Heckscher, *American Furniture*, cat. no. 173; Moses, *Master Craftsmen*, pl. 6, fig. 3.71. Examples of oriental furniture are in Wang Shixiang, *Classic Chinese Furniture* (London: Han-Shan Tang, 1986), pls. 55, 66, 72, 73, 79, 80, 99, 150, 165; Robert Hatfield Ellsworth, *Chinese Furniture: Hardwood Examples of the Ming and Early Ch'ing Dynasties* (New York: Random House, 1971), figs. 10, 11, 19, 22, 41, 52, 60, 64, 74, 75; for the influence of Chinese furniture on Western furniture, see Robert C. Smith, "China, Japan, and the Anglo-American Chair," *Antiques* 96, no. 4 (October 1969): 552–58; Robert W. Symonds, "The Chair with the 'Bended Back,'" *Antique Collector* (July/August 1951): 155–61; Nicholas Grindley, *The Bended-Back Chair* (London: Barling, 1990); Gertrude Z. Thomas, *Richer than Spices* (New York: Alfred A. Knopf, 1965), fig. 42, pp. 160–61.

## 77 ◆ Roundabout chair
**Southeastern New Hampshire; York County, Maine; or Essex County, Massachusetts**
**1760–80**

---

Spindles as decorative elements beneath the arm rails of roundabout chairs are rare. Horizontal stay rails, bowed to conform to the arms, are usually shaved thin to facilitate bending and framing, thus precluding the use of thick-tenoned spindles. The short spindles in this chair are actually split in half lengthwise, the flat surfaces forward and the round surfaces to the back, in the manner of banisters. (The small, narrow rectangular tenons are partially visible at the spindle bases, due to wood shrinkage.) A roundabout chair

of almost identical pattern was part of a Brookline, Massachusetts, collection early in this century. Modest differences in the two chairs appear in the bases. The front-leg baluster of the Brookline chair is longer, and the ornamental stretchers have single ball turnings and spool-like tips.[1]

Although the slim spindles in the extension piece of the Winterthur chair resemble those of No. 76 right, the differences in the back units of the two chairs are greater. Here, the design of the blunt-end rail cap and crest is aesthetically less pleasing than that of the southern New England roundabout chair, which is terminated by ogee tips. The long spindles, extended in height by the addition of elongated tips and rounded bases, lack the neck rings of No. 76 right. The profile generally correlates with that of the split banisters in the lower back, although the relationship is distorted by the compressed form of the short turnings. The banisters are actually copies of the posts, and the principal element is an unusual, double-ended baluster.

The double-ended post balusters and distinctive front stretchers, turned with two central balls and truncated tips, are the essential clues in establishing the origin of this chair. A small core group associated with coastal New Hampshire and vicinity—some banister-back chairs with an uncommon, flamboyant crest pattern distinguished by tall, opposing, tonguelike projections, others with triangular crests identified by double arches at the center top flanked by short hollows—have similar double-baluster ball-turned front stretchers. The majority have ball and cylinder–type front posts similar to the lower front leg of this chair. One chair has scroll-end arms mounted in a horizontal plane, much like the roundabout chair arms; another is turned with short, double-ended balusters in the lower back at the posts and banisters. Several chairs with carved, pierced crests and "Gaines"-type scroll arms (see No. 18) also have long, double-ended balusters in the back posts. The presence of birch in the legs of this chair further reinforces the northern New England ascription, since birch is more common in furniture originating in that part of the region than in the southern New England states.[2]

Splint seats appear to have been less common than rush bottoms in turned chairs, although they were cheaper. American side chairs, armchairs, and roundabouts constructed with banister, vase, spindle, and slat backs, and dating from the seventeenth century to the early nineteenth century, were sometimes fitted with splint woven around the seat rails. The comprehensive chairmaking accounts of Solomon Fussell of Philadelphia refer on many occasions during the late 1730s and the 1740s to chairs with "Checkt bottoms," a term that describes the appearance of the woven splint. Fussell also bottomed chairs with rush, as indicated by charges to customers and purchases of "bundles of Rushes," and occasionally he recorded an order for a "Superfine" rush-bottomed seat. William Barker and the Proud brothers of Providence also provided a "fine bottom" from time to time. Whereas rushes were harvested from

grasses that grew in meadows and marshes, splint was split out of newly felled timber. Hickory, ash, oak, basswood, and occasionally elm were used for this work. Bass-bottom chairs are itemized in three Boston inventories dating from the 1750s and 1760s. To produce a splint seat, uniform strips of wood usually about 1/2 inch in width were split to about a 1/16-inch thickness. The lengths were coiled for storage and soaked briefly before use. After warp strips were positioned from back to front, crosswise weft splints were woven over and under in patterns of ones, twos, or threes.[3]

*NGE*

---

**Construction:** The laterally curved extension crest, which is steeply rounded on the face and ends and flat at the back, is supported on the tenons of the four turned spindles; all spindles are pinned at the crest back. The spindle bases pierce through the heavy back rail and arms with large, exposed round tenons. The back rail, which is steeply rounded at the ends, slightly rounded at the front, and flat on the top and back, is extensively pinned: from the top, twice near the back edge and twice at each tip; and from the rail bottom, four times along the back edge, three times near the front edge, and four times surrounding the tip of the back post. The two-piece flat arm rail is lapped at the center back and secured by the tenon of the back post and the four back-post pins. The plain, relatively broad arms are terminated by large circular pads at the front supported on the tenons of the front posts. All post tenons are pinned from the outside edge of the rail. The large split spindles of the lower back are joined to the arm rail and the stay rails with slim rectangular tenons. The bent stay rails are flat on the front and rounded to a thin taper at the back, where tool marks are visible, especially at the reduced-tenon ends. The seat rails are oval in section; the tips are small rounded squares, which are tenoned into the posts. The right front rail is continuous with the front seat block. The front leg is tenoned into the seat block and pinned from the right face. Broad, impressed markings on the rails indicate that the seat was always made of splints. The long posts and front leg are scribed with faint lines marking the mortises. The stretchers are round tenoned into the adjacent members.

**Condition:** A diagonal break occurs in the lower lap of the center-back arm-rail joint. The left arm terminal is shattered and cracked through in a diagonal break behind the scroll at the post top. The damage is repaired with inset wooden strips, wooden pins, glue, and composition material; the top surface now slants downward toward the outside. The front of the left post is punctured and defaced at the double-ended turning. The center rings of all

the front stretchers are worn on the top surfaces, as are the bottoms of the feet. The splint seat is broken and chipped in places, with substantial losses along the right front edge. The seat could be original, as indicated by the ridges impressed into the top surface of the rails.

**Dimensions:**

| | | |
|---|---|---|
| H. | 42 3/4 in. | 108.6 cm |
| H. (seat) | 16 15/16 in. | 43.0 cm |
| W. (crest) | 19 1/8 in. | 48.6 cm |
| W. (seat, across center) | 22 1/2 in. | 57.1 cm |
| W. (arms) | 27 3/4 in. | 70.5 cm |
| W. (feet, across center) | 24 3/4 in. | 62.9 cm |
| D. (center seat) | 23 3/8 in. | 59.4 cm |
| D. (feet, front to back) | 24 5/8 in. | 62.5 cm |

**Materials:** *Microanalysis:* Primary: birch (leg, arm rail). Secondary: hickory (stretcher). *Finish:* medium brown color in resin over traces of brick-red wash or primer, which is possibly original.

**Accession history:** Bequest of H. F. du Pont, 1969. 66.1210

---

1. A rare and unusual roundabout chair with 10 turned spindles tenoned into thick, straight, inverted-ogee stay rails was advertised by Roger Gonzales and Frank Cowan, *Maine Antique Digest*, October 1990, p. 25-A. For the Brookline chair, see Nutting, *Furniture Treasury*, no. 1841. A third chair is virtually identical to the Brookline example except for the shaped tips of the feet; see Liverant-Wesley advertisement, *Maine Antique Digest*, September 1992.

2. For the chairs associated with New Hampshire and environs, see Nutting, *Furniture Treasury*, nos. 535, 1957; Fales, *Furniture of Historic Deerfield*, fig. 37; Kane, *Three Hundred Years*, no. 47; Estelle M. Glavey advertisement, *Antiques* 103, no. 3 (March 1973): 480; Nathan Liverant and Son advertisement, *Antiques and the Arts Weekly*, October 1, 1993; Gary Ludlow and Martha Ludlow advertisement, *Maine Antique Digest*, February 1994; Robert O. Stuart advertisement, *Maine Antique Digest*, February 1990; James B. Bell and Cynthia Dunn Fleming, "Furniture from the Atkinson-Lancaster Collection at the New England Historic Genealogical Society," *Antiques* 113, no. 5 (May 1978): 1080, fig. 2; Jobe, *Portsmouth Furniture*, pp. 287–91. For related chairs with "Gaines"-type arms, see Fales, *Furniture of Historic Deerfield*, fig. 32; Bishop, *Centuries and Styles of the American Chair*, fig. 52.

3. Solomon Fussell account book, 1738–48, Stephen Collins Papers, Library of Congress, Washington, D.C.; William Barker account book, vol. 1 (1750–72), Rhode Island Historical Society, Providence; William Proud, Daniel Proud, and Samuel Proud ledger, 1772–ca. 1825, Rhode Island Historical Society, Providence. A New York spindle-back "great chair" with an elm splint seat is illustrated in Forman, *American Seating Furniture*, cat. 9. Elias Delarues (1756), Joseph Wheeler (1761), and Elizabeth Hutchinson (1766) estate inventories, Suffolk County Probate Court, Boston (microfilm, Downs collection). For splint preparation and weaving, see John D. Alexander, Jr., *Make a Chair from a Tree: An Introduction to Working Green Wood* (Newtown, Conn.: Taunton Press, 1978), chap. 12.

## 78 ◆ Easy chair
Northeastern Massachusetts,
possibly Boston
1732–45

Richly upholstered chairs are detailed in
English noble and royal household inventories
made in the early sixteenth century. Soft,
upholstered seats of varied form were known
much earlier, however, including boarded
chairs upholstered with cloth and folding
chairs of ease with nailed coverings. During
the twelfth century, at the latest, the portable
X-form seat (folding chair) was enhanced by
the addition of a back and arms. This seat
remained the principal seating furniture of
ease in the genteel household into the early
seventeenth century, when it was accompanied
by chairs of low (Cromwellian) or tall back,
with and without arms. The true easy chair,
a tall padded seat with winglike side pieces
designed to provide comfort and offer
protection from drafts, was first introduced
during the reign of Charles II of England,
which commenced in 1660.[1]

In recent years furniture historians have
embraced the theory that easy chairs with
"wings" evolved from European mechanical
seats, also known as invalid, gout, and
"sleepeinge chayres." Designed with adjustable
backs and footrests, and sometimes with
movable arms and side flaps, such seating was
made as early as the late sixteenth century but
was limited in distribution, being the province
of the wealthy. The adjustable, boxlike flaps,
or wings, that appear on some chairs probably
were not actually introduced until the second
half of the seventeenth century and likely
were inspired by the upholstered daybed
with an adjustable backrest at one end or
the upholstered couch with two hinged arm
panels, such as the well-known example at
Knole, Kent, that dates to the second quarter
of the seventeenth century. A two-seated
upholstered settee of a contemporary date,
also at Knole, has large, quarter-round wings
above the arms. Fixtures such as these appear
to have influenced invalid chair design, but
whether updated models with large, draft-proof
flaps were in the market before the first easy

chairs were introduced is debatable. Examples
with histories appear to date no earlier than
the 1670s.[2]

Another possible design source for the
wings of the easy chair is the wicker chair,
which was used throughout Europe in the
seventeenth century. Woven with arms for
structural stability, many had hoods for the
protection and comfort of the sitter. Some
even occupied places of honor in the
bedchambers of the gentry until the easy
chair was introduced. Still another avenue of
investigation is the settle. Constructed with
side panels, a shallow roof, and backboards
extending to the floor, this commodious seat
was designed as a warm retreat. Reduced to
single size and reinterpreted as a chair for
stuffing with soft materials, the settle could
well have inspired this bold, new concept
in seating comfort. Since settles were used
everywhere in Britain, the prototypes were
close at hand—at the hearth in modest
cottages and below stairs in mansions.[3]

Through most of the eighteenth century
the easy chair continued in popularity with
British consumers, as examples with pad, claw,
Marlborough, and tapered supports indicate.
Drawings for easy chairs in the furniture
estimate books of the Lancashire firm of
Gillows, dated 1788 and 1795, further illustrate
the longevity of the form. American consumers
were introduced to the easy chair at a relatively
early date. In his pioneer essay on the easy
chair in America, William MacPherson Hornor
cites evidence from probate documents
originating in New York (1708), Boston
(1712), and Philadelphia (1720). During
the early eighteenth century, well-to-do
American merchants, lawyers, doctors, and
others ordered this expensive seating from
London. Some easy chairs were carried to
America in the household baggage of public
officials. Gov. William Burnet's furnishings,
which included an easy chair, were disposed
of at several Boston auctions in 1729. Patrick
Gordon's (d. 1736) "Plush easy Chair" may

Needleworkers also provided a finish cover for a new seat cushion, since the original cushion was missing when the chair was purchased. Wool for the repairs and the new cushion was "dyed to order and [the] pattern, copied exactly." The cushion cover is so faithful a representation of the original stitchery that the new work is hardly apparent. The brilliant colors of the faded original needlework are still preserved at the inside chair back where the original seat cushion protected the lower part of the panel from light, wear, and soil. The intense blue and red (now deep pink) that predominate were augmented by deep lemon yellow, lavender (now beige), green (now beige), and white. An illustration of the chair as purchased in 1930 shows tape around the arm tops and wing faces, presumably the original treatment. Tape may also once have embellished other seams and edges. The outside back needlework panel differs from the rest of the cover, being a loom-woven "flame"-patterned cloth of French origin dating to about the early eighteenth century, and was introduced to the chair sometime before 1930. The back may originally have been covered with a plain-woven woolen fabric, a common treatment for easy chairs covered with needlework and other costly materials.[2]

Boston probate inventories from the 1760s through the 1780s show that ownership of the expensive easy chair was principally, though not exclusively, concentrated in the hands of the wealthy and the elite, who are referred to by title or occupation as esquire, gentleman, merchant, doctor, and ship owner. Several women also possessed easy chairs. Other examples were in the hands of sea captains, a mariner, an apothecary, two clergymen, a bricklayer, a silk dyer, a goldsmith, and a vendue master. A few individuals, identified as esquire and doctor, owned more than one easy chair.[3]

Of the chairs listed by specific or determinable location, 80 percent were placed in a bedchamber. When more precise information is available, the front chamber, which generally represented the principal household bedroom, is named most frequently. Downstairs locations are generally unspecified, but both front and back parlors, which were rarely furnished with bedsteads, seem indicated. Crimson (or red), green, and yellow are the fabric colors mentioned and in that order of popularity. Specific fibers and weaves include the woolen mohairs, harateens, damasks, and

russels. Dark chintz is mentioned once and furniture check several times. One chair was specifically furnished with a removable case. Any mention of needlework is missing from the survey, an indication of the rarity of the cover and a conclusion borne out by the paucity of evidence from other regions (see No. 83).

NGE

---

**Construction:** (Frame upholstered; a photograph without upholstery is unavailable.) The interior frame has squared edges; the lower back is braced by a stay rail. The modified horseshoe-shape seat frame is curved inward along the sides and rounded at the front corners; the center front is flat. The front and side rails, which have a horizontal orientation, are joined with mortise and tenon and pinned. The front legs are attached with large dovetails exposed on the front and top surfaces and wedged. The rear legs are canted on the forward surfaces. The back corners are lightly chamfered from seat to base; the forward corners are chamfered below the side stretchers. The pad feet have narrow ledges at the ankle backs; the ogee knee brackets are secured with two nails each. The side stretchers are joined to the legs with vertical rectangular tenons (pinned, at back); the medial and rear stretchers are round tenoned into the adjacent members.

**Condition:** The exposed frame is marked by surface nicks and scratches. The pad feet are slightly chipped around the edges. The original stuffing of the seat deck and upper frame has been replaced with modern materials beneath the period cover. The cushion and the needlework cushion cover are modern restorations. Fabrication of the cushion cover and repairs to the fast cover of the chair frame were the work of Katharine Lee Grable's Lenox Hill Studio, New York, in 1930–31.

**Dimensions:**

| | | |
|---|---|---|
| H. | 47 in. | 119.4 cm |
| H. (seat) | 12 1/2 in. | 31.7 cm |
| W. (wings) | 28 3/4 in. | 73.0 cm |
| W. (seat front) | 30 in. | 76.2 cm |
| W. (seat back) | 24 1/4 in. | 61.6 cm |
| W. (arms) | 35 1/4 in. | 89.5 cm |
| W. (feet) | 31 1/8 in. | 79.1 cm |
| D. (seat) | 22 in. | 56.2 cm |
| D. (feet) | 25 in. | 63.5 cm |

**Materials:** *Macroidentification:* Primary: walnut. *Microanalysis:* Secondary: soft maple group (seat

**Fig. 1.** Detail, right front rail joint and leg attachment.

frame, rear leg). *Finish:* medium dark brown color in resin. *Upholstery:* Irish-stitch canvaswork in polychrome colors; America, 1750–75.

**Publications:** John Wanamaker, "An Important Collection of Antique American Furniture" (1930), lot 10. John Wanamaker advertisement, *Antiquarian* 15, no. 5 (November 1930): 15. Downs, *American Furniture*, fig. 74. Susan Burrows Swan, *Plain and Fancy: American Women and Their Needlework, 1700–1850* (New York: Holt, Rinehart, and Winston, 1977), pp. 89–90.

**Accession history:** Purchased by H. F. du Pont from John Wanamaker, New York, October 1930. Bequest of H. F. du Pont, 1969.
58.1505

---

1. For the Metropolitan Museum of Art chair, see Heckscher, *American Furniture*, cat. no. 72; for the SPNEA chair, see Jobe and Kaye, *New England Furniture*, no. 101.

2. Katharine Lee Grable to H. F. du Pont, November 15 and 21, 1930, and n.d.; H. F. du Pont to Katharine Lee Grable, November 18, 1930, Winterthur Archives. An illustration of the chair with tape in place is in John Wanamaker advertisement, *Antiquarian* 15, no. 5 (November 1930): 15. A set of needlework covers that was removed in the mid twentieth century from an easy chair with a Boston family history is also in the Winterthur collection; see Donald L. Fennimore et al., *Eye for Excellence: Masterworks from Winterthur* (Winterthur, Del.: Henry Francis du Pont Winterthur Museum, 1994), p. 96. Another easy chair of eastern Massachusetts origin that retains its original needlework upholstery is in the Bayou Bend collection, Museum of Fine Arts, Houston; see "Bayou Bend," *Antiques and the Arts Weekly*, March 11, 1994, p. 72 upper right.

3. Inventories in the survey include: William Skinner (1760), Dr. Hugh Kenedy (1760), Ebenezer Fisher (1760), Dr. Thomas Bulfinch (1761), Benjamin Pratt (1763), John Simpson (1764), Andrew Sigourney (1765), John Spooner (1765), Dr. Henry Crozier (1766), Rev. Dr. Jonathan Mayhew (1769), Nathaniel Rogers (1770), John Spooner (1771), Widow Sarah Comrin (1771), Edward Clarke (1771), William Hall (1771), James Otis (1772), Charles Hamock (1773), Mary Hubbard (1779), James Smithwick (1779), Robert Auchmuty (1779), Thomas Hubbard (1779), Henderson Inches (1780), Daniel Scott (1780), Isaac Gardner (Brookline, 1780), Rev. William Vinal (1781), Josiah Quincy, Jr. (1781), Newman Greenough (1781), Thomas Parker (1782), John Webb (1782), Thomas Thompson (1783), Josiah Quincy, Sr. (Braintree, 1784), Ezekial Goldthwait (1784), Enoch Brown (1787), Clement Collins (1787), Zachariah Brigden (1787), John Hinckley (1787), Benjamin Dolbeare (1787), Isaac Smith (1787), all in Suffolk County Probate Court, Boston (microfilm, Downs collection).

## 80 ◆ Easy chair
Boston, Massachusetts
1750–75

The easy chair was the product of two craftsmen—the chairmaker who constructed the frame and the upholsterer who stuffed it. Sometimes both skills were combined in one shop; otherwise, upholsterers appear to have employed journeymen chairmakers more frequently than chairmakers hired upholsterers. An upholsterer could purchase his frames outright from one or more chairmakers, and a chairmaker (or cabinetmaker) could subcontract upholstery work to a specialty shop. Regardless of the business or labor arrangement, fabrication of an easy chair was costly and almost always represented "bespoke," or ordered, work. Few examples are documented to their makers, and only a small number retain family histories.

Just as the bases of New England easy chairs are constructed in several styles, so the interior structures are subject to variation.

Many seat frames are rectangular with squared or rounded front corners. Some, like this chair, are horseshoe shape. The most successful are rounded across the entire front rather than only at the corners (fig. 1). Mortise-and-tenon joints secure the seat back. Square-front chairs are framed with squared leg extensions mortised to rectangular tenons cut in the narrow side and front rails. Seats with rounded fronts differ in two respects: the side and front rails are broad and framed with a horizontal orientation, and the front legs are not integral to the joints. The two common framing methods are the mortise-and-tenon joint, as on this chair, and a full lap secured by pins from the top surface. The front legs are joined to the frame in one of two ways: with a large tenon, usually quarter-round in shape and centered in the joint, or a large open dovetail centered above the knee at the forward edge of the joint. The latter technique is thought to be of German origin and also

appears in Philadelphia easy chair construction. Both leg attachments are used with either type of joint. The frame is frequently reinforced with triangular corner blocks.[1]

The tall back stiles in New England Queen Anne and Chippendale easy chairs are usually single pieces of wood continuous with the back legs; oftentimes the outside back corners are rounded to protect the finish cover. A moderate backward rake in the rear legs is essential to prevent the top-heavy seats from tumbling backwards. The stretchers and seat rails are attached near the bottom. Across the lower back a stay rail is tenoned to the inside stile faces (fig. 2). At the top, the crest is secured to tenons cut in the stile tops or mortised and tenoned between the stiles. In this example the crest has been chamfered on the upper forward edge of the arch to provide a thin sloping surface for feathering the stuffing while maintaining a precise top line.

The side framing members begin at the upper wing rails and terminate at the forward arm cones. The rear stile and wing-rail joint is either a mortise and tenon or a large, nailed dovetail as shown (see fig. 2). Mortise-and-tenon joints most commonly attach the wing rails to the wing stiles and the wing and arm stiles to the seat rails. Cones are formed at the arm stiles by nailing rounded tapered pieces to the outside surfaces. The flat scrolled pieces capping the cones are secured with nails; the rear extensions are joined to the wing stiles at inside rabbets and are either nailed or screwed in place.[2]

With a completed frame in hand, the upholsterer began his work. Strips of webbing, called "girth web" (also girt web), were tacked from front to back and crosswise on the seat frame. This chair originally had three-by-three interwoven strips supporting the seat deck. A coarsely woven piece of linen, or sackcloth, was tacked over the webbing on the top surfaces of the rails. Next, an edge roll, fabricated of finely woven linen and usually stuffed with cured grass, was formed and

**Fig. 1.** Detail, seat frame.

tacked to the top edge of the front seat rail (see figs. 1, 3). The roll protected the finish fabric and the sitter's legs and created a well to contain the loose cushion. A thin layer of meadow or marsh grass, sometimes with a skimmer of curled horsehair, tow, or unprocessed wool, was spread evenly over the sackcloth in this well. The stuffing was held in place by an undercover of finely woven linen. Tacked to the forward face of the front rail below the edge roll, the undercover was drawn back and secured to the top surfaces of the side and rear seat rails.[3]

The back was the second unit to be stuffed. The original webbing, which is retained on this chair, consists of two cross strips and a vertical strip tacked to the crest and stay rail faces (see fig. 2). A sackcloth was tacked in place across the lower crest-front face, down the stiles, and across the stay-rail face. The loose bottom was drawn behind the rear seat rail and baste-tacked (lightly tacked for easy removal). With the chair on its back atop the upholsterer's bench, the face was stuffed. The material (in this case, grass and a skimmer of horsehair) was feathered at the chamfered crest edge and stitched through at several points to hold it in place. As on the seat deck, an undercover was placed over the stuffing and tacked to the forward faces of the back stiles. The top was drawn over the crest and tacked to the upper back. The bottom was pulled through to the back rail where it and the sackcloth were baste-tacked on the outside face.

The wings and arms were stuffed last. Since these units receive no webbing, the sackcloth was attached directly to the inside surfaces. Tacking lines are present along the inside edges of the wings and arms, ending at the inside forward cone faces in vertical lines extending to the seat rails. The back edges were drawn across the outside faces of the back stiles and baste-tacked; the lower edges were pulled through to the outside and baste-tacked to the side seat rails (see fig. 2). Edge

**Fig. 2.** Three-quarter back view without slipcover.

rolls, like the one at the seat front, were tacked in place along the inside top edges of the wing rails, upper stiles, and arm rails to the vertical cones, where the rolls were feathered lightly around the forward faces and terminated (see fig. 3). The interior stuffing was again secured by undercovers, which were drawn over the edge rolls and tacked to the forward faces or outside surfaces of the wing rails, upper arm stiles, and arm tops; the lower front extensions were carried around the cones and tacked vertically along the outside creases at the cone backs. The loose edges extending above the cone tops were trimmed to a short length, snipped with perpendicular cuts, compass pleated, and, after final adjustments, tacked to the cone tops. Like the sackcloth, the back and bottom edges of the undercovers were drawn to the outside surfaces of the back stiles and side seat rails where they were baste-

tacked in double layers; final tacking would occur after installation of the finish covers.[4]

The rare survival of part of the original stuffing makes this chair a valuable instructional object. The fabric surfaces have been stabilized, and sewing strips have been stitched to the cloth edges at the outside seat rails and back stiles. A false deck has been placed over the seat frame. A fitted slipcover, similar to those used in the eighteenth century, protects the original upholstery, and a new cushion simulates the original one. All can be removed to study the frame and interior upholstery.

The stylistic attributes of the undercarriage of this chair, its construction features, and its similarities to a chair documented to the Boston shop of upholsterer Samuel Grant through records dated in 1759 suggest an eastern Massachusetts origin. The front knees

**Fig. 3.** Three-quarter front view without slipcover.

The frame retains much of its original upholstery: webbing on the back panel; sackcloths (liners), stuffing, and undercovers on the back and wing-arm panels; edge rolls around the seat front (repaired with later canvas) and interior edges of the wing and arm panels. The seat frame retains remnants of the original webbing strips. Bits of the original blue-green woolen finish cover remain beneath many of the upholstery tacks. The frame and stuffing are now tightly fitted with a loose cover of modern dark green wool moreen simulating fixed upholstery.

**Dimensions:**

| | | |
|---|---|---|
| H. | 47 in. | 119.4 cm |
| H. (seat frame) | 12 5/8 in. | 32.1 cm |
| W. (wings) | 29 5/8 in. | 75.2 cm |
| W. (seat front) | 31 in. | 78.7 cm |
| W. (seat back) | 24 in. | 61.0 cm |
| W. (arms) | 35 7/8 in. | 91.1 cm |
| W. (feet) | 30 3/4 in. | 78.1 cm |
| D. (seat) | 23 1/2 in. | 59.7 cm |
| D. (feet) | 25 5/8 in. | 65.1 cm |

**Materials:** *Microanalysis:* Primary: American black walnut. Secondary: birch (rear leg, rear stiles); beech (seat rails); soft maple group (wing stiles). *Finish:* dark brown color in resin.

**Accession history:** Museum purchase from Frank Cowan, Patterson, N.Y., 1989.
89.47

1. Morrison H. Heckscher, "Form and Frame: New Thoughts on the American Easy Chair," *Antiques* 100, no. 6 (December 1971): 886–93; Steven L. Pine, "Construction Traits of the Eighteenth-Century American Easy Chair" (Unpublished manuscript, Winterthur Museum and University of Delaware Program in Art Conservation, Spring 1986), pp. 1–11 and appendixes (copy courtesy of Mark Anderson, conservator, Winterthur); Jobe and Kaye, *New England Furniture*, nos. 101–4. For a discussion of the German attributes found in American chairmaking, see Désirée Caldwell, "Germanic Influences on Philadelphia Early Georgian Seating Furniture" (Master's thesis, University of Delaware, 1985).

2. I am grateful to Robert F. Trent for his helpful insights and explanations relative to the intricacies of easy chair construction and for his assistance in providing source materials for further study.

3. For a discussion of grasses used as stuffing material, see F. Carey Howlett, "The Identification of Grasses and Other Plant Materials Used in Historic Upholstery," in Marc A. Williams, ed., *Upholstery Conservation* (East Kingston, N.H.: American Conservation Consortium, 1990), pp. 66–91. For the use of unprocessed wool as occasional stuffing material, see Brock Jobe, "The Boston Upholstery Trade, 1700–1775," in Cooke, *Upholstery*, p. 83.

4. I am grateful to Robert F. Trent for his infinite patience in illuminating the "mysteries" of the upholsterer's art. Other helpful sources are Andrew Passeri and Robert F. Trent, "Two New England Queen Anne Easy Chairs with Original Upholstery," *Maine Antique Digest*, April 1983, pp. 26A–28A; Edward S. Cooke, Jr., "The Nathan Low Easy Chair: High-Quality Upholstery in Pre-Revolutionary Boston," *Maine Antique Digest*, November 1987, pp. 1C–3C; Andrew Passeri and Robert F. Trent, "More on Easy Chairs," *Maine Antique Digest*, December 1987, pp. 1B–3B; Morrison H. Heckscher, "Eighteenth-Century American Upholstery Techniques: Easy Chairs, Sofas, and Settees," in Cooke, *Upholstery*, pp. 97–108. See also Thomas G. Schwenke advertisement, *Antiques* 123, no. 5 (May 1983): 983.

5. On the Grant chair, now in the collection of the SPNEA, see Jobe and Kaye, *New England Furniture*, no. 101. Boston Fire Documents and Correspondence, vol. 1, p. 50, Boston Public Library, Boston.

and brackets of the two chairs are identical (the feet have been restored on the Grant chair), the front rail joints and leg attachments are similar, and the turned stretchers are closely related. The same wing-arm construction and high-crest arch are present in both chairs. The seat frame of the Grant chair is rectangular with rounded front corners, although that form and the horseshoe shape of the Winterthur chair were contemporary options. The chamfered rear legs of the Grant chair are stylistically earlier than the plain legs illustrated, suggesting that this chair dates slightly later. The supposition is reinforced by the lack of rounded edges on the outside rear corners of the stiles, a feature often present in early Queen Anne easy chairs. Grant did business with two Boston chairmakers—Clement Vincent and George Bright—in the year he billed Judge Jonathan Sayward of York, Maine, for the easy chair described above. Vincent suffered losses in the great fire of Boston in 1760, losing two easy chair frames, among other shop work. This easy chair is not necessarily from any shop mentioned, but a Boston origin seems almost certain.[5]

NGE

**Construction:** The arched crest, deeply chamfered on the upper front edge, is supported on rectangular tenons at the tops of the squared rear stiles; the stiles are continuous with the back feet. A horizontal, lower-back stay rail is tenoned into the stiles. The

vertical and horizontal members comprising the wing and arm units are united by joints of several types: open dovetails secured by rosehead nails (wing rails/ back stiles); mortises and tenons (wing rails/wing stiles; wing, arm stiles/side seat rails); and nailed rabbets (wing stiles/arm rails). The vertical arm stiles are rounded on the inside and forward faces and fitted with applied outside cones. The modified horseshoe-shape seat frame is curved inward along the sides and rounded across the front. The front and side rails, which have a horizontal orientation, are joined with mortise and tenon. The front joints are pinned from the top surface. The rear legs are canted on the forward surfaces; the front corners are chamfered to points below the stretchers. The front legs join the seat frame in open dovetails at the front corners; the knee brackets are nailed in place. The side stretchers are joined to the legs in vertical rectangular tenons (pinned); the creased-tip medial and rear stretchers are round tenoned into the adjacent members.

**Condition:** The right front foot is restored on much of the front surface to above stretcher level but forward of the joint pins; glue and a screw secure the new wood. The left front foot is chipped on the forward face. Modern wooden disks are applied to the bottoms of the feet. All knee brackets are replaced except one at the left side rail. The right side-stretcher column is severely cracked on the lower surface and repaired with glue and nails. The medial stretcher surfaces are considerably marred, and the left tip is splintered. The left side stretcher is cracked on the inside face at both ends. A piece has splintered off the inside front edge of the right side rail.

## 81 ✦ Easy chair
Northeastern Massachusetts
1750–75

Construction features are useful, frequently critical, complements to stylistic attributes in determining the regional origin of an easy chair, although it is not always possible to inspect the interior frame. Generally, the back stiles in New England examples are a continuation of the rear legs, in contrast to the spliced construction of Philadelphia and New York easy chairs. Philadelphia construction also frequently includes through, or exposed, tenons at the side rail joints with the rear stiles. New England continuous-stile legs are frequently made of maple and stained to match the rest of the undercarriage when it is constructed of walnut or mahogany.[1]

The nature of the front joints and the cabriole-leg connections is often of equal, if not greater, importance than regional characteristics in making proper identifications. Square-front frames have little interregional variation; blocklike leg extensions form the front corners and are mortised to receive the tenons of the front and side rails. New York chairs frequently have blocked leg extensions with rounded front corners in squared or rounded frames. Joints in rounded frames outside New York are more commonly formed exclusive of the front legs. The side and front rails are laid flat, the depth greater than the height. The broad joints are either lapped and pinned or secured with mortise and tenon. The front legs are merely inserted into the preformed joints with a large front dovetail or a through tenon of round, quarter-round, or pentagonal form. Round and pentagonal tenons are present in Pennsylvania work; the quarter-round tenon is found in New England construction. The dovetail connection is common in both Philadelphia and New England frames when the joint is lapped but, apparently, occurs only in New England work

when the front is mortised and tenoned. The New England quarter-round tenon appears to be limited to the lapped joint, while the Philadelphia round tenon accompanies mortise-and-tenon construction.[2]

This chair has lapped front rails to which the legs are attached with quarter-round tenons. Several wooden pins inserted from the top surface secure the rail connection. Several other chairs of similar construction have plain pad-foot front legs of slim proportions. Two are braced across the center with stretchers turned to the uncommon profile shown in the Winterthur chair: tipped ends flanked by large spools.[3]

The shells carved on the knees are unusual (fig. 1). An extensive search has failed to produce either a similar or related American example. The form differs significantly from recognized shell-carved ornament, which includes the broad convex shell on a beaded, double-scroll base and the modified scallop shell (see No. 24). The carved work may have

been executed by an emigrant British craftsman, but more likely the shell was copied or adapted from a piece of imported furniture. No exact prototypes have been located in British cabinetwork; closest in form is a haystack-shape shell centered in the front apron of a console table. The basic profile may have its roots in William and Mary–style carved crests (see No. 18, fig. 2). Another possibility is that the shape was adapted from a baroque shell used as a cast ornament on a piece of European or American silver, particularly on the salver form.[4]

Like No. 78, both the finish fabric and the cushion style are inappropriate for this eighteenth-century easy chair. Silk velvet was costly and impractical. More durable were the wool velvets, known by various names, including velour and plush. The most common cover fabrics until after the revolutionary war were the worsted wools, including calimanco, cheney, harateen, moreen, and damask. Cushions were made

**Fig. 1.** Detail, left front knee shell.

with boxed edges about four inches to six inches deep, producing trim edges that were visually compatible with the front surface of the seat frame.[5]

After stuffing an easy chair and securing the undercover (see No. 80), an upholsterer was ready to cut and fit the finish cover. Because textiles were expensive, as little as possible was wasted. First a panel was loosely fitted and baste-tacked temporarily at the back of the seat deck. The forward end was drawn over the front rail and tacked to the underside, the rounded front corners fitted with fine pleats or short horizontal seams at the edge roll from the knees to the arm cones. The side and rear edges were pulled over the rails and tacked on the outside faces; several tacks held the cover in place over the knees.

To permanently tack the long sides of the inside back panel to the outside faces of the back stiles, the baste-tacks temporarily securing the linings of the wings were loosened. The top of the back panel was carried over the crest and tacked to the back surface. The bottom was drawn through the lower back, and with the sackcloth and undercover that secured the back stuffing, was tacked to the outside surface of the seat rail over the edge of the seat cover.

The top edges of the inside wing covers were then tacked to the outside faces of the wing rails, wing stiles, and arm rails. The bottoms were secured to the sides of the seat rails, the tacks also piercing the wing linings and the finish cover for the seat deck. The front edges were drawn around the arm cones and tacked vertically along the outside back creases. The rear edges were permanently tacked, along with the wing linings, to the outside surfaces of the back stiles over the finish cover for the inside back panel. The raw fabric edges that extended above the arm cones were fitted to the curved surfaces with compass pleats and tacked in place, like the undercovers. The outside wing covers were

tacked to the wing and arm tops and the forward edges terminated in the creases of the arm cones. The bottoms were carried under the seat rails and tacked; the back edges were secured to the rear faces of the back stiles (see No. 80, fig. 2).

The outside back panel was fitted and held in place with pins while the upholsterer hand-seamed the cover to the front panel across the crest top and to the outside wing panels at the sides. The lower edge was drawn beneath the back rail and tacked (see No. 80, fig. 2). The forward and top edges of the wings and arms were covered with narrow panels. To achieve smooth surfaces at the cone tops, the upholsterer introduced a series of short, compass cuts around the panel circles before folding the edges to the inside and hand-stitching the panel lengths.[6]

To complete the basic upholstery, the chair needed a cushion. Stout linen or ticking woven in a twill pattern were the common interior casings. Fashioned from three pieces of cloth, the case consisted of top and bottom panels and a long narrow boxing forming the sides and was usually stuffed with feathers, frequently down. About three to four pounds were required to fill a plump cushion having a six-inch boxing. The stuffed cushion was either placed within a second case made of the finish fabric or the outside cover was stitched directly to the down case.[7]

Prior to delivery of the easy chair, seams and other edges had to be bound or concealed with tape. The effect of self welting could be

created at corded or raised seams around the wing and arm panels, across the crest, and around the cushion edges (see No. 82). The same seams could be concealed with a decorative tape that was also placed around the bottom of the frame and up the back creases of the cones (see No. 80). Tape at the lower edges was sewed, glued, or nailed in place. When nailed, polished-iron domed-head nails, widely spaced, were generally used. Few easy chairs appear to have been finished with closely spaced brass nails. The tuckaways at the inside back corners of the eighteenth-century easy chair were never true, as in modern work, because all the tacking was done on the basic frame without the use of special intermediate tacking strips.[8]

NGE

**Construction:** (Frame upholstered; a photograph without upholstery is unavailable.) The squared back stiles are shaved to rounded surfaces at the outside back corners. The modified horseshoe-shape seat frame is curved inward along the sides and rounded at the front corners; the center front is flat. The front and side rails, which have a horizontal orientation, are secured with lap joints at the front corners (pinned). The front legs are attached to the frame with large quarter-round tenons that pierce the top surface. The rear legs are canted on the forward surfaces; the lower bends are angled backward sharply. The rear corners are narrowly chamfered, top to bottom; the front corners are chamfered below the side stretchers. The front feet have thin disks beneath the pads and ledges at the ankle backs. The knee shells are carved in low relief; the brackets are attached with nails. The side stretchers are joined to the legs with vertical rectangular tenons (pinned); the medial and rear stretchers are round tenoned into the adjacent members.

**Condition:** Surface abrasion and dents mark the exposed wooden parts, including the carved shells; the right shell is chipped at the top of one lobe. Small chips occur in the front pad feet; caster holes are present in the bottoms of all four feet. The right front leg is repaired at the upper inside block. The knee brackets are renailed. Longitudinal cracks are present on the lower front section of the right side stretcher, extending into the front joint.

**Dimensions:**

| | | |
|---|---|---|
| H. | 48 1/2 in. | 123.2 cm |
| H. (seat frame) | 13 in. | 33.0 cm |
| W. (wings) | 27 1/2 in. | 69.8 cm |
| W. (seat front) | 31 in. | 78.7 cm |
| W. (seat back) | 23 3/4 in. | 60.3 cm |
| W. (arms) | 35 in. | 88.9 cm |
| W. (feet) | 31 1/4 in. | 79.4 cm |
| D. (seat) | 23 3/4 in. | 60.3 cm |
| D. (feet) | 25 in. | 63.5 cm |

**Materials:** *Microanalysis:* Primary: mahogany. Secondary: maple (seat rail). *Finish:* medium brown color in resin. *Upholstery:* dark green silk velvet; Europe, possibly Italy, 1700–1800.

**Publications:** Downs, *American Furniture*, fig. 80.

**Accession history:** Bequest of H. F. du Pont, 1969. 58.2218

---

1. Morrison H. Heckscher, "Form and Frame: New Thoughts on the American Easy Chair," *Antiques* 100, no. 6 (December 1971): 886–93; Steven L. Pine, "Construction Traits of the Eighteenth-Century American Easy Chair" (Unpublished paper, Winterthur Museum and University of Delaware Program in Art Conservation, Spring 1986; copy courtesy of Mark Anderson, conservator, Winterthur).

2. For a square-frame New York easy chair, see Bernard and S. Dean Levy, Inc., *Catalogue VI* (New York: By the company, 1988), p. 110; for a round-frame New York easy chair, see Heckscher, "Form and Frame," fig. 7.

3. The tipped-stretcher chairs are in Teina Baumstone advertisement, *Antiques* 83, no. 4 (April 1963): 362; Taylor B. Williams advertisement, *Antiques* 102, no. 3 (September 1972): 369.

4. The console table is in Kirk, *American Furniture*, fig. 1327. See also a shell-carved footstool in Cescinsky, *English Furniture*, 2:20. A silver salver with baroque shells is illustrated in Ian M. G. Quimby, *American Silver at Winterthur* (Winterthur, Del.: Henry Francis du Pont Winterthur Museum, 1995), p. 64.

5. Thornton, *Seventeenth-Century Interior Decoration*, pp. 111–12, 220–21.

6. I am indebted to Robert F. Trent for his guidance in understanding the idiosyncrasies of this work.

7. For cushions and their construction, see Forman, *American Seating Furniture*, p. 358; Brock Jobe, "The Boston Upholstery Trade, 1700–1775," and Morrison H. Heckscher, "Eighteenth-Century American Upholstery Techniques: Easy Chairs, Sofas, and Settees," in Cooke, *Upholstery*, pp. 71, 98, 100; Robert F. Trent, Robert Walker, and Andrew Passeri, "The Franklin Easy Chair and Other Goodies," *Maine Antique Digest*, December 1979, p. 29-B; Andrew Passeri and Robert F. Trent, "Two New England Queen Anne Easy Chairs with Original Upholstery," *Maine Antique Digest*, April 1983, p. 27-A. Between the late 1720s and the early 1740s, Samuel Grant, an upholsterer in Boston, recorded the cost of feathers per pound between 3s. 6d. and 4s., a figure that exceeded the cost of curled hair, which was used as a skimmer in various parts of the tight upholstery; Samuel Grant account book, 1736–60, American Antiquarian Society, Worcester, Mass. (microfilm, Downs collection).

8. For binding techniques, see Trent, Walker, and Passeri, "Franklin Easy Chair," p. 29-B; Passeri and Trent, "Two Easy Chairs," p. 28-A; Edward S. Cooke, Jr., "The Nathan Low Easy Chair: High Quality Upholstery in Pre-Revolutionary Boston," *Maine Antique Digest*, November 1987, p. 2-C; Andrew Passeri and Robert F. Trent, "More on Easy Chairs," *Maine Antique Digest*, December 1987, pp. 2-B, 3-B.

## 82 ◆ Easy chair
### Boston, Massachusetts
### 1750–75

Curved-stretcher easy chairs are rare. Only five have come to this writer's attention; three are at Winterthur. One of the Winterthur chairs is now thought to be English, and another was constructed originally with block-and-turned braces. The remaining chair at Winterthur and the other two, which are privately owned, are of Boston origin, although stylistically there are substantial variations. Two chairs are made of walnut and the third of mahogany. The secondary wood of the mahogany chair and this walnut chair at Winterthur is maple. The Winterthur chair was purchased from a Long Island family early in the twentieth century; the second walnut chair was purchased before 1930 in Warren, Rhode Island, from a descendant of the original owner.[1]

Curved-stretcher easy chairs, which probably were introduced slightly later than side and armchairs with curved braces (see No. 14), were sometimes made in suites with other seating forms of compatible design. In fact, the front feet on the other two curved-stretcher easy chairs are saucer-shape pads like those in No. 14, a Boston side chair, and the walnut easy chair has similar beads and scrolls at the knees. The walnut easy chair is said to have been made to accompany a set of six walnut side chairs with flat stretchers that are in the same private collection and were acquired from the same family source. The general prototypes for furniture with curved stretchers appear in Britain, but even there the easy chair with curved braces is a rarity. The two types are: a flat brace with angular offsets in the side supports and a rounded molded brace. One uncommon feature of the stretchers in this chair is the deep cove cut along the upper forward and outside edges, a detail of British cabinetwork from the late seventeenth century seen in elaborate upholstered seats and side tables with crossed and arched braces.[2]

Whereas the regional characteristics of this chair were once considered mixed

**Fig. 1.** Detail, left front knee shell.

between features associated with New York and others assigned to Rhode Island, recent scholarship has shown that the point of origin for this and related seating furniture with flat stretchers (aside from those made in Philadelphia) was Boston. Confusing the picture has been the presumed descent of a set of high-style flat-stretcher side chairs in a New York branch of the Apthorp family of Boston. The Apthorp chairs appear to be the only examples with a cove cut along the upper outside edges of the side stretchers in the manner of this easy chair. The Apthorp chairs also have blocked rear feet, a characteristic not associated previously with Boston chairmaking. Another feature of the easy chair found in the Apthorp chairs and previously thought to be the province of New York rather than Boston design is the knee-bracket profile with its pronounced scroll and spur (see Nos. 26, 27). The same profile appears in a roundabout chair (see No. 74). The slim front legs of this chair are characteristic of Boston easy chairs (see Nos. 79–81, 84), and the compressed, webbed foot also has been reassigned to that urban center (see No. 86). The elongated shell with alternating concave and convex lobes and a pendent bellflower is an uncommon interpretation of this ornament. The feature is also present on a side chair once owned by John Aspinwall of New York and now assigned to a Boston origin.[3]

Construction features of the easy chair reinforce the Boston provenance. The front and side rails are laid flat and joined with mortise and tenon, and the legs are attached with large dovetails, techniques common in New England easy chairs. In this frame, however, the dovetails of the front leg extensions are wedged (see No. 79, fig. 1)—an uncommon feature that also occurs in an easy chair with standard block-and-turned

stretchers. That chair, newly reassigned to Boston, has similar ankles and webbed feet; standard, ogee-type knee brackets; and broad, convex-lobed shells at the knees. Both chairs have a rounded-end crest with a flat top. Because of the height of the crest end curves in the two chairs, the wing rails are joined to the back frame at a low level and angled forward in pronounced slopes. A similar slope appears in the wings of the mahogany, curved-stretcher easy chair, although the crest has a normal low arch (see No. 84). The front legs of that chair pierce the flat mortise-and-tenon joints of the rails with rectangular tenons that appear to be wedged, and the rear legs are spliced to the rear stiles, an uncommon construction in New England easy chairs until the federal period. The construction technique employed at the back of this chair has not been determined.[4]

NGE

---

**Construction:** (Frame upholstered; a photograph without upholstery is unavailable.) The crest is probably chamfered on the upper forward edge; the back stiles have squared corners. The rails forming the horseshoe-shape seat frame are laid flat and joined by mortise and tenon. The front legs are attached with large dovetails exposed on the front and top surfaces and wedged. The rear legs, which are rectangular at the top, are rounded through most of the length; the feet are blocked to a rectangular form. The forward faces are flattened to receive the side stretchers. The cabriole front legs are carved with shells and pendent bellflowers; the knee brackets are attached with nails. The flat curved side stretchers are joined to the legs with vertical rectangular tenons (pinned). The medial stretcher is secured to the side stretchers with horizontal tenons (pinned). All flat stretchers are molded with a hollow cove on the upper outside or forward edges. The rear stretcher is round tenoned into the back legs; the conical tips are turned with scribed beads, rings, and collars at the inside faces.

**Condition:** The knee brackets, with the exception of one at the left front, appear to be replacements made at two different times. The front feet are worn away by at least 1/2"; the rear feet are slightly worn. The left rear foot is pieced out on the back half to an incorrect profile. Some stretchers are repinned.

**Dimensions:**

| | | |
|---|---|---|
| H. | 46 in. | 116.8 cm |
| H. (seat frame) | 12 1/4 in. | 31.1 cm |
| W. (wings) | 28 1/4 in. | 71.7 cm |
| W. (seat front) | 30 1/2 in. | 77.4 cm |
| W. (seat back) | 23 7/8 in. | 60.6 cm |
| W. (arms) | 28 1/4 in. | 71.7 cm |
| W. (feet) | 30 3/4 in. | 76.2 cm |
| D. (seat) | 23 in. | 58.4 cm |
| D. (feet) | 25 in. | 63.5 cm |

**Materials:** *Microanalysis:* Primary: American black walnut. Secondary: soft maple group (seat frame). *Finish:* medium dark brown color in resin. *Upholstery:* green and white worsted damask woven with vertical bands of spiraled lace and red and yellow brocaded flowers; England, probably Norwich, 1750–80.

**Publications:** Downs, *American Furniture*, fig. 79. Parke-Bernet Galleries, "The Americana Collection of the Late Mrs. J. Amory Haskell, Part 2" (May 17–20, 1944), lot 746. Keno, Freund, and Miller, "Very Pink of the Mode," fig. 15.

**Provenance:** Ex coll.: Mrs. J. Amory Haskell, Red Bank, N.J.

**Accession history:** Purchased by H. F. du Pont from John S. Walton, Inc., New York, 1951. Gift of H. F. du Pont, 1951.
51.21

---

1. The English-ascribed easy chair is in Downs, *American Furniture*, fig. 73; for the 2 easy chairs not at Winterthur, see *American Antiques from Israel Sack Collection*, 10 vols. (Washington, D.C.: Highland House, ca. 1969–), 6:1548–49; Moses, *Master Craftsmen*, p. 256. The privately owned walnut chair was sold at auction; see American Art Association Anderson Galleries, "Colonial Furniture, Silver, and Decorations: The Collection of the Late Philip Flayderman" (January 2–4, 1930), lot 493.

2. One walnut side chair from the set of 6 is illustrated in Moses, *Master Craftsmen*, p. 255; the chairs were formerly in the Flayderman collection; American Art Association Anderson Galleries, "Colonial Furniture," lot 492. For British curved-stretcher easy chairs, see Downs, *American Furniture*, fig. 73; John Bivins, "A Catalogue of Northern Furniture with Southern Provenances," *Journal of Early Southern Decorative Arts* 15, no. 2 (November 1989): 46; Kirk, *American Furniture*, fig. 1148. For British upholstered seating and side tables with molded coves, see Thornton, *Seventeenth-Century Interior Decoration*, pl. 204; Macquoid and Edwards, *Dictionary*, 3: frontispiece, pl. 3, p. 76 (figs. 11, 12); Cescinsky, *English Furniture*, 1: figs. 31, 58, 102, 107.

3. Keno, Freund, and Miller, "Very Pink of the Mode," pp. 271–85. An Apthorp side chair is illustrated in Heckscher, *American Furniture*, cat. no. 22. The new scholarship on New York–Boston chairs was first discussed in Sotheby's, "Important Americana" (October 23, 1994), lot 370. The Aspinwall chair is illustrated in Rollins, *Treasures of State*, cat. no. 11.

4. For the block-and-turned-stretcher easy chair, see Jobe and Kaye, *New England Furniture*, no. 103. For the mahogany curved-stretcher easy chair, see *American Antiques from Sack Collection*, 6:1548–49.

## 83 ◆ Easy chair
**Northeastern Massachusetts, probably Boston**
**1755–80**

Several stylistic features identify this chair as a product of northeastern Massachusetts, probably Boston. The manner in which the wings drop below the crest ends and slope along the top surface suggests a relationship with Nos. 79 and 80 and Massachusetts easy chairs in the Museum of Fine Arts, Boston, the Baltimore Museum of Art, and the former Adolph Meyer collection. The comparison continues in the understructure. A long-tipped medial stretcher also appears in No. 80 and in chairs in the above-named collections. The stretchers are a throwback to Queen Anne design (see Nos. 7, 8, 11), but the smooth styling of the front knees, as also seen in the Museum of Fine Arts, Boston, and Meyer chairs, is a reflection of the Boston chair market of the 1760s and 1770s (see Nos. 53, 55).[1]

The antique blue, wool moreen or harateen of this chair, although not the original upholstery, is appropriate, since worsted woolens were the most common easy chair covers during the first three-quarters of the eighteenth century. Cheney (also china), another worsted that was available in a range of colors and sometimes with a watered ground, was popular in the seventeenth century and continued in American demand for easy chair covers and room hangings until the early 1740s. After 1740, harateen became the favored textile for easy chairs, loose (slip) seats, and room hangings—in short, for complete room suites. Colors ranged from the reds (crimson, orange, and rose) to blue, green, and yellow. Harateen, in turn, was replaced by moreen, a worsted of similar appearance that was available in a greater range of colors, including black, brown, garnet, pink, and purple, although American consumers appear to have favored the primary colors listed for harateen. Following the revolutionary war, worsted covers and hangings went out of fashion and were replaced with printed linens and cottons imported in a variety of colors and

a profusion of patterns. The practicality of washable fabrics and a greater affluency among the general population encouraged the trade, and the use of cases and slipcovers to protect furniture with fixed upholstery increased.[2]

The calendering process by which patterns were impressed on harateens and moreens and other worsted woolens required specialized machinery. A watered effect, such as appears on this chair cover, was achieved by folding textile lengths into triangular blocks or placing the lengthwise folded fabric on rollers and then submitting the cloth to pressure from a heavy calender, causing the coarser threads to leave impressions on the facing surfaces.[3]

As indicated, the cost of an easy chair was substantial. Because many of upholsterer Samuel Grant's Boston accounts for easy chairs are itemized, it is possible to analyze chair cost in terms of labor and materials. The complete frame with its rough interior and finished undercarriage accounted for slightly less than 25 percent of the total cost, while the upholstery charges exceeded 75 percent. Upholstery expenses can be further broken down into three components: labor—about 20 percent; stuffing materials—about 25 percent; and finishing materials—about 34 percent. The prices charged at midcentury by John Elliott, a cabinetmaker in Philadelphia, were comparable; labor was slightly less, and the cost of finishing materials was somewhat more.[4]

A recurring item in Grant's easy chair accounts for 1 to 1 1/8 yards of "print" (fabric) in addition to the usual 6 1/2 to 7 yards of finishing material has peaked the curiosity of furniture scholars and led to speculation that the cloth was used to line the seat deck or the out back. At the time that Stephen Collins, a prosperous Quaker merchant in Philadelphia, acquired a copperplate upholstered easy chair from Plunket Fleeson in 1773 or 1774, he itemized in his accounts the "Coste of a Bed & Furniture of a Room" and in so doing provided an answer: "2 yd callico for Back of Ease Chair." Collins's expenses of almost 5 1/2s. per yard for the copperplate, 4s. for the calico, and 2s. for the linen permit certain speculative conclusions. The calico would not have been used as an interior lining when linen would have done as well at less cost. Calico was only slightly cheaper than copperplate; therefore, economy was not the reason for its use on the exposed chair back. Only the dictates of fashion appear to account for covering the out back with a print. The panel would have been on view, since a window or fireside location would have positioned the chair away from the wall.[5]

NGE

**Construction:** (Frame upholstered; a photograph without upholstery is unavailable.) The low-arched crest is rounded or chamfered on the upper forward edge. The rear stiles are squared. The rectangular seat frame is joined by mortise and tenon. The rear legs are canted on the forward surfaces; the upper legs and feet are chamfered on all four corners. The front legs have creased knees and claws with three-joint toes; the knee brackets are attached with nails. The side stretchers are joined to the legs with vertical rectangular tenons (pinned at rear). The long creased-tip medial and rear stretchers are round tenoned into the adjacent members.

**Condition:** Minor stress cracks occur in the rear legs. The side stretcher joints are repinned (or newly pinned) at the outside back. The left front knee bracket is replaced.

**Dimensions:**

| | | |
|---|---|---|
| H. | 46 in. | 116.8 cm |
| H. (seat frame) | 13 in. | 33.0 cm |
| W. (wings) | 27 7/8 in. | 70.8 cm |
| W. (seat front) | 30 7/8 in. | 78.4 cm |
| W. (seat back) | 23 3/4 in. | 60.3 cm |
| W. (arms) | 34 3/8 in. | 87.3 cm |
| D. (feet) | 32 1/2 in. | 82.5 cm |
| D. (seat) | 22 3/4 in. | 57.8 cm |
| D. (feet) | 26 3/4 in. | 67.9 cm |

**Materials:** *Macroidentification:* Primary: walnut. *Microanalysis:* Secondary: soft maple group (seat frame, rear leg). *Finish:* medium light brown color in resin. *Upholstery:* watered blue moreen; England, 1750–1800.

**Accession history:** Bequest of H. F. du Pont, 1969. 58.2770

1. For the Museum of Fine Arts chair, see Randall, *American Furniture,* no. 154; for the Baltimore Museum of Art chair, see William Voss Elder III and Jayne E. Stokes, *American Furniture, 1680–1880, from the Collection of the Baltimore Museum of Art* (Baltimore: By the museum, 1987), cat. no. 34; for the Meyer chair, see Sotheby's, "Important Americana from the Collection of Mr. and Mrs. Adolph Henry Meyer" (January 20, 1996), lot 173.

2. Florence Montgomery, *Textiles in America, 1650–1870* (New York: W. W. Norton, 1984), pp. 126–27, 199, 256–57, 300, 302–3.

3. Montgomery, *Textiles in America,* pp. 256–57, 300, 302–3; fig. D-26; pls. D-27A, B.

4. Forman, *American Seating Furniture,* p. 358. Jobe and Kaye, *New England Furniture,* p. 365. Brock Jobe, "The Boston Furniture Industry, 1720–1740," in *Boston Furniture,* p. 34. Andrew Passeri and Robert F. Trent, "Two New England Queen Anne Easy Chairs with Original Upholstery," *Maine Antique Digest,* April 1983, p. 27-A. Morrison H. Heckscher, "Eighteenth-Century American Upholstery Techniques: Easy Chairs, Sofas, and Settees," in Cooke, *Upholstery,* pp. 105, 107. Nancy Ann Goyne, "Furniture Craftsmen in Philadelphia, 1760–1780: Their Role in a Mercantile Society" (Master's thesis, University of Delaware, 1963), pp. 81, 83.

5. Forman, *American Seating Furniture,* p. 359. Passeri and Trent, "Two Easy Chairs," p. 27-A. Goyne, "Furniture Craftsmen," pp. 81, 83.

## 84 ◆ Easy chair
### Northeastern Massachusetts, probably Boston
### 1755–80

Many eastern Massachusetts easy chairs are braced by medial stretchers turned with conical tips. This chair represents a small group fitted with center braces terminated by blocks and rings. The ring pattern is varied from a single turning adjacent to the block to a series of rings extending two inches or more inside the end piece; disk- and knob-size rings appear. The typical cabriole front legs are moderate in breadth with cusped knee brackets and compressed ball feet grasped by well-defined, webless toes. Knees are both rounded and creased, and some are accented by acanthus-leaf carving. A few chairs have plain pad feet. Timothy Danielson (b. 1733)

of Brimfield, Massachusetts, originally owned an uncarved chair in this group turned with single rings adjacent to the medial stretcher blocks. Danielson was a major general during the revolutionary war and later became chief justice for the Court of Common Pleas in Hampshire County. As in this example, the Danielson easy chair has a low-arched crest, tall vertical arm cones, and rounded front seat corners secured by mortise and tenon; the legs are attached with dovetails.[1]

Although an easy chair, which cost from £7 to £10 when new, was expensive, mainly due to the cost of the upholstery materials, it was beyond public view in most homes. Household inventories, vendue notices, memoranda, and even literary references name the master, or principal, bedchamber as the most common location. As early as the Middle Ages, chairs were commonly placed in principal bedchambers in households of European nobility and substantial citizens. Many chairs had high backs and some were upholstered, but the seat recognized today as an easy chair probably was not developed until the late seventeenth century. By way of example, one of the prominent characters in the 1707 play *The Beaux Stratagem* directed, "Get my easie chair down stairs, put the gentleman in it." More than sixty-five years later in 1773 or 1774, Stephen Collins, a Philadelphia merchant, recorded at the back of his memorandum book an account of the "Coste of a Bed & Furniture of a Room," listing among the expenses an "Easey chair" for which he paid £7.10.0.[2]

Probate and other types of household inventories provide the greatest amount of information on easy chair use in America. An early record is the 1736 Philadelphia estate enumeration of Lt. Gov. Patrick Gordon; it lists a plush easy chair and bedding in a room also furnished with window hangings, four old cane chairs, and a dressing table. Boston inventories dating before 1740 identify the "Front" chamber, "Hall" chamber, and "Best" chamber as locations for easy chairs. During the 1760s the Honorable Benjamin Pratt of neighboring Milton furnished his "middle" chamber with a green harateen chair. The red harateen easy chair purchased by Timothy Orne of Salem in 1763 complemented a full-dressed bed and six loose-seat mahogany side chairs in the same cloth. Silk damask was the textile chosen before 1773 by John Apthorp, Esq., for his easy chair and matching bed and window hangings. Several households were furnished with two easy chairs. During the 1770s Samuel Shoemaker of Philadelphia placed a green damask easy chair in the back bedchamber on the first floor and an easy chair with a "Blue Cover" upstairs. John Spooner of Boston furnished an upstairs bedroom with an easy chair and installed another one, described as an "Easy harreteen Chair Carved feet," on the first floor in the harateen-curtained back parlor with his "Desk & Book Case Carvd" and a round tea table. During the early 1790s, a yellow wool damask easy chair stood in the "Great Chamber" of John Hancock's Beacon Hill mansion.[3]

The easy chair has been described as a haven for the aged, sick, and infirm. John Singleton Copley and other artists often painted elderly patrons seated in easy or other upholstered chairs. But the possession of easy chairs by affluent younger individuals indicates that age was not a criterion for ownership. John Cadwalader of Philadelphia and merchant Samuel Moffatt of Portsmouth purchased easy chairs before they were thirty. Judge Jonathan Sayward of York, Maine, bought an easy chair from Samuel Grant of Boston when he was forty-five years old.[4]

Some easy chairs were fitted as commode, or necessary, chairs. The framework for the pans or pots remains in some chairs, and evidence of a pot frame exists in others that were converted long ago for modern use. In England a charge for framing a "Close stool" in an easy chair was itemized as late as 1802 in the *Bolton Supplement to the London Book of Cabinet Piece Prices*. Since practicality was an important consideration when close-stool fittings were present, chairs stuffed in canvas to receive fitted removable cases for washing were likely the norm. Although commode easy chairs were unsuitable for use in rooms other than the bedchamber, evidence suggests that easy chairs without fixtures were sometimes moved to other locations in the house on a temporary basis. In the Philadelphia home of William Cooper and at Stenton, the suburban Germantown residence of the Logan family, easy chairs were placed in the parlor, likely as temporary accommodation for an elderly or sickly family member. John Spooner's harateen easy chair, however, appears to have been more permanently placed in the back parlor of his Boston home since the cover matched the cloth of the window hangings. Evidence also confirms that some bedchambers were furnished with upholstered side chairs made en suite with easy chairs. One customer purchased a chaney-covered easy chair and a cabriole-leg "low" chair with a "cushion seat" from upholsterer Samuel Grant in January 1731/32. The existence in a private collection of an easy chair and a low, upholstered backstool with identical undercarriages further substantiates the practice.[5]

NGE

---

**Construction:** (Frame upholstered; a photograph without upholstery is unavailable.) The squared back stiles are slightly rounded on the outside rear corners. The rectangular seat frame, joined by mortise and tenon, is rounded at the front corners. The front legs are attached with large dovetails exposed on the front and top surfaces. The rear legs are canted on the forward surfaces; the upper legs and feet are chamfered on all corners. The front legs, which are carved in low relief at the knees, have small claw feet with three-knuckle toes; the knee brackets are attached with nails. The side stretchers are joined to the legs with vertical rectangular tenons (pinned). The medial stretcher is secured to the side stretcher blocks with horizontal tenons. The creased-tip rear stretcher is round tenoned into the rear legs.

**Condition:** The rear legs are cracked through at the stretcher joints and repaired. The left rear leg joint is misaligned; a piece is reattached at the lower inside rear corner. The side stretcher joints are repinned (or newly pinned) at the outside back. The inside forward toe of the right front foot is broken off at the bottom and the piece lost. The feet were once fitted with casters. The right front knee bracket is replaced. The medial stretcher collar adjacent to the right block is chipped.

**Dimensions:**

| | | |
|---|---|---|
| H. | 46½ in. | 118.1 cm |
| H. (seat frame) | 12⅞ in. | 32.7 cm |
| W. (wings) | 29 in. | 73.6 cm |
| W. (seat front) | 32¼ in. | 81.9 cm |
| W. (seat back) | 23⅝ in. | 60.0 cm |
| W. (arms) | 36¼ in. | 92.1 cm |
| W. (feet) | 32½ in. | 82.5 cm |
| D. (seat) | 23 in. | 58.4 cm |
| D. (feet) | 26 in. | 66.0 cm |

**Materials:** *Microanalysis:* Primary: mahogany. Secondary: soft maple group (seat frame). *Finish:* medium brown color in resin. *Upholstery:* modern floral-stamped medium blue wool.

**Publications:** Downs, *American Furniture*, fig. 82.

**Accession history:** Bequest of H. F. du Pont, 1969. 58.2429

1. For the Danielson chair, see *American Antiques from Israel Sack Collection*, 10 vols. (Washington, D.C.: Highland House, ca. 1969–), 4:888.

2. George Farquhar, *The Beaux Stratagem* (1706–7), act 4, scene 1, as quoted in *Oxford English Dictionary* (Oxford, Eng.: Clarendon Press, 1933), 3:22. Nancy Ann Goyne, "Furniture Craftsmen in Philadelphia, 1760–1780: Their Role in a Mercantile Society" (Master's thesis, University of Delaware, 1963), pp. 81, 83. On early use of chairs in bedchambers, see Penelope Eames, *Furniture in England, France, and the Netherlands from the Twelfth to the Fifteenth Century* (London: Furniture History Society, 1977), pp. 198–202; Macquoid and Edwards, *Dictionary*, 3:356; Thornton, *Seventeenth-Century Interior Decoration*, pp. 193, 195–96.

3. Patrick Gordon estate inventory, 1736, Register of Wills, Philadelphia; John Spooner estate inventory, 1771, Suffolk County Probate Court, Boston (microfilm, Downs collection). The Boston inventories are those of Capt. Edward Pell (1737), Capt. John Welland (1737), James Townsend (1738), and Capt. John Hill (1739), as quoted in Lyon, *Colonial Furniture*, pp. 167–68. Information on the Pratt household is in Jobe and Kaye, *New England Furniture*, no. 102. Hannah Cabot, bill to Timothy Orne, July 19, 1763, Timothy Orne Papers, Peabody Essex Museum, Salem, Mass. Apthorp auction, as quoted in Dow, *Arts and Crafts in New England*, p. 126. For John Hancock, see Brock Jobe, "The Boston Upholstery Trade, 1700–1775," in Cooke, *Upholstery*, pp. 68, 80. "Estate of Samuel Shoemaker," 1778, as transcribed in "Forfeited Estates," in *Pennsylvania Archives*, ed. Thomas Lynch Montgomery, 6th series (Harrisburg: Harrisburg Publishing Co., 1907), 12:724–25.

4. The elderly Mrs. Nicholas Salisbury of Worcester, Mass., was painted by Christian Gullager while seated in a damask-covered easy chair; see Bishop, *Centuries and Styles of the American Chair*, fig. 216; John Singleton Copley painted Mrs. John Powell of Boston in 1764 seated in her red easy chair; see Elisabeth Donaghy Garrett, *At Home: The American Family, 1750–1870* (New York: Harry N. Abrams, 1990), p. 125. Nicholas B. Wainwright, *Colonial Grandeur in Philadelphia: The House and Furniture of General John Cadwalader* (Philadelphia: Historical Society of Pennsylvania, 1964), p. 41. Samuel Moffatt estate inventory, 1768, New Hampshire Archives, Concord; Jane C. Giffen, "The Moffatt-Ladd House at Portsmouth, New Hampshire, Part 1," *Connoisseur* 175, no. 704 (October 1970): 113. For Sayward, see Jobe and Kaye, *New England Furniture*, no. 102.

5. Grant information as quoted in Forman, *American Seating Furniture*, p. 360. *Bolton Supplement*, as reproduced in Christopher Gilbert, *English Vernacular Furniture, 1750–1900* (New Haven: Yale University Press for the Paul Mellon Centre for Studies in British Art, 1991), p. 262. Hornor, *Blue Book*, p. 228. The matching easy chair and backstool are in Moses, *Master Craftsmen*, fig. 1.53.

## 85 ◆ Easy chair
Northeastern Massachusetts,
probably Boston
1760–90

Easy chair crest profiles of arched and
rounded-end form were augmented by a
serpentine design about 1760. All three
patterns appear to have been marketed
simultaneously until the postwar years. The
major London furniture designers of the
1760s—Chippendale, Manwaring, and Ince
and Mayhew—embraced the serpentine line.
When viewed head-on, the new peaked-
terminal crest has a horizontal orientation
that modifies the verticality of the chair in
keeping with the new low, broad emphasis
prominent in Chippendale-style seating,
although the dimensions remain the same.
The serpentine curve of this chair is flatter
than most examples, both at the center and
the peaks. Chairs of the new pattern were
introduced with pad-foot supports, quickly
updated with carved claws that were
occasionally accompanied by ornament at
the knees, "modernized" with straight,
molded, Marlborough "feet," and, finally,
reinterpreted with tapered, federal-style,
cylindrical and square legs.[1]

Most New England serpentine-top easy
chairs originated in Massachusetts. Almost all
the pad-foot examples have thin disks resting
on cushioned bases. The cushioned variant of
the pad support was introduced in the slim,
Queen Anne vase-back chair (see No. 7).
The most extensive use of the cushioned
foot appears to have been in a small group
of owl's-eye chairs similar to that illustrated
in No. 31 and in the easy chair group that
includes this example. Throughout production
of the cabriole-leg styles, the cusped knee
bracket was far more common for serpentine-
top easy chairs than the plain returns on this
chair. The columnar side stretchers, which are
standard, were combined most frequently with
conical-tipped medial and rear braces.

It can be argued that claw-foot chairs
represent a maturation of the serpentine-crest
style in easy chairs. Of equal merit is the
theory that claw feet were available almost
from the introduction of the new pattern,
and customer choice was dictated by
preference or pocketbook. Supporting the
second argument is evidence documenting
the longevity of the pad-foot style. A receipt
dated 1771 from Boston was found in the
original stuffing of an easy chair with
cushioned-pad feet owned by the Old Gaol
Museum in York, Maine. A 1770 bill itemizes
two dining tables with similar feet made by
George Bright, a Boston cabinetmaker, for
Jonathan Bowman, a Bostonian who moved
to Pownalborough, Maine. Carved work on
the knees added a further premium to the cost
of the chair in either leg style. A pad-foot
example is embellished with carved shells;
handsome acanthus leaves complement

well-carved claw feet in two other chairs.
Plain knees were most common, however.[2]

The prevailing one-piece construction of
the rear supports and stiles in New England
cabriole-leg easy chairs necessitated the
substitution of a less expensive wood in
place of the walnut or mahogany generally
used in the front legs and stretchers. Maple
was the principal choice for these uprights
and for selected parts of the interior frame,
as seen in this example, but white pine,
birch, ash, beech, chestnut, cherry, and oak
were also used in New England easy chair
frames. Where exposed, the wood was stained
or colored and varnished to match the show
wood at the front.

This serpentine-top easy chair, along with
No. 86, has a square-front seat frame with
standard mortise-and-tenon joinery at the
front leg extensions. The chairs are part of a
group of eleven or more in the serpentine-crest

sample fitted with claw front feet; all but one has a square frame. Among the fourteen pad-foot examples (thirteen with cushioned pads, one standard), the round-front seat is more common by about two to one. The seat frame construction, when known, is mortise and tenon with dovetailed front leg connections.[3]

Leather covers, such as those used on this chair, appear to have been uncommon in American easy chair construction during the eighteenth century, judging by the absence of references in contemporary documents. Nor, as a rule, were the upholstered frames embellished with brass nails; woven tapes and binding were the usual treatment. The seat deck has been raised higher than normal to compensate for the absence of a loose cushion.

NGE

---

**Construction:** (Frame upholstered; a photograph without upholstery is unavailable.) The serpentine-arched crest is rounded or chamfered on the upper forward edge. The rear stiles are squared. The arm cones are extended to the bottoms of the seat rails. The rectangular seat frame is joined by mortise and tenon. The rear legs, which are canted on the forward surfaces below the seat rails, are chamfered at the upper front corners only. The feet flare backward and are chamfered at the outside forward corner. The front feet have three-knuckle claws;

the knee brackets are glued in place. The side stretchers are joined to the legs with vertical rectangular tenons (pinned at rear). The long, creased-tip medial and rear stretchers are round tenoned into the adjacent members.

**Condition:** The side rear stretcher joints are repinned. Minor cracks and nicks occur on the rear stretcher. The seat deck has been raised to compensate for the missing cushion. The chair frame is upholstered in modern leather.

**Dimensions:**

| | | |
|---|---|---|
| H. | 48 1/4 in. | 122.5 cm |
| H. (seat frame) | 13 3/8 in. | 34.0 cm |
| W. (wings) | 27 7/8 in. | 70.8 cm |
| W. (seat front) | 30 3/4 in. | 78.1 cm |
| W. (seat back) | 24 1/2 in. | 62.2 cm |
| W. (arms) | 33 1/8 in. | 84.1 cm |
| W. (feet) | 33 1/2 in. | 85.1 cm |
| D. (seat) | 22 7/8 in. | 58.1 cm |
| D. (feet) | 25 7/8 in. | 65.7 cm |

**Materials:** *Macroidentification:* Primary: mahogany. *Microanalysis:* Secondary: soft maple group (seat frame, rear leg). *Finish:* medium dark reddish brown color in resin.

**Accession history:** Gift of H. F. du Pont, 1965. 59.2834

---

1. Thomas Chippendale, *The Gentleman and Cabinet-Maker's Director* (3d ed., London: By the author, 1762); Robert Manwaring, *The Cabinet and Chair-Maker's Real Friend and Companion* (London: Henry Webley, 1765); Robert Manwaring and others, *The Chair-Maker's Guide* (London: Robert Sayer, 1766); William Ince and John Mayhew, *The Universal System of Houshold Furniture* (1762; reprint, Chicago: Quadrangle Books, 1960).

2. For the Old Gaol Museum chair and 1 of the Bright dining tables, see Jobe and Kaye, *New England Furniture*, nos. 15, 63, 104. The shell-carved chair is in John S. Walton advertisement, *Antiques* 71, no. 4 (April 1957): 292; the leaf-carved examples are in Heckscher, *American Furniture*, cat. no. 74; Israel Sack advertisement, *Antiques* 115, no. 3 (March 1979): inside front cover.

3. The serpentine-top easy chair group includes 2 at Winterthur and the carved examples cited in note 2. For the rest, see Greenlaw, *New England Furniture*, no. 67; *American Antiques from Israel Sack Collection*, 10 vols. (Washington, D.C.: Highland House, ca. 1969–), 3:751, 7:1998, 9:2479; Parke-Bernet Galleries, "The Notable American Collection of Mr. and Mrs. Norvin H. Green" (November 29–December 1, 1950), lot 503; R. W. Oliver advertisement, *Antiques and the Arts Weekly*, January 4, 1991, p. 168; Warren, *Bayou Bend*, nos. 90, 91; Fales, *Furniture of Historic Deerfield*, fig. 68; Jobe and Kaye, *New England Furniture*, no. 104; Kane, *Three Hundred Years*, no. 213; no. 66.1769; DAPC, Visual Resources Collection, Winterthur Library; C. W. Lyon advertisement, *Antiques* 60, no. 4 (October 1951): 225; H. and R. Sandor advertisement, *Antiques* 88, no. 3 (September 1965): 263; Heckscher, *American Furniture*, cat. no. 73; Bishop, *Centuries and Styles of the American Chair*, fig. 219; Morse, *Furniture of the Olden Time*, p. 185; Albert Sack, *Fine Points of Furniture: Early American* (New York: Crown Publishers, 1961), p. 66; Northeast Auctions, "The Collection of John Howland Ricketson III" (May 29, 1993), lot 84; Bernard and S. Dean Levy advertisement, *Antiques* 145, no. 3 (March 1994): 321.

## 86 ◆ Easy chair
### Northeastern Massachusetts, probably Boston or Salem
### 1760–90

The distinctive character of the peaked crest ends in this serpentine-top chair is repeated in the stylish flaring tips of the medial and rear stretchers that brace the lower frame. Similar stretchers appear in an easy chair at Colonial Williamsburg, which is also comparable in other features: front leg profiles and brackets, rear leg chamfers, upper back curves, and long tapering arm cones. The Williamsburg chair has cushioned pad feet in place of claws, a reminder that both leg options were available to consumers during the years the design was marketed; clearly, the same shops made both chairs.[1]

When received as a gift in 1970, this chair retained most of the original stuffing on the upper frame, including the webbing, sackcloth,

wing edge rolls, curled horsehair stuffing, and undercover (figs. 1, 2). The upholstery was subsequently stripped from the frame and replaced with new materials, although the undercover and horsehair of the wing interiors were retained for study purposes (fig. 3). The large "✳J✳" stenciled in dark brown (originally black) ink on the lower reverse surface of the right wing panel probably represents a shipper's identification that appeared originally on the outside of the linen bundle or on the wrapper from another commodity. The curled, springy stuffing consists of three colors of hair intermingled— blond, black, and medium brown. The edge rolls, visible in figure 2, were stuffed with grass. Edge rolls that once lined the front and side seat rail returns were stabilized at the upper forward corners of the frame by the low peaked projections at the leg posts; the projections form a shallow trough on the back face.

Name associations add another measure of interest to this chair, which according to tradition was owned in the Fiske family of Sturbridge, Massachusetts. Early census records confirm the presence of Fiske family members in that central Massachusetts community, although more detailed insights are unavailable. The chair is also branded inside the front seat rail with the name J:POPE in serif letters (fig. 4). Several lines of investigation are opened by the brand, although all remain speculative.

Joseph Pope (ca. 1750–1826) of Boston was a well-known instrument maker. Between 1776 and 1787 he built a spectacular twelve-sided orrery, which measures more than 6½ feet in diameter and is supported on a hexagonal mahogany stand with fluted Marlborough legs. An artisan capable of producing a complicated brass instrument such as this was sufficiently skilled to fabricate a simple branding iron for personal use.[2]

Essex County, Massachusetts, records identify a Folger Pope as an upholsterer. Between 1783 and 1790 he completed work for Elias Hasket Derby and the Sanderson brothers of Salem. Pope also made an easy chair for Capt. William Bartlett of neighboring Beverly. The 1790 Massachusetts census lists a Folger Pope as well as a John and a Joshua Pope in Salem, and all three were still there in 1800. Perhaps one of the latter two men also pursued the upholstery or woodworking trades in Salem and used the J:POPE iron to identify his work.[3]

NGE

Inscriptions or marks: *Branded inside rear seat rail:* "J:POPE" *in serif letters. Stenciled on reverse of inside right wing undercover:* "✳J✳".

Construction: The serpentine-arch crest is rounded or chamfered on the upper forward edge. The squared rear stiles are continuous with the rear legs. The frame is joined with mortise and tenon at: the crest and rear stiles; the stay rail and rear stiles; the wing stiles, top and bottom; the arm stiles and seat

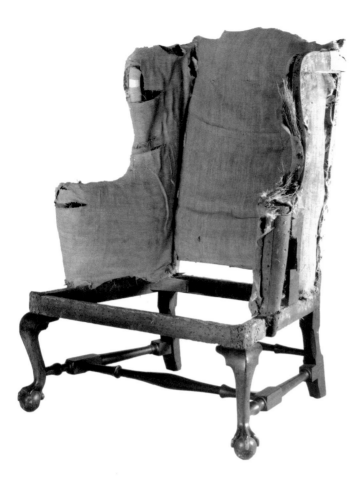

**Fig. 1.** Frame with stuffing materials.

**Fig. 2.** Detail, inside right-wing stuffing on frame.

rails; and the corners of the seat frame. The wing rails are rabbeted or dovetailed to the rear stiles and secured with nails. The outer halves of the conical arm supports are probably nailed to the inner halves and the side seat rails. The front corners of the seat frame are formed by extensions of the cabriole legs; the outside upper tips are raised in triangular peaks to stabilize the edge rolls. The rear legs, which are canted on the forward surfaces, are chamfered on all corners between the seat rails and stretchers and on the front corners of the feet below the side stretchers. The side stretchers are joined to the legs with vertical rectangular tenons (pinned, at back); the medial and rear stretchers are round tenoned into the adjacent members.

**Condition:** The lower 5/16" of each front foot has been restored, including the toenails. The knee brackets have been reattached. Corner blocks have been added to the interior seat frame and the upper corners of the back panel. The arms have been repaired, using a metal bracket and glueblock. The right seat rail is splintered along the bottom surface. A short crack occurs on the inside face of the right stretcher tip, and a piece has split off the lower inside edge of the left forward stretcher block. The original stuffing and undercovers have been replaced with modern materials.

**Dimensions:**

| | | |
|---|---|---|
| H. | 45 5/8 in. | 115.9 cm |
| H. (seat) | 13 1/8 in. | 33.3 cm |
| W. (wings) | 28 in. | 71.7 cm |
| W. (seat front) | 31 3/4 in. | 80.6 cm |
| W. (seat back) | 24 in. | 60.9 cm |
| W. (arms) | 35 in. | 88.9 cm |
| W. (feet) | 33 1/8 in. | 84.1 cm |
| D. (seat) | 22 5/8 in. | 57.4 cm |
| D. (feet) | 25 3/4 in. | 65.4 cm |

**Materials:** *Microanalysis:* Primary: mahogany (front legs, stretchers). Secondary: soft maple group (crest rail, wing stiles, seat rails). *Finish:* medium dark brown color with reddish to yellowish cast in resin. *Upholstery:* modern, floral-stamped medium blue wool.

**Publications:** Jobe and Kaye, *New England Furniture,* p. 98, no. III-33; Morrison H. Heckscher, "Eighteenth-Century American Upholstery Techniques: Easy Chairs, Sofas, and Settees," in Cooke, *Upholstery,* pp. 97–99, figs. 83–86.

**Accession history:** Gift of Mrs. Walter Salzenberg, 1970.
70.71

---

1. For the Williamsburg chair, see Greenlaw, *New England Furniture,* no. 67.

2. Museum of Fine Arts, Boston, *Paul Revere's Boston, 1735–1818* (Boston: By the museum, 1975), p. 73; Walter Muir Whitehill, Brock Jobe, and Jonathan Fairbanks, "Foreword," in *Boston Furniture,* pp. viii, x.

3. Folger Pope, bill to Elias Hasket Derby, March 11, 1790, Derby Family Papers, vol. 2, Peabody Essex Museum, Salem, Mass. Folger Pope, bill to Jacob Sanderson, September 1785, Papers of Elijah Sanderson, Peabody Essex Museum, Salem, Mass. Folger Pope, bill to Capt. William Bartlett, December 23, 1783, Papers of William Bartlett, Beverly Historical Society, Beverly, Mass. A fall-leaf dining table said to be similarly branded with large claw feet with prominently knuckled talons relate to those of No. 85; see Valdemar F. Jacobsen advertisement, *Antiques* 143, no. 3 (March 1993): 376.

**Fig. 3.** Detail, inside right-wing undercover and horsehair filling.

**Fig. 4.** Detail, brand on inside face of front seat rail.

## 87 ◆ Easy chair
### Rhode Island, probably Newport
### 1780–1800

When George Hepplewhite illustrated an "Easy Chair" of this general type in the first edition of *The Cabinet-Maker and Upholsterer's Guide* (1788), he further described it as a "Saddle Cheek Chair" (fig. 1). The reference is to the serpentine-contoured "wings" that give the chair a distinctive character. The plates in Hepplewhite's volume are dated 1787, the year the illustrations were engraved, although most patterns had probably been popular in Britain for a number of years. For instance, the saddle-cheek chair design is associated with the Chippendale style, although here the upholstery is leaner and trimmer than the stuffing in earlier chairs.[1]

Construction of the saddle-cheek chair varies from that of the easy chairs previously described (fig. 2). The flaring upper corners and broad cheeks of the stiles require thinner units than those used in earlier frames, which are frequently constructed so that the posts and rear legs are one continuous piece of wood. To achieve the stoutness necessary for the legs and yet accommodate the new back design, chairmakers used two-piece construction and spliced the units together above seat level. Screws or nails secure the joints in the Philadelphia manner. In this example the joints are further strengthened by beveling the lower stile tips and notching them into the seat rails. The ogee curves of the wings, which complement the cheeks of the back stiles, are sawed to the proper shape from short pieces of wood and are tenoned into the arms; the earlier construction technique extended the wing stiles to the seat rails. The horizontal arms rather than the vertical wing stiles are the major structural units of the side panels. The forward arm supports were framed in one of two ways. In the first method, small triangular panels of wood are added to the forward face of the

arm supports, the front edges abutting the front leg extensions, as seen in this chair. The hollow curve extending from the arms to the front legs provides a graceful transition between the two support levels. This type of framing accommodates a square cushion that fits entirely within the side panels. In the second method, single vertical sticks of wood or narrow planks positioned at or near the arm tips are terminated abruptly several inches behind the front seat rail. T-shape cushions are required with this type of framing. As illustrated by Hepplewhite, cushions could be omitted. The introduction to *The Cabinet-Maker and Upholsterer's Guide* suggests that saddle-cheek chairs should "be covered with leather, [or] horse-hair; or have a linen case to fit over the canvas stuffing." The choice of leather and horsehair covers reflects the new simplicity and practicality of furniture fashions. Both materials require brass nailing to hold the covers in place.[2]

In 1792 a group of Hartford, Connecticut, cabinetmakers formed a society for the purpose of regulating the prices of cabinetwork. The table they published contains the entry: "For an Easy Chair, with plain or fluted legs, stuffed," demonstrating the currency of chairs in the general style illustrated. An extra charge for claw feet indicates that the older form of support was also available. Several New England saddle-cheek easy chairs with carved feet and plain or carved knees are known; the cushions are T-shape. The group of saddle-cheek chairs supported on Marlborough legs is sizable. A few chairs have plain rectangular legs, including one with a history in the Whiton family of Hingham, Massachusetts. Some supports are fluted, but most are molded. The group is divided between seats for square and T-shape cushions. Saddle-cheek chairs of later design produced at the end of the eighteenth century and during the early nineteenth century often have tapered legs

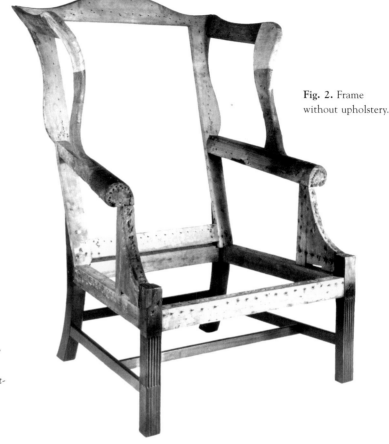

Fig. 1. Saddle-cheek easy chair. From [George] Hepplewhite, *The Cabinet-Maker and Upholsterer's Guide* (2d ed., London: I. and J. Taylor, 1789), pl. 15 left.

Fig. 2. Frame without upholstery.

Fig. 3. Detail, right front leg stop fluting.

of squared or cylindrical form. Some supports are plain, but many are patterned with turned rings, flutes, molding, or, occasionally, carving.[3]

Chances are slim that saddle-cheek easy chairs were made in America before the revolutionary war, given the substantial attention focused on this form in England during the late 1780s. The straight Marlborough leg remained popular in English easy chair design, as demonstrated in a drawing made by the Gillow firm of Lancashire dated in 1788. Marlborough supports used in American saddle-cheek chairs are usually molded; plain surfaces and stop fluting are rare (fig. 3). In fact, only one other saddle-cheek stop-fluted example has been located, although several fluted chairs are known with plain wings. The principal exponents of stop-fluted decoration resided in Newport, Rhode Island (see Nos. 124, 138), and there is every reason to believe that this chair came from that area. The quality and execution of the fluting relates closely to that on tables, upholstered seating, a bedstead, and a kneehole chest (bureau table) ascribed to that area; the work is virtually identical to the fluting in No. 47. A straight-leg roundabout chair with cross stretchers and interlaced-strap

splats in the Redwood Library, Newport, has similar stop-fluted embellishment.[4]

*NGE*

**Construction:** (Frame upholstered; some commentary based on a photograph of the bare frame.) The serpentine crest is supported on rectangular tenons at the tops of the rear stiles. The wing rails appear to be rabbeted to the outside faces of the rear stiles and are probably secured with nails. The forward ends of the wing rails are tenoned into the wing stiles, which in turn are tenoned into the arms. The joinery of the arm assembly is uncertain, but the arms, which are squared at the back, are either tenoned or nailed to the rear stiles. The forward ends rest on top of the front stiles, possibly secured with a tenon. The bases of the same supports are tenoned into the side seat rails. The triangular forward pieces, which are attached to the faces of the arm stiles with glue or nails, are probably glued at the front to the side rails and leg extensions. The rear stiles and feet are spliced together just above rail level, the joint secured by screws. The bottom tips of the stiles are also notched into the tops of the side rails. The seat rails and legs are joined with mortise and tenon. The rear legs are canted on the forward surfaces; the inside front corners are broadly chamfered, top to bottom. The rear surfaces flare backward, forming arcs. The front legs, which extend above the rails, are square in section with a wide chamfer on the inside rear corners, top to bottom. The outside surfaces are patterned with stop fluting. The narrow rectangular outside stretchers are tenoned into the adjacent members; the medial stretcher is dovetailed into the side stretchers from the bottom.

**Condition:** The exposed surfaces are marked by minor nicks and scratches.

**Dimensions:**

| | | |
|---|---|---|
| H. | 48 in. | 121.9 cm |
| H. (seat frame) | 14 in. | 35.6 cm |
| W. (wings) | 33 5/8 in. | 85.4 cm |
| W. (seat front) | 29 1/2 in. | 74.9 cm |
| W. (seat back) | 23 7/8 in. | 60.6 cm |
| W. (arms) | 33 1/2 in. | 85.1 cm |
| W. (feet) | 29 1/2 in. | 74.9 cm |
| D. (seat) | 24 1/4 in. | 61.6 cm |
| D. (feet) | 27 1/2 in. | 69.8 cm |

**Materials:** *Macroidentification:* Primary: mahogany (front and rear legs). *Microanalysis:* Secondary: birch (seat frame). *Finish:* medium to medium dark reddish brown color in resin; refinished. *Upholstery:* green, yellow, and pink striped silk bourette; Europe, 1800–1840.

**Provenance:** Ex coll.: Guy W. Walker, Jr., Beverly Farms, Mass.

**Accession history:** Purchased by H. F. du Pont from Guy W. Walker, Jr., Beverly Farms, Mass., 1958. Gift of H. F. du Pont, 1959.
58.135.8

---

1. [George] Hepplewhite, *The Cabinet-Maker and Upholsterer's Guide* (London: I. and J. Taylor, 1788), pl. 15 left. For British examples, see Kirk, *American Furniture*, figs. 1161, 1163.

2. Hepplewhite, *Cabinet-Maker and Upholsterer's Guide,* pl. 15 left. For a chair framed for a T-shape cushion, see *American Antiques from Israel Sack Collection*, 10 vols. (Washington, D.C.: Highland House, ca. 1969–), 2:381.

3. The Hartford price list is reproduced in Lyon, *Colonial Furniture*, pp. 267–70. The claw-foot chairs are in Bernard and S. Dean Levy, Inc., *Catalogue V* (New York: By the company, 1986), p. 51; David Stockwell advertisement, *Antiques* 141, no. 4 (April 1992): 529; Charles Woolsey Lyon advertisement, *Antiques* 95, no. 4 (April 1969): 459. For the Whiton chair, see Rodriguez Roque, *American Furniture*, no. 97; for molded-leg easy chairs, see *American Antiques from Sack Collection*, 4:1108, 5:1354.

4. For the Gillow drawing, see Kirk, *American Furniture*, fig. 1162. For the second stop-fluted easy chair, see *American Antiques from Sack Collection*, 4:976. For other Newport stop-fluted furniture, see Moses, *Master Craftsmen*, pp. 13, 51–54, 78–80, 106, 126–27, 157–58, 265, 291–92. For the Redwood Library chair, see Lorraine Dexter and Alan Pryce-Jones, eds., *Redwood Papers: A Bicentennial Collection* (Newport, R.I.: Redwood Library and Athenaeum, 1976), p. 86.

## 88 ◆ Easy chair
Coastal New Hampshire; or Essex County or Suffolk County, Massachusetts
1770–90

This easy chair is something of an enigma. Peripheral documentation and circumstantial evidence strongly suggest that the chair originated in northeastern New England, yet many design and construction features appear to be unique to this example or to the small group of easy chairs it represents. The chairs are outside the pattern ranges currently associated with seating furniture produced in southern New Hampshire and northeastern Massachusetts. The principal distinguishing characteristic of the group is the rear-leg profile: a squared cabriole with a hooflike terminal.

Six easy chairs constitute this unusual body of furniture. This example is the only one with cabriole front legs; the rest have plain, straight feet of Marlborough form with beads at the outside forward corners. A definite chronology of design is apparent within the group. This chair is earliest in date and is distinguished by curved front legs, vertical arm rolls, and straight-sided wings. A straight-leg chair with similar arms and wings is next in the design sequence. The remaining four chairs are constructed with Marlborough front legs, horizontal arm rolls, and saddle cheeks—the general form approximating that of No. 87.[1]

Three other features of the support structure of this chair are as unusual as the squared and curved rear legs: the pattern and character of the carved work of the front knees (fig. 1), the two-part knee brackets, and the profiles of the stretcher turnings. The front knee carving is confined to the leg proper without extending onto the brackets,

**Fig. 2.** Frame without upholstery.

**Fig. 1.** Detail, left front leg.

a detail that deviates from the norm (see No. 54). The decoration is also completely symmetrical and precisely defined in ridges, which are almost as regular as the raised wales in a corded textile. Surrounding the carving is a broad accent band of punchwork reminiscent of Boston ornament in placement (see No. 56, fig. 2) but more uniform and rigid in execution. The two-part knee brackets consist of flat ogee-end back pieces attached to the seat rails and backs of the leg blocks and plain, cheeked-and-rounded front blocks glued to the faces of the back units. The cusped tips of the front blocks extend below the back pieces. The delicate, plain, cylinder stretchers are unusual. The starkness of the pattern is relieved only by a centered swell flanked by fillets in the medial and rear braces and small blocks in the side stretchers. None of these three features has a known counterpart in other furniture. By contrast, the rectangular-braced chairs with Marlborough legs that constitute the rest of the group are relatively straightforward in design.

Other peculiarities of construction exist in this small group of easy chairs, especially in the earliest examples. The seat frame of this chair is oak, an uncommon material in American formal seating furniture but one encountered frequently in British work (fig. 2). The open corner braces notched into the interior faces of the seat rails are also more indicative of British than American construction. Broad panels, such as those forming the wing stiles, are seldom encountered in easy chair frames; even wider boards appear in the straight wings of the second chair in this group. That frame also includes a broad vertical board centered in the chair back. The remaining frames are fairly standard, except for unusually large corner braces inside the seat rails that form solid or open triangles with straight or curved diagonal edges.

Perhaps the most critical piece of construction evidence illuminating the background of this seating group is the design of the cones that form the vertical arm rolls of the two earliest chairs (see fig. 2). They vary from standard design in two significant ways: the rolls are slim cylinders rather than broad cones, and the cylinder tops are inset rather than flush with the edges of the circular arm pads. If these features occur in other American work, they are exceedingly rare; rolls of this type appear to be reasonably common in British chairmaking, however.

To hypothesize that this group of chairs was made by an immigrant British craftsman is probably close to the mark. The fact that the two vertical-arm chairs have several aberrant constructional characteristics while the later horizontal-arm chairs retain only the unusual corner braces of the earlier examples (aside from the "signature" legs), reaffirms this speculation. The acculturation process left tangible signs in the work of this artisan.[2]

The rear leg pattern of these easy chairs appears to have direct roots in English design. In the English furniture market of the 1710s and 1720s, fashionable side chairs and armchairs supported on cabriole legs of early design, some angular, often had rounded or squared tassel-like hoof feet. The style had died out in London by the early 1730s, although examples, some upholstered on both the backs and seats, remained in country estates and other residences. An American manifestation of this support pattern is the squared cabriole leg terminated by a Spanish, or tassel, foot (see No. 1). An immigrant craftsman from a provincial British center who was familiar with seating supports of this type likely adapted the curved line for use at the back of an easy chair, although by the time he introduced the pattern, the profile was considerably out of date. Nevertheless, the novelty of the design apparently obscured this fact from his customers, since he continued to use the pattern. The arrival in Portsmouth, New Hampshire, of the London upholsterer Henry Golden in 1763 and English cabinetmaker Robert Harrold in 1765 and the appearance of new designs for tables and chairs in the local market about that time may signal the arrival of still other British craftsmen. If documentation were available, similar patterns of immigration would likely emerge for other northeastern communities.[3]

Tangible links between the hoof-foot chairs and northeastern New England are varied. The background history of this chair is unknown. The easy chair with vertical arms and straight front legs was found in Warner, New Hampshire. One of the horizontal-arm chairs is signed "R. Hart" in chalk on the crest back—a name that is also branded on several postrevolutionary-style tables and that has been identified as that of Richard Hart, a Portsmouth merchant. A similar chair sold from the Philip Flayderman collection in 1930 is branded "J. FRANCIS," but the name has not been identified. Members of the Francis family were scattered over a broad territory in America, extending from the South to northeastern Massachusetts. A Joseph Francis is listed as a chairmaker in the 1789 Boston city directory. The 1790 census lists the Boston craftsman and a second Joseph Francis of Newburyport. It may be more than coincidental that a federal-style card table of a shape described as square with an elliptic front and serpentine ends is branded "J. FRANCIS" under the top. The shape of the table is identical to one labeled by Joseph Short, a Newburyport cabinetmaker; the decorative inlay is also related. Alternately, Col. John Francis (d. 1822) of Beverly, who served in the Revolution and later became a town selectman, may have been the owner of the brand.[4]

*NGE*

---

**Construction:** (Frame upholstered; some commentary based on a photograph of the bare frame). The serpentine crest is squared at the upper edges. The upper frame is joined with mortise and tenon at: the crest and rear stiles; the stay rail and rear stiles; the wing rails and rear stiles; and the wing stiles and wing rails. Many joints are secured

from the outside surfaces by single pins. The bottoms of the unusually wide wing stiles are tenoned into the side seat rails and pinned twice from the inside rail. The arms are attached to the wing stiles with inside rabbets fastened with single pins. The forward ends are supported on the tops of the rounded front posts, which they overhang, and are secured with large centered rosehead nails. The rear stiles and feet are spliced together just above rail level. The seat rails and front leg extensions are joined with mortise and tenon (pinned). In profile, the unusual rear legs are shaped to squared cabrioles with hoof feet slightly rounded at the back. The frame is strengthened by four open corner braces notched into the upper inside faces of the rails. The front legs, which are creased at the knees, are carved with stylized "corded" leafage outlined by double- and triple-stippled borders forming bands. The three forward toes are carved with knobby double joints and short nails; the plain back toes are angular. The balls are apple shape. The uncommon knee brackets are constructed in two parts. Flat-faced pieces of wood are butted against the bottom edges of the rails and tenoned into the inside faces of the knees; the exposed ends are ogee curved. To the faces of the brackets are glued rounded ornamental front pieces, the lower tips extending in points below the bases of the flat brackets. The side and rear stretchers are round tenoned into the adjacent members; the cylinder ends are slightly swelled. The medial stretcher is joined by mortise and tenon to the side stretcher blocks. The centers of the medial and rear stretchers are double scored and turned with filletlike rings. The rear stretcher is tenoned below the side stretchers.

**Condition:** Three of the four ornamental knee brackets have tooled surfaces; the left front bracket is smooth. Whether three brackets are original and one replaced, or vice versa, is unclear. The ball feet are slightly worn around the bottom edges. A chunk of wood is missing from the forward face of the left rear leg; the bottom edges of both rear feet are defaced. All legs have large caster holes in the bottom. The right end of the medial stretcher is poorly fitted to the side block.

**Dimensions:**

| | | |
|---|---|---|
| H. | 48³/₄ in. | 123.8 cm |
| H. (seat frame) | 12⁷/₈ in. | 32.7 cm |
| W. (wings) | 28³/₄ in. | 73.0 cm |
| W. (seat front) | 30³/₄ in. | 78.1 cm |
| W. (seat back) | 25³/₈ in. | 64.5 cm |
| W. (arms) | 36³/₄ in. | 93.3 cm |
| W. (feet) | 32³/₄ in. | 83.2 cm |
| D. (seat) | 24¹/₂ in. | 62.2 cm |
| D. (feet) | 28 in. | 71.1 cm |

**Materials:** *Microanalysis:* Primary: mahogany. Secondary: soft maple group (wing rail, arm rail); yellow pine group (wing stile); oak (seat rails, by macroidentification). *Finish:* medium reddish brown to medium dark brown (rear stretcher) color in resin. *Upholstery:* gold silk damask; Europe, 1725–50.

**Accession history:** Purchased by H. F. du Pont from Teina Baumstone, New York, 1955. Gift of H. F. du Pont, 1958.
55.20

---

1. Of the 5 straight-leg chairs, 1 is in a private collection and the others are illustrated as follows: *American Antiques from Israel Sack Collection*, 10 vols. (Washington, D.C.: Highland House, ca. 1969–), 3:749; "Interesting American Furniture from a Recent Sale," *The Antiquarian* 14, no. 5 (May 1930): 56; photographic files, Bernard and S. Dean Levy, Inc., New York; Northeast Auctions, "New Hampshire Memorial Day Weekend Auction" (May 29–30, 1993), lot 478. Another horizontal-arm easy chair that may relate to this group has square, tapered front legs, sweep arm returns at the front, and board-constructed back and wings; the signature back legs are lacking, however. See Fred and Jo Ann Cadarette advertisement, *Maine Antique Digest*, December 1990.

2. For British examples, see John Bivins, "A Catalogue of Northern Furniture with Southern Provenances," *Journal of Early Southern Decorative Arts* 15, no. 2 (November 1989): 46; Kirk, *American Furniture*, fig. 1157.

3. For English prototypes of the squared-hoof foot, see Macquoid and Edwards, *Dictionary*, 1: figs. 91, 98, 105, 106, 109, 114, 115, 130; Victoria and Albert Museum, *English Chairs* (2d ed., London: Her Majesty's Stationery Office, 1965), figs. 44, 46. Squared cabriole legs terminated by Spanish feet also appear on American easy chairs before 1740; see Forman, *American Seating Furniture*, pp. 18, 31, 33. On Henry Golden, Robert Harrold, and the appearance of new designs in Portsmouth, see Jobe and Kaye, *New England Furniture*, pp. 18, 31, 33; Myrna Kaye and Brock Jobe, "Robert Harrold: Portsmouth Cabinetmaker," *Antiques* 143, no. 5 (May 1993): 776–83.

4. For the Hart chair, see *American Antiques from Sack Collection*, 3:749; on Hart see Jobe and Kaye, *New England Furniture*, pp. 33, 405; Myrna Kaye, *Fake, Fraud, or Genuine?: Identifying Authentic American Antique Furniture* (Boston: Little, Brown, 1987), pp. 30–32; Myrna Kaye, "Marked Portsmouth Furniture," *Antiques* 113, no. 5 (May 1978): 1099–1100. For the Francis chair, see "Interesting American Furniture," p. 56. A photograph of the Francis card table is in the correspondence files of the American Decorative Arts Department, MFA, Boston. For the Short card table, see Benjamin A. Hewitt, Patricia E. Kane, and Gerald W. R. Ward, *The Work of Many Hands: Card Tables in Federal America, 1790–1820* (New Haven: Yale University Art Gallery, 1982), cat. 9. On John Francis, see Robert W. Lovett, "A Parish Weathers War and Dissension: The Precinct of Salem and Beverly, 1753–1813," *Essex Institute Historical Collections* 99, no. 2 (April 1963): 109.

**Fig. 1.** Robert Sayer and James Bennett, *The Toilet*, London, 1780. Mezzotint on laid paper hand-painted in opaque watercolors; H. 13 15/16 in. (35.4 cm), W. 9 13/16 in. (24.9 cm) to platemarks. (Winterthur 55.14.2)

## 89 ◆ Back stool

Boston, Massachusetts
1740–70

Catering to a desire for comfort, European craftsmen developed a range of upholstered seating furniture. One was the side chair with "stuft back and seat"—a design identified as a back stool. Chairs of this description "covered withe greene Velvett" stood in the great gallery of Leicester House, London, as early as 1588. For most of the following century, styles were short in height and open at the lower back between the posts (the Cromwellian and farthingale chairs of popular modern terminology). Backs were extended during the late seventeenth century, and by the turn of the eighteenth century, the area between the stay rail and the seat was often enclosed. The shape of the back and the exposed parts of the wooden undercarriage were subject to the vagaries of fashion as the eighteenth century

progressed. In England the cabriole leg was probably introduced to the tall, narrow, stuffed-back side chair during the 1710s, when block-and-turned, William and Mary–style back stools were occasionally produced in Boston. The cabriole leg was probably not used on the American back stool until the 1730s. The first curved supports were squared like those in No. 5. Boston chairmakers soon introduced the round cabriole leg (see No. 6). While not uncommon in households of the affluent in England and on the Continent, upholstered back stools are seldom listed in American inventories and then only in the households of prosperous individuals living in or near urban centers.[1]

In the English home, back stools were used in sets in a variety of rooms, from bedchambers to halls or reception rooms. In plate 2 from the series *Marriage à la Mode* (1743), William Hogarth, the prominent chronicler of eighteenth-century English taste

and manners, depicts the count and countess seated on back stools drawn up to a pedestal table in front of a fireplace. A set of back stools lines the wall of the adjacent reception room. The chair seats, like the seat illustrated, are loosely fitted in the frame to lift out rather than being upholstered over the rails. A pen-and-ink and watercolor drawing of about 1725 depicts a Dutch family at the Passover meal seated on back stools around a large circular dining table. In recent decades several authors have suggested that back stools were used primarily by women, citing visual representations of the form drawn up to a dressing table (fig. 1), but the inclusion of back stools in Hogarth's *Midnight Modern Conversation* (1733), depicting one of London's drinking clubs, confirms that the form was commonly used by both men and women (fig. 2).[2]

A 1746 Boston auction that included "Eight Walnut Tree Chairs, stuft Back and

**Fig. 2.** From William Hogarth, *A Midnight Modern Conversation*, London, 1733. Line etching on laid paper; H. 12⁷/₈ in. (32.7 cm), W. 17¹⁵/₁₆ in. (45.6 cm). (Winterthur 75.219)

**Dimensions:**

| | | |
|---|---|---|
| H. | 35⁵/₈ in. | 90.5 cm |
| H. (seat) | 13³/₄ in. | 34.9 cm |
| W. (crest) | 14¹/₄ in. | 36.2 cm |
| W. (seat front) | 20¹/₈ in. | 51.1 cm |
| W. (seat back) | 14¹/₄ in. | 36.2 cm |
| W. (feet) | 21 in. | 53.3 cm |
| D. (seat) | 17 in. | 43.2 cm |
| D. (feet) | 19⁷/₈ in. | 50.5 cm |

**Materials:** *Microanalysis:* Primary: American black walnut. Secondary: soft maple group (rear legs). *Finish:* medium orange-brown color in resin. *Upholstery:* light yellow, floral-medallion silk brocatelle; Europe, probably Italy, 1700–1740.

**Publications:** Downs, *American Furniture*, fig. 98.

**Provenance:** By tradition the chair was handed down in the family of President Franklin Pierce, although this history cannot be substantiated.

**Accession history:** Purchased by H. F. du Pont from Mrs. Frances M. Nichols, Glebe House, Inc., Marblehead, Mass., 1934. Bequest of H. F. du Pont, 1969.
58.2598

Seats cover'd with [crimson] Damask" en suite with bed hangings, window curtains, and an easy chair indicates that wealthy Americans placed sets of back stools in bedchambers as did their English counterparts. The expense of the finish fabric, which had to be imported, and the other materials and the cost of labor precluded the use of these stuffed frames by more than a limited segment of American society. Back stools remained popular in England into the immediate prerevolutionary period and probably somewhat longer in America. At the death of prominent London cabinetmaker William Linnell in 1763, several mahogany "back stool chairs" finished with nailed covers or removable cases stood in the "Back Ware Room." Similar mahogany seats in the "Chair Room" included one still in the frame and another stuffed in "Hessings" (hessians), a coarse linen canvas.[3]

Relatively few New England back stools survive, but those that do demonstrate that a range of design options was available. Family histories and traditions of ownership associated with these stuffed seats are about equally divided between Rhode Island and Massachusetts. Most back stools probably were made in Boston, however, and carried to Rhode Island in the lucrative coastal trade in Boston chairs.[4]

*NER/NGE*

**Construction:** (Frame upholstered; a photograph without upholstery is unavailable.) The round-cornered crest is chamfered or rounded on the upper forward edge. The stiles, which are continuous with the rear legs, are slightly canted in profile. The thick compass-shape seat has a rounded-sloping top lip and flat arches at the front and sides, which are slightly chamfered at the inside edges. The loose-seat frame is supported by interior rabbets. The rails are joined to the posts and front leg extensions with mortise and tenon (pinned). The rear rail is mounted above the level of the side rails; there is no stay rail. The rear legs are chamfered on all corners between the seat and rear stretcher; the feet are canted on the forward faces and chamfered at the front corners. The saucer-shape front feet have narrow back ledges and shallow disks. The ogee brackets are applied with rosehead nails. The side stretchers are joined to the legs with vertical rectangular tenons (pinned, at rear). The medial and rear stretchers have creased tips and are round tenoned into the adjacent members.

**Condition:** The seat frame has been repinned and probably reglued; the front rail is patched on the inside right end. The inside corner of the left knee block is split off from top to bottom. The right rear leg is cracked diagonally thorough both stretcher joints and reglued; both back feet are gouged and defaced. The left front knee bracket has been replaced; the others have been reattached. The left stretcher is cracked horizontally along the column into the long block, which has a piece broken out and reattached. Scribelike lines on the side stretchers near the back may have been created by a temporary brace, such as a metal wire or collars. The side stretcher joints may have been taken apart and reset. The medial stretcher has been apart; the round mortises in the side stretcher blocks have been enlarged, and the medial stretcher has been remounted or replaced. The bottoms of all feet have holes from former glides. Surface nicks and blemishes occur overall. The loose-seat frame is old but possibly not original to this chair.

1. For the Leicester House chairs, see Macquoid and Edwards, *Dictionary*, 1:26. Thornton, *Seventeenth-Century Interior Decoration*, pp. 185–92; Victoria and Albert Museum, *English Chairs* (2d ed., London: Her Majesty's Stationery Office, 1965), figs. 14, 22, 23, 25, 41, 42, 45, 47, 48, 50–52, 60, 61, 63, 66, 69; Forman, *American Seating Furniture*, cats. 85, 86.

2. For a discussion of back stools and *Marriage à la Mode*, pl. 2, see Venable, *American Furniture*, cat. 12. For the Dutch family drawing, see "Catalogue of the Exhibition," in Baarsen et al., *Courts and Colonies*, cat. 36.

3. *Boston News-Letter*, January 9, 1746, as quoted in Dow, *Arts and Crafts in New England*, p. 111. William Linnell estate inventory, 1763, Chancery Masters' Exhibits, Public Record Office, London.

4. Related chairs descended in the Cooper family of Cambridge, Mass., and the Capen family of Charlestown, Mass.; see Parke-Bernet Galleries, "Eighteenth- and Nineteenth-Century American Furniture" (November 16–18, 1972), lot 700; *American Antiques from Israel Sack Collection*, 10 vols. (Washington, D.C.: Highland House, ca. 1969–), 8:2078. Another chair was owned in the nineteenth and early twentieth centuries by a prominent Boston antiquarian, although a near mate has a tradition of ownership in the Maynard and Hazard families of Newport; see Venable, *American Furniture*, cat. 12. For another example ascribed to Rhode Island, see Ralph E. Carpenter, Jr., *The Arts and Crafts of Newport, Rhode Island, 1640–1820* (Newport: Preservation Society of Newport County, 1954), no. 22. Keno, Freund, and Miller, "Very Pink of the Mode," pp. 266–306.

## 90 ◆ Back stool
Boston, Massachusetts
1740–70

Assignment of this chair to Boston seems warranted, since the principal stylistic elements occur in furniture documented to or associated with that urban center. Easy chairs with serpentine crests were made in Boston. Some are supported on cabriole legs with disklike pad feet elevated on thick or thin cushion-type underpads resembling those illustrated here. The feet of this back stool also relate to the front supports in No. 7, a Boston compass-seat side chair possibly made as early as the 1730s. The medial stretcher is a distinctive Boston design that appears infrequently (see No. 25). The profile, with its rounded, bonelike knobs flanking the midsection, has its counterpart in English chairmaking and first appeared in Boston work

about the late 1720s at the introduction of the square cabriole leg. Boston seating furniture that dates as late as the claw-foot pierced-splat styles retains this feature. Furniture from the urban center also may be enhanced with ornamental, scroll-end knee brackets similar to those illustrated (see Nos. 74, 82).[1]

The numbers of American back stools made and used, even in comparison to the easy chair, were small due to the expense of the stuffing and cloth covers and the limited function of upholstered chairs without arms. The earliest known examples were made in the William and Mary style with block-and-turned bases, double-ogee–curved front rails, and high-arched crests. There followed a design with squared cabriole front legs and baluster side stretchers. Back stools of this style probably were constructed en suite with an easy chair. Indeed, Samuel Grant, a Boston upholsterer, drew an invoice in January

1731/32 for an easy chair covered with crimson wool cheney and a "Low chair horse bone foot cush'n seat." Pad-foot cabriole-leg back stools in the Queen Anne style with tall, narrow backs followed. Crests with rounded upper corners and straight or slightly depressed centers are stylistically the earliest (see Nos. 89, 91). The serpentine line of this chair probably was introduced to the back stool a few years later. Round-cornered and serpentine-back chairs also complemented easy chairs of similar, and even varied, tops (see Nos. 82, 85, 86). The survival of a back stool and a companion easy chair with identical undercarriages confirms the continuing use of these stuffed forms together. Back stools in Queen Anne and earlier styles probably all had low seats in the 12-inch to 16-inch range. Extant examples are about equally divided between loose seats and fixed bottoms.[2]

Several Boston inventories appear to document a modest use of back stools in that city. A reference to a "low Chair Stufft" in the household of Andrew Oliver, Esq., the beleagured administrator of the Stamp Act in 1765, is reasonably specific, since another city inventory identifies the alternative types of short-leg chairs as a "low mahogany Chair" (the loose-seat splat-back form) and a "low straw bottom chair." "Stuff Back" chairs in the inventories of lawyer Josiah Quincy, Jr.; Samuel Elliott, Jr., a merchant; and Capt. Joseph Cowdin probably were back stools as well. Most were listed with an easy chair, and one household contained a set of six—too many chairs to place in one bedroom if they were of a size framed with arms.[3]

*NGE*

---

**Construction:** (Frame upholstered; a photograph without upholstery is unavailable.) The serpentine-shape crest is chamfered or rounded on the upper forward edge. The stiles, which are continuous with the rear legs, are flared backward. The compass-shape seat is joined by mortise and tenon. The rear legs are chamfered on all corners between the seat and rear stretcher; the feet are canted on the forward faces and chamfered at the front corners. The rear surfaces of the feet are narrowly chamfered from the base to the rear stretcher. The flattened pads of the front feet are supported on low cushions. The knee brackets were probably nailed in place originally. The side stretchers are joined to the legs with vertical rectangular tenons; the medial stretcher has horizontal tenons. The rear stretcher is round tenoned into the adjacent members.

**Condition:** The triangular blocks attached with screws to the inside front corners of the seat frame are modern. The pads of the front feet are worn. All knee brackets have been reattached with glue and countersunk nails covered with composition material. The left front bracket is cracked at the scroll, defaced on the outer surface, and shallower than the other three brackets. The left side bracket is cracked on the inside surface. The left rear leg is cracked at the inside top and on the inside face at stretcher level. The side stretcher joints are repaired at the back and repinned inside and out. The right stretcher is cracked at the front, the damage continuing onto the adjacent leg surface. The left front leg is cracked at the ankle back. The pad foot of the same leg has broken off and the pieces (one large, two small) reattached. The medial stretcher is nicked on the lower forward face.

**Dimensions:**

| | | |
|---|---|---|
| H. | 40³/₄ in. | 103.5 cm |
| H. (seat) | 12 in. | 30.5 cm |
| W. (crest) | 16³/₈ in. | 41.6 cm |
| W. (seat front) | 21¹/₂ in. | 54.6 cm |
| W. (seat back) | 15³/₄ in. | 40.0 cm |
| W. (feet) | 22¹/₈ in. | 56.2 cm |
| D. (seat) | 18¹/₄ in. | 46.3 cm |
| D. (feet) | 20¹/₄ in. | 51.4 cm |

**Materials:** *Microanalysis:* Primary: mahogany. Secondary: soft maple group (rear legs, seat rails). *Finish:* mottled medium reddish brown color in resin. *Upholstery:* yellow wool serge with applied lace decoration; Europe, 1700–1750.

**Publications:** Downs, *American Furniture,* fig. 95.

**Accession history:** Gift of H. F. du Pont, 1965. 65.3091

1. For Boston-ascribed chairs with comparable feet, see Randall, *American Furniture,* nos. 147, 151, 153, 154; Warren, *Bayou Bend,* no. 91; Katharine Bryant Hagler, *American Queen Anne Furniture, 1720–1755* (Dearborn, Mich.: Henry Ford Museum and Greenfield Village, 1976), p. 17 bottom; Greenlaw, *New England Furniture,* no. 66; Rodriguez Roque, *American Furniture,* no. 85. On English and early Boston chairs with similar medial stretchers, see Jobe and Kaye, *New England Furniture,* no. 90, fig. 90a; for later examples, see Kirk, *American Chairs,* figs. 112, 128; see fig. 120 for a chair with similar knee brackets.

2. For early American back stools, see Forman, *American Seating Furniture,* figs. 85, 86. For the companion easy chair and back stool, see Moses, *Master Craftsmen,* fig. 1.53.

3. Andrew Oliver (1774), Isaac Smith, Esq. (1787), Josiah Quincy, Jr. (1781), Samuel Elliott, Jr. (1784), and Joseph Cowdin (1794) estate inventories, Suffolk County Probate Court, Boston (microfilm, Downs collection).

## 91 ◆ Back stools
### Boston, Massachusetts
### 1740–70

Except for the arms and arm supports, these chairs appear identical in all respects—size, elements, carving, and construction—and they almost certainly were made as part of the same set. The left chair is marked "II" on the front rail rabbet, and the right is marked "VII"; therefore the original set contained eight or more chairs. There are two known side chairs from this group numbered "VI" and "III" on the front rails. The first, which is in a private collection, has a history of ownership in the Maynard and Hazard families of Newport. The second chair is in the Bybee collection at the Dallas Museum of Art.[1]

Close inspection of the arms and supports of these chairs indicates that they were not part of the original design and framework. Several factors corroborate this. The arm assembly of the left chair is clumsy and poorly

executed compared to the rest of the frame, and the blocked bases of the supports extend well below the side rail arches, partially obliterating the feature. The recesses cut in the rails to accommodate the arm supports are larger by ¹/₂ inch than the posts, indicating that each side rail once supported different arms. The recesses are now patched, the repairs concealed by veneer on the outside surfaces. The bird's-head arms and supports of the right chair are made of mahogany, although the primary wood of the frame is walnut. Examination of the right arm and rear stile joint reveals that the arm is merely butted against the long post, and the tenon that fills the slot cut in the stile is a separate block of mahogany. Clearly, the arms and supports came from another chair and likely one that originated in the vicinity of Boston. When appropriated for this chair, the arms probably were already damaged.[2]

The arm restoration of the two chairs raises other questions. Both chairs were fitted

suggests an alteration rather than original construction. The theory is further substantiated by the shallow seat rails with flat arches, which would have maximized exposure of the special fitting. Perhaps the commode and first arm conversions were made at the same time in the late eighteenth or early nineteenth century, when some of the chairs in this outmoded set were adapted for use by an elderly owner.

The tall narrow backs and concave crests of these upholstered chairs, duplicated in the profiles of contemporary vase-back chairs, place the design squarely in the Queen Anne style (see Nos. 7, 10). The long slim lines of the vertical frame are reinforced by slender cabriole legs and thin rails cut in long flat arches. The distinctive shells and pendent bellflowers on the carved knees are particularly handsome representations of Boston design (fig. 1). Related shells and pendants occur on the knees of Boston vase-back side chairs (see No. 24).[3]

*NER/NGE*

**Inscriptions or marks:** (Left) *Incised on front seat-rail rabbet:* "II". (Right) *Chiseled on front seat-rail rabbet:* "VII".

**Construction:** (Left) Photographs taken when the chair was stripped for reupholstery provide details of the construction. The yoke-shape crest is supported on rectangular tenons at the post tops (probably pinned). The posts, which are continuous with the rear legs, are narrowly chamfered on the corners above the seat. A stay rail is tenoned between the posts about 2" above the back rail. The arms are let into long slots extending from front to back on the outside faces of the posts. The joints are held secure by single screws inserted from the inside faces of the posts. The arms are moderately curved from front to back, lightly contoured on the elbow tops, slightly rounded at the vertical sides, and poorly carved at the front scrolls. The arms and supports are butted and secured with mortise and tenon. The squared S-curve arm supports are slightly rounded at the corners. The rectangular base blocks are chamfered on the outside edges and rabbeted to the side rails at shallow, pseudo dovetails. The joints are secured by two screws from the inside rail surfaces. The thick, compass-shape seat has a rounded-sloping top lip and

with elbows prior to the installation of the new arms. Since the chairs appear to be from the same set, the first arms probably were alike. This conclusion is substantiated by the similarity of the back post slots that receive the arm tenons and the size, position, and configuration of the dovetail-type rabbets in the side seat rails. Another question concerns the originality of the first set of arms in either chair. Comparison of the seat measurements with those of the Bybee side chair indicates that all three are the same. In common practice, armchair dimensions are somewhat greater than those of companion side chairs (see No. 13); moreover, a tall, rounded, stuffed-back Queen Anne chair fitted with a loose seat and arms is unusual. Logic also suggests that if two chairs in the set had arms originally, the numbers chiseled on the front rails would be consecutive and fall at the beginning or end of the sequence. They do not. These chairs have been identified as back stools because evidence weighs more heavily

in favor of their having been constructed originally as side chairs.

During the nineteenth century, conversions in seating furniture were not uncommon. Older household furniture was frequently recycled for new use by making a few relatively simple alterations. A common modification was attaching rockers to chair legs, and side chairs of all types, made in formal and vernacular styles, were enhanced with arms. A common debasement of the Windsor chair was the introduction of a chamber pot to a hole cut in the seat center, and that conversion was not limited to wooden-bottom seating. The Bybee chair from the set of back stools represented here is fitted at the lower inside rail edge with six small blocks to support a frame for a chamber vessel. The blocks are so situated that the pot frame was inset below the seat rabbets. In this arrangement a second frame, or internal seat, with a central hole rounded at the sides was placed on top of the seat rabbets during use to support the weight of the sitter, a design that

flat arches at the front and sides. The interior rabbet supporting the loose seat frame is roughly gouged on the inner edges. The rails are joined to the posts and front leg extensions with mortise and tenon (pinned). The rear rail is mounted above the level of the side rails. The rear legs are chamfered on all corners between the seat and rear stretcher; the feet are canted on the forward faces and chamfered at the front corners. The shell-carved front legs have raised disks beneath the pad feet and slight insets at the ankle backs; the ogee brackets are applied with two rosehead nails. The side stretchers are joined to the legs with vertical rectangular tenons (pinned, at rear); the medial and rear stretchers are round tenoned into the adjacent members.

(Right) Visual inspection and photographs taken when the chair was stripped for reupholstery indicate that construction details are similar to those in the left chair, except for the arms and arm supports. The arms are let into slots extending from front to back on the outside faces of the posts. Unlike the left chair, the inside back corners of the arms also butt against the forward surfaces of the posts. The joints are held secure by screws. Further stability is provided by small blocks nailed to the post faces above and below the joints. The squared arms are curved from front to back; angular elbows are formed on the outside surfaces. The front scrolls are long, winged bird's heads modeled in low relief. The arms and supports are butted and secured with mortise and tenon (pinned, from inside). The S-curve supports are slightly rounded on the forward and back surfaces. The rectangular base blocks, which are deeply chamfered on the outside edges, are joined to the side rails with shallow sliding dovetails tapering outward from top to bottom. Narrow ledges at the top corners of the supports prevent the units from slipping further into the joints. The joints are secured on the inside rail by two screws of different sizes and by a single outside screw covered with composition material. (The left support is further secured by two additional outside fasteners.)

**Condition:** (Left) The arms and arm supports are not original to the chair. The interior rabbet of the seat frame is partially gouged away across the front and at the forward side cheeks, a condition that appears original to the construction for the better "seating" of the loose frame. The lower outside surfaces of the side rails have been patched and veneered at the arm support connections. The left front, side knee bracket has been repaired with a small wooden piece. An unexplained horizontal saw mark occurs at the back of each front leg behind the bellflower. The rear stretcher has a long gouge in the left tip. The loose seat frame has some age but is not original to the chair.

(Right) Like the left chair, the arms and arm supports are not original, and the interior rabbet is

**Fig. 1.** Detail of left chair, right front knee.

partially gouged away. The bird's head of the right arm has been broken off, reattached, and repaired with glue, small patches, and pins; the top surface is scratched. The left arm is cracked in the same general area and repaired with glue and a small patch; the joint with the support is also repaired. The right arm support has been damaged and repaired with a patch. Concealed wood blocks on the back posts above and below the arm joints are probably later additions rather than original construction. Small patches of finish missing from the back of the left arm on the inside top and bottom surfaces probably are evidence of an earlier joint. Triangular corner blocks held with screws at the front corners of the seat frame have age but are not original. The front and side rails are marked by stress cracks at the front corner joints. Stress cracks occur in the rear legs at the lower left stretcher joint and upper right rail joint. Horizontal saw cuts occur behind the knees. The front legs, pad feet, and medial stretcher are scarred and dented. The right side stretcher has various longitudinal cracks, and both side stretcher collars are chipped. The stretchers are reglued. The loose-seat frame has some age but is not original to the chair.

**Dimensions:**
Left

| | | | |
|---|---|---|---|
| H. | | 41 in. | 104.2 cm |
| H. (seat) | | 16 1/8 in. | 41.9 cm |
| W. (crest) | | 16 3/8 in. | 41.6 cm |
| W. (seat front) | | 22 in. | 55.9 cm |
| W. (seat back) | | 16 in. | 40.6 cm |
| W. (arms) | | 24 1/2 in. | 62.3 cm |
| W. (feet) | | 22 5/8 in. | 57.5 cm |
| D. (seat) | | 18 1/2 in. | 47.0 cm |
| D. (feet) | | 21 1/2 in. | 54.6 cm |
| Right | | | |
| H. | | 41 1/4 in. | 104.8 cm |
| H. (seat) | | 16 in. | 40.6 cm |
| W. (crest) | | 16 1/4 in. | 41.3 cm |
| W. (seat front) | | 22 in. | 55.9 cm |
| W. (seat back) | | 16 1/8 in. | 41.0 cm |
| W. (arms) | | 29 1/4 in. | 74.3 cm |
| W. (feet) | | 22 1/4 in. | 56.5 cm |
| D. (seat) | | 18 1/8 in. | 46.0 cm |
| D. (feet) | | 21 1/2 in. | 54.6 cm |

**Materials:** *Microanalysis:* (Left) Primary: American black walnut. Secondary: soft maple group (crest, stiles, stay rail). (Right) Primary: American black walnut (front legs); mahogany (right arm). Secondary: hard maple group (crest); soft maple group (rear leg, stiles, rear seat rail). *Finish:* (Left and right) mottled, medium dark, reddish brown color in resin. *Upholstery:* (Left and right) light yellow, floral medallion silk and linen(?) brocatelle; Europe, probably Italy, 1700–1750.

**Exhibitions:** (Right) "Flights of Fancy," University Hospital Antiques Show, Philadelphia, April 12–16, 1983.

**Publications:** Charles F. Hummel, "Queen Anne and Chippendale Furniture in the Henry Francis du Pont Winterthur Museum, Part 1," *Antiques* 97, no. 6 (June 1970): 902–3, figs. 14–19. (Left) Downs, *American Furniture*, fig. 15; Comstock, *American Furniture*, no. 143. (Right) Bishop, *Centuries and Styles of the American Chair*, fig. 121; Venable, *American Furniture*, cat. 12, fig. 3.

**Provenance:** (Left) Ex coll.: Philip Flayderman, Boston. (Right) The chair has a tradition of ownership in the Ellis family of Dedham, Mass.

**Accession history:** (Left) Purchased by H. F. du Pont at the Philip Flayderman sale, American Art Association Anderson Galleries, New York, 1930. Gift of H. F. du Pont, 1965. (Right) Purchased by H. F. du Pont from John S. Walton, Inc., New York, 1968. Bequest of H. F. du Pont, 1969. 65.3084, 68.771

1. For the privately owned chair, see David Stockwell, "Living with Antiques: Log Folly in Delaware," *Antiques* 119, no. 5 (May 1981): 1103, pl. 4; for the Bybee chair, see Venable, *American Furniture*, cat. 12.

2. The Boston area designation for the bird's-head arms of the right chair is based on related examples with local histories. This bird is plainly modeled with a beaklike crest, round eye, parrotlike beak, and a long crescent-tipped wing. A slightly more complex design with feathers at both ends of the wing and over the body surface is on a Boston claw-foot chair of the back pattern illustrated in No. 58, fig. 2. The bird's-head terminals on the arms of several cabriole-leg lolling chairs are finely feathered with striations overall, although 2 general designs are represented. One chair and a close mate now in the Museum of Fine Arts, Boston, descended from Elias Hasket Derby to Martha C. Codman (Mrs. Maxim Karolik). The bird's-head arms have been repositioned and reduced in length at the back, although they are probably original, since there is a close mate at the Henry Ford Museum, Dearborn, Mich. See *American Antiques from Israel Sack Collection*, 10 vols. (Washington, D.C.: Highland House, ca. 1969– ), 3:614; Hipkiss, *Eighteenth-Century American Arts*, no. 81, suppl. 81; Bishop, *Centuries and Styles of the American Chair*, figs. 220, 220a.

3. For another side chair, see *John Brown House Loan Exhibition*, cat. 8.

## 92 ◆ Upholstered armchair
Boston, Massachusetts
1745–65

It is speculated that this chair is one of two armchairs once owned by Abraham Redwood II (1709–88), a wealthy Quaker of Newport. The mate is in a private collection. The chairs are unusual, probably unique, in American chairmaking in combining bold hooplike arms with a short upholstered back of lobed profile. Both features are found on occasion in colonial American seating from other regions although not together. Inspiration may have flowed directly from English design, since Boston, the principal center of the furniture trade in the New World before the Revolution, maintained close commercial connections with the mother country. The Redwoods themselves had close ties with Britain. Abraham I, an Englishman, commanded a vessel that traded to the West Indies where he married and eventually, through his wife, acquired a large sugar plantation in Antigua that remained in the family for several generations. Redwood settled in Newport in 1712.[1]

Hooplike projections were introduced to British seating furniture somewhat before the feature was used for elbows as illustrated. Squared legs with bulging hoops at the knees and tall, hoof feet preceded squared cabriole supports in early eighteenth-century design. Hoop-ended crests were next in sequence, sometimes accompanied by straight-sided rather than curvilinear splats. Several chairs of this design, possibly produced by an immigrant English craftsman, were made in Boston during the 1730s (see No. 13). Hoop elbows appear to have been current in British chairmaking by 1720 but probably were introduced to American work only during the 1740s.[2]

The interior frame detail of the mate to this chair suggests that the two chairs are the work of an immigrant craftsman. As indicated by the light and dark wood, the sticks of mahogany forming the back legs are continuous with the rear stiles (fig. 1). From the arms up, the outer curves are pieced out, probably with maple, which is the wood of the seat rails and the lobed crest. The low, rounded curves of the top piece may derive from the tripartite arches in the crests of a group of early Georgian (Queen Anne–style) English chairs with splat backs. The English design appears to have also influenced the crests of a small group of late Boston leather chairs with turned bases and scroll arms and a tall back stool with cabriole legs and flat stretchers in the English style made in Philadelphia, a city where Redwood had many connections.[3]

Just as a prototype for the crest of this chair appears in British chairmaking, so that source is linked with the design of the narrow-waisted back, broad compass (horseshoe-shape) seat, and crook arm posts supporting hoop arms. The broad interior framing members of the seat resemble those of an easy chair. Given the multiplicity of influences that probably came to bear on the design of this chair and the absence of Redwood from Newport during a stay in Antigua from 1737 to 1740 or 1741, the seating probably was not acquired before the mid 1740s. The use of mahogany as the primary wood suggests an even later date, since comparable American chairs are made of walnut unless, of course, Redwood acquired a mahogany log directly from the Caribbean to construct the furniture. The choice of a bonelike medial stretcher and the use of a cylinder-and-block design for the rear legs, features now recognized as originating in Boston, would seem to preclude that Redwood ordered his chairs in Newport, Philadelphia, or New York. Providing reinforcement for this line of thinking is a letter to Redwood

**Fig. 1.** Frame of upholstered mate armchair, Boston, 1745–65. Mahogany, maple; H. 34 7/8 in. (88.6 cm), D. (seat) 19 1/2 in. (49.5 cm). (Collection of the late Joseph K. Ott; photo, Israel Sack, Inc.)

**Fig. 2.** Portrait of Abraham Redwood II (1709–88), attributed to Samuel King (1748/9–1819), Newport, R.I., ca. 1773–80. Oil on canvas; H. 42 1/2 in. (107.9 cm), W. 33 1/2 in. (85.1 cm). (Collection of Redwood Library and Athenaeum, Newport)

dated May 26, 1749, written by Stephen Greenleaf, a Boston merchant who was Redwood's agent: "I . . . have ordered 8 chairs and two roundabouts to be made which will be strong and neat and not high priced." It is conceivable that armchairs of the Redwood design were sometimes referred to as roundabouts in the mid eighteenth century.[4]

Chairs with low, upholstered backs, large stuffed seats, and open arms, sometimes known as French chairs, were still popular during the 1760s. Chippendale illustrated ten designs with variations in the 1762 edition of the *Director*. Most patterns retain the cabriole leg, and several crests have modified lobed profiles. Ince and Mayhew and Manwaring followed suit and published their own designs for "French Elbow Chairs," some with back profiles compatible with those in their back stools.[5]

The brown leather covers of this chair are original, as are the brass nails that finish the seat bottom and outline the back. The chair or its mate may be the one pictured in a portrait of Abraham Redwood II attributed to Samuel King (fig. 2). The painting was commissioned in 1773 or sometime thereafter by the Redwood Library and Athenaeum of Newport. In depicting Redwood's chair, the painter eliminated the chair back, although it can be argued that the sitter's body conceals the feature. What appears to be an extra structural support behind Redwood's elbow has been described as a sheaf of papers protruding

from one of his pockets but could be another small leather-bound volume like the one in his right hand. The entire area under question is ambiguously painted, and even the folds of Redwood's coat are unnatural in appearance.[6]

In 1743 Redwood purchased a large tract of land in neighboring Portsmouth, Rhode Island, from his father-in-law, Abraham Coggeshall, and set about building a splendid country house with extensive gardens maintained by a professional gardener brought from England. It has been written of Redwood that "by the time he was forty he had established an ample fortune and was one of the group of merchant princes whose prosperity, educated tastes, and cosmopolitan sympathies made the Newport of that day a notable center of wealth and culture." When his daughter, Mehetable, married Benjamin Ellery in 1769, Redwood bestowed upon her a handsome dowry of £5,000 sterling. Redwood was in a position to afford the very best in household appointments, and the choice of mahogany for the frame of this chair and its mate was clearly a conscious one. The selection of leather covers was perhaps a practical one, since Redwood may have

intended that the chairs serve the functional needs of a businessman. Rich cloth covers may also have seemed somewhat ostentatious in view of the Quaker sensibilities of the family.[7]

In all likelihood, this chair rather than its mate is the one depicted in the Redwood portrait because the mate appears to have passed to Redwood's son Abraham III, perhaps through his sister Mehetable Ellery, who was bequeathed her father's plate and household furniture. Abraham III married a Honeyman (Hunneman), and the chair may have passed into that collateral family line when Abraham III, who inherited the Antigua plantation, moved to the West Indies. The last owner of the mate chair was a Hunneman.[8]

This upholstered armchair, along with the Redwood portrait, probably descended lineally to Redwood's great-granddaughter Martha Maria Ellery, who married Elbert J. Anderson. A Philadelphia cousin of the Redwoods saw the portrait and "the old Redwood chair" during a Newport visit in 1874. A granddaughter of Martha Ellery Anderson bequeathed the portrait to the Redwood Library in 1950. The descent of the chair from Martha is uncertain. It was acquired by Henry Francis du Pont sometime between the mid 1920s and 1950, but no purchase record has been found.[9]

NGE

---

**Construction:** The crest is chamfered on the upper forward edge and shaped on the lower edge to conform to the outline. The crest is joined to the back posts with mortise and tenon. The posts, which are pieced at the shaped outer edges and sawed to a serpentine profile on the inner edges, are continuous with the rear legs. The pieced back members are secured with screws. A stay rail is tenoned to the back posts near the back rail. The hoop-shape arms are molded to an inward slope on the top surface and rounded at the bottom; both are secured to the back posts with plugged countersunk screws. The arms and supports are butted and secured with mortise and tenon. The arm-support bases, which are rectangular with rounded corners, are rabbeted to the seat rails and secured with double, countersunk, and plugged screws. The rails of the horseshoe-shape seat frame are joined with mortise and tenon (pinned, at front). The side and front rails are oriented horizontally; the interior edges are lightly chamfered. Rear side-rail returns are tenoned and glued to the back posts. The rear legs, which are raked backward, are rounded from several inches below the rails to the rear stretchers. The rectangular rear feet are canted on the forward surfaces below the side stretchers and chamfered at the front corners. The short cabriole front legs are terminated by flattened pads with slight ledges at the ankle backs and flat surfaces at the stretcher joints. The legs are joined to the seat frame with open dovetails at the front corners; the knee brackets are secured with four rosehead nails apiece. The side stretchers are joined to the legs with vertical rectangular tenons (pinned); the medial stretcher tenons are horizontal. The rear stretcher is round tenoned into the adjacent members.

**Condition:** The upper block of the right rear leg is cracked vertically at an outside corner; two chunks of wood are missing from the back of the foot. The left front foot has been shattered and repaired with three original pieces, composition material, and glue. Casters were once mounted on the rear feet. The chair retains the original upholstery, including the leather outer cover, webbing, sackcloth, and stuffing. The brass nails appear to be original; several are missing. The dark brown leather is split and patched. An outside back panel of oil cloth simulating crinkled leather was added in the late nineteenth or early twentieth century.

**Dimensions:**

| | | |
|---|---|---|
| H. | 34³/₄ in. | 88.3 cm |
| H. (seat) | 13³/₄ in. | 34.9 cm |
| W. (crest) | 16¹/₂ in. | 41.9 cm |
| W. (seat front) | 23 in. | 58.4 cm |
| W. (seat back) | 14¹/₄ in. | 36.2 cm |
| W. (arms) | 25¹/₄ in. | 64.2 cm |
| W. (feet) | 22⁷/₈ in. | 58.1 cm |
| D. (seat) | 19 in. | 48.2 cm |
| D. (feet) | 22¹/₄ in. | 56.5 cm |

**Materials:** *Microanalysis:* Primary: mahogany. Secondary: soft maple group (seat rails). *Finish:* dark reddish brown color in resin.

**Publications:** Downs, *American Furniture*, fig. 18. Elizabeth Bidwell Bates and Jonathan L. Fairbanks, *American Furniture: 1620 to the Present* (New York: Richard Marek Publishers, 1981), p. 98. Joseph K. Ott, "Abraham Redwood's Chairs?" *Antiques* 119, no. 3 (March 1981): 670, fig. 2.

**Accession history:** Bequest of H. F. du Pont, 1969. 58.2597

---

1. The pioneering article on the Redwood chairs is Joseph K. Ott, "Abraham Redwood's Chairs?" *Antiques* 119, no. 3 (March 1981): 669–73. Information on Abraham Redwood is in *Dictionary of American Biography*, 15:444–45. Gladys E. Bolhouse, "Abraham Redwood: Reluctant Quaker, Philanthopist, Botanist," *Newport History* 45, pt. 2, no. 146 (Spring 1972): 17–35.

2. For British prototypes, see Cescinsky, *English Furniture*, 1: figs. 60, 67, 83; Hinckley, *Directory*, ills. 9, 15, 17, 28, 36; Macquoid and Edwards, *Dictionary*, 1:254, fig. 84; p. 256, figs. 91, 92; Kirk, *American Furniture*, figs. 285, 286. Hoop elbows appear on a labeled, upholstered armchair made by Robert Webb, Sr. (w. 1712–32) of London; see Christopher Gilbert, *Pictorial Dictionary of Marked London Furniture, 1740–1840* (Leeds, Eng.: Furniture History Society and W. S. Maney and Son, 1996), p. 463.

3. This chair and its mate were published as walnut with cherry secondary wood in Downs, *American Furniture*, fig. 17; *American Antiques from Israel Sack Collection*, 10 vols. (Washington, D.C.: Highland House, 1969– ), 7:1724–25; Ott, "Abraham Redwood's Chairs?" For a typical lobed-top early Georgian chair, see Macquoid and Edwards, *Dictionary*, 3:255, fig. 86. For the Boston chair, see Forman, *American Seating Furniture*, cat. 81; for the Philadelphia back stool, see Downs, *American Furniture*, fig. 97.

4. See British prototypes in Macquoid and Edwards, *Dictionary*, 1:259, fig. 100; 1:262, figs. 111–13; pl. 15; Cescinsky, *English Furniture*, 1: figs. 88, 89; Hinckley, *Directory*, ills. 5–7, 36, 43–46. Ott, "Abraham Redwood's Chairs?" p. 672.

5. Thomas Chippendale, *The Gentleman and Cabinet-Maker's Director* (3d ed., London: By the author, 1762), pls. 19–23. William Ince and John Mayhew, *The Universal System of Houshold Furniture* (1762; reprint, Chicago: Quadrangle Books, 1960), pls. 58, 59. Robert Manwaring, *The Cabinet and Chair-Maker's Real Friend and Companion* (London: Henry Webley, 1765), pl. 21.

6. It has also been argued that Redwood is seated on a low-back, or roundabout, chair, but the hoop-arm design is incompatible with that construction. It is possible that King painted a structural support where one did not exist on Redwood's chair, since the chair arm might otherwise have appeared to hang in space. The Redwood Library and Athenaeum was named in recognition of Redwood's munificence to that institution in its early years.

7. *Dictionary of American Biography*, 15:445. Ott, "Abraham Redwood's Chairs?" pp. 670, 672; Redwood's Quakerism is reflected in the 1749 purchase of a plain looking glass rather than a gilt one; see p. 672. *New England Historical and Genealogical Register* (Boston: Samuel G. Drake, 1853), 22:353.

8. Ott, "Abraham Redwood's Chairs?" pp. 671, 673 n. 15.

9. Ott, "Abraham Redwood's Chairs?" pp. 669, 671, 673 n. 12.

## 93 ◆ Upholstered armchair
Massachusetts, Boston area
1750–70

Upholstered chairs with open arms were made in Europe from the beginning of the seventeenth century and perhaps, like the back stool, from the late sixteenth century. Backs were short in the Cromwellian style or of medium height and frequently open adjacent to the seat. Early examples were braced with stretchers positioned around the outside of the frame. By the reign of Louis XIV of France (beginning 1643), an H-plan turned-stretcher system was in place, and the chair had become larger overall. Chairs used for public functions or to seat prominent individuals frequently had tall backs, symbolic of the rank or stature of the sitter. Stuffed chairs became increasingly elaborate through the end of the century, as rich fabrics, carved surfaces, and intricately shaped stretchers and legs were introduced; sometimes the frame was gilt. Just such a set of chairs with arms terminated by dolphin's heads was inventoried in 1679 in the north drawing room of Ham House in Surrey and described as "Six arme Chayres with carved and guilded frames covered with rich Brocard fringd." Final statements in this somewhat ponderous style are designs for upholstered furniture published about 1700 by Daniel Marot, a French Huguenot who fled to the Netherlands (see No. 94, fig. 1), and a tall silver throne, imitative of a richly carved wooden seat, made for King Frederick IV of Denmark about 1715.[1]

The sinuous lines of the cabriole form began to prevail in the early eighteenth century and achieved full development during the reign of Louis XV. The style as interpreted in England was sometimes plainer; it was plainer still in America (see No. 90). The round-shouldered crest of this chair with its central depression is more than suggestive of the Queen Anne style (see No. 7). This profile and one of lobed form (see No. 92) were current in European upholstered seating

furniture before 1736, as indicated in six furniture plates for Gaetano Brunetti's book of ornament published that year in London. Crests of both types are included.[2]

There is little doubt about the Boston origin of this chair. The seat rails are birch, a common secondary material in northeastern New England furniture. The sweeping, wafer-thin feet raised on cushioned bases relate significantly in the lower curves, front and back, to No. 7. The creased knees and simply curved brackets are typical of eastern Massachusetts chairs dating to the third quarter of the eighteenth century (see Nos. 30, 31, 50 left, 53). Although cone-tipped medial stretchers were fashionable in splat-back armchairs and side chairs somewhat earlier (see Nos. 7, 8, 11, 23), use of this stretcher in fully upholstered seating furniture, especially the easy chair, generally occurs with the heavy, creased knee (see Nos. 83, 85, 86).

*NGE*

---

**Construction:** (Frame upholstered; a photograph without upholstery is unavailable.) The round-

cornered crest is chamfered or rounded on the upper forward edge. The canted stiles are probably spliced to the rear legs, which are made of mahogany. The narrow S-scroll arms are contoured to an inward slope on the upper surface behind the angular elbows, rounded at the sides, and flat on the bottom. The top forward surfaces are rounded and terminated by small scrolls carved with volutes. The arm-and-stile joints are concealed. The arms and forward supports are tenoned and pinned from the outside arm surfaces. The supports appear to be mortised and tenoned into the seat frame. The seat rails are joined to the back stiles and front leg extensions with mortise and tenon. The lower interior edges of the front and side rails are narrowly chamfered; the rear rail is shaved in a wide, irregular chamfer. The rear legs are canted on the forward surfaces. The back corners of the legs and the front corners of the feet are narrowly chamfered. The front legs have creased knees and flat feet supported on cushioned pads. There is a ringlike ledge at the back of each foot. The knee blocks are applied with nails. The side stretchers are joined to the legs with vertical rectangular tenons. The medial and rear stretchers have creased tips and are round tenoned into the adjacent members.

**Condition:** Both arm supports are repaired at the outside bases; the left arm-and-support joint is also repaired. The left arm is a replacement of some age; the color varies from that of the rest of the exposed wood. The right arm is damaged on the underside and at the elbow; nail holes along the sides indicate that the arm (and the original left one) was once stuffed (not original). The seat may have been fitted once with springs. The small triangular corner blocks at the seat front are later additions. Surfaces are nicked and blemished. All the feet are fitted with glides.

**Dimensions:**

| | | |
|---|---|---|
| H. | 40⅝ in. | 103.2 cm |
| H. (seat) | 13¼ in. | 33.6 cm |
| W. (crest) | 19 in. | 48.2 cm |
| W. (seat front) | 24⅜ in. | 61.9 cm |
| W. (seat back) | 19¾ in. | 50.2 cm |
| W. (arms) | 26⅝ in. | 67.6 cm |
| W. (feet) | 26 in. | 66.0 cm |
| D. (seat) | 20 in. | 50.8 cm |
| D. (feet) | 23⅝ in. | 60.0 cm |

**Materials:** *Microanalysis:* Primary: mahogany. Secondary: birch (seat rails). *Finish:* medium to medium light yellowish brown color in resin. *Upholstery:* watered red wool worsted, possibly moreen; Europe, 1750–1800.

**Publications:** Downs, *American Furniture,* fig. 19.

**Provenance:** By tradition, the chair descended in the Stacy family of Gloucester, Mass.

**Accession history:** Purchased by H. F. du Pont from Israel Sack, Inc., New York. Bequest of H. F. du Pont, 1969. 66.1034

1. Peter Thornton and Maurice Tomlin, "The Furnishing and Decoration of Ham House," *Furniture History* 16 (1980): 123. Development of the upholstered armchair can be followed in Helena Hayward, ed., *World Furniture: An Illustrated History* (New York: McGraw-Hill Book Co., 1965), figs. 170, 192, 205, 221, 223, 253, 267, 277, 278, 315, 353, 364, 393, 396; Gervase Jackson-Stops, "The Court Style in Britain" in Baarsen et al., *Courts and Colonies,* figs. 51, 52; "Catalogue of the Exhibition," in Baarsen et al., *Courts and Colonies,* cats. 137, 140, 141; Thornton, *Seventeenth-Century Interior Decoration,* pls. 170, 171, 186–93; Macquoid and Edwards, *Dictionary,* 1:245, 249, pls. 9, 10, 12; p. 249, figs. 70, 75, 76, 77–79, 128–30, 147, 159, 161, 197; Thornton and Tomlin, "Furnishing and Decoration," pp. 122–23, fig. 109; Victoria and Albert Museum, *English Chairs* (2d ed., London: Her Majesty's Stationery Office, 1965), pls. 17, 26, 27, 30, 35, 36, 68.

2. Peter Ward-Jackson, *English Furniture Designs of the Eighteenth Century* (London: Victoria and Albert Museum, Her Majesty's Stationery Office, 1958), nos. 27, 29.

## 94 ◆ Upholstered armchair
### Massachusetts, Boston area
### 1750–75

The eighteenth-century upholstered American armchair is generally tall and attenuated in profile. Although the form dates principally to the second half of the century, the figure derives from late seventeenth-century designs current in the Netherlands and England during the reign of William and Mary. Of French derivation, the style reached its zenith in the hands of Daniel Marot, a Huguenot who fled to Holland in 1685, where he was soon in the employ of William of Orange and members of the nobility residing on both sides of the Channel (fig. 1). The vertical style was first transferred to America in the tall cane chair and was followed by the leather chair and the banister-back chair. Perhaps the only tall stuffed chairs made in America during the first several decades of the eighteenth century were easy chairs and back stools.[1]

The tall upholstered armchair, also known later as a lolling chair, may have been introduced to the American furniture market only in the late 1740s. Unlike the back stool, there are no identified examples constructed with block-and-turned bases in the William and Mary style or with squared cabriole legs. In fact, prior to the federal period when the form came into its own, only a limited number of tall upholstered armchairs appears to have been made. Production occurred primarily in New England. The earliest examples are patterned in the Queen Anne style with horizontal, scrolled and contoured arms, modeled arm supports, cabriole legs terminated by pad feet, and turned columnar stretchers. Claw-foot examples were introduced slightly later. The ratio of pad-foot to claw-foot examples is perhaps one to one. As in the easy chair, the conical-tipped stretcher is the most common cross brace. A few chairs were constructed without any braces.[2]

The features of this chair, which are typical of those found in New England upholstered armchairs dating to the third quarter of the eighteenth century, provide a springboard for enlarging the discussion. Above stuffed seats of generous size, flat arms are curved in bold S shapes, frequently accented by pronounced angular elbows, as illustrated. The molded rear surfaces of the arms in this chair are rounded on the outside; alternative outer profiles are canted or straight. The flat, front scrolls vary in size; only infrequently are they carved with a volute on the top surface (see No. 93). Other scrolled front terminals are reoriented from the horizontal to the vertical. The plain, modeled posts that support the arms are curved in a segmental profile, as shown, or to an ogee form; the latter is somewhat more common. Chairs produced in the federal period frequently have posts articulating with the front legs rather than the side rails, and the front surfaces are frequently modeled, sometimes inlaid or carved. A few supports are turned.

Crest profiles are something of a guide to the stylistic maturity of the upholstered armchair. The earliest line is the oxbow of No. 93; the latest, and most common, is the serpentine sweep of No. 96. Between the two fall the straight-top crests of this chair and No. 95; a modified serpentine profile with rounded rather than pointed corners; a pinched double ogee that is an imitation of the front rail in No. 16; and a low segmental arch, such as appears in easy chair crests. At best, the selection of features throughout is a mix-and-match situation. In the federal period, the backs of tall stuffed chairs frequently have pronounced tapers from crest to seat rather than almost perpendicular sides. Comparison of the undercarriage in this chair with the support structure of No. 93 indicates that the two chairs originated in the same area.[3]

NGE

---

**Construction:** (Frame upholstered; parts of upholstery loosened for internal examination of the front.) The rectangular crest is chamfered or rounded on the upper forward edge and is secured

**Fig. 1.** Daniel Marot, *Werken van D. Marot* (Amsterdam, [1707]), pl. 81.

on top of the stiles with mortise and tenon. The rear legs are continuous with the canted rear stiles. A stay rail is tenoned between the stiles at the lower back. The S-scroll arms are contoured on the upper surface behind the angular elbows, rounded at the outside, canted on the inside, and flat on the bottom. The forward surfaces are squared and rounded and terminated by small uncarved scrolls. The arms are butted to the rear stiles and held with screws; the arms and forward supports are tenoned. The support bases, which are rectangular with chamfered edges, are rabbeted to the seat rails and secured with two countersunk plugged screws from the outside and one from the inside. The seat rails are joined to the stiles and front leg extensions with mortise and tenon. The rear legs are canted on the forward surfaces below the seat frame and the side stretchers. All the corners are chamfered between the seat frame and stretchers; the front corners of the feet are narrowly chamfered. The front legs have creased knees and flat feet supported on cushioned pads. A ringlike ledge occurs at the back of each foot. The knee brackets are applied with nails. The side stretchers are joined to the legs with vertical rectangular tenons (pinned). The medial and rear stretchers have creased tips and are round tenoned into the adjacent members.

**Condition:** The right arm is a replacement and was attached to the back frame with a screw inserted from the outside rather than from inside under the upholstery. The right arm has been broken and reattached to the stiles with two screws from the outside. The holes are covered with composition material. The left arm and support joint is cracked and newly pinned, inside and out. A piece has cracked off the forward top surface of the right arm support and has been reattached; the joint is pinned inside and out. The support bases have been reset; the screw holes have been gouged out and refilled with composition material. The left side knee

bracket is replaced; the right front bracket is cracked and repaired with glue and a small patch. The other brackets have been reset and renailed. The front feet are badly chipped around the edges. The arm support bases, front legs, and side and medial stretchers are considerably scratched and marred. All the feet have caster holes.

**Dimensions:**

| | | |
|---|---|---|
| H. | 39 1/2 in. | 100.3 cm |
| H. (seat) | 13 1/8 in. | 33.3 cm |
| W. (crest) | 19 1/2 in. | 49.5 cm |
| W. (seat front) | 23 3/4 in. | 60.3 cm |
| W. (seat back) | 20 in. | 50.8 cm |
| W. (arms) | 28 1/2 in. | 72.4 cm |
| W. (feet) | 25 7/8 in. | 65.7 cm |
| D. (seat) | 19 1/2 in. | 49.5 cm |
| D. (feet) | 23 1/2 in. | 59.7 cm |

**Materials:** *Microanalysis:* Primary: American black walnut. Secondary: hard maple group (seat rails). *Finish:* medium brown color with reddish cast, in resin. *Upholstery:* pale blue-green silk dress fabric brocaded with blue, peach, and yellow flowers; Europe, probably France or Italy, 1730–60.

**Exhibitions:** "Loan Exhibition of Eighteenth- and Early Nineteenth-Century Furniture and Glass," National Council of Girl Scouts, New York, September 25–October 9, 1929.

**Publications:** National Council of Girl Scouts, *Loan Exhibition of Eighteenth- and Early Nineteenth-Century Furniture and Glass* (New York: By the council, 1929), cat. 577. Downs, *American Furniture*, fig. 20. Comstock, *American Furniture*, no. 145.

**Accession history:** Bequest of H. F. du Pont, 1969. 58.2595

---

1. Reinier Baarsen, "The Court Style in Holland," Gervase Jackson-Stops, "The Court Style in Britain," and "Catalogue of the Exhibition" in Baarsen et al., *Courts and Colonies,* cat. 141. Gervase Jackson-Stops, "Daniel Marot and the Court Style of William and Mary," *Antiques* 134, no. 6 (December 1988): 1320–31. Lisa White, "The Furnishing of Interiors during the Time of William and Mary," *Antiques* 134, no. 6 (December 1988): 1362–69, pl. 1, fig. 5.

2. For back stools, see Forman, *American Seating Furniture,* cats. 85, 86; for upholstered armchairs without braces, see Warren, *Bayou Bend,* no. 88; David Stockwell advertisement, *Antiques* 98, no. 4 (October 1970): 473.

3. For modified serpentine and double-ogee crested chairs, see *John Brown House Loan Exhibition,* cats. 22, 23.

The rear legs are maple, like the seat frame, and continuous with the stiles rather than spliced on. Originally these plain supports were stained or colored to resemble the walnut of the front legs and arms. The creased knees and shallow pad feet of the cabriole supports suggest that eastern Massachusetts was the place of origin. The front leg profile, including the brackets, appears to be almost identical to that in a Massachusetts-ascribed chair with an arc-type crest. The arms are varied somewhat in curve and modeling, but the arm supports in both chairs are U shape at the base rather than rectangular. Another lolling chair with pad-foot legs of related profile was once owned by Samuel Allyne Otis (1740–1814) of Boston, member of the Continental Congress and first secretary of the U.S. Senate.[3]

*NGE*

## 95 ◆ Upholstered armchair
Massachusetts, Boston area
1750–75

Charles Montgomery, in his pioneering study of furniture of the federal period, discovered that the eighteenth-century term for tall chairs with open arms and stuffed backs and seats was *lolling chair*. Although the seating form was most common in America following the Revolution, references dating from the prewar years indicate that the term was current in the third quarter of the eighteenth century. Household furniture offered at auction from a Boston estate in 1758 included "A lolling chair frame." Merchant Nathaniel Rogers's 1770 estate inventory listed a "lolling Chair Lin[e]d [with] leather" valued at 30s. in the "West front Room," which was used as both a sitting and dining parlor. Jane Mecom, a Boston widow, and Elias Hasket Derby, Salem's preeminent merchant, also furnished their dining rooms with lolling chairs. Two such

chairs were in the Derby mansion dining parlor, a room considerably more sophisticated than that in the home of cordwainer Ezra Burril of Salem, where two lolling chairs were also part of the furnishings.[1]

The bedroom was, perhaps, an equally popular location for the lolling chair. Two cabinetmakers, Moses Adams of Beverly and Abraham Hayward of Boston, preferred the privacy of that setting for their reclining chairs. Among "Things in the Shop" also itemized in the Hayward inventory was a lolling chair, probably the frame only, valued at $4. Elizabeth Senter, widow of the prominent Newport, Rhode Island, physician Isaac Senter, favored the drawing room for her two lolling chairs with copperplate covers. The same fabric was also used for window curtains and on an upholstered sofa.[2]

The exposed frame of this lolling chair (fig. 1) illustrates the simplicity of the structure when compared to that of the French chair (see No. 92) or the easy chair (see No. 80).

**Construction:** (Frame upholstered; some commentary based on a photograph of the bare frame.) The rectangular crest appears to be squared on all edges and is secured on top of the stiles with mortise and tenon. The rear legs are continuous with the canted rear stiles, which are squared at the edges. A stay rail is tenoned between the stiles at the lower back. The S-scroll arms are flat, top and bottom, and rounded at the sides behind the angular elbows. The forward surfaces are rounded across the top and sides and terminated by uncarved scrolls. The arms appear to butt against the inside forward surfaces of the stiles and to slot into open mortises on the outside surfaces. The arms and forward supports are tenoned. The support bases, which are half circular, are rabbeted to the seat rails and secured with two countersunk plugged screws. The seat rails are joined to the stiles and front leg extensions with mortise and tenon. The rear legs are canted on the forward surfaces. The corners of the legs are chamfered between the seat frame and the stretchers and at the feet. The front legs have creased knees and saucer-type pad feet with narrow ledges at the ankle backs. The knee brackets are applied with nails. The side stretchers are joined to the legs with vertical rectangular tenons. The

**Fig. 1.** Frame without upholstery.

medial and rear stretchers have creased tips and are round tenoned into the adjacent members.

**Condition:** The left arm is pieced and repaired at the back joint and cracked at the front adjacent to the scroll. The left front support is restored at the top with a new piece secured with a pin from the outside. Gouges around the screw plugs at the base indicate the joint was taken apart. The right arm is repaired with a small piece at the outside back corner; the forward joint with the support is broken and repaired with glue, plugs, and other fasteners. The support has been reinforced at the rail attachment with an additional plugged screw; the other screw plugs are new. Reinforcing blocks were once in place inside the side rails at the arm support connections. Small blocks abutting the bases of the arm supports on the inside top surfaces of the side rails may not be part of the original fabric of the chair. Blocks have been added to all interior seat corners and nailed twice. The inside corners of the front leg-extension blocks have been restored. The knee brackets have been reattached, and the left side bracket has been restored on the back half. The brackets, knees, and feet are considerably bruised and defaced. The side stretchers are newly pinned (repinned?) at the outside back. The forward face of the left stretcher tip is marked by a gouge.

The medial and rear stretchers are reglued and possibly refitted. Casters, which were once on the feet, are now replaced by glides.

**Dimensions:**

| | | |
|---|---|---|
| H. | 41 in. | 105.4 cm |
| H. (seat) | 13 1/8 in. | 33.3 cm |
| W. (crest) | 19 1/2 in. | 49.5 cm |
| W. (seat front) | 22 5/8 in. | 57.5 cm |
| W. (seat back) | 18 in. | 45.7 cm |
| W. (arms) | 29 in. | 73.7 cm |
| W. (feet) | 24 7/8 in. | 63.2 cm |
| D. (seat) | 18 in. | 45.7 cm |
| D. (feet) | 22 1/4 in. | 56.5 cm |

**Materials:** *Microanalysis:* Primary: American black walnut. Secondary: soft maple group (rear legs, seat rails). *Finish:* medium dark brown color in resin. *Upholstery:* watered red wool worsted, possibly moreen; Europe, 1750–1800.

**Provenance:** Ex coll.: Guy W. Walker, Jr., Beverly Farms, Mass.

**Accession history:** Purchased by H. F. du Pont from Guy W. Walker, Jr., Beverly Farms, Mass., 1958. Gift of H. F. du Pont, 1959.
58.135.9

1. Joseph Grant, Jr., estate advertised in the *Boston Gazette*, November 13, 1758, as quoted in Dow, *Arts and Crafts in New England*, p. 118; Nathaniel Rogers estate inventory, 1770, Suffolk County Probate Court, Boston (microfilm, Downs collection). Montgomery, *American Furniture*, pp. 155–56. The Mecom chairs are described as "stuff'd back easy Chairs" (Mrs. Jane Mecom estate inventory, 1794, Suffolk County Probate Court, Boston [microfilm, Downs collection]). Elias Hasket Derby estate inventory, 1800, Essex County Probate Court, Salem, Mass. Ezra Burril estate inventory, 1797, Hathorne Family Manuscripts, Peabody Essex Museum, Salem, Mass.

2. Moses Adams estate inventory, 1796, Essex County Probate Court, Salem, Mass.; Abraham Hayward estate inventory, 1796, Suffolk County Probate Court, Boston (microfilm, Downs collection); Elizabeth Senter estate inventory, 1802, Newport County Probate Court, Newport, R.I. (microfilm, Downs collection). The lolling chairs may have been in the household long before Dr. Senter's death in 1800, since extensive family bills for the last 2 decades of the eighteenth century omit references to such purchases; see Joseph K. Ott, "Recent Discoveries among Rhode Island Cabinetmakers and Their Work," *Rhode Island History* 28, no. 1 (February 1969): 3–14.

3. For the arc-crest chair, see Kane, *Three Hundred Years*, no. 206; for the Samuel Otis chair, see John S. Walton advertisement, *Antiques* 123, no. 6 (June 1983): 1098.

another $4.50 to the cost. The price of a tight-fitting slip case was variable, depending upon the cloth selected and the use of trimmings. The labor charge for making trimmed cases was about $.75. Four yards of copperplate chintz, the most popular furnishing fabric in the postwar years, cost about $4.00. A 1783 bill from Ziphion Thayer to the widow Anne Doane of Boston calls for twelve yards of binding and two yards of fringe to trim a case at an additional charge for materials of $.82. Thus, the total cost of a plain, straight-leg mahogany lolling chair finished in canvas with a trimmed and fringed slip case of copperplate was about $15.00. The same amount of money at that time would have purchased a field bedstead and a small looking glass or two plain card tables and a large mahogany tea tray. The average craftsman earned $1.00 a day or less in the 1780s.[3]

*NGE*

## 96 ◆ Upholstered armchair
Massachusetts, Boston area
1755–85

The claw feet of this chair update the creased cabriole legs with bulging knees and simple ogee brackets illustrated in Nos. 93 and 94. From the standpoint of style, the serpentine crest that ornaments the top was the latest shape introduced to the back of the colonial lolling chair. It was also the most common one because this profile remained popular after straight legs and the later tapered supports became fashionable in seating furniture. When Henry Francis du Pont loaned this chair to the landmark exhibition sponsored by the National Council of Girl Scouts in 1929, it was described as "a very rare and dignified example."[1]

Through the 1760s and into the 1770s, John Singleton Copley often painted female subjects seated in serpentine-top lolling chairs of medium-tall height. Although Copley's straight-leg chair appears to be a studio prop, it was obviously considered an acceptable status symbol by the affluent Bostonians who sat for the artist. The upholstery, which also covers the arms, is a rich, light-colored floral-patterned damask with a tufted surface that is further embellished at the edges of the frame with closely spaced brass nails. The chair may have been made in England, since upholstered arms are less common in American lolling chairs. Whatever the origin of the chair, Copley's wealthy patrons, among them Mrs. Isaac Smith (painted 1769), found it acceptable.[2]

Like the back stool, easy chair, and sofa, the lolling chair was an expensive piece of furniture. A plain mahogany frame with straight or tapered, molded legs and plain rectangular stretchers cost about $5.00. (Cabriole frames with turned stretchers would have been slightly more expensive.) Stuffing the frame in canvas to receive loose covers (a separate purchase) added, on an average,

**Construction:** The serpentine crest is rounded on the upper forward edge and joined to the tops of the canted rear stiles with mortise and tenon. The rear legs are continuous with the rear stiles, which are squared at the edges except at the outside back where there is a narrow chamfer. A stay rail is tenoned between the stiles at the lower back. The S-scroll arms are contoured to an inward slope on the upper rear surfaces behind the angular elbows; the sides are canted, the bottoms flat. The top forward surfaces are rounded and terminated by uncarved scrolls flattened on the top. The arms are fastened to the rear stiles with screws. The arms and forward supports are tenoned (pinned). The support bases, which are rectangular with chamfered edges, are rabbeted to the seat rails and secured with two countersunk screws concealed with composition material. An additional countersunk screw penetrates each joint from the inside. The seat rails are joined to the stiles and front leg extensions with mortise and tenon, the joints pinned at the side back and either end of the front. The rear legs are canted on the forward surfaces. The feet are lightly chamfered at the front corners. The front legs have creased knees and claw feet with two or three knuckles and a single large toe at the back. The knee brackets, which are double nailed, have a narrow chamfer on the inner edge. The side stretchers are joined to the legs with vertical rectangular tenons. The medial stretcher is joined to the side stretcher blocks with horizontal rectangular tenons. The rear stretcher has coved inner tips and is round tenoned into the adjacent members.

**Condition:** The flaring tips of the crest are restored, the wood forming the projections held in place with glued cloth. The stiles and rails are mutilated from nail holes. Both arms are damaged and repaired at the back joints with the stiles (damage to the left joint is severe). The right arm is cracked and repinned at the front joint. The left arm-support joint is repaired, as is a crack on the outside upper half of the support. The left side and rear rails are cracked. Most toenails on the front feet have worn away. Small pieces that broke off the right front and side knee brackets have been reattached. The medial stretcher has been repaired with a new horizontal tenon at the right joint. The mortise of the left joint appears to have been cut too long initially or enlarged to effect repairs; a 1/2" slot on the forward inside surface of the side stretcher has been plugged.

**Dimensions:**

| | | |
|---|---|---|
| H. | 40 3/8 in. | 102.6 cm |
| H. (seat) | 13 1/8 in. | 33.3 cm |
| W. (crest) | 21 5/8 in. | 54.9 cm |
| W. (seat front) | 23 in. | 58.4 cm |
| W. (seat back) | 19 1/2 in. | 49.5 cm |
| W. (arms) | 26 3/4 in. | 68.0 cm |
| W. (feet) | 24 3/4 in. | 62.9 cm |
| D. (seat) | 18 1/4 in. | 46.3 cm |
| D. (feet) | 22 5/8 in. | 57.5 cm |

**Materials:** *Macroidentification:* Primary: mahogany. *Microanalysis:* Secondary: birch (seat frame, rear leg). *Finish:* medium reddish brown color in resin; the rear legs are streaky dark brown color over brick red primer. *Upholstery:* cream-colored floral-patterned silk damask; Europe, probably Italy, 1700–1740.

**Exhibitions:** "Loan Exhibition of Eighteenth- and Early Nineteenth-Century Furniture and Glass," National Council of Girl Scouts, New York, September 25–October 9, 1929.

**Publications:** National Council of Girl Scouts, *Loan Exhibition of Eighteenth- and Early Nineteenth-Century Furniture and Glass* (New York: By the council, 1929), cat. 605.

**Accession history:** Purchased by H. F. du Pont before 1929. Gift of H. F. du Pont, 1958. 58.2138

1. National Council of Girl Scouts, *Loan Exhibition of Eighteenth- and Early Nineteenth-Century Furniture and Glass* (New York: By the council, 1929), cat. 605.

2. Copley subjects include: Mrs. Thomas Boylston and Mrs. Isaac Smith (Jules David Prown, *John Singleton Copley, 1738–1815* [Washington, D.C.: National Gallery of Art, 1965], pl. 4, fig. 40); Mrs. Sylvanus Bourne and Miss Mary Warner (Bishop, *Centuries and Styles of the American Chair*, figs. 214, 217); Mrs. Timothy Rogers, Mrs. James Russell, and Mrs. Ebenezer Austin (Barbara Neville Parker and Anne Bolling Wheeler, *John Singleton Copley: American Portraits in Oil, Pastel, and Miniature with Biographical Sketches* [Boston: Museum of Fine Arts, 1938], pls. 17, 71). Merchant Isaac Smith's personal estate was valued at almost £2,218 at his death in 1787; Isaac Smith estate inventory, 1787, Suffolk County Probate Court, Boston (microfilm, Downs collection).

3. For cost of stuffing materials, see Jonathan Bright accounts of Jacob Sanderson, 1801–2, 1803, Elijah Sanderson Papers, Peabody Essex Museum, Salem, Mass. Brown and Thayer bill to Paul Revere, 1798, Revere Family Papers, Massachusetts Historical Society, Boston. Ziphion Thayer bill to Mrs. Anne Doane, 1783, David Greenough Papers, Massachusetts Historical Society, Boston. Comparative furniture prices are given in Benjamin Frothingham bill to William Erving, 1788; Moses Grant bill to William Erving, 1788; Alexander Edward account of Grant Webster, 1772–93, Greenough papers, Massachusetts Historical Society, Boston; and George Bright bill to Caleb Davis, 1787, Caleb Davis Papers, Massachusetts Historical Society, Boston.

## 97 ◆ Settee

Boston, Massachusetts
1760–75

"Ingenious Fancy . . . devised The soft settee; one elbow at each end." Like the sofa, Cowper's settee appears to have evolved from the double-ended couch to which a back was added. The settee can be distinguished from the sofa by its smaller size, which is suitable for two or three people and generally not of sufficient length for reclining. Although an English settee-couch at Knole Park, Kent, is datable to the early seventeenth century, both the settee and sofa were rarities until late in the century when long stuffed seats, especially the settee, were considered essential to the well-appointed household, judging by the numbers that survive. The Knole settee-couch may in fact have been described only as a couch in its day, although the short length and fixed vertical wings of the frame would have made it awkward for the user to recline. From this low form resembling an expanded, closed-back farthingale chair, the settee was altered to a high-back seat before 1700 and

often constructed as a double chair with two back arches and, occasionally, as a triple chair. It is no surprise that some settees were made en suite with sets of chairs, all lavishly upholstered and trimmed. Many double-chair settees had wings and rolled arms like the easy chair.[1]

Wings and stuffed arms remained features of many settees into the eighteenth century, when the cabriole leg was introduced to the elongated seat at an early date in Britain. Plain pad and hooflike feet were eventually exchanged for carved claws. A London advertisement of 1716 attests to the popularity of the settee by that date. Only a few years later, an on-site sale of household goods belonging to the "Honourable Brigadier General Munden, Deceased" in suburban Egham outside London disposed of furnishings in the "Chints Bed-Chamber," consisting in part of "Six chairs needle-work backs, seats [with] cases" and "A settee ditto." The reference makes several important statements: costly needlework was often used lavishly by the well-to-do in England, a practice mimicked to some extent in the American

colonies; and placement of a settee in a bedroom furnished with back stools may have had its counterpart, on occasion, in the homes of prosperous Americans and resident English officials. In the "great Parlour" of the same house, two settees, six chairs, and two stools were fitted with "false cases," suggesting the furniture was all of a suite or made to appear so by using similar covers.[2]

The French taste in stuffed furniture began to prevail by midcentury, promoted by designers such as Thomas Chippendale. One of the manifestations of this influence was the introduction of high, stuffed arms to terminate the back curves of the long seats, such as found in the sofa of No. 98. Chippendale published a handsome sofa of this design, which also has a double-ogee–arched back similar to that illustrated here. Despite the fashionable crest, this settee is *retardataire* in retaining vertical scrolled arms and cutaway wings; however, the American craftsman who produced this settee and a mate at the Metropolitan Museum of Art was well versed in the principles of good design. An American six-leg settee of similar date with high-scrolled arms is, by comparison, boxy and considerably less graceful. The new arm design required a frame of sofa length to achieve the maximum effect.[3]

Aside from the small size of this settee and the well-designed back, distinctive features are the knee carving of the front legs—asymmetrical at the corner supports and symmetrical at the center leg—and the vigorous shaping of the claw feet. These embellishments, along with the flaring feet of the rear supports, link the settee with a small but distinctive group of Boston furniture dating to the 1760s and 1770s that consists of several dozen chairs, a card table, and the matching settee. A few chairs in the group have hairy paws in place of claw feet (see No. 58). The carved work and the splat design of some chairs relate closely to English prototypes known to have been owned in Boston at the time this furniture was produced (see No. 58, fig. 2).[4]

Recent study of the bare frame of the mate to this settee has indicated that the original outer cover (found as a fragment beneath a tack) was a yellow worsted. Decorative brass nailing accented the crest, wing faces, and base of the seat frame at the front and sides. A projecting lip at the upper rear crest edge, conforming to the profile of that element, is also part of this settee's design. The amount of time expended on this feature suggests its use was more than merely that of a wall bumper to protect fragile unbraced rear legs. Both settees were possibly intended to stand away from the wall within the open space of a room.[5]

Early references to the settee in America date to the 1750s when craftsmen in New York and Philadelphia advertised the form and an auction house in Boston offered a settee at a local vendue. Several craftsmen who made settees in the prewar years made note of their London backgrounds. Long, upholstered seats were fashionable as early as the late seventeenth century in the Boston area, although it is unlikely that these low-back forms resembling extended farthingale chairs were called anything but couches when purchased by the local elite. One such seat later came into the possession of William Bentley, a Salem antiquarian, who described the "settle" he purchased at an Appleton family auction as "not far from the form of those now used in our houses being stuffed in the back & seat as our Settees & Sophias are, only open between the seat & back." Caution is in order when interpreting settee references since the splat-back double-chair form was current from the late Queen Anne period

through the end of the eighteenth century, and Windsor seating had a settee component by the 1750s and 1760s.[6]

*NGE*

―――――――

**Construction:** (Frame upholstered; some commentary based on a structural description and photograph of mate settee without upholstery and on an X-ray examination of this settee.) The crest consists of two pieces of wood—a board with a serpentine top and a plain arch on the lower surface, the face chamfered at the upper edge, and a projecting rounded lip applied with nails to the crest edge at the upper back. The crest, like the stay rail at the lower back, is tenoned into the back stiles. Pieces applied to the outside upper corners of the stiles form the rear terminals of the flaring wings. A short central post tenoned into the crest and stay rail provides additional structural strength; the crest joint is secured with two nails. The wing stiles are dovetailed to the side rails. The arm stiles, to which the outer sections of the cones are nailed (probably), are joined to the side rails with large through tenons pinned twice from the inside surfaces. The seat frame is joined to the back stiles and front leg extensions with mortise and tenon. Triangular blocks at the inside corners, attached with four rosehead nails, are narrowly chamfered at the exposed edges. The center front and back legs are tenoned through the rails and double-pinned. Two concave, front-to-back seat braces flanking the center legs are dovetailed to the seat frame from the bottom and nailed. Upholsterer's peaks occur at the upper outside front corners of the seat frame. The squared rear corner legs are slim through the center and flared at the base. The center rear leg curves backward near the bottom. The brackets of the front legs are secured with two countersunk screws apiece. The claw feet have prominent knuckled toes continued into the ankles, accompanied by long nails and high-domed balls. The knee carving of the end legs forms an asymmetrical design; the central leg carving is symmetrical.

**Condition:** The center rear leg has either been repaired at the top or replaced, as indicated by a large round hole in the interior frame immediately above it, which is filled with glue. The right rear leg was cracked or broken and repaired with an internal metal rod or bolt. The seat-rail mortises in the left rear leg have been cut larger than necessary and plugged, probably indicating later repairs. In 1977 the outside rear feet were treated for dry rot and worm damage and repaired with epoxy, wood dust, and stain. The right end rail is cracked on the inside at the arm-stile joint. The dovetails of the seat braces have been reglued and renailed; a reinforcement strip has been glued to the top of the front rail above the dovetail of the left brace. The dovetails are somewhat damaged from upholstery tacks. The corner blocks have been reattached on one or more occasions. Holes in the leg bottoms indicate the supports were once fitted with glides.

**Dimensions:**

| | | |
|---|---|---|
| H. | 36 in. | 91.4 cm |
| H. (seat) | 16 1/4 in. | 41.3 cm |
| W. (wings) | 56 1/2 in. | 143.5 cm |
| W. (seat front) | 54 1/4 in. | 137.8 cm |
| W. (seat back) | 50 in. | 127.0 cm |
| W. (arms) | 57 1/4 in. | 145.4 cm |
| W. (feet) | 56 3/8 in. | 143.2 cm |
| D. (seat) | 22 5/8 in. | 57.5 cm |
| D. (feet) | 25 1/2 in. | 64.8 cm |

**Materials:** *Microanalysis:* Primary: mahogany. Secondary: soft maple group (rear legs, seat rail, medial brace); white pine (corner blocks). *Finish:* dark brown color in resin. *Upholstery:* white silk woven in a pattern of meandering vines and lacey bands and brocaded with intersecting diagonal rows of floral vines in shades of rose and blue tied with green bows; France, 1750–60.

**Exhibitions:** On loan from Miss Ella Parsons, Philadelphia, to the Pennsylvania Museum (now Philadelphia Museum of Art), 1929–32.

**Publications:** Downs, *American Furniture*, fig. 270. Nutting, *Furniture Treasury*, no. 1689. Mary Ellen Hayward Yehia, "Ornamental Carving on Boston Furniture of the Chippendale Style," in *Boston Furniture*, pp. 201–6, fig. 145. Elizabeth Bidwell Bates and Jonathan L. Fairbanks, *American Furniture: 1620 to the Present* (New York: Richard Marek Publishers, 1981), p. 158.

**Provenance:** Ex coll.: Miss Ella Parsons, Philadelphia.

**Accession history:** Purchased by H. F. du Pont from Joe Kindig, Jr., York, Pa., 1935. Bequest of H. F. du Pont, 1969.
59.1877

―――――――

1. William Cowper, *The Task* (London, 1784), bk. 1, p. 75, as quoted in *Oxford English Dictionary* (Oxford: Clarendon Press, 1931), 9:553. For the Knole Park and other settees, see Macquoid and Edwards, *Dictionary*, 3:70–98, figs. 1, 2, 5–24, 37, 38, 42, 50, pl. 3. Thornton, *Seventeenth-Century Interior Decoration*, pp. 210–17.

2. *London Gazette*, no. 5494 (1716) and *The Free-Thinker* 44 (1718; reprint 1733): 317, as quoted in *Oxford English Dictionary*, 9:553. General Munden estate inventory, 1726, Chancery Masters' Exhibits, Public Record Office, London.

3. Thomas Chippendale, *The Gentleman and Cabinet-Maker's Director* (3d ed.; London: By the author, 1762), pl. 62 top. For the settee with high arms, see Warren, *Bayou Bend*, no. 95.

4. For the matching Boston settee, see Heckscher, *American Furniture*, cat. no. 83.

5. Kathryn Gill, "Minimally Intrusive Upholstery Treatments: A Case Study Concerning an Eighteenth-Century American Settee," in *Conservation of Furnishing Textiles* (conference proceedings, Burrell Collection, Glasgow, Scot., March 30–31, 1990), pp. 7–13.

6. Forman, *American Seating Furniture*, cat. 49, p. 212, including Bentley quotation. Thomas Griggs, *New-York Mercury*, April 15, 1754; George Richey, *New-York Mercury*, July 30, 1759; [Rita Susswein Gottesman, comp.], *The Arts and Crafts in New York, 1726–1776: Advertisements and News Items from New York City Newspapers* (1938; reprint ed., New York: Da Capo Press, 1970), pp. 113, 137–38. Edward Weyman, *Pennsylvania Gazette* (Philadelphia), January 28, 1755, as quoted in Hornor, *Blue Book*, p. 153. Auction notice, *Boston Gazette*, December 12, 1757, as quoted in Dow, *Arts and Crafts in New England*, p. 116.

## 98 ◆ Sofa
Newport, Rhode Island
April 1812
Adam S. Coe

Late colonial American sofa design is rooted in the upholstered furniture of Restoration England, where tall settees shaped like double easy chairs were popular appointments in the households of prosperous citizens. Within a short period the verticality of the late seventeenth-century seat was modified: the back was lowered, the double-arch top was eliminated in favor of a continuous sweep across the crest, and the side wings were discarded, leaving only the low, rolled arms. Expanding the frame from a six- to an eight-leg form completed the shift from the vertical to the horizontal line. The longer length provided more seating space or permitted a single occupant to recline. Although the sofa was relatively common in Britain during the early eighteenth century, it was unusual in American households until well after 1750, and even then it remained the province of the well-to-do.[1]

The earliest references to sofas in advertisements of American craftsmen date to the 1760s. John Brower, a New York upholsterer, offered to stuff and cover "Sophas, Couches, Easy Chairs, French [open arm] Chairs, back stools, &c." in May 1765. In Philadelphia, John Webster, "Upholsterer from London," promised customers "work executed in the best and newest taste" in 1767; sofas were enumerated among his products. During the 1770s such notices appeared with increasing frequency, and sofas were acquired and owned by prominent citizens. John Cadwalader of Philadelphia contracted with Plunket Fleeson for the upholstery of a "large" sofa in October 1770, and only three months later upholstered three more frames acquired from Thomas Affleck. The presence of four upholstered sofas in the Cadwalader household is little short of extraordinary based on present knowledge of furnishings in American homes of the colonial period. Bostonian John Apthorp, Esq., who died in 1773, owned a large suite of furniture including ten chairs, four window curtains, a "large Sopha," and a small sofa accompanied by five chairs fashioned in the "Chinese Taste," all covered in "crimson Silk-Damask."[2]

This sofa is a rarity: few such seats are distinguished by having family histories, and fewer still are documented to their makers. Were it not for the documentation, the straight molded legs would associate the form with eastern Massachusetts in the late eighteenth century, but in fact the sofa was signed and dated by Adam S. Coe in Newport, Rhode Island, in 1812 (fig. 1). Coe also included the name of his client, merchant Edward Lawton. Coe was only thirty years of age when he framed this piece of furniture; his client was several years younger. Since Lawton married Mary Engs in May 1812, the sofa was likely purchased to furnish their new home. Given the availability of newer cabriole and square-back frames, selection of a Chippendale-style "camelback" frame represented a conscious customer choice. Even a late-style camelback sofa with tapered legs and spade (thermed) feet made for Thomas Shaw of New London, Connecticut, is documented to 1790.[3]

A second, fainter inscription, written in another hand and located on the crest face below the client's name, reads "B Hadwen/ of[?] Newport" followed by additional characters that *may* include the date 1812. Rhode Island census records first list a Benjamin Hadwen (Hadwin) of Newport in 1830. In 1840 and 1850 an individual of that name is listed in South Kingston, a township in Washington County across Narragansett Bay from Newport. The logical explanation for the appearance of Hadwin's name on the sofa frame is that he was the original or a later

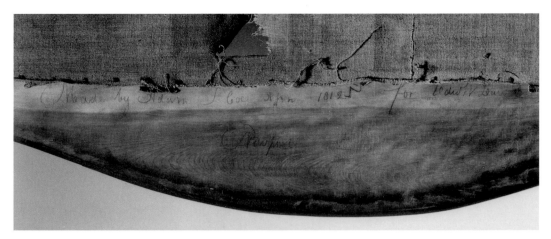

**Fig. 1.** Detail, maker's and other inscriptions.

upholsterer. The absence of his name from earlier documents may indicate that he was not yet head of a household. One further point of interest: a detail from an 1862 Rhode Island map based on earlier surveys pinpoints the locations of landholders in part of South Kingston (South Kingstown). A "B. Hadwin" occupied land east of Wakefield at a small coastal settlement called Narragansett Pier, a site providing good access to Newport by water.[4]

The geographic incidence of straight-leg New England camelback sofas is broad. A serpentine-top scroll-arm example with a curved front and molded legs is documented through a chalk inscription on the crest to John Harris (d. 1775) of Newburyport, Massachusetts. A nineteenth-century label further identifies the frame as descending in the Treadwell family from Gov. William Eustis (b. 1753) of Cambridge, Massachusetts. A serpentine-front sofa of similar profile, but

with plain, tapered legs, originally owned by Col. Daniel Putnam of Brooklyn, Connecticut, probably was purchased in New London or Norwich. Other furniture owned by Putnam, consisting of chairs and a pair of pembroke tables, is more closely associated with designs produced in Newport, Rhode Island. A second tapered-leg sofa, one with molded surfaces, is said to have descended from William Ellery, a Newport resident and signer of the Declaration of Independence for Rhode Island. Three sofas of two sizes (apparently representing an original matched set) with serpentine tops, straight fronts, and stop-fluted Marlborough legs, were once owned by Providence merchant John Brown, who is known to have made furniture purchases in Newport (see No. 47).[5]

The construction and upholstery methods employed in this sofa are typical of eighteenth-century practice. The back panels, arm panels, and bottom frame were built as four separate

units (fig. 2). Much of the framing is mortise and tenon, exceptions being the arm rolls, which are nailed in place, and the front-to-back seat struts, which are dovetailed. The range of fabrics available for use as finish covers on sofas was similar to that for easy chairs. The considerable depth of many eighteenth-century camelback sofas suggests that fitted seat cushions and accessory cushions stuffed with a soft material, such as down, were relatively common. Chippendale, who illustrated six sofas in the 1762 edition of the *Director*, recommended that "when made large" sofas should "have a Bolster and Pillow at each end, and Cushions at the Back." George Washington's green damask sofa was furnished with two cushions. Cushions and pillows are depicted in John Singleton Copley's 1771 portrait of an unidentified New York woman lounging on a floral-patterned damask-covered sofa. Given the vertical depth of the interior space of this sofa, it too was

**Fig. 2.** Frame disassembled and without upholstery.

likely fitted originally with a seat cushion and accessory pillows.[6]

NGE

---

**Inscriptions or marks:** *On front of crest rail:* "Made by Adam S Coe April 1812 for Edw W Law[ton]/ Newport" in red chalk. *On front of crest rail:* "B Hadwen/ of[?] Newport/ [?]" in pencil.

**Construction:** (Frame upholstered; some commentary based on a photograph of the bare frame.) The frame comprises four units: a serpentine-top back panel, two end panels with roll tops, and a long rectangular base. The chamfered crest, bottom rail, and three vertical stiles of the back panel are joined by mortise and tenon. The arm panels are framed with top rolls nailed between the forward and rear stiles. The stiles are tenoned into bottom rails. The triangular front pieces forming the forward sweeps of the arms probably are nailed to the front stiles and bottom rails. The seat rails are tenoned into the tops of the corner legs. The front seat rail is laminated across the center bulge. The inside frame corners are strengthened by four small triangular glueblocks. Embowed front-to-back seat braces, or struts, positioned at the intermediate legs are joined to the front and back rails with open dovetails. The intermediate back legs are double tenoned into the rails; the corresponding front legs are secured with rear tenons and open forward dovetails. All four rear legs flare backward and are canted on the forward surfaces. The end rear legs are chamfered on the inside forward corners; the center rear legs are chamfered on both forward corners. The forward faces of all the front legs and the outside faces of the end legs are molded in a serpentine profile with flanking beads. The slim rectangular stretchers are crowned on the top surface; all are tenoned into the adjacent members. The three units that compose the lengthwise medial stretchers are finished at the ends with projecting triangular points on the top surface to effect smooth transitions between crowned surfaces meeting at right angles. When the sofa is assembled, the back panel is positioned forward of the three vertical extensions located above the back rail and secured with screws. The end extensions are

part of the rear legs; the center extension is tenoned into the back rail. Long, round tenons (probably dowels) beneath the wing panels pierce the seat rails and are secured from below with key wedges. The panels were perhaps secured originally with bed bolts. The delicate tenons located near the bottom front probably served only to guide the panels into position. Where the back stiles of the side units are butted to the ends of the back panel, large screws are inserted from the back of the crest scrolls into the arm rolls to further secure the units.

**Condition:** The long, round tenon (dowel) and key wedge at the base of the right arm unit are replacements. The length of the tenon and that at the left end raises questions of originality, since the tips are clearly visible when the sofa is upholstered and assembled. The front rail is split for several inches on the inside face near the left end. The beaded corners of the end front legs have sustained damage and losses; the two center legs are patched on the lower left side. Nail holes mar the tops of all front legs. The second leg from the right was once braced at the upper back with an angle iron secured to the back face of the leg and the adjacent central strut. The left rear end leg has been broken and repaired with a new triangular piece spliced to the lower back. All the rear feet are chipped at the bottom on the back and side faces. The lack of extensive tacking on the frame may indicate that the sofa was originally finished in canvas to receive a slip cover. The substantial front-to-back taper of the arm rolls is probably more exaggerated than originally intended.

**Dimensions:**

| | | |
|---|---|---|
| H. | 41½ in. | 105.4 cm |
| H. (seat frame) | 14½ in. | 36.8 cm |
| W. (crest) | 91⅞ in. | 233.3 cm |
| W. (seat front) | 78½ in. | 199.4 cm |
| W. (seat back) | 77¾ in. | 197.5 cm |
| W. (arms) | 94 in. | 238.7 cm |
| W. (feet) | 78 in. | 198.1 cm |
| D. (seat) | 27¾ in. | 70.5 cm |
| D. (feet) | 26½ in. | 67.3 cm |

**Materials:** *Microanalysis:* Primary: mahogany. Secondary: birch (seat rails); cherry (seat braces);

white pine group (corner blocks). *Finish:* medium reddish brown color in resin; refinished. *Upholstery:* medium light green silk damask; Europe, 1700–1750.

**Publications:** Downs, *American Furniture*, fig. 276.

**Accession history:** Purchased by H. F. du Pont from John S. Walton, Inc., New York, 1951. Gift of H. F. du Pont, 1951.
51.33

---

1. Cescinsky, *English Furniture*, 1: figs. 40–52. Macquoid and Edwards, *Dictionary*, 3: pl. 3; 3:73–77, figs. 5, 7–16.

2. John Brower advertisement, *New-York Mercury*, May 20, 1765, as quoted in [Rita Susswein Gottesman, comp.], *The Arts and Crafts in New York, 1726–1776: Advertisements and News Items from New York City Newspapers* (1938; reprint ed., New York: Da Capo Press, 1970), p. 134; John Webster advertisement, *Pennsylvania Journal* (Philadelphia), August 20, 1767, as quoted in Alfred Coxe Prime, comp., *The Arts and Crafts in Philadelphia, Maryland, and South Carolina, 1721–1785: Gleanings from Newspapers* ([Topsfield, Mass.]: Wayside Press for the Walpole Society, 1929), pp. 214–15. Nicholas B. Wainwright, *Colonial Grandeur in Philadelphia: The House and Furniture of General John Cadwalader* (Philadelphia: Historical Society of Pennsylvania, 1964), pp. 40–42. The Apthorp sale is described in Dow, *Arts and Crafts in New England*, p. 126.

3. Downs, *American Furniture*, fig. 276. *New London County Furniture*, no. 94.

4. The map detail is reproduced in "Soldiers in King Philip's War," George M. Bodge, comp., *New England Historical and Genealogical Register* 40 (1886): facing p. 76.

5. For the Harris sofa, see John S. Walton advertisement, *Antiques* 81, no. 3 (March 1962): 240. Information about the Putnam sofa and other furnishings was transmitted to the author by Robert F. Trent; for the sofa, see *Connecticut Furniture*, no. 259. For the Ellery sofa, see Ginsburg and Levy advertisement, *Antiques* 87, no. 6 (June 1965): 639. One of the John Brown sofas is in the Rhode Island Historical Society, and 2 are still in private hands; see *John Brown House Loan Exhibition*, cats. 28, 29; Moses, *Master Craftsmen*, fig. 1.41.

6. Thomas Chippendale, *The Gentleman and Cabinet-Maker's Director* (3d ed.; London: By the author, 1762), pls. 29–31, 33, p. 4. Hornor, *Blue Book*, p. 152. For the Copley portrait, see Brock Jobe, "The Boston Upholstery Trade, 1700–1775," in Cooke, *Upholstery*, p. 64.

## 99 ◆ Couch
Portsmouth, New Hampshire
1765–90
Attributed to Robert Harrold (d. 1792)

This "double-headed," backless couch, which has close associations with Portsmouth, is perhaps unique among American furniture forms and is unknown in this size even in British furniture. Robert Harrold (d. 1792), an emigrant English craftsman and the probable maker of this long seat, likely based his design on that of a smaller, backless, English window stool with scroll ends dating from the third quarter of the eighteenth century. A form of the long, scroll-end seat was first introduced in England in the late seventeenth century. Designs for window stools, with and without a back and supported in part on two or three legs across the front, are included in Ince and Mayhew's 1762 furniture pattern book (fig. 1). The crucial feature that relates the Ince and Mayhew designs to the Portsmouth couch is the interior slope of the scroll ends at seat level. Although the stools are poorly delineated in the pattern book, there are clearly no tuckaways (crevices for the upholstery to pass through for tacking) separating the bed of the seat from the upright ends, or heads. The fabric line from scroll top to scroll top is continuous.[1]

During the early 1760s, Robert Sayer, a London map and print seller, also published closely related engravings for window stools in an anthology of furniture designs, which

appeared in several editions. William Ince and John Mayhew were among the leading furniture designers of the period who contributed drawings for the volume. Undoubtedly, they were responsible for the designs for the window seats, termed "French Stools" in both *Universal System of Houshold Furniture* and *Genteel Houshold Furniture in the Present Taste*.[2]

Photographs of several English window stools dating from the 1750s to the 1770s, with scroll ends sloping on the interior surface, are included in the Robert Wemyss Symonds Collection of Photographs in the Winterthur Library. A pair and a single example have cabriole legs terminated by scroll feet. Three related although longer examples with paneled legs at Paxton House, Berwickshire, Scotland, are securely attributed to Thomas Chippendale, Sr. (1718–79), and Thomas Chippendale, Jr. (1749–1822), who supplied much of the furniture for this country estate beginning in 1774. The "window seats" still stood in the dining room along with a suite of sideboard furniture with similar paneled legs when an inventory was made of the house in 1828.[3]

Aside from being inspired by an English design of limited execution and circulation, the Portsmouth couch is remarkable for its specialized function, that of supporting a lounging rather than a seated figure. The daybed, a single-ended version of the long seat made for lounging, was imported into or made in America from the late seventeenth century,

but it was found in small numbers and in affluent households where female occupants enjoyed some measure of leisure. By the time the Portsmouth couch was made, daybeds were out of fashion, and most had already been relegated to back rooms and garrets. The easy chair became the "lounge" of the elderly, sick, and infirm, and sofas could be made more comfortable with the addition of cushions, bolsters, and pillows. These accessories had long been popular in England and in France, which by the mid eighteenth century had a profound impact on English furniture design. Exotic foreign cultures also influenced household furnishings in affluent European circles. Turkish culture had some currency at midcentury and later and may have been the catalyst for renewed interest in lounging furniture fitted with stuffed accessories.

Mme de Pompadour had her bedroom at Bellevue decorated *à la turque* at midcentury, and in 1755 her portrait was painted in the costume of a sultana lounging on a low, cushioned platform, her back supported by a mound of draped pillows or bolsters. Aspects of the style appeared in England. Ince and Mayhew published a design for a "Turkish Soffa" in 1762, and as late as 1794, Thomas Sheraton produced a design for a "Turkey Sofa" set in an alcove. Most individuals of means furnished their homes with standard upholstered forms in the prevailing fashion (see No. 98), however, and added stuffed accessories to achieve greater comfort. The

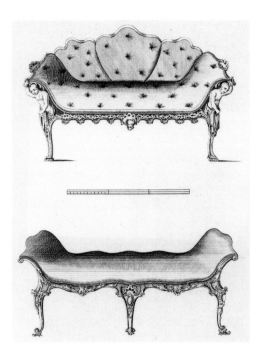

**Fig. 1.** From William Ince and John Mayhew, *The Universal System of Houshold Furniture* (London: Robert Sayer, 1762), pl. 61 bottom.

same interior slope found at the ends of this Portsmouth couch could be simulated with stuffed accessories used in any of several ways: a flat stack of square pillows or cushions of diminishing size from bottom to top; a cylindrical or quarter-round bolster covered by a pillow; or one or more upended pillows. No doubt the sofas in many American households were furnished in this manner in the second half of the eighteenth century.[4]

Harrold, the presumed maker of the Portsmouth couch, appears to have emigrated about 1765 from England, where he would have been exposed to a wide range of influences shaping furniture design. Harrold's arrival in Portsmouth coincides with the introduction of several new furniture forms and designs in the local market, including this double-headed couch. The cabinetmaker quickly secured the patronage of the royal governor of New Hampshire, Sir John Wentworth (1737–1820)—a testimony to his skills.[5]

The hand of Harrold is suggested by two construction techniques of English origin in the framework of the couch: open corner braces and blind-tenon stretcher-to-stretcher joints. Other features in the couch associated with Harrold are the use of short versus long scribe lines marking the cuts for the tenons and the boldly molded legs. The birch and white pine secondary woods of the couch identify it as an American product and point to a northern New England origin. A group of French-style chairs with upholstered seats and backs and open arms are also associated with Harrold through their construction features and design. Two that descended in the Wendell family have molded legs and casters identical to those in this couch.[6]

Family history and circumstantial evidence associate the Portsmouth couch with Jacob Wendell (1788–1865) of Portsmouth and his descendants. Wendell purchased his Pleasant Street house in 1815, and the furnishings remained relatively intact until their dispersal in 1988. How, when, or where the eighteenth-century furniture in the house was acquired remains a mystery. Some objects may have been purchased at auction. Inheritance may account for other acquisitions. Wendell's family tree includes members of several other prominent Portsmouth families. Perhaps the couch was originally owned by Sir John Wentworth, who fled the colony in 1775. Jacob Wendell's father, John, is reputed to have made several purchases at the sale of the governor's effects. Of these, a china table and a kettle stand, like the backless couch, are now ascribed to Harrold.[7]

*NGE*

---

**Inscriptions or marks:** *On the inner surface of a scrolled support:* "Reupholstered & repaired by John A. Stickney June 1 1887" in pencil.

**Construction:** The seat rails are tenoned into the tops of the corner legs and pinned; the inside legs are tenoned into the bottom surface of the seat rails. The inside corners of the seat frame are reinforced with open braces slotted into dovetails in the frame. The embowed front-to-back seat braces positioned above the intermediate legs are similarly framed. The slim, rectangular, front-to-back and longitudinal stretchers are crowned on the top surface. All are joined to their adjacent members with tenons. The tenons of the longitudinal stretchers are horizontal; the others are vertical. All exposed legs are molded on the outside surfaces in a serpentine profile; those at the four corners have a corner bead. The inner corners are chamfered (one chamfer on each corner leg, two on the inside legs). The original casters are attached by plates and screws to the bottoms of the legs. Above the seat frame, the front and rear panels of the scroll ends are tenoned into the seat rails and pinned. The projecting top scrolls are formed of half rolls set between the front and rear panels and nailed in place.

**Condition:** Before restoration in 1990, the frame was loose and several broken stretchers were repaired with metal straps and screws. The tops of all the corner legs were shattered by tacks used to secure successive changes of upholstery. Large, cut nails repaired the splits. One caster was replaced in the nineteenth century. In restoring the frame, the legs and stretchers were removed, and the joints, breaks, and cracks were reinforced with hot hide glue. Most of the original upholstery foundation— webbing, sackcloth, and stuffing of grass and curled horsehair—was intact. Two strips of webbing were missing, and the grass-stuffed linen rolls bordering the edges of the seat and scroll ends were torn in places. The foundation was stabilized and refurbished as needed.

**Dimensions:**

| | | |
|---|---|---|
| H. | 32³/₈ in. | 82.2 cm |
| H. (seat) | 15³/₄ in. | 40.0 cm |
| W. (seat rail) | 78 in. | 198.1 cm |
| W. (to scroll ends) | 90¹/₄ in. | 229.2 cm |
| W. (seat) | 30¹/₈ in. | 76.5 cm |

**Materials:** *Microanalysis:* Primary: mahogany. Secondary: birch (seat frame, braces, scroll frame); eastern white pine (scroll rolls). *Finish:* heavy, medium dark brown shellac of late nineteenth-century date over original resin. *Upholstery:* modern green silk damask.

**Publications:** Robert F. Trent, "The Wendell Couch," *Maine Antique Digest*, February 1991, pp. 34-D–37-D. Jobe, *Portsmouth Furniture*, pp. 338–40. Myrna Kaye and Brock Jobe, "Robert Harrold, Portsmouth Cabinetmaker," *Antiques* 143, no. 5 (May 1993): 780, pl. 10. Myrna Kaye, "Discovering Portsmouth, New Hampshire's Premier Cabinetmaker," *Maine Antique Digest*, July 1994, p. 3-B.

**Provenance:** Tradition of descent in the family of Jacob Wendell (1788–1865) of Portsmouth, N.H., until sent to auction in January 1989. (Sotheby Parke Bernet, "Important Americana" [January 26–28, 1989], lot 1445.)

**Accession history:** Museum purchase from Richard and Gloria Manney, New York, 1992, funds gift of the Henry Francis du Pont Collectors Circle. 92.103

1. An 1808 inventory of Temple Newsam describes a couch—which is part of a set of seating furniture that also contains 20 backstools and 4 settees and that was purchased from James Pascall of London for the Long Gallery at Temple Newsam, Leeds, Yorkshire, by Henry 7th Viscount Irwin in 1746—as "a large double headed couch with carved and gilt legs and stuffed and covered with fine needlework and 2 Bolsters." The reference documents the term used to describe this rare seating form. The set still has its original needlework covers, and the couch retains its cylindrical bolsters; see Christopher Gilbert, *Furniture at Temple Newsam House and Lotherton Hall: A Catalogue of the Leeds Collection*, 2 vols. (Leeds, Eng.: National Art-Collections Fund and the Leeds Art Collections Fund, 1978), 1:61–63. Representative examples of English scroll-end, backless seats from the seventeenth and eighteenth centuries are illustrated and discussed in Macquoid and Edwards, *Dictionary*, 2:139–42, figs. 10, 11, 13, 16, pl. 6; Ralph Edwards and Margaret Jourdain, *Georgian Cabinet-Makers, c. 1700–1800* (3d rev. ed., London: Country Life, 1955), pp. 44–47, pl. 45; Christopher Gilbert, *The Life and Work of Thomas Chippendale*, 2 vols. (New York: Macmillan Publishing Co., 1978), 2: fig. 58; Robert Wemyss Symonds Collection of Photographs, nos. 59.577, 59.1637, DAPC, Visual Resources Collection, Winterthur Library. William Ince and John Mayhew, *The Universal System of Houshold Furniture* (1762; reprint, Chicago: Quadrangle Books, 1960), pl. 61. Recent research brought to light the fact that Harrold made "2 Small Mahugony Coutchas With Castors" in 1767 for Gov. John Wentworth's pew in Queen's Chapel (now St. John's Church), Portsmouth. Thus, the cabinetmaker was familiar with the couch form, although the exact design of the governor's furniture is unknown; see Myrna Kaye, "Evidence from Robert Harrold's Hand, or Why I Write for M.A.D. and Read My Mail," *Maine Antique Digest*, August 1995, p. 6-B.

2. *Genteel Houshold Furniture in the Present Taste* (1764–65; reprint, East Ardley, Yorkshire, Eng.: EP Publishing, 1978), p. 10.

3. Symonds collection, nos. 59.793, 59.794, 59.1157; Gilbert, *Life and Work of Chippendale*, 1:268–70, 2: fig. 391. Chippendale probably supplied the window stools to Paxton in 1776.

4. Helena Hayward, ed., *World Furniture: An Illustrated History* (New York: McGraw-Hill Book Co., 1965), fig. 407; Ince and Mayhew, *Universal System*, pl. 65, p. 9; Thomas Sheraton, *The Cabinet-Maker and Upholsterer's Drawing-Book* (1793; reprint, New York: Dover Publications, 1972), pl. 52. Representative examples of long seats with stuffed accessories are in Macquoid and Edwards, *Dictionary*, 2:140–42, figs. 13, 16, pl. 6; 3:92–97, figs. 49, 51–54, 56–59, 61; Ince and Mayhew, *Universal System*, pl. 64.

5. Myrna Kaye and Brock Jobe, "Robert Harrold, Portsmouth Cabinetmaker," *Antiques* 143, no. 5 (May 1993): 776–83.

6. Kaye and Jobe, "Robert Harrold," pp. 776–83; Robert F. Trent, "The Wendell Couch," *Maine Antique Digest*, February 1991, pp. 34-D–37-D; Jobe, *Portsmouth Furniture*, pp. 335–40.

7. Jobe, *Portsmouth Furniture*, pp. 335–40; Gerald W. R. Ward and Karin E. Cullity, "The Wendell Family Furniture at Strawbery Banke Museum," in Luke Beckerdite, ed., *American Furniture 1993* (Milwaukee, Wis.: Chipstone Fndn., 1993), pp. 235–62.

## 100 ◆ Couch
### Coastal New England or Connecticut River valley
### 1730–70

The basic couch form—a long narrow seat with at least one end tall enough to provide a backrest—has existed since antiquity. This prominent article of ancient Greek and Roman household furniture was used for reclining at meals, resting during the day, and sleeping at night. Reintroduced in France in the Middle Ages as a simple double-headed bed, the design had been adopted by the English by the fifteenth century. English couches from the late Middle Ages were backless; conceptually, they were a bench with two outward slanting panelled ends fitted with cushions and pillows. By the early seventeenth century, the shape had become that of a broad Cromwellian-style armchair with hinged rests. Couches of this type were upholstered (seat, back, and rests) in leather, turkeywork, or assorted luxurious textiles. Not long after the restoration of the Stuart monarchy in 1660, a new design based on the French single-headboard *lit de repos* (literally, "bed of ease") appeared in England.[1] Conceptually, the new form was a contemporary side chair with an elongated seat frame, a basic shape that remained constant throughout the late seventeenth and early eighteenth centuries, although ongoing changes in taste were reflected in the details of the design.

Double-headed couches with hinged rests appear in American inventories in the late 1640s. America's introduction to the single-headed couch came with the importation of English cane seating furniture beginning late in the seventeenth century. The earliest examples—those with cane backs and bottoms—reached the colonies before 1688 and can be found listed in New England probate inventories by the mid 1690s.[2]

Boston upholsterer Thomas Fitch observed in 1707 that "Leather [armchair-style] couches are as much out of wear as steeple crown'd hats; cane [daybed-style] couches or others we make like them w^th a quilted pad are cheaper, more fash[ionable], easie & usefull," confirming that the daybed-style caned couch had already supplanted the upholstered armchair form in fashion-conscious urban centers. Ongoing importation of English cane furniture during the first three decades of the eighteenth century introduced new chair and couch designs to New England markets. One, based on Chinese models, featured a posture-conforming back described as a "crooked" back in contemporary accounts. One of the earliest references to this new shape appears in Fitch's accounts in a February 27, 1722/23, bill to Edmund Knight for "I doz crook'd back chairs" at £16.4.0. Other features introduced in the 1720s and 1730s include a yoke-shape crest rail, serpentine-shape stiles, a "banister" or baluster-shape splat, and "horsebone" or "crooked"—that is, cabriole—legs.[3] These motifs came to be associated with a style now commonly called "Queen Anne."

Between 1730 and the 1770s, at least two basic styles of couches with reclining backs were available contemporaneously. One featured the newly fashionable cabriole leg; the other, seen here, had the molded stiles and turned block-and-baluster base used on so-called Boston chairs. Leather-covered "Boston chairs" were made in quantity during the second quarter of the eighteenth century and were shipped by the thousands to cities on the Atlantic seaboard, to the West Indies, and even to inland centers such as Albany.[4]

This couch combines the turned base of the "Boston chair" with the newly fashionable crooked-back banister and yoke-shape crest. Although this blending of elements has, historically, been called *retardataire* or, at best, "transitional," it nevertheless represented a fashion preferred by numerous patrons. In joining earlier stylistic elements with more fashionable ones, chairmakers developed a design that enjoyed a long period of popularity, remaining available in seating furniture until late in the eighteenth century.

For the New Englander of means, owning a couch had both symbolic and practical implications. Even at the peak of fashion—in the first quarter of the eighteenth century—the

couch was never widely produced. Possession provided a concrete statement of the owner's prosperity. Couches generally were to be found in homes where the appraised value of the furnishings and apparel was more than £50. Most belonged to sea captains or prosperous merchants, but occasionally the form was owned by someone in one of the lucrative craft trades.[5] References in eighteenth-century probate inventories appear so infrequently that estimating the actual availability of the form is difficult, leading one perhaps to conclude that the form was not a widely popular one.

In eighteenth-century New England, couches generally were placed in a parlor or similar main floor room where they are presumed to have been used for resting during the day.[6] The adjustable backrest and thick, soft squab on the canvas seat afforded the user a heightened level of physical comfort. When they appear in inventories in a second- or third-floor chamber, they often are described as old and were of little value.

The design for this couch—with molded stiles, yoked crest, block-and-baluster–turned legs, and carved Spanish feet—is taken from a chair form popular throughout New England from about 1730 until almost the end of the century (see Nos. 3, 4). Its overall style and the peculiarities of its back construction are similar to a couch at Historic Deerfield.[7] On

both couches, although the back appears fixed as in a chair form, it is actually fashioned in such a manner to allow the back to recline. The crest rail lifts up and off tenons at the top of the stiles; the entire inner back unit—crest rail, inner stiles, banister (splat), and base rail—pivots on round tenons set in horizontal slots cut in the inner face of the stiles. The design of the turned leg and carved foot is especially unusual in that the top of the leg joins the seat rail with a block, and the block at the top of the foot is barely three quarters of an inch deep.

Although an early date often is given to this design, the chair form on which it was based was made almost until the end of the century. Hence, the couch could date as late as the 1760s or 1770s. Assigning a specific regional origin is difficult without documentary evidence because this chair design was produced throughout New England during the period.[8]

*NER with WAC*

---

**Inscriptions or marks:** *On the upper block of each turned leg:* small circular punches (●) numbering 1–6, running sequentially from front to back. *On left side rail at the front end:* similar double circle punch mark (●●).

**Construction:** The back, serpentine in profile, is adjustable by lifting the crest up and off the

tenons on the outside posts. The inner unit pivots on round tenons set into a long oval slot in the stiles. On the posts, the stiles above the rear seat rail are molded on the front and are flat behind. The rear legs are tapered below the stretchers on the front and back. The Spanish feet are carved from solid wood. The crest rail, chamfered on the upper back edge, is pegged to the inner stiles and splat. A rectangular bottom rail, ogee-molded on the front and chamfered on the back on either side of the inner stiles, has round tenons that slot into oval mortises in the inner face of the stiles. The splat is chamfered on the back. The seat rails are mortised and tenoned and pegged at all joints. A modern transverse brace is double pegged to the frame between the intermediate legs. All the stretchers are turned except the rear stretcher, which is rectangular. A modern linen and muslin sacking, blind tacked to the frame, supports a loose cushion.

**Condition:** The transverse brace is modern. The entire frame appears to have been apart and repegged. A line of tack holes on the underside of all seat rails suggests that the couch once was upholstered over the rails.

**Dimensions:**

| | | |
|---|---|---|
| H. | 40 1/2 in. | 102.9 cm |
| H. (seat) | 15 3/4 in. | 40.0 cm |
| W. (seat front) | 21 15/16 in. | 55.7 cm |
| W. (feet) | 22 7/16 in. | 57.0 cm |
| D. (seat) | 61 3/8 in. | 155.9 cm |
| D. (feet) | 62 1/8 in. | 157.8 cm |

**Materials:** *Microanalysis:* Primary: hard maple group. Secondary: tulip-poplar (replacement medial brace). *Finish:* surface has been heavily cleaned.

**Publications:** Downs, *American Furniture*, fig. 210.

**Accession history:** Purchased by H. F. du Pont from Harry Arons, Ansonia, Conn., 1947. Bequest of H. F. du Pont, 1969.
58.1509

1. Thornton, *Seventeenth-Century Interior Decoration*, p. 172; Macquoid and Edwards, *Dictionary*, 2:135–36, figs. 1, 3, pl. 5; Benno Forman cites an early reference to caned couches in London in the 1676/77 probate inventory of Capt. Francis Digby who owned "12 cane chairs with 12 cushions and backs of Damask" valued at £5 and "one couch and Squab of the same" worth £3.10 (Forman, *American Seating Furniture*, p. 248).

2. Forman, *American Seating Furniture*, pp. 210–11. The earliest known mention of a cane couch in America appears in the September 9, 1688, inventory of New York merchant Francis Richardson; and another is recorded in the 1695 inventory of merchant Capt. Andrew Cratey, of Marblehead, Mass. (formerly from London); see Forman, *American Seating Furniture*, p. 248. Sir William Phips's inventory, taken in Boston in 1696, lists "in the Hall, 12 cane chaires and 1 couch, £7" (Lyon, *Colonial Furniture*, p. 154). See David F. Wood, *The Concord Museum: Decorative Arts from a New England Collection* (Concord, Mass.: By the museum, 1996), pp. 59–61.

3. Thomas Fitch letterbook, April 22, 1707, American Antiquarian Society, as quoted in Jobe and Kaye, *New England Furniture*, p. 317. Fitch account book, Massachusetts Historical Society, Boston, as quoted in Forman, *American Seating Furniture*, p. 285. The accounts kept by Boston upholsterer Samuel Grant provide contemporary names for various features. An April 29, 1732, bill to John Beck included "8 Leathr Chairs horsebone feet & banist[er] backs" (see Brock Jobe, "The Boston Furniture Industry, 1720–1740," in *Boston Furniture*, p. 43). The term "horsebone" appeared in Grant's accounts on October 14, 1729; Grant used the term "crooked" in an August 16, 1739, entry. The designation "crooked" continued to be used until the late eighteenth century; see Jobe and Kaye *New England Furniture*, p. 185n. Entries for "chairs with crooked legs" appeared in the 1772 and 1786 Philadelphia price books.

4. Monkhouse and Michie, *American Furniture*, p. 153; see also Richard H. Randall, Jr., "Boston Chairs," *Old-Time New England* 54 (Summer 1963): 13; and Norman S. Rice, *New York Furniture before 1840 in the Collection of the Albany Institute of History and Art* (Albany, N.Y.: Albany Institute of History and Art, 1962), p. 20.

5. Examples from Suffolk County include Boston mason John Decosta, whose March 12, 1774, inventory listed more than £52 worth of household furnishings, and Boston "singlewoman" Mary Grice, who, according to her June 4, 1774, inventory, owned furnishings and apparel valued at £76.7.2; see Alice Hanson Jones, *American Colonial Wealth: Documents and Methods*, 3 vols. (New York: Arno Press, 1977), pp. 914–15, 931–33.

6. Cummings, *Rural Household Inventories*, pp. 120, 235.

7. Nutting, *Furniture Treasury*, no. 2101; Greenlaw, *New England Furniture*, no. 41; and Fales, *Furniture of Historic Deerfield*, nos. 52, 53, 55, 56; the similar Deerfield couch is no. 54.

8. Documented examples have been attributed to several Connecticut towns, the Connecticut River valley, eastern Massachusetts, Rhode Island, and New Hampshire; see Monkhouse and Michie, *American Furniture*, p. 155 n. 2.

## 101 ◆ Couch
### Probably Massachusetts or Rhode Island
### 1730–60

In his 1753 London imprint, *The Analysis of Beauty*, William Hogarth referred to the cyma, or reverse curve, as "the line of beauty"; American artisans used the slightly less elegant term "crook'd" to describe this serpentine signature of the Queen Anne and Chippendale styles. As can be clearly seen in this New England couch, the craftsmen who created it used this S-shape line in every surface plane he was working in, from the turned stretchers to the carved cabriole legs, the shaped seat rails, the curved stiles, shaped baluster splat, yoked crest rail, and scrolled tops of the stiles.

While No. 100 could well have been made at the same date, this couch represents the ultimate New England form.[1] Closely following the designs of new-fashion contemporary chairs, elongated chairs with movable, reclining backs were undoubtedly also being produced in the shops of chairmakers. Although this eighteenth-century form does not survive in great quantity, it would appear just from the number of related couches of this specific design that the form experienced its greatest popularity with the creation of the ultimate Queen Anne couch. Despite the availability of mahogany in urban areas, most New England couches are made of native woods. Surviving examples suggest that black walnut was the most desired wood (perhaps in coastal urban areas), although couches made of maple and cherry are also known.

This couch with double stiles in the back is related to at least five other similar examples, three of which (at Chipstone Foundation, Art Institute of Chicago, and Henry Ford Museum and Greenfield Village) are made of walnut and two (Museum of Fine Arts, Boston, and Metropolitan Museum of Art) are made of maple.[2] Comparison of design and construction details indicates that no two are identical, although they do share several design features, including the general outline of the crest, banister back, cabriole front and intermediate legs, and the chamfered rear legs. The preference seems to have been for seats with "shaped" rather than plain rails, even though the addition of this work would have made the couch more costly. The Winterthur, Art Institute of Chicago, and Chipstone couches all have seat rails cut with a lively pattern of opposing cyma curves joined by pendent half-circles. The skirt on the couch in the Museum of Fine Arts, Boston, is cut in a cyma–cyma-reverse shape at the front and sides, while the example at Greenfield Village employs a flat arch. The Metropolitan Museum of Art couch varies the most in its design, having plain seat rails; outer stiles that terminate in turned, flattened ball finials; and outer stiles that are more dramatically shaped than the coordinate inner ones. The rails on all of these couches are roughly rectangular in section, cut with either a shallow rabbet for sacking or a deeper one for a slip seat. The Winterthur and Chipstone couches also have a scratch bead on the upper face of the rail.

The variations in the construction details of the couches related to this couch indicate that the form was made in more than one locality and in more than one shop. The chair design on which these couches are based was popular in both Massachusetts and Rhode Island in the mid eighteenth century. Hence, without a firm provenance, a precise attribution is difficult since nothing in the design, construction, or choice of materials is area specific.

*NER with WAC*

**Inscriptions or marks:** *Stamped, in right rear knee block and adjacent rail:* "X".

**Construction:** The adjustable back is spoon-shape in profile. On the stiles, the flat volutes are pieced.

The stiles are flat on the front and stop-chamfered on the back; the rear legs are chamfered on four edges between the rail and the stretcher and on the front edges only below the stretchers. On the back unit, extensions of the crest rail (beveled on the back) lap into dovetail-shape notches on the back of the stiles. The rectangular stiles are pegged to the crest and to the shoe-shape base rail, which is attached to the posts on round tenons, allowing the back to pivot. The broad splat is chamfered on the back edges. The rectangular seat rails are tenoned and double-pegged to the rear and front legs. The intermediate legs are tenoned and double-pegged to the rails(?) All the rails including the rear rail are shaped on the lower edge. The rails have a decorative scratch bead on the upper outside edge; the inner edge is cut in a very shallow rabbet to house the canvas bottom. Saddle-shape transverse braces are tenoned to the rails above the intermediate legs. The cross stretchers are tenoned and pegged to the legs; the axial stretchers are round tenoned to the cross stretchers. The knee blocks are glued in place.

**Condition:** The couch has been refinished, although traces of a dark stain still are visible. The piece has

been apart, and many of the pegs are replaced. The shoe holding the splat is repaired. The left rear leg is repaired at the foot. The back left cabriole leg has been heavily repaired. Many of the knee brackets are replacements; all have been reglued. There are a series of filled peg holes and rectangular patches on the outside surface of the side rails, although neither set of holes extends through the rails. Both sets of holes are placed symmetrically on each side and match side to side. There once was a transverse brace (now missing) let into the top of the side rails between the intermediate legs. The couch now has a fabric sacking stitched to a 4" linen border mitered at the corners. The cushion and thin seat pad are covered in a late eighteenth-century canvaswork embroidery.

**Dimensions:**

| | | |
|---|---|---|
| H. | 38 in. | 96.5 cm |
| H. (seat) | 15 5/8 in. | 39.8 cm |
| W. (crest) | 23 3/4 in. | 60.3 cm |
| W. (seat front) | 21 3/4 in. | 55.2 cm |
| W. (feet) | 23 1/2 in. | 59.7 cm |
| D. (seat) | 63 in. | 160.0 cm |
| D. (feet) | 64 in. | 162.6 cm |

**Materials:** *Microanalysis:* Primary: American black walnut. Secondary: soft maple group (transverse braces). *Finish:* natural resin.

**Publications:** Downs, *American Furniture,* fig. 212.

**Accession history:** Bequest of H. F. du Pont, 1969. 58.2223

1. *Connecticut Furniture,* pp. 140–41, no. 255, illustrates a couch that combines a back like that in No. 101 with legs and stretchers similar to those in No. 100, clearly demonstrating the contemporaneous usage of various design elements and suggesting that the combinations might well have been patron driven.

2. Rodriguez Roque, *American Furniture,* no. 90; *The Antiquarian Society of the Art Institute of Chicago: The First Hundred Years* (Chicago: By the institute, 1977), no. 42; Katharine Bryant Hagler, *American Queen Anne Furniture, 1720–1755* (Dearborn, Mich.: Henry Ford Museum and Greenfield Village, 1976), p. 20; Randall, *American Furniture,* no. 190. The construction of the frame of the MFA, Boston, couch differs from the others. The rails are not joined to the front legs in the standard manner. Rather, the legs are tenoned into blocks reinforcing the join of the rails. Heckscher, *American Furniture,* cat. no. 65, pp. 113–14.

## 102 ◆ Couch

Possibly Connecticut or Connecticut
River valley
1740–90

Although closely related to No. 101, this
cherry couch, a less frequently seen variant
with scrolled stiles, differs primarily in the
configuration of the back, which has only
single stiles framing the splat and crest. This
couch is one of a small group of similarly
designed eight-leg couches fabricated in native
woods. It is related, though not identical, to
a beech couch formerly in the collection of
Henry W. Erving, and the two share several
construction peculiarities.[1] Unlike most
surviving Queen Anne couches, the backs
have a single set of stiles, which end in a flat
scroll. The adjustable backrest pivots on round
tenons attaching the shoe-shape base rail to
the stiles. Flat tenons at the ends of the crest
rail fit into cutouts on the back of the stiles.
The Winterthur couch has two saddle-shape
medial braces dovetailed to the side rails above
the legs. The seat rails once were cut with a

deep rabbet to hold a loose seat. Now a linen
sacking tacked to filling strips in the rabbet
supports the squab. The Erving couch appears
to have the same seat-frame construction,
although the braces and the loose seat are
missing in the photograph. Both have
scalloped skirt rails and swelled stretchers.

Another New England couch with single
stiles is less closely allied. Made of maple, it
is in the collection at Colonial Williamsburg.[2]
Unlike the Winterthur and Erving examples,
its stiles scroll to the rear rather than to the
side. Other variations in design include a fixed
banister back and straight seat rails.

In the absence of specific documentation,
attribution to a locale often is based on the
choice of materials and on regional preferences
in design and construction. Use of a native
timber rather than a more expensive imported
variety as the primary wood traditionally has
suggested manufacture away from the coastal
urban centers. Cherry, used here, often is
linked to a Connecticut or Connecticut River
valley provenance. Readily available in the

eighteenth century throughout the eastern half
of the United States, cherry was prized as an
easily worked, straight-grained hardwood that
could be finished smoothly to an attractive
red color or stained to simulate mahogany.
Also supporting a possible attribution to
Connecticut are such design features as the
shape of the banister and the profile of the
sharp cabriole legs, which appear on a group
of Connecticut chairs (see No. 20).[3]

*NER with WAC*

Inscriptions or marks: *On rear transverse brace:*
"321/ 210" in modern blue crayon.

Construction: The adjustable back, spoon-shape in
profile, was originally held by a chain through the
back posts (and is now secured with a modern cord).
The stiles are flat on both the front and back; the
rear legs rake backward below the stretcher. The
ends of the crest rail, flat on the back, terminate
in tenons that half lap into the stiles. The shoe is
integral with the base rail, which pivots on round
tenons. The splat, chamfered on the rear side at
outer edges, is tenoned to the base and crest rails

and held with four tiny wood pins at the top and bottom. The side seat rails, fillet-molded on the upper outside edge and originally cut with a deep rabbet on the inside, are tenoned and double-pegged to each corner leg. The end rails are tenoned and single-pegged. The intermediate legs are tenoned and double-pegged to the rails. Saddle-shape transverse braces are dovetailed to the rails above the intermediate legs. The knee blocks are nailed to the leg and rail.

**Condition:** Remnants of an old dark stain are still visible. A repair to the lower back of the splat is double-pegged. The transverse braces appear to be replacements. The couch once had a slip seat. Tacking strips have been pieced into the deep rabbet in the rails, and modern webbing now supports a wool and canvas sacking and a loose cushion covered in an eighteenth-century lace-appliquéd gold wool. Setting-out lines for the placement of the seat rails are still visible on the outside of the back posts.

**Dimensions:**

| | | |
|---|---|---|
| H. | 38$7/8$ in. | 96.2 cm |
| H. (seat) | 16$3/8$ in. | 41.6 cm |
| W. (seat front) | 21$1/2$ in. | 54.6 cm |
| W. (feet) | 23$1/4$ in. | 59.1 cm |
| D. (seat) | 62$1/2$ in. | 158.8 cm |
| D. (feet) | 64$1/4$ in. | 163.2 cm |

**Materials:** *Microanalysis:* Primary: cherry. Secondary: soft maple group (replacement transverse braces). *Finish:* natural resin.

**Publications:** Nutting, *Furniture Treasury*, no. 1608.

**Provenance:** Ex coll.: Edward F. Sanderson, Nantucket, Mass. Purchased by Collings and Collings, New York.

**Accession history:** Purchased by H. F. du Pont from Collings and Collings, New York, 1928. Bequest of H. F. du Pont, 1969.
66.777

---

1. Nutting, *Furniture Treasury*, no. 1601. Its present location is unknown.

2. Greenlaw, *New England Furniture*, no. 87.

3. Richard J. Preston, Jr., *North American Trees* (3d ed., Ames: Iowa State University Press, 1976), p. 261; Samuel J. Record and Robert W. Hess, *Timbers of the New World* (1943; reprint, Salem, N.H.: Ayer Co. Publishers, 1986), p. 452. For the Connecticut chairs, see Bishop, *Centuries and Styles of the American Chair*, fig. 80; Heckscher, *American Furniture*, cat. no. 5; *Great River*, cat. 119.

# Bedsteads

AS THE CENTERPIECE FOR THE PRIMARY EVENTS in life—birth, marriage, and death—the fully dressed bed was among the most important articles of furniture in a wealthy eighteenth-century household. Its size alone made it the principle focus in the room; more significant, it was often the highest valued item in an inventory. The bed "furniture," as the hangings were described in the period, was so important that frequently in advertisements and inventories the color and type of textiles defined the bed; for instance, "a fine Chints bed," "a fashionable yellow Camblet Bed lin'd with Satten," and "handsome red Harrateen-Bed."[1] The quality and cost of these textiles made the completely dressed bed a symbol of wealth and position, but they functioned more practically as well. They kept out cold drafts, conserved warmth in underheated rooms, and offered a degree of privacy in chambers that may have housed more than one bedstead or served as a passage to another room.

The actual piece of furniture consisted of two main parts—the "bed," a stuffed tick-covered sack or mattress on which one slept, and the "bedstead," a frame that supported the mattress off the floor. The two parts generally are listed separately in both English and American eighteenth-century inventories. This separation acknowledged the different artisans (upholsterers and cabinetmakers) involved in their manufacture as well as the relative cost to produce each part. The mattress was the more expensive part, often appraised at several times the value assigned to the frame. By the end of the eighteenth century, the term *bed* came to be used to identify both the mattress and the frame. Thomas Sheraton, in *The Cabinet Dictionary*, noted that "bed, taken in a general sense, includes the bedstead and other necessary articles incident to this most useful article of furniture."[2]

Eighteenth-century bedsteads were of three basic types, generally termed in the period *low-post*, *high-* or *four-post*, and *press*. The simplest, or low-post, form was a frame with rails mortised and tenoned into four low corner posts. The second type extended the corner posts into pillars, or high posts, that supported a tester frame and cornice from which was hung the "furniture." The press bedstead, or turn-up bedstead, had hinged side rails that allowed the lower two-thirds of the frame to fold up beneath an abbreviated tester frame.

The high-, or four-post, form survives in the greatest numbers from the eighteenth century. Its antecedents are the sleeping furniture of the sixteenth century, which grafted heavy corner pillars, a tall headboard, and a solid tester to the low, boxlike bedstead surrounded by draperies used during the Middle Ages. In the seventeenth century, these heavy bed frames were replaced by tall, slender posts supporting a flat, fabric-covered tester that usually was surrounded by a boldly molded or scrolled cornice. As the overall bulk of the frame diminished over time, the elaboration of the hangings seemed to increase. By the end of the century, the best beds in fashionable English households were lavishly dressed in a style inspired by the designs of Daniel Marot, a Huguenot architect and designer to Louis XIV and later to the court of William of Orange.[3] These richly draped bedsteads featured the artistry of the upholsterer more than the craft of the cabinetmaker.

During the first half of the eighteenth century, English furniture design reflected the dual influence of classical architecture, as espoused by Lord Burlington and William Kent, and contemporary French decorative designs in the style that now is called *rococo*. Beginning in the 1750s, publication of pattern books illustrating furniture in the rococo (or *modern* as it was then termed), Chinese, and Gothic tastes fostered the dissemination of these designs to English and American audiences.

Most pattern books were intended as guides for practicing craftsmen. They offered a range of patterns including designs for elaborate "state" beds, high-post bedsteads with full draperies, smaller canopied beds, folding beds, and other furniture forms (seating furniture, tables, and case pieces) that could be transformed into beds. American craftsmen replicated few of these designs exactly. New England craftsmen tended to borrow details selectively. This was especially true of the published patterns for bedsteads, many of which were deemed too elaborate for wide consumption in the relatively conservative, less aristocratic American market.

The standard bedstead, whether high- or low-post, generally was held together with bed screws, although some were secured with ropes. Interlaced cord, threaded through holes in the rails, was the least expensive support system for a mattress and bedding. A more costly treatment employed a sacking bottom held on turned pegs set in the rails. The typical sacking bottom consisted of a large, rectangular piece of linen or canvas edged with hand-sewn grommets that was laced with cords to the turned pegs on the rails or to narrow strips of linen or canvas which, in turn, were nailed along the rails of the bedstead.[4] Supporting narrow wooden slats, or lath, was a third construction method, although it was never as popular in America as it was in eighteenth-century England.

Fitting out a bedstead with appropriate bedding and hangings represented a major expense. Bedding was multilayered, consisting of a mattress, bed, sheets, blanket, bolster and pillow, and bedcover (or "counterpin," "coverlid," or "quilt," as it was called in the eighteenth century). The mattress, a canvas or linen sack stuffed with coarse materials such as straw, chopped wool flock, or marsh grass, lay directly on the sacking or the laced cord. Tufting prevented the filling from shifting. A thick, dome-shape bed of linen ticking filled with curled animal hair or feathers rested on the mattress. Forty to fifty pounds of feathers were needed for each bed with another twenty to thirty pounds for the bolster and two pillows. Most beds had sheets as well as pillow and bolster cases in fine linen or in soft but coarser tow, a cloth woven from the short and broken fibers of flax and hemp.[5] One or two wool blankets and a bedcover completed the assemblage. Wealthier households had more or better bedding, but the essential components remained the same.

The hangings completed the fittings for a fully dressed, high-post bedstead. Depending on the particular design, a complete set of hangings could include the following: two to six curtains (wide enough to enclose the bedstead fully and long enough to reach almost to the floor), outer and inner valances, a head cloth, tester, bedcover, and bases (skirt valances). This would require from forty to sixty yards of expensive imported textiles, substantiating the extraordinary value of beds in estate inventories of the period. Boston upholsterer Samuel Grant used "43 yards of cheney, 108 yards of binding, and 45 yards of braid" as well as an unspecified amount of buckram—a coarse, stiff linen—as a lining material when making a "Yellow bed" (without counterpane) for Samuel Ballard, a Boston bookkeeper. Purchases of the articles and hardware necessary to complete and hang the furniture included lining material; decorative trims; thread, tapes, and metal curtain rings; metal or wooden cornice rods; and pulleys, hooks, bed cords, and cloak pins. The absence of high posts did not preclude the use of bed hangings to enclose a low-post bedstead. Alternative methods of suspending the hangings from the ceiling were devised using hooks, rods, and cords, occasionally enclosed by a cornice molding attached to the ceiling. In 1830 Ellen Rollins described the "best room" in her grandparents' New Hampshire house, remarking that the "most noticeable of its furnishings was the bed, more for show than for use. It was a tall structure, built up of corn-husks and feathers, . . . Its blue and white checked canopy, edged with knotted fringe, suspended by hooks from the ceiling, was spun and dyed and woven by the women of the household."[6]

Few sets of American eighteenth-century bed furniture survive intact, although a variety of individual sections of valances, curtains, bases, and bedcovers are known. The crewel bed hangings made by Mary Bullman in York, Maine, about 1745, now owned by the Old Gaol Museum in York, are a rare exception. American eighteenth-century bed furniture was fashioned in serge, cheyney, harateen, camblet, calico, chintz, plate-printed cottons, and cotton checks; the most popular colors were red or crimson, yellow, green, and "blew."[7] The inclusion of both worsted and cotton fabrics suggests that most well-appointed New England households had both winter and summer bed dressings.

In great English houses, specialized room use is a product of the late sixteenth century. Until that time, bedsteads could be found in almost any room. In the seventeenth and eighteenth centuries, principal bedchambers in fashionable English homes served not only as areas for sleeping but also as reception rooms, where owners entertained family and close friends while completing their daily toilette.

Fashion-conscious Americans tended to pattern their behavior on English practice, and diaries as well as inventories document the inclusion of bedsteads in parlors and other first-floor rooms well into the eighteenth century in urban areas and into the early nineteenth century in some households in rural New England. In 1771 John Adams was startled still to find a "dining Room . . . crouded with a Bed and a Cradle, &c. &c." when he visited the Middletown, Connecticut, home of Dr. Eliot Rawson. This Connecticut doctor was an exception, however—by the third quarter of the eighteenth century, bedsteads were found primarily in chambers and garrets.[8]

Beds survive in fewer numbers proportionately than other eighteenth-century furniture forms. Clues to regional preferences in design and to contemporary designations for forms come largely from documentary evidence found in wills and probate inventories, craftsmen's account books, and cabinetmakers' price books. The earliest-known American furniture price book, the 1756 Providence, Rhode Island, "Rule and Price of Joyners Work," lists three styles of sleeping forms: "Beadsted with Long Posts @ £9"; "Palet beadsteds @ £14"; and "Trundel Beadsted @ £8." The precise identification of the "palet beadsted" as used in this price book is unclear. Contemporary sources define pallets as squares of ticking or canvas filled with straw, the type of sleeping accommodation usually given to servants. The meager value generally assigned to the form in eighteenth-century inventories indicates that it was probably the crudest bed frame in the house. However, the cost assigned in this price book is higher than that of the standard high-post bedstead, suggesting a more elaborate or more labor-intensive form. Listings for pallet bedsteads do not appear in any subsequent American or English price books. A revised schedule, issued the following year, repeated the three types (each costing £2 to £4 more) and added a "Palet Beadsted with Loe Posts @ £10." Two other eighteenth-century New England furniture price books are known: the Hartford Society of Cabinetmakers' price list printed in 1792 and the 1796 Hatfield, Massachusetts, cabinetmakers' agreement.[9] The Hartford price book lists the greatest variety of forms: plain cord, high-post, field and child's bedsteads, and bedsteads "to turn up against the wall," all with several decorative options.

Five of the eighteenth-century New England bedsteads in Winterthur's collection are of the high-post form, one is a diminutive, arched canopy field bedstead, and another is an unusual "press" bedstead that folds into the guise of a case of drawers. They exhibit a variety of faceted and fluted rectangular posts and architecturally inspired turned and carved columnar pillars set on cabriole and Marlborough legs. The collection illustrates the two types of mattress support most popular in the eighteenth century: cording and canvas sacking. Although most of the New England high-post beds at Winterthur were fitted with sacking, there is one New England rope bedstead (No. 106). One bedstead originally had narrow strips for sacking nailed to the rails (No. 104); the sacking was attached to turned pegs on the others. The press bedstead is the only example that retains its original sacking bottom.

*NER/WAC*

---

[1] Dow, *Arts and Crafts in New England*, pp. 108, 110, 121.

[2] Thomas Sheraton, *The Cabinet Dictionary* (1803; reprint in 2 vols., New York: Praeger Publishers, 1970), 1:42.

[3] [Daniel Marot], *Werken van D. Marot, Opperboumeester van Zyne Majiesteit Willem den Derden Konig van Groot Britanje* (Amsterdam, [1707]).

[4] Brock Jobe, "The Boston Upholstery Trade, 1700–1775," in Cooke, *Upholstery*, pp. 75, 77, fig. 53.

[5] Jobe, "Boston Upholstery Trade," pp. 75, 77, fig. 54. Pamela Clabburn, *The National Trust Book of Furnishing Textiles* (London: Viking Press in association with the National Trust, 1988), p. 255.

[6] On Grant, see Jobe, "Boston Upholstery Trade," p. 76. For alternative suspension methods, see Abbott Lowell Cummings, comp., *Bed Hangings: A Treatise on Fabrics and Styles in the Curtaining of Beds, 1650–1850* (Boston: Society for the Preservation of New England Antiquities, 1961), fig. 22; William Voss Elder III, *Maryland Period Rooms* (Baltimore: Baltimore Museum of Art, 1987), p. 7; Jane C. Nylander, *Our Own Snug Fireside: Images of the New England Home, 1760–1860* (New York: Alfred A. Knopf, 1993), p. 252.

[7] For the Bullman hangings, see Elizabeth Bidwell Bates and Jonathan L. Fairbanks, *American Furniture: 1620 to the Present* (New York: Richard Marek Publishers, 1981), p. 111. List developed from newspaper advertisements and Suffolk County (Massachusetts) probate inventories, 1725–75. See Dow, *Arts and Crafts in New England*, pp. 170–72; Cummings, *Rural Household Inventories*, pp. 121, 163, 201; Cummings, *Bed Hangings*, pp. 12–14.

[8] Cummings, *Bed Hangings*, p. 4. Entry for Sunday, June 9, 1771, in *The Diary of John Adams*, ed. L. H. Butterfield, Leonard C. Faber, and Wendell D. Garrett, vol. 2 (Diary 1771–81) (Cambridge: Harvard University Press, Belknap Press, 1961), p. 31. I am indebted to Barbara Carson for this reference. Cummings, *Rural Household Inventories*, pp. 150–262; Alice Hanson Jones, *American Colonial Wealth: Documents and Methods*, 3 vols. (New York: Arno Press, 1977), 2:607–800, 2:887–1022.

[9] *John Brown House Loan Exhibition*, p. 174. A manuscript copy of the February 19, 1756, agreement and the March 24, 1757, revision are at Rhode Island Historical Society. The prices listed are in the highly inflated Rhode Island currency of the day, where the exchange rate was £23.6.8 = £1 (sterling). The Hartford price book is cited in *Great River*, pp. 471–73; see also Lyon, *Colonial Furniture*, pp. 267–70. Hatfield price list (1796) is cited in Fales, *Furniture of Historic Deerfield*, p. 286.

## 103 ◆ Bedstead
**Eastern Massachusetts or Rhode Island**
**1740–70**

Many of the New England bedsteads that
survive from the eighteenth century are of
the high-post variety, although low-post
forms probably were made in equal, or
even greater, numbers. High-post bedsteads
range in design from examples with plain,
rectangular posts at all four corners to those
with four elaborately ornamented pillars on
curved cabriole or straight Marlborough
legs. Generally, however, the footposts of a
bedstead exhibited the most fashionable style,

and the headposts were plainer, presumably
because they would have been hidden by the
head cloth and curtains.

The production of a fully hung, high-post
bedstead was a cooperative venture requiring
the skills of several artisans from at least two
different shops. In the cabinetmaker's shop,
a turner and carver would have produced
the posts and the turned pegs to which the
sacking was laced. A journeyman or apprentice
may have produced the rails, headboard, and
cornice and tester frame, all of which required
a lesser degree of skill. An upholsterer would
fashion all the fabric parts of the bed—sacking
bottom, mattress, beds, bolster and pillows,

and the bed furniture, or hangings. The
upholsterer also set up and "dressed" the bed,
perhaps changing the hangings seasonally for
winter and summer if the patron could afford
such a luxury.

The cabriole leg (called "horsebone" or
"crooked" in contemporary documents) was
introduced into America on seating furniture
in the late 1720s and became a regular feature
on all furniture forms shortly thereafter. In
sleeping furniture, the cabriole shape appears
most frequently in combination with a ball-
and-claw foot. Cabriole-leg bedsteads on pad,
or "plain," feet from any region are rare.[1] None
of the extant eighteenth-century price books

lists the plain foot design in either a high- or low-post form.

Only three New England tall-post examples with plain, tapered pillars, cabriole legs, and pad feet are known to survive to date: one at Colonial Williamsburg, one in a private collection, and this one, which Henry Francis du Pont used as his own bed prior to 1951.[2] The three share several characteristics: in addition to the similar shape of the footposts, all use bed screws to join the rails to the posts, and all originally were fitted with sacking bottoms to support the bedding. In most other construction details there is less uniformity.

Footposts, as they were more visible, were often made from fashionable woods (such as mahogany or walnut), while less expensive woods (maple, birch, and pine) were used for headposts, rails, and headboards, which were usually covered by the hangings. The two other bedsteads follow this pattern: the footposts of the Williamsburg bedstead are mahogany; those on the privately owned bed are walnut. The tapered rectangular headposts and the rails of both beds are maple, but the headboard of the Williamsburg bed is white pine and the other is maple. The fabrication of Winterthur's bedstead is exceptional because all four posts are turned pillars with carved cabriole legs and pad feet and are made of mahogany, as are the head and foot rails; the side rails and headboard are made of soft maple. This bedstead was consequently extremely costly due to the expense of the mahogany and the amount of stock wasted in fashioning the pillars and cabriole legs from one seven-and-a-half-foot length of squared-off timber.

Despite the general similarity among these three New England beds, the shape of the footposts differs from bed to bed. A plain, tapered pillar rises directly from the square block at the rail on the Winterthur and the Williamsburg examples (fig. 1). The pillar on the privately owned bed has a more architecturally correct, classical base. The Winterthur and privately owned bedsteads have cabriole legs with sharp knees and deep pad feet on shallow disks. The knee on the Williamsburg bed is rounded, and the disk is a high ring.

Determining the regional origin of Winterthur's bedstead is difficult. Joseph Downs originally assigned it to Rhode Island, and an unconfirmed history indicates that it was purchased in the early 1900s by Israel Sack at the McFarland sale in Mansfield,

**Fig. 1.** Detail, footpost.

Connecticut.[3] The Williamsburg bedstead has an unsubstantiated history of ownership in Massachusetts. Only the privately owned bedstead has a pre-twentieth-century history—it descended in the family of Maj. Gen. John Thomas (1724–76) of Kingston, Massachusetts. The design and the choice of materials for all three bedsteads suggest a coastal New England provenance, and it seems likely that they were made in eastern Massachusetts or Rhode Island.

*NER/WAC*

---

**Inscriptions or marks:** *Incised on the rails and adjacent posts, at their juncture, clockwise, from left headpost:* "I"–"VIII".

**Construction:** The headboard is tenoned into two slots in the headposts but is not pinned. All four posts are identical and are plain, tapered columnar pillars above the rail, ending in cabriole legs with pad feet raised on shallow disks. The rectangular rails, higher than they are wide, are molded on the upper outside edge and cut with a deep rabbet on the inner edge to hold the turned pegs for a roped or sacking bottom. The rails are tenoned to the posts and held with bed bolts; the housed nuts for the bolts are mortised into the rails and plugged on the outside. The rectangular tester (not original) has mitered corners and rests on iron pins in the top of the posts.

**Condition:** All the posts have been extended 12 1/4". The foot on the right headpost is patched. Several knee brackets are replaced. The tester is not original.

**Dimensions:**

| | | |
|---|---|---|
| H. | 91 1/2 in. | 232.4 cm |
| H. (posts) | 90 3/4 in. | 230.5 cm |
| H. (rails) | 17 1/4 in. | 43.1 cm |
| L. (posts) | 77 1/2 in. | 196.9 cm |
| L. (feet) | 79 in. | 200.7 cm |
| W. (posts) | 57 1/2 in. | 146.1 cm |
| W. (feet) | 60 in. | 152.4 cm |

**Materials:** *Microanalysis:* Primary: mahogany (posts, head and foot rail); soft maple group (side rails, headboard [original]). Secondary: white pine group (tester rails [not original]). *Finish:* natural resin.

**Exhibitions:** "Loan Exhibition of Eighteenth- and Early Nineteenth-Century Furniture and Glass," National Council of Girl Scouts, New York, September 25–October 9, 1929.

**Publications:** National Council of Girl Scouts, *Loan Exhibition of Eighteenth- and Early Nineteenth-Century Furniture and Glass* (New York: By the council, 1929), cat. 562. Downs, *American Furniture*, fig. 1. Comstock, *American Furniture*, no. 138. Marshall B. Davidson, ed., *The American Heritage History of Colonial Antiques* ([New York]: American Heritage Publishing Co., [1967]), fig. 214. Butler, *American Furniture*, p. 31. Fitzgerald, *Three Centuries*, fig. III-7. Jay E. Cantor, *Winterthur* (New York: Harry N. Abrams, 1985), p. 105.

**Accession history:** Purchased by H. F. du Pont from Collings and Collings, New York, 1927. Gift of H. F. du Pont, 1955. 55.793

1. Jobe and Kaye, *New England Furniture*, p. 185. Of the 3 high-post and 3 low-post cabriole-leg bedsteads known to the author, all are of New England origin except for a Pennsylvania low-post frame at Colonial Williamsburg. A fourth high-post bedstead with 4 cabriole legs terminating in hoof feet, made entirely of mahogany, is owned by MESDA and thought to be of North Carolina origin; see Helen Gaines, "Collectors' Notes," *Antiques* 100, no. 2 (August 1971): 233–35; John Bivins, Jr., *The Furniture of Coastal North Carolina, 1700–1820* (Winston-Salem, N.C.: Museum of Early Southern Decorative Arts, 1988), pp. 386–87.

2. For the Williamsburg bed, see Greenlaw, *New England Furniture*, no. 6; for the privately owned example (formerly in the collection of Mrs. Walter B. Robb), see Edith Gaines, "The Robb Collection of American Furniture: Part I," *Antiques* 92, no. 3 (September 1967): 324, fig. 4; see also *American Antiques from Israel Sack Collection*, 10 vols. (Washington, D.C.: Highland House, ca. 1969–), 5:1217.

3. A research note in the object file at Winterthur states: "Sack got this in the early 1900's at an auction in Mansfield, Conn. McFarland the auctioneer, who wouldn't sell the bed early in the day, made Sack lose the last train to Boston, then pushed the bidding up and gave long orations until Sack got it for $130" (folder 55.793, Registration Office, Winterthur).

### 104 ◆ Bedstead
Eastern Massachusetts, possibly Salem
1765–95

One popular mid eighteenth-century footpost design, as seen here, featured an architecturally inspired, fluted pillar with turned capital and base set on a cabriole (or "crooked") leg with a ball-and-claw foot. Variations on this design were available in most urban centers. While there is no mention of the form in the abbreviated Providence cabinetmakers' price lists of 1756–57, a high-post bedstead "with Baces & Caps, Claw foot" valued at £2.12.6 is recorded in the 1772 Philadelphia price book. This design apparently remained popular until almost the end of the eighteenth century

because the form is also listed in the 1786 Philadelphia price book and the 1792 Hartford price book.[1]

New England high-post bedsteads with cabriole legs and claw feet are only slightly better represented today than are their plain (pad) foot counterparts. Of those known, only a small group exhibit the raked-back side talons favored by Massachusetts carvers and patrons. The cabriole legs on this bedstead are distinguished by linear, stylized, acanthus-leaf carving set off by a punched-star background— a decoration that appears with some frequency on furniture made in Salem in the federal period (fig. 1). Another bedstead, once owned by the firm of Bernard and S. Dean Levy, has similar decoration. A closely related example

now in the Museum of Fine Arts, Boston, has stop-fluted footposts, a star-punched and stippled background, and raked-talon ball-and-claw feet. Examples at Bayou Bend and Colonial Williamsburg also have the fluted columnar pillars, but the legs are uncarved.[2]

As is typical of most high-post bedsteads, this example has elaborately turned and carved mahogany footposts and simple, square, tapered, soft maple headposts and rails. The headboard is white pine, a less costly wood, because fabric hangings would no doubt have covered it. Although its original bed hangings have not survived, important evidence of cloak pin holes in the headposts suggest that festooned curtains originally hung from the tester frame. They were controlled by cords

**Fig. 2.** Bedstead, fully furnished.

**Fig. 1.** Detail, footpost leg.

through rings on the back of each curtain, drawn up by cords run through pulleys in the tester frame, and wrapped around cloak pins, or brass knobs, secured to the headposts. These hangings were fabricated in 1985 to illustrate the cord and pulley system for a set of "draw up" curtains (fig. 2). The design was taken from a partial set of curtains and valances at Winterthur owned in the third quarter of the eighteenth century by the Burnham family of Newburyport, Massachusetts.[3]

NER/WAC

**Inscriptions or marks:** *Incised on posts and rails at their juncture, clockwise, from left footpost:* "I"–"VII", "X".

**Construction:** The headboard is held between narrow quarter-round strips nailed to the inside of the square, tapered headposts. The footposts have turned, fluted, and tapered pillars above the rails; below the rails, the leaf carving on the knees is set off by a punched-star background. The plain rectangular rails are tenoned into the posts and bolted; nuts securing the bolts are inserted into the rails from the outside. A shallow rabbet cut in the inside top edge of the rails was intended to receive the strips of canvas for a sacking bottom. The bed bolt covers are cast and appear to be original.

**Condition:** The headposts and rails are grain-painted to simulate mahogany. The headboard,

which appears to be original (though possibly with some modification), has been refinished on the front, but on the reverse it retains the red base coat that forms the foundation for the grain-painted decoration on the headposts and rails. A second board has been added to bring the headboard to the required height. The bedstead was fitted with casters at one time. The tester and a frame for the sacking were constructed in 1985 when the new set of bed hangings was prepared.

**Dimensions:**

| | | |
|---|---:|---:|
| H. (fabric cornice) | 93 in. | 236.2 cm |
| H. (frame) | 90³/4 in. | 230.5 cm |
| H. (rail) | 16 in. | 40.6 cm |
| L. (top fabric cornice) | 78¹/2 in. | 199.4 cm |
| L. (frame) | 75 in. | 190.5 cm |
| L. (feet) | 75⁷/8 in. | 192.7 cm |
| W. (top fabric cornice) | 58 in. | 147.3 cm |
| W. (frame) | 56¹/4 in. | 142.9 cm |
| W. (feet) | 58¹/4 in. | 148.0 cm |

**Materials:** *Microanalysis:* Primary: mahogany (footposts). Secondary: soft maple group (headpost, rails); white pine group (headboard, modern tester, frame for sacking). *Finish:* headposts and all rails are grained to simulate mahogany.

**Exhibitions:** "The Cut of the Cloth," Tri Delta Antiques Show, Dallas, March 28–31, 1985.

**Publications:** Downs, *American Furniture*, fig. 4. Joseph Downs, "A Selection of American Furniture," *Antiques* 61, no. 5 (May 1952): 424–28. Florence M. Montgomery, "Eighteenth-Century English and American Furnishing Fashions," *Antiques* 97, no. 2 (February 1970): 270. Butler, *American Furniture*, p. 59. Kay Wilson, *A History of Textiles* (Boulder, Colo.: Westview Press, 1979), pl. 76. Nancy E. Richards, "The Cut of the Cloth: Style and Taste in

Eighteenth-Century Furnishing Fabrics," *Washington Antiques Show 1986* (Washington, D.C.), p. 70, fig. 6.

**Provenance:** Ex coll.: Grace Low. Inherited from the Russell family of Mass.

**Accession history:** Bequest of H. F. du Pont, 1969. 55.792

---

1. The 1772 Philadelphia price book is cited in Martin Eli Weil, "A Cabinetmaker's Price Book," in Ian M. G. Quimby, ed., *Winterthur Portfolio 13* (Chicago: University of Chicago Press for the Henry Francis du Pont Winterthur Museum, 1979), p. 192; the 1786 Philadelphia price book is cited in Harold E. Gillingham, "Benjamin Lehman: A Germantown Cabinet-Maker," *Pennsylvania Magazine of History and Biography* 54 (1930): 304; the Hartford price book is cited in *Great River*, p. 318, and Lyon, *Colonial Furniture*, p. 270.

2. The star-punch decoration appears on Salem furniture, especially pieces attributed to the carving shops of Samuel McIntire and his son, Samuel Field McIntire, and Joseph True; see Dean A. Fales, Jr., *Essex County Furniture: Documented Treasures from Local Collections, 1660–1860* (Salem, Mass.: Essex Institute, 1965), nos. 3, 60, 61, 65, 68. The bed once owned by Levy is no. 75.712, DAPC, Visual Resouces Collection, Winterthur Library; it has been attributed to the shop of Salem cabinetmaker Jacob Sanderson based on a card attached to the frame: "This Bedstead was the property of my Grandmother, Sarah Holmes. It was bought of Jacob Sanderson, March 27, 1786 for [£]4.10.0. April 7, 1890 [signed] Joseph Ropes, Salem." For the MFA, Boston, bed, see Christie's, "The Contents of the Lindens: The Collection of the Late Mrs. George Maurice Morris" (January 22, 1983), lot 353. For Bayou Bend's bed, see Warren, *Bayou Bend*, no. 138.

3. For Colonial Williamsburg's bed, see Greenlaw, *New England Furniture*, no. 7. Cummings, *Rural Household Inventories*, p. 126. Florence M. Montgomery, *Textiles in America, 1650–1870* (New York: W. W. Norton, 1984), p. 36.

## 105 ◆ Bedstead
New England, possibly the
Connecticut shore
1770–1800

While the relatively high survival rate of richly ornamented high-post bedsteads suggests they were numerous, it actually creates a distorted picture of eighteenth-century chamber furnishings. Even in wealthier homes, relatively few beds had elaborately carved decoration or other embellishment. The majority probably had simple turned or molded posts, which were relatively inexpensive to produce. One of the less expensive models was the corded high-post bedstead with square, tapered posts at all four corners. This design, described in the 1792 Hartford price book as "plain square high posts without screws and for a cord with plain teaster painted red," cost £1.3.0.[1]

Although this bedstead conforms to that price-book description, several features raise it above the standard. The footposts are fluted on four sides and the headposts on two; because this detail meant extra work, between 21s. and 42s. would have been added to the cost of the frame. The use of "screws" (bed bolts) to secure the frame instead of laced cords or ropes also increased the cost another 3s.

The addition of a shaped wooden cornice on this bed suggests the transfer of a design tradition found in richly appointed country houses in eighteenth-century England. Rarely were the elaborate pattern-book models reproduced in America. Exceptions include a state bed at Colonial Williamsburg and two bedsteads at the Metropolitan Museum of Art. American craftsmen, especially those in New England, generally favored less elaborate models with a simple undulating or scalloped

outline. Cornices of this type could be painted or covered with fabric.[2] The cornice and tester unit on this bed has wooden pulleys over which a cord could be drawn to raise and lower the drapery.

*NER/WAC*

**Inscriptions or marks:** *Incised on each end of each rail, beginning with the right headboard and moving counterclockwise:* "I", "II", "III", "IIII", "V", "VI", "VII", *and* "VIII". *On the posts, beginning with the left headpost and moving counterclockwise:* "III", "X", "XI", "II" [unmarked], "I" [unmarked], *and* "IIV".

**Construction:** All four posts are tapered rectangles. The headposts are fluted on the front and outside surfaces; the footposts are fluted on all four sides above the rail and on the front and outside surfaces below. The rectangular rails, slightly wider than they are high, are cut with a narrow chamfer on the outside lower edge and a wide chamfer on the inside lower edge. The rails are tenoned into the posts and secured by bed bolts, which are screwed into nuts inserted into the rails from outside slots. The mattress is supported by cord laced through horizontally drilled holes in the rails. The headboard is held by narrow strips nailed to the inside of the headposts. The original scalloped cornice boards are fabricated from 7/8" pine that is quarter round on the outer bottom edge. A cove cut on the backside in the area of the scalloping has reduced the stock thickness to 5/8", lightening the effect of the sawn shaped elements. The cornice sides are nailed through the outside into the tester and attached on the inside with chamfered, rectangular blocks that are nailed in place. Each cornice side rail and the cornice foot rail are fitted with three spool-shape pulleys. The cornice is held on the posts with iron pins.

**Condition:** Both headposts are split. The cornice sides are old, and the end is new. The cornice side rails show evidence of hand planing; the end is modern. The headboard and tester (end) are replacements. The bed bolts are replaced.

**Dimensions:**

| | | |
|---|---|---|
| H. (with cornice) | 85 in. | 215.9 cm |
| H. (posts) | 80 1/2 in. | 204.5 cm |
| H. (rails) | 19 1/2 in. | 49.5 cm |
| L. (cornice) | 77 3/4 in. | 197.5 cm |
| L. (posts) | 75 3/4 in. | 192.4 cm |
| L. (feet) | 76 1/8 in. | 193.4 cm |
| W. (cornice) | 53 3/4 in. | 136.5 cm |
| W. (posts) | 51 5/8 in. | 131.3 cm |
| W. (feet) | 51 in. | 129.5 cm |

**Materials:** *Microanalysis:* Primary: cherry (posts); birch (rails). Secondary: white pine group (headboard, cornice). *Finish:* headboard is stained to simulate the finish on the headposts; cornice has a thin coat of white paint.

**Publications:** Downs, *American Furniture*, fig. 9. Ralph Kovel and Terry Kovel, *American Country Furniture, 1780–1875* (New York: Crown Publishers, 1965), p. 4, fig. 4. Butler, *American Furniture*, p. 58.

**Provenance:** Ex coll.: Fred W. Fuessenick, Torrington, Conn.

**Accession history:** Purchased by H. F. du Pont through Israel Sack from Fred W. Fuessenick, Torrington, Conn., 1944. Gift of H. F. du Pont, 1955. 55.780

1. The Hartford price book is cited in *Great River*, p. 318, and Lyon, *Colonial Furniture*, p. 269; *Connecticut Historical Society Bulletin* 33, no. 1 (January 1968): 35. This price was roughly the cost of a plain breakfast table (£1.9.0).

2. Barbara Carson, *The Governor's Palace: The Williamsburg Residence of Virginia's Royal Governor* (Williamsburg, Va.: Colonial Williamsburg Fndn., 1987), p. 38; Jan Kirsten Gilliam and Betty Crowe Leviner, *Furnishing Williamsburg's Historic Buildings* (Williamsburg, Va.: Colonial Williamsburg Fndn., 1991), pp. 38–39, figs. 48, 51; Graham Hood, *The Governor's Palace in Williamsburg: A Cultural Study* (Williamsburg, Va.: Colonial Williamsburg Fndn., 1991), pp. 207, 209. For the beds at the Metropolitan Museum of Art, see Heckscher, *American Furniture*, cat. nos. 89, 90. For a painted cornice, see Greenlaw, *New England Furniture*, no. 12; for one covered in fabric, see Jobe and Kaye, *New England Furniture*, no. 141.

## 106 ◆ Bedstead
### North Shore, Massachusetts, or Portsmouth, New Hampshire
### 1770–1810

The frequent use of Marlborough legs on New England bedsteads in the last quarter of the eighteenth century was a handsome and economic alternative to the carved cabriole and ball-and-claw footposts. The introduction of the Marlborough leg is difficult to document, although it probably coincides with the revival of interest in chinoiserie and the Gothic during the 1740s. Furniture forms incorporating the straight-leg design (with and without a cuff) appear in most English pattern books of the 1750s and 1760s, including Haypenny's *New Designs for Chinese Temples* (1750), Chippendale's *Director* (1754), Ince and Mayhew's *Universal System of Houshold Furniture* (1762), Manwaring's *Cabinet and Chair-Maker's Real Friend and Companion* (1765), and Society of Upholsterers' *Genteel Houshold Furniture in the Present Taste* (1760–65). The design enjoyed a long period of popularity in England, extending from the mid eighteenth century into the second decade of the nineteenth century. A drawing of a Marlborough-leg table, identified as "An Oak Hall Table 4ft by 1ft 10," is included in a June 1816 entry in the Estimate Book of the Gillows firm.[1]

References to Marlborough-leg furniture appear in Boston records even before

publication of the design in the English pattern books: upholsterer Samuel Grant's account book includes an entry for Marlborough chairs on August 20, 1746.[2] The design grew in popularity in America during the third quarter of the eighteenth century and remained fashionable into the nineteenth century. One late example of the design can be seen on the serpentine-back sofa (No. 98) made by Adam S. Coe in April 1812.

How this straight-leg design came to be called "Marlborough" is unclear. British furniture scholars speculate that it may relate to the dedication of Ince and Mayhew's *Universal System of Houshold Furniture* to George Spencer, fourth Duke of Marlborough.[3] The term appears in the 1772 Philadelphia price book describing an alternative to "crooked" (cabriole) leg furniture and in subsequent editions of price books printed on both sides of the Atlantic until the early nineteenth century.

The straight Marlborough leg supporting a turned pillar and baluster adorned one of the most popular New England bedstead designs. Of those with unornamented footposts, two bedsteads are most closely related to Winterthur's example—one at the Society for the Preservation of New England Antiquities (SPNEA) and one at the Chipstone Foundation.[4] All three have similar, but not identical, cuffed footposts and octagonal, or "pencil" as they are called

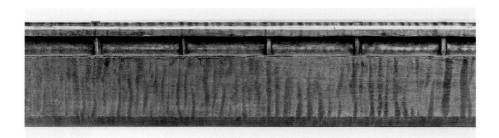

**Fig. 1.** Detail, rail.

today, headposts above Marlborough legs. All are made of native woods—maple (Winterthur and Chipstone) and birch (SPNEA)—rather than the more fashionable mahogany or walnut. However, they differ in the peculiarities of construction.

The Winterthur and SPNEA bedsteads are most alike. On both, the rails are mortised into the posts and secured with bed bolts. The rails on the Chipstone bedstead are tenoned into the legs, but the frame is held together by laced cord. The Winterthur and SPNEA bedsteads also share an unusual support system for the canvas sacking. Instead of the more common turned, mushroom-shape pegs set in a rabbet in the rails, the sacking was laced to cylindrical quarter-inch pins driven through the top of the rail into a concave slot (fig. 1). Of the three, Winterthur's

bedstead is unique in its use of a mitered cuff (fig. 2) on all four posts instead of the more traditional method in which the front and back sections of applied molding overlap the sides. The bedstead has lost its original tester and cornice, but holes for cloak pins in the footposts confirm that the bed once had draw-up curtains.

The question of provenance for this bedstead is not easily resolved. Because it was owned by descendants of Richard Derby in Salem, Joseph Downs assigned it to Massachusetts. A Massachusetts or Rhode Island origin also has been suggested for the Chipstone bedstead based on its similarity to Winterthur's frame and to more elaborately ornamented bedsteads commonly assigned to Newport. The SPNEA bedstead, once owned by James Rundlet, a Portsmouth merchant

**Fig. 2.** Detail, Marlborough leg.

and mill owner, is believed to have been made locally.[5] The construction similarities shared by the SPNEA and Winterthur examples suggest a strong probability that Winterthur's bedstead was made in coastal Essex County or in nearby New Hampshire.

*NER/WAC*

**Construction:** The slightly arched headboard has a quarter-round bead on the top edge and is held between strips nailed to the inside of the tapered, octagonal headposts. The octagonal headposts are set on square bases with applied molded cuffs, mitered at the corners. The rectangular rails, higher than they are wide, are molded on the upper outer edge and chamfered on the other edges; the inside face has a cut concave dado with wooden pins set in from the top to hold the ropes for a sacking bottom. The rails are tenoned into the posts and secured by bed bolts, which are screwed into nuts inserted into the rails from the outside. The bed bolt covers are of cast brass; they are old and appear to be original. On the outside of the footposts, $57^3/4$" from the floor on the left and $54^3/4$" from the floor on the right, are holes, now plugged, for cloak pins; there are no corresponding holes on the headposts.

**Condition:** All the posts have been extended by 7" at the top. The white pine headboard has been grained to simulate maple. The front strips holding the headboard are replaced.

**Dimensions:**

| | | |
|---|---|---|
| H. | $88^3/4$ in. | 225.4 cm |
| H. (original posts) | $81^3/4$ in. | 207.6 cm |
| H. (rails) | 20 in. | 50.8 cm |
| L. (posts) | $78^1/4$ in. | 198.8 cm |
| L. (feet) | $80^3/4$ in. | 206.6 cm |
| W. (posts) | $54^3/4$ in. | 139.1 cm |
| W. (feet) | 58 in. | 147.3 cm |

**Materials:** *Microanalysis:* Primary: soft maple group (posts, rails). Secondary: white pine group (headboard). *Finish:* headboard grained to simulate maple.

**Publications:** Downs, *American Furniture*, fig. 6. Butler, *American Furniture*, p. 66.

**Provenance:** The bed descended in the family of Richard Derby of Salem, Mass., and was sold by them in 1939.

**Accession history:** Purchased by H. F. du Pont from Joe Kindig, Jr., York, Pa., 1943. Gift of H. F. du Pont, 1955.
55.781

1. Kirk, *American Furniture*, fig. 1387.

2. The Samuel Grant accounts are cited in Jobe and Kaye, *New England Furniture*, p. 391.

3. John Gloag, ed., *A Complete Dictionary of Furniture* (1952; rev. ed., Woodstock, N.Y.: Overlook Press, 1991), p. 448.

4. For the SPNEA bed, see Jobe and Kaye, *New England Furniture*, no. 141; for the Chipstone example, see Rodriguez Roque, *American Furniture*, no. 191.

5. Downs, *American Furniture*, fig. 6. For the Newport bedsteads, see Ralph E. Carpenter, Jr., *The Arts and Crafts of Newport, Rhode Island, 1640–1820* (Newport: Preservation Society of Newport County, 1954), no. 3; *American Antiques from Israel Sack Collection*, 10 vols. (Washington, D.C.: Highland House, ca. 1969–), 3:699; Ginsburg and Levy advertisement, *Antiques* 78, no. 1 (July 1960): 17; and Greenlaw, *New England Furniture*, no. 11; on the SPNEA bed, see Jobe and Kaye, *New England Furniture*, pp. 445–47.

## 107 ◆ Field bedstead

Lower Housatonic River valley,
Stratford, Connecticut
1780–95
Possibly from the shop of Brewster
Dayton (w. 1762–d. 1796)

Narrow high-post bedsteads with hinged, arched testers were referred to in contemporary records as "camp," "tent," or "field" beds. They were historically thought to be one of the earliest high-post forms, and the name may derive from the type of light, folding bed frame (*lit de camp*) with a loose, one-piece bed dressing used in the late medieval period by military officers in the field. Because they could be dismantled quickly and folded for easy transport, these beds may also have been used by people of rank when they traveled. By the early eighteenth century, the field bed had been adapted for domestic use; in May 1735 Daniel Goffe of Boston advertised a "Publick Venue . . . at the Dwelling House of Mr. Jonathan Barnard," where among various household goods there was offered "a Field Bedstead and Bed, the covering a Blew Harrateen."[1]

Designs for various styles appeared in several English furniture pattern books in the 1760s. Examples in Chippendale's *Director*, Ince and Mayhew's *Universal System of Houshold Furniture*, and Society of Upholsterers' *Genteel Houshold Furniture in the Present Taste* featured elaborate single-headed couches with ornate hangings, but these rococo designs appear to have had little influence on the field beds produced by New England craftsmen. Examples that have survived are closer instead to the designs published by Hepplewhite and Sheraton.[2]

Field beds were used in New England households by at least the second quarter of the eighteenth century. The 1732 probate inventory of the estate of Col. William Tailer of Dorchester, Massachusetts, lists "Curtains

for a field Bed" valued at 70s.; the Reverend Thomas Harward of Boston left a "Field Bedstead" in his estate when he died in 1736; and the 1774 estate inventory of Massachusetts Lt. Gov. Andrew Oliver included a "Field Bed & Bedstead Bolster & pillow" valued at £5. The level of popularity of the form can be inferred from its inclusion in the 1772 Philadelphia price book, which lists "Popler field Bedsteds, Canopy Rales, £2.15.0." No comparable document exists for any New England city in the 1770s or 1780s, but the form is listed in the 1792 Hartford price book.[3]

**Fig. 1.** Detail, headboard.

Eighteenth-century field beds differ from the standard flat-tester high-post bedstead in several ways, including the shape of the tester, the relative lightness of the framing members, the degree of ornament, and the complexity of the "bed furniture," or hangings. The relative plainness of its design prompted Sheraton to declare the field bed suitable for use "for low rooms, either for servants or children to sleep upon."[4]

In its overall form Winterthur's bedstead is closer to Sheraton's model than to other pattern-book examples. The pillars are joined fast into the head and foot rails, which is a departure from standard bedstead construction, in which all the rails are mortise-and-tenoned and held with bolts; but the design lacks the hinged side rails and the strengthening lath recommended by Sheraton. The method of attaching the headboard also differs from standard practice—instead of being tenoned into the pillars or riding between narrow strips nailed to the posts, it slides into

channels cut in the post stock (fig. 1). This unusual method is also seen on a similar field bedstead once owned by Israel Sack.[5] Unlike Winterthur's example, the rails on that bed appear to disassemble.

According to the 1792 Hartford price book, a simple "Field Bedstead, plain turn'd posts, green" cost £2.5.0. "Screw caps," or bed bolts, added 3s. to the price; adding a headboard and painting (or staining) the frame red further increased the price by 12s. to £3. This was slightly more than the £2.18.0 charged for a simple chest of drawers with "plain" (pad) feet.[6]

Research on the joiners of Stratford, Woodbury, and Newtown, Connecticut, makes it possible to sharpen the attribution of Winterthur's bedstead. Its history of ownership in the Blakeman family of Stratford, along

with the general design and method of construction, support lower Housatonic River valley, specifically Stratford, as the place of origin. Design and construction similarities with products from the shop of Brewster Dayton, including the Spanish feet, clearly suggest the likelihood of its production in the shop of this known Stratford cabinetmaker (see No. 166). Additionally, a more thorough understanding of the tastes and styles embraced by craftsmen and patrons in the lower Housatonic River valley of Connecticut now allows us to date this bed to the late eighteenth century.[7]

*NER/WAC*

**Inscriptions or marks:** *Incised on left side rail and adjacent footpost:* "II". *Incised on right side rail and adjacent headpost:* "X".

**Construction:** All four identical posts are sawn from square stock. Above the juncture with the rails, the octagonal posts taper, and the chamfers stop to transition to a square top. Below the rail, the posts are cut in a stiff cabriole leg ending in a five-toed "Spanish" foot. The square rails have a bead molding on three sides and are chamfered on the inner lower edge. They are deeply rabbeted to receive turned, mushroom-shape pegs for roping or for a laced sacking bottom. The head and foot rails are fixed to the posts with double-pinned mortise and tenons. The side rails are detachable and are joined to the posts by bed bolts that screw into iron nuts slotted into the rails from the outside. The inner corners of the headposts (in the area of the headboard) have not been chamfered, to allow for a slot into which the removable headboard slides. The arched tester is hinged at the middle. Four cross ribs, or slats, are tenoned into the tester side rails. The tester's head and foot rails are separate; they are cut in a mitered rabbet and held at the top of the posts with iron pins.

**Condition:** The left headpost is patched in several places. The right headpost has a major crack at the rail. A section of the left footpost is replaced at the rail, and the right footpost is patched. The bedstead once was fitted with casters.

**Dimensions:**

| | | |
|---|---|---|
| H. | 84 7/8 in. | 215.6 cm |
| H. (posts) | 62 3/8 in. | 158.4 cm |
| H. (rails) | 17 3/4 in. | 45.1 cm |
| L. (posts) | 73 in. | 185.4 cm |
| L. (feet) | 73 in. | 185.4 cm |
| W. (posts) | 48 1/2 in. | 123.1 cm |
| W. (feet) | 49 1/4 in. | 125.1 cm |

**Materials:** *Microanalysis:* Primary: soft maple group (posts, rails). Secondary: tulip-poplar (headboard, tester). *Finish:* pigmented red stain.

**Publications:** John A. H. Sweeney, "New Rooms at Winterthur," *Antiques* 67, no. 2 (February 1955): 133. Edward S. Cooke, Jr., "Craftsman-Client Relations in the Housatonic Valley, 1720–1800," *Antiques* 125, no. 1 (January 1984): 276, fig. 6.

**Provenance:** The bed has a history of ownership in the Blakeman family of Stratford, Conn.

**Accession history:** Purchased by H. F. du Pont from John S. Walton, New York, 1952. Gift of H. F. du Pont, 1955.
52.97

1. On military beds, see Macquoid and Edwards, *Dictionary*, 1:67–68; Thornton, *Seventeenth-Century Interior Decoration*, p. 153. Dow, *Arts and Crafts in New England*, p. 110.

2. Thomas Chippendale, *The Gentleman and Cabinet-Maker's Director* (3d ed., London: By the author, 1762), pl. 44; William Ince and John Mayhew, *The Universal System of Houshold Furniture* (1762; reprint, Chicago: Quadrangle Books, 1960), pl. 28; *Genteel Houshold Furniture in the Present Taste* (1764–65; reprint, East Ardley, Yorkshire, Eng.: EP Publishing, 1978), p. 83. [George] Hepplewhite, *The Cabinet-Maker and Upholsterer's Guide* (1794; reprint 3d ed., New York: Dover Publications, 1969), pls. 102–4; and Thomas Sheraton, *The Cabinet Dictionary* (1803; reprint in 2 vols., New York: Praeger Publishers, 1970), 1: pl. 15.

3. Tailer cited in Cummings, *Rural Household Inventories*, p. 116; Harward cited in Abbott Lowell Cummings, comp., *Bed Hangings: A Treatise on Fabrics and Styles in the Curtaining of Beds, 1650–1850* (Boston: Society for the Preservation of New England Antiquities, 1961), p. 6; Oliver cited in Alice Hanson Jones, *American Colonial Wealth: Documents and Methods*, 3 vols. (New York: Arno Press, 1977), 2:968. The 1772 Philadelphia price book is reprinted in Martin Eli Weil, "A Cabinetmaker's Price Book," in Ian M. G. Quimby, ed., *Winterthur Portfolio 13* (Chicago: University of Chicago Press for the Henry Francis du Pont Winterthur Museum, 1979), p. 192. Benjamin Lehman's manuscript copy of the 1786 Philadelphia price book includes a similar entry at the same price; see Harold E. Gillingham, "Benjamin Lehman: A Germantown Cabinet-Maker," *Pennsylvania Magazine of History and Biography* 54 (1930): 304. The Hartford price book is cited in *Great River*, p. 473, and Lyon, *Colonial Furniture*, p. 269.

4. Sheraton, *Cabinet Dictionary*, 1:123–24.

5. Israel Sack advertisement, *Antiques* 75, no. 3 (March 1959): inside front cover; see also Comstock, *American Furniture*, no. 140.

6. Hartford price book cited in *Great River*, p. 473.

7. Edward Strong Cooke, Jr., "Rural Artisanal Culture: The Preindustrial Joiners of Newtown and Woodbury, Connecticut, 1760–1820" (Ph.D. diss., Boston University, 1984); Edward S. Cooke, Jr., "Craftsman-Client Relations in the Housatonic Valley, 1720–1800," *Antiques* 125, no. 1 (January 1984): 276.

## 108 ◆ Press bedstead
### Massachusetts
### 1780–1800

Folding furniture has existed since antiquity. The primary types of furniture designed to fold are those forms that are put aside or stored when not in use, such as chairs, tables, and even bedsteads. While portability is a distinguishing feature of folding chairs and tables, the great advantage of a folding bedstead is in maximization of room space. As early as the 1600s "press" and "turn-up" bedsteads appear in English records; they continued to be made into the nineteenth century.[1] They were "disguised" in a variety of forms: sofa- and chair-beds; table bedsteads; and press beds, which were designed to turn up and fit into a cupboard or other piece of case furniture (fig. 1).

Few examples of these innovative folding bedsteads appear in eighteenth-century furniture pattern books, presumably because they were more suitable for modest households where rooms were smaller and saving space was a significant consideration. Ince and Mayhew's *Universal System of Houshold Furniture* does offer a single design, the pattern for "A Sofa Bed," with diagrams of the bedstead folded and the frame extended. Neither *Genteel Houshold Furniture in the Present Taste* nor Chippendale's *Director* include designs for the form, but Chippendale's shop records cite references to the production of wainscot press beds as well as to bureau and table bedsteads. One explanation for the absence of design prototypes is offered in the introduction to the third edition of Hepplewhite's *Cabinet-Maker and Upholsterer's Guide*, which indicates that patterns were purposely omitted, "their general appearance varying so little from wardrobes, which piece of furniture they are intended to represent, that designs for them were not necessary." Eighteenth-century English examples are rare but include a chair-bed and a "Mahog'y Chest

Bedstead" originally at Nostell Priory and an unusual bureau-bed in which the frame folds out from the back of the case.[2]

Some folding bedsteads may have been held in reserve in secondary rooms, while others of simpler design may have been intended for use in servants' quarters, where space was limited. Among the Estimate Books of the cabinetmaking firm of Gillows in Lancaster, England, is a sketch for "a Buro Bedstead Made of deal with 5 sham drawers in front," as well as a simple beech and elm, turn-up stump bed, both of which English furniture historian Christopher Gilbert cites as quite probable examples of servant furniture.[3]

Folding bedsteads—specifically press beds—appear in American inventories and newspaper advertisements by at least the mid 1730s. Notice of the sale of "A Very good Press-Case for a Bed" appeared in the *Boston News-Letter* on October 28, 1736. Among the furnishings included in the 1737 inventory of the estate of Jacob Williams, a Roxbury, Massachusetts, sea captain, was a press bed valued at £12 located in "the Back Room." Williams's inventory included two other "beds and furniture": one in the "Great Chamber" was valued at £26; another in the "Little Chamber" was priced at £20. Listings for press beds appear in New England inventories

at least through the Revolution. When his estate was inventoried in 1774, Boston lawyer Andrew Oliver owned at least eight bedsteads at his houses in Boston and Dorchester, including "1 old Press Bedstead" valued at 8s. Despite their continuing availability, the form is not listed in any of the American price books from the second half of the eighteenth century; it does, however, appear in the 1791

*Leeds Cabinet and Chair Makers Book of Prices* and in the 1793 *Cabinet-Makers' London Book of Prices*.[4]

This press bedstead differs from the Gillows "Buro bedstead" as well as the type with doors resembling a clothes press, or wardrobe, in that it has a single lift-out front panel. The fold-out bedstead is very similar, however, to the English examples and to the

**Fig. 1.** Closed case.

illustrations that appear in the 1833 and 1839 editions of John Loudon's *Encyclopedia of Cottage, Farm, and Villa Architecture and Furniture*.[5] Winterthur's example retains its original canvas sacking as support for the straw and feather "beds." A large section of canvas is nailed to the head rail and one of the side rails; narrow canvas strips are nailed to the other side rail and to the foot rail. The three sections are joined by cord laced through holes reinforced with stitching. This arrangement differs from the more usual treatment in which a large piece of canvas is nailed to the head rail and then laced with cord to narrow strips of canvas that are nailed to the side and foot rails.

Once thought to have been made in Philadelphia, this press bedstead now is attributed to Massachusetts. The shape of the feet, especially the drawn-back side talons of the birdlike claws, is a design preferred by Massachusetts carvers but rarely seen elsewhere. The use of birch, a wood commonly used in northern New England, for the top and sides of the case supports the reattribution to New England. The unusual construction and character of the case itself suggests that this is probably the product of a joiner specializing in beds and not the work of a skilled cabinetmaker.

NER/WAC

---

**Inscriptions or marks:** *On the inside of the backboard:* "4" *in chalk. Stamped on some brass hardware plates:* "HJ"; these possibly were made by the firm of Thomas Hans and William Jenkins working in Birmingham between 1790 and 1803.

**Construction:** The case concealing the bedstead is built upon a heavy ash frame, mortised and tenoned at the corners. The corners are cut out to receive the leg posts of the feet, which are nailed in place and reinforced with glueblocks. The bottom edges of the sides are rabbeted, fitted to the base frame, and nailed. The three horizontal boards of the back are nailed to rabbets cut in the sides and top. The top of the case is made of two separate boards: the rear board is fixed to the case sides with interior glueblocks, and the front board is hinged to it in order to lift up and fold back. The front and sides of the top boards are trimmed with a wide molding,

which in the front forms a lip that holds the front panel. The front panel is further secured by a groove in the top front edge of the base formed by the front molding and a rabbet cut in the front of the base. Slip tenons mortised into the front edge of each side (2" from the top) fit into corresponding mortises in the top corners of the front panel. To open the bedstead the hinged top folds back, and the front panel is removed by pulling forward (away from the slip tenons) and lifting the panel up and out of the groove in the base to reveal the folded bed frame. The front panel consists of a frame with medial rail, all mortised and tenoned. All inside edges are rabbeted to receive thin (3/8") mahogany panels—simulating drawer fronts—which are held in place with small, triangular glueblocks. The upper drawer blade and lower drawer dividers are applied to the face, concealing the remaining seams between the panels. Linen strips glued to the back of the panel further reinforce the seams. The bedstead frame (mortised and tenoned at the corners) is slid into the case with the side rails resting on boards nailed to the case sides. The head rail is attached to the case with three wrought nails driven through the back of the case. The three-part side rails are hinged in two places. Just inside the front edge of the case they are hinged with a knuckle joint pivoting on the bed bolts driven through the sides of the case. Cast-iron hinges let into the underside of the rails articulate the second joint. The lower part of the bedstead is supported by four legs; the legs at the foot are fixed to the frame with mortise-and-tenon joints. These are angled back to clear the bottom rails of the case when folded inward. The intermediate legs are mortised to a rail that pivots on rosehead nails driven through the top of legs into the bed rails.

**Condition:** The front edge of the hinged top has been pieced. The right front and right rear knee brackets are replaced.

**Dimensions:**

| | | |
|---|---|---|
| H. (case) | 43 1/4 in. | 109.9 cm |
| H. (rails) | 17 1/2 in. | 44.5 cm |
| W. (case) | 49 in. | 124.5 cm |
| W. (bed frame) | 47 3/8 in. | 102.3 cm |
| W. (feet) | 51 1/8 in. | 129.9 cm |
| D. (case) | 22 in. | 55.9 cm |
| D. (feet) | 24 1/2 in. | 62.2 cm |
| L. (bed frame) | 75 3/4 in. | 192.4 cm |

**Materials:** *Microanalysis:* Primary: mahogany (legs, cornice molding, thin panels of case front); birch (top and sides of case). Secondary: white pine group

(backboard); ash (bed frame, rail on bottom of case). *Finish:* natural resin.

**Exhibitions:** "Now I Lay Me Down to Eat: A Contribution to the Art of Living," Cooper-Hewitt Museum, New York, November 18, 1980–February 22, 1981.

**Publications:** Downs, *American Furniture*, fig. 10. Charles F. Hummel, "Queen Anne and Chippendale Furniture in the Henry Francis du Pont Winterthur Museum, Part 1," *Antiques* 97, no. 6 (June 1970): 896–97, figs. 1, 2. Mark Dittrick, *The Bed Book* (New York: Harcourt Brace Jovanovich, 1980), p. 19.

**Accession history:** Purchased by H. F. du Pont from Joe Kindig, Jr., York, Pa., 1948. Gift of H. F. du Pont, 1963.
56.518

---

1. Macquoid and Edwards, *Dictionary*, 1:68–69.

2. William Ince and John Mayhew, *The Universal System of Houshold Furniture* (1762; reprint, Chicago: Quadrangle Books, 1960), pl. 27. On Chippendale, see Christopher Gilbert, *The Life and Work of Thomas Chippendale*, 2 vols. (New York: Macmillan Co., 1978), 1:53; [George] Hepplewhite, *The Cabinet-Maker and Upholsterer's Guide* (1794; reprint 3d ed., New York: Dover Publications, 1969), p. 20; on Nostell Priory, see Ralph Edwards and Margaret Jourdain, *Georgian Cabinet-Makers, ca. 1700–1800* (3d rev. ed., London: Country Life, 1955), pp. 174, 99; for the bureau-bed, see "News in Brief—Purchases for Temple Newsam at the Nostell Sale," in *Furniture History Society Newsletter* 99 (August 1990): 5–6; the piece is now at Temple Newsam in Leeds, Eng. Julia W. Torrey, "Old Furniture as the Collector Finds It," *Antiques* 3, no. 3 (March 1923): 119.

3. Christopher Gilbert, *English Vernacular Furniture, 1750–1900* (New Haven: Yale University Press for the Paul Mellon Centre for Studies in British Art, 1991), pp. 139–41.

4. Jacob Williams inventory, 1737, as cited in Cummings, *Rural Household Inventories*, p. 125; Andrew Oliver, Esq., inventory, March 16, 1774, as cited in Alice Hanson Jones, *American Colonial Wealth: Documents and Methods*, 3 vols. (New York: Arno Press, 1977), 2:968. *The Cabinet-Makers' London Book of Prices, and Designs of Cabinet Work* (London: W. Brown and A. O'Neil, 1793), pp. 38–40. *Leeds Cabinet and Chair Makers Book of Prices* (1791) as cited in Gilbert, *English Vernacular Furniture*, p. 139.

5. John C. Loudon, *Encyclopedia of Cottage, Farm, and Villa Architecture and Furniture* (London: Longman, Rees, Orme, Brown, Green, and Longman, 1833), p. 330, figs. 685–87.

# Tables

SINCE ANTIQUITY THE TABLE has been a requisite article of household furniture in all but the poorest homes. Its use traditionally has been associated with group gatherings. By defining the table as "a horizontal surface raised above the ground, used for meals and other purposes" in his 1755 *Dictionary of the English Language*, Dr. Samuel Johnson focused on the socializing functions of the form.[1] But tables had other roles as well. They offered a work surface for a full range of domestic activities from food preparation to sewing, reading, and writing. And they provided a suitable place to display objects.

Derived from the Latin *tabula* (a board or plank), tables take one of two general shapes based on the method of construction. In one design, the top is mounted on a rail frame supported on four (or occasionally three) long legs joined to the rails. Frame construction permitted great variety in table design. Tops were, to use the eighteenth-century terms, *square, square with rounded corners, scalloped, round*, or, occasionally, *octagonal*. Tops were solid or hinged; they overhung the rails or conformed to the frame. Legs were turned, straight, or carved in cabriole shapes. A second type—called a *stand table* or a *claw table* in the eighteenth century—had the top mounted on a central pillar that stood on a tripod base. Tops on this form were round or square with serpentine sides. On some the surface was flat; others had a raised, molded rim.

Although the eighteenth century marked the high point in the introduction of new table types, specialization in table use—and therefore design—began about the fifteenth century. What followed was a plethora of new forms made to meet the requirements of an increasingly leisured and pleasure-loving society. The title page of *Houshold Furniture in the Genteel Taste* for 1760, published in London by Robert Sayer for the Society of Upholsterers, Cabinetmakers, &c., listed "China, Breakfast, Side-board, Dressing, Toilet, Card, Writing, Claw, Library, Slab, and Night Tables."

English cabinetmakers' pattern books provided inspiration for new forms, but American eighteenth-century probate inventories offer few specifics on the table designs popular in New England at the time. Many entries simply record the form. When a table is described, it is identified by shape (square, round), size (small, four-foot), material (mahogany, painted, japanned), or use (tea, card, chamber, kitchen). Inventories confirm that although specialized table forms—tea and dining tables, card tables, toilet and chamber tables—often were assigned to specific areas, the ubiquitous "table" could be found in any room in a house. Often the generic table was multipurpose. Depending on size and surface height, the same table might hold food and/or beverages at one time during the day and serve as a work surface for writing or sewing at another.

Few events so transform patterns of living as did the introduction of tea to Europe through Holland early in the seventeenth century. Used initially for medicinal purposes, its consumption soon became a social activity. At first the cost and scarcity of the beverage and the expense of the equipment used to serve it limited its use to the well-to-do in private homes. Bohea (or black) tea was priced at 30s. per pound in England and as much as 40s. per pound in Boston; green tea was roughly half the cost. But as the century progressed, supplies of tea increased and costs declined, making the beverage available to a widening segment of the population in public tea and coffee houses as well as in private homes. By the middle of the eighteenth century, tea was an integral part of the morning meal. But its main popularity came as the centerpiece for afternoon gatherings. A whole set of manners and social behavior developed to coincide with tea drinking.[2]

The increased acceptance of tea as the primary social beverage encouraged the introduction of new furniture forms to serve and display the fragile accoutrements associated with its consumption. One popular form was the "square tea table," so called because its corners were square (although the tops were invariably rectangular). The earliest forms have broad board tops with a wide overhang, a design borrowed from the stretcher-base tables of an earlier period. As the eighteenth century progressed, the overhang disappeared, and tea table tops conformed more closely to the size and outline of the skirt rails. Tea tables almost invariably appear in New England probate inventories in proximity to ceramics. The itemized contents of a house belonging to John Jekyll, Esq., of Boston, in a 1732/33 inventory, included "1 Tea Table and Set of burnt China, £15" and assorted other china in the hall. The 1774 inventory of Andrew Oliver's Boston home contained "1 Japannd. Tea Table & set of Enamilld. China, £2.13.4."[3] It is commonly held that the raised rim found on most tea tables was intended to protect the tea set, although the barricade may also have served to restrain sewing or work implements.

Within the broad category of square tea tables is a distinctive subgroup known in the eighteenth century as the "china table." Introduced in the 1750s, this form is distinguished by the addition of a raised gallery inside the rim. In design, china tables relate to the wooden stands with removable lacquerwork trays imported from the Orient in the seventeenth century. Thomas Chippendale included two patterns for china tables in the 1754 edition of *The Gentleman and Cabinet-Maker's Director* (pl. 34), which he described as "tables for holding each a set of China, and may be used as Tea-Tables."[4]

Beyond the difference in their primary functions ("service" for the square tea table versus "display" for the china table), there was a substantial difference in the price of each type of table. The only New England price book for the third quarter of the eighteenth century, from Providence—"The Rule and Price of Joyners Work"—lists only three tea table designs: a "common tea table @ 10£," a "Mehogny Stand Table @ 30£," and "Do Black walnut @ 26.00.0." These prices are quoted in the highly inflated Rhode Island currency of the day with an exchange rate of £23.6.8=£1 (sterling). More illustrative are figures taken from the 1772 Philadelphia price book that fix the cost of a square, mahogany tea table with plain top, feet, and rails at £3.[5] A "china" table in the same material with plain (that is, Marlborough) legs, stretchers, bases, brackets, and fret top cost 50 percent more, or £4.10.0. The comparable cost of a mahogany pillar tea table with plain top and pad feet was £2.15.0.

Winterthur's collection includes a wide range of tables with both standard square and shaped overhanging tops. Among those with shaped tops are a group with projecting round corners (see

Nos. 111, 112)—a design identified in the twentieth century as a *porringer top*—and two with unusual octagonal tops (Nos. 116, 117). Also included are a stylish mahogany table with Marlborough legs (No. 138) from Rhode Island and an unusual, simple table on a triangular frame (No. 115).

The more traditional square tea tables at Winterthur illustrate a range of designs available from Rhode Island, Massachusetts, and New Hampshire craftsmen. The Rhode Island forms include a galleried "china table" (No. 125) attributed to John Townsend (1733–1809) and two tea tables made by John Goddard (1723/24–85) with the serpentine-shape square-corner rails (No. 123) favored in Newport. The Massachusetts tea tables include some of the more unusual designs: a tea table with a tile top (No. 119), one with a dished marble top (No. 120), and one with a ceramic tray inset in a frame (No. 124). Also in the collection is a mahogany tea table with an unusual, scalloped-edge top and rails in a design that has come to be called a *turret top* (No. 122). The traditional, square tea table form is represented by a New Hampshire example (No. 113).

Another specialized table form introduced in America in the eighteenth century featured a stationary, rectangular, four-leg frame with the skirt finished on three sides and a "stone" (that is, marble) or, occasionally, wood top. Its origins were Continental; the form was brought to England from France with the restoration of the monarchy in 1660. In England the form had two distinct uses. In one role, it could be found in most main rooms in a stylish house stationed in the pier between windows. This so-called pier table held lighting devices and other decoration and usually was displayed with a complementary looking glass above it. As illustrated in eighteenth-century pattern books, pier tables were intended to be fabricated in soft wood, elaborately carved and gilded, and finished with marble "slab" tops. The form afforded designers and carvers working in the rococo style—men such as Matthias Lock, Thomas Johnson, and Thomas Chippendale—opportunity to experiment with fantasy.

A second design, called a *sideboard table* in the eighteenth century, was intended for use in a dining room as the surface to display silver and gold plate, wine decanters, and elaborate knife boxes. Related to the pier table in overall conception, it also had a marble, scagliola, or mosaic slab top. Some English examples had fanciful, gilded, carved rococo decoration, but most sideboard tables were made in a more restrained fashion using mahogany throughout.

Physical and documentary evidence confirm that both forms were available in America. Although there is no comparable listing in the 1756–57 Providence cabinetmakers' price book, the 1772 Philadelphia price book includes both forms. "Sideboard" tables are listed in both mahogany and walnut but were available only with straight (Marlborough) legs and wooden tops. Frames for marble "slab" tables were listed both with "Marlboro fee[t]" and with cabriole legs on claw feet.[6]

Despite an exceptionally early reference to "a Marble table, In the Hall" in the 1665 inventory of Gov. John Endicott of Massachusetts, documentary evidence indicates that the slab table appeared in New England in the second quarter of the eighteenth century. Most contemporary inventory references describe the form as a "marble table and frame," and most place it in a hall, parlor, dining room (if the house had a space so designated), or chamber.[7] The variety of locations suggests that the form may have had more than one use. Once considered to be only the province of wealthy householders (merchants, mariners, and professional men) in major port cities such as Boston or Salem, its availability and use appears to have been more widespread than previously thought. Winterthur's collection includes cabriole-leg examples from the Portsmouth, New Hampshire/Berwick, Maine, area (No. 126); Norwich, Connecticut (No. 127); and Massachusetts (No. 128).

One of the greatest modifications in eighteenth-century table design came in those forms used for dining. During the middle of the previous century, round or oval, hinged-leaf gateleg tables (called "falling tables" in the eighteenth century) replaced the long, fixed dining tables and trestle-base tables with removable tops that had graced the medieval hall. These smaller tables made social entertaining more relaxed and convivial. They also had the advantage of offering an expansive surface when in use but occupying minimal floor space when stored. Round and oval dining tables continued to be available into the early eighteenth century but were gradually replaced by rectangular-shape models after the 1740s. The new design had a certain advantage over the round forms. Rectangular tables of similar height could be used separately or placed together to form a single, long table if needed. It is notable that neither Chippendale nor any of his contemporaries included designs for dining tables in their trade catalogues. Possibly this reflects a standardization of the form, allowing for only minimal experimentation with decoration.

Prices for dining tables were calculated on the length of the "bed," or frame, and whether the flaps (leaves) were cut with an old-fashioned butt joint or the newly fashionable "rule" joint. The difference in this feature, according to the 1756–57 Providence price book was an added 10s. for the rule joint: the 1756 price-per-bed-foot with rule joint was £4.10.0 and with the old-fashioned butt joint, £4. By 1772, when the Philadelphia price list was published, the rule joint was standard. The prices for dining tables are quoted with "plain feet crook=ed [cabriole legs] or Marlborough with bases 3 feet in the bed, 3.5.0." This is a standard four-leg table where two of the legs swing to support the leaves. The price increased by 10s. to 15s. for each additional six inches in bed length. There was also an increase in price when the length of the bed reached five feet and an additional pair of legs was needed for support.[8]

One by-product of the Restoration was the introduction in upper-class British homes of a room specifically set aside for dining where the table was left in situ. In more modest homes, dining was incorporated into one of the parlors; the table was moved into place for use and returned to the wall for storage. Formal meals were served at large, drop-leaf tables. Informal family meals, such as breakfast, were served on small tables of various forms. Popular designs included tables with two hinged flaps supported on gatelegs or, later, on hinged brackets. Breakfast tables and pembroke tables developed in response to the eighteenth-century practice among the British upper class of rising late and eating in an upstairs chamber. The origins of the breakfast table are unknown, but in his *Cabinet Dictionary* (1803), Thomas Sheraton credits the origin of the pembroke table to "the lady who first gave orders for one of them."[9]

Although we tend to use the names *breakfast table* and *pembroke table* interchangeably today, they were two distinct designs to Thomas Chippendale. He describes the breakfast table, the earlier of the two names, as having an enclosed lower shelf, while the pembroke table was distinguished by the inclusion of a drawer.[10] Chippendale included designs for both forms in the 1762 edition of his *Director* (pl. 53), although he titles the drawings "Breakfast Tables."

American eighteenth-century probate records show a decided preference for the term *breakfast table*, while the available post-1765 price books consistently use the designation *pembroke table*. As with other table forms, breakfast/pembroke tables were available in several designs. The 1772 Philadelphia price book offers the range of decorative options:

| Pembroke Tables | [mahogany] | [walnut] |
|---|---|---|
| *Breakfast Table plain* | *2.15.0* | *1.15.0* |
| *Ditto with a Drawer* | *3.0.0* | *2.0.0* |
| *Ditto with bases & bragets* | *3.5.0* | *2.5.0* |
| *Ditto with a plain Stretcher* | *3.10.0* | *2.10.0* |
| *Ditto with open Stretcher & 2 dra^(wer)* | *4.0.0* | *3.0.0* |
| *Ditto with Claw feet* | *3.15.0* | *2.15.0[11]* |

Winterthur has a wide variety of tables used for dining, both full-size and smaller tables, mostly from eastern Massachusetts. Of particular interest are a group of round or oval leaf tables (see Nos. 130–32), two single-leaf rectangular tables (No. 134), a full-size dining table labeled by Benjamin Frothingham, Jr. (1734–1809), of Charlestown, Massachusetts (No. 137), and a pembroke table in the Chinese taste labeled by John Townsend (1733–1809) of Newport (No. 138).

Completing the table forms considered essential in a well-appointed eighteenth-century English or New England home was the card table. Although Sheraton observed that it was "a piece of furniture oftener used than to good purpose," the form was not new to the eighteenth century. Card games had been popular in England since at least the fourteenth century. These early games did not require any special furniture beyond a small table with a flat surface that could be covered with a cloth or carpet on which the cards were spread. As the form developed, card tables were semicircular or rectangular with two identical leaves, one attached to the frame and the other folding on top of it. The unfolded leaf was supported on hinged rear legs. By the eighteenth century, the design had been modified to include projecting square or round front corners with shallow depressions that held candlesticks during evening play. Some card tables also had deeper depressions or holes, called *guinea pits*, for counters or money.[12] Most card tables had the playing surface covered with green baize, although a few were solid wood.

No date has been determined for the introduction of the form to New England, but scattered references to card tables (probably English) appear after about 1725. After midcentury, card tables become a standard listing in American cabinetmakers' advertisements. Early examples tend to favor projecting, rounded front corners; later examples are likely to have projecting square corners. Some card tables were fitted with drawers, but this was not an essential feature of the form in New England.

Card tables are listed in New England inventories primarily in parlors or in chambers that appear to have been used for entertaining. The form is listed singly or in pairs—an acknowledgment of the eighteenth-century emphasis on balance and order. Like other furniture forms, card tables were stored against a wall and brought out for use. When not in use, they provided a suitable surface for displaying other objects.

Winterthur's collection includes representative examples of two of the typical card table forms produced in Rhode Island. One relates to the classic Newport block-and-serpentine tea table form (No. 141) and is a product of the Townsend-Goddard school. The other (No. 142) has a chip-carved serpentine facade with square corners and fluted straight legs. A related card table in a similar design (No. 143) was made in nearby Massachusetts. The collection also includes a rare Boston card table with scroll feet (No. 140) and a labeled card table made by Benjamin Frothingham (No. 139).

The roots of the form known in the eighteenth century as the "stand table" or "claw table" are in the pedestal-base tables of ancient Greece and Rome.[13] The design—a round (or occasionally square) top supported on a single column or pillar that terminates below in three spreading feet or claws—was introduced into England about the time of the restoration of the monarchy. Its great period of popularity began about 1730 and continued for almost half a century, until the introduction of neoclassicism in the mid 1760s. The form enjoyed a revival in the nineteenth century.

The pillar and tripod table form afforded a wide range of decorative options. Tops could be plain (flat), dished (with a molded rim), or scalloped (in what has come to be called a "pie crust" rim). Decorative alternatives for the pillar ranged from simple turning to elaborate carving. On the cabriole legs, the knees could be either plain or carved and the feet plain or carved in a ball and claw, scroll, or paw. One advantage of the tripod base was that it effectively compensated for any unevenness in the floor.

English cabinetmakers offered the pillar table in a range of sizes intended to accommodate a variety of needs. Those with two- to three-foot-diameter tops generally were used as tea tables, although they also served in other capacities. Tables of a similar form, but ringed for as many as eight plates, were designated "supper tables."[14]

The pattern of use for tripod tables in America parallels that in England, although supper tables were considerably less common here. The form recognized today as the tripod table did not become numerous until the eighteenth century. It was produced concurrently with the square tea table and enjoyed its greatest popularity in New England between about 1730 and the end of the century.

In terms of construction the tripod table was a collaborative effort of the turner (who shaped the pillar and rounded the top), the carver (who ornamented the top, pillar, and legs), and the cabinetmaker (who assembled the component parts). The simplest and least expensive design featured a fixed top. Tables with fixed tops tended to be smaller in size. They were less versatile than comparable hinged-top models, which could be moved and stored more easily. Hinged-top pillar tables were of two designs. In one, the top was hinged by cleats fitted over pintles on one side of a block fixed to the top of the shaft; the top was held horizontal by a metal catch. In the second, the stationary block is replaced by a "box" composed of turned balusters tenoned between two square blocks; the same clasp mechanism was used to secure the tabletop to the top of the box. Use of the box allowed the top to tilt vertically and to rotate horizontally on the pedestal. Advertisements for tea table catches appear in Philadelphia and Boston by the 1740s.[15]

The prices for pillar tables reflect the choice of materials and the amount of ornament. The 1757 Providence price book lists:

> *Mehogeney Stand Table @ 30 £*
> *Do Black walnot @ 26.00.0*
> *Maple Do @ 20 £*

The 1772 Philadelphia price book details the level of ornament:

| Tea Tables | Mahogany | Walnut |
|---|---|---|
| Plain top & feet | 2.15.0 | 1.15.0 |
| Plain Tea table with Claw feet | 3.15.0 | 2.5.0 |
| Ditto Leaves on the knees | 4.0.0 | 2.15.0 |
| Ad for fluting the piller 5s.[16] | | |

The strength of Winterthur's collection is in the representation of Massachusetts examples with round (see Nos. 144, 145) and "square" tops (see No. 146). One of the round-top tables has an unusual box (No. 145). Boxes are standard on pillar tables from the middle colonies and the

South, but the feature is rare in New England. One of the most unusual round-top tables in the collection (No. 147) is a Rhode Island table with a cabinet support in place of the traditional pillar.

*NER with WAC*

1 Samuel Johnson, *A Dictionary of the English Language,* 2 vols. (London: J. F. and C. Rivington, 1755), s.v. "table."

2 The 1717 inventory of Capt. Walter Rosewell of Boston listed "10 lbs of Green Tea, at 20s., £10" and "5 lbs Bohee Tea at 40s., £10" (as quoted in Lyon, *Colonial Furniture,* p. 232). For a general survey of eighteenth-century tea drinking customs in America, see Rodris Roth, "Tea Drinking in Eighteenth-Century America: Its Etiquette and Equipage," *United States National Museum Bulletin,* no. 225 (Washington, D.C.: Smithsonian Institution, 1961): 61–91.

3 Lyon, *Colonial Furniture,* p. 217. Andrew Oliver inventory, March 16, 1774, as quoted in Alice Hanson Jones, *American Colonial Wealth: Documents and Methods,* 3 vols. (New York: Arno Press, 1977), p. 967.

4 Macquoid and Edwards, *Dictionary,* 3:206. Thomas Chippendale, *The Gentleman and Cabinet-Maker's Director* (3d ed., London: By the author, 1762), p. 7n, pl. 51.

5 "The Rule and Price of Joyners Work," Providence, R.I., 1756, and the March 24, 1757, revision are at Rhode Island Historical Society; revised list quoted in *John Brown House Loan Exhibition,* p. 175. John J. McCusker, *Money and Exchange in Europe and America, 1600–1775: A Handbook* (Chapel Hill: University of North Carolina Press for the Institute of Early American History and Culture, Williamsburg, 1978), p. 153. The Philadelphia price book is cited in Martin Eli Weil, "A Cabinetmaker's Price Book," in Ian M. G. Quimby, ed., *Winterthur Portfolio 13* (Chicago: University of Chicago Press for the Henry Francis du Pont Winterthur Museum, 1979), pp. 187–89.

6 Weil, "Cabinetmaker's Price Book," pp. 187, 189.

7 Lyon, *Colonial Furniture,* pp. 206–7.

8 "The Rule and Price of Joyners Work," Providence, R.I., 1756, as quoted in *John Brown House Loan Exhibition,* p. 174. Philadelphia price list cited in Weil, "Cabinetmaker's Price Book," p. 185.

9 Thomas Sheraton, *The Cabinet Dictionary* (1803; reprint in 2 vols., New York: Praeger Publishers, 1970), p. 284.

10 Christopher Gilbert, *The Life and Work of Thomas Chippendale,* 2 vols. (New York: Macmillan Co., 1978), 1:303, 306.

11 Weil, "Cabinetmaker's Price Book," p. 186.

12 Sheraton, *Cabinet Dictionary,* pp. 128–29. John Gloag, ed., *A Complete Dictionary of Furniture* (1952; rev. ed., Woodstock, N.Y.: Overlook Press, 1991), p. 182.

13 Gisela Marie Augusta Richter, *The Furniture of the Greeks, Etruscans, and Romans* (London: Phaidon Press, 1966), p. 70.

14 Macquoid and Edwards, *Dictionary,* 3:207, fig. 15.

15 Hornor, *Blue Book,* p. 143. The availability of "table ketches" may be inferred in Gilbert Deblois's advertisement of "Scutchions and all other Materials needed by cabinetmakers" in the *Boston News-Letter,* May 7, 1746, as quoted in Dow, *Arts and Crafts in New England,* p. 227.

16 "Rule and Price of Joyners Work," revision, 1757, as quoted in *John Brown House Loan Exhibition,* p. 175. Weil, "Cabinetmaker's Price Book," p. 187.

twentieth-century scholars, appears on chairs usually assigned to New York City, western Long Island, or the Hudson River valley, but it also can be found on chairs made in coastal Connecticut (see No. 42). A variation of this leg design also appears on New England and western Long Island–made tables.[2] In the absence of other region-specific designs or materials, the widest possible provenance has been assigned. The extended date range reflects the long term production of furniture with straight, turned legs and offset feet.

NER with WAC

**Construction:** The dished top is formed by a cyma-recto molding nailed to the outside edge of the solid, one-board top. The top is nailed to the corners of the frame. The tenons on the four rails are shouldered only on the outside surface and the top edge. They are fixed in the leg mortises with double pins. The legs are turned, but the feet are carved. Saw marks on the outside of each leg above the ankle are overcuts from when the blocks needed for carving the feet were roughed out.

**Condition:** Both side rails and one end rail are split at one end at the lower peg. Two of the foot pads are patched.

**Dimensions:**

| | | |
|---|---|---|
| H. | 25 in. | 63.5 cm |
| W. (top) | 24 3/8 in. | 61.9 cm |
| W. (frame) | 13 3/4 in. | 34.9 cm |
| W. (feet) | 19 1/2 in. | 49.5 cm |
| D. (top) | 17 in. | 43.2 cm |
| D. (frame) | 12 1/4 in. | 31.1 cm |
| D. (feet) | 17 1/8 in. | 43.5 cm |

**Materials:** *Microanalysis:* Primary: soft maple group (throughout). *Finish:* the primary layer appears to be a red stain with a resin coat; covering it are 2 different layers of green paint; the finish coat is a natural resin.

**Publications:** Downs, *American Furniture*, fig. 368. Butler, *American Furniture*, p. 53. Kirk, *American Furniture*, fig. 393.

**Accession history:** Bequest of H. F. du Pont, 1969. 66.780

1. John T. Kirk (*American Furniture*, pp. 152–53) has speculated that this shaping is the result of a wedge-shape cut above the ankle that permitted the foot to bend out. However, X-ray analysis contradicts this and indicates that this overcut defines the top of the block needed for carving the feet.

2. For New York chairs, see Charles F. Hummel, *With Hammer in Hand: The Dominy Craftsmen of East Hampton, New York* (Charlottesville: University Press of Virginia for the Henry Francis du Pont Winterthur Museum, 1968), p. 257, no. 188E; Dean F. Failey, *Long Island Is My Nation: The Decorative Arts and Craftsmen, 1640–1830* (Setauket, N.Y.: Society for the Preservation of Long Island Antiquities, 1976), pp. 81–83, nos. 94, 95, 98; John L. Scherer, *New York Furniture at the New York State Museum* (Alexandria, Va.: Highland House, 1984), p. 16, fig. 13, pp. 22–23, fig. 22. For New England tables, see Nutting, *Furniture Treasury*, nos. 1244 (no provenance), 1259 (Connecticut origin). See also Greenlaw, *New England Furniture*, no. 119. For western Long Island tables, see Failey, *Long Island Is My Nation*, no. 115.

## 109 ◆ Square table

Possibly coastal Connecticut or
New York
1740–90

While the development of gentility and affluence in the eighteenth century created a consumer demand for tables of increasing specialization, there was a continuing need for general, nonspecific forms. Small tables that could serve more than one function appear in most household inventories and were found in all rooms in a house; they were particularly useful where space or funds were limited. Both urban and rural eighteenth-century New England joiners produced a seemingly endless array of small, portable tables that filled a variety of needs. The form was descended from the small, stretcher-base table of 1690–1700. So generic were they that they often appear in period records identified simply as "table," without descriptive designation.

One group of these utilitarian tables features an overhanging top pinned to a simple frame with legs mortised and tenoned to the rails. Winterthur's example, a small, painted table with a single-board top and broadly splayed legs is among the more unusual

examples of this form. Its most distinctive feature is the design and execution of the turned legs, which taper to a thin ankle and end in a dramatically splayed, sloping pad foot. So abrupt is the transition from ankle to foot that the foot appears to extend beyond the plane of the block at the top of the leg.[1] The simple, unbroken reverse curve of the rails with such deep relief is quite different from the more conventionally shaped rails seen on No. 110.

This table would have probably been described in the eighteenth century simply as "square," a designation that referred to the shape of its corners rather than the outline of its rectangular top. The applied moldings on the sides of the top create a rim, indicating that it was probably intended to be used as a tea table.

Of all the table forms, the straight, turned-leg table with offset feet is the most difficult to assign to a particular region or time period. Often, nothing in the design, the choice of materials, or the method of construction is area or time specific. In the case of this table, the only clue to a possible provenance is in the design of the legs and feet. This type of support, called a "Dutch foot" by early

## 110 ◆ Square table
New England
1735–75

A common form of the New England splayed-leg, "square" table features a rectangular top that extends well beyond the conforming frame, a skirt cut in a flat-head arch, and straight, turned and tapered legs with offset, plain (pad) feet. This may be the form listed as a "common tea table" in the 1756 "Rule and Price of Joyners Work" in Providence, Rhode Island, where it was priced at a highly inflated cost of £7. In the same list, Providence joiners charged £8 for a "common house chest" or a maple "candel stand."[1]

A key feature in the success of the design of this table is the apparent thinness of the top, an illusion achieved by beveling the under edge of the top boards. The turned legs are set at a slight splay to provide optimum stability and to balance the top visually.

The spare simplicity of line and form give this very portable and functional table a stately elegance. Finished on all sides, it was clearly intended to be pulled away from the wall. Its twenty-six-inch–high top provided a comfortable level for serving food and beverages to seated family or guests. The absence of a raised rim suggests that, in addition to its possible use as a tea table, it could also have functioned as a work surface for a variety of activities from reading or sewing to possibly even game playing.

No distinctive design or construction features identify its specific place of manufacture, although the use of soft maple and birch confirm its New England provenance.

*NER/WAC*

**Inscriptions or marks:** *Inscribed in ink:* "33" *on modern gum paper label, on underside of top.*

**Construction:** The top is fashioned from two pieces of equal-width wood. Attached to the end rails from the top with four countersunk screws, the top has a slightly rounded edge and is beveled on the underside. The rails, incorporating the corner bracket, are double-tenoned into the legs. The turned, tapered cylindrical legs end in a thick, "plain" (pad) foot.

**Condition:** The top has been refinished. A split in the top has been repaired with four dowels; the countersunk screws probably were installed at that time. One long rail is split at the lower tenon.

**Dimensions:**

| | | |
|---|---|---|
| H. | 26 in. | 66.0 cm |
| W. (top) | 32 in. | 81.2 cm |
| W. (frame) | 19¹/₂ in. | 49.4 cm |
| W. (feet) | 22¹/₄ in. | 56.7 cm |
| D. (top) | 25⁷/₈ in. | 65.8 cm |
| D. (frame) | 15⁷/₁₆ in. | 39.4 cm |
| D. (feet) | 18³/₄ in. | 47.6 cm |

**Materials:** *Microanalysis:* Primary: soft maple group (top, rails, and 1 leg); birch (3 legs). *Finish:* table once painted black; top now unfinished; legs and frame retain black paint.

**Accession history:** Bequest of H. F. du Pont, 1969. 68.532

1. Quoted in *John Brown House Loan Exhibition*, pp. 174–75. Based on the 1756 rate of exchange between Rhode Island and London—that is, £23.6.8 = £1 (sterling)—a common tea table would cost between £0.6.6 and £0.7.0; see John J. McCusker, *Money and Exchange in Europe and America, 1600–1775: A Handbook* (Chapel Hill: University of North Carolina Press for the Institute of Early American History and Culture, Williamsburg, 1978), p. 153.

## 111 ◆ Square table
Newport, Rhode Island
1740–90

## Square table
Rhode Island or adjacent Connecticut
or Massachusetts
1740–90

Rectangular frame tables with projecting rounded corners may have been described as "scallop'd" in eighteenth-century records, although most likely they were simply included in the category of "square tables" or "square tea tables." Today they are commonly called *porringer-top tables*, a term introduced in the twentieth century. The form most likely derived from mid eighteenth-century folding English card tables with rounded corners or from similar colonial American card tables made in Boston, New York, and Philadelphia.[1]

As can be seen from these two examples, this innovative American form was further defined by variations in the design of the rails, the proportion of the top to the frame, and the shape of the feet. Additionally, this popular table form could be made to accommodate almost every pocketbook and hence was available in a variety of woods and finishes, including maple (usually stained or painted), walnut, or mahogany. Examples made in less expensive woods were, undoubtedly, popular items for the export trade.[2]

These two tables present a dramatic example of these different interpretations, contrasting the more costly urban taste (left) with a bolder, more lyrical expression (right) that suggests an origin outside a major urban center. The mahogany table (left) exhibits a carefully controlled delicacy in the thin, one-board top; the lightly relieved slender rails; and the beautifully turned, tapered legs terminating in perfectly shaped pad feet raised on thin disks. In contrast, the right table is made of hard (top) and soft (frame) maple, and originally the base was painted red. The tiger maple, two-board top with simple,

quarter-round, molded edge has a more pronounced overhang than its companion table fashioned of mahogany. The strong cyma-curve arched design of the rails boldly echoes and enhances the shape of the rounded corners.[3] The turned legs are thicker than those of the other table, and the feet are shaped more like clubs than delicate pads on disks. These features, combined with the unusually thick stock of the rails, suggest that it was not the product of an urban center like Newport but was made elsewhere in Rhode Island or in adjacent areas of Connecticut or Massachusetts.

Small tables of this type were movable and served many purposes. As breakfast or tea tables, they were ideal for serving food or drink to a small seated group. Additionally, they were probably used during evening entertainments such as card playing and carousing, with candlesticks placed on the protruding corners. Beyond these social functions, these tables were used in the business world as well. Samuel King's 1772 portrait of prominent Salem merchant David Moore shows him seated at such a table with

an open ledger inscribed "Newport Dec' 25 1772." About 1775 artist Gilbert Stuart portrayed Francis and Saunders Malbone, sons of a prominent Newport merchant family, using a similar table for studying and writing letters.[4]

*NER/WAC*

---

**Inscriptions or marks:** (Left) *On underside of top:* " . . . Property of/ the Misses/ . . . Allen" in ink, on fragment of gummed paper label.

**Construction:** (Left) The single-board top, rounded on the edge, is joined to the frame on the underside by countersunk screws. Each rail, with the corner bracket incorporated into the rail, is tenoned and double-pegged to the legs; the joint is reinforced with vertical glueblocks.

(Right) The two-board top is constructed of a wide and a narrow board now connected by three small slip tenons pegged to either side of the joint. The top, with slightly chamfered edge, is secured to the frame with wooden pegs (wedged) into all four rails. The 1 3/16"-thick rails are cut to include the corner brackets. The legs are tenoned (shouldered on inside and upper edges) and double-pegged to the rails.

**Condition:** (Left) There are several cracks in the top. All the leg extensions are split at the pegs. Layout lines for cutting the corners and positioning the legs are visible on the underside of the top.

(Right) The top is slightly warped and is lifting from the frame. There is a slight separation of the two top boards and a large crack in the edge of the wider board. One side rail return has been repaired.

**Dimensions:**

Left
| | | |
|---|---|---|
| H. | 25 1/2 in. | 64.8 cm |
| W. (top) | 35 in. | 88.9 cm |
| W. (frame) | 28 in. | 71.1 cm |
| W. (feet) | 28 1/2 in. | 72.4 cm |
| D. (top) | 23 1/4 in. | 59.1 cm |
| D. (frame) | 16 7/8 in. | 42.9 cm |
| D. (feet) | 18 1/4 in. | 46.4 cm |

Right
| | | |
|---|---|---|
| H. | 25 1/2 in. | 64.5 cm |
| W. (top) | 38 1/2 in. | 98.2 cm |
| W. (frame) | 24 1/2 in. | 62.3 cm |
| W. (feet) | 24 in. | 61.0 cm |
| D. (top) | 24 1/2 in. | 62.4 cm |
| D. (frame) | 18 1/2 in. | 47.0 cm |
| D. (feet) | 18 3/8 in. | 46.5 cm |

**Materials:** *Microanalysis:* (Left) Primary: mahogany. Secondary: red cedar (glueblocks). (Right) Primary:

hard maple group (top); soft maple group (rails, legs). *Finish:* (Left) natural resin. (Right) evidence of early red paint (iron oxide) on the base suggests that originally only the base was painted. The remnants of a later coat of black paint overall remain on the edges of the top and on the legs and feet. The top has been refinished, leaving the curled maple surface visible. The top is now coated with a natural resin.

**Publications:** (Left) Downs, *American Furniture*, fig. 302. (Right) Downs, *American Furniture*, fig. 301. Comstock, *American Furniture*, no. 227. Dean A. Fales, Jr., *American Painted Furniture, 1660–1880* (New York: E. P. Dutton, 1972), fig. 119.

**Provenance:** (Right) The table was discovered in New London, Conn.

**Accession history:** (Left) Bequest of H. F. du Pont, 1969. (Right) Purchased by H. F. du Pont from George Arons and Brothers, Ansonia, Conn., 1935. Bequest of H. F. du Pont, 1969.
64.1072, 59.1531

---

1. Also referred to as square tea tables in eighteenth-century Rhode Island were those with stop-fluted legs (No. 114) and cabriole legs with slipper feet or ball-and-claw feet (No. 123). For an English card table, see Macquoid and Edwards, *Dictionary*, 3:195–200, figs. 9,

12–18, 23, 25; for a Boston example, see Randall, *American Furniture*, no. 79; Museum of Fine Arts, Boston, *Paul Revere's Boston, 1735–1818* (Boston: By the museum, 1975), no. 95; for New York examples, see Downs, *American Furniture*, figs. 336, 337, 339; Heckscher, *American Furniture*, cat. nos. 104, 105. For a Philadelphia card table, see Downs, *American Furniture*, figs. 343, 346; Hornor, *Blue Book*, pls. 207, 234, 235.

2. For maple examples, see Greenlaw, *New England Furniture*, no. 125; Fales, *Furniture of Historic Deerfield*, figs. 301, 302; *American Antiques from Israel Sack Collection*, 10 vols. (Washington, D.C.: Highland House, ca. 1969–), 5:1352, 6:1517; Rodriguez Roque, *American Furniture*, no. 126. For walnut examples, see Max Webber advertisement, *Antiques* 81, no. 1 (January 1962): 33; *American Antiques from Sack Collection*, 2:495. For mahogany examples, see Nutting, *Furniture Treasury*, fig. 885; John S. Walton advertisement, *Antiques* 63, no. 3 (March 1953): 169; John Kenneth Byard advertisement, *Antiques* 69, no. 6 (June 1956): 473; *American Antiques from Sack Collection*, 1:20; 8:2324; Monkhouse and Michie, *American Furniture*, cat. 69; Christie's, "The Collection of the Late Jeannette R. Marks, Lexington, Kentucky" (June 5, 1987), lot 322. Joan Barzilay Freund, *Masterpieces of Americana: The Collection of Mr. and Mrs. Adolph Henry Meyer* (New York: Sotheby's, 1995), p. 24. On the export trade, see Jeanne Vibert Sloane, "John Cahoone and the Newport Furniture Industry," in *New England Furniture*, pp. 110–11.

3. For another example of a serpentine-shape skirt, see *American Antiques from Sack Collection*, 3:709.

4. William B. Stevens, "Samuel King of Newport," *Antiques* 96, no. 5 (November 1969): 728; *Gilbert Stuart: Portraitist of the Young Republic, 1755–1828* (Providence: Museum of Art, Rhode Island School of Design, 1967), pp. 36–37.

## 112 ◆ Square table
Coastal Connecticut or Long Island,
New York
1730–75

This is the largest of the "square" tables
with rounded corners at Winterthur, and it
is indeed a most unusual form. Wider than
most porringer-top tables (see No. 111), this
example has finely carved cabriole legs with
shod slipper feet rather than the usual turned
and tapered cylindrical legs with pad feet.
The extraordinarily deep rails with unusually
complex shaping are reminiscent of those seen
on New England high chests and dressing
tables from the 1710s to the 1740s (Nos. 156,
158). A variation on that elaborate shaping
also appears on a group of similar casepieces,
including a dressing table from the Windsor,
Connecticut, area (No. 161).[1]

More specifically, the frame of this
table relates closely to Rhode Island and
Connecticut chests-on-frames, although it is
about four or five inches wider than the frame
for a chest might be.[2] Another feature of this
table that relates it directly to case furniture
construction is the design and fabrication of
the rear legs. The back sides of the stiles on

the rear legs have not been cut away and
hence are heavier than those on the front.
Further indicative of frames for cases of
drawers is the fact that the rear rail, while
presently shaped to echo the front rail,
appears to have begun as a straight rail.
Although this table poses some perplexing
juxtapositions, one logical explanation is that
as a nonurban product it was fashioned in a
shop of craftsmen primarily producing case
furniture, and they created a distinctive table
based on their own specific traditions and
practices. Alternately, it could have been
fabricated according to a specific patron's
request, perhaps in order to match case
furniture already owned by that patron.

The association with coastal Connecticut
or Long Island is based primarily on the
specific shape of the legs and feet. Unlike
the cabriole legs with delicate slipper feet
found on Rhode Island furniture, these legs
lack the square shape and hard edges of those
examples, and the feet relate more directly to
the raised shod-pad feet seen on New York
furniture. Clearly not the product of an urban
cabinetmaker, this table represents a bold
break with tradition resulting in a dramatically
creative, very much out-of-the-mainstream

product that could well have originated in
coastal Connecticut where traditions from
Rhode Island as well as Long Island might
well have had an influence.

The only other table that bears a
resemblance to this design is a larger,
more sophisticated marble-top table in the
collection of Colonial Williamsburg.[3] It
has pad feet and an inset marble top, but
the skirt is vigorously shaped on all four
sides. It has a loose association with an early
Connecticut governor, Gurdon Saltonstall
(1666–1724).

*WAC/NER*

**Construction:** The shaped, one-board top with
chamfered edge overhangs the frame on all four
sides. The top is secured to the frame with pins at
the corners and at the center of the front and rear
rails. These latter pins are visible on the lower edge
of the skirt. The rails are tenoned and triple-pegged
to the legs. The stiles/legs are cut from 3"-square
maple; the front cabriole legs have fully developed
knees on the front and sides. The rear legs, though
fully profiled in their length, only have rounded
knees on the sides. Because the knees are not
rounded on the rear, the rear stiles are a full 3"
deep. The knee brackets are glued to the legs.
Platforms for turned drops are nailed to the skirt;

there is no evidence that the table ever was fitted with pendent drops.

**Condition:** The table once was painted or stained. Although the rear rail originally was plain, it has been cut to conform to the shape of the front rail. (This reshaping has considerable age and may predate the twentieth century.) Some of the knee blocks are replaced.

**Dimensions:**

| | | |
|---|---|---|
| H. | 28 1/2 in. | 68.9 cm |
| W. (top) | 42 in. | 106.7 cm |
| W. (frame) | 36 7/8 in. | 93.7 cm |
| W. (feet) | 38 in. | 96.5 cm |
| D. (top) | 24 in. | 61.0 cm |
| D. (frame) | 19 in. | 48.3 cm |
| D. (feet) | 20 in. | 50.8 cm |

**Materials:** *Microanalysis:* Primary: soft maple group (throughout). *Finish:* natural resin; an earlier paint or wash has been cleaned from the surface.

**Publications:** Downs, *American Furniture*, fig. 352.

**Accession history:** Bequest of H. F. du Pont, 1969. 58.2600

1. For the high chests and dressing tables, see Randall, *American Furniture*, nos. 50, 51; Fales, *Furniture of Historic Deerfield*, nos. 423, 424, 430; Jobe and Kaye, *New England Furniture*, fig. 29; Rodriguez Roque, *American Furniture*, no. 11; Flanigan, *American Furniture*, cat. no. 18; Monkhouse and Michie, *American Furniture*, cat. 23; Ward, *American Case Furniture*, cats. 94–96. For the Connecticut casepieces, see Heckscher, *American Furniture*, cat. 152; Lyon, *Colonial Furniture*, p. 87; for the table, see "Shop Talk," *Antiques* 67, no. 2 (February 1955): 104.

2. *John Brown House Loan Exhibition*, pp. 88–89, cat. 58; see also photographs from the Israel Sack, Inc., Archives, New York, of a maple, Rhode Island, slipper-foot chest-on-frame and a cherry, Connecticut, slipper-foot chest-on-frame.

3. Greenlaw, *New England Furniture*, no. 143.

## 113 ◆ Tea table
### New Hampshire
### 1740–80

Previously believed to have been made in Massachusetts, this table has been reassigned to New Hampshire based on similarities of certain details to known works. Most compelling, the relatively tight, vertical cabriole legs pointed at the knee and ending in a raised midrib pad foot on a large, coved disk are very similar to legs on furniture documented to Portsmouth cabinetmaker Joseph Davis. Davis, an apprentice to Boston cabinetmaker Job Coit, Sr., and his son Job, Jr., signed a customer's receipt in February 1726/27 that verifies his service.[1]

A comparable table with double-molded tray top with a large overhang and slim legs ending in hocked pad feet on large disks is attributed to John/William Trefethern of Rye, New Hampshire, now in the collection of Colonial Williamsburg. The Trefethern tabletop has an even greater overhang than Winterthur's example.[2]

Although no maker can be assigned to this table, the New Hampshire provenance is further supported by a chalk inscription on the underside of the top: "Cushman/ Tilton/ 9 Washington/ st." Tilton, New Hampshire, located approximately fifteen miles north of Concord, is the only New England town so named.

*NER/CGN*

**Inscriptions or marks:** *On underside of top:* "Cushman/ Tilton/ 9 Washington/ st." in chalk ("Tilton" is in much fresher chalk); and, partially visible: "Mrs Cushman House Tilton" in ink on lined paper, pasted.

**Construction:** An applied cavetto molding is nailed to the one-piece quarter-round-edge top board. The overhanging top is nailed to the corners of the frame. The rails are pegged to the legs with tiny pins. The shaped skirt is nailed to the face of the rails. The cabriole legs end in a midrib pad resting on a coved disk.

**Condition:** The top is split at one side. One leg extension is repaired on the inner edge. The finish is degraded, and the top is water damaged.

**Dimensions:**

| | | |
|---|---|---|
| H. | 25 5/16 in. | 64.3 cm |
| W. (top) | 27 1/4 in. | 69.3 cm |
| W. (frame) | 21 5/16 in. | 54.4 cm |
| W. (feet) | 24 1/4 in. | 61.7 cm |
| D. (top) | 18 5/8 in. | 47.4 cm |
| D. (frame) | 15 3/16 in. | 38.7 cm |
| D. (feet) | 18 1/8 in. | 46.5 cm |

**Materials:** *Microanalysis:* Primary: American black walnut (top, applied rim molding); soft maple group (rails, legs). *Finish:* natural resin.

**Publications:** Butler, *American Furniture*, p. 30.

**Accession history:** Bequest of H. F. du Pont, 1969. 60.584

1. Margaretta Markle Lovell, "Boston Blockfront Furniture," in *Boston Furniture*, pp. 98–99. Alexandra W. Rollins, "Furniture in the Collection of the Dietrich American Foundation," *Antiques* 125, no. 5 (May 1984): 1101.

2. Greenlaw, *New England Furniture*, pp. 148–49, no. 128. For a similar small tea table at Historic Deerfield, see Fales, *Furniture of Historic Deerfield*, fig. 308.

Fig. 1. Detail, leg.

## 114 ◆ Square table
Rhode Island, possibly Providence
1765–90

Straight-leg furniture was introduced in pattern books of the mid eighteenth century and was swiftly adopted by American craftsmen. Quite fashionable, this style was also less labor-intensive and therefore was cheaper to produce. Rhode Island cabinetmakers began using this type of leg on a variety of table forms perhaps a full decade prior to the Revolution. Unlike the fluted legs commonly used in other geographic regions, Rhode Island cabinetmakers defined their flutes by literally "stopping" the concave flute about six to eight inches from the base of the leg; hence the term *stop fluted*. Fashion-conscious consumers could choose the option of square (or Marlborough), stop-fluted legs on tea and china tables (No. 125), pembroke (breakfast) tables (No. 138), and card tables (Nos. 142, 143).

The stop-fluted Marlborough leg was also used in Rhode Island on a small group of square tables with overhanging tops.[1] Although they differ in the manner of decoration, all have mortise-and-tenoned frames with the top secured to the rails by a series of interior

glueblocks, a technique found on other styles of Rhode Island tables. The most unusual of the group is this example, with a solid mahogany top, figured mahogany veneer on the rails, carved interrupted bead molding at the lower edge of the skirt, pierced brackets, and stop-fluted legs finished with a thin platform (fig. 1). The highly figured stock of the rails and the top suggests that the table was intended to be placed in a prominent and highly visible room, such as a best parlor, where it could be adequately admired.

Several interesting features separate Winterthur's table from the group. It is the only one with mahogany veneer on solid maple rails. In a departure from the standard practice of gluing, the veneer facings on the long rails are glued and then nailed, with the projecting nail ends bent over on the inside of the frame. This technique is not used on the end rails. The brackets are nailed in place and also reinforced from behind with thin mahogany blocks instead of mortised and tenoned without any reinforcing blocks. Winterthur's table is also the only example raised on applied platforms and the only one to have been fitted with casters. The interrupted bead molding is not only unusual but is also handled in an irregular manner,

with the number of beads varying from seven to twelve.

Prior to the 1984 publication of Michael Moses's study of Newport furniture, most Rhode Island tables with stop-fluted legs and pierced knee brackets were assigned to the shop of John Townsend. These attributions were for the most part based on a visual similarity to such labeled pieces as Winterthur's breakfast table (No. 138). Despite this visual affinity, the method of construction among these tables is very different. The square tables lack the transverse bracing of the frame and the flat-filed, mortise-and-tenoned knee brackets that seem to be Townsend's preferred method of construction.[2] The stop-fluted legs of this table have only three flutes (as opposed to the four or five on documented Townsend pieces) and lack the steadiness indicative of the best Newport furniture. Furthermore, the workmanship on this table does not reflect the crisp precision and quality of most documented Townsend furniture. Although at first glance this square table appears to be a product of a Newport shop, closer examination suggests that more likely it was made outside Newport (perhaps in Providence) by a craftsman who either apprenticed in Newport or was visually familiar with the production of that style center. The closely related table in the collection of the Museum of Art, Rhode Island School of Design has a history of ownership in the Providence area (Cranston), and Christopher P. Monkhouse has suggested "the possibility that it was made at the northern end of the Narragansett Bay."[3]

*WAC/NER*

**Construction:** The one-piece top, ogee-molded on all four sides, has a deeper overhang on the ends than on the long sides. The top is attached to the frame with glueblocks on all the rails; it also now is nailed from the underside of the frame. The veneered rails are tenoned and double-pinned to the legs. A carved, interrupted bead molding is nailed to the lower edge of the frame. The pierced knee brackets, nailed to the legs and rails, are supported on the inside by triangular glueblocks. The stop-fluted legs are chamfered on the inner edge; a conforming platform is nailed to the bottom of the leg.

**Condition:** The highly figured top is warped and has several splits along the grain, including a crack on the front edge, which is held with a butterfly patch on the underside. In addition to the glueblocks, the top is nailed from the inside of the frame, possibly in an effort to correct the warp. Some of the brackets are repaired. Two of the platforms on the legs are original; two are replaced. The table once was fitted with casters.

**Dimensions:**

| | | |
|---|---|---|
| H. | 27 1/4 in. | 69.2 cm |
| W. (top) | 33 3/4 in. | 85.7 cm |
| W. (frame) | 27 7/8 in. | 70.8 cm |
| W. (feet) | 28 1/2 in. | 72.4 cm |
| D. (top) | 23 in. | 58.4 cm |
| D. (frame) | 18 in. | 45.7 cm |
| D. (feet) | 18 1/2 in. | 47.0 cm |

**Materials:** *Microanalysis:* Primary: mahogany; mahogany veneer. Secondary: soft maple group (rails); white pine group (glueblocks); mahogany (glueblocks supporting the brackets). *Finish:* natural resin.

**Publications:** *The Antiquarian* 15, no. 5 (November 1930): 14. Au Quatrieme, "Sale of the John Wanamaker (New York) Collection" (1930), p. 24, fig. 2. Downs, *American Furniture*, fig. 371.

**Accession history:** Purchased by H. F. du Pont at the exhibition and sale of the John Wanamaker (New York) collection at Au Quatrieme, New York, 1930. Bequest of H. F. du Pont, 1969.
59.2842

1. Rodriguez Roque, *American Furniture*, no. 127; Teina Baumstone advertisement, *Antiques* 90, no. 4 (October 1966): 402; Nutting, *Furniture Treasury*, no. 889; John S. Walton, Inc. (no. 70.3900, DAPC, Visual Resources Collection, Winterthur Library); Monkhouse and Michie, *American Furniture*, cat. 72.

2. Moses, *Master Craftsmen*, pp. 89–91.

3. Monkhouse and Michie, *American Furniture*, cat. 72.

## 115 ◆ Table
### New England
### 1730–80

Frame tables with triangular bases and round tops are considerably less common than those with rectangular bases. This unusual and rather diminutive table seems to derive from the popular oval or porringer-top tables with turned legs terminating in pad feet. However, the three legs of this table are turned the entire length instead of being square in the upper third where the rails are tenoned into the legs. This rare feature creates a visual continuity between the top and frame, almost suggesting that the rails should follow the same circular pattern. The rails instead echo those seen on numerous square tables with a broken cyma curve at each end, suggesting a bracket as it lightly relieves the rail. These shaped rails, along with ring turnings on the legs, provide the only decoration on the table.

Several unusual construction features add to the maverick quality of this table. In a

**Fig. 1.** Detail, underside of top.

departure from the standard method of mortise-and-tenon framing, the rails are joined to the cylindrical stiles with tenons shouldered only on the inside edge of the frame, and instead of pinning the top board to the frame or attaching it with glueblocks, the maker nailed wide cleats to cutouts in the rails and then to the underside of the top (fig. 1). These construction solutions and the combination of walnut top and legs with mahogany rails represents a distinctive approach that is not part of a currently identifiable shop tradition.

The exact function of this table is also difficult to ascertain given its unique size and characteristics. However, the unusually low height (just twenty-five inches) indicates that it was probably not used for serving tea or meals, nor would it have been used for writing or a leisure time activity. It might simply have been used in a passageway to hold candlesticks or in a chamber to hold miscellaneous personal items or a washbowl and pitcher.

*NER/WAC*

---

**Construction:** The top is pieced from one wide and two narrow boards. Three battens, nailed to notches cut into the top edge of the frame, are in turn attached to the underside of the top with rosehead nails. The edges of the battens are chamfered on the outside of the frame. The tapered legs are fully turned (on two axes) to resemble a true turned and carved cabriole leg. The rails are joined to the legs with mortise-and-tenon joints; they are secured with vertical glueblocks reinforced with wrought nails. Because adjacent rails join the legs at less than a ninety-degree angle, the tenons are flush with the outside of the rails (shouldered only on the inside) in order to leave as much wood as possible between the mortises for maximum strength. Layout lines for the placement of the legs are still visible on the underside of the top.

**Condition:** One leg, split at the top, has been repaired and has three plugged holes. Another leg has lost a section of the leg extension. All the legs have small reinforcing nails added to the tenons.

**Dimensions:**

| | | |
|---|---|---|
| H. | 25 in. | 63.5 cm |
| Diam. (with grain) | 26 in. | 66.0 cm |
| Diam. (across grain) | 25 1/2 in. | 64.8 cm |
| W. (feet) | 21 1/2 in. | 54.6 cm |

**Materials:** *Microanalysis:* Primary: American black walnut (top, legs, battens); mahogany (rails). Secondary: chestnut (glueblocks). *Finish:* multilayer natural resin finish with substantial crazing on the skirt rail.

**Accession history:** Museum purchase from Harry Arons, Ansonia, Conn., 1956. 56.94.3

## 116 ◆ Square table
### Eastern New England
### 1740–90

The captivating appeal of this simple birch table has been achieved through broken cyma-curve–shaped rails, an octagonal top with a quarter-round molded edge, and tapered, faceted legs that echo the unusual shaping of the top. Normally, a square frame table of this type would have plain rails, tapered cylindrical legs, and a rectangular top with a wide overhang on the ends. The faceted top visually lightens the entire aspect of the table and focuses the eye on the similarly faceted legs, which are bead molded on the outside edge of the top third, are chamfered below the rails, have clearly defined ankles, and end in midrib pad feet raised on disks. This unusual leg pattern and the support for the top also appear on a "square" table at the Museum of Art, Rhode Island School of Design. Several related tables with rectangular tops, similarly shaped skirts, and cabriole legs with pad feet offer interesting comparisons to Winterthur's example.[1]

Although the use of birch throughout suggests a possible northern New England or New Hampshire origin, this table's similarities to other examples from different regions makes it difficult to attribute it to any specific area. For example, similarly shaped rails and a related stance can be seen in an eastern Connecticut table and a Newport table, and the unusual faceted leg can be found on a tray-top tea table from Newport now at the Art Institute of Chicago.[2]

*NER/WAC*

---

**Construction:** The thumbnail-edge two-board top (one board slightly wider than the other) is joined by a full-depth cleat nailed to the underside of the top and notched into the long apron rails. The top is through-pinned into the frame and the stiles. The side and end rails are tenoned and double-pinned to the legs. The rails vary markedly in thickness, resulting in the tenons on three rails being shouldered on both surfaces and the tenons on one end rail shouldered only on the outside. The legs, molded on the outer edge at the skirt, are chamfered on four corners below the skirt and terminate at the foot. The pad foot has an unusual, raised midrib.

**Condition:** The top is warped. Butterfly patches let into the underside are used to rejoin the separating top boards. Two of the stiles and one end rail are split.

**Dimensions:**

| | | |
|---|---|---|
| H. | 26¼ in. | 66.7 cm |
| W. (top) | 32½ in. | 82.6 cm |
| W. (frame) | 17¼ in. | 43.6 cm |
| W. (feet) | 16¾ in. | 42.5 cm |
| D. (top) | 22⅝ in. | 57.5 cm |
| D. (frame) | 14¼ in. | 36.2 cm |
| D. (feet) | 13½ in. | 34.3 cm |

**Materials:** *Microanalysis:* Primary: birch (throughout). *Finish:* originally covered in a natural resin finish, the table has coats of green and gray paint covered by its present coat of brown paint.

**Publications:** Downs, *American Furniture*, fig. 300. Butler, *American Furniture*, p. 53.

**Accession history:** Bequest of H. F. du Pont, 1969. 63.620

1. For the more common form of square frame table, see Greenlaw, *New England Furniture*, pp. 142–43; for the Museum of Art, RISD example, see Monkhouse and Michie, *American Furniture*, cat. 68; for the related tables, see Jonathan Fairbanks, "A Decade of Collecting American Decorative Arts at the Museum of Fine Arts, Boston," *Antiques* 120, no. 3 (September 1981): 596, fig. 5; David Stockwell advertisement, *Antiques* 110, no. 1 (July 1976): 1.

2. For the Connecticut table, see Nathan Liverant and Son advertisement, *Antiques* 143, no. 1 (January 1993): 81; for the Newport table, see Albert Sack, "Regionalism in Early American Tea Tables," *Antiques* 131, no. 1 (January 1987): 255, fig. 4; the tea table is fig. 6.

## 117 ◆ Square table
Possibly Rhode Island or coastal Connecticut
1740–80

Although this octagonal-top square-frame table is related in concept to the preceding example, the resulting overall design is quite different. The octagonal top (which originally was as wide as it was long) is positioned atop a square frame in such a manner that the corners of the frame line up with the corners of the top. Additionally, the center of the flattened arch on each rail lines up with a corner of the top, creating a well-proportioned and balanced design. An unusually complex molding composed of a horizontal torus combined with cyma-reversa curve is applied to the edge of the top, suggesting that the table was used to serve tea or punch or perhaps simply displayed fashionable utilitarian wares. The slender, rather rigid cabriole legs are square in section with well-defined edges and are similar to those often seen on Rhode Island furniture. The pad feet have a steeply sloping upper profile atop a well-defined cup raised on a thin disk.

Tables with octagonal (or hexagonal) tops are infrequently seen in mid eighteenth-century English furniture pattern books. On rare occasions when the design does appear, it usually takes the form of a small candle- or kettle stand.[1] The absence of the form in high-style source books may suggest that they were more the creation of nonurban craftsmen breaking away from the norm.

Nothing in the method of construction of this table suggests a specific region of origin. The best clues to provenance are the square cabriole leg and the flattened-arch skirt. One or both of these features are present on a wide range of mid eighteenth-century Rhode Island and Connecticut furniture.

*NER/WAC*

**Inscriptions or marks:** *Incised on one rail:* "X"; *incised on another:* "V".

**Construction:** The two-board top, its applied molding both nailed and pinned (later), is pinned to the frame from the top; there are two pins on one pair of rails and a single pin on the other. The skirt rails are tenoned (shoulders on inside) and double-pinned to the legs. Small knee brackets are glued to the face of the skirt.

**Condition:** The table has been refinished. A major separation in the top has been repaired with a thin wood spline. Two adjacent leg posts are split and have portions replaced. Sections of top molding are split, and several have been reattached using small wood pegs. The nails used to hold the molding are older than the pegs. Several knee blocks are replaced.

**Dimensions:**

| | | |
|---|---|---|
| H. | 29 in. | 73.7 cm |
| W. (top, across grain) | 26⁷⁄₁₆ in. | 67.0 cm |
| W. (top, with grain) | 26³⁄₄ in. | 67.7 cm |
| W. (frame) | 14¹⁄₂ in. | 37.0 cm |
| W. (feet) | 16⁷⁄₁₆ in. | 41.8 cm |
| D. (frame) | 14¹⁄₂ in. | 36.5 cm |
| D. (feet) | 16 in. | 40.6 cm |

**Materials:** *Microanalysis:* Primary: soft maple group (throughout). *Finish:* painted or stained at one time; now covered with a natural resin finish.

**Publications:** Israel Sack advertisement, *Antiques* 40, no. 5 (November 1941): 262.

**Provenance:** Ex coll.: Guy W. Walker, Jr., Beverly Farms, Mass.

**Accession history:** Purchased by H. F. du Pont from Guy W. Walker, Jr., Beverly Farms, Mass., 1958. Gift of H. F. du Pont, 1959.
58.135.4

1. Thomas Chippendale, *The Gentleman and Cabinet-Maker's Director* (3d ed., London: By the author, 1762), pls. 144–46; William Ince and John Mayhew, *The Universal System of Houshold Furniture* (1762; reprint, Chicago: Quadrangle Books, 1960), pl. 14; *Genteel Houshold Furniture in the Present Taste* (1763; reprint, East Ardley, Yorkshire, Eng.: EP Publishing, 1978), p. 92.

## 118 ◆ Square tea table
**Eastern Massachusetts or possibly Portsmouth, New Hampshire**
**1730–70**

Tea was introduced into England through Holland early in the seventeenth century. Valued initially for its medicinal properties, by the middle of the eighteenth century it had become a much-sought-after social beverage enjoyed by all levels of society both in homes and in public establishments. Its popularity stimulated the introduction of a variety of new furniture forms, including tables with applied molded rims, or ornate galleries, designed to prevent the ceramic wares used in brewing and serving tea from slipping off the table edge.

The majority of eighteenth-century American high-style tea tables are patterned after English prototypes. The model for the square tea table appears to have been a stand with lacquer tray imported from the Orient. A late eighteenth-century variant can be seen in two American examples of the two-piece tea table featuring deep ceramic trays. One tray-top tea table (No. 124) is at Winterthur; a second, almost identical, example is at the State Department Diplomatic Reception Rooms.[1] By about the second quarter of the eighteenth century, tea tables with fixed tops had replaced those with removable trays as the fashionable form. A number of New England inventories suggest that imported tea tables, perhaps imitating the lacquered-tray-on-stand form, were fashionable possessions that reflected status.

The standard design featured on most high-style square tea tables produced in urban shops includes an applied rim or gallery, shaped skirt rails, and cabriole or Marlborough legs. The addition of a carved or molded rim to the edge of the top created the illusion of a tray, although fixed in place. Rails are usually scalloped on the lower edge or embellished by an applied, convex, plain or shaped skirt. The shape of the cabriole leg varies regionally and can sometimes offer a clue in establishing provenance, as can the shape of a pad or ball-and-claw foot.

Based on the incidence of survival, New Englanders appear to have preferred the "square tea table" to the circular pedestal-base "snap table" for the service of tea. This well-proportioned table, like many other New England examples, has a shaped, convex piece applied to the lower edge of the rail, giving greater depth and dimension to the skirt as the gentle curve of the knee is carried along the profile of the lower edge of the rails. This design and construction feature derives from

English (and no doubt oriental) precedents. An applied molded bead above the shaped apron minimizes the unusual depth of the skirt and visually balances the frieze and apron. The shaping of the applied convex apron (with a double drop on the long sides and a single one on the short sides) also appears on a marble slab table (No. 126) in the Winterthur collection that may have been made in Portsmouth or southern Maine.[2] The rather straight cabriole leg with restrained, almost blunt, knee seems to relate to those found on other northeastern New England tables, but without any specific provenance, it is difficult to identify this tea table's area of manufacture with certainty.

NER/WAC

---

**Construction:** The table is finished on four sides with an applied concave rim molding; there are carved insets at each corner. The one-piece top board extends over the frame as an exposed torus molding. A transverse medial brace, tenoned to the long rails and reinforced by a series of glueblocks, supports the top. Bead molding is glued to the rail above an applied, quarter-round, shaped skirt molding. The rails are tenoned and double-pinned to the legs.

**Condition:** A split in the top has been repaired with an applied wood batten and brown paper tape.

**Dimensions:**

| | | |
|---|---|---|
| H. | 27 1/8 in. | 68.9 cm |
| W. (top) | 29 7/8 in. | 75.9 cm |
| W. (frame) | 28 1/8 in. | 71.4 cm |
| W. (feet) | 30 1/4 in. | 76.8 cm |
| D. (top) | 20 1/4 in. | 51.4 cm |
| D. (frame) | 18 5/8 in. | 47.4 cm |
| D. (feet) | 20 3/4 in. | 52.7 cm |

**Materials:** *Microanalysis:* Primary: mahogany (top, legs, skirt molding); cherry (all rails). Secondary: white pine group (glueblocks, transverse brace). *Finish:* natural resin.

**Publications:** Downs, *American Furniture*, fig. 365. Comstock, *American Furniture*, no. 230.

**Accession history:** Gift of H. F. du Pont, 1965. 65.3092

---

1. Thornton, *Seventeenth-Century Interior Decoration*, p. 230; see also Barquist, *American Tables and Looking Glasses*, p. 230. For the State Dept. table, see Rollins, *Treasures of State*, cat. no. 96.

2. For other New England examples, see Albert Sack, "Regionalism in Early American Tea Tables," *Antiques* 131, no. 1 (January 1987): figs. 3, 5, 6, 9, 14, pls. 3, 4; for an English precedent, see Kirk, *American Furniture*, p. 331, fig. 1300; a tea table formerly owned by Mr. and Mrs. Bertram K. Little has a similar skirt design and a history of ownership in Hempstead, N.H.; see *The Decorative Arts of New Hampshire, 1725–1825* (Manchester, N.H.: Currier Gallery of Art, 1964), no. 31; Nina Fletcher Little, *Little by Little: Six Decades of Collecting American Decorative Arts* (New York: E. P. Dutton, 1984), fig. 284. The shaped, pendent drop also appears on a desk-on-frame at the Henry Ford Museum; see Katharine Bryant Hagler, *American Queen Anne Furniture, 1720–1755* (Dearborn, Mich.: Henry Ford Museum and Greenfield Village, 1976), p. 12 top.

## 119 ◆ Tile-top tea table

Boston or Marblehead,
Massachusetts, area
1735–70

---

In overall appearance, this well-proportioned square tea table is similar to other high-style examples with its applied, molded rim with carved, inset corners, and slender cabriole legs with delicate pad feet, but two very different features set it apart from most other New England examples. Instead of being made of a hardwood and finished with a natural resin, it is made entirely of white pine and was originally painted with red and black pigments. The top, composed of fifteen lead-glazed earthenware tiles, relates it to a small number of tile-top tables and two later eighteenth-century tables with tin-glazed earthenware tray tops imported from Sweden.[1] A marble or glazed earthenware top provided a stain-resistant surface that would not be damaged by spilled tea or punch or a hot kettle.

The original surface finish of red and black pigments may have been intended to resemble a variation of japanning. Tea tables described as "japanned" do occur in New England inventories, although they were most likely imported examples. In 1754 the inventory of Thomas Wright, a Portsmouth ship captain

and shopkeeper, listed "1 tea table japanned . . . £5" in the parlor. Bostonian Andrew Oliver's 1774 inventory noted that he owned "1 japanned tea table . . . £3." The present coat of black paint on this table appears to have been added in the third quarter of the nineteenth century, when the aesthetic movement dictated a style made popular by English designer Charles Eastlake. Incised floral decoration bearing traces of gilt are still visible on the rails of the table. A 1931 letter to Henry Francis du Pont from Frederick Whitwell, a descendant of the original owner, describes the condition of the table at the time of its sale:

> When I first knew the table nearly fifty years ago it was painted black and at one time I remember had plants kept on it on account of its tile top. At one time my aunt and uncle, to whom it then belonged not caring much for antiques as such, but wishing to keep this table on account of its tradition had some gilt hues put on it in the then fashionable East Lake manner. When the table came to my father from his brothers and sisters he had it again painted black as before and the traces of decoration are practically gone.[2]

**Fig. 1.** Detail, tile top.

Although today tables with earthenware tile tops are generally called mixing tables, period documentation tells us that in the eighteenth century the form was simply termed "a Tile Tea Table," such as that listed in the 1774 inventory of Ipswich yeoman John Berry. Rare in American furniture, only five of these tile-top tables are known today: Winterthur's example, a "square" table with turned William and Mary–style legs, two square tray-top tea tables with cabriole legs, and a tilt-top tripod stand. The top of Winterthur's example is set with fifteen tin-glazed earthenware tiles decorated with biblical scenes hand-painted in blue (fig. 1).[2] They appear to be Dutch from the first half of the eighteenth century, but they are of a type that was produced over a long period of time and widely copied by various makers. Further complicating the exact origin of the tiles is the fact that the English continually copied Dutch imports.

Of this small group of tile-top tables, one at the Henry Ford Museum is the closest in general appearance to Winterthur's table. Although it is larger, with twenty tiles, similarities suggest that the Henry Ford Museum table was made in the same shop as Winterthur's table. They are very close in form; they were both originally painted, presumably, to simulate japanning; the construction details are the same; and, most conclusive, the tiles are the same. A third table, at Deerfield, differs from the others both in design and construction: its wide overhanging top, inset with twelve aubergine floral tiles, is mounted on heavy rails molded on the lower edge, and the legs have sharp knees and an angular cabriole profile.[3] Its provenance in the Leffingwell family suggests a Norwich, Connecticut, origin.

The provenance of Winterthur's tea table confirms that it was made either for Rev. Simon Bradstreet (1670–1741) of Charlestown, or Rev. Simon Bradstreet IV (1709–71) of Marblehead. Based on the Queen Anne form and the date of the tiles, it most likely was owned by the latter. Congregational minister Bradstreet's ownership of a tea table with biblical tiles featuring themes of persecution and redemption most likely was not entirely coincidental.[4]

*WAC/NER*

---

**Inscriptions or marks:** *On inside front rail:* "Belonged to/ Governor Simon Bradstreet/ Black table with tiles" on early twentieth-century paper label.

**Construction:** The apron rails are joined to the legs with mortise-and-tenon joints. The lower molding is glued to the face of the apron. To support the heavy top, a 3" cross brace set on edge is mortised into the long sides, and longitudinal braces attach with sliding dovetails to the end rails and the cross braces. The fifteen tiles (with mortar between) rest on a 3/8"-thick board with rounded edge. The perimeter of the top is finished with an applied concave gallery molding; the shaped, concave corners are separately carved and inset.

**Condition:** Currently painted black, there are traces of gilt in the incised floral decoration on the front and rear rails. The end rails and legs once also had incised geometrical decoration picked out in gilt. The top is warped. A section of the molded gallery is missing. There are several long cracks in the subtop. There are repairs to all four legs at the knees requiring the addition of triangular reinforcing blocks.

**Dimensions:**

| | | |
|---|---|---|
| H. | 27 1/8 in. | 69.0 cm |
| W. (top) | 29 3/16 in. | 74.1 cm |
| W. (frame) | 25 3/16 in. | 65.4 cm |
| W. (feet) | 27 in. | 68.5 cm |
| D. (top) | 19 in. | 48.3 cm |
| D. (frame) | 17 11/16 in. | 45.0 cm |
| D. (feet) | 19 in. | 48.4 cm |

**Materials:** *Microanalysis:* Primary: white pine group (throughout). *Finish:* both red and black pigments were used in the initial finish, possibly in an attempt to ebonize the pine substrate; the current bluish black paint was added late in the nineteenth century.

**Exhibitions:** Museum of Fine Arts, Boston, 1931.

**Publications:** Downs, *American Furniture*, fig. 350.

**Provenance:** The table descended through the Bradstreet and Story families of Charlestown and Marblehead, Mass., until its acquisition in 1931 from the great-great-great-grandson of Rev. Simon Bradstreet IV. Formerly associated with Gov. Simon Bradstreet (1603–79), the table is more likely to have belonged to his grandson, Rev. Simon Bradstreet (1670–1741) of Charlestown, or Governor Bradstreet's great-grandson, Rev. Simon Bradstreet (1709–71) of Marblehead. The presumed descent is to the latter's daughter, Rebecca Bradstreet Story (1749–1823), wife of Rev. Isaac Story of Marblehead; to their daughter, Sophia Story Whitwell (1787–1867); to her son, Frederick Augustus Whitwell (1820–1912); and to his son, Frederick Silsbee Whitwell, the last private owner. Ex coll.: Frederick Silsbee Whitwell, Marblehead, Mass.

**Accession history:** Purchased by H. F. du Pont from Frederick Silsbee Whitwell, Marblehead, Mass., 1931. Bequest of H. F. du Pont, 1969. 58.1507

---

1. Nancy Reinhold, finish analysis report, January 14, 1988, folder 58.1507, Registration Office, Winterthur; one tray-top table is in the Winterthur collection (No. 124), the other is at the State Dept. Diplomatic Reception Rooms; see Rollins, *Treasures of State*, cat. no. 96.

2. Thomas Wright inventory, 1754, Portsmouth Probate Records, Downs collection; Andrew Oliver inventory, 1774, Suffolk County Probate Records, Downs collection. Frederick Whitwell to H. F. du Pont, September 7, 1931, Winterthur Archives.

3. John Berry inventory, 1774, as cited in Alice Hanson Jones, *American Colonial Wealth: Documents and Methods*, 3 vols. (New York: Arno Press, 1977), 2:618. Though listed as a yeoman, the use of "Mr." in front of his name suggests that he was more than just a farmer, and the high value of his estate, £564.8.9, suggests that his house was unusually well appointed—indeed, it also included a second tea table and "a tip table" in addition to the tile-top one. For the table with turned legs, see Lockwood, *Colonial Furniture*, 2: fig. 712; for the tables with cabriole legs, see Katharine Bryant Hagler, *American Queen Anne Furniture, 1720–1755* (Dearborn, Mich.: Henry Ford Museum and Greenfield Village, 1976), front and back covers; Fales, *Furniture of Historic Deerfield*, fig. 263; for the tilt-top table, see *American Antiques from Israel Sack Collection*, 10 vols. (Washington, D.C.: Highland House, ca. 1969–), 9:2409.

4. Hagler, *American Queen Anne Furniture*, front and back covers; Comstock, *American Furniture*, no. 226; Elizabeth Bidwell Bates and Jonathan L. Fairbanks, *American Furniture: 1620 to the Present* (New York: Richard Marek Publishers, 1981), p. 125. Fales, *Furniture of Historic Deerfield*, no. 263.

5. Ron Fuchs, "Catalogue Report," 1995, folder 58.1507, Registration Office, Winterthur.

## 120 • Square tea table
New England, probably Massachusetts
1740–80

The square tea table with a wooden top and with or without pull-out candle slides was a popular form in eighteenth-century New England as attested to by the survival of a significant number today.[1] The notable quantity of "square mahogany tea tables" listed in New England probate inventories of the last quarter of the eighteenth century further attests to the popularity of this essential form. The use of marble for the top instead of wood, however, is so rare that this example is the only one known to date to survive with its original top. Its production was a cooperative venture, requiring the skills of a cabinetmaker, a carver, and a marble cutter. This gray and white marble top with ovolo corners is dished in the same manner as a top on a raised-rim pedestal table. The cavetto molding applied at the top of the rail joins the top and the frame visually. The slender cabriole legs are flanked by carved C scrolls that flow onto the scalloped apron, producing a table unparalleled in design and execution.

These carved C scrolls, the most distinctive ornamental feature of this table, are a decidedly English Georgian characteristic, which can be found on other square tea tables and other forms of tables made in the eastern Massachusetts region. The rather diminutive size of this table compared with other similar tea tables is a rare characteristic. No doubt it was one of the aspects that most endeared Henry Francis du Pont to this particular table, as he wrote to Israel Sack on February 23, 1953:

One of my favorites is the little Queen Anne mixing table with its dish top of gray marble and candleslides at each end. That piece, you may remember, you telephoned me about during the height of the depression and when I said I was out of the market, you answered: "I shall bring it down in my car immediately." Needless to say, the minute I saw it, it was a "must."[2]

Although this table was originally published as a New York product by Joseph Downs and attributed by more recent writers to Rhode Island, family history links it to the Leach and Blaney families of eastern Massachusetts. Furthermore, extensive research by Alan Miller and Leigh Keno on Boston furniture of the first half of the eighteenth century attributes the Georgian, carved C scrolls to tables and chairs from the Boston area.[3]

*WAC/NER*

---

**Construction:** The thick marble top, cut with a molded rim and ovolo corners, is finished on the underside. The rails are mortised and tenoned to the legs. The shaped ovolo lower edge of the apron is glued to the face of the apron. The cavetto cornice molding is glued and nailed to the apron. The corners of the cornice molding are carved to conform to the shape of the marble top. A cross brace is dovetailed to the midpoint of the top of the long rails; the slides ride in grooved runners nailed to the end rails. These runners are further supported by blocks nailed to the end rails below the slide opening. Wooden pins in the tops of the leg posts fit into the corresponding holes in the marble top. Two vertical glueblocks reinforce each mortise-and-tenon joint of the frame. The thick marble top rests on the frame. The C scrolls that bracket the tops of the legs are carved from solid wood.

**Condition:** There is a split in the top of one post where a new pin was installed to hold the marble top. Band-saw marks on the edge of the top molding and the presence of wire nails indicate that the molding is replaced. One long rail is split at the leg join. The facings on the candle slides are reattached. The gray and white marble top is polished on the underside.

**Dimensions:**

| | | |
|---|---|---|
| H. | 27 in. | 68.4 cm |
| W. (top) | 28 11/16 in. | 73.1 cm |
| W. (frame) | 25 5/16 in. | 64.4 cm |
| W. (feet) | 27 5/16 in. | 69.6 cm |
| D. (top) | 16 3/4 in. | 42.4 cm |
| D. (frame) | 13 1/2 in. | 34.5 cm |
| D. (feet) | 15 1/4 in. | 38.7 cm |

**Materials:** *Microanalysis:* Primary: mahogany. Secondary: white pine group (glueblocks, runners for candle slides); mahogany (transverse brace, candle slides). *Finish:* natural resin.

**Publications:** Downs, *American Furniture*, fig. 351. Butler, *American Furniture*, p. 28. Harold Sack and Max Wilk, *American Treasure Hunt: The Legacy of Israel Sack* (New York: Ballantine Books edition, 1986), pp. 139–41. Harold Sack, "The United States Department of State: The Furniture," *Antiques* 132, no. 1 (July 1987): 254.

**Provenance:** According to family tradition, the table was first owned by John Leach (b. London ca. 1724; d. Boston, 1799) who married Sarah Coffin (daughter of Charles and Mary Coffin of Boston) on July 24, 1750. The table was inherited by their son, Thomas (1757–1828) and descended as an heirloom to his daughter, Sally Leach, the wife of William Blaney. Subsequently, it passed to her daughters, Sarah Coffin and Harriet Blaney, then to Charles Blaney, and finally to Charles P. Blaney, the last private owner.

**Accession history:** Purchased by H. F. du Pont from Israel Sack, New York, 1941. Bequest of H. F. du Pont, 1969.
57.718

1. *American Antiques from Israel Sack Collection*, 10 vols. (Washington, D.C.: Highland House, ca. 1969–), 4:975, 8:2196, 8:2263. See also Museum of Fine Arts, Boston, *Paul Revere's Boston, 1735–1818* (Boston: By the museum, 1975), p. 96, no. 122; Greenlaw, *New England Furniture*, pp. 148–50, no. 129.

2. For related tea tables, see Downs, *American Furniture*, fig. 367; Christie's, "The Collection of Mr. and Mrs. Eddy Nicholson" (January 27–28, 1995), lot 1045. For other tables, see Downs, *American Furniture*, figs. 347, 354.

3. Downs, *American Furniture*, fig. 351. Albert Sack, "Regionalism in Early American Tea Tables," *Antiques* 131, no. 1 (January 1987): 254–55. Sack's reattribution may have been based on the use of cove moldings on a table that descended in the Gardiner family of Newport (see *John Brown House Loan Exhibition*, cat. 31) and a Rhode Island table at Chipstone (see Rodriguez Roque, *American Furniture*, no. 125). Keno, Freund, and Miller, "Very Pink of the Mode."

## 121 ◆ Square tea table
### Boston, Massachusetts
### 1745–60

Several aspects of the form and carved details of this square tea table relate it to the three previous entries. Yet in overall form it is most closely associated with a small but distinctive group of Boston, or coastal New England, square tea tables distinguished by a carved rim with shaped corners, an applied convex apron cut in cyma-curves on the lower edge, carved C scrolls ornamenting the inner edges of the legs and apron, and comparatively straight cabriole legs with a blunt knee profiles and pad feet.[1] Winterthur's table stands apart from this group in three details: the molded rim is not applied but carved from solid wood, it has carved ball-and-claw feet, and the extraordinary foliate knee carving extends onto the ends of the convex applied apron just above the upper portion of the C scroll.

When this table was first published by Joseph Downs in 1952, it was thought to be of New York origin, presumably because of the "leafage on the legs and the heavy claws," even though its provenance related that it had come from the Jewett family of South Berwick, Maine. Only recently, with more focused attention and scholarship devoted to eighteenth-century Boston furniture, has this table been recognized as the product of a mid eighteenth-century Boston cabinetmaker whose patrons were strongly influenced by imported English Georgian furniture. Although no related English tea tables owned in Boston in the eighteenth century are known to date as sources of influence, the carved leafage, C scrolls, and ball-and-claw feet do relate to those seen on other Boston tables of the period. The stylized symmetry of the carving, the simple incised lines defining the veining of the leaves, the pendent bellflower with circular drop beneath, and the fishscale-like imbrication in the carved "V" of the knee relate to other Boston workmanship. Notable is the high relief of the carving as well as the unusual manner in which the leaf carving of the apron comes out of the flat of the apron to abut the knee carving, instead of flowing from the knee onto the apron. The distinctive central "V" carving on the knee is reminiscent of that seen on several related Portsmouth, New Hampshire, dressing tables and on the front skirt of an altar table attributed to Joseph Davis.[2]

Although in 1940 the recorded Sack provenance for this tea table related it to the Jewett family of South Berwick, Maine, it is not known whether it was originally owned by the Jewetts, acquired in the nineteenth century by the family, or collected in the early twentieth century by Dr. Theodore Jewett Eastman. In 1909, following the death of noted nineteenth-century author Sarah Orne Jewett, the Jewett family home in South Berwick was occupied by Sarah's sister Mary Rice Jewett (b. 1847) and her nephew, Theodore Eastman, son of Sarah and Mary's elder sister, Caroline Augusta Jewett Eastman. This tea table appears in a 1931 photograph of the parlor of the Jewett house taken following the deaths of Mary in 1930 and Eastman in 1931. It could easily be assumed that this table had descended in the Jewett family if it were not for the knowledge that Eastman, a Harvard graduate who practiced all his life in Boston (presumably traveling to South Berwick on weekends) apparently openly acknowledged "his 'dissipations' in the form of collecting rare New England antiques."[3] Consequently, we are left to wonder when, how, and from whence this tea table came to reside in South Berwick.

*WAC with NER*

---

**Inscriptions or marks:** *Inscribed:* "Dr. Eastman" in ink, on small twentieth-century paper label with blue edge.

**Construction:** The long rails are ³/₈" thicker than the shorter side rails. All rails are mortised and tenoned to the leg posts, and those joints are reinforced with vertical glueblocks. The convex lower portion of the apron is applied, as is the bead at the juncture between the upper part of the rails and the applied lower portion. A central brace is mortised into the upper inner edges of the long rails. The top with shaped and molded rim is carved from solid wood and secured with glueblocks; the applied cove molding just beneath the top is nailed and glued.

**Condition:** The top has split from shrinkage, and various remedial repairs can be seen beneath it; mattress ticking was glued to the underside at one time to contain the fissure, and a piece of poplar was also secured to the underside to contain the split. Some glueblocks have been reattached and about 5" of the rim has been replaced on one end. On one long side the lower edge of the shaped apron has suffered breaks and losses probably due to a flaw in the wood.

**Dimensions:**

| | | |
|---|---|---|
| H. | 27¹/₂ in. | 69.8 cm |
| W. (top) | 31 in. | 78.7 cm |
| W. (frame) | 28³/₄ in. | 73.0 cm |
| W. (feet) | 30¹/₂ in. | 77.5 cm |
| D. (top) | 19³/₄ in. | 50.2 cm |
| D. (frame) | 17³/₄ in. | 45.1 cm |
| D. (feet) | 20¹/₄ in. | 51.5 cm |

**Materials:** *Microanalysis:* Primary: mahogany. Secondary: white pine (glueblocks, medial brace). *Finish:* modern, natural resin.

**Publications:** Downs, *American Furniture*, fig. 367. Carolyn Hughes, "Sarah Orne Jewett House, South Berwick, Maine," *Antiques* 129, no. 3 (March 1986): 648–51.

**Provenance:** Ex coll.: Dr. Theodore Jewett Eastman, Boston and South Berwick, Maine; to H. H. Richardson, Brookline, Mass.; to Israel Sack.

**Accession history:** Purchased by H. F. du Pont from Israel Sack, New York, 1940. Gift of H. F. du Pont, 1965.
63.619

---

1. Christie's, "The Collection of Mr. and Mrs. Eddy Nicholson" (January 27–28, 1995), lot 1045; *American Antiques from Israel Sack Collection*, 10 vols. (Washington, D.C.: Highland House, ca. 1969–), 8:2196.

2. Downs, *American Furniture*, fig. 367. We thank Leigh Keno and Alan Miller for their insights and comments on this table and related Boston examples. For comparable Boston carving, see Leigh Keno advertisement, *Antiques* 143, no. 5 (May 1993): 649. Miller, "Roman Gusto," pp. 195–96. Hipkiss, *Eighteenth-Century American Arts*, no. 50. Rodriguez Roque, *American Furniture*, no. 150, pp. 320–21. Gerald W. R. Ward, ed., *American Furniture with Related Decorative Arts, 1660–1830: The Milwaukee Art Museum and the Layton Art Collection* (New York: Hudson Hills Press, 1991), cat. 67, pp. 180–82. For the related dressing and altar tables, see Jobe, *Portsmouth Furniture*, cat. nos. 17, 18, 52.

3. We thank Richard C. Nylander for his assistance in locating this photograph in the Archives of the SPNEA and for noting that it was published in Carolyn Hughes, "Sarah Orne Jewett House, South Berwick, Maine," *Antiques* 129, no. 3 (March 1986): 651. Eastman quotation from a typescript in the Archives of the SPNEA, History and Biography microfiche. We thank Richard C. Nylander for providing this information.

## 122 ◆ Tea table
Boston, Massachusetts
1745–65

This highly articulated, late baroque interpretation of a square tea table appears to be singularly a Boston creation. Twentieth-century collectors and scholars have come to call this form a *turret-top* or *scalloped-top* tea table, but those terms do not appear in eighteenth-century documents; they were probably just referred to as "square mahogany tea tables," or "mahogany tea tables." It appears that this innovative yet functional table was inspired by a combination of two other forms of English Georgian tables: the round-cornered card table and the circular, scallop-top pillar and claw tea table. The round-cornered card table was a form particularly popular in Massachusetts between about 1730 and 1760 and probably derived from imported English examples. English examples of the circular, scallop-top pedestal tea tables are known, as is an unusual eighteenth-century Chinese lacquered

example. A singular "square" lacquered tea table with ten turret projections exists, but its exact place and date of manufacture are unconfirmed, making it unfeasible to cite it as a precedent.[1]

Presently, six tea tables of this scalloped design are known. Two tables, this example and one at Deerfield, have twelve scallops, or turrets. The remaining four tables have fourteen turrets each; one is at Bayou Bend, two are in the Museum of Fine Arts, Boston, and one is in the collection of the late Dr. William S. Serri. Winterthur's table is identical in size and construction to the table at Deerfield and differs from it only in the inclusion of unusual, asymmetrical carving on the knees (fig. 1). It is one of only two tables in the group with decorative carving; the other, at the Museum of Fine Arts, Boston, has a very different type of carving consisting of acanthus leaves on the knees and knee brackets. Although the carving on Winterthur's table is quite unusual in its overall asymmetrical pattern, the character of the rounded, flowing leaves with simple

incising relates to the symmetrical carving seen on several rounded corner card tables.[2]

All six known tables are similar in overall configuration, but five have tops with molded rims cut from solid wood, and one has a plain top with no rim (but there is evidence that it once had an applied rim).[3] The plain-top table was also constructed in a different fashion than four of the other five (the Serri table has not been examined). Instead of a dovetailed frame box keyed into the turret (into which the leg has been tenoned), the table's rails are tenoned into the rounded turret block (into which the leg has been tenoned) and further secured with two triangular glueblocks. This variation in a construction solution to a rather challenging design clearly signals the work of a different cabinet shop; perhaps one outside the urban center that produced the other tea tables.

Of the six tables in the group, Winterthur's example has the clearest history of ownership prior to the twentieth century. Inherited in the Sever family of Kingston, Massachusetts, it is said to have been part of the furnishings of the house built by William Sever (1729–1809) in Kingston shortly after his marriage to Sarah Warren (d. 1797) on December 2, 1755. The eldest son of Kingston merchant Nicholas Sever, he joined his father's mercantile business following his graduation from Harvard in 1745. Sever prospered in the coastal trade and also held several political posts between 1754 and 1783, including naval agent for the southern district of Massachusetts. In that capacity he built, armed, supplied, and sent out ships of war and disposed of their prizes. After the war, Sever retired from public life.[4]

Sarah Warren Sever's brother James married Mercy Otis of Barnstable in 1754. Not only did Mercy Otis Warren own an impressive round-cornered card table (for which she wrought a brilliantly colored needlework top), but she also owned an unusual trefoil-lobed kettle stand. Did the sisters-in-law have similar tastes, or were they influenced by each other's acquisitions? Did

**Fig. 1.**
Detail, knee.

Mercy also have a turreted tea table to correspond to her kettle stand? Of further interest is the fact that the only other table with any history (the Deerfield example) was "found near Duxbury" and was reported in 1942 as having come from the Winslow-Pierce families. Since both the Winslows and Pierces are notable South Shore (Massachusetts) families, it is tempting to think that there might have been a local fashion for these tables south of Boston.

Curiously (and inexplicably), when Joseph Downs wrote about Winterthur's table in 1952, he cited the inventory of Elisha Doane of Wellfleet, in which there was "1 Mahog. Tea Table" valued at £4.4.0—the most expensive of three mahogany tables listed.[5] The table now in the Bayou Bend collection was acquired from Frederick Beck of Brookline, whose wife was Lucy Doane Beck, born at Eastham on Cape Cod. One of Lucy's ancestors was Elisha Doane of Wellfleet, although there is no documentation that Bayou Bend's turret-top tea table was an inherited Doane piece or one that the Becks had collected.

Some of the tables in the group have been dated as early as 1740 based on the profile of the leg, the absence of carving, and a general relationship to Boston round-cornered card tables. In the case of the Sever family table, a date between 1755 and 1760 seems more appropriate, based on the date of James's marriage and the completion of his house.

*WAC/NER*

**Construction:** The apron rails are dovetailed at the corners to form the frame. Of eight lathe-turned turrets (with integral ogee cornice molding), four were split in half and applied to the sides, and four were left whole. Turned legs were tenoned into the turrets, and the whole assemblage was notched out and applied to the dovetailed corner of the frame box, held in place with a large screw. Shaped knee brackets (glued in place) reinforce the corner joint and complete the design. A single piece of quarter-round molding is nailed to the lower edge of the frame and turrets. The single board tray top (that is, molded edge carved from solid wood) is attached to

the frame with glueblocks on the underside; nails through the top into the turrets may have been added later.

**Condition:** A section of the rim molding is patched on one corner. At one time, the table was fitted with casters. In 1985 the legs were stabilized by regluing; one split turret was repaired, and one leg split was repaired. At the same time, a water-damaged finish was removed from the top.

**Dimensions:**

| | | |
|---|---|---|
| H. | 27 1/2 in. | 69.9 cm |
| W. (top) | 30 in. | 76.2 cm |
| W. (frame) | 28 3/8 in. | 72.1 cm |
| W. (feet) | 28 3/8 in. | 72.1 cm |
| D. (top) | 19 3/8 in. | 49.2 cm |
| D. (frame) | 17 3/4 in. | 45.1 cm |
| D. (feet) | 18 1/8 in. | 46.0 cm |

**Materials:** *Microanalysis:* Primary: mahogany. Secondary: white pine group (glueblocks). *Finish:* natural resin.

**Publications:** Downs, *American Furniture*, fig. 370. Marshall B. Davidson, ed., *The American Heritage History of Colonial Antiques* ([New York]: American Heritage Publishing Co., [1967]), fig. 305. Fitzgerald, *Three Centuries*, p. 72, fig. IV-42.

**Provenance:** The table descended in the Sever family of Kingston, Mass. Sold in 1934 by Maj. George F. Sever and Mr. Francis Sever of New Bedford, Mass., to Hyman Kaufman, Antique Galleries, Boston.

**Accession history:** Purchased by H. F. du Pont from Hyman Kaufman, Antique Galleries, Boston, 1939. Bequest of H. F. du Pont, 1969.
58.2774

1. Although English card tables with eighteenth-century Massachusetts histories are not currently known, like English bombé case furniture and double chairback settees, they probably were imported to and owned in Boston. The number of surviving Massachusetts-made examples confirm their popularity; a number with "accordian action" support the fact that they were copied from English prototypes; see Warren, *Bayou Bend*, nos. 57, 58; Museum of Fine Arts, Boston, *Paul Revere's Boston, 1735–1818* (Boston: By the museum, 1975), no. 95; Leigh Keno advertisement, *Antiques* 143, no. 5 (May 1993): 649; Randall, *American Furniture*, no. 80; *American Antiques from Israel Sack Collection*, 10 vols. (Washington, D.C.: Highland House, ca. 1969–), 4:1068; Miller, "Roman Gusto," pp. 195–96. For English scallop-top tables, see Cescinsky, *English Furniture*, 1:202, 209. Ambrose Heal, *The London Furniture Makers from the Restoration to the Victorian Era, 1660–1840* (New York: Dover Publications, 1972), p. 154; for the Chinese lacquered example, see Carl L. Crossman, *The Decorative Arts of the China Trade* (Woodbridge, Eng.: Antique Collectors Club, 1991), frontispiece, pp. 263–65. For the table with 10 turrets, see Christie's, "The Contents of Godmersham Park, Canterbury, Kent, England" (June 6–9, 1983), lot 133.

2. For the Deerfield table, see Fales, *Furniture of Historic Deerfield*, fig. 315; for the Bayou Bend table, see Warren, *Bayou Bend*, no. 61; for the 2 tables at MFA, Boston, see Hipkiss, *Eighteenth-Century American Arts*, no. 60; Randall, *American Furniture*, no. 81. For the Serri table, see *Antiques* 71, no. 3 (March 1957): 258, fig. 17. For comparable carving on card tables, see Miller, "Roman Gusto," pp. 195–96; Leigh Keno advertisement.

3. Randall, *American Furniture*, no. 81. The table has a history of ownership in Medford, Mass., according to Charles Bemis Gleason, "History of My Old Furniture," December 1945, memorandum, MFA, Boston. According to family tradition, the tea table was possibly owned originally by one Ebenezer Hall (b. 1743) of Medford and his wife (a "Jones girl") of Weston or Concord. It descended to their daughter Susan M. Fitch (1808–1901) and appears in a list of her possessions (ca. 1890) as "a Mahog. scalloped table Grandmother Jones of Weston." Also in the file is an old letter with a penciled notation signed "KCB" (Kathryn C. Buhler) and dated 1937: "An office visitor claiming to be a relative of Mrs. Hayes told of the loan of this table to a dealer who the family believe returned not the original but a copy of it." We thank Gerald Ward, associate curator of American Decorative Arts and Sculpture, MFA, Boston, for this detailed information.

4. Clifford K. Shipton, comp., *Biographical Sketches of Those Who Attended Harvard College in the Classes 1746–1750* (Boston: Massachusetts Historical Society, 1962), 11:575–78. For William Sever's house in Kingston, see Mabel M. Swan, "Two Early Massachusetts Houses," *Antiques* 52, no. 2 (August 1947): 107–9.

5. Downs, *American Furniture*, fig. 370.

## 123 ◆ Tea table
Newport, Rhode Island
1763
John Goddard (1723/24–85)

**Tea table**
Newport, Rhode Island
1760–80
Attributed to John Goddard
(1723/24–85)

These distinctive Newport tables represent a brilliant variation on the simple square tea table form. With unusual "swelled" sides cut in opposing reverse-cyma curves from solid planks of mahogany, this design is as regionally individualistic as the Boston-made turret-top tea tables. It appears to have no known English or Continental prototypes, nor was it made in any other American urban center. The bold shaping of the sides is echoed by the conforming top, shaped from a solid board and carved with a molded rim. The cabriole legs are typical of Newport workmanship with their square profile, sharp edges, and symmetrical low-relief carving of a palmette-and-leaf pattern on either side of the knee (fig. 1). Variations of this distinctive Newport carving appear on a range of Newport furniture forms, including tables (No. 141), high chests, and dressing tables.[1] The finely carved ball-and-claw feet, with undercut or open talons, reflect the best (and most expensive) Newport workmanship.

This design was undoubtedly the most costly of all Newport tea tables, and it is significant that seven examples of the type survive today. Several have histories of ownership associated with Rhode Island families, but one of Winterthur's tables (left) has perhaps the most interesting documentation. Originally owned by Jabez Bowen (1739–1815) of Providence, the table was acquired by Boston collector Philip Flayderman directly from Bowen's great-great-

grandson. A letter written by John Goddard on June 30, 1763, to Moses Brown of Providence, verifies the maker: "Friend Brown/ I send herewith The Tea Table & common Chairs which thou spoke for with the bill. the other Work is in good forwardness hope to compleat in a short time. I Recd. a few lines from Jabez Bowen whom I suppose this furniture is for, Requesting me to make a pre. Case of Drawers. . . ./ Jnᵒ Goddard." Although the referenced bill does not survive, other correspondence between Goddard and Brown in October 1763 further supports Goddard's assumption that the furniture was made for Bowen. Just six months prior to the letter, in December 1762, Bowen had married Sarah Brown, Moses Brown's cousin.[2] Since Sarah's father, Obadiah, had died the previous June, the fact that her cousin Moses facilitated the acquisition of what must have been her wedding furniture is not unusual.

Not only was Sarah from one of Rhode Island's wealthiest and most prominent families, but Jabez Bowen was among the most eminent men of his day. He held numerous

elected offices, including that of deputy governor of Rhode Island in 1788. He commanded a Rhode Island regiment in the winter of 1777 and served as a member of the Constitutional Convention in 1790. An active mason and Grand Master, he also served as chancellor of Brown University from 1785 to 1815. The Bowens's status, wealth, and taste was not only represented by their fine Newport furniture but was also clearly evidenced in the portraits they commissioned from John Singleton Copley.[3]

John Goddard (1723/24–85) probably completed his apprenticeship to Newport cabinetmaker Job Townsend shortly before he married Townsend's daughter Hannah in 1746.[4] From the production of his earliest documented furniture in the mid 1740s to the commission for Bowen, Goddard's craft skills and reputation steadily increased, and his patrons included many of the most prominent citizens of Rhode Island.

Although Winterthur's tables are visually similar, the right one is slightly smaller. Furthermore, because it is fashioned in a

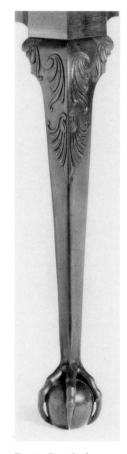

more highly figured, mottled mahogany (often described as "plum pudding"), the general aspect is different, and it is heavier than the left table. The dense, clearly grained mahogany of the left table seems to have a more defined form as the striations of the woods' growth rings define the curves of the sides. There are also subtle differences in the carving of the leaves and tendrils on the knees of the two tables, suggesting different carvers working within the same shop (fig. 2). Additionally, the ball-and-claw feet on the right table differ slightly: the ball is flatter, and there is less space between the ball and the open talon, but they retain the flat area between the tendons, the smooth knuckles, and the bulbous rear talons found on the other table (fig. 3). Variations between the two may simply reflect a difference in the journeymen/apprentices involved in their construction or a difference in the date of construction and are not significant enough to suggest any shop of origin other than Goddard's.

Although it is exceedingly rare to find visual documentation of specific furniture

forms in eighteenth-century paintings, Gilbert Stuart did record the presence of this specific type of tea table in a fashionable Newport home when he painted *Dr. William Hunter's Spaniels* about 1765.[5]

*WAC/NER*

---

**Construction:** (Left) Cut from solid wood, the one-piece top is let into the skirt frame and held on all four sides by a series of small, rectangular glueblocks. The rails are tenoned and double-pinned to the legs. Veneered facings on the stiles continue the grain pattern of the skirt. The knee blocks are glued in place. The talons on the feet are open.

(Right) Dished from solid wood, the one piece top is let into the skirt frame and now held by two transverse braces and a series of small, rectangular glueblocks on all four sides. The rails are tenoned to the legs and pegged in two places. Veneer facings covering the stiles continue the grain pattern of the skirt. The knee brackets are glued in place; one is reinforced with a rosehead nail. The feet have open talons.

**Condition:** (Left) There are several surface splits in the top and in the veneered facings. Two of the

knee blocks appear to be original; the others are replaced. The surface has been selectively cleaned and waxed.

(Right) There are several full-length splits in the top. Earlier efforts at stabilization included the use of a medial brace and diagonal cross braces from one long rail to the opposite corners. These have been replaced by two cross braces and a series of glueblocks inside the frame. The top has been reset, and all the glueblocks are replaced. The veneer facings on the posts are split in several places; it is patched on one post. One knee bracket is new; the

**Fig. 2.** Detail of right table, knee.

**Fig. 3.** Detail of right table, foot.

others appear to be old. A talon on one foot has been replaced.

**Dimensions:**
Left

| | | |
|---|---|---|
| H. | 26 7/8 in. | 68.4 cm |
| W. (top) | 32 1/4 in. | 82.0 cm |
| W. (skirt) | 31 5/8 in. | 80.4 cm |
| W. (feet) | 32 3/4 in. | 83.2 cm |
| D. (top) | 19 1/8 in. | 48.8 cm |
| D. (skirt) | 18 3/4 in. | 47.8 cm |
| D. (feet) | 20 3/8 in. | 51.8 cm |

Right

| | | |
|---|---|---|
| H. | 26 3/8 in. | 67.1 cm |
| W. (top) | 32 5/8 in. | 83.1 cm |
| W. (frame) | 32 1/8 in. | 81.8 cm |
| W. (feet) | 33 11/16 in. | 86.0 cm |
| D. (top) | 19 1/4 in. | 49.4 cm |
| D. (frame) | 19 1/16 in. | 48.6 cm |
| D. (feet) | 20 1/2 in. | 52.3 cm |

**Materials:** *Microanalysis:* (Left) Primary: mahogany. Secondary: tulip-poplar (glueblocks). (Right) Primary: mahogany. Secondary: white pine group (replaced glueblocks). *Finish:* (Left and right) natural resin.

**Publications:** (Left) American Art Association Anderson Galleries advertisement, *Antiques* 16, no. 6 (December 1929): 448. "Furniture Items from the Year's Sales," *Antiques* 17, no. 4 (April 1930): fig. 6. Thomas H. Ormsbee, "Block-Front Table by John Goddard," *American Collector* 6 (May 1937): 2. Albert Sack, *Fine Points of Furniture: Early American* (New York: Crown Publishers, 1950), p. 247. Downs, *American Furniture*, fig. 373. F. Lewis Hinckley, *A Directory of Antique Furniture* (New York: Crown Publishers, 1953), fig. 977, p. 306. Hugh Honour, *Cabinet Makers and Furniture Designers* (London: Weidenfeld and Nicolson, 1969), p. 152. Butler, *American Furniture*, p. 54. Liza Moses and Michael Moses, "Authenticating John Townsend's and John Goddard's Queen Anne and Chippendale Tables," *Antiques* 121, no. 5 (May 1982): fig. 5. Moses, *Master Craftsmen*, p. 204, pl. 7, fig. 4.4, pp. 217–18, figs. 5.4, 5.4a, 5.4b. Thomas E. Norton, *One Hundred Years of Collecting in America: The Story of Sotheby Parke Bernet* (New York: Harry N. Abrams, 1984), p. 112. (Right) Downs, *American Furniture*, fig. 327. Moses, *Master Craftsmen*, fig. 5.10, p. 222.

**Provenance:** (Left) Made by John Goddard in 1763 for Sarah and Jabez Bowen of Providence. The table descended in the family to Jabez Bowen's son, the Hon. Henry Bowen in 1815. It passed to Henry's son, William H. Bowen about 1866. On the death of William H. Bowen in 1897, the table passed to his son, Henry Bowen. Henry's son, Donald F. Bowen was the last family member to own the table before its purchase by Philip Flayderman. Ex coll.: Philip Flayderman, Boston. (Right) By tradition, the table descended from Charles Field of Providence. Intermediate owners may have included David Howell, whose daughter married a Burroughs; and a Mrs. Burroughs. This line of descent cannot be confirmed. Ex coll.: Charles Field Swain, Pomfret Center, Conn.

**Accession history:** (Left) Acquired by H. F. du Pont at the Flayderman sale, American Art Association Anderson Galleries, New York, 1930. Gift of H. F. du Pont, 1958. (Right) Purchased by H. F. du Pont from Charles Field Swain through Ella M. Bolt, Pomfret, Conn., 1930. Gift of H. F. du Pont, 1958. 58.2148, 58.2149

1. Moses, *Master Craftsmen*, figs. 3.21, 3.39, 3.73–3.75, 3.99, 3.100, 5.16–5.22.

2. The remaining 5 of the 7 tables are: one at Bayou Bend, see Warren, *Bayou Bend*, no. 106; Moses, *Master Craftsmen*, p. 223, fig. 5.11; one owned by Mrs. R. H. Ives Goddard, Providence, R.I., see Ralph E. Carpenter, Jr., *The Arts and Crafts of Newport, Rhode Island, 1640–1820* (Newport: Preservation Society of Newport County, 1954), no. 77; a table formerly in the George B. Lorimer collection and now owned by Eric M. Wunsch, see Ginsburg and Levy advertisement, *Antiques* 103, no. 1 (January 1973): 17; Moses, *Master Craftsmen*, p. 224, fig. 5.12; Bernard and S. Dean Levy, Inc., *An American Tea Party: Colonial Tea and Breakfast Tables, 1715–1783* (New York: By the company, 1988), cat. 8, pp. 14–15. Wendy A. Cooper, *In Praise of America: American Decorative Arts, 1650–1830/Fifty Years of Discovery since the 1929 Girl Scouts Loan Exhibition* (New York: Alfred A. Knopf, 1980), no. 215; and one in the Kaufman collection, see Flanigan, *American Furniture*, cat. no. 12; Moses, *Master Craftsmen*, frontispiece. American Art Association Anderson Galleries, "Colonial Furniture, Silver, and Decorations: The Collection of the Late Philip Flayderman" (January 2–4, 1930), lot 450. Goddard to Brown, June 30, 1763, RISD, as cited in Moses, *Master Craftsmen*, pp. 196–97. On other Goddard/Brown correspondence, see Carpenter, *Arts and Crafts of Newport*, p. 14; *The Chad Browne Memorial* (Brooklyn, N.Y., 1888), pp. 40–41.

3. Carrie Rebora et al., *John Singleton Copley in America* (New York: Metropolitan Museum of Art, 1995), p. 70, fig. 62.

4. Norman M. Isham, "John Goddard and His Work," *Bulletin of the Rhode Island School of Design* 15 (April 1927): 14–24; Moses, *Master Craftsmen*, pp. 195–245.

5. The painting does not appear to be a studio piece and probably records the furniture in Hunter's home; Carpenter, *Arts and Crafts of Newport*, no. 92; Lawrence Park, *Gilbert Stuart: An Illustrated Descriptive List of His Works* (New York: William Edwin Rudge, 1926), no. 250.

## 124 ♦ Tray-top tea table
### Salem or Beverly, Massachusetts
### ca. 1788

This plain but stylish table frame with its enormous Swedish earthenware tray is one of a small number of tray-mounted tea tables known and one of only two framed in America. The similarity of the American frames indicates that the two pieces of furniture are closely related, and circumstantial evidence further strengthens the connection. Winterthur's table was originally owned by John Tittle, a sea captain of Beverly, Massachusetts, in whose family it descended into the mid twentieth century. The second table, which was acquired at auction in 1987 for the collection of the United States Department of State, was owned by Augustus Flagg of Boston in the late nineteenth century and later by his descendants.[1]

Capt. John Tittle (1735–1800), who appears to have acquired the ceramic trays for both tables, commanded the schooner *Tryal* on a voyage to Virginia in 1764. During the revolutionary war he sailed several vessels under letters of marque, including the ship *Cato*. On a voyage to France in late spring 1782, the *Cato* encountered and fought off three British war vessels simultaneously. At various times before 1797, when Tittle became master and owner of the schooner *Nancy*, he commanded a number of large two-masted and three-masted vessels. One of the latter was Elias Haskett Derby's 330-ton ship *Astrea*.[2]

Tittle commanded the *Astrea* for two voyages to Sweden in 1788. The instructions from Derby for the first voyage were dated from Salem on March 26. The vessel was laden with a cargo of coffee, rum, tobacco, and flour and was to return with iron, steel, tea, and sheet glass. Following customary practice, Tittle in his capacity as captain was accorded special compensation in addition to

his wages: "Elias H. Derby is to allow me a priviledge of five per cent of what the Ship loads with ten Dollars per month wages, and as I am not to have a Comission, I am to receive One hundred dollars for Expenses—Jno Tittle." For the voyage to Gothenburg and return, Tittle was directed to "make all the dispatch in your power, I mean in prudance, so as to be here in July." He appears to have met the schedule because a cargo manifest for the homeward voyage was registered at the customhouse in Stockholm on June 18. The second voyage of the *Astrea* under Tittle in 1788 is identified in an insurance policy dated from Boston on August 26, covering the ship's return from Stockholm.[3]

With part of the anticipated profits from the trade goods stored in his 5 percent of the cargo space, Tittle could afford to indulge a whim and acquire an attractive tray destined to be a novelty at home. Although tray tops of this type were alien to the American culture, Tittle apparently ventured the purchase of a second tray at this time for resale in Massachusetts. The trays have been variously attributed to Marieberg and

Rorstrand—Sweden's two principal factories for the manufacture of ceramic wares—which were located near the capital city, but because they are unmarked, their precise origin may never be known. Both factories produced faience, the porous earthenware covered with thick white glaze, and both appear to have produced limited numbers of large specialty trays with deep wells (fig. 1). The Marieberg factory was bought out by Rorstrand in 1782, and in 1788 it closed its doors. At that time it probably sold off its remaining stock at reduced prices, either at the manufactory or a merchandising outlet in Stockholm.[4]

Where Tittle ordered the frame for the large tray is unknown, but a cabinet shop in Salem or Beverly would have been the most obvious choice. As a Beverly resident, Tittle may have had an established pattern of patronage at a local shop. However, since the *Astrea*'s cargo was landed at Derby's wharf in Salem harbor, an artisan located in the vicinity of the waterfront may have been a more practical selection. The tray is heavy, and when secured in a protective shipping crate, it would have required the services of

**Fig. 1.** Detail, tray top.

several men to move it. The similarity of the second table frame to this one and the probable sale of the second tray to a Salem resident support the theory of a Salem waterfront shop.

The design of this table frame is one of understated elegance. The lines are as streamlined as those of any twentieth-century functional furniture, yet the form is an effective complement to the ornamental ceramic it supports. The projecting lip and rounded corners of the frame top enhance and protect the fragile tray. The cabinetmaker superbly unified his design by continuing the rounded corners down the legs and introducing complementary curves at the outside edges of the delicate, pierced brackets. Individual elements are further united by scratch beads at the lower edges of the frame, which continue onto the brackets and along the forward corners of the quarter-round legs.

The design of the second table frame varies only in subtle details, except for the addition to the end rails of Chippendale-type brass carrying handles with shaped, solid backplates and bale grips. The large, triangular leg brackets are pierced in a one-inside-two slot pattern instead of the three-slot design that ornaments the open faces of the brackets on Winterthur's table. The leg design better integrates the brackets with the overall structure—the short returns at the bracket bases are continued onto the front edges of the legs, producing a flowing line from rail to floor. The rail, bracket, and leg edges are also finished with a bead.[5]

The large, white-glazed earthenware, or faience, tray of the tabletop is more particularly associated with Swedish ceramic production than that of other European factories. The decoration is hand-painted in bright pink over the opaque glaze. The outer guilloche, or continuous-loop, border was a

relatively common ceramic decoration in the second half of the eighteenth century and occurs on a number of Swedish trays. The bold "fish-scale" border around the sides of the deep well probably was adapted from Chinese porcelains, which were highly prized throughout Europe. Large format landscapes or marine scenes appear to have been popular subjects and were ideal for trays of this size. Several depict classical ruins in a harborscape; similar examples are painted with a view of Drottningholm Palace in Stockholm. The scenic focus of the companion tray is a classical ruin in a semirural landscape with a winding river in the foreground.[6]

Inspiration for the classical tray scenes likely derived from the decoration of other objects that circulated in trade throughout Europe—Continental porcelains, enameled metalware, textiles, and prints. The ultimate sources were the artistic works of painters such as Claude Lorrain and his imitators and the spectacular architectural theatrical backdrops produced for the courts of Europe by the prolific Bibiena family. Lorrain often painted harbor scenes featuring ruins elevated on quays with small fishing boats in the waters and bystanders on the shore. The itinerant Bibienas carried their art throughout Europe; Giovanni Carlo Bibiena (d. 1760) even traveled to Sweden.[7]

Sometime after John Tittle arrived in Salem about July 1788 and before his

departure for a second voyage to Sweden, on or shortly after August 26, he probably ordered the mahogany frame for his newly acquired tray and likely also disposed of the second tray he had purchased in Stockholm. The new owner may well have been Samuel Flagg, a Salem merchant, since the table was owned in the last part of the nineteenth century by one Augustus Flagg. Samuel Flagg was acquainted with Captain Tittle because nine years earlier he was one of several signers of a petition to the Massachusetts Council requesting that Tittle be commissioned commander of the ship *Marquis De La Fayette*, a privateer. Because he produced the second table frame sometime after the first one, the unknown cabinetmaker had an opportunity to appraise his initial work with a fresh eye, leading to the modest design changes described.[8]

Whether Captain Tittle had additional orders for large faience trays in his pocket when he sailed for Stockholm in August and whether he would have ventured other ceramic purchases while there are matters for conjecture, since the *Astrea* never completed her second voyage to Sweden, due to difficulties at sea. The Reverend William Bentley, Salem's indefatigable diarist, reported on October 29: "This day arrived Derby's Ship Astrea, which had been on a voyage to the North of Europe, & upon a leak, had put in at Newfoundland." When Captain Tittle died a dozen years later in 1800, his

"Mahogany fram'd Table cover'd with China" was appraised at $4.50, or 75 percent of the value of his mahogany desk.[9]

*NGE*

---

**Construction:** The rectangular wooden frame has rounded corners and an applied, molded top lip assembled from eight separate pieces glued together—two lengths, two ends, and four rounded corners. The applied lip is secured to the frame with glue and screws inserted from the interior surface. The tray top is supported on an interior rabbet. The corners of the frame, which are formed by extensions of the legs, are joined to the rails by mortise and tenon (not pinned). Each interior corner is reinforced with two vertical-grain blocks, the tops of which are scooped out with a chisel to accommodate the tray. Two flat 3 1/4"-wide interior braces abut the front and back rails, where each is secured with glue and reinforced with a large block abutting the lower surface. Glueblocks are fixed to the sides of the braces to further support the tray. Additional blocks are spaced along all interior rail surfaces just below the rabbet. The legs, which are rounded on the outside surfaces, are shaped in quarter circles; the interior corners are chamfered, top to bottom. Pierced triangular brackets, 3/8" thick and narrowly chamfered at the interior bottom edges, are attached with glue to the corners formed by the frame and legs and reinforced with two small interior glueblocks. A decorative scratch bead at the outside bottom edge of the frame is continued onto the brackets and down the outside corners of the legs. The rectangular ceramic tray has a deep, flat-bottomed well, curved sides, and flat, projecting lip. A shallow foot rim is present on the exterior bottom. The soft, porous earthenware body is buff colored with a white glaze.

**Condition:** Some reinforcing screws in the wooden frame are replaced; others are missing. The joints and interior corner blocks at the leg tops are reglued. A horizontal crack occurs in one end of the frame at the joint with the right leg. The top of one leg is cracked vertically at each side from the lip to the bracket. Five brackets have been repaired.

Residue from the earthenware body of the tray remains on the surfaces of some interior blocks to which the tray was glued. Diagonal, hairline glaze cracks extend across the upper right corner of the ceramic tray. Another surface crack extends in an arc from the lower center-right border area into the foreground of the scenic panel, and left towards the panel border. Some chips and glaze imperfections occur along the lip and sides. The decoration has sustained some surface abrasion. The exterior bottom has body losses at points where the tray was glued to the interior framing blocks of the table.

**Dimensions:**

Frame

| | | |
|---|---|---|
| H. | 27 5/8 in. | 70.2 cm |
| W. (lip to lip) | 37 1/4 in. | 94.6 cm |
| D. (lip to lip) | 25 5/8 in. | 65.1 cm |

Tray

| | | |
|---|---|---|
| H. | 2 1/4 in. | 5.7 cm |
| W. (lip to lip) | 35 1/2 in. | 90.1 cm |
| D. (lip to lip) | 24 in. | 61.0 cm |

**Materials:** *Microanalysis:* Primary: mahogany. Secondary: white pine (corner block, medial brace). *Finish:* medium reddish brown color with combed streaks of darker brown.

**Publications:** Nancy A. Goyne, "An American Tray-Top Table," *Antiques* 93, no. 6 (June 1968): 804–6. Nancy A. Goyne, "An American Tray-top Table," *Winterthur Newsletter* 12, no. 1 (January 5, 1966): 1–3; addendum, vol. 15, no. 10 (December 1969): 6.

**Accession history:** Purchased by H. F. du Pont from John S. Walton, Inc., New York, 1963, who acquired the table from a descendant of the original owner. Gift of H. F. du Pont, 1964. 64.1150

---

1. For the second American table, see Robert W. Skinner, "Fine Americana" (January 2, 1987), lot 184. Swedish trays in European frames are in Sotheby and Co., "Fine English and Continental Furniture, Rugs and Carpets, Tapestries and Clocks" (May 21, 1965), lot 111; Sotheby's, "French and Continental Furniture and Decorations" (September 29, 1990), lot 272; Sotheby's, "Important Americana: The Bertram K. and Nina Fletcher Little Collection, Part 2" (October 21–22, 1994), lot 768.

2. Secretary of the Commonwealth, comp., *Massachusetts Soldiers and Sailors of the Revolutionary War* (Boston, 1907), pp. 791–92. *Essex Institute Historical Collections* 40 (January 1904): 66; vol. 41 (April 1905): 157; vol. 69 (April 1933): 180; vol. 71 (July 1935): 292; vol. 80 (July 1944): 267.

3. Elias Hasket Derby, Instructions to Capt. John Tittle, March 26, 1788, Derby Family Papers, vol. 7, Peabody Essex Museum, Salem, Mass. Manifest of the ship *Astrea*, Stockholm, June 18, 1788, Derby Family Papers, vol. 7, Peabody Essex Museum, Salem, Mass. "Policy of insurance on the ship Astrea and cargo at and from Stockholm to Salem," August 26, 1788, Derby Family Papers, vol. 7, Peabody Essex Museum, Salem, Mass.

4. Carl Hernmarck, "The Marieberg Porcelain Factory," in Paul J. Atterbury, ed., *European Pottery and Porcelain* (New York: Mayflower Books, 1979), pp. 142–45. Carl Hernmarck, *Gammal Svensk Keramik* (Stockholm, 1951), pls. 17, 59.

5. Skinner, "Fine Americana," lot 184.

6. Sotheby's, "Fine English and Continental Furniture," lot 111. Carl Hernmarck, *Marieberg* (Stockholm: Wahlstrom and Widstrand, 1946), pls. 9, 10. Hernmarck, *Gammal Svensk Keramik*, pls. 17, 59. Skinner, "Fine Americana," lot 184.

7. Siegfried Ducret, *The Color Treasury of Eighteenth-Century Porcelain* (New York: Thomas Y. Crowell, 1976), fig. 62. Franz-Adrian Dreier, "Two Berlin Emamelplates from the Time of Frederick the Great," in *Yearbook of the Hamburg Art Collection*, 3 vols. (Hamburg, Ger.: Ernst Hauswedell, 1958), 3:137–44. Marcel Rothlisberger, *Claude Lorrain*, 2 vols. (New Haven: Yale University Press, 1961), 2: figs. 2, 32, 62, 74, 75, 106, 177, 201, 300, 361. Diane M. Kelder, *Drawings by the Bibiena Family* (Philadelphia: Philadelphia Museum of Art, 1968), esp. cats. 20, 38, 39. Guiseppe Galli Bibiena, *Architectural and Perspective Designs* (1740; reprint, New York: Dover Publications, 1964), esp. pt. 1, pp. 6, 10; pt. 2, pp. 7, 10; pt. 3, p. 10; pt. 4, p. 7.

8. Skinner, "Fine Americana," lot 184. Secretary of the Commonwealth, *Massachusetts Soldiers and Sailors*, p. 791.

9. *The Diary of William Bentley*, 4 vols. (Salem, Mass.: Essex Institute, 1905), 1:107. John Tittle estate inventory, 1801, Essex County Probate Court, Salem, Mass.

## 125 ◆ China table
Newport, Rhode Island
1785–1800
Attributed to John Townsend
(1733–1809)

As tea drinking became a ritualized social activity, new manners and specialized furnishings were required, including the tea table as the center of activity. Initially, tea tables, like other furniture forms, were kept against the walls and brought out only for use. For their protection, the fragile and expensive tea bowls were stored out of the way until they were required. By the middle of the eighteenth century, possession of a ceramic tea set became a status symbol. In affluent homes in England and in America it became customary to display all or part of the tea set on a table. One of the new forms introduced in the 1750s was the "china table" with a galleried edge, which Thomas Chippendale noted in his *Director* was for "holding each a set of China, and may be used as Tea-Tables." John Goddard of Newport presumably owned a copy of the 1762 edition of Chippendale's *Director*, so in October 1763, when Moses Brown wrote to Goddard about the "Cheney table and Leather chairs I sent

you Mony for," he was probably familiar with this fashion-conscious form.[1]

Purchase of a china table was not a small investment. In its simplest design, a china table—"with plain legs, 3 feet long, stretcher, bases (cuffs), bragets (brackets), and fret top—cost £4.10.0, roughly 50 percent more than a comparable square tea table.[2] A china table with "open stretchers" and stop-fluted legs, like this one, would cost several pounds more. In the colonies, china tables with pierced galleries were made from Williamsburg, Virginia, to Portsmouth, New Hampshire. However, judging by the small numbers that survive, their high cost meant that they were primarily status symbols owned by the wealthy in urban centers.

This rectilinear, galleried china table is very different in concept from the robust, sculptural, blocked tea tables (see No. 123) made in Newport at about the same time. As the only known Newport table of this form, Winterthur's example is part of a small group of stop-fluted straight-leg Newport furniture further distinguished by crosshatch decoration, molding let into the apron, openwork corner brackets, and cross stretchers in a Chinese motif. Except for a table at the Chipstone

Foundation, the group shares a common method of frame construction—a series of interior transverse braces with three dovetailed to the top of the long rails and two dovetailed to the bottom (fig. 1). On all the tables, the rails are tenoned and double-pegged to the leg, one peg set through the let-in skirt molding. The corner brackets are tenoned to the rails and legs instead of simply being glued and sprigged. These construction features are sufficiently discrete to the tables labeled by John Townsend to serve as one criteria in assigning a piece of furniture to his shop. Interestingly, listed in the personal estate inventory of Christopher Townsend in 1792 were three china tables: "1 old blacknut china table 6/" and "1 old blacknut china table 3/" and "1 mahog china table 10/."[3]

The unusually thin, highly figured top board of this table is rabbeted on the underside to fit inside the frame. The very shallow rabbet is cut broad enough to encompass the glueblocks that secure the top to the frame, and although rabbeting a tabletop to rest in a frame is not uncommon, this particular type of rabbet has no known parallels in eighteenth-century Newport furniture. This suggests either that the top is replaced or that the rabbet was cleaned and enlarged when the original top was reset. Supporting the latter hypothesis is a chalk "B" on the underside of the top, drawn in a style reminiscent of the calligraphy on other documented John Townsend furniture.[4]

NER/WAC

---

**Inscriptions or marks:** *On underside of top:* "B" in chalk.

**Construction:** The pierced tray frame, or gallery, is dovetailed at the corners and glued to the top. The top board, projecting on all four sides as an exposed torus molding and cut with a shallow rabbet on the underside, rests on the skirt rails. It is attached to the frame by a series of glueblocks that are set into the rabbet along all four sides. The frame has a series of transverse braces between the long side rails—three dovetailed to the top of the rails and two dovetailed to the bottom. The rails are tenoned and double-pegged to the legs; each joint is reinforced with two vertical glueblocks and a single horizontal block across the top. On the rails, the molding above the incised band of cross-hatching is let in and glued. The 1/2"-thick pierced corner brackets are tenoned to the legs and rails. The legs, chamfered on the inner edge, are stop fluted on two sides. The cross stretchers are deeply mortised into the legs and have an applied gadrooned molding screwed to the underside.

**Condition:** The table has been refinished. The pierced gallery is repaired in several places. The top board has been reset. The glueblocks holding it in place now are reinforced with screws. One of the upper transverse braces and both bottom braces are replaced.

**Dimensions:**

| | | |
|---|---|---|
| H. | 27 1/4 in. | 69.2 cm |
| W. (molding) | 34 1/2 in. | 87.6 cm |
| W. (frame) | 33 7/8 in. | 86.0 cm |
| W. (feet) | 34 in. | 86.4 cm |
| D. (molding) | 20 5/8 in. | 52.5 cm |
| D. (frame) | 20 1/2 in. | 52.1 cm |
| D. (feet) | 20 in. | 50.8 cm |

**Materials:** *Microanalysis:* Primary: mahogany. Secondary: soft maple group (original upper cross braces); white pine group (replaced lower cross braces); chestnut (glueblocks). *Finish:* natural resin.

**Fig. 1.** Detail, underside.

**Publications:** Israel Sack advertisement, *Antiques* 73, no. 2 (May 1958): inside front cover. Wendy A. Cooper, *In Praise of America: American Decorative Arts, 1650–1830/Fifty Years of Discovery since the 1929 Girl Scouts Loan Exhibition* (New York: Alfred A. Knopf, 1980), p. 142, no. 160. Liza Moses and Michael Moses, "Authenticating John Townsend's Later Tables," *Antiques* 119, no. 5 (May 1981): 1158, fig. 10. Moses, *Master Craftsmen*, figs. 3.79, 3.79a, 3.79b. Albert Sack, "Regional Characteristics of American Tea Tables," *Antiques* 31, no. 1 (January 1987): 257.

**Provenance:** The table descended in the Bullock family of Rhode Island. The original owners are thought to have been Jabez Bullock (1741–1808) and his wife, Mary (Richmond) Bullock (1740–1801). A statement of family history accompanying the table at the time of purchase (now on file at Winterthur) indicates a connection between the Bullock and the Townsend families although the relationship is not detailed.

**Accession history:** Acquired from the Bullock family by Nathan Liverant, Colchester, Conn. Museum purchase from Israel Sack, Inc., New York, 1958.
58.37

1. Thomas Chippendale, *The Gentleman and Cabinet-Maker's Director* (3d ed., London: By the author, 1762), pl. 51 nn, p. 7; Moses Brown to John Goddard, October 1763, Brown Papers, John Carter Brown Library, Brown University, as cited in Morrison H. Heckscher, "English Furniture Pattern Books in Eighteenth-Century America," in Luke Beckerdite, ed., *American Furniture 1994* (Milwaukee, Wis.: Chipstone Fndn., 1994), pp. 185.

2. Figures are taken from the prices listed in the 1772 Philadelphia price book because no comparable published lists exist for New England in this time period; see Martin Eli Weil, "A Cabinetmaker's Price Book," in Ian M. G. Quimby, ed., *Winterthur Portfolio 13* (Chicago: University of Chicago Press for the Henry Francis du Pont Winterthur Museum, 1979), pp. 188–89.

3. Included in the group are a pembroke table labeled by Townsend at Winterthur (see No. 138); a pembroke table at Chipstone (Rodriguez Roque, *American Furniture*, no. 137); a pembroke table with scrolled openwork stretchers in the Dietrich Americana Foundation collection (Moses, *Master Craftsmen*, p. 156, fig. 3.80); and a stretcherless card table labeled by Townsend at the Metropolitan Museum of Art (Heckscher, *American Furniture*, cat. no. 100). On construction details, see Moses, *Master Craftsmen*, p. 112, fig. 3.25. Christopher Townsend estate inventory cited in Wendell D. Garrett, "The Newport, Rhode Island, Interior, 1780–1800" (Master's thesis, University of Delaware, 1957). On Townsend attribution criteria, see Liza Moses and Michael Moses, "Authenticating John Townsend's Later Tables," *Antiques* 119, no. 5 (May 1981): 1152–63.

4. Moses, *Master Craftsmen*, fig. 3.79b, pp. 88, 102–3.

## 126 ◆ Marble slab table

Probably Portsmouth, New Hampshire, or Berwick, Maine
1730–60

The term *side table* is used generically to describe any table intended to stand against the wall of a room. The form, variously interpreted, has been in use since the Middle Ages for the display of such symbols of prosperity as silver plate and glassware. Early examples were made entirely of wood: usually oak and later walnut. But by the late seventeenth century, cabinetmakers offered side tables with "stone" (that is, marble) tops. At that time, the marble was imported from Italy, and its cost limited ownership of the form to affluent households. One of the earliest references to the presence of a marble-top side table in England appears in the circa 1700 travel diary of Celia Fiennes. She cites seeing in the long gallery at Hampton Court "two marble tables in two peers with great jars on each side each table" and at Windsor "marble tables in the peers between the windows" in a large anteroom and "a white marble table behind the doore as a sideboard" in the dining room.[1]

As the eighteenth century progressed, designers from William Kent to Robert Adam introduced new table designs incorporating marble tops. In their hands, the form consisted of a carved base—initially in gilded soft wood and later in mahogany—topped by a thick marble slab. These "marble slabs and frames," as they are cited in cabinetmakers' records and probate inventories, were generally decorative wall furniture reserved for use in reception halls, parlors, and dining rooms.

An isolated early example of the form is recorded in the probate inventory of Gov. John Endicott of Massachusetts in 1665 as "a marble table found in the hall." Clearly, this was an imported table. Probate inventory references in the Boston area in the 1740s confirm that the form was present, although the precise designs are unknown. References commonly list simply "a Marble Table and Frame." Owners generally were merchants or other gentlemen of property—few eighteenth-century New England homes could boast a table with a marble top since possession of such a specialized piece of furniture suggested both affluence and sophistication. The inventory of the estate of Benjamin Prat, Esq., of Milton, Massachusetts, taken July 8, 1763, records, in the middle parlor, "one Marble Slab and Frame . . . £6.0.0." This is the same value placed on a large mahogany desk. Boston merchant William Molineaux owned four marble slab tables. His inventory, dated December 20, 1774, lists "Marble Slab & frame, 20/," "Marble Slab & Stand, £1.16," "a large Marble Slab & Frame, £2.8," and "small Marble Slab & Stand, 10/" as well as "2 Marble Slabs broke, 8/."[2]

When this table was acquired, its delicate cabriole legs, seemingly simple frame, and white pine secondary wood—well-known features of Massachusetts tables—led Joseph Downs to attribute it to that state. Downs also considered the then-unidentified stamped brand "I•HILL," which appears on the underside of one of the rails, to be a maker's mark (fig. 1). Identification of the brand and a broader knowledge of craft practices north of Boston, however, has lead to the reattribution of the table to Portsmouth, New Hampshire, or possibly Berwick, Maine.[3]

The "I•HILL" brand now is considered an owner's mark. The table may have been made for John Hill (1703–72), a prominent Berwick, Maine, landowner whose probate inventory, valued at more than £1,134, included interest in fourteen pieces of property. Hill held several military and civic posts and, at the time of his death, was considered one of the wealthiest men in Maine.[4] The inventory of his estate includes references to several pieces of furniture, but this table is not mentioned.

If Hill was the original owner, then perhaps the maker was Timothy Davis III (ca. 1715–72), a Portsmouth-trained joiner who bought property in Berwick in 1729. Extant bills confirm that Davis made furniture for Hill and also provided a range of services generally offered by rural woodworkers. In April, 1754, Davis supplied "a Ovel table . . . £8.15.0" and "a Small Table . . . £2.10.0." On August 28, 1756, he billed Hill for "one Case of Draws without y^e locks & Brass work . . . £28.0.0 [old tenor]." He also provided "a large duftail Chest . . . £4.10.0" on October 25, 1763.[5]

Based on this evidence, for many years the table was reassigned to Berwick, Maine. Recent research provides insight into the idiosyncrasies of cabinetmaking in that area that suggests a further reattribution is appropriate. The standard model of most New England marble-top tables is finished on three sides with the marble slab resting on and overhanging the frame. In contrast, this table is finished on all four sides, and the marble top is partially recessed behind an applied molding, suggesting that perhaps it was originally made to be used as a freestanding piece of furniture in the center of a room.[6] Because of its size, this table could have been made for use as a communion table in a church.

NER/WAC

---

**Inscriptions or marks:** *Branded on inside surface of one long side of frame:* "I•HILL".

**Construction:** The apron is a composite construction consisting of inner pine rails tenoned and pinned to the leg posts; the joints are reinforced with vertical glueblocks. The lower ovolo molding is applied to the rails between the legs. The drops and brackets on the apron are applied and finished in place. The cavetto molding, mitered at the corners, is nailed in place and the seam covered

**Fig. 1.** Detail, rail.

with an applied bead. The uppermost molding is mitered and nailed to the cavetto forming a rabbet, which receives the marble top. Two transverse braces, between the long side rails, are held in place with vertical glueblocks.

**Condition:** The thickness of the marble top varies, hence it has been rough cut on three sides to sit level on the rails. One of the legs is patched above the ankle; another is patched at the knee. The inside of one of the leg posts is repaired. Some of the skirt returns are repaired. A section of the top molding is replaced.

**Dimensions:**

| | | |
|---|---|---|
| H. | 30 1/2 in. | 77.5 cm |
| W. (cornice) | 52 1/8 in. | 132.4 cm |
| W. (frame) | 49 1/4 in. | 125.1 cm |
| W. (feet) | 50 3/8 in. | 128.0 cm |
| D. (cornice) | 27 3/8 in. | 69.5 cm |
| D. (frame) | 24 3/8 in. | 61.9 cm |
| D. (feet) | 26 in. | 66.0 cm |

**Materials:** *Microanalysis:* Primary: American black walnut. Secondary: white pine group (inner rails, transverse braces). *Finish:* natural resin.

**Publications:** Downs, *American Furniture,* fig. 353. Helen Comstock, "Cabinetmakers of the Norwich Area," *Antiques* 87, no. 6 (June 1965): no. 217. Marshall B. Davidson, ed., *The American Heritage History of Colonial Antiques* ([New York]: American Heritage Publishing Co., [1967]), p. 153, fig. 201. Charles F. Hummel, "Queen Anne and Chippendale Furniture in the Henry Francis du Pont Winterthur Museum, Part 2," *Antiques* 98, no. 6 (December 1970): 900–901, 903, figs. 12, 13. Kirk, *American Furniture,* fig. 1292.

**Accession history:** Purchased by H. F. du Pont from Winsor White, Mamaroneck, N.Y., 1946. Gift of H. F. du Pont, 1965.
65.3093

---

1. Christopher Morris, ed., *The Journeys of Celia Fiennes,* as cited in John Gloag, ed., *A Complete Dictionary of Furniture* (1952; rev. ed., Woodstock, N.Y.: Overlook Press, 1991), p. 447; see also Macquoid and Edwards, *Dictionary,* 3:123.

2. John Endicott inventory, 1665, as cited in Lyon, *Colonial Furniture,* p. 206, see also p. 207. Benjamin Prat inventory, 1763, cited in Cummings, *Rural Household Inventories,* p. 199; William Molineaux inventory, 1774, cited in Alice Hanson Jones, *American Colonial Wealth: Documents and Methods,* 3 vols. (New York: Arno Press, 1977), 2:961–62.

3. Downs, *American Furniture,* fig. 353; Jobe, *Portsmouth Furniture,* p. 433.

4. Identification of Hill was made by John J. Evans and Charles F. Montgomery from manuscript and printed material in the Winterthur Library; see Charles F. Hummel, "Queen Anne and Chippendale Furniture in the Henry Francis du Pont Winterthur Museum, Part 2," *Antiques* 98, no. 6 (December 1970): 902–3. John Hill inventory, May 7, 1772 (photocopy, Downs collection).

5. Hummel, "Queen Anne and Chippendale Furniture," p. 903; see also Jobe, *Portsmouth Furniture,* p. 417. Davis to Hill, bill, collection 156, Downs collection.

6. Jobe, *Portsmouth Furniture,* p. 419. Examples of recessed marble tops include a freestanding table at Colonial Williamsburg (Greenlaw, *New England Furniture,* no. 143) and a table at the Metropolitan Museum of Art that is finished on 3 sides (Heckscher, *American Furniture,* cat. no. 95).

### 127 ◆ Marble slab table
Norwich, Connecticut, area
1770–95

Marble slab tables were an expensive luxury and were infrequently purchased. In New England the form generally was owned in affluent households where the value of household goods—excluding the plate (silver hollow- and flatwares)—was over £50. In the absence of comparable printed figures for New England, the Philadelphia price book for 1772 provides relative costs for the construction and decoration of slab tables. A plain "frame for marble slab" with undecorated cabriole legs and claw feet cost £4 in mahogany; adding carved leaves on the knees and a carved molding increased the cost to £5.[1]

One of the few examples with a known Connecticut history is this table with a tradition of ownership in the Trumbull (Trumble) family of New London County. The Trumbulls operated a prosperous mercantile business in the middle years of the eighteenth

century. From the early 1730s to about 1766, Capt. Joseph Trumble (1679–1755) followed by his son Jonathan (1710–85) carried on direct trade with Great Britain. In 1766 the business suffered a severe reversal from which it never recovered, and Jonathan Trumbull, already active in politics, transferred his focus from business to public service. That year he was appointed deputy governor under William Pitkin (1694–1769) and following Pitkin's death in 1769 he succeeded as governor.[2]

Several related pieces by an as-yet-unidentified Norwich-area craftsman descended in the Trumbull family, including a blockfront chest-on-chest with shell carving, a plain blockfront chest of drawers, a desk-and-bookcase, and three pedestal stands (including No. 149 right).[3] The marble slab table shares with this group several distinctive decorative motifs: a beaded wave-and-scroll apron, unusual leaf and double-scroll carving on the knees, and sloping, webbed ball-and-claw feet. The shaping on the skirt and the

treatment of the feet are repeated on the table, the chest-on-chest, the chest of drawers, and the desk-and-bookcase. The leaf and double-scroll carving on the legs of the table is similar to that on the three pedestal stands.

The knee carving with each leaf emerging under the one above in descending order and two sets ending in volutes is similar to carving on two candlestands (No. 149 right) (fig. 1). A paper label on one states that it was made about 1778 for Samuel Hunt of Charlestown, New Hampshire, by a soldier taken prisoner at the Battle of Bennington. Robert F. Trent has speculated that one possible New London County maker would be William Sprats, a Scots soldier captured by Gen. John Stark's troops.[4]

Two New London County craftsmen known to have made furniture for Jonathan Trumbull are Isaiah Tiffany (1723–1806) and Isaac Fitch (1734–91), who worked for Trumbull as builder and architect as well as cabinetmaker.[5] The New Hampshire–

New London County relationship is also strengthened by the wavelike scrolls approaching the center of the rails of this slab table that are not unlike the decoration found on furniture attributed to the Dunlaps of New Hampshire (No. 175).

Beyond its distinctive carved decoration, inset top, and unusually deep skirt, this table differs structurally from other New England marble slab tables. The front and side rails consist of a thick cherry board glued to an ash inner rail. The two are treated as a single board with tenons at each end cut from the combined stock. Supporting the heavy marble slab are two deep, transverse braces and drop-in supports placed diagonally from the braces to the rear corners; the latter are not usually found in New England slab table construction.

*NER/CGN*

---

**Construction:** The thick marble top, molded on three sides and fitting into a rabbet cut on the upper edge of the frame and legs, rests on the frame and a series of transverse and diagonal braces. Two deep transverse braces, shoulder-dovetailed to the front and back rails, are supported at the front by a batten nailed with rosehead nails to the lower inside of the front rail; there is no corresponding batten across the back. Drop-in braces from the transverse braces to the rear corners provide additional support; they are held by battens nailed with rosehead nails to the inside side rails. Rectangular blocks nailed with rosehead nails to the inside of the front and side rails reinforce the front corners. The front rail is tenoned and double-pegged to the legs; the side rails are tenoned and triple-pegged. The carved skirt and the adjacent carved brackets are nailed to the rails. On the rear legs, the feet are fully carved, but there is no leaf carving on the knee. The balls of the feet are decorated with a stipple punch.

**Condition:** The finish is thick and crazed. A diagonal brace is missing from the left side. The scrolling on the apron molding is cut using a center-lead side-spur bit. The molding itself is attached

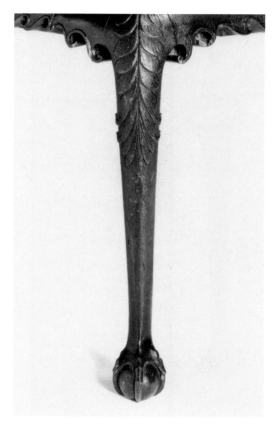

**Fig. 1.** Detail, leg.

with rectangular-shaft nails and does not appear to be replaced.

**Dimensions:**

| | | |
|---|---|---|
| H. | 28 in. | 71.1 cm |
| W. (marble top) | 42 11/16 in. | 108.4 cm |
| W. (frame) | 44 3/8 in. | 112.7 cm |
| W. (feet) | 45 1/8 in. | 114.6 cm |
| D. (marble top) | 20 1/2 in. | 52.1 cm |
| D. (frame) | 21 1/2 in. | 54.6 cm |
| D. (feet) | 21 7/8 in. | 55.6 cm |

**Materials:** *Microanalysis:* Primary: cherry (rails). Secondary: white pine group (transverse braces); ash (inner front rail). *Finish:* natural resin.

**Provenance:** The table has a history of ownership in the Trumbull family of Lebanon and Norwich, Conn.

**Accession history:** Purchased by H. F. du Pont from Harry Arons, Ansonia, Conn., 1955. Gift of H. F. du Pont, 1958.
55.15.1

1. Martin Eli Weil, "A Cabinetmaker's Price Book," in Ian M. G. Quimby, ed., *Winterthur Portfolio 13* (Chicago: University of Chicago Press for the Henry Francis du Pont Winterthur Museum, 1979), p. 189.

2. The family changed the spelling of the name from Trumble to Trumbull about 1766; Macquoid and Edwards, *Dictionary,* s.v. "Trumbull."

3. For the chest-on-chest, see William Voss Elder III and Jayne E. Stokes, *American Furniture, 1680–1880 from the Collection of the Baltimore Museum of Art* (Baltimore: By the museum, 1987), cat. no. 54; *New London County Furniture,* no. 48; for the chest of drawers, see *Connecticut Furniture,* no. 59; John T. Kirk, "The Distinctive Character of Connecticut Furniture," *Antiques* 92, no. 4 (October 1967): 525, fig. 3; for the desk, see Kemble's advertisement, *Antiques* 135, no. 1 (January 1989): 120; for the stands, see Heckscher, *American Furniture,* cat. no. 131.

4. Robert F. Trent, "The Colchester School of Cabinetmaking, 1750–1800," in Francis J. Puig and Michael Conforti, eds., *The American Craftsman and the European Tradition, 1620–1820* (Minneapolis: Minneapolis Institute of Arts, 1989), cat. no. 51.

5. *New London County Furniture,* pp. 106–32.

## 128 ◆ Marble slab table

Boston, Massachusetts
1745–55

On January 16, 1766, John Adams visited the mansion of wealthy Boston merchant Nicholas Boylston and was exceedingly impressed by "the Furniture, which alone cost a thousand Pounds sterling." Among the specific pieces he cited were "Marble Tables," which most likely were large mahogany frames with marble slab tops, possibly similar to this example. This strong, bold Boston interpretation of a "mahogany frame with slab" follows very closely the English Georgian preference for massive marble-top tables embraced by Boston merchants such as Thomas Hancock, Charles Apthorp, and Nicholas Boylston. Although Joseph Downs published this table in 1952 as a New York example, it is more directly related to several forms of early Georgian Boston furniture that have recently received extensive scholarly attention.[1]

Only a few extant examples of elegant English furniture owned by wealthy Bostonians have been identified to date, but there is no doubt that they were present in Boston mansions, probably beginning with the homes of the English royal governors of Massachusetts. Imported slab tables undoubtedly influenced the designs produced by Boston craftsmen, who copied the distinctive characteristics of English and Irish furniture.

English Georgian features are echoed on this table in the decidedly straight cabriole leg, the carved C scroll outlining the inside upper portion of the leg, the blunt, rounded knee with carved shell and pendent bellflower, and the relatively small, round ball foot squarely grasped by well-defined claws. The same profile of the leg and foot, as well as the shell carving, are seen on a Boston card table with a history of original ownership by Peter Roe Dalton of Boston. The simple concave, convex shell with circular bead linking the

pendent bellflower to the base of the shell is related to the shells on the knees of early Georgian Boston chairs (see No. 27). The C scrolls and the shape of the foot are similar to the central leg on a slab-top pier table at the Museum of Fine Arts, Boston, which is English in its derivation. The concave profile of the skirt is also characteristic of English examples and can be seen on a related New England example (see No. 126). Although there may still be some question regarding attribution to Boston or New York, the primary carved details (C scroll, shells and bellflowers, leg profile, and ball-and-claw feet) can be most directly associated with pieces of undisputable Boston origin.[2]

This table was formerly in the collection of noted nineteenth-century artist Robert W. Weir (1803–89). Born in New York City to Robert Weir, who had emigrated from Scotland in 1790, and Mary Catherine Brinkley from Philadelphia, Weir was destined for a mercantile career. At seventeen, his artistic instinct led him to abandon his clerk's position and begin studying art at the Academy of Design. In time, Weir became very much a part of the artistic community of young "classical" artists, and in 1834 he became the instructor of drawing at the United States Military Academy at West Point. Weir's interest in history and antiquarianism drew him to collecting, principally books, prints, and drawings but also old furniture and objects, some of which occasionally appeared in the backgrounds of his paintings. Two of his sons, John Ferguson and J. Alden, also became well-known artists, and in 1864 the former painted *The Studio*, depicting his father's artistic haven. In 1865 a critic described the scene: "One steps from brilliant sunshine into the quiet light and tranquil atmosphere of the artist's studio. Here are rare engravings, sketches of foreign scenes, furniture from overseas, bits of rare tapestry, armor, reminders of romantic achievement and feudal deeds." Indeed Weir did own imported furniture, but more important, he had some very fine eighteenth-century American furniture. In the lower right corner of the painting is a New York blockfront bureau table with ball-and-claw feet; this eighteenth-century piece is now in the Museum of Fine Arts, Boston.[3]

In addition to the bureau table and Winterthur's slab table, Weir also owned a triple-top New York card table now at the Metropolitan Museum of Art.[4] All three pieces were acquired by Ginsburg and Levy at the house auction of the estate of Susan Weir,

Garrison, New York, on August 21, 1937. Weir's antiquarian interests led him to collect locally available antiques presumably originally owned by New York families. His acquisition of a Boston table along with New York furniture indicates that this table may be an example of the export trade from Boston to New York in the mid eighteenth century.

*WAC with NER*

---

**Inscriptions or marks:** *On inside rear rail:* "GINSBURG & LEVY/ ANTIQUES/ 815 Madison Avenue/ New York" on small paper label, pasted.

**Construction:** The rear leg posts are not shaped on the back side; the back rail is mortised into the leg posts flush with the back surface. The side and front rails are mortised into the leg posts, set back from the outside surface of the leg posts, and faced with mahogany. The joints are reinforced with two-part vertical glueblocks. The applied upper facing has an integral bead beneath a broad cove that is surmounted by a flat frieze. The lower applied skirt is convex. Faceted corners are applied to leg posts and moldings. Scrolled knee brackets are applied between the legs and lower skirt.

**Condition:** An original medial brace is missing. The glueblocks are reset, with some possible replacements. A section of the lower bead on the front facing has been replaced.

**Dimensions:**

| | | |
|---|---|---|
| H. | 29 in. | 73.6 cm |
| H. (frame) | 27³/₈ in. | 69.5 cm |
| W. (top) | 53³/₄ in. | 136.5 cm |
| W. (frame) | 50⁷/₈ in. | 149.4 cm |
| W. (feet) | 50 in. | 127.0 cm |
| D. (top) | 29 in. | 73.6 cm |
| D. (frame) | 27 in. | 68.6 cm |
| D. (feet) | 26³/₈ in. | 67.0 cm |

**Materials:** *Microanalysis:* Primary: mahogany. Secondary: maple, tulip (probably replaced blocks). *Finish:* natural resin.

**Publications:** Downs, *American Furniture*, fig. 354.

**Provenance:** Ex coll.: Robert W. Weir (1803–89); to Susan Weir, Garrison, N.Y.; to Ginsburg and Levy, New York.

**Accession history:** Purchased by H. F. du Pont from Ginsburg and Levy. Gift of H. F. du Pont, 1963. 60.1068

---

1. L. H. Butterfield, ed., *Diary and Autobiography of John Adams*, 4 vols. (Cambridge: Harvard University Press, 1961), 1:294–95. We thank both Alan Miller and Leigh Keno for their help in recognizing this table as a product of a Boston shop and for their leadership role in the reexamination of a large body of eighteenth-century furniture; see Keno, Freund, and Miller, "Very Pink of the Mode," pp. 266–306.

2. For the Dalton card table, see Sotheby's, "Important American Furniture and Folk Art" (October 14, 1989), lot 321; for another closely related card table with similar legs, feet, and C scrolls, see Christie's, "Highly Important American Furniture from the Collection of Dr. C. Ray Franklin" (October 13, 1984), lot 397. For a Boston side chair with almost identical shell and bellflower carving on the knees, see Heckscher, *American Furniture*, pp. 43–44, 336. For the MFA, Boston, pier table, see Hipkiss, *Eighteenth-Century American Arts*, no. 50, pp. 92–93.

3. William H. Gerdts, *Robert Weir: Artist and Teacher of West Point* (West Point: Cadet Fine Arts Forum of the U.S. Corps of Cadets, 1976), p. 84, pl. 89. Irene Weir, *Robert W. Weir: Artist* (New York: House of Field-Doubleday, 1947), p. 58. On Weir's household, see Dorothy Weir Young, *The Life and Letters of J. Alden Weir* (New Haven: Yale University Press, 1960), p. 6.

4. For the bureau table, see Hipkiss, *Eighteenth-Century American Arts*, no. 25; for the card table, see Heckscher, *American Furniture*, pp. 171–72.

## 129 ◆ Slab table
Boston, Massachusetts
1750–70

Like No. 128, this similarly bold example exhibits several prominent features that echo English Georgian precedents. The cyma-curve shaping of the front skirt and central carved bellflower motif are reminiscent of English examples that have pendent shells centered on the skirt.[1] The feature most closely borrowed from English furniture of the period, however, is the carved hairy-paw feet. While presently no Boston-owned eighteenth-century English slab tables with hairy paw-feet are known, several pieces of English seating furniture with hairy-paw feet have good Boston histories.

Among the numerous objects Thomas Hancock ordered from London for his Beacon Street mansion about 1740 was a handsome double chair-back settee with hairy-paw feet and carved lions' masks on the knees; and William Phillips of Boston owned an English hairy-paw foot side chair in 1750. Variations of the hairy-paw foot are found on Boston seating furniture, tables, and case furniture of the period. The hairy-paw feet on a Boston blockfront desk at the Museum of Fine Arts, Boston, are quite similar to those

on Winterthur's table. A hairy-paw foot with distinct and separated hairy talons grasping a well-defined ball is seen on a Boston blockfront desk and several Boston blockfront desk-and-bookcases.[2]

The character of the foliate carving on all four legs is distinctly Boston and can be seen on numerous other pieces of Boston furniture. Very linear and stylized, it is characterized by simple lobed leaves with two or three long incised lines simulating veining. The central tapering midrib with beaded edge is also an identifying characteristic. One unusual feature (which may eventually identify a group) is the strong horizontal cuts flanking the midrib in the upper portion of the carving.

WAC

---

**Construction:** All rails are mortised into the leg posts with the lower, shaped, convex skirt glued and screwed to the face of the apron. The corners of front leg posts are rounded, echoing the rounded shape of the marble top. The central shaped drop is pieced out with an applied piece. The rear legs are only carved on the outside. Vertical two-part glueblocks reinforce the joints. A central cross brace is notched through the front and rear rails.

**Condition:** Glueblocks are replaced. Through-notching on the cross brace may not be original. The table has been refinished.

**Dimensions:**

| | | |
|---|---|---|
| H. (frame) | 27 3/4 in. | 70.5 cm |
| H. (to top of marble) | 28 3/4 in. | 73.0 cm |
| W. (top) | 48 in. | 121.9 cm |
| W. (frame) | 42 in. | 106.6 cm |
| W. (feet) | 45 1/2 in. | 115.3 cm |
| D. (top) | 23 7/8 in. | 60.6 cm |
| D. (frame) | 20 1/2 in. | 52.1 cm |
| D. (feet) | 23 in. | 58.4 cm |

**Materials:** *Microanalysis:* Primary: mahogany. Secondary: maple, pine (replaced glueblocks). *Finish:* modern; natural resin.

**Publications:** Edgar G. Miller, Jr., *American Antique Furniture: A Book for Amateurs,* 2 vols. (Baltimore: Lord Baltimore Press, 1937), 2:711, 709, no. 1306. Downs, *American Furniture,* fig. 358.

**Accession history:** Purchased from Joe Kindig, December 20, 1939. 59.2844

1. Kirk, *American Furniture,* p. 1325.

2. On Hancock and Phillips, see Museum of Fine Arts, Boston, *Paul Revere's Boston, 1735–1818* (Boston: By the museum, 1975), pp. 46–47, 50. Winterthur also owns an armchair with hairy-paw feet (51.80) that came from Frederick Beck of Brookline, Mass., and may have been owned in Boston by Beck's ancestors in the eighteenth century; Downs, *American Furniture,* fig. 55. For the Boston block-front desk, see Hipkiss, *Eighteenth-Century American Arts,* no. 25, pp. 42–43. For Boston desks with foot variants, see John S. Walton advertisement, *Antiques* 65, no. 9 (September 1954): 152; David Stockwell advertisement, *Antiques* 109, no. 1 (January 1976): 1. Jobe and Kaye, *New England Furniture,* pp. 241–46.

## 130 ◆ Table with round falling leaves

North Shore, Massachusetts, or
Portsmouth, New Hampshire
1760–90

Achieving flexibility in the size of a table's top was a phenomenon of the sixteenth century. One design—the draw table—fitted two subsidiary leaves to the traditional medieval long table. Set beneath the main board, the leaves could be pulled out to nearly double the length of the top. A massive piece of generally stationary furniture, the form faded from popularity late in the seventeenth century.

An alternative design introduced at about the same time featured hinged leaves and a gate support. Identified at the time as a table with "falling" leaves, or flaps, and now called a drop-leaf or gateleg table, the form was available in a variety of sizes and shapes. It enjoyed great popularity in the post-Restoration period, when the practice of dining at separate small tables became fashionable on both sides of the Atlantic.

Its eighteenth-century successor was the hinged-leaf table with cabriole legs. Period documents offer little assistance in determining the specific names or uses of the myriad hinged-leaf table forms made in a range of sizes and shapes. Larger tables were generally used for dining; smaller examples, identified today as "breakfast" tables, probably were multifunctional. The serving height of this table is a little low for eating a meal, and so it may have functioned as a tea table. Both sizes generally were placed against a wall with leaves down when not in use and were moved around the room as needed. The advantage of hinged-leaf tables over tables with fixed tops is the minimum amount of floor space occupied when folded, and yet they could be opened to afford the maximum accommodation.

Several details link this table with North Shore, Massachusetts, and Portsmouth, New

Hampshire. An unusual cabriole leg—its pronounced leading edge notched below the knee and tapered to a rounded, or pad, foot—once was cited as a distinguishing feature of Essex County furniture. That profile, which appears on a variety of table and tall-leg case forms including a dressing table at Winterthur (see No. 165), now is assigned more broadly to include North Shore, Massachusetts, and the Portsmouth, New Hampshire, area. Variations on the distinctive foot pattern, which is a five-eighths-inch pad ring incised on the top and resting on a half-inch disk, appear on tables (No. 133) and chairs from the same geographic region.[1] Another North Shore, Massachusetts, feature is the shaped skirt design in broken cyma and cyma-reverse curves.

Following the previously accepted dating chronology based on foot design (that is, the pad foot preceding the introduction of the ball-and-claw foot), Joseph Downs originally dated this table to the second quarter of the

eighteenth century. As the price books confirm, however, the pad foot remained an option well into the second half of the eighteenth century. Richard H. Randall has suggested that the block from which a ball-and-claw foot was carved could also produce the large, wide-spreading pad foot seen here.[2]

*NER/CGN*

---

**Inscriptions or marks:** *Incised on rail in block letters:* "BW".

**Construction:** The top, slightly beveled on the edge, is chamfered on the undersurface. When open, the top is nearly circular; when closed, it is a narrow rectangle. The center board, pegged to the stationary leg and to the end rails, meets the leaves on rule joints and is attached with pairs of iron butt hinges. The sides of the frame are double-railed. On each side, the outer rail, the same thickness as the stile, is sawed in two unequal sections attached by an eight-finger knuckle-joint hinge. The longer stationary part is tenoned and double-pegged to its adjacent leg and secured with five rosehead nails to a narrower inner side rail; the movable part, tenoned and double-pegged to its leg, swings to support the raised leaf. The inner side rail is dovetailed to one end rail and stops 1½" from the other. The heavy end rails are chamfered on the inner edge.

**Condition:** Once painted black, the table has been refinished. There are traces of paint on the underside of the top and on the bottom edge of the end rails. One of the leaves is split at the rule joint. One of the stationary legs is repaired behind the knee. One of the movable legs is repaired with a plugged screw at the knee. A portion of foot pad and disk is missing on one stationary leg. The other stationary leg has two splits, one repaired with a spline. The hinges are original, although some of the screws are replaced.

**Dimensions:**

| | | |
|---|---|---|
| H. | 25³/4 in. | 65.4 cm |
| W. (top open) | 27 in. | 68.6 cm |
| W. (top closed) | 9³/4 in. | 24.8 cm |
| W. (frame) | 7 in. | 17.8 cm |
| W. (feet) | 8⁵/8 in. | 22.0 cm |
| D. (top) | 27⁵/8 in. | 70.3 cm |
| D. (frame) | 18⁵/8 in. | 47.4 cm |
| D. (feet) | 19³/4 in. | 50.2 cm |

**Materials:** *Microanalysis:* Primary: American black walnut. Secondary: white pine group (inner rail). *Finish:* once painted black; now covered with a clear varnish.

**Publications:** Downs, *American Furniture*, fig. 308. Butler, *American Furniture*, p. 30.

**Accession history:** Bequest of H. F. du Pont, 1969. 66.776

1. On the Essex County leg, see Dean A. Fales, Jr., *Essex County Furniture: Documented Treasures from Local Collections, 1660–1860* (Salem, Mass.: Essex Institute, 1965), no. 248; on its reassignment, see Jobe, *Portsmouth Furniture*, cat. no. 55B, p. 244; Jobe and Kaye, *New England Furniture*, no. 61, pp. 273–75. Examples of tables include a slightly larger hinged-leaf table at Historic Deerfield (see Fales, *Furniture of Historic Deerfield*, fig. 248), one at Colonial Williamsburg (see Greenlaw, *New England Furniture*, no. 132), and one sold by Sotheby Parke Bernet (see "Important American Furniture and Related Decorative Arts" [November 22, 1980], lot 1322). For chairs, see Randall, *American Furniture*, nos. 151, 153, 154.

2. A breakfast table with plain feet was £1 cheaper than the same table with claw feet; see Martin Eli Weil, "A Cabinetmaker's Price Book," in Ian M. G. Quimby, ed., *Winterthur Portfolio 13* (Chicago: University of Chicago Press for the Henry Francis du Pont Winterthur Museum, 1979), p. 186. Randall, *American Furniture*, no. 154n.

## 131 ◆ Table with oval falling leaves

Portsmouth, New Hampshire, area 1755–85

During the fifteenth century, a number of new table forms were introduced to augment the medieval *table dormant*, the principal table in the house. Among the specialized forms in use was a small hinged-leaf occasional table that might double as a "breakfast" table, which was referenced in sixteenth-century documents. During the Stuart period, small turned-leg tables with flaps or of gate construction mentioned among the contents of parlor and eating rooms probably were used for this purpose. By the eighteenth century, the habit among the more leisured class of rising late and dining upstairs led to the introduction of small breakfast tables designed to complement the other furnishings of the room.[1]

Thomas Chippendale was familiar with the form, which he described as "a table with two hinged flaps and an enclosed lower shelf."[2] But these designs in his *Director* today are identified as *pembroke tables*. The term *breakfast table* today identifies a small round or oval hinged-leaf table with two fixed and two hinged cabriole legs.

The twenty-eight-inch surface height and roughly three-foot diameter of the open top of this table suggest that it may have been used as a traditional breakfast table. The most distinctive feature is the shape of the cabriole legs. They are rectangular in section with the back of the knee cut in a slight chamfer; they end in an oval ball clasped by thin elongated claws without articulated knuckles. This feature and its perceived relation to a tea table documented to John Goddard (see No. 123 left) probably led Joseph Downs to assign the table to Newport.[3] The combination of mahogany, white pine, and tulip-poplar (a timber indigenous to southern New England) would seem to support Downs's thesis.

**Fig. 1.** Detail, underside.

Although the table is fashioned in mahogany, the wood used for the top is not of uniform or particularly high quality. The center section is cut from less highly figured wood than the leaves, which have knotholes. Given the availability of the highest quality materials and the level of competence and craftsmanship of the Townsend-Goddard school, it is difficult to associate this table with that group.

More telling in determining provenance is the unusual method of attaching the top to the frame. Instead of following the traditional practice of pegging it to the frame, screwing it through the frame, or attaching it with a series of small glueblocks, the maker of this table joined the top to the base by long glueblocks inside each corner that are both glued to the top and pegged to the frame (fig. 1). This method of construction was identified by Brock Jobe and Myrna Kaye as common to a small group of Portsmouth area tables. Further

study of Portsmouth area tables confirms the provenance and assigns production of the design to a single unidentified shop working between 1755 and 1785.[4]

*NER/CGN*

---

**Inscriptions or marks:** *On underside of one leaf:* shopmark "XX2" in pencil. *On underside of other leaf:* shopmark "XX3" in pencil.

**Construction:** The edge of the top is slightly rounded. When open, the top is oval; when closed, the top is a narrow rectangle. The top board and its flanking leaves meet in rule joints and are secured with pairs of iron butt hinges. The center board is glued to long rectangular glueblocks which, in turn, are joined to the frame with wood pegs. The sides of the frame are double-railed. The outer rail is sawed into two unequal pieces with a five-part finger-joint hinge. Tenoned and double-pegged to its fixed leg, the longer part is secured with four rosehead nails to the inner rail and also is wood-pegged to the inner rail and to the glueblock; the shorter part, tenoned

and double-pegged to its leg, forms the swing action. The inner side rail is dovetailed to one end rail and stops 1 1/2" short of the other.

**Condition:** One leaf is severely cracked, and the other is pieced up on the outer edge. There is a deep burn mark on the center section of the top. There are several splits in the top following the line of the grain and several plugged holes where the screws from the hinges have pierced the top. One leg, fractured at the knee and post, has been repaired extensively; the stile on the swing leg on the same side also is repaired. One of the fixed rails is split at the knuckle hinge.

**Dimensions:**

| | | |
|---|---|---|
| H. | 28 in. | 71.1 cm |
| W. (top open) | 36 3/8 in. | 92.4 cm |
| W. (top closed) | 13 in. | 33.0 cm |
| W. (frame) | 10 1/2 in. | 26.7 cm |
| W. (feet) | 10 3/4 in. | 27.3 cm |
| D. (top) | 38 1/8 in. | 71.1 cm |
| D. (frame) | 26 3/8 in. | 67.9 cm |
| D. (feet) | 27 1/4 in. | 69.2 cm |

**Materials:** *Microanalysis:* Primary: mahogany. Secondary: tulip-poplar (outer rail); white pine group (inner rail). *Finish:* natural resin.

**Publications:** Downs, *American Furniture*, fig. 307.

**Accession history:** Bequest of H. F. du Pont, 1969. 60.718

---

1. Macquoid and Edwards, *Dictionary*, 3:190–91.

2. Christopher Gilbert, *The Life and Work of Thomas Chippendale*, 2 vols. (New York: Macmillan Co., 1978), 1:303.

3. Downs, *American Furniture*, fig. 307.

4. Jobe and Kaye, *New England Furniture*, no. 61 n. 1. Jobe, *Portsmouth Furniture*, cat. no. 55, p. 245. "A mahogany oval Table new Fashion" was advertised in the *Boston Gazette*, July 4, 1757 (Dow, *Arts and Crafts in New England*, p. 116).

## 132 ◆ Table with oval falling leaves

**Connecticut River valley**
**1780–1830**

Designs for straight-leg furniture reached America in the 1760s in English pattern books on forms inspired by Chinese furniture. The "Marlborough" leg, as it came to be called, was never as popular in America as it appears to have been in England, although American price books record the design on dining, card, pembroke, corner, sideboard, and china tables.[1] Rhode Island cabinetmakers, in particular, adopted the straight leg (plain, molded, or fluted) for use on pembroke and card tables (see Nos. 138, 142).

Because the design was cheaper to produce than its cabriole-leg counterpart, Marlborough-leg tables may have been more common than their survival rate indicates. Simple tables such as this one may have been considered too common to warrant preservation. In general, New England cabinetmakers used the Marlborough leg on breakfast and dining tables in combination with rectangular leaves.[2]

Its use here on an oval-top hinged-leaf table is rare—no other example is known.

This table form, like most others, was available in a variety of woods, including mahogany and walnut as well as local timbers. Paint or stain provided a uniform appearance when multiple woods were used, as seen on this table, which has a birch top and side rails but cherry end rails and legs.

Stylish tables with Marlborough legs have been dated as early as the 1760s, based on the introduction of the design. The motif reached its height of popularity in the 1780s and continued to be made into the first two decades of the nineteenth century. The quality of workmanship on this table suggests that the later date range probably is more accurate.

*NER/CGN*

---

**Construction:** The edge of the top is slightly beveled. The top board and the leaves meet in a rule joint and are linked by pairs of iron butt hinges. The center board is attached to the frame by rectangular glueblocks, three on each side and one on each end. The sides of the frame are double-railed. On each side, the outer rail, sawed in half,

has a five-part finger-joint hinge. One half, attached with four rosehead nails to the inner rail, is tenoned and double-pegged to the fixed leg; the other, tenoned and double-pegged to its leg, forms the swing action that supports the raised leaf. The inner side rail is dovetailed to one end rail and stops 1/2" from the other. The legs, molded on two sides, have a tapered chamfer on the inner edge.

**Condition:** The piece has been refinished although some remnants of the older finish remain. There are a series of dark circular stains on the top, which has a compound warp. One of the gateleg posts is patched, and a part of the other is missing. A small section of the swing rail also is missing. X-rays indicate that the mortise-and-tenon joints are poorly cut. The five-finger joint and one of the rule joints are poorly executed, and the dovetails are loose throughout. A modern, round tenon secures the finger hinge for one leaf. There is some worm damage to the birch top and rails.

**Dimensions:**

| | | |
|---|---|---|
| H. | 27³/₈ in. | 69.5 cm |
| W. (top) | 29⁵/₈ in. | 75.4 cm |
| W. (frame) | 22³/₄ in. | 57.8 cm |
| W. (feet) | 22¹/₄ in. | 57.2 cm |
| D. (top open) | 35¹/₄ in. | 89.5 cm |
| D. (top closed) | 10⁷/₈ in. | 27.6 cm |
| D. (frame) | 9⁷/₈ in. | 20.1 cm |
| D. (feet) | 10¹/₈ in. | 25.7 cm |

**Materials:** *Microanalysis:* Primary: birch (top); cherry (legs, end rails). Secondary: birch (swing rail, inner rail); white pine group (glueblocks). *Finish:* natural resin.

**Provenance:** Ex coll.: Charles K. Davis, Fairfield, Conn.

**Accession history:** Gift of Charles K. Davis, Fairfield, Conn., 1954.
54.74.4

---

1. Martin Eli Weil, "A Cabinetmaker's Price Book," in Ian M. G. Quimby, ed., *Winterthur Portfolio 13* (Chicago: University of Chicago Press for the Henry Francis du Pont Winterthur Museum, 1979), pp. 185–89.

2. For Marlborough-leg square-leaf dining tables, see Jobe and Kaye, *New England Furniture*, no. 65; Barquist, *American Tables and Looking Glasses*, cats. 58, 59.

## 133 ◆ Corner table with falling leaf

Eastern Massachusetts, possibly Boston or Salem
1740–60

An entry in the 1772 Philadelphia price book for "Corner Table Cruked legs . . . 3 feet Square" aptly describes this table. The price book lists its cost in mahogany with plain (pad) feet or "Marlbro feet with bases" at £3.10.0. The same table with "claw feet" was £1 more.[1]

The basic design—a triangular frame with three fixed legs and one hinged leg and a single leaf—relates to the triangular-top tables made in Georgian England.[2] The popularity of the form in England is difficult to measure, but an indication of its relative rarity is suggested by its absence from the major eighteenth-century English pattern books. Corner tables, like other single-leaf tables (see No. 134), were designed to be placed with the falling leaf facing out (much like a "snap" or tilt-top table) when not in use (fig. 1).

The corner table is a relatively rare furniture form in eighteenth-century America

as well. Most of the surviving examples are high-style, urban products with cabriole legs and pad feet. This table is among the most complex of the group, which displays molded-edge tops with indented corners and shaped skirt rails on the two sides opposite the falling leaf. On two of these, including Winterthur's table, the outline of the skirt is opposing cyma curves in an ogee arch; the skirt pattern on the third is simpler, combining C scrolls and flat arches. Two tables have plain-edge tops and straight skirts.[3] One of these has a sliding center leg supporting the leaf. Most, however, share the expected rear rail construction with the swing rail pivoting from a knuckle joint attaching it to the stationary rail.

Several of these tables have strong eighteenth-century histories in eastern Massachusetts. The one with the sliding center leg, probably made in Boston, was owned by the Higginson family of Boston and Deerfield. The table with the C scroll and flat-arch skirt descended in the Perley family, originally from Ipswich, Massachusetts. Although the eighteenth-century provenance of Winterthur's

**Fig. 1.** Table, leaf down.

table is fragmentary, paper labels confirm its late nineteenth-century ownership in the Chaney family of Salem, Massachusetts.

*NER with CGN*

Inscriptions or marks: Two gummed paper labels are attached to the underside of the top. *On the upper label:* "This table was bought [illegible]/ [missing] William Shano[illegible] [missing] 67 and given to his daughter Sarah/ on her [illegible] and then was given to her/ daughter Thankful Honis who married/ Jeremiah Gore and on her desc[missing]/ to [Ca]rolin Gore, to be retained in the/ Family C. Gore married Charles Rogers/ [illegible] Maine" in ink. *On second label:* "Given by Caroline Rogers to her sister Zakah/ May Smith, and by her to her daughter/ Annee M. Hackect[?] who presented it to Rev/ George L. Chaney her mother's beloved/ pastor and friend/ June 29th 1881" in ink. *Stamped on iron hinges:* "JP" or "IP" in a serrated rectangle.

**Construction:** The outside point of the triangle on both the top and the leaf has been pieced-up. Originally affixed to the frame with rectangular glueblocks, the top now is held with wood screws countersunk into the frame. The leaf meets the top in a rule joint and is held with a pair of iron butt hinges. On the triangular frame, with its obtuse front angle, the rails are double-pegged to the legs. The thick rear rail is cut to provide both the fixed rail and the gate action, which is divided into two unequal parts by a six-finger knuckle-joint hinge. The lower edge of the frame, cut in a scalloped pattern, is chamfered on the inner edge. The knee blocks are glued over the frame. The cabriole legs taper to an undercut ankle; the flattened foot rests on an unusually thick pad.

**Condition:** The top has been reset. On the leaf, there is a major repair below the rule joint: a thin triangular patch (approximately 8" long) at the left hinge and a much longer triangular patch at the right hinge. The right foot is repaired at the ankle. The center leg post is repaired. A water-damaged finish on the top was removed in 1972; the piece was treated with orange shellac and paste wax.

**Dimensions:**

| | | |
|---|---|---|
| H. | 26³/4 in. | 68.0 cm |
| W. (top) | 35³/8 in. | 88.7 cm |
| W. (frame) | 26³/8 in. | 67.0 cm |
| W. (feet) | 27¹/4 in. | 69.2 cm |
| D. (top open) | 35 in. | 88.8 cm |
| D. (top closed) | 17³/8 in. | 44.2 cm |
| D. (feet) | 15¹/2 in. | 39.4 cm |

**Materials:** *Microanalysis:* Primary: mahogany. Secondary: soft maple group (rear rail, swing rail). *Finish:* natural resin; orange shellac.

**Provenance:** Presented to the Reverend George L. Chaney, Salem, Mass., 1881; the table remained in the Chaney family until its sale.

**Accession history:** Purchased by H. F. du Pont from John S. Walton, Inc., New York, 1952. Gift of H. F. du Pont, 1952.
52.145

---

1. Martin Eli Weil, "A Cabinetmaker's Price Book," in Ian M. G. Quimby, ed., *Winterthur Portfolio 13* (Chicago: University of Chicago Press for the Henry Francis du Pont Winterthur Museum, 1979), p. 187.

2. Kirk, *American Furniture*, p. 324, fig. 1262.

3. An exception to the high-style corner table is a walnut example with turned, straight cabriole legs; see Elizabeth Bidwell Bates and Jonathan L. Fairbanks, *American Furniture: 1620 to the Present* (New York: Richard Marek Publishers, 1981), p. 127. For the other complex tables, see Greenlaw, *New England Furniture*, no. 134; Barquist, *American Tables and Looking Glasses*, cat. 55. For the 2 plain-edge tables, see Katharine Bryant Hagler, *American Queen Anne Furniture, 1720–1755* (Dearborn, Mich.: Henry Ford Museum and Greenfield Village, 1976), p. 52; Fales, *Furniture of Historic Deerfield*, fig. 251.

### 134 ◆ Table with single falling leaf
Boston, Massachusetts
1740–80

### Table with single falling leaf
Boston, Massachusetts, area
1750–90

The infrequent survival of eighteenth-century tables with one falling leaf suggests that the form was considerably less common than the two-leaf model, although documentary evidence from the period provides no confirming proof. In fact, inventory takers seldom specified the size of a table (beyond describing it as large or small, square, round, or oval), nor did they record the number of leaves.[1]

For the eighteenth-century cabinetmaker, the size of the frame or "bed" was a determining factor in the production and cost of tables with falling leaves. From midcentury, standard measurements for dining tables in American price lists began with a three-foot-long frame and progressed in six-inch increments to a six-foot-long bed.

Both of these tables represent the top-of-the-line in single-leaf tables. The left table displays an elaborately scrolled skirt on the front and end rails, delicate cabriole legs emphasized by molded C scrolls behind the knees, and well-articulated pad-on-disk feet. Its construction differs from standard practice only in the unusual pegging pattern of the rails: the front and rear rails are double-pegged in the usual manner, but the end rails are held by a single peg in front and double pegs at the back.

Few decorative details provide so clear an indication of place as does the claw foot with high rounded ball, articulated knuckles, and retracted side talons. This terminal appears most often on Boston furniture. Cabinetmaker Benjamin Frothingham, working in nearby Charlestown, Massachusetts, used this foot on a dining table (No. 137) and a card table (No. 139).

Apart from the carved feet, the right table appears deceptively simple. The top is "square" with an ogee-molded edge. The profile of the cabriole leg with its ridged knee softening at the ankle is characteristic of eastern Massachusetts furniture. An unusual detail is the way the knee flows into the block rather than stopping at the base in the standard manner; another is the treatment of

the skirt. On most single-leaf tables, all exposed rails are treated similarly. In this case, the long rail is plain, but the end rails are shaped in a pattern of broken cyma curves ending in an ogee arch. This design appears on three other Massachusetts tables. A fourth has simpler cyma–reverse-cyma end rails, and the side talons of its claw feet are less drastically retracted.[2]

The sophisticated design, the highly figured mahogany ogee-molded tops, the graceful legs and feet, and the shaping of the rails suggest these tables occupied rooms used for public entertaining. They probably served many purposes, such as serving tea, writing, and dining.

*NER/CGN*

---

**Construction:** (Left) The rectangular top has ogee molding on all four sides and consists of two boards (the center board wider than the leaf) meeting in a butt join and secured with iron butt hinges. The top is joined to the frame by rectangular glueblocks. The back side of the rectangular frame is double-railed. The outer rail, divided in half, has a five-part finger-joint hinge. The stationary section, tenoned and pegged to the adjacent leg, is secured with rosehead nails to the inner rail; the swing section,

tenoned and double-pegged to its leg, supports the raised leaf. The inner rail is dovetailed to one end rail and nearly abuts the other. The end rails are tenoned and double-pegged at one end of the back rail and single-pegged at the other. The finished front rail is tenoned and double-pegged at both ends. A skirt molding is applied to the front and end rails, its lower edge cutting into the supporting rails. The front and end rails are approximately ½" deeper than the rear rail.

(Right) The rectangular top, ogee-molded on four sides, consists of two boards (the center board slightly wider than the leaf) that meet in a rule joint and are attached with iron butt hinges. The top is attached with screws countersunk into the frame. The rectangular frame is double-railed on the back. The outer rail, sawed in two unequal parts, has a five-part finger-joint hinge. The stationary rail, tenoned and double-pegged to the adjacent leg, is screwed and secured with rosehead nails to the inner rail; the movable rail, tenoned and double-pegged to its leg, forms the swing action and supports the leaf. The underside of the leaf has a mahogany stop for the leg, secured with six rosehead nails. The inner back rail is dovetailed to one end rail and almost abuts the other end rail. A vertical glueblock once reinforced the dovetail join. The front and end rails are tenoned and double-pegged to the legs. The shaping on the end rails is sawn and finished with a chisel.

**Condition:** (Left) The top is slightly warped, and a large split along the grain has been filled. The swing leg is repaired at the rail joint. The hinges are old.

(Right) There is a 4½" split on the right side of the leaf below the hinge. The front rail also is split. Small pegs now reinforce the dovetails on the end rails.

**Dimensions:**

Left

| | | |
|---|---|---|
| H. | 26⅛ in. | 66.4 cm |
| W. (top) | 29⅜ in. | 74.6 cm |
| W. (frame) | 27⁵⁄₁₆ in. | 64.3 cm |
| W. (feet) | 29½ in. | 74.9 cm |
| D. (top open) | 29 in. | 73.6 cm |
| D. (top closed) | 12⅜ in. | 31.4 cm |
| D. (frame) | 14¹⁵⁄₁₆ in. | 37.9 cm |
| D. (feet) | 16½ in. | 41.9 cm |

Right

| | | |
|---|---|---|
| H. | 27⅞ in. | 70.8 cm |
| W. (top) | 28¾ in. | 73.0 cm |
| W. (frame) | 16 in. | 40.6 cm |
| W. (feet) | 17⅝ in. | 45.0 cm |
| D. (top open) | 28⅞ in. | 73.3 cm |
| D. (top closed) | 14¾ in. | 37.5 cm |
| D. (frame) | 12½ in. | 31.8 cm |
| D. (feet) | 15⅛ in. | 38.5 cm |

**Materials:** *Microanalysis:* (Left) Primary: mahogany. Secondary: soft maple group (outer rear rail); white pine group (inner rear rail, glueblocks). (Right) Primary: mahogany. Secondary: white pine group (rear rail). *Finish:* (Left and right) natural resin.

**Publications:** (Right) Downs, *American Furniture*, fig. 310.

**Accession history:** (Left) Purchased by H. F. du Pont from Charles F. Montgomery, Wallingford, Conn., 1948. Bequest of H. F. du Pont, 1969. (Right) Bequest of H. F. du Pont, 1969.
66.1033, 61.811

---

1. A rare exception is the "Walnut one leafd Table" recorded in the 1736 inventory of Gov. Patrick Gordon of Pennsylvania; Hornor, *Blue Book*, p. 60; see also Barquist, *American Tables and Looking Glasses*, cat. 54, p. 138.

2. For the 3 tables, see Florene Maine advertisement, *Antiques* 70, no. 3 (August 1956): 95; Sotheby Parke Bernet, "The Garbisch Collection: Volume 4" (May 23–25, 1980), lot 1166; Fales, *Furniture of Historic Deerfield*, fig. 252. For the fourth table, see Barquist, *American Tables and Looking Glasses*, cat. 54.

## 135 ◆ Dining table
Boston or North Shore, Massachusetts
1750–80

One piece of furniture found in virtually every home was a dining table. Its basic design consisted of a fixed center section secured to a "bed" or frame and two hinged leaves supported by hinged swing legs. Early in the eighteenth century, dining tables were generally oval in shape, adapting the new support systems developed for tables with cabriole legs to designs popular on earlier turned-leg styles. By about midcentury dining table tops had changed from oval (or occasionally round) to rectangular—the molded and rounded edges of earlier forms were replaced by square edges so that tables could be placed together as needed.

This particular dining table is smaller than the standard three-foot-"bed"-size listed in the price books, but its top was large enough for general utility purposes. With the leaves up it provided an adequate surface for serving breakfast, tea, or playing cards.

Several construction features of this table are unusual. The bed is unusually small for the size of the center board, which overhangs it by six inches at each end. The top, finished with a rounded edge and indented corners, is

chamfered on the underside of the fixed section and the outside edges of the leaves to create an illusion of delicacy to betray the actual thickness of the stock. The top and bed are joined by a series of internal glueblocks, but long horizontal glueblocks join the top to the outside of the frame at the stationary outer rail—a feature that may be unique.

The knee flows up onto the corner of the rail rather than stopping at the base just as in No. 134 right, a feature that seems to be a characteristic of some Massachusetts tables with falling leaves. The shape of the end rails—broken cyma curves, a flat arch, and pendent semicircle—also appears on other Massachusetts tables.[1] Confirming the Massachusetts provenance are the sharp cabriole knee and ball-and-claw foot with retracted talons characteristic of Boston-area furniture (see Nos. 134, 138, 140).

*NER/CGN*

---

**Inscriptions or marks:** *On underside of one leaf:* "Isaac Chum" in chalk. *Chiseled on all mortise-and-tenon joints on the side rails:* "I" – "IIII".

**Construction:** The round-edge top with indented corners is slightly chamfered on the underside to reduce the appearance of bulk. The top consists of three rule-jointed boards of equal size. The center board is attached to the frame with glueblocks;

there is also a single glueblock on the outside of the frame at each fixed rail. The leaves are joined with pairs of iron butt hinges. The rectangular frame has double side rails. The outer rail, tenoned to the legs, is divided into two unequal parts by a six-part finger-joint hinge. The longer part is secured with rosehead nails to the inner rail; the shorter part, tenoned to its leg, forms the swing action to support the raised leaf. The inner side rail is dovetailed to one end rail and stops 1 1/8" from the other end rail. The legs have a slight chamfer on the inner edge of the knee.

**Condition:** The top is sun bleached and has a series of dark circular stains. The ankle of one gateleg is repaired. A section of the side toe is missing from one fixed leg. The hinges and screws are old and may be original.

**Dimensions:**

| | | |
|---|---|---|
| H. | 26 1/8 in. | 66.4 cm |
| W. (top open) | 34 in. | 86.4 cm |
| W. (top closed) | 11 1/4 in. | 28.6 cm |
| W. (frame) | 9 5/8 in. | 24.6 cm |
| W. (feet) | 11 3/4 in. | 29.8 cm |
| D. (top) | 36 in. | 91.4 cm |
| D. (frame) | 24 1/8 in. | 61.3 cm |
| D. (feet) | 25 3/4 in. | 65.4 cm |

**Materials:** *Microanalysis:* Primary: mahogany. Secondary: birch (outer rail); white pine group (inner rail, glueblocks). *Finish:* natural resin.

**Provenance:** Descended in the Carver family of Marshfield, Mass., who may or may not have been descended from the "Mayflower" John Carver, first governor of Plymouth.

**Accession history:** Purchased by H. F. du Pont from Winsor White, Mamaroneck, N.Y., 1948. Bequest of H. F. du Pont, 1969.
64.1069

---

1. For other tables with knees flowing onto the corners of the rails, see Jobe and Kaye, *New England Furniture*, no. 64; Christie's, "The Collection of Mr. and Mrs. Eddy Nicholson" (January 27–28, 1995), lot 1068. Related examples with chaped end rails are owned by John S. Walton (no. 70.966, DAPC, Visual Resources Collection, Winterthur Library) and by Mrs. Hugh Cox, Alexandria, Va. (no. 77.128, DAPC, Visual Resources Collection, Winterthur Library).

## 136 ◆ Dining table
### Coastal Massachusetts
### 1750–80

Dining tables are one of the few table forms not included in eighteenth-century pattern books. This may be because although the form was an essential component of virtually every household, it offered relatively little opportunity for experimentation.

The classic New England Queen Anne–style dining table has a deceptively simple design. Its three-part top is mounted on a double-railed "bed" supported on cabriole legs, and ornamentation is minimal and generally restricted to the exposed end rails. Considered equally appropriate for use in urban or rural settings, the design was popular for more than half a century.

The carefully chosen striped maple in which this dining table is fashioned adds a decorative element to a relatively plain design. Its straight-edge top permitted it to be used singly or in conjunction with another square-edge table to create a large surface. The only decoration is a plain quarter-round molding applied on the lower edge of the skirt. Its angular cabriole legs have a sharp leading edge that continues from the knee onto the thick pad foot raised on a narrow disk.

This pattern of applied quarter-round skirt molding coupled with angular cabriole legs is indicative of eastern Massachusetts

manufacture. In a departure from standard Massachusetts construction practice in which the inner rail is dovetailed to the open end and stops short of the other end rail, here the inner rail is dovetailed to the end rail at both ends. This is possible because the end attached to the fixed leg is dovetailed only to the shoulder of the end rail. This technique has not been found on other hinged-leaf tables and may be idiosyncratic to the maker of this table.

The simplicity of design and construction kept the cost of this dining table reasonable. The 1757 "Rule and Price of Joyners Work" in Providence lists the cost for "Maple Rule Joynt tables @ 6 £ pr foot" in the bed. Based on its thirty-two-inch-long bed, this table would have cost £16, which is equivalent to the cost of a mahogany candlestand or a one-drawer pine chest.[1]

*NER/CGN*

---

**Inscriptions or marks:** *Scratched on underside of one leaf:* "X". *On underside of centerboard and adjacent leaf:* "X" *in chalk.*

**Construction:** The rectangular, flat-edge top consists of three boards, the center board wider than the leaves. The center board originally was pegged to the frame; now it also is attached from the underside with countersunk screws and triangular glueblocks. The rectangular frame has double side rails separated at the center by a deep spacer block. The outer rail, tenoned and double-pegged to the legs, is sawed in two unequal parts and has a five-

part finger-joint hinge. The shorter part has the swing action that supports the leaf. The inner rail is dovetailed to the end rail at both ends. A quarter-round skirt molding is nailed to the ends.

**Condition:** The table has been refinished; traces of a pigmented stain are still visible on the underside of the top. The top, which is slightly warped, has been resurfaced on the underside to sit better on the frame. It is reattached using countersunk screws and glueblocks, which have been reset. There is a long split in one of the leaves at the hinged edge.

**Dimensions:**

| | | |
|---|---|---|
| H. | 28 5/8 in. | 65.2 cm |
| W. (top open) | 41 1/2 in. | 105.4 cm |
| W. (top closed) | 16 3/8 in. | 41.6 cm |
| W. (frame) | 13 1/2 in. | 34.3 cm |
| W. (feet) | 14 7/8 in. | 37.8 cm |
| D. (top) | 47 3/4 in. | 121.3 cm |
| D. (frame) | 32 5/8 in. | 83.0 cm |
| D. (feet) | 34 1/8 in. | 86.7 cm |

**Materials:** *Microanalysis:* Primary: soft maple group. Secondary: soft maple group (outer rails); white pine group (inner rail); spruce (glueblocks). *Finish:* natural resin.

**Accession history:** Bequest of H. F. du Pont, 1969. 58.1738

---

1. "Rule and Price of Joyners Work" (1757) as cited in *John Brown House Loan Exhibition*, p. 175. The prices are given in the inflated Rhode Island currency of the day where the exchange rate was £23.6.8 = £1 (sterling).

## 137 ◆ Dining table

Charlestown, Massachusetts
1760–75
Benjamin Frothingham, Jr. (1734–1809)

From a time when few New England craftsmen marked their furniture, the pieces labeled by Benjamin Frothingham of Charlestown today provide insight into the range of forms and styles supplied by a single shop. His products included seating furniture, tables, and case furniture—chests, high chests, and desks—and although no documented pieces are known, records indicate that he also supplied beds.[1]

In many respects, Frothingham's career is one of the best documented. His father and grandfather were joiners. Benjamin Frothingham, Sr. (1708–65), owned a shop near Milk Street in Boston that is recorded as having burned in the great fire of March 20, 1760. No physical evidence remains of the elder Frothingham's craft skills, but a bill for furniture supplied to John Edwards in 1749 suggests that he was a well-qualified craftsman.[2]

Frothingham, Jr., probably began his career in Boston, apprenticed to his father. By the mid 1750s he had moved to Charlestown

where he set up a shop on Walker Street that he operated until his death in 1809. In 1756 Frothingham enlisted in Capt. Richard Gridley's artillery company and took part in the 1759 expedition to capture Quebec. He served in the army during the Revolution rising to the rank of major, a title he retained for the rest of his life, and was a member of the Society of the Cincinnati. His was one of twenty-nine cabinetmakers' shops destroyed in June 1775 when Gen. Thomas Gage ordered Charlestown burned. Forced to resign from active service in 1782, he rebuilt his house and shop on the west side of Main Street and returned to the business of cabinetmaking. In 1789 President George Washington honored him by visiting him at his residence.[3]

Most of the surviving documented furniture by Frothingham, Jr., is case furniture. Only two tables are known—this dining table and a card table (No. 139). The six-leg dining table with two swinging gates to support each leaf is an unusual design, especially for New England. Only one other is known: a six-leg mahogany table with rounded leaves originally owned by Daniel Henshaw (1701–81) of

Leicester, Massachusetts. Most New England hinged-leaf dining tables have four legs; the six-leg model is more common in New York.[4]

The construction of this table has no known New England parallels. The end rails are in two sections, tenoned into the fixed legs and dovetailed to the side rails. Each section of end rail has an applied quarter-round skirt cut in a cyma–reverse-cyma outline on the lower edge. The top is secured to the "bed" with small glueblocks and reinforced with countersunk screws. The legs are well shaped; the carved talons are not so acutely retracted as on the card table (see No. 139), and the rear talon is unarticulated except for the nail.

Labeled eighteenth-century New England furniture is very rare. The importance of this table as a benchmark for Boston/Charlestown cabinetmaking in the third quarter of the eighteenth century exists in the printed label on the outside of one of the side rails protected by the gate rail: "Benjⁿ Frothingham/ Cabbinet Maker/ IN/ CHARLESTOWN. N.E." (fig. 1). The label was engraved for Frothingham by Boston silversmith Nathaniel Hurd (1729–77), who printed labels in this design between 1760 and 1777. Frothingham continued to use this label until his death.

*NER/CGN*

**Inscriptions or marks:** *Outside of one fixed side rail:* "Benj^n Frothingham/ Cabbinet Maker/ IN/ CHARLESTOWN. N.E." on attached paper label. The original iron hinges are marked "RF"; the name of the English maker is unknown.

**Construction:** The rectangular top consists of three boards that were once of equal size. The center section is attached to the frame from the inside with countersunk screws and reinforced with glueblocks; the leaves are attached to the center section with three pairs of iron butt hinges. The rectangular frame has double side rails. The outer rails are divided by seven-finger knuckle-joint hinges into three parts: a stationary middle section attached with rosehead nails to the inner rail flanked by two movable ends mortised and tenoned to legs that form the swing action. The inner rails are dovetailed to each end rail. The two sections of the end rails are tenoned to stationary center legs. An applied, shaped skirt is glued to the end rail on either side of the leg.

**Condition:** One of the leaves is approximately 1" narrower than the other, having been cut down from the join of the bed in a repair. Both are warped. Butterfly patches are visible on the underside of the short leaf repairing an old break. There also are repaired breaks on both the inner edge of that leaf and the adjacent edge of the center section. Two of the applied skirt moldings are replaced. The original hinges are marked "RF."

**Dimensions:**

| | | |
|---|---|---|
| H. | 28¼ in. | 71.8 cm |
| W. (top) | 60 in. | 152.4 cm |
| W. (frame) | 51⅞ in. | 131.8 cm |
| W. (feet) | 53¾ in. | 136.5 cm |
| D. (top open) | 58⅝ in. | 149.0 cm |
| D. (top closed) | 20 in. | 50.8 cm |
| D. (frame) | 14 in. | 35.6 cm |
| D. (feet) | 54⅞ in. | 139.4 cm |

**Fig. 1.** Detail, label.

**Materials:** *Microanalysis:* Primary: mahogany. Secondary: soft maple group (outer side rails); white pine group (inner side rail, swing rail, glueblocks). *Finish:* natural resin.

**Publications:** Mabel Munson Swan, "Major Benjamin Frothingham, Cabinetmaker," *Antiques* 62, no. 5 (November 1952): 393. Charles F. Hummel, "Queen Anne and Chippendale Furniture in the Henry Francis du Pont Winterthur Museum, Part 3," *Antiques* 99, no. 1 (January 1971): 92, figs. 2, 3. Richard H. Randall, Jr., "Benjamin Frothingham," in *Boston Furniture*, p. 230, fig. 158. Elizabeth Bidwell Bates and Jonathan L. Fairbanks, *American Furniture: 1620 to the Present* (New York: Richard Marek Publishers, 1981), p. 167.

**Provenance:** Ex coll.: Mrs. Ernest Amos, Whiteoak, Md. According to tradition, Mrs. Amos inherited the dining table from her uncle, a Mr. Miller. Miller had inherited it from his uncle, who supposedly had paid $5.00 for it in a Washington, D.C., second-hand store. Ex coll.: Dr. D. B. Moffett, Washington, D.C.

**Accession history:** Purchased by H. F. du Pont from Israel Sack, Inc., New York, 1951. Gift of H. F. du Pont, 1952.
52.149

1. Frothingham's bill to Colonel Ervin dated June 12, 1788, records the purchase of 2 field bedsteads valued at £6; Mabel Munson Swan, "Major Benjamin Frothingham, Cabinetmaker," *Antiques* 62, no. 5 (November 1952): 394.

2. On August 3, 1749, Benjamin Frothingham, Sr., billed John Edwards for a case of drawers, a bureau table, a walnut table, and another table of unspecified wood. All these pieces were "casd" for shipment; Downs collection.

3. Biographical information is assembled from Richard H. Randall, Jr., "Benjamin Frothingham," in *Boston Furniture*, pp. 223–49; Dexter Edwin Spaulding, "Benj^n Frothingham of Charlestown: Cabinetmaker and Soldier," *Antiques* 14, no. 6 (December 1928): 536–37; and Swan, "Major Benjamin Frothingham," pp. 392–95.

4. Examples include an oval table with cabriole legs and slipper feet at Winterthur (Downs, *American Furniture*, fig. 318); an oval dining table with leaf-carved cabriole legs and ball-and-claw feet (Heckscher, *American Furniture*, cat. no. 110); a Marlborough-leg dining table at the New York State Museum (John L. Scherer, *New York Furniture at the New York State Museum* [Alexandria, Va.: Highland House, 1984], fig. 16); and the Henshaw table, now in a private collection, also has iron hinges stamped "RF."

## 138 ◆ Pembroke table
Newport, Rhode Island
1783–ca. 1795
John Townsend (1733–1809)

About the middle of the eighteenth century, a new table form with short, falling leaves was introduced. Unlike the tables with two hinged legs, this form had four fixed legs; its short leaves were supported on a hinged section of the side rails known as a "fly."

The terms *breakfast table* and *pembroke table* have come to be used interchangeably to identify this new form, but for Thomas Chippendale, they represented two separate designs. Chippendale described the breakfast table form as "a table with two hinged flaps and an enclosed lower shelf." He first included an illustration of it in the 1754 edition of his *Director*. That same plate also included the design for the form he called a *pembroke table*—"a small occasional table with two hinged flaps and a drawer." The precise origin of the term *pembroke table* is unclear. In *The Cabinet Dictionary*, Thomas Sheraton indicated that it was "a name given to a kind of breakfast table, from the name of the lady who first gave orders for one of them, and who probably gave the first idea of such a table to the workmen." English furniture historian John Gloag suggests that the term may be connected with Henry Herbert (1693–1751), ninth earl of Pembroke and a gifted amateur architect, who may have been responsible for the design.[1]

By 1772 American cabinetmakers had adopted both the form and the name. The pembroke table was available in Philadelphia and other urban centers in a variety of styles as outlined in a 1772 cabinetmaker's price list:

| Breakfast Table plain | 2.15.0 |
| Ditto with a Drawer | 3.0.0 |
| Ditto with baces & bragetes | 3.5.0 |
| Ditto with a plain Stretcher | 3.10.0 |
| Ditto with open Stretcher 2 draw | 4.0.0 |
| Ditto with Claw feet | 3.15.0 |
| Add for Scolloping the top | 4s |

One of the earliest examples of the pembroke form in New England is a table at the Society for the Preservation of New England Antiquities made by Boston cabinetmaker George Bright and sold to Jonathan Bowman for £2.0.0 in 1770.[2]

One style of pembroke table associated with Newport had a distinctive appearance. Strongly influenced by Chinese design, it had short, square leaves, fluted or stop-fluted square legs, open fretwork corner brackets, and pierced and gadrooned cross stretchers. In the hands of Newport master-craftsman John Townsend, the basic form was enhanced by an incised crosshatch border on the lower edge of the end rails beneath an inset astragal molding. This particular decorative motif appears on several Townsend tables including this labeled pembroke table (fig. 1), a labeled card table at the Metropolitan Museum of Art, and an unlabeled china table at Winterthur (No. 125).[3]

Because of its documentation, this Townsend pembroke table is a model against which construction features can be compared to identify the craftsman's work.[4] On tables with a drawer, the facing is cut from the end rail; an applied bead on the inside of the drawer opening masks the saw marks. Townsend employed a system of dovetailed cross bracing—three-over-two (as seen here) or three-over-three—on the center section of the frame. On tables with drawers, a long longitudinal brace attached to two of the upper cross braces holds the drawer level when it is pulled out. The pins used to join the legs are unusually thin, usually one-eighth to one-quarter inch in diameter. The pierced knee brackets are tenoned to the legs and frame rather than simply nailed in place. Each section of stretcher is in two parts—the pierced stretch unit and a separate strip of gadrooning attached with screws.

Winterthur's table is part of a small group of pembroke tables almost identical in size, construction, and decoration that includes one at the Museum of Fine Arts, Boston, and one in a Delaware private collection. Also part of this group, but with slightly different detailing, are tables in the Dietrich American Foundation collection and the State Department Diplomatic Reception Rooms with serpentine corners and saltire stretchers pierced in a scroll pattern.[5] In all other respects, the decoration on these tables is identical to that on Winterthur's example.

A second group of similarly designed breakfast tables lacks the crosshatch decoration and astragal molding on the end rails and varies in the pattern of the fretwork brackets and stretchers. Included are a labeled John Townsend table at the Colonial Society of Massachusetts and unlabeled examples at Chipstone Foundation and in three private collections.[6]

John Townsend (1733–1809) was a member of Newport's best-known cabinetmaking dynasty, joined through marriage to the cabinetmaking Goddard family. Townsend probably apprenticed with his father, Christopher, a cabinetmaker and ship's furnituremaker. John Townsend has left a rich legacy of signed and labeled work. His earliest documented work—a document chest and an oval dining table—is dated 1756.[7] His skills matured over the years, and during his long career he supplied furniture to some of the most prominent families in Rhode Island. His only period of restricted activity was during the revolutionary war when his Quaker heritage limited his ability to conduct business. With peace his business flourished. Between 1783 and about 1792, he produced most of the furniture that incorporated designs in the Chinese taste.

*NER/CGN*

---

**Inscriptions or marks:** *Inside drawer bottom:* "Made By/ John Townsend/ NewPort" on printed paper label with ink number "1743" added in the upper left corner. The ink number is not contemporary and is not the date of the table.

**Construction:** The straight-edge top consists of three boards, the center board more than twice the width of the leaves. The center board meets each leaf at a rule joint and is secured with paired iron butt hinges. The top is joined to the frame with long rectangular glueblocks. The rectangular frame has double side rails. The outer rail, divided into three parts, is tenoned and double-pegged to the legs. The center section—a short wing cut with a five-part finger joint at one end and diagonally with a finger grip at the other—swings out to support the raised leaves. The inner side rails, secured with rosehead nails to the outer rail and abutting the legs at both ends, are joined by five transverse braces, three dovetailed into the top edge of the rails and two dovetailed to the bottom. The corners of the inner frame are reinforced with vertical glueblocks. One end rail has an opening cut for a drawer with an applied bead surround; the other end rail is solid. The drawer slides on runners lapped at the front and nailed to the inner rail; a median guide above the drawer is nailed to two of the transverse braces.

**Fig. 1.** Detail, label.

The drawer sides are rounded on the upper edge and flat on the back; the drawer bottom is nailed to a rabbet in the front and flush across the sides and back. An applied strip of astragal molding is dadoed to each end rail. Below is an incised crosshatch band. The pierced knee brackets are tenoned to the legs and end rails. The legs, stop fluted on two sides, are chamfered on the inner edge. Tenoned and pegged into the corners of the legs are pierced cross stretchers. The gadrooned molding applied to the lower edge of the stretchers is held with screws.

**Condition:** The top is slightly warped. There is a small split in the center board and in the rail housing the drawer. The drawer sides are warped. Portions of the pierced stretcher are repaired. Layout lines for the tenons and the fluting are visible on the legs.

**Dimensions:**

| | | | |
|---|---|---|---|
| H. | | 26 3/8 in. | 67.0 cm |
| W. (top open) | | 36 1/2 in. | 92.7 cm |
| W. (top closed) | | 20 1/8 in. | 51.1 cm |
| W. (frame) | | 18 15/16 in. | 48.1 cm |
| W. (feet) | | 18 13/16 in. | 47.8 cm |
| D. (top) | | 33 1/2 in. | 85.1 cm |
| D. (frame) | | 30 7/8 in. | 78.4 cm |
| D. (feet) | | 31 in. | 78.7 cm |

**Materials:** *Microanalysis:* Primary: mahogany. Secondary: soft maple group (transverse braces); tulip-poplar (drawer linings). *Finish:* natural resin.

**Exhibitions:** Boston Antiques Exposition, 1929.

**Publications:** Thomas H. Ormsbee, "Chippendale as Followed at Home and in America," *American Collector* (January 1938): 10. Downs, *American Furniture*, fig. 311. Wendell D. Garrett, "The Newport Cabinetmakers: A Corrected List," *Antiques* 73, no. 2 (June 1958): 561. Butler, *American Furniture*, p. 61. Elizabeth Bidwell Bates and Jonathan L. Fairbanks, *American Furniture: 1620 to the Present* (New York: Richard Marek Publishers, 1981), p. 173. Liza Moses and Michael Moses, "Authenticating John Townsend's Later Tables," *Antiques* 119, no. 5 (May 1981): 1152, figs. 1, 1a, 1b. Moses, *Master Craftsmen*, figs. 3.18, 3.18a, 3.23, 3.28, 3.45.

**Provenance:** Owned originally by Col. John Cooke, Middletown, R.I. Ex coll.: Philip Flayderman, Boston.

**Accession history:** Purchased by H. F. du Pont at the Flayderman sale, American Art Association Anderson Galleries, New York, 1930. Gift of H. F. du Pont, 1958.
58.2147

1. Christopher Gilbert, *The Life and Work of Thomas Chippendale*, 2 vols. (New York: Macmillan Co., 1978), 1:303, 306. Thomas Sheraton, *The Cabinet Dictionary* (1803; reprint in 2 vols., New York: Praeger Publishers, 1970), 2:284. John Gloag, ed., *A Complete Dictionary of Furniture* (1952; rev. ed., Woodstock, N.Y.: Overlook Press, 1991), p. 502.

2. The 1772 Philadelphia price book is cited in Martin Eli Weil, "A Cabinetmaker's Price Book," in Ian M. G. Quimby, ed., *Winterthur Portfolio 13* (Chicago: University of Chicago Press for the Henry Francis du Pont Winterthur Museum, 1979), p. 186. Jobe and Kaye, *New England Furniture*, no. 66.

3. Heckscher, *American Furniture*, cat. no. 100. An advertisement in the December 1929 *Antiques* showed a photograph of Winterthur's table along with the label now glued onto the drawer surface (see **Inscriptions or marks**). However, the Flayderman catalogue (American Art Association Anderson Galleries, "Colonial Furniture, Silver, and Decorations: The Collection of the Late Philip Flayderman" [January 2–4, 1930]) pictured the same printed label with the table, but one with a scripted date "1794" in the lower right corner. The label now on Winterthur's table was shown below one of a pair of federal-style card tables, also made by Townsend and also originally owned by Col. John Cooke. Either the labels or their photographs were switched between the 1929 advertisement and the January 1930 catalogue, which would seem to indicate they were not glued to the drawer at the time.

4. For a thorough explanation of the construction and decoration prerequisites for identifying the work of John Townsend, see Moses, *Master Craftsmen*, pp. 89–93.

5. For the MFA, Boston, table, see Hipkiss, *Eighteenth-Century American Arts*, no. 66; for the table in the Delaware private collection, see Ralph E. Carpenter, Jr., *The Arts and Crafts of Newport, Rhode Island, 1640–1820* (Newport: Preservation Society of Newport County, 1954), no. 56; for the table in the Dietrich collection, see Charles Woolsey advertisement, *Antiques* 94, no. 3 (October 1968): 447; and Moses, *Master Craftsmen*, fig. 3.80; the scroll piercing on the stretchers of this entry is a simpler version of the gallery on a straight-leg china table (see No. 125) at Winterthur. For the State Dept. table, see Rollins, *Treasures of State*, cat. no. 97.

6. For the Colonial Society table, see Moses, *Master Craftsmen*, fig. 2.8; for the Chipstone example, see Rodriguez Roque, *American Furniture*, no. 137; Col. John Cooke, reported to have been one of the richest men in colonial Rhode Island, owned this Chipstone pembroke table as well as Winterthur's table. For the 3 privately owned tables, see Christie's, "Highly Important American Furniture: The Collection of Mr. and Mrs. Hugh B. Cox" (June 16, 1984), lot 412; *John Brown House Loan Exhibition*, cat. 45; Carpenter, *Arts and Crafts of Newport*, no. 57; John S. Walton advertisement, *Antiques* 109, no. 1 (February 1976): 220.

7. For the most recent biographical information on John Townsend, see Moses, *Master Craftsmen*, pp. 65–70. For the document chest, see *Antiques* 121, no. 2 (May 1982): 1144; for the dining table, see Moses, *Master Craftsmen*, fig. 9.

## 139 ◆ Card table
Charlestown, Massachusetts
1755–90
Benjamin Frothingham, Jr. (1734–1809)

In England, the tradition of engaging in games of chance involving cards dates to the fourteenth century. Most early card games were designed for either two or four players, and no elaborate equipment was involved. The only furniture requirement was a small table that could be covered with a cloth or carpet on which to lay the cards.[1] Tables specifically intended as card tables, however, were not introduced until early in the seventeenth century. These forms had two identical leaves, one fixed to the frame and the other hinged to the fixed leaf. The early designs generally were semicircular or rectangular in shape with turned and tapered supports stabilized by stretchers. One leg, hinged to the back rail, swung out to support the open leaf. When open, the table was asymmetrical and somewhat unstable.

Early in the eighteenth century, a new form was introduced in which cabriole legs replaced turned supports, stretchers disappeared, and square tops became the accepted design. Some card tables were made with the plain, flat playing surface, but as the century progressed, tables with a carved depression on the interior surface to receive a permanent playing cloth and candlesticks at the corners replaced the earlier style. Some card tables also had deeper depressions, called "guinea pits" in the eighteenth century, to hold either coins or counters.[2]

Card playing and gambling at cards was generally discouraged in seventeenth-century New England, but by the eighteenth century, this leisure activity had gained wider acceptance. Card playing was not restricted to any particular social or economic group and

was enjoyed both in the privacy of the home and in public inns and taverns. The earliest references to American card tables in the style that has come to be called Queen Anne appear about 1730 with the introduction of cabriole leg furniture. By the middle of the eighteenth century, a card table was considered a key feature of a fashionable American home. Portable and versatile, card tables might be found anywhere in a house, but they generally were used in formal rooms intended for entertaining.[3]

One popular Massachusetts card table design with cabriole legs featured a blocked facade with projecting square corners for candlesticks. The form was available with either pad or ball-and-claw feet.[4] Most card tables in this design, including this one, are relieved on the inside to accommodate a baize or an embroidered playing surface and on the corners to accept candlesticks. Unornamented

except for the carved ball-and-claw feet with the side talons drawn back in the characteristic eastern Massachusetts manner, the table relies on form rather than decoration for effect. This table has a printed paper label inside the drawer (fig. 1) that identifies the maker as Benjamin Frothingham of Charlestown, Massachusetts; he also made and labeled a mahogany dining table (see No. 137).[5] These two tables have similarly shaped legs and feet. The label also identifies the engraver: "N H. Sc\[P\]" refers to Boston silversmith and engraver Nathaniel Hurd (1730–77). It was the only style of printed label used by Frothingham.

*NER/CGN*

**Inscriptions or marks:** *Inside drawer:* "Benj\[n\] Frothingham/ Cabbinet Maker/ IN/ CHARLESTOWN. N.E./ N H. Sc\[P\]" on printed paper label.

**Fig. 1.** Detail, label.

Frothingham, Cabinetmaker," *Antiques* 62, no. 5 (November 1952): 393. Hugh Honour, *Cabinet Makers and Furniture Designers* (London: Weidenfeld and Nicolson, 1969), pp. 162–63. Richard H. Randall, Jr., "Benjamin Frothingham," in *Boston Furniture*, figs. 156, 157, p. 226. Elizabeth Bidwell Bates and Jonathan L. Fairbanks, *American Furniture: 1620 to the Present* (New York: Richard Marek Publishers, 1981), p. 171. Jobe and Kaye, *New England Furniture*, no. I-26, p. 27.

**Provenance:** Ex coll.: Joe Kindig, Jr., York, Pa.

**Accession history:** Purchased by H. F. du Pont from Joe Kindig, Jr., York, Pa., 1948. Gift of H. F. du Pont, 1960.
59.1880

---

1. Macquoid and Edwards, *Dictionary*, 3:192.

2. John Gloag, ed., *A Complete Dictionary of Furniture* (1952; rev. ed., Woodstock, N.Y.: Overlook Press, 1991), pp. 182, 377.

3. For an overview on card playing in America, see Gerald W. R. Ward, "'Avarice and Conviviality': Card Playing in Federal America," in Benjamin A. Hewitt, Patricia E. Kane, and Gerald W. R. Ward, *The Work of Many Hands: Card Tables in Federal America, 1790–1820* (New Haven: Yale University Art Gallery, 1982), pp. 15–38.

4. For pad-foot examples at Yale and Deerfield, see Kirk, *American Furniture*, fig. 1374; Fales, *Furniture of Historic Deerfield*, fig. 268. Tables with ball-and-claw feet include examples with dished tops: "American Furniture in the Collection of Mr. and Mrs. Edward H. Tevriz," *Antiques* 89, no. 1 (February 1966): 259; and *American Antiques from Israel Sack Collection*, 10 vols. (Washington, D.C.: Highland House, ca. 1969–), 2:395; tables with solid tops: *American Antiques from Sack Collection*, 7:1869; and one at the MFA, Boston (MFA 65.26); and a table with an inset embroidered playing surface at Chipstone: Rodriguez Roque, *American Furniture*, no. 150.

5. For additional biographical information on Benjamin Frothingham, see Dexter Edwin Spaulding, "Benjⁿ Frothingham of Charlestown: Cabinetmaker and Soldier," *Antiques* 14, no. 6 (December 1928): 536–37; Mabel Munson Swan, "Major Benjamin Frothingham, Cabinetmaker," *Antiques* 62, no. 5 (November 1952): 392–95; Richard H. Randall, Jr., "Benjamin Frothingham," in *Boston Furniture*, pp. 223–49.

**Construction:** The two halves of the top are hinged at the back. A tenon centered on the back edge of the stationary lower half keys into a slot in the upper half. The upper half unfolds to rest on the left rear leg, which extends to support it. The stationary lower half is secured to the frame by a series of rectangular glueblocks. The inner surface of the top is cut away on the playing surface to accommodate a green baize lining and in squares on the corners to hold candlesticks. The thick skirt boards, flat on the inside, are tenoned to the legs. The inner rear rail is dovetailed to the left side and attached from the inside with four rosehead nails. The outer rear rail is divided in half by a seven-finger knuckle-joint hinge. The stationary part is tenoned to the right rear leg; the swing part is tenoned to the left rear leg. The front rail is cut to accommodate a drawer that rides on two-piece L-shape runners tenoned to the front and rear rails. The drawer has a thumb-molded edge and no overhang. The bottom is rabbeted to the front and sides and nailed across the back. The drawer sides and back are rounded slightly on top. The knee brackets are glued and reinforced with nails.

**Condition:** The top has been reset; it now is secured by two screws in the outside of the back rail and a single screw on the left side rail in addition to reinforcing nails in the glueblocks. There is a split in the right rear post and a small patch on the stationary top at the left hinge. The swing leg was nailed closed at one time. The drawer interior has been coated. The drawer handle is old but may not be original. The hinged top is severely light bleached. The baize lining is a replacement.

**Dimensions:**

| | | |
|---|---|---|
| H. (closed) | 28 in. | 71.0 cm |
| H. (open) | 27³/₁₆ in. | 69.1 cm |
| W. (top) | 34 in. | 86.3 cm |
| W. (frame) | 32 in. | 81.3 cm |
| W. (feet) | 33¹/₈ in. | 84.1 cm |
| D. (open) | 33¹/₂ in. | 85.0 cm |
| D. (closed) | 16⁵/₈ in. | 42.2 cm |
| D. (frame) | 13³/₈ in. | 34.0 cm |
| D. (feet) | 17¹/₂ in. | 44.4 cm |

**Materials:** *Microanalysis:* Primary: mahogany. Secondary: white pine group (drawer linings, back rail, glueblocks); yellow pine group (left drawer support). *Finish:* natural resin.

**Publications:** *Antiques* 45, no. 2 (April 1944): inside front cover. Downs, *American Furniture*, fig. 349. Mabel Munson Swan, "Major Benjamin

## 140 ◆ Card table
### Boston, Massachusetts
### 1740–60

During the second half of the eighteenth century, a key element of social intercourse was entertaining friends in the evening. One of the activities often provided was card playing. Contemporary inventories indicate that card tables were appropriate in any room used for entertaining. Their decoration was expected to complement the other furniture in the room, and often they were purchased in pairs and placed symmetrically. When not in use, they were folded up and stored at the sides of a room or in an adjacent passage where they could be used for other purposes.

The blocked card table with square corners often is associated with the Boston area. This card table, almost identical in shape to the preceding Frothingham-labeled table (No. 139), is enhanced by a bold, elongated carved shell and pendent husk

**Fig. 1.**
Detail, leg.

on the knees and an inner C scroll (fig. 1). Card tables formerly in the Robb and Taradash collections are very similar except for their ball-and-claw feet.[1]

Both the knee treatment and the graceful scroll-foot termination on Winterthur's table are derived from English design, but the slimmer shape of the leg is a Boston feature. The scroll foot does appear more frequently on Philadelphia forms than on New England furniture, where the preferred terminal for cabriole legs was a "plain" (pad) or a ball-and-claw foot. A Boston walnut side chair with similar scroll feet is in the Museum of Fine Arts, Boston. Perhaps it was this rarity of the scroll foot in New England furniture that influenced the attribution of the table to Philadelphia at the time of its sale in 1935. The elaborately carved shell and pendent husk (or bellflower) on the knee and the raised C scrolls on the knee brackets, decorative details formerly associated with Rhode Island, undoubtedly influenced Joseph Downs's reattribution of the table to that region. Those decorative motifs are now thought to have been first used in Boston.[2]

The stylized leaf carving and stipple punchwork on the knee brackets is another decorative feature generally associated with Massachusetts, however. This type of carving is found on a group of furniture including a bombé desk-and-bookcase at the Museum

of Fine Arts, Boston, made by Boston cabinetmaker George Bright.[3] Stipple carving is not found on Rhode Island furniture.

*NER/CGN*

---

**Inscriptions or marks:** *On outside back of drawer:* "R x G" in ink. The inscription appears to be in an eighteenth-century hand, but the initials have not been identified.

**Construction:** The halves of the top are two solid boards hinged together at the back. The upper half unfolds to rest on the left rear leg, which swings out to support it. The lower half is attached to the frame with glueblocks on the sides and rear rail. The inner surface of the top is cut away: on the playing surface, to accommodate a fabric lining; on the corners, in squares to hold candlesticks; and on the right of each side, in ovals to hold the counters. The thick, solid skirt boards, flat on the inside, are tenoned to the front legs. The front rail is cut to receive a drawer. On the drawer, the front is thumbnail molded but has no overlapping lip; the sides and back are slightly rounded on the upper edge; and the bottom is rabbeted at the front and nailed flush over the sides and back. The drawer runners now are nailed to the supporting rail at the front and lapped at the back. The inner rear rail is dovetailed to one side rail and nearly abuts the other. The thick outer rear rail, divided into two equal parts by a five-part knuckle-jointed hinge, is tenoned and double-pegged to the rear legs. The stationary part is secured with rosehead nails through spacer blocks to the inner rear rail; the movable part swings to support the leaf.

**Condition:** The front rail has sustained extensive damage. In repairing it, the frame and the top were disassembled and rejoined. Much of the internal framing—the rails behind the front skirt, the drawer runners, and the glueblocks—is replaced. There are new glueblocks holding the legs. The bracket for the left rear leg now is supported by a block nailed to the inside of the side rail, which reinforces a shattered nail. The brackets may be old replacements. A portion of the C scroll on the left front leg is patched below the knee. The leaf is slightly warped. The hinges are replaced. The fabric lining is replaced.

**Dimensions:**

| | | |
|---|---|---|
| H. (open) | 27 1/2 in. | 69.9 cm |
| W. (top) | 31 1/8 in. | 79.1 cm |
| W. (frame) | 29 7/8 in. | 75.9 cm |
| W. (feet) | 31 3/8 in. | 79.7 cm |
| D. (top open) | 30 1/2 in. | 77.5 cm |
| D. (top closed) | 15 1/4 in. | 38.7 cm |
| D. (frame) | 14 1/4 in. | 35.9 cm |
| D. (feet) | 15 3/4 in. | 40.0 cm |

**Materials:** *Microanalysis:* Primary: mahogany. Secondary: white pine group (inner and outer rear rails, drawer lining). *Finish:* natural resin.

**Publications:** Downs, *American Furniture*, fig. 347. Marshall B. Davidson, ed., *The American Heritage History of Colonial Antiques* ([New York]: American Heritage Publishing Co., [1967]), fig. 316. John A. H. Sweeney, *Winterthur Illustrated* (New York: Chanticleer Press for the Henry Francis du Pont Winterthur Museum, 1963), p. 69.

**Provenance:** Ex coll.: Mr. and Mrs. Stanley H. Lowndes, Northport, Long Island, N.Y.

**Accession history:** Purchased by H. F. du Pont at the sale of the Stanley H. Lowndes Collection, American Art Association Anderson Galleries, New York, 1935. Gift of H. F. du Pont, 1960. 61.815

---

1. Edith Gaines, "The Robb Collection of American Furniture, Part II," *Antiques* 93, no. 4 (April 1968): fig. 3; *American Antiques from Israel Sack Collection*, 10 vols. (Washington, D.C.: Highland House, ca. 1969–), 7:1951.

2. Ginsburg and Levy advertisement, *Antiques* 82, no. 4 (October 1962): 339; Philadelphia examples include a marble slab table made for John Cadwalader at the Metropolitan Museum of Art (Heckscher, *American Furniture*, cat. no. 97) and a pair of side chairs at Winterthur (Downs, *American Furniture*, fig. 135); for the walnut side chair, see Randall, *American Furniture*, no. 148. American Art Association Anderson Galleries, "Sale of the Stanley H. Lowndes Collection of American Furniture and Decorations" (April 29–May 4, 1935), lot 1235. Downs, *American Furniture*, fig. 347. Keno, Freund, and Miller, "Very Pink of the Mode," attributes C scrolls on knee brackets and carved shells and pendent husks on legs to Boston-made furniture and emphasizes that large amounts of Boston furniture were shipped in coastal trade.

3. Randall, *American Furniture*, no. 65; see also Mary Ellen Hayward Yehia, "Ornamental Carving on Boston Furniture of the Chippendale Style," in *Boston Furniture*, pp. 200–201.

## 141 ◆ Card table
### Newport, Rhode Island
### 1760–80

In card tables, Newport cabinetmakers favored two basic designs. One with cabriole legs incorporates a blocked, sculptural facade with square corners. The other, on straight legs, has a simple serpentine front with square corners (Nos. 142, 143). Both designs are thought to have been developed in Newport, and neither is recorded in eighteenth-century English pattern books, nor are any English prototypes known.

This table is an example of the sculptural design. It has an elaborate recessed and cyma-shape facade, and in overall outline it relates to the design used by John Goddard on a tea table he made for Jabez Bowen (see No. 123 left). It is one of a small group of similarly designed card tables that share a number of features distinctive to Newport: highly figured woods, facades cut from solid mahogany planks, square-section legs with crisp edges that soften somewhat at the ankle, ball-and-claw front feet with high ridged ankles and smooth knuckles, rear pad feet raised on disks, and knees carved with a stylized leaf

and palmetto design; however, the legs are slimmer and the rear knuckles smoother than documented Goddard tables.[1]

The outline of the top and conforming skirt of Winterthur's table has extended cyma curves and a relatively narrow block across the center. It shares this design feature with one of the tables in the group; on the others, the center block is longer, and the cyma curves are more compressed. The tables also vary in the treatment of the playing surface. On five of the tables in the group, including Winterthur's, the top is solid. The remaining two have carved candle recesses and baize playing surfaces.[2]

All the tables have the leaf-and-palmetto–carved knees used on the Goddard tea table, although there is considerable variety in the execution of the design. The carving on Winterthur's table is largely intaglio and relates most closely to carving attributed by Michael Moses to John Townsend (fig. 1). The carving on most other tables is both relief and intaglio.[3]

Winterthur's table also has the dovetailed cross braces found on most tables assigned to the Townsend-Goddard school: there are two braces across the top of the long rails, and originally there was one at the center bottom. The top is secured by screws through the frame and reinforced by a long glueblock on each rail. This does vary from the bracing pattern of three-over-two used by Moses as a criteria in assigning objects to Townsend. Citing this and a difference in the treatment of the rear talon on the ball-and-claw feet, Moses has assigned Winterthur's table to "Christopher Townsend or one of his apprentices."[4] The lack of documented examples by Christopher Townsend, however, makes confirmation of this attribution difficult. The smaller dimensions of this table may have necessitated the two-over-one construction, thus the possibility of John Townsend as maker should not be ruled out.

Like so many pieces of furniture in collections today, this table has no eighteenth-century history, although a nineteenth-century paper label indicates that it was owned by A. M. Greene and was passed to his daughter Catharine. Their identities have not been determined, although Greene is a prominent Rhode Island name.

NER/CGN

**Inscriptions or marks:** *Inside front skirt rail:* "for my daughter/ Catharine E. B. Greene/ from A. M. Greene" in ink on paper label, attached.

**Construction:** The two halves of the solid top are hinged together at the back. Two tenons in the back edge of the leaf key into slots in the stationary lower half. The upper half unfolds to rest on the rear legs, which swing out to support it. The lower half is attached to the frame with screws—two through the front and rear skirt rails and a single screw in each side—and by long glueblocks on each of the four rails. The frame has three transverse braces: two dovetailed to the top edge of the front and inner rear rails and one (now missing) originally

**Fig. 1.** Detail, leg.

dovetailed to the bottom. The front and side skirts, serpentine on the outer surface and flat on the inner, are tenoned into the front legs, the joints reinforced by vertical glueblocks. The thick outer rear rail is divided by a pair of five-fingered knuckle-joint hinges into three parts: the stationary middle part, which is attached to the inner rear rail with rosehead nails, and two swinging parts, which are tenoned and double-pegged to the legs. The side rails are rabbeted at the back to accommodate the rear legs. The knees on the rear legs are uncarved. All the knee brackets are the thickness of the legs.

**Condition:** The table has been refinished. A transverse brace is missing from the bottom of the frame. Several glueblocks are missing, and some of the existing ones are replacements. A knee block is missing from the left rear leg. There is considerable insect damage on the rear rails.

**Dimensions:**

| | | |
|---|---|---|
| H. (closed) | 26 3/4 in. | 67.9 cm |
| H. (open) | 25 15/16 in. | 65.9 cm |
| W. (top) | 33 5/8 in. | 85.5 cm |
| W. (frame) | 32 3/4 in. | 83.2 cm |
| W. (feet) | 34 1/2 in. | 87.6 cm |
| D. (top open) | 33 in. | 83.8 cm |
| D. (top closed) | 16 1/2 in. | 41.9 cm |
| D. (frame) | 16 1/4 in. | 41.3 cm |
| D. (feet) | 18 1/2 in. | 47.0 cm |

**Materials:** *Microanalysis:* Primary: mahogany. Secondary: soft maple group (rear rails, transverse braces); chestnut (glueblocks). *Finish:* natural resin.

**Publications:** Downs, *American Furniture*, fig. 348. Liza Moses and Michael Moses, "Authenticating John Townsend's and John Goddard's Queen Anne and Chippendale Tables," *Antiques* 121, no. 5 (May 1982): 1142, fig. 31.

**Accession history:** Gift of H. F. du Pont, 1960. 59.2647

1. The group includes examples in: the State Dept. (Rollins, *Treasures of State*, cat. no. 70; Liza Moses and Michael Moses, "Authenticating John Townsend's and John Goddard's Queen Anne and Chippendale Tables," *Antiques* 121, no. 5 [May 1982]: 1135, fig. 15; Moses, *Master Craftsmen*, p. 45, fig. 1.31); Stratford Hall, Stratford, Va. (Moses and Moses, "Authenticating," p. 1138, fig. 23); a private collection (Moses, *Master Craftsmen*, p. 228, fig. 5.17); Historic Deerfield (Fales, *Furniture of Historic Deerfield*, fig. 271); one owned by Flayderman and Kaufman (Nutting, *Furniture Treasury*, no. 1016); one sold at auction (American Art Association, "American Furniture Property of Benjamin Flayderman" [October 6, 1932], lot 256); one owned by Leigh Keno (*Antiques* 131, no. 1 [January 1988]: 52–53); and one once owned by Dr. Karl C. Smith (*Antiques* 31, no. 2 [June 1937]: frontispiece).

2. The 5 are from the State Dept., Stratford Hall, the private collection, and Deerfield; the 2 with carved recesses are the Keno table and the one sold at auction.

3. Comparable carving can be found on: a card table signed by John Townsend and dated 1762 (Moses and Moses, "Authenticating," pp. 1131, 1133, figs. 2, 8); the State Dept. card table authenticated to John Townsend (Moses, *Master Craftsmen*, fig. 1.31), a card table assigned to Townsend in a private collection (Moses, *Master Craftsmen*, fig. 3.75); and a high chest at Rhode Island Historical Society (Moses, *Master Craftsmen*, fig. 100).

4. Moses and Moses, "Authenticating," p. 1142, fig. 31.

## 142 ◆ Card table
Newport, Rhode Island
1780–1800

Another card-table design popular with Newport cabinetmakers features a serpentine facade with square corners and straight legs. Presumed to have been developed in Newport, the form has no known English prototypes and is not represented in eighteenth-century English pattern books. This table is one of a group of seven nearly identical examples notable for the serpentine shape of both the facade and bottom edge of the skirt. On all, an incised bead outlines the top and edge of the folding leaf and is decorated with gouged notches on the edge; the fixed leaf has a cavetto chamfer on the underside; and a band of chip-carved bead or rope carving—cut as part of the serpentine portion of the rail and let into the square corners and across the stiles—finishes the lower edge of the skirt. On Winterthur's table, the bead carving on the square corners is applied so deftly that it takes close examination to see the join between the carving on the lower edge of the solid skirt and the applied section on the corners. The

brackets are pierced in a common chinoiserie pattern and nailed with sprigs to the rail and legs. On Winterthur's example, the stop-fluted legs are finished with a plain cuff (or "base" as it was called in the eighteenth century) and slightly chamfered on the outside leg (fig. 1). Two related tables not in the group have stop fluting that carries to the bottom of the leg.[1]

Traditionally all these tables have been assigned to the Goddard-Townsend school based on their similarity to the straight-leg furniture labeled by or attributed to John Townsend (see Nos. 125, 138). Despite the high quality of craftsmanship demonstrated in their construction, they lack the specific features thought to characterize Townsend's work, including the dovetail bracing of the frame-and-tenoned brackets.[2] Although they are clearly the work of Newport craftsmen, they cannot be attributed more specifically at this time.

*NER/CGN*

---

**Inscriptions or marks:** *On underside of top:* "No. 2" in chalk. *On inside of inner rear rail:* "No. 2" in

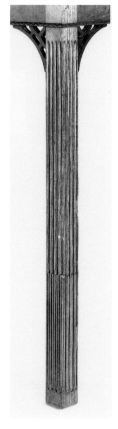

**Fig. 1.** Detail, leg.

pencil, upside down. *Scratched on back and bottom of stationary outer rear rail and on back of both right and left rear legs:* "X".

**Construction:** The two halves of the solid top are hinged together at the back. The upper half has a conforming incised bead outlining the top. A tenon centered in the back edge of the stationary lower half keys into a slot in the upper half. The upper part unfolds to rest on the left rear leg, which swings out to support it. The lower half is attached to the frame with glueblocks on each of the four sides. The front and side skirts, serpentine on the outer surface and flat on the inner, are tenoned to the front legs. The inner rear rail is dovetailed to one end rail, the joint reinforced with a quarter-round vertical glueblock, and abuts the other end rail. The thick outer rear rail, divided in half by a five-part finger-joint hinge, is tenoned to the rear legs. The stationary part is attached with rosehead nails through a spacer block to the inner rear rail; the other part forms the swing action. The chip-carved skirt edge is cut as part of the serpentine rail. A similar chip-carved strip is nailed onto the square corners and stiles and overlaps the join of the serpentine edge. The front legs, stop fluted on two sides, and the rear legs, stop fluted only on the outside edge, are chamfered on the inner corner; the fluting terminates 1" from the floor. The pierced knee brackets are nailed with sprigs to the rails and legs.

**Condition:** The table has been refinished. The right rear leg is slightly warped. The top retains some of the original glueblocks. The forged nails in the rear rail have been reset. The left side bracket is cracked.

**Dimensions:**

| | | | |
|---|---|---|---|
| H. (closed) | 29¹/₂ in. | 74.9 cm |
| W. (top) | 32 in. | 81.3 cm |
| W. (frame) | 31⁵/₈ in. | 80.5 cm |
| W. (feet) | 30¹/₂ in. | 77.5 cm |
| D. (top open) | 31 in. | 78.7 cm |
| D. (top closed) | 15¹/₂ in. | 39.4 cm |
| D. (frame) | 14³/₄ in. | 37.5 cm |
| D. (feet) | 14¹/₄ in. | 36.2 cm |

**Materials:** *Microanalysis:* Primary: mahogany. Secondary: white pine group (inner rear rail, glueblocks); soft maple group (outer rear rail). *Finish:* natural resin.

**Accession history:** Museum purchase from David Stockwell, Wilmington, Del., 1953. 53.93.2

1. The remaining 6 of the 7 are: a table at SPNEA (Jobe and Kaye, *New England Furniture*, no. 70); a pair of card tables now in a private collection (Ralph E. Carpenter, Jr., *The Arts and Crafts of Newport, Rhode Island, 1640–1820* [Newport: Preservation Society of Newport County, 1954], no. 67; *Antiques* 95, no. 2 [April 1969]: inside front cover; and Sotheby Parke Bernet, "Important Americana" [January 28–30, 1988], lot 1876); a table formerly in the collection of Mrs. Henry Riker (National Council of Girl Scouts, *Loan Exhibition of Eighteenth- and Early Nineteenth- Century Furniture and Glass* [New York: By the council, 1929], cat. 657); one advertised by John S. Walton in *Antiques* 105, no. 5 [May 1974]: 948; and one sold in 1996 (Sotheby's, "Important Americana from the Collection of Mr. and Mrs. Adolph Henry Meyer" [January 20, 1996], lot 77). One of the 2 related tables, formerly in the collection of Katrina Kipper, has pierced brackets in a curved chinoiserie design (no. 66.1327, DAPC, Visual Resources Collection, Winterthur Library); the other, formerly in the Charles K. Davis collection, has brackets in a simpler chinoiserie pattern and 5 stopped flutes on the legs (*American Antiques from Israel Sack Collection*, 10 vols. [Washington, D.C.: Highland House, ca. 1969–], 5:1316).

2. Liza Moses and Michael Moses, "Authenticating John Townsend's and John Goddard's Queen Anne and Chippendale Tables," *Antiques* 121, no. 5 (May 1982): 1130–43; Moses, *Master Craftsmen*, pp. 89–91, 142–43.

## 143 ◆ Card table
South Shore, Massachusetts
1785–1800

Variations on the straight-leg serpentine-facade card table indicate that the design was available from more than one shop and in more than one locale. Confirmation comes from a related card table signed by Providence cabinetmaker Judson Blake, which differs from the standard format only by the appearance of plain tapered legs. A serpentine-front card table with molded legs and a Portsmouth, New Hampshire, provenance was auctioned in 1945.[1]

The design of this table is one of the most successful interpretations, with molded rather than stop-fluted legs (fig. 1). An unusual feature is the profile of the outer edges of the stile, which are less thick than the leg itself, indicating that the leg was molded its full length and the outer portion cut away. This card table has another version of the incised and carved decoration found on No. 142, but the rope carving and the gouges on the edge of the leaf are smaller. The knee brackets are cut in a similar pattern and are nailed with sprigs. Both Winterthur card tables have soft maple outer rear rails and white pine inner rear rails, but they differ in their method of construction. On this table, the stationary outer rail is secured directly to the inner rail with rosehead nails; on No. 142, there is a spacer block separating the inner and outer fixed rails. The methods of securing the tops are also different. On this table, the top is held by five large screws countersunk into the frame; No. 142 is secured by a series of small glueblocks on all four rails.

A small, unusual stamped mark, "HM" (or possibly "WH"), appears on the top of the swing leg. This same mark appears three times on a Massachusetts bow-front chest of drawers at the Worcester Art Museum.[2] Although it has yet to be assigned to a specific individual, it may be the mark of a lumber dealer supplying piecework bits—a more plausible explanation than interpreting it as an owner's or craftsman's mark.

*NER/CGN*

**Inscriptions or marks:** *Stamped on top of swing leg:* "HM" (or possibly "WH"). *On underside of top:* "2034/ A-32" in black marker.

**Construction:** The two halves of the solid top are hinged together at the back. A tenon centered in

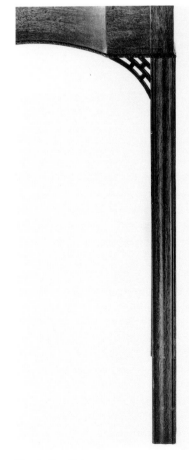

**Fig. 1.** Detail, leg.

the back edge of the stationary half keys into a slot in the upper half. The upper half, decorated with a conforming incised bead on the top and chisel cuts on the edge, unfolds to rest on the left rear leg, which swings out to support it. The lower half is attached with screws countersunk into the frame. The front and side skirt rails, serpentine on the outer surface and flat inside, are tenoned to the front legs, the joint reinforced with a quarter-round vertical glueblock. The inner rear rail is dovetailed to one end rail and abuts the other; both corners are reinforced with quarter-round vertical glueblocks. The thick outer rear rail, divided in half by a five-part finger-joined hinge, is tenoned to the rear legs. The stationary part is attached with rosehead nails to the inner rail; the other part forms the swing action. The carved skirt edge is cut from solid wood across the front and side rails and is let into the legs as a separate piece. The pierced brackets are nailed to the legs and rails with cut sprigs. All the legs are molded on two sides.

**Condition:** The top is slightly warped. There are minor splits in the hinged portion of the top. The right rear leg is split at the rail. A hole through the inner rear rail and partially through the outer rear rail held a pin, making the swing leg immovable. The bracket on the left side is broken. Some glueblocks are replaced.

**Dimensions:**

| | | |
|---|---:|---|
| H. (closed) | 28 1/2 in. | 72.4 cm |
| W. (top) | 33 in. | 83.8 cm |
| W. (frame) | 31 1/4 in. | 79.4 cm |
| W. (feet) | 31 3/8 in. | 79.7 cm |
| D. (top open) | 32 1/2 in. | 82.6 cm |
| D. (top closed) | 16 1/4 in. | 41.3 cm |
| D. (frame) | 14 7/8 in. | 37.8 cm |
| D. (feet) | 15 in. | 38.1 cm |

**Materials:** *Microanalysis:* Primary: mahogany. Secondary: soft maple group (outer rear rail); white pine group (inner rear rail); spruce (glueblocks). *Finish:* natural resin.

**Accession history:** Purchased by H. F. du Pont from John S. Walton, Inc., New York, 1965. Gift of H. F. du Pont, 1965. 65.2905

1. Moses, *Master Craftsmen*, p. 113, fig. 3.29. Judson Blake (w. 1823–38) was a Providence cabinetmaker and lumber merchant with warerooms on President Street. The Judson Blake card table is in a private collection; see Ethel Hall Bjerkoe with John Arthur Bjerkoe, *The Cabinetmakers of America* (Garden City, N.Y.: Doubleday, 1957), p. 43. For the Portsmouth card table, see *Antiques* 47, no. 1 (January 1945): 5.

2. The mark appears on the back edge of the keys used to secure the top to the sides and on the exposed end of a section of base molding. The Worcester Art Museum chest of drawers (acc. no. 1935.209) exhibits the design and construction features characteristic of eastern Massachusetts, including large ball-and-claw feet with well-articulated knuckles and bulbous rear talons, huge glueblocks supporting the knee brackets, dovetailed blades with a beaded facing covering the join, and an ogee-molded top attached to the sides on sliding dovetails.

## 144 ◆ Round tea table
### Coastal Massachusetts
### 1770–90

Tripod tables with pivoting tops, today called tilt-top tables, are described in eighteenth-century English records as *claw, pillar and claw, screen,* or *snap* tables. American craftsmen generally referred to the form simply as a *tea table*—occasionally with the added descriptor *round*—but other contemporary names include *stand table, fly tea table,* and *turn-up table.*[1]

The hinged pillar table had obvious advantages over similarly sized frame tables. The tripod form was physically lighter and was more easily transported. It was also a space saver—when not in use, the top could swing vertically for easy storage against a wall or in a corner.

**Fig. 1.** Detail, foot.

The turned pillar and spiral-fluted urn shape of this table is one favored in Massachusetts design. Like most pedestal tables made in the region, the top tilts on a maple block wedged to the tenoned end of the pillar. The style of deeply carved acanthus leaf decoration on the knees also is in the tradition of eastern Massachusetts, especially Essex County, carving. Carved, hairy, animal paw feet are uncommon in New England but do appear occasionally on Boston tables and case and seating furniture (fig. 1).[2]

One of the features that sets this mahogany table apart is its large, thirty-six-inch single-board top. Although probably used for tea, its size and unmolded top suggest it also may have been used as a dining table, a presumption supported by the fact that the table originally was fitted with casters. An eighteenth-century English painting depicts a seated couple with a sewing basket and implements on a similar table.[3] Obviously, such forms were versatile.

*NER/CGN*

---

**Construction:** The plain one-board top tilts vertically. A pair of large trapezoidal-shape cleats, chamfered on the ends and with thin chamfers on the bottom, are screwed to the underside of the top. Between them is a thick block, chamfered on the lower edge, which is attached to the cleats with round hinge pins. A round catch holds the top in a horizontal position. The top of the pillar continues through the block as a square tenon and is wedged

on four sides. The legs are dovetailed into the base of the pillar, the joints reinforced by a three-arm iron brace attached with screws. The platforms under the carved feet are cut from solid wood as they are on a Winterthur fire screen (No. 155).

**Condition:** The tabletop has been refinished; the pillar and legs retain an old finish. The top once was screwed to the block. The catch that holds the top horizontally is replaced. An old break at the base of the shaft was repaired in 1988. The table once was fitted with casters.

**Dimensions:**

| | | |
|---|---:|---|
| H. | 27¹⁄₂ in. | 69.9 cm |
| Diam. (with grain) | 36 in. | 91.4 cm |
| Diam. (across grain) | 35¹⁄₂ in. | 90.1 cm |
| W. (feet) | 27¹⁄₂ in. | 69.9 cm |

**Materials:** *Microanalysis:* Primary: mahogany. Secondary: hard maple group (block). *Finish:* natural resin.

**Publications:** Edgar G. Miller, Jr., *American Antique Furniture: A Book for Amateurs,* 2 vols. (Baltimore: Lord Baltimore Press, 1937), 2:735, no. 1379.

**Provenance:** Tradition of ownership in the Beck family of Brookline, Mass.

**Accession history:** Purchased by H. F. du Pont from the Colonial Antiques Shop, Boston, 1952. Gift of H. F. du Pont, 1952.
52.21

1. For references to *pillar and claw,* see Macquoid and Edwards, *Dictionary,* 3:207–9. Ince and Mayhew use the term *claw table* to identify plain-top tripod-base tables; see William Ince and John Mayhew, *The Universal System of Houshold Furniture* (1762; reprint, Chicago: Quadrangle Books, 1960), pl. 13. References to *screen* and *snap* tables appear in a 1764 manuscript agreement between the cabinetmakers and joiners in York, Eng.; see Christopher Gilbert, "An Early Cabinet and Chair Work Price List from York," *Furniture History* 21 (1985): 227–28. The term *snap* is used in Suffolk County (Boston) inventories beginning in the 1780s. For the term *tea table,* see Martin Eli Weil, "A Cabinetmaker's Price Book," in Ian M. G. Quimby, ed., *Winterthur Portfolio 13* (Chicago: University of Chicago Press for the Henry Francis du Pont Winterthur Museum, 1979), p. 187. Listings for *stand tables* in various woods appear in the 1757 Providence price list; see *John Brown House Loan Exhibition,* pp. 174–75; Lyon, *Colonial Furniture,* p. 266. Job Townsend, Jr., used the term *fly tea table* throughout the period 1756–75; see Moses, *Master Craftsmen,* pp. 346–49. Peter Minot's inventory taken in Boston in 1757 lists a "Mahogany Turn up Table" (Downs, *American Furniture,* fig. 385).

2. Fales, *Furniture of Historic Deerfield,* figs. 318, 319. Related knee carving appears on a smaller pedestal table formerly in the collection of Mrs. Edward F. Hutton (Sotheby Parke Bernet, "The Collection of Mrs. Edward F. Hutton" [June 10, 1972], lot 875) and a fire screen at Winterthur (see No. 155). Examples of hairy-paw feet include a desk-and-bookcase by George Bright at the MFA, Boston (Randall, *American Furniture,* no. 64), a Benjamin Frothingham desk at Historic Deerfield (Fales, *Furniture of Historic Deerfield,* fig. 464), and a side chair (No. 58) and a slab table (No. 129) at Winterthur.

3. The painting is *Mr. and Mrs. Robert Dashwood, 1750;* see Charles Saumarez Smith, *Eighteenth-Century Decoration, Design, and the Domestic Interior in England* (New York: Harry N. Abrams, 1993), p. 187.

## 145 ◆ Round tea table
Coastal Massachusetts
1760–90

If the incidence of survival is a direct reflection of use, customer preference in the design of Massachusetts tripod tea tables was for a "falling" (or tilting) top without a raised rim. The hinged top allowed the table to be stored compactly until needed, and the flat surface accommodated work or play as well as dining or taking tea. Eighteenth-century English paintings and prints record the use of a cloth on plain-top tripod tables.[1] The practice probably was followed in fashionable

**Fig. 1.** Detail, box.

American homes, but no comparable American genre scenes are known.

In Massachusetts, the standard tilting mechanism on such a table included a block at the top of the pillar attached to cleats on the underside of the top with round hinge pins. A metal spring catch at the opposite end of the block held the top horizontal. In an unusual variation on that system, this table operates on a pillared "box" (today called a "birdcage"), which permitted the top to revolve as well as tilt (fig. 1). The box is a common feature on New York and Pennsylvania pedestal tables but is rare in New England. Also unusual, the pillars on this box are columnar rather than the more traditional baluster shape and are shorter than those generally found on New York or Philadelphia tables.[2]

Although the tapering pillar and plain or swirl-carved urn pedestal is more readily identified with coastal Massachusetts, cabinetmakers in that area also used a tapering, fluted column with a Doric capital and base as a pillar support. Also characteristic of eastern Massachusetts pedestal tables are the attenuated birdlike talons on the carved feet. The presence of naturalistic scallop-shell

**Fig. 2.** Detail, leg.

carving on the knees is unusual (fig. 2). Based on survival, Massachusetts patrons and craftsmen seem to have preferred the knees plain or with leaf carving.

*NER/CGN*

**Construction:** The one-board top, rounded on the edge, tilts vertically and, when horizontal, rotates freely. A pair of trapezoidal-shape cleats, chamfered on the ends and edges, are screwed cross-grain to the underside of the top. Fixed between them is an open box that consists of two square boards connected by four small columnar pillars, their round through-tenons fitted with a wedge. At one end of the top board, round tenons fit into holes in the cleats, forming a hinge so that the top can be tilted; a round, brass spring catch holds the top fast in the horizontal position. The box, which rests on a flange at the top of the pillar, is held in place by a wooden wedge slotted through the pillar. The pillar continues through the box and into its top board as a round tenon. The legs, chamfered from under the knees to the ankles, are dovetailed to the bottom of the pillar and the joints covered by an iron Y-shape brace held with rosehead nails.

**Condition:** A fragment remains of a leather pad attached between the underside of the top and the top of the box. The box has been taken apart; a break in the top board near the hinge pins has been reglued. A loose veneer collar has been added to the tenoned end of the pillar to provide a tighter fit. The wedge securing the box is new. Layout marks for positioning the pillars are visible on the underside of the top of the box and the upper side of the bottom.

**Dimensions:**

| | | |
|---|---|---|
| H. | 27¼ in. | 69.2 cm |
| Diam. (with grain) | 35⅛ in. | 89.2 cm |
| Diam. (across grain) | 34¾ in. | 88.3 cm |
| W. (feet) | 28½ in. | 72.4 cm |

**Materials:** *Microanalysis:* Primary: mahogany (throughout). *Finish:* natural resin.

**Publications:** Downs, *American Furniture*, fig. 385.

**Accession history:** Purchased by H. F. du Pont from Maurice Rubin, Colonial Antiques Shop, Boston, 1951. Bequest of H. F. du Pont, 1969. 58.2778

1. See Johann Zoffany's "Lord Willoughby de Broke and Family"; William Hogarth's "Shortly after the Marriage" from *Marriage à la Mode*; Hogarth's "The Strode Family"; and Robert Dighton's mezzotint engraving *December*.

2. For another example with a pillared box in a private collection, see "Shop Talk," *Antiques* 69, no. 1 (January 1956): 14; English cabinetmakers used columnar pillars on pedestal table boxes, but the design is rare on American turn-up tables from any area; Macquoid and Edwards, *Dictionary*, 3:208, fig. 17.

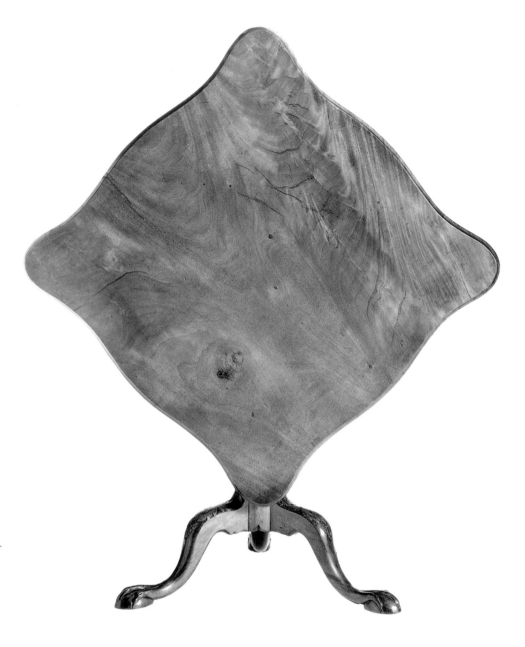

## 146 ◆ Square tea tables
**Coastal Massachusetts**
**1760–1800**

Tripod tables with large serpentine-shape square tops were only slightly less popular in New England than those with round tops. Boston and Newport inventories describing tables as "square" could have referred to these plain-top tables with tapering pillar-on-urn pedestals, somewhat horizontal S-curve legs, and attenuated claw feet on egg-shape balls. In Philadelphia this sort of table would have been called pillar-and-claw, although most would have had round tops. Today we refer to tilt-top tables as ones whose top can be brought vertical when not in use to save space.

The left table has well-articulated asymmetrical leaf carving on the knees and upper leg surrounded by a snowflake-shape punchwork ground more commonly found on neoclassical Salem-area furniture (fig. 1). The base price for a tripod mahogany tea table with "claw" feet and "leaves on the knees" was £4.0.0. One with this much carved ornament was even more expensive. One wonders how it would compare to the "Mahogany Turn up Table" in Peter Minot's 1757 Boston inventory valued at £10.[1] In the process of refinishing, the carving has lost some of its crispness, but it still reflects the effort of a highly skilled craftsman.

The makers of both tables chose fine figured mahogany from very large trees for the single-plank tops and edged the serpentine sides with ogee molding. The heights of both (twenty-eight inches) suggests that they may have been used for a variety of functions, such as dining, writing, and tea-drinking.

A serpentine-shape square table with a swirl-molded urn as its pedestal base but with no knee carving belonged to Benjamin and Cora Ginsburg; another also without carving sold at a Skinner auction in June 1994.[2]

*NER/CGN*

**Construction:** (Left) The one-board ogee-molded serpentine-shape top tilts vertically. A pair of arched

cleats, flat on the bottom and ends, are placed diagonally across the grain and screwed to the underside of the top. The top of the pillar is through-tenoned to a thick block chamfered on the under edge. The block has round hinge pins at one end set into the cleats that allow the top to tilt; a round, brass spring catch at the other end holds the top horizontal. The legs are dovetailed to the base of the pillar, the joints covered by a three-arm iron brace secured with cut nails.

(Right) The serpentine-shape ogee-molded top tilts vertically. A pair of arched cleats, flat on the bottom and rounded on the ends, are screwed diagonally across the grain to the underside of the top. The top of the pillar is a square through-tenon wedged to a thick block. Round hinge pins at one end of the block fit into holes in the cleats forming a hinge for the top; a teardrop-shape brass spring catch at the other end of the block holds the top horizontal. The legs are dovetailed into the bottom of the pillar, the joints covered by a three-arm iron brace held with round-head screws.

**Condition:** (Left) The table has been refinished. The top has several splits along the grain; one of the splits has been filled on the underside. There

also are patched knotholes on the underside of the top. A repair to one of the legs is reinforced by a brass brace.

(Right) The table has been refinished. The block has warped, and the top no longer can be locked in a horizontal position. The underside of the top has been cut out to accept the lock plate on the catch. The block also is repaired at the hinge. The spring catch is a replacement. The base of the pillar is cracked; the repair is old. The iron plate covering the join of the legs is original; the screws are not. The table once was fitted with casters.

**Dimensions:**

Left

| | | |
|---|---|---|
| H. | 28¼ in. | 71.8 cm |
| W. (top with grain) | 32½ in. | 82.6 cm |
| W. (top across grain) | 32¼ in. | 81.9 cm |
| W. (feet) | 25½ in. | 64.8 cm |

Right

| | | |
|---|---|---|
| H. | 28 in. | 71.1 cm |
| W. (top with grain) | 34½ in. | 87.6 cm |
| W. (top across grain) | 34 in. | 86.4 cm |
| W. (feet) | 27½ in. | 69.9 cm |

**Materials:** *Microanalysis:* (Left) Primary: mahogany. Secondary: soft maple group (block). (Right)

Primary: mahogany. Secondary: white pine group (cleats, block). *Finish:* (Left and right) natural resin.

**Accession history:** (Left and right) Bequest of H. F. du Pont, 1969.
59.1878, 57.546

1. The 1772 Philadelphia price book is cited in Martin Eli Weil, "A Cabinetmaker's Price Book," in Ian M. G. Quimby, ed., *Winterthur Portfolio 13* (Chicago: University of Chicago Press for the Henry Francis du Pont Winterthur Museum, 1979), p. 187; for the Minot inventory, see Downs, *American Furniture*, fig. 385.

2. Christie's, "The Contents of Benjamin Ginsburg, Antiquary, Including the Property of Cora Ginsburg" (October 14–15, 1983), lot 714. Robert W. Skinner, "Americana" (June 12, 1994), lot 168.

## 147 ◆ Round tea table
Probably Rhode Island
1750–80

This round "snap" table with five graduated drawers exemplifies the connoisseur's collecting goal: a very rare form, the best example extant, and the use of a rare combination of exotic woods. Only five other tables in this unusual design are known: one at the Lyman Allyn Museum in New London, Connecticut; one at the Newport Restoration Foundation; one formerly owned by Herbert Newton (present location unknown); and two others offered at auction in 1969 and 1981.[1]

All tables in the group have dished tops, slightly concave cabinet sides, columns that contrast in color with the cabinet panels, triangular platforms, and cabriole legs. Despite the similarity of design, the tables vary considerably in their size, materials, construction, and decoration. On most, the cabinet is fitted with five graduated, recessed blockfront drawers (fig. 1). The exception is the table formerly in the Newton collection,

which has four recessed, blockfront drawers with a shell-carved drawer on top. The sides of the pie-shape drawers are straight on Winterthur's table (fig. 2); those from the tables at the Lyman Allyn Museum and the Newport Restoration Foundation are bow-shaped. Winterthur's table is the largest of the group and is the only one with a shaped lower edge to the platform. It shares with the Newton table undecorated knees and raised midribbed, pointed pad feet; the tables at the Lyman Allyn Museum and the Newport Restoration Foundation both have the five-toed paw feet found on some Newport stands (see No. 152). Newport cabinetmakers also produced a similar triangular platform with four-toed paw feet that was used extensively on fire screens. The platform base is an English design—Ince and Mayhew included a teakettle stand with a platform base in *The Universal System of Houshold Furniture*. Used in the colonies mainly in Newport, it also can be found on some Massachusetts tables and stands.[2]

Tables with the platform cabinet design generally are assigned to Rhode Island based on their visual similarity to a related triangular platform table with four columnar supports in the Karolik collection at the Museum of Fine Arts, Boston; it has a tradition of manufacture by John Goddard as a gift for his daughter Catherine. Of the six cabinet tables in the group, only the one at the Lyman Allyn Museum has a pre-twentieth-century history—it was owned in the late eighteenth century by John and Sarah (Starr) Deshon of New London.[3] Both Winterthur's table and the Newton table were recovered in the Connecticut River valley. Winterthur's table descended in the Davis family of Plantsville, Connecticut, and the Newton table was found near Springfield, Massachusetts. The Newport Restoration Foundation table was acquired at auction without a history.

Perhaps the most surprising feature of Winterthur's table is the number of tropical woods used in its manufacture. As expected, the top, cabinet sides, and platform are made of mahogany, as are the drawer fronts, sides, and bottoms, and the blades between the drawers. The legs, however, are fashioned of *Astronium*, a reddish brown hardwood striped with black. Similar in appearance to rosewood, *Astronium* was used as veneer in some eighteenth-century European furniture. Native to Central and South America, it is better known as "Goncalo alves" and may be the timber referred to as *kingwood* in eighteenth-century ship manifests. The columns are fabricated from West Indies satinwood, a very dense light-colored wood with a strong ray fleck.[4] The golden columns effectively contrast the mahogany. Even the cleats are made of a tropical hardwood; the only native wood in the table is the red cedar used for the drawer backs.

*NER/CGN*

**Inscriptions or marks:** *Inside front of top drawer:* "M. A. [Nor]ton/ Loan" in pencil, on red-bordered

**Fig. 1.** Table open.

**Fig. 2.** Detail, drawer.

**Exhibitions:** Morgan Memorial, Hartford, Conn., 1926.

**Publications:** Malcolm A. Norton, "The Cabinet Pedestal Table," *Antiques* 4, no. 4 (November 1923): 224–25, fig. 2. Nutting, *Furniture Treasury*, no. 1314. Downs, *American Furniture*, fig. 384.

**Provenar.ce:** The table descended in the Davis family of Plantsville, Conn. Ex coll.: Malcolm A. Norton, Hartford, Conn.

**Accession history:** Purchased by H. F. du Pont from Walter A. Crabtree, Norton's son-in-law, Hartford, Conn., 1932. Gift of H. F. du Pont, 1960. 59.2648

1. The Lyman Allyn Museum, Newton collection, and Winterthur tables were published in Malcolm A. Norton, "The Cabinet Pedestal Table," *Antiques* 4, no. 4 (November 1923): 224–25. For the Newport Restoration Foundation table, see Moses, *Master Craftsmen*, fig. 1.36. Parke-Bernet Galleries, "Important Eighteenth-Century American Furniture" (October 25, 1969), lot 84. Sotheby Parke Bernet, "Fine Americana" (September 26, 1981), lot 445.

2. For fire screens, see *John Brown House Loan Exhibition*, cat. 93; Rodriguez Roque, *American Furniture*, no. 196; Heckscher, *American Furniture*, cat. no. 133; Flanigan, *American Furniture*, cat. no. 33. For English designs, see Macquoid and Edwards, *Dictionary*, 3:68, 149, 150, figs. 1, 12, 13, 15, 16, 19. William Ince and John Mayhew, *The Universal System of Houshold Furniture* (1762; reprint, Chicago: Quadrangle Books, 1960), pl. 14 extreme left. For Massachusetts tables and stands, see Randall, *American Furniture*, no. 112.

3. For the Karolik collection table, see Hipkiss, *Eighteenth-Century American Arts*, no. 50; see also Ralph E. Carpenter, Jr., *The Arts and Crafts of Newport, Rhode Island, 1640–1820* (Newport: Preservation Society of Newport County, 1954), no. 32; and Moses, *Master Craftsmen*, fig. 1.35. Catherine Goddard married Perry Weaver, and the table descended in the Weaver family of Rhode Island. On the history of the Lyman Allyn Museum table, see Norton, "Cabinet Pedestal Table," p. 224.

4. Samuel J. Record and Robert W. Hess, *Timbers of the New World* (1943; reprint, Salem, N.H.: Ayer Co. Publishers, 1986), pp. 39–41; David A. Kribs, *Commercial Foreign Woods in the American Market* (New York: Dover Publications, 1968), pp. 6–7. The columns originally were thought to be of sycamore, another light-colored wood with a strong ray fleck.

gummed label, pasted. *On label:* "286.26" in red crayon.

**Construction:** The tabletop is made of a wide board pieced at one side with a 6 3/4" strip cut from the same log. The molded rim is cut from solid wood, and there is an incised bead on the lower outside surface of the edge. The top tilts vertically. A pair of trapezoidal-shape cleats, rounded on the ends and bottom, are screwed to the underside of the top. Between them is a thick triangular block with round tenons that forms the plate for the enclosed, slightly concave-sided triangular cabinet. The three-quarter full columns at each corner are screwed to the block from the top and rest on the platform. Behind each of the front columns there are full-length triangular blocks to which the framing for the door is nailed. Beaded on two edges, a hinged door, cut slightly shorter than the sides to clear the cleats, opens to reveal a series of five graduated triangular drawers. The drawer fronts are cut in a concave block; the sides are nailed to rabbets in the front and across the back; the bottoms, rabbeted at the front, are nailed over the sides and back. The raised, thumbnail-molded panels on the sides of the platform are cut from solid wood and are shaped on the lower edge. The legs are dovetailed to the platform from below, the joints covered with a Y-shape iron brace held with modern screws.

**Condition:** A split in the top has been repaired and the cleats refastened. The upper plate is split at the hinge pins. The left side of the cabinet is cracked. The door is patched at the lower hinge and repaired below the lock. The platform is patched on two sides. The right leg has broken out at the dovetail. The right ankle has been reconstructed with new wood added. The backs of three of the drawers are replaced. The hinges, escutcheon, and the latch are replaced; the door originally had snipe hinges. All but one drawer pull are original.

**Dimensions:**

| | | |
|---|---|---|
| H. | 28 1/4 in. | 74.3 cm |
| Diam. (with grain) | 33 in. | 83.8 cm |
| Diam. (across grain) | 32 1/4 in. | 81.9 cm |
| W. (feet) | 20 1/4 in. | 51.4 cm |

**Materials:** *Microanalysis:* Primary: mahogany (top, cabinet sides, drawer fronts); *Astronium* sp. ["Goncalo alves"] (legs). Secondary: West Indies satinwood (columns); mahogany (drawer sides and bottoms, blades); red cedar (original drawer backs); tropical hardwood (cleats). *Finish:* natural resin.

# Stands and Fire Screens

THE UNDERLYING DESIGN OF THE ROUND or "claw" tea table is replicated on several new furniture forms popularized in the eighteenth century, including small pillar stands, basin and kettle stands, and pole screens. So similar are the design and construction of pillar stands and round tea tables that the distinction, traditionally, is one of size. The term *stand* usually is reserved for a form with a less than two-foot-diameter top. Entries in the 1772 Philadelphia price book listing folding stands of "22 inches with a box" and "fixed 18 inches" support this differentiation.[1] Like the larger models, stands were made with either folding or fixed tops.

As a discrete form, the stand was introduced into England from Italy, France, and Holland about the time of the Restoration. In well-to-do English households, pairs of stands were part of an en suite parlor or hall grouping with an ornamental pier (side) table and a complementary looking glass. The stands were intended to hold lighting devices to supplement the fixed lighting in a room. The form especially captured the fancy of mid eighteenth-century English designers. Patterns based on French and oriental models appeared in Edwards and Darly's *New Book of Chinese Designs* (1754); Ince and Mayhew's *Universal System of Houshold Furniture* (1762); Thomas Johnson's *One Hundred and Fifty New Designs* (1758, 1761); *Genteel Houshold Furniture in the Present Taste* (1760, ca. 1765), compiled by a "Society of Upholsterers"; and Robert Manwaring's *Cabinet and Chair-Maker's Real Friend and Companion* (1765). Thomas Chippendale was an enthusiastic proponent of the form; he included seventeen designs for stands in the third edition of his *Director* (1762). Many of the proposed rococo designs were highly fanciful and difficult to implement. Relatively few were executed, most in a modified form.

Entries for small movable stands appear in most eighteenth-century inventories on both sides of the Atlantic. Stands for lighting devices were appropriate for use in virtually any room in a house. The more elaborately carved designs were intended for display in public spaces in the grand English houses. More restrained interpretations, those not generally included in the design books, were reserved for family areas. It was these more conservative designs that appealed to the English middle class and to Americans.

Production of candlestands was sufficiently common in America to warrant inclusion in the cabinetmaker's price books of the period. Listings in the 1757 Providence price book include:

*maple Candel Stand @ 10 £*
*Do walnot 12 [£] & mehogny @ 16 £.*[2]

The prices listed are in the inflated Rhode Island currency of the day. The adjusted prices of the stands in the applicable sterling standard are approximately £7.6.0 in maple, £10.0.0 in walnut, and £13.0.0 in mahogany. The quoted prices are roughly half the cost of a round tea table in the same materials. Winterthur's collection includes representative examples of candlestand forms from eastern Massachusetts; Newport, Rhode Island; and Norwich, Connecticut.

The eighteenth century witnessed the generation of a number of other specialized stand forms. The conventions surrounding the preparation and service of tea in the late seventeenth century stimulated the need for stands to hold the hot water kettle and its heating element. Eighteenth-century design books illustrate two pattern types: the tripod stand and a four-leg variety. Both styles were produced in England and America. References to kettle or urn stands do not appear in the 1757 Providence price book, but by 1772 the form was sufficiently popular in Philadelphia to be included in that price book:

*Tea Kettle Stand with Gallery top*
 *& plain feet*           *2.10.0*

*Tea Kettle Stand with Claw feet*
 *leaves on Knees Carved & fluted piller*
 *with turned banesters*        *3.10.0*[3]

There is no American eighteenth-century listing for the rectangular form on four legs. Winterthur's collection includes an example of each design. The tripod form was made in Newport and is attributed to John Townsend (No. 150). The four-leg form comes from southeastern New England or nearby Long Island (No. 151).

Another new stand form was the basin stand. Until the second half of the sixteenth century, washing was performed in a bed chamber with the basin and ewer placed on any convenient flat surface. Not until the middle of the eighteenth century did designers introduce a specialized form for this purpose. Chippendale included three patterns in the 1762 edition of the *Director*. The form was further popularized at the end of the eighteenth century in designs by Hepplewhite, Sheraton, and Shearer. Winterthur has a single New England basin stand; it was made in Newport (No. 152).

Movable screens to control household drafts and reduce excessive heat or light have been in use since the Middle Ages. In English homes they appeared in at least three distinct designs: tall panels, standing singly or hinged together as a folding screen; a sliding panel screen on four short feet called "a horse fire screen" by Chippendale; and the tripod form with an adjustable panel mounted on a pole that Chippendale described as "screens that stand on a Pillar, and slide up and down."[4]

The pole screen became popular in England about 1730 as an alternative to the "horse" or cheval screen. The design itself was not new. An iron "stick screen" with tripod base and sliding screen was inventoried at Ham House in 1679 as part of the chimney furnishings in the Queen's Bedchamber.[5] What was new in the eighteenth century was the fabrication of the design in wood. Appropriate for use in any room with a fireplace, the pole screen generally was placed in proximity to the fireplace opening.

Probate inventories offer scant references to the use of the pole screen in eighteenth-century New England. That the form was produced and used here is certain. Less clear is its popularity.

Proportionately fewer New England examples survive than do pole screens from the middle colonies. The form is not included in either the 1757 Providence price book or the 1792 Hartford price list. However, it does appear in the 1772 Philadelphia price book:

|  | *mahogany* | *walnut* |
|---|---|---|
| *fire Screenes with plain feet* | *1.15.0* | *1.5.0* |
| *ditto.with Claw feet* | *2.2.6* | *1.12.6* |
| *ditto with Leaves on the knees* | *2.10.0* | *2.0.0*[6] |

All of the New England fire screens at Winterthur are the tripod form, and all were made in Massachusetts.

*NER*

---

[1] Martin Eli Weil, "A Cabinetmaker's Price Book," in Ian M. G. Quimby, ed., *Winterthur Portfolio 13* (Chicago: University of Chicago Press for the Henry Francis du Pont Winterthur Museum, 1979), p. 187.

[2] "Rule and Price of Joyners Work," March 24, 1757, Rhode Island Historical Society, Providence, as quoted in *John Brown House Loan Exhibition*, p. 175.

[3] Weil, "Cabinetmaker's Price Book," pp. 187–88.

[4] Thomas Chippendale, *The Gentleman and Cabinet-Maker's Director* (1762; reprint 3d ed., New York: Dover Publications, 1966), pl. 152n.

[5] Macquoid and Edwards, *Dictionary*, 3:62, fig. 15.

[6] Weil, "Cabinetmaker's Price Book," p. 190.

decorated on the outside edge with a pair of incised lines. A single wide cleat, its bottom trapezoidal with chamfered edges and rounded ends, is screwed to the underside. The stop-fluted and swirl-fluted pillar is tenoned and pegged into the cleat. The legs are dovetailed into the bottom of the pillar, the joints covered with an iron Y-shape brace held with screws.

**Condition:** The table has been refinished, causing a loss of definition in the knee carving. The cleat has been repositioned in an effort to correct a warp in the top and has been secured with new screws; it now is set with the grain. The base of the pillar is repaired where one leg broke out at the dovetail join. One foot is replaced and the ankle repaired with added wood on another leg. The screws in the brace are modern, and the brace may be a replacement.

**Dimensions:**

| | | |
|---|---|---|
| H. | 26 in. | 66.0 cm |
| Diam. (with grain) | 17 in. | 43.2 cm |
| Diam. (across grain) | 16⅞ in. | 42.9 cm |
| W. (feet) | 17 in. | 43.2 cm |

**Materials:** *Microanalysis:* Primary: mahogany (throughout). *Finish:* natural resin.

**Publications:** Downs, *American Furniture*, fig. 285. Butler, *American Furniture*, p. 54.

**Accession history:** Purchased by H. F. du Pont from Frances M. Nichols, Glebe House, Marblehead, Mass., 1935. Gift of H. F. du Pont, 1960. 59.2651

## 148 ◆ Stand
### Boston, Massachusetts, or Rhode Island
### 1780–1800

Patterned after contemporary English models, the turned urn-and-column pillar was a universal design on New England pedestal tables in the second half of the eighteenth century.[1] Artisans in each colony adapted the design in their own way so that the shape of the pillar, like the shape of the foot, indicated regional origin. Massachusetts carvers apparently preferred a lean design with tight spiral carving on the urn and a plain pillar above (see No. 144). On Connecticut stands (see No. 149), the column is an architecturally correct order. In the hands of the finest Rhode Island carvers, the design was fuller with a broad spiral-carved vase topped by a fluted or stop-fluted column.

Executing the fluted pillar design was labor intensive and costly. This unusual treatment is known on a relatively small group of Rhode Island stands. A mahogany falling-top example has a simple dished top, undecorated legs, and plain pad feet. A related stand in a Rhode Island private collection has a similar spiral urn and fluted pedestal. Its mahogany top is octagonal with a candleslide at one end; the legs have a single leaf carved on the knee with C-scroll marginal borders and end in a ribbed snake foot on a platform. Winterthur's stand is the only one of the group with a fixed top, and although the stop fluting relates it to Rhode Island examples, its molded rim has an unusual profile not found on other Rhode Island pedestal tables or stands. The shell-and-husk carving on the knees is a derivative of that first used on Boston-made furniture.[2]

*NER/CGN*

**Construction:** The one-board top is stationary; its shallow molded rim is cut from solid wood and

1. Macquoid and Edwards, *Dictionary*, 3:205–8, figs. 7, 10, 11, 12, 15, 18; Ralph Edwards and Margaret Jourdain, *Georgian Cabinet-Makers, c. 1700–1800* (3d rev. ed., London: Country Life, 1955), p. 237, pl. 226; Victoria and Albert Museum, *Georgian Furniture* (3d ed., revised, London: Her Majesty's Stationery Office, 1969), figs. 48, 83.

2. For the falling-top example, see Rodriguez Roque, *American Furniture*, no. 171; for the stand in the private Rhode Island collection, see Ralph E. Carpenter, Jr., *The Arts and Crafts of Newport, Rhode Island, 1640–1820* (Newport: Preservation Society of Newport County, 1954), no. 53; Moses, *Master Craftsmen*, fig. 1.37. On Boston carving, see Keno, Freund, and Miller, "Very Pink of the Mode."

## 149 ◆ Candlestand
Charlestown, New Hampshire
ca. 1778

## Candlestand
Norwich, Connecticut, area
1778–1800

All eighteenth-century New England cabinetmakers, whether urban or rural, were expected to be fully conversant with the classical orders of architecture. As Thomas Chippendale noted:

> Without an Acquaintance with this Science, and some Knowledge of the Rules of Perspective, the Cabinet-Maker cannot make the Designs of his Work intelligible. . . . These, therefore, ought to be carefully studied by every one who would excel in this Branch, since they are the very soul and Basis of his Art.[1]

One of the most direct applications of architectural orders to table furniture is in a series of three stands associated with the Norwich, Connecticut, area. Two of the stands, shown here, are at Winterthur. Previously catalogued as a pair, the right stand is slightly larger, the edge of the platform has fewer and larger scallops, and the fish-scale carving on the legs is less defined. A third, at the Metropolitan Museum of Art, shares the same design but differs from these two in size and detail.[2] Each features an elaborately carved lathe-turned top, a separate scalloped support screwed to the underside of the top, an architecturally correct Corinthian column and spiral-reeded-vase pillar, and unusual flat-leaf-carved cabriole legs attached to a platform base.

The design is at once sophisticated and naive. Instead of a pillar tenoned to a cleat under the top and to the platform base, the post has die-cut wooden screws at both ends threaded into the scalloped top support and the turned base block. The decoration on the top and pillar uses motifs found in furniture design books of the period and in builders' manuals as well. The fluting on the inner surface of the top has some parallels in English furniture, but the unusual knee carving—a series of flat leaves flanking either side of a central vein with the two lower leaves extending to the edge of the leg as volutes—seems to be particular to these three stands and to a marble slab table that descended in the Trumbull family of Lebanon, Connecticut (see No. 127).[3] The richly detailed carving lacks the dimension of the finest New England examples, but stipple punching on the background emphasizes the row of leaves edging the rim and the Corinthian capital.

Attached to the underside of the platform of the left stand is a paper label inscribed:

> This stand was made about the year/ 1778, for Samuel Hunt of Charlestown/ No. 4, [by] an [English] soldier taken/ prisoner at [the battle of] *Bennington*/ Aug 16, 177[7] [by the] NH and Vt/

Militia under John Stark/ [a sentence effaced]/ The old Secretary is also his make.

The reference to "Charlestown" caused Joseph Downs to assign the stand to Charlestown, Massachusetts, which he further supported by citing the shape of the pillar and the carved rat-claw foot grasping an egg-shape ball—features found on some coastal Massachusetts tables and stands (see No. 146 left). Robert F. Trent, however, has identified "Charleston No. 4" as Charlestown, New Hampshire, a town on the east bank of the Connecticut River that served as fort no. 4 of the Massachusetts defenses during the French and Indian War. Samuel Hunt, Jr. (1734–99), for whom the stand was made, was a distinguished Charlestown, New Hampshire, politician and landholder married to Esther Strong of Northampton, Massachusetts, sister of Massachusetts Governor Caleb Strong.[4]

Although scholars have doubted the veracity of the label, it is lent credibility by a letter dated December 11, 1777, from Jonathan Starr, Jr., a New London cabinetmaker, to Jeremiah Wadsworth:

Dear Sir—I am Under a Necessity of beging the favour of you to Let me Know Whether there is any of the British Soldiers Prisoners now at Hartford that are Cabinetmakers by Trade as I am Under Necessity of hirieing a Journeyman. [I] will take it as a favour if you will make a Little inquiry if any one is to be had there and Let me Know next week by Post . . . if a good Serviseable fellow is to be had Mr. Edward Hall begs the favour of you to Procure one for him.

The identity of the craftsman is unknown, but Trent speculates that one possible candidate is William Sprats (1747–1810), a Scots joiner taken prisoner by General Stark's troops at the capture of Fort Edward. In 1779 and 1781 Sprats was listed as a prisoner of war in Connecticut, although his place of confinement is not known. He later worked for the Cowles, Deming, and Champion families in Connecticut.[5]

Made of cherry and assembled in the same manner, the right stand is similar but not identical to the left. Comparison of the treatment of individual motifs shows that the carving is less precise and probably is by

another hand. Differences in size and in the turnings and carved detail along with Starr's letter and the Trumbull family provenance that includes similar furniture all suggest that the stand may have been made by a New London County craftsman to match the previous example. Possible New London County makers include Isaiah Tiffany (1723–1806), a New London and Lebanon craftsman known to have made furniture for Jonathan Trumbull, Sr.; Isaac Fitch (1734–91) of Lebanon, who worked for the Trumbull family over the years as cabinetmaker, builder, and architect; Samuel Edgecomb (d. 1795) of New London, who made a range of furniture forms; and New London cabinetmaker Jonathan Brooks (1745–1808), who advertised a variety of case furniture and tables. Of these craftsmen, only Fitch is documented by known work—a desk traditionally believed to have been made for Gov. Jonathan Trumbull (1740–1809) in 1769.[6] Unfortunately the desk has no construction or decorative features comparable to the stand.

Regardless of the identity of the craftsman, the stand affirms a level of sophistication enjoyed in the major towns in New London County and demanded by prominent citizens such as Trumbull. It also confirms the availability of skilled artisans to produce stylish furniture comparable to that produced in major metropolitan areas in the late eighteenth century.

*NER/CGN*

---

**Inscriptions or marks:** (Left) *On base:* "This stand was made about the year/ 1778, for Samuel Hunt of Charlestown/ No. 4, [by] an [English] soldier taken/ prisoner at [the battle of] *Bennington*/ Aug 16, 177[7] [by the] NH and Vt/ Militia under John Stark/ [a sentence effaced]/ The old Secretary is also his make" in ink, on paper label, attached.

**Construction:** The crimped inner edge and the three-dimensional acanthus leaf outer edge of the tops of both stands are cut from solid wood. The tops are screwed to circular collars scalloped on the lower edge with fourteen lobes (nine lobes on right table). The turned and fluted pillars have a carved Corinthian capital and spiral-reeded urn. The shafts, threaded at both ends, are screwed into a circular collar and into a drum-shape platform topped with an ogee-molded cap. The lower edges of the platforms are shaped between the cabriole legs dovetailed into them. No braces cover the dovetail joins.

**Condition:** (Left) The top has been reset and reglued. There is a small split in the platform.
(Right) The platform has been repaired at one of the leg joints.

**Dimensions:**
Left
| | | |
|---|---|---|
| H. | 27 5/8 in. | 70.2 cm |
| Diam. (with grain) | 8 7/8 in. | 22.9 cm |
| Diam. (across grain) | 8 13/16 in. | 22.4 cm |
| W. (feet) | 17 in. | 43.1 cm |

Right
| | | |
|---|---|---|
| H. | 28 1/16 in. | 71.4 cm |
| Diam. (with grain) | 9 3/8 in. | 23.9 cm |
| Diam. (across grain) | 9 3/8 in. | 23.9 cm |
| W. (feet) | 16 3/16 in. | 41.1 cm |

**Materials:** *Microanalysis:* (Left and right) Primary: cherry (throughout). *Finish:* (Left and right) natural resin.

**Publications:** (Left) Downs, *American Furniture,* fig. 284. Comstock, *American Furniture,* no. 353. Joseph T. Butler, "American Furniture," in Phoebe Phillips, ed., *The Collectors' Encyclopedia of Antiques* (New York: Crown Publishers, 1973), fig. 398a. Robert F. Trent, "The Colchester School of Cabinetmaking, 1750–1800," in Francis J. Puig and Michael Conforti, eds., *The American Craftsman and the European Tradition, 1620–1820* (Minneapolis: Minneapolis Institute of Arts, 1989), cat. no. 51.

**Accession history:** Bequest of H. F. du Pont, 1969. 59.1874.1, .2

---

1. Thomas Chippendale, *The Gentleman and Cabinet-Maker's Director* (1762; reprint 3d ed., New York: Dover Publications, 1966), preface.

2. Heckscher, *American Furniture,* cat. no. 131; also *Connecticut Furniture,* no. 154.

3. Drawings for capitals are included in Batty and Thomas Langley, *The Builder's Jewel* (1746; 2d ed., London, 1757), pls. 40, 41. For fluting on English furniture, see Macquoid and Edwards, *Dictionary,* 3:207, fig. 16; Christopher Claxton Stevens and Stewart Whittington, *Eighteenth-Century English Furniture: The Norman Adams Collection* (Woodbridge, Eng.: Antique Collectors' Club, 1983), p. 307.

4. Downs, *American Furniture,* fig. 284. Trent, "Colchester School," cat. no. 51.

5. For doubts about the label, see Heckscher, *American Furniture,* cat. no. 131. Letter, Wadsworth Papers, Connecticut Historical Society, as quoted in *New London County Furniture,* p. 127. On Sprats, see Trent, "Colchester School," cat. no. 51.

6. See checklist of New London County cabinetmakers in *New London County Furniture,* pp. 106–32. For Fitch desk, see Gerald W. R. Ward, ed., *Perspectives on American Furniture* (New York: W. W. Norton for the Henry Francis du Pont Winterthur Museum, 1988), no. 180. See also William Lamson Warren, "Isaac Fitch Revisited (as Cabinetmaker)," *Connecticut Antiquarian* 31, no. 1 (June 1979): 21–27.

## 150 ◆ Teakettle stand

Newport, Rhode Island
1770–95
Attributed to John Townsend
(1733–1809)

Eighteenth-century English family portraits, such as Joseph Van Aken's *English Family at Tea* (ca. 1720) and *Thomas Smith and His Family* (1733), document the presence of a special stand placed near the tea table to hold the kettle and its spirit lamp as part of the equipment for the tea ceremony in a well-appointed English household.[1] Comparable illustrations of eighteenth-century American interiors are not available, but documentary evidence and surviving examples of the form suggest that the practice was followed in at least some fashionable New England homes.

Teakettle stands or, as the form later became, urn stands were introduced about the same time as the specialized tea table. English teakettle stands were of two basic types—the tripod and pillar form, as seen here, or the tray-top stand on four legs (No. 151). In general, English kettle stands were lower than the surface of the tea table, usually under twenty inches high. By the 1760s, designs for the form were included in Chippendale's *Director*, Ince and Mayhew's *Universal System of Houshold Furniture*, and *Genteel Household Furniture in the Present Taste*. Hepplewhite's *Cabinet-Maker and Upholsterer's Guide* also includes six designs for urn stands.[2] The form continued to be made in England until about 1800, when it was replaced by the small occasional table. Craftsmen in America generally followed these precedents, although kettle stands usually are about twenty-eight inches tall.

Kettle stands appear less frequently in eighteenth-century American documents than in English ones; however, the form seems to have been sufficiently well known to warrant inclusion in the 1772 Philadelphia cabinetmaker's price book. The design described is the pillar and tripod base form:

Tea Kettle Stand with Gallery top & plain feet, £2:10:0

Tea Kettle Stand with Claw feet, leaves on knees, carved and fluted pillar with turned banesters, £3:10:0[3]

The traditional form took on a distinctive appearance in Newport, Rhode Island, where cabinetmakers frequently used a triangular platform base supported on three dovetailed cabriole legs for pillar forms such as tables (see No. 147), stands (see No. 148), and fire screens. Winterthur's kettle stand is attributed to John Townsend (1733–1809) based on its distinctive pierced fretwork gallery and the crosshatch frieze also found on a labeled pembroke table (see No. 138) and a labeled card table at the Metropolitan Museum of Art. A related kettle stand has a similar pillar and base, but its shallow case lacks the distinctive pierced gallery and crosshatch frieze found on this example.[4]

*NER/CGN*

---

**Construction:** The pierced gallery, dovetailed at the corners and mitered on the upper edge, has an incised double bead on the upper edge of each side. The gallery is let into a dado cut in the top board. The top board, cut with a filleted torus molding on all sides, extends over a crosshatch frieze that functions as the frame. The three-piece block, mitered on the back corners, is cut diagonally, paralleling the crosshatch ornament to form a pull-out shelf dished to hold a teapot or saucer. The shaped solid base is attached through the frieze to the top board with screws. The top of the fluted and swirl-reeded pillar is tenoned to the top and to the platform base. The thumbnail-molded panels on the sides of the platform are cut from solid wood. The legs are dovetailed into the platform from below, the joints reinforced by a triangular iron plate held with screws.

**Condition:** The pierced gallery has numerous repairs. The base of the top is split along the figured grain at the left front. The hardware is replaced.

**Dimensions:**

| | | |
|---|---|---|
| H. | 29¹/₈ in. | 74.0 cm |
| W. (box, with grain) | 8¹/₂ in. | 21.6 cm |
| W. (box, across grain) | 8¹/₄ in. | 21.0 cm |
| W. (feet) | 19 in. | 48.3 cm |

**Materials:** *Microanalysis:* Primary: mahogany (throughout). *Finish:* natural resin.

1. Rodris Roth, "Tea Drinking in Eighteenth-Century America: Its Etiquette and Equipage," *United States National Museum Bulletin*, no. 225 (Washington, D.C.: Smithsonian Institution, 1961): frontispiece; see also Elizabeth Einberg and Judy Egerton, *The Age of Hogarth: British Painters Born 1675–1709* (London: Tate Gallery, 1988), no. 159; Charles Saumarez Smith, *Eighteenth-Century Decoration, Design, and the Domestic Interior in England* (New York: Harry N. Abrams, 1993), fig. 90.

2. Thomas Chippendale, *The Gentleman and Cabinet-Maker's Director* (1762; reprint 3d ed., New York: Dover Publications, 1966), pl. 55; William Ince and John Mayhew, *The Universal System of Houshold Furniture* (1762; reprint, Chicago: Quadrangle Books, 1960), pl. 14; *Genteel Household Furniture in the Present Taste* (1763; reprint, East Ardley, Yorkshire, Eng.: EP Publishing, 1978), pls. 85, 92; [George] Hepplewhite, *The Cabinet-Maker and Upholsterer's Guide* (London: I. and J. Taylor, 1788), pls. 55, 56.

3. Martin Eli Weil, "A Cabinetmaker's Price Book," in Ian M. G. Quimby, ed., *Winterthur Portfolio 13* (Chicago: University of Chicago Press for the Henry Francis du Pont Winterthur Museum, 1979), pp. 187–88.

4. On Newport platform bases, see Rodriguez Roque, *American Furniture*, nos. 196, 198; Heckscher, *American Furniture*, cat. no. 133; Flanigan, *American Furniture*, cat. no. 33. For card table, see Heckscher, *American Furniture*, cat. no. 100; for related stand, see Sotheby Parke Bernet, "The Garbisch Collection: Volume 4" (May 23–25, 1980), lot 1091.

## 151 ◆ Teakettle stand
### Coastal southern New England or Long Island, New York
### 1790–1830

Like its pedestal-based companion, the four-leg kettle stand generally has a working surface only large enough to hold the hot water kettle used to brew and dilute tea. A narrow raised rim around the top serves, as it does on tea tables, to keep the kettle in place. A small sliding shelf mounted below the top supports a small teapot during the brewing process. Most kettle stands have either stretchers or a platform shelf for stabilization.

American examples of this form are relatively rare.[1] This simple fluted-leg kettle stand is a variation on the standard rectangular design. Incorporating an open storage cabinet and drawer, its design suggests parallels to chamber or night tables rather than to traditional kettle stands. The marble top and the slide for the pot or cup indicates that it probably was used to prepare hot punch and posset as well as tea.

Stylistic features including the fluted Marlborough legs and plain rose and bail handle probably influenced Joseph Downs's decision to date the stand 1760–80. However, the use of cut nails throughout indicates that a post-1790 date is more appropriate. Assuming that the primary wood was maple and recognizing no clear regional design or construction features, Downs assigned the stand broadly to New England. Microscopic identification of the woods—tulip-poplar and white and yellow pine—has helped to narrow the possible provenance to coastal southern New England (Connecticut and Rhode Island) and Long Island based on the natural growth range for these woods.[2]

*NER/CGN*

**Construction:** An ogee-molded retaining rim surrounding the inset marble top is nailed to the frame with cut nails. The marble, rough cut on the underside, rests only on the ends of the stiles. The side and back rails are tenoned and double-pegged to the legs; the front rails are tenoned and single-pegged. The top front rail is cut to receive a pull-out slide. A fixed shelf, nailed from the top to a transverse batten, is secured on the underside with glueblocks. The drawer hangs from rails nailed with cut nails to the inside of the legs. Applied rails are nailed to the drawer sides with cut nails. The drawer bottom, deeply chamfered and set into grooves on the front and sides, is nailed across the back. The drawer sides, back, and bottom are made with 1/2" stock. The front legs are fluted on two sides; the rear legs are fluted only on the outside surface.

**Condition:** Except for the interior of the drawer, the entire surface is grained in red and black paint. A series of missing glueblocks around the upper inside edge of the frame that originally supported the marble top are replaced. There is a 1/4" separation between the side and rear rails and the top molding. A replaced transverse brace supports the pull-out slide.

**Dimensions:**

| | | |
|---|---|---|
| H. | 29 1/8 in. | 71.4 cm |
| W. | 12 in. | 30.5 cm |
| D. | 12 in. | 30.5 cm |

**Materials:** *Microanalysis:* Primary: yellow pine group (legs); tulip-poplar (drawer front, fixed shelf). Secondary: tulip-poplar (drawer bottom); white pine group (medial brace). *Finish:* grained in red and black casein paint. Although there are several layers of paint, all parts of the stand have the same finish history. Fluorescence microscopy determined that the stand originally was painted, not finished with the traditional natural resin.

**Publications:** Downs, *American Furniture*, fig. 289.

**Accession history:** Purchased by H. F. du Pont from Joe Kindig, Jr., York, Pa., 1947. Bequest of H. F. du Pont, 1969.
67.1378

1. Examples include a Philadelphia stand with plain, straight legs and pierced brackets (Hornor, *Blue Book*, pl. 284) and 2 molded square-leg Portsmouth stands (Jobe, *Portsmouth Furniture*, cat. no. 50; James Biddle, *American Art from American Collections* [New York: Metropolitan Museum of Art, 1963], no. 84).

2. Downs, *American Furniture*, fig. 289. Richard J. Preston, Jr., *North American Trees* (3d ed., Ames: Iowa State University Press, 1976), pp. 234, 8, 18.

## 152 ◆ Basin stand
Newport, Rhode Island
1760–90

Until the introduction of indoor plumbing about the middle of the nineteenth century, basins and ewers offered the primary method of personal hygiene.[1] Until the seventeenth century, these utensils were placed on any convenient flat surface. The most common support form probably was a small table with a single drawer that held the soap, cloth, razor, and implement (often leaves or soft twigs) for cleaning the teeth. By the late seventeenth century, in the more affluent English homes, the basin and ewer were stored out of view in an enclosed chamber table.

One of the new special-purpose furniture forms introduced in the mid eighteenth century was the "bason stand" or washstand. Plate 55 of the 1762 edition of Chippendale's *Director* included three designs (fig. 1). Produced both as a tripod and as a four-leg form, the stand had a circular hole in the top for the wash basin. Below were one or two

drawers or a shelf to store soap and other toilet articles and, at the bottom, a platform with a dished depression to hold the water bottle. The intent, as Thomas Sheraton later claimed, was to produce a functional object "which may stand in a genteel room without giving offence to the eye."[2] Following this injunction, several later designers, including Hepplewhite and Shearer, provided washstands that were ingeniously constructed to disguise their real purpose.

Craftsmen in this country rarely produced the form before the federal period, although the 1772 Philadelphia price book includes two entries for the form:

| | |
|---|---|
| Bason Stand with three pillers & 2 drawers | £2 10 0 |
| Ditto Square with 2 drawers | 1 10 0 |

Cabriole-leg models are uncommon. Joseph Downs included two examples (figs. 277, 278) in *American Furniture*, his 1952 survey of the Winterthur collection. One fits the general description for the three-pillar two-drawer

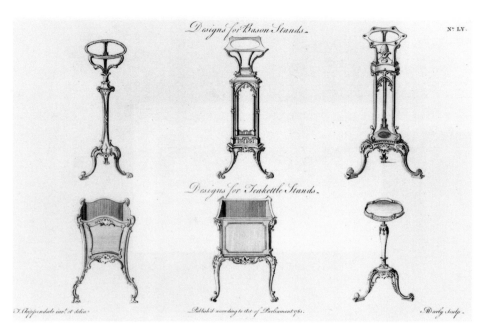

**Fig. 1.** From Thomas Chippendale, *The Gentleman and Cabinet-Maker's Director* (3d ed., London: By the author, 1762), pl. 55.

stand in the Philadelphia price book. The other, seen here, builds on the design model used for pedestal forms in Rhode Island. It incorporates the fluted supporting pillar, raised panel platform, and well-carved five-toe animal feet found on several Rhode Island round tea tables, fire screens, and kettle stands (No. 150). This basin stand is one of two examples in this design; the other is owned by Mr. and Mrs. Philip Holzer.[3] Unfortunately, the eighteenth-century histories of the stands are unknown.

While the Rhode Island provenance of this stand is clear, attribution to a specific cabinet shop is less certain. In 1952 Downs attributed the basin stand to John Townsend based largely on its similarity to other forms assigned to his shop. More recently, Michael Moses has reassigned the basin stand to John Goddard based on its similarity to the feet of a tea table that Goddard made for James Atkinson in 1774.[4] Insufficient historical or construction evidence exists to assign the basin stand to either shop with any degree of certainty.

NER/CGN

**Construction:** The upper portion consists of three tiers: a molded-edge ring for the wash basin, a disk with three circular cutouts for soap dishes, and a disk dished at the center for the water bottle. The ring, turned from a solid board, has incised double beads on the top surface. Separating the ring from the ovolo-edge disk below are three small, turned pillars round-tenoned to the ring and the disk. The disk is decorated with incised double beads around each opening and around the rim. Three fluted columns are attached with round tenons to the solid, ovolo-edge disk. Turned *lignum vitae* caps cover the lower end of the tenon. The lower disk has incised double beads around the center depression and the rim. A circular collar is screwed to the underside of the bottom disk. The turned and fluted pillar is round-tenoned into the collar and wood-threaded to the triangular platform and secured with a large old screw. The applied thumbnail molding, cut from solid wood, embellishes the platform sides. The legs are dovetailed into the platform from below, the joints covered individually with metal braces held by rosehead nails.

**Condition:** There is a repaired break in the top ring. The shelves are slightly warped. A section is missing from one of the small turned pillars. The caps covering the round tenons on the fluted columns are replaced. The center pillar is split. There is a small split in one leg. The three iron braces holding the legs are original.

**Dimensions:**

| | | |
|---|---|---|
| H. | 31⅞ in. | 90.0 cm |
| Diam. (with grain) | 11 in. | 27.9 cm |
| Diam. (across grain) | 11 in. | 27.9 cm |
| W. (feet) | 17¾ in. | 45.1 cm |

**Materials:** *Microanalysis:* Primary: mahogany (throughout). *Finish:* natural resin.

**Publications:** Downs, *American Furniture*, fig. 278. Comstock, *American Furniture*, no. 352. Joseph T. Butler, "American Furniture," in Phoebe Phillips, ed., *The Collectors' Encyclopedia of Antiques* (New York: Crown Publishers, 1973), fig. 394a. Carol Bohdan, "Cabriole Legs," *Fine Woodworking* 18 (September/October 1979): 78. Moses, *Master Craftsmen*, p. 240, fig. 5.28.

**Accession history:** Purchased by H. F. du Pont from Joe Kindig, Jr., York, Pa., 1939. Bequest of H. F. du Pont, 1969.
59.2650

1. Macquoid and Edwards, *Dictionary*, 3:328–32.

2. Macquoid and Edwards, *Dictionary*, 3:367, figs. 7–12. Thomas Sheraton, *The Cabinet-Maker and Upholsterer's Drawing-Book* (1793; reprint, New York: Dover Publications, 1972), pp. 91–92.

3. The 1772 Philadelphia price book is cited in Martin Eli Weil, "A Cabinetmaker's Price Book," in Ian M. G. Quimby, ed., *Winterthur Portfolio 13* (Chicago: University of Chicago Press for the Henry Francis du Pont Winterthur Museum, 1979), p. 188. Downs, *American Furniture*, fig. 277. Although Downs originally assigned this stand to Massachusetts, the exclusive use of tulip-poplar as the secondary wood suggests that a New York provenance is more appropriate. For Rhode Island tea tables, see Malcolm A. Norton, "The Cabinet Pedestal Table," *Antiques* 4, no. 4 (November 1923): 225, figs. 1, 3; Hipkiss, *Eighteenth-Century American Arts*, no. 59; Ralph E. Carpenter, Jr., *The Arts and Crafts of Newport, Rhode Island, 1640–1820* (Newport: Preservation Society of Newport County, 1954), no. 79; Moses, *Master Craftsmen*, p. 49, fig. 1.36. For Rhode Island fire screens, see Wendy A. Cooper, "The Furniture and Furnishings of John Brown, Merchant of Providence, 1736–1803" (Master's thesis, University of Delaware, 1971), figs. 33, 34; *John Brown House Loan Exhibition*, cat. 93; Rodriguez Roque, *American Furniture*, no. 196; and Heckscher, *American Furniture*, cat. no. 133. For the Holzer stand, see Barquist, *American Tables and Looking Glasses*, p. 268, fig. 59; it was formerly in the Garbisch collection, see Sotheby Parke Bernet, "The Garbisch Collection: Volume 4" (May 23–25, 1980), lot 1160.

4. Downs, *American Furniture*, fig. 278; Moses, *Master Craftsmen*, p. 240, fig. 5.28; on the Goddard tea table, see Carpenter, *Arts and Crafts of Newport*, no. 79; and Moses, *Master Craftsmen*, p. 208, fig. 4.7.

## 153 ◆ Fire screen
### Eastern Massachusetts
### 1760–80

The primary source of heat in most eighteenth-century English and American homes was an open fireplace that burned logs or coal in a grate or, at the end of the century, an iron stove. Each vented uneven warmth into a room. Early efforts to control the distribution of heat and minimize drafts included the introduction of movable tall panel screens, either singly or in multiple sections hinged together. The cumbersome and unwieldy nature of these tall screens prompted the introduction of two new forms—the tripod fire screen, or pole screen as it is known in England, and the "horse" (or later, cheval) fire screen with fixed panel or folding and sliding leaves.[1]

Both tripod and horse fire screens appear in eighteenth-century inventories on both sides of the Atlantic, although mention of any type of fire screen is relatively rare in New England documents of the period. A survey of 1774 probate inventories for Suffolk County, Massachusetts, lists only seven screens: "2 mohogony Fire Screens, £1," in the estate of Capt. Barnabas Binney of Boston; a fire screen, its specific value unlisted, in the estate of the Honorable Andrew Oliver of Boston; a fire screen (appraised with "2 stone Potts" and "1 pine Leaf" at £6.6.0), "1 Chair Screen, 2/0," and "1 sconce, 1 carpet & 1 screen, £1:2.0"

owned by Boston widow Mary Hubbard; and "a skreen frame 1/4d" listed in the front upper chamber of Boston shopkeeper Isaac Cozneau's house.[2] The absence of the form from the majority of Suffolk County households suggests that they were considered a luxury rather than a necessity.

Extant examples indicate that the preferred form for fire screens in New England was the tripod stand with adjustable panel. Its relatively uncomplicated construction, similar to that of a pillar stand but substituting a slender pole and panel for the circular top, may have been a contributing factor in its popularity. This design could be assembled by combining a stock pillar, provided by a turner, with carved legs and a framed panel, supplied by a cabinetmaker's own shop. The panel could be of solid wood, textile, paper, or even tin set into a frame. Thomas Chippendale favored the use of tapestry for the sliding panel. This example has a solid panel covered by needlework on the front and a wove, block-printed paper on the back.[3]

The most common style of American pole screen has a thin, plain pole mounted above the pillar. In the variation shown here, the thin pole is screw-threaded, and the screen is adjusted by rotating it on compensating threads. This particular design is uncommon in New England furniture, although two other

very similar fire screens are known—each has a flame finial, a screw-threaded pole, a bulbous pillar, and plain cabriole legs. One with an embroidered panel screen was owned by Dr. William Samuel Johnson (1727–1819), president of King's College (now Columbia University) in New York. The embroidery has been attributed to Dr. Johnson's daughters. A second pole screen differs from the other two: it has no embroidered covering and has the pointed "snake foot" popular along the North Shore of Massachusetts in place of the rat's-claw foot.[4] The elongated bulbous shape of the pillar, the high arch of the legs, and the rat's-claw feet are features found on a variety of Massachusetts pillar-and-claw furniture (see No. 146).

*NER/CGN*

---

**Construction:** The large, urn-and-flame carved finial screws to the top of the spiral-turned pole, which is fitted into the pillar above a metal collar. The legs are dovetailed into the bottom of the pillar, the joints reinforced by three iron braces overlapping at the center and held by rosehead nails. The screen, a solid panel covered on the front by needlework and on the back with a late eighteenth-century or early nineteenth-century wove block-printed paper, is attached to the pole by two arched cleats.

**Condition:** The finial, painted white with traces of gilding, is a replacement. The dovetail joint on one leg has been reglued. The needlework dates from the late eighteenth century but may not be original to the screen. The block-printed wove paper backing on the screen is torn in several places; it covers an earlier eighteenth-century laid paper, also block printed. The cleats holding the screen are replaced.

**Dimensions:**

| | | |
|---|---|---|
| H. | 57 3/4 in. | 146.7 cm |
| W. (screen) | 18 in. | 45.7 cm |
| L. (screen) | 17 3/4 in. | 45.1 cm |
| W. (feet) | 19 7/8 in. | 50.5 cm |

**Materials:** *Microanalysis:* Primary: cherry (throughout). *Finish:* natural resin.

**Accession history:** Bequest of H. F. du Pont, 1969. 58.1506

---

1. "Fire-screens, which stand on four Feet, and are commonly called Horse-Fire-screens" (Thomas Chippendale, *The Gentleman and Cabinet-Maker's Director* [1762; reprint 3d ed., New York: Dover Publications, 1966], pl. 152n).

2. Alice Hanson Jones, *American Colonial Wealth: Documents and Methods*, 3 vols. (New York: Arno Press, 1977), 2:893, 966, 942, 912, inventories dated August 3, March 16, March 11, August 4, 1774.

3. The April 9, 1776, inventory of Joshua Loring lists 2 paper fire screens in the lower front room; Joshua Loring inventory, 1776, Suffolk County Probate Court, Boston (microfilm, Downs collection). Christopher Gilbert, *The Life and Work of Thomas Chippendale*, 2 vols. (New York: Macmillan Co., 1978), 1:56. Report by John Krill, paper conservator, Winterthur, May 30, 1996.

4. Rodriguez Roque, *American Furniture*, no. 195. Attribution of embroidery is cited in Morse, *Furniture of the Olden Time*, p. 309. For second pole screen, see *American Antiques from Israel Sack Collection*, 10 vols. (Washington, D.C.: Highland House, ca. 1969–), 4:945.

The supporting frame of this fire screen—its legs, pillar, and shaft—is original. The adjustable panel is replaced and probably contained needlework rather than the eighteenth-century hand-painted Chinese silk fabric shown here, although it does suggest an embroidery design source.[3]

This fire screen entered the Winterthur collection with a hinged shelf suggestive of the federal-style pole screens in Charles F. Montgomery's *American Furniture: The Federal Period in the Henry Francis du Pont Winterthur Museum*.[4] The shelf had been fashioned from a portion of the top of a small neoclassical stand and was therefore removed. A larger fire screen would be more appropriate proportionally to the pole.

*NER/CGN*

**Construction:** The pole is fitted into the top of a plain column and twist-reeded urn pillar. The legs are dovetailed into the bottom of the pillar. The adjustable screen is attached to the pole by a brass guide ring at the top and a brass ring and spring bracket at the bottom.

**Condition:** The pillar is repaired at the base. One foot is new. Although the hand-painted eighteenth-century silk covering the screen is old, the supporting board and the silk covering on the back of the screen panel are modern. The molding applied to the screen is new.

**Dimensions:**

| | | |
|---|---|---|
| H. | 51 3/8 in. | 130.5 cm |
| W. (screen) | 12 1/2 in. | 31.8 cm |
| L. (screen) | 14 5/8 in. | 36.5 cm |
| W. (shelf) | 12 1/4 in. | 31.1 cm |
| D. (shelf open) | 7 3/4 in. | 19.7 cm |
| W. (feet) | 17 3/4 in. | 45.1 cm |

**Materials:** *Microanalysis:* Primary: mahogany. Secondary: cherry (modern frame by macroidentification). *Finish:* natural resin.

**Publications:** Downs, *American Furniture*, fig. 240.

**Accession history:** Purchased by H. F. du Pont from Joe Kindig, Jr., York, Pa., 1941. Gift of H. F. du Pont, 1960.
59.2649

## 154 ◆ Fire screen
Boston, Massachusetts, area
1765–90

In *The Cabinet Dictionary*, Thomas Sheraton identified the screen as "a piece of furniture used to shelter the face or legs from the fire. Hence the more common name is fire-screen, of which there are a great variety, as tripod fire-screens, horse or safe fire-screens, folding, and sliding fire-screens, and table fire screens."[1]

The price of any piece of eighteenth-century furniture was determined by combining the cost of materials and the labor required for its fabrication with an additional sum for profit. After the middle of the eighteenth century, American price books and their London prototypes regularized labor costs by establishing the rates for specific piecework. By identifying each modification to the basic form, they also codified what furniture scholars have

come to call "a language of workmanship" common to all eighteenth-century English-speaking cabinetmakers. Comparing the similarities and differences among price books affords documentary evidence concerning regional preferences in design and construction. None of the extant printed price books list the specific features needed to determine the precise cost of this fire screen, however. The January 1786 *Prices of Cabinet and Chair Work* by Benjamin Lehman lists £1.15.0 as the basic price for "mohogany fire screens with plain feet."[2] Ornamenting the pillar with a spiral-twisted urn would have been an additional cost.

The spiral turnings of the twist-reeded urn and plain pillar are design features associated with Boston and coastal Essex County tea tables, stands, and fire screens (No. 148), as is the elongated rat's-claw foot (No. 146).

1. Thomas Sheraton, *The Cabinet Dictionary* (1803; reprinted in 2 vols., New York: Praeger Publishers, 1970), 2:302.

2. Harrold E. Gillingham, "Benjamin Lehman: A Germantown Cabinet-maker," *Pennsylvania Magazine of History and Biography* 54, no. 4 (1930): 301.

3. For spiral turnings, see Randall, *American Furniture*, nos. 110, 111.

4. Montgomery, *American Furniture*, nos. 202–5.

## 155 ♦ Fire screen
### Massachusetts, probably the Boston-Salem area
### 1775–1810

While not as obvious a status symbol as the "dressed" bedstead or a large looking glass, the presence of a fire screen in the parlor of an eighteenth-century New England home implied affluence. Beyond controlling the heat from a fireplace and softening the glare of light, its panel provided a prominent place to display the "tapestry" covering recommended for the form by Thomas Chippendale.[1] This might be a piece of professional embroidery or a sample of the needlework skills of a family member.

The type of "fancy work" used in creating a fire screen panel required training beyond the traditional skills of "plain sewing" (hemming, seaming, and the construction of simple garments such as aprons) and "marking" (working cross-stitch numbers,

initials, or dates on household linens) expected of every eighteenth-century woman. Fancy needlework generally was practiced by women with available leisure time and often was learned in a private embroidery school. Advertisements for private instruction appear in Boston newspapers from as early as 1719 and are more prevalent in the third quarter of the eighteenth century.[2] The canvaswork panel on this fire screen, a repeating flame design in Irish stitch, probably was worked by a member of the Bromfield family of Boston, the family in which the fire screen descended.

Supporting the needlework panel is an unusual stand distinguished by its distinctive spiral-turned pillar, which incorporates a bead line in the recess of the turning—a pattern that appears on several pieces of furniture associated with Salem, Massachusetts. It is used on the pillar of a fire screen that descended in the family of Salem merchant

Elias Hasket Derby. Two stands, one with a slightly longer shaft, have similar beaded spiral turnings.[3]

The pillar and pole of Winterthur's fire screen are turned as a unit, a departure from common practice. The raised carving on the legs is in unusually high relief, and the carved volutes extend almost one-eighth inch beyond the finished plane of the leg. The feet are finished in an unusual four-toed animal foot, which is related in design to the animal foot on a large Massachusetts tripod table (No. 144).

*NER/CGN*

---

**Construction:** The pole and pillar are turned as a unit from the same block of stock. The legs are dovetailed into the bottom of the pillar, the joints covered by a metal plate held by screws. The platforms under the animal-claw feet are carved from solid wood. The adjustable screen is attached to the pole by a plain brass guide ring at the top and a brass ring and spring bracket at the bottom. The screen, a solid board framed by an applied molding, has an eighteenth-century needlework covering on the front surface.

**Condition:** A major split in the base of the pillar where one of the legs broke out has been repaired and reinforced with four plugged screws (or nails) and a new metal plate. The eighteenth-century needlework is reapplied to a new screen board; the surrounding molding is new. A wooden collar has been added to the pole below the lower bracket to fix the screen height. A pair of modern brass candle arms has been removed.

**Dimensions:**

| | | |
|---|---|---|
| H. | 51 in. | 129.5 cm |
| W. (screen) | 18 in. | 45.7 cm |
| L. (screen) | 16½ in. | 41.9 cm |
| W. (feet) | 18 in. | 45.7 cm |

**Materials:** *Microanalysis:* Primary: mahogany. *Finish:* natural resin.

**Provenance:** The fire screen once stood in the Bromfield-Phillips house on Beacon Street in Boston and is thought to have belonged originally to Col. Henry Bromfield. It descended through Colonel Bromfield's daughter, Elizabeth (Mrs. Nathaniel Rogers), to her daughter, Elizabeth (Mrs. John Tilton Slade), and to Mrs. Slade's son, Daniel Denison Slade. It was purchased by the dealer from Mrs. Daniel Denison Slade's granddaughter.

**Accession history:** Purchased by H. F. du Pont from Harry Arons, Ansonia, Conn., 1964. Gift of H. F. du Pont, 1964.
63.1013

---

1. Christopher Gilbert, *The Life and Work of Thomas Chippendale*, 2 vols. (New York: Macmillan Co., 1978), 1:56.

2. Dow, *Arts and Crafts in New England*, pp. 273–76.

3. For the Derby fire screen, see *American Antiques from Israel Sack Collection*, 10 vols. (Washington, D.C.: Highland House, ca. 1969–), 5:1119, 1156–57. For the 2 related stands, see Rodriguez Roque, *American Furniture*, no. 162; and (longer shaft) *American Antiques from Sack Collection*, 5:1251.

# Dressing Tables and High Chests of Drawers

THE DRESSING TABLE AND HIGH CHEST OF DRAWERS are considered together in this catalogue because they were frequently purchased en suite in the eighteenth century. Few remain together today, but evidence points to the commonness of the practice. In a survey of ninety-six household inventories from Boston and vicinity dating from 1754 to 1797, thirty-three enumerate a tall chest and low table together in a chamber, or bedroom. Four households contained two sets of chamber furniture, making a total of thirty-seven suites. The list of owners includes merchants and gentlemen of means, doctors and widows, manufacturers, shopkeepers, and craftsmen. Estate valuations are better indicators than occupations, however, of the financial standing of these individuals in the community. Owners whose assets exceeded £1,000 constitute almost half the number. True to expectations, members of this group include most of the gentlemen and merchants and one of the two doctors on the list. The group is broadened by a chocolate maker, a goldsmith, and a "mariner" entrepreneur. The remaining owners, who were successful businessmen, including a tobacconist, stationer, and shipwright, left estates valued between £500 and £1,000. No estate in the survey valued below £100 contained a high chest of drawers and companion dressing table or even a suite of furniture described as "old."[1]

Terminology in inventories that identifies the tall chest and low table combination appears as two equally popular terms: "A Case of Draws & Table" or a "Chest of Draws & Table." Combined valuations range from less than £1 to about £7, depending upon the age, condition, and features of the furniture. A few suites valued at higher figures probably were almost new. The term *case of drawers* may have been the one more commonly used by craftsmen. When accounting for their losses after the great fire of Boston in 1760, cabinetmakers Benjamin Frothingham and Thomas Foot referred to their "cases of Drows" and accompanying "Tables." *Case* was also preferred in a "Particular Price of Joinnery Work" drawn up in Providence in 1756. The word "High" further identifies the larger piece of furniture, and in the following year a revised price list added a "Crown" to the tall chest. By 1792, when furnituremakers in Hartford drew up their "Table of Prices for Cabinet Work," listings for high cases of drawers had given way to those for chests-on-chests. When listed independently of a table, both *case of drawers* and *chest of drawers* may have identified a low chest with three or four drawers.[2]

Two terms, *chamber table* and *dressing table*, describe the form accompanying the high chest of drawers, and a third, *toilet table*, identifies a closely related piece of furniture; each may have had a specific or a generic meaning, depending on who used it. Of the tables associated with dressing listed in the Boston inventory survey (exclusive of bureau tables), the greatest number described further (twenty-eight) are *chamber tables*, six of them in combination with a chest/case of drawers. After the Boston fire, both Frothingham and Foot identified the low tables that accompanied their cases of drawers as chamber tables. Foot's furniture was made of black walnut. Mahogany chamber tables are listed in the 1756 and 1757 price lists for joiner's work at Providence.[3]

In a 1987 study, Benno Forman identified the seventeenth-century chamber table as a significant bedroom form. It was a lift-top storage box usually fitted with a long drawer across the bottom, the whole supported on tall legs. Although appraisers in Boston usually gave the highest valuations to the chamber tables in the documents surveyed, it is doubtful that the form referred to had a lift top by the early eighteenth century. More likely the enumerators identified a "table with draws," such as the one that accompanied the "black walnut chest draws" in the home of William Taylor, Esq., in Milton, south of Boston.[4]

Only seven entries identify dressing tables in the survey. One table made of walnut and described in 1765 as "old" accompanied a "Chest draws" in the household of Alexander Hunt, a shipwright of Boston whose estate was worth a substantial £891. Undoubtedly, other dressing tables in Boston households were called simply *tables*, indicated by the sizable number of small bedroom accessories identified as *dressing* accoutrements by appraisers, including dressing boxes and dressing glasses. The term "Dressing Draw" used in 1760 by appraisers at Boston when enumerating the household contents of William Skinner, Esq., probably provides a reasonable description of this piece of furniture. The valuation range, which is lower than that of the chamber table, supports the suggestion that the dressing table had one rather than two tiers of drawers, as illustrated in Nos. 156 and 157. The one-tier design is rare among surviving tables.[5]

The third table—the *toilet table*—is not identified as an accompaniment to the tall chest in the Boston inventories. Independent references to this piece of furniture are greater, however, than the total for the dressing tables. The general price/value appears to have been lower than that of the dressing table, suggesting that the design was a simple one, probably a tablelike frame made in inexpensive, painted wood. Further supporting evidence occurs in the papers of Isaac Senter (1753–99), a prominent physician of Newport, Rhode Island, who in 1778 married Elizabeth Arnold, daughter of a prosperous Cranston family. Among the Senter furniture bills is listed the 1783 purchase of a "mahogany dressing table" for £3.12.0, a cost comparable to that for one of the two "square mahogany dining tables" purchased the same year. Seven years later Senter paid Job Gibbs, a local joiner and handyman, 10s.6d. for a "toilet table." It was priced the same as a "cross legged table" acquired from Gibbs in 1787, inviting speculation that they were related in design. That speculation is enhanced by an item in Senter's estate inventory of 1800 for "2 Toilet Tables and C" valued together at a modest $2 (about 12s.). The mysterious "C" almost certainly refers to a cover or cloth—a decorative and protective accessory in common use with the simple toilet table and mentioned on occasion in the surveyed Boston inventories. Frequently, the cloth completely covered the toilet table, thereby concealing its simple construction.[6]

Two other pieces of chamber furniture that appear with regularity in the survey are the bureau table and the bureau. As low chests of drawers, they are larger than dressing and chamber tables, and their value in general was greater. Both served as modest storage units, but their usual function was to organize the equipment and accessories used in dressing and personal adornment. The bureau table has a central recess to accommodate the knees of a seated user; the bureau might be fitted at the top with a partitioned dressing drawer. Although both pieces of furniture were relatively new in the mid eighteenth century, the numbers recorded in the inventory survey—twenty-two bureau tables and thirty-seven bureaus itemized from the 1760s to the 1790s—indicate that they were replacing the shallow-frame table on tall legs, which had been fashionable since early in the century.[7]

The New England high chest of drawers exists in sufficient numbers today to demonstrate its enormous popularity during the second and third quarters of the eighteenth century. The storage potential is obvious, and part of its great demand was due to the lack of closets in eighteenth-century houses. The absence of a chest of drawers in the furniture market from the late 1720s until the maturation of the Georgian style in the third quarter of the century further heightened the marketability of the tall case piece on high legs.

*NGE*

[1] Survey based on Boston estate records, 1755–95, Suffolk County Probate Court, Boston (microfilm, Downs collection); Boston Fire Documents and Correspondence, vols. 1 and 2, 1760, Boston Public Library, Boston; and Confiscated Loyalist Estates, 1770s, Boston (photostats, Downs collection).

[2] Elias Delarues and William Skinner, estate records, 1756 and 1760, Suffolk County Probate Court (microfilm, Downs collection); Benjamin Frothingham and Thomas Foot, accounts of losses, 1760, Boston Fire Documents, vol. 2, pp. 29, 37; "Particular Price of Joinnery Work," Feb. 19, 1756, and "Rule and Price of Joyners Work," March 24, 1757, Rhode Island Historical Society, Providence; the Hartford price list is transcribed in Lyon, *Colonial Furniture*, pp. 267–70.

[3] Frothingham and Foot, accounts of losses; "Particular Price of Joinnery Work" and "Rule and Price of Joyners Work."

[4] Benno M. Forman, "Furniture for Dressing in Early America, 1650–1730," *Winterthur Portfolio* 22, nos. 2/3 (Summer/Autumn 1987): 149–64; William Taylor estate records, 1789, Suffolk County Probate Court (microfilm, Downs collection).

[5] Alexander Hunt and William Skinner, estate records, 1765 and 1760, Suffolk County Probate Court (microfilm, Downs collection).

[6] Isaac Senter background, bill, and inventory in Joseph K. Ott, "Recent Discoveries Among Rhode Island Cabinetmakers and Their Work," *Rhode Island History* 28, no. 1 (February 1969): 3–11, 25.

[7] Boston estate records; Boston Fire Documents; Confiscated Loyalist Estates.

## 156 ◆ Dressing table
Northeastern Massachusetts,
possibly coastal New Hampshire
or adjacent region
1730–45

This frame may have been the type that
appraisers in Boston called a dressing table,
as distinguished from the frame with two
tiers of drawers, which they may have termed
a chamber table. Although the skirt of this
shallow frame is sawed with eye-catching
William and Mary–style curves, the most
interesting feature of the table is the feet.

Hocked feet are rare in American furniture
(fig. 1). English prototypes, which are also
rare and date to the early eighteenth century,
usually are formed as fairly naturalistic hoofs. A
few of the "horsebone feet" (legs) introduced in
the Boston furniture market late in the 1720s
may have had hooflike or hocked terminals,
but the new support quickly matured into a
full-blown Queen Anne cabriole leg with a pad
foot of fairly standard profile. The feet of this
table are rare in their large size, pronounced
rear hocks, and long funnel-like pads. The
thick disks with canted sides below the pads
heighten the effect. Only two close mates have
been located—a maple flat-top high chest of
drawers and a dressing table owned early in the
twentieth century by Boston collector Dwight
Blaney. The high chest has other features in
common with the dressing table: a similar
skirt profile, legs thickened for a considerable
distance below the knees, and molding profiles
at the waist that in the lower part appear to
approximate the edges of the tabletop. Flat
arches in the Blaney table replace the ogee
profiles below the drawers of Winterthur's
table, and small hooklike knee blocks, similar
to those in the high chest, flank the tops of
the legs. Acorn drops and small, plain wing-
type brasses ornament the facade. The double-
lipped top of the Blaney table is illustrated
only in profile, so whether the edging is solid
or applied or possibly forms a tray top cannot
be determined.[1]

A search for other early furniture with
hocked feet has produced examples that
can be divided into three style groups. Each
example has a supporting disk below the foot.
One group, which has feet that are flatter than
those on this table and of a cuplike profile,
includes two high chests of drawers, a dressing
table with two tiers of drawers, a rectangular
tea table (all ascribed to Massachusetts),
and a table with drop leaves that may have
originated in New Hampshire. Another
group, one with sloping disklike feet and less
pronounced hocks, consists of five rectangular
tables with shallow frames and a high chest of
drawers. The legs of all the tables are marked
by a pronounced crease down the center, as is
seen on Winterthur's table. The tops of three
are distinctive because of their long overhang
and applied raised molding around the edges;
two of these are dressing tables. One of them
has a front skirt that appears to duplicate that
of Winterthur's in profile; two small, although
deeper, drawers are also present. The other
dressing table has a history of descent in a

family that resided in southeastern New
Hampshire. The remaining two tables, without
raised moldings, have unusual cabriole legs
with short, quirky bulges at the high knees.
They are attributed to Samuel Sewell of York,
Maine, and were part of the furnishings of a
local home. The high chest is ascribed to
Massachusetts. The third group of hocked-foot
furniture is made up entirely of chairs that
probably originated in Portsmouth, New
Hampshire. They are ascribed to a member
of the Gaines family of craftsmen. The flat
disklike feet are distinctive—the "hock" is
produced by a deep V cut at the lower back
(see No. 19, fig. 1).[2]

The general profile of this table frame—a
central round-headed arch flanked by flattened
ogee arches, which are repeated at the sides—is
one encountered throughout New England in
high chests of drawers and companion tables.
The pattern, which originated in England,
probably was first produced in America in
Boston. It was popular from the William and
Mary style through the early Queen Anne

style. The subtle variation of the profile of this table, namely the slightly skewed inside ogee of the projections supporting pendent drops (missing), is rarely encountered. Other examples include the hocked-foot dressing table with a wide overhanging top mentioned above and a three-drawer dressing table with plain pad feet once in the collection of Bertram K. Little and Nina Fletcher Little. The Little table descended in the Sheldon family of Deerfield, Massachusetts.[3]

In a departure from the standard method of construction, the front of the table is a single board with holes cut for the drawer openings, a technique later applied occasionally to card table construction for both visible and hidden drawers. The construction enhances the delicacy of the form. Another notable feature is the profile of the molded edge of the top board. Rising above the thumb-molded lip of early design is a straight-sided fillet of unusual depth. Perhaps this feature is a signature of the craftsman or the region where he worked.

From an early date, a cover or cloth concealed the dressing table or at least protected the top. The practice was common in Europe during the early seventeenth century, when a carpet was the usual covering in households of the well-to-do. A small linen cloth termed a *toilet* (also a toilette, twilet, twilight, etc.) protected the carpet and eventually gave its name to the dressing accessories placed on it and even to the table itself. In time, the carpet dropped from fashion and the linen cloth was replaced by rich toilet covers made of silk or velvet trimmed with lace or fringe. Engraved prints of the period chronicle these changes.[4]

Toilet covers used in America were much simpler. In his study of furniture for dressing in early America, Benno Forman found "Twilights," or dressing table cloths, listed in Boston inventories beginning in 1711. The term continued in use among Boston appraisers as late as the 1750s and 1760s. When not covering a piece of furniture, these cloths are itemized with the household linens and clothing. During the 1760s, terminology

**Fig. 1.** Detail, right rear leg.

such as "1 Toilet & covering" or "Cover for Toilet Table" became more common. In a survey group of ninety-six inventories drawn up between 1754 and 1797, only two identify the material of the toilet cover. Both Jonathan Snelling (d. 1755) and Andrew Oliver, Esq. (d. 1774) used oilcloths on their dressing furniture. A 1763 advertisement in a city newspaper, "Handsome Oyl-Cloths for Tables," attests to the fashionable appearance of the Snelling and Oliver tables. Cloth when treated with oil was rendered waterproof, thus oilcloths protected vulnerable surfaces from stains. Some may have been painted with designs. Winterthur's table has nail holes on the underside of the top, suggesting it may have had a fixed cover of unknown type at some point in its history.[5]

Other covers were less utilitarian than the oilcloth. Forman found a reference to a fine muslin twilight trimmed with lace in a Boston inventory of 1720. Philadelphia records identify "Chests of Drawer Cloaths Damask," probably a worsted fabric, and "Diaper"-patterned covers woven of linen or linen and cotton. A calico cloth may have been printed or plain. The opulent city residence of Gen. John Cadwalader, which was furnished extensively in mahogany, was enriched by a toilet table with a "worked

cover" and "yellow silk to go round" it (see No. 89, fig. 1).[6]

NGE

---

**Inscriptions or marks:** *On inside of both drawers:* "M R Shaw" in pencil. *On outside of one drawer:* "Williams boots $11" and several mathematical calculations. *On underside of top:* "Joseph J s[?]/ For/ F[?]/ Joseph J[ose]ph" in white chalk, partially legible.

**Construction:** The single board top, with a deeply stepped ogee molding and a substantial overhang on all four sides, is pinned to the frame. The entire case, including the front, is tenoned to the leg posts and double-pinned (except for the left front, which has only a single pin). The one-piece case front has cutouts for two small drawers. An applied bead is nailed to the lower edge of the front and side case skirts. The drawer runners are rabbeted and nailed to the case front and tenoned to the backboard. The drawer sides are secured to the front with a single large dovetail; the back corners are also joined with dovetails. The tops of the drawer sides are cut with a heavy outside bead (missing from one drawer top); the tops of the drawer backs are flat. The drawer bottoms are set into very deep grooves on the front and sides; one is unusually thick and has heavy chamfers, the other is thin and relatively flat. A narrow thumbmolding finishes the front edges of the drawers; only the side lips butt against the case. The hooflike feet have prominent hocks at the inside corners from which extend single ridges up the backs of the legs. The leg fronts are creased from the knees to the upper ankles. The feet are supported on thick disks with canted sides.

**Condition:** A series of nails and nail holes on the underside of the top suggests that it once had a cover. The lower edge of one of the drawer fronts has broken off, and all the drawer sides have been reinforced with nails. All the knee blocks and the turned pendent drops at the skirt front are missing. The exterior surface has been painted black.

**Dimensions:**

| | | |
|---|---:|---|
| H. | 25 3/8 in. | 64.4 cm |
| W. (top) | 30 in. | 76.2 cm |
| W. (case) | 24 3/8 in. | 61.9 cm |
| W. (feet) | 25 1/2 in. | 64.8 cm |
| D. (top) | 18 in. | 45.7 cm |
| D. (case) | 15 in. | 38.1 cm |
| D. (feet) | 16 1/8 in. | 40.9 cm |

**Materials:** *Microanalysis:* Primary: soft maple group. Secondary: white pine group (drawer linings). *Finish:* black paint, possibly covered with a yellowed varnish.

**Accession history:** Bequest of H. F. du Pont, 1969. 69.766

1. English prototypes with hoof feet are in Macquoid and Edwards, *Dictionary*, 1:253, fig. 82, 3:225, fig. 6. The term "horsebone feet" appears in the account book of Samuel Grant, a Boston upholsterer, in 1730 and is thought to be an early reference to the introduction of the cabriole leg; see Forman, *American Seating Furniture*, pp. 286–87. For the high chest of drawers, see Northeast Auctions, "New Hampshire Auction" (March 2–3, 1996), lot 763. For the Blaney table, see Lockwood, *Colonial Furniture*, fig. 88. The missing knee blocks in Winterthur's table may have duplicated those in the high chest and the Blaney table. In the Colonial Williamsburg Foundation is a single-drawer dressing table with a double-lipped top similar to that in the Blaney table; the edge is an applied molding that forms a tray surface; see Greenlaw, *New England Furniture*, no. 128. A high chest of drawers with a flat top ascribed to Salem, Mass., and of about contemporary date with Winterthur's dressing table has tall funnel feet without hocks; see *American Antiques from Israel Sack Collection*, 10 vols. (Washington, D.C.: Highland House, 1969–), 3:698.

2. Examples in group 1 are: Bernard and S. Dean Levy, Inc., *Catalogue IV* (New York: By the company, 1984), p. 25 (high chest); *American Antiques from Israel Sack Collection*, 1:167 (high chest); 6:1644 (dressing table); Bernard and S. Dean Levy, Inc., *An American Tea Party: Colonial Tea and Breakfast Tables, 1715–1783* (New York: By the company, 1988), p. 13 (tea table); *The Decorative Arts of New Hampshire: A Sesquicentennial Exhibition* (Concord: New Hampshire Historical Society, 1973), fig. 56 (table). For a painted 4-drawer dressing table of Massachusetts origin with especially large hocked pad feet, see Joseph Sprain advertisement, *Antiques* 108, no. 4 (October 1975): 579. Examples in group 2 are: Parke-Bernet Galleries, "Important Eighteenth-Century American Furniture and Decorations: Property of Mrs. Francis P. Garvan" (October 31, 1970), lot 157 (dressing table); Greenlaw, *New England Furniture*, no. 128 (dressing table); Fales, *Furniture of Historic Deerfield*, fig. 305 (tea table); Myrna Kaye, "Mix and Match: A Study of the Furniture in One Household," in *New England Furniture*, pp. 228, 240.

3. Parke-Bernet Galleries, "Important Eighteenth-Century American Furniture," lot 157; Sotheby's, "Important Americana: The Bertram K. Little and Nina Fletcher Little Collection, Part 1" (January 29, 1994), lot 349.

4. Macquoid and Edwards, *Dictionary*, 3:226, 343–44; Benno M. Forman, "Furniture for Dressing in Early America, 1650–1730," *Winterthur Portfolio* 22, nos. 2/3 (Summer/Autumn 1987): 157–58; Thornton, *Seventeenth-Century Interior Decoration*, pp. 243, 302–3, pls. 131, 289, 290, 309.

5. Forman, "Furniture for Dressing," p. 158. References to twilights, toilet covers, and oilcloths in estate records of Jonathan Snelling (1755), John Legg (1762), William Henry Crozier (1766), Thomas Green (1766), Henderson Inches (1780), and Andrew Oliver (1774), Suffolk County Probate Court, Boston (microfilm, Downs collection). Advertisement for oilcloths in *Boston Gazette*, March 21, 1763, as quoted in Dow, *Arts and Crafts in New England*, p. 121.

6. Forman, "Furniture for Dressing," p. 158; Hornor, *Blue Book*, p. 113; Nicholas B. Wainwright, *Colonial Grandeur in Philadelphia: The House and Furniture of General John Cadwalader* (Philadelphia: Historical Society of Pennsylvania, 1964), pp. 72–73.

## 157 ◆ Dressing table
### Northeastern Massachusetts
### 1730–50

Several features of this rare, shallow-frame Queen Anne table recall the William and Mary style. The low, rounded arch centered in the front skirt was a common profile in high chests of drawers and dressing tables made in England during the seventeenth century, and the feature appeared in American production at the start of the eighteenth century. The broad, flat arches flanking the center section are more commonly associated with the Queen Anne style, but the astragal pendants between the three arches appear to simulate projections with turned drops, which became popular with the William and Mary style. Small astragals such as these usually are reserved for the shallow skirts of cabriole-leg tea, side, and center tables and the straight bottom rails of cases of drawers and desks (see Nos. 118, 126, 204).[1]

The single long drawer of this table is another holdover from earlier styles. Long drawers appeared in English dressing tables of early baroque design with bold strapwork legs before they became part of the better-known William and Mary form supported on trumpet-turned legs. Equally, if not more, popular for shallow William and Mary frames were three small drawers in a single tier. The long drawer appears only occasionally in single-tier tables of the Queen Anne period.[2]

Also uncommon in Queen Anne dressing tables is inlaid decoration. Here, bands of stringing in a light-dark-light pattern border the tabletop and drawer face. In William and Mary tables, banding was used with veneer rather than solid wood surfaces.

The rituals of dressing the hair and body and applying "unguents and cosmetics" to the face were entrenched in Europe from an early date and gave rise to a multitude of accessories to accomplish these tasks (see No. 89, fig. 1). Written references to the accoutrements of dressing appear in British records by the sixteenth century. Using probate inventories, Benno Forman documented the use of dressing equipment in seventeenth-century America. The chamber table, dressing table, and dressing box, usually fitted with a looking glass inside the lid, are all mentioned. By the early eighteenth century, two more pieces of dressing furniture were added to the group. One was a freestanding swinging glass for the tabletop, and the other was the toilet table, also termed a "toilette" or, phonetically, a "twilight."[3]

By the mid eighteenth century, the tall dressing box known from the previous century was passing out of fashion. A survey of ninety-six Boston probate and related records dating between 1750 and 1800 yields few references. In 1755 a dressing box valued at 12s. was located in the hall chamber of Jonathan Snelling's home. The "mariner" entrepreneur's box probably stood on the "Table" that accompanied the high "Case Drawers" because that was the only furniture in the room aside from fourteen caned chairs and a case with bottles. Snelling almost certainly occupied this bedroom, as it contained his clothing. Edward Brattle Oliver, a gentleman, owned two dressing boxes in 1760 when the great fire of Boston destroyed much of his property. One box was in the north chamber, the principal bedroom, where it stood on either a "Mohogeny Baurow Table" or a "Large Stand Table Mohogeny." The older black walnut box in the kitchen chamber (the room over the kitchen) probably stood on the "Chamber Table" that accompanied the high "Case of Draws Black Walnutt." Conveniently, a looking glass hung on the wall above the table.[4]

Taking the place of the dressing box by the 1750s was the dressing glass. Sometimes this was simply a small framed mirror mounted in an easel-like stand. Of greater convenience was the looking glass supported on a low box with small drawers (see Nos. 215, 216). It is not always possible to distinguish between the two in records, however.

A dozen references to dressing glasses emerge from the documents in the survey. This piece of equipment stood most commonly on a table, described variously as a toilet, dressing, or chamber table, which was frequently made en suite with a high chest of drawers. Both walnut and japanned furniture is identified. In three households, the dressing glass stood on a mahogany bureau or bureau table; one glass was identified as mahogany. The toilet table supporting the dressing glass in the home of Boston merchant John Merchant was furnished with a "covering," although the material is not identified. Undoubtedly, dressing cloths were included in the "furniture" of the two toilet tables in Oliver Smith's south front chamber. This gentleman of means placed his dressing

glass on one of them. The dressing glass and "appurces" (appurtenances) listed following the bureau table in the middle chamber of Benjamin Pratt, Esq.'s, home appears from its valuation at £1 to have constituted the complete set of equipment.[5]

Dressing boxes, dressing glasses mounted on low boxes, and the tables fitted with drawers that supported them served as receptacles for the equipment of grooming and dress. Small compartments might hold salves, cosmetics (including rouges and powders), essences, oils, patches, and "pomatums" (pomades— perfumed ointments, especially for the hair). Boxes and drawers also contained soap, scissors, jewelry, miscellaneous trinkets, and shaving equipment. A "Shaving box Compleate" stood on the mahogany bureau in Dr. Joseph Gardner's north chamber before his death in 1788. Dressing sets, comprising combs, brushes, pincushions, and assorted boxes, sometimes en suite with a dressing glass, first came into fashion in England during the Restoration (1660–85). These were laid out for display on the cloth covering the table and were fabricated of such materials as silver, japan, tortoiseshell, wood, and base metal (see No. 89, fig. 1). Writing equipment might also be included in the "furniture" or "appurtenances" of the dressing table.[6]

*NGE*

---

**Inscriptions or marks:** *On bottom of drawer and underside of one batten:* "F Lo__" in white chalk.

**Construction:** The top, made of two equal boards and finished with a thumbmolding on all four sides, overhangs the case; the overhang is wider on the sides than on the front or back. The top is pinned to the leg posts and along the sides and is reinforced by small glueblocks. The case sides and back are tenoned and double-pinned to the posts, the lower pin at the knees. The front skirt rail is tenoned to the posts and held by single pins. Two battens supporting the drawer are notched into the front rail and tenoned to the backboard. Drawer stops are glued to the backboard, and runners are glued and nailed to the case sides. The knee brackets are glued over the skirt, front and sides. The drawer is dovetailed, and the tops of the sides and back are flat. The bottom board, the grain running from front to back, is let into a rabbet in the front and nailed flush at the sides and back. A narrow thumbmolding finishes the front edges of the drawer. A narrow three-string inlay (light, dark, light) forms a rectangular panel near the edges of the case top and on the face of the drawer.

**Condition:** The knee brackets are replaced, and sections of the string inlay are repaired. These repairs were made in 1945 when the dressing

table was acquired, as indicated in a letter from H. F. du Pont to Winsor White, December 14, 1945 (Winterthur Archives). Several glueblocks are missing from the inside back, and the two center blocks on the left side have been replaced. The top has been better secured with some additional pins near the side edges. The brass hardware is original.

**Dimensions:**

| | | |
|---|---|---|
| H. | 29 in. | 73.7 cm |
| W. (top) | 33 in. | 83.8 cm |
| W. (case) | 28 7/8 in. | 73.3 cm |
| W. (feet) | 30 3/4 in. | 78.1 cm |
| D. (top) | 20 1/2 in. | 52.1 cm |
| D. (case) | 17 3/4 in. | 45.1 cm |
| D. (feet) | 18 3/4 in. | 47.6 cm |

**Materials:** *Microanalysis:* Primary: American black walnut. Secondary: birch (rear rail); white pine group (drawer lining). *Finish:* muddy, dark reddish brown color in resin.

**Exhibitions:** "The Past Perceived," Washington Antiques Show, Washington, D.C., January 1986.

**Publications:** Downs, *American Furniture*, fig. 369.

**Provenance:** This dressing table appears to have emerged from a private family in the area of Boston. It passed through the hands of several local dealers before being purchased by H. F. du Pont.

**Accession history:** Purchased by H. F. du Pont from Hyman Grossman, Boston, 1945. Bequest of H. F. du Pont, 1969.
58.2225

---

1. For furniture with low, rounded arches, see Kirk, *American Furniture*, figs. 539, 540, 547, 553, 1460, 1463, 1466; Ward, *American Case Furniture*, cats. 93, 126, 127. For furniture with astragal drops, see Rollins, *Treasures of State*, cat. nos. 13, 99; Fales, *Furniture of Historic Deerfield*, fig. 465.

2. Kirk, *American Furniture*, figs. 1454, 1455, 1457–61, 1463–67, 1476, 1478.

3. Benno M. Forman, "Furniture for Dressing in Early America, 1650–1730," *Winterthur Portfolio* 22, nos. 2/3 (Summer/Autumn 1987): 149–64; Macquoid and Edwards, *Dictionary*, 3:224, 226, 343–44.

4. Jonathan Snelling estate records, 1755, Suffolk County Probate Court, Boston (microfilm, Downs collection); claim of Edward Brattle Oliver, Boston Fire Documents and Correspondence, vol. 2, 1760, Boston Public Library, Boston.

5. References to dressing glasses are in the estate records of Dr. Hugh Kenedy (1760), Benjamin Pratt, Esq. (1763), Nathaniel Rogers (1770), Newman Greenough (1781), Benjamin Pemberton, Esq. (1782), John Williams, Esq. (1782), Isaac Smith, Esq. (1787), John Merchant (1787), Zackariah Brigden (1787), Stephen Greenleaf, Esq. (1795), Thomas Russell (1796), and Oliver Smith (1797), Suffolk County Probate Court (microfilm, Downs collection).

6. Forman, "Furniture for Dressing," pp. 157, 163; Macquoid and Edwards, *Dictionary*, 3:224, 226, 343–44; Joseph Gardner estate records, 1788, Suffolk County Probate Court (microfilm, Downs collection).

## 158 ◆ Dressing table

Northeastern Massachusetts,
possibly Salem
1730–50

The profiles of the front and side skirts of this table duplicate those of No. 156. Beyond the limited storage of that table, however, this form offers a full complement of drawers; the alteration in case depth is balanced by shorter legs. The skirt profiles are those first encountered in English William and Mary–style high and low cases augmented by veneered surfaces, double- or single-bead moldings around the drawers, and trumpet-type turned legs.[1]

High and low cases with beaded drawers were introduced in Boston perhaps as early as the 1690s, when John Brocas emigrated from England and settled in the city. Handsome figured walnut and other wood veneers appear to have ornamented the facades of the most costly examples. From Boston, specimens of the new high chest and dressing table forms and knowledge of their construction were disseminated to an extensive regional market where enterprising local craftsmen emulated the urban style.[2]

Sometime during the early 1730s, the William and Mary high chest and dressing table acquired cabriole legs and pad feet in the Queen Anne style, and craftsmen added to many examples a second tier of drawers above the three that formed the lower row. As illustrated, the beaded moldings around the drawer openings at first remained, along with the figured veneers. In this table, veneer covers the case and drawer fronts and the tabletop. Further enriching the facade are wide bands of herringbone veneer bordering the drawers. Inside the applied, thumb-molded edge of the top, the flat surface exhibits several rich embellishments (fig. 1). A wide outer border of cross-banded veneer surrounds a narrow herringbone band, which in turn encloses a large central panel divided into four sections. The four flitches, or strips, of veneer

are book matched in pairs and balanced lengthwise in symmetry. Two solid walnut boards form each case side. Curiously, the joint in the left panel is formed on the diagonal. In another material-saving measure, the cabinetmaker pieced the stock for the left front leg at the knee.

Variation is characteristic of the skirt profile in early Queen Anne veneered and beaded dressing tables and companion high chests. A round central arch flanked by smaller ogee arches beneath the side drawers, as in this example, was a popular choice. Equally common was the round arch flanked by flat arches. A slight modification of the round arch introduced a cusped figure similar to two lobes of a melon. The usual accompaniment at the side front was a flat arch, although a few ogee-arch examples and a triple-cusped-arch table are known. Cases with a central ogee arch or a flat arch cut high into the skirt are considerably less common, particularly the flat-arch cases. Examples of later date are sawed with three flat arches, all at the same level.[3]

During the 1730s, cases framed with lipped drawers supplanted those with flush drawers and beaded surrounds. Some examples retained

veneered surfaces with banded drawers and tops, but plainer, solid surfaces were coming into vogue. Skirt profiles are divided between high-cut and low central arches.[4]

The two-tiered five-drawer arrangement of this example is the most common one among veneered and beaded Queen Anne dressing tables. When cabriole legs were introduced to the dressing case, the one-tier three-drawer arrangement was on the wane. Rising in popularity, however, was a two-tier plan with four drawers, the upper level comprised of one long drawer.[5]

Although the engraved brass hardware of this table dates from the period of the case, it is not original to this piece of furniture. Small brasses embellished with engraved or stamped decoration were common to the early Queen Anne high chest and matching dressing table, however. In a survey group of sixteen cases said to retain original hardware, only one has plain brasses. Over the years, hardware on early furniture has fallen victim to abuse, damage, and loss—thus it is remarkable that so many cases reportedly have their original fittings. Another embellishment that has perished over time is the pair of drops on the skirt front. These decorations, which socket into the base, apparently began to disappear or sustain damage at an early date. Solomon Fussell, a chairmaker and turner in Philadelphia, recorded an order from a customer in 1741/44: "To an ornament: Ball for a Dressing Table." The charge was 4d.[6]

The cushioned pad feet of this dressing table are distinctive and bear a decided relationship to those on several groups of chairs originating in northeastern Massachusetts. A contemporary group of chairs has solid splats in the Queen Anne style (see No. 7); slightly later cushioned-foot seating is part of a large double-loop, or owl's-eye, splat group (see No. 30). A tea table with closely related feet has a history in the Gideon White (1717–79) family of Plymouth County. Another piece of furniture with similar feet—a high chest of drawers retaining its original japanned surfaces (see No. 159)—is associated with Boston because of the finish. Furniture ascribed to New Hampshire sometimes has cushioned feet supported on disks, but the several identified foot types are distinctly different. Most of the veneered Massachusetts cases with drawers supported on cushioned feet have front skirts sawed with a high, round arch at the center. Even the Gideon White table is sawed all around the skirt with a series of negative and positive round arches.[7]

Several veneered dressing tables with the standard cup-shape pad foot found in eastern Massachusetts are accompanied by family histories. A table sawed in a cusped arch at the center front is associated with the Shaw family of Boston. Tables with ogee-centered skirts descended in the family of Maj. Gen. Benjamin Lincoln of Hingham and the Dawes family of Cambridge. A dressing table with a distinctive flat-arch skirt accompanied by a matching high chest is identified by its chalk inscription as having belonged to the Reverend Ebenezer Gay of Salem. That table is also distinguished by a veneered top of the

**Fig. 1.** Detail, top.

pattern in Winterthur's table, complete with cross and herringbone bands and book-matched flitches forming a large central panel.[8]

*NGE*

**Inscriptions or marks:** *On outside backs of all drawers:* shop mark and one-digit number in white chalk. *Lower left drawer:* calculations in pencil and red crayon on outside left side. *Lower right drawer on outside back:* "Perley" in pencil.

**Construction:** The veneered rectangular top with applied, mitered quarter-round moldings on all four sides is pinned to the top of the leg posts. The veneer consists of a large central panel of crotch wood in four sections forming mirror and inverted mirror patterns. The panel is bordered by narrow chevron and wide perpendicular bands, both mitered at the corners. The case front is veneered, and the drawer fronts are banded in a simpler version of the top. The drawer openings are framed by double-arch moldings, and the skirt edge is finished with an applied bead secured by rosehead nails (central arch) and sprigs. The two-board case sides (the left one butted on the diagonal) are also tenoned and pinned to the leg posts. The lower edges have applied beading. The backboard, cut with four tenons, is double-pinned to the rear posts. The horizontal blade between the upper and lower tiers of drawers is slotted into the leg posts. The vertical divider between the top drawers is slotted into the blade and tenoned to the backboard. Runners for the upper tier of drawers are tenoned at the back and half-lapped and nailed to the blade at the front; the runners for the lower tier of drawers are tenoned to the back and bevel-slotted and nailed at the front. Drawer stops are glued to the case back. The drawers are dovetailed, front and back, and the upper edges of the sides and back are roughly rounded. The grain of the bottom boards runs from

front to back; the boards are rabbeted at the front and nailed flush on all sides. The legs are one piece with the corner posts; the rear legs extend beyond the back of the case. The knee brackets are glued over the skirt, front and sides.

**Condition:** The stock for the left front leg was pieced originally at the knee front. The side panels have been disassembled, reglued, and repinned; a narrow strip has been added to the top of each panel to account for shrinkage. There is a wood loss at the front in the butt joint of the right panel. The left rear leg post is repaired with a replacement block at the top. The backboard, which appears to be original, has been extended at the top with two strips of wood, side by side, that appear to have been reworked or replaced. Scribe marks are visible on the inside surface along with two unused mortise holes, which may represent an original mistake by the cabinetmaker. The center left runner in the lower tier of drawers has been replaced. The left foot is cracked on the top surface of the pad foot. The veneer has been patched and repaired. A large replacement piece is centered behind the hardware on the upper left drawer. The pendent drops, small tablets, and supporting glueblocks on the back are replaced. The hardware, which is old, is replaced.

**Dimensions:**

| | | |
|---|---|---|
| H. | 30¹/₂ in. | 77.4 cm |
| W. (top) | 33⁷/₈ in. | 86.0 cm |
| W. (case) | 29⁵/₈ in. | 75.2 cm |
| W. (feet) | 31¹/₂ in. | 80.0 cm |
| D. (top) | 20³/₈ in. | 51.8 cm |
| D. (case) | 17³/₄ in. | 45.1 cm |
| D. (feet) | 19¹/₄ in. | 48.9 cm |

**Materials:** *Microanalysis:* Primary: American black walnut and walnut veneer. Secondary: white pine group (subtop, backboard, drawer linings). *Finish:* variegated light to dark reddish brown color in resin.

1. English prototypes are in Kirk, *American Furniture*, figs. 552, 1464, 1465; Macquoid and Edwards, *Dictionary*, 3:225, fig. 2.

2. Examples are in Gerald W. R. Ward, ed., *American Furniture with Related Decorative Arts, 1660–1830: The Milwaukee Art Museum and the Layton Art Collection* (New York: Hudson Hills Press, 1991), cat. 26; Ward, *American Case Furniture*, cats. 94–96; *American Antiques from Israel Sack Collection*, 10 vols. (Washington, D.C.: Highland House, 1969–), 2:461, no. 1139, 5:1265, 7:1992; Bernard and S. Dean Levy, Inc., *Vanity and Elegance* (New York: By the company, 1992), pp. 8–10; Jobe and Kaye, *New England Furniture*, no. 29.

3. Examples are in Kenneth E. Tuttle advertisement, *Antiques* 142, no. 1 (July 1992): 14 (round/flat arches); G. K. S. Bush advertisement, *Antiques* 128, no. 6 (December 1985): 1071 (cusped/flat arches); Robert W. Skinner advertisement, *Antiques* 138, no. 4 (October 1990): 636 (cusped/ogee arches); Rodriguez Roque, *American Furniture*, no. 14 (cusped arches); Greenlaw, *New England Furniture*, no. 145 (ogee arch); Jobe and Kaye, *New England Furniture*, no. 35 (flat arch); Leigh Keno advertisement, *Antiques* 143, no. 4 (April 1993): 501 (low flat arches).

4. Examples are in Israel Sack advertisement, *Antiques* 135, no. 5 (May 1989): inside front cover; C. C. Deininger Gallery advertisement, *Antiques* 94, no. 3 (September 1968): 287.

5. A 4-drawer example is in Cinnamon Hill advertisement, *Antiques* 134, no. 6 (December 1988): 1234.

6. Cases with engraved brasses are in Tuttle advertisement; *American Antiques from Sack Collection*, 7:1944–45. Solomon Fussell account book, 1738–48, Stephen Collins Papers, Library of Congress, Washington, D.C. (microfilm, Downs collection).

7. Gideon White tea table in Jonathan Fairbanks, "A Decade of Collecting American Decorative Arts and Sculpture at the Museum of Fine Arts, Boston," *Antiques* 120, no. 3 (September 1981): 596. New Hampshire cushioned feet include examples with flat pads, creased pads, and pads supported on diminutive disks, as in Jobe, *Portsmouth Furniture*, pp. 244, 47, 134, 136.

8. On Shaw family table, see Margaret J. Moody, *American Decorative Arts at Dartmouth* (Hanover, N.H.: Dartmouth College Museum and Galleries, 1981), p. 1; for Lincoln family table, see Israel Sack advertisement, *Antiques* 102, no. 6 (December 1972): inside front cover; for Dawes family table, see Peter H. Eaton advertisement, *Antiques* 123, no. 5 (May 1983): 961; for Gay family table, see *American Antiques from Sack Collection*, 7:1944–45.

## 159 ◆ High chest of drawers
### Boston, Massachusetts
### 1730–50

The cushioned feet of this chest relate to the supports in No. 158, a dressing table. Other features compare with those in a small group of flat-top japanned high chests of drawers originating in the Boston area. The projecting base molding was introduced in the William and Mary period and appears on a number of trumpet-leg chests, some with japanned surfaces. One of the decorated examples was painted and signed by William Randle (also Randall), who worked as a japanner in Boston from 1714 to 1735. The molding also is duplicated in a Queen Anne chest offered for sale in 1954 that shares similar front and side skirt profiles with this chest. A third cabriole-leg chest with the same waist molding is of slightly later date. The drawers are lipped rather than flush in a beaded surround, and the arches of the front skirt are of equal height. Printed in black ink on a drawer in that case is the name "Brocas," which identifies the Boston cabinetmaker as either John Brocas, Sr. (d. 1740), or Jr. (d. 1751). The painted initials "RD" under the top may be those of Boston japanner Robert Davis.[1]

The complex cornice of this chest is duplicated in a chest at the Museum of Fine Arts, Boston. Painted reserves accent the deeply coved bases of both cornices, which are actually drawers, although the chests were not decorated by the same hand. The cornices in other flat-top japanned chests lack the center stage seen on these two chests, which consists of a shallow, almost horizontal, ogee and a deep, vertical fillet. Above this profile the top of the cornice projects in another ogee finished with a wafer-thin fillet.[2]

Of greater importance than the structural features of this chest, however, is the japanned surface finish, which at the time the chest was constructed had been a fashionable option in England for three-quarters of a century. Japanwork is a greatly simplified imitation of oriental lacquerwork, an exotic product known in select European circles from before the start of the seventeenth century, when both the English East India Company (chartered 1600) and the Dutch East India Company (chartered 1602) embarked upon their enormously profitable commercial intercourse with the Far East. Even so, the English and Dutch were relative latecomers to this lucrative business; the Portuguese had established an Eastern presence decades earlier.[3]

Both genuine lacquerware and European imitations appeared in English households in modest numbers during the early seventeenth century. By 1614 Lord Northampton had furnished his London residence with several items of "China worke," including a work table and a field bedstead. The Countess of Arundel apparently owned articles of genuine lacquer. An inventory of Tart Hall made in 1644 lists "Indian" chests, looking glasses, a cabinet, and a table. There was little distinction among Japan, China, and India or their goods in the minds of Europeans at this date since few had traveled to the Orient and printed descriptions were rare. Better known among Far Eastern commodities were spices, textiles, and porcelain. But that was soon to change.[4]

On June 9, 1662, following the marriage of Charles II and Catherine of Braganza and only two years after the restoration of the monarchy, John Evelyn, the wealthy diarist and intimate of court circles, wrote: "The Queen brought over with her from Portugal such Indian cabinets as had never before been seen here." This began the frenzy to own similar cabinets or copies.[5]

Ship size and the distance to the Far East prevented the supply of decorated lacquerware cabinets from meeting the demand. Enterprising craftsmen and patrons circumvented the problem in part by cutting panels from other imported lacquered articles to create fashionable furniture and accessories. Folding screens were an especially popular commodity used for this purpose, and in a number of instances they became the wainscot of rooms. One observer commented on the practice of the joiners, who "never consider the situation of their figures; so that . . . you may observe the finest hodgepodg and medly of Men and Trees turned topsie turvie." It was the development of japanwork in imitation of the costly lacquer, however, that created a boon for the European craftsman and popularized the surface finish. In the conversion, polished surfaces created

Sandelands owned two looking glasses in japanned frames at his death in 1708. The "Japan'd Cabinet" that stood on a "black painted Table" in the Edward Shippen house three years later may have also been made in England.[7]

Japanning, as practiced in Boston and other American centers, was a simpler process than that followed in England. The use of fine-grained maple rather than porous oak for cases eliminated the need for gessoed surfaces. Vermilion paint formed the base in japanned finishes that simulated tortoiseshell, as in this example. Over this surface, the japanner streaked a coat of lampblack in resin to complete the ground pattern. Chinoiserie decoration was executed both as flat and raised ornament on the case surface. The raised figures were built up with gesso, then gilded and detailed with fine black lines. The finished product was then covered with several coats of varnish.[8]

A japanned chest was the product of two sets of craftsmen—the cabinetmaker, who framed the case, and the japanner, who decorated it. Rarely is it possible to identify either artisan, although the names of many Boston cabinetmakers and japanners are known. In this instance, the chalk inscription "Nat____" on a drawer in the upper case offers one clue; several cabinetmakers with the given name of Nathaniel worked in the city during the 1730s and 1740s. The most plausible candidate is Nathaniel Holmes (w. 1725–40), who paid William Randle to japan a high chest and dressing table in 1734. Another possibility is Nathaniel Rogers, a joiner and cabinetmaker working in Boston between 1720 and 1749. The poor condition of the painted surfaces of this chest and the general anonymity of japanwork on most cases makes identification of the decorator impossible, although daisylike figures on the side panels of the lower case may relate to decoration of the same type on the side panels of a high chest of drawers in the New Haven Colony Historical Society.[9]

*NGE with NER*

---

**Inscriptions or marks:** *On left side of bottom drawer in upper case:* "Nat____" *in white chalk. On outside back of second drawer from bottom in upper case: a number. Heavy scribe marks on the bottom of the upper case:* "⊞⊞ I."

in the East from dozens of layers of hard, clear, colored lacquer (*Rhus vernicifera*) were replaced by color in varnish made from gum-lac or seed-lac and usually applied over a ground of whiting and size to conceal the pores in the wood. In 1688 in Oxford, John Stalker and George Parker published the first popular treatise on japanning. The text is directed principally to the amateur, and the illustrations, or patterns, depict oriental life and motifs from a European viewpoint.[6]

Knowledge of japanning appears to have been transferred to the colonies from Britain in several ways: through immigrant craftsmen, through furniture imported by merchants and private individuals, and through circulation in the craft community of publications containing practical information and designs. Japanners are known to have worked as early as 1712 in Boston, which, with New York, became the principal center for this work in America. In April 1716 the *Boston News-Letter* carried William Gent's advertisement for "a Parcel of very fine Clocks" imported from London, some "in Japan Cases." Evidence of imported goods dates even earlier in Philadelphia, where James

**Construction:** (Upper case) The top and bottom boards are dovetailed to the case sides. The mitered cornice molding is formed in three parts, from top to bottom: three thicknesses of boards at the top, a long cavetto in the middle, and a double bead at the bottom. At the case front, the cavetto molding is attached to the face of a wide, shallow drawer. The molding forms 2 1/2" returns at the drawer sides, and the side panels of the case are cut away to accommodate this structure. The other moldings are applied to the case top with nails. The interior of the case top is stabilized with a center-front glueblock and thin battens running from front to back that are secured with rosehead nails to the case sides. Between the shallow drawer of the cornice and the two small drawers of the upper case is a full dust board attached to the case sides at shallow grooves. The drawer blades, faced with an applied double bead (nailed), are slotted into the case sides. The ends of the center blade project through the sides on a sliding half-dovetail; the other blade ends are blind. A vertical, double-beaded facing strip is nailed to the front edge of the case sides. The vertical divider between the small upper drawers has an applied double-beaded facing. The divider slots into the bottom of the dust board and the top of the upper drawer blade and is further secured from the bottom of the blade by a rosehead nail. The back of the divider has a rear facing that extends almost to the backboard. The front of the bottom board is faced with a molding that joins similar side moldings at front miters; the side moldings are applied with sprigs. Drawer runners nailed to the case sides abut the drawer blades and backboard. Small vertical glueblocks at the back of the case interior serve as drawer stops. The backboard, made of two wide, horizontal, lap-joined boards with a narrow butt-joined board above, is nailed to rabbets in the sides and top and nailed flush across the bottom to the back edge of the bottom board. The wide upper board is planed; the lower wide board retains handsaw marks on the back.

(Lower case) The back and sides of the case are tenoned to the corner posts. A shallow, projecting, mitered waist molding, inside which the upper case rests, is nailed to the upper edge of the frame. Four front-to-back boards are slotted to the waist molding at the front and nailed to the upper back of the case. The drawer blades, long and short, are slotted into the corner posts and the lower drawer dividers, respectively. The dividers, each with a long back extension tapering on the lower edge from front to back, are tenoned to the backboard; the top tenon extends through to the outside surface. The front of the upper divider is glued in place at the top and slotted to the long drawer blade at the bottom. The lower dividers are slotted to the underside of the long blade and nailed near the bottom to the inside faces of the skirt. Double-beaded moldings are applied to the drawer blades, the vertical dividers between the drawers, the inside edge of the front corner posts, and the bottom of the drawer openings just above the skirt. Each side skirt is sawed in a double-ogee arch and finished with an applied, nailed bead. The front skirt is also finished with an applied, nailed bead. The drawer runners, which are centered below the drawers, are tenoned to the backboard. They are lapped and nailed at the front

to the long drawer blade or the skirt. The back extensions of the drawer dividers serve as inside guides. Outside guides are glued to the case sides. Drawer stops are glued near the backs of the dividers. The pad feet have raised center ribs; they rest on rounded pads and raised disks. The legs and the corner posts are one piece. The knees of the rear legs extend beyond the back of the case. The skirt pendants support small tablets and drops and are faced on the back with small glueblocks. The corners of the drawers of both cases are dovetailed; the bottoms are set into a rabbet at the front and nailed flush at the sides and back. The grain of the bottoms runs from side to side in the long drawers and in the bottom tier of small drawers, and from front to back in the others. The drawer sides are ogee-molded at the upper edge in the cornice drawer and double-chamfered on the other drawers; the top edge of the back has a thin, rear chamfer. Front shims are applied to the bottoms of all drawers.

The high chest is entirely painted in a tortoiseshell pattern of black on a vermilion ground. Raised gesso ornament appears on the drawer fronts, the sides of the upper case, and the front skirt. Other ornament is painted in gold directly on the tortoiseshell ground.

**Condition:** The two top backboards of the upper case are replaced. A filler strip has been added below the cornice drawer to close a gap between the dust board and the bead. The left interior batten above the cornice drawer is missing, as are the battens covering the joint of the bottom board and sides, on which the upper case rested. Both side waist moldings on the upper case are replaced. The outside drawer backs in the upper case retain handsaw marks; the drawer backs in the lower case are planed. The bottoms of several drawers are split, and several of the drawer stops have been replaced. Some of the moldings around the drawers have been replaced, and most of the battens (and the shims) on the drawer bottoms have been replaced. The tablets above the pendent drops on the front skirt are new; the glueblocks behind the pendants may be old replacements. The present brass hardware is the third set. The japanned surface was treated in June 1951 by Susumu Hirota of Rockport, Massachusetts, and New York City. The front surface of the case has been filled and colored to provide a visual continuity. The sides of the lower case have a stable but degraded surface that appears to have less restoration than the front. The sides of the upper case are considerably deteriorated, and the ornament applied over the tortoiseshell ground is indistinct. The surface of the raised ornament is flaking, particularly at the left side, exposing the gesso ground.

**Dimensions:**

| | | |
|---|---|---|
| H. | 69 3/8 in. | 176.2 cm |
| W. (cornice) | 40 1/2 in. | 102.9 cm |
| W. (upper case) | 35 1/8 in. | 89.2 cm |
| W. (lower case) | 37 in. | 94.0 cm |
| W. (feet) | 39 in. | 99.1 cm |
| D. (cornice) | 22 1/8 in. | 56.2 cm |
| D. (upper case) | 19 1/2 in. | 49.5 cm |
| D. (lower case) | 20 1/4 in. | 51.4 cm |
| D. (feet) | 22 5/8 in. | 57.4 cm |

**Materials:** *Microanalysis:* Primary: soft maple group; ash (legs). Secondary: white pine group (backboards on both cases, top and bottom boards on upper case, top board on lower case, drawer linings, drawer runners); yellow poplar (middle backboard of upper case). *Finish:* japanned surface with a tortoiseshell ground, some raised gesso ornament, and handpainted motifs.

**Publications:** Downs, *American Furniture*, fig. 187. Jay E. Cantor, *Winterthur* (New York: Harry N. Abrams for the Henry Francis du Pont Winterthur Museum, 1985), p. 105.

**Accession history:** Purchased by H. F. du Pont from Harry Arons, Ansonia, Conn., 1950. Gift of H. F. du Pont, 1952.
52.255

1. A high chest of drawers similar in form, cornice, waist molding, and cushioned feet but with ogee arches at the sides of the front skirt and veneered rather than japanned surfaces is in the Yale University Art Gallery; see Ward, *American Case Furniture*, cat. 129. William and Mary chests with similar waist molding are in Randall, *American Furniture*, nos. 50, 51; Dean A. Fales, Jr., "Boston Japanned Furniture," in *Boston Furniture*, fig. 45; Richard H. Randall, Jr., "William Randall, Boston Japanner," *Antiques* 105, no. 5 (May 1974): 1128–29; Morrison H. Heckscher and Frances Gruber Safford, "Boston Japanned Furniture in the Metropolitan Museum of Art," *Antiques* 129, no. 5 (May 1986): 1046–47. For the Queen Anne chest with similar skirt, see Florene Maine advertisement, *Antiques* 65, no. 2 (February 1954): 103. For the Brocas chest, see John S. Walton advertisement, *Antiques* 115, no. 5 (May 1979): 830.

2. The chest with a similar cornice is in Randall, *American Furniture*, no. 52. Chests with related crests are in Maine and Walton advertisements; Alexandra W. Rollins, "Furniture in the Collection of the Dietrich American Foundation," *Antiques* 125, no. 5 (May 1984): 1105; Heckscher, *American Furniture*, cat. no. 153.

3. Macquoid and Edwards, *Dictionary*, 2:266–71; Gertrude Z. Thomas, *Richer than Spices* (New York: Alfred A. Knopf, 1965), chap. 6; Reinier Baarsen, "Japanese Lacquer and Dutch Furniture in the Seventeenth and Eighteenth Centuries," *Antiques* 141, no. 4 (April 1992): 632–41.

4. Macquoid and Edwards, *Dictionary*, 2:266–67.

5. Evelyn diary as quoted in Thomas, *Richer than Spices*, p. 76.

6. Macquoid and Edwards, *Dictionary*, 2:266–69. For quotation on joiners, see John Stalker and George Parker, *A Treatise of Japanning and Varnishing* (Oxford, 1688), as quoted in Gertrude Z. Thomas, "Lacquer: Chinese, Indian, 'Right' Japan, and American," *Antiques* 79, no. 6 (June 1961): 574.

7. Esther Stevens Brazer, "The Early Boston Japanners," *Antiques* 43, no. 5 (May 1943): 208–13; Randall, "William Randall," p. 1127; William Gent advertisement, *Boston News-Letter*, April 9–16, 1716, as quoted in Dow, *Arts and Crafts in New England*, p. 146; Hornor, *Blue Book*, p. 12.

8. John H. Hill, "The History and Technique of Japanning and the Restoration of the Pimm Highboy," *American Art Journal* 8, no. 2 (November 1976): 59–84; Dean A. Fales, Jr., *American Painted Furniture, 1660–1880* (New York: E. P. Dutton, 1972), pp. 58–69.

9. On Holmes, see Elizabeth Rhoades and Brock Jobe, "Recent Discoveries in Boston Japanned Furniture," *Antiques* 105, no. 5 (May 1974): 1088, see also pp. 1084–85 for the New Haven Colony Historical Society high chest. On Rogers, see Myrna Kaye, "Eighteenth-Century Boston Furniture Craftsmen," in *Boston Furniture*, p. 295.

## 160 • High chest of drawers

Boston, Massachusetts
1740–50
Case by John Pimm

Identifiable japanned furniture of Boston origin numbers about three dozen examples and includes high chests of drawers, dressing tables, tall case clocks, looking glasses, and a bureau table. Japanned tea tables are mentioned frequently in early records, but none have been identified. Surface condition varies from complete loss of original paint and decoration to minimally damaged or modestly restored surfaces, but because of the impact of climate on japanning, few objects have survived in near original condition. During the past several decades, this has led several museums, guided by current restoration philosophy, to undertake the consolidation and restoration of painted surfaces on selected objects in their collections to return to them a measure of their original integrity. This chest was restored in the mid 1970s.[1]

One of three japanned "Piddement Chest[s] . . . Tortoiseshell & Gold" enriched with meticulously carved shells and swagged ornament finished in gilt, this example stands alone in the use of floral swags rather than drapery and the introduction of unusual, square claw feet reminiscent of Spanish-type supports in place of rounded pads.[2]

Esther Stevens Fraser presented much of what is known about the background of this high chest in an article written in 1929. She discovered the chalk letters "Pim" written on the backs of the drawers, and her investigation revealed the connection between the inscription and Boston cabinetmaker John Pimm (fig. 1). Biographical information on Pimm is sketchy; where he was born and received his training is unknown. He was an established craftsman by 1735, the year he billed Michael Trowlett, a merchant and shipowner, for eight pieces of furniture: a

mahogany tea table, a five-foot table, two card tables, a stand table, two bedsteads, and a clotheshorse. Records show that in 1736 Pimm purchased two parcels of land in Boston—one property, which was in Fleet Street near Scarlet's Wharf in the commercial district, may have housed his business since the following year he advertised from a location

"near Scarlet's Wharfe." The cabinetmaking business appears to have flourished because he purchased additional real estate in 1747. Pimm's will, in which he calls himself a "Cabinet Maker," is dated September 30, 1773, about two months before his death, but no inventory of his estate has been discovered. The only signed example of his cabinetwork is this high chest. The identity of the japanner of the case is less certain.[3]

A black ground was common on japanned furniture in the William and Mary period, but with the introduction of the Queen Anne style, a simulated tortoiseshell surface composed of a painted vermilion ground streaked with lampblack in resin became increasingly popular. On this surface was dispersed flat and raised gold decoration. Ornamentors drew inspiration for this fantastic decoration from varied sources, including imported japanwork; design books and illustrated volumes, such as Stalker and Parker's *Treatise of Japanning and Varnishing* (1688) and Johan Nieuhoff's *Embassy from the East-India Company* (1665, 1669 in English); and in some cases their own European backgrounds. "Sundry old Draughts of Japan Work" were part of the shop equipment itemized in 1739 by appraisers of Robert Davis's estate in Boston. Imagination was also given free rein: japanners clustered or scattered their motifs across painted surfaces, although they generally produced balanced, if somewhat eclectic, compositions in which the ornaments vary in size and subject, and repetition is common.[4]

Diaperwork, the finely patterned figure on the scrollboard of this high chest, is an elegant embellishment on several japanned Queen Anne high chests, its immediate antecedent found in border ornament on William and Mary cases. Winged cherubs, although not part of the decoration of this chest, are present on the pediments and shell drawers of a larger number of tall chests. Virtually all japanned chests have floral compositions on the drawer fronts, some of them large and bold. Garden shelters abound, frequently dwarfed by large-scale animals, ranging from more common

Fig. 1. Detail, back of center bottom drawer.

dogs and lions to exotic camels and dragons. Long-legged cranes wander through many compositions, vying with robed human figures for attention. More ambitious decoration introduces hunt scenes and chariotlike carriages drawn by pairs of swans or teams of fantastic four-legged animals (see No. 159). Remnants of once-brilliant landscape or floral vignettes fill the side panels of many cases.

Furniture historians have identified a total of ten japanners who practiced their craft in Boston before 1750, including Jean Berger, a Huguenot, whose presence in the community was revealed following the discovery of his manuscript design book. Six of the drawings attest to Berger's familiarity with the flora, fauna, figures, and structures of the Far East, although the source of his inspiration remains unknown. The work of two Boston japanners—William Randle (w. 1714–35) and Robert Davis (d. 1739)—has been identified through documented examples. They appear to have shared a similarity of technique in the way they scattered ornament across the drawer fronts of high chests without much regard for unifying the design. Davis became Randle's son-in-law in 1735 and apparently took over the business about that time, when Randle became an innkeeper. Stephen Whiting, Sr. (b. 1720), probably belongs to this group as well because he likely served an apprenticeship with Davis in the late 1730s.[5]

The raised and flat chinoiserie decoration of this chest relates generally in motif and execution to that on at least seven other high chests, including one at the Baltimore Museum of Art signed by Robert Davis. An attribution to Davis for any of the unsigned chests seems unwise, however, given the surface conditions of the entire body of Boston japanwork: paint and gesso losses, old retouching, and late twentieth-century restoration. The Davis chest, in particular, has lost a substantial amount of its decoration. The recurring motifs on this group of chests are worth noting, however. Large animals appear with regularity (fig. 2); sizable birds, such as roosters, are less common. Blossoms forming clusters, sprays, or small petal-like groups spread across many surfaces; trees accompany buildings, fences, and other motifs. Long-necked birds resembling cranes are part of all the decoration and are frequently paired; small birds are always airborne. Human figures, which are present on every chest, are engaged in various activities: crossing bridges, bobbing about in small boats, traveling in sedan chairs, or lounging in garden settings. Winterthur's chest has the only carved shells in the group; three other chests have gilt shells accented by raised gesso. Diaperwork also ornaments four other chests.[6]

This chest retains its original brass hardware, chased with ornamental patterns on the front and cast with the maker's initials "I.P." on the back (fig. 3). The founder has been tentatively identified as John Pulley of London, who in 1731 gained his "freedom" to work at the trade.[7]

By tradition, the high chest belonged to "Commodore" Joshua Loring (1716–81) and his wife, Mary Curtis. Loring, born in Boston and apprenticed as a tanner, became

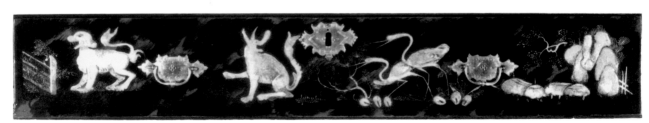

Fig. 2. Detail, front of top long drawer in upper case.

a privateer in the 1740s during the conflict between England and France. In 1747 he was captured by the French and incarcerated in the Fortress of Louisburg for several months. He again entered naval service in 1757 during the French and Indian War, when he was commissioned a captain in the British navy and commanded naval operations on lakes George and Champlain in 1759 and on Lake Ontario the following year. He participated in the seige and capture of Quebec and was severely wounded in 1760; thereafter he retired on a King's pension to his Georgian mansion in Jamaica Plain, Roxbury (now part of Boston). He held several public posts until the beginning of the Revolution, when as a Loyalist he and his wife were forced to flee to England, where they died in exile.[8]

Inventory evidence links other prosperous residents in the Boston area with ownership of japanned furniture. Before 1700 Capt. Andrew Craty possessed what may have been an imported japanned case of drawers. In the early eighteenth century, a japanned looking glass, table, and high chest furnished the home of Henry Guineau. His furniture may have shared a similar origin with Judge Peter Oliver's "London clock with Japan case." Esquires Newman Greenough, Benjamin Pemberton, and Josiah Quincy, Sr., owned japanned cases of drawers probably purchased in Boston about midcentury or earlier. Dressing tables accompanied all three high chests.[9]

*NGE with NER*

**Fig. 3.** Detail, back of brass escutcheon from lower case.

**Inscriptions or marks:** *On outside back of most drawers:* "Pim" *in white chalk. On back of top shell drawer and top long drawer: indecipherable markings. On inside back of upper case on top board:* "Top", *inverted, in pencil. On inside back of upper case, on lower board:* "Back". *Stamped on back of one of original brasses:* "I.P."

**Construction:** (Upper case) The case sides and bottom board are dovetailed. The scrollboard is tenoned to the case sides and nailed flush at the center to the vertical dividers in the top tier of drawers. The pediment backboard is rabbeted to the case sides and nailed; it is also rabbeted to the top of the backboard proper. The vertical boards of the box behind the scrollboard are nailed flush to the edges of the cutout in the backboard and abut the scrollboard at the front. The floor of the pediment box is nailed to the bottom edges of the vertical boards, to the bottom of a square cutout in the

backboard, and to a horizontal batten nailed behind the scrollboard. The pediment roof is nailed to the top edges of the scrollboard, backboard, case sides, and box. The mitered cornice molding is nailed to the scrollboard and case sides. The short returns at the top center front are nailed and supported by small corbel-like blocks. The blade below the top tier of drawers runs the full depth of the case; the other blades are approximately 7" deep. All are slotted to the case sides; the joints are covered by applied facings. The base rail is nailed to the top of the bottom board. The vertical dividers in the top row of drawers are slotted at the bottom to the drawer blade; that in the second tier is slotted to the drawer blades and nailed, top and bottom. Drawer guides above the outside edges of the small drawers in the top tier are nailed to the case sides. Inside guides extend three-quarters the depth of the case and are glued to the dust board. The drawers run on the dust board. The interior runner on the second tier is tenoned to the blade and to a batten across the back of the case, which in turn is tenoned to the case sides. Runners for the remaining drawers, except the bottom one, are nailed to the case sides; the runners for the bottom drawer are nailed to the bottom board. The backboard proper is formed of two lapped, horizontal boards nailed to rabbets in the case sides; part of the mitered waist molding is nailed to the lower edge of the upper case.

(Lower case) A second mitered waist molding is nailed to rails on the front and sides. The front rail is nailed to the top of the corner posts; the side rails are nailed to the upper edges of the case sides and the tops of the rear corner posts. Top boards, the grain running from front to back, are nailed to rabbets in the rails and rest on top of the backboard. The sides and back are tenoned to the corner posts and pinned. The deep drawer blade is joined to the corner posts with exposed, shouldered half-dovetails; the skirt is tenoned and pinned to the posts. The vertical divider between the upper drawers is joined to the top rail and drawer blade with exposed, shouldered dovetails; the dividers between the lower drawers are slotted at the top and joined to the skirt with exposed half-dovetails. Slotted behind the

upper divider is a vertical guide extending almost the full depth of the case. The outer guides are glued to the top of the drawer blade, which serves as a runner for the small upper drawers. The L-shape outer runners of the lower drawers are rabbeted and nailed to the corner posts, and guides are glued to the top surface. The interior runners are bevel-lapped in front and tenoned to the backboard; guides are glued to the top surface. The knee blocks are applied over the skirt and case sides. An applied beading is secured with rosehead nails to the lower edge of the front and sides. Both shell drawers are carved from solid 1¼" stock; the other drawer fronts are sawed from 1" stock. The corners are dovetailed. The drawer sides and back, made of ½" stock, are chamfered/rounded on one or two edges. The drawer bottoms, the grain running from front to back, are rabbeted and nailed at the front and nailed flush at the back; applied battens are glued in place. The drawer fronts are thumb molded on the edges. The side lips (and probably the others originally) abut the case facade. The original brasses with bail handles are held with cotter pins. There are functional locks on all drawers in the upper case except the top tier; there are no locks on the drawers in the lower case.

**Condition:** Portions of the japanned finish were restored in 1930–31 and the legs touched up in 1932 by Elizabeth Fritscher, a restorer and glass painter in New York City. The high chest underwent conservation in 1975–76 by John H. Hill, a private restorer. At that time, loose portions of the gesso decoration were reattached, the original decoration was protected by an isolating film, and the optical appearance of the surface was improved by replacing missing sections of raised decoration with a treated microcrystalline wax compound and by in-painting some lost sections of flat decoration. The brasses were cleaned and lacquered. When acquired, the high chest had only a center finial; this was replaced by the present, modern, gilt-antiqued urn-shape finial sometime after 1929. The thumb-molded top lip of the left side cornice and a similar section near the front on the right case side are replacements. A long crack in the right side panel of the upper case extends from top to center. The floor of the pediment box is cracked from front to back. A break in the scrollboard at the upper right neck has been repaired. The upper lip of the shell drawer in the lower case is replaced. Some drawer bottoms have cracks or separations. Sections of the skirt beading have been replaced using a mahogany bead. The knee brackets are mahogany replacements except for those at the left rear and right front. The drops are replacements.

**Dimensions:**

| | | |
|---|---|---|
| H. (with finial) | 85¼ in. | 216.5 cm |
| H. (case) | 83¾ in. | 212.7 cm |
| W. (cornice) | 42 in. | 106.7 cm |
| W. (upper case) | 36⅞ in. | 93.7 cm |
| W. (lower case) | 38⅞ in. | 98.7 cm |
| W. (feet) | 41⅛ in. | 104.4 cm |
| D. (cornice) | 24⅝ in. | 62.5 cm |
| D. (upper case) | 22 in. | 55.9 cm |
| D. (lower case) | 23¼ in. | 59.1 cm |
| D. (feet) | 25¼ in. | 65.4 cm |

**Materials:** *Microanalysis:* Primary: soft maple group (drawer fronts); American black walnut (legs); white pine group (case sides). Secondary: white pine group (pediment top, scroll board, backboards, bottom board upper case, top board lower case, drawer linings); mahogany (replacement finial, replacement applied skirt beading, replacement knee brackets). *Finish:* originally a thin coat of red lead was applied over the whole case. This was covered with black shellac worked in a tortoiseshell pattern and covered with a layer of clear or orange shellac. Raised decoration containing white lead was applied. Flat and raised gilt decoration covered by shellac provided a ground for the painted decoration. The surface was covered with several protective layers of shellac. Since restoration, several coats of synthetic varnish protect the finish.

**Publications:** Esther Stevens Fraser, "A Pedigreed Lacquered Highboy," *Antiques* 15, no. 5 (May 1929): 398–401. Downs, *American Furniture*, fig. 188. Helena Hayward, ed., *World Furniture: An Illustrated History* (New York: McGraw-Hill Book Co., 1965), facing p. 192. John H. Hill, "The History and Technique of Japanning and the Restoration of the Pimm Highboy," *American Art Journal* 8, no. 2 (November 1976): 59–84. Elizabeth Bidwell Bates

and Jonathan L. Fairbanks, *American Furniture: 1620 to the Present* (New York: Richard Marek Publishers, 1981), p. 136. Jay E. Cantor, *Winterthur* (New York: Harry N. Abrams for the Henry Francis du Pont Winterthur Museum, 1985), p. 123.

**Provenance:** The high chest probably was purchased during the 1740s following Joshua Loring's marriage to Mary Curtis of Roxbury. By tradition, the chest was given to Mrs. Loring's brother, the Reverend Phillip Curtis, when the Lorings went into exile at the beginning of the Revolution. Curtis and his wife, in turn, gave the high chest to their daughter Susanna (1752–1833) when she married Judge Daniel Cony in 1776. Cony and his wife moved from Massachusetts to Hallowell, Maine, in 1778, taking the high chest with them. It passed to their second child, Sarah Lowell Cony (1784–1867), wife of Reuel Williams of Augusta, U.S. Senator from Maine. The high chest was inherited by their youngest daughter, Ann Matilda Williams (1825–1907) and on her death passed to her niece, Helen Williams Gilman Nichols (1839–1914). It was inherited by her sons, John T. Gilman Nichols and Henry A. Nichols, the last private owners. The high chest is pictured in a late nineteenth-century photograph of the parlor of the Williams House in Augusta (photograph in Maine Historical Society, Portland).[10]

**Accession history:** Purchased by H. F. du Pont from John T. G. and Henry A. Nichols, of Boston, with Esther Stevens Fraser as agent for H. F. du Pont, 1929. Gift of H. F. du Pont, 1963. 57.1084

---

1. John H. Hill, "The History and Technique of Japanning and the Restoration of the Pimm Highboy," *American Art Journal* 8, no. 2 (November 1976): 59–84.

2. The other 2 high chests with carved shells are in Heckscher, *American Furniture*, cat. no. 155; Warren, *Bayou Bend*, no. 68.

3. Esther Stevens Fraser, "A Pedigreed Lacquered Highboy," *Antiques* 15, no. 5 (May 1929): 398–401; Downs, *American Furniture*, fig. 188. John Pimm will, 1773, Suffolk County Probate Court, Boston (microfilm, Downs collection).

4. John Stalker and George Parker, *A Treatise of Japanning and Varnishing* (Oxford, 1688); Johan Nieuhoff, *An Embassy from the East-India Company, of the United Provinces, to the Grand Tartar Cham or Emperour of China* (London, 1669), as illustrated and discussed in Leslie B. Grigsby, "Johan Nieuhoff's Embassy: An Inspiration for Relief Decoration on English Stonewares and Earthenwares," *Antiques* 143, no. 1 (January 1993): 172–83; Esther Stevens Brazer, "The Early Boston Japanners," *Antiques* 43, no. 5 (May 1943): 210.

5. Brazer, "Boston Japanners"; Sinclair H. Hitchings, "Boston's Colonial Japanners: The Documentary Record," in *Boston Furniture*, pp. 71–75; Robert A. Leath, "Jean Berger's Design Book: Huguenot Tradesmen and the Dissemination of French Baroque Style," in Luke Beckerdite, ed., *American Furniture 1994* (Milwaukee, Wis.: Chipstone Fndn., 1993), pp. 137–61; Elizabeth Rhoades and Brock Jobe, "Recent Discoveries in Boston Japanned Furniture," and Richard Randall, "William Randall, Boston Japanner," *Antiques* 105, no. 5 (May 1974): 1082–91 and 1127–31; Morrison H. Heckscher and Frances Gruber Safford, "Boston Japanned Furniture in the Metropolitan Museum of Art," *Antiques* 129, no. 5 (May 1986): 1046–61. The documented Randle high chest is in Randall, "William Randall," pp. 1128–29. The documented Davis high chest is in Rhoades and Jobe, "Recent Discoveries," p. 1089.

6. The 7 high chests with related decoration are located as follows: Baltimore Museum of Art, SPNEA, Colonial Williamsburg, Shelburne Museum (see Rhoades and Jobe, "Recent Discoveries," pp. 1083, 1086–87, 1089–91); MFA, Boston, and a private collection (see Randall, "William Randall," pp. 1130–31); and the Dietrich American Foundation (see Alexandra W. Rollins, "Furniture in the Collection of the Dietrich American Foundation," *Antiques* 125, no. 5 [May 1984]: 1105).

7. Donald L. Fennimore, *Metalwork in Early America: Copper and Its Alloys from the Winterthur Collection* (Winterthur, Del.: Henry Francis du Pont Winterthur Museum, 1996), cat. 303.

8. Fraser, "Pedigreed Highboy," p. 399; *Dictionary of American Biography*, ed. Allen Johnson and Dumas Malone (New York: Charles Scribner's Sons, 1930), s.v. "Loring, Joshua."

9. Lyon, *Colonial Furniture*, pp. 90, 94; Peter Oliver confiscated estate, ca. 1776, source unknown (photostat, Downs collection); Newman Greenough, Benjamin Pemberton, and Josiah Quincy, Sr., estate records, 1781–84, Suffolk County Probate Court, Boston (microfilm, Downs collection). The Quincy high chest is discussed and illustrated in Jobe and Kaye, *New England Furniture*, no. 36.

10. Fraser, "Pedigreed Highboy," p. 399. We are indebted to Mrs. Charles Tillinghast and Mr. H. LeBrec Micoleau for confirmation of the line of descent and to Philip Zea for bringing to their attention the photograph of the Williams House parlor.

## 161 • High chest of drawers
South Windsor, Connecticut
1736

The body of this chest, comprising two cases with drawers, is basically a William and Mary form updated by the addition of tall cabriole supports. The simple ogee cornice and the bold, stepped and projecting waist moldings are other features of the early style. No. 159 retains similar waist fittings, but its ogee cornice is part of a complex elevated crown, which with the addition of a second tier of drawers in the lower case emphasizes the tall stature of the new Queen Anne style. This chest also compares to the dressing table in No. 158, which has sawed skirt profiles of almost identical form and retains similar early eighteenth-century double-beaded moldings around the drawers. An uncommon feature of the tall chest is the paired ogee arches at the case sides separated by pendants supporting turned drops. Completing the early design are the original cotter-pin brasses.

Vying for attention with the painted decoration of the chest are the bandy legs. The crease down the front sharpens and emphasizes the exaggerated curve at the knees (fig. 1). The outsize pad feet, reduced to the basics in form, anchor the structure firmly to the ground. The articulation of legs and feet is abrupt, suggesting in the frontal view a leafless stalk rising from the earth.

Inspiration for the design of the double case and its japanwork derives from Boston, although the exact mode of transmittal to the Connecticut River valley is unknown. In the eighteenth century, inland towns located on waterways or on major roads were less isolated and insular than previously thought. Many enjoyed an active trade with the seaboard entrepots, serving both as a supplier of commodities and as an outlet for goods. Often these goods reflected styles and trends popular in the larger urban centers. This high chest is an excellent example of the transfer of an urban idea and its translation by craftsmen in a less cosmopolitan setting. The date "1736"

painted on the left side of the chest at the top indicates that the transfer occurred reasonably early. Neither the case nor the painted decoration would be mistaken for the work of urban artisans, however. The selection, random placement, and eclectic juxtaposition of the forms and figures on the simulated tortoiseshell ground exhibit much of the same naïveté as the design of the legs. The decoration is neither gessoed nor gilded; instead it is executed in cream-color paint now yellowed with old varnish.

A chest almost identical in form is in the Metropolitan Museum of Art. Of subtle variation is the cornice, which has a cove rather than an ogee beneath the thumb-molded edge. The escutcheons also vary in profile. Related decoration is scattered in the same manner over the painted surfaces. Both chests likely had companion dressing tables.

An example that duplicates Winterthur's chest in design from the waist down, although its drops are missing, is grain-painted to imitate cedar and is in the Shelburne Museum in Shelburne, Vermont. The tall chests and dressing table share an unusual construction feature—the top and side edges of the drawer fronts are slanted backward slightly to ensure a tight fit.[1]

Through the years other furniture has been discovered with decoration that relates to that of this high chest and the one at the Metropolitan Museum of Art. To date, the group includes two chests of drawers, the tops of three high chests converted to chests of drawers, and a small, table-top lidded chest with one drawer. Painted dates on the furniture range from 1735 to 1738.[2]

The decoration peculiar to this group of vernacular chests is broad-based, encompassing flora, fauna, human figures, and miscellaneous buildings. Among the animal/bird subjects are giraffes, stags, hounds, hares, foxes, squirrels, unicorns, parrots, and peacocks. The unusual crowned lion passant on the bottom long drawer of this chest may have its inspiration in heraldry. Of the more complex scenes centering on the human figure, this chest features a huntsman with bow and arrow on the center long drawer, another huntsman and his dog with a treed fox on the left side panel, and a kneeling falconer and his falcon on the right front skirt (a rare motif). A strange combination is the three-story building and giraffe at the right on the bottom long drawer. One early twentieth-century writer has likened the floral and animal subjects of these chests to figures found on Indian painted calicoes and crewel embroideries. Another claims, "The figures, singly and collectively, suggest Chinese inspiration, but have been metamorphosed into the American vernacular, with a distinctly provincial flavor."[3]

The origin of this group of chests is the Connecticut River valley from Wethersfield, Connecticut, north to Hadley and Amherst, Massachusetts, a distance of about fifty miles, with a concentration in the town(ship) of Windsor. This chest descended in the Higley family of South Windsor until its sale at auction, possibly in the 1920s. Its close mate at the Metropolitan Museum of Art was owned in Hartford in 1891 and is said by Irving W. Lyon, a prominent late nineteenth-century antiquarian, to have come from neighboring Windsor. Two of the low chests in the group were purchased in East Windsor. Most of the other objects were discovered by J. L. Cummings in central Massachusetts during the 1930s.[4]

In addition to structure, decoration, and place of origin, the secondary wood—yellow pine—links several of the chests in this Connecticut River valley group. It is used in the case shell and the secondary elements. This includes the two high chests and probably the chests examined by Cummings, although Cummings described the material as *pitch pine*, a term often used interchangeably with *yellow pine*. A 1981 study of Connecticut River valley board chests associates five chests also made of yellow pine with towns ranging from Wethersfield to Hadley, a circumstance that confirms the availability of the material and its selection by area craftsmen.[5]

*NGE with NER*

---

**Inscriptions or marks:** *On left side upper left corner:* "1736" *in creamy yellow paint. On inside of left drawer in lower case:* "JH", "L" (?), *and* "H" *in pencil, among other miscellaneous scribbling*

**Fig. 1.** Detail, right front leg.

*and numerical notations on inside and outside of drawers. On inside of some drawers:* miscellaneous looped marks in black crayon. *Gouged deeply on lower backboard of upper case:* "HH" *and two vertical strokes. On modern gummed paper label with dark blue border inside bottom drawer of upper case and center drawer of lower case:* "CONNECTICUT TERCENTENARY" *printed in dark blue ink. Inscribed on same label:* "C.T. 296B/ Mrs. Olive A. Jones/ for Jones Estate" *in black ink.*

**Construction:** (Upper case) The single-board top and bottom are dovetailed to the single-board case sides. The mitered thumb-and-ogee–molded cornice is applied flush with the top board to the case sides and facade using nails. The back has two horizontal lap-joined boards nailed to rabbets in the sides and nailed flush across the bottom to the back of the bottom board. A double half-round molded facing is applied to the front edge of the case sides. The drawer blades, which are of varying depth and slotted into the case sides, have a similar molding worked from solid wood. The vertical dividers between the small drawers, which are glued to the top board and the drawer blade, are similarly molded on the front edge. The mitered, ogee base molding, nailed to the front and sides, extends slightly below the bottom board and provides support for the upper section. Drawer runners for the long drawers and the outside top drawers are nailed to the case sides. Inner runners for the top drawers are nailed to both faces of the full-length dividers at a bottom extension behind and level with the drawer blade. Front to back battens at the interior joints of the case sides and bottom board are nailed in place. The exterior surface of the case sides and top bear visible plane marks.

(Lower case) Nailed at the front and sides and overlapping the two-board top is a projecting, mitered thumbmolding that secures the upper case. The top boards are planed, chamfered at the front and side edges, and nailed to the upper surface

of the case sides. The front rail, case sides, and horizontal backboard are tenoned and pinned to the corner posts. Double-ogee arches separated by a turned pendant on the shaped case sides are echoed on the front skirt, with the addition of a rounded arch at the center. A beading applied with rosehead nails outlines the lower edge of the skirt front and the case sides. Double half-round molding similar to that on the upper case is applied to the drawer openings on three sides. The drawer dividers, which are extensions of the skirt, are reinforced on the back with full-length vertical battens secured with wrought nails. The side drawers slide on medial runners tenoned to the backboard and notched and nailed to the front skirt. Outer guides are notched to the corner posts and nailed to the case sides. The center drawer slides on runners tenoned to the backboard and notched into the vertical battens behind the dividers. Guides are glued to the top surface. A drawer stop is nailed to the case at the center back. The legs and corner posts are one piece. The knee brackets are applied with sprigs. The drawer fronts are beveled slightly at the upper and outside edges for a tight fit. The drawer sides, rounded on top, are attached to the front and back with one or more large dovetails. The grain of the bottom board runs from side to side on the long drawers and from front to back on the small drawers. The drawer bottoms are rabbeted at the front and nailed flush at the back; some of the flush side edges have applied battens.

**Condition:** The drawer runners of the upper case and the battens nailed to the bottom board have been replaced. The left runner and guide of the lower case have been replaced. Some battens on the underside of the drawers have been replaced. A small ³⁄₄"-by-¹⁄₄" piece of wood has been let into the face of the center drawer, lower case, at the upper left of the hardware. The molding above the drawer was cut to receive a lock that was never installed. The beading that lines the skirt bottom, front, and sides has repairs, small losses, and restorations. Replaced sections include: right side, the forward ogee arch; left side, the forward ogee arch and the forward section of the rear ogee; front, the inside half of the extreme right ogee arch. The drops are replaced, and the areas of their attachment have been repaired. The right front foot has been repaired. There is worm damage on the back legs and knee blocks. The brasses appear to be original. Extra "holes" of irregular placement on the interior of the drawer fronts appear to be points where the ends of the cotter pins were once embedded.

**Dimensions:**

| | | |
|---|---|---|
| H. | 61 in. | 154.9 cm |
| W. (cornice) | 35⁵⁄₈ in. | 90.5 cm |
| W. (upper case) | 33⁵⁄₈ in. | 85.4 cm |
| W. (lower case | 37⁵⁄₈ in. | 95.6 cm |
| W. (knees) | 41³⁄₈ in. | 105.1 cm |
| W. (feet) | 40¹⁄₈ in. | 101.9 cm |
| D. (cornice) | 20¹⁄₈ in. | 51.1 cm |
| D. (upper case) | 19 in. | 48.2 cm |
| D. (lower case) | 21⁷⁄₈ in. | 55.6 cm |
| D. (knees) | 25⁵⁄₈ in. | 65.1 cm |
| D. (feet) | 24⁵⁄₈ in. | 62.6 cm |

**Materials:** *Microanalysis:* Primary: soft maple group (drawer fronts, legs). Secondary: yellow pine group (drawer linings). *Finish:* black paint streaked over a red ground to simulate tortoiseshell; cream-color (or white) painted decoration. An old varnish finish gives the basic surface a yellow cast and the decoration a pale yellow color. The basic decoration consists of floral forms—stems, leaves, blossoms—augmented by individual motifs, including birds, animals, human figures, and a building.

**Exhibitions:** "Three Centuries of Connecticut Furniture," Tercentenary of Connecticut, Hartford, June 15–October 15, 1935.

**Publications:** Downs, *American Furniture*, fig. 186. First National Bank of Hartford advertisement, *Antiques* 50, no. 3 (September 1946): 147. Charles F. Hummel, "Queen Anne and Chippendale Furniture in the Henry Francis du Pont Winterthur Museum, Part 1," *Antiques* 97, no. 6 (June 1970): 897.

**Provenance:** Descended in the Higley family of South Windsor, Conn. Purchased at auction by Oliver Jones before 1935.

**Accession history:** Purchased by H. F. du Pont from the First National Bank of Hartford, Conn., executors for a Jones estate, with Winsor White acting as agent for H. F. du Pont, 1946. Bequest of H. F. du Pont, 1969.
54.507

---

1. Heckscher, *American Furniture*, cat. no. 152; Alice Winchester, ed., *The Antiques Treasury* (New York: E. P. Dutton, 1959), p. 286 left. A related high chest at the Wadsworth Atheneum in Hartford, Conn., with a heavy cornice and an extra tier of drawers in the lower case, which has lost its original painted finish, shares the same drawer construction feature.

2. J. L. Cummings, "Painted Chests from the Connecticut Valley," *Antiques* 34, no. 4 (October 1938): 192–93. *Connecticut Furniture*, nos. 54–56. Dean A. Fales, Jr., *American Painted Furniture, 1660–1880* (New York: E. P. Dutton, 1972), fig. 87.

3. Joseph Downs, "American Japanned Furniture," *Bulletin of the Metropolitan Museum of Art* 28, no. 3 (March 1933): 48; Cummings, "Painted Chests," p. 193.

4. The Higley family history is related in a letter from Helen K. Pelton to the curatorial department at Winterthur, February 12, 1974, Winterthur Archives. Lyon, *Colonial Furniture*, p. 87; *Connecticut Furniture*, nos. 55, 56; Cummings, "Painted Chests," pp. 192–93. In the eighteenth century, the town(ship) of Windsor bridged the Connecticut River and included the communities that are now Windsor, East Windsor, South Windsor, and Windsor Locks.

5. William N. Hosley, Jr., and Philip Zea, "Decorated Board Chests of the Connecticut River Valley," *Antiques* 119, no. 5 (May 1981): 1146–51.

## 162 ◆ High chest of drawers
Charlestown, Massachusetts
1760–85
Benjamin Frothingham, Jr. (1734–1809)

The chalk signature "Bena$^n$ Frothingham" written across the outside bottom of the long drawer in the lower case of this chest (fig. 1) identifies the maker as a prominent craftsman of Charlestown, a community located across the Charles River from Boston. As a youth Frothingham likely trained with his father,

Benjamin, Sr. (1708–65), a cabinetmaker of Boston. By the mid 1750s, Benjamin, Jr., had relocated to Charlestown, where he purchased real estate and joined an artillery company. He saw active service at the end of the decade in the British expedition to Quebec and again in the American Revolution, when he rose to the rank of major. Frothingham was among the more than four hundred residents of Charlestown whose property was destroyed when the British set fire to the town on June 17, 1775 (also the date of a fierce battle

**Fig. 1.** Detail, outside bottom of long drawer in lower case.

**Fig. 2.** Detail, brass cabinet handle from lower right drawer of lower case.

at Bunker Hill). Frothingham rebuilt his house and shop after the war and in 1784 became a member of the Society of the Cincinnati. Of Frothingham's seven children, only one, Benjamin, was a son; he followed his father's trade.[1]

Benjamin, Jr., is one of a few eighteenth-century cabinetmakers represented by a sizable body of documented furniture and a modest number of attributable objects, in his case, more than twenty items. Furniture that bears Frothingham's name, whether in chalk, pen, pencil, or on a label, attests to his skill as a craftsman and designer. In addition to this high chest and its companion dressing table (see No. 163), the forms associated with Frothingham include a single example each of a side chair, dining table (see No. 137), and a sideboard. Forms represented by more than one example, and sometimes by variant designs, are card tables (see No. 139), chests of drawers, chests-on-chests, desks, and desk-and-bookcases. Three pieces of furniture—the side chair, sideboard, and one card table—are in the federal style. The body of signed or attributed work falls into Frothingham's early and middle working years, however, when pad-foot cabriole legs and bracket feet were the norm. Nathaniel Hurd, a silversmith of Boston, engraved the cabinetmaker's label and enclosed the text within a fancy rococo border (see No. 139, fig. 1).[2]

Winterthur's high chest is one of a large group of eastern Massachusetts high chests fashioned with three flat arches across the front skirt, a fan-carved drawer in the base (and frequently a second one in the center top drawer), and cabriole legs with pad feet. Less common are two of the profiles at the top of the chest: the sweep-top edges of the small

side drawers, which follow the curve of the cornice molding, and the rounded projections in the circular cutouts of the scrollboard just beneath the tips of the cornice. The finials with a corkscrew on a covered urnlike cup with a midrib, which are original to the chest, appear on other tall casepieces by Frothingham. The original midrib drops of the skirt have a comparable profile. Other finials on eastern Massachusetts furniture are similar but not exact; it is possible, of course, that a turner specialist was responsible for the ornaments, and he could also have worked for other cabinetmakers.

A slightly larger subgroup of eastern Massachusetts chests with flat-arch front skirts and rounded projections in the scrollboard openings have low, flat side drawers at the top that lack the consonance with the scrollboard achieved by sweep-top drawers. A still greater number of chests of flat-arch skirt design are without either feature. Other variations include carved shells, plain recesses without a carved feature, cushioned pad feet, claw feet, and pilasters. The central plinth supporting the finial is frequently not as well shaped as the one on this example. Some plinths are cut off abruptly to form low, flat platforms without a rounded bulge. In a few chests with flat-arch skirts, lipped drawers are replaced by flush drawers, which returned to popularity in the late eighteenth century.

Customers of eastern Massachusetts high chests could choose from a variety of woods. Mahogany and walnut were the more expensive options; a few cases are veneered in walnut. Maple and cherry were less frequent choices in urban areas. The highly figured primary wood of this chest, first identified as curly walnut in the 1930s and as mahogany

in more recent decades, has been determined microscopically to be sabicu. The lustrous, variegated surface prompted use of the term *horseflesh mahogany* to describe this hardwood in the eighteenth century. Sabicu appears to have been harvested and merchandised as a variety of mahogany, and probably few timber merchants and cabinetmakers were aware that it was not actually a wood of that species. Use of the wood probably was more widespread than previously recognized. The companion dressing table to this chest (see No. 163) is made of sabicu, as are a pair of chairs (see No. 46), a desk-and-bookcase (see No. 206), and a blockfront chest of drawers (see No. 179).[3]

The name "I.GOLD" stamped on one of the plates of the brass hardware on this chest was discovered as early as 1936, but the manufacturer has been identified only in recent years (fig. 2). Donald L. Fennimore has determined that the mark is that of John Gold, a brassfounder of Birmingham working in the mid 1760s and possibly earlier and later. The basic pattern appears in several trade catalogues in the Winterthur Library. Of closest profile is item number 926 in a Birmingham catalogue once inscribed "Boohe [sp. ?] & Barker" on the front flyleaf (now crossed through), which probably is datable to the 1770s or early 1780s. The same pierced brasses are on the Frothingham dressing table. Although furniture hardware was imported into America in vast quantities from the manufacturing centers of England both before and after the Revolution, only now is significant attention being focused on this neglected subject.[4]

The design of the eastern Massachusetts high chest had considerable influence on cabinetmakers working in other areas of New England, from New Hampshire to Connecticut. Within eastern Massachusetts, family histories pinpoint original ownership of chests in Boston and the surrounding communities of Marblehead, Salem, Ipswich, Newburyport, and Kingston.[5]

NGE with NER

**Inscriptions or marks:** (Upper case) *On inside back of center top drawer:* "Mary" *in white chalk. On outside back of center top and right small drawers:* "12" *and* "13", *respectively. On outside back of upper to lower long drawers:* "14", "15", "16", *and* "17", *respectively. On upper or lower sides of top to third drawer blades:* "II", "III", *and* "IIII", *respectively.* (Lower case) *On outside bottom of long drawer:* "Na" *and* "Bena^n Frothingham" *written from side to side, the latter intersecting at right angles the name* "Nathanal Richards", *all in white chalk. On outside bottom of center small drawer:* indecipherable name in script, "W B rson"(?). *On outside back of long drawer:* a script "S" above an "X" in pencil. *On outside bottom of the small drawers, right to left:* "X" *accompanied by* "2", "3", *and* "4", *respectively. On the inside back of the front of the center small drawer:* "3". *Stamped beneath the bail handle on the brass plate of the right small drawer:* "I.GOLD".

**Construction:** (Upper case) The case top and bottom are dovetailed to the sides, which are formed of one wide and one narrow board. The scrollboard laps over the case sides and is nailed to the front edges and the vertical drawer dividers. Horizontal and vertical glueblocks support the center pediment opening. The vertical boards and roof of the enclosed pediment are secured with nails. The cornice molding and its side and center returns are nailed in place. The center returns are further supported below by corbel-like brackets nailed in place. The outer finial plinths are glued in place. The drawer blades are dovetailed to the case sides, the joints at the front edge concealed with facing strips. The blades are backed with secondary wood, the backing at the top forming a full dust board. The vertical dividers in the upper tier of drawers are rabbeted to the scrollboard at the top and slotted into the upper drawer blade at the bottom and

nailed. Runners for the top three long drawers are fitted into slots in the case sides and glued; runners for the lower drawers are glued to the case bottom. Vertical blocks nailed at the back corners of the case serve as drawer stops. Drawer guides flanking the center top drawer are glued in place on the dust board. The three horizontal boards that form the backboard are set into rabbets and nailed; the uppermost board has a rectangular cutout behind the pediment.

(Lower case) A mitered molding is nailed to the case sides and front rail. The case top, made of two boards, is set into a groove in the front rail and nailed to the upper edge of the backboard. The case sides, backboard, upper front rails, medial drawer blade, and front skirt are tenoned to the corner posts. The vertical dividers between the drawers slot into the drawer blade at the top and are rabbeted to the skirt at the bottom. The runners flanking the center bottom drawer are tenoned to the backboard and rabbeted at the front to the skirt, the center front notched to pass around the drawer dividers. The interior drawer guides, which are marked by three spaced semicircular notches, are glued to the runners. The outside drawer runners are notched and nailed to the front and back posts, and guides are glued to the top surface. Battens at the case top are nailed to the sides between the posts. Facing blocks support the front skirt at the knees and behind the pendent drops. The legs and posts are one piece. The rear knees do not extend beyond the backboard. The knee brackets are glued to the face of the skirt and sides. The drawers in both cases are finely dovetailed; the tops of the sides and back are rounded. The grain in all drawer bottoms runs from front to back; the bottoms in the large drawers are made of two boards. The bottoms are set into rabbets at the front and sides and nailed flush across the back. Most bottoms have a narrow chamfer across the back. Battens are glued to the lower surface of the bottoms at the sides. The carved drawer has a rounded reinforcing block on the back of the front panel. The drawer fronts are thumb molded on four sides, and the side lips butt against the case facade.

**Condition:** The right center cornice return has been replaced. The scrollboard is split near the top. The facing strip on the front edge of the right case side is split. The upper left small drawer has a section of molding missing and a repair to the drawer back. The upper right corner of the second long drawer is patched. There are splits in the bottoms of all the long drawers; most have been repaired with splines. There is a split in the left side panel of the upper

case and a spline patch on the right side of the lower case. The bracing block behind the left skirt drop and the tablet above the left drop are replacements. The tablet above the right drop has been repaired and partially restored. The front lip of the left finial plinth has been restored. The foot rings for the corkscrews of the left and center finials have been broken and restored. The brass hardware, finials, and drops are original.

**Dimensions:**

| | | |
|---|---|---|
| H. (case) | 83⁵⁄₈ in. | 212.4 cm |
| W. (cornice) | 42 in. | 106.7 cm |
| W. (upper case) | 38¹⁄₄ in. | 97.1 cm |
| W. (lower case) | 40¹⁄₈ in. | 101.9 cm |
| W. (feet) | 42¹⁄₈ in. | 107.0 cm |
| D. (cornice) | 22 in. | 55.9 cm |
| D. (upper case) | 19⁷⁄₈ in. | 50.5 cm |
| D. (lower case) | 21 in. | 53.3 cm |
| D. (feet) | 22 in. | 55.9 cm |

**Materials:** *Microanalysis:* Primary: mahogany (legs, finials); sabicu (drawer fronts, case sides). Secondary: white pine group (drawer linings, top panel); red pine group (support panel for cornice return). *Finish:* medium reddish brown color in resin on the cases; similar darker color in resin on the legs, drops, finials, and plinths.

**Exhibitions:** Detroit Institute of Arts, Detroit, 1935.

**Publications:** Thomas H. Ormsbee, "Matched Highboy and Lowboy Found with Frothingham Signature," *American Collector* 5, no. 11 (December 1936): 1, 17. Alice Winchester, "Antiques in Domestic Settings: The Home of Mr. and Mrs. Charles K. Davis, Part 2," *Antiques* 39, no. 3 (March 1941): 128. Alice Winchester, *Living with Antiques* (New York: Robert M. McBride, 1941), p. 58. Albert Sack, *Fine Points of Furniture: Early American* (New York: Crown Publishers, 1952), p. 185. Helen Comstock, "Frothingham and the Question of Attributions," *Antiques* 63, no. 6 (June 1953): 502; Charles F. Hummel, "Queen Anne and Chippendale Furniture in the Henry Francis du Pont Winterthur Museum, Part 3," *Antiques* 99, no. 1 (January 1971): 100; Richard H. Randall, Jr., "Benjamin Frothingham," in *Boston Furniture*, pp. 224–26. Harold Sack and Max Wilk, *American Treasure Hunt: The Legacy of Israel Sack* (New York: Ballantine Books, 1987), pp. 122–24.

**Provenance:** Ex coll.: George S. Mottley, Lowell, Mass., to Israel Sack, Inc., New York. Ex coll.: Mitchell Taradash, Ardsley-on-Hudson, N.Y., to Israel Sack, Inc., New York, 1936. Ex coll.: Charles K. Davis, Fairfield, Conn.

**Accession history:** Purchased by H. F. du Pont from Charles K. Davis, Fairfield, Conn., 1967. Bequest of H. F. du Pont, 1969.

67.1445

1. Dexter Edwin Spalding, "Benjⁿ Frothingham of Charlestown: Cabinetmaker and Soldier," *Antiques* 14, no. 6 (December 1928): 536–37; Mabel Munson Swan, "Major Benjamin Frothingham, Cabinetmaker," *Antiques* 62, no. 5 (November 1952): 392–95; Mabel M. Swan, "Furnituremakers of Charlestown," *Antiques* 56, no. 4 (October 1944): 203–6; Richard H. Randall, Jr., "Benjamin Frothingham," in *Boston Furniture*, pp. 223–49.

2. Furniture documented and attributed to Frothingham is in Randall, "Benjamin Frothingham," pp. vi, 114, 142, 224, 227–28, 230–31, 233–34, 237–39, 242, 244, 245, 246, 249; Swan, "Major Benjamin Frothingham," pp. 392–95; Margaret Rose Ingate, "History in Towns: Mobile, Alabama," *Antiques* 85, no. 3 (March 1964): 309; Helen Comstock, "Frothingham and the Question of Attributions," *Antiques* 63, no. 6 (June 1953): 503–4; Greenlaw, *New England Furniture*, no. 98; Ethel Hall Bjerkoe with John Arthur Bjerkoe, *The Cabinetmakers of America* (Garden City, N.Y.: Doubleday, 1957), pl. 17, no. 2; *American Antiques from Israel Sack Collection*, 10 vols. (Washington, D.C.: Highland House, 1969–), 4:1056–57; Rollins, *Treasures of State*, cat. no. 13; Douglas P. Maier advertisement, *Antiques* 101, no. 2 (February 1972): 319 (the authenticity of this inscription cannot be confirmed); David Stockwell advertisement, *Antiques* 109, no. 1 (January 1976): 1; Cinnamon Hill advertisement, *Antiques* 128, no. 2 (August 1985): 218; no. 91.624, DAPC, Visual Resources Collection, Winterthur Library. A second chalk signature in the drawer with the Frothingham signature in Winterthur's high chest is thought to be that of Nathaniel Richards (1712–88), a saddler, innkeeper, and magistrate of Roxbury (now part of Boston).

3. We are indebted to Harry A. Alden for his assistance in identifying this wood; see also Eleanor H. Gustafson, "Collectors' Notes," *Antiques* 135, no. 5 (May 1989): 1102, 1106.

4. Donald L. Fennimore, "Brass Hardware on American Furniture, Part 1: Cast Hardware, 1700–1850," *Antiques* 139, no. 5 (May 1991): 953, pl. 5; Donald L. Fennimore, *Metalwork in Early America: Copper and Its Alloys from the Winterthur Collection* (Winterthur, Del.: Henry Francis du Pont Winterthur Museum, 1996), cat. 307; see also Charles F. Hummel, "Queen Anne and Chippendale Furniture in the Henry Francis du Pont Winterthur Museum, Part 3," *Antiques* 99, no. 1 (January 1971): 98, 100–101, fig. 4. Pioneering work on furniture hardware identification by Hummel is "Samuel Rowland Fishers's Catalogue of English Hardware," in Milo M. Naeve, ed., *Winterthur Portfolio 1* (Winterthur, Del.: Henry Francis du Pont Winterthur Museum, 1964), pp. 188–97. The newly identified trade catalogue by Boohe(?) and Barker is listed in E. Richard McKinstry, comp., *Trade Catalogues at Winterthur: A Guide to the Literature of Merchandising, 1750 to 1980* (New York: Garland Publishing, 1984), no. 273.

5. Furniture with family histories is in Gerald W. R. Ward, ed., *American Furniture with Related Decorative Arts, 1660–1830: The Milwaukee Art Museum and the Layton Art Collection* (New York: Hudson Hills Press, 1991), cat. 63 (Boston); Elisabeth Donaghy Garrett, "A Houston Collection of American Antiques," *Antiques* 108, no. 3 (September 1975): 504 (Boston); *American Antiques from Sack Collection*, 8:2176–77 (Boston); Bernard and S. Dean Levy, Inc., *Vanity and Elegance* (New York: By the company, 1992), p. 40 (Boston); *American Antiques from Sack Collection*, 6:1504–5 (Marblehead); John S. Walton advertisement, *Antiques* 112, no. 5 (November 1977): 784 (Salem); *American Antiques from Sack Collection*, 3:758–59 (Salem); Venable, *American Furniture*, cat. 8 (Ipswich); C. L. Pricket advertisement, *Antiques* 114, no. 3 (September 1979): 529 (Newburyport); Sara Greene advertisement, *Antiques* 104, no. 4 (October 1973): 555 (Kingston).

## 163 ◆ Dressing table
Charlestown, Massachusetts
1760–85
Attributed to Benjamin Frothingham, Jr. (1734–1809)

This dressing table forms a suite of furniture with the high chest of drawers of No. 162. Estate inventories from eastern Massachusetts provide ample evidence that dressing tables and high chests were commonly used together in the bedchamber, further suggesting that many were made and purchased en suite. Many suites have been broken through the years, however, as estates have been dispersed. In a survey of more than seventy New England dressing tables of the flat-arch skirt pattern with a feature in the center drawer (a fan, shell, or plain recess), of which this table is representative, six suites, or about 9 percent of the sample, remain intact.

Although a close comparison of this dressing table with its companion high chest reveals subtle differences, there seems little question that they were meant to complement one another. The original pierced brasses of uncommon pattern are the same on both chests, as are the turned, midrib pendants of the skirts. Construction materials also compare favorably—the secondary wood is white pine, the legs are fashioned from mahogany, and the figured wood used for the exposed surface of the case is sabicu, a tropical hardwood that looks like mahogany and is uncommon in eighteenth-century furniture.

The fan-carved drawers and the leg tops vary in the two pieces. The broader dimensions of the high chest dictated a larger fan, which is composed of twenty-eight flutes, as compared to the twenty-two flutes of the dressing table fan. The ends of the flutes, which are carved in crescents, are noticeably deeper and thicker in the high chest, and the base lines of the two ornaments also differ slightly in their proximity to the bead of the drawer lip. The pattern variation at the leg

tops is less subtle. A single sweep from knee to bracket tip marks the legs of the high chest, but the sweep of the dressing table knees and returns is interrupted by a cusp (fig. 1), and the bracket tips are rounded instead of pointed. These differences may represent the work of different journeymen in the shop of Benjamin Frothingham, Jr. (1734–1809), or the hand of more than one outside carver, in the case of the fans. The customer may also have ordered the furniture at different times, permitting variation to creep into the details. The pendent drops, which duplicate those on the high chest, may represent a pattern peculiar to Frothingham's shop. The ornaments merely slip into holes drilled in the skirt pendants, and they would have been stockpiled in sufficient quantity to meet shop demand, ensuring continuity of design.

The more than seventy flat-arch dressing tables surveyed for this study permit a few generalizations about the form. Examples with square-cornered tops outnumber those with notched front corners by three to two. As expected, the carved fan is the most common feature of the center drawer, accounting for 63 percent of the total. Shell-carved (large lobes) or leaf-carved drawers represent 27 percent of the sample, and plain recesses are a modest feature in the remainder. Walnut was the favored wood (40 percent). Mahogany ranks second (29 percent), and cherry is a close third (24 percent); maple was an uncommon choice (3 percent). A thumb-molded drawer lip, such as that found on this dressing table, was the popular framing choice (78 percent). The alternative framing, which employs a flush drawer, probably was most common at the beginning and end of the period, when the William and Mary style was dying out, and later, when federal furniture began to exert an influence. Only three tables surveyed have ball-and-claw feet; one also has leaf-carved knees. Banded veneer appears on a few tables at the beginning of the style period, but only one surveyed table has a painted surface.

As early as 1944 Mabel M. Swan studied the claims submitted by the residents of Charlestown, the location of Frothingham's shop, for losses sustained when the British burned the community in June 1775. She noted that twenty-nine of the petitioners (7 percent) were members of the town's furnituremaking community and observed that the number more than exceeded that required to sustain an urban population numbering only several thousand. She suggested that the woodworkers supplemented local sales by constructing furniture for both the domestic and foreign export trades. Part of Charlestown's waterfront stands on Boston harbor, and in the eighteenth and early nineteenth centuries the community shared the status of a port of entry with the larger urban center. Even as late as 1839, chairs and cabinetware were enumerated among the leading manufactures of the town.[1]

The extensive claims of several woodworkers reinforce Charlestown's role in the export furniture trade and explicate the survival of so many pieces of furniture documented to Benjamin Frothingham, Jr. At the time of the Charlestown fire, benches for four workmen stood in Frothingham's shop, and furniture either under construction or completed consisted of a bureau table, four cases of walnut and mahogany drawers, twelve tables of different types, and six chairs. Frothingham was no stranger to the furniture export business. As a boy in Boston, he had seen his father, Benjamin Frothingham, Sr., constructing furniture and "Caceing" it for export. Among the elder Frothingham's customers for cased furniture was the rich merchant Thomas Hancock.[2]

Venture furniture was just one part of the export trade. Coastal customers near and far who placed orders with Frothingham wisely paid for shipping cases to protect their purchases in transit. Gen. Henry Knox acquired mahogany bedsteads, card tables, pembroke tables, and a large wardrobe from Frothingham in 1797. Presumably, the furniture was cased and shipped, as Knox resided in Thomaston, Maine. Eight years earlier Nathaniel Gorham, merchant, statesman, land speculator, and native of Charlestown, had directed Frothingham to make a mahogany desk-and-bookcase, for which he paid £19.10.0. A shipping case cost another 10s.[3]

The production of coffins and mundane articles of household furniture, such as the "pine Kitchen Table" constructed for "Col° Ervin" (Maj. William Erving) in 1788 by Frothingham, Jr., formed another substantial part of every cabinetmaker's business. Erving also acquired two field bedsteads at the same time, and when he died in 1791, "two feild Bedsteads with curtains" were itemized among the household furnishings offered at a public auction held at his house on Jamaica Plain, Roxbury (now part of Boston).[4]

NGE

---

**Construction:** The top, which is made of one broad and one narrow board and ogee molded on the front and side edges, is attached to the frame with glueblocks on all four sides. The sides of the case, their lower edges cut in a stepped flat arch echoing the front skirt, and the one-piece backboard are tenoned to the posts; no pins are visible. The top rail and the front skirt rail are also tenoned to the corner posts; the drawer blade is attached with shouldered dovetails. The vertical partitions between the small drawers are attached to the drawer blade and skirt with shouldered dovetails. All drawer runners are beveled; they are lapped and nailed at the front and tenoned to the backboard. The outside guides are glued to the runners and case sides. The guides flanking the center bottom drawer are tenoned to the backboard and glued to the top of the runners. Each has a large, squared notch cut out near the front. The knee brackets are glued over the skirt. The rear knees extend beyond the backboard. The legs and corner posts are one piece. The drawers are dovetailed. The bottoms, the grain running from front to back, are nailed flush with the sides and back and to a rabbet at the front; they have applied battens. The top edges of the sides are rounded. A narrow thumbmolding finishes the front edges of the drawers; the side lips butt against the case.

**Condition:** There are splits in the top near the right rear corner and in the backboard. The top has been reset and a thin spline inserted at the upper edge of each side panel below the top. The left front leg post is split above the blade. The left rear knee has split along the grain and is reglued. The right front and rear knee brackets are replaced; the other knee brackets are reglued. The upper right corner of the right small drawer is replaced. The pendent drops and hardware appear to be original.

**Dimensions:**

| | | |
|---|---|---|
| H. | 31 3/8 in. | 79.7 cm |
| W. (top) | 33 3/4 in. | 85.7 cm |
| W. (case) | 29 3/4 in. | 75.5 cm |
| W. (feet) | 31 3/8 in. | 79.7 cm |
| D. (top) | 20 3/4 in. | 52.7 cm |
| D. (case) | 17 3/4 in. | 45.1 cm |
| D. (feet) | 19 1/2 in. | 49.5 cm |

**Materials:** *Microanalysis:* Primary: sabicu (top, drawer fronts, case sides, blades); mahogany (legs). Secondary: white pine group (drawer linings, backboards, glueblocks). *Finish:* medium reddish brown color and resin on the case and top. Similar darker color in resin on the legs and drops. Evidence of the original reddish brown stain on unexposed wood surfaces.

**Exhibitions:** Detroit Institute of Arts, Detroit, 1935.

**Publications:** Thomas H. Ormsbee, "Matched Highboy and Lowboy Found with Frothingham Signature," *American Collector* 5, no. 11 (December 1936): 1, 17. Alice Winchester, "Antiques in Domestic Settings: The Home of Mr. and Mrs. Charles K. Davis, Part 2," *Antiques* 39, no. 3 (March 1941): 128. Helen Comstock, "Frothingham and the Question of Attributions," *Antiques* 63, no. 6 (June 1953): 502. Helen Comstock, "The American Lowboy: An Antiques Survey," *Antiques* 80, no. 6 (December 1961): 571, fig. 5. Richard H. Randall, Jr., "Benjamin Frothingham," in *Boston Furniture*, p. 227. Harold Sack and Max Wilk, *American Treasure Hunt: The Legacy of Israel Sack* (New York: Ballantine Books, 1987), pp. 122–24.

**Provenance:** Ex coll.: George S. Mottley, Lowell, Mass., to Israel Sack, Inc., New York. Ex coll.: Mitchel Taradash, Ardsley-on-Hudson, N.Y., to Israel Sack, Inc., New York, 1936. Ex coll.: Charles K. Davis, Fairfield, Conn.

**Accession history:** Purchased by H. F. du Pont from Charles K. Davis, Fairfield, Conn., 1967. Bequest of H. F. du Pont, 1969.
67.1446

---

1. Mabel M. Swan, "Furnituremakers of Charlestown," *Antiques* 46, no. 4 (October 1944): 203–6; Mabel Munson Swan, "Major Benjamin Frothingham, Cabinetmaker," *Antiques* 62, no. 5 (November 1952): 392–95; John Hayward, *The New England Gazetteer* (Boston: By the author, 1839), s.v. "Charlestown, Mass."

2. Swan, "Furnituremakers," p. 203; Benjamin Frothingham, Sr., bills to Thomas Hancock, June 28 and October 12, 1746, Private and Business Papers (Boston), vol. 1, Boston Public Library, Boston; Benjamin Frothingham, Sr., bill to John Edwards, August 3, 1749, Downs collection.

3. Benjamin Frothingham, Jr., bill to Gen. Henry Knox, January 16, 1797, Henry Knox Papers, Maine Historical Society, Portland, as quoted in Richard H. Randall, Jr., "Benjamin Frothingham," in *Boston Furniture*, p. 247; Benjamin Frothingham, Jr., bill to Nathaniel Gorham, December 1, 1789, Phelps-Gorham Collection, New York State Library, Albany.

4. Swan, "Major Benjamin Frothingham," p. 394. Swan did not give her source for Benjamin Frothingham, Jr.'s, bill to "Colo Ervin" dated June 12, 1788; that document is here identified as in the David Greenough Papers, Massachusetts Historical Society, Boston. Other documents in the Greenough papers make it clear that William Erving attained only the rank of major.

## 164 ◆ Dressing table

Northeastern Massachusetts, probably
Essex County or Middlesex County
1755–85

The design of this dressing table is a subtle variation of the flat-arch skirt pattern of No. 163. The small lunette centered at the front complements the curves of the carved fan and reinforces the central focus of the design. The curves are repeated in the small, scroll-like brackets flanking the knees. In this example, the pendants supporting the turned drops are ogee-sided rather than hollow-sided as in No. 163—an alternative, although less common, profile found in tables both with and without the small lunette. The quality of the carved fan in the drawer recess varies significantly from that in No. 163. The execution is perfunctory, with only token modeling at the creases between the segments. Complementary creases mark the front corners of the top.

A survey of published sources revealed 82 percent fewer lunette-embellished tables than plain examples. All the lunette-type tables have plain pad feet, and most have thumb-molded, lipped drawers and square-cornered tops. Simple, gouge-carved fans appear in several other examples, although the greater number are modeled. A few tables have a plain recess in the center drawer. Walnut is the material of two-thirds of the examples surveyed; cherry and maple are equally divided in the rest.

The style survey also produced a group of high chests of drawers with the lunette feature in the skirt. By tradition one tall chest descended in the family of William Dudley, a son of Gov. Joseph Dudley of Massachusetts, and is thought to have been made in the Boston area. A second high chest, one with a flat top, descended in the Freeman family, probably from Enoch Freeman (1734–1824), a shipbuilder. Freeman was a resident of

Brunswick, Maine, a seacoast community with direct access to Massachusetts's North Shore. Two other tall chests with family histories have companion dressing tables. One suite, which descended in the Chandler family of Petersham in central Massachusetts, has several unusual features: the knees of both pieces of furniture are carved with an attenuated shell, and the drawers in the upper case of the high chest are flanked by pilasters. Of more particular note is a vertical recess in the tall case, which extends from the center top shell drawer to the waist molding and balances the recessed shell in the base. The effect is that of a blockfront case.[1]

The second suite of furniture, which is made of walnut, descended in the Gilbert family of Salem and is of standard design. The scrolled pediment of the high chest relates closely to that in No. 162 by Benjamin Frothingham, Jr., of Charlestown, although there is variation in the upper tier of drawers;

it also has a shell-carved center top drawer but lacks the sloping profile of the side drawers in the Frothingham chest. The Salem chest and table also relate to this dressing table. The scroll-end knee brackets are the same, and the skirt pendants supporting the turned drops repeat the double-ogee pattern. In quality of execution, the carved fans on the Salem chest and table fall somewhere between those on the Frothingham suite and the ornament of this dressing table. The character of the carved work on this table probably precludes its origin in a sophisticated urban center.[2]

A group of Boston-area blockfront bureau tables, a parallel development in chamber furniture design, has similar centered lunettes in the ogee-ended hoods above the kneehole recesses. Most of the eight examples located for this study are made of mahogany, and both round- and flat-blocked facades are represented. Prominent cusps similar to those in the knee brackets of No. 163 are the principal elements of the returns flanking the straight-bracket feet. Six cases have flush drawers; the others are lipped. Four of the bureau tables have family backgrounds. One was owned in the Little family of Salem from at least the late nineteenth century; another is associated with Gen. Henry Knox, whose home was Thomaston, Maine. Two cases have Boston provenances: one, which descended in the Dering family of Shelter Island, New York, probably was purchased originally by Thomas Dering (1720–85), a Boston merchant, and the other was owned by Maj. Thomas Melville (1751–1832), who participated in the Boston Tea Party and in 1774 married a daughter of Boston merchant John Scollay.[3]

Because bureau tables were sometimes made en suite with dressing tables and high chests of drawers to create three-piece sets of case furniture, a group of Boston-area estate records dating from 1754 to 1797 was examined for this study. Eight households that contained all three forms as bedchamber furnishings have been identified. Another four residences were furnished with a bureau table in company with a high chest of drawers. In one home, that of John Simpson, a Boston merchant, the evidence is clear that all three pieces of furniture—a "Chest of draws & Table" and a "Mehogony Bureau Table"—were used together in the same room. Presumably, the cases complemented one another, although they were not necessarily of the pattern under consideration. The "Chamber Glass" in the room probably hung above the bureau table or the dressing table.[4]

Two inscriptions on the drawers of this table, which appear to be contemporary, provide additional insights on its origin and further explicate period terminology. The place name "Dracut," which identifies a small town in Middlesex County near the New Hampshire border, is written on one small drawer. The words "S[h]ell draw," probably by the same hand, appear on the back of the center drawer. Although this type of carved ornament is generally designated a fan today to distinguish it from the naturalistic, lobed variety, some eighteenth-century craftsmen may have indiscriminately placed all such carvings in

the category "Shell." That other terminology was current, however, is demonstrated by an entry for a "phanned" dressing table in the accounts of a Wethersfield, Connecticut, resident in the mid eighteenth century.[5]

*NGE*

---

**Inscriptions or marks:** Various shop marks in white chalk on outside backs of all drawers. *On outside back of center bottom drawer:* "S[h]ell draw" in white chalk. *On outside back of right small drawer:* "Dracut" in white chalk.

**Construction:** The top, notched on the front corners and made of one wide and one narrow board, is ogee molded on the front and sides and thumb molded on the back. It overhangs the case on all sides and is screwed to the frame from the top. The connection with the backboard is reinforced with glueblocks. The case back and side boards are tenoned and double-pinned to the posts, and the front skirt rail is tenoned and single-pinned. The horizontal blade between the upper and lower tiers of drawers is dovetailed (exposed) to the front posts. The vertical dividers are slotted to the blade at the top and dovetailed to the skirt at the bottom. The drawer runners are tenoned to the backboard and bevel-lapped at the front. The drawers are dovetailed, front and back, and the upper edges of the sides have a thin bead on the outside. The back of the long drawer is chamfered at the top, and the backs of the small drawers are flat. The drawer bottoms, which are chamfered at the sides and front, are set into grooves in the front and sides and nailed flush across the back. The grain runs side to side in the top drawer and from front to back in the small drawers. The drawer fronts are lipped on four sides (except the top of the long drawer), and the side lips butt against the case. The fanlike shell of the center drawer has fifteen lobes and a bead along the lower edge. The knee brackets are applied over the skirt front and sides.

**Condition:** The exterior surface has been refinished. The top has been reset at least once; the screw holes are concealed with plugs. The upper lip has been restored on all the small drawers. The left side-front knee bracket has been replaced; some of the others have been reattached. The drops are replacements. A large patch is inset at the upper right corner of the backboard. Several glueblocks at the connection of the top and backboard are missing. One glueblock has been introduced to the right side. The brass hardware and the lock are replacements and represent at least the third set.

**Dimensions:**

| | | |
|---|---|---|
| H. | 28 3/4 in. | 73.0 cm |
| W. (top) | 31 3/16 in. | 79.2 cm |
| W. (case) | 28 1/4 in. | 71.7 cm |
| W. (feet) | 29 3/4 in. | 75.6 cm |
| D. (top) | 19 1/2 in. | 49.5 cm |
| D. (case) | 17 in. | 43.2 cm |
| D. (feet) | 18 5/8 in. | 47.3 cm |

**Materials:** *Microanalysis:* Primary: American black walnut. Secondary: white pine group (drawer back, back of blade); yellow pine group (backboard). *Finish:* medium brownish orange color in resin.

**Accession history:** Bequest of Mrs. Francis B. Crowninshield, Marblehead, Mass., 1958. 58.140.1

1. Fales, *Furniture of Historic Deerfield*, fig. 435; Robert W. Skinner, "American Furniture and Decorative Arts" (March 24, 1996), lot 110; Sotheby's, "Important Americana: The Bertram K. Little and Nina Fletcher Little Collection, Part 1" (January 29, 1994), lots 428, 429.

2. Christie's, "The Collection of Mr. and Mrs. Eddy Nicholson" (January 27–28, 1995), lot 1064.

3. The bureau tables are in Greenlaw, *New England Furniture*, no. 147; Robert W. Skinner, "Americana" (October 27–28, 1989), lot 323; Sotheby's, "Fine American Furniture, Silver, Porcelain, and Related Decorative Arts" (June 28–30, 1984), lot 572; Wayne Pratt advertisement, *Antiques* 143, no. 4 (April 1993): 512; Sotheby's, "Important Americana: The Bertram K. and Nina Fletcher Little Collection, Part 2" (October 21–22, 1994), lot 889 (Little family); James Julia auction advertisement, *Antiques and the Arts Weekly*, August 20, 1993 (Knox family); Heckscher, *American Furniture*, cat. no. 134 (Dering family); American Art Association Anderson Galleries, "Collection of Herbert Lawton" (April 2–3, 1937), lot 375.

4. Estate records of Samuel Miller, Esq. (1761), John Simpson (1764), Thomas Green (1766), John Spooner (1771), Edward Clarke (1771), Benjamin Andrews (1773), James Smithwick (1779/82), Benjamin Pemberton, Esq. (1782), John Williams (1782), and William Coffin (1787), Suffolk County Probate Court, Boston (microfilm, Downs collection); Edward Brattle Oliver claim, Boston Fire Documents and Correspondence, vol. 2, 1760, Boston Public Library, Boston; Joseph Green confiscated loyalist estate, 1776, Boston (photostat, Downs collection).

5. A "phanned" dressing table is itemized in the account book of Elisha Williams, Jr., 1738–56, Wethersfield Historical Society, Wethersfield, Conn., as quoted in Kevin M. Sweeney, "Furniture and Furniture-Making in Eighteenth-Century Wethersfield, Connecticut," *Antiques* 125, no. 5 (May 1984): 1156.

## 165 ◆ Dressing table

Coastal Essex County, Massachusetts,
possibly Newbury area
1755–85

The front recess with carved fan links this
dressing table to Nos. 163 and 164, but the
design is rare. Only one close mate has been
located, although the patterns of the principal
elements—the knees, feet, shell, and front
skirt—are tied to furniture originating in
northeastern Massachusetts from Boston to
coastal New Hampshire and the surrounding
region. The mate dressing table may have
originated in the same shop, although it is
wider by about an inch and a half, resulting in
slightly flatter but more graceful skirt curves
and a broader shell. The character of the
knees, feet, shell, and skirt is the same in both
tables, but the mate lacks the indented top
front corners of Winterthur's example. Maple is
the principal wood of both pieces of furniture.[1]

A distinctive feature of this table is the
undercut base of the creased knees (fig. 1). Of
an assembled group of twenty-seven objects
with this feature, eight are linked to specific

places through family history, recovery
location, or relationship. The provenances
range from Boston to Salem and Rowley in
Essex County to South Berwick and York,
Maine, in the Portsmouth area. Seven
furniture forms are represented. In addition
to the dressing table and high chest, there
are small and medium-size tables with falling
leaves (see No. 130) and corner chairs, side
chairs, an armchair, and an easy chair. The
undercut knee is confined to the top part of
the leg in most examples, although in several
long-leg tables the crease extends to midleg.[2]

The high, steep-sided cup-shape pattern
of the feet of this dressing table represents
a subtle yet substantial departure from the
standard design of Nos. 163 and 164. A thin
disk, sharply defined top edge, and shaved
heel with a suggestion of a hock are other
distinctive characteristics of this foot. Making
comparisons among feet on casework is
considerably more subjective than making
other design identifications. The supports of
as few as six high chests and dressing tables
exhibit a close resemblance to those on this
table. Three have provenances: a high chest

with several features relating closely to profiles
in No. 162 descended in the Edmands family
of Boston, and two tall cases with flat tops are
associated with Newbury. One of these, a chest
at the Society for the Preservation of New
England Antiquities, Boston, is thought to
have been made in Newbury and owned in
neighboring Byfield. It is said to be almost
identical to another chest in the Historical
Society of Old Newbury that has a provenance
in a local family. The legs and feet of the
two chests compare favorably with those on
another flat-top chest that is signed by its
makers, Joshua Morss and Moses Bayley; the
cabinetmakers also added dates in January
and February 1748/49 and the place name
"Newbury" to the chest.[3]

In proficiency of execution, the shell in
this table falls between those of Nos. 163 and
164. The most distinctive characteristic is
the blunt lunette-shape tips of the radiating
segments. Also notable is the way the
segments angle forward sharply at the ends
rather than rising gradually from the center
to the outside. None of twelve high chests,
dressing tables, and chests-on-chests with
comparable shells has a specific background
history, although two have a presumed
association with Boston. The high chests in
the group have the flat-arch skirt, pediment
features, and related details associated with
northeastern Massachusetts furniture.[4]

The profile of the skirt of this table is rare;
the only comparable form found among case
furniture or tables is the mate dressing table.
Patterns related to the multiple ogee curves
and small central arch are found in a group of
five tea tables and a marble-top side table with
provenances from Hingham, Massachusetts, to
York, Maine. Two tables descended in Salem
families, and the original owner of the table in
Maine is known to have had business ties to
Portsmouth, Newbury, and Boston. The skirt
figure may also be likened to that in No. 158,
with all of the curves pulled down to a single

horizontal baseline. Thus, the profile is not new but is simply redefined.[5]

A group of seven objects emerges from the furniture surveyed whose provenances place them in the coastal Essex County towns of Salem, Newbury, Rowley, and Byfield. One of the chests is also signed by craftsmen who worked in Newbury. Given the similarity of features between these objects and this table, attribution to that area is reasonable. The materials and several unusual construction characteristics reinforce the attribution and further narrow the area of origin to towns north of Salem.

The primary woods of the dressing table are maple and birch. All the furniture in the survey associated with Newbury, Byfield, and Rowley is made of maple, and birch was also a popular cabinet wood in the same region. A birch desk at the Society for the Preservation of New England Antiquities was originally owned by a resident of Ipswich, a town just south of Rowley. In contrast, furniture in the surveys linked with Salem is made of mahogany and walnut. Also pointing to a semirural origin for the dressing table are several structural features: the case back is fashioned from a board that has bark on both the upper and lower edges; the pegs joining the case sides to the legs are set in an unconventional pattern, with two pegs near the top and a single peg at the knee; and the small drawers have thick sides double beaded on the upper edge, and the shell drawer has an unusually thin back.[6]

The exterior surfaces have been refinished to a light wood color, which was atypical in the eighteenth century. Remnants of an old, possibly original, medium reddish brown stain remain, however. It was common practice to stain inexpensive woods, including maple and birch, to imitate costly materials such as walnut and mahogany. The stain on this table would have also concealed the use of different woods in the case and top. When the stain coat dried, the furnituremaker applied a clear finish selected by the customer: oil, wax, or varnish. Whatever the finish, the surface would have been polished to provide a high gloss.[7]

*NGE with NER*

**Inscriptions or marks:** *On right small drawer on outer sides:* remnants of illegible white chalk inscriptions.

**Construction:** The top, ogee molded on the front and side edges and flat on the back, has notched front corners. The top is screwed to the frame from the outside: twice at the top of the backboard and once at the top of each side panel. The backboard

**Fig. 1.** Detail, right front leg.

and case sides are tenoned and pinned to the corner posts. The case sides are sawed on the lower edge with a double-ogee curve. The top front rail is tenoned to the post tops; the drawer blade and skirt are tenoned and pinned to the posts. The vertical drawer dividers are tenoned to the blade and skirt rail. The runners for the long drawer are bevel-lapped at the front to the blade and lapped and nailed at the rear posts. The guides immediately above them and those for the small drawers are nailed to the case sides. The runners for the lower drawers are lapped at the front and tenoned to the backboard. Bracing blocks at the upper side panels adjacent to the top are lapped at the backposts and glued in place. The rear knees project beyond the back of the case. The legs and corner posts are one piece. The knee brackets are glued over the skirt. The drawers are dovetailed, finely at the front. The grain of the bottom board runs from side to side in the long drawer and from front to back in the small drawers. The bottoms are set into grooves on the front and sides and nailed flush at the back. The upper edges of the sides and back in the long drawer are flat; the upper edges of the sides in the small drawers are double beaded. A narrow thumbmolding finishes the front edges of the drawers; the side lips butt against the case. The front board of the center small drawer is thicker than the others to accommodate the shell, which is carved from solid wood.

**Condition:** The exterior has been refinished, and an old medium reddish brown stain has been removed. The left front and rear legs have one or two gouges on the inside surfaces. The drops are replaced, and new knee brackets have been added on the back of the rear legs. There is some worm damage on the left bottom edge of the backboard. The hardware is original.

**Dimensions:**

| | | |
|---|---|---|
| H. | 32 in. | 81.3 cm |
| W. (top) | 34 7/8 in. | 88.6 cm |
| W. (case) | 30 1/2 in. | 77.5 cm |
| W. (feet) | 32 3/4 in. | 83.2 cm |
| D. (top) | 19 1/4 in. | 48.9 cm |
| D. (case) | 15 7/8 in. | 40.3 cm |
| D. (feet) | 18 1/8 in. | 46.3 cm |

**Materials:** *Microanalysis:* Primary: maple (case, drawer fronts, legs); birch (top). Secondary: white pine group (backboard, linings on small drawers); chestnut (bottom long drawer). *Finish:* light orange color in resin.

**Publications:** Downs, *American Furniture*, fig. 328.

**Accession history:** Bequest of H. F. du Pont, 1969. 59.839

1. Mate table is in G. K. S. Bush advertisement, *Antiques* 139, no. 6 (June 1991): 1016.

2. Survey examples in Bush advertisement; Jobe and Kaye, *New England Furniture*, nos. 61, 96, 112; *American Antiques from Israel Sack Collection*, 10 vols. (Washington, D.C.: Highland House, 1969–), 2:387, 3:654, 4:1013, 5:1256, 6:1556, 1562, 8:2083, 2166; no. 66.683, DAPC, Visual Resources Collection, Winterthur Library; Albert Sack, *Fine Points of Furniture: Early American* (New York: Crown, 1950), p. 197 bottom; Ward, *American Case Furniture*, cat. 134; John S. Walton advertisement, *Antiques* 83, no. 4 (April 1963): 409; Nutting, *Furniture Treasury*, no. 2077; Dean A. Fales, Jr., *Essex County Furniture: Documented Treasures from Local Collections, 1660–1860* (Salem, Mass.: Essex Institute, 1965), no. 76; Fales, *Furniture of Historic Deerfield*, fig. 248; Randall, *American Furniture*, nos. 153–54; Heckscher, *American Furniture*, cat. no. 108; Greenlaw, *New England Furniture*, nos. 131, 132; Christie's, "Fine American Furniture, Silver, Folk Art, and Decorative Arts" (January 23, 1988), lot 382.

3. Survey examples in Bush advertisement; *American Antiques from Sack Collection*, 3:761, 4:1004, 6:1590–91; Jobe and Kaye, *New England Furniture*, no. 39; Sotheby's, "Important Americana" (January 28–30, 1988), lot 1203.

4. Survey examples in Bush advertisement; Sack, *Fine Points*, p. 116 bottom, p. 197 bottom; *American Antiques from Sack Collection*, 2:466–67, 5:1325, 7:1704, 1925, 2104–15, 9:2486–87, 10:2650; Herbert F. Schiffer advertisement, *Antiques* 95, no. 1 (January 1969): 81; New England Gallery advertisement, *Antiques* 130, no. 2 (August 1986): 213.

5. Survey examples in Bush advertisement; *American Antiques from Sack Collection*, 10:2633; Jobe and Kaye, *New England Furniture*, no. 68; Greenlaw, *New England Furniture*, no. 129; Jobe, *Portsmouth Furniture*, cat. no. 47; Comstock, *American Furniture*, no. 228; Rodriguez Roque, *American Furniture*, no. 125.

6. For the Ipswich desk, see Jobe and Kaye, *New England Furniture*, no. 48.

7. Jobe and Kaye, *New England Furniture*, pp. 94–95, 237; Robert D. Mussey, Jr., "Transparent Furniture Finishes in New England, 1700–1825," in *New England Furniture*, pp. 287–305; Benno M. Forman, "Salem Tradesmen and Craftsmen, Circa 1762: A Contemporary Document," in *Essex County Essays* (Salem, Mass.: Newcomb and Gauss, [1971]), pp. 30–33.

## 166 ◆ High chest of drawers
Stratford, Connecticut
August 1784
Brewster Dayton (w. 1762–d. 1797)

A chalk inscription inside the backboard of this high chest reads: "August 1784 Brewster Dayton made theese draws at Stratford" (fig. 1). The discovery of a piece of eighteenth-century furniture so fully documented is rare. The inscription identifies the work of a little-known craftsman and documents the longevity of the Queen Anne style in case furniture in southern New England.

Little is known of Brewster Dayton's background and training. In 1755 he moved from Brookhaven, Long Island, probably his birthplace, to Stratford. By 1762 his shop was operational, and he was prepared to offer a full range of products. An inventory of his estate, taken after his death in 1797, details the shop equipment, which included two benches, a lathe, planes, and other hand tools. The inventory also lists chair slats and rounds (stretchers) and a quantity of rush for seats. Turned chair frames both partly assembled and finished in paint stood in the shop. Chairs documented or attributable to Dayton are unknown, but his skill as a craftsman is recorded in three signed and dated high chests.[1]

The earliest example of his work is a flat-top cherry high chest. It is inscribed in chalk under the top board of the upper case: "Brewster Dayton/ maker april ye 1=1775" and on the bottom of the lower drawer of the upper case: "mayd may the 12, 1775." Aside from the differences at the case top, the chest is remarkably similar to this high chest in construction and design. The legs of both are thick through most of the length and have pointed knee blocks and comparable flangelike projections below the knees. Centered above the flat-arch skirt is a fan similar in character to that on this chest.[2]

A second tall pedimented chest made by Dayton appears to vary from Winterthur's only in the addition of carved C scrolls at the leg tops in place of flanges. It has the same distinctive plain pediment, drawer arrangement, waist molding, fan carving (fig. 2), and brass hardware. Like Dayton's other work, the chest has several chalk inscriptions. Inside the top board of the upper case is the date "Jan thee 24 1784" and Dayton's name. The cabinetmaker identified himself again on the bottom of the shell

drawer and on another small drawer in the lower case, "Right Hand draw/ B. Dayton/ 1784." There also is a scratched inscription, "BD 1784," in the bottom of the upper case.[3]

Stratford, the agriculture-centered coastal Connecticut town in which Dayton practiced his craft, has been described by Edward S. Cooke, Jr., as a closely knit community dominated by cultural conservatism. The plain style of Dayton's cases apparently met local requirements of taste and appealed to a sense of status on an individual basis. Cooke suggests

**Fig. 1.** Detail, inside surface of backboard, upper case.

that Dayton trained locally with a joiner of English provincial background, whose work he has identified. He attributes a casepiece with features rooted in English design to the early years of Dayton's career. Several construction features of this chest also appear in Dayton's later work. Drawer sides are beveled on the top on both edges, and the dovetail sequence is similar. On the case front, yellow poplar backs the drawer blades, and strips of primary wood conceal the blade joints at the forward edges of the case sides. Many interior and secondary surfaces are finished with a toothing plane.[4]

**Fig. 2.** Detail, center bottom drawer.

As identified by Cooke, elements of the Stratford style were transferred to other locations in the Housatonic River valley, especially to the town of Woodbury. Relating to one of the Woodbury chests of drawers is a flat-top cherry high chest that has a similarly carved spoon-handle shell. The knees are marked with the same unusual flange that is found on some of the Dayton furniture (fig. 3). A dressing table with this feature, the only other example located, relates to other Woodbury work through its shell. Several high chests associated with the inland community are supported on thick legs that taper sharply near the bottom in the manner of Winterthur's chest. The feature may have originated before 1750 in Newport, where high chests and tables on long legs with pointed- or rounded-pad feet are noticeably thick at the knees and slim at the ankles. The transfer may have been direct along Long Island Sound or by way of neighboring New London County, Connecticut (see No. 20). Connecticut–Rhode Island border influence is also suggested by the particular selection of woods in Winterthur's high chest, especially the use of sycamore and butternut. Both materials, which are uncommon in eighteenth-century furniture, appear again in border work in the postwar years, when they are used as planks in large-size Windsor chairs.[5]

The carved fan centered at the bottom of this chest is distinctive and appears on two of the three documented Dayton chests (see fig. 2). A slight curve along the length of each radiating segment completes the illusion of an open fan with overlapping sticks. The outer boundary, precisely detailed with crescentlike cuts of the carver's tool, is further defined by the arch of the recess. Related, though not identical, fans appear in a few other Connecticut cherrywood chests and a dressing table. The delicate ornament is a sharp contrast to the plain scrollboard at the top of the case. The board, of uncommon depth for a Boston-type high chest, may represent a cross between Massachusetts and Rhode Island design (see Nos. 162, 172).[6]

Winterthur's high chest probably was purchased from Dayton by Nathan Wheeler of New Stratford (now Monroe) in the Housatonic River valley at about the time of his second marriage in 1784, to Elizabeth Hawley. Wheeler (1747–1817) was a farmer and possessed forty-four acres of land. At the time of his death his estate was valued at $18,000. He was sufficiently affluent to have purchased a high chest in the most fashionable local style, and his selection of a traditional design speaks to the "selective conservatism" that extended even beyond Stratford to encompass the Housatonic River valley.[7]

*NER/NGE*

---

**Inscriptions or marks:** *Inside backboard of upper case behind top long drawer:* "August 1784 Brewster Dayton made theese draws/ at Stratford" in white chalk; *on batten at upper back:* "1784 made". *Inside bottom long drawer of upper case:* miscellaneous numerical jottings. *On top of second blade in upper case:* "August 1734" and

1888
1734
154

in pencil (a later misreading of the chalk inscription, presumably written in 1888). *Scratched inside left side of upper case:* "X". *On outside back of top left small drawer of upper case:* "PS" or "RS". *On outside back of right small drawer of upper case:* "R". *On inside of backboard in lower case:* "X". Modern penciled numbers on many drawers. *On inside of bottom long drawer in upper case:* series of number jottings in no particular order in white chalk.

**Construction:** (Upper case) The case top and two-board bottom are dovetailed to the one-board sides. The scrollboard is lapped to the case sides and further supported by the vertical dividers between the top drawers to which it is nailed at slotted and butted joints. The dividers are dovetailed at the bottom to the upper drawer blade. The pediment backboard is rabbeted to the case sides and nailed. Further reinforcing the front and back structures of the pediment is a central interior strut lapped to the scrollboard above the center drawer and tenoned to the backboard. Supplementary struts, tenoned front and back, are positioned at the upper left and right inside the pediment beneath the hollow curve of the roof. The rear tenons pierce through the backboard. The floor of the box behind the pediment opening is rabbeted, pinned, and nailed to the bottom of a square cutout in the backboard. At the front it is rabbeted and nailed to a horizontal brace attached to the inside of the scrollboard. The floor of the box supports vertical sides that are butted and pinned to the side edges of the cutout in the backboard. At the front the vertical boards are fastened to vertical braces attached to the inside of the scrollboard. The central plinth of the scrollboard is reinforced on the back with a glueblock. The mitered cornice molding is attached to the scrollboard and case sides with nails. The short returns at the top center front are glued and nailed to supporting blocks fixed to the box sides and further supported at the base by small corbels. The pediment roof is nailed to the top edges of the scrollboard, backboard, case sides, and box. The shallow drawer blades, backed with secondary wood, are slotted into the case sides, the joints and those of the scrollboard covered by facings that are pinned and nailed (later) in place. The bottom rail is pinned to the top of the bottom board. The center runners for the small top drawers are lapped to a batten across the back of the case and bevel-lapped to the top drawer blade. Guides are pinned to the top surface. Runners for the long drawers and the outer small drawers are butted and glued to the case sides, except those for the bottom drawer, which are nailed to the bottom board. The interior surfaces of the case sides and bottom board retain the marks of a toothing plane. The horizontal backboard, composed of a wide and a narrow board, is rabbeted and nailed to the case sides and nailed flush across the bottom to the back of the bottom board.

(Lower case) An applied waist molding is nailed to the upper edge of the front and sides. The two-piece backboard and the two-board sides are tenoned and pinned to the corner posts. The front rail, molded slightly on the upper edge, is dovetailed to the top of the front corner posts. The upper edge of the posts and sides is similarly molded. The blade is slotted into the posts. The vertical partitions between the drawers are dovetailed to the blade and to the bottom rail, or skirt. The bottom rail is tenoned to the posts and pinned. Front-to-back battens, lapped and pegged to the front rail and notched and pegged to the backboard at the case ends, provide additional support. A series of rectangular glueblocks under the battens reinforce the joint with the case sides. The outer drawer runners, lapped to the posts and tenoned to the backboard, are nailed to a spacer board that serves as a guide and is attached to the case sides. The inner drawer runners are lapped to the bottom rail and tenoned to the backboard; a supplemental guide is pinned to the top. Knee brackets are nailed and glued to the lower edge of the front rail and case

**Fig. 3.** Detail, right front leg.

sides. The outside of the backboard retains marks of a toothing plane. The drawers in both cases are dovetailed. The tops of drawer sides are chamfered on both edges; the backs are flat or chamfered on the outer edge. The grain in the bottom of the long drawers runs from side to side and in the small drawers from front to back. The chamfered bottoms are set into grooves at the front and sides and either nailed or pinned across the back. The drawer faces are thumb molded on all sides; the side lips butt against the case facade.

**Condition:** The finial, which has been repaired, appears old and may be original. The pediment was cut to house side finials, but there is no evidence that these were used. The scrollboard is cracked at both neck extensions. The cornice molding is patched at the right front corner. The left cornice return (case side) is replaced, and the right return is cracked and repaired. The plinth tablet beneath the finial is broken and repaired. A supporting glueblock in the upper case is missing from the upper right inside corner. Several drawer runners in the upper section are replaced. Most runners are replaced in the lower section due to extensive insect damage. Some drawers are reinforced with glueblocks on the bottom or patched or restored at the sides. The applied strip facing the front edge of the bottom board, upper case, is replaced. The right side waist molding is new. All legs show evidence of insect damage. The left front corner post has been repaired at the bottom. Portions of bark

remain in the lower case on the inside of the skirt and on two of the corner posts. Some knee brackets have been replaced: left rear, left side front, right front, and right rear. The lower left drawer is marred by a large circular mark. The lower case was once severely twisted out of shape, a condition now corrected. The hardware on the two small drawers in the lower case is replaced; all other hardware is original, although variation in the size of the piercings is evident. An original escutcheon, which once lapped over the upper part of the shell, has been removed. The drops are replaced.

**Dimensions:**

| | | |
|---|---|---|
| H. (case) | 82¼ in. | 208.9 cm |
| W. (cornice) | 40 in. | 101.6 cm |
| W. (upper case) | 37⅛ in. | 94.3 cm |
| W. (lower case) | 39¾ in. | 101.0 cm |
| W. (feet) | 41⅝ in. | 105.7 cm |
| D. (cornice) | 20¾ in. | 52.7 cm |
| D. (upper case) | 18⅞ in. | 48.9 cm |
| D. (lower case) | 20⅜ in. | 51.8 cm |
| D. (feet) | 21 in. | 53.3 cm |

**Materials:** *Microanalysis:* Primary: sycamore (upper case: left side); cherry (lower case: side panels, legs, drawer blades). Secondary: yellow poplar (backboards, drawer linings); butternut (bonnet boards). *Finish:* variegated orange-brown color in resin.

**Publications:** Edward S. Cooke, Jr., "Craftsman-Client Relations in the Housatonic Valley, 1720–1800," *Antiques* 125, no. 1 (January 1984): 275, fig. 4.

**Provenance:** The high chest has a history of ownership in the Wheeler family of New Stratford (later Monroe), Conn. A misreading of the chalk date as "1734" instead of "1784" led to the assumption that the high chest was once owned by Nathan and Charity (Beach) Wheeler and had previously belonged to her mother. Charity Wheeler died in 1773, and it is more likely that the high chest was purchased by Wheeler for his second wife, Elizabeth Hawley, about the time of their marriage in 1784. The high chest was inherited by Betsey Wheeler (b. 1803), the elder child of Wheeler and his third wife, Eunice (Nichols) Edwards. According to family history, Betsey Wheeler never married and, after her mother's death in 1853, went to live with her younger brother Nathan Nichols Wheeler. The high chest was acquired by Mrs. John Williamson in 1931 from the de Forest family. Although no specific record exists of when the high chest was inherited by the de Forests, the families were neighbors, and Betsey Wheeler's older half sister, Mehetabel, married Lockwood de Forest in 1793.

**Accession history:** Purchased by H. F. du Pont from Mrs. John D. Williamson, Ramsey, N.J., 1968. Bequest of H. F. du Pont, 1969.
68.772

1. In 1762 Dayton billed Henry Curtiss for "on Case of Drawes £ 5:12:0, one Round Tabell £ 1:6:0, one ditto 8/ , 6 Chares £ 3, 6 Ditto £ 1:16:0, and 6 Ditto £ 1," Curtiss account book, vol. 2 (1749–93), Stratford Historical Society, Stratford, Conn., and Stratford Probate Court Records, vol. 3, p. 267, Stratford Town Hall, Stratford, Conn., as quoted in Edward Strong Cooke, Jr., "The Selective Conservative Taste: Furniture in Stratford, Connecticut, 1740–1800" (Master's thesis, University of Delaware, 1979), pp. 45, 273.

2. The flat-top chest was discovered by Edward S. Cooke, Jr.; see no. 78.2413, DAPC, Visual Resources Collection, Winterthur Library.

3. The second pedimented chest is in Edward S. Cooke, Jr., "Craftsman-Client Relations in the Housatonic Valley, 1720–1800," *Antiques* 125, no. 1 (January 1984): 276, fig. 5.

4. Cooke, "Craftsman-Client Relations," pp. 272–75.

5. Cooke, "Craftsman-Client Relations," pp. 275–79; C. L. Prickett advertisement, *Antiques* 137, no. 2 (February 1990): 373; Edward S. Cooke, Jr., *Fiddlebacks and Crooked-backs: Elijah Booth and Other Joiners in Newtown and Woodbury, 1750–1820* (Waterbury, Conn.: Mattatuck Historical Society, 1982), fig. 29; *American Antiques from Israel Sack Collection*, 10 vols. (Washington, D.C.: Highland House, 1969–), 7:1750; Moses, *Master Craftsmen*, figs. 1.20, 1.24, 1.25, 1.30, 1.33, 2.2, 5.15; Trent with Nelson, "A Catalogue of New London County Joined Chairs," nos. 5, 6, 21, 29, 30.

6. Furniture with related fans is in Ronald A. De Silva advertisement, *Antiques* 108, no. 6 (December 1975): 1063; Bernard and S. Dean Levy advertisement, *Antiques* 114, no. 1 (July 1978): 15; Herrup and Wolfner advertisement, *Antiques* 137, no. 4 (April 1990): 833.

7. Cooke notes that despite opportunities for exposure to new ideas and styles, consumers in the Housatonic River valley displayed a preference for designs popular earlier in the century; see Edward Strong Cooke, Jr., "Rural Artisanal Culture: The Preindustrial Joiners of Newtown and Woodbury, Connecticut, 1760–1820" (Ph.D. diss., Boston University, 1984), p. 275. Writing of the furnishings in Nathan Wheeler's home, Emily Johnston de Forest described the high chest: "But the glory of the whole room was the beautiful highboy! This was a particularly handsome one, whith the two parts of the hooded top bending toward each other, while between them stood erect a slender carved flame. On the drawers were unusually beautiful handles and escutcheons. This highboy still has in one of its drawers the inscription 'August 1734 Brewster Dayton made theese draws at Stratford'" (Mrs. Robert W. De Forest, *A Walloon Family in America*, 2 vols. [Boston: Houghton Mifflin, 1914], 1:290).

# 167 ◆ High chest of drawers
## Probably Concord, Massachusetts
## ca. 1769–76

One of the more idiosyncratic interpretations of the high chest form surrounds this blocked example long assigned to Joseph Hosmer (1735–1821), a cabinetmaker of Concord. Several generations of the Hosmer family were engaged in the building and furniture trades, but Joseph Hosmer remains one of the elusive artisans of eighteenth-century Concord. Present knowledge of his life and work is based, in large part, on a memoir written in the late nineteenth century by a granddaughter and several articles and notes published in the early to mid twentieth century. These sources cite the craftsman's training with Robert Rosier, a Frenchman married to Hosmer's cousin, his patriotic stance during the Revolution, and his subsequent public service. One author identified thirteen pieces assigned to Hosmer that had been owned in Concord families for generations. Until the early 1980s these were the core of all attributions to this Concord craftsman.[1]

The body of furniture currently associated with Hosmer falls into four distinct groups. The first group closely parallels the products of Boston and coastal Massachusetts craftsmen and includes a fall-front desk and chest of drawers, both with swelled serpentine facades; joined pad-foot seating furniture consisting of single round-shouldered and square-shouldered mahogany side chairs upholstered over the seat rail, a maple easy chair, and a maple couch (daybed); and a mahogany table with a single drop leaf. The desk and chest of drawers have an oral tradition of manufacture and use by Hosmer; the remaining pieces were owned in the Hosmer family and, by tradition, have been assigned to Joseph Hosmer. Based on the use of construction methods commonly associated with Boston-area craftsmen, however, it seems likely that this furniture was imported from the coastal center rather than made in Concord.[2]

Second and third groups of furniture are best described as functional and substantial. Nine rush-seat chairs with scrolled strapwork splats representing three patterns, the legs square or turned, form the second group. Two chairs are associated with the family of Capt. James Barrett of Concord; the others have no particular local history. Group three comprises six tall chests of singular design, including this example. Most have local histories; several are associated with dates in the 1760s and 1770s. A pedimented high chest once owned by Ebenezer Stow of Concord, who married in 1775, and a similarly embellished chest-on-chest belonging to Hugh Cargill, who settled in Concord in 1774, are in the Concord Museum. The Society for the Preservation of New England Antiquities owns a flat-top high chest that was introduced to the furnishings of a house in neighboring Weston probably during the late nineteenth century. Of the other pedimented high chests, one is in the Isaac Royall house in Medford, a town east of Concord, and another, which descended in the Wheeler family of Concord, is privately owned. By tradition, Winterthur's chest was made for Phoebe (Bliss) and William Emerson, grandparents of Ralph Waldo Emerson, in the 1770s, when the young minister of Concord and his bride moved into their new house, later called the Old Manse. Emerson died seven years later near Ticonderoga from a fever while serving as a chaplin during the revolutionary war. The six chests, which are related in design and construction, have in the past been assigned to Hosmer based on the conclusion that he made the Emerson family chest, which is said to have always stood in the upper hall of the Old Manse.[3]

Common to the six tall chests are features often associated with artisans working at a distance from a major coastal center. Design

below appears on two other chests, although the position varies.[4]

The curved, convex blocking that projects beyond the line of the drawer front in the Emerson chest is characteristic of case furniture made in eastern Massachusetts, although its use in the high chest form is rare. Here, the shape of the blocking is idiosyncratic and not particularly well integrated into the overall design. Also unusual are the size and arrangement of drawers. Three small drawers in the upper and lower tiers of a high chest are the norm. In the base, the shallow and deep units are generally reversed from the arrangement seen here.[5]

A single chest-on-chest, now in the Concord Museum, constitutes the fourth group of furniture associated with Hosmer. In modern times the chest has been linked with the Tarbell family of Acton, a town adjacent to Concord. An old inscription reading "made by Joseph Hosmer Concord Mass/ 1782" is now identified as being of nineteenth-century date, although it probably has validity. More important are the names "Louina Davis" and "Abel Davis 1782" that are written in chalk on the backs of two drawers and are probably contemporary with the chest. The Davises ran a tavern near Concord; Louina was the daughter of Hosmer. The chest-on-chest, an accomplished piece of cabinetry, exhibits none of the peculiarities of construction and design associated with the chests in group three, heretofore considered the work of Hosmer.[6]

In conclusion, the body of furniture assigned to or associated with Joseph Hosmer through the years runs the gamut from sophisticated to vernacular examples, based on exterior design and interior construction. Although much of the furniture has a strong association with Concord or Concord families, no piece is signed or otherwise documented to Hosmer. Only a chest bearing the names of Hosmer's daughter and son-in-law appears

and construction solutions often appear labored, the work of a joiner rather than a cabinetmaker, and the cases are overengineered and overbuilt. Posts are common at the interior corners of the chests, and diagonal braces frequently strengthen the tops of the lower cases. Some backboards are chamfered at the edges, and some drawers exhibit construction peculiarities. The knee brackets, which are distinctive in pattern, are tenoned into the leg

tops; pins secure the joints in Winterthur's chest. A small, inverted triangular overlay is another prominent design feature, which in this chest appears both top and bottom (fig. 1). As in other chests with pediment tops, the central finial of Winterthur's chest should rest directly on the pedestal without benefit of a secondary plinth—the restoration, made in the early twentieth century, is incorrect. The decorative brass plate centered in the fan

to have a reasonable chance of coming from his shop. Given the long association of Winterthur's chest with Concord, the casepiece probably originated in the town or its vicinity. Until more work is done on the local cabinetmaking community, however, even speculation as to the chest's maker is indefensible.

NER/NGE

**Fig. 1.** Detail, pediment facade.

**Inscriptions or marks:** *Scratched on all drawer blades in upper section from top to bottom:* "IIII", "III", "II", and "I". *Chiseled on top front of fourth drawer in upper case:* "V". *Deep drawer in lower case:* "V". *On bottom of deep drawer in lower case:* "I" *in chalk. On upper surface of right cornice molding and adjacent pediment roof; on top and bottom surfaces at left end of drawer blades in upper case, and in same locations on bladelike front rail at top of lower case; and on top and bottom surfaces at right end of drawer blade in lower case: an original shop mark consisting of an incised compass circle with a center point.*

**Construction:** (Upper case) The case top, which consists of one deep and one shallow board, is joined to the case sides from the back in a sliding half-dovetail that is positioned about 2 1/2" below the top edge of the side panels. The top supports the pediment, which is faced with a scrollboard rabbeted to the front faces of the side panels and nailed. A backboard mounted at the same level is rabbeted to the back of the case sides. The vertical sides of the boxlike opening centered in the pediment are slotted to the scrollboard and backboard. Additional structural strength is provided by thick two-board battens nailed from front to back along the upper edge of the box sides and reinforced with nails driven in through the backboard. The mitered, cavetto cornice molding is nailed to the scrollboard, case sides, and front part of the battens. The pediment roof is secured with rosehead nails to a rabbet in the scrollboard and to the top of the battens and the backboard. A supplementary row of nails extends down the roof center to the side panels, secured to an internal medial brace. A false bottom at the pediment center behind the top of the carved fan is slotted into the scrollboard and nailed to the lip of a boxlike opening in the backboard. The

central plinth of the scrollboard supports an inverted triangular-shape ornament at the front that is slotted to the cap piece and nailed at the bottom. The cap piece, which is secured with sprigs, supports a small removable square plinth and finial. Similar plinths supporting finials are mounted at the outer front corners of the pediment. The thirty-one-ribbed carved fan at the front of the scrollboard is faced at the center bottom with an applied double-ogee-shape brass plate secured with two brass nails. The four beaded and blocked drawer blades are slotted to the front faces of the side panels, the joints concealed with vertical double-beaded facing strips nailed in place. The upper edge of the top drawer opening has an applied bead nailed in place. The two-board case bottom is dovetailed to the case sides. It is supported on the underside by an X-shape brace lapped at the center and tenoned to the sides of the lower case. Thin drawer runners are nailed to the case sides behind all drawer blades. The bottom drawer runs on thin facing strips nailed to the bottom board. The two-board lapped backboard (the upper board chamfered on four edges, the lower board chamfered only on the sides) is rabbeted and nailed to the case sides and nailed to the back of the bottom board. Thin, vertical bracing strips are nailed in place at the inside back corners. Incised layout lines for blocking the drawer blades and the front rail of the lower case occur on the top and bottom surfaces of those elements.

(Lower case) The case sides and back are tenoned and pinned. The bladelike rail at the case top fronts the bottom board of the upper case but is not attached to it. The rail is lap-joined at the front corners to the side moldings, which are nailed to the top edge of the case sides, providing a shallow well to secure the upper case. The drawer blade is attached to the front corner posts with sliding

dovetails concealed by applied beaded facings nailed in place. The skirt is tenoned to the front posts and leg tops and pinned. The upper edge of the skirt is finished with a nailed bead that corresponds to the bead lining the bottom edge of the scrollboard. The flat-arch skirt of the side panels complements that of the case front. The central pendant of the front skirt supports a second triangular-shape ornament nailed in place. A small molding nailed to the bottom of the pendant accommodates a turned drop. The legs and corner posts are one piece. The knees of the rear legs extend beyond the back of the case. The knee brackets facing the front skirt and side panels are tenoned to the leg tops and pinned and nailed to the skirt boards. The drawer runners, which are nailed to the case sides, are also lap-joined and nailed to the corner posts. Guides are glued to the outer top surface. Thin, vertical strips are nailed in place at the back corners of the case.

The drawers in both cases are dovetailed. The blocked drawer fronts are cut from solid wood and shaped on the interior to conform to the exterior profile. Layout marks are present. The drawer sides, which are lower than the front, have a tiny chamfer on both edges. The thick drawer back has a chamfer on the outside edge. The two-board drawer bottoms are set into rabbets at the front and nailed flush at the sides and back; the grain runs from side to side in those of the upper case and from front to back in those of the lower case. The drawers of the lower case are partitioned to form three sections. The partitions are slotted to the upper drawer back and secured with nailed, U-shape braces that pierce the drawer bottom at the front.

**Condition:** The central plinth block of the pediment and the molding and turned drop of the skirt pendant are replaced (an old photograph shows the chest without these elements; see folder 52.256, Registration Office, Winterthur). The right finial is pieced on either side of the post; the left one has a chip missing from the base. Although old, the side finials may be replacements of two different periods; the left finial has a tighter spiral than the right one. The center finial is a later copy of the left finial. The scrollboard is split in the upper left neck. The upper left case side is split at the top front corner, and there are gouge marks across the center. The left cornice molding has been reset after case repairs. The top left molding of the lower case has been repaired. The locks are missing from the upper two of the top three drawers, upper case, which were fitted for locks. A punched mark similar to that on a nine-spot domino appears on the right front surface of the fourth drawer from the top in the upper case. The left front interior bracket supporting the drawer partition in the bottom drawer, lower case, is replaced; it is also secured with rosehead nails instead of sprigs like the others.

**Dimensions:**

| | | |
|---|---|---|
| H. (with finials) | 89 1/8 in. | 226.4 cm |
| H. (case) | 82 3/8 in. | 209.2 cm |
| W. (cornice) | 41 1/4 in. | 104.8 cm |
| W. (upper case) | 38 1/4 in. | 97.2 cm |
| W. (lower case) | 40 in. | 101.6 cm |
| W. (feet) | 40 1/2 in. | 102.9 cm |
| D. (cornice) | 21 in. | 53.3 cm |
| D. (upper case) | 19 1/2 in. | 49.5 cm |
| D. (lower case) | 19 3/4 in. | 50.2 cm |
| D. (feet) | 20 3/8 in. | 51.7 cm |

**Materials:** *Microanalysis:* Primary: cherry (case front, drawer fronts); soft maple group (case sides). Secondary: white pine group (upper case: backboard, drawer linings); soft maple group (lower case: backboard). *Finish:* dark reddish orange-brown color in resin worn to a mottled surface on the drawer fronts; crackled resin on all surfaces is worn smooth around the hardware and the brass plate of the scrollboard; the maple sides of the case were probably colored originally to approximate the hue of the cherrywood facade.

**Exhibitions:** From 1930 until its sale, the high chest was exhibited at the Concord Antiquarian Society (now Concord Museum) for 10 months each year by the owners of the Old Manse, Concord, Mass.

**Publications:** Nutting, *Furniture Treasury,* no. 342. Hazel E. Cummin, "The Concord Antiquarian Collection and Its Setting, Part 2," *Old-Time New England* 22, no. 2 (October 1931): 61. Russell H. Kettell, "Joseph Hosmer, Cabinetmaker: His Work," *Antiques* 73, no. 4 (April 1958): 359, fig. 6. Lester Margon, *More American Furniture Treasures, 1620–1840* (New York: Architectural Book Publishing Co., 1971), p. 242. Myrna Kaye, "Concord Case Furniture: Cabinetry Twenty Miles from the Bay," in Peter Benes, ed., *The Bay and the River, 1600–1900,* Dublin Seminar for New England Folklife Annual Proceedings, 1981 (Boston: Boston University Scholarly Publications, 1982), p. 35, fig. 4. Downs, *American Furniture,* fig. 189. Kirk, *American Furniture,* fig. 395. Margaretta Markle Lovell, "Boston Blockfront Furniture," in *Boston Furniture,* p. 130. David F. Wood, ed., *The Concord Museum: Decorative Arts from a New England Collection* (Concord, Mass.: By the museum, 1996), fig. 11.1.

**Provenance:** According to tradition, the high chest was made for Phoebe Bliss (1741–1825) of Concord on the occasion of her marriage to the Reverend William Emerson (1743–76) of Concord. It stood in the second floor hall of the "Old Manse," the home Emerson built in Concord in 1770. Emerson died in 1776, and 4 years later his widow married his successor, the Reverend Ezra Ripley (1751–1841). The high chest passed to their granddaughter, Sophia Ripley, wife of James B. Thayer, and then to their youngest child, Sarah Ripley Thayer, who married John W. Ames. Ames, who inherited the high chest from his wife in 1939, remembers seeing the piece in the second-floor hall of the "Old Manse" in 1878. An old photograph inscribed on the reverse, "Reginald Lewis Coll," suggests that the high chest was owned by Lewis prior to its purchase by Charles Woolsey Lyon (folder 52.256, Registration Office, Winterthur).

**Accession history:** Purchased by H. F. du Pont from Charles Woolsey Lyon, Inc., New York, 1949. Gift of H. F. du Pont, 1952.
52.256

1. Citing "the design, wood, and history" of Winterthur's chest, Joseph Downs asserted that "this unique high chest was almost certainly made by Joseph Hosmer in Concord, Massachusetts"; Downs, *American Furniture,* fig. 189. Cabriole-style furniture has been assigned to Joseph Hosmer (1735–1821), a cousin John (1752–1814), and to another cousin Rufus (1809–33); see Nancy Cooper, "A Family of New England Cabinetmakers," *House Beautiful* 66, no. 6 (December 1929): 729, 764, 766–67. Kenneth Scott, "Joseph Hosmer, Cabinetmaker: His Life," and Russell H. Kettell, "Joseph Hosmer, Cabinetmaker: His Work," *Antiques* 73, no. 4 (April 1958): 356–59; Josephine Hosmer, "Memoir of Joseph Hosmer," in *The Centennial of the Social Circle in Concord* (Cambridge: Riverside Press, 1882), pp. 114–19; Myrna Kaye, "Concord Case Furniture: Cabinetry Twenty Miles from the Bay," in Peter Benes, ed., *The Bay and the River, 1600–1900,* Dublin Seminar for New England Folklife Annual Proceedings, 1981 (Boston: Boston University Scholarly Publications, 1982), pp. 29–42; Ethel Hall Bjerkoe with John Arthur Bjerkoe, *The Cabinetmakers of America* (Garden City, N.Y.: Doubleday, 1957), s.v. "Hosmer, Joseph." For the 13 attributions, see Kettell, "Joseph Hosmer," pp. 358–59.

2. Christie's, "Fine Americana: Metalwork, Folk Art, Memorabilia, and Furniture" (March 10, 1978), lots 156–58; Dean A. Fales, Jr., "Hosmer Family Furniture," *Antiques* 83, no. 5 (May 1963): 548–49.

3. Scott, "Joseph Hosmer," and Kettell, "Joseph Hosmer," pp. 357–59, fig. 7; Kaye, "Concord Case Furniture," pp. 30–31, 33–34; Hazel E. Cummin, "The Concord Antiquarian Collection and Its Setting, Part 2," *Old-Time New England* 22, no. 2 (October 1931): 60.

4. Kaye, "Concord Case Furniture," pp. 29–31, 40–41; Jobe and Kaye, *New England Furniture,* no. 38.

5. For other blockfront high chests, see Jobe, *Portsmouth Furniture,* cat. no. 16; Sotheby's, "Important Americana: The Bertram K. Little and Nina Fletcher Little Collection, Part 1" (January 29, 1994), lot 428; Kenneth and Paulette Tuttle advertisement, *Antiques* 123, no. 1 (January 1983): 36; Leigh Keno advertisement, *Antiques* 138, no. 6 (December 1990): 1166; David F. Wood, ed., *The Concord Museum: Decorative Arts from a New England Collection* (Concord, Mass.: By the museum, 1996), cat. 10A.

6. Kaye, "Concord Case Furniture," pp. 38, 42; telephone conversation with David Wood, curator, Concord Museum, December 18, 1995.

## 168 ◆ Dressing table
### Northeastern Massachusetts
### 1745–65

The dressing table is among the earliest case forms embellished with blocking on the facade. Tables with both flat-blocking, as seen on this example, and round-blocking (see No. 169) are known, although they are uncommon. The stylistic features of this table date it sometime after the introduction of the early Queen Anne style in the 1730s and probably into the third quarter of the century, when the chest of drawers reemerged as a popular household form. The emphasis on depth and verticality in the introduction of a third row of brass handles to simulate a drawer front suggests that the maker was strongly influenced by the multidrawer facade of the chest of drawers.[1]

Several other features support this dating range. The steep, ogee-molded edge of the tabletop is a profile introduced between the thumb-molded lip of the William and Mary and early Queen Anne tabletop (see No. 158) and the projecting ogee of the mature blockfront chest of drawers (see Nos. 176, 179) and some later dressing tables (see No. 164). The lipped drawer with its narrow thumb-molded edge abutting the case replaced the flush drawer of the William and Mary–style case during the 1730s and remained popular in the dressing table and tall chest forms until after the Revolution. The broad, flat arches of the skirt separated by pendants supporting turned drops identify a profile introduced after those on No. 159, which is marked by a high central arch, and No. 160, a type also embellished with large ogee-sided pendants; both designs appeared in the 1730s. Integrating the various elements of the facade is the overhanging top with its patterned forward edge, which reverses the profile of the skirt.

The feet of the dressing table are distinctive. The edges of the large pads are precisely defined, even at the back, which is scored with a scribe line. The heel above has been chamfered, leaving a small hock behind the ankle. This feature is also present in rudimentary form in No. 169.

Counting Winterthur's example, eight tables with flat-blocking have been located, including the three earliest known blockfront tables. These were made in New Hampshire possibly in the mid 1730s by a Boston-trained craftsman. The three raised panels of the facades are poorly integrated into the cases, which also include carved, central shells and fluted pilasters at the corners, suggesting that the design and execution of blockfront furniture was still in the experimental stage.[2]

Another early table, one with well-integrated blocking, also has strong earmarks of 1730s design but differs subtly from the New Hampshire examples. The facade of three drawers—two deep and one shallow—is organized like the plain-front dressing tables and high chest bases of the 1720s and 1730s (see Nos. 158, 161). The thumb-molded edge of the top and the high-arch center of the skirt complement the early three-drawer theme. The applied bead of the skirt edges, front and sides, is a delicate feature that continues as a scratch bead down the outside edges of the cabriole legs terminated by squarish pad feet.[3]

Next in date stylistically is a blockfront dressing table that has walnut-veneered surfaces with inlaid checkered borders and a centered, high-relief inlaid shell. The shaped top has a complex molded edge, but the hocked feet relate closely to those in Winterthur's table. The blocked facade, organized in the usual way with two raised and one central recessed panel, includes a long top drawer and three relatively shallow lower drawers. The table has an eastern Massachusetts provenance.[4]

Another dressing table with the same drawer arrangement and blocked facade but none of the ornamental embellishments of the veneered example was executed with a plain case. The feet again follow the pattern of those in Winterthur's table, as does the lip of the tabletop. Thus, within a basic framework, craftsmen were innovative and could produce cases of individual character. The plain table is the only one among the eight in the sample that is made of mahogany; the rest are walnut.[5]

An eighth table, the blocking more angular than in the others, has six small flush drawers in two tiers. Because the drawers are deeper than those in Winterthur's table, the skirt is shallow and inappropriate for garnishing with an extra row of brass hardware.[6]

Winterthur's dressing table first came to public notice at the beginning of the twentieth century when it turned up in Saco or Kennebunk, Maine, and was purchased by a dealer named Miller. The table passed into the hands of Israel Sack, located at that date in Boston, who sold it to Boston collector Arthur W. Wellington for the then-substantial sum of $300. According to Sack, "At the time it was the talk of Boston that someone would pay that much for an old piece of furniture." The table was purchased by Henry Francis du Pont in 1927, in time to be exhibited in the prestigious Girl Scout loan exhibition of 1929.[7]

*NGE*

---

**Inscriptions or marks:** *On backboard:* "Back/ X" inverted, in white chalk. *On drawer openings and some drawers:* modern penciled numbers.

**Construction:** The two-board top, with notched corners and ogee-molded edges on all four sides, overhangs the case on all sides. Originally secured in part by glueblocks, the top currently is pinned to the frame. Screws secure the top to the top rail at the front. The case sides and backboard are tenoned and pinned to the posts, six pins at each post. The lower front rail, or skirt, its blocking cut from solid wood, is tenoned and double-pinned. The top rail is tenoned into the top of the posts. The drawer blade is attached to the corner posts on an inset (shouldered) dovetail. The vertical drawer dividers

are one piece, notched to pass behind the blade; they are dovetailed at the bottom and inset dovetailed at the top. The outer drawer runners are secured with rosehead nails to the case sides, lapped to the drawer blade or skirt at the front, and tenoned to the backboard. The inner runners are tenoned to the backboard and half-lapped to the front members. The drawers, which are dovetailed front and back, have projecting fronts that are cut from solid wood and are flat on the inside surface. The drawer sides are slightly rounded on the upper edge; the backs are flat on top. The drawer bottoms, the grain running from front to back, are chamfered on three sides, slotted into the front and sides, and nailed flush with rosehead nails across the back. A narrow thumbmolding finishes the front edges of the drawers; the side and top lips butt against the case. The legs are one piece with the case posts. The rear legs are finished on the back and project beyond the frame. The knee brackets are glued to the skirt and case sides.

**Condition:** The top has been refinished, but the case retains remnants of an old finish. The top has warped causing the old pins to fail. The right rear knee bracket is missing; the one at the right front is cracked at the inside tip. The pendent drops are replaced, and the forward half of the left cap above the drop has been replaced. Several drawer lips have been repaired. Glueblocks securing the top are missing at the left side and renewed at the right side. There are deteriorated and missing knots in the backboard. The brass hardware on the upper left drawer once was placed closer to the top to accommodate the lock, which is modern.

**Dimensions:**

| | | |
|---|---|---|
| H. | 32⁷⁄₈ in. | 83.5 cm |
| W. (top) | 36¹⁄₈ in. | 91.7 cm |
| W. (feet) | 33¹⁄₈ in. | 84.1 cm |
| D. (top) | 21 in. | 53.3 cm |
| D. (feet) | 20 in. | 50.8 cm |
| W. (case) | 30³⁄₄ in. | 78.1 cm |
| D. (case) | 18¹⁄₁₆ in. | 46.2 cm |

**Materials:** *Microanalysis:* Primary: American black walnut. Secondary: white pine group (backboard, drawer linings, drawer runners). *Finish:* mottled medium to dark reddish brown color in resin, the resin heavy and crackled in many places.

**Exhibitions:** "Loan Exhibition of Eighteenth- and Early Nineteenth-Century Furniture and Glass," National Council of Girl Scouts, New York, September 25–October 9, 1929.

**Publications:** Lockwood, *Colonial Furniture*, fig. 101. National Council of Girl Scouts, *Loan Exhibition of Eighteenth- and Early Nineteenth-Century Furniture and Glass* (New York: By the council, 1929), cat. 616. John T. Kirk, *Early American Furniture* (1970; reprint, New York: Alfred A. Knopf, 1981), fig. 99. Downs, *American Furniture*, fig. 325. Butler, *American Furniture*, p. 33. Margaretta Markle Lovell, "Boston Blockfront Furniture," in *Boston Furniture*, p. 97, fig. 67. Don Nicholson De Marino, "In the Eye of the Beholder," in *Delaware Antiques Show 1975* (Wilmington, Del.), p. 54, fig. 4.

**Provenance:** The dressing table is reported to have turned up in Saco or Kennebunk, Maine, about 1902. It was acquired by Israel Sack and sold to Arthur W. Wellington of Boston. Sack reacquired the dressing table in 1916 and sold it to Samuel Galston King of Boston. It was reacquired by Sack in 1927.

**Accession history:** Purchased by H. F. du Pont from Israel Sack, Boston, through Collings and Collings, New York, 1927. Bequest of H. F. du Pont, 1969. 63.975

---

1. One idiosyncratic high chest of drawers with a blocked facade, made in New Hampshire, 1735–50, is known; see Jobe, *Portsmouth Furniture*, cat. no. 16.

2. Jobe, *Portsmouth Furniture*, fig. 29, cat. nos. 17, 17a.

3. The dressing table is in Bernard and S. Dean Levy advertisement, *Antiques* 129, no. 3 (March 1986): 455.

4. The dressing table is in Flanigan, *American Furniture*, cat. no. 21.

5. The dressing table is in Charles Navis advertisement, *Antiques* 106, no. 2 (August 1974): 201.

6. The dressing table is in Helen Comstock, "The American Lowboy: An Antiques Survey," *Antiques* 80, no. 6 (December 1962): 572, fig. 8.

7. Folder 63.975, Registration Office, Winterthur; National Council of Girl Scouts, *Loan Exhibition of Eighteenth- and Early Nineteenth-Century Furniture and Glass* (New York: By the council, 1929), cat. 616.

## 169 ◆ Dressing table
Northeastern Massachusetts,
probably Boston
1745–65

The dressing table form offered a range of possibilities for case development, from flat surfaces of solid wood or banded veneer to baroque facades laid out in projecting and receding planes. One of the most innovative cases is this example with round blocking, a six-drawer format, and a row of supplemental brass hardware on the skirt simulating a third tier of drawers. The interplay and repetition of curved lines in the round blocking, shaped top, ogee side skirts, crescentlike knee brackets, and cabriole legs illustrate the principles of order and variety put forth by William Hogarth in *The Analysis of Beauty* (London, 1753). The painter-engraver and social commentator considered the wavy profile (S curve) the "line of beauty." Its undulations added grace and intricacy to a form, leading the eye on "a wanton kind of chace."[1]

From the steeply curved ogee lip of the tabletop and the chamfered heels of the pad feet to the extra row of brass hardware below the drawers and the diminutive pendants in the skirt, this dressing table shares many features with No. 168. It is one of seven similarly designed and scaled round-blocked dressing tables that appear to have come from the same or nearby shops. Of the group, this is the only table made of mahogany; the rest are walnut. Except for the ball-and-claw feet on one example and the lack of brass hardware on the skirt of another, there is little difference in design among the seven. The brasses and turned drops vary, but some are replacements. Modest variation is also discernable in the hooklike tips of the knee brackets and the lip of the tabletop. Two tables have histories in New England families. In date these round-blocked dressing tables appear to be contemporary with the square-blocked table of No. 168. Like the blockfront chest of drawers,

the flat-blocked table probably preceded the rounded one in the consumer market.[2]

This dressing table, inscribed "Cushing" in pencil on the backboard (fig. 1), has a tradition of ownership in one of eighteenth-century Boston's influential mercantile families. Three generations of Cushings—Thomas I (1663–1740), Thomas, Jr. (1693–1746), and Thomas III (1725–88)—were prominent importers, and all held important public offices. Thomas I was a member of the King's Council in Massachusetts. His son, a Harvard graduate, became speaker of the Massachusetts House of Representatives before the Revolution. Thomas III served in the same capacity and was a delegate to the First Continental Congress in 1774. He later became lieutenant governor of Massachusetts. The Cushings were linked to another eminent trading family through Thomas, Jr.'s, marriage to Mary Bromfield, the youngest daughter of Boston

merchant Edward Bromfield. Thomas Cushing, Jr., is known to have patronized many of Boston's leading cabinetmakers. His waste book lists purchases from Job Coit, Thomas Sherburne, and Nathaniel Holmes; however, no documentary evidence has been found to link this dressing table to a specific craftsman. Furthermore, its design is more sophisticated and the construction technically more competent than that of the blockfront desk-and-bookcase in No. 205, the only documented example of Coit's work.[3]

Like many pieces of early American furniture that were relegated to attics and other storage places once they became unfashionable and were replaced with more current patterns and forms, Winterthur's dressing table was eventually rescued from its hideaway by a member of a later generation and "modernized" for further use. Sometime during the nineteenth century, someone refurbished it

**Fig. 1.** Detail, outside surface of backboard.

**Dimensions:**

| | | |
|---|---|---|
| H. | 31 1/8 in. | 79.1 cm |
| W. (top) | 33 5/8 in. | 85.4 cm |
| W. (case) | 29 3/4 in. | 75.6 cm |
| W. (feet) | 31 in. | 78.7 cm |
| D. (case) | 18 1/4 in. | 46.4 cm |
| D. (top) | 21 11/16 in. | 52.1 cm |
| D. (feet) | 18 3/4 in. | 47.6 cm |

**Materials:** *Microanalysis:* Primary: mahogany. Secondary: white pine group (drawer linings, backboard). *Finish:* medium reddish brown color in resin, the legs somewhat darker.

**Publications:** Butler, *American Furniture*, p. 33. Margaretta Markle Lovell, "Boston Blockfront Furniture," in *Boston Furniture*, pp. 96–97. Charles F. Montgomery and Patricia E. Kane, eds., *American Art, 1750–1800: Towards Independence* (Boston: New York Graphic Society for Yale University Art Gallery and Victoria and Albert Museum, 1976), p. 150.

**Provenance:** Ex coll.: Reginald M. Lewis, Easton, Md.

**Accession history:** Purchased by H. F. du Pont, 1964.
61.142

with a stationary dressing glass—two plugged holes and the outline of rectangular fittings attest to the transformation.

*NER/NGE*

**Inscription or marks:** *On the outside backboard:* "Cushing" in pencil. The drawer openings are numbered in modern pencil from 1 to 6, out of sequence. Miscellaneous chalk and modern pencil markings are on all the drawers.

**Construction:** The top, made of a broad and a narrow board with four notched corners, is ogee molded on the front and side edges and rounded slightly on the back. The top conforms to the shape of the case and overhangs slightly on all four sides. It is nailed to the top rail from below and further reinforced on the interior by small glueblocks on all four sides. The case sides, their lower edges shaped in a double ogee, are tenoned and double-pinned to the posts. The backboard is also tenoned and pinned to the posts. The drawer blade is dovetailed to the posts. The top rail is tenoned into the corner posts; the bottom rail, or skirt, is tenoned and double-pinned. The swelled fronts of the skirt are formed from solid wood. The one-piece vertical dividers, notched to pass in front of the drawer blades, are dovetailed to the top rail and skirt. The

outside drawer runners are fixed with rosehead nails to the case sides; the interior runners are bevel-lapped to the front members and tenoned into the backboard. The knee brackets are glued over the skirt and case sides. The legs are one piece with the corner posts. The knees on the rear legs do not project beyond the back of the case. The drawers are dovetailed, front and back, and the fronts of the outer drawers are hollowed roughly on the inside to conform to the facade. The drawer sides are rounded on the upper edge; the backs are slightly chamfered on the outer edge. The drawer bottoms are chamfered on three sides, set into grooves in the front and sides, and nailed flush across the back with rosehead nails. A narrow thumbmolding finishes the front edges of the drawers; the side and top lips butt against the case.

**Condition:** The top has two plugged holes and bears the outline of rectangular fittings that once mounted a dressing glass. The upper backboard and a large portion of the upper right drawer runner are heavily damaged by insects. Many drawer lips have been repaired, patched, or renewed. The pendent drops are replacements. The hardware has been replaced at least twice; ghosts of a larger set of similarly shaped brasses and single holes for central pulls remain. The outer surface has been refinished.

1. Edward T. Joy discusses Hogarth's *Analysis of Beauty* in "Furniture," in *The Connoisseur Period Guides: The Early Georgian Period, 1714–1760* (London: The Connoisseur, 1957), p. 39.

2. The other 6 round-blocked dressing tables are in Alexandra W. Rollins, "Furniture in the Collection of the Dietrich American Foundation," *Antiques* 125, no. 5 (May 1984): 1109, pl. 10; Robert W. Skinner advertisement, *Antiques* 137, no. 5 (May 1990): 1085; Ruth Davidson, "Auction Notes," *Antiques* 86, no. 3 (September 1964): 324; Albert Sack, *Fine Points of Furniture: Early American* (New York: Crown Publishers, 1950), p. 193 top; Sotheby Parke Bernet, "The American Heritage Society Auction of Americana" (November 16–18, 1978), lot 948; Weschlers Auctioneers' advertisement, *Antiques and the Arts Weekly*, April 14, 1995, p. 175. The only other round-blocked dressing table known is of New York origin with a distinctively different overall design; see *American Antiques from Israel Sack Collection*, 10 vols. (Washington, D.C.: Highland House, 1969–), 9:2458–59.

3. The Thomas Cushing, Jr., waste book is in the Baker Library, Harvard University, Cambridge, Mass., as cited in Margaretta Markle Lovell, "Boston Blockfront Furniture," in *Boston Furniture*, p. 95.

## 170 ◆ Dressing table
Probably Rhode Island, possibly
Washington County
1750–75

The challenges of attributing this piece of
furniture, one of three known low cases
produced in the same shop, are many,
ranging from place of origin to identification
of "J. Larkin," who inscribed a drawer in one
of the two related dressing tables. A broad
survey of visual sources has failed to produce
additional pieces of furniture from this shop
or work bearing similar shells on the knees or
related carved ornament centered in the skirt.[1]

The dressing tables from the hand of the
craftsman who made this piece of furniture
share several distinctive features, yet each
has independent characteristics. The visual
articulation of the cabriole legs and their
extensions at the case corners are the same in
all three tables. The knee brackets attach to
the leg tops but neither face nor abut the case
skirts in the usual way, producing a delicate
balance between support and case somewhat
in the manner of a William and Mary dressing
table. The same elongated ribbed shell with
volute extensions at the sides ornaments the
knees of each table (fig. 1), although subtle
variation occurs in the design of the shell
drops, volutes, and bracket edges—the shells
of this example have two fewer ribs than
the others. The legs of all three tables
sweep forcefully, yet gracefully, into bold,
competently carved claw feet that have more
the character of Philadelphia than New
England craftsmanship.

Other features of Winterthur's dressing
table set it apart from the two related tables.
The interrupted-ogee profile of the edges and
complex double-ogee front corners of the
top contrast with the deep, shallow-molded
edges and single forward notches of the other
two tables. The depths of the cases and
organization of the facades are also different.
The drawers in the other tables form a single

tier—a broad, shallow drawer at the center
and two deep ones at the sides. The large,
centered shells of those cases fill the void
below the broad drawer rather than the
confined space of a shallow skirt, somewhat
in the manner of a Newport dressing table
(see No. 173). Although the shells of all
three tables are set within shallow arches,
Winterthur's differs in its smaller size and
composition from the other two, which are
more closely related in detail. Rather than
having scroll-sawed skirts, those tables are
flat at the lower edges with only simple ogee
cutouts flanking the open bottoms of the
shells. In one, a bead finishes the front corners
of the case and the bottom edge of the skirt.

The assignment of a definite place of
origin to these tables, although based on
circumstantial evidence only, permits a more
focused examination of relevant materials
than previous general associations with New
England and the Middle Atlantic region have
allowed. The construction materials provide
some insights. The primary wood of two
tables is black walnut; that of the third is
cherrywood. Yellow poplar and chestnut are

present in all three tables as secondary
woods. Oak occurs in two tables; it is further
identified in Winterthur's example as red
oak. Chestnut is usually associated with
furniture made in eastern Connecticut and
Rhode Island (see Nos. 172, 173), although it
appears occasionally in eastern Massachusetts
cabinetwork (see No. 165). Red oak is
considerably less common, but a survey of
published information on the collections of
two prominent institutions identifies red oak
as a secondary wood in Queen Anne– and
Chippendale-style casework from Connecticut
to Maine.[2]

"J. Larkin," which is inscribed in chalk on
a drawer in one of the related dressing tables
and appears to be contemporary with the piece
of furniture, offers another clue to the origin
of Winterthur's table. Although the federal
census of 1790—the only comprehensive body
of data for tracking families over broad areas
in the eighteenth century—is of late date and
perhaps as much as two generations removed
from the maker of the dressing tables, it
pinpoints concentrations of Larkin family
members in two areas of New England. Other

records confirm that family representatives were resident in both locations from the late seventeenth century.[3]

Twelve Larkins were heads of households in Massachusetts in 1790; eight of them were in the greater Boston area. Of the twelve, two men are known to have made furniture: John (1724–98) in Charlestown and Boston and Thomas (1730–99) in Charlestown and Marlborough. Both are listed in records as chairmakers, however, indicating that the focus of their trade was turnery rather than cabinetwork. The men were likely descendants of Edward Larkin (d. 1677), a turner in Charlestown.[4]

A second concentration of Larkins numbering twenty-five heads of households, was located in Washington County, Rhode Island, in 1790, with an additional member each in the communities of Newport and Providence. Washington County is bounded west by Connecticut, south by the Atlantic Ocean, and east by Narragansett Bay. Family members resided in the towns (or townships) of Charlestown, Hopkinton, Richmond, South Kingstown (now South Kingston), and Westerly. Three family heads were among the "free Inhabitants of the towne of westerle" in 1669.[5]

A search of town records for Hopkinton, Richmond, South Kingstown, and Westerly has yielded mixed information, although one circumstance appears reasonably certain: the J. Larkin who signed one of the dressing tables was not a furniture craftsman. No evidence was uncovered to support an attribution. Several candidates as owners emerge from the records, but again the evidence is inconclusive. Most prominent among these men is John Larkin of Westerly, who died in 1773 and was titled *esquire* at times. His son John (d. 1777?) resided in neighboring Hopkinton, a town formed from part of Westerly in 1757. These men were principally farmers. Another John Larkin (1755–1821) resided in South Kingstown. His life dates

**Fig. 1.** Detail, right front leg.

appear too late to make him the original owner of the dressing table; he also was a farmer. The paucity of furniture in the inventories of these men probably is explainable in light of the bequests made to family members. The bequeathed household furnishings were removed or set aside before the appraisers made their estate evaluations.[6]

Washington County's fifty-mile coastline provided a strong and profitable maritime economy supported by fertile, productive land. The region was famous for its breed of Narragansett pacing horses; dairying and grain cultivation were equally important. Fish stocked in an abundance of salt- and freshwater ponds were exported in quantity. The Pawcatuck River, which divides into the Charles and Wood rivers above Westerly, was the site of numerous mills, an area that by the early nineteenth century was devoted principally to the manufacture of cotton and woolen goods. Shipbuilding was another local industry. In short, Washington County was a prosperous and productive rural region whose citizens were well able to afford luxury furniture constructed of fine cabinet woods embellished with rich sawed, molded, and carved ornament. The county's coastal

location and ease of access to the urban centers of Newport, Providence, Boston, New York, and even Philadelphia likely encouraged a cross fertilization of ideas that contributed to the eclectic, idiosyncratic design of these tables.[7]

The complex, molded double-ogee corners of the top of Winterthur's table are uncommon. Occasionally tea or dining tables ascribed to Connecticut or Rhode Island have this feature. The shell of the skirt relates to those of the other two tables, and yet each is distinctly different. The compact form recalls Philadelphia work, although the open base likely reflects the influence of the Newport dressing table form with its broad, fluted shell sometimes contained within a scribed arc (see No. 173). The sawed skirt of Winterthur's table has no known prototype. The intricacy of the pattern again suggests Philadelphia craftsmanship; however, an unusual tall chest on a scroll-sawed frame assigned to Rhode Island in the early twentieth century, based perhaps on family descent, indicates that there may have been a more local source for the feature.[8]

The curve of the legs in the three dressing tables is generous but not exaggerated; the knees may bulge somewhat more in this example than the others. The profile is not unlike that found on some fully developed Newport card, tea, and dining tables with claw feet. A rare Newport side table with marble top, pad feet, and pronounced leg curves has the similar leg and corner post articulation in which the brackets are attached solely to the knees.[9]

The ornament of the knees, which is similar in the three dressing tables except for the small drop below the shell, is of singular design (see fig. 1). The basic element, the elongated ribbed shell of the center, is a general type with a broad distribution— Philadelphia, New York, Rhode Island, Boston. The sweep of the outer ribs into the volutes of the brackets is rare and possibly unique to the work of this craftsman. In other examples, the scrolls terminate at the arched tips of the ribs, and many are no more than a slim bead (see No. 24). Symmetrical three-petal bellflower drops frequently accompany these shells. The drops on the three tables are of independent design, however. That on Winterthur's table is a scored ellipse on a stem, and those on the other two tables are tapered, slightly curved rootlike pendants. Of closest comparison is the central element in a floral drop on the legs of a Newport tripod table. Skirts with carved or scratch beads, as found in one of the related tables, are uncommon in cabriole-leg case furniture, although general examples occur in Philadelphia and New York work. The carved feet of the three tables duplicate profiles associated variously with Philadelphia, New York, and Boston. Dating of this group of tables is based on the latest features—claw feet, the use of a scribed bead, and the presence of a two-tier drawer plan and scrolled skirt in one example.[10]

*NGE*

---

**Inscriptions or marks:** *On inside back of all drawers:* "4" in chalk.

**Construction:** The two-board top with cove- and thumb-molded edges on three sides and indented double-ogee–shape front corners overhangs the case deeply at the sides and more shallowly at the front; it is pinned to the frame. The sides of the case and the backboard are tenoned and double-pinned to the posts. The top rail, drawer blade, and bottom rail (or skirt) are tenoned into the front posts—the blade and bottom rail held with single pins. The vertical drawer divider is through-tenoned to the drawer blade at the top. The divider bottom is tenoned in part to the skirt; a back extension butts against the back of the skirt. The runners for the top drawer are tenoned to the drawer blade and nailed at the back to the case sides. The outer runners for the bottom drawers are notched to fit around the posts and nailed. The center runner is notched at the front to fit around the extension of the vertical divider and nailed; the back end is supported on a batten. Battens are nailed across the

inside of the backboard below each tier of drawers; the batten at the top is much narrower than the one at the bottom. The legs are one piece with the corner posts; the brackets are glued to the inside faces of the knees. The drawers are dovetailed, front and back, and the upper edges of the sides and back are rounded. The drawer bottoms, the grain running from front to back, are deeply chamfered on three sides, set into grooves, and nailed flush across the back with rosehead nails. A narrow thumbmolding finishes the front edges of the drawers; the side and top lips butt against the case.

**Condition:** There are minor blemishes on the front legs. The exterior surface has been refinished. The center escutcheon has been replaced with old, compatible hardware. The other hardware, which represents two closely related patterns, may all be original to the table.

**Dimensions:**

| | | |
|---|---|---|
| H. | 31³/4 in. | 80.6 cm |
| W. (top) | 39⁷/8 in. | 101.3 cm |
| W. (case) | 32 in. | 81.3 cm |
| W. (feet) | 33⁷/8 in. | 86.0 cm |
| D. (top) | 22³/16 in. | 56.3 cm |
| D. (case) | 20 in. | 50.8 cm |
| D. (feet) | 22 in. | 55.9 cm |

**Materials:** *Microanalysis:* Primary: American black walnut. Secondary: chestnut (drawer bottoms); red oak group (backboard); yellow poplar (drawer sides, backing on vertical divider, drawer runners). *Finish:* orange-brown color in resin.

**Publications:** Downs, *American Furniture*, fig. 326.

**Accession history:** Bequest of H. F. du Pont, 1969. 58.2775

---

1. The other 2 dressing tables in this group are in Sotheby's, "Important Americana: The Collection of Dr. and Mrs. Henry D. Deyerle" (May 26–27, 1995), lots 420, 634. Occasionally other furniture is carved with elongated shells on the knees flanked by detached scrolls that could have served as sources of inspiration; see a pair of early Georgian chairs in a Malcolm Franklin advertisement, *Antiques* 123, no. 6 (June 1983): 1106; and a high chest of drawers attributed to a Providence cabinetmaker in Eleanore Bradford Monahon, "The Rawson Family of Cabinetmakers in Providence, Rhode Island," *Antiques* 118, no. 1 (July 1980): 134.

2. Survey material in Jobe and Kaye, *New England Furniture*, nos. 33, 36, 38, 41; Ward, *American Case Furniture*, cats. 78, 132, 135. Some New England

Windsor furniture also contains red oak; it was used for bows, spindles, stretchers, posts, crest pieces, and cross rods.

3. The "J. Larkin" inscription was discussed with the present owner of the dressing table in a telephone conversation with the author, December 30, 1995.

4. Ethel Hall Bjerkoe with John Arthur Bjerkoe, *The Cabinetmakers of America* (Garden City, N.Y.: Doubleday, 1957), p. 142; Myrna Kaye, "Appendix A: Eighteenth-Century Boston Furniture Craftsmen," in *Boston Furniture*, p. 286.

5. J. D. Champlin, Jr., "Early Settlers of Westerly, Rhode Island," in *New England Historical and Genealogical Register for the Year 1858* (Boston, 1858), 12:237–38.

6. Larkin family probate and land records, town clerks' offices in Hopkinton, Richmond, South Kingstown, and Westerly, R.I. James N. Arnold, comp., *Vital Records of Rhode Island, 1636–1850*, 1st ser., vol. 5, Washington Co. (Providence: Narragansett Historical Publishing Co., 1894), pt. 2, p. 22; pt. 4, pp. 41, 113; pt. 6, pp. 14, 30; pt. 7, p. 43. *Chronicle of the Larkin Family of the Towne of Westerlie and Colony of Rhoad Island in New England*, no. 1 (LaPorte, Ind.: William H. Larkin, Jr., for the Larkin Family Assoc., 1908), p. 4; Alden Gamaliel Beaman, comp., *Rhode Island Vital Records*, n.s. (Princeton: By the compiler, 1977), 3:175, 4:197; Jay Mack Holbrook, comp., *Rhode Island 1782 Census* (Oxford, Mass.: Holbrook Research Institute, 1979), p. 76; Gary Boyd Roberts, comp., *Genealogies of Rhode Island Families* (Baltimore: Genealogical Publishing Co., 1989), 1:626; John R. Bartlett, comp., *Census of the Inhabitants of Rhode Island and Providence Plantations, 1774* (Lambertville, N.J.: Hunterdon House, 1984), p. 223.

7. John Hayward, *New England Gazetteer* (Boston: By the author, 1839), s.vv. "Pawcatuck River" and "Washington County, R.I."

8. *American Antiques from Israel Sack Collection*, 10 vols. (Washington, D.C.: Highland House, 1969–), 5:1276, 7:1867, 8:2229–31, 2:401, 3:636; Moses, *Master Craftsmen*, figs. 1.25, 3.105, 5.22; Nutting, *Furniture Treasury*, no. 356.

9. *American Antiques from Sack Collection*, 1:221.

10. Downs, *American Furniture*, fig. 192; Dean F. Failey, *Long Island Is My Nation: The Decorative Arts and Craftsmen, 1640–1830* (Setauket, N.Y.: Society for the Preservation of Long Island Antiquities, 1976), no. 142; *American Antiques from Sack Collection*, 7:1922, 1951–52, 2035, 9:169, 10:73, 5:1350; Jobe and Kaye, *New England Furniture*, nos. 99, 103; Bernard and S. Dean Levy, Inc., *Vanity and Elegance* (New York: By the company, 1992), fig. 41; Israel Sack advertisement, *Antiques* 147, no. 5 (May 1995): inside front cover; Moses, *Master Craftsmen*, fig. 1.36; *American Antiques from Sack Collection*, 1:219; Levy, *Vanity and Elegance*, figs. 41, 42; Kirk, *American Chairs*, figs. 70, 114, 143.

## 171 ⬥ Dressing table
Northampton, Massachusetts, area
1760–80

The Connecticut River valley was a center of patronage and furnituremaking as early as the seventeenth century. The river, a source of regional prosperity, served to convey goods, people, and ideas easily. During the early eighteenth century, coastal Massachusetts, particularly Boston, became a strong influence on Connecticut River valley furniture. Local residents acquired knowledge of new forms and fashions as furnishings were imported from the coast and craftsmen trained in urban centers migrated inland. Before 1750, Wethersfield and Windsor in Connecticut and Northampton in Massachusetts had become small centers for the fabrication and distribution of furniture in styles reflecting their urban prototypes.[1]

During the third quarter of the century, a form of furniture embellishment rare elsewhere emerged from the river communities as cabinetmakers began to fit a number of small tables and low cases with tops shaped on three or four sides in highly curvilinear profiles (fig. 1). This costly consumer option may have been offered first to customers in Wethersfield, but soon Northampton and Deerfield became small production centers of the new style. Tops shaped with complex compass curves appear to have been termed "Scallop'd" from the start. Inspiration for the ornament probably derived from the furniture itself, much of which has intricate sawed curves in the skirts.[2]

Although scalloped-top furniture, comprising tables, dressing tables, and chests of drawers (many on frames), numbers more than thirty examples, the group is small compared to furniture production in general in Connecticut River valley shops. Cherry was the wood of choice by the mid eighteenth century, and it frequently was stained to imitate mahogany. The secondary woods of Winterthur's table—white pine and yellow pine—also reflect common choices. White pine was popular throughout New England for

secondary construction, but yellow pine was more regional, and it had served valley woodworkers since the seventeenth century.[3]

Tea tables of Connecticut River valley origin with scalloped tops are rare. Chests of drawers are more common, and almost a dozen are known. The predominant design is a case supported in a frame on short cabriole legs. Five small drawers form the upper tiers—two shallow, stacked storage units flanking a deep one carved with a fan. Single or double drops ornament the skirts of most frames. A modest version of the scalloped-top chest was made as late as circa 1802 in West Hartford, Vermont, on the Connecticut River, attesting to the longevity of the ornamental form in the conservative climate of the valley.[4]

Probably as many as two dozen dressing tables with scalloped tops are known. They form an eclectic group based on the treatment of the principal features—the scroll-edge top, case skirt, number and arrangement of drawers—and the particular combination of features from table to table. There are as many as eight patterns for the scalloped tops, and few within a pattern are exactly alike. The top on this table is one of the two most common

profiles (see fig. 1). Short double ogees at the center front are flanked by longer ogees terminating at double-lunette corners. Only a few tops are as complex because in addition to the tightly scalloped pattern on three sides, the edges have been finished in a compound curve comprising a fillet and a deep, oblique ogee. Instead of scrapers, the cabinetmaker used carving tools to form the edge, a labor-intensive, costly procedure. The other popular pattern was one with three long, shallow arcs across the front and corners rounded in large, single lobes.[5]

The most common drawer combination in the scalloped-top dressing table is one with a long unit across the upper case and three small ones in the second tier. Variety is introduced in the small drawers—most are equal in size, the center one carved with a fan or related device that is sometimes placed in a recess extending through the skirt. The arrangement in Winterthur's table, which is both unique and the most intricate in the group, is necessitated by the design of the skirt. Its profile has a high, central arch in the manner of William and Mary and early Queen Anne work (see No. 158). The curves of the

**Fig. 1.** Detail, top.

tabletop and the skirt perfectly complement each other, producing an integrated, aesthetically satisfying design that is one of the most successful.

The attribution of scalloped-top dressing tables to Northampton, Massachusetts, and vicinity appears to hinge on the background history of this table. Penciled on several drawers are names identified as those of Jerusha Ann Williams and Mary A. Woodruff, mother and daughter. These names and the table's recovery in Northampton in the 1930s prompted a genealogical investigation that placed the table in the same locale.[6]

*NGE*

*Inscriptions or marks:* On right side of right small drawer: "Mary A. Woodruff/ from Mother" in pencil. *On bottom of center small drawer:* "J. A. Williams/ Mary A. Woodruff/ from Mother" (see **Provenance**). The small drawers and drawer openings are numbered in modern pencil from 1 to 3.

**Construction:** The shaped, two-board top, with a stepped ogee molding and a substantial overhang on all four sides, is straight across the center back. It is pinned to the frame. The backboard and case sides are tenoned and pinned to the posts, two pins at each side and back tenon. The skirt rail is single-tenoned and pinned to the front posts; the top rail is tenoned to the top of the front posts. The drawer blade and the vertical dividers between the small drawers are half-dovetailed to their adjacent elements. The two sets of one-piece outer drawer runners are secured with rosehead nails to the case sides; the two sets of one-piece inner drawer runners are tenoned at the back and rabbeted at the front to the vertical dividers. The legs and posts are one piece. The knee brackets are glued to the case front and sides. The stock used for the drawer sides, backs, and bottoms is unusually thick. The drawer sides, rounded on the upper edge, have several

small, closely spaced dovetails at the front and large, more widely spaced dovetails at the back; the drawer sides extend beyond the back of the drawer. The grain of the top drawer bottom runs from side to side; the grain of the small drawers runs from front to back. The drawer bottoms are rabbeted at the front and sides and nailed flush across the back with wrought nails; they have applied battens. A narrow thumbmolding finishes the front edges of the drawers; the side and top lips butt against the case.

**Condition:** A full-length split across the front of the tabletop has been repaired at either side of the case with a long, shaped stabilizing cleat that is screwed to the underside of the top. The knee brackets have been reattached. The upper left lip of the left small drawer is repaired. The table has a multilayered crackled finish. The escutcheon of the long drawer is a replacement.

**Dimensions:**

| | | |
|---|---|---|
| H. | 32 in. | 81.3 cm |
| W. (top) | 39 in. | 99.0 cm |
| W. (feet) | 33 5/8 in. | 85.4 cm |
| D. (top) | 24 in. | 61.0 cm |
| W. (case) | 32 in. | 81.3 cm |
| D. (case) | 17 in. | 43.2 cm |
| D. (feet) | 18 3/4 in. | 47.6 cm |

**Materials:** *Microanalysis:* Primary: cherry. Secondary: white pine group (backboard); yellow pine group (drawer bottoms). *Finish:* medium reddish orange color in resin.

**Exhibitions:** "The Great River: Art and Society of the Connecticut River Valley, 1635–1850," Wadsworth Atheneum, Hartford, Conn., September 22, 1985–January 6, 1986.

**Publications:** Downs, *American Furniture*, fig. 327. Marshall B. Davidson, *The American Heritage History of Colonial Antiques* ([New York]: American Heritage, [1967]), fig. 216. Butler, *American Furniture*, fig. 62. Michael K. Brown, "Scalloped-top Furniture of the Connecticut River Valley," *Antiques*

117, no. 5 (May 1980): 1096, fig. 8. Philip Zea, "Furniture," in *Great River*, cat. 103.

**Provenance:** The dressing table originally belonged to a member of the Williams or Stoddard families of Hampshire County, Mass. Purchased from a Northampton home in the 1930s, its history can be traced though the names "J. A. Williams" and "Mary A. Woodruff" inscribed on the drawers. Mary Woodruff (b. 1864) was the daughter of Jerusha Ann Williams Woodruff (1835–1915) and the great-granddaughter of John Williams (1767–1845) of Conway who married Nancy Stoddard of Northampton in 1799. The dressing table dates a generation earlier.

**Accession history:** Bequest of H. F. du Pont, 1969. 58.589

1. Philip Zea, "Furniture," in *Great River*, pp. 185–91; Kevin M. Sweeney, "Furniture and Furniture-Making in Mid-Eighteenth-Century Wethersfield, Connecticut," *Antiques* 125, no. 5 (May 1984): 1156–63.

2. Zea, "Furniture," cats. 102–4; Michael K. Brown, "Scalloped-top Furniture of the Connecticut River Valley, *Antiques* 117, no. 5 (May 1980): 1092–99; Sweeney, "Furniture and Furniture-Making," pp. 1159–60.

3. Zea, "Furniture," cats. 102–4; Brown, "Scalloped-top Furniture," 1092–99; William N. Hosley, Jr., and Philip Zea, "Decorated Board Chests of the Connecticut River Valley," *Antiques* 119, no. 5 (May 1981): 1146–51.

4. For tea tables and chests of drawers, see Brown, "Scalloped-top Furniture," pp. 1092–94, 1095–99 respectively. Kenneth Hammitt advertisements, *Antiques* 98, no. 5 (November 1970): 667, *Antiques* 107, no. 4 (April 1975): 593, *Antiques* 122, no. 3 (September 1982): 358; Bernard and S. Dean Levy, Inc., *Catalogue IV* (New York: By the company, 1984), p. 23; Kenneth Joel Zogry, *The Best the Country Affords: Vermont Furniture, 1765–1850* (Bennington, Vt.: Bennington Museum, 1995), cat. 65.

5. For dressing tables, see Brown, "Scalloped-top Furniture," pp. 1094–97; Sweeney, "Furniture and Furniture-Making," pp. 1159–60; Christie's, "Fine American Furniture, Silver, Folk Art, and Decorative Arts" (January 23, 1988), lots 304, 378; *American Antiques from Israel Sack Collection*, 10 vols. (Washington, D.C.: Highland House, 1969–), 3:635; Fales, *Furniture of Historic Deerfield*, fig. 444; Sotheby's advertisement, *Antiques* 127, no. 1 (January 1985): 43; Levy, Inc., *Catalogue IV*, p. 22; George E. Schoellkopf advertisement, *Antiques* 114, no. 3 (September 1978): 459; Kenneth Hammitt advertisement, *Antiques* 89, no. 1 (January 1966): 65; Albert Sack, *The New Fine Points of Furniture: Early American* (New York: Crown Publishers, 1993), p. 210; Garth's Auctions advertisement, *Antiques* 132, no. 1 (July 1987): 83; Kenneth and Paulette Tuttle advertisement, *Antiques* 129, no. 1 (January 1986): 38; no. 71.82, DAPC, Visual Resources Collection, Winterthur Library; Paul W. Cooley advertisement, *Antiques* 83, no. 1 (January 1963): 71; Barquist, *American Tables and Looking Glasses*, cat. 38.

6. Brown, "Scalloped-top Furniture," pp. 1095–96, 1098 n. 12; Zea, "Furniture," cat. 103.

## 172 • High chest of drawers
Newport, Rhode Island
1755–75

The classic Newport high chest lends itself, as Ralph Carpenter has pointed out, to "seemingly endless degrees of similarity." The arched pediment with raised panels, the standardized molding profiles, the reverse curves of the undulating front and side skirts, and the squared cabriole legs with ball-and-claw or pad feet appear to be almost a

formula. There is, however, considerable variety within this general design—specifically the inclusion of fluted quarter columns on the upper case, the introduction of carving to the legs, and especially the treatment of the shell carving in the skirt. Based on surviving examples, which number more than thirty-six, two general designs were available. The largest group, which includes this high chest, has a plain upper case and shell carving on the skirt; the usual supports are unornamented cabriole legs terminated by ball-and-claw

front feet and pad rear feet. A second, smaller group is characterized by the addition of fluted quarter columns in the upper case, frequently accompanied by carving on the front legs.[1]

The thirty-six-chest sample illuminates the range of options beyond the basic design represented by Winterthur's chest. Occasionally the pediment is fitted with three finials instead of a single one at the center, although side finials are more common on cases with quarter columns. The standard two-over-three drawer arrangement of the upper case is sometimes altered to three-over-three or -four, or two-over-four. In two examples with three drawers in the top tier, the center drawer is taller than the others, and the raised panels in the tympanum are eliminated. The distinctive carved shell of the skirt, although similar in general form from chest to chest, varies in the number of flutes and the treatment of the center element and outer arch. The shell on Winterthur's chest is an example of the plain-rather than scalloped-arch type. Carved knees are present in only 20 percent of the cases without quarter columns but are featured in 50 percent of the high chests with quarter columns. Three of the chests without quarter columns have four carved feet, and one of them also has four carved knees; seven are supported on four pad feet. Two cases have pointed rather than rounded leg terminals. The prevailing primary wood of the chests is mahogany; however, walnut is present in at least three examples.[2]

More than one-third of the high chests in the sample have a known family history or other type of provenance. Most are associated with Rhode Island, although two chests were owned on Long Island, a trading partner of Rhode Island located across Block Island Sound. Two chests are documented by penciled or chalked inscriptions to their makers. One, signed by John Townsend in 1759, is in the Yale University Art Gallery, and Benjamin Baker inscribed a chest now at the Newport Restoration Foundation. Both have pad feet at the back and the celebrated Newport open-talon claws at the front, the supports similar to those on Winterthur's chest (fig. 1). The Townsend chest is the most ornate, with three finials, quarter columns in the upper case, and carved knees on the front legs. The Baker chest also has carved knees, but the top tier in the plain upper case consists of three small drawers. The shells differ from that in Winterthur's example, and construction details are variable as well. Winterthur's chest cannot be linked with a specific craftsman based on either design details or construction.

Newport cabinetmakers differed from their New England counterparts both in their choice of design elements and in method of assembly. Most New England craftsmen used dovetail construction for the upper case and joined the lower section with mortise and tenon, but Newport artisans used dovetail construction for both sections. As a result, the leg assembly on a Newport high chest is distinct: the leg extensions above the cabrioles are not integral to the construction of the lower case. The legs are detachable, and the extensions form short posts of reduced size that slide into place inside the corners. Covering the front corners of the case are thin facings, which on most Newport high chests are of vertical grain to simulate a continuous leg and stile. On Winterthur's high chest, however, the grain is horizontal. Newport high chests also vary from common New England practice in the method of joining the two case sections. Rather than securing the waist molding to the top of the lower case, Newport craftsmen usually attached it to the lower edge of the upper case, permitting it to overlap the lower case to provide a visually neater fit. Winterthur's chest is an exception, as the waist molding is nailed to the lower case.

Other tall chests of Rhode Island origin demonstrate a close relationship with the Rhode Island pedimented chest in elements of their design. Long ogee curves are a feature of the skirt in a substantial number of flat-top

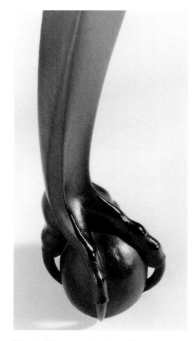

**Fig. 1.** Detail, right front foot.

chests, many with pointed pad feet, which date slightly earlier. The center of the skirt either rises in a double-lobed arch with pendant or is filled with a carved shell of the general type found in Winterthur's chest. One chest with the open arch was signed and dated by its maker, Christopher Townsend, in 1748. A few chests of this type also have pedimented tops faced with raised panels. Cornice profiles are similar or are related to that on Winterthur's chest. The long-ogee profile of the skirt in the Rhode Island high chest was not new with the Queen Anne style. The addition of a shell to the center arch merely redefined a pattern with roots in William and Mary design. For example, a few four-legged, cross-stretcher William and Mary high chests have front skirts with sweeping ogee curves of this type flanking a central arch.[3]

Of contemporary date with Winterthur's high chest are a small number of chests-on-chests with raised-panel pedimented tops, several of which are further embellished with quarter columns in the upper and lower cases. Family histories associate two examples with the Gibbs and Almy families of Newport and a third one with Moses Brown of Providence.[4]

Rhode Island casework also had considerable impact on furniture produced in adjacent regions. In particular, the sweeping ogee curves of the front skirt, which are frequently notched, are present on high and low cases made on Long Island and in eastern and southern Connecticut, including New London and Windham counties, the Connecticut River valley around Wethersfield and Hartford, and the greater Housatonic River valley. Similar design impulses are found in cabinetwork originating in Salem,

Massachusetts, and along the North Shore. A high chest inscribed by Simeon Pomeroy, who worked in the interior of Massachusetts at Northampton or Amherst in the Connecticut River valley, reflects Rhode Island influence transmitted from Salem in the east or Wethersfield in the south.[5]

Winterthur's high chest bears two family associations that appear to be independent of one another. One, in the Tripp family, is inscribed in black ink on a drawer blade. The other, in the Wheaton/Debon-Hunter-Birckhead family, is on the back of a mid twentieth-century (or earlier) photograph of the chest (see **Provenance**). As the Wheaton/Debon association with the chest dates only to the early nineteenth century, that family probably either inherited the chest or acquired it at a sale of Tripp family furnishings.

The names of the three members of the Tripp family that are inscribed on the chest are in a hand that appears to date to the late eighteenth or early nineteenth century. The first, Martha L. Tripp, may identify the original owner. A widow of this name, without middle initial, is listed in the 1790 federal census of Rhode Island as a resident of Exeter, Washington County. The town, incorporated in 1743 and devoted principally to dairy herding, is located across Narragansett Bay from Newport and about five miles inland from North Kingstown (now Wickford). Situated on a good harbor, North Kingstown was "a place of considerable trade" particularly of the coastal type. Ownership of Newport furniture likely was a source of personal pride among affluent local inhabitants and an inspiration to area craftsmen anxious to emulate the richness of the Newport style (see No. 170). In 1790 the Tripp household consisted of two white males sixteen years or older and three white females, including the head of the household. Tripp's name is absent from the 1800 and later censuses.[6]

Other records shed additional light on the Tripp family and reinforce their strong bond with Washington County. A census of Rhode Island made as early as 1774 lists Tripp family members as residents of the town of Exeter only. Vital and family records identify other Tripp women with the given names of Martha and Mary (Mary L. is the second name in the inscription). Thomas Tripp, of Tiverton, a town south of Newport, whose will was proved in 1766, had a daughter Martha. A Martha Wall and an Isaac Tripp of East Greenwich, located just north of Washington County, married before 1763 and had children named Mary (b. 1765) and Martha (b. 1781). Peregrine Tripp of Exeter married Martha Boss of Richmond, Washington County, in 1760. He may have been the son of Job, whose married daughter Phebe Boss inherited her father's "high Case of Drawes, Large Ovel Table and one Set of Callico Curtains" in 1779. Ezekiel Tripp, another of Job's children, married Mary Lawton of Exeter in 1765. Of more than passing interest is the existence of another Newport high chest with features, including the brass hardware, close to those of Winterthur's chest; the first owners are said to have been Christopher Lawton (1728–52) of South Kingstown (now Wakefield), Washington County, and Elizabeth Tripp. Lending credence to this tradition is the existence of a needlework pocketbook with a silver clasp bearing the initials of Elizabeth's second husband, which descended with the high chest. Although the foregoing discussion points up the complexities of making family identifications, it also suggests the value Rhode Island families placed on owning a Newport high chest, even several generations after its purchase.[7]

NGE/NER

**Inscriptions or marks:** *On underside of top board in upper section:* "Top" *in white chalk. On inside back of all long and several short drawers:* an arabic number or letter. *On outside back of upper right drawer:* miscellaneous markings. *At center top of lower drawer blade in upper case:* "Martha/ L Tripp", "Mary/ L Tripp", *and* "T[or F]/ Tripp" *written on a diagonal, in black ink. Some of the brass backplates have cast marks* "B" *and* "36" *on the reverse side.*

**Construction:** (Upper case) The case top and bottom are dovetailed to the sides. The scrollboard is rabbeted to the case sides and to the vertical divider between the top drawers. The center plinth of the scrollboard is reinforced on the back with a conforming glueblock; a small tablet at the top is secured with sprigs. The tablet supports a removable rectangular plinth fluted on the front face only. Its sprigged tablet supports the finial, which is carved with narrow flutes in the urn, except at the center back. The pediment backboard is glued to the case top and further secured inside with glueblocks. Dovetailed battens link the scrollboard and backboard at the pediment top. Heavy battens abutting the scrollboard and case backboard are secured with rosehead nails to the upper case sides below the case top. The pediment molding is applied with small nails to the front of the scrollboard, the upper case sides, and the top battens. The pediment top is nailed to rabbets on the scrollboard and to the top of the backboard. Thumb-molded conforming panels are applied to the face of the scrollboard. The three drawer blades are joined to the case sides with shouldered dovetails. The vertical divider between the top drawers is tenoned to the case top and the upper drawer blade. The bottom rail is slotted into the case sides and reinforced with three glueblocks along the inside edge. The underside of the case is reinforced at both ends with nailed battens running from front to back. The back of the case consists of three lap-joined horizontal boards nailed to rabbets in the case sides. Inside the case beneath the top board, rails reinforce the joints of the top and sides. A batten across the upper back at the level of the top drawer blade is slotted to the case sides. A wide, central vertical batten, which reinforces the backboards, extends from the horizontal batten to the bottom board, passing behind both at notches. Drawer runners are attached to the case sides with rosehead nails. The runner centered between the top small drawers is rabbeted to the top drawer blade and the corresponding batten at the back. A guide is glued and nailed to the top surface.

(Lower case) A mitered waist molding, which is nailed to the case front and sides, helps to secure the upper case. There is no top board; the upper case rests on the front rail and backboard of the lower case. The case sides, sawed in curves complementing the front skirt, are dovetailed to the backboard. At the front, the top rail, drawer blade, and skirt are dovetailed to the case sides. Wood strips of horizontal grain face the front corners from skirt to top rail. The shell centered in the skirt is carved from solid wood. The legs, once detachable, continue part way up the interior case as posts and are reinforced with nailed glueblocks. The runners for the top drawer are tenoned to the backboard and rabbeted to the drawer blade. Guides, which are glued to the top surface, are notched and nailed at the front to interior bracing blocks. Runners for the small drawers, which are centered beneath the bottoms, are tenoned to the backboard and lapped and nailed to the front skirt. Outside guides are notched and nailed to blocks securing the leg extensions. The short vertical dividers between the small drawers are slotted and nailed at the top to the underside of the drawer blade and rabbeted and nailed at the bottom to the case skirt, with a rear extension continuing downward below drawer level. The extension is reinforced with flanking glueblocks. Interior drawer guides are tenoned to the backboard and rabbeted and nailed to the vertical dividers. Short interior front corner blocks extend between the drawer blade and the tops of the leg extensions. The knees of the rear legs extend beyond the back of the case. The knee brackets are glued to the leg tops. The talons of the front feet are undercut.

The drawers in both cases are finely dovetailed. The sides are rounded at the top edges; the back edges are flat. The grain of the drawer bottoms runs from front to back in the small drawers and from side to side in the large drawers. The bottoms of the drawers in the upper case and the long drawer in the lower case are chamfered on three sides, slotted into the drawer front, and butted to the sides and back. The back is nailed flush; the sides are nailed flush through applied battens. The flat bottoms of the small drawers in the lower case are nailed flush at the sides and back and to a rabbet at the front. The drawers fronts, which are thumb molded on four sides, abut the case facade at the sides and top.

**Condition:** Through-cracks are centered in the right side of the upper case. A split in the skirt from the lower left drawer through the carved shell has been repaired. Cracks have been repaired at the back of the left front leg, in the facing of the left front post, and in the left front foot. The right front foot has a repaired talon. The right leg has a long hairline crack on the upper outside face. The knee brackets of the left front leg are new, and the bracket at the right rear knee may also be replaced. A section of waist molding on the lower right rear side is replaced. The drawer blades in the upper case have been patched at the center front. Many drawers have been repaired at the upper front corners; the bottom right drawer is patched at the lower left corner. The surface of the chest has been refinished. The brass hardware appears to be original except for the backplates on the two outside bottom drawers, which are modern fabrications, and some of the bail handles (larger in size). The drawers with the replaced brasses once had larger plates (shadows visible). The brasses on the two small drawers of the upper case were repositioned upward when locks were installed; the old holes are plugged. The finial and its supporting fluted plinth are replacements.

**Dimensions:**

| | | |
|---|---|---|
| H. (case) | 80⅝ in. | 204.8 cm |
| W. (cornice) | 39¼ in. | 99.7 cm |
| W. (upper case) | 36¾ in. | 93.3 cm |
| W. (lower case) | 38⁵/₁₆ in. | 97.3 cm |
| W. (feet) | 40¾ in. | 103.5 cm |
| D. (cornice) | 21⁵/₁₆ in. | 54.1 cm |
| D. (upper case) | 19¾ in. | 50.2 cm |
| D. (lower case) | 20⅞ in. | 53.0 cm |
| D. (feet) | 22½ in. | 57.1 cm |

**Materials:** *Microanalysis:* Primary: mahogany. Secondary: white pine group (backboard); yellow poplar (bonnet board, backing on blades, drawer bottoms); chestnut (outside drawer guides, center drawer runner, blocks facing inside of knees, except at left rear). *Finish:* modern coat of medium reddish brown color in resin; the legs and especially the feet are darker.

**Publications:** William S. Ayres, "Contrasts: Philadelphia and Newport Furniture Styles, 1755–1780," in *Delaware Antiques Show 1982* (Wilmington, Del.), p. 65, fig. 5.

**Provenance:** When purchased, the high chest was accompanied by a photograph with a family history inscribed on the back by one of the last private owners. According to the history, the original owner was the Reverend Solomon Wheaton, rector of Trinity Church, Newport, from 1810 to 1840, or his wife Anne Debon of Boston. The chest descended to their daughter Anne Wheaton, who never married, to her sister Mrs. David King of Newport,

to Mrs. King's daughter Mrs. William Birckhead, and to Mrs. Birckhead's son Malbone. Mrs. Malbone Birckhead of Baltimore was the last owner.

**Accession history:** Purchased for the museum by H. F. du Pont from John S. Walton, Inc., New York, 1951.
51.32

1. Ralph E. Carpenter, Jr., *The Arts and Crafts of Newport, Rhode Island, 1640–1820* (Newport: Preservation Society of Newport County, 1954), p. 67.

2. The remaining 35 chests are in Moses, *Master Craftsmen*, figs. 1.19, 1.23, 3.99, 3.100, 3.102, 3.103, 3.109, 3.110, 5.29, 7.20, pl. 22; nos. 66.1715, 66.2530, 66.2674, 68.2012, 68.2768, 68.2791, DAPC, Visual Resources Collection, Winterthur Library; Plaza, "Fine Americana" (February 1, 1968), lot unknown; Northeast Auctions, "New Hampshire Auction" (November 4–5, 1995), lot 760; American Art Association Anderson Galleries, "Fine American Furniture, Property of Hyman Kaufman" (April 12–14, 1934), lot 446; Sotheby's, "Important Americana from the Collection of Mr. and Mrs. Adolph Henry Meyer" (January 20, 1996), lot 170; Israel Sack advertisement, *Antiques* 57, no. 2 (February 1950): 83; Bernard and S. Dean Levy advertisement, *Antiques* 141, no. 5 (May 1992): 681; Donald R. Sack advertisement, *Antiques* 135, no. 5 (May 1989): 1016–17; Eleanor H. Gustafson, "Museum Accessions," *Antiques* 131, no. 5 (May 1987): 980; Eden Galleries advertisement, *Antiques* 91, no. 1 (January 1967): 15; Ralph E. Carpenter, "Newport, a Center of Colonial Cabinetmaking," *Antiques* 147, no. 4 (April 1995): 555; Leigh Keno advertisement, *Antiques* 136, no. 4 (October 1989): 675; Joseph K. Ott, "Some Rhode Island Furniture," *Antiques* 107, no. 5 (May 1975): 945, fig. 9; "In the Museums," *Antiques* 86, no. 4 (October 1964): 472; Latimer House advertisement, *Antiques* 63, no. 4 (April 1953): 331; Bernard and S. Dean Levy, Inc., *Vanity and Elegance* (New York: By the company, 1992), cat. 26; Joseph Downs, "The Furniture of Goddard and Townsend," in Alice Winchester, ed., *The Antiques Book* (New York: A. A. Wyn, 1950), p. 92, fig. 10; Rodriguez Roque, *American Furniture*, no. 12; Katharine Bryant Hagler, *American Queen Anne Furniture, 1720–1755* (Dearborn, Mich.: Henry Ford Museum and Greenfield Village, 1976), p. 25.

3. For representative, related high chests of drawers, see Moses, *Master Craftsmen*, figs. 1.21, 1.24 (Townsend chest); Robert O. Stuart advertisement, *Antiques* 133,

no. 5 (May 1988): 1007. A four-legged, William and Mary chest with a long-ogee skirt is in Nutting, *Furniture Treasury*, no. 339.

4. The chests-on-chests with family histories are in Bernard and S. Dean Levy advertisement, *Antiques* 138, no. 6 (December 1990): 1115; Israel Sack, Inc., *Celebrating Our Ninetieth Anniversary* (Alexandria, Va.: Hennage Creative Printers, 1993), p. 38; Ott, "Some Rhode Island Furniture," p. 942.

5. Representative high chests of drawers are in Ward, *American Case Furniture*, cats. 130, 136, 139; Albert Sack, *The New Fine Points of Furniture: Early American* (New York: Crown Publishers, 1993), p. 188 bottom, 198–99; *New London County Furniture*, nos. 21–23; *Connecticut Furniture*, nos. 79, 81, 83, 94, 113–16, 158, 179, 181; Greenlaw, *New England Furniture*, no. 82; Kevin M. Sweeney, "Furniture and Furniture-Making in Mid-Eighteenth-Century Wethersfield, Connecticut," *Antiques* 125, no. 5 (May 1984): 1156–61; Nathan Liverant and Son advertisement, *Antiques* 123, no. 2 (February 1983): 339; C. L. Prickett advertisement, *Antiques* 144, no. 6 (December 1993): 746; G. K. S. Bush advertisement, *Antiques* 144, no. 3 (September 1993): 236; Dean Wilson advertisement, *Antiques* 104, no. 4 (October 1973): 532; Philip Zea, "Furniture," in *Great River*, cat. 98 (Pomeroy chest).

6. John Hayward, *The New England Gazetteer* (Boston: By the author, 1839), s.vv. "Exeter, R.I." and "North Kingston, R.I."

7. John R. Bartlett, comp., *Census of the Inhabitants of the Colony of Rhode Island and Providence Plantations, 1774* (Lambertville, N.J.: Hunterdon House, 1984); *Tripp Wills, Deeds, and Ways with Key to Tripp Descents, Via New England, and also New York* (Washington, D.C.: Valentine Research Studio, 1932), pp. 100–101; Arthur D. Dean, *Genealogy of the Tripp Family Descended from Isaac Tripp of Warwick, R.I., and Wilkes-Barre, Pa.* (Scranton, Pa.: By the author, 1903), pp. 42–43; James N. Arnold, comp., *Vital Records of Rhode Island, 1636–1850*, 1st ser., vol. 5, Washington County (Providence: Narragansett Historical Publishing Co., 1894), pt. 4, p. 20; Exeter Births, Marriages, and Deaths, vol. 1, p. 203, vol. 3, p. 170, and Exeter Council and Probate Books, vol. 4, pp. 102–5, Office of the Town Clerk, Exeter, R.I. For the Christopher Lawton chest, see *American Antiques from Israel Sack Collection*, 10 vols. (Washington, D.C.: Highland House, 1969–), 6:8.

## 173 ◆ Dressing table
Newport, Rhode Island
1760–80

The same source material that produced thirty-six examples of the Newport high chest of drawers for study (see No. 172) yielded twenty examples of the shell-carved dressing table. Originally, a bureau table may have taken the place of a dressing table in some households.[1]

Like the Newport high chest, the design of the Newport dressing table is far from static. Of the surveyed examples, only two tables appear to be alike in all points of design, including the arrangement and size of the drawers. The two cases differ, however, in the construction of the front corners—in one, the facing strips above the legs are vertically grained; in the other, the grain is horizontal. This uncommon feature, also seen on some high chests (see No. 172), occurs in a total of three dressing tables, or 15 percent of the sample.[2]

In more than half of the shell-carved dressing tables, a deep cove, or cavetto, molding is attached to the case immediately below a top board finished with ogee-molded edges, as seen in this example. The profile echoes that in the cornice of the high chest, with the top element inverted (see No. 172).

A second group of tables, which lack the cornice molding below the top board, is stylistically earlier in date. A variant in this group has a thumb-molded edge in place of the ogee profile, and the front corners are notched. The drawer arrangement in the case facade ranges from a one-tier plan similar to that in early eighteenth-century dressing tables and high-chest bases (see No. 161) to a three-tier scheme comprised of two long drawers over two small narrow ones. The two-tier plan, as seen on Winterthur's table, is the most common pattern, although the lower drawers can vary in width and depth and occasionally in number.

The common profile of the skirt front is the notched ogee of Winterthur's table. About one-third of the examples surveyed have the alternative plain-ogee skirt. The dressing table shell, which duplicates the carved shell common to the high chest, also varies in number of flutes and treatment of the center element and outer arch; one example is of small size. Just one table has carved decoration on the front knees. The feet exhibit as much variety as the drawer arrangement. Most common are four rounded pads and a combination of claw feet and rounded pads; pointed pad feet appear on about one-third

of the examples. One table has four claw feet, and, atypically, they support a case with an early-style one-tier drawer arrangement.[3]

Shell-carved Newport dressing tables range in date from the 1740s to perhaps as late as the 1780s. An early example now at the Chipstone Foundation is documented to Job Townsend by a bill of sale addressed to Samuel Ward of Newport and dated 1746. As expected, the table has pointed pad feet and a plain top without an applied cavetto molding. The front skirt is sawed in plain ogees without notches. Four of six dressing tables with pointed feet and five of the six examples with plain skirts are part of the early group, and all have plain tops.

Townsend's bill to Ward (1725–76), governor of Rhode Island during the 1760s and a delegate to the First and Second Continental Congresses, charges £13.10.0 for a "Mahogony Dressing Table," which apparently was made en suite with a mahogany high chest of drawers costing £30. The currency of the period was inflated, although comparison of the price ratio in Townsend's bill with that in a table of prices for joiners' work drawn at Providence in 1757 suggests that the high case had a flat top. In the Providence list, the cost of a mahogany high chest is twice that of a mahogany dressing ("chamber") table. The addition of a "Crown and Claws" to the tall case increased the price by 50 percent.[4]

This dressing table is close in pattern and feature to the high chest in No. 172, although the two did not form an original suite of furniture, as has been suggested. Three comparisons are significant. The drawer plan of the table varies from that in the base of the high chest, although the arrangement in the tall chest was an option. The wood grain in the facing strips at the case corners above the front legs is vertical in the dressing table but is of the rarer horizontal orientation in the high chest. The small arched element in the center of the dressing-table shell is flat across the bottom; the narrow border around the arch rises from the end lobes of the shell proper.

The same element in the high chest is curved along the bottom, and the raised border band springs from the small centered volutes.

As a group, the Newport shell-carved dressing tables have extensive background histories. Ward was not the only governor of Rhode Island to own one of these handsome tables—Stephen Hopkins (1707–85), who held the same office and was also a signer of the Declaration of Independence, is said to have owned the claw-foot example with carved knees now in the Diplomatic Reception Rooms of the U.S. Department of State. Other tables descended in the Brenton, Easton, Pearce, and Perry families of Rhode Island. Nicholas Easton, an affluent landowner, inscribed and dated his table in 1771. Winterthur's dressing table was owned in the eighteenth century by Dr. William Hunter, who purchased the architecturally prominent Hunter house on Washington Street in Newport and in 1761 married Deborah Malbone, a daughter of Col. Godfrey Malbone, a wealthy merchant in the town. The dressing table may have been acquired at the time of Hunter's marriage. It descended on the distaff side through Hunter's daughter and son-in-law and remained in the family until purchased by Winterthur. In cases such as this, changes of family name from generation to generation frequently have clouded and even obliterated the early histories of much household furniture. Oral and written traditions and inscriptions on the furniture itself have preserved some of these associations (see No. 46).[5]

Preceding the shell-carved dressing table in the Newport furniture market during the 1740s and 1750s were tables, many made of mahogany, marked by a double-lobed arch and pendant at the center of the front skirt, a design with a counterpart in the high chest. Other standard features include a notched and molded-edge top without a cornice, pointed feet, and ogees in the front skirt (some notched). A prototype exists in English dressing furniture of the second quarter of the century. As discussed in the entry for the Newport high chest (see No. 172), the sweeping ogee curves in the front skirts of Newport chamber furniture influenced furniture design in adjacent regions.[6]

NGE

**Inscriptions or marks:** *On underside of top:* in white chalk, a three-column sum in pounds, shillings, and pence (the total being £4.19.0). *On inside of backboard at upper left:* "4"; *at upper right:* "1".

**Construction:** The one-piece top with ogee-molded front and side edges overhangs the case slightly at the back. The case interior is lined with glueblocks at the top of all four sides, the largest also secured with sprigs. Rosehead nails through the long side blocks secure the top to the case. The rear blocks are secured with rosehead nails from the outside of the backboard. A coved cornice molding with mitered corners is nailed to the case top. The one-piece backboard is dovetailed to the sides. The top rail, drawer blade, and skirt of the case front are dovetailed to the case sides. Two shallow blocks of secondary wood are set between these elements at the front corners, and the corners are covered with facing strips of vertically grained wood to conceal the construction. The drawer blade is faced with secondary wood on the back and through the center passes behind the skirt above the shell, forming a rabbet. The broad runners for the upper drawer abut the case sides and are tenoned into the backboard and rabbeted into the front blade. The centered runners for the small drawers are tenoned to the backboard and dovetailed to the front skirt. The drawer guides, which flank the shell, are tenoned to the backboard and dovetailed to the skirt at the inside faces of the drawer openings. The shell in the skirt is carved from solid wood. The legs, once removable, continue halfway up the case as interior stiles and are secured with glueblocks. All four talons of the front feet are undercut. The sides of the dovetailed drawers are rounded on the top; the backs are flat. The bottom board on the long drawer, the grain running from side to side, is chamfered on the front edge and set in a groove; it is mounted flush along the sides, which are secured by applied battens, and nailed flush along the back. The bottoms of the small drawers, the grain running from front to back, are lapped at the front and nailed flush at the sides and back. A narrow thumbmolding finishes the front edges of the drawers; the side and top lips butt against the case.

**Condition:** The top is badly warped and probably has been reattached. Reinforcing strips and guides have been applied to the runners supporting the upper drawer. A small block that served as a stop for the upper drawer is missing from the upper center of the backboard, although the rosehead nail that secured it from the outside remains. The rear legs have been reinforced with screws and nails inserted through the backboard. Some of the glueblocks flanking the leg extensions are missing; the rest appear to be old replacements. All knee blocks except the right rear side block are replaced. The left small drawer is restored at the upper right inside corner; the right small drawer is restored along the entire upper lip. The front and outside toes on the left front foot have been replaced. The current hardware is the fourth set. Central holes indicate that a set of knoblike pulls were last in place. Plugged holes and stains and shadows on the wood identify the former presence of solid plates with bails and circular post-and-bail handles on the case. The finish is partly deteriorated and partly restored.

**Dimensions:**

| | | |
|---|---|---|
| H. | 31⅞ in. | 80.9 cm |
| W. (top) | 34⅞ in. | 88.5 cm |
| W. (case) | 32⅞ in. | 83.5 cm |
| W. (feet) | 34⅞ in. | 88.6 cm |
| D. (top) | 20⅛ in. | 51.1 cm |
| D. (case) | 18⅞ in. | 47.9 cm |
| D. (feet) | 20⅛ in. | 51.1 cm |

**Materials:** *Microanalysis:* Primary: mahogany (top, legs, sides, drawer fronts). Secondary: chestnut (drawer sides and back); white pine group (drawer bottom); spruce (replaced glueblocks). *Finish:* beneath the medium light to medium dark brownish orange color in resin, the old finish on case and the legs is deteriorated; modern oil finish on top.

**Publications:** Ralph E. Carpenter, Jr., *The Arts and Crafts of Newport, Rhode Island, 1640–1820* (Newport: Preservation Society of Newport County, 1954), no. 60.

**Provenance:** The dressing table is said to have been used in the Hunter house on Washington Street in Newport and to have descended in the Hunter and Birckhead families.

**Accession history:** Purchased by the museum from Elizabeth D. Birckhead (Mrs. Philip G.) of New York, 1955.
55.36

1. The remaining 19 dressing tables are in Ralph E. Carpenter, Jr., *The Arts and Crafts of Newport, Rhode Island, 1640–1820* (Newport: Preservation Society of Newport County, 1954), no. 61; Moses, *Master Craftsmen*, figs. 1.25, 6.7; *John Brown House Loan Exhibition*, cats. 63–65; Bernard and S. Dean Levy, Inc., *Vanity and Elegance* (New York: By the company, 1992), cat. 25; Katharine Bryant Hagler, *American Queen Anne Furniture, 1720–1755* (Dearborn, Mich.: Henry Ford Museum and Greenfield Village, 1976), p. 24; Bernard and S. Dean Levy advertisement, *Antiques* 36, no. 5 (November 1989): 899; Florene Maine advertisement, *Antiques* 89, no. 1 (January 1966): 56; Harry Arons advertisement, *Antiques* 95, no. 1 (January 1969): 29; Rollins, *Treasures of State*, cat. no. 50; Gary C. Cole advertisement, *Antiques* 109, no. 5 (May 1976): 846; *American Antiques from Israel Sack Collection*, 10 vols. (Washington, D.C.: Highland House, 1969– ), 5:1152; Ann Woods advertisement, *Antiques* 118, no. 4 (October 1980): 672; Warren, *Bayou Bend*, no. 115; G. K. S. Bush advertisement, *Antiques* 147, no. 4 (April 1995): 476; Rodriguez Roque, *American Furniture*, nos. 17, 18.

2. The tables with horizontally grained facing strips are in *John Brown House Loan Exhibition*, cat. 63; Rollins, *Treasures of State*, cat. no. 50; Woods advertisement.

3. The table with carved knees is in Rollins, *Treasures of State*, cat. no. 50; the table with 4 claw feet is in Warren, *Bayou Bend*, no. 115.

4. Townsend's bill, which is in the Ward Papers, Rhode Island Historical Society, Providence, is reproduced in *Rhode Island History* 5, no. 2 (April 1946): 58; "Providence, March ye 24th 1757 made By us Subscribers the Price of Joyners work," as reproduced in Lyon, *Colonial Furniture*, app.

5. On the Brenton, Easton, Pearce, and Perry tables, see Hagler, *American Queen Anne Furniture*, p. 24; Levy, Inc., *Vanity and Elegance*, fig. 25; Bush advertisement; *John Brown House Loan Exhibition*, cat. 65.

6. For a representative double-lobed–arch dressing table, see Nathan Liverant and Son advertisement, *Antiques* 137, no. 3 (March 1990): 582; for an English prototype, see Kirk, *American Furniture*, fig. 1473. Representative dressing tables from adjacent regions are in Kevin M. Sweeney, "Furniture and Furniture-Making in Mid-Eighteenth-Century Wethersfield, Connecticut," *Antiques* 125, no. 5 (May 1984): 1157–58, 1160; Israel Sack advertisement, *Antiques* 132, no. 3 (September 1987): inside front cover.

## 174 ◆ High chest of drawers

East Windsor, Connecticut
1775–90
Attributed to the shop of
Eliphalet Chapin (1741–1807)

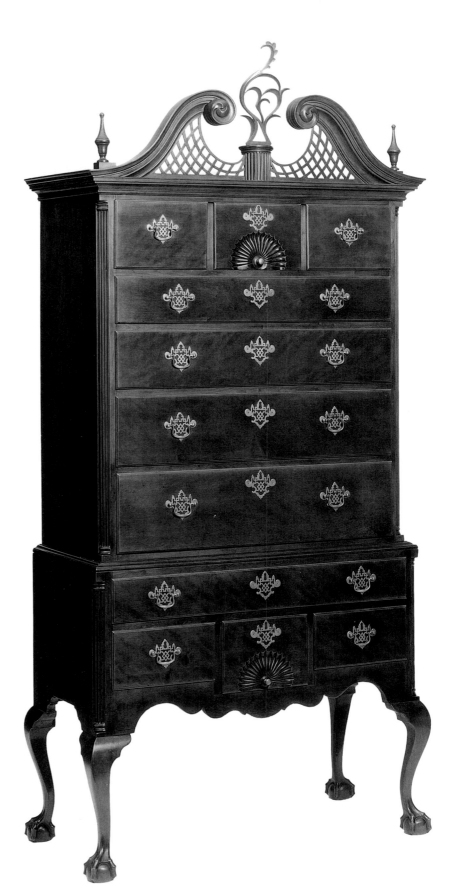

Based on recent and ongoing scholarly studies of case furniture believed to have originated in the greater Hartford area, much of it long associated with cabinetmaker Eliphalet Chapin (1741–1807) of East Windsor, this high chest can be assigned to the Chapin shop, although it is likely the product of several shop hands, including Aaron Chapin (1753–1835), who worked with his second cousin Eliphalet from 1774 to 1783. Twelve criteria have been established to distinguish between lattice-work high chests produced in Eliphalet Chapin's shop and those made by other craftsmen working in the Chapin manner. The critical points cover material, joints, internal and external constructional characteristics, and the quality and nature of the carved features. This chest is notable for the pediment cartouche (fig. 1), which is the only original one of its type (the others are copies); the original pierced brasses; and the East Windsor family provenance, which can be reasonably documented.[1]

Eliphalet Chapin's working experience in Philadelphia between 1767 and 1771 had a substantial influence on furniture design in the Connecticut River valley from the greater Hartford area north into central Massachusetts for several decades beginning in the early 1770s. Heretofore, regional furniture had borne the stamp of Boston design liberally infused with features borrowed from Rhode Island furniture. Although Chapin's tall chests are smaller than comparable Philadelphia cases, there is no mistaking the source of influence that helped to shape the design. Notable Philadelphia characteristics are the short cabriole legs and somewhat compressed ball feet; the scrolled, apronlike figure of the front skirt; the use of quarter columns at the case corners; the carved volutes and latticework of

the pediment; and the asymmetrical rococo form of the cartouche. Some cases attributed to the Chapin shop are embellished with carved vines in place of the fanlike shells seen on this chest. In several respects the vine decoration is better integrated into the overall design because its flowing quality echoes that of the ogee-scrolled pediment and the carved ornament above the central plinth. The

looplike protuberances along one side of the cartouche tip are repeated in the vines.[2]

Despite the general visual similarity in lattice-top high chests ascribed to the Chapin shop and the Chapin school, the cabinetmaker and consumer had considerable lattitude in choice of decorative elements. The volutes of all the chests located to date are carved in different scroll patterns (see fig. 1), and the spirelike side finials exhibit a range of variation. The original cartouches likely represented greater variety than is apparent today—many are copies of the ornament on Winterthur's chest. The face of the plinth that supports the cartouche is decorated in one of several carved patterns. The fluted surface of the Winterthur example is equally common as one carved with a large, low-relief rosette centered with an X; the rarest pattern is a latticelike blind fret. Quarter columns were a costly option on many chests; one distinctive example has caps, bases, and stop fluting fabricated of brass. The carved work of the chest proper is divided between fanlike shells and delicate vines, both ornaments confined to the surface of the small center drawers. One chest has vines in the upper case and a shell at the bottom. The brass hardware exhibits considerable variety; some are pierced, some are plain. Two methods of positioning the brasses on the case were popular: the hardware was aligned in three vertical rows or the outer handles on the long drawers of the upper case were inset, as was the fashion in Philadelphia. Inset brasses have been found on all the lattice-top high chests attributed to the Chapin shop, although the feature cannot be considered an infallible guide in making an attribution.[3]

The pierced brasses on Winterthur's high chest are original to the case. Brass furniture handles and escutcheons are among the many items of hardware routinely imported from England during the eighteenth and early nineteenth centuries. Most local merchants stocked a supply for cabinetmakers' use; occasionally a customer supplied his own furniture hardware, especially if he was involved in trade. These handsome examples, stamped on the reverse with the number "1064" (fig. 2), have been located under the same pattern number in an English trade catalogue probably published in Birmingham in the 1770s or early 1780s (fig. 3). Inscribed in ink on a flyleaf at the front is the notation "Rabais 15%," indicating that the catalogue was in French hands at one point and probably explaining why another inscription at the top of the page was cancelled with penned flourishes. Careful examination has revealed the cancelled name to read: "Boohe [sp. ?] & Barker." One of the partners likely was John

**Fig. 1.** Detail, cartouche and pediment volutes.

Barker of Birmingham, who signed another trade catalogue, probably dating to the 1770s, containing several closely related handle patterns.[4]

In many instances the ornament on a Chapin-like chest represents a mere borrowing by another craftsman of a successful design feature, and the furniture itself has no meaningful relationship with Chapin's work. The decoration, which usually appears in multiples, represents the full vocabulary of features found on Chapin's shop work and includes carved crest volutes, vines, shells, and claw feet; latticework; half-round cartouche plinths; turned finials; fluted quarter columns; and scrolled skirts. The furniture ranges in form from dressing tables and a small desk-on-frame to chests-on-chests and desk-and-bookcases. A flat-top high chest and a high chest with a solid scrollboard are also part of the group. The latticework pediments of Chapin-ascribed furniture may also have inspired a filigree-like open fret in the pediments of a small group of cherrywood chests-on-chests and a desk-and-bookcase dating to the late eighteenth century.[5]

The starting point for establishing the criteria to aid in distinguishing between the work of the Chapin shop and the Chapin school among extant lattice-top high chests was a group of chairs made in the late eighteenth century for two heads of households who resided in East Windsor. Alexander King ordered a set of ball-and-claw-foot chairs similar in pattern to the chair in No. 48, as documented in a bill of sale dated in 1781. King was the brother-in-law of Aaron Chapin, who worked with his second cousin Eliphalet in East Windsor before establishing a shop in Hartford in 1783. Other chairs, including a set with "molbor'o" legs (see No. 49), were made for Ebenezer Grant, as recorded in his account book in

December 1775. The chairs were part of the dowry Grant provided for his daughter Ann when she married the Reverend John Marsh; the chairs descended in the Marsh family.[6]

Two lattice-top high chests have histories in the King family—one in the Yale University Art Gallery and this one. The chest and a companion dressing table at Yale likely were made for Alexander King and his wife after their marriage in 1781. The furniture was sold out of the family in the 1920s by a great-granddaughter (or her heirs) of the Kings. Family tradition asserts that this high chest of drawers was purchased by a member of the King family at an early date from a neighbor in East Windsor. The chest came into the possession of Cornelia King, who willed it to her grandniece Deborah King Walker (1911–93), the last King family owner of the chest. The case was already in Deborah's possession in 1935 when she loaned it to the landmark Connecticut Tercentenary Exhibition at the Wadsworth Atheneum in Hartford. No less than three Chapin-type lattice-top chests were included in the exhibition (all assigned to Aaron Chapin), a testimony to their desirability among New England collectors, even at that early date.[7]

NGE

---

**Inscriptions or marks:** *On upper case, on underside of top board:* "2" at left end and "1" at right end, in period (?) pencil. *On case sides:* "L" at upper left side front and "R" at upper right side front. *On top surface of case bottom:* "3" at left end and "4" at right end. Various modern pencil markings. *On outside drawer backs near bottom:* X-like shop mark, in white chalk. *Inscribed on inside right side surface of long drawer and outside left side surface of left small drawer:* indecipherable words in lower-case letters. *On inside right side surface of bottom drawer in upper case:* "____NARY [printed]/____B/____King Jr./____s King" in black ink on remnants of a white gummed label with a dark blue border from the Connecticut Tercentenary Exhibition. *Stamped on reverse of one brass backplate:* "1064".

**Construction:** (Upper case) The case top and bottom are dovetailed to the sides. The pediment is supported, in part, in a rabbet at the front of the case top; above the rabbet the top is roughly chamfered. The pediment S scrolls are fastened at the outer ends with countersunk screws extending into the top of the case moldings. The fretwork forms a facing behind the scrolls, and a solid section of it passes behind the center plinth, which is half-cylindrical in form. The plinth and fret are reinforced on the back by a glueblock. The plinth is formed in two pieces: a lower barrel and an upper capital.

The cartouche above the plinth is supported at the bottom by a rectangular extension that is inset into an open mortise in the back of the plinth and secured by a metal screwplate. Behind the pediment at either end small low blocks without caps support the finials. The mitered-corner molding is applied to the case with sprigs. The side returns are one piece from the bottom through the ends of the S scrolls; an internal core of pine is triangular in section. The turned and fluted quarter-columns of the case are formed of three pieces—a capital, shaft, and base—and set into recesses in the front corner posts; the posts, case sides, drawer blades, and top and bottom front rails are secured by mortise and tenon. The vertical dividers between the upper drawers tenon into the top rail and the top drawer blade. Behind them, runners for the small drawers are lapped to the blade and tenoned through the backboard. Drawer guides glued to the top surface of the runners are butted to the dividers at the front and tenoned at the back. The top long drawer runs on a full dustboard behind the drawer blade; guides are nailed to the case sides behind the front stiles. The other long drawers and the outer small drawers are supported on combination runners and guides butted to the front and back corners and nailed to the case sides.

(Lower case) The two-piece case sides, which are shaped in a flat arch at the bottom, and the backboard are tenoned into the rear corner posts and pinned. The case sides, front posts, top rail, drawer blade, and skirt are secured by mortise and tenon. The fluted quarter-columns are formed like those in the upper case. The case has no top board. The mitered waist molding appears to be glued in place, except at the right case side, where a few nails are visible. Front-to-back battens at the case top and vertical glueblocks at the front and back corners further strengthen the case interior. The vertical drawer dividers are tenoned, top and bottom. The one-piece centered drawer runners and guides accommodating all three lower drawers are rabbeted to the front skirt and tenoned through the backboard. The one-piece outside runners and guides for the long drawer are rabbeted to the drawer blade, butted to the case back, and nailed to the case sides. The outer supports for the small drawers are butted to the front and back corners and nailed to the case sides. The legs and corner posts are one piece. The knees of the rear legs extend beyond the case; the knee brackets are glued and nailed in place.

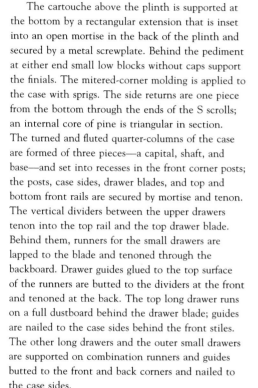

Fig. 2. Detail, back surface of handle.

Fig. 3. Attributed to Boohe(?) and Barker, catalogue of furniture hardware, probably Birmingham, Eng., ca. 1770s–80s, pattern no. 1064, p. 31. (Winterthur Library)

The drawers in both cases are finely dovetailed at the corners. The upper side edges are beaded on the outside; the back edges are flat. The bottom board runs from side to side in the long drawers and from front to back in the small drawers. The drawer bottoms are chamfered on three sides, set into grooves at the front and sides, and nailed flush at the back. The drawer fronts are thumb molded on four sides; the top and side lips butt against the case facade. The pierced brass handles and escutcheons are original.

**Condition:** The upper right batten of the upper case has been replaced. Most drawer bottoms have been reset, and the battens have been replaced except in the three small top drawers. The center bottom drawer has been rebuilt at the upper back. Blemishes on the wood surface have been puttied and sanded; the present finish dates from about the mid twentieth century.

**Dimensions:**

| | | |
|---|---|---|
| H. (case) | 81¹/₄ in. | 203.9 cm |
| W. (cornice) | 40 in. | 101.6 cm |
| W. (upper case) | 36³/₁₆ in. | 91.9 cm |
| W. (lower case) | 38¹/₄ in. | 97.2 cm |
| W. (feet) | 40¹/₄ in. | 102.2 cm |
| D. (cornice) | 19¹/₈ in. | 48.5 cm |
| D. (upper case) | 17 in. | 43.2 cm |
| D. (lower case) | 18³/₈ in. | 46.7 cm |
| D. (feet) | 20¹/₈ in. | 51.1 cm |

**Materials:** *Macroidentification:* Primary: cherry (drawer fronts, case sides, pediment and finials, legs). Secondary: white pine group (drawer linings, interior supports, top and bottom boards, backboards). *Finish:* medium reddish orange brown color in resin.

**Publications:** *Three Centuries of Connecticut Furniture, 1635–1935* (Hartford: Tercentenary Commission of the State of Connecticut, 1935), no. 164. Robert F. Trent, "Furniture," in Donald L. Fennimore et al., *Eye for Excellence: Masterworks from Winterthur* (Winterthur, Del.: Henry Francis du Pont Winterthur Museum, 1994), pp. 84–85. Philip Zea, "Diversity and Regionalism in Rural New England Furniture," in Luke Beckerdite and William N. Hosley, eds., *American Furniture 1995* (Milwaukee, Wis.: Chipstone Fndn., 1995), pp. 92–93.

**Provenance:** By tradition the chest was purchased from a neighbor by a member of the King family of East Windsor, Conn. The original purchaser may have been Alexander King (1749–1831), a brother-in-law of Aaron Chapin, although King already owned a high chest purchased from Eliphalet Chapin in 1781 (now at the Yale University Art Gallery, New Haven). Just as likely, the chest was purchased by one of Alexander's sons. The casepiece descended to Cornelia King, probably a great-granddaughter of Alexander King, and was bequeathed by her to her grandniece Deborah

Olcott King Walker (1911–93), the last family member to own the chest.

**Accession history:** Purchased by the museum from the heirs of Deborah Olcott King Walker (Mrs. Norman A. Walker), West Hartford, Conn., 1993.
93.55

---

1. Alice Kugelman, Thomas Kugelman, and Robert Lionetti, "The Chapin School of East Windsor, Connecticut," *Maine Antique Digest*, January 1994, pp. 12D–14D; Joseph Lionetti and Robert F. Trent, "New Information about Chapin Chairs," *Antiques* 129, no. 5 (May 1986): 1082–95. Winterthur's chest lacks only 1 of the 12 identifying characteristics associated with Chapin shop work—the dovetailed back brace of the upper case. A full dustboard occurs below the top long drawer, however. The dovetails of the drawers are of the same general type as those associated with the Chapin shop, although they are more finely done.

2. Kugelman, Kugelman, and Lionetti, "Chapin School"; Lionetti and Trent, "New Information"; Hornor, *Blue Book*, pls. 120–23, 126, 134, 138, 139, 141, 144.

3. Kugelman, Kugelman, and Lionetti, "Chapin School." Other examples are in Leigh Keno advertisement, *Antiques* 141, no. 5 (May 1992): 707; Albert Sack, *Fine Points of Furniture: Early American* (New York: Crown Publishers, 1950), p. 188 right; Nutting, *Furniture Treasury*, no. 374; *Connecticut Furniture*, no. 93; *Three Centuries of Connecticut Furniture, 1635–1935* (Hartford: Tercentenary Commission of the State of Connecticut, 1935); Ward, *American Case Furniture*, cat. 146.

4. The basic trade catalogue search is courtesy of Jason Samuel Hackler. The newly identified trade catalogue by Boohe(?) and Barker and the signed John Barker catalogue are in the Winterthur Library collection of trade catalogues, as listed in E. Richard McKinstry, comp., *Trade Catalogues at Winterthur: A Guide to the Literature of Merchandising, 1750 to 1980* (New York: Garland Publishing, 1984), nos. 257, 273; see also no. 256, which is attributed to Barker.

5. For examples of other case forms, see Ward, *American Case Furniture*, cats. 108 (dressing table, Chapin shop), 155 (desk-on-frame); Kugelman, Kugelman, and Lionetti, "Chapin School," fig. 3a (dressing table, Chapin shop), fig. 6 (desk-and-bookcase); Philip Zea, "Furniture," in *Great River*, cats. 112–14 (chest-on-chest, desk-and-bookcase, high chest); Nathan Liverant and Son advertisement, *Antiques* 145, no. 5 (May 1994): 671 (flat-top high chest); Florene Maine advertisement, *Antiques* 138, no. 4 (October 1965): 471 (chest-on-chest). A representative filigree-pediment chest-on-chest is in Ward, *American Case Furniture*, cat. 86.

6. Lionetti and Trent, "New Information," pp. 1083–91; Henry P. Maynard, "Eliphelet Chapin, the Resolute Yankee, 1741–1807," *Wadsworth Atheneum Bulletin*, 6th ser., vol. 1, no. 2 (Fall 1965): 12.

7. Robert F. Trent, "Furniture," in Donald L. Fennimore et al., *Eye for Excellence: Masterworks from Winterthur* (Winterthur, Del.: Henry Francis du Pont Winterthur Museum, 1994), pp. 84–85. For information about the King family and the descent of the 2 high chests that accompanied this chest when acquired by Winterthur, see folder 93.55, Registration Office, Winterthur.

## 175 ◆ High chest of drawers
Probably Goffstown, New Hampshire
ca. 1773–77
Probably Maj. John Dunlap (1746–92)
with the assistance of William Houston
(1755–1830)

The initial question prompted by the study of this casepiece is whether it is properly termed a *high chest of drawers* or a *chest-on-chest*. Rural New Hampshire furniture of this general design, which is associated with the Dunlap family or the broader Dunlap school of craftsmen, tends to have a lower center of gravity than tall casework from other areas of New England. The accounts of Maj. John Dunlap, kept at Goffstown and Bedford during a twenty-year period from the late 1760s to the late 1780s, provide little insight into specific nomenclature. Dunlap's term for all tall furniture formed of two stacked cases was *case of drawers*, regardless of the style or height of the legs. Bracket-foot and short–cabriole-leg cases qualify today as chests-on-chests (see No. 196). Those with either long or medium-high cabriole supports, as seen in this example, are probably better termed *high chests*, although appreciable variation in leg height occurs in the medium range.[1]

Dunlap's accounts do provide somewhat greater insights into the *price* of a case of drawers, although product options and therefore final cost varied slightly from order to order, determined in part by the number of drawers in the case, the amount and nature of the carved work, and the selection of plain or claw-carved feet. Sometimes a customer supplied his own brass hardware. Other factors to consider were the extra charges for the selection of a highly figured wood and the introduction of painted accents, as represented in this example. During the recording of Dunlap's accounts, currency fluctuated widely due to inflation from the war and its aftermath. Computations in "old tenor," "lawful money," and even dollars further confuse the picture.

Thus, equivalents rather than actual currency are the best indicators of the relative value of these large two-case chests. A case of drawers that cost £54 in 1780 was equal to 22 3/4 days' pay for Dunlap. Actual construction time was somewhat less because materials and profit above labor are calculated in the price. In the commodities market the same case was worth eighteen bushels of corn—a staple that figured prominently in the barter economy of the region. In comparison to other furniture forms, the case of drawers cost 18 to 27 percent more than a fall-front desk with fitted interior, about 80 percent more than a plain cherrywood tea table, and 55 percent more than a set of six banister-back chairs.[2]

At least forty tall cases are recorded in Dunlap's accounts. Customers were located principally in Goffstown and adjoining Bedford, although towns ranging from northwest to southeast of those locations are mentioned, including Dunbarton, Deering, New Boston, Litchfield, Windham, and Derry. Three chalk inscriptions on this chest are critical supporting evidence of the attribution to Dunlap. One is the signature of William Houston, a young man from Bedford who worked intermittently for Dunlap between 1773 and 1777 (fig. 1). In a formal indenture of apprenticeship between the two men, dated March 9, 1775, Houston agreed to serve Dunlap for two years to learn the trades of cabinetmaker and joiner. In later years Houston is named in deeds as practicing those trades. The account book does not detail Houston's shop activities, although on one occasion in April 1775, the apprentice worked with Samuel Dunlap, John's brother who assisted in the shop, for a period of ten and a half days. The place name "Goftstown" (Goffstown) also appears with Houston's name on the bottom board inside the upper case of the chest.[3]

Dunlap was a resident of Goffstown during the period of Houston's association. The community was also the home of Thomas

identical brasses, which is slightly more embellished and has coordinated shells in the gallery and base section, is in the New Hampshire Historical Society in Concord. That chest is linked with Dunlap's shop through its family history. Both the original owner, Jean Walker, and her sister Susanna, who also acquired a tall chest, are recorded in Dunlap's accounts on March 17, 1782. The Walker chests, along with two made the following year for a customer in New Boston, New Hampshire, all for about £120 apiece, appear to be the most costly furniture recorded by Dunlap. The prices must be viewed with caution, however, as the New Boston cases were paid for with currency valued in the "old Way." In noninflated currency, the prices of all four chests probably represent no more than a modest increase in Dunlap's usual charge for extra-embellished cases, such as that at Winterthur.[5]

Thomas Miller appears to have been in a financial position to afford an expensive piece of furniture. Land records from as early as 1768 identify him as a "Gentleman"—a title reserved in early documents for affluent individuals. Miller sold his farm in Goffstown in 1781 and moved to Hillsborough, a community about twenty miles distant, presumably taking his high chest with him. A "Case of Drawers" was one of the highest valued items (at $8) in the inventory of his estate made in 1805.[6]

Winterthur's chest displays a rich vocabulary of ornament. The carved flowered-ogee and bead-and-reel moldings of the upper cornice below the gallery are more precisely executed than comparable moldings in the bases of Nos. 187 and 196, chests associated with the shop of Dunlap's brother Samuel. The pierced basket-weave panels, or frets, of the front and sides of the gallery are one of several patterns used by the Dunlaps (fig. 2). Many examples, including this one, retain evidence of the laying-out lines that guided the hands of the carver and the workman who pierced the

Miller, a customer of Dunlap's who purchased a case of drawers on May 21, 1773. On the same date Dunlap charged Miller for two and a half days of unspecified work by Houston. That Winterthur's chest could be the one purchased by Miller is suggested by the third inscription in the upper case of the chest, which reads "Jennet M_ller," and is accompanied by the date "1780." The second letter of the surname could be read as an *i*, *o*, or *u*. The name could be that of a family member, legatee, or descendant of Thomas Miller, and the date, which has been enhanced in the twentieth century, may be original.[4]

Winterthur's chest is one of almost twenty tall cases from the Dunlap school constructed with a deep, ornamental gallery above the cornice. A second chest of close design with

**Fig. 1.** Detail, inside bottom board of upper case.

panels. The scribe lines, including those around and within the shells (or fans), are more prominent today because the original finish has been removed from the smooth surfaces of the surrounding wood. The backs of the pierced panels are slotted to receive thin tablets, which create blind frets (here removed for photography). Few galleries are finished with a top molding, as are this example and the chest in Concord; the scroll ends terminate in tiny carved and applied rosettes. The paired projections accenting the corners and center front of the gallery are acroteriumlike, and with the gallery proper they emphasize the architectural qualities of the chest. Originally, the effect of the decoration was heightened by contrasting colors in the gallery molding, shells, fretwork, and facing tablets. Items in Dunlap's shop inventory indicate that he was well equipped to embellish his furniture in this manner: "stone to grind paint," "lampblack," and "paint pots."[7]

The decorative features of the lower case are in some measure at odds with those in the upper case, although both shell and scroll forms are part of the ornament and the balanced arrangement anchors the mass (fig. 3). The "spoon-handle" shells with their astragal-like tips vary in number of lobes and carved detail from the shell in No. 196. The central fan of the shell in the chest-on-chest is better modeled. The tips are rounded instead of blunt and create a more convincing illusion of stop fluting. The paired, partially silhouetted S scrolls are a distinctive addition to this and several dozen other Dunlap-type cases, both high and low. The most ornate examples, as represented here, are detailed with a cushioned surface outlined by a flat bead—the two elements separated by a heart-shape cutout. Color contrasts likely were also a feature of this ornament, as in the gallery. The distinctive half ball and webbed talons of the carved feet compare with those in Nos. 187 and 196.[8]

Few craftsmen's accounts provide more than token information about how furniture was transferred from a craftsman's shop to a customer's home. Small items could be hand carried, but heavy case furniture was another matter. Arranging transport appears to have

been principally the responsibility of the purchaser. Dunlap referred to furniture deliveries in his accounts on four occasions: three customers lived several towns away, and another was a local sawmill owner. In each instance, a case of drawers was all or part of the load. Dunlap charged a customer who lived in Litchfield, a community to the south along the Merrimack River, for "Carreing one Case of Drawers to Coll [Colonel?] Nicholeses," perhaps a halfway point where the customer could collect his purchase more easily. Curiously, all the recorded deliveries were made in February and may have been transported via a yoke of oxen and a sleigh; at his death in 1792 Dunlap owned both in addition to a cart and two horses. Account-book entries also make it clear that Dunlap had access to transportation through barter activity.[9]

*NGE*

---

**Inscriptions or marks:** (Upper case) *Inside backboard:* "Jennet M_ller/ 1780" in white chalk, date added to or enhanced in twentieth century. *Inside bottom board:* "Will^m Houston" and "Gofstown" in white chalk. *Inside back of top small drawers:* "L", "MID", "R" left to right, all modern. *Inside back of top small drawers, left and center:* shop mark in form of vertical stroke. *Inside back of all long drawers:* "‡" near either end. *Outside right of right small drawer:* "Gu[ ? ]" in dark red crayon. *Outside right of second and third long drawers from top:* "B[ ? ]" and "Gu[ ? ]/ W[ ? ]" respectively. *On drawer blades:* "1" to "4" centered, top to bottom, in modern pencil. (Lower case) *On inside back of both long drawers:* vertical shop mark, centered, in white chalk. *Outside back of small drawers:* "L", "Shell", and "R" left to right. *Inside left and right small drawers:* modern marks. *Inside bottom of top long drawer:* illegible inscription in pencil.

**Construction:** (Upper case) The top and bottom of the case are dovetailed to the sides. The mitered gallery and cornice are formed of three horizontal units, the lower two constituting the cornice and nailed to the case. The top molding of the cornice, which is carved, is rabbeted to receive the gallery, which is also nailed in place. The gallery projections, or scrolls, at the center front and corners are pieced up to height. The entire top edge of the gallery is finished with a delicate ogee molding that is terminated at each projection by a tiny applied

rosette. The basket-weave panels are fitted with thin wooden tablets that slot into openings behind the piercings. Laying-out marks formed with rule and compass remain highly visible at each fan and basket-weave panel. The top rail of the case is slotted into the sides. The blades are attached to the sides with exposed shouldered dovetails that pierce the sides. The vertical dividers are slotted into the top rail and top blade. The bottom rail abuts the case sides and is secured with rosehead nails from the bottom of the bottom board. The outer drawer runners are nailed to the case sides. Inner runners for the small drawers are bevel-lapped in front and tenoned through the back; guides are glued to the top surface. The two-board backboard extends above the top board. It is rabbeted and nailed to the case sides and nailed to the back edge of the top and bottom boards.

(Lower case) The mitered waist molding is nailed on top of the frame. The two-board case sides, sawed with a flattened arch on the lower edge, and two-board backboard are tenoned and pinned to the corner posts. The top rail is dovetailed to the corner posts from the top. The blades and the ornamented skirt rail are tenoned and pinned to the corner posts. The vertical dividers are slotted into their adjacent members. The runners for the long drawers are lapped in front and tenoned in the back; the inner runners for the small drawers are bevel-lapped in front and tenoned through the backboard. Guides are glued to the top surface of all runners. The joints of the two-board sides are reinforced on the interior with large glueblocks. The legs and corner posts are one piece. The knee brackets are glued over the front skirt and the case sides. The drawers in both cases are dovetailed; the tops of the sides and back are flat. The bottom boards, running side to side in the long drawers and front to back in the small drawers, are chamfered on four edges, slotted into the front and sides, and nailed flush along the back. The drawer fronts are thumb molded on four sides; the side and top lips abut the case.

**Condition:** The right front basketwork tablet has been replaced. A patch in the backboard of the upper case covers a knothole. A large open crack extends across the upper right side of the lower case; a hairline crack is at the upper rear corner of the left side. The right rear corner post is cracked near the top. The second long drawer from the chest top is pieced at the lower right lining and split in the bottom. All drawers in the lower case have internal repairs. Some brasses have been replaced. The case surface has been refinished.

**Fig. 2.** Detail, gallery.

**Fig. 3.** Detail, shell drawer and skirt front.

**Dimensions:**

| | | |
|---|---|---|
| H. | 83 1/8 in. | 211.1 cm |
| W. (gallery) | 41 7/8 in. | 106.4 cm |
| W. (upper case) | 36 5/8 in. | 93.2 cm |
| W. (lower case) | 39 1/8 in. | 99.4 cm |
| W. (feet) | 42 in. | 106.7 cm |
| D. (gallery) | 20 7/8 in. | 53.0 cm |
| D. (upper case) | 17 5/8 in. | 44.8 cm |
| D. (lower case) | 19 3/8 in. | 49.2 cm |
| D. (feet) | 20 1/8 in. | 51.1 cm |

**Materials:** *Microanalysis:* Primary: soft maple group. Secondary: white pine group (throughout). *Finish:* yellowish brown color in resin with dark streaks of former finish.

**Publications:** "The Editor's Attic," *Antiques* 13, no. 1 (January 1928): 26–28, frontispiece. Charles Messer Stow, "Northern New England Furniture," *The Antiquarian* 10, no. 4 (May 1928): 34. Alice Winchester, "The Dunlap Dilemma," *Antiques* 46, no. 5 (December 1944): 337, fig. 2. Downs, *American Furniture*, fig. 193. Elizabeth Stillinger, *The Antiques Guide to Decorative Arts in America, 1600–1875* (New York: E. P. Dutton, 1972), p. 158. Butler, *American Furniture*, p. 60. *Plain and Elegant, Rich and Common: Documented New Hampshire Furniture, 1750–1850* (Concord: New Hampshire Historical Society, 1979), no. 15. Harold Sack,

"The Development of the American High Chest of Drawers," *Antiques* 133, no. 5 (May 1988): 1120, fig. 6. Jay E. Cantor, *Winterthur* (New York: Harry N. Abrams, 1985), p. 143. Marshall B. Davidson, *The American Heritage History of Colonial Antiques* ([New York]: American Heritage Publishing Co., [1967]), p. 228. *Dunlaps and Their Furniture,* fig. 5. Ethel Hall Bjerkoe with John Arthur Bjerkoe, *The Cabinetmakers of America* (Garden City, N.Y.: Doubleday, 1957), pl. 10, no. 1. Charles F. Hummel, "Queen Anne and Chippendale Furniture in the Henry Francis du Pont Winterthur Museum, Part 1," *Antiques* 97, no. 6 (June 1970): 898. Jobe and Kaye, *New England Furniture*, p. 68. Zea and Dunlap, *Dunlap Cabinetmakers*, p. 137. Victoria Kloss Ball, *Architecture and Interior Design: Europe and America from the Colonial Era to Today* (New York: John Wiley and Sons, 1980), p. 219, fig. 5.45.

**Provenance:** Ex coll.: Mrs. Austin Palmer (formerly Mrs. DeWitt Clinton Howe [Katherine B.]), Hopkinton, N.H. Ex coll.: Katharine Prentis Murphy, Westbrook, Conn.

**Accession history:** Purchased by H. F. du Pont from Collings and Collings, New York, 1926. Bequest of H. F. du Pont, 1969.
57.1391

1. "Major John Dunlap's Account Book," as transcribed in *Dunlaps and Their Furniture*, pp. 171–310.

2. "Major John Dunlap's Account Book," p. 75, figs. 1–50.

3. "Major John Dunlap's Account Book," pp. 18, 53, 55.

4. "Major John Dunlap's Account Book," p. 220.

5. On the tall cases with galleries, see *Dunlaps and Their Furniture*, figs. 1–15; Nutting, *Furniture Treasury*, no. 354; Christie's, "Important American Furniture, Silver, Folk Art, and Decorative Arts" (October 10, 1987), lot 243; Kenneth E. Tuttle advertisement, *Antiques* 139, no. 1 (January 1991): 125; John S. Walton advertisement, *Antiques* 108, no. 3 (September 1975): 308. Zea and Dunlap, *Dunlap Cabinetmakers*, p. 19; "Major John Dunlap's Account Book," pp. 218, 282.

6. Thomas Miller land and probate records, Registry of Deeds and Probate, Hillsborough County, Nashua, N.H.

7. Other fret patterns and Dunlap's inventory are in *Dunlaps and Their Furniture*, figs. 1, 7, pp. 36–37.

8. Other cases with paired S scrolls are in *Dunlaps and Their Furniture*, figs. 1–4, 7, 8, 10, 11, 13, 14, 20–22, 25–27, 29, 30, 38, 40–44, 46–49, 51, 58, 73.

9. "Major John Dunlap's Account Book," pp. 196, 206–7, 230–31, 282. Dunlap inventory in *Dunlaps and Their Furniture*, pp. 36–37. See also Ann W. Dibble, "Major John Dunlap: The Craftsman and His Community," *Old-Time New England* 68, nos. 3–4 (January–June 1978): 50–58.

# Chests of Drawers, Bureau Tables, and Chests-on-Chests

THE EIGHTEENTH-CENTURY CABINET FORMS known in American furniture as chests of drawers, bureau tables, and chests-on-chests derived from English prototypes, which in turn had their roots in Continental furniture. Furniture craftsmen in London in the early seventeenth century adapted the earliest English chest of drawers, a type with the drawers concealed behind cupboard doors, from a Netherlands *kas*, or cupboard, whose doors opened to interior shelves. References to the chest of drawers appear in 1640s inventories from both London and eastern Massachusetts, an indication that the form had already been in use for some time and was known from an early date in America. From the mid 1660s onward, references are common in London records. Documents originating in Massachusetts indicate that some chests of drawers used there at an early date were transported from England in the household baggage of affluent emigrants. Other chests appear to have been made in Boston by furniture craftsmen from London, some of whom were trained in the use of dovetail construction—a technique transferred to London from northern Germany by 1600. London craftsmen had also introduced the chest of drawers and dovetail construction to the New Haven colony and other areas of New England before 1700, but the technique probably was not in common use in America until about 1700.[1]

By the time Thomas Chippendale published the bureau dressing table in his *Director* (1754), the form had been available in England for almost half a century. Figure 71a illustrates a starkly rectangular case with minimal ornament consisting of a wide frieze drawer atop pedestals, or columns, of narrow drawers flanking a recessed cabinet. Obviously, Chippendale thought in architectural terms since he began his *Director* with a listing of classical orders. Designs for the form in subsequent editions of the *Director* are more curvilinear, reflecting the introduction of the rococo taste. On some English models the long drawer is divided and fitted with a dressing glass, boxes, and compartments; other examples have a baize-covered pull-out writing slide. Bureau tables relate visually to chests of drawers.[2]

The forerunner of the chest-on-chest is the double chest of drawers, introduced to America from England in the second half of the seventeenth century. The two stacked boxes of this early footed chest fitted with drawers, or drawers and a cupboard, are secured by vertical tenons in the top of the lower box but can be separated for ease in moving. Sometime before the second quarter of the eighteenth century, a true chest-on-chest (literally a chest of drawers placed on top of a chest of drawers) was introduced to the Boston furniture market. The English appearance and construction of this rectilinear chest point to an immigrant craftsman as the maker, and indeed several candidates settled in the community in the mid 1710s. Early Georgian chests-on-chests and complementary chests of drawers with flat surfaces sometimes relieved by figured veneers or painted ornament were rare in early America. The more common chests associated with the Georgian style, called the Queen Anne style in America, are flat-front plain-finished chests of drawers or, in urban centers, ones whose surfaces are modeled or swelled instead of flat, although the form was not current much before the mid eighteenth century.[3]

The striking feature of most of the chests of drawers and bureau tables in the catalogue entries that follow, and to some extent of the chests-on-chests, is the baroque quality of their facades. The swelling, projecting, and receding surfaces exhibit a considerable sense of movement that is heightened by the play of light and shadow across their modeled features. Carved, sawed, and inlaid accents of shells, pinwheels, volutes, and compass stars in company with bold moldings, pilasters, and scroll pediments further enhance the visual impact.

Local woods were predominantly used in cabinetmaking throughout New England preceding the Revolution and even later, especially in inland, rural, and lightly populated areas. Regional preferences can be explicated from wood analyses. Maple is the primary construction material of the cases made in New Hampshire. The curled figure of one example was undoubtedly a more expensive option than the common maple of several other chests. Cabinetmakers and consumers in Connecticut favored cherrywood; it was even the primary wood in a stylish labeled chest of drawers made in Hartford in the postrevolutionary period. Mahogany was more easily obtained in the seacoast centers of Boston and Newport than in less commercial areas, and eventually it became the choice of style-conscious consumers, even to the exclusion of other woods. Underscoring this point is a note from a Boston merchant included with a shipment of a mahogany bureau and chest of drawers to a consignee in Wilmington, North Carolina: "It has not been in our power to procure the Beareau & Chest Drawers made of Cherrytree, our Cabinet makers having done working in that Kind of wood. We have therefore sent Mahogney. Should they not Suit your J[ohn] Bergwin Esqr. you will please to sell them for our accot." The catalogue also includes a black walnut case made in the early eighteenth century by an English emigrant craftsman accustomed to working in that material and a later chest made in coastal Massachusetts from the exotic tropical wood sabicu, a hardwood that passed for mahogany in the eighteenth century.[4]

The terminology that identifies eighteenth-century chests in their variety in period records is flexible and confusing. The clearest term describes a tall double chest, called a "Chest upon Chest of drawers" by Daniel Rea, a painter of Boston, when crediting the account of cabinetmaker Alexander Edwards in 1773. William MacPherson Hornor, Jr., has documented the use of the term as early as 1747 in a Philadelphia estate that contained a "Chest of Drawers Walnut, Chist upon Chist." Forty-five years later the 1792 price book of the Hartford, Connecticut, Society of Cabinetmakers still included a section dealing with the chest-on-chest. Other terms for the stacked form, such as chest with drawers, can be misleading unless accompanied by a price or a valuation in the £10 range. A Nantucket inventory of 1787 introduces another term in describing a "Case of Draws," which is further qualified by the phrase "called Chest upon Chest."[5]

Descriptions of the chest of drawers, an open-front frame containing a set of three or four drawers, are less certain. Terminology varies with date, place, and author and applies to more than one furniture form. In Boston "Chests of Drawers" were among the "fashionable Furniture" offered at auctions of household goods in 1751 and 1760. The term could just as easily have been applied to the tall double case on high cabriole legs, however, because inventories often describe a dressing table en suite. A chest with only one or two drawers probably is a frame with a lift top. In some areas, *low chest of drawers* identifies the standard form, but in Pennsylvania the term describes a medium-tall chest with five or six ranks of drawers supported on a low frame.[6]

*Case* was at times a substitute for the word *chest*. The "Case of Draws" that Nathan Bowen of Marblehead, Massachusetts, made for £2.8.0 in 1777 was probably relatively plain because the "Swelld Case Draw[ers] with Plasters [pilasters]" made the following year for the same customer cost about a pound more. The prices of both compare with that for a swelled-front desk from the same shop. In another sense of the word *case*, Benjamin Baker of Newport, Rhode Island, priced his "Chist of drawes" at slightly less than one-third the cost of a "Case of Draws of mehogni," indicating that the mahogany piece was a tall chest on high legs. This is also the form described in a 1756 auction notice in Boston as "a beautiful Mehogany Case of Draws, with an Oger [ogee] Top [pediment] . . . brass'd off in the best manner."[7]

The "bureau table" or "bureau dressing table" was known by the end of the eighteenth-century as a "kneehole dressing chest." Today it is often called a kneehole desk. The origin of the name *bureau table* is somewhat confusing. The *Oxford English Dictionary* states that the term was borrowed from the French *bureau*, a word originally used to identify the woolen cloth used for covering writing desks and later associated with the writing desk itself. In England, *bureau* was used loosely in the early eighteenth century to identify writing furniture, including a chest of drawers with a writing slide. Later, the term also applied to a chest of drawers with four (occasionally three) long drawers.[8]

A "neat Beauro" was offered for sale in Boston in 1760, although at that date the form may have been a bureau table. Both terms appear in New England records through the end of the century, sometimes together. Price books for furniture from Hartford, Connecticut (1792), and Hatfield, Massachusetts (1796), use the term *bureau* to identify a chest of drawers. Thomas Sheraton in 1803 noted that the contemporary French definition of *bureau* was a small chest of drawers but that the English reserved the term for a desk, as the French had earlier in the century. *Commode* is also of French origin and generally describes forms with swelled facades. Some commodes, as illustrated by Chippendale, Ince and Mayhew, and Hepplewhite, were chests of drawers, and some, like the bureau, were fitted with a dressing drawer.[9]

As expected, chests of drawers, chests-on-chests, and bureau tables were commonly used in bedrooms. The back chamber, middle chamber, kitchen chamber, and front, or best, chamber (today's master bedroom) are all locations for these three forms of storage furniture, as listed in probate records. In Boston-area inventories dating to the second half of the eighteenth century, both black walnut and mahogany furniture are itemized. Black walnut construction was of long standing by that date and probably also included furniture described as old and veneered. In households containing several chest forms, the item "Small Case of draws" likely identified the chest of drawers. Toward the end of the century, *bureau* became the common term for the same form in these records. A bureau table was present in about 21 percent of the ninety-six estates surveyed and almost always in company with another storage or dressing form.[10]

*NGE*

---

1   Benno M. Forman, "Chest of Drawers in America, 1635–1730: The Origins of the Joined Chest of Drawers," and Robert F. Trent, "The Chest of Drawers in America, 1635–1730: A Postscript," *Winterthur Portfolio* 20, no. 1 (Spring 1985): 1–30, 31–48.

2   Thomas Chippendale, *The Gentleman and Cabinet-Maker's Director* (London: By the author, 1754), pl. 61.

3   Trent, "Chest of Drawers," pp. 40–41; Edward S. Cooke, Jr., "The Warland Chest: Early Georgian Furniture in Boston," *Maine Antique Digest*, March 1987, pp. 10C–13C.

4   Caleb Davis bill of lading for brigantine *Juno*, invoice of cargo for brigantine *Juno*, and letter to Bergwin, Jukes, and London, December 15, 1784, Caleb Davis Papers, vol. 11, Massachusetts Historical Society, Boston.

5  Daniel Rea ledger, 1764–99, Baker Library, Harvard University, Cambridge; Hornor, *Blue Book*, pp. 68, 104; The Hartford price list is transcribed in Lyon, *Colonial Furniture*, p. 268; Davis invoice; Matthew Barnard, Jr., inventory, 1787, Registry of Probate, Nantucket Co., Mass.

6  *Boston Evening Post*, July 29, 1751, and *Boston Gazette*, June 9, 1760, as quoted in Dow, *Arts and Crafts in New England*, pp. 112, 119; "chests of drawers" with accompanying tables are listed in the inventories of Dr. Thomas Bullfinch (1761), Isaac Gardner (1780), and Joseph Webb (1787), Registry of Probate, Suffolk Co., Mass. (microfilm, Downs collection); Elisha Hawley account book, 1781–1805, Ridgefield, Conn., and Isaiah Tiffany account book, 1746–67, Lebanon and Norwich, Conn., Connecticut Historical Society, Hartford; Benjamin Lehman, "Prices of Cabinet and Chair Work," Philadelphia, 1786, as transcribed in Harrold E. Gillingham, "Benjamin Lehman, A Germantown Cabinetmaker," *Pennsylvania Magazine of History and Biography* 54, no. 4 (1930): 295.

7  Nathan Bowen account book, 1775–78, Downs collection; Benjamin Baker account book, 1760–88, Newport Historical Society, Newport, R.I.; *Boston Gazette*, September 27, 1756, as quoted in Dow, *Arts and Crafts in New England*, p. 115.

8  Brock Jobe and Myrna Kaye link the reference "2 Mahogany Buroe Tables" in Boston cabinetmaker George Bright's bill of August 10, 1770, to Jonathan Bowman to a rounded blockfront chest of drawers at SPNEA; see Jobe and Kaye, *New England Furniture*, no. 15.

9  *Boston News-Letter*, August 7, 1760, as quoted in Dow, *Arts and Crafts in New England*, p. 119; entries for bureaus in the Hartford and Hatfield price books are transcribed in Montgomery, *American Furniture*, p. 179; Thomas Sheraton, *The Cabinet Dictionary* (1803; reprint in 2 vols., New York: Praeger Publishers, 1970), 1:111; Thomas Chippendale, *The Gentleman and Cabinet-Maker's Director* (1762; reprint 3d ed., New York: Dover Publications, 1966), pl. 69; William Ince and John Mayhew, *The Universal System of Houshold Furniture* (1762; reprint, Chicago: Quadrangle Books, 1960), pl. 43; [George] Hepplewhite, *The Cabinet Maker and Upholsterer's Guide* (1794; reprint 3d ed., New York: Dover Publications, 1969), pl. 77.

10  Samuel Miller inventory, 1761, Registry of Probate, Suffolk Co., Mass. (microfilm, Downs collection).

## 176 ◆ Chest of drawers
Boston, Massachusetts, or area
1750–75

The origin of the blocked facade as first interpreted on case furniture made in Boston in the second quarter of the eighteenth century has been debated for three-quarters of a century. In 1928, discovery of a massive twenty-five-foot five-bay blockfront storage chest in the sacristy of the cathedral in Havana, Cuba, triggered speculation that this piece of furniture (probably made in the early eighteenth century) was the source of inspiration for the blockfront style as introduced in Newport, Rhode Island, then considered the center of American development of the form. The extensive commercial traffic between New England and the Caribbean islands in the eighteenth century seemed to support this theory.[1]

Today it is more obvious that the design of the Havana chest and the adoption of blocked surfaces in New England casework were independent developments. With the discovery of a desk-and-bookcase made by Job Coit of Boston in 1738, the identification of related casepieces, and recent scholarship on another early group of blockfront furniture made in Boston by Richard Walker and probably others, initial development of the blockfront style in America has been reassigned to Boston.[2]

Both the Havana and the New England furniture described above have their stylistic roots in European cabinetry. Specifically, the blockfront style in Boston reflects the influence in the local market of immigrant English craftsmen or imported English blockfront furniture or perhaps a combination of the two. The English blockfront style itself was a transplant, transferred to London from the Continent in the late seventeenth century by immigrant craftsmen. Given the sophisticated character of blockfront casework

in England and America, the style appears to have originated in France and was carried to London in the cultural baggage of displaced Huguenot artisans or Dutch craftsmen exposed to French design. The earliest use of bulging and recessed surfaces in French casework probably was in the writing table, an elegant form already well known in French court circles in the late seventeenth century when curved facades began to replace flat ones. By the turn of the century, the popular commode form was updated in like manner. Diffusion of the blockfront style was rapid: writing tables in the French manner were apparently made in London by the 1690s. By the time blockfront casepieces were produced in Boston in the 1730s, the style had spread throughout western Europe, where regional interpretations occur in Germany, Scandinavia, and on the Iberian peninsula.[3]

This example is typical of eastern Massachusetts construction and design of the blockfront chest of drawers. The top, grooved at the ends on the underside, is fitted to the case sides on sliding dovetails, and

the drawer blades, or horizontal dividers, are also dovetailed to the case sides. These joints are not usually exposed, as they are here; more typically, the ends of the dovetails are concealed within the side panels, and facing strips are applied to the front edges of the panels to cover the entry slots, a technique that follows British practice. The front base molding is secured to the case bottom with a central oversize ("giant") dovetail (fig. 1).[4]

Common to early Boston blockfront work is flat-face blocking rounded abruptly at the block ends, as found on this chest. The style, with its emphasis on verticality, is also common to the Massachusetts blockfront desk, desk-and-bookcase, bureau table, and chest-on-chest. A conforming, overhanging case top and a base blocked at the molding and front brackets integrates the design. The greatest variation occurs in the base—at the feet, brackets, and central drop. A straight foot is the most common support, and occasionally the base blocking continues onto the inside edge of the front feet. The cheeked swells of these feet are considerably less common than

**Fig. 1.** Detail, oversize dovetail.

plain, straight feet although not as rare as an ogee-curved support.

Variation in the foot brackets includes depth, length, and sawed profiles, but a cusp is the prominent feature of each pattern. Chests without a central drop may outnumber those so ornamented by as many as two to one, although some examples probably have lost their pendants over the years. A curved piece centered by a single astragal or inverted arch is most common; the double-lobed profile of this example is rare.

A gift to the museum, this chest has a history of ownership in a New England family, although the family originated in Rhode Island rather than in Massachusetts. The remnants of a Portsmouth, New Hampshire, 1841 newspaper were found on the three-piece backboard of the chest, but at least one board and probably all three have been recycled. Several related chests have associations, histories, or documentation linking them with Massachusetts; at the beginning of the twentieth century, one was owned in Boston. Others descended in the Cushing family of Newburyport and in the family of Dr. William Whiting. A virtual mate chest with similar feet, drop, and molded top lip and brasses of close design descended in the Barrett family of Concord. Of greatest historical significance, however, is a chest of drawers once owned by John Hancock (d. 1793) that was purchased through auction of his estate in the nineteenth century by a Petersham, Massachusetts, resident. That chest exhibits the same side-exposed dovetail construction of the drawer blades as found on the Winterthur chest. Still another Massachusetts blockfront chest, one with an astragal drop at the center front, bears the label of Benjamin Frothingham, a Charlestown cabinetmaker.[5]

*NGE*

**Inscriptions or marks:** *On backboard:* "HS" and "34" in crayon. *On upper surface of bottom board:* script "B"

in pencil. Each blade, from near bottom to top, has a scratched roman numeral from "I" to "III".

**Construction:** The top and sides of the chest are joined in sliding dovetails. The top, which overhangs the case, extends ½" farther at the sides than at the front and is flush at the back. The top conforms to the case blocking at the front and is ogee molded at the front and side edges. The horizontal drawer blades, or dividers, which are backed with pine and beaded at the front edges, are attached to the case sides with through dovetails; layout lines for the blocking are visible. There is no top rail. Vertical beads are nailed to the inside faces of the case sides. Runners nailed inside the case sides support the three upper drawers; the bottom drawer runs on the bottom board. The sides and bottom of the chest are joined with dovetails. The bottom is further supported on the lower surface by cleats extending from front to back at either end and across the front behind the base molding. A heavy cyma-reversa base molding is attached with a large dovetail to the front of the case; conforming moldings are nailed to the sides. The straight-bracket front feet are formed of two facing pieces mitered vertically at the corners and reinforced on the inside surface with vertical and horizontal glueblocks. The side rear foot facings are similarly reinforced, and each is further supported by a plain board at the back canted on the inside edge and secured with a single horizontal glueblock. The front pendant is glued to the base and reinforced on the back with a glueblock. The three horizontal backboards are set into rabbets at the back of the case sides and nailed. The drawers are dovetailed at the corners and sawed on the inside front to conform to the exterior blocking. The sides of the drawers are double-beaded on the top edge; the back is thicker than the sides and chamfered at the top. The drawer bottoms, which run from side to side, are set into rabbets at the sides and front and nailed; the back edge is nailed flush. Vertical blocks glued to the outside drawer backs serve as stops. All drawers are fitted with locks.

**Condition:** Facings on all four feet have been repaired (left front) or replaced (lower part of both outside rear feet and right front foot); some glueblocks have been replaced. Cavetto moldings have been added to the upper case sides to stabilize

the top. There are splits in the top and the left side board. The exposed dovetails of some drawer blades are broken and pieced. The drawer runners are replaced. The worn lower edges of the drawer sides are patched with strips of yellow poplar, and all drawers are lined with canvas on the bottom. The brasses are not original. The exterior surface has been refinished.

**Dimensions:**

| | | |
|---|---|---|
| H. | 31 in. | 78.9 cm |
| W. (top) | 35 ³/₄ in. | 90.8 cm |
| W. (case) | 32 ³/₄ in. | 83.2 cm |
| W. (feet) | 34 ³/₈ in. | 87.3 cm |
| D. (top) | 21 ¹/₄ in. | 54.0 cm |
| D. (feet) | 20 ⁷/₈ in. | 53.0 cm |

**Materials:** *Microanalysis:* Primary: mahogany. Secondary: white pine group (drawer linings, backing on blades, backboard, bottom board, glueblocks behind feet); yellow poplar (replaced drawer runners). *Finish:* medium light reddish brown resin.

**Publications:** Margaretta Markle Lovell, "Boston Blockfront Furniture," in *Boston Furniture*, p. 81.

**Provenance:** The chest descended through 5 generations of the Selfridge family of Rhode Island to Duncan I. Selfridge, the last family owner.

**Accession history:** Gift of Mrs. Duncan I. Selfridge, Wayne, Pa., 1957.
57.32.1

1. Wendell D. Garrett, comp., "Speculations on the Rhode Island Block-front in 1928," *Antiques* 99, no. 6 (June 1971): 887–91.

2. R. Peter Mooz, "The Origins of Newport Block-front Furniture Design," *Antiques* 99, no. 6 (June 1971): 882–86; Brock Jobe, "A Boston Desk-and-Bookcase at the Milwaukee Art Museum," *Antiques* 140, no. 3 (September 1991): 413–19; Miller, "Roman Gusto," pp. 160–200; Philip D. Zimmerman and Frank M. Levy, "An Important Block-front Desk by Richard Walker of Boston," *Antiques* 147, no. 3 (March 1995): 436–41.

3. Helena Hayward, ed., *World Furniture: An Illustrated History* (New York: McGraw-Hill Book Co., 1965), figs. 240, 242, 264, 265, 307, 383, 388, 542, 560, 561, 614, 625, 626, 643.

4. The pioneering work on the Massachusetts blockfront style and still the principal source is Margaretta Markle Lovell, "Boston Blockfront Furniture," in *Boston Furniture*, pp. 77–135.

5. Morse, *Furniture of the Olden Time*, p. 42; David Stockwell advertisement, *Antiques* 134, no. 5 (November 1988): 883; *American Antiques from Israel Sack Collection*, 10 vols. (Washington, D.C.: Highland House, 1969–), 2:449; David F. Wood, ed., *The Concord Museum: Decorative Arts from a New England Collection* (Concord, Mass.: By the museum, 1996), cat. 7B. Nathan Liverant and Son advertisement, *Antiques* 133, no. 5 (May 1988): 966; "The Editor's Attic," *Antiques* 17, no. 3 (March 1930): 211 left.

## 177 ◆ Chest of drawers
### Northeastern Massachusetts
### 1755–80

A combination of features makes this chest rare. Its diminutive size—the case proper is a full three inches narrower than No. 176—the blocked panels, and the narrow feet increase the vertical emphasis, which the designer cleverly offset by introducing a large fan-shape drop in the base. The substantial overhang of the top, an inch greater at each end than in No. 176, also helps to anchor the form. Construction features match those found in northeastern Massachusetts—sliding dovetail joints on the top and an oversize dovetail on the bottom front molding. The dovetails of the drawer blades are exposed on the front face but are otherwise concealed within the side panels, unlike those of No. 176.

A fan-shape drop is uncommon in the Massachusetts chest of drawers with flat blocking, and one this size may be unique (fig. 1). A blockfront chest of drawers with a small fan descended in the Moulton family of Newburyport, Massachusetts; a small fan is also featured in a 1770 round-blocked chest made by George Bright of Boston. A related fan forms a pendant at the base of a Massachusetts blockfront mahogany desk in the collection of the Chipstone Foundation, and a fan-shape drop appears occasionally in the high chest form. The crest ornament in a Massachusetts side chair is also comparable (see No. 30, fig. 1). The strong reeded character of the chest fan also relates well to the beading of the drawer openings, a common feature on mid and late eighteenth-century case furniture.[1]

The cabinetmaker took full advantage of the ornamental properties of mahogany across the face of this chest. The choice of richly figured wood and the care taken to create a harmonious pattern with the four separate pieces of wood likely cost the customer a premium. In the mid eighteenth

century, mahogany was only just beginning to achieve prominence as a cabinet wood in American seaport cities, although there are instances of its limited use in cabinetwork half a century earlier.[2]

Passage of the Naval Stores Act in Britain in 1721 marked the turning point in the popularity and use of tropical woods. Duties were lifted on stores imported from America, which included wood and lumber from the West Indies. For the first time it became profitable to import Virginia walnut and West Indian mahogany to supplement the primary trade in naval stores, sugar, and tobacco. The result was an immediate rise in English importation of ornamental woods for furniture and architectural interiors. American interest in tropical timbers paralleled that in Britain—by at least 1737, mahogany and other imported woods were offered for sale on Long

Wharf in Boston. Recent scholarship has also identified a sizable group of mahogany furniture constructed in Boston before 1750, including a desk, desk-and-bookcases, clock cases, and a card table.[3]

The original brass hardware of this chest is notable because it has survived intact. Size, intricacy of design, and number of metal plates determined the cost of the trimming. Most hardware used on American furniture in the eighteenth century was imported from England; by midcentury the principal centers of manufacture were London, Birmingham, and Sheffield. In a Birmingham brassfounder's catalogue of the 1780s owned by Samuel Rowland Fisher, a Philadelphia merchant, comparable unpierced plates of large size were priced at 5s. 9d. per dozen. Allowing for importation costs, the retailer's markup, and the cabinetmaker's charge for mounting the

**Fig. 1.** Detail, fan-shape drop.

hardware on the case drawers, the cost to the consumer for trimming likely was almost doubled. The scarcity of Boston furniture records and the general nature of most chest references that exist permit only a general estimate of the cost of a blockfront chest of this quality when new, but a range of £5 to £6 is probably reasonably accurate (see No. 179). Thus, the hardware on this chest represented between 9.5 and 11.5 percent of the purchase price.[4]

NGE

**Construction:** The top and sides of the chest are joined in sliding dovetails. The top, which overhangs the case, extends farther at the sides than at the front and back; it conforms to the case blocking at the front and is ogee molded on the front and side edges. The horizontal drawer blades, or dividers, which are backed with pine and beaded at the front edges, are attached to the case sides with dovetails that almost pierce the outer side surfaces; there is no top rail. Vertical beads at the inside faces of the case sides form miters with those of the drawer blades. Runners nailed inside the case sides support the three upper drawers; the bottom drawer runs on the bottom board. Drawer stops are glued and nailed to the case sides. The sides and bottom of the chest are joined with dovetails. The bottom is further supported by wide cleats extending from front to back at either end on the lower surface and by glueblocks across the front behind the base molding. A heavy cyma-reversa base molding is attached with a large dovetail to the front of the case; conforming moldings are nailed to the sides. The straight-bracket front feet are formed of two facing pieces mitered vertically at the corners

and reinforced on the inside surface with vertical and horizontal glueblocks. The rear foot facings are similarly reinforced, and each is further supported by a plain board at the back canted on the inside edge and secured with a single horizontal glueblock. The fan pendant is glued to the base and reinforced on the back with stacked horizontal glueblocks. The two horizontal lap-jointed backboards are set into rabbets at the back of the case sides and nailed. The drawers are dovetailed at the corners and sawed on the inside front to conform to the exterior blocking. The sides of the drawers are beaded on the inner top edges. The drawer bottoms, which run from front to back and are chamfered on three sides, join the sides and front with sliding dados and are nailed flush at the back.

**Condition:** Facings on all four feet have been cracked (right end), repaired (left rear), or replaced (left front). The vertical supports inside the corners of the feet are replaced. The tip of the lower cusp in some leg brackets has been broken off and replaced. The sides and back of the bottom drawer have been rebuilt using some original materials. All the drawer battens are replaced. A long crack in the right side base molding has been repaired. Both side case panels are cracked, and short gougelike marks appear on the frame and molding at the lower front flanking the shell. The exterior surface is refinished.

**Dimensions:**

| | | |
|---|---|---|
| H. | 31 5/8 in. | 80.5 cm |
| W. (top) | 34 3/4 in. | 88.2 cm |
| W. (case) | 29 9/16 in. | 75.1 cm |
| W. (feet) | 31 1/4 in. | 79.5 cm |
| D. (top) | 22 5/8 in. | 57.5 cm |
| D. (feet) | 20 7/8 in. | 53.2 cm |

**Materials:** *Microanalysis:* Primary: mahogany. Secondary: white pine group (backboard, bottom

board, blade extensions, drawer linings). *Finish:* medium orange color in bright resin, which emphasizes the figure of the wood.

**Publications:** Downs, *American Furniture*, fig. 168.

**Provenance:** Ex coll.: Mr. and Mrs. Arthur L. Kelley, Worcester, Mass.

**Accession history:** Purchased by H. F. du Pont from Israel Sack, Boston, 1928. Bequest of H. F. du Pont, 1969.
57.508

---

1. For Moulton chest, see Israel Sack advertisement, *Antiques* 94, no. 3 (September 1968): inside front cover; for Bright chest, see Jobe and Kaye, *New England Furniture*, no. 15; Rodriguez Roque, *American Furniture*, no. 25; for high chest, see *American Antiques from Israel Sack Collection*, 10 vols. (Washington, D.C.: Highland House, 1969–), 10:2599. See also chest of drawers in Sotheby's, "Important Americana" (January 30–February 1, 1986), lot 544.

2. Appraisers of the estates of 2 Philadelphia cabinetmakers listed mahogany in their 1708 and 1711 inventories; see Hornor, *Blue Book*, pp. 8–9, 13–14.

3. Adam Bowett, "The Commercial Introduction of Mahogany and the Naval Stores Act of 1721," and John M. Cross, "The Changing Role of the Timber Merchant in Early Eighteenth-Century London," *Furniture History* 30 (1994): 43–56, 57–64; Dow, *Arts and Crafts in New England*, p. 129; Philip D. Zimmerman and Frank M. Levy, "An Important Block-front Desk by Richard Walker of Boston," *Antiques* 147, no. 3 (March 1995): 436–41; Miller, "Roman Gusto," pp. 160–200, figs. 7, 15, 20, 36, 37, 51, 55.

4. Charles F. Hummel, "Samuel Rowland Fisher's Catalogue of English Hardware," in Milo M. Naeve, ed., *Winterthur Portfolio I* (Winterthur, Del.: Henry Francis du Pont Winterthur Museum, 1964), pp. 188–97, fig. 3 upper left; Donald L. Fennimore, "Brass Hardware on American Furniture, Part I: Cast Hardware, 1700–1850," *Antiques* 139, no. 5 (May 1991): 948–55.

## 178 ◆ Chest of drawers
### Portsmouth, New Hampshire
### 1750–75

Several stylistic and structural characteristics point to a Portsmouth origin for this piece of furniture, one of five blockfront chests of drawers now associated with that community. Several features in this chest also appear in a group of dressing tables made slightly earlier in Portsmouth.[1]

The broad, blocked feet are uncommon in blockfront cases, although a variant appears in two other Portsmouth chests, both with regional histories. Visible on the exterior of the case is a narrow thumbmolding that finishes the four edges of the drawers (except the top edge of the upper drawer) and extends to form lips at the sides, causing the drawers to butt against the front edges of the case frame. By the third quarter of the eighteenth century, this

construction and feature was out of fashion in Boston, replaced by beaded drawer blades and flush drawer facades (see Nos. 176, 177, 179). The case dimensions are also higher and narrower than is common in Massachusetts prototypes of this date (see No. 177).[2]

Other regional or non-Boston features of this chest are concealed within the case. The base molding abuts the case bottom and lacks the large connecting Boston dovetail; the drawer runners are secured to the case sides with rosehead nails, and a bead and a chamfer finish outside top edges of the drawer sides and a chamfer extends across the back, respectively. Inside the drawers, the blocked front ends have been hollowed out with chisels to the depth of the drawer bottoms; the usual hollow, or depression, is sawed from top to bottom as is characteristic in Boston practice.[3]

Attachment of the case top to the sides differs from that of Massachusetts blockfront

chests and three of the four other New Hampshire examples. Structural problems created by warping of the case sides led to the removal, alteration, and reattachment of the case top in the late nineteenth or early twentieth century, and consequently it was thought in recent years that the top was a replacement. Careful examination and analysis now offers an explanation for the exposed nail holes in the case sides and top adjacent to the present molding strips and for the peculiar profile of the molding itself. The molding that originally secured the top to the case was broader and deeper and was held in place by nails that entered the now-exposed holes. The current molding is unusual in profile, with a flat outer face and lipped bottom edge ending in a front return. Further examination has revealed that the lipped edges are identical to those of the case top, including the narrow fillet that separates the flat upper surface from the ogee edges. Originally, the chest top overhung the back and, like the sides and front, was finished with a lip. This also explains the presence of old glueblock shadows on the case backboard adjacent to the top.[4]

A finished rear overhang is unusual on a mid eighteenth-century chest of drawers. Also uncommon is the fillet that separates the ogee-molded edges from the flat upper surface of the top. Both features are found, however, in Portsmouth dressing tables of contemporary or earlier date. Although the dressing table tops generally are thumb molded at the edges, the blockfront chests in the New Hampshire group are finished with an ogee.[5]

A family history confirms this structural and stylistic analysis of origin: the chest was made in New Hampshire. When consigned to auction in 1931, it was accompanied by an affidavit signed by the last private owners, two brothers who were born in Exeter, New Hampshire. They identified Joseph Pearson (b. 1737) of Exeter and Concord, a brother of their great grandfather, Maj. Edmund Pearson, as the original family owner of the chest. Joseph Pearson, who was secretary of state for New Hampshire between 1786 and 1804, was a Harvard graduate and began his public career as master of the Exeter school in 1760. The potentially modest circumstances of a schoolmaster coupled with his birth date raises doubts about Pearson as the chest's first owner; he may have acquired it secondhand at a later date.[6]

This example is the only one of the five New Hampshire blockfront chests that is made of maple—the others are mahogany. Maple was abundant in New England and was often obtained by both urban and rural cabinetmakers as barter in exchange for services and products. Common maple was sometimes stained to imitate more expensive wood, but the curled variety with its prominent figure was held in some esteem, as indicated by the quality and variety of furniture produced from it.

*NGE*

---

**Construction:** The top of the chest is screwed to the side moldings, which, in turn, are screwed to the case sides from the inside. Wooden plugs in the top cover the screw holes. The top overhangs the case and conforms to the case blocking at the front. The front and side edges are ogee molded. The horizontal drawer blades, or dividers, are attached to the case sides with dovetails; there is no top rail. Runners fixed with rosehead nails inside the case support the three upper drawers; the bottom drawer runs on the bottom board. The sides and bottom of the chest are joined with dovetails. The bottom is further supported by wide cleats extending across the front on the lower surface. An ogee base molding is glued to the front of the case; the molding continues at the sides. The straight-bracket front feet are formed of two pieces mitered vertically at the corners and reinforced on the inside surface with vertical and horizontal glueblocks. The side foot facings, front and back, are cut in one piece. The rear feet are each further supported by a plain board at the back arched on the inside edge and secured with glue and nails to the case bottom. The back of the case, consisting of two planed, horizontal lap-jointed boards, is set into rabbets at the back of the case sides and secured with rosehead nails. The drawers are dovetailed at the corners and chiseled at the front behind the blocking to conform to the exterior. All drawers have four thumb-molded edges, except the top one, which has three (side and bottom edges). The side moldings of the drawers butt against the case sides. The sides of the drawers are beaded on the inner top edges, and the back is chamfered on the rear edge. The drawer bottoms, which run from side to side, are set into rabbets at the front and sides and are flush at the back; rosehead nails secure the construction. Battens are applied to the bottoms of the drawers.

**Condition:** The right rear foot, the arched board at the back of the left rear foot, and a section of the right side base molding are replaced. The vertical glueblocks inside the front feet are missing. The side moldings beneath the case top have been replaced with strips of wood removed from the back edge of the top. The moldings are attached to the case and the top to the moldings with modern screws. The worn drawer runners have been reversed, and worn sections on the blades have been patched. The bottom blade also is patched at the lock. The top three drawers have burlap strips covering the separation between the drawer front and the drawer bottom; the bottom drawer has a portion of the bottom replaced. Several drawers are patched on the corners, and replacement battens have been added to the bottoms of most drawers. The top front edge of the top drawer is crudely chamfered, probably to relieve binding when the case sides warped. The brass hardware is replaced; at one time the case had a set of single-post pulls. The exterior surface is refinished.

**Dimensions:**

| | | |
|---|---|---|
| H. | 30 3/4 in. | 78.1 cm |
| W. (top) | 35 3/4 in. | 90.8 cm |
| W. (case) | 31 3/4 in. | 80.7 cm |
| W. (feet) | 33 1/4 in. | 84.5 cm |
| D. (top) | 18 3/4 in. | 47.6 cm |
| D. (feet) | 18 1/2 in. | 47.0 cm |

**Materials:** *Microanalysis:* Primary: soft maple group. Secondary: white pine group. *Finish:* yellowish brown resin over the residue of a former finish containing color or stain.

**Publications:** Downs, *American Furniture*, fig. 167.

**Provenance:** The chest has a history of ownership in Exeter, N.H., by Joseph Pearson, first secretary of state of New Hampshire. It descended in the family of his brother Edmund to Edmund's granddaughter Mary Moses Ricker and to her sons Henry M. and Charles E. Ricker of Malden, Mass., the last private owners.

**Accession history:** The chest was purchased by H. F. du Pont at the National Art Galleries, New York, in 1931, at the sale of the collections of King Hooper, Inc., Hyman Kaufman, and Herbert Lawton. Bequest of H. F. du Pont, 1969. 58.1741

---

1. For the other blockfront chests, see Jobe and Kaye, *New England Furniture*, nos. 16, 17; Jobe, *Portsmouth Furniture*, cat. nos. 6, 7. Portsmouth dressing tables are in Brock W. Jobe, "An Introduction to Portsmouth Furniture of the Mid-Eighteenth Century," in *New England Furniture*, pp. 165–87.

2. Jobe and Kaye, *New England Furniture*, no. 16; Jobe, *Portsmouth Furniture*, cat. no. 6.

3. For a blocked drawer front similarly hollowed out, see Jobe, *Portsmouth Furniture*, p. 105.

4. I am grateful to Michael S. Podmaniczky for his insights during the examination of this chest.

5. Jobe, "Introduction to Portsmouth Furniture," pp. 168–86; Jobe and Kaye, *New England Furniture*, nos. 16, 17; Jobe, *Portsmouth Furniture*, cat. nos. 6, 7.

6. National Art Galleries, "Seventeenth and Eighteenth-Century American Furniture . . ." (December 3–5, 1931), lot 470; Clifford K. Shipton, comp., *Biographical Sketches of Those Who Attended Harvard College in the Classes, 1746–1750* (Boston: Massachusetts Historical Society, 1962), 14:306–7.

## 179 ◆ Chest of drawers
Northeastern Massachusetts,
probably Boston
1760–90

A survey of eastern Massachusetts chests of drawers with rounded or flat blocking on the facade that have been illustrated in publications during the past thirty years demonstrates the overwhelming popularity (in a ratio of about two to one) of the rounded form in the eighteenth century, although the flat-blocked chest was in the market first. Chests with rounded blocking coincide in production with the period of rising prosperity that preceded the Revolution.

The modest differences in the date ranges of the two types of blocking are apparent in the supports of the chests. Straight-bracket feet are most common on flat-blocked chests but appear on only about half the chests with rounded blocking. Flat-blocked examples with ogee-bracket ("swelled") feet or carved claw supports are rare. A conservative round-blocked example supported on tall, narrow, straight brackets is made of walnut rather than mahogany and is said to be dated "1765" on the back of the bottom drawer. A rounded mahogany example with straight feet and a more complex base molding ascribed to the shop of Benjamin Frothingham of Charlestown descended in the Otis family of Boston and perhaps was not made until 1764, the marriage date of the original owner.[1]

Round-blocked chests with either ogee-bracket or claw feet are later in style than the straight-bracket examples. A few chests with ogee supports originated in eastern Connecticut and Rhode Island; the construction material is more commonly cherry. A striking Massachusetts example in mahogany is fully documented: it was made in 1770 by George Bright of Boston for Jonathan Bowman, a cousin of John Hancock, and is a rare example of a round-blocked chest of drawers ornamented with a fan-shape drop at the center front (although the carved feature is still only half the size of that in No. 177).[2]

This round-blocked chest, with its overhanging top and molded base conforming to the undulating rhythm of the facade and its robust support structure carved to form four substantial claws (fig. 1), is a powerful expression of the cabinetmaker's art. A group of this type represents slightly less than one-third of the ninety blockfront illustrations collected for this survey. A shaped drop centered below the base molding is a feature in about half of the claw-foot chests. Of these, the most common profile is an astragal. Many examples are plain, as illustrated.

Family histories are associated with about 14 percent of the rounded blockfront sample, a substantial figure after two hundred years, and, as expected, many are centered in Boston or other eastern Massachusetts communities, including Marblehead, Newburyport, and Plympton. In other instances, Massachusetts round-blocked chests are known to have been part of the household furnishings of individuals located at a substantial distance from Boston but who maintained close

commercial and cultural ties with the New England center. One owner, Benjamin Rolfe, son-in-law of the first minister to settle in Concord, New Hampshire, maintained ties with his native Newbury. Jonathan Bowman, a Bostonian who purchased his chest from George Bright, a Boston cabinetmaker, moved to Pownalborough, Maine, before the revolutionary war to act as business agent for his wealthy uncle Thomas Hancock. That other Boston round-blocked chests of drawers were exported as venture cargo to southern coastal and Caribbean destinations by entrepreneur/merchants is suggested by the Danish histories of two chests, possibly a pair. One is known to have been removed to Europe from the Danish Virgin Islands about 1860 by a legatee.[3]

The Bowman chest of drawers mentioned above, which is in the collection of the Society for the Preservation of New England Antiquities, is accompanied by a bill of sale from Bright. It is one of two "Mahogany Buroe Tables" purchased by Bowman in 1770 at a cost of £5.6.8 apiece. The term *bureau table* was also applied to the chest form with a deep center-front recess, demonstrating the flexibility of terminology in the period. Other use of the word *bureau* in contemporary records occurs in the papers of Boston merchant Caleb Davis. A mahogany case purchased locally in 1769 from cabinetmaker John Cogswell was priced the same as Bowman's chest. During the next fifteen years, Davis purchased other mahogany bureaus for area clients or for exportation—one was made by Boston cabinetmaker Alexander Edwards. Davis's shipping interests ranged from Baltimore to the Carolinas to the Caribbean, demonstrating further the distribution potential of Boston furniture.[4]

This chest is constructed of sabicu, a hard, durable tropical timber also known as "horse-flesh" in the eighteenth century, and is part of a growing body of New England furniture identified as employing this wood (see also Nos. 46, 162, 163, 206). Imported from Cuba and the Bahamas, sabicu served as a substitute for mahogany, although it usually passed as the better-known wood. The relevance of sabicu to furniture history is only just being explored and understood. Its importance to the furniture trade was likewise not fully comprehended in the eighteenth century, as noted by Johann David Schoepf, a German physician and scientist, when visiting the Bahama Islands in 1784:

> The mahogany wood which is sent to Europe [and America] from this and the other West India islands does by no means come from one and the same variety of tree. . . . Several kinds of . . . related trees are marketed under this name. . . . An uncommon sort is called here, from its color and coarse wood-fibre, the 'Horse-flesh Mahogany' . . . [It] passes in Europe [and America] for mahogany.[5]

*NGE*

**Inscriptions or marks:** *Scratched, on inside left side of case and at left top of each drawer blade, from top to bottom:* "III", "II", *and* "I".

**Construction:** The top and sides of the chest are joined in sliding half dovetails. The top, which is made of two boards butted near the back and is ogee molded on the front and side edges, overhangs the case and conforms to the case blocking at the front. The horizontal drawer blades, or dividers, which are

**Fig. 1.** Detail, right front foot.

backed with pine and beaded at the front edges, are attached to the case sides with exposed dovetails; there is no top rail. Vertical beads at the inside faces of the case sides form miters with those of the drawer blades. Runners nailed inside the case support the three upper drawers; the bottom drawer runs on the bottom board. The sides and bottom of the chest are joined with dovetails. The bottom is further supported by cleats extending from front to back at either end and by five butted pieces of wood across the front, all secured originally with small rosehead nails. A heavy cyma-reversa base molding is attached with a large dovetail to the front of the case; conforming moldings are nailed to the sides. The cabriole legs and flanking thick knee brackets are glued and nailed to the bottom board. The rear feet are identical, except they lack an inside talon and have a plain glueblock instead of a shaped bracket at the rear. The back of the case, consisting of two horizontal lap-jointed boards, is nailed into rabbets at the case sides and top and nailed flush at the bottom. The drawers are dovetailed at the corners and sawed at the inside front to conform to the exterior blocking. The sides of the drawers are double-beaded on the top edges; the upper edge of the back has a heavy chamfer. The drawer bottoms, which run from front to back, are nailed into rabbets at the front and sides and nailed flush at the back. Battens on the bottoms of the drawers are applied.

**Condition:** The top has multiple scratches, several circular burn marks, a small, deep gouge, and a repaired break at the back. The third drawer from the top has several deep scratches on the face. The boards are separating on both sides of the case. New full-length battens screwed to the backboard serve as drawer stops. The right rear knee bracket is replaced. The bottoms of the three lower drawers are split. All the drawers are fully lined with an old marbleized paper (not original) except the top drawer, which has paper only on the sides. The chest has a multilayer finish of some age; the feet have been refinished. The brasses and the locks are old but not original.

**Dimensions:**

| | | |
|---|---|---|
| H. | 32 1/2 in. | 82.6 cm |
| W. (top) | 36 in. | 91.5 cm |
| W. (case) | 33 3/8 in. | 84.7 cm |
| W. (feet) | 36 1/8 in. | 91.8 cm |
| D. (top) | 21 1/8 in. | 53.6 cm |
| D. (feet) | 20 7/8 in. | 53.0 cm |

**Materials:** *Microanalysis:* Primary: sabicu. Secondary: white pine group (backboard, bottom board, blade backings, drawer linings). *Finish:* remnants of reddish brown color in resin. The top is cleaned off, the case front and sides are mottled, and the feet and brackets are a dark color.

**Publications:** American Art Association Anderson Galleries, "Colonial Furniture, Silver, and Decorations: The Collection of the Late Philip Flayderman" (January 2–4, 1930), lot 429. Downs, *American Furniture*, fig. 169.

**Provenance:** Ex coll.: Philip Flayderman, Boston. The American Art Association sale of the collection of Philip Flayderman, January 2–4, 1930, lot 429.

**Accession history:** Purchased by H. F. du Pont from Israel Sack, Boston, 1930. Bequest of H. F. du Pont, 1969.
65.1623

1. Nutting, *Furniture Treasury*, no. 274; Jobe and Kaye, *New England Furniture*, no. 14.

2. On Bright round-blocked chest, see Jobe and Kaye, *New England Furniture*, no. 15. For a claw-foot round-blocked chest with a differently shaped drop, see Albert Sack, *The New Fine Points of Furniture: Early American* (New York: Crown Publishers, 1993), p. 110.

3. Jobe and Kaye, *New England Furniture*, nos. 14, 15; Walter Muir Whitehill, Brock Jobe, and Jonathan Fairbanks, "Foreword," in *Boston Furniture*, fig. 4; *American Antiques from Israel Sack Collection*, 10 vols. (Washington, D.C.: Highland House, 1969–), 2:513, 10:2676; Venable, *American Furniture*, cat. 27; David A. Schorsch advertisement, *Antiques* 136, no. 4 (October 1989): 702; Sotheby's, "Important American Furniture and Folk Art" (December 8, 1984), lot 265; Israel Sack advertisement, *Antiques* 105, no. 3 (March 1974): inside front cover; Leigh Keno advertisement, *Antiques* 143, no. 5 (May 1993): 648; Donna-Belle Garvin, "Concord, New Hampshire: A Furniture-Making Capital," *Historical New Hampshire* 45, no. 1 (Spring 1990): 12; Heckscher, *American Furniture*; Rollins, *Treasures of State*, cat. no. 74.

4. Jobe and Kaye, *New England Furniture*, no. 15; Caleb Davis, bills from John Cogswell, 1769, and Alexander Edwards, 1773, invoice for cargo of brigantine *Juno*, 1784, Caleb Davis Papers, Massachusetts Historical Society, Boston.

5. Johann David Schoepf, *Travels in the Confederation, 1783–1784*, trans. and ed. Alfred J. Morrison, 2 vols. (Philadelphia: William J. Campbell, 1911), 2:273–74.

## 180 ♦ Chest of drawers
Newport, Rhode Island
1765–85

The European-inspired blockfront style in furniture first developed in America in Boston during the 1730s apparently found its way to Newport about two decades later. How the transfer occurred remains a mystery, although bonds of kinship, commerce, and religious persuasion and even interaction among craft communities all likely played a part. The earliest known blockfront furniture of Newport origin dates only to the start of the 1760s; however, John Goddard's oft-quoted letter of 1763 describing case furniture of a "Costly" pattern with a "Sweld front" suggests that the style, though uncommon, was not new. By that date, the integrated facade that elevates the Newport blockfront pattern to an art form had been perfected. Among low case forms in the market, the three-drawer chest was more common than the chest of four drawers, but neither appears to have been as popular with consumers as the bureau table, based on the numbers of surviving examples.[1]

In the Newport blockfront style, the rhythmic play of projecting and receding panels on the front of the case is punctuated by bold arched shells at the top and a heavy conforming molding at the bottom that integrates the blocked ogee feet. The close-fitting case top with a deep cavetto molding visually balances the base. Newport's unique contribution to the blockfront style is the addition of baroque-type convex and concave carved shells to the panel tops. Well before its integration into the blockfront facade, however, the Newport shell was a feature of the plain furniture case. A dressing table with this lobed shell centered in the skirt front descended in the family of Samuel Ward, a governor of Rhode Island, and is thought to be the "Mahogany Dressing Table" itemized in a 1746 bill from John Townsend to Ward.[2]

Development of the Newport shell is still a mystery. Some Boston case furniture of contemporary or earlier date decorated with fanlike shells of inlaid, trompe l'oeil, or carved form may have been a source of inspiration. Closer at hand, however, were locally made built-in cupboards, or buffets, with ribbed-shell ceilings, one of which still stands in an upper room of the Nichols-Wanton-Hunter House built in Newport in the second quarter of the eighteenth century. Contemporary with the earliest Newport case shells are the distinctive, small, bulging convex shells that ornament the crests of some round-shouldered Queen Anne–type joined chairs made in Boston from the 1730s and exported in quantity along the northern American coast to destinations ranging from New York to Canada (see No. 24). A prominent bead, not unlike that forming the central C scroll in the Newport case shells, finishes the bottom edge of the chair shells. European design books may have also contributed to the distinctive character of the Newport shell.[3]

In comparing this chest with documented and related blockfront low-case examples executed by members of the Townsend and Goddard families of Newport, it seems closest in component design to furniture ascribed to Edmund Townsend (b. 1736). The small, carved C scroll at the center of the shell on Winterthur's chest relates closely to the same feature on four bureau tables (one signed by Edmund Townsend) and a three-drawer chest. The carved figure, although subtly varied in each example, is a fanned cluster of seven slender petals, or narrow leaves, each hollowed to its short stem with the gouging tool (fig. 1). In two of the bureau tables, a heavy horizontal bar, or bead, extends across the base of the petals. Of the primary shells in the two bureau tables, one has more lobes and the other fewer than the shell in Winterthur's chest, which has eleven convex lobes in the end shells and ten hollow lobes in the center one. In three examples, the molding beneath the case top has an additional short fillet below the bottom bead. The closest mate to Winterthur's chest is a three-drawer example in the Kaufman collection, which is comparable in the profile and scroll of the swelled foot brackets, the flush construction of the drawers in the case (as opposed to lipped construction), the carved shell lobes, and the profile of the top molding.

**Fig. 1.** Detail, top drawer.

The C-scroll arch of the center shell is slightly higher in the Kaufman chest, however, resulting in longer stems on the fanned petals. Obviously, exact duplication of elements from chest to chest, even among close mates, is not characteristic of Newport blockfront case furniture.[4]

The shell centers in other low cases of Newport origin are of several types. Perhaps the earliest are those that are plain or carved with a stylized fleur-de-lis. The petal-carved examples vary greatly in form as well as petal count. A sizable number have petal clusters with stop-fluted stems; some of the documented John Townsend cases fall into this category. A later design found on several cases labeled by Townsend introduces crosshatching below a wide spray of short petals, and a few examples substitute a diaper pattern for the crosshatching.[5]

The delicate petal ornament of the Newport blockfront shell is also found on other carved work of Newport origin. Slender, hollow loops are a component of the leafy decoration found on a group of local chairs, tables, and high chests. Although the hollow figure is common in carved work, its interpretation in particular motifs, such as the shell centers, is more personalized. Inspiration may have come from imported furniture or a printed design source—a related figure of clustered loops termed *Godrons* was published in Jean Lepautre's 1751 *Deisseins de Divers Ornemens et Moulures*.[6]

NGE

---

**Inscriptions or marks:** *On underside of top:* "Frunt Top" *in pencil. On each drawer blade:* "1", "2", *and* "3". *Inside the case sides at the upper front:* "Top".

**Construction:** The solid board top, which has ogee-molded edges and overhangs the front and sides of the case, with a short overhang at the back, is attached with rosehead nails to a full subtop. The subtop is nailed at the ends to horizontal cleats nailed to the case sides. Below the top a cavetto molding is nailed to the front and sides of the case. The horizontal drawer blades, or dividers, which are backed with pine and beaded at the front edge, are attached to the case sides with exposed dovetails. The top and bottom rails of the case front are also dovetailed, the top joints concealed. Vertical beads

at the inside faces of the case sides are applied. Runners nailed or glued inside the case sides support three drawers. The sides and bottom of the case are joined with dovetails. A mitered ogee molding is attached with nails to the base of the case at the front and sides, and a quarter-round molding is nailed between the legs at the front and sides. The ogee-bracket feet are formed of two mitered facing pieces reinforced on the inside surface with vertical and horizontal glueblocks. The rear foot facings are attached with sliding dados to the chest base and are further reinforced with vertical interior glueblocks and shaped boards at the back. The case back, consisting of two horizontal lap-jointed boards, is set into rabbets and secured with rosehead nails on all edges. The drawers are dovetailed at the corners. The thin sides are roughly rounded at the top; the backs are chamfered at the forward and rear edges. The drawer bottoms, which run from front to back and are chamfered on three sides, are set into sliding dados on the front and sides and nailed flush at the back. The projecting shells of the top drawer are applied; the inside surface is flat. The other drawer fronts are worked from solid wood and blocked inside and out.

**Condition:** The blade between the top and center drawers is patched where the lock was broken out. That blade and the lower one are also repaired at the dovetails on the left side. Cracks in the cornice molding are repaired in several places. All the drawer bottoms are split, and the bottom two drawers have 1"-wide patches. The larger backboard is cracked in several places. The drawer stops are modern additions. The exterior surface is refinished.

**Dimensions:**

| | | |
|---|---|---|
| H. | 32 in. | 81.3 cm |
| W. (top) | 35 3/4 in. | 91.0 cm |
| W. (case) | 34 in. | 86.9 cm |
| W. (feet) | 37 in. | 94.0 cm |
| D. (top) | 20 5/16 in. | 51.6 cm |
| D. (case) | 18 7/8 in. | 48.0 cm |
| D. (feet) | 21 in. | 53.0 cm |

**Materials:** *Microanalysis:* Primary: mahogany. Secondary: white pine group (subtop, backboard, blade extensions, drawer linings). *Finish:* medium reddish brown color in clear resin that emphasizes the variegated wood grain.

**Publications:** Charles F. Hummel, "Queen Anne and Chippendale Furniture in the Henry Francis du Pont Winterthur Museum, Part 3," *Antiques* 99, no. 1 (January 1971): 101–3, fig. 8. David Stockwell, "American Blockfront Furniture," *America in Britain* 9, no. 2 (May 1971): 12–15.

**Provenance:** The chest of drawers descended in the West-Minturn families of Bristol, R.I., as related by the last private owners, who were descendants. Its history can be traced back to Jonas and Abigail West Minturn (ca. 1825). The chest passed to their daughter, Gertrude Minturn Sanford (b. 1850), and to her daughter, Mrs. William Wallbridge, the last private owner. (See also **Provenance** of No. 47.)

**Accession history:** Gift of Mr. and Mrs. William K. Wallbridge, Short Hills, N.J., 1958. 58.18.1

---

1. Moses, *Master Craftsmen*, pp. 4–9; R. Peter Mooz, "The Origins of Newport Block-front Furniture Design," *Antiques* 99, no. 6 (June 1971): 882–86; Margaretta M. Lovell, "'Such Furniture as Will Be Most Profitable': The Business of Cabinetmaking in Eighteenth-Century Newport," *Winterthur Portfolio* 26, no. 1 (Spring 1991): 27–62; Philip Zea, "Rural Craftsmen and Design," in Jobe and Kaye, *New England Furniture*, p. 53.

2. Rodriguez Roque, *American Furniture*, no. 17.

3. Miller, "Roman Gusto," pp. 165, 169, fig. 10; 170, fig. 11; 173, fig. 16; 177, 178, fig. 23; 179, fig. 26; 191, fig. 47; 196, fig. 54; 197, fig. 55; Margaretta Markle Lovell, "Boston Blockfront Furniture," in *Boston Furniture*, pp. 92, 103; for Nichols-Wanton-Hunter House cupboard, see Dorothy Pratt and Richard Pratt, *The Treasury of Early American Homes* (New York: Hawthorne Books, 1959), p. 79; and Moses, *Master Craftsmen*, p. 24; Mooz, "Origins of Newport Block-front Furniture Design."

4. For the 4 bureau tables and the chest of drawers, see Moses, *Master Craftsmen*, pp. 34, 285, 287, figs. 15, 19. See also Flanigan, *American Furniture*, cat. no. 24.

5. For a survey of shell-center types, see Moses, *Master Craftsmen*, pp. 27, 32, 64, 130, 164, 259, 286, fig. 3; Rodriguez Roque, *American Furniture*, nos. 4, 34; "Living with Antiques: The Cape Cod Home of Mrs. Charles D. Cook," *Antiques* 52, no. 2 (August 1947): 104; Herbert Cescinsky and George Leland Hunter, *English and American Furniture* (Garden City, N.Y.: Garden City Publishing Co., 1929), p. 156 bottom; Albert Sack, *Fine Points of Furniture: Early American* (New York: Crown Publishers, 1950), p. 103 bottom; G. K. S. Bush advertisement, *Antiques* 127, no. 1 (January 1985): 35; Lockwood, *Colonial Furniture*, p. 134 top; Nutting, *Furniture Treasury*, no. 269; Sotheby's, "Fine American Furniture, Silver, Porcelain, and Related Decorative Arts" (June 28, 30, 1985), lot 691; National Council of Girl Scouts, *Loan Exhibition of Eighteenth- and Early Nineteenth-Century Furniture and Glass* (New York: By the council, 1929), fig. 602; *John Brown House Loan Exhibition*, cat. 51; Morrison H. Heckscher, "John Townsend's Block-and-Shell Furniture," *Antiques* 121, no. 5 (May 1982): 1144–52.

6. For related Newport carved work, see Moses, *Master Craftsmen*, pp. 223, 224, 231–32, 236, 241–42, fig. 21. For the Lepautre design, see Mooz, "Origins of Newport Block-front Furniture Design," p. 884, fig. 5.

## 181 ◆ Chest of drawers
Colchester–Norwich area, northern New London County, Connecticut
1770–90

After more than three-quarters of a century of discovery and investigation, knowledge of case furniture made in New London County, Connecticut, remains far from comprehensive. As early as the 1920s, furniture connoisseurs suggested that eastern Connecticut blockfront cases, which are divided between cherrywood and mahogany construction, were the prototypes for the even-then-celebrated Newport shell-carved chests. That theory was later refuted as it became better recognized that members of the eastern Connecticut school of blockfront cabinetmaking were followers rather than regional leaders. By the mid 1930s when the Connecticut tercentenary was celebrated with an exhibition of Connecticut furniture and a catalogue was prepared by Luke Vincent Lockwood (then the leading authority on colonial furniture), there was demonstrated interest in associating known regional cabinetmakers with some of the exhibited furniture. Significant contributions to the core of basic information on Connecticut cabinetmaking were still two decades away, however. From the mid 1950s to the mid 1960s, Houghton Bulkeley singlehandedly laid the groundwork for the several studies of eastern Connecticut cabinetwork that followed, among them a major exhibition in 1974 focusing attention on the furniture of New London County. More recently, the Colchester school of cabinetmaking and its principal exponents identified to date, Benjamin Burnham and Samuel Loomis, have been the subject of an interpretive reappraisal. Still, in-depth knowledge of New London County cabinetwork is limited.[1]

To place this blockfront chest of drawers in a local New London County context, a review of pertinent features is necessary.

Associated with the Colchester school is the highly stylized, bold interpretation of the regional ogee-bracket foot, characterized in Winterthur's chest by its large size, prominent bead forming a volute at the base, and inward-projecting knee scroll. Three chests of drawers (including this one), a chest-on-chest, and a fall-front desk exhibit this support. Two other cases—a chest-on-chest and a fall-front desk—associated with Norwich have related, bead-enhanced ogee feet supplemented by a double-cusp bracket common to casework from that community.[2]

Fluted pilasters appear on the facades of cases associated with both Colchester and Norwich. All five of the cabinets with beaded ogee feet like those of Winterthur's chest have pilasters; three examples are stop fluted. The stop-fluted variation is sometimes featured in other forms made in Colchester. Without a capital or base, however, the ornament has been used in a nonarchitectural way, a criticism that, in this case, extends to the presence of a double dentil course in the

"cornice" (fig. 1) and a single dentil above the base molding.[3]

The inclusion of shell-crowned blockfront panels in the facade of this chest and in other cases of eastern Connecticut origin demonstrates the overwhelming influence of Rhode Island cabinetmaking on the region (see No. 180). A characteristic (and a shortcoming) of the three chests of drawers in this group is the abrupt termination of the blocking on the case proper above the base molding. This feature also occurs on a scroll-top chest-on-chest with fluted pilasters in the upper case that has several features associated with Norwich cabinetmaking (including a shallow, wavelike scrolled skirt below the base molding and deeply webbed claw feet elongated in the horizontal plane) and a history in the Trumbull family of that community.[4]

Two three-drawer chests relate closely to the Winterthur example—one is owned by the Antiquarian and Landmarks Society of Connecticut and the other by the Connecticut Historical Society. In ornament, assembly

**Fig. 1.** Detail, top drawer.

method, and construction materials (cherry with chestnut and maple), the Winterthur and antiquarian society chests are virtually identical, and their hardware is similar as well. The historical society chest, although a reasonably close visual mate, differs slightly in several aspects. The profiles of the top edge and molding vary, the case lacks applied dentil moldings and a bead outlining the case front, and the flute count of each shell is one less than that of the other two chests. The primary wood is mahogany, with secondary materials of pine and yellow poplar. The case top is attached to its interior subtop with a dovetail-key technique (a constructional feature found in Rhode Island cabinetmaking) instead of with nails, as in the Winterthur chest. The historical society chest also has stop fluting in the pilasters, a decorative element also found on a desk and a chest-on-chest with similar feet. Like the stop fluting on the double chest, that of the historical society low chest is unusual in forming a panel elevated above the pilaster base with plain fluting both above and below the panel. The breadth and depth measurements of the low chest are also slightly less than those of Winterthur's example.[5]

Of the three low chests, only the one owned by the antiquarian society has a known history. It is believed to have been part of the furnishings brought to the Amasa Day House by Day (b. 1808) and his first wife, Ursula Maria Gates, both of the Westchester section of Colchester, or possibly by Day's second wife, Sarah Spencer, who came from nearby Hadlyme. Justin Day of Colchester, father of Amasa, is presumed to have been the first owner of the chest. These three related shell-carved beaded-foot chests of drawers, which are supported only by a single circumstantial background history, display a sufficient number of features identified with two localized centers

of cabinetmaking in New London County to negate a precise determination of their origin at this time.[6]

*NGE with NER*

---

**Inscriptions or marks:** *Inside front of top drawer:* "CONNECTICUT TERCENTENARY" [printed] and "C. T. 212/ Wᵐ B. Goodwin" inscribed in black ink, all on blue-bordered paper label.

**Construction:** The two-board top, which has rounded edges and overhangs the front and sides of the case, is attached by rosehead nails to a full subtop. Below the top an ogee molding with fillets is nailed to the front and sides of the case. On the front only, two rows of dentil molding are glued across the top rail and upper stiles, and a single dentil molding is attached above the base. The horizontal drawer blades, or dividers, which are backed with yellow poplar and have applied beaded facings at the front edges attached with small wooden pegs, join the case sides with sliding dovetails. Vertical beaded facings are attached to the stiles flanking the drawer openings. The blades are cut out at the sides to receive the fluted stiles, which are secured by the top and base moldings. The wide drawer runners nailed to the interior case have glued strips inset from the sides behind the stiles, which serve as drawer guides. The two-piece case sides are dovetailed to the bottom board. A mitered, ogee base molding is nailed to the front and sides of the case. The ogee-bracket front feet are formed of two mitered facings glued and nailed to thick supporting foot posts that consist of two rectangular, half-lapped vertical blocks further reinforced with large horizontal, triangular glueblocks. The rear feet are supported by thick single foot posts and triangular horizontal glueblocks between the exposed facing and the rear footboard, which is a single board arched at the center and nailed in place. An applied bead molding is nailed between the feet on the front and sides of the case. The case back, consisting of three horizontal lap-jointed boards (one narrow board between two wide boards), is set into rabbets

and secured at the sides with large-headed nails. The drawers are joined at the corners with large dovetails and chamfered in two directions on the upper edges of the sides and back. The drawer bottoms, which run from side to side and are chamfered on three sides, join the sides and front with sliding dados and are nailed flush at the back. The drawer fronts, which are flat on the inner surface, are built up of two thicknesses of cherry on a maple board. The applied carved shells are screwed to the front of the top drawer; the applied blocking on the other two drawers is nailed in place. The posts for the hardware are imbedded in the drawer fronts instead of piercing the entire thickness to the inside surface. Most of the cast hardware, which is patterned with an intaglio leaf design, is original.

**Condition:** The case top is sun bleached and marked by several dark circular stains; a series of concentric compass circles appears on the left front corner. Old splits in the sides have been repaired on the interior with cloth tape. The front stiles are slightly warped because the drawer runners have pushed out the blades. The facings at the back of the drawer blades are broken and pieces are missing. The front right foot facing is cracked horizontally and repaired; the right rear foot is pieced out on the bottom third. The right rear glueblock is missing. An 8" strip of beading between the front feet is replaced. The lower edges of several drawer sides have been pieced out. The bottom dentil molding and each outside third of the double top dentil molding are replaced. The left bail handle on the bottom drawer is replaced.

**Dimensions:**

| | | |
|---|---|---|
| H. | 35⅛ in. | 89.2 cm |
| W. (top) | 40⅛ in. | 101.9 cm |
| W. (case) | 36⅞ in. | 93.6 cm |
| W. (knees) | 40 in. | 100.9 cm |
| D. (top) | 20 in. | 50.8 cm |
| D. (case) | 18¾ in. | 47.6 cm |
| D. (knees) | 20¼ in. | 51.5 cm |

**Materials:** *Microanalysis:* Primary: cherry. Secondary: chestnut (subtop, backboard, drawer bottoms, foot posts); yellow poplar (drawer sides and backs, blade extensions). *Finish:* muddied medium reddish brown color in resin.

**Exhibitions:** Connecticut Tercentenary, Wadsworth Atheneum, Hartford, 1935. Norwalk Historical Society, Norwalk, Conn., July 1979.

**Publications:** Malcolm A. Norton, "More Light on the Block-Front," *Antiques* 3, no. 2 (February 1923): 63, fig. 3. Nutting, *Furniture Treasury*, no. 276. *Three Centuries of Connecticut Furniture, 1635–1935* (Hartford: Tercentenary Commission of the State of Connecticut, 1935), no. 212. Charles F. Hummel, "Queen Anne and Chippendale Furniture in the Henry Francis du Pont Winterthur Museum, Part 3," *Antiques* 99, no. 1 (January 1971): 102–3, fig. 9. *Connecticut Furniture, 1700–1800* (Norwalk, Conn.: Norwalk Historical Society, 1979), [p. 23]. Margaretta Markle Lovell, "The Blockfront: Its Development in Boston, Newport, and Connecticut," *Fine Woodworking*, no. 23 (July/August 1980): 45, fig. 3.

**Provenance:** Ex coll.: William B. Goodwin, Hartford, Conn.; Arthur G. Camp, Farmington, Conn.; Harry Arons, Ansonia, Conn.; L. E. Brooks, Marshall, Mich.

**Accession history:** Purchased by H. F. du Pont from John S. Walton, Inc., New York, 1960. Gift of H. F. du Pont, 1960. 58.2426

1. Malcolm A. Norton, "More Light on the Block-Front," *Antiques* 3, no. 2 (February 1923): 63–66; *Three Centuries of Connecticut Furniture, 1635–1935* (Hartford: Tercentenary Commission of the State of Connecticut, 1935), no. 212; Houghton Bulkeley, *Contributions to Connecticut Cabinetmaking* (Hartford: Connecticut Historical Society, 1967), esp. pp. 7–27; Robert F. Trent, "The Colchester School of Cabinetmaking, 1750–1800," in Francis J. Puig and Michael Conforti, eds., *The American Craftsman and the European Tradition, 1620–1820* (Minneapolis: Minneapolis Institute of Arts, 1989), pp. 112–23, 128–29.

2. For the 4 examples with beaded ogee feet, see *New London County Furniture*, nos. 90–92; Arthur Liverant, "New London County Furniture," *The Forum* 5, no. 4 (December 1991): 3, as published in *Antiques and the Arts Weekly* (Newtown, Conn.), December 1991. For the 2 cases with related feet, see *New London County Furniture*, nos. 56, 58.

3. For representative furniture with fluted pilasters, see *New London County Furniture*, nos. 31–33, 39, 48, 55, 90–92; *Frederick K. and Margaret R. Barbour's Furniture Collection* (Hartford: Connecticut Historical Society, 1963), pp. 48–51.

4. *New London County Furniture*, nos. 48, 90–92.

5. *New London County Furniture*, nos. 90–92; Liverant, "New London County Furniture," p. 3.

6. Frederic Palmer, "The Amasa Day Chest of Drawers," *The Antiquarian* 20, no. 2 (December 1968): 20–24; *New London County Furniture*, no. 90; Ronna L. Reynolds, *Images of Connecticut Life* (Hartford: Antiquarian and Landmarks Society of Connecticut, 1978), pp. 136–39, 144.

## 182 • Chest of drawers
Chatham Township, Middlesex County, Connecticut, or vicinity
1789
James Higgins (1766–1827)

A question about the originality of the top of this chest led to the discovery of the maker and date of construction. A narrow strip of wood at the back bearing hinge marks on the bottom surface indicated that repairs had been made. Because a full subtop lies beneath the finished top, it was impossible to inspect the bottom surface of the finished top by removing the drawers and examining the case interior. The basic two-board construction of the top (without the added piece) is correct and the profile of the edge compares with that in similar chests. Some doubts remained, however, and a decision was made to remove the finished top, which was nailed in place. The two wide boards proved to be original, and the strip at the back appears to have been added to compensate for shrinkage and the correction of warp in the boards. Upon

removal of the top, it was discovered that the signature of the maker (twice) and the date were written in white chalk on the upper surface of the subtop (fig. 1).[1]

James Higgins was about twenty-three years of age when he constructed this chest in 1789. Whether he worked independently or as a journeyman is unknown, but the concealed location of the inscription implies that he may not have been his own master at that date. The style of the chest and the competency of the work suggest that he served his apprenticeship with a master in the vicinity of Chatham Township, Middlesex County, where he was raised, or in the neighboring community of Colchester, a regional center of the furnituremaking trade. Nine children were born to Higgins (married 1780 or 1790) and his wife Lydia (Smith) before they left Chatham in 1809–10 for Hamilton in eastern central New York. An early settler of Hamilton, Higgins built a brick house and a cabinet shop on Madison Street. He later kept a hotel in East Hamilton, and at

**Fig. 1.** Detail, cabinetmaker's signature and date on top of subtop.

his death in 1827 he was the proprietor of a tannery in neighboring Earlville. The interior parts of New York State, which were just being developed in the early nineteenth century, attracted many New Englanders. Higgins's first cousin Sylvester (1776–1860), son of Heman and Eunice Higgins, who also grew up in Chatham and became a cabinetmaker, worked briefly in Duanesburg near Schenectady, but he did not enjoy the same success as James. He and his Connecticut partner, Samuel Silliman, erected a shop in 1804 where they produced tables, "buroes," desks, clock cases, and other furniture before trade stagnated and they returned to Connecticut.[2]

Ten or more chests, including this one, are known in this distinctive blockfront style with tall cabriole legs at the case front and high ogee-bracket feet at the back. With one exception in this group, the scrolled knee returns at the front have the same profile from chest to chest, although the through-pierced scrolls of Winterthur's chest were less common than the blind scrolls of other chests. The front feet are precise in execution, with two-knuckle toes, squared ankle bases, and deep hollows emphasizing the sinews of the lower part of the legs (fig. 2). Drawer openings are beaded, a deep cove molding forms a cornice, and the edges of the top consist of a deep fillet, a flat projecting ogee, and a thumb-molded return.[3]

The greatest individuality in chest design occurs in the shells (fig. 3). Twenty-one lobes and flutes are common in the side shells, but as few as nineteen and as many as twenty-five are also found. The central vertical lobe sometimes has an hourglass shape (see No. 183, fig. 2). Ten lobes are usual in the center shell, although one example has eleven slim lobes with tips that project farther than normal. The central carved figure of the shells is a cluster of gouge-formed petals on raised stems. Five is the common number of petals, but as many as

**Fig. 2.** Detail, right front leg and bracket.

seven occur. Occasionally, the center shell has more petals than the side ones. The center shell is further detailed by an inset border around the tips of the lobes. In several chests a second, outer, arclike border is laid out in punchwork on the flat surface of the drawer beyond the lobes, as seen in this chest.

No other chest in the survey group of ten is identified by maker or date. Several have Connecticut family histories, however. One was purchased from the Post family of Haddam; another has a history in the Carew family of Norwich. A former owner of a third chest acquired the casepiece from a descendant of the presumed original owner, Thomas Harland, a silversmith and clockmaker who settled in Norwich in 1773 and died in 1807. Antiquarian Frances Clary Morse owned Winterthur's chest of drawers at the beginning of the twentieth century. She published an illustration of it in *Furniture of the Olden Time* and indicated that it had come from Colchester. In the mid twentieth century, however, Israel Sack claimed that the chest actually was found in Wethersfield, presumably by a Mr. Maggott (probably Meggat), an

undertaker, collector, and antiques dealer, who sold it to Morse for $85.[4]

The evidence presented to date suggests that the geographic boundaries of this type of chest are defined by the Connecticut River valley south of Hartford and the region eastward to Norwich. Stylistic evidence present in the Carew family chest reinforces this hypothesis. That case has the extra lobe in the center shell and the variant knee brackets, but the particularly unusual feature is the carved work of the front knees, which forms a grooved surface accented by a large volute. The decoration relates closely to carved work on a desk dated 1769 and documented to the Colchester cabinet shop of Benjamin Burnham (ca. 1737–73 or later). The two pieces of furniture share a general relationship in the design of the front brackets and claw feet, and the desk is also supported on large ogee-bracket feet at the back, although they are not as high as those in the chest of drawers. Still other furniture relates to the group of ten chests, including two chests-on-chests, one with tall cabriole feet at the front and ogee-bracket feet at the back and another with four cabriole supports and a background history in Colchester. The bottle chest of No. 183 has front and rear feet that are similar to those in this chest, and the brackets and shells are closely related. There is also evidence in the shell-carved, blocked facade of the low chests of the unmistakable influence of Newport cabinetmaking associated with the Townsend-Goddard school.[5]

James Higgins's shop location near the Connecticut River may have afforded him the opportunity to vend some of his furniture in the export trade to supplement local sales. Middletown, a few miles upriver, was a port of entry engaged in the coastal and Caribbean trades. By the late eighteenth century, Middle Haddam had a developed landing, and shipbuilding and navigation were flourishing businesses for several decades.[6]

**Fig. 3.** Detail, top drawer.

Higgins's removal to the interior of New York in 1810 may have been prompted by the availability of cheap land in that developing region. Almost certainly, economic conditions in Connecticut loomed large in the decision. National relations with Great Britain were deteriorating, and French spoliation played havoc with American shipping. The local economy, which relied heavily on the coastal and Caribbean trades, was already suffering when Higgins left. How long the cabinetmaker followed his trade in Madison County, New York, is unclear. At his death in 1827, the furniture and tools of the Hamilton shop remained: "1 Turning Lathe & Tools belonging to it"; "Cabinet Tools & 2 Table Benches"; "1 Box Stove & Pipe." The presence of "2 Table Frames" in the facility suggests that Higgins continued to make furniture on a part-time basis after he established other businesses. An intriguing entry among the household goods in his inventory is that for "2 old Bureaus." With nine children in tow, the family certainly carried some household furniture from Connecticut to New York State in 1809–10.[7]

NGE

**Inscriptions or marks:** *On top surface of subtop:* (left rear corner) "1789"; (across right end) "James __iggins"; (right front corner) "James Higg__" (cut off by edge of board); (center) partial date "17__" and "25380" all in white chalk. *Inside backboard:* "v" (twice) in white chalk. *Underside of subtop:* "x" (once and a diagonal stroke) in white chalk. *Inside all drawer backs:* "x" in white chalk. *On backboard:* (upper left outside corner) "111.112.1" in red crayon.

**Construction:** The two-piece top (with a third narrow piece added later at the back) is nearly flush at the back. The distinctive molded front and side edges of the top form, in profile, a fillet and an ogee with a thumb-molded base. The top is nailed to a full subtop that is dovetailed to the two-board side panels of the case and planed on the top and bottom surfaces. A cleat butted to the front edge of the subtop and extending below it supports the nailed front cornice molding; the side moldings are nailed to the side panels. The drawer blades, beaded on both edges, are joined to the front edge of the case sides with dovetails concealed by applied facing strips. The top and bottom rails are single-beaded adjacent to the drawer openings. Single beads adjacent to the drawer sides are inset into the case sides. The bottom board, which is planed on the top and bottom surfaces, is dovetailed to the case sides. Like the subtop, it has a butted cleat at the front extending above the surface to provide a nailing surface for the front base molding; the side moldings are nailed to the side panels. An additional thin, deep molding (quarter-round on the front edge) is nailed between the front legs to the case bottom with roseheads. The top extensions of the front legs are reinforced by small vertical glueblocks. Horizontal blocks nailed to the bottom of the case provide a support to which the knee brackets are glued (with some later nailings). The side rear foot facings and returns, which are one piece, are dovetailed to the rear foot boards. The rear foot boards are planed on the front and back surfaces and reinforced by a vertical interior glueblock; they have a diagonal inside return ending in a projecting finger adjacent to the case. The two 1"-inch thick backboards, which are lapped horizontally and planed on the front and back surfaces, are slotted into grooves at the back of the side panels and nailed across the top and bottom with roseheads. Drawer runners (replaced) are nailed to the inside surfaces of the side panels; originally they were joined to the case sides from the back on sliding dovetails. The drawers are dovetailed front and back. The thick drawer sides are slightly rounded at the top; the tops of the drawer backs are flat. The drawer bottoms are single, lengthwise boards set into grooves at the front and sides and nailed with roseheads across the back; reinforcing battens are applied. The projecting shells of the top drawer are nailed to the drawer front; the recessed center shell has a narrow 3/16" inset border around the scalloped edge accompanied by an arc on the flat surface of the drawer formed of small continuous punchwork triangles. The inside front surface of the top drawer is flat. The other drawer fronts are blocked inside and out, the inside surfaces sawed at canted angles that do not correspond to the rounded exterior surfaces.

**Condition:** A 1" piece of wood has been added at the back of the two-board finished top; the undersurface of this strip bears the marks of two old hinge mountings. The finished top is water damaged and has two small central nail holes into the subtop, now filled with a composition material, which probably represent a former repair to the finished top. The cornice molding has been off and reattached. The raised shells of the top drawer are secured with countersunk nails, the holes filled with composition material; the original attachment method may have been glue. The side panels are damaged: (right) hairline cracks along the front edge and a short vertical crack at the upper back corner; (left) a short crack near the upper front corner and a long vertical crack near the center bottom. The bottom case molding, which is cracked at the left forward side, has been renailed. Both front legs are cracked and repaired behind the knees. The front leg brackets have been restored in part: (right) the scroll adjacent to the leg, which is secured with glue and several small glueblocks at the back; (left) the scroll adjacent to the leg and the central scroll. Of the three glueblocks on the rear legs, two at the left and one at the right are replaced; the vertical block on the left leg is also missing. All the drawer runners are replaced. All drawer interiors are coated with a resin finish. All hardware is replaced except perhaps for the round knobs on the top drawer. Three of the bail handles appear to be later castings of the fourth one (lower left). The posts of the bails and the escutcheons do not match in pattern.

**Dimensions:**

| | | |
|---|---|---|
| H. | 36³⁄₄ in. | 93.3 cm |
| W. (top) | 38¹⁄₂ in. | 97.8 cm |
| W. (case) | 35⁵⁄₈ in. | 90.5 cm |
| D. (top) | 20¹⁄₂ in. | 52.1 cm |
| D. (case) | 18⁵⁄₈ in. | 47.3 cm |
| D. (feet) | 20¹⁄₄ in. | 51.4 cm |

**Materials:** *Microanalysis:* Primary: cherry. Secondary: white pine group (throughout). *Finish:* medium reddish brown to medium reddish orange (2 lower drawer faces) color in resin.

**Publications:** Morse, *Furniture of the Olden Time,* pp. 44–46, ill. 30. Downs, *American Furniture,* fig. 172.

**Provenance:** Ex coll.: Mrs. Frances Clary Morse. By tradition, the chest was found in Wethersfield, Conn., by a Mr. Maggott (probably Meggat) and was acquired by Mrs. Morse in the early 1900s.

**Accession history:** Purchased by H. F. du Pont from Collings and Collings, New York, 1928. Bequest of H. F. du Pont, 1969.
59.775

1. The chest top was removed by furniture conservator Michael S. Podmaniczky, Winterthur.

2. Mrs. Katharine Chapin Higgins, *Richard Higgins . . . and His Descendants* (Worcester, Mass.: By the author, 1918), pp. 179–81, 280; Samuel Silliman account book, 1804–7, New York State Historical Association, Cooperstown, N.Y. (microfilm, Downs collection).

3. For 7 chests in the survey group, see Sotheby Parke Bernet, "The American Heritage Auction of Americana," vol. 2 (November 27–December 1, 1979), lot 1701; Warren, *Bayou Bend*, no. 128; Sotheby's, "Important Americana from the Collection of Mr. and Mrs. Adolph Henry Meyer" (January 20, 1996), lot 215; Comstock, *American Furniture*, no. 300; David Stockwell advertisement, *Antiques* 127, no. 1 (January 1985): 1; Houghton Bulkeley, *Contributions to Connecticut Cabinetmaking* (Hartford: Connecticut Historical Society, 1967), p. 44; Israel Sack advertisement, *Antiques* 88, no. 2 (August 1965): inside front cover. Two other chests are in private/corporate collections.

4. For Post family chest, see Warren, *Bayou Bend*, no. 128; for Carew family chest, see Sotheby's, "Important Americana . . . Meyer," lot 215; for Harland chest, see Bulkeley, *Contributions*, p. 44; Morse, *Furniture of the Olden Time*, pp. 44–46, ill. 30. Alice Kugelman suggested the correct spelling for the Meggat name.

5. For Carew family chest, see Sotheby's, "Important Americana . . . Meyer," lot 215; for Burnham desk, see Heckscher, *American Furniture*, cat. no. 178; for bracket-foot chest-on-chest, see *Connecticut Furniture*, no. 100; for Colchester background chest, see Fales, *Furniture of Historic Deerfield*, fig. 439.

6. *History of Middlesex County, Connecticut* (New York: J. B. Beers, 1884), p. 181.

7. James Higgins inventory and estate papers, 1827–28, Surrogate's Court, Madison County, N.Y.

## 183 ◆ Bottle box on case of drawers
Colchester, New London County, Connecticut, area
1775–95

This unusual form was once thought to be a blanket chest over drawers despite the small size of the upper box section. The discovery of vertical channels on the interior walls that accommodated interlocking dividers to form fifteen compartments indicated its true function. "Cases of cabinet work" to store bottles of wine or spirits, originally called *cellars* but by the mid eighteenth century termed *cellarets*, came into use in Europe early in the century. The usual form was a box of variable shape with a hinged lid, sometimes elevated on legs or a low frame. The cellaret appears to have been uncommon in America before the mid eighteenth century and came into general use only after the Revolution, although rough utilitarian cases to protect glass bottles were common at an earlier date. That the original hardware on this chest was apparently of oval form substantiates the date attribution of this example.[1]

Like No. 181, this bottle box and drawers bears a strong stylistic relationship to New London County furniture associated with Colchester and Norwich, although the secondary woods of the two chests are different. The tall cabriole-style front supports of the chest relate it closely to a group of blockfront chests of drawers similarly elevated at the front and supported at the back on oversize ogee-bracket feet (see No. 182). These chests, too, are associated with eastern Connecticut. One is said to have descended from clockmaker Thomas Harland, who settled in Norwich in 1773, and another is associated with the Carew family of Norwich. Others have been linked in recent years with the Burnham-Loomis shop tradition of Colchester. No. 182 likely was made in Chatham Township, Middlesex County. The claw feet on many of the chests of drawers have the same squared ankle termination at the ball that is prominent in this example (fig. 1). Typically, the two-joint talons form sharp, precise angles (see No. 182).[2]

Bordering the knee brackets of the bottle box, the tight, volute-type scrolls are typical in general of those found on a range of case furniture now associated with northern New London County. In this example the cylindrical piercings do not penetrate the complete depth of the wood. A peculiarity of the bracket profile in this chest is the pairing of two opposing volutes. In general, the pierced volutes in a single bracket face are in the same direction. These paired volutes also appear on a mahogany fall-front desk (now identified as the bottom of a desk-and-bookcase) originally owned by Eliphalet Bulkeley of Colchester and inscribed in pencil "Lomis," suggesting a now generally accepted relationship with Colchester cabinetmaker Samuel Loomis. The Bulkeley desk is also related in its exterior design and unusual triple-tier desk interior to a desk signed and dated by Benjamin Burnham of Colchester in 1769. The Bulkeley desk has the same squared ankle and ball articulation as the bottle box, although the cabriole supports are shorter. One of the comparable chests of drawers has the same short legs, which are further carved on the knees in an unusual incised volute pattern similar to that found on the Burnham desk.[3]

The stacked cases and narrow dimensions of the bottle box and drawers determined the unusually long, slim proportions of the blocked panels on the facade. In turn, the panel width dictated the high, narrow proportions of the shells, which somewhat distort the carved features. The alternating convex and concave pattern of wavy flutes in the outer shells follows in general the classic design developed in Rhode Island, with the addition at the center top of a slim lily-shape flute of a type seen in New London County work (fig. 2). The center shell is marked by a scratch-groove

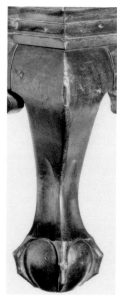

Fig. 1. Detail, right front foot.

border around the outside and single incised lines in alternating flutes, the latter technique another subtlety of regional carving. The shell centers are distinctive and uncommon: a flat, raised arc-shape border terminated by tiny volutes at a straight crossbar forms a lunette that encloses five rough-cut beads, from which rise a like number of squared, gouge-carved petals. No exact mate has been located. Closest in design are the beaded shell centers in a large chest-on-chest and a chest of drawers from the Norwich area that has a gadrooned skirt between ogee-bracket feet. The chest-on-chest has short cabriole front feet squared at the base of the ankle like those on the bottle box but with the added embellishment of carved work in the manner of Benjamin Burnham. Stop-fluted shell-ended pilasters in the lower case relate closely to those in a chest of drawers on cabriole feet that are also carved in the Burnham manner.[4]

A final notable decorative feature on this bottle box is the horizontal band of alternating flutes and fillets below each shell. The bands are a light-catching embellishment that lengthens the shells and better integrates them into the case facade. Banded decoration beneath carved shells is another occasional feature of New London County cabinetwork.[5]

Painted in black on the outside bottom surface of the bottle box and drawers is the name "E. Foote," which appears to be the name of an owner and contemporary with the case. Although Connecticut census records for 1790, 1800, and 1810 list individuals of this initial, none are located in New London County; Foote family records indicate, however, that many individuals of this surname resided in Colchester in the late eighteenth century. Ephraim Foote (1716–1800), son of Ephraim (d. 1765), probably died in Stockbridge, Massachusetts; all three of his wives were from

Lyme, Connecticut. Eli Foote (1747–92) married Roxanna Ward; they were the grandparents of Harriet Beecher Stowe and Henry Ward Beecher. Eli was educated for the bar, practiced for awhile in Guildford, and became a merchant trading to the South. Cabinetmaker Joseph Foote (1755–1834) also lived in the community, and his only known advertisement dates to 1800, when he indicated that he kept "All kinds of CABINET WORK, constantly for sale," at his shop. Joseph, Ephraim, and Eli were all descendants of Nathaniel Foote III (d. 1703), the first of the family to settle in Colchester. Other owner candidates include: Elisha (b. 1757) and Elias (b. 1766), sons of Charles Foote of Colchester; Ephraim (1765–1838) and Epaphroditus (1769–1845), sons of Adonijah Foote of Colchester; and Enoch Foote of Colchester, appointed guardian in 1766 to one Joseph Foote, a minor. Records

**Fig. 2.** Detail, right shell.

of the First Congregational Church of Colchester provide several other appropriate names. A Joseph Foote, Jr. (1777–1814), who appears to have been a nephew of Joseph Foote, the cabinetmaker, was also a woodworker. His probate inventory lists "part Sett Joiners Tools" and a small stock of pine and cherry boards.[6]

NGE

**Inscriptions or marks:** *On outside bottom surface of lower case:* "E. Foote", "No15", and "This Side up" all in black paint. *On backboard of upper case:* "Ballroom/ 18th Century/ Mahogany Chest/ 2 drawers below" in black ink on masking tape, attached.

**Construction:** (Upper case) An applied cavetto molding with mitered corners is nailed to the underside of the molded hinged top. The case sides are joined to the horizontal backboard and the front in exposed dovetails. The blocking on the front is shaped and carved from solid wood. The bottom board is set in a channel at the front and sliding dados at the sides and nailed across the back. Inside, all four sides are channeled vertically to receive interlocking dividers.

(Lower case) The mitered midmolding is nailed to cleats affixed to the front and sides of the case top to form a well. The case sides are dovetailed to the top and bottom boards. The horizontal backboard is set in sliding dados in the case sides from a bottom mounting; the upper back is nailed flush to the top. The top and bottom front rails have single-beaded edges; the single drawer blade is double-beaded. The beading on the sides of the drawer openings is set into the case sides. Runners nailed inside the case sides support the drawers. The base molding is nailed to the bottom board. Between the front leg brackets, an applied quarter-round molding is nailed in place from the bottom. The thick knee brackets, nailed to the case bottom, are reinforced by horizontal glueblocks flanking the front legs, which are tenoned into the leg blocks and nailed. The large ogee-bracket rear legs are attached with sliding dados to the chest base and are each further reinforced with a shaped board at the back and a large triangular, horizontal glueblock. The drawers are dovetailed at the corners and sawed on the inside front to conform to the exterior blocking. The sides of the drawers are rounded on top; the thick back is chamfered slightly on both edges of the top. The drawer bottoms, which run from side to side and are chamfered on three sides, join the sides and front with sliding dados and are nailed across the back edge, which projects slightly.

**Condition:** The left side of the upper case is cracked horizontally the full depth of the box, with another short crack at the back; the right side has several smaller cracks. The left cavetto molding is split at the back. The interior bottle dividers are missing. The right side of the lower case is split vertically; the forward corner has a large gouge mark. The glueblocks reinforcing the legs appear to have been reglued. The brass handles and escutcheons are replacements; there is evidence of a former set of oval backplates. Rectangular metal plates on the inside of the lid and on the facade of the recessed panel of the upper case have been removed.

**Dimensions:**

| | | |
|---|---|---|
| H. | 39 3/4 in. | 100.9 cm |
| W. (lid) | 28 in. | 71.2 cm |
| W. (upper case) | 25 7/8 in. | 65.7 cm |
| W. (lower case) | 28 in. | 71.2 cm |
| W. (feet) | 31 in. | 78.7 cm |
| D. (lid) | 16 3/8 in. | 41.6 cm |
| D. (upper case) | 15 9/16 in. | 39.5 cm |
| D. (lower case) | 16 1/2 in. | 41.9 cm |
| D. (feet) | 18 1/4 in. | 45.7 cm |

**Materials:** *Microanalysis:* Primary: cherry. Secondary: white pine group (back and bottom board of upper case, top board, back and bottom board of lower case, drawer linings). *Finish:* medium dark to dark reddish brown color in resin.

**Exhibitions:** On loan from Margaret Sherwood Patterson to the Colonial Dames of America, New York, before 1931.

**Publications:** "The Editor's Attic," *Antiques* 19, no. 6 (June 1931): frontispiece, 435–36. John A. H. Sweeney, *The Treasure House of Early American Rooms* (New York: Viking Press, 1963), p. 59.

**Provenance:** Ex coll.: Margaret Sherwood Patterson. Given by Mrs. Patterson's daughter to the Colonial Dames of America, New York, before 1931.

**Accession history:** Museum purchase from the Colonial Dames of America, New York, 1956. 56.91

1. Macquoid and Edwards, *Dictionary*, 1:221–22; Dow, *Arts and Crafts in New England*, p. 99. Another bottle box on a case of drawers, constructed of cherry and pine and said to be one of 3 related cases, varies considerably from this example: the frame is wider; the front is plain; 3 small drawers fill the lower tier, the center one carved with a fan; the astragal-scalloped front skirt has a small, carved pinwheel at the center; the long cabriole legs have flute-carved knees and flute-carved pad feet with hocked ankles. The case may be of eastern Connecticut origin; see Bernard and S. Dean Levy, Inc., *In Search of Excellence* (New York: By the company, n.d.), p. 36.

2. For chests of drawers supported by cabriole legs of related design, see Houghton Bulkeley, *Contributions to Connecticut Cabinetmaking* (Hartford: Connecticut Historical Society, 1967), p. 44; *New London County Furniture*, nos. 33, 34; Francis J. Puig and Michael Conforti, eds., *The American Craftsman and the European Tradition, 1620–1820* (Minneapolis: Minneapolis Institute of Arts, 1989), cat. no. 47; Sotheby's, "Important Americana from the Collection of Mr. and Mrs. Adolph Henry Meyer" (January 20, 1996), lot 215.

3. The bit that cut the cylindrical holes in the knee brackets had a lead screw and produced a flat-bottom cavity, but according to Michael S. Podmaniczky, furniture conservator, Winterthur, it does not appear to have been a center bit. Bulkeley, *Contributions*, pp. 28–33; *New London County Furniture*, pp. 32–36; Robert F. Trent, "The Colchester School of Cabinetmaking, 1750–1800," in Puig and Conforti, *American Craftsman*, pp. 113–15.

4. For furniture with shells featuring a lily-shape flute or incised lines, see *New London County Furniture*, nos. 34, 35, 55, p. 104 upper right, lower left; Bulkeley, *Contributions*, p. 44; *Frederick K. and Margaret R. Barbour's Furniture Collection* (Hartford: Connecticut Historical Society, 1963), pp. 51, 61, 67; *Connecticut Furniture*, no. 99. For the chest of drawers and a detail of its bead-centered shells, see *Frederick K. and Margaret R. Barbour's Furniture Collection*, p. 39; *New London County Furniture*, p. 104 upper left. For the chest-on-chest, see David Stockwell advertisement, *Antiques* 113, no. 5 (May 1978): 893. For chest of drawers with Burnham-type carving, see *New London County Furniture*, no. 33.

5. For furniture with banded decoration, see *New London County Furniture*, no. 40; *Connecticut Furniture*, no. 88; Stockwell advertisement.

6. For genealogical information on Foote family, see Townley McElhiney, "A Block Front Cellarette as an Icon of Connecticut Culture" (Summer Institute paper, 1973, folder 56.91, Registration Office, Winterthur), p. 20; Phyllis Kihn, comp., "Connecticut Cabinetmakers, Part I," *Connecticut Historical Bulletin* 32, no. 4 (October 1967): 123; Abram W. Foote, *Foote Family, Comprising the Genealogy of Nathaniel Foote of Wethersfield, Conn., and His Descendants* (Rutland, Vt.: Marble City Press/ Tuttle Co., 1907), pp. 34, 48–49, 51–52, 89, 99, 110, 118. See also card file of church records, inventory of Joseph Foote, Jr. (Colchester, 1814), and guardianship of Enoch Foote (Colchester, 1766) in Genealogical Section, Connecticut State Library, Hartford.

## 184 • Chest of drawers
Boston, Massachusetts
1770–90

Some years ago, Gilbert T. Vincent traced the European roots and development of the bombé form. A key influence was the Italian *cassone*, or marriage chest, which by the sixteenth century had assumed characteristics of Renaissance design: craftsmen introduced carved classical ornament to the chest surface in place of painted folk decoration and gave the form an architectural focus by adopting the bulging profile of the classical Roman sarcophagus. The form fit the emerging baroque aesthetic, which during the late seventeenth century was embraced by French designers and disseminated via design books and exchanges of craftsmen within the European community. The commode, a bulging case of two or three drawers, emerged in France as the premier expression of the new design in room furnishing and quickly influenced other case forms and stimulated further innovation throughout Europe. Transfer of the bombé profile from England to America, specifically to the Boston area, was accomplished within a few decades, probably during the 1740s and likely through exported furniture.[1]

Of the almost sixty pieces of surviving bombé furniture, slightly more than half, or thirty-one, are chests of drawers; nineteen are desk-and-bookcases; four are chests-on-chests; and four are desks. The bombé style also appears in dressing glasses (see No. 215), although they are not included in the surveyed group. In the more than twenty years since Vincent's study was published (which included four documented tall casepieces), no additional documented examples have been discovered.[2]

Based on the evidence of the two earliest documented pieces of bombé furniture (one constructed in 1753) and other examples that can be dated before the Revolution with

assurance, the first form that appeared in the market was a bulging case with straight-sided drawers. This construction seems to have been limited to some desk-and-bookcases and a small number of desks. In the most common form, the drawers (or at least the drawer fronts) follow the contours of the bulging case sides, as seen in this example.[3]

Several other design options for the chest of drawers accompanied the bombé swell. A few chests are straight-sided in the entire upper case, with an abrupt transition to the bombé form at the top of the third drawer (see No. 185). More commonly, the curve begins above the lower corners of the second drawer and forms a gradual transition from a flat to a curved case surface, as seen in this chest.

Winterthur's chest exhibits still another case option available to consumers: a bulging facade shaped in two dimensions—top to bottom and side to side—sometimes described as double serpentine. This, too, has its variation. The crease that marks the drawer ends from top to bottom and follows the

contours of the case sides is either narrow, as illustrated, or broad. The chest top is shaped across the front in imitation of the case curves, thus integrating the design.

About a dozen double-serpentine bombé chests of drawers are known. One of the prominent makers was John Cogswell of Boston, whose serpentine bombé case production also included desks and desk-and-bookcases. Based on a review of Cogswell's work, Winterthur's chest falls outside the body of furniture that can be attributed to his shop. The curve of the case sides varies subtly from the one common to Cogswell's work: the bulge is more pronounced, and the start of the curve is more abrupt. The thick ankles of the Winterthur example are hunched to a greater degree than found in Cogswell's work, although the long, slim talons are better defined.[4]

Construction techniques in the Winterthur and Cogswell examples also vary. The dovetails of the drawer blades in Cogswell's work are exposed; here they are

**Fig. 1.** Detail, case interior.

concealed. Cogswell used large triangular glueblocks under the base to support the corners; Winterthur's chest is reinforced with rectangular blocks along the front and sides. The interior case and drawer construction of the two shops coincides in part, however. Cogswell hollowed the interior of his cases to follow the outside curve and then used one of several methods to construct the drawers. The lower drawers in two cases have angled sides, as in the Winterthur example, and the front boards form lips at the ends to butt against shallow rabbets cut into the inside front edges of the case sides (fig. 1).[5]

Based on Cogswell's work, it appears that production of the double-serpentine bombé case in Boston began only in the early 1770s, although it continued for at least two decades, as indicated by the evidence of patronage and other factors. The refinement of workmanship in Cogswell's cases progressed as his experience with the form increased. The variety of brass hardware found on double-serpentine bombé chests of drawers varies from the standard solid backplate with cusped projections to the simple post-and-bail postwar style of this example. Falling between the two in dates of introduction are the chinoiserie and rococo brasses found on two chests in the group. Identical patterns appear in catalogues issued by brass founders in England during the 1770s. Serpentine bombé chests are also built consistently in figured mahogany with white pine as the secondary wood.[6]

Bombé furniture, considered both ornamental and novel, was also expensive due to the size of the mahogany planks required to create the bulges of the case

and drawers and the labor-intensive nature of the construction. This restricted purchasers to wealthy families or at least to the most prosperous segments of society. The list of identified owners, which reads like a Who's Who, principally comprises Boston and North Shore merchants and includes Thomas Amory, Jr.; Joseph Barrell; Elias Hasket Derby (Salem); Jeremiah Lee (Marblehead); Josiah Quincy, Jr.; John Hancock; and Gardiner Greene. Greene, whose third wife was Elizabeth Clarke (daughter of artist John Singleton Copley), was worth more than $1 million at his death in 1832.[7]

*NGE*

---

**Construction:** The top and sides of the chest are joined in sliding half dovetails. The top, which overhangs the case, conforms to the case blocking at the front and is ogee molded on the front and side edges. The horizontal drawer blades, or dividers, which are backed with pine and beaded at the front edges, are attached to the case sides with dovetails; there is no top rail. Vertical beads at the inside faces of the case sides form miters with those of the drawer blades. Each side panel of the case is shaped on the inner surface to conform in general to the outer bombé profile, although the interior surfaces at the bulge are canted rather than rounded. Runners glued and nailed inside the case sides support the three upper drawers; the bottom drawer runs on the bottom board, which has been planed on the outside. Vertical drawer stops are glued to the corners of the backboards. The sides and bottom of the chest are joined with dovetails. The bottom is further supported on the lower surface by large rectangular glueblocks along the front and sides. A heavy cyma-reversa base molding is attached to the front and sides of the case. The pendent drop

is glued to the base molding and reinforced on the back with a glueblock. The cabriole front legs are flanked by knee brackets glued in place and reinforced on the back by glueblocks. Stacked glueblocks reinforce the inside rear faces of the back legs. The case back, consisting of two planed horizontal butted boards held together with sprigs, is secured to the case sides with the glueblocks that serve as drawer stops. The drawers are dovetailed at the corners and sawed on the inside front to conform to the exterior curves. The sides of the drawers are chamfered on both edges of the top; the sides of the two drawers at the bottom are also set at an angle that conforms to the inside of the case. The heavy drawer backs are chamfered on the outside edge. The drawer bottoms, which run from front to back, are rabbeted and nailed.

**Condition:** The top drawer has been partitioned to form three compartments; the second drawer was similarly modified, but the partitions are missing. The left rear leg has been repaired at the knee. The left rear knee block and the left side glueblock are replacements; the left side front glueblock is also replaced. The base molding on the left side has been repaired and reattached. A small piece broken from the left corner of the second drawer from the top has been reattached. Some of the drawer runners are new, and all are nailed in place. The brass carrying handles at the case sides are not original. The exterior surface is refinished.

**Dimensions:**

| | | |
|---|---|---|
| H. | 33 1/4 in. | 84.4 cm |
| W. (top) | 36 in. | 91.0 cm |
| W. (case) | 35 7/8 in. | 90.8 cm |
| W. (knees) | 36 in. | 91.0 cm |
| D. (top) | 21 1/8 in. | 53.7 cm |
| D. (case) | 20 3/8 in. | 51.7 cm |
| D. (knees) | 20 5/8 in. | 52.4 cm |

**Materials:** *Microanalysis:* Primary: mahogany. Secondary: white pine group (backboard, bottom board, backing on blades, drawer linings). *Finish:* variegated light to medium dark reddish brown color in resin, in part over residue of former coats.

**Publications:** Downs, *American Furniture*, fig. 165.

**Provenance:** Ex coll.: Mr. and Mrs. Arthur L. Kelley, Worcester, Mass.

**Accession history:** Purchased by H. F. du Pont from Collings and Collings, New York, 1927. Bequest of H. F. du Pont, 1969. 59.1881

1. Gilbert T. Vincent, "The Bombé Furniture of Boston," in *Boston Furniture*, pp. 137–96; Eric Mercer, *Furniture, 700–1700* (London: Weidenfeld and Nicolson, 1969), pp. 93–99, 130, pls. 108, 144; Helena Hayward, ed., *World Furniture: An Illustrated History* (New York: McGraw-Hill Book Co., 1965), figs. 394, 627, 648; Kirk, *American Furniture*, figs. 482, 571, 572, 630; Baarsen et al., *Courts and Colonies*, pp. 166–67, 233, 240. Macquoid and Edwards, *Dictionary*, 1:136, fig. 30, p. 221, fig. 2; 2:109.

2. Vincent, "Bombé Furniture," figs. 97, 101, 124, 125.

3. Vincent, "Bombé Furniture," pp. 137–96; for examples of straight-sided drawer construction, see figs. 97, 101, 108.

4. Robert Mussey and Anne Rogers Haley, "John Cogswell and Boston Bombé Furniture: Thirty-Five Years of Revolution and Politics in Design," in Luke Beckerdite, ed., *American Furniture 1994* (Milwaukee, Wis.: Chipstone Fndn., 1994), pp. 73–105. For double-serpentine bombé chests of drawers, see Harold Sack, "The Bombé Furniture of Boston and Salem, Massachusetts," *Antiques* 135, no. 5 (May 1989): 1178–89, pls. 2, 11, 13, 15, 16, 20; Mussey and Haley, "John Cogswell," p. 97, fig. 40, p. 98, fig. 43; Albert Sack, *The New Fine Points of Furniture: Early American* (New York: Crown Publishers, 1993), p. 108; H. and R. Sandor advertisement, *Antiques* 102, no. 6 (December 1972): 945; Sotheby's, "Important American Furniture, Folk Art, Folk Paintings, and Chinese Export Porcelain" (October 24–25, 1986), lot 208; Northeast Auctions, "The Collection of John Howland Ricketson III" (May 29, 1993), lot 95.

5. Mussey and Haley, "John Cogswell," pp. 86–87.

6. Mussey and Haley, "John Cogswell," p. 83, fig. 12, pp. 94–95.

7. On Greene, see *American Antiques from Israel Sack Collection*, 10 vols. (Washington, D.C.: Highland House, 1969–), 6:1466–67.

## 185 ◆ Chest of drawers
**Salem, Massachusetts**
**1760–80**
**Probably Henry Rust (1737–1812)**

Equally as impressive as the serpentine bombé chest of No. 184 is this chest of drawers, which was made in Salem rather than Boston. The base pendant is embellished with a small, delicately carved scallop shell of a type associated with cabinetwork originating in that community (fig. 1). Two pieces of blockfront furniture that bear inscriptions linking them to Salem have similar shell pendants flanked by long, swelled knee brackets sawed to comparable, modified astragal profiles. A fall-front desk supported on cabriole legs is incised on the case bottom with the name "H x Rust," a Salem cabinetmaker. A desk-and-bookcase with a base section that appears to be identical to that of the Rust desk, down to the use of the same brass hardware, bears an inscription ("Nath Gould not his work") that has linked it with the shop of another Salem cabinetmaker.

Recent research has suggested that the desk-and-bookcase is in fact the work of Henry Rust (1737–1812), who may have worked at one time in the Gould shop. Another fall-front desk, signed and dated by Rust in 1770, has a plain facade and straight-bracket feet with astragal returns. The desk interior relates to the so-called Gould desk-and-bookcase and to an almost identical piece of tall case furniture in the Bybee collection at the Dallas Museum of Art, which is now attributed to Rust.[1]

Tentative ascription of the bombé chest of drawers to the Rust shop also seems warranted. Aside from the close relationship of the shell pendant and knee brackets to those in the blockfront furniture discussed above, there is a remarkable similarity in the feet: the short cabriole legs have the same thick ankles, slim knuckled talons with toenails, and deeply scooped webs between the talons (fig. 2). The brasses on the bombé chest, the Rust blockfront desk, and the two desk-and-bookcases are all of the same pattern. Charles Venable has found the construction

**Fig. 1.** Detail, base pendant.

techniques of the blockfront furniture and the bombé chest (and other bombé furniture in the group) to be closely related, given the necessary modifications dictated by differences in the basic shapes of the cases.[2]

Bombé furniture associated with Rust's shop includes several fall-front desks—one has a history in the Derby family of Salem. The base of a second chest of drawers, including the feet, brackets, and shell drop, is similar in design to the Winterthur chest and the documented furniture and is in the Bayou Bend collection at the Museum of Fine Arts, Houston. The brasses appear to have been replaced, and the dimensions vary modestly from those in the Winterthur chest, but the primary difference occurs in the curve of the case sides. Although the arcs of the bulges are the same, those in the Bayou Bend chest begin gradually at the level of the second drawer from the top rather than abruptly at the third drawer, as in the Winterthur chest. The Bayou Bend chest may represent a refinement of the original shop design since the curve is more pleasing aesthetically. On both chests the drawer sides are double-beaded on the upper inside edge, and the pins and tails of the dovetails in the drawer backs are reversed from the normal pattern. A nearly identical chest in the Marblehead Historical Society descended in the Osgood family of Salem. Winterthur's chest was owned at the beginning of the twentieth century by a member of the Waters family of Salem, but it also is thought to have descended in the Osgood family.[3]

Rust, the supposed maker of this chest, was born in Ipswich and probably trained in Salem with cabinetmaker Joseph Gavit (1699–1765). Rust probably was practicing his craft by the time he married in 1759, and three years later in 1762 his name appeared on a list of master craftsmen in Salem, indicating his independent status. By 1765 he was sufficiently secure financially to purchase the house and shop of cabinetmaker Thomas Needham at the corner of Federal and Washington streets. The location, four or five blocks from the waterfront and about the same distance from the Salem common, was in the heart of the town's developing residential district.[4]

**Fig. 2.** Detail, right front foot.

Rust began to invest in shipping ventures during the 1770s and apparently was reasonably successful. One of his occasional partners was Joseph Sprague (1739–1808), a Salem merchant, distiller, and landholder. Sprague was the first owner of the blockfront desk-and-bookcase attributed to Rust, which is now at the Dallas Museum of Art. During his early mercantile career, Rust also became acquainted with the Reverend William Bentley, who in 1784 settled in Salem as minister of the East Church. At Rust's death in 1812, Bentley commented favorably in his diary on the character and success of the man, a departure from his usual critical observations about Salem craftsmen who abandoned their trades for the uncertain risks of mercantilism: "He was a man of great integrity & of steady habits, so that through his life he passed commonly by the name of Elder Rhust. He has a considerable interest in Lands in Norway, Maine, & two Sons, settled there. . . . He has several dwelling houses, stores, & wharves & other real estate in Salem."[5]

*NGE with NER*

---

**Inscriptions or marks:** *On outside back of drawers, top to bottom:* "B4" *to* "B7" *in white chalk. Gouged on inside front of bottom drawer:* "IP".

**Construction:** The top and sides of the chest are joined in sliding dovetails. The top overhangs the case and is ogee molded on the front and side edges.

The horizontal drawer blades, or dividers, which are moderately shallow and beaded at the front edges, are attached to the case sides with exposed dovetails. The rails, top and bottom, are beaded on the edge adjacent to the drawer opening. Vertical beads at the inside faces of the case sides form miters with those of the drawer blades and rails. The side panels of the case are shaped on the inner surface to conform to the outer bombé profile. Runners nailed inside the case support all four drawers; vertical drawer stops are nailed to the case sides behind the runners. The sides and bottom of the chest are joined with dovetails. The bottom is further supported by end cleats extending from front to back on the lower surface. A heavy cyma-reversa base molding is applied with nails at the front and sides. The pendent drop with applied, carved shell is reinforced on the inside surface with a heavy glueblock; both are attached to the case with rosehead nails. The cabriole front legs are flanked by brackets supported by heavy, shaped horizontal glueblocks; both the brackets and blocks are nailed. Large, glued, wedge-shape blocks reinforce the joint of the rear legs and case and are further secured with nails. The case back, consisting of two horizontal lap-jointed boards chamfered at the sides on the inside surface, are nailed to rabbets at the sides and top and nailed flush at the bottom. The drawers are dovetailed at the corners, the pins and tails at the back reversed from the normal configuration. The sides of the drawers are double-beaded on the top edge and planed on the outside surface. The drawer bottoms, which run from side to side and are chamfered on three sides, join the sides and front with sliding dados and are nailed flush at the back.

**Condition:** There are splits along the grain in the top, at the base of each case side, and in the bottom board. An old split in the bottom of the lowest drawer is covered with modern paper tape. A reinforcing screw secures the top rail to the underside of the top. The left rear leg block is severely degraded. The underside of the top bears marks from a regulated reciprocating saw, reflecting an early use of this tool. The exterior surface is refinished.

**Dimensions:**

| | | |
|---|---|---|
| H. | 35 1/4 in. | 89.5 cm |
| W. (top) | 40 in. | 101.6 cm |
| W. (case) | 37 7/8 in. | 96.5 cm |
| W. (knees) | 37 1/2 in. | 95.2 cm |
| D. (top) | 22 1/2 in. | 57.1 cm |
| D. (bombé) | 21 1/4 in. | 54.0 cm |
| D. (knees) | 21 1/4 in. | 54.0 cm |

**Materials:** *Microanalysis:* Primary: mahogany. Secondary: white pine group (throughout). *Finish:* resin over residue of variegated medium to medium dark reddish brown color.

**Publications:** Morse, *Furniture of the Olden Time,* p. 44. Downs, *American Furniture,* fig. 166. Gilbert T. Vincent, "The Bombé Furniture of Boston," in *Boston Furniture,* pp. 192–94, fig. 136.

**Provenance:** Tradition of ownership in the Osgood family of Salem, Mass. Ex coll.: Charles R. Waters, Salem, Mass. (ca. 1902). The Waters and Osgood families were intermarried. Other Waters family furniture includes a blockfront desk-and-bookcase (No. 208). Ex coll.: Helen Temple Cooke, Wellesley, Mass.

**Accession history:** Purchased by H. F. du Pont from Israel Sack, Inc., New York, before 1930. Bequest of H. F. du Pont, 1969.
57.509

1. Venable, *American Furniture,* cat. 28. For Rust and "Gould"-inscribed furniture, see Benjamin Ginsburg advertisement, *Antiques* 111, no. 5 (May 1977): 845; Heckscher, *American Furniture,* cat. no. 181; *American Antiques from Israel Sack Collection,* 10 vols. (Washington, D.C.: Highland House, 1969–), 4:898–99.

2. Venable, *American Furniture,* cat. 28.

3. Venable, *American Furniture,* cat. 28; Gilbert T. Vincent, "The Bombé Furniture of Boston," in *Boston Furniture,* pp. 192–95. For Derby family desk, see Harold Sack, "The Bombé Furniture of Boston and Salem, Massachusetts," *Antiques* 135, no. 5 (May 1989): pl. 9; for Bayou Bend chest, see Warren, *Bayou Bend,* no. 127.

4. Venable, *American Furniture,* cat. 28.

5. Venable, *American Furniture,* cat. 28. Bentley quoted in Margaret Burke Clunie, "Furniture Craftsmen of Salem, Massachusetts, in the Federal Period," in *Dr. Bentley's Salem: Diary of a Town* (Salem, Mass.: Essex Institute, 1977), p. 45.

## 186 ◆ Chest of drawers
Hartford, Connecticut
1793
Samuel Kneeland (1755–1828) and
Lemuel Adams (d. 1821)

The flowing serpentine line as a decorative embellishment in the facades of case furniture pervaded European design by the mid eighteenth century. In England the serpentine profile appeared on many furniture forms, from chairs (seat fronts) and sofas to tables and almost all kinds of cases with drawers. Helping to popularize this bold figure in English furniture and likely in American furniture as well were the books of engraved furniture designs that circulated in the English and colonial markets in the 1750s and 1760s. A design for a "Comode Chest of Drawers" published by Ince and Mayhew is closer in plan and size to serpentine chests produced by American cabinetmakers than the designs for commode forms drawn by Chippendale. As late as 1794, Hepplewhite still illustrated a plain serpentine chest, although the updated feet are flared in the French style.[1]

Produced from Maine to Charleston, the chest of drawers with a serpentine facade was popular in America from the 1760s to the end of the century. Massachusetts chests are the most numerous followed by examples made in Philadelphia and Connecticut. Chests with ogee-bracket feet, including the massive canted-corner ogee foot, substantially outnumber those with cabriole feet; chests with straight brackets are uncommon. A few chests have one or more special decorative features, including a pendent drop centered in the base, carved work, fluted canted corners, and quarter columns. Chests with post-and-bail brasses somewhat outnumber those with solid, cusped backplates, and mahogany is by far the most common material. Inlay on a few examples is evidence of the particular popularity of the serpentine form in the postrevolutionary period. Brasses of special form enhance a few cases. Only a few serpentine chests are documented to a maker, and the example in this entry is the only one of the documented group that is associated with a Connecticut shop. That serpentine chests were a recognized local commodity is confirmed in a 1792 price list from Hartford, which describes bureaus of "plain" or "swell'd front" and special features, including "claw feet" and "columns."[2]

Connecticut serpentine chests of drawers are usually made of cherry, as is this case by Samuel Kneeland and Lemuel Adams of Hartford. Perhaps even more popular within the region was the cherrywood chest of reverse serpentine, or oxbow, facade, a form pictured in a stock illustration accompanying one of the firm's advertisements. Many more cases of reverse-serpentine design are embellished with quarter columns at the front corners than are serpentine forms, although brass fittings, such as on the columns of this case, which are adapted from clock parts, are a rarity (fig. 1). Cherrywood oxbow chests are usually supported on cabriole feet, and, like on the Kneeland and Adams case, they appear in conjunction with post-and-bail–style brasses dating to the late eighteenth century. A pair of cabriole-foot oxbow chests also have similar heavy ogee-bracket rear feet, a regional feature found in New London County work (see No. 183), although they are without documentation or family association. Oxbow chests of mahogany are usually associated with

Fig. 1. Detail, right front foot.

Massachusetts; in European construction the profile is rare.[3]

The breadth of this case is substantial; it is a full five or six inches greater than the largest chests of drawers in this catalogue. Built-up extensions at the front corners permit the drawer blades to slot into the case sides in the traditional manner and at the same time create a stylish flair. The way in which the ankle is squared off, or creased, adjacent

to the talons is distinctive and may prove the basis for establishing other relationships (see fig. 1). The cherrywood apparently was colored originally to imitate mahogany, a more expensive material.

Kneeland and Adams were business partners for only two and a half years, from September 10, 1792, to March 5, 1795. Their products, of which a number are known, can therefore be dated accurately; further, they demonstrate the lingering popularity of the cabriole support in Connecticut in the federal period. This chest of drawers was accompanied by a loose trade card inscribed in pencil across the top "bought Dec 23[d] 1793" (fig. 2). The same family also purchased a set of six early federal-style side chairs with modified Georgian backs now at Winterthur, which were also accompanied by a Kneeland and Adams trade card. A second chest, bearing the firm's label in an upper drawer, is of more conservative design—it has a flat facade and straight-bracket feet bellied on the inside face, but the brasses appear to be similar to those on this chest.[4]

One of the several looking glasses labeled by Kneeland and Adams is featured in this catalogue (No. 213). Three other fret-sawed glasses of related design are known but lack pierced crests and gilded ornament. Several pieces of furniture are also documented to either Kneeland or Adams separately. The earliest, made by Kneeland for Jeremiah Wadsworth, a prominent Connecticut figure in political and business circles, is a low box supported on ogee-bracket feet that functioned as a storage container for a porcelain bowl. The label in the box is dated 1786, and the inlaid stringing and oval top ornament attest to its postrevolutionary construction. Kneeland also stamped a pedestal table with a large square top, each side sawed to a serpentine profile. He is recorded in the accounts of Daniel Burnap as supplying seven clock cases between 1788 and 1792, but they are as yet unidentified.[5]

At the close of the partnership both Kneeland and Adams were awarded large contracts by the state of Connecticut to construct furniture for the new statehouse in Hartford. Kneeland made five tables of varying length—the largest was twenty-nine feet. Adams constructed twenty-two chairs, ten window seats, a desk, and two vote boxes. Some of the shield-back urn-splat armchairs with inlaid tapered legs survive, and they represent the most fully developed federal design identified with either man or the partnership. Whether the cabinetmakers were

Fig. 2. Kneeland and Adams trade card. (Winterthur)

reluctant to fully embrace the new federal style or their clientele leaned toward conservatism in household furnishings is unclear, but the late construction dates of two oxbow, or reverse-serpentine, chests documented to Connecticut craftsmen point to the latter explanation. One, with cabriole legs, was made in Hartford no earlier than 1790, based on the 1769 birthdate of the maker; the other, made in neighboring Wethersfield, has ogee-bracket feet and is inscribed with a date in 1796. A second serpentine chest, similar to No. 186 but with ogee-bracket feet, is said to be dated January 7, 1800, on the backboards. The work for the statehouse, a public commission, may have afforded the local gentry who directed the project the opportunity to address the new style on an experimental basis without committing personal funds or household space.[6]

Little is known about the size and organization of the Kneeland and Adams shop or the extent of their business, but their "compleat assortment of well seasoned Stuff" and announced production of "all kinds of Cabinet Work . . . in the newest fashions," ranging from parlor chairs to card tables and desk-and-bookcases to sideboards, describes their expectations. The partners' facility in silvering, framing, and gilding looking glasses and their advertisements for "a good workman at Common Chairs" and for "two or three Journeymen Cabinet Makers . . . and two likely active Lads . . . as apprentices" suggest an extensive operation or the potential for one.[7]

Within a few years of the dissolution of their partnership both Adams and Kneeland left Connecticut. Adams sold Windsor chairs and cabinetwares in Norfolk, Virginia, in 1801 and may have moved to New Hampshire at some point thereafter. Kneeland is thought to have been born in Colchester, Connecticut, and to have received his training there. If true, the relationship between the Kneeland and Adams chest and No. 183, a case associated with that community, becomes significant. Both chests are supported on cabriole front feet and large ogee-bracket rear feet, an unusual dual leg system. Kneeland is presumed to have left Connecticut for New York State in 1800; a man of that name died in Geneseo in 1828.[8]

NGE with NER

---

**Inscriptions or marks:** *On printed trade card:* "bought Dec 23d 1793" across top, in pencil; "Dec 23d 1793" across bottom (retouched) and "100 years 1893" (in a different hand). *Inside back of all drawers (marking upper edge):* "v" in pencil. *Underside bottom of third drawer:* "3" in pencil. *Inside bottom of bottom drawer:* "4" in pencil. *Underside of bottom board:* "X" in pencil. *At center top of all three drawer blades:* "X" accompanied by "I", "II", and "III" from top to bottom, in pencil.

**Construction:** The top and sides of the chest are joined on a sliding channel, the chest top inserted from the front and secured on the inside with trapezoidal glueblocks. The two-board top, which overhangs the case, conforms to the case curves and is molded at the front and side edges. The two-board case sides are flat on the inside and built up on the outside to form flared square corners. Fluted quarter columns with brass capitals and bases and blocking top and bottom are glued to the case sides. The top rail is glued to the underside of the case top and is not joined to the case sides. The horizontal drawer blades, or dividers, which are roughly finished on the inside back, are slotted into the case sides; wedge-shape front facing strips cover the joints. The drawer runners are glued into slots in the case sides. The sides and bottom of the chest are joined with dovetails. The bottom is further supported on the lower surface at the ends by wide front-to-back cleats shaped on the outer edge to form the side base moldings; a similarly molded board is nailed across the front. The shaped knee brackets flanking the front legs are unusually thick and are reinforced with shaped horizontal glueblocks. The front leg posts are reinforced with vertical glueblocks. On the rear legs, shaped vertical blocks inside and out reinforce the joint of the outside facing and the rear board-type bracket, which has a canted inside edge and is set in from the case back. Horizontal triangular glueblocks secure the feet to the case bottom. The case back, consisting of two horizontal lapped boards, is set into rabbets at the case top and sides, secured with nails, and nailed flush at the bottom. The drawers are dovetailed at the corners. The fronts are pieced on the inside and conform in general to the shape of the exterior. The drawer faces are scratch-beaded on all four edges; the sides and back are flat at the top edges. The two-board drawer bottoms, which run from side to side, are chamfered, set into dados, and nailed flush at the back.

**Condition:** The drawer runners have been reversed. The top two drawer blades are patched on the upper left where they meet the case side, as is the lower rail. Battens applied to all drawer bottoms have been restored with facing strips. The right rear footboard is cracked and repaired. The vertical glueblock on the left rear leg is a replacement. All the glueblocks were reset or replaced long ago. The brasses are original.

**Dimensions:**

| | | |
|---|---|---|
| H. | 35 7/8 in. | 91.1 cm |
| W. (top) | 45 3/4 in. | 116.2 cm |
| W. (case) | 43 3/8 in. | 110.6 cm |
| W. (knees) | 45 3/4 in. | 116.2 cm |
| D. (top) | 20 5/8 in. | 52.7 cm |
| D. (case) | 19 3/4 in. | 50.1 cm |
| D. (knees) | 21 1/8 in. | 53.9 cm |

**Materials:** *Microanalysis:* Primary: cherry. Secondary: yellow poplar (drawer linings, backboard); white pine group (glueblocks). *Finish:* old, possibly original orange-brown color in resin, considerably marred; probably meant to simulate mahogany.

**Exhibitions:** "The Great River: Art and Society in the Connecticut River Valley," Wadsworth Atheneum, Hartford, Conn., August 1985–February 1986.

**Publications:** Downs, *American Furniture*, fig. 173. Philip Zea, "Furniture," in *Great River*, cat. 144.

**Provenance:** In a letter of March 19, 1968, noting the source of a set of 6 Kneeland and Adams chairs at Winterthur (67.151.1–6), John C. R. Tompkins wrote: "The labeled chest by the same makers with free columns which the Museum acquired from Ginsburg & Levy also came from this house, and which I had purchased. . . . Miss Peck told me that her Mother & Father brought all the pieces by covered wagon from Hartford early in the 19th century." By tradition the furniture was purchased for Miss Peck's grandmother at the time of her marriage in 1793. The trade card accompanying the chair was inscribed as a bill by one of the partners and dated December 23, 1793. Ex coll.: Anna W. Peck, Pittsfield, Mass.; John C. R. Tompkins, Worcester, Mass.; Ginsburg and Levy, New York.

**Accession history:** Purchased for the museum by H. F. du Pont from Ginsburg and Levy, New York, 1951.
51.66.1

---

1. Helena Hayward, ed., *World Furniture: An Illustrated History* (New York: McGraw-Hill Book Co., 1965), figs. 408, 421, 497, 498, 515, 520, 521, 578, 580, 597, 616, 627, 631, 680, pl. facing p. 161; Macquoid and Edwards, *Dictionary*, 2:46–47, 49, fig. 49, pp. 51, 113; William Ince and John Mayhew, *The Universal System of Houshold Furniture* (1762; reprint, Chicago: Quadrangle Books, 1960), pl. 43; Thomas Chippendale, *The Gentleman and Cabinet-Maker's Director* (1762; reprint 3d ed., New York: Dover, 1966), pls. 66, 68 right, 70 right; [George] Hepplewhite, *The Cabinet-Maker and Upholsterer's Guide* (1794; reprint 3d ed., New York: Dover, 1969), pl. 77.

2. Table of prices for cabinetwork in Hartford is quoted in Montgomery, *American Furniture*, p. 179.

3. Kneeland and Adams advertisement, *Connecticut Courant* (Hartford), October 8, 1792, as illustrated in Phyllis Kihn, comp., "Connecticut Cabinet-makers, Part I," *Connecticut Historical Society Bulletin* 32, no. 4 (October 1967): 141; the pair of oxbow chests is in John S. Walton advertisement, *Antiques* 134, no. 4 (October 1988): 600.

4. "The Wadsworth Punch Bowl, ca. 1780," *Connecticut Historical Society Bulletin* 20, no. 2 (April 1955): 33–41; Kihn, "Connecticut Cabinetmakers," pp. 99–102, 137–44; Nancy E. Richards, "Furniture of the Lower Connecticut River Valley: The Hartford Area, 1785–1810," in Richard K. Doud, ed., *Winterthur Portfolio 4* (Charlottesville: University Press of Virginia for the Henry Francis du Pont Winterthur Museum, 1968), pp. 4–13; Philip Zea, "Furniture," in *Great River*, cat. 144.

5. Richards, "Furniture of Lower Connecticut River Valley," pp. 4–13, figs. 2, 10, 14. Two of the looking glasses are in private collections.

6. Kihn, "Connecticut Cabinetmakers," pp. 101–2, 139–40, figs. 2, 3. The Hartford oxbow chest was made by John I. Wells; see Richards, "Furniture of the Lower Connecticut River Valley," p. 14. The Wethersfield chest was made by Oliver Deming; Jairus B. Barnes and Moselle Taylor Meals, *American Furniture in the Western Reserve, 1680–1830* (Cleveland: Western Reserve Historical Society, 1972), p. 55. For the 1800 chest, see Phil and Jeanne Jessee advertisement, *Maine Antique Digest*, December 1995, p. 6-C.

7. Kneeland and Adams advertisement, *Connecticut Courant*, October 8, 1792, as cited in Kihn, "Connecticut Cabinetmakers," p. 141; Kneeland and Adams advertisement, *American Mercury* (Hartford, Conn.), September 10, 1792, October 14, 1793, as cited in William Stuart Walcott, Jr., "A Kneeland and Adams Mirror," *Antiques* 13, no. 1 (January 1928): 31.

8. Kihn, "Connecticut Cabinetmakers," pp. 99–102, 137–40; Adams advertisement, *Norfolk Herald*, July 11, 1801, as transcribed for citation file, Museum of Early Southern Decorative Arts, Winston-Salem, N.C.

## 187 ◆ Chest of drawers
New Hampshire
1795–1810
Possibly Lt. Samuel Dunlap (1752–1830)

Of the furniture that can be attributed with some assurance to the Dunlap family and their circle, chests survive in the largest quantity, with tall chests outnumbering chests of drawers. "Low chests" (that is, chests of drawers and chests-on-frames) were produced with either four or five drawers. Four-drawer models, like this example, generally are decorated with double-beading on the edge of the top, the leading edge of the case sides, and the drawer blades, and they share a distinctive base molding carved in a pattern that Maj. John Dunlap, Samuel's brother, identified as "flowered O G." The tops are secured on sliding dovetails in the manner of Massachusetts low chests. The cabriole legs have an unusually sharp knee and a pronounced inward sweep to a thin ankle, and the feet may be either simple pads or truncated claws-and-balls with well-defined knuckles and webbing and the lower portion of the ball removed, as in this example (fig. 1). The knee brackets are boldly scrolled, and the lower edge is undercut to reduce the bulk. This particular leg pattern is carved consistently in basswood without regard for the primary wood of the case.[1]

In his 1976 revised survey of Dunlap furniture, Charles Parsons located twenty-six "low chests," nine of which were of the four-drawer variety. Winterthur's example relates most closely to a chest of drawers in the Garvan collection at Yale. Both products of the Dunlap school, they share the same overall design and construction, varying only slightly in size and detail of carving. Even the drawers have the same chalk "B" on the inside of the back. The Winterthur chest has been loosely associated with the shop of Lt. Samuel Dunlap because it relates closely in the design of the

base to No. 196, a chest-on-chest, which is inscribed in chalk on one drawer "Salisbury" (a community Dunlap called home in 1797 and later) and which also bears a script letter "B" in white chalk on the inside back of the drawers. Two other features of this chest—cut nails in the construction and original oval brass hardware—date the case to the end of the eighteenth century.[2]

Archibald Dunlap (1713–54), the progenitor of the Dunlap family in America, was an Irish weaver of Scots ancestry who immigrated to Chester, New Hampshire, before 1741. Two of his sons, Maj. John Dunlap (1746–92) and Lt. Samuel Dunlap, were cabinetmakers, and eleven other family members in succeeding generations also were engaged in the woodworking trades in the postrevolutionary era. Although their work is rarely signed or labeled, much early New Hampshire furniture has been attributed to the Dunlaps.[3]

Samuel Dunlap, the fifth son, may have received his training in Chester, which was home to several cabinetmakers. By 1773 he had married and moved to Goffstown, where he worked briefly for his older brother John before enlisting in the army in 1775 at the rank of sergeant. During the next two years he served in campaigns in Quebec, New York, and Bennington, and by the time he left the militia in 1792, he had attained the rank of lieutenant. Throughout his military service, Samuel worked intermittently with John before settling in Henniker in 1780, where he was appointed surveyor of lumber and served as a selectman. In 1783 he assisted John in building pulpits for churches in Temple and Londonderry, New Hampshire. He moved to Salisbury in 1797 and continued the cabinetmaking business until his death.[4]

Both John and Samuel Dunlap trained several apprentices, some of whom continued to work for them after completing training.

**Fig. 1.** Detail, left front foot.

Each of them also had one or more sons who worked as cabinetmakers well into the nineteenth century. Because of the complex interrelations between family shops, there are few criteria for assigning furniture to a specific craftsman. Samuel and his son Samuel II (1783–1853) are the only family cabinetmakers who lived in Salisbury.[5]

*NER with NGE*

---

**Inscriptions or marks:** *On inside back of all drawers:* "B" in white chalk.

**Construction:** The one-board top, with double-bead-molded edges, overhangs the case on the front and sides and is flush at the back. The top is attached to the sides on sliding half dovetails. Long reinforcing blocks are nailed inside along the joint of the top and sides. The single-board case sides are double-bead-molded on the leading edge. The top rail is nailed to the underside of the top board; the bottom rail is pegged to the bottom board. Each has a single bead. The drawer blades, or dividers, are dovetailed to the case sides; all have double-beads. Across the inside back of the case, a batten corresponding to the bottom front rail is pegged to the bottom board.

Drawer runners are nailed to the inner sides of the case. The bottom board is dovetailed to the case sides. The base molding is nailed to the case, the joint mitered at the front. The backboard, made of two wide and one narrow horizontal boards lap-jointed, is nailed into rabbets on the top and sides of the case and nailed flush at the bottom. The legs are tenoned though the case and wedged from the top; the knee brackets are nailed in place. The drawers are dovetailed at the corners. The top of the drawer sides are shaped in an astragal; the backs are flat. The drawer bottoms, which run from side to side, join the front and sides with sliding dados and are nailed across the chamfered back. The drawer bottoms have applied battens.

**Condition:** The chest, which once had several layers of paint, has been stripped to reveal the maple surface. Remnants of the finish remain on the feet. The battens on all the drawer bottoms are repaired or replaced. Dressing boxes and a dressing glass once were attached to the top (not original). A front scroll adjacent to the right front leg bracket is broken off and lost. All the drawers had two sets of hardware; the two top drawers give evidence of three sets.

**Dimensions:**

| | | |
|---|---|---|
| H. | 38³/₄ in. | 98.4 cm |
| W. (top) | 40³/₄ in. | 103.5 cm |
| W. (case) | 37 in. | 94.0 cm |
| W. (knees) | 38¹/₂ in. | 97.2 cm |
| D. (top) | 20⁵/₈ in. | 52.4 cm |
| D. (case) | 19 in. | 48.2 cm |
| D. (knees) | 19¹/₂ in. | 49.5 cm |

**Materials:** *Microanalysis:* Primary: soft maple group; basswood (legs, knee brackets). Secondary: white pine group (drawer linings). *Finish:* clear, light yellowish brown resin over the refinished wood.

**Publications:** Alice Winchester, "The Dunlap Dilemma: Notes on Some New Hampshire Cabinetmakers," *Antiques* 46, no. 6 (December 1944): 338, fig. 7. *Dunlaps and Their Furniture*, fig. 54. Charles S. Parsons, "The Dunlaps of New Hampshire and Their Furniture," in John D. Morse, ed., *Country Cabinetwork and Simple City Furniture* (Charlottesville: University Press of Virginia for the Henry Francis du Pont Winterthur Museum, 1970), pp. 109–50. Zea and Dunlap, *Dunlap Cabinetmakers*, fig. 76.

**Accession history:** Purchased from Collings and Collings, New York, 1926. Bequest of H. F. du Pont, 1969.
56.523

---

1. *Dunlaps and Their Furniture*, pp. 8–9. Identification of the flowered ogee motif is taken from John Dunlap's plans for church pulpits constructed at Temple and Londonderry, N.H., in 1783; see pp. 45–52.

2. Charles S. Parsons, "More Dunlap" (Yale University Art Gallery Furniture Study, New Haven, 1976, typescript); Ward, *American Case Furniture*, cat. 64; Zea and Dunlap, *Dunlap Cabinetmakers*, pp. 28, 126.

3. *Dunlaps and Their Furniture*, pp. 4–6, 10–15, 35.

4. *Dunlaps and Their Furniture*, pp. 3–4, 6, 26 n. 60. Cabinetmakers Daniel Hodgkins, Moses Marshall, and Wilkes West resided in Chester in the late 1760s and early 1770s. Charles S. Parsons and David S. Brooke, "The Dunlap Cabinetmakers," *Antiques* 98, no. 2 (August 1970): 225.

5. *Dunlaps and Their Furniture*, pp. 6–7, 17–18, 35, 55–56.

## 188 ◆ Bureau table
Stratford, Connecticut
ca. 1720–30
Attributed to Samuel French (1687–1763)
or Thomas Salmon (1693–1749)

Tracing the dissemination of designs from England to eighteenth-century New England, conventional wisdom plots a path from London to Boston or New York and from there to other areas. This bureau table illustrates the fallacy of that assumption. Constructed of American black walnut with white pine and white cedar secondary woods, it has a history of eighteenth-century ownership in the Curtiss family of Stratford, Connecticut. Virtually indistinguishable from English case furniture of comparable date, its "English" conventions include a writing slide just under the top, thin drawer linings, glued-up boards with the grain perpendicular to the drawer front of the top drawer, and the use of black walnut (not native to the Stratford area) rather than readily available cherry.[1] Dating from the late 1710s or 1720s, it is one of the earliest American-made examples of the form surviving today.

Edward F. Cooke, Jr., and Robert F. Trent persuasively argue that this bureau table is the work of a provincially trained English joiner working in Stratford early in the eighteenth century because of the English characteristics described above. They propose Samuel French (1687–1763) or Thomas Salmon (1693–1749) as possible artisans attracted by the economic opportunities in the area. French, born in Bradford Abbas, Dorset, arrived in Boston in 1715 but moved to Stratford and was in business there by 1718. Salmon, the more prolific of the two, came to Connecticut directly from Wiltshire, England, and set up shop in Stratford in 1719. Over the next two decades, he and his apprentices produced case furniture and chairs that influenced the area for a generation.[2] A cherry chest-on-chest with very thin drawer sides and similar but slightly

less well-articulated feet made in Stratford about 1730–45 (see No. 192) also could have been made by Salmon.

*NER/CGN*

---

**Inscriptions or marks:** *Inside back long drawer:* script "3" horizontal or on side, in chalk. *Inside back left top small drawer:* script "T" in chalk. *Inside back left bottom small drawer:* "L" and "B" in chalk. *Inside back right top small drawer:* "R" in chalk. *Inside back right bottom small drawer:* "R" and "6" in chalk.

**Construction:** The two-board top has an overhanging thumbnail-molded front and side edges; the back edge is flush with the backboard. The top is attached to the sides on sliding half dovetails and is reinforced by plugged nails through the top. The back is a single horizontal board nailed to a rabbet in the sides. The blades, double-beaded on the edge, are let into the sides on grooves. The rails, backed with pine, extend almost the full depth of the case. The pull-out shelf, mitered on the front, is made of two boards joined by an internal tenon and

reinforced by a single butterfly patch. Both the blade (rail) supporting the shelf and the rail below the long drawer are reinforced with plugged screws through the sides. The recessed cabinet section, built as a self-contained box and slid into place, has one concave and one plain shelf. The arched door is two layers thick; a single panel backboard is attached to a framed panel door. The arched rail in front of the cabinet is glued to the case; a modern reinforcing nail has been added through the rail above. The one-piece bottom board is dovetailed to the sides; the join is reinforced on the underside by wide battens. The base molding is nailed to the front and sides; the piecing of the left side molding is original. The legs, tenoned into the case, are reinforced by heavy shaped knee brackets; there are no supplemental glueblocks. The drawer fronts, cut from solid wood, are flat on the inside. The upper edge of the drawer sides is rounded; the drawer backs are flat on the top. The drawer bottoms, with grain running front to back, are set into grooves on the front and sides and attached with rosehead nails across the back. Each of the small drawers has a lock inserted into the stock of the drawer front. Four of the small drawers have quarter-sawn sides; the other two are plain sawn.

**Condition:** The top has been reset, and the nails holding the top to the sides probably were added at that time. The rear board of the writing slide may be replaced. A spline has been inserted in the right side of the case to fill a split. The left side is cracked at the top front and a portion replaced at the top back. The backboard is split and has been renailed and a supplemental board added at the bottom. The left rear leg is cracked above the knee; the left front leg now is secured with a reinforcing screw. The toe on the right front foot has been reglued. The front of the long drawer has been pieced along the entire upper edge. The brass drawer handles are replacements; the small drawers once were fitted with center pulls. The lock on the cabinet door and one of the mushroom-shape pulls on the writing slide are replaced.

**Dimensions:**

| | | |
|---|---|---|
| H. | 31¼ in. | 79.4 cm |
| W. (top) | 34¾ in. | 88.2 cm |
| W. (case) | 30½ in. | 77.4 cm |
| W. (feet) | 33 in. | 83.8 cm |
| D. (top) | 20 in. | 50.8 cm |
| D. (case) | 18½ in. | 46.3 cm |
| D. (feet) | 20⅛ in. | 51.1 cm |

**Materials:** *Microanalysis:* Primary: American black walnut (top, sides, drawer fronts, front of writing slide). Secondary: white pine group (backboard, sides of long drawer); northern white cedar (drawer bottoms); yellow pine group (sides of small drawers, back of writing slide). *Finish:* natural resin.

**Publications:** John A. H. Sweeney, "New Rooms at Winterthur," *Antiques* 67, no. 2 (February 1955): 133. Edward S. Cooke, Jr., "Craftsman-Client Relations in the Housatonic Valley, 1720–1800," *Antiques* 125, no. 1 (January 1984): 272, fig. 1. Peter Arkell and Robert F. Trent, "A New American Bureau Table," *Maine Antique Digest* (October 1986), p. 36-C, fig. 11. Edward S. Cooke, Jr., "The Warland Chest: Early Georgian Furniture in Boston," *Maine Antique Digest* (March 1987), p. 13-C, fig. 14.

**Provenance:** Descended in the Curtiss family of Stratford, Conn.

**Accession history:** Purchased by H. F. du Pont from John S. Walton, Inc., New York, 1952. Gift of H. F. du Pont, 1952.
52.148

---

1. Edward S. Cooke, Jr., "Craftsman-Client Relations in the Housatonic Valley, 1720–1800," *Antiques* 125, no. 1 (January 1984): 272–80.

2. Cooke, "Craftsman-Client Relations." Robert F. Trent, "A New American Bureau Table," *Maine Antique Digest* (October 1986), p. 36-C. The Boston furniture industry in the early eighteenth century was not welcoming to outsiders; Edward S. Cooke, Jr., "The Warland Chest: Early Georgian Furniture in Boston," *Maine Antique Digest* (March 1987), p. 12-C. On Salmon, see Trent, *Hearts and Crowns*, pp. 39–42.

## 189 ◆ Bureau table
Massachusetts
1740–75

---

The form known as the bureau dressing table is an English invention, introduced early in the eighteenth century; it has no Continental prototype. Considered a piece of chamber furniture, it was intended as an alternative to the cabriole-leg dressing table. According to the dimensions recommended in Chippendale's *Director*, English bureau tables were comparatively small in size: thirty-two inches high, thirty-nine inches wide, and twenty-five inches deep. Many were rectilinear, favoring the straight facade shown in Chippendale's 1754 designs, and were offered by the Gillows firm of Lancaster, England, as late as the 1790s.[1]

One of the earliest references to a Boston-made bureau table is in a 1737 account between Boston cabinetmakers Nathaniel

Holmes and Richard Woodward in which Holmes paid Woodward £6 for making a bureau table. The precise form of Woodward's bureau table is unknown, but it probably was similar in appearance to a walnut bureau table at Gore Place (Waltham, Massachusetts) decorated with stringing and inlaid stars, ornament popular on Massachusetts furniture of the 1730s and 1740s. By the 1750s, bureau tables had become sufficiently well known that no description or explanation was included in newspaper advertisements:

> Made and sold by Thomas Sherburn, at his shop in Back Street, Boston; all sorts of Cabinet-Ware, in the neatest manner; such as Desks and Bookcases; Cases of Drawers, Buroe Tables, Chamber Tables, Dining Tables, Tea-Tables, Screens.[2]

Not content simply to copy English models, Boston cabinetmakers experimented with reshaping the front facade of the bureau table (and other case forms) with alternating concave and convex panels in a vertical pattern, a design known today as the "blockfront." This modern term is used to identify one type of shaping that, in the eighteenth century, was grouped with bombé, oxbow, and serpentine shapes under the imprecise term "swelled." Blocking appeared on New England furniture shortly after its introduction in England. The earliest documented piece of American block-facade furniture is a desk-and-bookcase made by Boston cabinetmakers Job Coit and Job Coit, Jr., dated 1738 (see No. 205). Over the next six decades, New England cabinetmakers experimented with blocked shaping. Massachusetts craftsmen developed two different styles: rounded blocking (of which a large number are known today), as seen here, and flat blocking, which appears more frequently on chests of drawers (see Nos. 177, 178). The rounded-block bureau table form, though common in Boston and preferred in New York, was not especially popular in other areas of New England where flat blocking was favored.[3] Massachusetts cabinetmakers also developed a proportional division of the facade in which the recessed area was broader than the relatively narrow drawer sections. Cabinetmakers in Rhode Island, where the bureau table form enjoyed great popularity, adopted another proportional arrangement in which the drawer sections were wider than the kneehole (see No. 190).

Throughout the eighteenth century, Massachusetts cabinetmakers continued to experiment, although their choice of materials, methods of case and drawer construction, foot types, and decorative and design motifs remained within a predictable range of design possibilities. The preferred primary wood for Massachusetts bureau tables was mahogany with white pine as the predominant secondary wood. Straight-bracket feet with shaped knee brackets are used on most bureau tables; other forms have ogee-bracket or carved ball-and-claw feet. Massachusetts case construction is readily identifiable. On the majority of low case forms, the top is secured to the upper edge of the case side on a sliding dovetail. The underside of the top is grooved to slide onto the case sides; occasionally there is a plug in the sliding dovetail to secure the join. There is no exterior molding below the top and no rail separating the top from the upper edge of the top drawer. Drawer blades are slotted into the case sides from the front and the join covered with a facing strip. Dovetails joining the fronts, sides, and backs of the

drawers tend to be coarse and somewhat irregular. Most drawers are supported within the case on narrow strips nailed to the case sides. Drawers generally run on the edge of the drawer side or on an applied batten.

The maker of this bureau table carefully selected matched mahogany panels for the fronts of the small drawers. His decision to use a 1 3/4-inch mahogany board for the top long drawer necessitated piecing the center section of the rounded blocking with a half-inch board, which may reflect economic considerations or the availability of materials. The side drawer fronts are cut from a 2 1/4-inch board, apparently the board width limit. The treatment of the cabinet door is an unusual departure from the standard arched field-panel and may be an example of the construction referred to as "a cupboard in the kneehole with a flat pannel'd door, on ovolo stuck on the framing the base moulding continued round under the door, £0.5.0." A frame in the kneehole to receive the door cost an extra 3s.; base price was £4.10.0.[4]

A number of similarly designed bureau tables, all fashioned in mahogany with shaped tops, shallow tray drawers above the cabinet, arched field-paneled cabinet doors, and straight-bracket feet with elaborately shaped knee brackets, share similar construction details. Included is a bureau table at the Museum of Fine Arts, Boston, that descended in the Amory family of Boston. Most of the rounded blockfront bureau tables with eighteenth-century histories can be traced to Massachusetts families—the Amorys of Boston, the Littles of Newburyport, the Metcalfs of Salem, and the Winslows of Plymouth. Newport lawyer and signer of the Declaration of Independence, William Ellery, also owned a Boston bureau table.[5]

The blockfront bureau table was an expensive piece of furniture to build. It was time-consuming and difficult to construct, as well as wasteful of expensive mahogany. These factors probably limited its sale to prosperous merchants, professional men, and men of affairs. On the rare occasions when the form is listed in a room-by-room inventory, it is always found in a chamber and is sometimes noted in proximity to a dressing glass.[6]

*NER/CGN*

---

Inscriptions or marks: *Long drawer, outside back:* "1" in chalk. *Upper left small drawer, outside back:* "O1" in chalk. *Upper left small drawer, inside bottom:* "5" in chalk. *Middle left small drawer, outside back:* "3" in chalk. *Lower left small drawer, outside back and inside:* "4" in chalk. *Upper right small drawer,*

inside bottom: "2" in chalk. *Middle right small drawer, outside back:* "6" in chalk. *Lower right small drawer, outside back:* "7" in chalk. *Lower right small drawer, right side:* script "T___".

**Construction:** The two-board top, conforming to the shape of the case, overlaps slightly on all sides and is molded on the front and side edges. It is attached to the two-board sides on sliding dovetails. The back is three horizontal, lapped boards nailed to rabbets in the sides. The rail below the long drawer extends the full depth of the case; it is slotted into the sides and has exposed ends. The blades between the drawers, cut with a double cock-bead, are dovetailed to the sides; the join is covered by a double-beaded facing strip. Above the central recess is a shallow sliding tray drawer; its front is cut from solid wood. It rides on a double-ogee–shape thin pine rail on the front edge. The inner surface of the front of the drawers conforms to the outer blocking. The convex blocking on the long drawer is pieced up on the outside; the blocking on the small drawers is cut from solid wood. The drawer sides are rounded on the top; the top of the drawer back is flat. The drawer bottoms, the grain running front to back, are nailed flush to the front, sides, and back. The cabinet door is a solid board, flat on the back and cut to simulate an arched field-panel on the front. The top and bottom rails surrounding the door are tenoned to stiles, which are nailed to cabinet walls. Two pine shelves behind the cabinet door are cut in a concave pattern on their fronts. The skirt molding attaches to the edges of the bottom board of the case and is reinforced with pine strips. The bracket feet are glued to the skirt; each foot is reinforced with a vertical glueblock butted to two horizontal blocks. The back bracket on the rear feet is cut on a diagonal. There is provision for a pin lock on the top drawer; similar locks for the top and middle small drawers are reached from inside the cabinet.

**Condition:** Splits in the top and case sides are repaired. The upper edge of the top drawer is split and the lock replaced. The bottom board of the sliding tray drawer is split. The right stile beside the prospect door is cracked. The lower right front of the prospect section is damaged from an iron gall ink spill. All feet have been repaired. The glueblocks on the rear brackets are replaced.

**Dimensions:**

| | | |
|---|---|---|
| H. | 31 1/2 in. | 80.0 cm |
| W. (top) | 34 3/16 in. | 87.0 cm |
| W. (feet) | 34 in. | 86.3 cm |
| D. (top) | 20 1/4 in. | 54.2 cm |
| D. (feet) | 18 15/16 in. | 48.0 cm |

**Materials:** *Microanalysis:* Primary: mahogany. Secondary: white pine group (throughout). *Finish:* natural resin.

**Publications:** Nancy A. Goyne, "The Bureau Table in America," in Milo M. Naeve, ed., *Winterthur Portfolio 3* (Winterthur, Del.: Henry Francis du Pont Winterthur Museum, 1967), fig. 5, p. 33.

**Accession history:** Purchased by H. F. du Pont from the Bonsal estate, 1955. Bequest of H. F. du Pont, 1969.
55.136.97

1. Thomas Chippendale, *The Gentleman and Cabinet-Maker's Director* (London: By the author, 1754), fig. 71a; Christopher Gilbert, *The Life and Work of Thomas Chippendale*, 2 vols. (New York: Macmillan Publishing Co., 1978), 2: figs. 415–17. Kirk, *American Furniture*, figs. 533–35.

2. Bourn Papers, Baker Library, Harvard University, as cited in Brock Jobe, "The Boston Furniture Industry, 1720–1740," in *Boston Furniture*, p. 20, see also fig. 18, p. 23; and Wendy A. Cooper, *In Praise of America: American Decorative Arts, 1650–1830/Fifty Years of Discovery since the 1929 Girl Scouts Loan Exhibition* (New York: Alfred A. Knopf, 1980), no. 233, p. 201 for the Gore Place bureau table. *Boston Gazette*, April 22, 1765, as quoted in Dow, *Arts and Crafts in New England*, p. 122.

3. This undulating form was inspired by European furniture articulated by Frenchman Jean Bérain; see Kirk, *American Furniture*, p. 127. Nancy A. Goyne, "The Bureau Table in America," in Milo M. Naeve, ed., *Winterthur Portfolio 3* (Winterthur, Del.: Henry Francis du Pont Winterthur Museum, 1967), pp. 32–33.

4. *Journeyman Cabinet and Chair-Makers Philadelphia Book of Prices*, 1795, Downs collection, p. 12.

5. On the Amory chest, see Hipkiss, *Eighteenth-Century American Arts*, no. 40. Brock Jobe and Myrna Kaye attributed the Amory chest to the shop of Benjamin Frothingham; see Jobe and Kaye, *New England Furniture*, p. 141. For the rest of the group of bureau tables, see Charles Woolsey Lyon advertisement, *Antiques* 59, no. 2 (February 1951): 85; R. Peter Mooz and Carolyn J. Weekly, "American Furniture at the Virginia Museum of Fine Arts," *Antiques* 113, no. 5 (May 1978): 1054; Israel Sack advertisement, *Antiques* 37, no. 6 (June 1940): 271; C. W. Lyon advertisement, *Antiques* 46, no. 1 (July 1944): 1; John S. Walton advertisement, *Antiques* 53, no. 3 (March 1948): 167; and *American Antiques from Israel Sack Collection*, 10 vols. (Washington, D.C.: Highland House, ca. 1969–), 3:764. For Ellery bureau table, see *American Antiques from Sack Collection*, 7:1796–97.

6. Inventories of Pryam Blowers (1739), John Phillips (1747), and William Clark (1760) as cited in Lyon, *Colonial Furniture*, pp. 131–32; also Goyne, "Bureau Table," pp. 35. Cummings, *Rural Household Inventories*, p. 201.

## 190 ◆ Bureau table
Newport, Rhode Island
1785–95
Attributed to John Townsend
(1733–1809)

The blockfront design capped with carved shells remains the most admired blockfront design. This form, developed by Newport craftsmen, added shell carving to the flat-blocked facade to create a unique design for which no direct English or Continental prototype is known. The Newport block-and-shell design was copied by Connecticut cabinetmakers, but the two interpretations differ sufficiently in choice of materials, method of construction, and quality of carving to admit no confusion.

The concept behind the blockfront design is three vertical panels: two convex outer panels separated by a concave panel. For Newport craftsmen, these projecting and receding surfaces lent themselves to the presentation of carved decoration. Nowhere is the integration of form and ornament handled more successfully than on the block-and-shell case furniture made in Newport from the 1760s to the 1790s. In the hands of the Townsends and the Goddards—the city's two most prominent cabinetmaking families—the resulting design was architectural in concept and sculptural in presentation.

The Newport bureau table was available in two basic designs. All have a long blockfront drawer with a concave shell flanked by two that are convex. Below this are two rows of three convex blocked drawers flanking a recessed cabinet. In one model, the cabinet door has a simple chamfered panel; in the other, the cabinet door has a concave block-and-shell motif. The latter form appears to have been preferred since more than half of the roughly fifty Newport bureau tables known are the four-shell variety, as shown here.

In Newport, mahogany was the primary wood of choice; secondary woods varied in combinations of chestnut, tulip-poplar, cedar, and white pine. The style and quality of the carving has been used as an important feature in identifying Newport furniture, but construction is a much more accurate criterion because it represents the "workmanship of certainty" rather than the "workmanship of risk."[1] One distinctive feature is the attachment of the top, which is secured to one or two wide cross braces running the full width of the case and dovetailed or mortised to the top of the sides. On Massachusetts examples, in contrast, a long, sliding dovetail joins the top and sides.

This bureau table is one of three examples that share distinctive decorative and construction details. They are identical in shell carving, profile of the cornice and base moldings, method of attaching the top, and construction and assembly of the feet. Even the brass hardware is identical. A fourth bureau table shares many of these characteristics but differs slightly in design and construction specifics, including a top held with screws and not keyed, as the others are, to battens; lack of the small spacer molding between the front legs found on the others; and fluting on the reserve of the cabinet shell instead of crosshatching.[2]

Only four documented Newport bureau tables are known: one labeled by and another signed by Edmund Townsend, one labeled by John Townsend, and an elaborately ornamented example signed by Daniel Goddard. Until recently, all Newport block-and-shell furniture not specifically labeled or inscribed generally was assigned to the Townsend-Goddard school. Patricia Kane, Morrison Heckscher, and Michael Moses, however, have provided a method for separating the work of individual craftsmen using the construction and decorative details of the four documented examples as keys.[3] Winterthur's bureau table conforms most closely to the decorative characteristics assigned to John Townsend's postrevolutionary work, including crosshatching on the center core of the central C scrolls within the shells, which end with buttonlike volutes; no ribs between the recesses between the lobes of the concave shells; a scratch-bead with scroll ends surrounding the entire concave shell; and an even number of lobes on the convex shells and an uneven number on the concave.

The applied moldings beneath the top's molded edge on Townsend case furniture, consisting of a narrow fillet, a cove, a bead, a fillet, and a cavetto molding, are architectural rather then structural and visually integrate the top with the case. The subtop, made up of two boards dovetailed to the sides, join the mahogany top board with two butterfly-shape dovetail keys, the bottom half hidden by the backboard. This is distinctive to Townsend's later work.[4] Blades supporting case-wide drawers are dovetailed to the case sides with exposed dovetails. Most examples are supported on ogee-bracket feet reinforced by shaped glueblocks that follow the contours of the bracket. In all but a few instances

(see No. 193), the convex shells are carved separately and applied. Blocking on the small drawers on Townsend bureau tables is always cut from solid wood.

Like their counterparts elsewhere in New England and the Middle Colonies, Newport bureau tables are included with chamber furnishings in probate inventories of the period, but precisely how this form functioned is unclear. The proportional spacing of the recessed kneehole is considerably narrower than on examples from other areas, making its comfortable use as a dressing table questionable. It may therefore have served as a chest of drawers with cabinet in Newport households.

*NER/CGN*

---

**Inscriptions or marks:** *On bottom rails, lower right and lower left:* partially legible early markings "A" and "B", respectively. Markings on the rails above are illegible.

**Construction:** The solid top board, which is ogee molded and overhangs the front and sides but is flush on the back, is keyed to battens across the back and front that are dovetailed to the top of the sides. Below the battens, three blocks are glued along the front; continuous glueblocks are nailed to the sides. An applied cove cornice molding is nailed to the case. An applied cock-bead is nailed to the underside of the top rail with rosehead nails. The top blade, backed with maple and attached to the sides on a long sliding dovetail, runs the full depth of the case. The rails between the small drawers are of solid wood. The rails have beaded edges around the drawers; the beading on the side boards is applied. The drawer fronts have a flat inner surface; the top edges of the sides are rounded; the bottoms overlap the sides and back and have applied battens. The projecting shells are applied on the top drawer; the grain of the drawer bottom runs side to side. The blocking on the small drawers is cut from solid wood; the grain of the drawer bottom runs front to back. The drawer runners are nailed to the sides and to the internal stiles forming the cabinet. Behind the recessed block-and-shell–carved solid cabinet door is a single plain medial shelf with rounded front edge. The bottom board is joined to the case sides with large, even dovetails with narrow throats. A deep rail from which the base molding is carved separates the drawer from the bottom of the case leaving an open space of more than an inch. The base molding is glued to the case. The bracket feet are glued to the bottom of the base molding; each front foot is reinforced with a shaped vertical glueblock flanked by horizontal blocks. The side of the rear legs projects beyond the back of the case. The rear feet have a shaped rear bracket attached on a sliding dovetail. Quarter-round moldings are applied between the front legs and on the sides; the molding below the recessed cabinet is a shaped continuous piece. The back is two lap-joined horizontal boards attached with wrought nails to rabbets in the sides.

**Condition:** All the legs are repaired at the ankle. Some of the original chestnut drawer runners are replaced with pine. Both sides of the case are

split. The bottom board of the shell-carved top drawer is split in two places. The brasses are original, but the plate on the middle right drawer has a portion missing. The brasses are attached in an unusual manner, with the posts treated as if they were nailed in.

**Dimensions:**

| | | |
|---|---|---|
| H. | 34½ in. | 87.8 cm |
| W. (top) | 36¾ in. | 93.4 cm |
| W. (feet) | 37½ in. | 95.5 cm |
| D. (top) | 20¼ in. | 51.3 cm |
| D. (feet) | 21 in. | 53.3 cm |

**Materials:** *Microanalysis:* Primary: mahogany. Secondary: chestnut (backboard, bottom board, front batten, side glueblocks for top); tulip-poplar (drawer linings); white pine group (walls of cabinet); hard maple group (backing on top blade); soft maple group (rear batten). *Finish:* natural resin in several shades of orangish brown.

**Exhibitions:** "Loan Exhibition of Eighteenth- and Early Nineteenth-Century Furniture and Glass," National Council of Girl Scouts, New York, September 25–October 9, 1929.

**Publications:** National Council of Girl Scouts, *Loan Exhibition of Eighteenth- and Early Nineteenth-Century Furniture and Glass* (New York: By the council, 1929), cat. 629. Downs, *American Furniture*, fig. 175. Wendell D. Garrett, "The Newport Cabinetmakers: A Corrected Checklist," *Antiques* 73, no. 6 (June 1958): 558–61. Helena Hayward, ed., *World Furniture: An Illustrated History* (New York: McGraw-Hill Book Co., 1965), fig. 712. John Kenworthy-Browne, "The Line of Beauty: The Rococo Style," in *The History of Furniture* (rev. ed., New York: Crescent Books, 1982), p. 137. Jay Cantor, *Winterthur* (New York: Harry N. Abrams for the Henry Francis du Pont Winterthur Museum, 1985), p. 143. Moses, *Master Craftsmen*, p. 161, fig. 3.84.

**Accession history:** Gift of H. F. du Pont, 1960. 59.2645

---

1. See David Pye, *The Nature and Art of Workmanship* (1968; 2d ed., Cambridge, Eng.: Cambridge University Press, 1982), p. 4.

2. For the 2 other examples, see Warren, *Bayou Bend*, no. 123; and Ward, *American Case Furniture*, cat. 109. See also Nutting, *Furniture Treasury*, no. 272; Morrison H. Heckscher, "John Townsend's Block-and-Shell Furniture," *Antiques* 121, no. 5 (May 1982): 1151, fig. 20. For the fourth, see John S. Walton advertisement, *Antiques* 110, no. 1 (July 1976): 4.

3. For the 4 documented bureau tables, see Hipkiss, *Eighteenth-Century American Arts*, no. 38; Moses, *Master Craftsmen*, pl. 5, figs. 3.59, 6.13; and *American Antiques from Israel Sack Collection*, 10 vols. (Washington, D.C.: Highland House, ca. 1969–), 3:792–93. Patricia Kane introduced her method of identifying the work of analysis in a workshop at Yale in May 1979. Heckscher, "John Townsend's Block-and-Shell Furniture," pp. 1144–52; Liza Moses and Michael Moses, "Authenticating John Townsend's Later Tables," *Antiques* 119, no. 5 (May 1982): 1130–43; Moses, *Master Craftsmen*, pp. 65–194.

4. Moses, *Master Craftsmen*, pp. 293–94; Margaretta Markle Lovell, "Boston Blockfront Furniture," in *Boston Furniture*, pp. 83–84, figs. 53, 54; Heckscher, "John Townsend's Block-and-Shell Furniture," pp. 1148–49.

## 191 ◆ Bureau table

Newport, Rhode Island
1785–95
Attributed to John Townsend
(1733–1809)

Despite subtle variations in carving and in the method of assembly, there is a remarkable uniformity in the overall appearance of the roughly fifty Newport bureau tables that are known today. Cabinetmakers in that city appear to have been less inclined to experiment with standard designs than were their counterparts in Massachusetts or Connecticut. Perhaps this is a result of the family interrelationships of the three generations of Goddards and Townsends working in close proximity to one another. Or it may indicate a sharing of patterns and templates within the city's cabinetmaking community.

One notable exception is this rare, and possibly unique, bureau table. It is a cross between the traditional kneehole bureau table and a chest with cabinet. Close reference to standard design is evident in the blocking on the recessed panel that continues through the bottom rail and the rail itself that is constructed in three pieces as it would be if the bureau table had the center legs required for a recessed cabinet. The shell design and carving and the construction details of the top, cornice molding, and legs match those on chests by John Townsend dated 1790 and 1792 and provide the basis for the attribution. A diminutive document cabinet at Chipstone Foundation, signed in pencil by John Townsend, also has a concave cabinet door flush with the convex drawers. Earlier in date, it differs in proportion (it is taller than it is wide), has a plain board top dovetailed to the sides, a carved shell based on the fleur-de-lis, and bun feet.[1]

Townsend probably thought of the "bureau" of this entry as a chest of drawers with cabinet. One clue is in the division of space across the facade. Instead of two wide sections separated by a narrow one, the panels are relatively equal in size, the same treatment used on standard Newport blockfront chests of drawers (see No. 180).

*NER/CGN*

---

**Inscriptions or marks:** *Brand, left top drawer on inner right side:* "IV". *Brand, left middle drawer on inside bottom:* small "V". *Brand, left bottom drawer on inside bottom:* large "X". *Brand, right middle drawer on inside bottom:* "X". *Brand, right bottom drawer on inside bottom:* small "V". *Scratched on top backboard:* "B" and "W".

**Construction:** The solid board top, ogee molded on the front and sides and flat on the back, overhangs the back slightly. It is attached with wooden dovetail keys to front and back battens, which, in turn, are dovetailed to the top of the sides. Below the front batten are three long glueblocks; an original, single, continuous glueblock at the sides is now missing. An applied cove cornice molding is glued to the case. An applied bead is nailed to the underside of the top rail. The full-depth drawer divider below the long drawer is a mahogany blade backed with chestnut and is joined to the case sides on sliding dovetails and nailed to the top of the internal stiles. The rails below the small drawers are solid wood. All the rails have beaded edges; the beading on the sides of the drawer openings is applied. On the drawers, the carved, projecting twelve-lobe shells are applied, and the blocked drawers are cut from solid wood; the drawer fronts have flat inner faces; the dovetail pins are small and closely spaced; the top edge of the drawer sides is rounded. The drawer bottoms, chamfered all around, overlap the sides and back and have applied battens. On the top drawer, the grain of the bottom board runs side to side; on the other drawers, it runs front to back. The drawer runners are nailed to the sides and to the internal stiles forming the walls of the cabinet. The concave cabinet door is cut from solid wood. Behind the door are two straight, fixed, mahogany shelves backed with tulip-poplar. A board has been inserted in the bottom of the cabinet section bringing it level with the top of the bottom rail. The base molding is attached to the front edge of the bottom board; it is nailed over the dovetailed lower edge of the sides. The bracket feet are glued to the bottom of the base molding and reinforced with shaped vertical blocks flanked by horizontal blocks. The side brackets on the rear legs project beyond the back of the case. The back bracket on the rear legs is cut in an ogee shape and is butted to the side bracket; the joint is reinforced with glueblocks. The back is two horizontal boards: the top board is cut for a lap join, the lower board is butt. Both boards are nailed to rabbets in the sides, the top with cut nails and the bottom with rosehead nails.

**Condition:** The cabinet door has been reinforced with keyed wooden braces at the top and bottom; a third brace reinforces the repair to the upper hinge. The drawer bottoms on the small drawers have been reset. There is worm damage on the right top drawer and the large drawer bottom, which is also split. The upper section of the backboard is replaced, and the lower portion is cracked. The continuous glueblocks under the top are replaced as is the outside drawer runner on the lower right small drawer. The "roses and bail" pulls are original. Both rear feet are repaired.

**Dimensions:**

| | | |
|---|---|---|
| H. | 33 1/2 in. | 85.2 cm |
| W. (top) | 36 5/8 in. | 93.0 cm |
| W. (feet) | 38 in. | 96.5 cm |
| D. (top) | 19 in. | 48.5 cm |
| D. (feet) | 20 in. | 51.0 cm |

**Materials:** *Microanalysis:* Primary: mahogany. Secondary: tulip-poplar (drawer linings, battens supporting top, internal stiles); chestnut (top blade, bottom board, glueblocks on feet); white pine group (backboards). *Finish:* natural resin.

**Exhibitions:** "Loan Exhibition of Eighteenth- and Early Nineteenth-Century Furniture and Glass," National Council of Girl Scouts, New York, September 25–October 9, 1929.

**Publications:** National Council of Girl Scouts, *Loan Exhibition of Eighteenth- and Early Nineteenth-Century Furniture and Glass* (New York: By the council, 1929), cat. 607. Downs, *American Furniture,* cat. 176. Morrison H. Heckscher, "John Townsend's Block-and-Shell Furniture," *Antiques* 121, no. 5 (May 1982): 1151, fig. 21. William S. Ayres, "Contrasts: Philadelphia and Newport Furniture Styles, 1755–1780," in *Delaware Antiques Show 1982* (Wilmington, Del.), p. 67, fig. 7. Moses, *Master Craftsmen,* p. 161, fig. 3.82.

**Accession history:** Purchased by H. F. du Pont from Israel Sack, Boston, 1928. Gift of H. F. du Pont, 1958.
58.2139

---

1. Morrison Heckscher considers this bureau an example of Townsend's postwar production and has dated it ca. 1790; "John Townsend's Block-and-Shell Furniture," *Antiques* 121, no. 5 (May 1982): 1151.

## 192 ◆ Chest-on-chest
### Connecticut, probably Stratford
### 1730–50

This chest-on-chest has been identified by Edward S. Cooke, Jr., as a product of the same shop that produced the bureau table in No. 188. The distinctive square, ribbed feet with prominent center toes are similar, the brackets are related (fig. 1), and the dovetail pattern of the drawers with a characteristic horizontal base to the bottom dovetail is the same. Structural and ornamental details and choice of materials in the two chests indicate that the craftsman, who settled in southern coastal Connecticut at the mouth of the Housatonic River in the early eighteenth century, was an immigrant Englishman. Several artisan candidates have emerged from contemporary records, and later examples of furniture influenced by this shop have been identified with craftsmen in Stratford and the Housatonic River valley.[1]

After constructing the bureau table in black walnut, the traditional choice for furniture among English craftsmen and their patrons in the early eighteenth century, the immigrant artisan or his customer selected cherrywood, the regional preference in cabinetwork, for this chest-on-chest. Stock used for the drawer linings was also increased in thickness from that used in the bureau table. The form itself, a chest on top of a chest of drawers, was uncommon in American cabinetwork before the mid eighteenth century. Among the few known are this example and one made in Boston a few years earlier (probably for a member of the Warland family) by another émigré English craftsman of more sophisticated skills. The craftsman's English background is also evident in several decorative features, including the recessed

inlaid ornament centered at the bottom of the chest. Rare in American work before the 1740s and even then uncommon, the rayed device in a coved arch was used in England on the chest-on-chest and other tall case forms, usually in company with a handsome burlwood facade or at the least one with string inlay outlining the drawer fronts, as here. The molding at the bottom of these chests has a deep vertical profile. Before midcentury, other craftsmen, principally a small group in the Boston area, introduced a recessed ornament of inlaid, gilded, or carved form to the facades of several dressing tables and to the upper cases of a few elegant desk-and-bookcases. This decorative device remained in use in Stratford into the late eighteenth century and from there was carried inland via the Housatonic River valley to Woodbury.[2]

The canted chest corner accented by a fluted pilaster is another English feature transferred to Stratford. The same feature

**Fig. 1.** Detail, right front foot.

appears on the Warland chest made a few years earlier by an immigrant craftsman in Boston. As interpreted in the Stratford chest, the diagonal terminals of the pilaster at the case top and base are unusual.

The inlaid ornament of the scrollboard, in a combination of light and dark wood, is frequently referred to as a sunburst or as starlike. The inlay at the base of the chest is comparable. These devices likely derived from nautical use—the familiar compass rose found on maps. The feature appears on English furniture from at least the seventeenth century and is said to be of Dutch origin. Considering its nautical roots, the motif likely had no single point of origin in Europe and came into use in various locations independently when inlay became a fashionable surface embellishment, although it may have been interpreted earlier in paint.[3]

The chip-carved rosette in the top drawer of this chest is somewhat inconsistent with the inlaid decoration, although the combination is not unique in Connecticut cabinetmaking. No exact mate for the carved motif has been located, but comparable ornaments abound in regional work of slightly later date. Closest in design are the pediment rosettes in a high chest also ascribed to the lower Housatonic River valley. In introducing this ornament to the chest-on-chest, the transplanted English artisan drew again on his own background: rosettes are common in the seventeenth-century English carved furniture that would have been familiar to him. The decorative antecedents are found in Continental work of the previous century.[4]

Another notable feature of this chest is the construction of the recessed ornament in the base. The dark-shaded lunette of the central area marks the point where a small slab of wood was added to the back of the

**Fig. 2.** Detail, lower drawer interior.

drawer face to provide sufficient depth to accommodate the ornament. Inside the drawer, the rounded block of wood, which is nailed to the drawer front, intrudes somewhat on the storage space (fig. 2). At the top of the case the considerable height and steep ramp of the pediment, which balance the arch of the base ornament, are modified by the introduction of a subtle flare to the lower ends of the molding, a feature found on other Connecticut tall chests.

In an era when household closets were a rarity, chests of all sizes were essential storage units. The chest-on-chest represented the maximum use of household space because two stacked cases doubled the capacity of the chest without requiring additional floor space. Clothing, bedding, and miscellaneous textiles were commonly stored in these chests. An advantage of the chest of drawers over the lidded chest was its front access and the ability to better organize the contents to minimize rummaging. Although the tall case was a space saver, its height was sometimes a drawback. As late as 1808 George Smith commented in *Household Furniture* about the "disagreeable" task of "getting onto chairs to place anything in the upper drawers." Several decades earlier, when Mary Kenyon of London wrote to her mother describing the family's new house in Lincoln's Inn Fields, she remarked on the new

chest-on-chest in her bedroom: "so high that I must have a step-ladder to look into the five top drawers."[5]

Due to size, the tall case of drawers was an expensive piece of furniture, and the cost was increased when the case was embellished with fashionable ornament, as seen in this example. Clearly, this chest was meant to be seen. Probably installed in a chamber, most likely the best one, or the hall if the house was of suitable size, this chest would not have gone unnoticed. Overnight stays during visits by friends and members of the extended family were not uncommon, and even strangers were sometimes accommodated overnight when they could not obtain lodging at a local inn.

*NGE*

---

**Inscription or marks:** *Stenciled on upper case backboard and lower case top board:* "d8714". *On top drawer blade upper case, left, center, right:* "I", "II", *and* "III", *respectively, in black crayon. On outside drawer bottom, left, center, and right small drawers:* "III", "II", "III", *respectively, in black crayon. On long drawers, upper case:* modern numbers in pencil. *On lower case, underside of drawer, top, second, third, bottom:* "I", "II", "III", "IV" *respectively, in black crayon. Incised on back of third drawer, lower case:* "X".

**Construction:** (Upper case) The pediment is enclosed except at the center. An elaborate cornice

molding is nailed to the scrollboard and case sides. The scrollboard and case sides are secured at the front by lap joints. The vertical plinth at the center of the scrollboard is capped by a flat tablet that supports the finial. A complex molding following the top of the upper row of drawers is pegged to the scrollboard. The center top drawer is supported by two short vertical dividers at the front and horizontal rails from front to back at the upper and lower drawer level, each side. The long top drawer blade, with its attached dust board running the full depth of the case, slots into the case sides and at the front secures the dovetails of the stiles supporting the center top drawer. The other blades, made of primary wood only, are laid into grooves in the case sides. Drawer guides/runners are nailed to the case sides above the blades of the long drawers and near the base. The case bottom is reinforced with broad framing rails at the front and sides. The fluted pilasters, angled on the facade, are pegged in place. The two-board sides are joined to the bottom board, probably with dovetails. The backboard is a shaped horizontal board above four vertical boards. The upper board laps over the case sides; the lower boards (not original) are set into rabbets in the case sides and nailed. A waist molding is pegged to the lower edge of the case.

(Lower case) A second waist molding is pegged to the upper edge of the case. The two-piece top and bottom boards are dovetailed to two-board case sides; the joint at the bottom is covered by wide framing battens secured with rosehead nails, which abut a framing member across the front similarly secured. The drawer blades, runners, and pilasters are framed as in the upper case. The lowest drawer is built up on the interior with an applied rounded piece of wood to form the inner part of the concave fan; the bottom board is concave at the center of the leading edge. The front base molding and the blocking behind it are cut in three pieces to follow the shape of the bottom drawer; the base and side moldings are applied with pegs. The legs are tenoned into the case; the shaped, one-piece knee brackets are glued in place. The rear legs are positioned so that the outer edge of the knee is even with the backboard. The backboard is formed of four vertical boards set in side rabbets and nailed on four sides. The drawers are dovetailed at the corners. The thumbnail edges overlap the case facade only on the top edge. The drawer sides are rounded on the top; the top of the drawer back is flat; there is some evidence of a narrow chamfer at the edges. The drawer bottoms are chamfered on three sides, set into dados in the front and sides, and secured across the back with rosehead nails. In the small drawers, the bottom boards run from front to back; in the long drawers the grain runs from side to side. The long drawer bottoms are made of two boards. The inlays are composed of light and dark wood. The stringing on the drawers consists of a dark string flanked by light strings.

**Condition:** (Upper case) The finial is old but probably not original to this case. The enclosed part of the pediment has several replaced boards. The cornice molding is split in several places; there are patches on both the left and right front corners. The lower half of the right side cornice molding at the back is a replacement; the right center cornice return has been reattached and a small piece of wood is missing at the bottom. All the drawer runners, now nailed to the case sides, have been repaired to compensate for wear. Those for the outer small drawers are ramped, rising from front to back to compensate for torque in the case. On the top long drawer, the upper portion of the back and the lower portion of the left side are pieced out; the upper left front corner is patched. Second long drawer: the back dovetails have been reglued; the drawer sides have been pieced out at the bottom. Third long drawer: the sides have been pieced out and the back corners reglued. The boards on both

sides of the case have separated along the glue joint; there are small splits on the upper left side and on the lower right side. The vertical sections of the backboard are replaced. The back section of the case bottom board has been replaced because of insect damage. The side framing rails are also damaged (right) and missing a piece (left).

(Lower case) All the drawer runners have been augmented with thin facing strips. The top drawer has worm damage; the upper left front corners of the other drawers have been repaired. All the feet are cracked, and there are repairs at the inside leg posts. There is considerable insect damage to the legs and brackets; all the knee brackets have been reglued. The front base molding is split on the right side; there is a new facing piece behind the left front molding. The backboard has been reattached. The runners on the drawer bottoms have been augmented. The drawers of both cases have been repaired at the joints, and all have a surface coating on the interior. All the long drawers have unexplained wrought nail holes surrounded by black iron stain in the drawer backs. The backs do not appear to be replaced, aside from the obvious repairs. Some of the hardware is replaced. The case surfaces have been refinished.

**Dimensions:**

| | | |
|---|---|---|
| H. (case) | 86 1/2 in. | 219.1 cm |
| W. (cornice) | 40 1/8 in. | 101.9 cm |
| W. (upper case) | 36 1/4 in. | 92.1 cm |
| W. (lower case) | 39 1/4 in. | 99.7 cm |
| W. (feet) | 42 1/4 in. | 107.3 cm |
| D. (cornice) | 21 3/4 in. | 55.2 cm |
| D. (upper case) | 19 1/2 in. | 49.5 cm |
| D. (lower case) | 21 1/4 in. | 54.0 cm |
| D. (feet) | 23 1/8 in. | 58.7 cm |

**Materials:** *Microanalysis:* Primary: cherry. Secondary: butternut (pediment top, top section of backboard in upper case, drawer sides and bottoms, lower case backboard); white pine group (vertical backboards in upper case); sweet gum (support for cornice return, upper case bottom board, lower case top and bottom boards); yellow poplar (drawer backs); birch (front and rear leg brackets). *Finish:* mottled orange-brown resin.

**Publications:** Downs, *American Furniture*, fig. 179. Edward S. Cooke, Jr., "Craftsman-Client Relations

in the Housatonic Valley, 1720–1800," *Antiques* 125, no. 1 (January 1984): 273. Edward S. Cooke, Jr., "The Wayland Chest: Early Georgian Furniture in Boston," *Maine Antique Digest*, March 1987, p. 13-C, fig. 15. Kirk, *American Furniture*, fig. 636.

**Provenance:** Ex coll.: Wallace Nutting, Framingham, Mass. Ex coll.: Gale H. Carter, Old Greenwich, Conn.

**Accession history:** Purchased by H. F. du Pont from Gale H. Carter, Old Greenwich, Conn., 1946. Bequest of H. F. du Pont, 1969.
58.1742

1. Edward S. Cooke, Jr., "Craftsman-Client Relations in the Housatonic Valley, 1720–1800," *Antiques* 125, no. 1 (January 1984): 272–80; Edward S. Cooke, Jr., "The Work of Brewster Dayton and Ebenezer Hubbell of Stratford, Connecticut," *Connecticut Historical Society Bulletin* 51, no. 4 (Fall 1986): 196–224. Edward S. Cooke, Jr., *Fiddlebacks and Crooked-backs: Elijah Booth and Other Joiners in Newtown and Woodbury, 1750–1820* (Waterbury, Conn.: Mattatuck Historical Society, 1982), pp. 57, 65, 68–78, 83, see also figs. 25, 27 with square-headed pediments that imitate stylistically the molded figure above the top drawers in Winterthur's chest.

2. Edward S. Cooke, Jr., "The Warland Chest: Early Georgian Furniture in Boston," *Maine Antique Digest*, March 1987. English prototypes for the recessed, rayed ornament of the chest base are in Macquoid and Edwards, *Dictionary*, 1:140, 2: fig. 36; Kirk, *American Furniture*, fig. 625. Examples of dressing tables with recessed ornament are in *American Antiques from Israel Sack Collection*, 10 vols. (Washington, D.C.: Highland House, 1969–), 4:959, 7:1834, 1197. Examples of desk-and-bookcases with recessed ornament are in Miller, "Roman Gusto," pp. 165, 168–69, 173, 177, 186, 191, 194–97.

3. For English furniture with inlaid adaptations of the compass rose, see Macquoid and Edwards, *Dictionary*, 1:139, fig. 37, p. 172, fig. 18, 2:17, 3:242, fig. 4.

4. For Housatonic River valley high chest with pediment rosettes, see Jobe and Kaye, *New England Furniture*, no. 41. For English and European rosettes, see Macquoid and Edwards, *Dictionary*, 2:17, fig. 27; p. 18, fig. 34; p. 154, fig. 2; p. 191, fig. 4; pl. 8. Kirk, *American Furniture*, figs. 198, 199, 221–26, 285, 436, 440, 585.

5. Benno M. Forman, "The Chest of Drawers in America, 1635–1730," *Winterthur Portfolio* 20, no. 1 (Spring 1985): 16, 25; Ward, *American Case Furniture*, pp. 343–44; Macquoid and Edwards, *Dictionary*, 2:41, 45.

## 193 ◆ Chest-on-chest
Rhode Island, possibly Providence
1760–85

This extraordinary blockfront, shell-carved chest-on-chest first came to public attention with its publication in the inaugural issue of *The Magazine Antiques* (January 1922). Illustrated in a column called "Little Known Masterpieces," the chest was described as "one of the best . . . block-front pieces of the Rhode Island type." One of six known Rhode Island blockfront double chests, it is taller than most and is the only one to have a row of inverted shells at the base of the upper case. Its majestic height and the vertical emphasis of the facade also link it to a group of ten blockfront, shell-carved desk-and-bookcases that tower even higher.[1]

The unusual boxed pediment of this chest-on-chest relates directly to a similar feature in two casepieces made for members of the Brown family, prominent Providence merchants. The closest parallel is the nine-shell desk-and-bookcase made for Joseph Brown (1733–85) shortly after his marriage to Elizabeth Powers in 1759. Also related is a four-shell chest-on-chest, which by tradition was owned originally by John Brown, Joseph's younger brother. Winterthur's chest-on-chest has an unconfirmed oral history of ownership by Joseph Brown's daughter, Eliza (Elizabeth) Ward, wife of Richard Ward (1765–1800), a New York merchant, and perhaps was owned earlier by Brown himself.[2]

In addition to their boxed pediments and Brown family connection, these three pieces of furniture share several other design and construction features, including the profiles of the cornice and base moldings, the shape of the feet, especially the tiny and unusual astragals of the brackets (fig. 1), and particularly the design and execution of the carved shells (fig. 2). Unlike most shell carving on Rhode Island blocked furniture, the raised ornaments are cut from solid wood rather than applied. The shells, which are distinctive, are carved in several relief planes; those on the raised surfaces appear to be recessed in hollow arches. Variation in the dimensions, number of rays, and petal centers of the shells is a result of differences in the form and structure of the three pieces of furniture, but the character of the work is similar. The design of the drawer fronts also sets these cases apart from the rest: all the drawers are lipped to butt against the case, whereas those in the other chests and desks slide into beaded openings and are flush with the case facade.[3]

The bold, carved rosettes terminating the pediment scrolls on this tall chest (fig. 3) appear on three other blockfront chests-on-chests and four desk-and-bookcases. Two basic patterns are represented. A small eight-petal floret within a larger eight-petal floret, with a bead at the center, is the ornament of six tall cases. The rosettes in the Winterthur chest and the Joseph Brown desk-and-bookcase (both cases constructed with boxed pediments) are carved in a different though related pattern: an outer circle of beadlike petals encloses a daisylike flower with a nub center. The petal count drops from sixteen in Winterthur's chest to twelve in the Brown desk, and the center nub of the latter is scored like a melon. The second boxed-pediment chest-on-chest has no rosettes.[4]

The original brass hardware on Winterthur's chest is unique within the two groups of blockfront furniture. Pierced brasses of this type were offered in English trade catalogues of the 1770s and 1780s. With one exception, the brasses on the other cases have solid, cusped plates—a chest with post-and-bail handles also varies substantially from others in having a pitched pediment. The finials of Winterthur's chest are replacements, but they obviously were copied from an

**Fig. 1.** Detail, left front foot.

appropriate model sometime after the chest was pictured in a 1941 advertisement.[5]

The three casepieces with boxed pediments, including this one, traditionally have been assigned to the Townsend-Goddard school of cabinetmaking in Newport. The attribution must be reassessed, however, in light of the major variations from documented Goddard and Townsend furniture that occur in design and construction: shells worked from solid wood, boxed pediments, astragal foot brackets, lipped drawers, and an atypical interior in the Joseph Brown desk-and-bookcase. The thesis that the furniture is the work of another Newport cabinetmaker or an as-yet-unidentified Providence craftsman appears to have validity. A plain fall-front desk with astragal foot brackets was made and dated in 1785 by Providence cabinetmaker John Carlile, Jr., and a tall case clock with similar supports has a dial inscribed "Spaulding, Providence." Caleb Wheaton and Edward Spaulding of Providence signed movements fitted in cases with boxed pediments. Some of the owners were also known residents of Providence.[6]

Who were the people who originally purchased the costly and pretentious blockfront shell-carved chests-on-chests and desk-and-bookcases that relate to the tall case at Winterthur? Three of the four wealthy Brown brothers—John, Joseph, and

Nicholas—merchants of Providence, owned seven of the sixteen pieces of furniture. Another chest in the group and a tall case clock with boxed pediment were handed down in the family of Jabez Bowen of Providence, a first cousin by marriage of the Brown brothers. Clearly, in the late eighteenth century a small group of Rhode Islanders whose members stood at the top of the economic ladder and possibly all resided in Providence was able to commission furniture of commanding size and select design because money was no object and a skilled craftsman or craftsmen existed who could meet the groups' expectations.[7]

*NER/NGE*

**Inscriptions or marks:** *On underside of upper case:* "Bottom/ xx" in chalk. *On underside of lower case:* "Bottom" in chalk. *Incised on right side of bonnet top:* "XI" or "IX". *On all blades in both cases:* sequential numbering from bottom to top, in chalk. *On all blades in both cases:* sequential numbering from top to bottom, in pencil. *On most drawer bottoms, backs, and/or sides:* various arabic numbers and roman numerals in chalk, pencil, or incised mark. *On outside bottom of top long drawer in lower case:* a sketch of the back of a shield-back federal-style chair depicting four slim, spaced banisters springing from a lunette at the shield base, in white chalk. (It has been suggested that the drawing is contemporary with the construction of the chest, but there is no way of knowing this. The sketch could just as easily have been placed there by a later repairer who found

**Fig. 2.** Detail, chest midsection.

the flat drawer surface a convenient drawing board. Also to be raised is the question of why the chair's original owner would have paid a substantial sum for an old-fashioned Georgian chest, undoubtedly destined for one of the best rooms in the house, and then introduced chairs of a currently fashionable but unrelated pattern.)

**Construction:** (Upper case) The front scrollboard and case sides extend above the elaborate pediment molding, which is nailed to their surfaces creating the illusion of a box pediment. The enclosed bonnet is nailed to a rabbet in the scrollboard and to the upper backboard. The edges of the top boards of the boxes are finished with an applied molding. The circular openings of the scrollboard flanking the central plinth are finished with a face molding. The fluted plinth is reinforced on the back by a long vertical block. The rosettes are carved from solid wood and appear to be one piece with the pediment molding. Inside the case behind the pediment there are vertical glueblocks at each corner and on either side of the central top drawer; the blocks flanking the central drawer are also attached with rosehead nails. Thin vertical partitions frame the front opening for the center top drawer, secured with dovetails and nails. The drawer blades are joined to the one-piece sides on a sliding dovetail, the joints covered by a plain facing strip. The top blade is butted by a thin dust board; the others have a 6" pine backing. Behind the blades, thin runners are nailed to the sides of the case. The backboard consists of three horizontal boards, the lower two chamfered and rabbeted together. The entire back unit is rabbeted to the

case sides. The two-piece bottom board is dovetailed to the sides and reinforced with framing battens on the bottom. A waist molding is nailed to the lower edge of the case.

(Lower case) A second, complex, waist molding is nailed to the upper edge of the case. The top and bottom boards are dovetailed to the sides. The rails and blades are dovetailed to the case sides, the joints covered by plain facing strips. Internal runners are nailed to the sides of the case (reversed because of wear). The two lapped horizontal boards of the backboard are rabbeted to the case sides and attached with rosehead nails. The bottom molding is nailed to the case. The blocked-ogee front foot facings and brackets are mitered at the corners and glued to vertical support blocks chamfered on the inside. Shaped horizontal glueblocks parallel the front and side brackets. At the back, an ogee-shape bracket is glued to a vertical support block; both the bracket and the rear ogee-curved foot panel are held by a series of horizontal glueblocks. The drawer fronts are lipped and beaded all around. The shells and blocking are formed from solid wood; the area behind the projecting shells is hollowed out to reduce the weight of the drawer. The drawer sides are flat on the upper edge; the backs are chamfered slightly. The dovetails joining the drawer sides to the front and back have unusually thin throats. The drawer bottoms, the grain running front to back, are rabbeted to the sides, nailed front and back, and further secured by battens. The elaborate pierced hardware is original.

**Condition:** All the finials are replaced. There is a long split across the neck of the scrollboard that

extends into the right side box. The scrollboard is pieced above the center shell drawer (which may be part of the original construction). The scrollboard is bowed out of plumb. The left divider between the small drawers, which is ¼" shy of reaching the top corner and is held with a modern nail, may be a replacement. Some of the drawer runners have been reversed and are renailed to the sides. Reinforcing battens have been added to several drawers. The lips on several drawers are patched. The left front foot is cracked at the side and repaired; the side volute is pieced out. The glueblocks on the underside of the lower case have been reset and some are nailed as well. The carrying handles on the case sides are not original. The surface is refinished.

**Dimensions:**

| | | |
|---|---|---|
| H. (case to scroll top) | 91 in. | 231.0 cm |
| W. (cornice) | 40³⁄₈ in. | 102.7 cm |
| W. (upper case) | 35⁷⁄₈ in. | 91.1 cm |
| W. (lower case) | 37¹⁄₂ in. | 95.2 cm |
| W. (feet) | 40¹⁄₄ in. | 102.3 cm |
| D. (cornice) | 22 in. | 55.8 cm |
| D. (upper case) | 19¹⁄₂ in. | 49.7 cm |
| D. (lower case) | 20¹⁄₈ in. | 51.1 cm |
| D. (feet) | 21⁵⁄₈ in. | 54.9 cm |

**Materials:** *Microanalysis:* Primary: mahogany. Secondary: chestnut (bonnet boards, drawer linings, backboards in lower case and two lower backboards in upper case); white pine group (top backboard upper case, top board lower case, backing on blades, drawer battens, interior glueblocks). *Finish:* medium reddish brown color, somewhat variegated, in resin.

**Fig. 3.** Detail, pediment.

**Exhibitions:** On loan to the Museum of Art, Rhode Island School of Design, Providence, 1939–43, by the last private owner.

**Publications:** "Little Known Masterpieces," *Antiques* 1, no. 1 (January 1922): 17–18. Lockwood, *Colonial Furniture*, 1:353. William B. Spooner, Jr., advertisement, *Antiques* 40, no. 3 (September 1941): 131. David Robb, *Art in the Western World* (rev. ed., New York: Harper and Brothers, 1963), p. 710. Alice Winchester, "Perspective," *Antiques* 51, no. 1 (January 1972): 148. Doreen Beck, *Book of American Furniture* (London: Hamlyn Publishing Group, 1973), p. 56, fig. 62. Butler, *American Furniture*, p. 50. David Stockwell, "American Blockfront Furniture," *America in Britain* 9, no. 2 (May 1971): 15. Julia Raynsford, *The Story of Furniture* (London: Hamlyn Publishing Group, 1975), p. 78. Lanto Synge, *Furniture in Color* (Poole, Eng.: Blandford Press, 1977), p. 132, fig. 56. Henry Hawley, "Two Newport Chests-on-Chests," *Bulletin of the Cleveland Museum of Art* 65 (October 1977): 278. Victoria Kloss Ball, *Architecture and Interior Design: Europe and America from the Colonial Era to Today* (New York: John Wiley and Sons, 1979), p. 218, fig. 5.43. Robert Bishop and Patricia Coblentz, *American Decorative Arts: Three Hundred Sixty Years of Creative Design* (New York: Harry N. Abrams, 1982), p. 107, pl. 121. John Cordor, *The Museologist* 155 (Winter 1981): cover. William S. Ayres, "Contrasts: Philadelphia and Newport Furniture Styles, 1755–1780," in *Delaware Antiques Show 1982* (Wilmington, Del.), p. 69, fig. 9. Moses, *Master Craftsmen*, p. 35, fig. 1.18. Jay E. Cantor, *Winterthur* (New York: Harry N. Abrams, 1985), p. 148.

Fitzgerald, *Three Centuries*, p. 75, figs. IV-49, IV-50. Nutting, *Furniture Treasury*, no. 317.

**Provenance:** Ex coll.: Mrs. Henry W. Burnett, Providence (pre-1922). Ex coll.: Mrs. John R. Gladding, Providence and East Thompson, Conn. (1922–39). At Mrs. Gladding's death in 1939 the chest-on-chest was inherited by Mrs. Burnett, a relative. That year it was offered to H. F. du Pont by Miss Ella M. Boult, a Pomfret, Conn., dealer acting as agent for Mrs. Burnett. According to a letter from Miss Boult, Mrs. Gladding had purchased the chest-on-chest and other items from "a Mrs. Burnett, who had inherited them. With a generous justice characteristic of Mrs. Gladding, she returned them in her will to Mrs. Burnett" (Ella M. Boult to H. F. du Pont, August 28, 1939, Winterthur Archives).

**Accession history:** Purchased by H. F. du Pont from Joe Kindig, Jr., York, Pa., 1944. Bequest of H. F. du Pont, 1969.
57.1394

1. "Little Known Masterpieces," *Antiques* 1, no. 1 (January 1922): 17–18. For the other 5 blockfront chests-on-chests, see Flanigan, *American Furniture*, cat. no. 26; Rodriguez Roque, *American Furniture*, no. 13; Sotheby Parke Bernet, "Americana Week" (January 24–27, 1973), lot 947; Henry Hawley, "A Townsend-Goddard Chest-on-Chest," *Bulletin of the Cleveland Museum of Art* 65 (October 1977): frontispiece; Comstock, *American Furniture*, no. 305. All 10 blockfront desk-and-bookcases are in Moses, *Master Craftsmen*, pls. 1, 2, figs. 8.5, 8.10–8.14, 8.16, 8.18.

2. The Joseph Brown desk-and-bookcase is discussed in *John Brown House Loan Exhibition*, cat. 67. The John

Brown chest-on-chest is discussed in Flanigan, *American Furniture*, cat. no. 26.

3. Three other pieces of furniture have astragal foot brackets: a plain fall-front desk in Joseph K. Ott, "Lesser-known Rhode Island Cabinetmakers: The Carliles, Holmes Weaver, Judson Blake, the Rawsons, and Thomas Davenport," *Antiques* 121, no. 5 (May 1982): 1157, fig. 2; a blockfront chest of drawers in Ward, *American Case Furniture*, cat. 58; and a tall case clock in *John Brown House Loan Exhibition*, cat. 77.

4. For the 3 other blockfront chests with rosettes, see Rodriguez Roque, *American Furniture*, no. 13; Sotheby Parke Bernet, "Americana Week," lot 947; and Comstock, *American Furniture*, no. 305. The 4 blockfront desk-and-bookcases with rosettes are in Moses, *Master Craftsmen*, pls. 1, 2, figs. 8.16, 8.18.

5. For related English brass hardware patterns, see Charles F. Hummel, "Samuel Rowland Fisher's Catalogue of English Hardware," in Milo M. Naeve, ed., *Winterthur Portfolio 1* (Winterthur, Del.: Henry Francis du Pont Winterthur Museum, 1964), fig. 6; Robert Mussey and Anne Rogers Haley, "John Cogswell and Boston Bombé Furniture: Thirty-five Years of Revolution in Politics and Design," in Luke Beckerdite, ed., *American Furniture 1994* (Milwaukee, Wis.: Chipstone Fndn., 1994), p. 83, fig. 12. For the pitched-pediment chest, see Hawley, "Townsend-Goddard Chest-on-Chest," frontispiece. William B. Spooner, Jr., advertisement, *Antiques* 40, no. 3 (September 1941): 131.

6. On the boxed-pediment attribution dilemma, see Flanigan, *American Furniture*, cat. no. 26. For the Carlile desk, see Ott, "Lesser-known Rhode Island Cabinetmakers," p. 1157. For the Spaulding clock, see *John Brown House Loan Exhibition*, cat. 77.

7. The Brown brothers owned 4 of the chests-on-chests and 3 of the desk-and-bookcases. The Jabez Bowen chest is in Rodriguez Roque, *American Furniture*, no. 13; for the clock, see Kenneth and Paulette Tuttle advertisement, *Antiques* 125, no. 5 (May 1984): 989.

## 194 ◆ Chest-on-chest
Eastern Massachusetts, possibly
Concord area
1765–90

The number of tall, rectangular double cases
of drawers with pilasters and a scroll pediment
that survive suggests that the form was a
popular storage item among householders in
eastern Massachusetts in the late eighteenth
century. The form appears to have been a
salable commodity for about four decades,
given the combined evidence of stylistic
attributes and family histories. As constructed
in eastern Massachusetts, the chest probably
had a dual ancestry: the high case of drawers
with pilasters and an "ogee top," or scroll
pediment, standing on tall legs; and the
multidrawer double chest with flat top
introduced from England to the Boston area
before the second quarter of the century,
probably by an immigrant craftsman. The
flat-top form remained common in English
provincial centers as late as the 1790s, the
date of several drawings in the estimate
book of the Gillows firm of Lancashire.
Outside Massachusetts the domestic form
with pilasters and ogee top had some currency
in Connecticut, where cherrywood examples
with regional features are known.[1]

The flat facade of this chest-on-chest was
one of several structural options available to
consumers, and although it was the cheapest,
it was by no means the most common. Many
more chests have lower cases swelled in one
of the several late baroque patterns popular
in eastern Massachusetts in the last half of
the eighteenth century. Most prominent is
the flat-blocked facade (see No. 176). A
variant seen occasionally is the case with a
recessed center like that in the bureau table.
Another occasional choice was a lower case
with an oxbow, or reverse-serpentine, facade.
The bombé lower chest is rare (see No. 185).
These cases were supported on straight-

bracket, ogee-bracket, or cabriole feet, depending upon the date of construction and customer choice. Patrons could also choose from a range of ornamental features: fluted pilasters, shells, fans, finials, rosettes in the pediment scrolls, and a pendant centered below the base molding.

There are five special ornamental features of this chest-on-chest: the fan in the center top drawer; the heads of the pilasters; the plinth centered in the pediment; the finials; and the foot brackets. The fan is distinctive and rare in its emulation of the actual object—complete with sticks, a folding leaf (fig. 1), and a pendent ring at the pivot. Four chests have been located with similar or related carving. One is a chest with a bureau table base; two are close mates to this chest and share other special features. The fourth chest, once associated with Concord cabinetmaker Joseph Hosmer (1736–1821), has a flat top and stands on tall legs and is a provincial interpretation. The fan drawer is centered at the bottom of the case and is interpreted in a simplistic manner.[2]

The Concord chest and Winterthur's chest both have a rounded, bosslike element worked from solid wood to form a pulvinated, or swelled, frieze above the pilaster capitals (this element is interpreted differently and repeated at the base of the pilasters in the Concord chest). Bosses of this size also occur on the three chests-on-chests with related fans and three other straight-front double cases. Pulvinated bosses of about half this size are features of eight other chests-on-chests in the assembled sample. Five of this number have blocked facades, three of which are either labeled by or attributed to Benjamin Frothingham (1734–1809) of Charlestown. Another chest descended in the Hall family of Medford, and one is associated with the Lawrence family.[3]

Another rare feature confined to a few chests is the flared-top plinth in the scrollboard

**Fig. 1.** Detail, fan and center of pediment.

that supports the center finial. Six other flat-front chests with pilasters are so embellished. In four chests, the scrollboard is also sawed with a swelling and notch at the opposite ends of the circles directly below the molding, and two of these also have a related fan. One of the chests without the sawed feature is inscribed "Concord 1786" on the concealed pine top of the bottom case. Still another straight-front chest, one without pilasters, has a flared central plinth, which supports an urn and "flame" finial that duplicates those of the pilaster-case group, except the one inscribed from Concord. The finial pattern is so close from chest to chest that it must represent the work of a particular carver or of a small number of cabinetmakers working in one area. These six are the only chests in the entire sample, which contains almost four dozen examples, with finials of this pattern.[4]

The sawed profile of the bracket feet is again an uncommon feature among the double chests. Starting at the inside edge, the profile is a steep diagonal ogee with a small return at the base molding and a large cusp at the opposite end. The profile is often combined with a bellied foot, which itself repeats the swelled profile of the pilaster boss, as seen

on this chest. Surprisingly, this bracket is also often found on chests of drawers and occasionally on fall-front desks of eastern Massachusetts origin.[5]

Of the five straight-front chests-on-chests (one maple and four cherry) that relate most closely to Winterthur's maple chest, four have brasses of the same pattern and all the drawer fronts are beaded around the edges. The next two chests of closest feature are both made of cherry. The choice of construction materials and the rarity of several ornamental features suggest that the Winterthur chest and its close mates originated outside Boston, where mahogany was preferred for household furniture in the postrevolutionary period.[6]

Other chests-on-chests with scroll pediments and pilasters have family associations that place them in Marshfield, Marblehead, and Worcester. One chest of oxbow facade in the lower case supported on cabriole feet was signed and dated by its makers Nathan Bowen (1752–1837) and Ebenezer Martin (d. 1800) of Marblehead in 1780. Locations plotted on a map form a partial ring around Boston beginning at Marshfield in the southeast, arching as far north as Newburyport, and ending at

Worcester in the west. Only Concord is mentioned specifically in relation to one of the chests closely associated with Winterthur's example.[7]

*NGE*

---

**Inscriptions or marks:** *On blades in both cases:* "1" to "8" from bottom to top, in pencil (numbering old but probably not original). *On bottom board:* "1" in pencil. *Inscribed on underside of right small drawer bottom, upper case:* "R". *On outside back of right small drawer:* indecipherable chalk mark. *On the underside of left small drawer bottom:* "L" in pencil. *On outside back of left small drawer:* "2" in chalk. *On top long drawer, on back:* shop mark and "4" in white chalk; *on the outside bottom:* a script "M" three times in different sizes in white chalk and "8" in pencil. *Inscribed on second long drawer, on bottom and outside back:* "1" in pencil and "3" in chalk, respectively. *On third long drawer, on bottom and outside back:* "6" in pencil and "2" in chalk, respectively. *On bottom drawer, upper case, on bottom and outside back:* "5" in pencil and "1" in chalk, respectively. (Many chalk numbers in both cases are accompanied by a caret symbol.) *On drawers in lower case, on bottom and outside back:* "4" to "1" in descending order, in pencil. (The chalk marks appear to be original; the pencil is probably later.)

**Construction:** (Upper case) The scrollboard is half-lapped to the front stiles and reinforced from the back with large rectangular glueblocks. The pediment is enclosed on either side of the central opening by vertical walls that support ogee-curved roofs. A deep cavetto molding is applied to the case sides and face of the scrollboard, with 5 3/4" returns at the pediment opening. The central plinth is supported at the back with a vertical glueblock. The fluted finial plinths above the pilasters are glued to the case top. Vertical partitions at either side of the top center drawer are nailed at the top to the scrollboard and dovetailed at the bottom to the upper drawer blade. All drawer blades and the bottom rail of the upper case are slotted into the case sides. The joints in the upper case are covered by stiles faced with fluted pilasters, the bosslike friezes cut from solid wood. The vertical strips are nailed in place. Slotted into the case sides, the wide drawer runners are attached at the back to flat, vertical posts fixed on end to the backboard with long glueblocks. Small cleats nailed to the top surface of the drawer runners and flush with the front stiles prevent the drawers from wobbling since they stand away from the case sides. The backboard of the upper case is made of three horizontal lap-joined boards rabbeted and nailed to the case sides; the shaped top board has a rectangular cutout behind the pediment. The bottom board is dovetailed to the case sides.

(Lower case) The waist molding is nailed to the top of the lower case. The top and bottom boards are dovetailed to the case sides; the top board has a maple facing at the front. The bottom rail rests on the bottom board, faced at the front and side with applied molding. The drawer runners are lap-joined to the blades at the front and nailed to the case sides. Vertical blocks between the drawer runners glued and nailed to the case sides at the back act as drawer stops. The bracket foot facings are attached to heavy vertical posts and reinforced with horizontal blocks. The rear feet are reinforced at the back with plain boards canted on the inside edge. The backboard of the lower case is made of two horizontal boards rabbeted and nailed to the case sides. The drawers are dovetailed. The drawer fronts are decorated with an incised bead. The upper edge of the drawer sides are rounded; that of the back is flat. The drawer bottoms, the boards running from side to side on the long drawers and front to back on the small drawers, are rough sawn with the high spots planed off and the edges chamfered. The bottoms are set into grooves on the drawer fronts and sides and nailed across the back. The brasses are original.

**Condition:** The surface has been refinished. The disk below the central finial is cracked across. Splits in the left side of both the upper and lower cases have been patched with a spline or composition fill. There are short vertical cracks on the right side of the upper and lower cases. The scrollboard is cracked on the left side in the upper projection and pieced out at the stile above the left small drawer. This appears to have been the result of a miscalculation on the part of the maker. Cracks in the foot facings (left side front, right front and side front, right rear) are repaired with splines.

**Dimensions:**

| | | |
|---|---|---|
| H. (case) | 82 in. | 208.3 cm |
| W. (cornice) | 40 3/8 in. | 102.5 cm |
| W. (upper case) | 37 in. | 94.0 cm |
| W. (lower case) | 39 3/4 in. | 101.0 cm |
| W. (feet) | 41 3/8 in. | 105.1 cm |
| D. (cornice) | 21 in. | 53.3 cm |
| D. (upper case) | 19 7/8 in. | 50.5 cm |
| D. (lower case) | 21 1/4 in. | 54.0 cm |
| D. (feet) | 22 3/8 in. | 56.8 cm |

**Materials:** *Microanalysis:* Primary: soft maple group. Secondary: white pine group (drawer linings, top board of lower case). *Finish:* clear resin over remnants of reddish brown color in resin; possibly mahoganized originally.

**Publications:** Downs, *American Furniture*, fig. 182. Robert Bishop, *Guide to American Antique Furniture* (New York: Galahad Books, 1973), p. 66, fig. 70.

**Accession history:** Bequest of H. F. du Pont, 1969. 59.1318

---

1. For design precedents for the ogee-top chest-on-chest with pilasters, see *American Antiques from Israel Sack Collection*, 10 vols. (Washington, D.C.: Highland House, 1969–), 9:2486–87; Edward S. Cooke, Jr., "The Warland Chest: Early Georgian Furniture in Boston," *Maine Antique Digest*, March 1987, pp. 10-C–13-C. "Oger [ogee] Top" in advertisement in *Boston Gazette*, September 27, 1756, as quoted in Dow, *Arts and Crafts*

*in New England*, p. 115; for Gillows's drawings, see Kirk, *American Furniture*, figs. 567–68. For a Connecticut cherrywood chest, see Fales, *Furniture of Historic Deerfield*, fig. 446.

2. For the chest with bureau-table base, see Parke-Bernet Galleries, "Early American Furniture and Decorations: Collection of Mr. and Mrs. R. Jay Flick" (November 16–17, 1945), lot 349. One straight-front chest is discussed and illustrated in Robert W. Skinner, "Americana and American Indian Art" (January 15–16, 1988), lot 284; for the second straight-front chest, see Anthony S. Werneke advertisement, *Maine Antique Digest*, August 1996, p. 23-B; on the Concord chest, see Jobe and Kaye, *New England Furniture*, no. 38.

3. For 3 chests-on-chests with large pulvinated bosses but different fans, see *American Antiques from Sack Collection*, 7:1925; Sotheby's, "Important Americana" (January 24–27, 1990), lot 1195; Christie's, "The Collection of Mr. and Mrs. Eddy Nicholson" (January 27–28, 1995), lot 1096. For the 8 chests with pulvinated bosses of half size, see Robert W. Skinner, "Fine Americana" (January 6, 1984), lot 181; Sotheby Parke Bernet, "Notable Americana" (May 10–11, 1974), lot 457; Israel Sack advertisement, *Antiques* 68, no. 1 (July 1955): inside front cover; *American Antiques from Sack Collection*, 6:23; Kenneth Hammitt advertisement, *Antiques* 95, no. 3 (March 1969): 325; Walter Muir Whitehill, Brock Jobe, and Jonathan Fairbanks, "Foreword," in *Boston Furniture*, p. vi; Sotheby Parke Bernet advertisement, *Antiques* 111, no. 4 (April 1977): 621; *American Antiques from Sack Collection*, 4:1056.

4. The related chests with pilasters are in Skinner, "Americana," lot 284; Skinner, "Fine Americana," lot 181; *American Antiques from Sack Collection*, 7:1925; Sotheby's, "Important Americana," lot 1195; Werneke advertisement; Christie's, "Collection of Mr. and Mrs. Eddy Nicholson," lot 1096. The chest without pilasters is in Philip H. Bradley advertisement, *Antiques* 128, no. 6 (December 1985): 1083.

5. One chest of drawers descended in a Boston family and is illustrated in *American Antiques from Sack Collection*, 5:1187; another likely originated in Newburyport and is branded "E•HUSE"; see *American Antiques from Sack Collection*, 9:2396.

6. The 7 related chests are in: Skinner, "Americana," lot 284; *American Antiques from Sack Collection*, 7:1925; Sotheby's, "Important Americana," lot 1195; Werneke advertisement; Christie's, "Collection of Mr. and Mrs. Eddy Nicholson," lot 1096; Skinner, "Fine Americana," lot 181; Parke-Bernet Galleries, "Early American Furniture," lot 349.

7. For Marshfield chest, see G. S. Sloan advertisement, *Antiques* 112, no. 2 (August 1977): 166; for Marblehead chest, see *American Antiques from Sack Collection*, 8:2097; for Worcester chest, see Good and Hutchinson advertisement, *Antiques* 99, no. 1 (January 1971): 77; for Bowen and Martin chest, see Randall, *American Furniture*, no. 41. A chest-on-chest and high chest in the Concord Museum, both with local family associations but without pilasters on the cases, have carved fans of a pattern closely related to that on Winterthur's chest. The chest-on-chest also has swelled bracket feet, a similar flared-top plinth, and identical finials, although the latter while old are thought not to be original to the case. This double chest was owned originally by a daughter and son-in-law of local cabinetmaker Joseph Hosmer. Two other tall chests in the Concord Museum have pilasters with pulvinated capitals and bases. Both have strong local family associations, and both relate to chest No. 167 in their use of applied triangular ornament in the pediment plinth; see David F. Wood, ed., *The Concord Museum: Decorative Arts from a New England Collection* (Concord, Mass.: By the museum, 1996), cats. 10A–B, 11A–B.

## 195 ◆ Chest-on-chest

New Marlborough, Massachusetts
1795–1805
Reuben Beman, Jr. (b. 1772)

Select features of this distinctive chest-on-chest describe both the craftsman's activity on a local level and his broader exposure to design impulses. Reuben Beman, Jr., is the maker; his name is inscribed in white chalk inside the backboard of the upper case (fig. 1). The signature is accompanied by a three-line penciled inscription that chronicles the repairs made to the chest in the late nineteenth and early twentieth centuries, and between the two appears the penciled inscription "Bought Dec 1801," which has heretofore been accepted as contemporary with the chest. Two factors call the notation into question: first, the lower-case *e* of the month is written with two open half loops in the manner of an upper-case *E*, which is atypical of period calligraphy; second, the inscription is crowded into a space between the maker's signature and the restorers' notations, overlapping in part the top line of the latter. It seems unlikely that the first restorer would have crowded an existing inscription in this manner with the entire remaining backboard available for use.

Almost nothing is known of Beman's background or career, nor is he the Reuben Beman identified previously as the maker of this chest. Earlier research associated Reuben Beman (b. 1742) of Kent, Connecticut, with this casepiece, and the mid twentieth-century vendor of the chest so inscribed one of the small drawers. The chest interior is inscribed twice with the place-name "Newmarlborough," however—once in white chalk and once in pencil. Reuben Beman of Kent was the son of Ebenezer and therefore not a junior of the name. He appears, however, to have been the father of the Reuben Beman, Jr., to whom the chest is now ascribed. Reuben, Sr., is identified as a cabinetmaker in a Kent town record; his

**Fig. 1.** Detail, inside backboard of upper case.

**Fig. 2.** Detail, upper left pilaster.

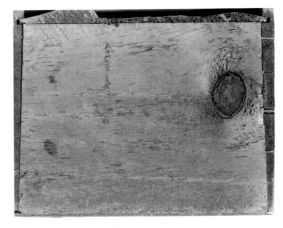

**Fig. 3.** Detail, drawer framing.

brother Ebenezer, Jr. (b. 1747 or 1756), also was a woodworker, as indicated by the large number of woodworking tools in his 1802 probate inventory. Either man could have served as master to Reuben, Jr.[1]

Beman, Sr., and his wife Meriam (also Mariam, Miriam) appear to have been residents of New Marlborough, Massachusetts (a rural village of Berkshire County about thirty-five miles from Kent), by 1764, when town records list the birth of their first child. Beman acquired land in the community a year later. By the time the senior Beman left Massachusetts for western New York State, Reuben, Jr., had reached adulthood and had married Mercy (also Marcy, Mary) Baker in 1792. One record gives the elder Beman's removal to New York State as 1799 or 1800, but entries for a Lt. Reuben Beman dated 1796 and 1803 in the New Marlborough accounts of Richard and Gilbert Smith appear to pertain to him. Beman is listed in the federal census as a resident of Lima, Ontario County, New York, in 1810. What happened to Reuben, Jr., is unknown. He may have followed his father and many other pioneers westward in search of cheap land. Men named Reuben Beman are listed in Ohio census records from 1820 to 1840 and in New York State records from 1830 to 1850.[2]

In the early 1980s, a second chest-on-chest similar to the Winterthur one and almost certainly from the same shop was

offered for sale at auction. That chest, the later of the two, had been modestly changed and simplified in design. The base supports are short cabriole legs with ball-and-claw feet, and the rope molding extends the entire width and depth of the case. The front corners of the stacked cases are embellished with spiraled quarter columns rather than diagonal pilasters, and the ogee heads and bases are much smaller in size. The drawer construction has been updated from the thumb-molded style of Winterthur's chest to the stylish flush design of the late eighteenth century that is surrounded by beading at the drawer openings. More obvious changes are in the pediment: the small pierced heart below the central plinth is absent, and to compensate, the plinth is longer; the slender double-lobed (heart-shape) strips between the plinth base and the slotted side panels have been eliminated. The slim spiraled cones of the side finials remain, but they are elevated above the plinths on short double-spool-and-disk stems. Cherry is the principal construction material.[3]

Two of the many unusual decorative features and three distinctive structural details of the Winterthur chest are shared by a three-drawer cherrywood chest of drawers of oxbow facade signed and dated by its maker, Bates How (b. 1776), in 1795. The How chest substitutes rope-twist quarter columns for the canted pilasters of the double chest but retains the bold ogee-shape terminals of the same

uncommon profile at the top and bottom (fig. 2). In Winterthur's chest, the ogee is repeated in the foot brackets. The second shared feature is the rope-twist base molding, the center point forming an inverted V. The feet of the How chest are similar to those in the Beman chest-on-chest that was sold at auction.[4]

The backboards of Winterthur's tall chest and the How low chest are dovetailed to the case sides instead of the common rabbeted construction, and the drawer runners tenon into the backboards. The bottom of the How chest does not extend the full depth of the case—a structural feature that in Winterthur's chest occurs at the bottom of the top section and the top of the bottom section. An uncommon feature in Winterthur's chest that is absent in How's work is the taper of the drawer sides from bottom to top, a construction that strengthens the joints of the drawer bottoms with the sides (fig. 3).[5]

Several other pieces of furniture have been ascribed to How based on their close stylistic relationship to the documented chest. One is a chest of drawers in the Connecticut Historical Society that appears to be a close mate; it shares, in addition to the distinctive quarter columns and base molding, an overhanging oxbow top with a deep fillet-and-thumb-molded edge, short cabriole legs with small squarish claw feet, and plain post-and-bail brasses. The backboard is dovetailed, and the

**Fig. 4.** Detail, upper drawers and pediment.

runners are tenoned into it. Several plainer chests of drawers on similar claw feet are known. A flat-top chest-on-chest is remarkable for the similarity of its quarter columns (top and bottom cases), base molding, and feet. It is further embellished in the center top drawer with a large swirled pinwheel that is similar in design to the ones in the Beman chests except for the substantially greater number of ribs. Whether these chests share the construction features described is unknown, but additional structural oddities of Winterthur's chest may help to identify related furniture, including the horizontal scribe marks on the interior case sides at the levels of the drawer blades and rails used as guides for framing; the tapered form of the drawer sides, as described above; and the rounded top edges of the drawer sides.[6]

How is as elusive a figure as Beman. He was born Bates Hoyt How in 1776 in Canaan, a small community in northwestern Connecticut. His family was in New Marlborough as early as 1785, when he and his twin, James, were baptized. Like the elder Beman, How is mentioned in the New Marlborough accounts of the Smith family; entries are dated in 1799 and 1800. Other How family members recorded in the Smith accounts include brothers James and Bowers (b. 1769), sister Lois (b. 1771), and possibly the father, Samuel (b. 1732). Bowers was in New Marlborough as late as 1803 when a child was born to him and his wife. Before 1810 he had migrated to New York State, where he is listed in the federal census that year and later. Brother James probably followed suit, as he was married in New York State. What happened to Bates remains a mystery. He may have migrated westward, but his name does not appear in New York or Ohio census records. The How(e) family genealogy indicates that Bates died unmarried but

provides no death date. An inscription in the North Canaan, Connecticut, cemetery is said to state that a Mrs. Bates How died May 27, 1801. Perhaps the report is in error and the recorded death was that of the cabinetmaker himself. Puzzling also is the date on the documented chest of drawers that indicates How was only about nineteen years of age when he inscribed the backboard. It is possible that he signed the piece while in the employ of a master; other instances of this are known. Certainly, How and Beman shared a close working relationship, and they appear to have been of similar age rather than of two different generations, as previously identified.[7]

Curiously, this group of furniture has a strong design relationship to case furniture made in the eastern part of Connecticut, particularly in New London County. There, rope columns, rope moldings, and pinwheels—some with swirling ribs of jagged tip as in Winterthur's Beman chest (fig. 4)—are also common decorative features. Several patterns of the plinth foot—the flaring, squarish support of this chest—also appear in eastern Connecticut work, and they were part of the vocabulary of Boston design as early as the mid eighteenth century.[8]

Canted pilasters are less common on eastern Connecticut casepieces, although one notable example is a chest-on-chest inscribed "Lisbon, 1796." From its stylish ogee-bracket feet to the low rise of its broken-scroll pediment with paneled scrollboard, the chest resembles Rhode Island case furniture; however, the narrow, fluted corners of the double case are terminated at the ends by diminutive lamb's tongues of bold ogee profile that strongly resemble those in Winterthur's Beman chest. Several cabinetmakers are known to have worked in Lisbon township

but none whose cabinetwork can be identified. The most prominent was Ebenezer Tracy, Sr. Among cabinetmakers active in neighboring Preston, John Wheeler Geer (1753–1828) initialed a lidded chest with the backboard dovetailed to the case sides. A chest-on-chest also ascribed to him through its family descent has flaring plinth feet of the type found on Winterthur's Beman chest.[9]

The most outstanding feature of Winterthur's chest is the pediment design (see fig. 4). The principal motif is a stylized double heart flanking a small inverted piercing of the same shape. Small pinwheel rosettes that repeat the form of the drawer ornament add another dimension to the design, serving as the "heavenly bodies" in figures that appear to represent comets, complete with trailing tails. The central element above the small heart may imitate an inverted tapeloom but falls short of the imaginative quality of the rest of the design. The elliptic "handle" of the loom is delicately patterned with chip carving along the top edge and fine stipplework on the face. Rounding out the design of the pediment are finials that can be described only as bizarre, but then incongruities are frequently part and parcel of vernacular furniture design.

*NGE*

**Inscriptions or marks:** *On inside backboard of upper case behind the top and second long drawers:* "Reuben Beman Junr" *in white chalk. Inside right side upper case:* "Newmarlborough" *in white chalk. Inside backboard behind small drawers:* "Sold + repaired by/ John S Walton, Riverside, Conn,/ June 6, 1949" *in pencil. Inside back behind second long drawer:* "Bought Dec 1801" (hand no. 1), "Repert April 1889 Watkins Bros" (hand no. 2), *and* "[Repaired] March 1927 [Watkins Bros]" (hand no. 3), *all in pencil. Inside backboard behind third long drawer:* "Repaired by Watkins Bros/ March 1927/ E H Buckland" (hand no. 4) in pencil. (The Watkins firm was in Hartford, Conn.) *Inside top of backboard, upper case:* "Newmarlborough" in pencil. *On bottom board of upper case:* indecipherable inscription. *On most drawer openings in the upper case:* numbers (modern), in pencil. *On outside back of lower right small drawer:* "Sold + refinished by John S Walton/ Post Rd. Riverside, Conn/ June 6, 1949. all original except/ brass on 3 long drawers/ Made by Rueben Beman, Kent, Conn./ in 1790–1800" in pencil.

**Construction:** (Upper case) The fully enclosed pediment is covered with thin oak boards nailed to the scrollboard and upper backboard with many rosehead nails. The two-piece top board is half-blind dovetailed to the one- (left) and two-board (right) case sides. The scrollboard is glued and nailed to a $1^5/8$"-thick top rail that is notched into the front corner posts; the joint is further reinforced on the back surface with glueblocks resting on the top board. The pinwheel rosettes are screwed to the scrollboard. The top piece of the reeded plinth centered in the scrollboard is notched in a sawtooth pattern around the top edge and stipple-patterned to form an ellipse on the face. The finials are original. All drawer blades and rails are notched into the front corner posts (and in the lower case). The fluted corner posts are cut from solid wood; glueblocks reinforce their joints with the case sides. The bottom board, which is planed, does not extend the full depth of the case; it is dovetailed to the case sides. The bottom rail is glued to the front of the bottom board and screwed to the stiles. The drawer runners, which stand away from the case sides, are tenoned into the backboard and rabbeted to the drawer blades; those supporting the center top drawer are similarly secured. There are no dust boards. The horizontal backboards are lap-jointed, except for the shaped upper backboard, which is butt-jointed to the other boards. The upper backboard is secured to the top board with rosehead nails. The three lower boards are dovetailed to the case sides and reinforced with rosehead nails. Horizontal scribe marks are scratched into the interior case sides, front to back, top and bottom, to mark the installation points of the drawer blades and rails.

(Lower case) The midmolding is secured with rosehead nails to the top rail from the inside. The top board, which does not extend the full depth of the case, and the planed bottom board are half-blind dovetailed to the double-board case sides. The top and bottom rails are glued to the front of the top and bottom boards. Many small rectangular glueblocks reinforce the joint of the bottom board and sides on the case bottom. The base molding is glued to cleats below the case bottom. Long, deep molding strips with gadrooned, or rope-twist, facings are glued to the lower edge of the case on the front and sides. The mitered foot facings are nailed in place. The case is supported on two-piece, shaped vertical blocks glued and nailed together in front and on single vertical blocks at the rear. Board-type brackets with canted inside edges are dovetailed to the rear foot facings and screwed to the vertical supports. The backboard, made of three horizontal sections, is lapped and dovetailed, as in the upper case. All the drawers are dovetailed and have tapered sides rounded on the top edge; the back is a thick flat-edged board. The dovetail pins at the

front are small; those at the back are thick. The drawer bottoms, the boards running from side to side, are planed on the outside bottom. They are chamfered at the side and front edges, set into sliding dadoes, and nailed flush at the back; applied battens are attached.

**Condition:** (Upper case) The cap on the left plinth block is chipped. A split in the upper right side panel has been patched with a wood spline. All the blades in the upper case are repaired at the joint with the left corner post.

(Lower case) Sections of the midmolding have been patched. Splits in the right and left side panels are repaired with wood splines. The top rail is pieced at both ends at the joints; the top blade is pieced on the right, and the second blade and bottom rail are pieced on the left. All foot facings are cracked through once or twice at the ankles and replaced from the crack to the bottom. A 1" piece at the bottom of the right rear footboard is replaced. One of the glueblocks on the bottom board is missing. The lips of all drawers in the lower case are patched. The hardware is replaced; the surface has been refinished.

**Dimensions:**

| | | |
|---|---|---|
| H. (case) | $87^7/8$ in. | 223.2 cm |
| W. (cornice) | 40 in. | 101.6 cm |
| W. (upper case) | $38^1/4$ in. | 97.2 cm |
| W. (lower case) | $40^1/4$ in. | 102.2 cm |
| W. (feet) | $43^1/2$ in. | 110.5 cm |
| D. (cornice) | 20 in. | 50.8 cm |
| D. (upper case) | 19 in. | 48.2 cm |
| D. (lower case) | $19^7/8$ in. | 50.5 cm |
| D. (feet) | $22^1/4$ in. | 56.5 cm |

**Materials:** *Microanalysis:* Primary: cherry. Secondary: white pine group (top boards both cases, backboards of both cases, drawer linings); white oak group (pediment top). *Finish:* clear resin of medium light reddish brown color.

**Publications:** Downs, *American Furniture*, fig. 181. "A Selection of American Furniture," *Antiques* 61, no. 5 (May 1952): 428. Butler, *American Furniture*, p. 65. Charles F. Montgomery, "Country Furniture," *Antiques* 93, no. 3 (March 1968): 358.

**Provenance:** The chest-on-chest was discovered by Florene Maine, a Ridgefield, Conn., dealer, who sold it to a Long Island collector. It was later acquired by Charles Woolsey Lyon.

**Accession history:** Purchased by H. F. du Pont from John S. Walton, New York, 1949. Gift of H. F. du Pont, 1951.
51.22

---

1. Gwen Boyer Bjorkman, comp., *The Descendants of Thomas Beeman of Kent, Connecticut* (Seattle, Wash.: By the author, 1971); Ethel Hall Bjerkoe with John Arthur Bjerkoe, *The Cabinetmakers of America* (Garden City, N.Y.: Doubleday, 1952), pp. 41–42; Clarence E. Beeman, comp., *Beeman Genealogy* (Goble, Ore.: By the author, 1954), pp. 8–9.

2. Beman family vital records, Office of the Town Clerk, New Marlborough, Mass.; Beman family, Probate Court and Registry of Deeds, Berkshire Co., Mass.; Bjorkman, *Descendants of Thomas Beeman*, p. 21; Richard and Gilbert Smith account book, 1796–1811, Downs collection; Emily Beamon Wooden, *The Beamon and Clark Genealogy: A History of the Descendants of Gamaliel Beamon and Sarah Clark of Dorchester and Lancaster, Mass.* (N.p.: By the author, 1909), pp. 149–50. Records

pertaining to eligible men named Reuben Beman are scattered and sometimes contradictory. For example, the family genealogy by Bjorkman names Ebenezer Beman, Sr., as the father of Reuben, Sr., yet Berkshire Co., Mass., land and probate records suggest that Reuben's father was named John. In both cases the name of Reuben's wife was Meriam (Miriam). The Beman genealogy also identifies a Reuben Beman (b. 1771), son of Friend Beman, as a carpenter, cabinetmaker, and farmer who was a resident of Milton, Vt., although his birth is recorded in the Kent, Conn., vital records; he died in Ohio. Another Reuben Beman (b. 1767) and his wife Elizabeth were residents of Hartland, Conn., near the Berkshire Co., Mass., border, at least between 1804 and 1823, according to local church records; see card file of church records, Genealogical Section, Connecticut State Library, Hartford, and Rollin H. Cooke Collection, vol. 55, Local History Room, Berkshire Athenaeum, Pittsfield, Mass.

3. For the second chest-on-chest, see Christie's, "Important American Furniture, Silver, and Decorative Arts" (June 2, 1983), lot 375. This chest also was published in Edward S. Cooke, Jr., "The Social Economy of the Preindustrial Joiner in Western Connecticut, 1750–1800," in Luke Beckerdite and William N. Hosley, eds., *American Furniture 1995* (Milwaukee, Wis.: Chipstone Fndn., 1995), p. 122, where it is said to be signed by Beman. That statement has not been confirmed by Cooke or by the individuals who supposedly supplied the information. Nor does Christie's catalogue indicate that the chest is documented.

4. The How chest of drawers is in the Yale University Art Gallery; see Ward, *American Case Furniture*, cat. 63. Christie's, "Important American Furniture," lot 375; the chest is also illustrated in Cooke, "Social Economy," p. 122.

5. Ward, *American Case Furniture*, cat. 63.

6. For the Connecticut Historical Society chest, see *Frederick K. and Margaret R. Barbour's Furniture Collection: A Supplement* (Hartford: Connecticut Historical Society, 1970), pp. 14–15. Plainer chests of drawers are in the Mattatuck Museum, Waterbury, Conn., and represented in no. 81.1218, DAPC, Visual Resources Collection, Winterthur Library. A related chest is in a Nathan Liverant and Son advertisement, *Antiques* 105, no. 5 (May 1974): 1027. For the chest-on-chest, see *American Antiques from Israel Sack Collection*, 10 vols. (Washington, D.C.: Highland House, 1969–), 2:331.

7. Ward, *American Case Furniture*, cat. 63; baptisms of How brothers at New Marlborough in records of St. James Church, Great Barrington, Mass., and marriage of James How in records of Congregational Church, New Lebanon, N.Y., both as compiled in Cooke Collection, vols. 15, 63; Smith account book; Daniel Wait Howe, *Howe Genealogies* (rev. ed., Boston: New England Historic Genealogical Society, 1929), pp. 431, 450; card file of newspaper death notices and cemetery inscriptions, Genealogical Section, Connecticut State Library, Hartford.

8. For Connecticut case furniture with rope ornament and/or pinwheels, see Ward, *American Case Furniture*, cats. 106, 107, 136; *American Antiques from Sack Collection*, 7:1705; John S. Walton advertisement, *Antiques* 109, no. 4 (April 1976): 614; Nathan Liverant and Son advertisement, *Antiques* 122, no. 4 (October 1982): 656; Phillip Johnston, "Eighteenth- and Nineteenth-Century American Furniture in the Wadsworth Atheneum," *Antiques* 115, no. 5 (May 1979): 1020–21; Marshall B. Davidson, ed., *The American Heritage History of Colonial Antiques* ([New York]: American Heritage Publishing Co., [1967]), p. 229, fig. 326. Examples with plinth feet are in *American Antiques from Sack Collection*, 5:1359; John S. Walton advertisement, *Antiques* 124, no. 5 (November 1983): 810; Kenneth Hammitt advertisement, *Antiques* 95, no. 2 (February 1969): 207; Rollins, *Treasures of State*, cat. no. 13.

9. For the Lisbon chest, see *New London County Furniture*, no. 70; see also a chest of drawers in *Connecticut Furniture*, no. 58; for the Geer furniture, see *New London County Furniture*, nos. 63, 64.

## 196 ◆ Chest-on-chest

Salisbury, New Hampshire
1797–1810
Probably the shop of Lt. Samuel Dunlap
(1752–1830)

The Dunlap family of woodworkers and their associates—apprentices, journeymen, and craft peers—worked in south central New Hampshire, the site of a substantial settlement of Scots-Irish immigrants in the early eighteenth century. Recent studies have explored their work in light of cultural antecedents found in Scottish furniture, particularly as those antecedents relate to the selection and organization of design motifs and the massing of form. In that respect, the most significant elements of this chest-on-chest are the spoon-handle shell (fig. 1), as it has come to be called, and the carved molding at the top of the cornice, which is repeated below the shell. Close prototypes for the shell and a general interpretation of the molding are found in several seventeenth-century chairs carved with craft symbols at Trinity Hall, the guildhall of Aberdeen, Scotland. In another comparison, the arrangement of the deep lower drawer with its false three-drawer facade perhaps recalls a structural feature of a case form known in Scotland at least from the nineteenth century as a "Scotch Chest." The top chest is usually divided into a deep, narrow, central drawer flanked by two shallow, stacked units on either side. Although not identical in form or position, the central focus and depth of this arrangement may be related; however, the arrangement was in use by other craftsmen (see No. 195).[1]

The chest-on-chest as designed and constructed by members of the Dunlap family and their circle varies substantially in appearance from one example to the next, a result of the number of craftsmen involved in their production and the long period during which the chests were made (ca. 1770 to 1810

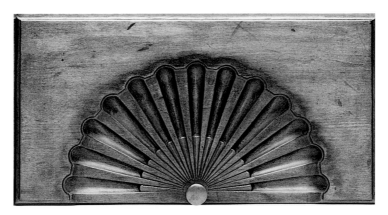

**Fig. 1.** Detail, bottom drawer.

and later). Of a sizable sample of twenty-eight chests-on-chests supported on short or medium short legs, the majority (82 percent) have flat tops with projecting cornices. The rest have gallery tops similar to that in No. 175. Slightly less than half of the total are supported at the bottom by a separate frame that, unlike the fixed base of this example, provides a deep skirt for the introduction of additional ornament. The feet range from sawed-bracket to modeled styles. As the most expensive option, the claw foot is rare; the pad foot is the most common. Drawer size and number also vary. Throughout the sample the upper case consists of five graduated unit levels. Most common are three separate drawers across the top range. Five long single drawers were another option, the top one sometimes made to look like three separate units. A few customers opted for an expensive arrangement of five small drawers in the top range in the manner of the Scotch chest. Choices for the lower case were even more extensive. Slightly more common than the four long, graduated units of this chest, which include a false front at the bottom, was the three-unit case with a similar bottom drawer. Other chests have three and four plain, graduated drawers. The two-drawer case and a chest with a range of three individual small drawers across the bottom are rare.[2]

The lower case of Winterthur's chest, which is similar to that of a Dunlap-style chest of drawers, is unusual (see No. 187). The facade is varied by the addition of a false drawer front at the bottom. Although the elimination of a gallery and separate base frame in this case greatly reduced the decorative options available to the consumer, the tall chest exhibits two of the most common embellishments found in Dunlap furniture: a "flowered OG[ogee]" molding and

a spoon-handle shell, although this one is unusual with thirteen rather than nine or eleven lobes. Visual emphasis is heightened in the cornice by the addition of a bold dentil molding; however, the impact is minimized by the introduction of the shell in the base. The shell also lowers the visual center of gravity in the chest, creating a somewhat bottom-heavy piece of furniture. The double-scroll brackets flanking the knees of the cabriole legs are fairly common in Dunlap chests of drawers and fall-front desks but are almost unknown in the tall chest.[3]

Several features of this piece of furniture support a guarded attribution to the workshop of Lt. Samuel Dunlap. Foremost is the chalk inscription "Salisbury" on the back of the second long drawer from the top in a hand that appears contemporary with the construction of the chest. Salisbury, New Hampshire, was Samuel's home from 1797 until his death in 1830. The similarity of the lower case to a chest of drawers also ascribed to Dunlap's shop (No. 187), based on other features, is another factor. The half-ball webbed feet, pointed knees, double-scroll brackets, and flowered-ogee moldings are close in both concept and execution. Rabbeted drawer construction, an uncommon structural feature of this tall chest, also is associated with Samuel Dunlap and furniture he made in Salisbury and with the work of a craftsman who trained with him during the 1790s.[4]

The Dunlap brothers—Samuel and John—were housebuilders and carpenters as well as cabinetmakers. The flowered-ogee molding so prominent in their furniture is also found in interior woodwork that can be documented or ascribed to them. They usually worked independently but collaborated in 1783 to build pulpits in churches in Temple and Londonderry. Plans for these fixtures and

related work, which survive, call for the use of flowered-ogee moldings. Earlier, in 1777, John built a house in Bedford for Zachariah Chandler that displayed flowered-ogee moldings on an arch surrounding a corner cupboard and a cornice above the cupboard. Samuel appears to have used a flowered-ogee molding in independent work, as well—the Elkins house in Salisbury, which he acquired in 1797, has a paneled room with fireplace in which both a flowered-ogee molding and a pierced-dentil molding of the pattern on the chest-on-chest are prominent elements of the cornice.[5]

The tall chest retains some evidence of its original red stain surface finish on the drawer sides and case interior. Whether this was an orange stain or a mahogany stain, for which there are recipes in the papers of John Dunlap, is unclear, but a mahogany finish seems more likely. Mahogany stain was made in part from logwood chips, a material also used by Samuel, who purchased a small quantity from his brother in 1784. The remnants of a dark residue, possibly black paint, still remain on the carved moldings, shell, and feet of the chest. Evidence of the original use of contrasting surface treatments on furniture ascribed to the Dunlap circle of craftsmen exists in two documented cases: a 1782 John Dunlap high chest of drawers had a green-painted ogee course and gilded rosettes in the gallery, and a 1770s high chest with gallery, made in John Dunlap's shop with the assistance of William Houston, originally had a mahoganized surface that contrasted with blue-green paint in portions of the cornice and base moldings (see No. 175).[6]

*NGE*

**Inscriptions or marks:** (Upper case) *On left small drawer, inside back:* "L" *in white chalk. On center* *small drawer, inside back:* "M" or "W" in white chalk; *on outside left side:* "Miss Beullah [or 'Budlah'] H" in an eighteenth- or early nineteenth-century hand; *on outside back:* "Moly [or 'Mols'] piteree [or 'pitee' or 'pitere']"; *on outside right side:* "T sophene[?] Boufait/ St. Helen[a?]"; *on outside right side:* "2" in pencil. *On right small drawer, inside back:* illegible chalk. *On inside back of all long drawers:* "B" in script in white chalk, accompanied by a short vertical stroke. *On underside of bottom:* "from upper part" in modern black crayon. *On outside back of second long drawer:* "Salisbury" in white chalk, in hand contemporary with the construction. *On upper edge of drawer blades:* "1" to "4" in modern pencil. (Lower case) *On inside back of all long drawers except top one:* script "B" in white chalk, accompanied by a short vertical stroke. *On underside of bottom of all long drawers except bottom one:* "to lower part" in modern black crayon. The chalk inscriptions appear to be by more than one hand, but all could be contemporary with the chest or nearly so.

**Construction:** (Upper case) The top is dovetailed to the sides. The two-piece mitered cornice molding, consisting of a separate carved border and a band of dentiling, is nailed over a molded board that forms the frieze. The top rail is slotted into the case sides. The vertical partitions between the drawers are slotted into the top rail and the top blade. The drawer blades are joined to the case sides with exposed shouldered dovetails. The drawer runners are nailed to the case sides. The bottom rail is pegged to the top of the bottom board. The bottom board is dovetailed to the case sides. The backboard consists of three horizontal lapped boards nailed to rabbets in the sides. The drawers are dovetailed, with overcut dovetails at the front. The upper edges of the sides and back are flat. The drawer bottoms, which are planed on the outside surface and run from side to side, are rabbeted on the front and sides; they are let into a rabbet at the front and grooves in the sides and are narrowly chamfered at the back and nailed flush. Only the top three long drawers are fitted with locks.

(Lower case) The waist molding is nailed to the top board. The top rail is glued to the front of the top board. The top and bottom boards are dovetailed to the case sides. The drawer blades and runners are secured as above. The bottom rail and a corresponding batten at the back of the case are pegged to the top of the bottom board. The carved base molding is nailed to the bottom board. The

legs are tenoned through the bottom board and rail, and the rectangular leg posts are exposed on the inside of the case. The knee brackets are glued and nailed to the case bottom. The backboard consists of two wide and one narrow board lapped on the inside and nailed to rabbets in the case sides. The drawers are constructed in the same manner as those in the upper case. The bottom drawer, which is full width, is molded on the front to simulate three small drawers. The brasses are original.

**Condition:** The backboard of the upper case is replaced with reused boards painted on the inside. Sections of the carved cornice molding are patched; some of the dentil molding is replaced. The lower surface of the top rail above the right small drawer was considerably chewed by a rodent. Holes in the bottoms of all the long drawers in the upper case are patched with facing pieces; the third and fourth drawers were chewed at the upper back by a rodent, and the third drawer is patched at the lock. The second and third drawer blades are patched above the locks. The top long drawer in the lower case is patched on the upper right corner and in the bottom. A section of the left waist molding is replaced. One or more drawer runners appear to be replaced. Several of the drawers have been patched on the side bottom. Both right legs are broken at the ankles. The right front leg is repaired with a stainless-steel rod; the right rear foot is patched with a vertical piece above the inside claw. The large scrolls of the knee brackets adjacent to the feet are replaced at the left front and right front and side. The chest, once stained and painted, has been refinished. Traces of red stain remain on the inside of the case and on the drawer sides; traces of black paint are still visible on the carved moldings, shell, and feet.

**Dimensions:**

| | | |
|---|---|---|
| H. | 80¾ in. | 205.1 cm |
| W. (cornice) | 42¼ in. | 107.3 cm |
| W. (upper case) | 36⅜ in. | 92.4 cm |
| W. (lower case) | 38⅝ in. | 98.1 cm |
| W. (knees) | 40½ in. | 102.9 cm |
| D. (cornice) | 20¾ in. | 52.7 cm |
| D. (upper case) | 17½ in. | 44.5 cm |
| D. (lower case) | 18¾ in. | 47.6 cm |
| D. (knees) | 19⅞ in. | 50.5 cm |

**Materials:** *Microanalysis:* Primary: soft maple group. Secondary: white pine group (drawer linings, backboards); basswood (feet, cornice frieze, dentil).

*Finish:* light honeybrown resin over remnants of original (?) mahogany stain and original (?) contrasting dark painted highlights.

**Publications:** Alice Winchester, "The Dunlap Dilemma: Notes on Some New Hampshire Cabinetmakers," *Antiques* 46, no. 6 (December 1944): 338, fig. 5. *Dunlaps and Their Furniture*, fig. 24. Charles S. Parsons, "The Dunlaps of New Hampshire and Their Furniture," in John D. Morse, ed., *Country Cabinetwork and Simple City Furniture* (Charlottesville: University Press of Virginia for the Henry Francis du Pont Winterthur Museum, 1970), p. 127. Zea and Dunlap, *Dunlap Cabinetmakers*, fig. 16.

**Accession history:** Bequest of H. F. du Pont, 1969. 56.524

1. Zea and Dunlap, *Dunlap Cabinetmakers*, pp. 38–45; David Learmont, "The Trinity Hall Chairs, Aberdeen," *Furniture History* 14 (1978): 1–8, pls. 4, 5, 9, 10, 12, 15–20; Philip D. Zimmerman, "Regionalism in American Furniture Studies," in Gerald W. R. Ward, ed., *Perspectives on American Furniture* (New York: W. W. Norton for the Henry Francis du Pont Winterthur Museum, 1988), pp. 33–38; David Jones, "Scotch Chests," *Regional Furniture* 2 (1988): 38–47. Motifs found on furniture of the Dunlap craftsmen also bear comparison with those on a carved wainscot armchair produced in 1695 by Scottish-born craftsman Robert Rhea, who settled in central New Jersey. Rhea's chair has a fanlike shell centered in the crest immediately below a pair of elevated, facing scrolls forming an open pediment–type arch in the manner of the double, projecting scrolls in the crest of No. 175, another Dunlap chest. The Rhea chair is in the Monmouth County Historical Assoc., Freehold, N.J.; see Zea and Dunlap, *Dunlap Cabinetmakers*, fig. 27.

2. The 28 chests-on-chests are gathered in *Dunlaps and Their Furniture*, figs. 1, 2, 9, 10, 15, 22–26, 28–33, 37, 40–50.

3. For John Dunlap's use of the term *flowered OG*, see *Dunlaps and Their Furniture*, pp. 45–52; for chests of drawers and desks with double-scroll brackets, see cats. 52–54, 64, 68, 74, 75.

4. *Dunlaps and Their Furniture*, p. 6; Zea and Dunlap, *Dunlap Cabinetmakers*, pp. 34, 36.

5. *Dunlaps and Their Furniture*, pp. 16–17, 45–52, figs. 100, 102.

6. *Dunlaps and Their Furniture*, pp. 19, 57, 249; Zea and Dunlap, *Dunlap Cabinetmakers*, pp. 29–32, 137, figs. 6, 80.

# Desks and Desk-and-Bookcases

THE ORIGIN OF THE WORD *DESK* CAN BE TRACED back to the Latin *discus*, meaning a table or a board for writing, reading, studying, or holding books, manuscripts, and writing paper. The earliest types of desks known through illustrations were probably used by ecclesiastical scholars and can be seen in illuminated manuscripts, woodcuts, and engravings that depict scholars seated at variously constructed sloped surfaces on which books or papers rest. By the end of the seventeenth century, *desk* referred to a simple writing surface, as in Samuel Pepys's 1666 mention of "the desk which he hath [made] to remove, and is fastened to one of the armes of his chayre"; or it might actually refer to a piece of case furniture in which books were stored. The desk and the desk-and-bookcase, as we know them in eighteenth-century American furniture, evolved from English and European forerunners, which were combinations of flat- or sloped-lid desk boxes and chests of drawers. The desk interior or "head" fitted with numerous pigeonholes and drawers derives from the sixteenth- and seventeenth-century sloped-lid boxes that had similar interiors.[1]

The addition of a case or "press" set on top of a "desk" to hold books came into fashion abroad by the first decade of the eighteenth century and was in Boston at least by 1715, when japanner William Randle advertised "at the Sign of the Cabbinett, a Looking-Glass Shop in Queen Street near the Town-House" that he sold "Escrutoires, Chests of Drawers, Tables, Beaufetts, Writing Desks, [and] Bookcases with Desk." It is possible that Randle's broad selection of goods were imported from England, as were the "Lately come from England . . . , Desks and Bookcases with Glass Doors" advertised three years later by William Hutchinson, Esq., of Boston. However, there is no doubt that once English precedents arrived in Boston, or any other colonial center, the form and style would soon be copied by quite capable cabinetmakers whose wealthy patrons were desirous of emulating the most fashionable taste abroad.[2]

During the second quarter of the eighteenth century, wealthy Bostonians desired extremely rich and stylish furniture. Patrons and cabinetmakers often looked to émigré craftsmen and imported furniture to inform them of the latest London taste and fashion. The production of Job Coit, Sr.'s, 1738 blockfront desk-and-bookcase (No. 205) and the extraordinarily creative example once owned by Josiah Quincy (No. 206) attest to the popularity of stylish and expensive desk-and-bookcases with affluent Boston merchants. By the third quarter of the century, Boston was eclipsed by Philadelphia in population, wealth, and emulation of the latest

London furniture fashions. In the 1752, 1754, and 1762 editions of Thomas Chippendale's *Gentleman and Cabinet-Maker's Director* are a number of designs for "Writing Tables," "Library Tables," and "Desk and Bookcases," as well as two versions of "A Lady's Writing Table and Bookcase." By that time, Boston's mercantile wealth was declining, and it is not surprising that none of these designs seem to have inspired any New England desks or desk-and-bookcases. The closest example to Chippendale's designs in Winterthur's collection can be seen in the upper section of No. 210, which is slightly reminiscent of plate 110. By the 1760s and 1770s, Philadelphians were even more enamored with these highly sophisticated and stylish rococo designs, and one known Philadelphia desk-and-bookcase is closely based on plate 108.[3] Perhaps if an English printed design source had been available twenty years earlier, at the height of Boston's economic ascendancy, the result would have been different.

The abundance of surviving eighteenth-century New England desks and desk-and-bookcases might seem disproportionate in comparison to examples from other regions, but the acquisition and ownership of desk-and-bookcases presupposes a level of education and economic means more readily attainable in New England. In the seventeenth century, an ample number of scholars, merchants, and ministers in New England were prospective purchasers of desks or desk-and-bookcases. Beginning in 1636 with the founding of Harvard, New England produced well-educated men who entered professions such as religion, education, law, medicine, and mercantilism. Add to this the fact that Boston became the major trading center in the colonies during the first four decades of the eighteenth century, as its population grew from more than 6,000 in 1690 to more than 16,000 in 1740. Although the majority of the population of New England was agrarian, tremendous fortunes were amassed by merchants and other tradesmen in Newport, Boston, Salem, and Portsmouth prior to the revolutionary war. This affluence was accompanied by a demand for functional furniture by the comfortably well-to-do and luxury goods and objects of status by those with greater wealth. Just as the architecture of the residences of merchant princes reflected their accomplishments and positions, so their desks or monumental desk-and-bookcases proclaimed their prosperity. While most frequently it was the merchants, entrepreneurs, and ministers who owned handsome desk-and-bookcases, it is not uncommon to find desks and desk-and-bookcases listed in the inventories of successful craftsmen or manufacturers. For example, in 1782 the inventory of Boston bricklayer Thomas Parker included "1 mahogany desk & Bookcase" valued at £8; the 1781 inventory of Dorchester chocolatemaker John Hannon, listed "1 desk" at £2.8.0; the 1780 inventory of Boston sugar refiner John Baker, noted "1 mahogany desk and bookcase . . . £18"; and Boston blacksmith Samuel Emmes left a "mahogany desk and bookcase" worth £8 when he died in 1783.[4]

Regardless of regional background, the furniture these men chose may have served a specific function relative to their professions, but it certainly announced a level of status to their respective peers. These pieces of furniture should not be defined as urban or nonurban but should be assessed in terms of what they represented within the context of their individual regional milieu. For example, the impressive cherry desk-and-bookcase (No. 203) owned by Preston, Connecticut, lawyer and entrepreneur Jeremiah Halsey was no doubt quite costly, perhaps the height of style in that region of the colonies. Likewise, the desk-and-bookcase that successful urban merchant Daniel Henchman purchased from Job Coit, Sr., in 1738 was the height of new fashion in Boston. Present-day perspective and breadth of knowledge might lead some to judge the Halsey desk-and-bookcase "provincial," but within its own context in the eighteenth century, it would never have been perceived as less fashionable or inferior.

New England desks and desk-and-bookcases provide an abundant resource illustrative of a wide variety of factors impacting regional styles, choices based strictly on economic concerns, and the more abstract indicators of status and social order. The choice of primary wood was most often economically based, although regional preference was sometimes a determining factor. For instance, the use of maple in the New Hampshire desk discussed in No. 200 was probably determined by regional preference as well as availability, while the choice of maple (instead of mahogany) in the Massachusetts desk-and-bookcase in No. 204 was perhaps more an economic decision. In the earliest known colonial "Cabinetmakers' Agreement," recorded in Providence, Rhode Island, on February 19, 1756, and revised March 24, 1757, a "Mehogany Desk with 2 Draws" cost £90, while a "walnot Do with 2 tear of Draws" cost £75. Other cost choices included: the type of feet (straight-bracket, ogee-bracket, pad, or claw); whether the front was "swelled" (blocked or serpentine) or straight; amount and detail of carving on the exterior or interior; and how the interior was configured. In the 1792 Hartford price list, "a plain Desk, 3 feet 3 inches in length, and plain feet, with 3 drawers in the head" cost £4.7.0. Extras that added to the list price included additional length, "swell'd feet," "swell'd front," "claw feet and carv'd moulding," and "quarter columns." The basic desk-and-bookcase on the same price list cost £6.5.0 and was described as "a Secretary, made plain, with swell'd feet, length 3 feet 8 inches." The addition of "doors and trays" increased the cost by 5s., while a "swell'd front" added £2 to make a total price of £8.10.0. Although this very specific listing does not mention the type of wood used, it may be assumed that the pieces are made of cherry, the wood of choice in Connecticut. Type of hardware and large carrying handles (in 1757 a "Plane Desk with Polished handels" cost £3 more), a broken scroll top, and pilasters in the bookcase section also added cost.[5]

Without specific primary references it is difficult to determine whether most desks and desk-and-bookcases of considerable cost were special orders or whether a cabinet shop might be likely to have one or two costly and fashionable pieces on hand at any one time. While it is most reasonable that the more costly examples were "bespoke" work—that is, special orders—some evidence suggests that makers might have had fashionable pieces on hand, and if they did not sell quickly, they were sent to auction. Most auction notices offered "pre-owned" household furniture, but occasionally some described new furniture, as in "A choice new Mahogany Desk, made after the best Manner." John Goddard of Newport either sometimes made desk-and-bookcases on speculation or had clients fail to purchase a piece that had been ordered, as revealed in a letter sent to Nicholas Brown of Providence on October 3, 1766. Goddard hopefully wrote, "P.S. I should be glad if thou or some of thy Brothers & I could agree abought a desk & Bookcase which I have to dispose of."[6]

Precisely where, how, and how often desks and desk-and-bookcases were used, as well as by whom, are difficult questions to answer. Presumably those of great cost and visual appeal were domestic pieces, for to be seen and to make an imposing impression were primary functions. Less costly, plainer examples might have been used in a merchant's counting house or office or a lawyer's or minister's library or office. Room-by-room inventories are useful resources, but they are rare survivals usually only completed for considerable estates. More impressive pieces generally would be found in the best parlor. Desk-and-bookcases with mirrored doors enclosing the upper section (Nos. 205, 206, 210) would have greatly enhanced the shimmering quality of any candlelight in the room at night, especially if candlesticks were positioned on the small slides that pull out beneath the mirrored doors (No. 206).

Just as the configuration of the drawers and pigeonholes within the interior of the desk can vary greatly, so too can the arrangement of shelves and dividers in the bookcase. Sometimes these vertical and horizontal parts are fixed, and sometimes they are movable, allowing for greater flexibility. Depending on the needs of the owner, these upper cases could be designed to accommodate everything from large, slim account ledgers to rows of smaller bound imprints. It is difficult to know exactly what level of collaboration might have existed between client and cabinetmaker before the piece was fabricated. The drawers below the writing surface could be used to store anything, from maps and papers to folded linens and clothes to unused fabric or scraps of fabric. For example, Providence merchant John Brown, who owned an impressive Newport block-and-shell desk-and-bookcase, wrote to his daughter in 1782, "Your Mar told me the pieces like your Brocade frock is in the Lore Draw of the Book Case[;] if they can be found, they shall be Sent you with this."[7] It is reasonable to conclude that the majority of desk-and-bookcases in the eighteenth century were made for men, as the heads of households and main financial managers. Some women and children used desks, however; a carefully conceived slant-front desk quite likely was made specifically for a woman, the drawers below designed for linen and clothing storage (No. 200).

Winterthur's collection contains a wide range of New England desks and desk-and-bookcases, and together the fourteen examples selected for this volume exhibit significant diversity in overall form, regional origin, design, materials, and function. The desks range from a diminutive painted desk-on-frame most likely used by a young person to a simple functional example with "claw feet and carv'd moulding" to one with a "swell'd" front. The desk-and-bookcases are some of the finest examples from Connecticut, Rhode Island, and Massachusetts—four blockfront pieces provide an enlightening study of this form, beginning with the earliest known dated Boston example. Two bombé desk-and-bookcases made in Boston conclude this section, illustrating variations on this important form.

WAC

---

1  For early desks, see Macquoid and Edwards, *Dictionary*, 2:203. On Pepys, see *Oxford English Dictionary*, s.v. "Pepys, Samuel." For the terms *head* and *pigeonholes*, see the 1792 Hartford price list, as cited in *Great River*, pp. 471–73; for a fuller discussion of the evolution of desks, see Macquoid and Edwards, *Dictionary*, 2:203–13.

2  Randle is cited in Dow, *Arts and Crafts in New England*, pp. 106–7. When Royal Governor William Burnet left Boston in 1729, "a Scriptore with Glass doors" that he owned was sold by Public Vendue in October 1729 (Dow, *Arts and Crafts in New England*, pp. 108–9). The desire to emulate English styles is embodied in the Karolik Collection Boston desk-and-bookcase; see Hipkiss, *Eighteenth-Century American Arts*, no. 18.

3  Flanigan, *American Furniture*, pp. 90–93.

4  For relevant inventories, see Thomas Parker (1782), John Hannon (1781), John Baker (1780), and Samuel Emmes (1783) estate inventories, Suffolk County Probate Court, Boston (microfilm, Downs collection).

5  A manuscript copy of the February 19, 1756, agreement and the March 24, 1757, revision is at Rhode Island Historical Society and is cited in *John Brown House Loan Exhibition*, pp. 174–75. See the Hartford price list as cited in *Great River*, p. 471.

6  Dow, *Arts and Crafts in New England*, p. 115. John Goddard to Nicholas Brown, October 3, 1766, Brown Papers, Misc. 1765–67, John Carter Brown Library, Brown University, Providence, R.I.

7  Ward, *American Case Furniture*, pp. 339–44. John Brown to Salley Brown, December 19, 1782, Brown Papers.

## 197 ◆ Desk-on-frame
Rhode Island or Eastern Connecticut
1725–50

Small desks made specifically for children in eighteenth-century New England are a varied and interesting group of case furniture. The most frequent interpretation is a plain three-drawer desk with a base molding and straight-bracket feet. Other versions, more closely related to this example, feature a desk section with one, two, or three drawers raised on a frame with either straight, turned legs or cabriole legs with pad or trifid feet.[1] The interiors of these desks are usually quite plain, and often they were originally painted with a pigmented stain even when a wood such as maple was used.

This diminutive fall-front desk-on-frame represents one variation of a child's three-drawer desk raised on a simple frame with straight, turned legs, pad feet, and a lively shaped apron on the front and sides. That it was not the product of an urban cabinet shop is suggested by a combination of features: rather thick construction of the drawers, random use of a variety of secondary woods, use of maple finished with a pigmented red stain, and less-refined dovetails and joinery. The original stamped, engraved brasses, secured with iron cotter pins, may indicate a date in the 1720s or 1730s; but if the piece was made in the 1750s, the earlier, less-fashionable brasses may suggest a lingering tradition indicative of more rural areas.

This desk-on-frame is closely related to two other almost identical children's desks, one of which is in the Museum of Fine Arts, Boston, and the other, formerly in the collection of Mr. and Mrs. Mitchell Taradash, is now privately owned. All three desks are approximately the same size; the Museum of Fine Arts desk has slightly shorter legs and is about 1 1/2 inches shorter than the other two. They all have what appear to be identical

brasses, and only the two top drawers on each have locks. The shaped aprons of the frames are reminiscent of those often seen on dressing tables and tea tables and are all identical except for a slight variation in the center of the front rail of Winterthur's desk. All three have the same interior arrangement of four plain drawers surmounted by a series of eight open compartments with arched valances that appropriately echo the shaped apron of the frame (fig. 1). The primary wood of all three desks is maple; Winterthur's example retains its pigmented red stain, as does the Museum of Fine Arts desk, which also has legs painted black. Richard Randall correctly observed that the two desks are likely the products of the same shop.[2] The third desk, which also may originally have been painted with a red pigment, is certainly from the same hand.

Because none of these desks have any known history of original ownership, it is more difficult to determine the precise region of origin. An area of manufacture can be deduced from specific design features as well as the use of secondary woods, however. The tapering cylindrical legs ending in pad feet are reminiscent of those found on numerous square (porringer-top) tea tables, a round table (see Nos. 111, 115), and some dining tables attributable to Rhode Island, as well as eastern Connecticut case furniture. The deeply shaped apron of the frame is also echoed on Rhode Island and Connecticut tea tables, high chests, and dressing tables. The simple yet lively presentation of the interior with plain drawers and shaped headers can similarly be seen in other Rhode Island and eastern Connecticut desks.[3] The random use of chestnut as a secondary wood is frequently seen in Rhode Island and eastern Connecticut manufacture, and although it is not conclusive evidence, it strongly suggests an origin in southeastern New England.

WAC

**Fig. 1.** Desk open.

---

**Inscriptions or marks:** All of the drawers in the desk have faint scratched numbers. *Inside back and on top of the far left drawer front:* "1". *Inside back of the second from left drawer front:* "C". *On top of second from left drawer front:* "2". *On back of second from left drawer:* "134" *in pencil. Scratched on top of second from right drawer front:* "3". *Scratched on top, sides, and back of far right drawer:* "4".

**Construction:** The top and bottom boards are through-dovetailed to the sides; the bottom dovetails are concealed by a molding applied to the top edge of the base of the frame. The interior writing surface and the top two drawer blades are joined to the sides with exposed half dovetails. The bottommost blade is simply dadoed into the sides. The drawer runners are nailed to the case sides with two forged nails on each runner. The top drawer and loper runners are nailed at the side at the rear, and the loper guides are nailed to the top of the runners with forged nails. The vertical loper blade is set into the leading edge of the interior writing surface and the uppermost drawer blade with exposed dovetails. The four horizontal, lap-joined backboards (pine) are rabbeted to the top and sides and fastened with forged nails. The lipped drawer fronts have a quarter-round molded edge; the sides are dovetailed front and back. The bottom boards (three boards lap joined, grain running front to back) are chamfered on the bottom front and sides and fit into grooves on the sides and front. The bottom is nailed flush to the back of the drawer with five forged nails. The engraved brasses are secured with cotter pins and appear to be original. The top two drawers retain their original locks; there is no lock on the bottom drawer. The fall-front lid is lipped on three sides with a quarter-round molding. The sides of the interior drawers have one large dovetail front and back; the bottoms are nailed flush at back and rabbeted to the drawer sides and front. The shaped valances of the

pigeonholes are glued in place and additionally secured with small blocks on their interior sides. The rails of the frame are mortised and tenoned to leg posts, and all joints are double-pinned. The lower edge of the front and side rails are cut with elaborate cyma-curve arches; the back rail is straight. A molding, mitered at the corners, is nailed to the top edge of the front and side rails of the frame.

**Condition:** One bottom board is replaced in lowest drawer. The hardware appears to be original, except for one bail handle and cotter pin.

**Dimensions:**

| | | |
|---|---|---|
| H. | 36 1/8 in. | 91.8 cm |
| H. (writing surface) | 28 3/8 in. | 72.1 cm |
| H. (case) | 23 1/4 in. | 59.1 cm |
| H. (frame) | 13 11/16 in. | 39.8 cm |
| W. (case) | 24 in. | 61.0 cm |
| W. (frame) | 26 in. | 66.0 cm |
| W. (feet) | 26 in. | 66.0 cm |
| D. (case) | 11 3/4 in. | 29.8 cm |
| D. (frame) | 13 in. | 33.0 cm |
| D. (feet) | 13 in. | 33.0 cm |

**Materials:** *Microanalysis:* Primary: soft maple group. Secondary: white pine group (bottom board of top

long drawer, sides of some long drawers); chestnut (bottoms and sides of some long drawers); yellow pine (backboard); beech (front rail, blades). *Finish:* reddish brown color in resin, probably original.

**Publications:** Downs, *American Furniture*, fig. 216.

**Accession history:** Bequest of H. F. du Pont, 1969. 59.2114

1. Ward, *American Case Furniture*, pp. 300–301; see also Heckscher, *American Furniture*, pp. 264–65. Bernard and S. Dean Levy, Inc., *In Search of Excellence* (New York: By the company, 1995), p. 9; Albert Sack, *The New Fine Points of Furniture: Early American* (New York: Crown Publishers, 1993), p. 149; Sotheby's, "Important Americana from the Collection of Mr. and Mrs. Adolph Henry Meyer" (January 20, 1996), lot 40.

2. For the MFA, Boston, desk, see Randall, *American Furniture*, no. 56; for the privately owned desk, see *American Antiques from Israel Sack Collection*, 10 vols. (Washington, D.C.: Highland House, ca. 1969–), 7:1919. Randall, *American Furniture*, p. 72.

3. For eastern Connecticut case furniture, see *New London County Furniture*, nos. 8, 19; for Rhode Island desks, see Jeanne Vibert Sloane, "John Cahoone and the Newport Furniture Industry," in *New England Furniture*, figs. 5, 8; for eastern Connecticut desks, see *New London County Furniture*, no. 18.

## 198 ◆ Desk
Northeastern Massachusetts or
New Hampshire
1770–1810

When this desk was first published in 1952 by Joseph Downs, it was thought to have been made in Newport, Rhode Island, around the middle of the eighteenth century. This attribution was based in large part on the shell carving, the ambitious design of the interior, and the bold shell and C-scroll carving on the knees. The early date of 1740–50 was in keeping with the then-current belief that the Queen Anne style was produced within a specific time frame. Years of study, research, and discovery have revealed that this desk is probably not the product of a stylish urban center like Newport, nor does the presence of pad feet restrict the date of manufacture specifically to the prerevolutionary period.

It is now well documented that throughout the second two-thirds of the eighteenth century and into the early nineteenth century, the Queen Anne style, and elements thereof, were produced in nonurban areas. The prevalence of pad feet on desks, chests, chairs, and tables made in rural areas well after the end of the Revolution may indicate that this feature was not considered so much a measure of fashion as a measure of means.

The overall form of this desk is similar to a number of others that have histories of ownership in northeastern Massachusetts and New Hampshire, suggesting that geographic region as a place of origin. The squat, bandy legs and pad feet relate in a general design sense to the work of the Dunlap family and their followers and hence also point to a possible New Hampshire provenance. The shell-carved knees and the elaborately configured and executed interior are the most distinctive characteristics of this otherwise rather simple slant-front desk. The shell

carving has nine alternating concave-convex lobes over a rather stylized pendent leaf, or bellflower, and is flanked with a C scroll on either side (which does not continue onto the brackets)—a feature not found on other related casepieces (fig. 1). Because the carved scrolls do not continue on the brackets, it is reasonable to think that all the brackets have been replaced; yet the front brackets appear to retain layers of original finish. One possible explanation might be that the turned and carved feet came from a separate shop, and when they were assembled on the desk and the brackets were added, there was no carver (or appropriate tools) available to execute the complementary scrolls on the brackets. The exaggerated cabriole of the bandy leg lacks the hock on the inside back that is associated with the "Bartlett" school in Salisbury, New Hampshire. Although the overall forms are similar, specific design, ornamentation, and construction features, including the very regular and meticulous dovetails, also argue

against an association with the shop of Levi or Peter Bartlett.[1]

Like many desks and desk-and-bookcases from the New England region, the interior of this desk is a variation on the five-part theme, always featuring a central section with major ornamentation, usually flanked with narrow document drawers faced with turned pilasters (fig. 2). With special care, the maker has shaped the top edges of these document drawers in a cyma-curve pattern. Instead of a central prospect door, this example has two plain drawers over a deep drawer with a concave shell carving. Beneath the central and two flanking compartments there is a long open space that might have been designed to hold a ledger or account book. The thin board dividing this space from the drawers above is skillfully and elaborately shaped. The overall execution of this interior is very refined and shows great attention to detail and design.

Unfortunately no provenance survives for this desk to provide some clues regarding the

**Fig. 1.** Detail, leg.

owner or maker. The dark reddish stain over the exterior surface suggests that it may have been finished in imitation of the more expensive mahogany desks produced in major urban areas, where imported woods would have commanded greater prices than locally available native woods.

WAC

**Inscriptions or marks:** *Painted in black on backboard:* "J762". *Incised on the underside of the writing surface:* "IV". The second, third, and fourth long drawers have a chalk shop mark "6" or "9". *Inside the front of the left convex drawer on paper label:* partial postmark "[BO]STON MASS" and in ink "48/ 437608".

**Construction:** The top is half-blind dovetailed to the sides. The hinged slant top, a solid piece with three tenons double-pegged to batten ends, opens to rest on narrow lopers cut on the front with a thumbnail molding. The desk interior, in a modified amphitheater design, is divided into five vertical sections. At each end, paired valanced pigeonholes surmount a convex blocked drawer with a plain drawer below. On either side of the prospect section, a single large pigeonhole rests above a convex blocked drawer. The prospect section consists of two plain drawers above a deep shell-carved drawer; the whole is flanked by narrow document drawers. The drawers in the desk section have rounded sides and flat backs, and the bottoms are set flush into a rabbet on all four sides. Each desk side has a wide and a narrow board. Plain blades are set into the sides on half dovetails with the ends exposed. The vertical dividers surrounding the top drawer are set into the rails on shouldered dovetails; the lower end of the divider pierces the blade. There are no dust or security boards. The drawer runners are set into grooves in the sides. The bottom board is dovetailed to the sides. The base molding is nailed to the case. The backboard, three vertical lapped boards with pit-saw marks still visible, is nailed to rabbets in the top and sides and flush across the bottom with rosehead nails. The legs appear to be joined to the case on small tenons. Wide, shaped knee brackets are nailed to the case. The rear legs project beyond the back of the case. On the long drawers, the sides are cut in a quarter-round-and-fillet molding on the upper edge; the back is flat; the bottoms, their grain running side to side, are set into grooves on the front and sides and nailed flush across the back with rosehead nails.

**Condition:** The piece has several layers of finish; the outer layer is heavily pigmented with a red stain. Several of the knee brackets may be replaced. All the brasses are new; the piece had at least two earlier sets of hardware. The hinges holding the slant lid appear to be old.

**Dimensions:**

| | | |
|---|---|---|
| H. | 41 3/8 in. | 105.1 cm |
| H. (writing surface) | 31 3/8 in. | 79.7 cm |
| W. (case) | 34 3/4 in. | 88.3 cm |
| W. (feet) | 37 1/4 in. | 94.6 cm |
| D. (case) | 18 1/4 in. | 46.4 cm |
| D. (feet) | 20 1/4 in. | 51.4 cm |

**Materials:** *Microanalysis:* Primary: soft maple group. Secondary: white pine group (throughout). *Finish:* dark reddish brown color in resin.

**Publications:** Downs, *American Furniture*, fig. 215.

**Accession history:** Purchased March 10, 1930, from Collings and Collings, New York. Bequest of H. F. du Pont, 1969.
58.2224

---

1. For related pieces with regional histories, see American Art Association Anderson Galleries, "American Furniture from the Collection of Benjamin Flayderman" (April 17–18, 1931), lot 180; Randall, *American Furniture*, no. 56; Sotheby Parke Bernet, "The American Heritage Auction of Americana," 2 vols. (November 27–December 1, 1979), lot 1244; Robert W. Skinner, "Americana" (October 29, 1988), lot 72; Northeast Auctions, "New Hampshire Auction" (March 3, 1996). Thanks to Robert F. Trent for calling my attention to Walter A. Backofen, *Some Queen Anne Furniture from New Hampshire's Federal Period* (East Plainfield, N.H.: Lord Timothy Dexter Press, 1988).

**Fig. 2.** Detail, interior.

## 199 ◆ Desk

New Hampshire
1790–1815
Probably by Maj. John Dunlap (1746–92),
John Dunlap, Jr., or Lt. Samuel Dunlap
(1752–1830)

Although desks of this form are often
referred to today as slant-lid or fall-front
desks, in the account books of Maj. John
Dunlap and his brother Samuel, they were
simply called "desks." John Dunlap's account
book indicates that from 1769 through 1785,
he made eleven desks, although two were
referred to as "one Comon Desk old Way"
and "one Shop Desk." Samuel recorded
making nine desks from 1783 to 1806. In
past studies at least twenty-five desks have
been identified and related to the work of the
Dunlaps, so presumably not all the desks they
made were contemporaneously recorded.[1]

Like all New England desks of the second
half of the eighteenth century, the group
associated with the Dunlaps vary in stylistic

details and decorative features. There were
four options exercised for the style of foot—
ogee-bracket, straight-bracket, cabriole with
plain (pad) foot, and cabriole with ball-and-
claw foot. Clearly there were different costs
associated with each, ranging from the least
expensive straight-bracket foot to the most
costly ball-and-claw. Other ornamental
features that would increase cost included
the addition of a central carved pendant, the
Dunlap "trademark" flowered-ogee molding,
and interior carved drawer fronts or pigeonhole
valances.[2] Stamped rococo brasses, oval brasses,
or simple bail brasses are all found on the
surviving desks, although it is not known if
Dunlap procured the brasses or if the client
was responsible for adding the hardware. The
generic term *desk* in the John Dunlap accounts
combined with the unstable fluctuation of
currency during this period make it impossible
to determine specific costs for these details
based on the total cost of each desk.

At least one other known desk appears
to be identical to Winterthur's example, with

ball-and-claw feet, scrolled brackets, flowered-
ogee molding, bail brasses, and an upper
tier of alternating fan- and shell-carved
interior drawers. Neither desk has any
history of ownership, but an almost identical
privately owned desk, which lacks the carved
ornamental details, has "a strong history of
ownership that suggests Samuel Dunlap was
its maker." A similarly unornamented desk
at Yale University has been attributed to
Samuel Dunlap based on the privately owned
example. Another desk with almost identical
interior is inscribed "JD" and attributed to
either Maj. John Dunlap or John Dunlap, Jr.
The distinctive technique employed on
Winterthur's desk of the square tenon of
the feet extending up through the bottom
board and the interior rail appears to be a
construction feature common to both Dunlap
brothers.[3] Consequently, it is impossible
without specific documentation to assign
the authorship of this desk to one particular
Dunlap shop or craftsman.

The scrolled brackets that flank the
legs on this desk also appear on many pieces
of furniture associated with the Dunlaps
(fig. 1). Quite similar brackets are found
on furniture made in the region of New
London County, Connecticut (see No. 127).
In the purest design sense, this can be
interpreted as a manifestation of Palladian,
or specifically Kentian, influence. But how
does one explain the exact manner of
transmission from London in the first quarter
of the eighteenth century to New Hampshire
or Connecticut in the last quarter of the
eighteenth century? Recent scholarship
surrounding some of the Connecticut pieces
of furniture (see No. 149) suggests that
perhaps these strongly architectural design
elements might have been disseminated
by a Scottish prisoner of war (and trained
architect), William Sprats, who was confined
at Hartford, Connecticut, in 1779.[4]

**Fig. 1.** Detail, leg.

Like much of the furniture produced by the Dunlap shops, this desk originally was stained to resemble mahogany. Among John Dunlap's accounts are several recipes for finishes. Presumably, the following was used on this desk: "*To stain wood to Resemble Mehogany*—Take 2 pounds of Logwood chipd fine put it in a Clean Brass kettle add 1 Gallon of water Boil this 4 hours then take out your chips—evaporate to 1 quart—strain and brush your maple 3 times over let it dry between each Brushing—Then take 1 oz. of Curkmy root—1 oz. of Dragons Blood—1 Oz. of logwood all made fine put it in a quart bottle add to this 1 pint of Spirits of wine let it steep 24 hours—turn it of Clear—brush it once over after the Logwood is brushed—and so Done."[5]

WAC

---

**Inscriptions or marks:** *On the small drawers in each row of the desk section, on inside back:* "R/1", "2", "3", "4", "5" *in ink; on the top row, bottom of drawers:* "1"–"5" *in modern pencil; and on second row, bottom of drawers:* "6"–"10". *Inscribed on the lower tier of drawers, inside back:* "L", "M", *and* "R" *in ink; and on the bottom:* "11", "12", *and* "13" *in pencil. Some of the desk drawers also have chalk shop marks.*

**Construction:** The top is joined to the sides with many small half-blind dovetails. Presumably the bottom is joined to the sides with fully exposed dovetails. Drawer blades are set into the front edge of the sides with fully exposed dovetails; the bottom blade is not dovetailed but simply pinned to the bottom board. The legs are through-tenoned and wedged. The carved molding is nailed to the bottom board, and the thick scroll-shape brackets are each secured with two nails to the bottom board. The two horizontal backboards are nailed to rabbets in the top board and sides and nailed flush to the bottom board. The vertical loper blades are notched in; the lopers are probably replaced. The drawer fronts are lipped with a quarter-round molded edge; the drawer sides are dovetailed front and back. The drawer bottoms are one board, with grain running side to side, with front and sides chamfered and set into grooves and nailed flush to the backboard. The top edges of the drawer sides are beaded. The hinged slant top, a solid piece with mitered battened ends, opens to rest on plain lopers chamfered on the front edge. The desk interior is divided into two horizontal sections. The upper section has two tiers of five drawers, the upper tier in two patterns of carved shell, the lower tier plain. The rail between the sections is cut with a broken-ogee molding. The lower section has three plain drawers. The drawers in the desk section have flat upper sides and backs; the bottoms are set into grooves in the front and sides and held with wood pegs across the back; the drawer fronts have long kerf marks where the dovetails are overcut.

**Condition:** The piece appears to have originally been stained to simulate mahogany. There is also evidence of a later coat of paint. The front edge of the right side has a repaired break. The writing surface is repaired at the hinges, and the hinges are replaced. Both front knee brackets are repaired; the left bracket has a section replaced. The sides of the top and third long drawers are repaired. The brass hardware is the second set.

**Dimensions:**

| | | |
|---|---|---|
| H. | 44 1/4 in. | 112.4 cm |
| H. (writing surface) | 34 1/4 in. | 87.0 cm |
| W. (case) | 37 5/8 in. | 95.7 cm |
| W. (feet) | 39 1/4 in. | 99.7 cm |
| D. (case) | 18 3/4 in. | 47.6 cm |
| D. (feet) | 19 in. | 48.3 cm |

**Materials:** *Microanalysis:* Primary: soft maple group. Secondary: white pine group (drawer bottoms, backboard); basswood (fronts of shell drawers in desk section, knee brackets). *Finish:* light brown color in resin.

**Publications:** Nutting, *Furniture Treasury*, no. 608. Alice Winchester, "The Dunlap Dilemma: Notes on Some New Hampshire Cabinetmakers," *Antiques* 46, no. 6 (December 1944): 338, fig. 6. *Dunlaps and Their Furniture*, fig. 68.

**Accession history:** Purchased by H. F. du Pont from Collings and Collings, New York, 1926. Bequest of H. F. du Pont, 1969.
65.1405

---

1. *Dunlaps and Their Furniture*, pp. 202, 218. Ward, *American Case Furniture*, p. 311.

2. Zea and Dunlap, *Dunlap Cabinetmakers*, p. 152; *Dunlaps and Their Furniture*, fig. 65. The one documented desk with pad feet is actually a desk-on-frame made by John Dunlap for Thomas Shirley of Bedford and listed in the account book on May 5, 1774, at £48. Recent research suggests that the inspiration for Dunlap's flowered-ogee molding may have come from the carved mantelpiece in Council Chamber Gov. Benning Wentworth's mansion near Portsmouth or some related architectural interior; see Zea and Dunlap, *Dunlap Cabinetmakers*, p. 27.

3. For the identical desk and the privately owned desk, see *Dunlaps and Their Furniture*, figs. 75, 71; for the Yale desk, see Ward, *American Case Furniture*, p. 311. For the desk inscribed "JD," see Zea and Dunlap, *Dunlap Cabinetmakers*, p. 151; see also p. 95 for construction techniques.

4. Zea and Dunlap, *Dunlap Cabinetmakers*, pp. 40–43; Robert F. Trent, "The Colchester School of Cabinetmaking, 1750–1800," in Francis J. Puig and Michael Conforti, eds., *The American Craftsman and the European Tradition, 1620–1820* (Minneapolis: Minneapolis Institute of Arts, 1989), pp. 132–33.

5. *Dunlaps and Their Furniture*, p. 57.

## 200 ◆ Desk
Probably southern New Hampshire
1780–1820

The most pronounced feature of this desk is the unusual and unconventional nonurban tour de force of ornamentation. Yet as one begins to understand this desk in its totality, it becomes clear that form, function, and design have been very carefully and consciously considered and conceived in its creation. Here we see the thoughtful collaboration between craftsman and patron from both a design and a usage standpoint. Unlike some desks where a major and expensive feature of ornamentation might be prominently placed on the face of the slant-front lid (and seen only when the desk was closed), the vocabulary of ornament displayed here was consciously placed low on the facade of the case so that it can still be admired when the fall-front is open (fig. 1).

As flashy and expensively ornamented as the lower part of the desk facade is, the interior represents almost the opposite extreme of simplicity and economy. With just two tiers of plain drawers and pigeonholes behind the fall-front, the only ornament is carved in the center of the two long drawers and echoes the hearts and pinwheels seen in bolder measure on the exterior.

Just as the maker and client must have carefully decided on where to place the most expensive aspect of ornamentation on this desk, so they also must have specifically discussed the visual presentation of the facade and how it would actually function. The desk appears to have three long drawers over a central, deep drawer flanked by two stacked, narrow, deep drawers. The division of drawers is more simplistic and functional than the facade suggests, however, as there are actually only three drawers: what appear to be two long drawers beneath the topmost narrower drawer is one deep drawer, and the lower

complex of five carved drawers is also only one deep drawer. This arrangement appears to be designed more for the storage of clothing and linens than for the containment of papers, maps, or charts and is reminiscent of some eighteenth-century chests over drawers that actually look like chests of drawers.

Another aspect of the design of this desk that may be directly related to its function as a work surface is the less-than-normal height of the desk interior and hence the shallow depth of the writing surface. The fall-front is about two to four inches shallower than the standard desk of this general form. This small proportion results in a smaller writing surface and less interior drawer or storage space. The type of storage space provided by the deep drawer arrangement, the diminished work space more appropriate for diary and letter writing rather than account and ledger work, and the inclusion of diminutive hearts in the

decoration leads to the speculation that this desk was made specifically for a woman's use.

The question still remains as to where this ambitious and innovative desk was made. No provenance survives to provide a clue for regional association, although the materials employed—maple, white pine—do suggest northern New England, probably New Hampshire. The placement of the ornament at the base, the concept of multidrawer facades on the face of one deep drawer that looks like five, and the ornament of fans and pinwheels are features related to the work of the Dunlaps, as well as that of Moses Hazen, Jr., of Weare, New Hampshire. It has been cited, however, that the construction of this desk is unlike that of the Dunlaps' work.[1] The massive lobed shell is reminiscent of great shell-carved corner cupboards, and it is possible that the joiner who worked on this desk was also involved

**Fig. 1.** Desk open.

with architectural work (fig. 2). Although specific authorship is at present difficult to ascertain, there is no doubt that this desk was specially commissioned and represents an innovative and thoughtful approach to a standard eighteenth-century form.

WAC

---

**Construction:** The top is half-blind dovetailed to the sides. The hinged slant-top lid, a solid board with batten ends, opens to rest on plain lopers rounded on the front. The interior of the desk is fitted with two wide central drawers, the upper drawer decorated with a carved, inverted, fanlike heart and the lower drawer ornamented with a leafy cluster of fanlike flowers. The upper drawer has an unusual locking mechanism operated from the drawer below. Flanking these drawers are two pigeonholes with plain drawers below. The drawers are flat on the upper edge of the sides and back; the bottoms are dadoed on the front and sides and secured across the back with tiny wood pegs. The top rail is joined on an exposed half-dovetail; the one-piece blades are joined on exposed dovetails. The vertical dividers are joined to the rails by exposed dovetails. The bottom rail is half-blind dovetailed to the sides and attached with rosehead nails to the bottom board. The sides are dovetailed to the bottom board. The drawer runners are secured with rosehead nails to the sides. The long drawers are flat on the upper edge of the sides and back. The drawer bottoms, the grain side to side, are chamfered and set into grooves on three sides; they are secured across the back with tiny wood pegs. Three horizontal tongue-and-groove boards forming the backboard are attached with rosehead nails to rabbets in the sides. The bracket feet and base molding are cut as a unit and nailed to the case; vertical glueblocks reinforce the mitered join. On each rear leg, the back bracket, its inner edge arched, is butted to the side bracket.

**Condition:** The desk has been refinished, although traces of the red and black stain (paint) are visible on the case. A split in the top rail has been repaired. The fall-front lid is a replacement. The blades show little evidence of wear and may be replaced. All the drawer sides have been patched on the lower edge. The front base molding is patched. The left front and right side brackets are repaired. The left and right rear brackets are pieced out. The vertical glueblock is missing from the right front foot; the right rear foot has a replaced glueblock. The hinges are replaced, and the brasses are not original. There is a series of holes on either side of the bottom board set approximately 2" from the side; wide battens have been removed from the underside of the case.

**Dimensions:**

| | | |
|---|---|---|
| H. | 42 1/4 in. | 107.3 cm |
| H. (writing surface) | 33 15/16 in. | 86.2 cm |
| W. (case) | 36 5/8 in. | 93.2 cm |
| W. (feet) | 38 in. | 96.5 cm |
| D. (case) | 17 3/4 in. | 45.1 cm |
| D. (feet) | 18 3/4 in. | 47.6 cm |

**Materials:** *Microanalysis:* Primary: soft maple group. Secondary: white pine group (drawer linings, backboard). *Finish:* light brown color in resin; once had polychrome decoration.

**Publications:** Helena Hayward, ed., *World Furniture: An Illustrated History* (New York: McGraw-Hill Book Co., 1965), fig. 721. Fitzgerald, *Three Centuries*, p. 153. Lester Margon, *More American Furniture Treasures, 1620–1840* (New York: Architectural Book Publishing Co., 1971), p. 48.

**Accession history:** Bequest of H. F. du Pont, 1969. 56.522

---

1. Zea and Dunlap, *Dunlap Cabinetmakers*, pp. 26–27, 29, 152–53, 196. I thank Donna-Belle Garvin of the New Hampshire Historical Society and Philip Zea of Historic Deerfield for their references with regard to the work of Moses Hazen, Jr. In 1972 Dunlap scholar Charles Parsons examined this desk and said that it was not by the Dunlaps, based on construction; Nancy Evans to Nancy Richards, memorandum, August 20, 1972, folder 56.522, Registration Office, Winterthur.

**Fig. 2.** Detail, lower drawer.

## 201 • Desk
Marblehead, Salem, or Newburyport,
Massachusetts
1780–1810

In 1795 Newburyport, Massachusetts, cabinetmaker Abner Toppan (1764–1836) made and branded a mahogany desk for Capt. William Little. The accompanying bill of sale was receipted by Toppan for the sum of £10.10.0 "To One Mahogany Swell front Desk" paid for by William's brother, Michael. The serpentine shape, or "swell front," of Little's desk was a popular form in the decades following the Revolution and was produced throughout New England into the first decade of the nineteenth century. Variations on the form included ball-and-claw feet or ogee-bracket feet and the addition of an upper bookcase section with either a flat top or an ogee top. Fall-front desks and desk-and-bookcases of this form were made in mahogany, cherry, maple, or birch, depending on the regional, aesthetic, and economic choices of both client and craftsman. Many of these desks or desk-and-bookcases documented as owned or made in the major port towns of coastal Essex County, Massachusetts (Marblehead, Salem, or Newburyport), have a distinctive carved shell pendant at the center of the base rail and shaped knee brackets like those seen on this striped maple example.[1] In addition to Toppan, Nathan Bowen from Marblehead and Abraham Watson, William King, and Elijah Sanderson of Salem all produced similar desks and chests with related shell pendants and shaped brackets. It is possible that the distinctive carved shell pendants and the bold, sharply defined ball-and-claw feet on these related pieces were supplied by one or two carvers in Essex County who either maintained a shop and sold piecework or traveled from shop to shop working on site.

Interior arrangements in desks of this form vary enormously, ranging from simple, plain drawer fronts with no ornament to costly interiors embellished with one or more carved or inlaid shells, fans, or paterae on the drawer fronts and valances. The 1792 price list printed in Hartford, Connecticut, noted the cost of "a plain Desk, 3 feet 3 inches in length, and plain feet, with 3 drawers in the head" as £4.7.0. The addition of five inches in width and a "swell'd front and 8 drawers in the head" and "claw feet and carv'd moulding" and "quarter columns" would raise the price to £9. The interior (or "head") of Winterthur's desk is quite plain—the only embellishment is a carved fan or shell on the front of the topmost central drawer (fig. 1). A closely related mahogany desk with an interior almost identical to Winterthur's desk, although completely unornamented, lacks the carved pendant at the base rail. The dated Toppan desk has a similarly plain interior, but three drawer fronts are embellished with inlaid paterae. The most costly type of interior can be seen on a related mahogany desk with an upper tier of blocked drawers, a shell-carved prospect door, flanking shell-carved drawers on the ends, four shell-carved valances, and turned, applied pilasters on the drawers flanking the prospect door.[2]

Winterthur's desk most closely resembles a birch desk with an identical interior owned by the Society for the Preservation of New England Antiquities. The carved pendant, feet, and measurements of the two desks vary only slightly. Originally, most desks of this form would have had simple bail brasses, but these two examples have elaborate replacement rococo brasses.[3] Both share the same distinctive pattern of construction with the base molding nailed beneath the bottom of the case and the legs tenoned into the case. The birch desk was originally owned by Richard Lakeman (1749–1841), of Ipswich, who was a fisherman, shipmaster, captain, and trader. Whether it was made in nearby Newburyport or further down the Essex County shoreline in Salem or Marblehead is unknown. However, like the Winterthur example it is made of a less costly wood and with a less expensive interior, making it an

impressive yet affordable possession for a middling sort of person.

Desks and desk-and-bookcases of this form are generally ascribed to makers in coastal Essex County, but an intriguing group of maple and cherry casepieces with similar carved pendants, ball-and-claw feet, shaped brackets, and related interiors have either histories of ownership in New Hampshire or inscriptions relating them to Gilmanton, New Hampshire. A striped maple desk-and-bookcase owned by the Currier Gallery of Art, Manchester, is closely related to the Winterthur example and is inscribed in chalk on the lower backboard, "Gilmanton/ June 5, 1799." Another desk-and-bookcase, made of cherry, is similar to the Winterthur and Currier pieces and is inscribed with the name Cogswell and 1799 and "_____manton" on the back.[4] It has been conjectured that a cabinetmaker trained in Essex County brought these specific regional characteristics to the Gilmanton area of New Hampshire, but, to date, the exact craftsman has not been identified. One possible source for the transmittal of these Essex County features might be through Gilmanton cabinetmaker Jonathan Ross, who was first noted in Stratford County land records in 1776 as a "cabinetmaker" of Salem, Massachusetts.[5] Jonathan also had two sons and a nephew (Jonathan, Jr., b. 1772; Stephen, b. 1785; and Samuel Dudley, b. 1773) who were all cabinetmakers in Gilmanton and might have had some familial North Shore contacts that led them to admire and copy the forms and ornament from that region. Given the presumed New Hampshire origin of these related examples, there is the possibility that Winterthur's striped maple desk might be the product of a shop in the Gilmanton, New Hampshire, area.

WAC

---

**Inscriptions or marks:** (Desk section) *On long drawer, upper left, on drawer back:* "8" *in pencil. On long drawer, upper right, on drawer back:* "3" *in pencil. On outer left small drawer, drawer back and inside front:* "5" *in pencil. On inner left small drawer, drawer back and inside front:* "9" *in pencil. On inner right small drawer, drawer back and inside front:* "6" *in pencil. On outer right small drawer, drawer back:* "7" *in pencil. On middle drawer, center section, drawer back and inside front:* "2" *in pencil. On bottom drawer, center section, drawer back and inside front:* "1". (Lower case) *On top drawer, inside back:* "x" *in chalk. On second drawer, inside back:* "1" *in chalk. On third drawer, inside back:* "x" *in chalk. On bottom drawer, inside back:* "x".

**Construction:** The desk top is half-blind dovetailed to the sides. The hinged slant top, a solid piece of figured wood with batten ends, opens to rest on solid lopers. The desk interior is unornamented except for the top center drawer, which is carved with a fluted shell. The center tier of drawers is flanked by two tiers of plain drawers above a series of four pigeonholes. On the drawers in the desk section, the bottom boards are set into rabbets on all four sides. Each desk side has two boards. Beaded edged blades are slotted into the side boards; the joints are covered by a facing strip beaded on the inside edge. There are no dust or security boards. The drawer runners are nailed to the side boards. On the long drawers, the solid fronts are contoured on the inside. The bottom boards, their grain front to back, are set into grooves in the front and sides and nailed across the back; a series of rectangular glueblocks act as an applied runner. The backboard, made of four horizontal boards (two wide and two narrow), is attached on all four edges with rosehead nails. Thick battens cover the dovetailed join of the sides and two-piece bottom board. The front base molding is nailed to the underside of the bottom rail with rosehead nails. The legs are tenoned to the case. The knee brackets, glued to the base molding, are reinforced with conforming horizontal glueblocks. The rear feet have fully articulated talons on three sides and a partial talon on the back. The carved pendent drop, nailed to the case, is reinforced by a supporting glueblock.

**Condition:** The desk has been heavily refinished, leaving patterns of abrasion indicating that the surface has been sanded. The lopers are replaced. The right front leg is repaired behind the knee. The brass hardware is old but not original. Portions of the escutcheons are missing on all the long drawers.

**Dimensions:**

| | | |
|---|---|---|
| H. | 44 1/4 in. | 112.4 cm |
| H. (writing surface) | 33 1/8 in. | 84.1 cm |
| W. (case) | 42 in. | 106.7 cm |
| W. (feet) | 45 1/4 in. | 114.9 cm |
| D. (case) | 20 3/4 in. | 52.7 cm |
| D. (feet) | 22 1/8 in. | 56.2 cm |

**Materials:** *Microanalysis:* Primary: soft maple group. Secondary: white pine group (drawer linings, backboard, bottom board, drawer runners). *Finish:* warm brown color in resin.

**Accession history:** Purchased by H. F. du Pont from John S. Walton, Inc., New York, 1952. Gift of H. F. du Pont, 1952. 52.254

1. Dexter Edwin Spaulding, "Abner Toppan, Cabinetmaker," *Antiques* 15, no. 6 (June 1929): 493–95. For other related examples, see Israel Sack advertisement, *Antiques* 59, no. 4 (April 1951): 249; *Antiques* 1, no. 3 (March 1922): frontispiece, 121–22; Christie's, "Important American Furniture, Silver, Folk Art, and Decorative Arts" (June 21, 1995), lot 240; Flanigan, *American Furniture*, cat. no. 23, pp. 66–69; Rollins, *Treasures of State*, pp. 128–29.

2. The Hartford price list is cited in *Great River*, pp. 471–73. For the related mahogany desk, see "Pedigreed Antiques IV: A Governor Winthrop Desk with an Adventurous Owner," *Antiques* 1, no. 3 (March 1922): 121–22. For the desk with expensive interior options, see Christie's, "Important American Furniture," lot 240. A desk with only slight variations in the interior has a nineteenth-century inscription in an interior drawer: "G.W. Pitman/ Madison/ N.H." (no. 69.1263, DAPC, Visual Resources Collection, Winterthur Library).

3. The birch desk originally did have federal-style brasses; Jobe and Kaye, *New England Furniture*, no. 48. The surface of the Winterthur desk has been so heavily cleaned that evidence of the original brasses no longer exists.

4. M. Ada Young, "Five Secretaries and the Cogswells," *Antiques* 88, no. 4 (October 1965): 478–85.

5. For the group of related casepieces, see Comstock, *American Furniture*, no. 332; M. Ada Young, "Five Secretaries," figs. 1, 1a, 2, 2a. On the Essex County craftsman, see *Plain and Elegant, Rich and Common: Documented New Hampshire Furniture, 1750–1850* (Concord, N.H.: New Hampshire Historical Society, 1979), pp. 18, 150–51; a large Salem-type desk-and-bookcase is illustrated in Stephen Ross advertisement, *Concord Gazette*, February 9, 1813.

## 202 ◆ Desk-and-bookcase
Lower Housatonic River valley,
Woodbury, Connecticut, area
1765–90

The unusual proportions and ambitious
ornamentation on this intriguing desk-and-
bookcase are a prominent expression of
nonurban fashion. The diverse quantity of
carved ornament, from the stylized Spanish
feet, the various shell and rosette carvings on
the lower drawer to the top of the pediment
and finials, and the pinwheel and lamb's
tongue motifs at the base and top of the
fluted pilasters, all add up to a specific
regional statement. But what region? With
no known provenance to suggest ownership
in a specific area, we must define stylistic
features similar to casepieces that do have
histories and associations with a discreet
region. Such a search brings us to the Lower
Housatonic River valley and specifically to
the towns of Woodbury, Southbury (a part
of Woodbury until 1787), and Newtown. As
one scholar has written, "Housatonic Valley
cases with more than one shell usually have
shells of more than one design. . . . An almost
endless vocabulary of decorative motifs was
used in central and western Connecticut. . . .
Whatever else may have been dull about living
in western Connecticut, looking at this
furniture (or doorways) was not."[1]

The distinctive, carved Spanish feet
(fig. 1) are at first reminiscent of those seen
on some Stratford-area pieces (see Nos. 107,
188, 192), but closer comparison relates
them more directly to casepieces attributed
to Woodbury, Connecticut. The bold
undulating shell carved in the front of the
bottom drawer and echoed in the concave
of the base molding is another distinctive
decorative feature seen on other casepieces
from the Lower Housatonic River valley. The
markedly odd proportion of a full-height lower
desk section topped with a squat bookcase

section can be seen in another desk-and-bookcase that also shares many of the same unusual characteristics of this example. When the related desk-and-bookcase was advertised in *Antiques* in December 1953, it was cited as "Noteworthy for its individuality and distinction. . . . Purchased from an early Woodbury, Connecticut family . . . we feel that the secretary was made in that vicinity as well."[2] Although it has a number of features quite dissimilar from Winterthur's example (ogee-bracket feet, pediment with central fan, fluted quarter columns, gadrooned base molding), the related piece does have a large carved rosette on the fall-front and an almost identical interior configuration (fig. 2).

Another casepiece with related features and a strong Woodbury history is a high chest in the collections of the Society for the Preservation of New England Antiquities. Although a distinctly different form, this high chest has a broken-scroll pediment and carved rosettes and finials that are almost identical in form to those on Winterthur's desk-and-bookcase. While no specific maker can be cited as the author of any of these related pieces of furniture, it seems clear that there were a number of makers working in this nonurban Connecticut region producing pieces that echoed familiar motifs and themes also often found in the architecture of the area.[3]

Several construction features support an attribution to a shop removed from a major urban center. The extensive use of wood pins implies that the maker was without a ready supply of nails, or that he was following a tradition of craftsmanship rooted in European precedents. Also unusual is the lack of a latch or other locking mechanism on the prospect section and on the doors to the bookcase section. An old photograph shows that originally there were no locks on the drawers in the desk section.[4]

WAC

Inscriptions or marks: *On small drawer in prospect section:* "Anitti" *in pencil, partially legible. On*

**Fig. 1.** Detail, foot.

*pigeonhole drawers:* "1"–"8" *in sequence, in blue crayon, and* "2/ B" *and* "2"–"8" *inscribed in pencil. Inscribed on one pigeonhole drawer:* "Left" *in chalk. On one pigeonhole drawer, underside:* "x" *twice. On desk drawers, left side:* "II" *scratched on one;* "9" *in pencil on a second; a scratched* "I" *and* "3" *in pencil on a third; the fourth has no inscription. On desk drawers, right side:* "8" *in pencil and* "5" *in ink on one;* "6" *in pencil and scratch* "V" *on a second;* "5" *in pencil on a third; the fourth has no inscription. Incised, on inner backboard of the desk section:* "XI III"; *on top left side board of the upper section:* "V"; *and on the bottom right drawer runner:* "IIV".

**Construction:** (Upper case) The form is basically a box with top and bottom dovetailed to the sides. Wide battens mitered at the front corners frame three sides of the bottom board and are attached with large wood pins. The tympanum is half-lapped with the side pilasters and backed up with a cornerpost to hold the half-lap together. The carved convex shell on the tympanum is applied, and the ogee cornice molding is attached with wooden pins. The top boards are nailed to the top of the tympanum with sprigs and secured to the backboards in the same manner. The backboards (three horizontally oriented) are secured to a rabbet in the sides with wire and cut nails; the top of the backboard is relieved in the center to echo the sweep and curve of the tympanum. The carved rosettes are one piece with the ogee cornice molding. The tympanum is braced by vertical front-to-back boards to which the top boards are also nailed. Each of these vertical boards is pierced by a 4"-by-4" opening suggesting secret compartments. The doors are typical panel-and-frame construction, through-tenoned on all corners. The raised-and-fielded panel is rabbeted into the face of the frame and held in place by the applied molding. This molding is held in place by wooden pins that pass through the molding and completely through the door frame. The interior is divided into a series of

vertical compartments with some dividers shaped on their front edges and some straight. The center finial may be a replacement, although the side ones appear to be original. On the upper case, a waist molding the same height as the battens is affixed to the battens presumably with small wood pegs.

(Lower case) The top and bottom are dovetailed to the sides. The bottom board consists of a wide pine board trimmed on the leading edge with cherry of the same dimension as the drawer blades; the cherry is tied to the pine with butterflies cut into the inside surface—these are partially covered by a second blade that is wood pinned to the first, doubling the thickness of the leading edge. This front rail assemblage is somewhat unorthodox due to the fact that the concave shell in the lower drawer continued onto the front lower molded edge and at the center reveals the leading edge of the bottom board, hence necessitating the cherry facing. The face of the front assembly is partially covered with an applied molding on either side of the central concavity. The feet are tenoned into the bottom, and the replaced knee brackets are nailed and applied, strengthened with rectangular glueblocks flush on the bottom board. Drawer runners are attached to the bottom board with wooden pins. The drawer blades are let into the case sides, and the fluted corner pilasters cover the joint. There are no dust boards between the drawers. The backboards (three) are horizontally oriented and nailed (with wrought and cut nails) into a rabbet in the sides and top. The original drawer runners appear to have been mortised into the backboards. One-inch-thick dividers are dovetailed in place forming a housing for the lopers. The fall-front and writing surface were damaged when the hinges split out, and the repair was carried out with a new piece of 1⁵⁄₈" on the writing surface and 3" on the fall-front. The fall-front also has been reworked with a 2⁷⁄₈" strip replacing the top edge. The long drawers have horizontal chamfered bottom boards and appear to have originally been set into a groove in the sides and the front. The drawers are dovetailed front and back and have third-generation hardware. The drawers of the desk interior are dovetailed front and back, nailed into a rabbet in the front, and nailed sides and back. The writing surface is half-depth and the baseboard of the interior compartment section is pinned to it. The drawer compartments and pigeonholes are formed by ¹⁄₄" dividers, dado-jointed together. The upper valances are actually

**Fig. 2.** Desk open.

drawer fronts. Behind the prospect door there is a compartment that slides out completely to reveal secret drawers in the back, which appears to have once had a rear enclosure. The vertical dividers between the pigeonholes are elaborately shaped to form stylized birds' heads. The waist molding is applied to lower case top edges with wooden pins.

**Condition:** A crack in the scrollboard has been repaired, and the support for the central finial has been repaired and reinforced. The middle board of the upper backboard is replaced. Both the lower 2 1/2" of the fall-front and the front section of the top blade are replaced. The upper edge of the middle drawer has been replaced. Several of the full drawers in the lower case have had applied battens reinforced. There is extensive wear on all the drawer runners. The feet are badly degraded from rot, possibly from standing on a moist or damp floor; the feet are tenoned into the bottom of the case; the tenons are new. (It appears that at one time the feet were cut off and the case rested on its base molding. When the feet were reattached, new tenon extensions were let into the back corner and reestablished in the original mortises.) Also, a repair piece has been let into the "toes" of the rear proper right foot. The brackets on the feet as well as all glueblocks (except rear) are replaced. The proper right waist molding is replaced. All of the hardware except the hinges on the bookcase doors is replaced. The present set of drawer pulls on the desk section are at least the third set of handles. There is evidence of a single hole knob and the ghost of an earlier set of "Queen Anne" brasses that were installed upside down. The old photograph shows that the piece originally had no keyhole escutcheons. The black paint highlighting the piece was added to cover old wear or new wood, possibly in the twentieth century.

**Dimensions:**

| | | |
|---|---|---|
| H. (with finials) | 87 13/16 in. | 223.0 cm |
| H. (case) | 85 7/16 in. | 216.9 cm |
| H. (writing surface) | 34 in. | 86.5 cm |
| W. (cornice) | 38 3/4 in. | 98.5 cm |
| W. (upper case) | 36 1/4 in. | 92.1 cm |
| W. (lower case) | 39 1/2 in. | 100.4 cm |
| W. (knees) | 42 1/2 in. | 108.1 cm |
| D. (cornice) | 11 7/8 in. | 28.4 cm |
| D. (upper case) | 9 3/4 in. | 24.7 cm |
| D. (lower case) | 21 7/16 in. | 54.6 cm |
| D. (knees) | 22 15/16 in. | 58.3 cm |

**Materials:** *Microanalysis:* Primary: cherry. Secondary: white pine group (drawer linings, backboards). *Finish:* dark, reddish brown color in resin; ebonizing not original.

**Publications:** Downs, *American Furniture*, fig. 231. Philip Zea, "Diversity and Regionalism in Rural New England Furniture," in Luke Beckerdite and William N. Hosley, eds., *American Furniture 1995* (Milwaukee, Wis.: Chipstone Fndn., 1995), pp. 100–101.

**Accession history:** Bequest of H. F. Pont, 1969. 58.1510

1. Jobe and Kaye, *New England Furniture*, pp. 213, 216.

2. For the Woodbury casepieces, see Edward Strong Cooke, Jr., "Rural Artisanal Culture: The Preindustrial Joiners of Newtown and Woodbury, Connecticut, 1760–1820" (Ph.D. diss., Boston University, 1984), p. 277, fig. 8. *Litchfield County Furniture*, 1730–1850 ([Litchfield, Conn.: Litchfield Historical Society, 1969]), pp. 62–63, nos. 37, 40; Christie's, "Highly Important American Furniture from the Collection of Dr. C. Ray Franklin" (October 13, 1984), lot 455. Although the last piece has been attributed to Brewster Dayton of Stratford, the profile of the feet and the carved shell in the lower drawer relate it to the work being produced further up the Housatonic River away from the coast. For the related desk-and-bookcase, see Florene Maine advertisement, *Antiques* 64, no. 6 (December 1953): 430; and Robert W. Skinner, "Fine Americana including the Private Collection of Kenneth Hammitt of Woodbury, Connecticut" (October 30, 1993).

3. Jobe and Kaye, *New England Furniture*, pp. 213–17. Edward S. Cooke, Jr., "The Social Economy of the Preindustrial Joiner in Western Connecticut, 1750–1800," in Luke Beckerdite and William N. Hosley, eds., *American Furniture 1995* (Milwaukee, Wis.: Chipstone Fndn., 1995), pp. 112–44.

4. The preference for wood pins "seems to be a selective reliance upon the Low Country tradition of securing moldings and drawer bottoms with pins" (Edward S. Cooke, Jr., "New Netherlands' Influence on Furniture of the Housatonic Valley," in Joshua W. Lane, *The Impact of New Netherlands upon the Colonial Long Island Basin* [New Haven and Washington, D.C.: Yale-Smithsonian Seminar on Material Culture, 1993], pp. 36–43). Photograph in folder 58.1510, Registration Office, Winterthur.

## 203 ◆ Desk-and-bookcase
Norwich, New London County,
Connecticut, area
1770–95

The overall design and aesthetic presentation
of this cherry desk-and-bookcase is complex
and sophisticated with distinctive nonurban
overtones. The facade of the bookcase section
is markedly architectural, reminiscent of
eighteenth-century interior paneling.[1] The
four arched-and-fielded panels that compose
the doors enclose a simple interior divided into
nine compartments of equal size. The H hinges
on the doors, often the type used on built-in
cupboards, echo interior architecture of the
period. Closer examination reveals several
unconventional construction techniques
that belie not only its nonurban origins but
perhaps suggest that the maker may have been
as equally involved with the joinery associated
with the construction of houses and interiors as
that used in furniture.

The lower case, or desk section, is
simple in design with a straight front and
plain ogee-bracket feet yet is bold and
strong both aesthetically and structurally.
The large original brasses and side carrying
handles follow urban precedents. The interior
exhibits meticulous construction and intricacy
with a double tier of undulating blocked
drawers surmounted by eight pigeonholes
with shaped dividers, small drawers above each
pigeonhole, two central vertical drawers with
ornamental fluting and carved pinwheels, and
a commanding central stack of six graduated
shaped-front drawers (fig. 1). For all the
external refinement and sophistication of this
desk section, the construction is substantial.
In a manner commonly employed in the
eighteenth century, the top and bottom are
dovetailed to the sides. As in other pieces of
New London County case furniture, the sides
extend to the floor and are relieved at the
center of each side beneath the base molding.[2]
The base molding and bracket feet are cut

from one piece of cherry and nailed to the front and sides of the case, not actually reaching the floor, but allowing the case sides to carry the weight.

As is often seen on other Norwich area (or New London County) case furniture, the influence of the work of Newport, Rhode Island, cabinetmakers is evident. The overall shape of the broken-scroll pediment, with carved rosettes above what appears to be an applied plaque in the tympanum, echoes Newport designs. Their unconventional methods of construction and design suggest a nonurban hand, however. The tympanum, or scrollboard of the pediment, is carved from a solid board to resemble an applied plaque. That the four arched panels of the doors intrude upon the lower portion of the tympanum is unusual but nevertheless successfully creates a rhythm of curves that are reflected in the top portion of the tympanum. The carved rosettes are applied to the fronts of solid cherry cylinders, and it is evident that the top of the bonnet was once completely covered across the central portion. A tapered strip of wood about ³/₈-inch thick is dovetailed into the back of the central portion of the pediment, suggesting that the present finial treatment is not original.

This desk-and-bookcase has a tradition of ownership by Jeremiah Halsey (1743/44–1829) of Preston, Connecticut, near Norwich, and therefore may have been made in the New London County area. Halsey was admitted to the bar in 1770 and practiced law in New London County. Commissioned a lieutenant in the militia in 1775, he served in the "Northern Department" under Ethan Allen and took an active part in the Revolution, rising to the rank of lieutenant colonel in 1780. After the war he commissioned a ship engaged in trade with Ireland. Halsey is best known today for his part in financing the construction and furnishing of the State House in Hartford, completed in 1796.[3] Halsey could have had this desk made prior to the

Fig. 1. Desk open.

Revolution, while a successful lawyer. The arrangement of the interior of the upper case suggests that it might have been designed for books and not the high, narrow ledgers that bookcase sections were often intended to hold. It is equally plausible, however, that Halsey's wealth increased following the war and he commissioned this desk-and-bookcase in the late 1780s or early 1790s.

WAC

---

**Inscriptions or marks:** *On top section, inside left door:* "James Bannister, 416 Bergen Street, Brooklyn" *in pencil. Scratched on inside drawer front on all pigeonhole drawers:* "I"–"VIII". *Inside bottom pigeonhole drawers:* (left to right) "1", "2", "3", "pen Drawer/ pay[illegible]ng", "M", "B", and "4" *all in pencil. On outside bottom of pigeonhole drawer left of prospect section:* "Amount due/ Hasbroach/ 8450/ 824/ 27423" *in pencil. On back of top far left blocked drawer inside desk:* "W. C. Caywood" *in ink. Inside top near left blocked drawer in desk:* "Miss Caywood/ Basco/ Hancock Co Ill/ Charleston Bently Station/ Ills" *in pencil; and on outside drawer bottom:* "Marlboro/ N Y". *On side of top near right drawer in the desk:* "A. J. Caywood" *and* "2" *in pencil. On inside back of top far right blocked drawer in desk:* "5" *in pencil. On inside bottom of far left blocked drawer in desk:* "1" *in pencil. On inside bottom of near left blocked drawer in desk:* "X" *in pencil. Inside back of near right bottom drawer in desk:* "[illegible] Daniel" *and* "4" *in pencil. On inside bottom of far right blocked drawer:* "5" *in pencil. On bottom of top drawer of the prospect section:* "Section/ 27-³/₄ x 41-¹/₂"/ canvas/ 21 x 41-¹/₂" *in pencil. On inside bottom of next to top drawer in*

**Fig. 2.** Detail, underside.

*prospect section:* "E. J. DeLaGarde/ M[illegible] P[illegible] Exhibition/ Rue de Richelieu/ Paris" in pencil. *On third drawer in prospect section, both outside back and interior:* "Mrs. E. J. Mayernick/ 1520 Broadway near 47th St/ New York" in ink and in pencil, respectively. *On inside back fourth drawer in prospect section:* "[illegible]/ 46 Leroy St/ New York" in pencil. *Inside back of fifth drawer prospect section:* "3" in pencil. *Inside bottom of bottom drawer prospect section:* "3" in pencil. *Inside top long drawer of lower section:* "15 cork elm (Ulmus elata)/ 2 coral berry (Sumphora carpum)/ 3 Virginia agave (Agave Virginiana)/ 1 black currant (Staphylea trifolia)/ 1 golden Hypericum (Hypericum dureum)" in pencil.

**Construction:** (Upper case) The primary form is a square box with the top and bottom boards dovetailed to the sides. The bottom board is deeply dovetailed to raise it 1¹/₂" higher than the bottom of the sides. A bottom face rail is dovetailed to the leading edges of the sides. The sides extend to the top of the side cornice. The tympanum is dovetailed to the sides; an upper rail behind the tympanum is tenoned to the sides and nailed to the top. The cornice molding and carved rosettes are applied to the face of the tympanum and nailed. Behind the rosettes, solid cherry cylinders of the same diameter extend to the backboard. The top of the bonnet was originally entirely covered with ¹/₄" white pine nailed to the top of the backboard and to a rabbet behind the cornice; the center section was removed some time ago. The blocks and finials are probably replacements; on the backside of the center of the tympanum is a long, tapered, sliding dovetail that may relate to the original pediment ornament. The fielded tympanum panel is carved from solid wood. The doors are of typical frame-and-panel construction with a central muntin separating two raised-and-fielded panels. The interior is divided into nine compartments by grooved and mitered ³/₈"-thick cherry shelves and dividers. All hardware is original, including the brass H hinges on the doors.

(Lower case) The top and bottom boards are dovetailed to the sides. The two board sides extend to the floor at the front and back, forming the

blocking behind the applied bracket feet. Similar to the sides, the two half-lapped horizontal backboards extend almost to the floor and are nailed to rabbets in the sides with rosehead nails. The 2"-wide blades are dovetailed to the sides, and there are no dust boards; the bottom rail is likewise dovetailed to the sides but on edge and is nailed to the bottom board. Drawer runners for the top drawer are in an inverted T-shape tenoned through the backboard; all others are nailed to the sides with rosehead nails. In the desk section, the drawer sides are slightly rounded on the upper edge and flat on the back. The drawer bottoms, chamfered on three sides, are set into grooves and secured with nails at the back. On the front and sides, the base molding and bracket feet are all cut from the same board and mitered at the corners. One-inch-thick dividers are dovetailed in place forming a housing for the lopers. The fall-front has tenoned breadboard ends. The hinges appear to be original but have been reset due to shrinkage of the fall-front. (Interior, lower case) The writing surface is composed of two boards, continuous to the back. The bottom board of the interior compartment assembly is nailed to the full-depth writing surface. The pigeonhole and drawer compartments are formed by ¹/₄" dividers dado-jointed together. Drawers are dovetailed at front and rear with chamfered bottoms set in grooves at front and sides, nailed at rear. The valances above the pigeonholes are actually drawer fronts. Waist molding is mitered and nailed in place.

**Condition:** All finials are probably replaced, but the central one differs from the side ones in that it is not completely carved on the back. The desk-and-bookcase was not fitted with side finials originally. The left side waist molding is replaced. The applied blocks on the front of the document drawers are replaced, and the hardware is new. There is a patch on the upper left corner of the middle long drawer. The front facing on the right front leg is pieced out as is the side facing on the right rear leg. The side facing on the right and left front legs have been reglued. Only the glueblock on the left rear foot is original. Those on both right feet are replaced, and

the glueblock on the left front foot is old but probably not original.

**Dimensions:**

| | | |
|---|---|---|
| H. (with finials) | 92¹/₈ in. | 234.1 cm |
| H. (case) | 87⁷/₈ in. | 223.4 cm |
| H. (writing surface) | 30⁷/₈ in. | 78.2 cm |
| W. (cornice) | 38¹/₂ in. | 98.0 cm |
| W. (upper case) | 36⁵/₁₆ in. | 92.3 cm |
| W. (lower case) | 38¹/₁₆ in. | 96.9 cm |
| W. (feet) | 40¹/₄ in. | 102.2 cm |
| D. (cornice) | 10³/₄ in. | 27.3 cm |
| D. (upper case) | 9⁵/₁₆ in. | 23.9 cm |
| D. (lower case) | 20¹³/₁₆ in. | 53.0 cm |
| D. (feet) | 23 in. | 58.4 cm |

**Materials:** *Microanalysis:* Primary: cherry. Secondary: white pine group (drawer linings, backboards); tulip-poplar or basswood (desk section interior drawers). *Finish:* dark brown color in resin.

**Publications:** Downs, *American Furniture*, fig. 230. Helen Comstock, "Cabinetmakers of the Norwich Area," *Antiques* 87, no. 6 (June 1965): 698, fig. 3. Houghton Bulkeley, *Contributions to Connecticut Cabinetmaking* (Hartford: Connecticut Historical Society, 1967), fig. 12, p. 38.

**Provenance:** The desk-and-bookcase has a tradition of original ownership by Jeremiah Halsey (1743/44–1829) of Preston, Conn. The subsequent history of the piece is unclear. None of the several names inscribed on the piece can be connected to the Halsey family. However, some may have been later owners.

**Accession history:** Purchased by H. F. du Pont from Charles Woolsey Lyon, New York, 1927. Gift of H. F. du Pont, 1960.
58.2427

1. I am aware of only 1 other Connecticut desk-and-bookcase that is similar to this example—it has 4 fielded panels in the upper section and a carved (or applied) panel in the tympanum; see Sotheby Parke Bernet, "Fine Americana" (September 26, 1981), lot 416.

2. During his own current research, Robert Lionetti has seen other Connecticut casepieces with similar side construction to this desk-and-bookcase. A 4-drawer chest of drawers from New London County has this same side construction; see Christie's, "Important American Furniture, Silver, Prints, Folk Art, and Decorative Arts" (January 21, 1994), lot 330.

3. On Halsey, see Emma C. Brewster Jones, *The Brewster Genealogy, 1566–1907*, 2 vols. (New York: Grafton Press, 1908), 1:230; Joseph Lafayette Halsey and Edmund Drake Halsey, *Thomas Halsey, of Hertfordshire, England, and Southampton, Long Island, 1591–1679, with His American Descendants to the Eighth and Ninth Generations* (Morristown, N.J.: Jerseymen Office, 1895), pp. 57–59. Halsey reportedly went into debt as a result of the project; see Newton Brainard, *The Hartford State House of 1796* (Hartford: Connecticut Historical Society, 1964), pp. 41–42.

## 204 ◆ Desk-and-bookcase
Eastern Massachusetts
1762

The form of this desk-and-bookcase was popular throughout coastal New England from the 1730s to about 1800 and was made in both urban and nonurban areas. Depending on the client's resources and preferences and regional availability, these desk-and-bookcases might be fashioned in mahogany, cherry, or maple. The upper section is distinguished by a broken-scroll pediment surmounting a pair of arched, raised panel doors enclosing a bookcase section with concave carved (or inlaid) shells (or fans) (fig. 1). It surmounts a fall-front desk with straight-bracket feet. Variations did occur in the lower section, where a more costly serpentine or blockfront might be substituted for a straight front, and the feet could be ogee-bracket, pad, or ball-and-claw in form. This desk-and-bookcase is the humblest, and was also probably the least expensive, of the four in the Winterthur collection with broken-scroll pediments, arched panel doors, and concave interior shells or fans. The other three (Nos. 205, 206, and 208), all made of mahogany, have blockfronts; the two prerevolutionary desks have straight-bracket feet, and the late eighteenth-century Salem example has ball-and-claw feet. Together they illustrate a range of choices available to eighteenth-century consumers.

One of the most intriguing features of this rather plain desk-and-bookcase can be seen not on the facade but on the back of the upper backboard. An eighteenth-century inscription is scrawled across this pine board in four lines, with one of the most recognizable portions being the date "1762" at the very end of the last line. Although somewhat illegible, the inscription appears to read: "Purch [illegible]/ of (?)/ Framingham Ju<sup>r</sup>/ An[no]dominy 1762." No Massachusetts cabinetmaker named Framingham is known, but it is tempting to think that the purchaser who wrote that inscription misspelled the maker's name and actually was referring to Benjamin Frothingham, Jr., of Charlestown, Massachusetts. Several desk-and-bookcases with broken-scroll pediments, arched panel doors, and straight-bracket feet bear the label of Frothingham, in addition to an unusual blockfront chest-on-chest with similar features and carved fans in the pediment and inscribed

"Charlestown/ B. Frothingham/ 1763."[1] The quality of construction of this casepiece does not compare favorably, however, with that of a signed Frothingham high chest and a dressing table in the Winterthur collection (see Nos. 162, 163).

The inscription "Framingham" may refer instead to the place where this piece was purchased and would therefore indicate a regional origin outside a major urban area, although the design conventions echo those of cabinetmakers in the closest urban style center—Boston. Another maple desk-and-bookcase with almost identical design features, proportions, and interior descended in the Capen family of Dedham, Massachusetts, and is inscribed "John Capen" on the base in contemporary chalk.[2] So similar is this piece to Winterthur's example that one might propose that they both came from the same shop. Wherever that shop was in eastern Massachusetts, at least the date of fabrication, 1762, provides a significant piece of documentation for this characteristic New England form.

WAC

**Fig. 1.** Desk open.

---

**Inscriptions or marks:** *On backboard of upper case:* "Purch [illegible]/ of (?)/ Framingham Ju[r]/ An[no]dominy 1762" in chalk. *On bottom board of the lower case:* "Bottom" in chalk. *Chiseled on drawers in bookcase section:* "I"–"IIII". *On drawers in bookcase section and on drawer openings:* "1"–"4" in pencil. *On long drawers in lower case:* "1"–"4" in both chalk and pencil. *On the next to the bottom drawer:* "G FIELD" in pencil (modern).

**Construction:** (Upper case) The sides are dovetailed to the bottom; the tympanum is half-lapped and nailed to the front edge of the sides. The back top board, which defines the profile of the pediment, is notched into the back edge of the sides. Backboards are horizontal and nailed into rabbets on the sides and across the bottom. The carved pediment moldings are face nailed to the tympanum. The top board is nailed into a rabbet on the top edge of the sides. The top boards of the pediment are nailed to the backboard and tympanum. Carved concave shells are set into arched cutouts and glued in place. The interior dividers are set into grooves from behind. All hinges are replaced. The doors with raised-and-fielded panels are set in a frame that is mortise and through-tenoned. Cock-beading is cut from solid wood on the edges of the major dividers. There are four drawers across the bottom, like the interior drawers. There are unexplainable screw holes in the bottom board. The long drawers have sides and backs of unusually thin (1/4") pine stock. The sides are double-chamfered slightly on the upper edge, and the back has a single chamfer on the outside edge. The dovetails joining the sides to the back have unusually thick throats. The plain drawer bottom, set into grooves on three sides, is reinforced on the front edge with small glueblocks. The grain of the drawer bottom runs front to back.

Except for the top drawer, the drawer runners are nailed to the sides. The runner for the top drawer is supported by a block glued to the side; it is not attached to the back.

(Lower case) The top and bottom boards are dovetailed to the sides; the two lap-joined chestnut horizontal backboards are nailed into a rabbet all around except the bottom, which is nailed flush to the bottom board. A 5/8"-by-2 1/2" frame is nailed and glued to the bottom of the bottom board; simple ogee molding is nailed to bottom board front and sides; straight-bracket feet are mitered at the corners with a vertical block behind, up to the bottom board, with bracket blocks butted against vertical support blocks. Solid maple blades are half-dovetailed completely through the sides, 1 1/8" deep. The fall-front has breadboard ends, tongue-and-grooved on, with a 1/4" round edge all around that is not lipped. The simple interior with a central prospect door (removable), which has a lock on the top edge, is flanked by four pigeonholes surmounting a pair of drawers over one long drawer on each side. Behind the prospect is a valance drawer and one concave blocked drawer. The prospect door is a fielded arched panel in frame. Symmetrical turned colonettes (stretcherlike) are applied to the face of the vertical drawers flanking the prospect. The drawers are dovetailed front and back; the bottoms are nailed to the sides and back and set into a rabbet in the front. Simple arched valances echo the arch of the fielded panel. Midmolding is nailed to the lower case front and sides of top board.

**Condition:** All the finials are new. The upper case has been apart. The bonnet is patched on the left side. The bonnet cover has been off and is reattached; possibly the new supports for the bonnet and the long glueblock were installed at that time. The left and right cornice moldings are replaced. The shelves in the bookcase section are of different sizes. The top shelf is patched at the center; it may

be a replacement. There are some unexplained holes in front of the drawer openings on the bottom board; these may have been to hold the drawers in place for moving. The right door has been pieced on the bottom rail; the center edge of the left door has been pieced with veneer. The door hinges are new, as is the left door latch. The metal prongs holding the prospect door are the ends of ten-penny nails. The loper dividers are replaced. Several of the battens on the long drawers have been repaired. There is a patch in the upper right corner of the bottom long drawer. There is a set of filled holes for a pull below the escutcheon on the slant lid; the escutcheon is a later addition. The key catch on the top long drawer has been repositioned, and the lock on the middle drawer is a replacement. There are functional escutcheons only on the top and middle drawers. All the glueblocks on the feet have been reglued and nailed. All the brass handles are replaced; one other set of holes is visible.

**Dimensions:**

| | | |
|---|---|---|
| H. (with finials) | 86 3/4 in. | 220.1 cm |
| H. (case) | 83 3/4 in. | 212.8 cm |
| H. (writing surface) | 30 5/16 in. | 76.9 cm |
| W. (cornice) | 37 9/16 in. | 95.6 cm |
| W. (upper case) | 34 9/16 in. | 87.9 cm |
| W. (lower case) | 36 7/8 in. | 92.5 cm |
| W. (feet) | 37 15/16 in. | 96.3 cm |
| D. (cornice) | 11 1/4 in. | 28.8 cm |
| D. (upper case) | 9 1/2 in. | 24.2 cm |
| D. (lower case) | 19 5/8 in. | 49.9 cm |
| D. (feet) | 20 9/16 in. | 52.4 cm |

**Materials:** *Microanalysis:* Primary: soft maple group. Secondary: white pine group (drawer linings, upper case backboard); chestnut (lower case backboard). *Finish:* light brown color in resin; modern finish.

**Publications:** Downs, *American Furniture,* fig. 229.

**Accession history:** Purchased by H. F. du Pont from Collings and Collings, New York, 1928. Bequest of H. F. du Pont, 1969.
59.771

---

1. For Frothingham desk-and-bookcases, see nos. 63.218, 63.216, DAPC, Visual Resources Collection, Winterthur; Mabel Munson Swan, "Major Benjamin Frothingham, Cabinetmaker," *Antiques* 62, no. 5 (November 1952): 392–95; Israel Sack advertisement, *Antiques* 61, no. 1 (January 1952): 4–5. For the chest-on-chest, see no. 91.624, DAPC, Visual Resources Collection, Winterthur Library.

2. *American Antiques from Israel Sack Collection,* 10 vols. (Washington, D.C.: Highland House, ca. 1969–), 3:816–17.

## 205 ◆ Desk-and-bookcase
Boston, Massachusetts
1738
Job Coit, Sr. (1692–1741) and Job Coit, Jr. (1717–45)

This desk-and-bookcase provides important evidence in tracing the introduction and development of the American blockfront form to the Boston region in the 1730s. Inscribed "J Coit/ 1738" and "Job Coit jr/ 1738" on two drawers of the interior of the desk section, it documents the production of two eighteenth-century Boston craftsmen working in this new style who might have otherwise remained unknown. With the exception of the blocking on the facade of the lower section, the overall design and limited ornamentation of this desk-and-bookcase are derived from English desk-and-bookcases of the 1710s and 1720s and are related to the Queen Anne style seen in a number of earlier veneered and inlaid Boston desk-and-bookcases.[1]

What prompted Coit, an experienced craftsman then in his forty-fifth year, to attempt this rather complex facade construction? Had he seen pieces from another shop with this design, or did a longtime client request something similar to a piece he had seen in the home of a friend or associate? In broader terms (assuming that this idea of "blocking" the facade did not originate with Coit), what design concept inspired Boston craftsmen or patrons to initiate this innovative "swelled front" technique?[2]

The abundance of late seventeenth-century baroque designs incorporating shells, swags, scrolls, arched panels, and particularly elaborate strapwork might well have provided the inspiration for this Boston innovation. These designs were indirectly translated onto a variety of sophisticated objects in the first quarter of the eighteenth century. A few surviving lively shaped valances for eastern

**Fig. 1.** Desk open.

Massachusetts beds perhaps offer the best example of how the strapwork motif could have been adapted to the facades of casework.[3] Although Coit's arched-top blocking is unusual, it does echo the rounded arches of the mirrored panels in the doors of the bookcase section. The central concave section is reminiscent of ornamented drawers in high chests and dressing tables of the period. Perhaps aping other early blocking he had seen in Boston, Coit likewise flattened the line between the convex and concave curves in order to minimize the thickness of the board used for the drawer fronts.

That Coit was not trained in the shop of an English immigrant craftsman and was not following high-style London designs is demonstrated by the construction of this desk-and-bookcase. It differs noticeably from English examples in the case and drawer construction. Following English models, the lower case is fashioned of dovetailed boards, but instead of using the dovetailed blades as would English craftsmen, Coit through-tenoned the blades to the sides and applied

a facing to cover the join. On English case furniture, drawer sides and backs often are relatively thin, but American craftsmen generally used heavier stock for drawer linings. On this desk-and-bookcase the drawers have relatively thin sides, but the backs are made of half-inch stock. Instead of the English practice of using full "dust boards" to support the drawers, the drawers ride on narrow runners nailed to the case sides.

Although the name "Job Coit" was known long before this desk-and-bookcase was acquired by Henry Francis du Pont in 1961, the details of his career remain sketchy. Apprenticed to an as-yet-unknown master, Coit (1692–1741) probably was just beginning his cabinetmaking career when he married Lydia Amie (or Amy) of Boston in 1713. Within three years he had acquired the property on Ann (North) Street that would serve as his home and shop until his death. By 1725 his shop included the services of at least one apprentice, Joseph Davis. Coit probably also trained his three sons—Nathaniel; Job, Jr.; and Joseph—each of whom is listed in legal

documents as a joiner or cabinetmaker. Only this piece of furniture is known to have been made by Coit, and relatively few bills have been discovered to document his business activities. One, submitted on February 28, 1742 (a year after Coit, Sr.'s, death) by son Joseph Coit on behalf of his mother, lists work done between 1734 and 1740 for Daniel Henchman, a prosperous Boston stationer, bookseller, and merchant. Included is an entry dated May 10, 1738, for a desk-and-bookcase sold to "Capt Daniel Hinksman" for £50.[4] While the inscribed Coit signature and date on the desk-and-bookcase and this 1738 bill for a very costly desk-and-bookcase is not conclusive documentation that Winterthur's example is the Henchman desk-and-bookcase, it is a strong probability further supported by circumstantial and genealogical evidence.

Coit's success as a craftsman is suggested by the inventory of his real and personal property, taken on September 25, 1742, which was valued at £1747.9.0. This sizable estate included his personal furniture, shop fixtures, tools, lumber, and new furniture. Job Coit, Jr. (1717–45), whose name also appears on the desk-and-bookcase, is even more elusive than his father. This desk-and-bookcase is the only piece of furniture that can be credited to him. That he was a cabinetmaker is confirmed by the inventory of his estate filed April 16, 1745, which listed "Joyners work not finisht and Joyners Tools" valued at £31.4.0.[5]

Daniel Henchman (1689–1761), for whom the desk-and-bookcase was presumably made in 1738, began his career as a stationer and bookseller in Boston. As this business prospered, Henchman expanded his mercantile activities to include trade in agricultural products, tropical merchandise, cured fish and whale oil, and a variety of manufactured articles.[6] Eventually his mercantile enterprises encompassed a broad network of trade with London, Madeira, Surinam, Barbados, and the southern colonies. By 1738, when the

**Fig. 2.** Detail, inlay.

desk-and-bookcase was made, Henchman had amassed a considerable fortune. It is not known *why* Henchman chose Coit over another craftsman—perhaps they attended the same church, lived in the same area, or were related in some way.

As the earliest dated example of the blockfront style yet discovered, this desk-and-bookcase is an important example of the form. Presumably at the same time (and probably even earlier), other craftsmen were producing more refined and ornamented designs employing related blockfront shapes. Closest in appearance is a mahogany slant-top desk that shares the domed blocking on the top drawer but has a more traditional prospect section with columns on the document drawers and a fan-carved door simulating drawer fronts (fig. 1). The desk differs structurally in the addition of a separate stile to hold the blades attached to the front inside edge of the sides. This construction feature is also found on a group of much more highly ornamented desk-and-bookcases that appear to have originated in the shop of a London-trained cabinetmaker.[7] They are related by the unusual projecting cornice molding on the sides of the upper case, applied carving in the pediment, fluted pilasters with carved capitals, ornamental shells in gold or silver leaf in the recesses behind the mirrored glass doors, an abundance of string inlay on all surfaces, rectangular blocking on the top drawer, full dust boards, thin drawer linings, and fine dovetailing (fig. 2).

For all of the circumstantial documentation, this desk-and-bookcase still holds some mysteries. With whom did Coit apprentice, and what were his sources of contact and realm of influence? What did he see that made him (or his client) break from the standard English format of a straight front and attempt the very avant-garde convention of the blocked or swelled facade? Did Coit produce other as-yet-

unidentified blockfront pieces, and was this experimentation with a new design concept carried any further by any of his three sons? With continuing scholarship, rethinking and revision, and new discoveries, in time the mystery of the innovation of the blockfront in Boston furniture will be more fully understood.

WAC

---

**Inscriptions or marks:** *On one side of right document drawer:* "J Coit/ 1738" in ink; *on other side of right document drawer:* "2" in ink. *On underside of valance drawer in prospect section:* "Job Coit jr/ 1738" *in pencil. On left document drawer:* "R. T. W. Thorndike Aug 24, 1876/ S. H. Thorndike, March 10, 1883/ M. D. Thorndike, March 1893/ R. D. (Fiske) Sanderson Feb 8th 1927/ (200th Anniversary of/ this desk)" in ink. *On outside back of top long drawer:* "XB" in chalk. *On outside drawer back of second drawer:* "BX" in chalk. *On outside drawer back of third drawer:* "BX1" in chalk. *On outside drawer back of bottom drawer:* "BXX" in chalk. *Inside drawer bottom, top long drawer desk section:* "For Mary Duncan Fiske. Belonged to great-great-great-aunt Black (Rosanna Duncan). From her came to great/ great aunt Esther Duncan (Black) in 1786. From her to grandmother Mary Duncan Wells in 1828. From her to Rosanna Wells Thorndike 1859" on modern paper label. *On underside of third long drawer:* pencil drawing of the framing for the mirrored portion of a dressing glass.

**Construction:** (Upper case) The backboard is of three horizontal lap-joined boards attached to a rabbet in the sides with large wrought nails. The waist molding is nailed to the top of the lower case. The hinged slant-top lid opens to rest on unornamented lopers. In the interior, two rows of drawers shaped in a broken cyma curve flank the open prospect section. The inside of the drawer fronts conform to the outside shape; the drawer sides and back are rounded on the upper edge; the sides are attached to the back with a single large dovetail; the flush drawer bottoms are set into a rabbet on all four sides. Above these drawers are three valanced pigeonhole compartments. The prospect section consists of a valanced pencil drawer above a pigeonhole compartment with

two concave drawers below; the whole is flanked by blind document drawers. The fronts of the concave drawers are reinforced on the inside with a chamfered rectangular block. The prospect case, held by a wooden spring lock in the top, slides forward to reveal four small secret drawers placed between the back wall of the prospect section and the backboard of the case. There are also hidden document drawers accessible from the back of the prospect case. The two-board sides are dovetailed to the top and to the two-board bottom board. The double-beaded blades are backed with 3" pine boards. The top and second blades are joined to the sides with exposed dovetails; the third blade has a blind dovetail. There are no security or dust boards. The drawer fronts are cut from solid wood. The drawer sides are rounded on the top edge; the drawer back is flat on top with a slight chamfer on the outer edge. The drawer bottom is chamfered on the front only; the bottom boards run front to back. The drawer runners are nailed to the sides. The base molding is glued and nailed to the bottom board; there is an additional fillet on the upper edge of the side molding not present on the front molding. The front feet facings, mitered at the corners, are attached to vertical blocks and reinforced with two layers of horizontal glueblocks. The rear legs have a thin horizontal glueblock at the bottom board and a shaped vertical block on the side that supports the case; there is a simpler shaped bracket on the rear that functions similarly.

(Lower case) Full vertical stiles from the scrollboard to the backboard support the partially closed bonnet. The bonnet boards are fastened to a rabbet in the cornice and to the top of the backboard with large wrought nails. The complex cornice molding returns at the center front to the backboard; the cornice return is nailed to a spacer rail rather than directly to the bonnet support. The two-board scrollboard laps over the sides and is nailed to the top board at the center and ends. The scrollboard has a scratch bead on the upper edge outlining the circular openings and the support for the center finial. The top rail is tenoned through the sides; it is double-beaded on the leading edge and is cut in semicircular recesses behind the arched doors. Thumbnail molded on both the inner and out edges, the mortised frame of the rounded-arch door panels is held by a single pin at each tenon.

Flat backing panels secured with cut nails hold the mirrored glass in place. Inside, behind the arched tops, are concave inlaid fans in bands of light and dark wood. Below the fans, the space consists of a row of valanced cubicles across the top and down the sides, a row of plain drawers across the bottom, and a single movable shelf dividing the central area. There are two flat candle slides set in the front rail below the through-tenoned bottom blade. The backboard has five lap-joined horizontal boards fastened by rosehead nails to the rabbet in the sides.

**Condition:** The finials are new. The upper surface of the cornice molding has been chiseled out to provide space for the plinth blocks on the outer corners; these side finials may be later additions. The interior of the bookcase section was replaced in 1962. The silvered glass in the doors and the backing panels are modern; internal evidence indicates that the mirrored glass replaces clear glazing installed in the nineteenth century. A nail hole in the center of the scrollboard indicates that the desk-and-bookcase once had an applied ornament. The fall-front lid has been pieced out on the top and right side. There is a patch on the center rail of the left door where the lock was broken out. There is an old trapezoidal patch on the lower right side of the lower case. All of the feet facings have been pieced out: 1⅝" has been added to the front feet and 1⅞" to the rear feet. There is a good deal of abrasion on the underside of the lower case suggesting that the piece sat for some time without feet. All the handles and escutcheons were replaced by the dealer before the piece was acquired. The ghosts of large Chippendale-style plates and escutcheons are visible behind the current set of Queen Anne–style hardware. The drawers in the lower case have been lined with a composition wood paper.

**Dimensions:**

| | | |
|---|---|---|
| H. (with finials) | 100⅛ in. | 253.5 cm |
| H. (case) | 95⅛ in. | 241.8 cm |
| H. (writing surface) | 31⅜ in. | 79.8 cm |
| W. (cornice) | 39⅛ in. | 99.5 cm |
| W. (upper case) | 35¾ in. | 91.2 cm |
| W. (lower case) | 37⅞ in. | 95.8 cm |
| W. (feet) | 39½ in. | 100.7 cm |
| D. (cornice) | 14¼ in. | 36.3 cm |
| D. (upper case) | 12½ in. | 32.0 cm |
| D. (lower case) | 22½ in. | 57.3 cm |
| D. (feet) | 24½ in. | 62.2 cm |

**Materials:** *Microanalysis:* Primary: American black walnut. Secondary: white pine group (drawer linings, blade extensions). *Finish:* reddish brown color in resin.

**Publications:** Plaza Art Galleries, New York, sale catalogue (1960). *Antiques* 86, no. 4 (October 1964): frontispiece. David Stockwell, "American Blockfront Furniture," *America in Britain* 9, no. 2 (May 1971): 12. Nancy Goyne Evans, "The Genealogy of a Bookcase Desk," in Ian M. G. Quimby, ed., *Winterthur Portfolio* 9 (Charlottesville: University Press of Virginia for the Henry Francis du Pont Winterthur Museum, 1974), p. 214. Margaretta Markle Lovell, "Boston Blockfront Furniture," in *Boston Furniture*, figs. 62–64, pp. 90–95. Minor Myers, Jr., "The Migration of a Style: Blockfront Furniture in Connecticut Towns," *Art and Antiques* 3, no. 2 (March–April 1980): 81–82. Elizabeth Bidwell Bates and Jonathan L. Fairbanks, *American Furniture: 1620 to the Present* (New York: Richard Marek Publishers, 1981), p. 118. Fitzgerald, *Three Centuries*, p. 45. Kirk, *American Furniture*, fig. 322. Mary Jean Madigan and Susan Colgan, eds., *Early American Furniture from Settlement to City: Aspects of Form, Style, and Regional Design from 1620 to 1830* (New York: Billboard Publications, 1983), p. 54. Moses, *Master Craftsmen*, figs. 1.6, 1.6a. Miller, "Roman Gusto," pp. 163, 167.

**Provenance:** The desk-and-bookcase was made for Daniel Henchman, a Boston stationer, bookseller, and later merchant, and billed to him on May 10, 1738. It passed through Henchman's widow to their daughter Lydia, the widow of Thomas Hancock, and through her to Hancock's nephew and heir, John Hancock. Dorothy Quincy Hancock, John's widow, sold the desk-and-bookcase at auction sometime between 1793 and 1796. Purchased by Moses Black, a well-to-do Boston merchant, sometime before his death in 1810, the desk-and-bookcase was inherited by his widow, Esther Duncan Black, and descended in her family to her niece, Mary Duncan Wells. It passed from Mrs. Wells to her daughter, Rosanna Wells Thorndike, and from Mrs. Thorndike to her daughter and subsequently her granddaughter, the last private owner. It was sold from her estate at the Plaza Art Galleries, New York, in 1960.

**Accession history:** Purchased by the museum from John S. Walton, Inc., New York, 1961.
62.87

1. Macquoid and Edwards, *Dictionary*, 1:139, fig. 37; Ralph Edwards and Margaret Jourdain, *Georgian Cabinet-Makers, ca. 1700–1800* (3d rev. ed., London: Country Life, 1955), p. 230, pl. 213. Hipkiss, *Eighteenth-Century American Arts*, pp. 28–30; Israel Sack advertisement, *Antiques* 54, no. 3 (September 1948): 131; Israel Sack advertisement, *Antiques* 89, no. 5 (May 1966): inside front cover; Israel Sack advertisement, *Antiques* 91, no. 3 (March 1967): inside front cover.

2. Alan Miller has suggested that Coit, inexperienced and unfamiliar with this design and technique, made a layout error in the cutting of the leading edge of the bottom board; see Miller, "Roman Gusto," pp. 163. For a thorough discussion of the Boston blockfront form, see Margaretta Markle Lovell, "Boston Blockfront Furniture," in *Boston Furniture*, pp. 77–136.

3. Baarsen et al., *Courts and Colonies*, pp. 188–89.

4. Notices for the settlement of the estates of Job Coit (*Boston News-Letter*, December 16, 1742) and Job Coit, Jr. (*The Boston Gazette*, October 22, 1751), are cited in Dow, *Arts and Crafts in New England*, p. 105. Mabel Munson Swan listed Job Coit as living in Ann Street, Boston, in 1731; see Mabel Munson Swan, "Boston's Carvers and Joiners, Part I, Pre-Revolutionary," *Antiques* 53, no. 3 (March 1948): 198–201. The extensive genealogical research on Job Coit and on the line of descent of this desk-and-bookcase is taken from Nancy Goyne Evans, "The Genealogy of a Bookcase Desk," in Ian M. G. Quimby, ed., *Winterthur Portfolio* 9 (Charlottesville: University Press of Virginia for the Henry Francis du Pont Winterthur Museum, 1974), pp. 213–22. A February 3, 1725/26 bill is signed by Joseph Davis "for my Master Mr. Job Coit" for £8.15.0 for work done for Joseph Baxter of Medford (MS 63x69, Downs collection). Shortly after completing his apprenticeship, it is thought that Davis went to work in Portsmouth, N.H., and may have brought the idea of the blockfront form there; for a signed Portsmouth blockfront dressing table by Davis (and related examples), see Jobe, *Portsmouth Furniture*, cat. no. 29. Bill from the estate of Job Coit to Daniel Henchman, Boston, February 28, 1742 (Baker Library, Harvard University).

5. Evans, "Genealogy," p. 216.

6. William T. Baxter, "Daniel Henchman, A Colonial Bookseller," *Essex Institute Historical Collections* 70, no. 1 (January 1934): 1–30.

7. For the slant-top desk, see *American Antiques from Israel Sack Collection*, 10 vols. (Washington, D.C.: Highland House, ca. 1969–), 4:1020. For the group of desks, see Miller, "Roman Gusto."

## 206 ◆ Desk-and-bookcase
Boston, Massachusetts
1740–50

In 1972 the Colonial Society of Massachusetts sponsored a conference and subsequent publication titled *Boston Furniture of the Eighteenth Century*, resulting in a profusion of new primary research and enlightening scholarship about the patrons, craftsmen, and production in this wealthy commercial center.[1] This event spurred new and continuing research on upholsterers, japanners, and carvers, along with deeper investigations into the origins and manifestations of blockfront and bombé case furniture made in eastern Massachusetts. The wealth and cosmopolitan sophistication that pervaded Boston in the second quarter of the eighteenth century created a climate conducive to the importation and production of the most fashionable material possessions available. Not only were Boston's merchants economically poised to spend great sums on luxury items, but the very nature of their businesses demanded that they have fashionable furniture to house account books and to provide a writing surface when open and proclaim their status when closed.

Over the past ten years, the relationship between an important early group of Boston blockfront desk-and-bookcases, presumably made by an immigrant English cabinetmaker, has been recognized, researched, and published.[2] They are of monumental stature and superior quality, but, significantly, although they embrace British Burlingtonian classicism, they also display a new and individual Boston blockfront design expression. In 1946 Henry Francis du Pont purchased one of these desk-and-bookcases—the most highly ornamented example now known—directly from Edmund Quincy, descendant of an eighteenth-century owner, Josiah Quincy (1704–84) of Boston and Braintree.

Although scholars still do not know who introduced the blockfront design into Boston

**Fig. 1.** Detail, left foot and column.

or when, the 1738 Coit desk-and-bookcase (No. 205), along with the group under discussion, provide clues for unraveling this mystery. Presumably, this major design innovation was introduced in the early 1730s, and it is conceivable that the Coit desk-and-bookcase and this undated blockfront example were made within a few years of each other. It has been noted that both Coit and the unknown immigrant English cabinetmaker seem to have been struggling with the execution and join of the blocked base molding to the bottom board, signaling that it was a new concept for both of them.[3]

Winterthur's blockfront desk-and-bookcase stands out in this group for a number reasons, foremost among which is its extensive carving (attributed to John Welch [1711–89]), certainly a factor that added considerably to its original cost. While it is not thought to be among the earliest of this blockfront group, it is the most classical, with engaged fluted columns with Corinthian capitals framing the lower section, three fluted pilasters capped with Corinthian capitals flanking the mirrored doors, and fluted half-colonettes with diminutive Corinthian capitals facing the document drawers on either side of the prospect compartment of the interior. The straight-bracket feet are unlike any others; the front feet are fully carved on the fronts and sides, and scrolls ornament the brackets at both front and rear (fig. 1). The design of the carving is unusual, with a stippled background and a chain of foliate bellflowers and flowers and leaves suspended from a ring. The bracket is similarly punched and carved with a wispy, trailing bellflower and foliage. The outer edges of the feet and brackets are outlined with a flat bead that resembles baroque strapwork.[4] A stippled background is a theme carried throughout the piece, from the feet through the interior, where the thick prospect door has been scooped out in an arched configuration echoing the shape of the bookcase doors. The area framing the plain concave arch is carved with flowing foliage and bellflowers and is stippled (fig. 2). Above the arched door the face of a small drawer is also punched and

carved with winged cherubs, similar to those seen in clock spandrels and architectural work. The carved rosettes with trailing garlands, applied carving on the scrollboard, and elaborately carved finials add a central element of ornamentation at the apex of the bookcase, balancing the heavily ornamented base and carved pendent shell (fig. 3).

The bookcase section of Winterthur's example is almost identical to those on three other desk-and-bookcases, two with bombé bases that are related to the signed and dated 1753 Benjamin Frothingham bombé desk-and-bookcase in the collection of the Department of State and one with a straight front.[5] The bombé desk at Bayou Bend does not have carved rosettes, and the other has rosettes but lacks trailing garlands. The central prospect doors and drawers on the Bayou Bend example and the straight-front example are the same as those on Winterthur's desk-and-bookcase, but they lack the carving and stippled background. While most of the related blockfront examples have painted and gilt shells in the coved areas behind the arched mirrored doors, Winterthur's example (like the two bombé ones) has carved fluted shells with scroll and foliate bases and a stippled background.

The similar construction features of the group tie their fabrication to the same shop and suggest the hand of an English-trained cabinetmaker. The use of exotic woods (sabicu for the backboards and dividers of the bookcase

and red cedar for the drawer sides and backs) is consistent within the group. Thin quarter-inch stock for the drawer linings, finely cut dovetails, full dust boards between the drawers, and layered or stacked support blocks behind the straight-bracket feet are the London craft techniques found in this furniture.

The circumstances surrounding the commissioning of this desk-and-bookcase are not known. However, three different inscriptions on the piece provide some specific provenance information as well as data for speculation about its original owner. On the backboard of the prospect section is probably the earliest inscription in iron gall ink; a scrolled surround encircles the difficult-to-read script that could be interpreted as "Josiah Q_____ / his desk August 1748(?)." Another inscription written in 1879 on the bottom of the prospect drawer by Eliza Susan Quincy states, "This desk was/ purchased by Josiah Quincy/ o Braintree/ 1778." A third inscription is incised into the top board of the desk section and states, "John Allen His Desk/ Made . . . [illegible]." The Allen inscription has been interpreted as eighteenth-century in origin and as referring to the original owner, presumably John Allen (1671–1760), a goldsmith. Both these interpretations are questionable, however. In 1736, at age sixty-five, Allen wrote his will declaring to be "weak in Body, but of perfect mind and memory."[6] Although he did not die until 1760, it is doubtful that a man in his seventies would have ordered a piece of furniture of this style and stature when a few years before he thought he was on the brink of death. The John Allen of this inscription may have been a different person, most likely a later owner.

Because the desk-and-bookcase was acquired directly from the Quincy family, at least part of its provenance is firm; the 1879 inscription recording Josiah Quincy as purchaser in 1778 by Eliza Susan Quincy is believed to be authentic and correct. Eliza was Josiah's great-granddaughter and the inveterate chronicler of family possessions. Her 1879 "Memorandum relative to pictures,

**Fig. 2.** Detail, desk interior.

**Fig. 3.** Detail, pediment.

China & furniture" noted that in the west chamber on the second floor was "a carved desk-and-bookcase, bought by a farmer in the neighborhood [that] was bought back in 1840." Upon Josiah's death in 1784, the furnishings of his house were "left to the ladies of the family who divided between them and sold what they did not want." Who then owned this desk between 1784 and 1840? Because Eliza was relating information that had been conveyed by family oral tradition, we can reasonably question whether the purchase date of 1778 is correct. A purchase date of 1748, however, would certainly have been more in keeping with Josiah's circumstances for several reasons. In 1778 he was seventy-one years old and perhaps was not acquiring much new furniture; in 1748, however, he and his business partners, Edmund Quincy and Edward Jackson, had an extraordinary financial windfall, making them the wealthiest men in Boston. It was also at this time that Josiah was about to "retire" to Braintree to become a gentleman farmer on his family's estate, a far more appropriate time for such an acquisition. Josiah's brother-in-law Edward Jackson also owned a desk-and-bookcase similar to this one, although it is unknown whether he acquired it soon after

his marriage in 1738 or following the windfall of 1748.[7] Although two fires burned Quincy's houses in 1759 and 1769, some of his finest English furniture was rescued from those tragic circumstances. This costly desk-and-bookcase could have been saved as well.

Clearly future research and discoveries will continue to shed light not only on the shop and craftsmen who produced this desk-and-bookcase but also on the early history of this remarkable example of British classicism and Bostonian innovation.

WAC

---

**Inscriptions or marks:** *Incised into the top side of the top board of the lower case:* "John Allen His Desk/ Made . . . [illegible]." *Incised on back of left drawer in bookcase section:* "I". *Incised on back of middle, middle-right, and right drawers in bookcase section:* "X". *On bottom of valance drawer in prospect section of desk:* "This desk was/ purchased by Josiah Quincy/ o Braintree/ 1778" in ink. *Incised on left side of the valance drawer:* "V". *On left secret document drawer in back of prospect section:* illegible numbers. *Incised on right secret document drawer:* "X" (twice) and "226/ new/ bills". *On top drawer of secret compartment:* "226/ 160/ / 386" and "1" in pencil. *Incised on second drawer secret compartment:* "V". *Incised on third drawer secret compartment:* "X" and "I". *Incised*

*on bottom drawer secret compartment:* "X", "IX", and "I". *On back of case holding secret drawers:* "Josiah Q_____ / his desk August 1748(?)" in ink. *On drawer bottom, lower far left drawer desk section:* "L" in pencil. *On drawer bottom, lower near left drawer desk section:* "4" in pencil. *On top right drawer desk section:* "3", "8", and "Boston May 12th 1623" in pencil. *On drawer bottom, lower near right drawer:* "2" in pencil. *On drawer bottom, lower far right drawer:* "1" in pencil. *On reverse of brass plates on drawer handles:* cast mark "J•C".

**Construction:** (Upper case) The bonnet is enclosed except in the center. The bonnet boards are nailed to a rabbet in the scrollboard, flush to full supports between the pediment and backboard, and flush to the upper edge of the backboard. The cove cornice molding, cut from a single board, is nailed to the case. Unornamented frieze blocks and a carved floral and acanthus leaf motif are glued to the scrollboard. Below, Corinthian pilasters with separate capitals and bases are attached to the outer stile of both doors; a similar pilaster is affixed to the inner stile of the right door. The rounded arched doors are glazed with beveled mirrored panels, which are supported by shaped boards held in place with wire brads (as the backing on a looking glass). Inside, behind the arched doors, are carved thirteen-lobe concave shells on a stipple background. The interior has a series of pigeonholes across the top and down each side and a row of plain drawers across the bottom. At the center is a large open space with adjustable shelves. A dished candle slide is centered below each door. The backboard, composed of three lapped horizontal boards (the lower two chamfered on the outside edges), is nailed to a rabbet in the sides. The sides are dovetailed to the bottom board.

(Lower case) A molding is nailed to the upper edge of the case. The top is half-blind dovetailed to the sides. The hinged slant-top lid, a solid board with batten ends mitered at the top, opens to rest on plain lopers. Inside, the carved prospect section is flanked by a row of four pigeonholes over two rows of shaped cyma drawers. The upper row has two small drawers now joined in a single long drawer; the lower row has two small drawers on each side. There is a carved valance drawer held on a spring above the prospect door and a plain drawer inside. The drawer fronts are shaped on the inside to conform to the exterior; the upper edge of the sides and back is flat; the drawer bottoms are set flush into rabbets on all four sides. Below the writing surface, beaded rails are dovetailed to the sides. The join is covered by a facing that includes a carved engaged Corinthian column. Vertical glueblocks reinforce the join with the sides. There are full dust or security boards between the drawers, which serve as drawer runners. The blocked drawer fronts, cut from solid wood, are conforming on the inside. The drawer sides are flat on the upper edge; the back is slightly chamfered. The drawer bottoms, the grain running from front to back, are set into rabbets on three sides; there are reinforcing battens on the sides. The backboard, chamfered across the top, is made of two horizontal boards nailed to rabbets. The bottom board is dovetailed to the sides. The bottom rail and front base molding are cut as a single piece; the side legs and side base molding are a unit. The bracket legs are reinforced by a vertical block; horizontal blocks reinforce the knee brackets. The back bracket on the rear legs is arched and is slotted into the side. The pendent drop has a reinforcing block.

**Condition:** The molding above the left pilaster is a replacement. The mirrored glass is replaced. The lower right side of the upper case is patched. The waist molding on the left and right sides is new. Several of the valances in the desk section have been reglued. The upper drawers in the desk section have been joined to make a single drawer; the left drawer has been broken and a portion of the back is missing. The base of the right column is patched. The centers of the scrolls on the front knee brackets have been reduced. The lower part of the right front foot facing is new.

**Dimensions:**

| | | |
|---|---|---|
| H. (with finials) | 97 1/4 in. | 246.8 cm |
| H. (case) | 94 in. | 238.7 cm |
| H. (writing surface) | 30 3/4 in. | 78.0 cm |
| W. (cornice) | 42 5/8 in. | 108.4 cm |
| W. (upper case) | 38 1/2 in. | 98.0 cm |
| W. (lower case) | 39 3/4 in. | 101.3 cm |
| W. (feet) | 42 7/8 in. | 109.0 cm |
| D. (cornice) | 14 1/2 in. | 36.8 cm |
| D. (upper case) | 12 in. | 30.5 cm |
| D. (lower case) | 21 1/4 in. | 54.0 cm |
| D. (feet) | 23 1/2 in. | 59.7 cm |

**Materials:** *Microanalysis:* Primary: mahogany; sabicu (upper case backboard, middle shelf of bookcase, some partitions in upper case). Secondary: white pine group (drawers in secret compartment, top board and backboard of lower case); eastern red cedar (drawer bottoms in lower case); ash (spring lock on secret compartment). *Finish:* dark brown color in resin.

**Publications:** Downs, *American Furniture*, fig. 226. Elizabeth Stillinger, *The Antiques Guide to the Decorative Arts in America, 1600–1875* (New York: E. P. Dutton, 1972), p. 162. Joseph Downs, "A Selection of American Furniture," *Antiques* 61, no. 5 (May 1952): 427. Joseph T. Butler, "American Furniture," in Phoebe Phillips, ed., *The Collectors' Encyclopedia of Antiques* (New York: Crown Publishers, 1973), p. 9. Margaretta Markle Lovell, "Boston Blockfront Furniture," in *Boston Furniture*, pp. 126, 128, 131. Elizabeth Bidwell Bates and Jonathan L. Fairbanks, *American Furniture: 1620 to the Present* (New York: Richard Marek Publishers, 1981), p. 183. Moses, *Master Craftsmen*, p. 26, fig. 1.7. Brock Jobe, "A Boston Desk-and-Bookcase at the Milwaukee Art Museum," *Antiques* 140, no. 3 (September 1991): 415. Miller, "Roman Gusto," pp. 170–74. Philip D. Zimmerman and Frank M. Levy, "An Important Blockfront Desk by Richard Walker of Boston," *Antiques* 147, no. 3 (March 1995): 440. Keno, Freund, and Miller, "Very Pink of the Mode," fig. 20.

**Provenance:** Although the identity of the original owner is not known, a nineteenth-century inscription indicates that the desk was acquired by Josiah Quincy (1704–84) in 1778. It passed out of the Quincy family and was reacquired from "a farmer in the neighborhood . . . in 1840." The desk remained in the Quincy family until it was sold by a descendant in 1946.

**Accession history:** Purchased by H. F. du Pont through J. A. Lloyd Hyde from Edmund Quincy of Boston, 1946. Gift of H. F. du Pont, 1960. 60.1134

1. *Boston Furniture.*

2. Alan Miller ("Roman Gusto") cites Joe Kindig III as the first furniture scholar to recognize this group of desk-and-bookcases (see Joseph Kindig III, "The Renaissance Influence in Boston" [unpublished ms. in the possession of Miller, n.d.); for a thorough discussion of this group,

see Miller, "Roman Gusto"; Brock Jobe, "A Boston Desk-and-Bookcase at the Milwaukee Art Museum," *Antiques* 140, no. 3 (September 1991): 412–19; Philip D. Zimmerman and Frank M. Levy, "An Important Blockfront Desk by Richard Walker of Boston," *Antiques* 147, no. 3 (March 1995): 436–41. While Walker has been proposed as the maker of several desks in this group, it seems more likely that he—recorded as a "ship carpenter" through the decade of the 1730s—might have done some piecework (for example, the carved, twisted pilasters on the face of the document drawers) or been an apprentice for cabinetmaker William Hunt in 1739.

3. If the early blockfront dressing table signed by Joseph Davis (*Boston Furniture*, fig. 68) was made in Portsmouth, N.H., after Davis's apprenticeship to Coit, then Davis must have seen blockfront pieces in Boston prior to his leaving Boston and moving to Portsmouth in 1733–34. Furthermore, the fluted pilasters employed by Davis on several dressing tables suggests that he was familiar with that design feature as rendered on casepieces like the Chipstone desk-and-bookcase and clock and the clock at the Art Institute of Chicago; see Miller, "Roman Gusto," figs. 20, 27, 32. Jobe, "Boston Desk-and-Bookcase," p. 416; and Miller, "Roman Gusto," p. 164.

4. For the earlier examples, see Miller, "Roman Gusto," pp. 160–69. There is an unlocated fall-front desk (p. 167) supposedly dated 1739 and the seemingly identical signed Walker fall-front desk (see Zimmerman and Levy, "Important Blockfront Desk"), both of which relate to the lower cases of the desk-and-bookcases and probably date about the same. Winterthur's desk-and-bookcase is the only one known with Corinthian columns on the outer corners of the lower case. Of 2 related tall clock cases presumably from the same shop, 1 retains its Corinthian capitals; see Miller, "Roman Gusto," figs. 27, 32. Two other known pieces have carved feet, although they are ogee-bracket feet and totally different with carved foliate motifs that seem almost three-dimensional. One was illustrated in Morse, *Furniture of the Olden Time* (see Miller, "Roman Gusto," fig. 40). The other, incorrectly cited in Miller (fig. 42) as the piece in Morse, is privately owned; it is illustrated in Jobe, "Boston Desk-and-Bookcase," fig. 5; no. 90.177, DAPC, Visual Resources Collection, Winterthur Library. Similar edge carving resembling strapwork is seen on 2 round-cornered card tables (1745–55); see Miller, "Roman Gusto," figs. 51, 52; Leigh Keno advertisement, *Antiques* 143, no. 5 (May 1993): 649; and on a small slab-top pier table in the Karolik collection (Hipkiss, *Eighteenth-Century American Arts*, no. 50).

5. The first desk-and-bookcase with a bombé base is in Miller, "Roman Gusto," figs. 45, 46 (now at Bayou Bend); the second is in Miller, "Roman Gusto," fig. 50; also illustrated in Marshall B. Davidson, ed., *The American Heritage History of Colonial Antiques* ([New York]: American Heritage Publishing Co., [1967]), p. 220. For the Frothingham desk, see Rollins, *Treasures of State*, pp. 94–95. The straight-front example is in Miller, "Roman Gusto," fig. 40.

6. On Allen inscription, see Miller, "Roman Gusto," pp. 170–71. John Allen will, Suffolk County Probate Court, 1759–60 (microfilm, Downs collection).

7. Eliza Susan Quincy, "Memorandum relative to pictures, China & furniture," Quincy, Mass., 1879 (photostat copy of unpublished manuscript [location unknown], pp. 31–32, 20, Downs collection). Clifford K. Shipton, comp., *Biographical Sketches of Those Who Attended Harvard College in the Classes 1746–1750* (Boston: Massachusetts Historical Society, 1962), 8:466–67. For Jackson's desk-and-bookcase, see Sotheby's, "Important Americana from the Collection of Mr. and Mrs. Adolph Henry Meyer" (January 20, 1996), lot 218.

## 207 ♦ Desk-and-bookcase
Newport, Rhode Island
1760–85

Newport block-and-shell desk-and-bookcases represent the zenith of a very distinct regional interpretation that seems to be singularly American in its fulfillment, if not its inspiration. The exact source of influence has never been specifically identified, although German, French, Dutch, and Chinese export precedents have been cited as possibilities, and an acknowledged French Huguenot presence in the eighteenth-century Newport community may eventually provide some leads to this mystery.[1] That the blockfront form was first produced in Boston by the 1730s is indisputable, and its transmission to Newport is explained by the export trade routes along the North American coast. But what inspired Newport craftsmen to incorporate boldly shaped shells on the upper case panels and fall-front lid and double applied plaques on the pediments?

The quality of design and craftsmanship evidenced in these pieces far exceeds that found in similarly elite productions from other major centers at the time, evidenced in the architectural quality, attention to detail, and selection of the finest materials possible. Perhaps because these desk-and-bookcases were the major emblems of commerce and success, to be displayed and revered within their own community (although sometimes exported), the makers and owners lavished great attention and resources on them.

These monumental Newport desk-and-bookcases have captivated connoisseurs since the first antiquarians began collecting American furniture. As early as about 1870, collector of eighteenth-century furniture Thomas Mawney Potter of Kingston, Rhode Island, bought a six-shell desk-and-bookcase in Newport. Potter's early acquisitions may have influenced Charles Pendleton, another Rhode Island collector and dealer, who also

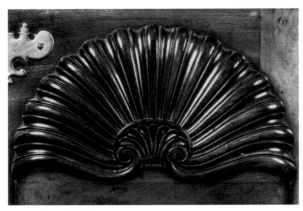

**Fig. 1.** Detail, shell.

acquired, among numerous other items, a Newport six-shell desk-and-bookcase. Pendleton bequeathed his collection to the Museum of Art of the Rhode Island School of Design upon his death in 1904; Potter's desk-and-bookcase descended in the family and was given to the same institution in 1967. Important collectors are often trendsetters, and Potter and Pendleton may have inspired two other early connoisseurs, Richard Canfield (1855–1914) and Marsden Perry (1850–1935), to acquire similar Newport desk-and-bookcases.[2] One year after Canfield's death in 1914, his desk-and-bookcase was bought by the Metropolitan Museum of Art, and in 1939 Maxim Karolik acquired the Perry desk-and-bookcase for the Museum of Fine Arts, Boston. Although all four desk-and-bookcases mentioned above are in museum collections today, their original histories of ownership have not been preserved.

In Luke Vincent Lockwood's 1913 edition of *Colonial Furniture in America*, he illustrated a nine-shell desk-and-bookcase originally owned by Joseph Brown (now thought to have possibly been made in Providence instead of Newport), with five of the six-shell desk-and-bookcases. In addition to the Pendleton, Canfield, and Perry examples, he included two others then still owned by descendants of the original owners—John Brown (1736–1803) of Providence and Elisha Potter of Kingston, Rhode Island. In 1918 the John Brown desk-and-bookcase was acquired by Francis P. Garvan (now in the Yale University Art Gallery), and in 1940 the Potter piece was given to the Museum of Fine Arts, Boston.[3]

The notoriety of Newport block-and-shell furniture was further heightened in 1927 when the Rhode Island School of Design presented the exhibition "John Goddard and His Work." Two years later, Garvan lent his six-shell desk-and-bookcase to the landmark Girl Scouts Loan Exhibition, held in New York at the American Art Association Galleries. In 1932 Henry Francis du Pont was presented with the opportunity to acquire one for his own

collection, and he wrote to his trusted New York agent Albert J. Collings asking him to look over a desk owned by his wife's cousin, Mrs. Walter Hidden—parenthetically indicating that he thought a suggested price of $30,000 was too much. Collings immediately realized that the feet had been replaced, and du Pont responded, "Do you think that Mrs. Hidden's desk is really good enough for my collection, in as much as it would have two new feet? Every piece I have is perfect, with no restorations, but of course these pieces are so scarce that I might make an exception of this one." Collings answered, "I need not tell you these desks are considered among collectors possibly the most desirable of any pieces produced in America. Mr. Garvan always considered his the 'piece de resistance' in his entire collection. It has always been my desire to see one of them in your collection." At that time, Collings speculated that the only others that might come on the market were the Thomas Potter one (given to Museum of Art, Rhode Island School of Design in 1967) and the Perry one (which Karolik subsequently bought). On Collings's advice, du Pont purchased the desk-and-bookcase from Mrs. Hidden.[4]

The piece had descended in Walter Hidden's family and is believed to have been originally owned by Lodowick Updike II (1725–1804). Lodowick II was the son of Daniel Updike (1694–1757), a lawyer and attorney general for Rhode Island, who lived in Newport, where Lodowick was born. The family also owned a substantial "plantation" of more than one thousand acres called "Cocumscussoc" on the west side of Narragansett Bay. Lodowick II inherited these lands and a mansion called "Smith's Castle," the house that had been the family's country home for generations, in 1757. Although schooled in law, he chose the life of a country gentleman and married Abigail Gardiner in 1760, together raising eleven children at Cocumscussoc. Because of his "high character and social prominence as a great landed

proprieter," he was among the most esteemed citizens of Rhode Island in his time. Under his direction, Cocumscussoc became a center for social activity in the area.[5]

Winterthur's desk-and-bookcase is one of nine six-shell desk-and-bookcases known today. In 1952 Miss Ima Hogg purchased a six-shell desk-and-bookcase that had been found in England; it is reputed to have been offered to du Pont, but he refused it because it had Victorian carving added to the tympanum, the base molding, and the feet. With the later carving removed, it is now in the Bayou Bend collection of the Museum of Fine Arts, Houston. Only one is not in a public collection; in 1989 the last example known and still owned by descendants of the original owner, Nicholas Brown, was sold to a private collector for an all-time record price for any piece of American furniture—$12.1 million. Despite the similarities within the group of nine, there is also great diversity in size and proportion, bonnet design, details of the bracket feet, carving of the shells and finials, and arrangement of the bookcase interior. In general design, they can be divided into two groups; the first comprises five with closed bonnets (the Winterthur, Bayou Bend, and Metropolitan Museum of Art desks, the Potter desk at the Rhode Island School of Design, and the E. Potter desk at the Museum of Fine Arts, Boston) plus one closely related open-bonnet example (Rhode Island School of Design's Pendleton desk). Three with open bonnets that have broken scroll cornice moldings terminating in carved rosettes constitute the second group (the one at Yale, the Perry desk at Museum of Fine Arts, Boston, and the privately owned example).[6]

Winterthur's desk-and-bookcase is most similar to two in the first group—the Metropolitan's and Bayou Bend's. All three are of approximately the same size and proportion and differ primarily in the interiors of the bookcase section.[7] Although the shells on the other two seem to be closely related and have the same number of lobes, those on Winterthur's desk-and-bookcase differ in number of lobes and the character of the central petal motif (fig. 1).

The interior of Winterthur's desk has sliding panels at the sides that enclose "secret" compartments between the case sides and the inner cedar lining (fig. 2). Discovered hidden behind these panels were twenty-four paper-wrapped packets of handmade eighteenth-century needles in several lengths ($^{11}/_{16}$ inch to 1¹/₂ inch) as well as several sizes of wire gages and eye openings. One packet is inscribed with the dates "January 23, 1761" and "1762." Needles were among the dry goods imported from England, and there are persistent references to the difficulties of obtaining them in New England.[8]

Although we know with certainty the original owners of four of these desk-and-bookcases (Nicholas Brown, John Brown, Elisha Potter, and Lodowick Updike II), none of them are signed or labeled by their makers, and both Morrison H. Heckscher and Thomas S. Michie have speculated that within the groups there appears to be the work of two or more shops. While the Thomas Potter desk-and-bookcase at the Museum of Art, Rhode Island School of Design bears an inscription, "Made by John Goddard 1761 and repaired by Thomas Goddard his son 1813," this was probably added in 1813 and can only suggest an attribution to John Goddard. It has been speculated that perhaps one of the Brown desk-and-bookcases might also have been made by Goddard, since in 1766 Goddard wrote to Brown and added, "P.S. I should be glad if thou or some of thy Brothers & I could agree abought a desk & Bookcase which I have to dispose of." One fact that remains undisputed is that none of these desk-and-bookcases appear to bear any distinct relationship to the work of John Townsend.[9]

The ornamental variations among these desk-and-bookcases raise several questions about Newport block-and-shell furniture. Were the different carvers and turners who prepared the shells, quarter columns, and finials working as integral journeymen within the shops? Or was this high-end block-and-shell furniture such a small percentage of the shop's output that these craftsmen were preparing specialized piecework for several trades, including architectural building, shipbuilding, cabinetmaking, and chairmaking? Is it possible that John Goddard specialized in these monumental desk-and-bookcases, and were all of them perhaps made prior to the Revolution? John Goddard (1723–85) would have been at his prime between 1760 and about 1774, and in the years immediately following the 1783 Treaty of Paris, the economic situation of Newport and much of Rhode Island was quite depressed.[10] The Brown brothers, John and Nicholas, as well as Lodowick Updike II, were also at their peak and flourishing financially prior to the Revolution. These recently introduced block-

**Fig. 2.** Desk open.

and-shell designs were presumably the height of fashion, and for prosperous merchant/entrepreneurs, cultured landowners, and respected lawyers alike, a great shell-carved desk-and-bookcase could only further announce social position and wealth.

WAC

---

**Inscriptions or marks:** *Chisel-marked on the inside drawer fronts of the original drawers in the desk interior:* Roman numerals. *Chiseled inside the drawer fronts and inside the backs of the four original valance drawers:* Roman numerals. *On underside of top section and on underside of bottom board of lower section:* "Bottom" in chalk. *On the backboard of the bonnet:* "Aday?/Back" in chalk.

**Construction:** (Upper case) The basic unit is composed of sides with laminated top and bottom boards (thinner cedar on full thickness maple) half-blind dovetailed to the sides. The bonnet is attached to a foundation of two heavy front-to-back pine glueblocks secured at the upper edges of the sides with glue and wrought nails. The back of the bonnet is enclosed with a horizontally oriented piece of maple. The front is enclosed with a complex laminated unit composed of an outer tympanum of ¹/₄" mahogany glued to a heavier

⁵/₈" maple board; the circular cutouts are built up behind with a thick pine blocking cut to the circular openings and faced on the curved surface with thin mahogany veneer. Finally, the cutout area is backed, or closed, with ¹/₂" maple, stained to match. Attached to the face of the tympanum and conforming to the shape of the bonnet is a pair of double applied plaques, circular moldings outlining the cutouts, and the carved cyma-curve cornice molding. The straight side cornice is nailed to the side. The top of the bonnet is enclosed with thin tulip boards nailed in place. The replacement plinths and finials are attached to the top front corners and center of the bonnet. The engaged columns and front stiles are attached to heavy pine glueblocks that are secured to the sides of the case with glue and wrought nails. The stop-fluted column was turned in three sections: shaft, plinth, and cap. The replacement midmolding is applied to the front and sides, extending ³/₄" below the bottom board, thus forming a lip that originally positioned the upper case on three cleats glued to the top board of the desk section. The interior is divided vertically into three sections and has fixed shelves. The interior shelves and thin vertical dividers (front edges are double-beaded) slide into grooves from the back; the vertical dividers, shaped on the leading edge, can be adjusted. The space behind the

columns and door stiles is enclosed with thin cedar panels, which slide in from the front, thus forming secret compartments. On the proper right side two shelf grooves were cut by mistake—laid out from the wrong end of the side board—and filled, possibly providing a motive for the creation of these enclosed compartments. The vertically oriented backboards are lapped and secured in a rabbet all around with wrought nails. The two outer doors are frame-and-panel construction with double tenons at the top; the convex panels and carved shells are separate pieces and applied to the face of the frame (from the inside, screws secure the shell and quarter-round molding on the panel). The center concave door with carved shell was cut from solid wood and reinforced on the back with a 1/8" mahogany board. The center door is hinged to the door on the left.

(Lower case) The top and bottom boards are half-blind dovetailed to the sides. The fall-front is solid with batten ends and thumbnail-molded edge; the central concave shell is carved from solid wood, and the flanking convex shells and blocked panels are made in two pieces and applied to the front. All edges have repairs; the hinges have been replaced. When the fall-front is open, the top drawer can be accessed through an opening (well) in the writing surface made of a thin panel that slides in grooves of the mortise-and-tenoned frame construction on three slides. The bottom board of the interior compartment is maple faced with mahogany, molded to echo the shaping of the blocked section above (which follows the shape of the facade). The vertical and horizontal dividers of the five part interior are slid in from the back and have rounded front edges. The interior drawer slides are half-blind dovetailed to the front and full dovetailed at back. The bottoms of all but the valance drawers are set into rabbets in the front and glued up to the sides and back; the valance drawer bottoms are set into a groove in the front and rabbets on the sides and back and glued. All drawer blades are maple (approx. 3 3/4" deep) edged with 1 3/4" mahogany (cock-beaded), and half-blind dovetailed to the sides. The front base molding (rabbeted on the lower back edge) laps over the leading edge of the bottom board; the bottom blade sits on top of the base molding and is dovetailed to the sides in the same manner as the upper blades. Cock-beading is applied to the sides of the case and to the underside of the writing surface. Replacement runners are secured to the sides of the case with modern screws. All drawer fronts are blocked and cut from solid mahogany. The bottoms are set into grooves on the side and rabbets in the front and nailed to the underside of the backs. The two bottom drawers are conventionally dovetailed (half-blind dovetailed in front, fully dovetailed in the back). The construction of the top drawer is different to accommodate the lopers. In order that the facade of the top drawer remain uninterrupted and hence consistent with the lower drawers, there are no loper dividers; the lopers ride in cutout maple blocking in the interior. Hence, the drawer sides are set in to accommodate the maple blocking and are attached to the drawer front with vertical sliding dovetails. The resulting end lip of the drawer front

is cut out around the loper. The horizontal backboards (three) are nailed into rabbets on the top and sides.

**Condition:** According to family history, the original feet were removed to lower the writing surface to a more acceptable level; the present feet are new and were installed about 1932. The waist molding is a replacement. In the desk interior, two of the valance drawers are replaced. The lower right blocked drawer is a replacement. A major split in the prospect door has been repaired and is reinforced with wooden splines top and bottom. All the drawers in the desk section are stained on the inside. The top rail of the lower case has been pieced out. The drawer fronts are original, but all the drawer sides, backs, and bottoms are replaced. The middle drawer has been repaired in the recessed section presumably due to the lock having broken out. The drawer runners are new and are held in place with modern screws. The left base molding is replaced by a thin strip of mahogany over white pine. The bottom board has been reset and the dovetails reinforced with wire nails. The brass back plates, handles, and escutcheons are replacements.

**Dimensions:**

|  |  |  |
|---|---|---|
| H. (with finials) | 97 7/8 in. | 248.7 cm |
| H. (case) | 93 7/8 in. | 244.1 cm |
| W. (cornice) | 42 3/4 in. | 108.5 cm |
| W. (upper case) | 40 in. | 101.8 cm |
| W. (lower case) | 42 1/4 in. | 107.2 cm |
| W. (feet) | 45 3/8 in. | 115.2 cm |
| D. (cornice) | 14 in. | 35.7 cm |
| D. (upper case) | 12 1/2 in. | 32.0 cm |
| D. (lower case) | 23 7/8 in. | 60.5 cm |
| D. (feet) | 25 1/2 in. | 65.0 cm |

**Materials:** *Microanalysis:* Primary: mahogany. Secondary: red cedar (backboard of top section, interior divider, sliding panel of top case); soft maple group (board behind scrollboard, support for drawer divider bottom section); white pine group (backboard lower case, bottom of small desk drawer, bonnet board); tulip-poplar (replacement long drawer sides, backs, and bottoms). *Finish:* medium brown color in resin.

**Publications:** Downs, *American Furniture*, fig. 232. William S. Ayres, "Contrasts: Philadelphia and Newport Furniture Styles, 1755–1780," in *Delaware Antiques Show 1982* (Wilmington, Del.), fig. 11, p. 71. Moses, *Master Craftsmen*, pp. 318–19.

**Provenance:** The desk-and-bookcase has a direct descent in the Updike and Hidden families. Originally owned by Lodowick Updike II (1725–1804), it passed to Lodowick's son, Wilkins (1784–1867) and then to Wilkins's daughter Abigail, who married Henry Hidden. It was inherited by Walter Hidden, their third son, passed to his daughter Mary (Hidden) Lee, wife of Howard Lee, and eventually to her son Walter, whose name was legally changed from Lee to Hidden.

**Accession history:** Purchased by H. F. du Pont from Mrs. Walter Hidden, Providence, R.I., 1932. Gift of H. F. du Pont, 1960.
59.2646

1. R. Peter Mooz, "The Origins of Newport Block-front Furniture Design," *Antiques* 99, no. 6 (June 1971): 882–86; Kirk, *American Furniture*, pp. 125–28; Carl L. Crossman, *The Decorative Arts of the China Trade* (Woodbridge, Eng.: Antique Collectors' Club, 1991), frontispiece, pp. 220–21, pls. 76, 77.

2. For Potter's desk-and-bookcase, see Monkhouse and Michie, *American Furniture*, pp. 17, 96–99; see also pp. 21–22 for collecting influences. For Canfield's desk-and-bookcase, see Heckscher, *American Furniture*, pp. 282–84; for Perry's, see Hipkiss, *Eighteenth-Century American Arts*, no. 19.

3. On reattribution to Providence, see Ralph E. Carpenter, "A Comparative Study of the Work of John Carlisle, Jr., of Providence and the Townsends and Goddards of Newport," *The Walpole Society Notebook* (Cambridge: Walpole Society, 1991–92), pp. 79–86; Lockwood, *Colonial Furniture*, pp. 246–52. For the John Brown desk, see Ward, *American Case Furniture*, pp. 342–43; for the Potter desk, see Randall, *American Furniture*, no. 62.

4. "John Goddard and His Work," *Bulletin of the Rhode Island School of Design* 15, no. 2 (April 1927): 14–24. H. F. du Pont to Albert J. Collings, May 31, 1932, and June 6, 1932, box 15, Winterthur Archives. Albert J. Collings to H. F. du Pont, June 7, 1932, box 15, Winterthur Archives.

5. For more on the Updike family, see Carl R. Woodward, *Plantation in Yankeeland* (Chester, Conn.: Pequot Press, 1971), pp. 24–159. The genealogy of the Updike-Hidden families (see also **Provenance**) was supplied by Mr. N. D. Scotti, of Providence, from Howard M. Chapin's manuscript "Ancestral Line of Old Rhode Island Families." Sincerest thanks to Mr. Scotti for making this information available.

6. For the Bayou Bend desk, see Warren, *Bayou Bend*, p. 69. Christie's, "The Magnificent Nicholas Brown Desk-and-Bookcase" (June 3, 1989), lot 100. For the characteristics within these groups, see Heckscher, *American Furniture*, pp. 282–84; Ward, *American Case Furniture*, pp. 339–44; all 9 examples are illustrated in Moses, *Master Craftsmen*, pp. 309–31.

7. For a comparison of these 3 desk-and-bookcases, see Heckscher, *American Furniture*, p. 284.

8. Similar compartments are in Yale's, Bayou Bend's, Rhode Island School of Design's Potter, and MFA's E. Potter desk-and-bookcase. Only those on RISD's are accessible; the others have been nailed shut. William Greene Roelker, "Governor Samuel Ward, Farmer and Merchant," *Rhode Island History* 6, no. 2 (April 1947): 56.

9. John Goddard to Nicholas Brown, October 3, 1766, Brown Papers, Misc. 1765–67, John Carter Brown Library, Brown University, Providence, R.I. Heckscher, *American Furniture*, p. 184. Monkhouse and Michie, *American Furniture*, p. 97.

10. On the unlikely use of outside "pieceworkers" by the Goddards and Townsends, see Margaretta M. Lovell, "'Such Furniture as Will Be Most Profitable': The Business of Cabinetmaking in Eighteenth-Century Newport," *Winterthur Portfolio* 26, no. 1 (Spring 1991): 27–62. It is Lovell's opinion, as well as Moses's, that the Goddard and Townsend shops were very strictly made up of family members and that various outside "pieceworkers" were not employed for specialized functions such as turning and carving, as we know to be the case in other urban centers. Presumably there were journeymen within the shop who were highly skilled carvers, and they worked only for that shop. (Moses, *Master Craftsmen*, p. 1; Lovell, "Such Furniture," pp. 61–62).

## 208 • Desk-and-bookcase
Probably Salem, Massachusetts
1770–90

The design of this commanding blockfront desk-and-bookcase evidences strong architectural influence in the upper case through the fluted pilasters flanking arched panel doors surmounted by a broken-scroll pediment. Produced with numerous variations in both urban and rural New England from the 1730s throughout the eighteenth century, the popularity of this particular design must have emanated from its balanced symmetry and carefully combined classical elements.

The most distinctive design features include the carved and applied shell projecting from the center of the tympanum, the fluted pilasters flanking each door, the rounded blocking on the fall front and facade of the lower case, and the pendent drop with central piercing applied to the lower edge of the base molding. As direct descendants of the blockfront desk-and-bookcases first made in Boston in the 1730s and 1740s (see No. 206), the Essex County examples have also been influenced by a number of design and ornamental details on the great Newport desk-and-bookcases (see No. 207). The small, almost square, lopers are similar to those found on Newport blockfront desks and are designed to intrude less on the blocking of the topmost drawer front. Another Newport detail is the circular molding applied to the tympanum around the circumference of the central cutouts. These two features, along with the rounded blocking, a flat pierced pendent drop instead of a carved scallop-shell pendant, and a very different interior with an unusual linear blocked lower section and fluted pilasters on the document drawers, distinguish this desk-and-bookcase from four other closely related Salem examples; one in the Bybee collection at the Dallas Museum of Art, one at the Metropolitan Museum of Art, one in the

**Fig. 1.** Desk open.

Mead Art Gallery at Amherst College, and one at the Art Institute of Chicago. The ball-and-claw feet on this example are not of the high ovoid type with massive, well-defined claws, as are seen on the Dallas and Metropolitan examples and No. 201; rather, they are smaller and flatter, with little semblance of knuckles on the claws. Although the rounded blocking might be interpreted as a Boston feature, the large dovetail usually seen on Boston blockfronts is not employed here; the bottom board is notched out instead (with ninety degree angles) to receive the front base molding.[1]

Winterthur's desk-and-bookcase differs markedly from the other examples in the group in the treatment of the interiors of the bookcase and desk (fig. 1). The domed recesses behind the arched panels of the doors are devoid of carving, and the valances over the pigeonholes are elaborately shaped. This bookcase is the only one with a central shell-carved, recessed blocked drawer over a narrow concave blocked drawer. An unusual original locking system for the document drawers in the desk interior necessitated the removal of the middle drawer behind the prospect door to release spring locks that then allowed the prospect drawers to be removed. Perhaps the most unusual feature of the interior is the treatment of the bottom tier of drawers. Elaborately blocked bases for the pilasters are applied to the front of a very wide center drawer that runs under the pigeonholes and the prospect section, flanked by narrow drawers (with similarly blocked fronts) beneath the end stacks of drawers with concave fronts. The linear profile created across the facade is in direct contrast to the more usual curvilinear-shape blocking and base molding.

Because more than a dozen or so cabinetmakers and shop joiners were working in Salem at the time this desk-and-bookcase was made, it is difficult to assign it to a particular shop. In general design and some construction features it relates to a group of desk-and-bookcases recently attributed to Henry Rust (1737–1812) of Salem, but overall there are not enough correlations to warrant attribution to the Rust shop.[2] However, some of the unusual design and construction features

of this desk-and-bookcase may eventually help to ascribe it to a specific Salem or Essex County shop.

Little is known about the original owner of this desk-and-bookcase, Joseph Waters (1758–1833) of Salem, who was married to Mary Dean (1759–98). The Reverend William Bentley made frequent mention in his diary of a Capt. Joseph Waters, presumably the same person. According to Bentley, he was apparently involved in the slave trade, for the Reverend recorded "property attached of Cap. J. Waters for this 'infamous trafick.'" In April 1805 Bentley noted that "Capt. Joseph Waters has bought at 4010 D. the Dean Estate on Derby Street, corner of Turner's street, north side of Derby street. It was the best House [as] to appearance which was in that part of Town when I came to Salem & had the best gardens around it. It is much decayed & has been long neglected."[3] This desk-and-bookcase descended in the Waters family and is seen in a late nineteenth-century photograph with a young lady (identified as Mary Mott) in colonial dress posed before it. The photograph is identified as being taken at the "Waters House, Washington Square,"

presumably not the same neglected property bought in 1805. The house was probably owned by Joseph Gilbert Waters (1796–1878), one of the captain's eight children and a noted attorney and judge who had an interest in history and was the secretary of the Essex Historical Society for twenty-one years.

WAC

---

**Inscriptions or marks:** *On outside back of next-to-bottom drawer:* "2" *in pencil. On outside back of bottom drawer:* "1" *in pencil. On left drawer side of top drawer:* "x" *or* "4" *in chalk. Pasted on the inside of the prospect door:* printed table of weights for silver coins and their value, inscribed "Engraved Printed and Sold by Nat. Hurd".

**Construction:** (Upper case) The top board (pine with 3" of mahogany applied to the leading edge) of the case fits in grooves in the sides; the bottom board is half-blind dovetailed to the sides. The bonnet is formed by a backboard cut to the arched shape and a tympanum cut to the same shape and applied to the front and back. The backboard is nailed to a rabbet cut in the sides. The lower edge of the tympanum is cut with two arches that are filled from the back with heavy mahogany blocking; the blocking and leading edge of the top board have been carved into shallow domed recesses.

The pediment is finished with straight and scrolled cornice molding and molding applied to the circular cutouts and a freestanding carved shell applied to the center of the tympanum. Front-to-back pine braces connect the top edges of the tympanum and backboard; the bonnet is closed from the outside cornice up to these braces with thin pine boards nailed into a rabbet in the front and sides and to the top of the backboard and braces. Behind the side plinths there is a molding identical to that at the waist. The interior is divided into three horizontal sections. The top section has four valanced pigeonholes flanking concave shell-carved drawers. Shaped dividers form eight compartments on the middle shelf and seven on the lower shelf. The interior shelves are grooved into the sides, slid in from behind, double cock-beaded on front edges. The vertical dividers slide into V grooves from behind. Drawers are dovetailed, front and back; the bottoms are chamfered and slide into grooves side and front, nailed to the underside of the back. The doors are frame-and-panel construction with raised-and-fielded panels and applied fluted pilasters (bases and caps are separate pieces). Thin candle slides are housed between the bottom board and the bottom shelf. Backboards are horizontal and secured with wrought nails into rabbets, top and sides.

(Lower case) The top board is half-blind dovetailed to the sides, and the bottom is through-dovetailed to the sides (with side molding covering the dovetails). A thin batten (white pine) is glued to the underside of the leading edge of the bottom board to build up the thickness to that of the base molding; the base molding is applied to this leading edge, notching in (with straight sides, not dovetailed) at the center to accommodate the concave blocking. The joint between the front molding and the bottom board is covered by the bottom blade, which is glued in place. The feet are tenoned into the bottom board; the pendant in the center of the base molding is applied with a supporting glueblock behind. The remaining cock-beaded blades (mahogany backed with pine) are half-blind dovetailed to the sides, which are cock-beaded on the inner edge. The sides of the top drawer are set in and attached to the drawer front with sliding dovetails. The fall-front lid has blocking on the face cut from solid wood, with batten ends presumably tenoned on; there is no lip on the fall-front, instead the surround is cock-beaded. The interior surface is mahogany (where visible) edge-glued to pine beneath the interior drawer section. The baseboard for the interior drawer assembly is similarly pine faced with molded mahogany blocked in a linear manner. The central prospect door,

carved from solid wood with a fielded arched panel, opens to reveal three concave blocked drawers, the top one with a carved shell. Remaining evidence suggests that the flanking pilasters (document drawers) originally could only be accessed when the middle interior drawer was removed, hence releasing wooden spring locks, only remnants of which remain today. (However, there is no wear on the drawer sides from these catches; the implications of this observation remain unclear.) All interior drawers are conventionally dovetailed, and bottoms are chamfered, set into grooves in the sides and fronts. The document drawers are pine; all other drawers have oak sides and pine bottoms (with composite mahogany fronts). The desk drawers are oak (running front to back) double-beaded on the top edges; they are dovetailed front and back, with bottoms chamfered on three sides, set in grooves front and sides and nailed up flush to the back of the drawers. There are no dust or security boards. The drawer runners now are screwed to the sides. Mahogany drawer fronts are blocked, cut from solid wood. The back is made of three butt-joined horizontal boards nailed to rabbets in the sides. The hardware is original. The second drawer from the bottom is the drawer front on which the blocking was originally planned; layout lines on the top edge reveal a cabinetmaker's change of plans regarding the amount of material he would remove for the blocking.

**Condition:** The side finials are replacements. There are extra cuts on the inside of the upper case suggesting either a craftsman's error or that the interior was configured differently. Some of the pigeonhole valances are replaced. A section of the molding is missing from the right front corner. The fall-front lid is cracked. Several of the blades have patched beading. The base molding is repaired at the center front. The left rear knee bracket is a replacement, and the left rear leg has been repaired. The brass pulls on document drawers may be additions.

**Dimensions:**

| | | |
|---|---|---|
| H. (with finials) | 90³⁄₄ in. | 229.4 cm |
| H. (case) | 88⁵⁄₈ in. | 225.2 cm |
| H. (writing surface) | 30¹⁄₄ in. | 77.0 cm |
| W. (cornice) | 40⁷⁄₈ in. | 104.1 cm |
| W. (upper case) | 38¹⁄₄ in. | 96.6 cm |
| W. (lower case) | 40 in. | 102.0 cm |
| W. (feet) | 43¹⁄₄ in. | 110.0 cm |
| D. (cornice) | 13¹⁄₂ in. | 34.2 cm |
| D. (upper case) | 12¹⁄₄ in. | 31.3 cm |
| D. (lower case) | 21¹⁄₂ in. | 53.9 cm |
| D. (feet) | 22³⁄₄ in. | 58.0 cm |

**Materials:** *Microanalysis:* Primary: mahogany. Secondary: white pine group (bottom board, backboard on upper case); white oak group (linings on long drawers). *Finish:* dark brown color in resin.

**Publications:** Newton W. Elwell, *Colonial Furniture and Interiors* (Boston: Geo. H. Polley, 1896), pl. 61. Downs, *American Furniture*, fig. 225. Morse, *Furniture of the Olden Time*, p. 128. Margaretta Markle Lovell, "Boston Blockfront Furniture," in *Boston Furniture*, pp. 122–23, fig. 86.

**Provenance:** By family tradition, the desk-and-bookcase was purchased originally by Joseph Waters (1758–1833) of Salem about 1780. A photograph of the desk-and-bookcase taken about 1870 is captioned: "Great grandfather Joseph Waters's Desk: Sold by Sarah W." and "From Cousin Fitz. Photo of Great Grandfather Waters's Desk-and-bookcase. Molly Mott leaning against it, Waters's House, Washington Square [Salem]." Ex coll.: Charles R. Waters, Salem, Mass., Israel Sack, New York. Ex coll.: Helen Temple Cook, Wellesley, Mass., Israel Sack, New York.

**Accession history:** Purchased by H. F. du Pont from Israel Sack, New York, 1941. Bequest of H. F. du Pont, 1969.
58.2771

---

1. On the transfer of Newport characteristics to Salem shops, see Venable, *American Furniture*, p. 61; Margaretta Markle Lovell, "Boston Blockfront Furniture," in *Boston Furniture*, p. 120. For the Dallas Museum of Art's example, see Venable, *American Furniture*, cat. 28; for the Museum of Modern Art desk, see Heckscher, *American Furniture*, cat. no. 181; for the Mead Art Gallery example, see Benjamin Ginsburg advertisement, *Antiques* 111, no. 5 (May 1977): 845; Lewis A. Shepard, *American Art at Amherst: A Summary Catalogue of the Collection at the Mead Art Gallery* (Middletown, Conn.: Wesleyan University Press, 1978), p. 245. The carved, applied shells and the straight-bracket feet on this desk-and-bookcase are incorrect replacements. For the Art Institute of Chicago desk, see Meyric R. Rogers, *American Interior Design: The Traditions and Development of Domestic Design from Colonial Times to the Present* (New York: W. W. Norton, 1947), p. 67. For a related blockfront desk-and-bookcase with a large dovetail, see Ward, *American Case Furniture*, cat. 174.

2. Benno M. Forman, "Salem Tradesmen and Craftsmen Circa 1762: A Contemporary Document," *Essex Institute Historical Collection* 107, no. 1 (January 1971): 65. On Rust, see Venable, *American Furniture*, cat. 28.

3. "The Diary of Wm. Bentley, D.D., pastor of the East Church, Salem, Mass., 1905–14," 1:385, 3:150, Peabody Essex Museum.

## 209 ◆ Desk-and-bookcase

Boston, Massachusetts
1780–90
Attributed to John Cogswell (1738–1818)

The mahogany "ogee top swelled desk and bookcase" with ball-and-claw feet must have been the eighteenth-century zenith of not only cabinetmaking but also status and style in Boston. Its popularity stretched over almost half a century—one of the earliest known dated Boston bombé desk-and-bookcases was made in 1753 and signed by Boston cabinetmaker Benjamin Frothingham, Sr.[1]

A number of design and ornamentation choices had to be made by either the craftsman or the patron; if the latter was making these decisions, cost as well as personal taste might have been a critical consideration. Carved ball-and-claw feet were more costly than simple ogee-bracket feet. A pitched pediment cost less than an ogee top since the former could be produced with a molding plane, but the latter was hand-carved, thus requiring more time and skill. Mirrored panels instead of crotch-grained mahogany panels in the doors of the upper section would also have increased the cost, as would gilding on the carved serpentine edge of the door frame surrounding the panels and additional carving or applied cut fretwork in the pediment, framing the upper case, or on the edges and base molding of the lower desk section.[2] And if one desired a carved and gilt phoenix bird as the crowning central ornament on a desk-and-bookcase, along with pendant garlands trailing from the carved rosettes, that indeed would increase the cost.

Two of the finest and most esteemed Boston cabinetmakers working in the second half of the eighteenth century were John Cogswell (1738–1818) and George Bright (1726–1805). According to period documentation, both produced superior bombé furniture, and this desk-and-bookcase relates closely to well-known pieces by each of them. A desk-and-bookcase made for Samuel Barrett of Boston and given to his daughter Ann upon her marriage to Isaac Green in 1792 is signed by George Bright.[3] Although the bookcase lacks the upper and lower bands of cut and applied fretwork, the desk has carved knees and brackets, carving around the inner edge of the door frame (which has mirrored panels), and carved pendants hanging from the rosettes. Enough "signature" features differ from Winterthur's example, however, to conclude that the makers are not the same.

Stylistically the case of Winterthur's desk-and-bookcase most closely relates to a chest-on-chest made (and signed) by John Cogswell in 1782 for Elias Hasket Derby. Based on close comparison, Winterthur's desk-and-bookcase can be attributed to John Cogswell. The most striking design similarities are seen in the height and stance of the carved feet, cabriole legs, and brackets (fig. 1); the lower and upper bands of cut and applied fretwork in the upper case; the fluted pilasters with carved Ionic capitals; and the distinctive shape of the tympanum with unusual applied carving and almost identical carved rosettes with trailing pendants. The trailing pendants are missing on the rosettes of Winterthur's desk-and-bookcase, but remnants of them remain. Evidence of a carved pendant ornament applied to the center of the lower edge of the base molding suggests that one similar to that on the 1782 chest-on-chest must have once existed on Winterthur's desk-and-bookcase. Because the door frames have been heavily cleaned, it is difficult to ascertain whether the carved serpentine edges of the frames were ever gessoed and gilded. The depth of the carving suggests that they may have been, although that feature usually occurs when the panels in the frames are mirrored, to enhance the reflective quality, and it is unclear whether the crotch-grained mahogany panels are original (fig. 2).[4] Unlike the Cogswell chest-

**Fig. 1.** Detail, foot.

on-chest, the profile of the inner surface of the case sides and the drawer sides is straight and vertical (see also No. 210). The interior of the desk section, typical of many Massachusetts desk-and-bookcases, is composed of a five-part plan with a concave, shell-carved central prospect door flanked on each side by pairs of pigeonholes with shaped valances over blocked drawers; and on the outermost extremes are tiers of three concave drawers, the top one having a carved fan or shell (fig. 3). The only major difference in this interior arrangement is in the omission of narrow document drawers faced with pilasters flanking the central prospect compartment.

John Cogswell was originally from Ipswich, Massachusetts, where his father Francis, a graduate of Harvard College, was a merchant of some prominence. In 1762 he married Abigail Gooding, who came from a sixth-generation family of artisans centered around Charlestown, Boston, and Cambridge. Presumably Cogswell had apprenticed with a member of this family and thus gained entry into the relatively closed community of Boston cabinetmakers. From 1763 until his death in 1818, he held minor town offices and appointments including constable, scavenger, surveyor of boards, surveyor of shingles, and surveyor of mahogany. As was the case with other artisans of this period, the economic

depression following the French and Indian War and that surrounding the revolutionary war meant that they often had to pursue several sources of income. While period records suggest that Cogswell was not quite as successful as some of his contemporary cabinetmakers, when he died in 1818 the value of his estate was $4,218.65, reflecting a moderate level of success. Much still remains to be learned about the size of Cogswell's shop throughout his working career as well as the other artisans he contracted with, particularly the carvers whose work is so prominently evidenced on pieces like this one.[5]

WAC

**Inscriptions or marks:** *Inscribed on underside of bottom of lowest drawer:* "1786 A.D./ Yorkshire" in pencil (this does not appear to be a period inscription). *Scratched on inside bottom board of lower case:* "X". *On upper drawer blade of lower section:* "X" *in pencil. Scratched, on underside of drawer front of middle drawer on right side of desk:* "V". *In bottom drawer on right side of desk:* "School Money" *in pencil on lined paper.*

**Construction:** (Upper case) The interior has a central shell-carved prospect door (concealing a large pigeonhole and upper and lower interior drawers), flanked by pairs of pigeonholes surmounting single-blocked drawers; at the extremes are three stacked drawers, the top of

**Fig. 2.** Detail, bookcase.

**Fig. 3.** Desk open.

which is shell-carved. Drawers are dovetailed front and back; bottoms are set into rabbets front and sides; drawer sides have an astragal molding on upper edges.

(Lower case) The top and bottom boards are dovetailed to the sides; the two horizontal backboards are lap-joined and nailed into a rabbet (straight and plumb on sides) on sides and top and directly to the bottom board. The single-board sides have not been carved out on the inside. The bottom board is framed out with 1" by 2" secondary wood on the sides and front and mitered at the front corners; the feet posts are square-mortised into the undersides through the framing. The feet are strengthened with knee brackets, outside molding, and inside glueblocks, which follow the shape of the brackets. The rear feet are not fully carved on the back. Above the front base molding, the drawer blade is half the thickness of the blades above, and runners support the bottom drawer. The blades are composite, pine, 4³/4" deep with a facing of mahogany; they are grooved into the sides with the mahogany facing dovetailed and visible on the outside. All drawer and loper openings have cock-beading cut from solid wood. Drawer runners are glued and nailed to the case sides and tongue-and-grooved into the back edge of the drawer blade (the grooves are only cut in the ends of the blade). The loper dividers are full thickness and just cut in. The drawers are fitted to the inside width of the case, having vertical sides; the sides are dovetailed to the

front and backboards. The drawer front ends have a deep rabbet cut to receive the dovetails of the vertical drawer sides. The rabbet creates a lip, the end of which follows the curve of the side. This thin lip is backed by a vertical block (mahogany) glued to the back of the lip and side of the drawer. The top edges of the drawer sides are rounded (after assemblage), and the top back edge is chamfered. The drawer bottoms run front to back and slide into grooves in the sides and back with additional battens (angles at the back) glued on and nailed across the back.

**Condition:** The surface of the upper case has been refinished. All finials and plinth blocks are replaced; glue lines indicate that the outer plinths on the desk-and-bookcase originally were larger. The carved rosettes have lost a portion of their pendent swags. Framing behind the scrollboard has been modified. There are splits in the left side cornice molding where it was reattached. The capital above

the left pilaster is replaced. The waist molding has been repaired; there is a patch on the right side. The fall-front lid is a replacement; it appears to have been a tabletop or a table leaf. The hinges on the lid are replaced, and there are patches on the desk rail. The hinges on the prospect door are replaced, and the door is pieced on the lock side. Both valances on the right pigeonhole compartments in the desk are replaced. The battens on the bottoms of all the long drawers are replaced, and the drawer runners have been repaired. There are repairs to the blades where locks have broken out. A glue line at the center of the base molding indicates the earlier presence of a pendent drop. The brasses on the carved shell drawers in the desk are replacements; there is evidence of a larger plugged hole. The exterior handles are old but not the first set. There is evidence of at least two earlier sets of pulls (a stamped oval rosette and a threaded wood or glass knob).

**Dimensions:**

| | | |
|---|---|---|
| H. (with finials) | 99 1/4 in. | 252.4 cm |
| H. (case) | 95 1/4 in. | 241.9 cm |
| H. (writing surface) | 34 3/4 in. | 88.2 cm |
| W. (cornice) | 44 9/16 in. | 113.2 cm |
| W. (upper case) | 40 11/16 in. | 103.3 cm |
| W. (lower case) | 45 1/4 in. | 115.0 cm |
| W. (feet) | 45 1/8 in. | 114.7 cm |
| D. (cornice) | 13 in. | 33.0 cm |
| D. (upper case) | 11 1/16 in. | 28.2 cm |
| D. (lower case) | 22 9/16 in. | 57.3 cm |
| D. (feet) | 22 7/8 in. | 58.2 cm |

**Materials:** *Microanalysis:* Primary: mahogany. Secondary: white pine group (all drawer linings, lower case top board, backboard, backing of blades); soft maple group (upper case backboard). *Finish:* light reddish brown with dark brown color in resin.

**Publications:** Nutting, *Furniture Treasury*, no. 717. Downs, *American Furniture*, fig. 228. Helena Hayward, ed., *World Furniture: An Illustrated History* (New York: McGraw-Hill Book Co., 1965), fig. 725. Gilbert T. Vincent, "The Bombé Furniture of Boston," in *Boston Furniture*, figs. 126–27.

**Provenance:** Ex coll.: Willoughby Farr, Edgewater, N.J. Israel Sack, Boston and New York, 1928.

**Accession history:** Purchased by H. F. du Pont, 1928. Gift of H. F. du Pont, 1969. 59.3414

---

1. Rollins, *Treasures of State*, cat. no. 13.

2. The "1 mahogany desk and bookcase with glass doors" listed in the 1782 inventory of John Williams, Esq., of Dorchester was valued at £20, when the value of mahogany desk-and-bookcases in other inventories about the same time was in the range of £7 to £12; see John Williams, Esq., estate inventory, 1782, Suffolk County Probate Court, Boston (microfilm, Downs collection).

3. On Cogswell, see Joseph Downs, "John Cogswell," *Antiques* 61, no. 4 (April 1952): 322–24; M. Ada Young, "Five Secretaries and the Cogswells," *Antiques* 88, no. 4 (October 1965): 482–85; Robert Mussey and Anne Rogers Haley, "John Cogswell and Boston Bombé Furniture: Thirty-Five Years of Revolution and Politics in Design," in Luke Beckerdite, ed., *American Furniture 1994* (Milwaukee, Wis.: Chipstone Fndn., 1994), pp. 73–106; on George Bright, see Richard Randall, "George Bright, Cabinetmaker," *Art Quarterly* 27, no. 2 (1964): 134–49. Randall, *American Furniture*, no. 64.

4. For the Cogswell chest-on-chest, see Mussey and Haley, "John Cogswell," p. 84, fig. 13. As illustrated in Nutting, *Furniture Treasury*, no. 717, the desk had a replacement carved pendant attached to the base molding and a Philadelphia-style cartouche and flame finials. Perhaps at that early date it was believed to be a Philadelphia desk-and-bookcase because of the carved and applied ornament in the pediment and a provenance maintaining that it belonged to the Carroll family of Carrollton in Maryland.

5. Mussey and Haley, "John Cogswell," pp. 77–81; these authors suggest that William Burbeck (1716–85) may have been one of the carvers doing piecework for Cogswell, but the fact that he died in 1785 prompts the question of who his apprentice/successor might have been.

## 210 ◆ Desk-and-bookcase
### Massachusetts, probably Boston
### 1780–95

In October 1928, Henry Francis du Pont purchased this exceptional serpentine bombé desk-and-bookcase through his agent Collings and Collings at the Anderson Galleries sale of the George S. Palmer Collection, "with additions of fine American pieces by I. Sack." The preceding spring, Israel Sack had written to du Pont inviting him to visit the Palmer House, in New London, noting: "I have in the collection. . . . a Chippendale Kettle-front secretary which I believe was made by Goddard in Newport. This would be an excellent piece for you to buy for Mrs. du Pont as it is a regular lady's desk, small in size with the original mirror in the door. It was evidently made to order for some special customer." This "Rhode Island Mahogany Kettle Bottom Secretary" was illustrated as the frontispiece in the auction catalogue for the sale, and the entry for Lot 277 transcribed the inscription on the inside of the left loper: "Bought this desk Oct. 15, 1828, of my Father . . . Total.—— Edward Brinley." It was referred to as "unquestionably one of the most important and rare examples of Colonial furniture extant." While today our knowledge of the desk's regional origin and design sources is quite different, its status as "most important and rare" has certainly not changed.[1]

In contrast to the bombé desk-and-bookcase of No. 209, the lower case of this example is related to a group of slant-front desks, desk-and-bookcases, and chests of drawers (see No. 184), all with bombé sides and double-serpentine fronts. None of the casepieces with this distinctive form are documented to a specific maker, though it has been strongly argued that Cogswell is the maker of Winterthur's Brinley desk-and-bookcase. Although the lower case is a distinctive Boston design, the upper mirrored bookcase section relates to English design sources of the period. While it is reminiscent of plate 110 in Chippendale's *Director*, it appears to have been directly derived from plate 44 in the 1760 edition of *Houshold Furniture in Genteel Taste*, published in London in four editions between 1760 and 1765 by the Society of Upholsterers. Fluted pilasters capped with Corinthian columns appear on other Boston bombé desk-and-bookcases (the earliest example is signed and dated 1753 by Benjamin Frothingham, Sr.), but the design of the foliate ogee top, central acanthus ornament, and scrolled foliage combined with thin rococo columns on the bookcase door is the only one of this form known to date (fig. 1). A Boston vendor or owner of this specific design book has not been identified, but the source is known to have been sold in New York, Philadelphia, and Baltimore and so may have been transported to Boston by an enterprising craftsman or patron.[2]

The design and execution of this desk-and-bookcase seems to be an expression of high-style rococo, or Chippendale, taste. The upper case is a triumph of the art of the carver, while the complexity of the curves of the lower case embody the best workmanship of the Boston cabinetmaking trade after the Revolution.[3] But why would this desk-and-bookcase have been made in the rococo style in the very decade that a new classical style was introduced to fashionable Bostonians? Does it not then seem rather *retardataire*? Several plausible explanations can be put forward to reinforce the postrevolutionary date, as well as to suggest that the form of the lower case embodies both rococo and classical aesthetics.

Beginning in the early 1770s, and certainly by 1774, the advent of the war halted almost all major craft production of luxury items, a result not only of the wartime fiscal situation but also the decreased artisan

labor force due to involvement in the war.[4] Even after the war, many of Boston's merchant patrons were still deeply rooted in the prerevolutionary aesthetic and taste that had prevailed as their fortunes matured. Design books such as *Houshold Furniture in the Genteel Taste* were still available after the war, yet it was not until the 1788 posthumous publications in London of George Hepplewhite's *Cabinetmakers' and Upholsterers' Guide* and Thomas Sheraton's *Cabinet-Maker and Upholsterers' Drawing-Book* between 1791 and 1793 that a new style was formally disseminated through published drawings.

The serpentine shape came into fashion in England with the emerging popularity of the French commode form just prior to 1740, and by the 1760s and early 1770s it was employed on most fashionable veneered commodes ornamented in the classical taste with colorful inlaid ovals, flowers, bowknots, and bellflower chains. Serpentine-shape fronts on American case furniture (chests, chest-on-chests, and sideboards) may have appeared in limited numbers in the early 1770s but were not widely popular until the 1780s and early 1790s, suggesting they were more an expression of the early classical than the eighteenth-century rococo style. Dated American examples can be identified from 1780, 1783, 1784, and from 1791, when Stephen Badlam made an impressive chest-on-chest for Elias Hasket Derby. Derby's chest-on-chest incorporates classically inspired ornament on a serpentine-front lower case, but the rectilinear upper case is still rooted in the eighteenth-century aesthetic. It has been suggested that the Joseph Barrell desk-and-bookcase (see No. 225), the lower case of which is almost identical to this example, was probably ordered at the time that Barrell's new mansion in Charlestown, Pleasant Hill, designed by Charles Bulfinch, was being completed in 1794.[5] This probable date of construction also roughly coincides with that of the

Derby-Badlam chest-on-chest and numerous American serpentine-front sideboards.

In 1928 the provenance for the original ownership of this desk-and-bookcase suggested by the citation of the inscription on the left-hand loper was offered, and almost seventy years later scholars are still not certain of the original owner. Francis Brinley (1690–1765), the progenitor of the family, was born in England and immigrated to New England in 1710. First settling in Newport, he eventually moved to Boston where he married Deborah Lyde in 1718. He inherited a substantial fortune from his grandfather, along with a tract of high land in Roxbury, where he built a house for his expanding family. Determining which Edward Brinley bought this desk in 1828 is made difficult because Edward (1730–1809), the third son of Francis, and Edward II (1765–1823), grandson of Francis, both died before the inscription date.[6]

WAC

---

**Inscriptions or marks:** *On the inside of the left loper:* "Bought this desk Oct. 15, 1828, of my Father . . . Total.—— Edward Brinley" in ink. *On backboard of lower case, partially legible:* "Attention/ this has [illegible]ty been Vo[illegible]/ Please not to meddle" in chalk. *On the bottom board:* "Bottom/ X" in chalk. Drawers in the bookcase section: (Top left) *Scratched on inside drawer front:* "X"; *chiseled on inside drawer front:* "IIII"; *on outside right side:* "4" in pencil. (Second left) *Scratched on outside left side:* "X III"; *scratched on inside front:* "X I". (Third left) *Scratched on inside front:* "X II"; *chiseled on top front:* "II"; *on outside right side:* "2" in pencil. (Bottom left) *On back:* "B" in chalk; *on right side:* "1" in pencil. (Top right) *Chiseled on drawer front:* "XX"; *on side:* "5" in pencil. (Second right) "6" in pencil; *and chisel [illegible].* (Third right) *Chiseled on inside front:* "IV/ X"; "7" in pencil. (Bottom right) *Chiseled on inside front:* "II"; "8" in pencil.

Inside desk section: (Top left) *Scratched inside drawer front:* "I". (Second row, far left) *Scratched inside drawer front:* "I"; *inside drawer front:* "X" in pencil. (Second row, inside left) *Scratched inside drawer front:* "I". (Bottom row, far left) *Chiseled*

*inside drawer front:* "I". (Bottom row, inside left) *Scratched inside drawer front:* "I". (Second row, inside right) *Chiseled inside drawer front:* "IV". (Second row, far right) *Chiseled inside drawer front:* "II". (Bottom row, inside right) *Chiseled inside drawer front:* "IV". (Bottom row, far right) *Chiseled inside drawer front:* "I". *On lower case blades:* "I", "II", "III", with scribe marks on upper surface. *Stamped on reverse of (some) brass back plates:* "669" (probably a style number).

**Construction:** (Upper case) The boards of the fully enclosed stepped bonnet—the upper level now covered in fabric—are secured to a rabbet in the scrollboard and to the upper edge of the backboard. Three butt-joined horizontal boards form the backboard. The upper board, shaped to conform to the top of the scrollboard, extends to the top blade; it is reinforced inside the case (on the outer edges only) by triangular vertical glueblocks joining the

**Fig. 1.** Detail, bookcase.

side and the back. The backboard is nailed to a rabbet in the sides. The cornice molding, shaped in a broken scroll with projecting leafage, is nailed to the scrollboard; a plain molding in the same profile is nailed above the pilasters and across the sides. The scrollboard, arch-shaped on the lower edge and decorated with an incised bead above the door, is nailed to the sides. In lieu of the more traditional flame finial, at the center is an acanthus leaf carving that scrolls forward above the top of the case. Below the pediment, the case is divided into three sections: a large mirrored center door flanked by hinged smaller doors decorated with fluted pilasters. The smaller doors are hinged to the sides of the case; the center door is hinged to the right pilaster door. The rails of the center door are through-tenoned. An applied decorative carving surrounds the nonconforming beveled glass on the front; a beveled mahogany backing panel that holds the glass is secured with screws. The smaller doors are solid panels with the pilasters applied. Behind the central door are three adjustable shelves with a fixed shelf at the top. The shelves are of pine with a narrow mahogany facing; they are double-beaded on the leading edge. Behind the small doors, there are two tall cubby holes, each topped with a shell-carved drawer and two plain drawers below. The bottom board is let in approximately 1¹/₂" above the lower edge of the side. The upper case rests on battens joining the sides and the underside of the bottom board.

(Lower case) The waist molding is nailed to the top of the lower case. The hinged, slant-top lid, a solid board with batten ends, opens to rest on lopers faced with a plain mahogany block. In the interior, three rows of drawers in a pattern of broken cyma curve and recessed block flank the prospect door. The upper row has a single drawer; the lower rows have two drawers. The drawers in the writing section are similarly constructed: the drawer fronts are straight across the inside; the sides are rounded on the top; the back has a slight chamfer on the outer edge; the bottoms are set flush into a rabbet on the front and sides and nailed to the back. On the prospect door, the shell and recessed block are cut from solid wood. Behind the prospect door is a fixed valance. The one-board sides are bombé-shaped on the exterior and straight on the interior. The bead on the outside edge of the drawer opening is cut from solid wood. Double-beaded mahogany blades backed with 4" pine boards are dovetailed to the sides. The drawer runners are nailed to the sides; drawer stops are nailed to the sides between the runners. There are no dust boards. The bottom rail, beaded on the upper edge, is dovetailed to the sides. A complex broken-cyma base molding is nailed to the bottom rail in front and to the lower edge of the sides covering the dovetailed join of the sides and bottom. On the front, the base molding is reinforced on the underside of the case by a series of tightly spaced glueblocks. The pendent drop is glued to the base molding and reinforced behind by a large horizontal glueblock. Unusually large triangular blocks, cut out for the leg posts, are glued to the one-piece bottom board. The leg is braced with large horizontal blocks that reinforce the knee brackets. The backboard is of two lap-joined horizontal boards nailed to the side rabbets with cut nails. All of the long drawers have similar dovetail construction front and back. The drawer fronts are shaped on the inside to conform to the exterior. The drawer sides are straight with a double-bead on the top edge. The drawer back is chamfered on the outer edge. The flat drawer bottoms are set into rabbets on the front and sides and nailed flush at back; the boards run front to back.

**Condition:** The top section of the central finial above the case line is replaced. The cornice molding has been repaired. There is a split on the right side of the scrollboard at the top of the lower cornice. The glass appears to have been resilvered. Sections of the molding around the glass have been reglued. The capital on the left pilaster is of lesser quality than that on the right and appears to be a replacement. The far right carved column is a replacement. There is a patch on the right pilaster door where the hinge has been reset. On the desk section, the waist molding is a replacement. The slant-top lid is patched on the right side and there is a break on the lower left edge. The hinges on the prospect door are replacements. The top right drawer in the desk section has an interior glueblock reinforcing a broken dovetail; cloth tape repairs a split in the drawer bottom. The top long drawer has a patch on the lower right corner. Sometime in the nineteenth century, the legs were cut approximately 3" below the bottom of the case (presumably to reduce the writing height to a more acceptable level). The original feet were saved and reattached prior to 1928. The present Chippendale-style handles and escutcheons are old but may not be original. The large carrying handles on the upper and lower case are not original.

**Dimensions:**

| | | |
|---|---|---|
| H. (with finials) | 82¹/₁₆ in. | 233.1 cm |
| H. (case) | 80¹/₁₆ in. | 228.9 cm |
| H. (writing surface) | 33⁹/₁₆ in. | 85.2 cm |
| W. (cornice) | 33³/₄ in. | 86.0 cm |
| W. (upper case) | 33¹/₂ in. | 82.5 cm |
| W. (lower case) | 36⁵/₈ in. | 93.0 cm |
| W. (feet) | 37¹/₄ in. | 94.4 cm |
| D. (cornice) | 10¹/₁₆ in. | 25.6 cm |
| D. (upper case) | 8³/₄ in. | 22.3 cm |
| D. (lower case) | 19¹³/₁₆ in. | 50.5 cm |
| D. (feet) | 20⁹/₁₆ in. | 52.8 cm |

**Materials:** *Microanalysis:* Primary: mahogany. Secondary: white pine group (drawer linings, lower case backboard); yellow pine group (upper case backboard). *Finish:* light reddish brown color in resin.

**Publications:** American Art Association, "George S. Palmer Collection with Additions of Fine American Pieces by I. Sack" (October 18–20, 1928), frontispiece, lot 227. "The Israel Sack Collections of American Antiques" ([Boston], 1928), pp. [7–8]. Aaron Mark Stein, "French Influences in American Furniture," *The Antiquarian* 17 (October 1931): 15. Downs, *American Furniture*, fig. 227. *The Britannica Encyclopedia of American Art*, p. 201. Harold Sack, "The Bombé Furniture of Boston and Salem, Massachusetts," *Antiques* 135, no. 5 (May 1989): 1178–89. Michael S. Podmaniczky and Philip D. Zimmerman, "Two Massachusetts *Bombé* Desk-and-Bookcases," *Antiques* 145, no. 5 (May 1994): 724–31. Robert Mussey and Anne Rogers Haley, "John Cogswell and Boston Bombé Furniture: Thirty-Five Years of Revolution and Politics in Design," in Luke Beckerdite, ed., *American Furniture 1994* (Milwaukee, Wis.: Chipstone Fndn., 1994), pp. 87–94.

**Provenance:** Sold at the American Art Association, October 18–20, 1928.

**Accession history:** Purchased by H. F. du Pont from the American Art Association with Collings and Collings, New York, as agents, 1928. Gift of H. F. du Pont, 1960.
57.1396

1. American Art Association, "George S. Palmer Collection with Additions of Fine American Pieces by I. Sack" (October 18–20, 1928). Israel Sack to H. F. du Pont, May 7, 1928, Winterthur Archives. In a letter dated September 11, 1928, Sack told du Pont, "The Sofa and Secretary will go into the sale of the Palmer Collection," which indicates that the secretary was not originally part of the Palmer Collection (Winterthur Archives). Monkhouse and Michie, *American Furniture*, p. 100.

2. For the group of serpentine bombé furniture, see Robert Mussey and Anne Rogers Haley, "John Cogswell and Boston Bombé Furniture: Thirty-Five Years of Revolution and Politics in Design," in Luke Beckerdite, ed., *American Furniture 1994* (Milwaukee, Wis.: Chipstone Fndn., 1994), pp. 73–105. The design book was discovered by Nancy E. Richards and subsequently published in Mussey and Haley, "John Cogswell." For the Frothingham desk, see Rollins, *Treasures of State*, pp. 94–95. The pediment of this desk is related to that on 2 desk-and-bookcases; see Gilbert T. Vincent, "The Bombé Furniture of Boston," in *Boston Furniture*, p. 161; Ralph Edwards and Margaret Jourdain, *Georgian Cabinet-Makers, c. 1700–1800* (3d rev. ed., London: Country Life, 1955), p. 166. On transmission of design sources, see Morrison H. Heckscher, "English Furniture Pattern Books in Eighteenth-Century America," in Beckerdite, *American Furniture 1994*, pp. 195–97.

3. Mussey and Rogers, "John Cogswell," p. 92, suggests William Burbeck (1716–85) as the carver, but he would have been 64 years old in 1780. The similarity of the carving to that executed by Burbeck on the Brattle Square Church pulpit in 1772–73 suggests either Burbeck or an apprentice trained by Burbeck as maker.

4. Mussey and Haley, "John Cogswell."

5. For the 1780 serpentine example, see Randall, *American Furniture*, no. 41; for 1783 example, see Wendy A. Cooper, *In Praise of America: American Decorative Arts, 1650–1830/Fifty Years of Discovery since the 1929 Girl Scouts Loan Exhibition* (New York: Alfred A. Knopf, 1980), pp. 31–32; for the 1784 example, see *New London County Furniture*, p. 53; on the Derby chest, see Ward, *American Case Furniture*, pp. 171–77; for the Barrell desk-and-bookcase, see Michael S. Podmaniczky and Philip D. Zimmerman, "Two Massachusetts *Bombé* Desk-and-Bookcases," *Antiques* 145, no. 5 (May 1994): 724–31.

6. Portraits of Francis and Deborah Brinley by John Smibert (painted in 1731) are owned by the Metropolitan Museum of Art; see John Caldwell and Oswaldo Rodriguez Roque, *American Painting in the Metropolitan Museum of Art* (New York: Metropolitan Museum of Art in association with Princeton University Press, 1994), 1:13–16. On the Edwards Brinley, see Mussey and Haley, "John Cogswell," p. 94.

# Looking Glasses and Dressing Glasses

WHEN IN 1719 THE PROPRIETOR of the "Glass-Shop in Queen Street, Boston" offered for sale "a fresh Parcel of Looking-Glasses of divers Sorts and Sizes" imported from London, "silvered" glass had been produced in England for only slightly more than one hundred years. Until immigrant Venetian workmen provided the technology necessary to produce mirror glass in Britain, only royalty, nobility, and the affluent were in a position to purchase these costly glass plates imported from Italy and France. To a considerable degree, the looking glass remained a luxury item in Europe well into the eighteenth century and in America until after the Revolution.[1]

The technology of manufacturing mirrors from blown glass, first introduced in continental Europe about the early sixteenth century, was practiced in England until the late eighteenth century: blown cylinders of glass were cut open, flattened under heat, ground smooth and polished on both flat surfaces, and "silvered" on one side by the application of tinfoil affixed with mercury. In 1773 a commercially feasible method of casting glass plates was introduced from France, but another three-quarters of a century passed before entrepreneurs in America commenced the manufacture of plate glass. Meanwhile, manufacturers in England and on the Continent happily filled the void.[2]

Mirror glass was also expensive to produce until the labor-intensive tasks of grinding and polishing the plates were mechanized in the late eighteenth century. Because of its value, both householders and workmen carefully salvaged old glass for new service. In 1777 Timothy Loomis reframed a looking glass for a customer in rural Connecticut, and Samuel Kneeland regularly resilvered and reframed looking glasses in Hartford during his postwar career there, just as William Randle, a japanner from Boston, had done almost seventy-five years earlier.[3]

Large numbers of English looking glasses were in the American market during the eighteenth century despite their substantial cost. English export records for the early years of the trade document the shipment of framed glasses, valued at a total of almost £1,600, to the American colonies between 1697 and 1704. In 1718 Capt. James Pitts offered English glasses from twenty-three to forty-three-inches long at his house in Clark Square, Boston. "Looking-glasses of several sizes in Mahogany Frames" were available at midcentury. Two decades later, looking glasses "in any Sort of Frames that will suite the Buyer" could be purchased from Stephen Whiting's shop.[4]

The considerable trade in European looking glasses in America during the eighteenth century is further attested by the substantial number of glasses that have histories of ownership in American families or that carry other evidence of use here (exclusive of examples that bear labels of American makers/dealers). A comprehensive, though not exhaustive, survey of published sources reveals sixty-one looking glasses with family associations (counting pairs of looking glasses as one unit). No less than eight of these were looking glasses of individual design from the Sayward-Wheeler House in York, Maine, all of which are believed to have been part of the household furnishings acquired by Jonathan Sayward (1713–97) during his lifetime. Had the furnishings of other eighteenth-century houses remained intact over the years, evidence of this type would be more plentiful.[5]

Labeled work by American looking-glass makers and dealers constitutes another body of material closely linked with the American home in the eighteenth century. Three documented glasses are discussed in this catalogue, and labels identify the glasses of six other individuals or firms whose products or merchandise fall within the stylistic purview of the catalogue examples. It was long thought that looking glasses labeled by American craftsmen were domestic products. In recent decades microanalysis of the woods used for the frames has suggested that many were imported along with the glass plates American manufacturers needed for their own production. Most looking-glass makers/dealers also stocked a general selection of fancy goods to augment their income, including maps, prints, scientific instruments, and drawing supplies.[6]

In stocking these imported looking glasses, American craftsmen bowed to the pressures of competition from import merchants and auctioneers and the preferences of some customers for foreign goods. Many craftsmen doubtless felt the same frustration as Stephen Whiting of Boston, who in 1767 announced that he "does more at present towards manufacturing Looking-Glasses than any one in the Province, or perhaps on the Continent, and would be glad of Encouragement enough to think it worthwhile to live." The tide gradually turned during the third quarter of the eighteenth century as carvers in the principal American cities—Boston, New York, Philadelphia, and Charleston—were sought by important clients to produce exquisite frames for their newly painted family portraits. From there, the production of ornate looking-glass frames required only a lateral step.[7]

Documents of several types, written and pictorial, describe the placement of looking glasses in the home. Primary locations were the parlor, the back parlor (dining room), and the chambers (bedrooms). As the principal room of the house for entertaining, the parlor was the repository of the best furnishings. A looking glass was frequently hung above a table on a pier wall between windows and sometimes above the mantel or on other walls. The reflective qualities of mirror glass helped to brighten a room in daylight or candlelight. In some well-appointed parlors, looking glasses were large, formed a pair, or had candle arms attached to the base. Glasses in other household locations were often plainer, especially those in the secondary bedrooms, where painted frames might suffice.

The range of options available to purchasers and some idea of the distribution of this luxury item in society can be gleaned from an analysis of a body of probate records related by place and time—in this instance documents from Nantucket Island dating between 1776 and 1805. Although isolated somewhat by location, Nantucket was a microcosm of society in the late eighteenth century because of its principal economic focus on trade and the fisheries, and the period under scrutiny encompasses households established there in the third quarter of the eighteenth century. Fifty-two looking glasses have been tallied in thirty-two estates.

The occupations or statuses of the owners in the sample range from gentleman and merchant to widow, schoolmaster, and mariner. The trades are well represented: cabinetmaker, joiner, boat builder, cooper, butcher, miller, blacksmith, shoemaker, and sailmaker. Looking-glass values range from as little as 1s. to 90s. About 38 percent of the glasses listed are valued but not further described. More than half are identified by size, with large glasses outnumbering small ones three to two. The remaining examples are identified by a special feature and frequently also by size. Small black walnut frames were appraised at 12s. and large examples at 60s. (At this time, 6s. was a high daily wage for a man with a trade.) A small gilt-frame looking glass was worth 24s.—two times the value of the small walnut one. Large gilt-frame glasses were appraised at 60s. and 84s. Five of the looking glasses described only as large were also valued at 60s. or more, suggesting that some were probably gilded or embellished with special ornament.[8]

Eleven looking glasses in the sample were valued at 60s. (£3) or more. A look at the occupations and worth of the owners is revealing since most individuals had estates valued in excess of £790. One man was titled "esquire," and two were identified as merchants. The estates of the two mariners exceeded £1,100 apiece, suggesting they were sea captains. Of the four "traders," an occupation probably a step below that of merchant, one was a widow and another was a blacksmith who was part owner of two sailing vessels. The individual identified as a "yeoman" was probably a large landholder on the island, since his real estate alone was valued at £605. The one puzzle is the schoolmaster, whose estate was worth only £89. Besides the looking glass, he owned several other valuable pieces of furniture, perhaps acquired by inheritance or from admiring friends.

Complementary to the production of looking glasses for the wall was that of glasses for the toilette, the ritual of personal grooming practiced by both women and men. The first dressing glasses of record were hand-held mirrors that, like the earliest looking glasses in use during the Middle Ages, had a reflective surface of polished metal. Gradually, two forms of dressing glass evolved: a mirror hung on the wall at a forward cant and a mirror mounted in a stand. The dressing glass supported in a stand or by struts appears to have become common in England by the late seventeenth century, although it was in use considerably earlier on the Continent. It usually stood on a table or chest in a bedchamber and was frequently draped with a cloth complementing that on the dressing table.

Some dressing glasses suspended between upright posts mounted on a box that survive in England date from 1700 or earlier. The form appeared in America shortly thereafter, as demonstrated in early Philadelphia records: James Sandlelands died in 1708 possessed of a "Looking Glass & Dressing box," and only five years later in 1713 James Logan, personal agent to the Penn family and member of the governor's council, imported a "Swinging glass with draws." In September 1737 the *Boston News-Letter* carried an advertisement for "SWINGING GLASSES with drawers and without." The design of the box and mirror frame kept pace with changing fashions through the eighteenth and early nineteenth centuries. Gradually, however, use of the dressing box was discontinued in England in favor of the fitted dressing table accompanied by a looking glass, although the form remained popular in America into the second quarter of the nineteenth century.[9]

*NGE*

---

[1] *Boston News-Letter*, August 31–September 7, 1719, as quoted in Dow, *Arts and Crafts in New England*, p. 127; Macquoid and Edwards, *Dictionary*, 2:309–53.

[2] Macquoid and Edwards, *Dictionary*, 2:309–27, 350–51; Helen Comstock, *The Looking Glass in America, 1700–1825* (New York: Viking Press, 1968), pp. 14–16; Barquist, *American Tables and Looking Glasses*, p. 295.

[3] Macquoid and Edwards, *Dictionary*, 2:350–51; Timothy Loomis account book, 1768–1804, Connecticut Historical Society, Hartford; Kneeland advertised in *Connecticut Courant* (Hartford), August 10, 1789, as reproduced in "The Wadsworth Punch Bowl, ca. 1780," *Connecticut Historical Society Bulletin* 20, no. 2 (April 1955): 38; Comstock, *Looking Glass*, pp. 14–15.

4 Barquist, *American Tables and Looking Glasses*, p. 294; Boston references in *Boston News-Letter*, June 30–July 7, 1718, November 12, 1767, and *Boston Gazette*, April 9, 1754, as quoted in Dow, *Arts and Crafts in New England*, pp. 20–21, 32, 127.

5 The looking glasses are illustrated or noted in: Hornor, *Blue Book*, pl. 454; Bernard and S. Dean Levy, Inc., *Catalogue V* (New York: By the company, 1986), p. 42; *American Antiques from Israel Sack Collection*, 10 vols. (Washington, D.C.: Highland House, 1969–), 1:113; 2:343, 363, 395, 476, 563; 3:639, 701, 845; 4:905, 1015, 1047, 1097, 1101; 5:1151, 1179, 1353; 7:2016; 9:2417, 2484; 10:2707; Rollins, *Treasures of State*, p. 175; Downs, *American Furniture*, figs. 242, 243, 245–48, 256, 265; Comstock, *Looking Glass*, figs. 12, 15, 18, 27, 30; Clement E. Conger, "Decorative Arts at the White House," *Antiques* 96, no. 1 (July 1979): 122, pl. 24; Myrna Kaye, "Mix and Match: A Study of the Furniture in One Household," in *New England Furniture*, pp. 199–204; Barquist, *American Tables and Looking Glasses*, cat. 168; *The Decorative Arts of New Hampshire: A Sesquicentennial Exhibition* (Concord: New Hampshire Historical Society, 1973), fig. 45; Peter Benes, ed., *Two Towns: Concord and Wethersfield: A Comparative Exhibition of Regional Culture, 1635–1850* (Concord, Mass.: Concord Antiquarian Museum, 1982), cats. 119, 120; Penny J. Sander, ed., *Elegant Embellishments: Furnishings from New England Homes, 1660–1860* (Boston: Society for the Preservation of New England Antiquities, 1982), no. 13; *Great River*, cat. 132; Nina Fletcher Little, *Little by Little: Six Decades of Collecting American Decorative Arts* (New York: E. P. Dutton, 1984), p. 207; Heckscher, *American Furniture*, cat. no. 210; Montgomery, *American Furniture*, no. 218; Herbert F. Schiffer, *The Mirror Book: English, American, and European* (Exton, Pa.: Schiffer Publishing, 1983), fig. 200.

6 The 6 other looking-glass makers are Barnard Cermenati, Newburyport, Mass.; Cermenati and Bernarda and Cermenati and Monfrino, both of Boston; Nicholas Geffroy, Newport, R.I.; and Edward Lothrop of Boston—all the looking glasses are illustrated in Schiffer, *Mirror Book*, figs. 397, 404, 421, 423, 428; and Joseph Grant of Boston, as illustrated in Sander, *Elegant Embellishments*, no. 12.

7 Whiting in *Boston News-Letter*, November 12, 1767, as quoted in Dow, *Arts and Crafts in New England*, p. 129; Morrison H. Heckscher and Leslie Greene Bowman, *American Rococo, 1750–1775: Elegance in Ornament* (New York: Metropolitan Museum of Art, 1992), pp. 137–42, 155–58, 170–73, 186–90.

8 Estate inventories of George Macy (1776), Andrew Worth (1781), Silvanus Coffin (1784), Andrew Myrick (1783), Dinah Jenkins (1788), Benjamin Barnard (1789), Zebulon Butler (1790), John Waterman (1792), John Ramsdell (1790), Henry Clark (1792), Matthew Barnard, Jr. (1787), Caleb Gardner (1793), Mary Pease (1793), Barzillai Macy (1793), Benjamin Coffin (1794), Jethro Starbuck, Jr. (1796), Elisha Bunker (1797), Francis Brown (1797), John Hall (1797), Thomas Delano (1800), Grindel Gardner (1802), Alexander Gardner (1802), Benjamin Fosdick (1801), Jonathan Barney (1802), Ebenezer Raymond (1802), Joseph Russell (1802), Thomas Marshall (1803), Alexander Gardner (1803), Charles Swain (1805), John Clasby (1805), Davis Coleman (1805), and Stephen Hussey (1805), Registry of Probate, Nantucket County, Mass.

9 Hornor, *Blue Book*, pp. 272–73, 281–82; *Boston News-Letter*, September 22–29, 1737, as quoted in Dow, *Arts and Crafts in New England*, p. 127; Macquoid and Edwards, *Dictionary*, 2:357–69; Venable, *American Furniture*, cat. 57.

## 211 ◆ Looking glass
Probably Boston, Massachusetts
ca. 1809–10
Elisha Tucker (ca. 1784–1827)

Looking glasses with relatively simple fret-sawed frames were common in American households from the mid eighteenth century into the early nineteenth century, judging by the numbers that have survived. The typical frame consists of a crest, a base, and side pieces mounted at the four corners, all butted to a basic rectangular framework consisting of narrow stiles and rails concealed by an applied picture-frame molding on the face.

As a small and simple frame of its type, this example is relatively uncommon. Three other frames are particularly close in profile, proportions, and breadth of the glass opening. Two have histories: one was recovered by an early twentieth-century owner at a farm in Carlisle, Middlesex County, Massachusetts; the other, which is gilded on the inner cove of the picture molding (possibly original), is part of the original furnishings of the Sayward-Wheeler House built in York, Maine, by Jonathan Sayward (1713–97), the town's leading citizen, who maintained close ties with Boston. The Sayward glass and the fourth one differ slightly from Winterthur's example in their fuller arches in the center crest and center base elements, although the basic character of the profile is the same: pendent, cusped scrolls that are attached to the crest arch are linked to larger, upright cusped scrolls by long, cusped hollows. The small, finial-like upright scrolls at the upper corners become pendants when inverted at the base. The repeating motifs integrate the design.[1]

This basic vocabulary of elements is somewhat altered in the more elaborate fret-sawed looking glasses of longer length that survive in greater numbers. The center of the crest is again arched high, but the entire base is deeper, with large inverted and inward

curving scrolls like those flanking the center crest element replacing the cusped projections. A gouge-carved border adjacent to the glass is gilded. Some crests are embellished with gilded wood or composition ornament, such as a spread-wing bird or a trio of featherlike plumes in a vase, that is applied to the solid wood or over a pierced opening. Three frames in the group are labeled by Boston craftsmen. Another looking glass of slightly modified design bears the label of a London maker, identifying the general source of the basic fret pattern.[2]

Winterthur's example is documented by a label from the shop of Elisha Tucker, a cabinet and chair manufacturer of Boston (fig. 1). The

text implies that Tucker (who worked at 40 Middle Street, ca. 1809–10) either produced his own frames or acquired them locally. An even simpler looking glass, the decoration confined to a fret-sawed crest above a plain picture frame, was labeled by Barnard Cermenati of neighboring Newburyport (w. 1807–9), who styled himself a "Carver, Gilder, Picture Frame, and Looking-Glass MANUFACTURER." The labels that associate five craftsmen working in the Boston area with the body of material described and the identification of white pine as the secondary wood in several frames helps reinforce the American origin assigned to the Tucker looking glass. The early

**Fig. 1.** Detail, label.

nineteenth-century dates of the craftsmen—
four of them working from about 1806 to 1810
and the fifth one slightly later—speaks to the
longevity of eighteenth-century–style fret-
sawed frames in the marketplace.[3]

The simplicity of this looking glass and
the Cermenati looking glass suggests that these
frames were displayed in a bedchamber. This
hypothesis is further supported by a small
unlabeled glass mounted in a dressing stand
with a similar fret-sawed crest above a simple
picture-type frame and the Sayward-Wheeler
House looking glass, which still hangs in a
bedchamber over the parlor where it perhaps
was first placed in the eighteenth century.[4]

*NGE*

**Inscriptions or marks:** Printed label of Elisha
Tucker on backboard (see fig. 1).

**Construction:** The stiles and rails of the basic
framework are secured at the corners with open-end
mortises. The crest and baseboards of horizontal
grain and the outward flaring side pieces of vertical
grain are butted and glued to the frame, and the
joints are reinforced on the back with rectangular
glueblocks. On the front, an applied, mitered picture
molding surrounds the mirror opening. A rough-
sawed backboard protects the silvered glass.

**Condition:** The frame has been refinished. Breaks at
the center top of the crest and in the upper left side
piece have been repaired. The applied front molding
has been reglued. The backboard is split vertically at
one side.

**Dimensions:**

|   |   |   |
|---|---|---|
| H. | 17 1/2 in. | 44.5 cm |
| W. | 11 1/2 in. | 29.2 cm |
| D. | 5/8 in. | 1.7 cm |

**Materials:** *Microanalysis:* Primary: mahogany.
Secondary: white pine group (framework,
backboard). *Finish:* shaded, light yellowish brown
color in resin (the coat is mostly removed).

**Publications:** Montgomery, *American Furniture*,
no. 223. Herbert F. Schiffer, *The Mirror Book:
English, American, and European* (Exton, Pa.:
Schiffer Publishing, 1983), figs. 431, 432.

**Accession history:** Museum purchase from Parke-
Bernet Galleries, New York, October 1955.
55.92.1

1. Russell Hawes Kettell, *The Pine Furniture of Early New
   England* (1929; reprint, New York: Dover Publications,
   1959), pp. 203–4; Myrna Kaye, "Mix and Match: A
   Study of the Furniture in One Household," in *New
   England Furniture*, pp. 197–98, 203; Albert Sack, *Fine
   Points of Furniture: Early American* (New York: Crown
   Publishers, 1950), p. 206 upper left.

2. Sack, *Fine Points*, p. 206 center; Greenlaw, *New
   England Furniture*, no. 109; Barquist, *American Tables
   and Looking Glasses*, cat. 171; Montgomery, *American
   Furniture*, no. 224; Herbert F. Schiffer, *The Mirror Book:
   English, American, and European* (Exton, Pa.: Schiffer
   Publishing, 1983), figs. 421–29 (including glasses
   labeled by Cermenati and Monfrino, Cermenati and
   Bernarda, and Edward Lothrop, all of Boston); *Litchfield
   County Furniture, 1730–1850* ([Litchfield, Conn.:
   Litchfield Historical Society, 1969]), no. 48 (a looking
   glass labeled by George Kemp and Son, London,
   w. ca. 1785–97).

3. Betty Ring, "A Checklist of Looking-Glass and
   Frame Makers and Merchants Known by Their Labels,"
   *Antiques* 119, no. 5 (May 1981): 1194; Schiffer, *Mirror
   Book*, figs. 397, 398.

4. *American Antiques from Israel Sack Collection*, 10 vols.
   (Washington, D.C.: Highland House, ca. 1969–),
   8:2125.

## 212 ◆ Looking glass
Newport, Rhode Island
1781–1800
John Townsend (1733–1809)

This looking glass has a bolder frame design than either No. 211 or its larger, more elaborate counterparts with deep bases and carved gilt inner borders. Some fretwork motifs reappear here, however: the crest scrolls, which are now larger and higher; the scrolls of the lower side pieces; and the cusped lunette of the center base, which is more deeply curved. Treelike side pieces at the upper corners have replaced the scrolls.

John Townsend, the maker of this glass and an accomplished cabinetmaker of Newport, carefully took full advantage of handsomely figured mahogany veneers to maximize the effect of light and shade on the flat surfaces of the frame. The swirling patterns in the crest and base are contained by the diagonals of the side pieces, which draw the eye inward. The gilded composition leaf-and-dart molding applied to the inner edge of the frame surrounding the glass is considerably more intricate than the usual incised or gouge-carved band. Importers of European composition ornament regularly advertised a "great variety of mouldings and beads, for glass and picture frames, surpassing the best carving," and apparently many domestic looking-glass makers used these rich ornaments to enhance their best work. Leaf-and-dart moldings of similar if not identical pattern are found on at least two other documented glasses made or retailed in America—one branded by Stephen Badlam (w. ca. 1785–1815), a furniture maker of Dorchester, Massachusetts, the other labeled by James Stokes (w. ca. 1785–1811), a merchant of Philadelphia.[1]

The design of this looking glass, with a central plinth supporting a finial, is uncommon in preclassical patterns with fret-style crests. The central element in a glass of this type is usually a large lunette with small pendent side scrolls, an enlarged version of the motif in No. 211. No evidence remains of the original finial on this glass; however, it likely was a gilded wooden or composition spread-wing bird. Baskets and sprays of flowers were less common options for this style of glass. In a folk-type portrait of Mrs. Reuben Humphreys painted by Richard Brunton in Connecticut about 1800, the subject is seated next to her tea table above which hangs a looking glass of the general type illustrated. The central feature of the crest is a brightly gilded urn.[2]

Lavish use of gilt carved and composition ornament is typical of more expensive fret-sawed plinth-type looking glasses, most of which probably were made in England. Decorative choices included: leafy overlays on the crest scrolls, intaglio-carved floral motifs below the plinth, long, vinelike floral pendants on the sides, crouching-bird finials grasping chains fastened to rosettes at the crest scrolls, and pendent composition balls.[3]

John Townsend's label is applied to the backboard of this glass (fig. 1). A member of a prominent, multigenerational family of woodworkers, he was a descendant through

**Fig. 1.** Detail, label.

his mother of a founding family of Newport. The looking glass is one of an unusual number of documented cabinetwares produced by family members. Townsend used hand-inscribed identification, some of it on labels, during the first part of his career. Sometime after the revolutionary war he began to use printed labels of the type illustrated, which are inscribed in ink with a number. Of those numbers that can be read, all but one fall between 1789 and 1797. Whether these represent dates has yet to be determined. Unfortunately, the number on this label cannot be read beyond the first two digits.[4]

NGE

---

**Inscriptions or marks:** *On printed label, glued to upper backboard:* "MADE BY/ JOHN TOWNSEND/ NEWPORT", with ink number in lower right corner "17__".

**Construction:** The stiles and rails of the basic framework are lapped and pegged at the corners. The veneered crest, base, and outward flaring side pieces are butted and glued to the frame, the joints reinforced on the back with glueblocks: three long vertical braces and two small horizontal blocks on the crest; one long and two short vertical braces and two horizontal blocks on the base; and large triangular blocks behind each side piece. The mirror opening, framed with applied, mitered picture molding, has a patterned and gilded composition liner; the gilding has been executed

over a reddish brown bole or sizing. Applied facings finish the side edges between the side pieces. The backboard is made of three horizontal butted or bevel-lapped boards.

**Condition:** The frame has been refinished. The original finial is missing. There are several minor patches and cracks in the veneer and a long crack in the veneer of the base. The gilt molding has minor cracks and losses. The left vertical brace on the crest is a replacement, and the left glueblock on the base is missing. A late nineteenth-century tinned sheet-iron hanger is attached with screws to the top rail of the frame.

**Dimensions:**

| | | |
|---|---|---|
| H. | 42 in. | 106.7 cm |
| W. | 21¹/₂ in. | 54.6 cm |
| D. | 1¹/₄ in. | 3.2 cm |

**Materials:** *Microanalysis:* Primary: mahogany veneer. Secondary: Atlantic white cedar (frame, backboard); white pine group (backing of base, glueblocks). *Finish:* medium yellowish brown color in resin.

**Publications:** John A. H. Sweeney, *The Treasure House of Early American Rooms* (New York: Viking Press, 1963), p. 53. Charles F. Hummel, "Queen Anne and Chippendale Furniture in the Henry Francis du Pont Winterthur Museum, Part 3," *Antiques* 99, no. 1 (January 1971): 101. Herbert F. Schiffer, *The Mirror Book: English, American, and European* (Exton, Pa.: Schiffer Publishing, 1983), figs. 407, 408.

**Accession history:** Museum purchase from Harry Arons, Ansonia, Conn., 1956. 56.94.5

---

1. Helen Comstock, *The Looking Glass in America, 1700–1825* (New York: Viking Press, 1968), p. 11; for the Badlam glass, see *American Antiques from Israel Sack Collection,* 10 vols. (Washington, D.C.: Highland House, ca. 1969–), 6:1645; for the Stokes glass, see Herbert F. Schiffer, *The Mirror Book: English, American, and European* (Exton, Pa.: Schiffer Publishing, 1983), fig. 447.

2. For the Brunton portrait, see Elisabeth Donaghy Garrett, *At Home: The American Family, 1750–1870* (New York: Harry N. Abrams, 1990), p. 256.

3. For examples, see Albert Sack, *The New Fine Points of Furniture: Early American* (New York: Crown Publishers, 1993), p. 227; Geoffrey Wills, *English Looking-Glasses: A Study of the Glass, Frames, and Makers, 1670–1820* (London: Country Life, 1965), fig. 49; *American Antiques from Sack Collection,* 1:67, 4:908; Albert Sack, *Fine Points of Furniture: Early American* (New York: Crown Publishers, 1950), p. 205; Schiffer, *Mirror Book,* fig. 447; Nutting, *Furniture Treasury,* nos. 2911, 2918, 2936, 2965; Montgomery, *American Furniture,* no. 217.

4. Moses, *Master Craftsmen,* pp. 65–69; Margaretta M. Lovell, "'Such Furniture as Will Be Most Profitable': The Business of Cabinetmaking in Eighteenth-Century Newport," *Winterthur Portfolio* 26, no. 1 (Spring 1991): 44, 48. A pembroke table at Winterthur (see No. 138), probably dating after the Revolution, bears the printed label of John Townsend inscribed in ink "1743," thereby raising doubts that the numbers refer to the year of manufacture.

## 213 ◆ Looking glass
Hartford, Connecticut
1792–95
Samuel Kneeland (1755–1828) and
Lemuel Adams (d. 1821)

The fret pattern of this looking glass—a pierced lunette with winglike extensions centered in the crest and a large lobed pendant in the base—was popular with consumers. The majority of these glasses are of English origin; a few appear to have been made in America. The use of yellow poplar in the backboard of this glass is a strong indication that the frame was made in America. The other secondary wood, white pine, was used in looking-glass manufacture on both sides of the Atlantic. The makers, Samuel Kneeland and Lemuel Adams of Hartford advertised "elegant LOOKING-GLASSES, of their own manufacturing" (fig. 1).[1]

This fret pattern varies subtly in profile from glass to glass. The majority of frames have rounded and indented corners above the mirror rather than the square corners of this glass. In a few examples, the profile of the upper side pieces is that of an inward facing scroll rather than the illustrated flamelike figure. A flame replaces a scroll in the lower side pieces in only two examples from a comparative survey of sixty-seven looking glasses of this pattern.[2]

Looking glasses embellished with special ornament, aside from the gilt crest feature and gilt glass liner common to this pattern, probably originated in England. Such special treatments are uncommon but include: incised and gilt carving on the broad surface of the crest, gilt composition and wire pendants down the sides, intaglio gilt shells or other ornament centered in the base, and incised work edging the frets. A few late eighteenth-century or early nineteenth-century looking glasses have a flat picture-frame molding centered with a string inlay.

A spread-wing bird, the prominent feature of this pattern, outnumbers a pierced-and-ruffled–leaf crest ornament on comparable frames by three to two. The typical bird associated with furniture in the last half of the eighteenth century resembles the modern description of a phoenix—a lean body; long neck, beak, and tail; and outstretched wings. Eighteenth-century furniture sources make no mention of the phoenix, although these birds frequently ornament engraved furniture designs. Period sources refer to such ornaments and finials simply as "birds." In one rare instance, an old penciled inscription (probably original)

on the backboards of a pair of looking glasses close in profile to this glass reads: "22 13 Edge & Bird." The numbers refer to the size of the glass plates in the frames, and the "edge" is the gilt liner adjacent to the glass.[3]

Kneeland and Adams first announced their partnership on September 10, 1792, but the business association continued only until March 5, 1795. This looking glass and another of slightly different fret pattern that also bears their pictorial label, therefore, can be assigned a tight date range. The second glass, in the collection of the Connecticut Historical Society, Hartford, has a closely related base profile with a similar, centered three-lobe

**Fig. 1.** Detail, label.

Press of Virginia, 1968), p. 11, fig. 11. Herbert F. Schiffer, *The Mirror Book: English, American, and European* (Exton, Pa.: Schiffer Publishing, 1983), figs. 402, 403. William Adair, *The Frame in America, 1700-1900: A Survey of Fabrication Techniques and Styles* (Washington, D.C.: American Institute of Architects Fndn., 1983), cat. 28.

**Provenance:** Purchased by William Walcott, Litchfield, Conn., in 1930 from the Thomas Bagg family of West Springfield, Mass. Ex coll.: William Walcott, Litchfield, Conn.

**Accession history:** Purchased by H. F. du Pont from John C. R. Tompkins, Worcester, Mass., 1951. Bequest of H. F. du Pont, 1969.
59.794

1. On looking-glass construction and materials, see Barquist, *American Tables and Looking Glasses*, pp. 294–341. Kneeland and Adams's advertisement also appears in the *American Mercury* (Hartford), July 22, 1793.

2. Looking glasses in the survey include: Herbert F. Schiffer, *The Mirror Book: English, American, and European* (Exton, Pa.: Schiffer Publishing, 1983), figs. 337, 339, 342, 346, 347, 356; Barquist, *American Tables and Looking Glasses*, cats. 167–69; Edgar G. Miller, Jr., *American Antique Furniture: A Book for Amateurs*, 2 vols. (Baltimore: Lord Baltimore Press, 1937), 2:1124, 1130, 1131; *American Antiques from Israel Sack Collection*, 10 vols. (Washington, D.C.: Highland House, ca. 1969–), 1:22, 167, 222, 268; 2:300, 384, 388, 392, 475; 3:846 (upper and lower left); 4:908 (upper and lower left), 946, 950, 952, 953, 1018, 1079; 5:1149, 1168, 1194, 1281; 6:1442, 1686 (top left); 7:1720; 8:2089, 2115 (bottom), 2171, 2350; 9:2406, 2496; 10:2597, 2598, 2634, 2707 (left and right); Nutting, *Furniture Treasury*, nos. 2903, 2946, 2947, 2953, 2966; Albert Sack, *Fine Points of Furniture: Early American* (New York: Crown Publishers, 1950), p. 205 (left and right); Rodriguez Roque, *American Furniture*, no. 113; Fales, *Furniture of Historic Deerfield*, figs. 540, 542; Bernard and S. Dean Levy, Inc., *Catalogue IV* (New York: By the company, 1984), pp. 40–41; Bernard and S. Dean Levy, Inc., *Catalogue V* (New York: By the company, 1986), p. 45 right; Bernard and S. Dean Levy, Inc., *Catalogue VI* (New York: By the company, 1988), pp. 96, 146; Myrna Kaye, "Mix and Match: A Study of the Furniture in One Household," in *New England Furniture*, p. 201.

3. Macquoid and Edwards, *Dictionary*, 2:337, 340. For references to "birds," see Minshull advertisement, *New-York Journal or the General Advertiser*, March 16, 1775, as quoted in [Rita S. Gottesman, comp.], *The Arts and Crafts in New York, 1726–1776: Advertisements and News Items from New York City Newspapers* (1938; reprint ed., New York: Da Capo Press, 1970), pp. 132–33; *American Antiques from Sack Collection*, 4:1018.

4. Betty Ring, "Check List of Looking-glass and Frame Makers and Merchants Known by Their Labels," *Antiques* 119, no. 5 (May 1981): 1187. William Stuart Walcott, Jr., "A Kneeland and Adams Mirror," *Antiques* 13, no. 1 (January 1928): 30–32.

5. The craftsmen are John Elliott, James McGlathery, James Stokes (Philadelphia); Biddle and Cooper (Boston); Nicholas Geffroy (Newport); and Joseph and John Vecchio (New York); see Schiffer, *Mirror Book*, figs. 347, 382, 390, 404, 405, 414, pl. 16. Kaye, "Mix and Match," p. 201. The English glasses are illustrated in Schiffer, *Mirror Book*, figs. 380, 383.

pendant. The S-scroll side pieces of the base are inverted and repeated at the top corners, where they replace the flame pieces of this glass. The center of the crest has a solid rather than a pierced crown and lacks a gilt ornament, and the secondary scrolls vary somewhat in pattern. A gilt liner finishes the mirror opening.[4]

Looking glasses labeled by craftsmen in Philadelphia, Boston, Newport, and New York relate to the Kneeland and Adams glasses in fret profile and, where applicable, gilded ornament. Some were made by the craftsmen who labeled them; others were imported from Europe and retailed. Among related English glasses, one in the Sayward-Wheeler House in York, Maine, was purchased by Jonathan Sayward before his death in 1797. Two others are labeled by London craftsmen Matthew and George Kemp (w. ca. 1785–97) and Thomas Aldersey (w. ca. 1754–73). Between foreign importations and glasses exchanged in the coastal trade, there were plenty of examples for craftsmen to copy.[5]

The family history of Winterthur's looking glass begins with the last private owner, who indicated in 1930 that he had obtained the glass from the Thomas Bagg family of West Springfield, Massachusetts, a community less than twenty-five miles north of Hartford. Census records list a Thomas Bagg there from 1790 to 1820.

*NGE*

**Inscriptions or marks:** *On backboard:* printed label of Kneeland and Adams (see fig. 1). *On a new stabilizing rail at the lower back:* "From Thomas Bagg/ family West Springfield/ Mass./ 1930" in modern pencil.

**Construction:** The stiles and rails of the basic framework are mitered at the corners. The crest, base, and lower side pieces are butted and glued to the frame; the upper side pieces are butted and glued to the frame and crest. The base is secured with four small triangular blocks abutting the framework and once had a long vertical stabilizing brace (now missing). The crest, base, and side pieces are veneered. The mirror is framed with an applied mitered picture molding carved and gilded on the inner edge. The carved, three-dimensional bird is formed of a piece with the crest proper to which is applied the high-relief bulk of the body and the free-standing head. The wing edges and tail that overlap the veneered crest surface are carved in intaglio. A vertical-grain backboard protects the silvered glass.

**Condition:** The backboard, once held with nails, now has retaining slats screwed across the top and bottom. The carved bird has been repaired at the neck. The veneer is patched in several places; the veneer on the pendant is checking.

**Dimensions:**

| | | |
|---|---|---|
| H. | 37 3/4 in. | 95.9 cm |
| W. | 18 3/4 in. | 47.6 cm |
| D. | 1 in. | 2.5 cm |

**Materials:** *Microanalysis:* Primary: mahogany veneer. Secondary: white pine group (frame); yellow poplar (backboard). *Finish:* variegated medium to medium dark reddish brown color in resin.

**Publications:** Montgomery, *American Furniture*, no. 218. Nancy E. Richards, "Furniture of the Lower Connecticut River Valley: The Hartford Area, 1785–1810," in Richard K. Doud, ed., *Winterthur Portfolio 4* (Charlottesville: University

## 214 ◆ Looking glass

(one of a pair)
England, probably London
1750–65

Fine looking glasses were greatly prized throughout the eighteenth century, as confirmed by the high values assigned to them in inventories. Production in America was limited before the revolutionary war because craftsmen lacked the technical background to make glass plates of satisfactory quality, and the duties levied on unframed glass imported from England were restrictive. Most glasses available in the American market were manufactured in Europe.

Both craftsmen and merchants imported looking glasses. In 1771 James Reynolds, a carver in Philadelphia, was invoiced for twenty-eight walnut glasses shipped from London ranging in description from "Plain" to "Gilt Edge & Shell." Some importers, among them John Elliott, Sr., who opened a looking-glass store in Philadelphia as early as 1756, supplied local merchants with looking glasses for the coastal trade. One group shipped to Portsmouth, New Hampshire, included two mahogany framed glasses "with Birds, side pieces &c." priced at a substantial £10.9.0 apiece in 1762. Years earlier in 1749, Stephen Whiting, a Boston craftsman, advertised a "Variety of large Sconce and Pier Looking Glasses, also small Looking Glasses by the Dozen &c. suitable for Traders and others." Whiting sold looking glasses to John Hancock in 1770: one fitted with candle arms is described as a "Large Sconce Looking Glass with Ornaments Carved & Gilt."[1]

This English looking glass is one of a pair owned by another prominent Bostonian, William Phillips, a wealthy merchant who purchased them for his three-story home on Beacon Street, which stood next to that of Gov. James Bowdoin. Phillips, a member of the Massachusetts aristocracy, was an outstanding patriot during the struggle for American independence and held many high political positions in Massachusetts before and after the revolutionary war. He served on committees with John Hancock, Samuel Adams, and Adams's cousin John Adams, later president of the United States. Phillips's looking glasses hung between two pairs of windows in a large room to the left of the entry when his eldest daughter, Abigail, married Josiah Quincy in 1769, as noted in a catalogue compiled in 1879 by the Quincys' great granddaughter Eliza Susan Quincy.[2]

Large vertical looking glasses, such as this one, generally are called *pier glasses* in period documents and design books. The bird finials on this glass and its mate are mounted to face each other when hung on the same wall. Pairs of looking glasses are recorded in the parlors of several Boston-area homes in the late eighteenth century. Those of Capt. William Downes Cheever, who in 1788 owned a store on State Street and a "mansion house" in west Boston, were valued at £3. The large glasses "with gilt frames" in the household of Hannah Winthrop, widow of doctor John Winthrop of Cambridge, were worth a substantial £10 two years later.[3]

These looking glasses derive from early Georgian architectural, or "pediment," frames popular in the second quarter of the eighteenth century. Typically, rococo overlays, here mounted asymmetrically in the crest, obscure much of the basic top profile but emphasize the bulging scrolls at the lower corners. Long side pendants and a scrolled and gilt border at the glass opening as well as carved and gilt intaglio ornament in the crest, sometimes in the base, usually adorn these glasses. A bird or a vase of flowers are the most common finials; other options were a basket of flowers, an urn, or a shell.[4]

NGE/NER

**Construction:** The crest and base are lap-joined and glued to the stiles. The backboard, which is planed on the exposed surface and chamfered on the four edges, is glued up from many horizontal boards. The lower part of the crest and the upper backboard bear remnants of an old Boston newspaper dating to the mid nineteenth century (after 1852). Figured walnut veneer embellishes the face of the frame, and cross-cut veneers cover the secondary wood at the side edges. The molding that edges the facade adjacent to the side pendants is applied. The silvered glass is bordered by a narrow, shaped molding accented by shallow carving and punchwork. The side pendants are nailed to the frame. The foliate ornament edging the base and the crest shoulders is carved from wood and is gessoed and gilded; it is fixed to the frame with screws inserted from the back. The finial, which is part of the center top ornament, is also carved of wood, then gessoed and gilded. The

wings are separate units inserted into the body. The mirror, which has rough-cut edges, appears to be original.

**Condition:** There are many cracks and imperfections in the burl veneer, and small pieces have been replaced. The gilding has been retouched. The backboard has been reset, as have some of the wedges securing the glass. There is a wide horizontal crack near the center back of the backboard, and a narrow horizontal piece is missing from the top.

**Dimensions:**

| | | |
|---|---|---|
| H. | 80 1/2 in. | 204.5 cm |
| W. | 36 3/8 in. | 92.4 cm |
| D. | 2 in. | 5.1 cm |

**Materials:** *Macroidentification:* Primary: European burl walnut veneer. *Microanalysis:* Secondary: spruce (frame, backboard, bird, carved decoration). *Finish:* remnants of clear resin over veneer, which now is a medium yellowish brown color; secondary wood is covered with a dull yellowish mustard pigment.

**Publications:** Downs, *American Furniture*, fig. 265. Helen Comstock, *The Looking Glass in America, 1700–1825* (New York: Viking Press, 1968), fig. 25.

**Provenance:** The looking glass and its mate came from the house on Beacon Street, Boston, owned by William Phillips (1722–1804) and his wife Abigail (Bromfield) Phillips. The glasses were inherited in 1805 by Phillips's only son, William Phillips (1750–1827), a merchant and later lieutenant governor of Massachusetts, who gave one to his sister Sarah Phillips Dowse (Mrs. Edward Dowse) and the other to his sister Hannah Phillips Shaw (Mrs. Samuel Shaw). At some point the looking glasses were reunited and for many years hung in Mrs. Dowse's home in Dedham. They were inherited by Mrs. Dowse's nephew, the Hon. Josiah Quincy (1772–1864), and passed through his son, Edmund Quincy (1808–77), to his grandson, Henry Parker Quincy (1838–99). Inherited by Henry Quincy's widow, Mary Adams Quincy (1846–1928), a granddaughter of President John Quincy Adams, the looking glasses passed to her daughter, Dorothy Quincy Nourse

(Mrs. Frederick Russell Nourse) in 1928. In 1945 they were sold by Mrs. Nourse's daughter, Dorothy Quincy Nourse Pope (Mrs. Henry V. Pope), and daughter-in-law, Margaret Dunn Nourse (Mrs. Frederick R. Nourse, Jr.) to Harry Arons.

**Accession history:** Purchased by H. F. du Pont from Harry Arons, Ansonia, Conn., 1945. Bequest of H. F. du Pont, 1969.
60.1075.1

---

1. William Barrell invoice book, 1771–75, and Stephen Collins accounts, box 13, Stephen Collins Papers, Library of Congress, Washington, D.C.; John Reynell account book, 1760–76, private collection; business papers, 1763–67, Reynell Papers, Coates Collection, Historical Society of Pennsylvania; Stephen Whiting advertisement, *Boston Gazette*, May 23, 1749, as quoted in Dow, *Arts and Crafts in New England*, p. 128; John Hancock domestic bills, 1768–70, Hancock Collection, Baker Library, Harvard University, Cambridge.

2. Hamilton Andrews Hill, "William Phillips and William Phillips, Father and Son, 1722–1827," *New England Historical and Genealogical Register* 39, no. 2 (April 1885): 109–17; Eliza Susan Quincy, "Memorandum relative to pictures, China & furniture," Quincy, Massachusetts, 1879 (photostat copy of unpublished manuscript [location unknown], pp. 49–50, Downs collection); "Genealogy of the Quincy Family," in Parke-Bernet Galleries, "Adams-Quincy Heirlooms" (January 12, 1946).

3. William Downes Cheever inventory, 1788, Caleb Davis Papers, Massachusetts Historical Society; John Winthrop (d. 1779)/Hannah Winthrop inventory, 1790, Winthrop Papers, Boston Public Library, Boston.

4. Survey of Phillips-Quincy–type looking glasses drawn from Bernard and S. Dean Levy, Inc., *Catalogue V* (New York: By the company, 1986), p. 63 left and right; Albert Sack, *Fine Points of Furniture: Early American* (New York: Crown Publishers, 1950), p. 209 right; Clement E. Conger, "Decorative Arts at the White House," *Antiques* 116, no. 1 (July 1979): 122, pl. 24; Herbert F. Schiffer, *The Mirror Book: English, American, and European* (Exton, Pa.: Schiffer Publishing, 1983), figs. 200, 201, 203, 204, 208; Barquist, *American Tables and Looking Glasses*, cat. 173; Geoffrey Wills, *English Looking Glasses: A Study of the Glass, Frames, and Makers, 1670–1820* (London: Country Life, 1965), fig. 51; Helen Comstock, *The Looking Glass in America, 1700–1825* (New York: Viking Press, 1968), figs. 22–24, 26, 27; Rodriguez Roque, *American Furniture*, no. 118.

## 215 ◆ Dressing glass
Boston, Massachusetts
1760–85

By the time this dressing accessory was made, the form was reasonably common in upper-middle-class households in England and America, and its usual place of use was on a dressing table or a chest of drawers in a bedchamber. Walnut construction gave way to mahogany framing by the mid eighteenth century. The usual term for a box and attached glass at this date was *dressing glass*, although glasses supported on a framework without a box probably were similarly identified. Only a few references are more specific: Samuel Moffatt of Portsmouth, New Hampshire, had "1 Dressing Glass, 1 Pine Table" located in a bedchamber in 1768, suggesting that the glass stood on a simple frame hung with a fabric skirt, a form popular in the third quarter of the century (see No. 89, fig. 1). The "Toilet" that accompanied the "Mahogany Dressing Glass, 1 Table" in another chamber may have been a richly embellished cloth or a set of small boxes and other accoutrements that accompanied the dressing glass. Of more certain description are the "Dressing Glass frame & Stand" sold by Townsend Goddard of Newport, Rhode Island, to Christopher Champlin in 1787 and the "1 draw dressing glass" that was part of the house furnishings of William Chenery, a cabinetmaker and upholsterer of London, when his estate was assigned to auction in 1785.[1]

Initially, American demand for dressing glasses was met by imports from England, but by the third quarter of the eighteenth century, domestic stands were also available. This dressing glass unites an imported mirror with a Boston-fabricated bombé chest, or box. The high-relief gilt-framed mirror recalls English looking-glass designs of the early eighteenth century. The box echoes the profiles of bombé-shape furniture made in Boston and Salem

from the 1750s and is closely linked in form with a fall-front desk bearing the owner's brand "G.CADE" and a desk-and-bookcase signed and dated by Benjamin Frothingham, Jr., in 1753. Like this box, both chests have drawer sides that are straight rather than swelled to follow the case contours and a plain, bulging front surface without a secondary serpentine curve across the breadth.[2]

Four American bombé-case dressing glasses supported on ogee-bracket feet are known, and three have spiral-turned posts supporting the looking glass. The boxes of three examples are similar in profile but vary in detail. The drawer sides in a dressing glass at the Metropolitan Museum of Art are straight like those in this example, although

there are three short drawers instead of one long one. A second box at Winterthur has a long drawer with sides that conform to the bulging case profile. Another example, illustrated by Wallace Nutting, also has a single drawer with shaped ends, but that drawer is considerably taller than the rest, and the case has a swelled rather than a bulging bombé profile.[3]

Spiral-turned posts appear only on bombé-shape dressing glasses. Equally rare but found on dressing boxes of several shapes is the gilt looking glass. Its appearance and use in America is confirmed in the inventory of wealthy Philadelphian Stephen Carmick: "1 Dressing Glass Mahoy [mahogany] Stand & Gilt Frame." Reinforcing this is the existence of another stand with gilt glass used slightly later in Philadelphia and attributed to cabinetmaker Jonathan Gostelowe.[4]

The dressing box was a convenient place to store items used in dressing, and some boxes even had drawers fitted with compartments. The affluent Edward Brattle Oliver of Boston described a "Mohogany Dressing Box with things of Value" when reporting his losses after the Great Fire in 1760. Generally, the dressing box was a handy place for cosmetics, combs, essences, patches, hair powders and ornaments, and pincushions. Men might add razors and brushes to the contents.[5]

*NGE/NER*

**Construction:** The one-piece crest board of the glass frame is lapped and glued to the narrow vertical side stiles. The base is mitered to the stiles, and a diagonal reinforcing spline is laid into the back surface of both joints. The front of the frame is decorated with gilded, carved, gesso ornament. The vertical backboard is chamfered on all edges and nailed to the frame. The spiral-turned uprights cant backward and are tenoned into the top of the chest. The glass frame pivots on two thumbscrews that can be tightened to hold the glass at a desired angle. The solid bombé side boards of the box are straight on the inside and dovetailed to the top and bottom boards. The horizontal, bombé-shape backboard, flat on the inside, is nailed to the top and sides. The beading around the drawer opening is worked from solid wood. An applied mitered molding is attached to the front and side edges of the bottom board. The mitered front feet are supported by one vertical and two shaped horizontal glueblocks; the rear feet have one vertical and one shaped horizontal glueblock. The pendent drop is glued to the case and has no supporting block. The drawer front is straight on the inside. The straight drawer sides are cut with a heavy bead on the top lip; the straight drawer back has a narrow chamfer on the upper rear edge. The four corners are dovetailed. The drawer bottom is set flush into rabbets on four sides. The drawer rides on the bottom board of the box.

**Condition:** The box and upright supports for the framed glass have been refinished. The box is cracked across the drawer front from the left side through the center and on the top of the case at the left post. The front molding is patched above the right front foot. The right rear foot is replaced, and the molding above it has been repaired. The horizontal glueblock on the left rear foot has been reattached with nails; the molding above the foot has been shattered and repaired. Some of the gilding of the glass frame has been retouched. The present hardware is not original.

**Dimensions:**

| | | |
|---|---|---|
| H. | 23 in. | 58.4 cm |
| H. (glass frame) | 16 1/4 in. | 41.3 cm |
| H. (box) | 6 5/8 in. | 16.8 cm |
| W. (glass frame) | 9 5/8 in. | 24.6 cm |
| W. (box) | 18 in. | 45.7 cm |
| W. (feet) | 18 3/4 in. | 47.6 cm |
| D. (box) | 9 in. | 22.9 cm |
| D. (feet) | 9 1/2 in. | 24.1 cm |

**Materials:** *Microanalysis:* Primary: mahogany. Secondary: white pine group (box bottom, drawer bottom); red cedar (drawer side); white oak group (box backboard); poplar/cottonwood/aspen group (mirror frame). *Finish:* (Case) medium to medium dark reddish brown color in resin.

**Publications:** Joe Kindig, Jr., advertisement, *American Collector* 9, no. 5 (June 1940): inside front cover; Gilbert T. Vincent, "The Bombé Furniture of Boston," in *Boston Furniture*, p. 174.

**Accession history:** Purchased by H. F. du Pont from Joe Kindig, Jr., York, Pa., 1943. Gift of H. F. du Pont, 1959.
58.2270

1. Samuel Moffatt account of sales of estate, 1768, New Hampshire Archives, Concord; Christopher Champlin account with Townsend Goddard, 1787, Wetmore Papers, vol. 15, Massachusetts Historical Society, Boston; John Phillips, *A Catalogue of . . . Household Furniture . . . of William Chenery, Cabinet-Maker and Upholsterer* (London: By the author, 1785), Chancery Masters' Exhibits, Public Record Office, London.

2. Macquoid and Edwards, *Dictionary*, 2:357–69. The Cade and Frothingham desks are in the Diplomatic Reception Rooms at the U.S. State Department; see Harold Sack, "The Bombé Furniture of Boston and Salem, Massachusetts," *Antiques* 135, no. 5 (May 1989): 1179, pl. 3, 1180, pl. 4.

3. Bondome, "The Home Market," *Antiques* 3, no. 3 (March 1923): 133–34; Heckscher, *American Furniture,* cat. no. 204; Winterthur 59.640; Nutting, *Furniture Treasury,* no. 3210.

4. Hornor, *Blue Book,* p. 282; Barquist, *American Tables and Looking Glasses,* cat. 207.

5. Edward Brattle Oliver claim, 1760, Boston Fire Documents and Correspondence, Boston Public Library; Barquist, *American Tables and Looking Glasses,* p. 354.

## 216 ◆ Dressing glass
Massachusetts
1785–1800

This dressing glass represents a blending of new and outdated features. A slanted, hinged desklike fall, or leaf, first appeared in English dressing boxes at the beginning of the eighteenth century. Behind the fall was a miniature desk interior, complete with drawers, pigeonholes, vertical document boxes, and a prospect door. In this example, the slanted, fixed board is the front panel of a long, plain drawer.[1]

The shield-, vase-, or urn-shape mirror is the most up-to-date feature of the dressing glass. Although objects that incorporate this form, either in shape or design appear sporadically in England from about 1760, the profile was uncommon in furniture until well into the 1770s. The Thomas Chippendales, Sr. and Jr., began to show considerable interest in the motif at that time as demonstrated in their drawings and executed work. George Hepplewhite illustrated a number of vase-back chairs in his *Cabinet-Maker and Upholsterer's Guide* with plates engraved in 1787. The following year, the first designs for vase-shape looking glasses were published in *The Cabinet-Makers' London Book of Prices*. Probably about that time Barnard Baker, an upholsterer and cabinetmaker of London, began to produce bow-front dressing boxes with vase-shape glasses.[2]

The mirror in this example is close in profile and detail to that in Baker's dressing box. The style is one that probably was produced in many London shops at the end of the eighteenth century, both for domestic consumption and for export. This mirror and one in a second dressing stand that is almost identical to it likely were imported. The cross-banded mahogany veneer and gilt beading of the frame contrast markedly with the plain, solid wood of the box and posts. White pine,

the secondary wood of the frame, is found in English as well as American looking glasses, and the fir of the backboard is rare in American work, although the thin sheet of wood could have been recycled from a packing case. The scratch beads of the posts complement the beads outlining the looking glass and the drawers of the box. The Winterthur dressing case differs from its close mate only in the height of the glass and the addition of two leaflike pendants at the base of the glass frame.[3]

The revised *London Cabinet Book of Prices* of 1793 lists piece rates as 6s. for a basic box

of the dimensions of this one with one beaded drawer; plain feet; a square, veneered looking glass; and straight posts. That figure is more than doubled by the addition of labor charges for extras such as substituting ogee-bracket feet, adding an extra drawer, making a vase-pattern glass frame with appropriate standards, and oiling and polishing. Some charges are not given, such as that for carving the four miniature claw feet and working the swelled lower drawer facade. The closest charge is that for "Sweeping the front of the box serpentine." Add to these charges those for materials—mahogany, glass plate, and hardware—and a fair markup and the cost to the consumer was no less than 24s. This figure may be compared with an urban craftsman's daily wage of about 6s. in the federal period.[4]

Whether of English or American fabrication, eighteenth-century, dressing stands were available in a variety of patterns. The oxbow, or reverse-serpentine, facade of this box is rare (as is the bombé facade of No. 215). The two most common patterns were the bow front and the plain serpentine front, followed by a flat facade and a flat facade sweeping forward at the base to form a low ledge. Probably the most expensive boxes to produce were those shaped at the front in compound curves. At the beginning of the century, desk-type boxes were fashionable, and a simulated sideboard was a new option at the end of the century.

The similarity of dressing boxes to large pieces of case furniture is not coincidental. Strong evidence indicates that some dressing boxes were made en suite with the chest or dressing table they stood upon. A serpentine box at Yale University Art Gallery attributed to Jonathan Gostelowe of Philadelphia descended in his family with a serpentine-front chest of drawers. A serpentine chamber table of Salem, Massachusetts, origin with reeded and leaf-carved cylindrical legs is still paired with its four-drawer serpentine dressing box framed with legs of comparable pattern. Other boxes and chests are known that were acquired separately but used together. An English dressing box with a facade composed of compound curves descended in the Otis family of Boston with a blockfront chest of drawers attributed to the Charlestown, Massachusetts, shop of Benjamin Frothingham, Jr. Although the Winterthur looking glass would not have stood on top of a fall-front oxbow desk, it was certainly inspired by that form and may have stood in the same room as a full-size desk of that design.[5]

The construction of this dressing box generally follows that of full-scale desks of Massachusetts origin, including the use of a "giant" dovetail to join the front molding to the bottom board. The ball-and-claw feet relate to those commonly found on eastern Massachusetts furniture. In an unusual

departure from common practice, the rear supports are not fully formed—the knees and ankles are complete, but the feet are cut in half.

*NGE/NER*

---

**Inscriptions or marks:** *On backboard:* "B" in white chalk. *On top of drawer blade:* pencil stroke. *On top of bottom board:* two pencil strokes.

**Construction:** The shield-shape glass frame is made from four rails lapped at the top, bottom, and upper sides below the arch. The facade is faced with cross-cut veneer, gilded on the inner coved edge and beaded and gilt on the outer edge. The applied pendent leaves are gilded wood. The conforming vertical backboard is thin. The backward canted posts, which are scratch-beaded on the front face and chamfered on the outer rear edge, are tenoned to the case. The glass frame pivots on two thumbscrews that can be tightened to hold the glass at a desired angle. The top board of the box is joined to the sides with a mitered dovetail. The blade between the drawers is attached to the sides with a sliding dovetail, the joint covered by an applied facing. The glides supporting the upper drawer are nailed in place on the box sides behind the blade. The bottom drawer runs flush on the bottom board, which is dovetailed to the sides. A large dovetail joins the front base molding to the bottom board. The side moldings are applied and meet the front molding in miters. The horizontal backboard is set into rabbets at the sides and top and nailed; the bottom is nailed to the bottom board and further secured with interior glueblocks. The legs and knee brackets are glued to the bottom board. The rear supports are half feet of semicircular shape. The top drawer face is thumb molded; the bottom drawer has an incised bead around the edge. The bow-shape drawer front is cut from solid wood but hollowed inside at the bulges. The dovetailed drawers are flat on the upper edge of the sides and back. The cross-grained drawer bottoms, set into rabbets at the front and sides and nailed, are reinforced with a single, centered glueblock on the front. Both drawers have broad, applied runners. The drawers are fitted with brass locks and pulls.

**Condition:** There are several patches in the veneer and bead molding of the glass frame. The applied facing on the front edge of the left side panel of the box is replaced. The top drawer is split at the left front, and the upper right corner is patched. The finials are replaced, and the brass drawer pulls are at least the second set of hardware.

**Dimensions:**

| | | |
|---|---|---|
| H. (with finial) | 27 3/8 in. | 69.5 cm |
| H. (glass frame) | 18 in. | 45.7 cm |
| H. (chest) | 7 7/8 in. | 20.0 cm |
| W. (glass frame) | 14 1/8 in. | 35.9 cm |
| W. (box) | 14 1/2 in. | 36.8 cm |
| W. (front feet) | 15 1/2 in. | 39.4 cm |
| D. (box) | 7 5/8 in. | 19.4 cm |
| D. (feet) | 7 1/8 in. | 18.1 cm |

**Materials:** *Microanalysis:* Primary: mahogany; mahogany veneer (mirror). Secondary: white pine group (mirror frame, box backboard and bottom, drawer linings); fir (backboard on mirror). *Finish:* variegated medium yellowish brown color in resin.

**Publications:** Montgomery, *American Furniture*, no. 251. Herbert F. Schiffer, *The Mirror Book: English, American, and European* (Exton, Pa.: Schiffer Publishing, 1983), p. 201, fig. 524.

**Accession history:** Purchased by H. F. du Pont from Ginsburg and Levy, New York, 1939. Gift of H. F. du Pont, 1960. 58.2431

1. For desk-type dressing glasses, see Macquoid and Edwards, *Dictionary*, 2:361–62.

2. Barquist, *American Tables and Looking Glasses*, p. 357; Christopher Gilbert, *The Life and Work of Thomas Chippendale*, 2 vols. (New York: Macmillan Co., 1978), 2: figs. 28, 29, 33, 53, 152, 153, 350, 351; [George] Hepplewhite, *The Cabinet-Maker and Upholsterer's Guide* (1794; reprint 3d ed., New York: Dover Publications, 1969), pls. 1–7, 9–11, 14; *The Cabinet-Makers' London Book of Prices, and Designs of Cabinet Work* (London, 1788), pl. 14. For a Baker dressing glass, see Charles B. Wood III, "Some Labeled English Looking Glasses," *Antiques* 93, no. 5 (May 1968): 649; the Bedford St. address on the label establishes a date range of 1778–96.

3. For the mate to the Winterthur dressing glass, see Craig and Tarlton advertisement, *Antiques* 97, no. 3 (March 1970): 339. The glass was sold at auction; Northeast Auctions, "The estate of John Howland Ricketson III" (May 29, 1993), lot 104.

4. *The Cabinet-Makers' London Book of Prices, and Designs of Cabinet Work* (Rev. ed., London: W. Brown and A. O'Neil, 1793), as reproduced in *Furniture History* 18 (1982): 214–16.

5. Barquist, *American Tables and Looking Glasses*, cat. 207; Flanigan, *American Furniture*, cat. no. 81; Jobe and Kaye, *New England Furniture*, nos. 14, 142. A dressing glass and dressing table associated for many years during their descent in the Wendell family of Portsmouth, N.H., are now at Strawbery Banke Museum; see Gerald W. R. Ward and Karin E. Cullity, "The Wendell Family Furniture at Strawbery Banke Museum," in Luke Beckerdite, ed., *American Furniture 1993* (Milwaukee, Wis.: Chipstone Fndn., 1993), p. 252.

# Case Studies

## 217 ◆ Armchair

Portsmouth, New Hampshire, or vicinity;
possibly northeastern coastal
Massachusetts
Style of 1730–60

At first encounter, this chair appears to be a straightforward example of "Gaines"-type seating furniture; however, close inspection reveals major structural problems.

The rounded splat, whether old or a copy, is the most common type found with this seating and undoubtedly predates the "hook"-type splat illustrated in No. 17. The carved crests of the two chairs are comparable, although the crest of this example is flatter. The crest dimensions are proportional rather than similar, due to the greater overall breadth of the armchair. The carved crest scrolls in the larger chair are terminated just short of the back posts rather than above them. In a related armchair at the Metropolitan Museum of Art, the carved work is narrower, the central hollow is shorter and rises to pronounced points, and the scroll ends have hollow rather than shouldered extensions.[1]

Like this example, the Metropolitan Museum of Art chair has carved and molded scroll arms supported on short posts set back from the seat front, although the post profiles beneath the scrolls are varied. The front stretcher tips are also longer and more pointed, and the rear brace has a heavy profile like that of No. 17. A closer comparison to this chair is an armchair with set-back arm posts that was once in the Mitchell Taradash collection. The rear stretcher is centered with an oval swell similar to the one illustrated, although the tips are tapered cylinders. The proportions of all three armchair splats vary. The Taradash chair banister is comparable in profile to this chair, although shorter in length. The splat in the Metropolitan Museum of Art chair is considerably slimmer, and the adjacent crest arches are higher.[2]

More significant modification of the design is to be noted in two other armchairs of this crest type. Both have forward arm posts that are extensions of the front legs. One chair has a splat with pointed upper corners in the baluster (see No. 18), a sawed rear stretcher, and a rectangular drop centered in the seat front with hollow stepped ends. Similar drops occur in a related pair of side chairs with splats comparable to that of No. 1; the rear stretchers are turned. A second armchair at the Metropolitan Museum of Art is fitted with a rush seat woven on rails socketed into the legs rather than onto a loose seat fitted

into a joined frame. As confirmed by the survey, variability is a characteristic of the general pattern.[3]

*NGE/NER*

**Construction:** The carved and pierced crest is supported on rectangular tenons at the sawed and molded post tops and splat. A rectangular tenon secures the splat and molded stay rail. The stay rail is tenoned into the back posts. The arms, which are molded to a bell shape with the deep bases chamfered at the edges, are secured by rectangular tenons at the back posts and round tenons at the front posts. The seat rails and side stretchers are joined to the legs and back posts with rectangular tenons. The lower edge of the front rail is ornamented with an incised bead. The front and rear stretchers are round tenoned into the legs.

**Condition:** The chair has been highly compromised. The crest and the back posts above the feet are old and probably original to one another, although there are no pins securing the crest joints. The splat is unusually thin and without tool marks; the contour varies from that of the posts. The splat may be a later addition or a part taken from another chair. The arms, which are old but not original to this chair, are pierced along the bottom by nails and have nail holes that once secured former padding (not original). The attachment to the back posts occurs at points above old patched holes for other arms. The long overhang of the forward scrolls is original, since there is only one set of round mortises to socket the short front posts, which could be replacements. The arms probably were cut off at the back; overall they are 2" shorter than those of No. 18. The front stretcher appears to be new; it has no wear, and the ends are too large for the leg blocks. The rear stretcher is probably old, since it is round-tipped internally and marked by appropriate lathe centers (through X-ray examination); however, the exposed rounded tips are atypical of the few ball-centered stretchers found on Gaines-type chairs. Whether the stretcher is original to this chair is questionable. The front legs are original down to the replaced feet. The rear feet, which are spliced on, are thin in profile and incorrect in their backward angles. The rush seat is new. Nail holes on the tops of the seat rails indicate that applied facings were once in place.

**Dimensions:**

| | | |
|---|---|---|
| H. | 43 1/4 in. | 109.8 cm |
| H. (seat) | 17 13/16 in. | 45.2 cm |
| W. (crest) | 17 7/16 in. | 44.3 cm |
| W. (seat front) | 23 1/4 in. | 59.1 cm |
| W. (seat back) | 17 3/4 in. | 45.1 cm |
| W. (arms) | 26 5/8 in. | 67.6 cm |
| W. (feet) | 27 in. | 68.6 cm |
| D. (seat) | 16 3/8 in. | 41.6 cm |
| D. (feet) | 21 in. | 53.3 cm |

**Materials:** *Microanalysis:* Primary: soft maple group (throughout). *Finish:* streaked reddish to dark brown color in resin (mahoganized).

**Accession history:** Purchased by H. F. du Pont before 1954. Bequest of H. F. du Pont, 1969. 54.513

---

1. For the Metropolitan Museum of Art chair, see Helen Comstock, "An Ipswich Account Book, 1707–1762," *Antiques* 66, no. 3 (September 1954): 191 upper left.

2. The Taradash chair is illustrated and discussed in Jobe, *Portsmouth Furniture*, cat. no. 77.

3. For the first armchair, see Jairus B. Barnes and Moselle Taylor Meals, *American Furniture in the Western Reserve, 1680–1830* (Cleveland: Western Reserve Historical Society, 1972), cat. 4; on related side chairs, see Israel Sack advertisement, *Antiques* 135, no. 2 (February 1989): inside front cover; for the second armchair, see Marshall B. Davidson and Elizabeth Stillinger, *The American Wing at the Metropolitan Museum of Art* (New York: Alfred A. Knopf, 1985), fig. 144.

## 218 ◆ Side chair
### Boston, Massachusetts, or vicinity
### 1760–85

A piece of furniture with a major element replaced is generally deemed unsuitable by fine collecting standards. The splat, the principal feature of this chair, is new. The initial clues pointing to this condition are the newly inset pieces of wood in the crest face and plinth back. The centered crest repair includes the lower third of the carved ornament. The violent impact, probably a backward fall of the chair, that caused the splat to break out of its mortises, front and back, could hardly have left this delicate, pierced element undamaged, yet there are no repairs on the splat. Close examination reveals that the splat is unusually thin (5/16-inch), and while the front surface finish blends well with the rest of the chair, the color of the back is uniformly light. Of unusual character are the saucered depressions that appear in the upper volutes at the splat front. Generally these roundels, when not carved, are flat or continue in a slight concavity up the straps toward the crest.

Chairs with looped, pierced splats of this pattern and a carved, foliated crest ornament on a punched ground are generally ascribed to the Boston area, based upon the descent of a chair through an Andover, Massachusetts, family. A plain example without carving or punchwork is branded inside the front seat rail with the name of a late eighteenth-century Boston merchant or his son. The carved crest ornament common to chairs within this subgroup of the owl's-eye pattern occurs in several variations and with either an upright or inverted orientation. The punched grounds are also varied, from the stars on this chair to stipples or O's. The seat frame is usually plain; a rare variant has a scalloped front. Many plain frames are shallower than this one, whether the rails were made for a loose seat or over-the-rail upholstery. The group is about equally divided between pad-foot supports with plain knees and claw feet with leaf-carved knees. Some pad feet are embellished with incised vertical lines, but all, whether plain or scored, are elevated on "cushion" bases in the manner of No. 7. Stretcherless chairs are more common than those with braces; chairs without stretchers have flared and blocked rear feet. Prototypes for the splat, leaf-carved crest ornament, and flared rear feet (in stretcherless chairs) appear in English chairmaking.[1]

NGE

---

**Inscriptions or marks:** *Chiseled, on front seat-rail rabbet, centered:* "V".

**Construction:** The crest is supported on rectangular tenons at the flat-faced backward flaring posts (pinned) and splat. The crest face is cheeked adjacent to the carved terminals. The centered foliate ornament, which is carved in low relief, has an incised surface and star-punched ground. The crest back is rounded at the ends, tips, and center top; the flat center has a chamfered base. The splat is lightly modeled on the face, canted at the edges and piercings, front to back, and tenoned into the plinth. The plinth is hollow on the front and side faces, finished with a shallow top bead, and nailed to the back rail. The rear post edges are chamfered from the seat to the upper back, where the surfaces are rounded. The rectangular seat has a flat lip with an adjacent quarter-round bead; an interior rabbet supports the loose-seat frame. The rails, which are joined to the posts and front leg extensions with vertical rectangular tenons (pinned), are flat at the bottom. Small ogee brackets are nailed at the side-rear corners. The rear legs are chamfered on all corners between the rails and the rear stretcher; the feet are canted on the forward faces and broadly chamfered at the front corners. The front knees have pronounced creases and shallow carving. The ankle backs are flat; the claws have three-knuckle toes with long nails. The side stretchers are joined to the legs with vertical rectangular tenons (pinned at back); horizontal rectangular tenons secure the medial stretcher to the side braces. The rear stretcher is round tenoned into the adjacent members.

**Condition:** The crest face has been repaired by a new 7"-by-1¼" piece of wood at the lower center, including part of the carved ornament. Another facing piece has been inserted at the plinth back. The splat is replaced. The seat-rail bottoms and seat-rail brackets are punctured by tack holes from over-the-rail upholstery. The rear stretcher is probably a replacement, as indicated by its color and poorly defined tips. The loose-seat frame is modern.

**Dimensions:**

| | | |
|---|---|---|
| H. | 34¼ in. | 87.0 cm |
| H. (seat) | 16½ in. | 41.9 cm |
| W. (crest) | 20 in. | 50.8 cm |
| W. (seat front) | 19¾ in. | 50.2 cm |
| W. (seat back) | 16¼ in. | 41.3 cm |
| W. (feet) | 21¾ in. | 55.2 cm |
| D. (seat) | 16¾ in. | 42.5 cm |
| D. (feet) | 20½ in. | 52.1 cm |

**Materials:** *Microanalysis:* Primary: mahogany. *Finish:* medium dark reddish brown color in resin. *Upholstery:* blue-gray cut, uncut, and voided silk velvet; Europe, 1750–1800.

**Publications:** Downs, *American Furniture*, fig. 152.

**Accession history:** Bequest of H. F. du Pont, 1969. 59.2312

---

1. The Andover family chair, now in the Colonial Williamsburg collection, is in Greenlaw, *New England Furniture*, no. 54. The chair, which is scored with lines on the pad feet, is stretcherless and has blocked rear feet. For the plain chair with a branded name, now in the collection of SPNEA, and an English chair of the same pattern, see Jobe and Kaye, *New England Furniture*, no. 109. A stippled ground surrounding the crest ornament appears in the Colonial Williamsburg chair; a ground of O's is illustrated in Randall, *American Furniture*, no. 146. For a scalloped-front seat variant, see *American Antiques from Israel Sack Collection*, 10 vols. (Washington, D.C.: Highland House, ca. 1969–), 2:349.

## 219 ◆ Side chair
United States, possibly New England
1890–1920

The designs of this chair and a close variant with a slimmer baluster splat on a moundlike, rather than an ogee, base are convincing eighteenth-century rural patterns until closely inspected, whereupon it becomes apparent that the chairs are too mechanically regular to be of the period. Most pins that secure the joints are perfectly round. The triple-grooved surfaces are precise, bearing none of the subtle irregularities of handwork (fig. 1). An even quality of execution is also characteristic of the minor ornament: the narrow channels around the edges of the splat and crest top, the horizontal bead across the base of the crest, the rows of gouges at the bottoms of the back feet (fig. 2) and inside faces of the front feet. The narrow- to medium-width chamfers at the back edges of the crest, splat, and posts have a regularity difficult to achieve with hand tools. However, X-ray examination indicates that the mortise-and-tenon joints of the front stretcher and legs are hand-formed, and the cylindrical rear-stretcher tips, which socket into the back legs, are hand-tooled with hollow necks that form a locking device. Another notable feature is the subtle simulated wear on the front stretchers of both chairs. The top surfaces are rounded forward except at the ends, where there are slight rises (fig. 3).

At present, there are six chairs known in the two splat patterns, three identical to that in this chair and three of the second profile. The Shelburne Museum, Shelburne, Vermont, owns one chair of each pattern. The Shelburne mate of Winterthur's chair bears similar first and second finishes on the wood in dark brown and medium blue-green, respectively. The outer surface is painted medium yellowish brown. The alternative pattern may have been the first in the market,

since the rounded splat base is less successful aesthetically than the ogee base of this chair, and the bottoms of the feet lack any trace of gouged ornament. One pin, rather than two, secures the splat-crest joint, and the front seat blocks are "pillowed" on the top surface rather than flat with a decorative hollow channel around the edges, as illustrated. Formerly referred to as Dunlap-school chairs, the only feature common with furniture made by members of the Dunlap family is the hooklike ornament of the splat top. Similar, though not identical, decorative detail occurs on the pediments of several Dunlap chest-on-chests.[1]

*NGE*

**Construction:** The sawed crest is supported on rectangular tenons at the grooved back posts (pinned) and splat (pinned twice). The crest is beaded at the lower front edge and channeled at the top and sides; the rear surface is chamfered across the top and around the tips. The front edges of the splat are defined by a shallow groove of mechanical quality; the rear edges are lightly

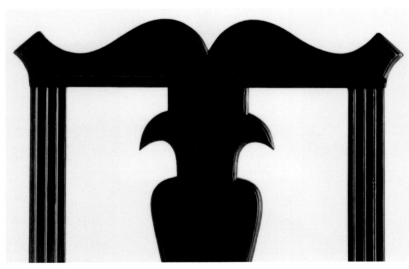

**Fig. 1.** Detail, upper back.

**Fig. 2.** Detail, right rear foot.

**Fig. 3.** Detail, front stretcher.

chamfered. The splat tenons into the stay rail (pinned). The grooved stay rail, which is inset at the back, is tenoned into the back posts (pinned). The post edges are lightly chamfered at the back and along the front edges below the seat. The rounded seat rails are tenoned into the posts and legs; the ends of the front rail are terminated by the seat blocks. The front legs, which are grooved on the outside faces, are tenoned into the seat blocks (pinned). The grooved front stretcher is joined to the legs with rectangular tenons (pinned); the side and rear stretchers are round tenoned into the legs and posts. The back feet are finished with rows of mechanically regular gouges on all faces. Similar gouges occur on the inside faces of the front legs.

**Condition:** The wood surfaces are like new. The chair was repainted in 1965 to match the original finish.

**Dimensions:**

| | | |
|---|---|---|
| H. | 41 in. | 104.1 cm |
| H. (seat) | 17⁵/₈ in. | 44.7 cm |
| W. (crest) | 15³/₄ in. | 40.0 cm |
| W. (seat front) | 18⁵/₈ in. | 47.3 cm |
| W. (seat back) | 14 in. | 35.5 cm |
| W. (feet) | 18 in. | 45.7 cm |
| D. (seat) | 14¹/₈ in. | 35.8 cm |
| D. (feet) | 15¹/₂ in. | 39.3 cm |

**Materials:** *Microanalysis:* Primary: soft maple group. *Finish:* originally painted dark brown covered with glaze; later painted medium-light blue-green, stripped, and painted white; present dark brown color in resin streaked lightly on the wood.

**Publications:** Bishop, *Centuries and Styles of the American Chair*, fig. 210. Marshall B. Davidson, ed., *The American Heritage History of Colonial Antiques* ([New York]: American Heritage Publishing Co., [1967]), fig. 333.

**Accession history:** Museum purchase from Charles F. Montgomery, Wilmington, Del., 1955. 55.104

1. Another chair of the pattern illustrated is in a private collection; a second chair of the alternative splat design was advertised by Jeanne Kendall, *Maine Antique Digest*, May 1983, p. 5-B; a third chair of the alternative design was offered in Northeast Auctions, "Important Americana and Folk Art" (August 3–4, 1991), lot 465.

## 220 ◆ Side chair
Massachusetts or England
Style of 1760–85

No recorded images relate to the splat of this chair. Close examination provides the reason: the splat is a replacement. The "pattern" appears to be a pastiche of elements drawn from several sources, particularly designs such as those in Nos. 50 and 51. The telltale evidence is substantial. The front edges of the splat are sharp, and the surfaces have few signs of wear (fig. 1). The back edges and piercings are narrowly chamfered, leaving little flat surface area (fig. 2). The splat front is colored

yellowish brown, while the other chair parts are reddish brown. The splat back has a bright, smeary, sticky-looking brown finish. Two small triangular piercings have been added to the crest center above the outer splat straps. The alteration is more obvious at the back than the front. Careful inspection indicates that the piercings have broken into the mortise-and-tenon joints securing the splat. The base of the crest adjacent to the splat-top ovals also appears to be somewhat reworked.

In considering whether the rest of the frame is American or British, the evidence is mixed and could be skewed in either direction.

The crest profile with extra peaks is an uncommon one (see fig. 1); it appears in some British chairs with splats similar to that in No. 51. The small, perfectly round crest aperture and delicate ribbonlike carved loops that flank it are unusual and appear to have no close prototypes, not even in British chairmaking. Stop-fluted back posts are rare in both British and American seating furniture. A set of chairs thought to be of Boston origin and a close copy of an English pattern have stop-fluted posts; the feature also appears in plain side chairs with diamond-centered splats like that of No. 58. The delicate chip-carved borders in the splat center could have been copied from a British or an American model. The Boston chairs and British prototype with stop fluting have similar carving. The carved gouges in the British example are long, slim ellipses, as illustrated in this chair; those in the American chairs are small nicks. Again, the feature is uncommon. The over-upholstered oak seat frame and open interior corner braces of this chair are more common in British than in American furniture. Oak is present in another Boston chair (see No. 58), and the set of American chairs mentioned above has open seat-front braces (see also Nos. 52 right, 88). Although the braces of this chair are made of American white pine, documentary sources identify that material as an export product.[1]

*NGE*

**Construction:** The crest is supported on rectangular tenons at the posts and splat. The face is slightly rounded and embellished with delicate, low-relief carving. The rear surface is flat at the center and rounded at the center top and at the ends into the terminals; the center base is chamfered and molded to conform to the upper splat piercings. The crest is curved laterally. The splat face is flat with C scrolls and volutes carved in low relief. The central elements are outlined with borders formed of small, continuous elliptic gouges. The central

**Fig. 1.** Detail, front surface of splat and crest.

**Fig. 2.** Detail, rear surface of splat and crest.

strapwork is delineated in low relief at the crossings and junctures of elements. A pointed ridge is centered in the stem of the large central oval element. The splat edges and piercings are slightly canted, front to back; the back surface is flat with a narrow chamfer around all edges and openings. The three-sided plinth is hollow on the face and sides, finished with a top bead, and nailed to the rear seat rail. The canted back posts have stop-fluted faces with outer beads; the rear surfaces are rounded from crest to seat. The seat rails are joined to the posts and front leg extensions with vertical, rectangular tenons. The back rail, measuring in section 2 1/8" by 1 1/4", is positioned with the broad dimension forming the depth; the front and side rails are thinner. The front seat corners are strengthened with open braces notched into the rails. A 1/8" mahogany veneer is applied to the outside back rail. The rear legs are canted on the forward surface. The front corners of the back feet are chamfered, the inside chamfer continuing to seat level; the back tips are rounded. The front legs are square in section with a chamfer at the inside back corner, top to bottom. The thin rectangular stretchers with crowned tops are tenoned into the adjacent members, except for the medial stretcher, which is dovetailed into the side stretchers from the bottom.

**Condition:** The left crest-post joint is cracked and repaired at the back. The right post top is cracked through and repaired. A narrow full-width piece is broken out of the crest base at the center front forward of the mortise and reattached. Triangular holes at the crest center flanking the circle are newly pierced and partially expose the internal mortise holes. The crest edge is probably also reworked to accommodate the replaced splat. A long, horizontal stress crack occurs on the inside face of the left seat rail. The side seat rails are wider than the front legs by 1/4", the overhang occurring on the inside faces. The side stretchers are repaired with inset wooden pieces on the inside faces adjacent to the medial stretcher dovetails; the left dovetail is chipped.

**Dimensions:**

| | | |
|---|---|---|
| H. | 38 7/8 in. | 98.7 cm |
| H. (seat) | 15 3/4 in. | 40.0 cm |
| W. (crest) | 21 1/8 in. | 53.6 cm |
| W. (seat front) | 22 3/4 in. | 57.8 cm |
| W. (seat back) | 17 3/4 in. | 45.1 cm |
| W. (feet) | 22 1/2 in. | 57.1 cm |
| D. (seat) | 18 in. | 45.7 cm |
| D. (feet) | 21 1/4 in. | 54.0 cm |

**Materials:** *Microanalysis:* Primary: mahogany; mahogany veneer (rear seat rail facing). Secondary: white oak group (rear seat rail); white pine group (left front brace). *Finish:* yellowish brown color in resin (splat face); medium dark brown color with reddish cast, in resin (rest of chair). *Upholstery:* white silk with brocaded vines and floral forms in a diagonal pattern; Europe, 1745–75.

**Accession history:** Purchased by H. F. du Pont from Carl Jacobs, Southwick, Mass., 1956. Bequest of H. F. du Pont, 1969.
56.61

1. For comparable British examples, see Kirk, *American Furniture*, figs. 904, 906, 919, 930–32 (see also fig. 929). For the set of Boston-attributed chairs and the English prototype, see Luke Beckerdite, "Carving Practices in Eighteenth-Century Boston," in *New England Furniture*, pp. 127–33; the Boston chair with oak secondary wood is illustrated on p. 134. White pine for mast use by the British Royal Navy was removed from the area of Goffstown, N.H., before the revolutionary war. Undoubtedly, some logs were judged unfit for that purpose in Britain and sold to timber merchants; *Dunlaps and Their Furniture*, pp. 18–19.

## 221 ◆ Settee
### Boston, Massachusetts
### 1770–85

Chairback settees are rare in eighteenth-century American furniture. The form is also uncommon in British chairmaking, where preference was given to long, fully upholstered seats. Of the major English furniture designers who published during the 1750s and 1760s, only Manwaring pictured settees with backs divided into chair sections, and those were illustrated among his designs for rural seating. Manwaring, along with Chippendale and Ince and Mayhew, probably intended that single chair designs be adapted for use in expanded seating.[1]

The chairback settee, which first appeared in English households during the reign of

Charles II (1660–85), was probably identified initially by size—a double chair or a "treble" chair—since the term *settee* appears to have become current only in the early eighteenth century. When Queen Anne and Chippendale styles provided greater design flexibility, chairback settees generally were produced as part of a suite of furniture with side chairs and armchairs. Splats ranged from Gothic, Chinese, and ribbon patterns to slotted and interlaced-loop styles. Several New England families are known to have owned English settees in the Chinese and slotted-back patterns. The "two Settees, with chairs suitable to them" sold from the Boston household of Thomas James Grunchy in 1758 could also have been of English origin, since Grunchy was "intending shortly for Europe." American production of chairback

settees was centered principally in eastern Massachusetts, where several owl's-eye (see No. 31) and diamond-centered figure-eight examples (as illustrated) have family histories.[2]

Although this settee is closely related to the side chair of No. 58, there are notable pattern differences, including carved versus plain crests and leaf-patterned plain-claw legs versus asymmetrically carved, hairy-paw supports. Less obvious are the splat differences: the absence of small projecting scrolls, top and bottom, in the settee; the longer vertical points of the chair diamond; and the tapering figure-eight strap crossings within the settee diamonds (fig. 1). Comparison of the carved work in the settee crest with that in side chairs of carved, open-arch crest identifies two leafy patterns. One approximates a continuous ruffle; the other consists of five, slightly irregular, modeled points resembling tongues of fire. The settee, which falls into the latter category, is also patterned with a single line of punchwork triangles between the leaf tongues and the C scroll bordering the open arch (see fig. 1). The same leaf-and-punchwork pattern appears in a side chair at the Museum of Art, Rhode Island School of Design, Providence. That chair has similarly oriented over-and-under splat crossings, tapered figure-eight straps within the diamond, and carved knees and claws. If the two pieces of furniture were not once part of the same suite, they originated in the same shop. The side chair was purchased by the donor's grandfather in Boston at one of the many sales of household furnishings from the John Hancock mansion on Beacon Hill.[3]

Unlike its matching side chair, the settee was substantially altered and later restored. Sometime during the second half of the nineteenth century, it was "Victorianized" by the installation of a high sprung seat. This led to removing the arms and internal seat brace and shortening all the legs by about 1 1/4 inches. The feet are now pieced out (fig. 2), and the arms and supports are replaced with old parts. In converting the settee to what was, perhaps, a Turkish-style sofa, narrow wooden strips forming a rectangular frame extending above the seat rails were glued to the front and side rabbets and along the inside face of the back rail, the latter reinforced with screws. Three-inch webbing strips were nailed crosswise and front to back to the bottom edges of the rails. To the webbing were sewed the base coils of upright helical springs tied in compression with twine. A sack cloth covered the coils and was nailed to the outside faces of the new seat frame. Stuffing and an undercover were placed over the sackcloth, and the cover was nailed in place. The undercovers and stuffing were quilted on the top, and the side edges were stitched to provide rigidity and a square edge. The new

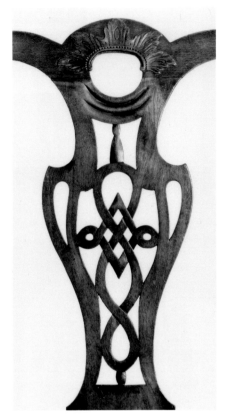

**Fig. 1.** Detail, right crest center and splat.

seat possibly extended as much as two inches above the present seat rails. The finish cover may have had a ruffled flounce attached to the face of the new seat frame; fabric was perhaps draped over the settee back. The open dovetails on the back posts suggest that padded arms likely were attached at the old joints (fig. 3).[4]

The existence of two other settees in this pattern provides information concerning the arm restoration. The elbows of one settee have long, overhanging scrolls at the front, similar to those in No. 31. The arms of the second settee are a broader version of the pattern illustrated, complete with ogee-curved and molded supports. The scroll ends of the arms are placed on the support tops; the support bases are attached toward the front on the side rails. Chippendale delineated "French Chairs" with similar elbows in the 1762 edition of the *Director*. However, arms of this style are more common in postwar American neoclassical chairs than in prewar seating, suggesting that Winterthur's settee dates toward the end of the Chippendale style period in Massachusetts.

**Fig. 2.** Detail, right front leg.

A review of four settees in the owl's-eye pattern substantiates this statement. Three settees, which are supported on cabriole legs, have scrolled arms with long overhangs at the front and posts mounted midway from front to back on the side rails. A fourth example, constructed with straight Marlborough legs—a support type that was introduced after the cabriole leg was in vogue—has French arms.[5]

The original settee arms and supports were replaced using old mahogany parts; the "new" elbows were attached at the original joints, necessitating their agreement in style with the original elbows. The parts probably came from another settee or a large English chair, since

**Fig. 3.** Detail, right rear post and arm joint.

**Fig. 4.** Detail, right arm front and support post.

**Fig. 5.** Detail, right arm support base.

the settee depth is several inches greater than that of the average late eighteenth-century American armchair. The fit is close but not perfect. The arms are loose in the post joints, the gaps partially filled with composition material. The supports are angled backward from the vertical ever so slightly, and there is a sizable gap in the rail at the forward edge of the right post (fig. 4). The scroll-and-post connection has also been reworked slightly. Approximately 1/16-inch to 1/8-inch has been removed from the scroll base, flattening the bottom curve and causing the post top to project slightly all around the connection. The post bases have also been shortened, perhaps by as much as half an inch, and unevenly chamfered. Half of an old screw hole remains at the base of the right post (fig. 5).[6]

*NGE*

**Construction:** The crest is supported on rectangular tenons at the canted posts and splats. The flat crest face is slightly cheeked at the tips and carved with low-relief ornament at the center arches. The carved leafy ornaments are incised for accent and separated from the inner C scrolls by single continuous bands of punchwork triangles. The back surface is flat across the center from tip to tip and rounded, top and bottom, except at the center arches, which are flat. The flat splat faces are modeled at the channels forming the drapery and at the central strap crossings. The upper tassels and lower beads are rounded; the pointed central diamond tips are cushioned and rounded backward. The splat edges and piercings are canted, front to back; the bases are tenoned into the plinths. The plinths are hollow on the front and sides, finished with low top beads, and nailed to the rear seat rail. An extra piece of wood is inserted at the center between the posts and nailed to the seat rail. The back posts are flat on the front surfaces and rounded at the back, crest to seat. The contoured arms are rabbeted to the back posts and secured by screws concealed by wooden plugs. The arm fronts are supported on tenons at the support tops and nailed or pinned from the inside faces; both scroll faces are carved with volutes. The contoured arm supports are molded on the forward faces to a serpentine profile flanked by beads. The bases are rabbeted to the side rails and secured by two countersunk screws (modern) from the inside surfaces; the lower outside edges are chamfered. The shallow seat rails are tenoned into the corner back posts and the front leg extensions (double-pinned). The flat top lip is finished with a quarter-round bead at the outside edge; the interior frame is rabbeted at the front and sides to support the loose-seat frame. Ogee brackets at the side rear and back rail corners are nailed twice; the side brackets are chamfered on the inside edges. All back legs are canted on the forward surfaces; the lower legs flare backward. The center back leg is wider than the end legs. The front legs are carved in low relief on the knees and brackets. The brackets are attached with two nails and chamfered on the inside edges. The claw feet have two-knuckle toes.

**Condition:** Unexplained nail or screw holes centered in each upper-back crest arch may have once supported small wall bumpers. Composition material secures a loose joint at the left rear arm and back post rabbet. A nail possibly secures the front post joint from the inside scroll face. A modern wooden pin secures the right front arm joint from the inside scroll face; the arm tip is cracked diagonally across the face in two places. The right arm support fits loosely in the rail rabbet. The interior screws securing the arm supports to the seat rails are modern but fitted into the original countersunk holes. Both arms and arm supports have been replaced using old parts. A full-length cleat (a later addition) was once glued and screwed to the inside face of the back rail, the top at rabbet level. A central, front-to-back, saddled seat brace, dovetailed at the front and tenoned at the back, is a modern replacement. Spaced clusters of holes (from nailed girt web) occur on the inside faces of the end rails and the lower edges of all rails. A small piece of wood is missing from the flat seat lip at the right front leg extension; the left leg extension is patched at the same place. The center back leg, which apparently cracked at the tenon, appears to have been repaired with a double-tongue pinned once on the rail, inside and out, and twice on the inside upper leg. The front leg extensions are cracked vertically through the pins, once at the right end and twice at the left. The front and rear legs are pieced out at the bottom to a height of 1 1/8" to 1 1/4". The loose-seat frame is modern.

**Dimensions:**

| | | |
|---|---|---|
| H. | 39 in. | 99.0 cm |
| H. (seat) | 16 1/2 in. | 41.9 cm |
| W. (crest) | 57 5/8 in. | 146.3 cm |
| W. (seat front) | 58 1/4 in. | 147.9 cm |
| W. (seat back) | 54 1/4 in. | 137.8 cm |
| W. (arms) | 60 in. | 152.4 cm |
| W. (feet) | 60 1/4 in. | 153.0 cm |
| D. (seat) | 23 1/2 in. | 59.7 cm |
| D. (feet) | 27 1/4 in. | 69.2 cm |

**Materials:** *Microanalysis:* Primary: mahogany. *Finish:* muddied, medium brown color with reddish cast, in resin. *Upholstery:* modern blue wool moreen.

**Publications:** Wendy A. Cooper, "American Chippendale Chairback Settees: Some Sources and Related Examples," *American Art Journal* 9, no. 2 (November 1977): 40, fig. 7.

**Accession history:** Museum purchase from John S. Walton, Inc., New York, 1957, with funds given by H. F. du Pont. 57.31.5

---

1. Robert Manwaring, *The Cabinet and Chair-Maker's Real Friend and Companion* (London: Henry Webley, 1765), pls. 29–32.

2. Sale notice in *Boston Newsletter*, November 2, 1758, as quoted in Dow, *Arts and Crafts in New England,* pp. 117–18. Macquoid and Edwards, *Dictionary,* 3:70–101. Wendy A. Cooper, "American Chippendale Chairback Settees: Some Sources and Related Examples," *American Art Journal* 9, no. 2 (November 1977): 34–45.

3. A chair carved in the leafy-ruffle pattern is illustrated in Kirk, *American Chairs,* fig. 118. For the side chair, see Monkhouse and Michie, *American Furniture,* cat. 113.

4. I am indebted to Robert F. Trent for his insights on this transformation.

5. Cooper, "Chairback Settees," figs. 8, 9, 11–15. Thomas Chippendale, *The Gentleman and Cabinet-Maker's Director* (3d ed.; London: By the author, 1762), pls. 19, 22, 23. For neoclassical chairs with related arms, see *John Brown House Loan Exhibition,* cat. 15; *American Antiques from Israel Sack Collection,* 10 vols. (Washington, D.C.: Highland House, ca. 1969–), 1:179; 4:1076.

6. I am indebted to Michael S. Podmaniczky, Robert F. Trent, and Clare G. Noyes for their helpful insights in working out the thorny details of the arm restoration.

## 222 ◆ High chest of drawers
### Eastern Massachusetts
### 1735–55

This tall chest is part of a small number of expensive, ornate cases produced by Boston cabinetmakers and allied artisans during the mid eighteenth century for a select group of affluent customers. Forms include high chests of drawers, dressing tables, desk-and-bookcases, and clock cases. Surface interest was achieved through the use of fine cabinet woods, handsome veneers, and colorful japanwork (see No. 160). Structural variety extended to blocked and bombé shapes. Customers could also choose from a range of special decoration that included bold carving, rich gilding, intricate inlay, applied and freestanding turned work, fluting, and fretwork.[1]

**Fig. 1.** Detail, lower right case side.

Among the ornate forms, this chest is somewhat restrained, however. Surfaces are extensively inlaid, although aside from the prominent fans in the drawers and the stars (compass roses) on the tympanum and case sides (fig. 1), the decoration is subtle. Narrow bands, composed of one dark and two light strings, border all drawers, divide the large drawers in half, outline the tympanum and side panels, and form a vertical stripe on the front corners of the lower case. Small quarter circles of banding mark the inlaid corners of the side panels. Fluted pilasters provide visual definition for the upper case just as the vertical inlays above the legs distinguish the lower case.

Eastern Massachusetts high chests with plain, arched recesses in the center top and bottom drawers are relatively common, but examples with ornamented recesses are unusual. Rarest are chests with carved and gilded shells; cases with fan-inlaid recesses are only slightly more common. The inlaid device is one copied from English casework, principally the chest-on-chest and desk-and-bookcase, forms that were uncommon with this decoration in American cabinetmaking (see No. 192). American craftsmen transferred the feature to the high chest and its matching dressing table. The pattern illustrated appears more frequently than others and in versions with seven, eight, or nine ribs. A dressing table in the Cincinnati Art Museum, which is a close mate to Winterthur's chest, appears to have originated in the same shop. The fan and banded inlay are the same, except in one

respect: the dressing table lacks an inlaid border at the drawer's edge below the fan. The profiles of the legs and skirt pendants also vary slightly.[2]

Inlaid stars were a popular case ornament among woodworkers and consumers in Boston and vicinity when Winterthur's chest was made, and two basic patterns are present here. On the tympanum, eight-pointed stars are fabricated of light and dark wood. The thick, diamond-shape points are divided into four compartments of opposing color. The figure creates the illusion of a circle at the center. On the case sides, eight-pointed stars of similar color and shape have slimmer, longer points, minimizing the circular figure (fig. 1). Confirming contemporary terminology appears in a Nantucket, Massachusetts, estate inventory describing "a Mahogany Desk with a Star in the fall."[3]

Two star-inlaid casepieces contemporary with this high chest are documented to Boston cabinetmakers—both are dated "1739." William Parkman (1685–1776) constructed a fall-front desk with a large star in the style of that on the sides of Winterthur's chest. Ebenezer Hartshorne (also Hartshern; 1690–1781), a resident of Charlestown (later of Boston), made and dated an elegant chest of drawers veneered with figured walnut and carved with gilt shells in the arched recesses. The sides of Hartshorne's case have inlaid stars similar to those in the Parkman desk.[4]

Despite the glories of Winterthur's high chest, it has been compromised to a "degree . . . approaching a critical level"—

raising questions about its desirability for the Winterthur collection and negating its former status as an icon of Boston material culture in the Queen Anne period.[5] A substantial loss is the closed hood that once filled the space behind the scrolled pediment. An irregularly trimmed backboard and thin sheets of wood forming a crudely installed flat roof are evidence that it once existed (fig. 2). The pediment molding is patched adjacent to the central finial and completely replaced above the left pilaster and along the left side. Cracks in the scrollboard (tympanum) include those formed where the board was originally pieced to size at the upper necks. All the finials are replaced; only a central turning was in place originally.

Serious problems also exist at the waist of the high chest where the upper and lower cases meet. Extensive abrasion on the outside surface of the bottom board of the upper case indicates that the top of the chest was removed from the base and placed on a rough surface for a period of time. The waist moldings were removed and later restored incorrectly. The upper case probably was originally elevated above its present position so that a walnut facing attached to the front of the bottom board was exposed above the moldings of the lower case. As now indicated, those moldings included forward projecting plinths for the pilasters at the front corners, but the plinths were linked by a front molding of the same height; the side returns were also mounted at plinth level. The pilasters, which have been shortened at the bottom (fig. 3),

**Fig. 2.** Detail, case top and back of pediment.

may once have had plain facing blocks at the bases corresponding to those at the top. Given the unusual piecing of the pilaster tops at the level of the fluting, the pilasters probably were cut down at both ends.[6]

Other problems, when considered collectively, further erode the integrity of this piece of furniture. Two of the two- or three-board case sides have split at their butted joints, defacing the star inlays (see fig. 1). In many areas, the banded inlay is repaired or replaced. The finials are new, as are the turned drops below the front skirt. The brass hardware is not original, and an unidentified former fitting in the upper shell drawer left four small holes, which are now plugged. One rear foot is defaced.

NGE

**Fig. 3.** Detail, waist molding and bottom of left pilaster.

**Inscriptions or marks:** *On inside front of fan drawer in upper case:* indecipherable scrolls in white chalk. *Stamped on back of replaced escutcheons:* "IC".

**Construction:** (Upper case) The vertical two-board sides (the individual board widths inconsistent, right and left) are joined to the two-board bottom with irregularly spaced dovetails. The three-board scrollboard (the neck areas pieced near the top) is lapped to the front of the case sides and reinforced on the back with several vertical blocks. The backboard is now level with the side cornices (cut down). A cove molding nailed to the case sides and scrollboard has short returns at the top of the pediment. Behind the pediment, the flat case top is covered with thin boards nailed to the top of the backboard, case sides, and internal bracing members of the front. Large quarter-round glueblocks at the

inside upper corners of the case reinforce the construction. The top drawer blade is let into the sides on a sliding groove and extends the full depth of the case, providing a dust board below the top row of drawers. The remaining blades are let in the front of the case sides. The joints are covered by vertical stiles notched into the blade ends and possibly nailed to the front faces of the case sides. The fluted pilasters, which have separate heads, are nailed to the stiles. The bottom front rail is nailed to the top of the bottom board. The vertical dividers between the small drawers are joined to their adjacent members with shouldered dovetails. The top dividers are further nailed to the inner edges of the scrollboard. Four drawer guides in the upper tier are nailed to the dust board. In the second tier, the center runner is butt-lapped

to the front and butted to the backboard, secured with a nail from the back; a guide is glued and nailed to the top surface. Side runners and guides are glued to the case sides. In the third and fourth tiers, runners with guides nailed to the top are nailed at the back from the outside surface of the backboard. At the front, the runners are lapped and nailed to the drawer blades. Runners for the bottom drawer are nailed to the case bottom; guides are nailed to the runners. The backboard, made of three lap-joined horizontal boards, is nailed to a rabbet in the case sides.

(Lower case) The top is open; top boards, once slotted into the front rail and set in a rabbet on the backboard, are missing. The backboard and the horizontally butted two-board and three-board (left) case sides are tenoned and pinned to the corner posts. A waist molding, shaped at the corners to form bases for the pilasters, is nailed to the upper edge of the case front and sides. The case sides are shaped in a double-ogee curve at the lower edge; an applied beading is secured with rosehead nails. The top rail and skirt are tenoned to the corner posts. The blade is secured to the corner posts with shouldered dovetails. Shouldered dovetails also secure the vertical drawer dividers to their adjacent members. Inside the case, a series of three random-width boards nailed to the sides provide additional support for the frame. Outer drawer runners are attached to the bracing boards with wrought nails. Inner drawer runners behind the dividers are bevel-lapped to the blade and skirt at the front and tenoned to the backboard at the back. Guides are glued or nailed to the top surface. The legs and corner posts are one piece. Knee blocks are glued to the case front and sides. All drawers are similarly constructed. The corners are dovetailed. The sides are double-beaded on the top edge; the backs are flat on the top. The drawer bottom boards, which run from front to back, are rabbeted and nailed at the front, set into grooves on the sides, and nailed flush at the back. The drawer fronts are thumb molded on four sides, and the side lips butt against the case facade. Banded inlay, composed of light-dark-light strings, outlines the scrollboard, all four edges of the upper case sides (with open quarter-circles at the corners), the sides and top of the lower case sides (with open quarter-circles at the top corners), and the drawer fronts. Double vertical bands accent the centers of the long drawers, and single bands accent the front faces of the corner posts in the lower case. Arched bands surround the fans on the small drawers. The rays of the fans are formed of dark bands flanked by light ones. The stars of the scrollboard and the case sides, top and bottom, are formed of alternating light and dark wedges forming elongated diamonds.

**Condition:** The side finials and plinths are new (the pediment originally had only a center finial), and the center finial has been replaced. The original roofed enclosure behind the pediment has been removed and the backboard behind it cut off, leaving an irregular edge. The present case top reutilizes some original roof boards and some new and recycled wood. There are several splits in the upper portion of the scrollboard; two are caused by the separation of the pieced boards in the upper necks. The glueblocks behind the scrollboard are replacements. The right front cornice molding is patched at the center front. The left side cornice molding and the section (two pieces) above the left pilaster are replaced; the right side cornice molding

and the section above the right pilaster have been renailed. The backboard at the top of the upper case has been cut down; the two lower boards are replaced. Four plugged holes on the shell drawer in the upper section probably once accommodated an interim pull; the holes do not penetrate the drawer front. One drawer guide is missing from the upper tier. A corner block is missing from the inside upper right case front. There is an unusual amount of wear on the bottom of the upper case, suggesting that the case was apart for some time. The waist molding on the lower case is replaced; the present plinth blocks, which are now part of the lower case, are made of mahogany rather than walnut. All case sides, upper and lower, have split at their butted-board joints; the separations have defaced the inlaid ornament, except at the upper right side. The drawer runner behind the center divider in the second top tier has been reworked. The applied beading is missing from the front skirt. The drops are new. The knee brackets at the right front, left rear, and left side front are replacements; the other knee brackets have been reglued. The right rear foot is severely worn away at the outside of the pad. Several drawer bottoms are split: upper case—left top drawer and two long drawers; lower case—fan drawer. The drawer interiors are lined with paper, except in the top tier of the upper case. There are numerous repairs to the banding and to the inlays of the stars. The hardware is replaced.

**Dimensions:**

| | | |
|---|---|---|
| H. (case) | 83 1/4 in. | 211.4 cm |
| W. (cornice) | 42 in. | 106.7 cm |
| W. (upper case) | 39 in. | 99.1 cm |
| W. (lower case) | 41 1/2 in. | 105.4 cm |
| W. (feet) | 43 1/4 in. | 109.8 cm |
| D. (cornice) | 21 5/8 in. | 54.9 cm |
| D. (upper case) | 20 1/4 in. | 51.4 cm |
| D. (lower case) | 21 1/4 in. | 53.9 cm |
| D. (feet) | 22 3/4 in. | 57.7 cm |

**Materials:** *Microanalysis:* Primary: American black walnut. Secondary: white pine group (drawer linings, backboards of upper and lower case); cherry (replacement drops); mahogany (replacement cornice molding, plinth blocks). *Finish:* medium orange-brown color in resin.

**Publications:** Downs, *American Furniture*, fig. 190. Helena Hayward, ed., *World Furniture: An Illustrated History* (New York: McGraw-Hill Book Co., 1965), p. 185, fig. 693. Lester Margon, *More American Furniture Treasures, 1620–1840* (New York: Architectural Book Publishing Co., 1971), p. 243. Walter Muir Whitehill and Norman Kotker, *Massachusetts: A Pictorial History* (New

York: Charles Scribner's Sons, 1976), p. 62. Hazel Harrison, ed., *World Antiques* (London: Hamlyn Publishing Group, 1978), p. 58, fig. 176. Victoria Kloss Ball, *Architecture and Interior Design: Europe and America from the Colonial Era to Today* (New York: John Wiley and Sons, 1980), p. 216, fig. 5.42. Jay E. Cantor, *Winterthur* (New York: Harry N. Abrams, 1985), p. 148. Marshall B. Davidson, *The American Heritage History of Colonial Antiques* ([New York]: American Heritage Publishing Co., [1967]), p. 124. Brock Jobe, "The Boston Furniture Industry, 1720–1740," in *Boston Furniture*, p. 22, fig. 17.

**Accession history:** Purchased by H. F. du Pont from Joe Kindig, Jr., York, Pa., 1948. Gift of H. F. du Pont, 1965.
54.522

1. Brock Jobe, "The Boston Furniture Industry, 1720–1740," in *Boston Furniture*, pp. 13–24; Jobe and Kaye, *New England Furniture*, pp. 3–26. Representative furniture is in Heckscher, *American Furniture*, pp. 236–45; Flanigan, *American Furniture*, cat. No. 20; Randall, *American Furniture*, no. 54 and frontispiece; Miller, "Roman Gusto," pp. 160, 165, 167–69, 172–77, 180–81, 183–85, 189–94; Christie's, "Property from the Estate of Mrs. Lansdell K. Christie" (January 27, 1996), lot 329.

2. Representative examples of high chests with plain recesses are in Benjamin Ginsburg advertisement, *Antiques* 110, no. 5 (November 1976): 865; Wayne Pratt advertisement, *Antiques* 136, no. 3 (September 1989): 372. A representative example of a high chest with gilded shells is in Flanigan, *American Furniture*, cat. 20. English chests with inlaid fans are in Macquoid and Edwards, *Dictionary*, 2:43, fig. 36; Kirk, *American Furniture*, fig. 635. A Massachusetts double chest with inlaid fan is in Edward S. Cooke, Jr., "The Warland Chest: Early Georgian Furniture in Boston," *Maine Antique Digest*, March 1987, p. 10-C; this chest and No. 192, which is similarly embellished, have decidedly English constructional features. The related dressing table is in Nutting, *Furniture Treasury*, no. 400.

3. Peter Coffin estate inventory, 1800, Registry of Probate, Nantucket Co., Mass.

4. The Parkman desk is in Dorothy E. Ellesin, ed., "Collectors' Notes," *Antiques* 107, no. 5 (May 1975): 952–53. The Hartshorne high chest is in Randall, *American Furniture*, no. 54.

5. An initial formal statement about the condition of this chest was made by Michael S. Podmaniczky, furniture conservator, Winterthur, on March 30, 1988, in an examination report; see folder 54.522, Registration Office, Winterthur.

6. Representative examples of high chests having waist moldings and pilaster bases that probably reflect the original treatment of Winterthur's chest are in Heckscher, *American Furniture*, cat. no. 157; Flanigan, *American Furniture*, cat. no. 20; Sara Greene advertisement, *Antiques* 104, no. 4 (October 1973): 555.

## 223 ◆ Chest of drawers
New England, in the style of Connecticut Style of 1750–75, probably made late in the nineteenth century

A fantasy of this magnitude is a worthy subject of study on many levels: technical, artistic, historical, and so on. However, the most intriguing angle is humanistic. That is, to look back at ourselves, the viewers, in order to shed some light on our own skills and standards of connoisseurship. That we now happen to be on the enlightened side of that moment in history when a researcher first noticed that the chest was not what it appeared should give little comfort since we are almost certainly on the *wrong* side of another, similar discovery that has not yet been revealed. Thus, to condemn an earlier generation for such a misunderstanding requires self-condemnation when something now in our midst is exposed.

This chest has indeed been made from whole cloth. However, since we are unable to ever look at it again with the eye of the uninitiated, we can never know exactly what was seen before the secret was out. How did so many eyes pass favorably over so many inconsistencies? How could filled holes and shadows of drawer hardware on the boards making up the sides be more obvious? There is no answer (fig. 1).

Although the connoisseur can claim a lack of technical understanding in having overlooked these glaring pieces of physical evidence, what of the inconsistency of overall design or the individual design details? As plain as the filled holes is the visual disunity of the facade design. How could so many viewers not be jarred by shells without their accustomed lower blocking or not be confused by the tortured irresolution of the concave blocking? Alongside another legitimate block-and-shell chest, this piece simply does not measure up. And yet, for a time it did.

Every break, loss, mark, abrasion, or discoloration on an object had a moment of creation, and the task of the examiner is to unravel the story woven into this texture. This is a holistic task, sometimes requiring technical expertise, sometimes historical understanding or design sensitivity, but always requiring dogged insistence that each detail under consideration be justifiable, that is, understood for what it is and how it was induced. And finally, any examination that does not question previous observations and assumptions will rarely root out false assumptions independently.

Once the eyes are opened, this chest can easily be seen for what it is—namely, an object made up from parts of other, disassembled objects, overly embellished with added carving

and enriched with never-before-seen decorative details in order to produce a seriously overdone expression. Furthermore, it would be difficult to imagine any motivation for this hoax other than deceit for unethical gain.

*MSP*

**Inscriptions or marks:** *On the inside of the back of all drawers:* shop mark "∧" in chalk.

**Construction:** The three-board top has stepped ogee-molded front and side edges. It is attached from the underside to battens fastened across the front and back. A series of applied glueblocks are attached on the inside edge of the battens and along the join of the top and sides. Below the top, a separate cornice molding is nailed to the front and sides. Two tongue-and-groove horizontal boards—one very wide and one narrow—form the backboard and are nailed to rabbets in the sides. The top and bottom rails and the blades are slotted into the sides; the join is covered by an applied facing beaded on the inside edge. On the drawers the projecting shells are applied and the recessed shells cut from solid wood; the inside surface of the drawer front is flat. The drawers are of dovetail construction with the drawer back thicker than the sides. The top edge of the sides is flat; the top of the back is chamfered on the outer edge. The drawer bottoms, the grain from side to side, are set into a rabbet in the front and grooves on the sides; battens have been applied. The drawer runners are attached to the sides with countersunk wood screws. The bottom board is dovetailed to the sides. A 1/2"-thick spacer board has been inserted to fill a gap between the bottom board and the front base molding. An elaborately scrolled skirt is applied below the front base molding. Heavy horizontal glueblocks above a shaped vertical block reinforce the join of the leg facings and the case. These blocks are nailed in place.

**Condition:** The case has been constructed reusing old materials and incorporating some new wood. The sides are fabricated from old drawer fronts. The drawers have been rebuilt. Patches indicate where other furniture hardware was placed. The feet have been reworked. The skirt is new. A photograph of the piece taken before its purchase in 1929 shows the original skirt and foot pattern.[1] The hardware also is replaced.

**Dimensions:**

| | | |
|---|---|---|
| H. | 33 1/4 in. | 84.5 cm |
| W. (top) | 35 5/8 in. | 90.6 cm |
| W. (case) | 33 1/8 in. | 84.1 cm |
| W. (feet) | 36 in. | 91.4 cm |
| D. (top) | 19 in. | 48.3 cm |
| D. (case) | 17 5/8 in. | 44.9 cm |
| D. (feet) | 19 in. | 48.3 cm |

**Materials:** *Microanalysis:* Primary: cherry. Secondary: white pine group (drawer linings, backboard, bottom board, battens, glueblocks). *Finish:* orange-brown color in resin.

**Fig. 1.** Detail, interior.

**Exhibitions:** Worcester Art Museum, Worcester, Mass., March 1929.

**Publications:** Downs, *American Furniture*, fig. 171.

**Provenance:** Ex coll.: Miss Frances H. Butler. Concerning the history of the chest, Mrs. George Lincoln wrote: "It may amuse you to know how my mother came into possession of the bureau. A middle-aged lady by the name of Miss Frances Butler of New Haven once visited a friend in Woodstock with the intention of staying three weeks. She extended her visit, and finally stayed thirty years! During Miss Butler's old age my mother frequently called upon her, and Miss Butler eventually bequeathed the bureau to my mother as a token of appreciation. We regret that we do not know how Miss Butler obtained the piece."[2]

**Accession history:** Purchased by H. F. du Pont from Mrs. Rufus B. Richardson, Woodstock, Conn., 1929. Bequest of H. F. du Pont, 1969. 57.507

1. Describing the chest, the New York dealer Albert Collings wrote: "I went up to Worcester yesterday and saw the block front. It is a genuine old piece but was put in order perhaps twenty-five years ago by a very unskilled cabinet maker. The feet have been very poorly pieced out about three inches on the bottoms. These pieces have to come off and the work properly done. It has had a little patching up in other places that can be improved. For all its faults it is a mighty attractive piece and there is nothing else like it. It will be an addition to any good collection" (Albert Collings to H. F. du Pont, dated May 22, 1929, Winterthur Archives).

2. Mrs. George Lincoln to H. F. du Pont, June 21, 1921, Winterthur Archives.

## 224 ◆ Desk-on-frame
New England
1735–60, with later alterations

Wood identification can occasionally help assign a region or date to an object. For example, the use of beech usually indicates European origin, and ash is found more commonly in nineteenth-century rather than eighteenth-century furniture. But what to do with the appearance of a wood species that is simply not used at all? Elm is one of these woods.

Although "English" elm was (and is) used extensively in Great Britain, its American counterpart is so difficult to work that it is usually found only as wooden wheel hubs, heavy equipment handles, or flooring in horse stalls.

This is because of the anatomical feature of interlocked grain. That is, the gentle spiral twist to the grain seen in the trunk of many species of trees is disrupted in elm. Every few years, the twist changes direction, resulting in grain that is so woven together that it is literally impossible to split and very difficult to shape or plane. This is not the case in the English species.

Although the various species of elm (genus *Ulmus*) cannot be separated by microscopic examination, when elm appears in a piece of furniture it nearly always implies English origin, with reliquary objects such as furniture made from Liberty Tree or the Penn Treaty Elm being notable exceptions.[1] This vernacular desk presents a problem because elm is used for the legs of the frame, which has raised the question, Could the frame be a later addition/replacement? However, the use of elm at *any* time, either by the original maker or a later restorer, is a questionable act, making the point of authenticity moot. The sheer naïveté required to use elm could in fact be argued to

support the originality of the frame. A restorer would almost certainly use the same woods throughout so as not to draw attention to his handiwork, but a rural cabinetmaker would be familiar with the use of elm in farm implements or other heavy-duty construction and so may have chosen it as an acceptable alternative to the more usual cabinet woods.

The originality of the frame to the desk is also called into question by the drawer construction since the drawer in the frame does not exhibit the same details as those above it. Strangely enough, the drawer in the

frame does correspond to the small interior drawers. The bottoms of the large desk drawers are set into grooves in the fronts and sides, but the bottoms of the frame drawer and interior drawers sit in rabbets, flush with the lower edges. Because these questions cannot be fully resolved, this desk remains, for the moment, in curatorial limbo.

*MSP*

**Inscriptions or marks:** *On underside of upper row of desk drawers:* "I", "II", "III" *left to right, in pencil. On underside of lower row of desk drawers:* "4", "5",

"6" left to right, in pencil. *On the bottom of the upper left drawer, desk section:* "Mr/ Sam/ olB/ 663" in chalk. *On right side of top left and lower left drawer:* "2" *in chalk. On bottom lower middle drawer:* "7-10-0" *or* "5-10-9" *in chalk.*

**Construction:** (Desk section) The top is full-blind dovetailed to the sides. The hinged fall-front lid, made of a solid board with batten ends, opens to rest on small undecorated lopers. Inside, the desk is divided into three vertical sections, each with two pigeonholes above two tiers of blocked drawers. The drawer fronts have an unlipped thumbnail-molded edge. The sides are rounded on the upper edge; the back has a tiny chamfer. The drawer bottoms, rabbeted on the front and flush over the sides and back, are nailed on four sides; the back edge has a tiny chamfer. A well in the writing surface gives access to the space below. The top rail is joined to the sides on an exposed shouldered dovetail; the blades are joined on an exposed shouldered half-dovetail. The ends of the top rail and the blades pierce the sides. The drawer runners are nailed to the sides. The long drawers are double-beaded on the upper edge of the sides and flat on the back. The drawer bottoms, the grain front to back, are dadoed to the front, rabbeted to the sides, and nailed across the back; battens are glued in place. The bottom board is dovetailed to the sides. The backboard, two thick horizontal tongue-and-groove boards chamfered on all four edges, is nailed to rabbets in the top and sides and flush to the back edge of the bottom board.

(Lower case) A molding is nailed to the top of the frame. The sides and rear rail are double-tenoned to the legs. The front rail is single-tenoned. The drawer runners are bevel-lapped to the front rail and tenoned to the backboard. The drawer is constructed in the same manner as those in the case above.

**Condition:** The stock used for the desk is not of high quality. The right front corner of the top is repaired. The molded-edge rail above the writing surface of the desk may be replaced. There are several ink stains on the desk top and writing

**Fig. 1.** Desk open.

surface. On the frame, a section of the front molding above the lock has been patched, and a split in the right side molding has been repaired. A portion of the right rear foot is missing. The lock is missing from the long drawer in the frame. The brass backplates and bail handles are original.

**Dimensions:**

| | | |
|---|---|---|
| H. | 38 3/4 in. | 98.4 cm |
| H. (writing surface) | 30 1/8 in. | 76.5 cm |
| W. (upper case) | 23 7/8 in. | 60.6 cm |
| W. (lower case) | 25 7/8 in. | 65.7 cm |
| W. (feet) | 25 1/2 in. | 64.8 cm |
| D. (upper case) | 13 5/8 in. | 34.7 cm |
| D. (lower case) | 14 1/2 in. | 36.8 cm |
| D. (feet) | 14 3/4 in. | 37.5 cm |

**Materials:** *Microanalysis:* Primary: cherry (desk, frame); elm (legs). Secondary: white pine group (drawer linings, backboard, back rail of frame). *Finish:* reddish brown color in resin.

**Accession history:** Bequest of H. F. du Pont, 1969. 63.618

1. Elm was used for a drawer bottom in a dressing table attributed to Samuel Sewell of York, Maine (Jobe and Kaye, *New England Furniture,* no. 33) and for drawer dividers, drawer sides, and some drawer fronts and backs on a high chest also attributed to Sewell (Jobe and Kaye, *New England Furniture,* no. 37).

2. Private correspondence with Harry A. Alden, wood anatomist, Forest Products Lab, Madison, Wis.

## 225 ◆ Desk-and-bookcase
Boston-Salem, Massachusetts, area
1785–1800, with late nineteenth-century
alterations

Heavily compromised, and indeed, with its
original appearance barely recognizable, this
desk-and-bookcase is nonetheless one of
the most intriguing objects ever collected
by Henry Francis du Pont.[1] Even though
formal analysis would condemn this desk, it
nonetheless strongly champions the notion
that tremendous artistic, historical, and
educational value may still be obtained from
certain objects that may have come down to
us in imperfect states.

There is no question that the present upper
case is a replacement for an original bookcase
and that the interior desk drawers and their
surrounding joinerwork of dividers and blades
are replaced. Unfortunately, the originality
of the lower desk drawers also can be called
into question albeit without the conclusive
evidence uncovered in the upper case. There
is optimism that the beautiful figurative
carvings, be they European or American,
may have surmounted the original bookcase.

The most important key to this desk
is the similar, so-called Brinley desk-and-
bookcase (see No. 210). Direct comparison
reveals that the bombé swells and the
serpentine drawer patterns of both desks
are of the exact same configuration, which
usually indicates use of the same templates
in the same shop environment.

Notably, however, this desk lacks the
supporting lopers for the writing surface
that exist on the Brinley desk-and-bookcase.
V-notches, filled with wood, in the underside
of the writing surface either indicate a
"craftsman's error," or are the remains of
original loper dividers. Craftsman's error
implies that a change from the original loper
design to the present hanger system was made

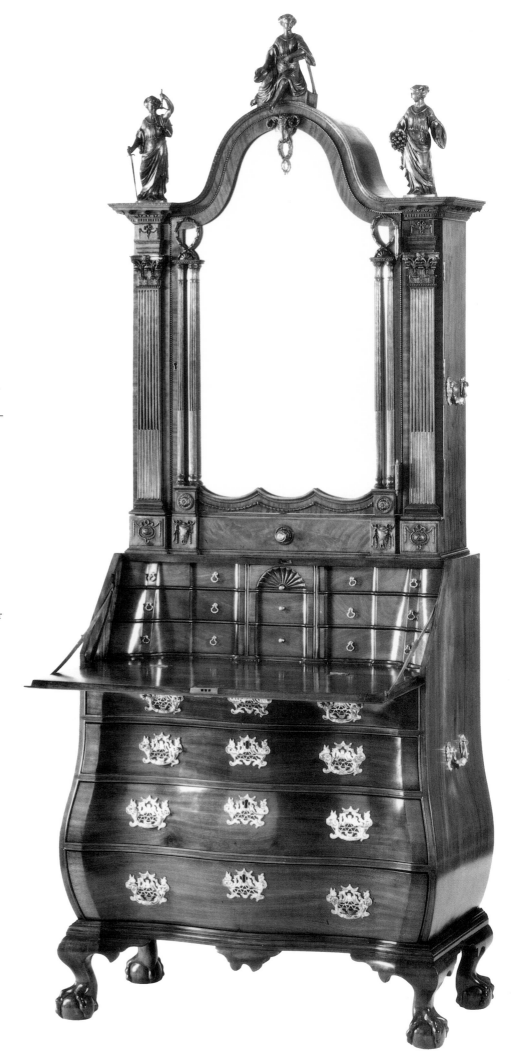

**Fig. 1.** Detail, interior of desk side.

during construction, an unlikely scenario given the virtually universal application of lopers in this period. Furthermore, from a cabinetmaker's perspective, the vertical grain direction of the filler wood in these notches is the least favorable orientation for a repair, suggesting instead that the pieces are the off-cut remains of original, vertical dividers. Since there are no corresponding notches in the blade below, the implication is that not only is the full-width top drawer replaced, but the blade is also replaced. Because the wood in all the desk drawers is identical, one is forced to consider the possibility that all are replaced.

Although questions remain about the lower drawers, there is no doubt that interior drawers have been replaced: examination of the inner surfaces of the desk sides above the writing surface reveals crudely filled notches, which indicates that the interior drawer blades originally extended much further out (fig. 1), a configuration very similar to that of the Brinley desk-and-bookcase. Also, barely visible scribe lines on the writing surface strongly support the proposition that the original drawer blocking was at much more of a dramatic slope than it is now.

As indicated by tool marks around the back edges of the upper case, it is clear that it began life as a square box, at least a few inches deeper than it now is. It was cut down in depth, built up into a "camel-back" shape on top (fig. 2), and heavily ornamented on the facade. Although this arbitrarily chosen bookcase could be cut down to fit front-to-back on the desk top, it was too narrow to fit well within the original waist molding. The solution was to remove the molding and partially veneer the desk top along the front and both sides to conceal the dovetailing and the nail holes left from the molding. Thus the bookcase sits freely, without any locating devices and without the expected waist molding as seen on the Brinley desk-and-bookcase.

Despite the beautifully carved and applied ornamentation, the bookcase could easily be disregarded as historically insignificant. However, a *design* comparison with the Brinley immediately reveals fundamental similarities, including the decoratively carved swagging below and double columns flanking the mirror. Even the unique camel-back shape of the pediment echoes the early rococo top of the Brinley. It is unimaginable that this

richly classical version was executed with no knowledge of either the Brinley or the presumably similar bookcase that was original to the desk.

The relief carving behind the central pediment figure representing Hope demonstrates that it, and by inference the other figures of Justice and Commerce, had previously surmounted a similar, architectonic object. It is tempting to conclude that they are original to the desk-and-bookcase for a number of reasons. Joseph Barrell, Charlestown merchant and the original owner of the desk-and-bookcase, was a fervent competitor with other successful Boston merchants for ever grander lifestyles. He and Elias Hasket Derby both were known for importing carved garden statuary and other articles of European decorative arts to enhance their richly decorated mansions. Barrell's bookplate includes allegorical figures in the same posture as two of the three carvings.

*MSP*

---

**Inscriptions or marks:** *Engraved on brass plate attached to the inside of bookcase section:* "Joseph Barrell/ Hannah Barrell Joy (wife of Benjamin Joy)/ John Benjamin Joy/ Charles Henry Joy/ Benjamin Joy". *Scratched inside the long drawer, bookcase section:* "BEARING BROTH". *On underside of bottom board, lower case:* "Botom" *and a shop mark* "V" *in chalk. Scribe marked on inside drawer fronts, left tier of drawers, desk section:* "I"; *on inside drawer fronts, right tier of drawers:* "II". *On drawer below shell drawer:* floral motif designed with a compass; *on the inside drawer back:* "II". *On secret drawer behind the middle drawer, prospect section:* shop mark "V". *Scratch marked on drawer front of bottom drawer, prospect section:* "III"; *on secret drawer behind bottom drawer:* "V" *on bottom and* "X" *on drawer front. Inside top long drawer, on compartment lids:* (far left) "37 & 38"; (second left) "39"; (right of center) "41"; (third from right) "35"; *and* (second from right) "42", *all in pencil. On bottom board:* "37 1111ᵉ £64" *in pencil.*

**Fig. 2.** Detail, construction of pediment.

**Construction:** (Upper case) The figures surmounting the pediment are fully carved. The mahogany boards of the fully enclosed top are coopered together and supported on the inside of the scrollboard by a series of glueblocks; sections of molding along the sides are held in place by wood screws countersunk from the top and filled. The two-board mahogany top board runs the full width of the case and is dovetailed to the sides. The panel-in-frame backboard is screwed flush to the case. The front of the upper case is mahogany veneer on mahogany. The carved cornice molding and the other carved decoration is glued to the case. The arched central door has two layers of glass; the inner layer is flat and the outer layer is mirrored plate glass cut with a wide, nonconforming bevel. Narrow flanking doors are covered by Corinthian pilasters. Behind the large door, the compartment is open; the sections behind the small doors are divided by two movable shelves.

(Lower case) The hinged slant-top lid, a solid board with batten ends, is held by steel lid hinges and brass butt hinges, probably added later. There are no lopers. The interior, in an amphitheater design, is divided into five vertical sections, each with three drawers. Behind the two lower drawers of the prospect section are secret drawers. The lower desk drawers run the full width of the case. The top drawer is divided into eight compartments across the back, each with sliding tops, and three open compartments across the front. The second drawer originally was fitted with compartments, but these are now missing. The blades between

each drawer, cut with a thick double-bead, are joined to the sides with exposed dovetails. There are full dust or security boards between each drawer. The bottom board is dovetailed to the sides. The base molding is nailed to the case. The backboard, two lap-joined horizontal boards, is nailed to rabbets in the sides. The legs are tenoned into the bottom of the case and reinforced by large, flat, triangular blocks and shaped vertical glueblocks. The knee brackets have supporting glueblocks. There are a series of glueblocks behind the bottom rail and the pendent drop. The drawer sides conform to the shape of the bombé and have a double-bead on the upper edge; the back, of thicker stock, is chamfered on the outer edge; the bottom, the grain front to back, is set into grooves on the front and sides and nailed at the back.

**Condition:** This desk has undergone major alterations, modifications, and additions; see main entry text for full interpretation.

**Dimensions:**

| | | |
|---|---|---|
| H. (with finials) | 95 1/2 in. | 242.8 cm |
| H. (case) | 87 in. | 220.9 cm |
| H. (writing surface) | 33 7/16 in. | 85.0 cm |
| W. (cornice) | 35 1/2 in. | 90.1 cm |
| W. (upper case) | 31 7/16 in. | 80.2 cm |
| W. (bombé) | 36 15/16 in. | 93.8 cm |
| W. (feet) | 37 5/16 in. | 95.0 cm |
| D. (cornice) | 10 3/4 in. | 27.4 cm |
| D. (upper case) | 8 1/16 in. | 20.6 cm |
| D. (bombé) | 19 3/8 in. | 49.4 cm |
| D. (feet) | 20 in. | 51.4 cm |

**Materials:** *Microanalysis:* Primary: mahogany. Secondary: white pine group (drawer lining top section, drawer lining bottom section, backboard lower case). *Finish:* reddish brown color in resin.

**Publications:** Montgomery, *American Furniture*, no. 176. Gilbert T. Vincent, "The Bombé Furniture of Boston," in *Boston Furniture*, p. 191, fig. 135. Wendy A. Cooper, *In Praise of America: American Decorative Arts, 1650–1830: Fifty Years of Discovery since the 1929 Girl Scouts Loan Exhibition* (New York: Alfred A. Knopf, 1980), pp. 132–33, detail no. 151. Michael S. Podmaniczky and Philip D. Zimmerman, "Two Massachusetts *Bombé* Desk-and-Bookcases," *Antiques* 145, no. 5 (May 1994): pls. 2, 3, 5–9, 11–14, figs. 1, 2.

**Provenance:** When acquired, the desk-and-bookcase had a history of original ownership by Joseph Barrell, a prosperous Boston merchant, and later ownership by Hannah Barrell Joy; John Benjamin Joy; Charles Henry Joy; and Benjamin Joy, the last private owner.

**Accession history:** Purchased by H. F. du Pont from Israel Sack, Inc., New York, 1956. Gift of H. F. du Pont, 1958.
56.23

---

1. For a detailed discussion, see Michael S. Podmaniczky and Philip D. Zimmerman, "Two Massachusetts *Bombé* Desk-and-Bookcases," *Antiques* 145, no. 5 (May 1994): 724–31.

# Short-Title Bibliography

Baarsen et al., *Courts and Colonies.*
>   Reinier Baarsen et al. *Courts and Colonies: The William and Mary Style in Holland, England, and America.* Washington, D.C.: Smithsonian Institution, 1988.

Barquist, *American Tables and Looking Glasses.*
>   David L. Barquist. *American Tables and Looking Glasses in the Mabel Brady Garvan and Other Collections at Yale University.* New Haven: Yale University Art Gallery, 1992.

Bishop, *Centuries and Styles of the American Chair.*
>   Robert Bishop. *Centuries and Styles of the American Chair, 1640–1970.* New York: E. P. Dutton, 1972.

*Boston Furniture.*
>   *Boston Furniture of the Eighteenth Century.* Publications of the Colonial Society of Massachusetts, vol. 48. Boston: By the society, 1974.

Butler, *American Furniture.*
>   Joseph T. Butler. *American Furniture from the First Colonies to World War I.* London: Triune Books, 1973.

Cescinsky, *English Furniture.*
>   Herbert Cescinsky. *English Furniture of the Eighteenth Century,* 3 vols. London: George Routledge and Sons, 1909–11.

Comstock, *American Furniture.*
>   Helen Comstock. *American Furniture: Seventeenth-, Eighteenth-, and Nineteenth-Century Styles.* New York: Viking Press, 1962.

*Connecticut Furniture.*
>   *Connecticut Furniture: Seventeenth and Eighteenth Centuries.* Hartford: Wadsworth Atheneum, 1967.

Cooke, *Upholstery.*
>   Edward S. Cooke, Jr., ed. *Upholstery in America and Europe from the Seventeenth Century to World War I.* New York: W. W. Norton, 1987.

Cummings, *Rural Household Inventories.*
>   Abbott Lowell Cummings, ed. *Rural Household Inventories: Establishing the Names, Uses, and Furnishings of Rooms in the Colonial New England Home, 1675–1775.* Boston: Society for the Preservation of New England Antiquities, 1964.

Dow, *Arts and Crafts in New England.*
>   George Francis Dow, comp. *The Arts and Crafts in New England, 1704–1775: Gleanings from Boston Newspapers.* 1927. Reprint. New York: Da Capo Press, 1967.

Downs, *American Furniture*.
> Joseph Downs. *American Furniture: Queen Anne and Chippendale Periods in the Henry Francis du Pont Winterthur Museum*. New York: Macmillan Co., 1952.

*Dunlaps and Their Furniture*.
> *The Dunlaps and Their Furniture*. Manchester, N.H.: Currier Gallery of Art, 1970.

Fales, *Furniture of Historic Deerfield*.
> Dean A. Fales, Jr. *The Furniture of Historic Deerfield*. New York: E. P. Dutton, 1976.

Fitzgerald, *Three Centuries*.
> Oscar P. Fitzgerald. *Three Centuries of American Furniture*. Englewood Cliffs, N.J.: Prentice-Hall, 1982.

Flanigan, *American Furniture*.
> J. Michael Flanigan. *American Furniture from the Kaufman Collection*. Washington, D.C.: National Gallery of Art, 1986.

Forman, *American Seating Furniture*.
> Benno M. Forman. *American Seating Furniture, 1630–1730: An Interpretive Catalogue*. New York: W. W. Norton, 1988.

*Great River*.
> *The Great River: Art and Society of the Connecticut Valley, 1635–1820*. Hartford, Conn.: Wadsworth Atheneum, 1985.

Greenlaw, *New England Furniture*.
> Barry A. Greenlaw. *New England Furniture at Williamsburg*. Williamsburg, Va.: Colonial Williamsburg Fndn., 1974.

Heckscher, *American Furniture*.
> Morrison H. Heckscher. *American Furniture in the Metropolitan Museum of Art*, Vol. 2, *Late Colonial Period: The Queen Anne and Chippendale Styles*. New York: Metropolitan Museum of Art and Random House, 1985.

Hinckley, *Directory*.
> F. Lewis Hinckley. *A Directory of Queen Anne, Early Georgian, and Chippendale Furniture Establishing the Preeminence of the Dublin Craftsmen*. New York: Crown Publishers, 1971.

Hipkiss, *Eighteenth-Century American Arts*.
> Edwin J. Hipkiss. *Eighteenth-Century American Arts: The M. and M. Karolik Collection*. Cambridge: Harvard University Press, 1941.

Hornor, *Blue Book*.
> William MacPherson Hornor, Jr. *Blue Book, Philadelphia Furniture: William Penn to George Washington*. 1935. Reprint. Washington, D.C.: Highland House, 1977.

Jobe, *Portsmouth Furniture*.
> Brock Jobe, ed. *Portsmouth Furniture: Masterworks from the New Hampshire Seacoast*. Boston: Society for the Preservation of New England Antiquities, 1993.

Jobe and Kaye, *New England Furniture*.
> Brock Jobe and Myrna Kaye. *New England Furniture, The Colonial Era: Selections from the Society for the Preservation of New England Antiquities*. Boston: Houghton Mifflin Co., 1984.

*John Brown House Loan Exhibition*.
> *The John Brown House Loan Exhibition of Rhode Island Furniture*. Providence: Rhode Island Historical Society, 1965.

Kane, *Three Hundred Years*.
> Patricia E. Kane. *Three Hundred Years of American Seating Furniture: Chairs and Beds from the Mabel Brady Garvan and Other Collections at Yale University*. Boston: New York Graphic Society, 1976.

Keno, Freund, and Miller, "Very Pink of the Mode."
> Leigh Keno, Joan Barzilay Freund, and Alan Miller, "The Very Pink of the Mode: Boston Georgian Chairs, Their Export, and Their Influence." In *American Furniture 1996*, edited by Luke Beckerdite. Milwaukee, Wis.: Chipstone Fndn., 1996.

Kirk, *American Chairs.*
John T. Kirk. *American Chairs: Queen Anne and Chippendale.* New York: Alfred A. Knopf, 1972.

Kirk, *American Furniture.*
John T. Kirk. *American Furniture and the British Tradition to 1830.* New York: Alfred A. Knopf, 1982.

Lockwood, *Colonial Furniture.*
Luke Vincent Lockwood. *Colonial Furniture in America,* 3d ed., 2 vols. 1901. Revised. New York: Charles Scribner's Sons, 1926.

Lyon, *Colonial Furniture.*
Irving Whitall Lyon. *The Colonial Furniture of New England: A Study of the Domestic Furniture in Use in the Seventeenth and Eighteenth Centuries.* 1891. Reprint. New York: E. P. Dutton, 1977.

Macquoid and Edwards, *Dictionary.*
Percy Macquoid and Ralph Edwards. *The Dictionary of English Furniture from the Middle Ages to the Late Georgian Period,* 3 vols. 1924–27, 1954. Revised. London: Barra Books, 1983.

Miller, "Roman Gusto."
Alan Miller. "Roman Gusto in New England: An Eighteenth-Century Boston Furniture Designer and His Shop." In *American Furniture 1993,* edited by Luke Beckerdite. Milwaukee, Wis.: Chipstone Fndn., 1993.

Monkhouse and Michie, *American Furniture.*
Christopher P. Monkhouse and Thomas S. Michie. *American Furniture in Pendleton House.* Providence: Museum of Art, Rhode Island School of Design, 1986.

Montgomery, *American Furniture.*
Charles F. Montgomery. *American Furniture: The Federal Period in the Henry Francis du Pont Winterthur Museum.* New York: Viking Press, 1966.

Morse, *Furniture of the Olden Time.*
Frances Clary Morse. *Furniture of the Olden Time.* Revised. New York: Macmillan Co., 1917.

Moses, *Master Craftsmen.*
Michael Moses. *Master Craftsmen of Newport: The Townsends and the Goddards.* Tenafly, N.J.: MMI Americana Press, 1984.

*New England Furniture.*
*New England Furniture: Essays in Memory of Benno M. Forman,* Vol. 72, no. 259. Boston: Society for the Preservation of New England Antiquities, 1987.

*New London County Furniture.*
*New London County Furniture, 1640–1840.* New London, Conn.: Lyman Allyn Museum, 1974.

Nutting, *Furniture Treasury.*
Wallace Nutting. *Furniture Treasury.* 1928–33. Reprint. New York: Macmillan Co., 1966.

Randall, *American Furniture.*
Richard H. Randall, Jr. *American Furniture in the Museum of Fine Arts, Boston.* Boston: By the museum, 1965.

Rodriguez Roque, *American Furniture.*
Oswaldo Rodriguez Roque. *American Furniture at Chipstone.* Madison: University of Wisconsin Press, 1984.

Rollins, *Treasures of State.*
Alexandra W. Rollins, ed. *Treasures of State: Fine and Decorative Arts in the Diplomatic Reception Rooms of the U.S. Department of State.* New York: Harry N. Abrams, 1991.

Thornton, *Seventeenth-Century Interior Decoration.*
Peter Thornton. *Seventeenth-Century Interior Decoration in England, France, and Holland.* New Haven: Yale University Press for the Paul Mellon Centre for Studies in British Art, 1978.

Trent, *Hearts and Crowns.*
Robert F. Trent. *Hearts and Crowns: Folk Chairs of the Connecticut Coast, 1720–1840.* New Haven: New Haven Colony Historical Society, 1977.

Trent, "New London County Joined Chairs."
  Robert F. Trent. "New London County Joined Chairs: Legacy of a Provincial Elite." *Connecticut Historical Society Bulletin* 50, no. 4 (Fall 1985): 15–36.

Trent with Nelson, "A Catalogue of New London County Joined Chairs."
  Robert F. Trent with Nancy Lee Nelson. "A Catalogue of New London County Joined Chairs." *Connecticut Historical Society Bulletin* 50, no. 4 (Fall 1985): 37–195.

Venable, *American Furniture*.
  Charles L. Venable. *American Furniture in the Bybee Collection*. Austin: University of Texas Press, 1989.

Ward, *American Case Furniture*.
  Gerald W. R. Ward. *American Case Furniture in the Mabel Brady Garvan and Other Collections at Yale University*. New Haven: Yale University Art Gallery, 1988.

Warren, *Bayou Bend*.
  David B. Warren. *Bayou Bend: American Furniture, Paintings, and Silver from the Bayou Bend Collection*. Houston: Museum of Fine Arts, 1975.

Zea and Dunlap, *Dunlap Cabinetmakers*.
  Philip Zea and Donald Dunlap. *The Dunlap Cabinetmakers: A Tradition in Craftsmanship*. Mechanicsburg, Pa.: Stackpole Books, 1994.

# Index

drawers, 361; couches, 190; dressing tables, 330, 332; easy chairs, 147, 148, 158; high chests of drawers, 327; settee, 483; side chairs, 19, 38, 65; tables, 228, 254, 260, 271

Champion family of Conn., 286

Champlin, Christopher, owner, 467

Champlin, Christopher, Sr., chairs descended from, 62

Champlin family of Charlestown, R.I. armchairs owned by, 63

Chandler family of Petersham, Mass., 319

Chandler, Zachariah, 406

Chaney family of Salem, Mass., owner, 257

Chaney, George L., owner, 258

"Change and Choice in Early American Decorative Arts," exhibition, IBM Gallery of Science and Art, New York, 8, 13, 15, 104

Chapin, Aaron, cabinetmaker, 84, 85, 345, 346, 347
  chairs made by, 86

Chapin, Eliphalet, cabinetmaker, 87, 347
  furniture made by: chairs, 3, 60, 84, 86; high chest of drawers, 345–46
  influence on furniture design in Conn., xiv, 345
  life of, 84
  shop of: characteristics of furniture from, 345–46; furniture associated with, 346

Chapin school, 345, 346

Chapin-type chairs, 84–85, 87

Charleston, S.C., xi, 78, 379, 456

Charlestown, Mass., 113, 258, 262, 286, 313, 317, 447, 470
  chairs associated with, 53
  export trade in, 317
  furniture made in: card table, 266; dining table, 262; dressing table, 316; high chest of drawers, 313–14

Charlestown, N.H., 286
  stands made in, 285–86

Cheever, William Downes, owner, 466

Chelsea, Mass., 96

Chenery, William, cabinetmaker and upholsterer, 467

cheney, 16, 18, 149, 153, 167, 197, 244

Cheney, Benjamin, carpenter, 39

cherry
  as primary wood: in bedstead, 204; in bottle box, 374; in chairs, 4, 13, 39, 40, 61, 62, 86, 87, 88, 109, 118, 121, 124, 126, 129; in chests of drawers, 368, 371, 381; in chests-on-chests, 393, 404; in couch, 193; in desk, 491; in desk-and-bookcases, 425, 428; in dressing tables, 334, 338; in fire screen, 291; in high chests of drawers, 325, 329, 347; in stand, 286; in tables, 231, 249, 256
  as secondary wood: in chairs, 35; in fire screen, 292; in high chests of drawers, 487, 489; in sofa, 185; in table, 256
  furniture made of (see also herein as primary wood; as secondary wood): "Boston chairs," 18; chairs, 61, 63, 67, 73, 85, 123, 127, 156; chests of drawers, 363, 367, 368, 380, 402; chests-on-chests, 346, 384, 390, 398, 399, 402; couches, 55, 190, 192; desk-and-bookcases, 346, 410, 421, 422, 426, 429; desks, 421, 422; dressing tables, 316, 319, 324; high chests of drawers, 314, 323, 324; seating, 84 (see also herein chairs; couches); stand, 286; table, 249

regions used in, 120, 128, 192, 337, 354, 390, 411

chestnut
  as secondary wood, 387, 414: in bureau tables, 388, 390; in chairs, 33, 124; in chest of drawers, 368; in chests-on-chests, 396; in desk-and-bookcases, 430; in desks, 414; in dressing tables, 322, 334, 336, 344; in high chests of drawers, 342; in tables, 228, 245, 270
  furniture made of (see also herein as secondary wood): chairs, 156; chests of drawers, 368
  regions used in, 334, 414

children's chairs, 1, 118–19

China
  designs from (see also Chinese furniture design; oriental design): bended-back chairs, 24
  furniture from: cabriole legs on, 27, 28; chairs, 24; tables, 28, 236
  cabriole-leg chairs from, 138
  goods from, 304

china tables, 187, 214, 215, 244–45, 264
  Marlborough legs on, 226, 256
  price of, 244

Chinese furniture design
  chair crests, 28, 107
  chairs, 86, 183: construction techniques, 107
  in pattern books, 196, 256
  incorporation into Townsend furniture, 265
  tables, 217: cross stretchers, 244

Chinese influence
  from: Chinese porcelains, 242; Chinese vase profiles, 27
  on: American furniture, 138; English furniture, 28, 138; japanned figures, 312; New England chair design, 188; Newport block-and-shell desk-and-bookcases, 439; Newport pembroke tables, 264

Chinese splats, 481

chinoiserie, 204, 271, 305
  brasses, 376
  decoration on high chests of drawers, 308

Chippendale, Thomas, designer, xiv, 5, 81, 110, 181, 215, 216, 285. See also Gentleman and Cabinet-Maker's Director, The
  designs by, 410: breakfast tables, 216, 264; bureau tables, 353, 385; chairs, 92, 481; chests of drawers, 355; china tables, 214, 244; commodes, 379; dressing glasses, 469; "French chair," 172, 482; Gothic, 99; hinged-leaf tables, 254; pembroke tables, 216, 264; screens, 282, 291, 293; serpentine crest, 156; sofas, 6, 181, 184; stands, 281, 282; window stools, 186
  shop records, 208

Chipstone Foundation
  furniture in: bedstead, 204–5; cabinet, 389; chair, 67; couches, 190; desk, 359; dressing table, 343; tables, 244, 265

Cincinnati Art Museum, dressing table in, 485

Clap, Thomas, president of Yale College, 30

club feet
  on: chairs, 70; tables, 222

Coe, Adam S., xiv, 183
  sofa made by, 183–84, 204

Coffin family of Mass., owner, 65

Coffin, Sarah, owner, 234

Coffin, Silvanus, owner, 65

Coffin, Tristram, I, owner, 65

Cogan, Lillian B., owner, 74, 75, 76, 77, 121, 124

Cogswell, John, cabinetmaker, 364, 375, 446, 449
  construction techniques used by, 375–76
  desk-and-bookcase made by, 446–47
  life of, 447

Cogswell, Martha (née Lathrop), owner, 37

Coit, Job, Jr., cabinetmaker, 432
  apprentices of, 225
  desk-and-bookcase made by, 332, 386, 431–33

Coit, Job, Sr., cabinetmaker, 332, 433
  apprentices of, 225
  career of, 432
  desk-and-bookcase made by, 357, 386, 409, 410, 431–33, 436
  inventory of, 432

Coit, Joseph (son of Job, Sr.), 432

Coit, Nathaniel (son of Job, Sr.), 432

Colchester, Conn., 381
  as center of furnituremaking trade, 369
  chair recovered from, 117
  furniture made in: bottle box, 372–74; cases, 367; chest-on-chest, 370; chests of drawers, 367–68, 370, 372; desk-and-bookcase, 372; desks, 370, 372

Colchester school of cabinetmaking, 367

Collings, Albert J., agent, 440

Collins, Stephen, merchant and owner, 153, 155

Colonial Society of Massachusetts conference, 435
  table in, 265

Colonial Williamsburg
  furniture in: bedsteads, 200, 201, 203; chairs, 102, 158; couch, 192; tables, 224, 225

compass seats, xiv, 3, 4, 14, 15, 16, 17, 26, 28, 39, 43, 44, 45, 48, 53, 54, 59, 63, 78, 80, 130, 132, 167, 171

Concord Antiquarian Society. See also Concord Museum
  exhibit, 329

Concord, Mass.
  furniture made in: by J. Hosmer, 326; chest-on-chest, 398–99; high chest of drawers, 326–27

Concord Museum. See also Concord Antiquarian Society
  chest-on-chest in, 326, 327

Connecticut. See also Branford; Colchester; Connecticut, eastern; East Hartford; East Windsor; Ellington; Fairfield; Fairfield County; Greenwich; Guilford; Hartford; Housatonic River valley; Meriden; Middlesex County; Middletown; Milford; New Haven; New Haven County; New London County; Newtown; Norwich; Preston; Saybrook; South Windsor; Southbury; Stamford; Stratford; Wallingford; Wethersfield; Windham County; Windsor; Woodbury
  as center of chairmaking, 1
  chair designs, 78, 119, 120: balusters, 123, 137; banisters, 192; crests, 70; cross slats, 117; "Dutch foot," 220; knees, 41; legs, 41, 117, 192; stretchers, 41, 122
  craftsmen in, 18, 390, 424: cabinetmakers, 354, 389; joiners, 207
  furniture associated with: chairs, 10; chests of drawers, 370; roundabout

chairs, 129; side chairs, 59, 72; tables, 224, 248
  furniture designs: block-and-shell, 387; cabriole legs, 380; carved rosette, 391; chairs, 108; decorative motifs, 423; dressing tables, 413; feet, 224; high chests, 413; legs, 224, 230; table skirts, 230; tea tables, 413
  furniture made in: banister-back chairs, 72; bedstead, 203; casework, 340; chairs, 37, 60, 84, 192, 220; chests, 324, 381; chests of drawers, xii, 379, 380, 488; chests-on-chests, 390–92, 398; couch, 192; desk-and-bookcases, xii, 412; dining tables, 335; dressing table, 324; "red" chairs, 75; roundabout chair, 125–26; stands, 284; tables, 220, 222, 224, 229; tea tables, 335; Windsor chairs, 138
  influence from: Boston furnituremaking, 59; eastern Mass. high chest, 315; New York furnituremaking, 73
  woods used in, 288, 324: cherry, 18, 192, 354, 380, 411; red oak, 334

Connecticut, eastern: chair designs, 125; cabriole legs, 14; solid splats, 39; stretchers, 59
  furniture associated with: chairs, 61; chests of drawers, 372; couch, 55; vernacular chairs, 63; Windsor chairs, 138
  furniture designs: blockfront cases as prototypes, 367; blockfront facade, 367; decorative features, 403; feet, 403, 413; legs, 413
  furniture made in: blockfront cases, 367; casework, 340; chairs, 3, 39; desk-on-frame, 413; round-blocked chests, 363; roundabout chairs, 123–24, 127; side chairs, 61, 117; tables, 228
  woods used in: chestnut, 334, 414; cherry, 39

Connecticut Historical Society. See also "Legacy of a Provincial Elite: New London County Joined Chairs, 1720–1790"
  furniture owned by: chest of drawers, 367, 402; looking glass, 463

Connecticut River, xiii, 286, 337, 370

Connecticut River valley
  as center of furnituremaking, 337
  furniture associated with: chairs, 85; tables, 278
  furniture made in: casework, 340; chairs, 3, 86; chests, 312; couches, 188–89, 192; tables, 256; tea tables, 337
  influence from: E. Chapin, 345; Mass. furnituremaking, 337
  introduction of japanwork to, 311

Connecticut Tercentenary Exhibition, Wadsworth Atheneum, Hartford, 346, 369

contoured back, 3, 7, 22, 24, 28, 42. See also crooked back

Cony, Daniel, 310

Cony, Sarah Lowell, owner, 310

Cook, Helen Temple, owner, 445

Cooke, Edward S., Jr., 125, 323–24, 384, 390

Cooke, Helen Temple, owner, 379

Cooke, John, original owner, 265, 288

Cooper, William, owner, home of, 155

Copley, John Singleton, artist, 376
  portraits by, 58, 155, 179, 184, 238

Coutant, David, 72

Cowdin, Joseph, owner, 167

Cowles family of Conn., 286

190; desk-and-bookcase, 440, 443; dressing glass, 467; high chest of drawers, 311–12; settee, 181; side chairs, 89; stand, 285; tables, 251, 264, 287
Michie, Thomas S., 441
Middlesex County, Conn., chest of drawers made in, 369–70, 372
Middlesex County, Mass., dressing table made in, 319
Middletown, Conn.
　as trade port, 370
　chairs associated with, 85
Milford, Conn.
　chair owned in, 119
　furniture made in: chairs, 72, 73, 74–75; side chair, 76
Miller, Alan, 233
Miller, Thomas, original owner, 349
Minnigerode (sp?), Meade, owner, 86
Minot, Peter
　inventory of, 276
Minturn, Abigail West, owner, 366
Minturn family of Bristol, R.I., owner, 82
Minturn, Gertrude, 83. See Sanford, Gertrude Minturn
Minturn, Jonas, owner, 83, 366
Moffatt, John, merchant, 36
Moffatt, Samuel, merchant and owner, 155, 467
Moffett, D.B., owner, 263
Moffett, Dr. and Mrs. Daniel Bruce, owners, 27
Molineaux, William, merchant, 246
Monkhouse, Christopher P., 227
Montgomery, Charles F., owner, xi, 177, 259, 292, 478
Moore, David, merchant, 222
Moorehouse, Mrs. Louis, 79
moreen, 5, 16, 18, 98, 149, 153
Morgan, Charles, family of, owner, 29
Morgan Memorial, exhibition, Hartford, Conn., 279
Morse, Frances Clary, antiquarian and owner, 370
Morse, Mrs. Frances Clary, owner, 372
Morss, Joshua, cabinetmaker, 321
Moses, Michael, 226, 269, 270, 290, 388
Mottley, George S., owner, 315, 318
Moulton family of Newburyport, Mass., owner, 359
Murphy, Katharine Prentis, owner, 351
Museum of Art, Rhode Island School of Design, Providence, 397
　furniture in: chairs, 93, 134, 482; desk-and-bookcase, 440–41; table, 227, 228
Museum of Fine Arts, Boston. See also Karolik Collection
　exhibition, 232
　furniture in: bedstead, 201; bureau table, 251, 386; chair, 29; couches, 190; desk, 413; desk-and-bookcase, 440; easy chairs, 153; high chest of drawers, 304; pembroke table, 264; side chairs, 89, 103, 105, 113, 268; slab-top table, 250; tea tables, 236
Museum of Fine Arts, Houston. See Bayou Bend collection

# N

Nantucket, Mass., 65
　trade in, 65, 456
Narragansett Bay, 183, 227, 335, 340, 440
Narragansett Pier, R.I., 184
National Council of Girl Scouts. See "Loan Exhibition of Eighteenth- and Early Nineteenth-Century Furniture and Glass"
Needham, Thomas, cabinetmaker, 378

needlework, 181, 293
　on: chair covers, 5, 49, 62, 81, 144; pocketbook, 341; screens, 291, 292; table covers, 236
　pictures, 10
　upholstery, 38
needleworkers, 145, 293. See also M. Fayerweather
Netherlands
　armchair designs, 175
　cupboard from, as model for chests of drawers, 353
New Bedford, Mass., 52
New England. See individual regions and cities
New Hampshire. See also Bedford; Charlestown; Dunbarton; Goffstown; Henniker; Londonderry; Manchester; Piscataqua region; Plaistow; Portsmouth; Salisbury; Temple; Tilton
　craftsmen, 215: cabinetmakers, 315; furnituremakers, 68; woodworkers, 405
　furniture associated with: chairs, 10, 29, 63, 65, 66; desks, 415; dressing table, 298
　furniture designs, 303: chairs, 141, 162; chests, 348; dressing tables, 321; influence from Boston, 107; tables, 248
　furniture made in: bedstead, 205; blockfront chests, 362; blockfront tables, 330; chairs, 69 (see also herein easy chair; roundabout chair; side chairs); chest of drawers, 382; construction techniques, 361; desk-and-bookcases, 422; desks, 417, 419, 422; dressing tables, 298; easy chair, 162; roundabout chair, 140–41; seating, 1; side chairs, 8–9, 68–69; tables, 215 (see also herein dressing tables; tea tables); tea tables, 225; vernacular seating, 3; woods used, 120, 228, 354, 362, 411, 419
New Hampshire Historical Society, Concord, high chest of drawers in, 349
New Haven Colony Historical Society, high chest of drawers in, 305
New Haven, Conn. See also Yale University Art Gallery
　furniture associated with: chairs, 137; table, 126
　chests of drawers made in, 353
　furniture trade in, xiii
New Haven County, Conn.
　inventories, 72
New London County, Conn., 39, 138, 324
　as: center of commerce, 3; center of culture, 3
　craftsmen, 248, 286
　furniture associated with: chairs, 76; joined seating, 117; table, 248
　furniture designs, 372, 417: cabinetwork, 373; case furniture, 403, 426; chairs, 41, 107, 108; chests, 380; stands, 286
　furniture made in: chairs, 107, 123; chest of drawers, 367; exhibition of, 367
New Marlborough, Mass., chest-on-chest made in, 401–3
New York, 370, 402, 403. See also Hamilton; Long Island; New York City; Poughkeepsie
　craftsmen in, 403: japanners, 305
　dissemination of designs from, 384

furniture associated with: chairs, 28, 48; side chairs, xii, 152; tea table, 234
furniture designs: ankles, 125; blockfront bureau tables, 386; cabriole legs, 82; chairs, 52, 60, 72, 91, 113; dining tables, 262; dressing tables, 335; easy chairs, 143; feet, 224; pedestal tables, 275; splats, 39, 76, 78, 80, 84
furniture made in: blockfront bureau table, 251; card tables, 251; construction techniques, 149; easy chairs, 149; influence of English design books on, 2; influence on Conn. design, 2; influence on R.I. design, 2; table, 220; woods used, 46
prototypes from: chairs, 75; "york" chair, 73
trade in, 251, 365
New York City, 2, 134
　craftsmen in, 182: carvers, 456
　chairs associated with, 48
　furniture designs: chair feet, 220; chairs, 74; "york" chairs, 119
　furniture made in: card tables, 222; looking glasses, 464
　rush-bottom chairs from, as prototypes, 70
Newbury chairs, 65
Newbury, Mass., 68
　furniture associated with, 322: tall cases, 321; woods used on, 322
　furniture made in: chairs, 65; chest, 321; dressing table, 321
Newburyport, Mass.
　as seaport, xiii
　furniture associated with: blockfront chests, 363; chairs, 65, 99; chests-on-chests, 399; desk-and-bookcases, 421; desks, 421; high chests, 315
　furniture made in: desk-and-bookcases, 421; desks, 421–22
Newport, 134. See also Newport Restoration Foundation; Redwood Library and Athenaeum, Newport
　as: center of chairmaking, 1; center of commerce, 2; center of furnituremaking, 39
　cabinetmakers in, influence on Norwich case furniture, 427
　craftsmen in, xiii, 464
　economy of, 80
　furniture associated with: chairs, 24, 26; roundabout chairs, 132
　furniture designs, 184: block-and-shell, 387, 388, 439; blockfront, 357, 365; card tables, 269, 271, 335; chairs, 80, 83, 132; chests of drawers, 389; dining tables, 335; dressing tables, 334, 335, 343; legs, 324; pembroke table, 264; shell-carved chests, 367; shells, 365; stands, 278, 287; tea tables, 215, 217, 335; tripod stands, 282
　furniture made in: bedsteads, 205; bureau tables, 387–88, 389; card tables, 269, 271, 335; chairs, 3, 42 (see also herein easy chairs; roundabout chairs; side chairs; Windsor chairs); chest of drawers, 365–66; china table, 244; construction techniques, 340; decorative features of, 161; desk-and-bookcases, 412, 439–41, 443; desks, 443; dressing tables, 343–44; easy chairs, 160–61; exhibition of, 132; high chests of drawers, 339–40; influence from British models, xiv;

looking glasses, 461–62; pembroke table, 264; roundabout chairs, 132; side chairs, 52, 62–63, 80, 82; sofa, 183–184; stands, 282, 287, 289–90; study of, 226; tables, 222 (see also herein bureau tables; card tables; china tables; dressing tables; pembroke table; tea tables; tripod table); tea tables, 228, 238–39, 244; tripod table, 336; use of mahogany, 354; Windsor chairs, 70; woods used, 387
introduction of blockfront style to, 365
trade, 410
Newport Restoration Foundation
　furniture in: high chest of drawers, 340; table, 278
Newton, Herbert, owner, 278
Newtown, Conn., 207
　casepieces associated with, 423
　chairs made in, 125
　social and economic development of, 125–26
Nichols, Frances M., owner, 284
Nichols, Helen Williams Gilman, owner, 310
Nichols, Henry A., owner, 310
Nichols House, Newport, 365
Nichols, John T. Gilman, owner, 310
Nichols, Mrs. Frances M., owner, 166
Norfolk, Va., 381
North Carolina, 354
　splat designs, 108
North Kingstown, R.I., coastal trade in, 340
North Shore, Mass.
　furniture made in: bedstead, 204–5; features of, 253, 291; table, 253, 260
Northampton, Mass., 340
　as center of furnituremaking, 337
　dressing table made in, 337–38
　side chair owned in, 89
Northend, Mary H., illustrator, 11
Northrop, Marion, owner, 75
Norton, Malcom A., owner, 279
Norwalk Historical Society, exhibition, Norwalk, Conn., 369
Norwich, Conn.
　as: center of chairmaking, 107; center of commerce, 2
　furniture designs: cabinets, 367; cases, 367; features of, 372
　furniture made in: chairs, 39; chest of drawers, 367–68, 373; chest-on-chest, 373; desk-and-bookcases, xii, 426–27; features of, 39; marble slab tables, 215, 248; side chairs, 37, 39, 59–60; stands, 282, 285–86
Nostell Priory, 209
Nourse, Dorothy Quincy, owner, 466
Nourse, Margaret Dunn, owner, 466
"Now I Lay Me Down to Eat: A Contribution to the Art of Living," exhibition, Cooper-Hewitt Museum, New York, 210
Nutting, Wallace, owner, 393, 467

# O

oak
　as secondary wood in chairs, 164
　furniture made of (see also herein as secondary wood): chairs, 156, 163, 479; tables, 246
　in splint seats, 141
oak, red
　as secondary wood: in casework, 334; in dressing tables, 336; in tables, 334